CLASSICAL AND MEDIEVAL LITERATURE CRITICISM

Guide to Gale Literary Criticism Series

For criticism on	Consult these Gale series
Authors now living or who died after December 31, 1999	*CONTEMPORARY LITERARY CRITICISM (CLC)*
Authors who died between 1900 and 1999	*TWENTIETH-CENTURY LITERARY CRITICISM (TCLC)*
Authors who died between 1800 and 1899	*NINETEENTH-CENTURY LITERATURE CRITICISM (NCLC)*
Authors who died between 1400 and 1799	*LITERATURE CRITICISM FROM 1400 TO 1800 (LC)* *SHAKESPEAREAN CRITICISM (SC)*
Authors who died before 1400	*CLASSICAL AND MEDIEVAL LITERATURE CRITICISM (CMLC)*
Authors of books for children and young adults	*CHILDREN'S LITERATURE REVIEW (CLR)*
Dramatists	*DRAMA CRITICISM (DC)*
Poets	*POETRY CRITICISM (PC)*
Short story writers	*SHORT STORY CRITICISM (SSC)*
Black writers of the past two hundred years	*BLACK LITERATURE CRITICISM (BLC)* *BLACK LITERATURE CRITICISM SUPPLEMENT (BLCS)*
Hispanic writers of the late nineteenth and twentieth centuries	*HISPANIC LITERATURE CRITICISM (HLC)* *HISPANIC LITERATURE CRITICISM SUPPLEMENT (HLCS)*
Native North American writers and orators of the eighteenth, nineteenth, and twentieth centuries	*NATIVE NORTH AMERICAN LITERATURE (NNAL)*
Major authors from the Renaissance to the present	*WORLD LITERATURE CRITICISM, 1500 TO THE PRESENT (WLC)* *WORLD LITERATURE CRITICISM SUPPLEMENT (WLCS)*

ISSN 0896-0011

Volume 47

CLASSICAL AND MEDIEVAL LITERATURE CRITICISM

Excerpts from Criticism of the Works of World Authors from Classical Antiquity through the Fourteenth Century, from the First Appraisals to Current Evaluations

Elisabeth Gellert
Jelena O. Krstović
Editors

GALE GROUP

THOMSON LEARNING

Detroit • New York • San Diego • San Francisco
Boston • New Haven, Conn. • Waterville, Maine
London • Munich

STAFF

Janet Witalec, Lynn M. Zott, *Managing Editors, Literature Product*
Kathy D. Darrow, Ellen McGeagh, *Content-Product Liaisons*
Elisabeth Gellert, Jelena Krstović, *Editors*
Mark W. Scott, *Publisher, Literature Product*

Madeline S. Harris, *Associate Editor*
Jenny Cromie, Mary Ruby, *Technical Training Specialists*
Deborah J. Morad, Joyce Nakamura, Kathleen Lopez Nolan, *Managing Editors, Literature Content*
Susan M. Trosky, *Director, Literature Content*

Maria L. Franklin, *Permissions Manager*
Kim Davis, *Permissions Associate*
Debra J. Freitas, *IC Coordinator*

Victoria B. Cariappa, *Research Manager*
Sarah Genik, *Project Coordinator*
Tamara C. Nott, *Research Associate*
Nicodemus Ford, *Research Assistant*

Dorothy Maki, *Manufacturing Manager*
Stacy L. Melson, *Buyer*

Mary Beth Trimper, *Composition and Prepress Manager*
Carolyn Roney, *Composition Specialist*

Randy Bassett, *Imaging Supervisor*
Robert Duncan, Dan Newell, Luke Rademacher, *Imaging Specialists*
Mike Logusz, *Graphic Artist*
Pamela A. Reed, *Imaging Coordinator*
Kelly A. Quin, *Imaging Content Editor*

Library of Congress Catalog Card Number 88-658021
ISBN 0-7876-5156-7
ISSN 0896-0011
Printed in the United States of America

10 9 8 7 6 5 4 3 2 1

Contents

Preface vii

Acknowledgments xi

Literary Criticism Series Advisory Board xiii

Preface

Since its inception in 1988, *Classical and Medieval Literature Criticism* (*CMLC*) has been a valuable resource for students and librarians seeking critical commentary on the works and authors of antiquity through the fourteenth century. The great poets, prose writers, dramatists, and philosophers of this period form the basis of most humanities curricula, so that virtually every student will encounter many of these works during the course of a high school and college education. Reviewers have found *CMLC* "useful" and "extremely convenient," noting that it "adds to our understanding of the rich legacy left by the ancient period and the Middle Ages," and praising its "general excellence in the presentation of an inherently interesting subject." No other single reference source has surveyed the critical reaction to classical and medieval literature as thoroughly as *CMLC*.

Scope of the Series

CMLC provides an introduction to classical and medieval authors, works, and topics that represent a variety of genres, time periods, and nationalities. By organizing and reprinting an enormous amount of critical commentary written on authors and works of this period in world history, *CMLC* helps students develop valuable insight into literary history, promotes a better understanding of the texts, and sparks ideas for papers and assignments.

Each entry in *CMLC* presents a comprehensive survey of an author's career, an individual work of literature, or a literary topic, and provides the user with a multiplicity of interpretations and assessments. Such variety allows students to pursue their own interests; furthermore, it fosters an awareness that literature is dynamic and responsive to many different opinions. Early commentary is offered to indicate initial responses, later selections document changes in literary reputations, and retrospective analyses provide the reader with modern views. The size of each author entry is a relative reflection of the scope of the criticism available in English.

An author may appear more than once in the series if his or her writings have been the subject of a substantial amount of criticism; in these instances, specific works or groups of works by the author will be covered in separate entries. For example, Homer will be represented by three entries, one devoted to the *Iliad,* one to the *Odyssey,* and one to the Homeric Hymns.

CMLC continues the survey of criticism of world literature begun by Gale's *Contemporary Literary Criticism* (*CLC*), *Twentieth-Century Literary Criticism* (*TCLC*), *Nineteenth-Century Literature Criticism* (*NCLC*), *Literature Criticism from 1400 to 1800* (*LC*), and *Shakespearean Criticism* (*SC*).

Organization of the Book

A *CMLC* entry consists of the following elements:

- The **Author Heading** cites the name under which the author most commonly wrote, followed by birth and death dates. Also located here are any name variations under which an author wrote, including transliterated forms for authors whose native languages use nonroman alphabets. If the author wrote consistently under a pseudonym, the pseudonym will be listed in the author heading and the author's actual name given in parenthesis on the first line of the biographical and critical information. Uncertain birth or death dates are indicated by question marks. Single-work entries are preceded by a heading that consists of the most common form of the title in English translation (if applicable) and the original date of composition.

- The **Introduction** contains background information that introduces the reader to the author, work, or topic that is the subject of the entry.

- A **Portrait of the Author** is included when available.

- The list of **Principal Works** is ordered chronologically by date of first publication and lists the most important works by the author. The genre and publication date of each work is given. In the case of foreign authors whose works have been translated into English, the list will focus primarily on twentieth-century translations, selecting those works most commonly considered the best by critics. Unless otherwise indicated, dramas are dated by first performance, not first publication. Lists of **Representative Works** by different authors appear with topic entries.

- Reprinted **Criticism** is arranged chronologically in each entry to provide a useful perspective on changes in critical evaluation over time. The critic's name and the date of composition or publication of the critical work are given at the beginning of each piece of criticism. Unsigned criticism is preceded by the title of the source in which it appeared. All titles by the author featured in the text are printed in boldface type. Footnotes are reprinted at the end of each essay or excerpt. In the case of excerpted criticism, only those footnotes that pertain to the excerpted texts are included. Criticism in topic entries is arranged chronologically under a variety of subheadings to facilitate the study of different aspects of the topic.

- A complete **Bibliographical Citation** of the original essay or book precedes each piece of criticism.

- Critical essays are prefaced by brief **Annotations** explicating each piece.

- An annotated bibliography of **Further Reading** appears at the end of each entry and suggests resources for additional study. In some cases, significant essays for which the editors could not obtain reprint rights are included here. Boxed material following the further reading list provides references to other biographical and critical sources on the author in series published by Gale.

Cumulative Indexes

A **Cumulative Author Index** lists all of the authors that appear in a wide variety of reference sources published by the Gale Group, including *CMLC*. A complete list of these sources is found facing the first page of the Author Index. The index also includes birth and death dates and cross references between pseudonyms and actual names.

Beginning with the second volume, a **Cumulative Nationality Index** lists all authors featured in *CMLC* by nationality, followed by the number of the *CMLC* volume in which their entry appears.

Beginning with the tenth volume, a **Cumulative Topic Index** lists the literary themes and topics treated in the series as well as in *Nineteenth-Century Literature Criticism, Twentieth-Century Literary Criticism,* and the *Contemporary Literary Criticism* Yearbook, which was discontinued in 1998.

A **Cumulative Title Index** lists in alphabetical order all of the works discussed in the series. Each title listing includes the corresponding volume and page numbers where criticism may be located. Foreign-language titles that have been translated into English are followed by the titles of the translation—for example, *Slovo o polku Igorove* (*The Song of Igor's Campaign*). Page numbers following these translated titles refer to all pages on which any form of the titles, either foreign-language or translated, appear. Titles of novels, dramas, nonfiction books, and poetry, short story, or essay collections are printed in italics, while individual poems, short stories, and essays are printed in roman type within quotation marks.

Citing *Classical and Medieval Literature Criticism*

When writing papers, students who quote directly from any volume in the Literary Criticism Series may use the following general format to footnote reprinted criticism. The first example pertains to material drawn from periodicals, the second to material reprinted from books.

T. P. Malnati, "Juvenal and Martial on Social Mobility," *The Classical Journal* 83, no. 2 (December-January 1988): 134-41; reprinted in *Classical and Medieval Literature Criticism,* vol. 35, ed. Jelena Krstović (Farmington Hills, Mich.: The Gale Group, 2000), 366-71.

J. P. Sullivan, "Humanity and Humour; Imagery and Wit," in *Martial: An Unexpected Classic* (Cambridge University Press, 1991), 211-51; excerpted and reprinted in *Classical and Medieval Literature Criticism,* vol. 35, ed. Jelena Krstović (Farmington Hills, Mich.: The Gale Group, 2000), 371-95.

Suggestions are Welcome

Readers who wish to suggest new features, topics, or authors to appear in future volumes, or who have other suggestions or comments are cordially invited to call, write, or fax the Managing Editor:

Managing Editor, Literary Criticism Series
The Gale Group
27500 Drake Road
Farmington Hills, MI 48331-3535
1-800-347-4253 (GALE)
Fax: 248-699-8054

Acknowledgments

The editors wish to thank the copyright holders of the excerpted criticism included in this volume and the permissions managers of many book and magazine publishing companies for assisting us in securing reproduction rights. We are also grateful to the staffs of the Detroit Public Library, the Library of Congress, the University of Detroit Mercy Library, Wayne State University Purdy/Kresge Library Complex, and the University of Michigan Libraries for making their resources available to us. Following is a list of the copyright holders who have granted us permission to reproduce material in this volume of *CMLC*. Every effort has been made to trace copyright, but if omissions have been made, please let us know.

COPYRIGHTED MATERIALS IN *CMLC*, VOLUME 47, WERE REPRODUCED FROM THE FOLLOWING PERIODICALS:

COPYRIGHTED MATERIALS IN *CMLC*, VOLUME 47, WERE REPRODUCED FROM THE FOLLOWING BOOKS:

PHOTOGRAPHS AND ILLUSTRATIONS APPEARING IN *CMLC*, VOLUME 47, WERE RECEIVED FROM THE FOLLOWING SOURCES:

Literary Criticism Series Advisory Board

The members of the Gale Group Literary Criticism Series Advisory Board—reference librarians and subject specialists from public, academic, and school library systems—represent a cross-section of our customer base and offer a variety of informed perspectives on both the presentation and content of our literature criticism products. Advisory board members assess and define such quality issues as the relevance, currency, and usefulness of the author coverage, critical content, and literary topics included in our series; evaluate the layout, presentation, and general quality of our printed volumes; provide feedback on the criteria used for selecting authors and topics covered in our series; provide suggestions for potential enhancements to our series; identify any gaps in our coverage of authors or literary topics, recommending authors or topics for inclusion; analyze the appropriateness of our content and presentation for various user audiences, such as high school students, undergraduates, graduate students, librarians, and educators; and offer feedback on any proposed changes/ enhancements to our series. We wish to thank the following advisors for their advice throughout the year.

Aeschines
c. 390 B.C.-c. 314 B.C.

Athenian orator.

INTRODUCTION

Considered one of the greatest Athenian orators, second only to his rival, Demosthenes, Aeschines used his verbal skills to try to convince the leaders of Athens to seek peace with Macedonia. Demosthenes was ultimately more persuasive in their bitter debates, however, and the defeated Aeschines exiled himself to Rhodes. Only three of Aeschines's speeches are now extant but they demonstrate Attic rhetoric at its finest and are important to the historical study of the rise of Philip II of Macedonia.

BIOGRAPHICAL INFORMATION

Little is known of Aeschines's life except for what may be gleaned from his speeches and those of Demosthenes. Although Aeschines's parents were not poor, they had to work for their living. His father, Atrometus, taught reading and writing; his mother, Glaucothea, took part in religious purification ceremonies. Atrometus's profession of schoolteacher was not well respected, but Aeschines benefitted from associating with his father's students. Before entering politics, he worked as undersecretary to assorted magistrates and then was elected public secretary. In this post he read laws out loud to the Council and the Assembly. Aeschines next worked as an actor. As secretary and as an actor, he gained experience in using his voice in front of crowds. He married a woman from a fairly wealthy family sometime around 348 B.C., and the couple eventually had three children. No longer having to struggle for a living, Aeschines entered politics. Although he was not trained professionally in rhetoric, he was familiar with all the intricacies of the craft and took advantage of his excellent voice and impressive physique in addressing the Assembly. After a devastating rhetorical defeat at the hands of Demosthenes in 330 B.C., Aeschines left Athens for Rhodes, where he lived his remaining years, teaching rhetoric.

MAJOR WORKS

Aeschines's first surviving speech is *Against Timarchus* (345 B.C.) While serving as an ambassador for Athens, Aeschines was either outmaneuvered or bribed by King Philip II. Although Aeschines was able to make the terms of the

peace agreement with Macedonia less harsh than Philip had at first declared, the citizens of Athens were not pleased. Demosthenes, also involved in the peace agreement, charged Aeschines with treason. One of the planned witnesses for the prosecution was Timarchus. Aeschines successfully brought a countersuit against Timarchus, thus weakening Demosthenes's case. Although *Against Timarchus* accomplished what Aeschines had sought, Demosthenes went ahead with his case. *On the Embassy,* sometimes referred to as *On the False Embassy* (343 B.C.), preserves Aeschines's defense. Aeschines survived the battle but his political power waned, while Demosthenes's grew. The two men became even more bitter foes, and over the years neither missed an opening to attack the other. *Against Ctesiphon* (330 B.C.) is the last of Aeschines's surviving speeches. Although the speech's target is nominally Ctesiphon, who proposed that Demosthenes be given a crown for his services to Athens, its main purpose is to attack Demosthenes. Aeschines charges Ctesiphon with violations of Athenian law, but the infractions are minor, technical, and really just an excuse to discuss

Demosthenes's career and argue why he does not deserve the award. Demosthenes replies with a speech known as *On the Crown,* considered a masterpiece, and prevails in the contest.

CRITICAL RECEPTION

Numerous critics have analyzed Aeschines's speeches for his debating tactics. Charles Darwin Adams explains that he makes use of accusations, slanders, and personal attacks, much as Demosthenes does, but falls short of his rival in the area of broad statesmanship. "In the two speeches of Aeschines in which we should expect a review of the whole field of international relations during the critical period of the rise of the Macedonian power, we find nowhere any large grasp of the situation, no broad view of either Athenian or Hellenic interests, nothing statesmanlike in the discussion of policies." He believes this deficiency was largely responsible for Demosthenes gaining the advantage over Aeschines. J. F. Dobson praises *On the Embassy* overall, but is critical of its occasional vagueness and writes that sometimes "Aeschines seems to aim not at refuting but eluding the accusations." E. Badian and Julia Heskel contend that Aeschines constructed misleading chronologies in *On the Embassy* in order to deceive his audience; a similar use of the trick is explained by Edward M. Harris. Cecil W. Wooten credits Aeschines for using the simple and effective technique of enumerating his arguments in the beginning of his speech and then consistently following through on them. Despite some reservations concerning their nastier elements, critics agree that the speeches of Aeschines are superb examples of Athenian oratory.

PRINCIPAL WORKS

Against Timarchus (speech) 345 B.C.
On the Embassy (speech) 343 B.C.
Against Ctesiphon (speech) 330 B.C.

Principal English Translations

The Speeches of Aeschines (translated by C. D. Adams) 1919
Greek Orations (translated by W. Robert Connor) 1966
Aeschines (translated by Chris Carey) 2000
Aeschines: Against Timarchos (translated by Nick Fisher) 2001

CRITICISM

J. F. Dobson (essay date 1919)

SOURCE: "Aeschines," in *The Greek Orators,* Books for Libraries Press, 1967, pp. 163-98.

[*In the following excerpt, originally published in 1919, Dobson offers an overview of Aeschines's life, including evaluations of his public character, personality, and oratorical style.*]

1. LIFE

Aeschines was for twenty years a bitter enemy of Demosthenes. This enmity was perhaps the chief interest in his life; at any rate it is the dominant motive of his extant speeches. Demosthenes on his side could not afford to despise an enemy whose biting wit and real gift of eloquence assured him an attentive hearing, whether in the courts or before the ecclesia, and thus gave him an influence which the vagueness of his political views and the instability of his personal character could never entirely dissipate. Aeschines had no constructive policy, but he had just the talents which are requisite for the leader of a captious and malicious opposition. To the fact of the long-maintained hostility between these two men we owe a good deal of first-hand information about each of them, both as regards public and private life. It is true that we cannot accept without reservation the statements and criticisms made by either speaker about his rival; but in many cases they agree about facts, though they put different interpretations on them, and so, with care, we may arrive at a substratum of truth.

Aeschines was born about 390 B.C.[1] His father Atrometus, an Athenian citizen of pure descent,[2] was exiled by the Thirty, and fled to Corinth, with his wife. He served for some time as a mercenary soldier in Asia, and finally returned to Athens, where he kept a school. His wife, Glaucothea, filled some minor religious office, initiating the neophytes in certain mysteries, apparently connected with Orphism. Aeschines seems to have helped both his parents in their work, if we may suppose that there is a grain of truth mixed with the malice of Demosthenes:

> 'You used to fill the ink-pots, sponge the benches, and sweep the schoolroom, like a slave, not like a gentleman's son. When you grew up you helped your mother in her initiations, reciting the formulas, and making yourself generally useful. All night long you were wrapping the celebrants in fawn-skins, preparing their drink-offerings, smearing them with clay and bran,' etc.[3]

The whole of the description from which the foregoing passage is taken is an obvious caricature, and its chief value is to show that Demosthenes, if circumstances had not made him a statesman, might have been a successful writer of mediocre comedy; but it seems to point to the fact that Aeschines' parents were in humble circumstances, that he himself had a hard life as a boy, and did not enjoy the usual opportunities of obtaining the kind of education desirable for a statesman.[4] After this, at an age when other aspirants to public life would have been studying under teachers of rhetoric, he was forced to earn his living. He was first clerk to some minor officials, then an actor—according to Demosthenes he played small parts in an inferior company, and lived chiefly on the figs and olives with which the spectators pelted him.[5] He also served as a hoplite, and, by his own account, distinguished himself at Mantinea and Tamynae. In 357 B.C. he obtained political employment, first under Aristophon of Azenia, then under Eubulus, and later we find him acting as clerk of the ecclesia.

He married into a respectable family about 350 B.C., and in 348 B.C. he first appears in a position of public trust, being appointed a member of the embassy to Megalopolis in Arcadia. On this occasion he went out admittedly as an opponent of Philip, but came back a partisan of peace. The reasons for this change of view will be discussed later. His own explanation, that he realized war to be impracticable, is reasonable in itself.[6] Two years later he was associated with Demosthenes in the famous embassies to Philip, which, after serious delays, resulted in the unsatisfactory peace of Philocrates. The peace was pronounced by Demosthenes to be unworthy of Athens,[7] though he urged that, good or bad, it must be upheld; and besides uttering insinuations against the conduct of Aeschines as an ambassador, he prepared to prosecute him for betraying his trust by taking bribes from Philip. He associated with himself as a prosecutor one Timarchus. Aeschines prepared a counter-stroke. He prosecuted Timarchus on the ground that he was a person of notorious immorality, and, as such, debarred from speaking in public. Timarchus appears to have been found guilty. In 343 B.C. Demosthenes brought the action in which his speech *de Falsa Legatione* and that of Aeschines bearing the same title were delivered, and Aeschines was acquitted by the rather small majority of thirty votes. In the next year Aeschines prepared for reprisals, but when on the point of impeaching Demosthenes he in his turn was thwarted by a counter-move on his rival's part.[8]

In 339 B.C. Aeschines was a *pylagorus* at the Amphictyonic Council, and an inflammatory speech which he made there led to the outbreak of the Sacred War.

In 337 B.C., the year after the battle of Chaeronea, the proposal of Ctesiphon to confer a crown on Demosthenes for his services to Athens gave Aeschines a new weapon with which to strike at his enemy. He impeached Ctesiphon for illegality. The case was not actually tried till 330 B.C., when Aeschines, failing to obtain a fifth of the votes, was fined a thousand drachmae, and, being unable or unwilling to pay, went into exile. He retired to Asia Minor, and lived either in Ephesus or Rhodes. He is said by Plutarch to have spent the rest of his life as a professional Sophist, that is to say, no doubt, as a teacher of rhetoric; but we have no further information about his life or the manner or date of his death.

2. PUBLIC CHARACTER

Aeschines cannot be considered as a statesman, since he had no definite policy. He was, as he admitted himself, an opportunist. 'Both individual and state,' he says, 'must shift their ground according to change of circumstances, and aim at what is best for the time'; and though he claims to be 'the adviser of the greatest of all cities,' he never had in public matters any higher principle than this following of the line of least resistance.

It is necessary, however, to consider whether he was actually the corrupt politician that Demosthenes makes him out to be.

Athenian opinion with regard to corrupt practices was less strict than ours; Hyperides admits that there are various degrees of guiltiness in the matter of receiving bribes; the worst offence is to receive bribes from improper quarters, *i.e.* from an enemy of the State, and to the detriment of the State.[9]

This principle implies a corollary that to receive bribes for doing one's duty and acting in the best interests of one's country is a venial offence, if indeed it is an offence at all; in which case a man's guilt or innocence may be a matter for his individual conscience to determine.

Demosthenes definitely accused Aeschines of changing his policy in consequence of bribes received from Philip. It is known that at the beginning of his public life he was an opponent of Macedon, and we have his own account of his conversion on the occasion of the embassy to Megalopolis:

> 'You reproach me for the speech which I made, as an envoy, before ten thousand people in Arcadia; you say that I have changed sides, you abject creature, who were nearly branded as a deserter. The truth is that during the war I tried to the best of my ability to unite the Arcadians and the rest of the Greeks against Philip; but when I found that nobody would give help to Athens, but some were waiting to see what happened and others were marching against us, and the orators in the city were using the war as a means of meeting their daily expenses, I admit that I advised the people to come to terms with Philip, and make the peace which you, who have never drawn a sword, now say is disgraceful, though I say that it is far more honourable than the war.'[10]

After the conclusion of the peace of Philocrates the accusations were more definite. Demosthenes asserts that Aeschines had private interviews with Philip when on the second embassy, and that for his services he received certain lands in Boeotia;[11] he recurs to this charge in the *de Corona*, many years later. Aeschines does not deny or even mention this charge either in the speech ***On the Embassy*** or in the accusation of Ctesiphon. Demosthenes, having, apparently, little direct evidence, tries to establish his case by emphasizing the relations of Aeschines with the traitor Philocrates; but this is a weak argument, for though Aeschines at one time boasted of these relations, on a later occasion he repudiated them, and even ventured to rank Demosthenes himself with Philocrates.[12] Perhaps we should attach more importance to the other fact urged by Demosthenes, that Aeschines from time to time urged the city to accept Philip's vague promises of goodwill; but before we condemn him on this ground we must recollect that Isocrates, a man of far greater intelligence than Aeschines, and of undoubted honesty, had come so completely under the spell of Philip's personality as to place a thorough belief in the sincerity of his professions.[13] Aeschines may have been duped in the same manner.

But the most severe condemnation of Aeschines' policy is contained in his own speeches.

During a visit to the Macedonian army in Phocis he was guilty of a gross piece of bad taste by joining with Philip in dancing the paean to celebrate the defeat of Phocis. He admits the charge, and maintains that it was even a proper thing to do.[14] His conduct at the Amphictyonic Council was far more serious.[15] He was invited to make a speech, and as he began, was rudely interrupted by a Locrian of Amphissa. In revenge it 'occurred to him' to recall the impiety of the Amphissians in occupying the Cirrhaean plain. He caused to be read aloud the curse pronounced after the first Sacred War, and by recalling the forgotten events of past generations worked up his audience to such a pitch of excitement that on the following morning—for it was too late to take action that night—the whole population of Delphi marched down to Cirrha, destroyed the harbour buildings, and set fire to the town. Though this action undoubtedly plunged Greece into an Amphictyonic War, Aeschines, quite regardless of the awful consequences, can only dwell upon the remarkable effects of his own oratory.

3. PERSONALITY

Something of the personal characteristics of Aeschines may be gathered from his own writings and those of Demosthenes. He must have been a man of dignified presence, for even if he only played minor parts, as Demosthenes so frequently asserts, he acted, on occasion, in good company, as his enemy, in an unguarded moment, admitted. The conditions under which Greek tragedy was performed required a majestic bearing even in a tritagonist, and the taunt of Demosthenes, who calls him 'a noble statue,' makes it certain that Aeschines did not fall short of these requirements.[16] The words of Demosthenes probably imply that the dignity was overdone, that the statuesque pose of the ex-actor appeared pompous and exaggerated in a law-court. Aeschines himself condemned the use of excited gestures by orators. He urged the necessity of restraint, and often insisted that an orator should, while speaking, hold his hand within his robe.[17] This declared prejudice on his part gave Demosthenes his opportunity for a neat retort—'You should keep your hand there, not when you are speaking, but when you go on an embassy.'[18] On this occasion Demosthenes scored a point, but where wit and repartee were in question, the honours generally rested with Aeschines.

Another striking characteristic of Aeschines was his magnificent voice, which he used with practised skill; Demosthenes, who had serious natural disabilities as a speaker, envied him bitterly, and in consequence was always trying to ridicule his delivery. Conscious, no doubt, of his natural advantages, to which Demosthenes had once paid a more or less sincere tribute, Aeschines was apparently unmoved by these taunts; but he seems to have been deeply injured when Demosthenes compared him to the Sirens, whose voices charm men to their destruction. His indignation can find no repartee; he can only expostulate that the charge is indecent, and even if it were true, Demosthenes is not a fit man to bring it; only a man of deeds would be a worthy accuser; his rival is nothing but a bundle of words. Here, recovering himself a little, he delivers himself of the idea that Demosthenes is as empty as a flute—no good for anything if you take away the mouthpiece.

In the case of other orators I have laid but little stress on personal characteristics, because as a rule the orator must be judged apart from his qualities as a man. In considering Isaeus, for instance—an extreme case, certainly—personal qualities and peculiarities are of no importance at all. But so many personal traits appear in the writings of Aeschines that we cannot afford to neglect them; they form important data for our estimate of him, both as a speaker and a public character. There is some excuse, then, for dealing at greater length with his personality than with that of any other of the Attic orators. The question of his public morality has already to some extent been discussed;[19] an examination of his more private qualities may possibly throw further light on the question of his culpability.

He was, as we saw, to some extent a self-made man; he had at least risen far above the station in which he was born. All through his speeches we find traces of his pride in the position and the culture which he has attained—his *vanité de parvenu,* as M. Croiset styles it. He is proud of his education, and boasts of it to excess, not realizing that he thus lays himself open to the charge of having missed the best that education can give. Demosthenes is just, though on the side of severity:

> 'What right have you,' he asks, 'to speak of education? No man who really had received a liberal education would ever talk about himself in such a tone as you do; he would have the modesty to blush if any one else said such things about him; but people who have missed a proper education, as you have, and are stupid enough to pretend that they possess it, only succeed in offending their hearers when they talk about it, and fail completely to produce the desired impression.'[20]

Aeschines considered . . . want of education, almost as a cardinal sin, and could never conceive that he himself was guilty of it. He displays his learning by quotations from the poets, which are sometimes, it must be admitted, very appropriate to his argument, and by references to mythology and legend, which are sometimes frigid. His use of history betrays a rather superficial knowledge of the subject; it is hardly probable that he had studied Thucydides, for instance. Still, he possessed a fair portion of learning; what leads him astray is really his lack of taste. He is at his best in the use of quotation when he adduces the lines of Hesiod on the man whose guilt involves a whole city in his own ruin—the passage will be quoted later.[21] The verses give a real sting to his denunciations, and the opinion which he expresses on the educational influence of poetry is both solemn and sincere. But he cannot keep to this level. His much boasted education results generally in an affectation of a sort of artificial propriety in action and language, and a profession of prudery which is really foreign to his nature. He professes an admiration for the self-restraint of public speakers in Solon's time, and during the greatness of the republic, and speaks with disgust of Timarchus, who 'threw off his cloak and performed a *pancration* naked in the assembly.'[22] In the opening of the same speech he makes a strong claim to the merit of 'moderation'; in the prosecution of Timarchus his moderation consists in hinting at certain abominable practices, which he does not describe by name.

> 'I pray you, Gentlemen, to forgive me if, when forced to speak of certain practices which are not honourable by nature, but are the established habits of the defendant, I am led away into using any expression which resembles the actions of Timarchus. . . . The blame should rest on him rather than on me. It will be impossible to avoid all use of such expressions, . . . but I shall try to avoid it as far as possible.'[23]

Notice again the hypocritical reticence or 'omission' (*paraleipsis*)—a rhetorical device familiar to readers of Cicero—which insinuates what it cannot prove:

> 'Mark, men of Athens, how moderate I intend to be in my attack on Timarchus. I omit all the abuses of which he was guilty as a boy. So far as I am concerned they may be no more valid than, say, the actions of the Thirty, the events before the archonship of Euclides, or any other limitation which may ever have been established.'[24]

> 'I hear that this creature' (an associate of Timarchus) 'has committed certain abominable offences, which, I swear by Zeus of Olympus, I should never dare to mention in your presence; he was not ashamed of doing these things, but I could not bear to live if I had even named them to you explicitly.'[25]

In spite of the prosecutor's modesty, particular references to the offences of Timarchus are frequent enough throughout the speech; the reticence is assumed for the purpose of insinuating that only a tithe of the offences are really named. The whole tone of the speech, therefore, is disingenuous and dishonest.

On the other hand, the orator's tribute to the judges' respectability is at times overdrawn. They are informed that 'Timarchus used to spend his days in a gambling-house, where there is a pit in which cock-fights are held, and games of chance are played—I imagine there are some of you who have seen the things I refer to, or if not, have heard of them.'[26] No large assembly could ever take quite seriously such a compliment to its innocence, and it must have been meant as a lighter touch to relieve the dark hues

around it. Such playful sallies are not infrequent, and, like this one, are often quite inoffensive.[27]

A far more serious arraignment of the character of Aeschines is brought by Blass, who, having made a very careful study of the speech against Timarchus, finds a strong presumption, on chronological grounds, that the majority of the charges are false. It is certainly remarkable that the charges of immorality rest almost entirely on the statements of the prosecutor. He expresses an apprehension that Misgolas, a most important witness, will either refuse to give evidence altogether, or will not tell the truth. To meet trouble half-way like this is a very serious confession of weakness, which is confirmed by the orator's further comment on the state of the case. He has, he says, other witnesses, but 'if the defendant and his supporters persuade them also to refuse to give evidence—I think they will not persuade them; at any rate not all of them— there is one thing which they never can do, and that is to abolish the truth and the reputation which Timarchus bears in the city, a reputation which I have not secured for him; he has earned it for himself. For the life of a respectable man should be so spotless as not to admit even the suspicion of offence.'[28]

Blass considers that the minor charges, directed against the reckless extravagance with which Timarchus had dissipated his inherited property, are better substantiated; but these alone would have been hardly enough to secure his condemnation.

Against Blass' theories we must set the little that we know about the facts. Timarchus was certainly condemned and disfranchised.[29] Now an Athenian jury was not infallible, and whether in an ordinary court of justice or, as for this case, in the high court of the ecclesia, political convictions might triumph over partiality; nevertheless, a man who was innocent of the charge specifically brought against him, especially if he had not only committed no real political offence, but had played no part in political affairs—a man, moreover, who had the powerful influence of Demosthenes behind him—might reasonably expect to have a fair chance of being acquitted. Aeschines himself was acquitted a few years later on a political charge, though his political conduct required a good deal of explanation, and he had all the weight of Demosthenes not for him, but against him.

Aeschines might well feel a legitimate pride at the high position to which he had climbed from a comparatively humble starting-point; but to reiterate the reasons for this pride is a display of vanity. He likes to talk of himself as 'the counsellor of this the greatest of cities,' as the friend of Alexander and Philip. 'Demosthenes,' he says, 'brings up against me the fact of my friendship with Alexander.'[30] Demosthenes retorts that he has done nothing of the sort. 'I reproach you, you say, with Alexander's friendship? How in the world could you have gained it or deserved it? I should never be so mad as to call you the friend of either Philip or Alexander, unless we are to say that our harvesters and hirelings of other sorts are "friends" and "guests" of those who have hired their services.'[31]

And again—'On what just or reasonable grounds could Aeschines, the son of Glaucothea, the tambourine-player, have as his host, or his friend, or his acquaintance, Philip?'[32] Demosthenes' estimate of the position is probably the truer one; Aeschines, with all his cleverness, was not the man, as Isocrates was, to meet princes on terms of equality.

His vanity about his speeches and the effect which they produced is attested by the various occasions on which he quotes them, or refers to them. He gives a summary of a speech which he made as an envoy to Philip;[33] a speech delivered before the ecclesia is epitomized;[34] a speech made before 'thousands and thousands of Arcadians' is mentioned.[35] The notorious speech delivered to the Amphictyons is quoted at some length,[36] and its disastrous effect described, the speaker's delight in his own powers blinding him completely to the serious and far-reaching consequences of his criminal indiscretion.

His private life, in spite of some damaging admissions in the *Timarchus,* seems to have been satisfactory according to Athenian standards. Demosthenes accused him of offering a gross insult to an Olynthian lady. Whether or not the statement was an entire fiction, we are not in a position to judge. Aeschines indignantly denies the charge, and asserts that the Athenian people, when it was made, refused to listen to it, in view of their confirmed respect for his own character:

> 'Only consider the folly, the vulgarity of the man, who has invented so monstrous a lie against me as the one about the Olynthian woman. You hissed him down in the middle of the story, for the slander was quite out of keeping with my character, and you knew me well.'[37]

Whatever his origin may have been, he was not ashamed of it. He more than once refers with affectionate respect to his father.[38] His love for his wife and children is on one occasion ingeniously introduced in an eloquent passage to influence the feelings of his hearers. This use of 'pathos' was familiar enough to Greek audiences, but Aeschines shows his originality by the form in which he puts the appeal—aiming directly at the feelings of individual hearers for their own families, rather than asking the assembly collectively to pity the victims of misfortune:

> 'I have by my wife, the daughter of Philodemus and sister of Philon and Echecrates, three children, a daughter and two sons. I have brought them here with the rest of my family in order that I may put one question and prove one point to my judges; and this I shall now proceed to do. I ask you, men of Athens, whether you think it likely that, in addition to sacrificing my country and the companionship of my friends and my right to a share in the worship and the burial-place of my fathers, I could betray to Philip these whom I love more than anything in the world, and value his friendship higher than their safety? Have I ever become so

far the slave of base pleasures? Have I ever yet done anything so base for the sake of money? No; it is not Macedon that makes a man good or bad, but nature; and when we return from an embassy we are the same men that we were when you sent us out.'[39]

Lastly, he could speak of himself with dignity, as in the passage, quoted above,[40] where he rebuts a charge against his private character, and in the following:

> 'My silence, Demosthenes, is due to the moderation of my life; I am content with a little; I have no base desire for greatness; and so my silence or my speech is due to careful deliberation, not to necessity imposed by habits of extravagance. You, I imagine, are habitually silent when you have got what you want; when you have spent it, you raise your voice.'[41]

4. STYLE

The vocabulary of Aeschines consists mostly of words in ordinary use which require no comment. Though he was a great admirer of poetry, his ordinary writing does not display more poetical or unusual words than that of any other orator.

The difference between his style and that of a writer such as Lysias is, essentially, a difference not of vocabulary but of tone; the tones of Aeschines are raised. He tends to use words which are stronger than they need be, to be 'angry' when only surprise is called for; to be 'excessively indignant' when a moderate resentment would meet the case, to 'detest' when to dislike would be enough. He makes unnecessary appeals to the gods more frequently than any other orator except Demosthenes. Exaggeration is part of the secret of his *splendor verborum,* as the Roman critic described it; but by far the greatest part is his instinct for using quite ordinary words in the most effective combinations. His best passages, if analysed, contain hardly any words which are at all out of the common, and yet their vigour and dignity are unquestionable.[42] The ancients, however, denied purity of diction to Aeschines, perhaps on account of the characteristics just described.

He is, as Blass observes, occasionally obscure; that is, it is possible to find sentences which are not quite easy to understand; but on the whole these are very rare. No writer, even a Lysias, can be at all times perfectly lucid.[43] As a rule Aeschines is as simple in the construction of his sentences as he is in the arrangement of his speeches, and he is much easier to understand than, for instance, Demosthenes.

He has not the consummate grace and terseness which critics admire as the chief beauties of Lysias; sometimes unnecessary repetitions of a word are to be found, sometimes two synonyms are used where one word would suffice; but such repetitions often give us lucidity, though at the expense of strict form, and the accumulation of synonyms increases the emphasis. Only the great artist, who is perfectly confident that he has found the right word to express adequately his whole meaning in exactly the right way, can afford to do without all superfluous strokes. Aeschines is not a perfect artist in language; he aims not at artistic beauty but effect, to which style is nothing but a subordinate aid. The composition of artistic prose is, for him, far from being an end in itself.

His speeches were designed not to be read by literary experts, but to be delivered from the platform, and he aimed, not at pleasing the critics' taste but at working on the passions of the ordinary citizen. Some of his most important orations were not written at all, though he probably preserved notes of them,[44] and the three which he did write out in full were preserved not for their literary beauty but for their subject-matter. The time for the rhetoric of culture was past; the course of events required the kind of oratory that would stir men to action. As to the effectiveness of his speeches, there can be no doubt. We know—on his own authority, certainly; but it has never been disputed—how his harangue moved the Amphictyons; and we know that, without any conspicuous moral qualities, with no advantages from family influence and no definite political principles, he became a power in Athens solely by virtue of his eloquence.

Aeschines varies the length of his sentences very considerably; some of them are long, and consist of strings of participial and relative clauses. These, however, occur mostly in narrative passages, where such discursive style is excusable: for instance, the long sentences in the *de Legatione,* §§ 26-27, §§ 75-77, and §115, contain reports of Aeschines' own earlier speeches. The first of these (§§ 26-27) is monotonous owing to the series of genitives absolute which compose an inordinately long protasis, the main verb not occurring till near the end of the sentence, and then being followed by another genitive clause.

A long sentence early in the **Ctesiphon** gives a *résumé* of the circumstances by which the orator is impelled to speak; the clauses are mostly connected by *kaí,* though all depend on a relative at the beginning. No skill is displayed in the structure of such sentences, and their possible length is limited only by the amount of water in the *clepsydra.* Up to a certain length, they are forcible, but if the limit is exceeded, the effect is lost, for the point which the orator wishes to make is too long deferred, since the main clause, containing the statement which the preceding relative clauses illustrate or explain, is not reached until the heavy accumulation of relative clauses has wearied the perception.

In general, however, Aeschines is moderate in length; his sentences, on the average, are shorter than those of Isocrates, and he tacitly adheres to the rule that a period should not be so long that it cannot be uttered in one breath.

Though not pedantic, he was far from being without a taste for composition. In all the speeches we find examples of the deliberate avoidance of hiatus, and in the **de Legatione** he bestowed some care on the matter.

The avoidance may generally, though not always, be traced in an unusual order of words.[45] Examples of harsh hiatus are rare, though there are many unimportant instances. Quite apart from theoretical rules, a good orator will instinctively avoid awkward combinations of letters, for euphony is necessary for fluent speaking. Aeschines, secure in the possession of a perfect delivery, might admit sounds which Isocrates and other theorists considered harsh; it was with practical declamation that he was concerned.

The use of the rhetorical 'figures' is a prominent characteristic of Aeschines. The verbal contrasts which Gorgias and the Sophists affected, many of which seem to us so frigid and tedious, have too much honour from Aeschines; for instance, the purely formal antithesis—'He mentions the names of those whose bodies he has never seen,'[46] where the sound of the jingle . . . is more important than the sense. The effect of such 'like endings' (*homoeoteleute*) cannot as a rule be reproduced, though sometimes a play upon words will indicate it: . . . 'he has changed, not his habits, but only his habitation.'[47] In such assonance there is an undoubted aiming at comic effect. A forcible repetition of words is found in such sentences as the following: 'What I saw, I reported to you as I saw it; what I heard, as I heard it; now what was it that I saw and heard about Cersobleptes? I saw . . .' etc.[48] Repetitions of this and similar kinds seem to break at times from the speaker's control, and pass all measure.[49]

Aeschines does not seem to have paid any attention to rhythmical writing; his style is too free to be bound by unnecessary restrictions; verses and metrical passages occur sporadically, but they are rare. He seems to have fallen into them by accident, since they occur in positions where no special point is marked by an unusual rhythm.[50]

Direct quotations of poetry, for which he had a great liking, are, on the other hand, very frequent. No other orator, except Lycurgus, is comparable to him in this respect, and Lycurgus uses his power of quotation with much less force than Aeschines, who often employs it aptly. He gives us the impression that serious religious conviction is at the back of his quotation from Hesiod:

> 'Often the whole of a city must suffer for one man's sin.'[51]

In other cases the quotations are excessively long and, like those of Lycurgus, have hardly any bearing on the point.

His metaphors are sometimes vivid and well chosen—'to strip the city like a vineyard'; 'it was dinned into everybody's ears.' Some of the most forcible occur in passages which purport to be quotations or paraphrases of Demosthenes: *e.g.* 'to bridle' the war-party; 'to sew up Philip's mouth.'[53] These are probably caricatures of Demosthenes' daring phrases.

Turning now from the consideration of the materials to the finished product, we find that Aeschines can attain a high level of style. His denunciation of the sharp practices prevailing in the course of his day is impressive; we know that he is speaking the truth, and he does not make the mistake of exaggerating. The seriousness is relieved, but not impaired, by the light thread of sarcasm which runs through the whole fabric:

'The hearing of such cases, as my father used to tell me, was conducted in a way very different from ours. The judges were much more severe with those who proposed illegal measures than the prosecutor was, and they would often interrupt the clerk and ask him to read over again the laws and the decree; and the proposers of illegal measures were found guilty not if they had ridden over all the laws, but if they had subverted one single clause. The present procedure is ridiculous beyond words; the clerk reads the illegal decree, and the judges, as if they were listening to an incantation or something that did not concern them, keep their minds fixed on something else. And already, through the devices of Demosthenes, you are admitting a disgraceful practice; you have allowed the course of justice to be changed, for the prosecutor is on his defence, and the defendant conducts his prosecution; and the judges sometimes forget the matter of which they are called on to be arbiters, and are compelled to vote on questions which they ought not to be judging. The defendant, if he ever refers to the facts at all, tells you, not that his proposal was legal, but that somebody else has proposed similar measures before his time, and has been acquitted.'[53]

The following passage has been many times pointed out, and justly, as a fine example of the higher style of Aeschines' rhetoric. Taken apart from its context, and without any consideration of the truth of the insinuations which it makes, it is a notable piece of 'pathetic' pleading. The Romans, with a fondness for epigrammatic contrast, attributed to Aeschines more of sound and less of strength than to Demosthenes. This is true if we regard their works as a whole; but in isolated passages like this, Aeschines finds his level with the best of Attic orators:

'Thebes, our neighbour Thebes, in the course of a single day has been torn from the midst of Greece; justly, perhaps, for in general she followed a mistaken policy; yet it was not human judgment but divine ordinance that led her into error. And the poor Lacedaemonians, who only interfered in this matter originally in connection with the seizure of the sanctuary, they who once could claim to be the leaders of the Greeks, must now be sent up to Alexander to offer themselves as hostages and advertise their disaster; they and their country must submit to any treatment on which he decides, and be judged by the clemency of the conqueror who was the injured party. And our city, the common asylum of all Greeks, to whom formerly embassies used to come from Greece to obtain their safety from us, city by city, is struggling now not for the leadership of the Greeks but for the very soil of her fatherland. And this has befallen us since Demosthenes took the direction of our policy. A passage in Hesiod contains a solemn warning appropriate to such a case. He speaks, I believe, with the intention of educating the people, and advising the cities not to take to themselves evil leaders.

I shall quote the lines, for I conceive that we learn by

heart the maxims of the poets in childhood, so that in manhood we may apply them:—

'"Often the whole of a city must suffer for one man's sin,
Who plotteth infatuate counsel, and walketh in evil ways,
On such God sendeth destruction, by famine and wasting plague,
And razeth their walls and armies, and shatters their ships at sea."'[54]

We know that Aeschines took education very seriously—more seriously, in fact, than anything else—and his reference here to the educative influence of the poets gives proof of his earnestness, which may have been a transient emotion, but was, for the moment, a strong one.

Setting apart a few such serious passages, Aeschines is at his best when he is directly accusing Demosthenes. His attacks are nearly always characterized by a humorous manner which does not make them any the less forcible, and they generally contain just enough truth to make their malice effective. The fact that Aeschines himself had too deep a respect for the truth to be prodigal in the use of it does not diminish the virulence of his attack on his rival's veracity, while any question as to the exactitude of his statements would be drowned in the laugh that followed the concluding paragraph:

'The fellow has one characteristic peculiarly his own when other impostors tell a lie, they try to speak vaguely and indefinitely, for fear of being convicted of falsehood; but when Demosthenes seeks to impose upon you, he first of all enforces his lie with an oath, invoking eternal ruin on himself; secondly, though he knows that a thing never can happen at all, he dares to speak with a nice calculation of the day when it is going to happen; he utters the names of people whose faces he has never seen, thus cheating you into hearing him, and assuming an air of truthfulness; and so he thoroughly merits your detestation, since, being such a scoundrel as he is, he discredits the usual proofs of honesty.

After talking in this way he gives the clerk a decree to read—something longer than the *Iliad,* and more empty than the speeches he makes or the life he has led; full of hopes that can never be realized, and armies that will never be mustered.'[55]

The pleasing custom followed by the orators of antiquity, whether Greek or Roman, of defiling the graves of the ancestors of their political opponents, and defaming their private lives, can be as well exemplified from Aeschines as from his rival. Aeschines shows no great originality in particular terms of abuse—Dinarchus has a greater variety of offensive words—but the following extract from his circumstantial fictions about Demosthenes is more effective, because more moderate in tone, than the incredible insults with which the latter described the family circumstances and the career of Aeschines:[56]

'So, on his grandfather's account, he must be an enemy of the people, for you condemned his ancestors to death; but through his mother's family he is a Scythian, a barbarian, though he speaks Greek; so that even his wickedness is not of native growth. And what of his daily life? Once a trierarch, he appeared again as a speech-writer, having in some ridiculous fashion thrown away his patrimony; but as in this profession he came under suspicion of disclosing the speeches to the other side, he bounded up on to the tribunal; and though he took great sums of money from his administration, he saved very little for himself. Now, however, the king's treasure has drowned his extravagance—but even that will not be enough; for no conceivable wealth can survive evil habits.

Worst of all, he makes a living not out of his private sources of income, but out of your danger.'[57]

But he is really at his best where some slight slip on the part of his opponent gives him the opportunity of magnifying a trivial incident into importance. In the following caricature the indecision of Demosthenes is better expressed by the vacillating language thrust into his mouth than it could have been by the most eloquent description in the third person:

'While I was in the middle of this speech, Demosthenes shouted out at the top of his voice—all our fellow-envoys can support my statement—for in addition to his other vices he is a partisan of Boeotia. What he said was something to this purpose:—"This fellow is full of a spirit of turbulence and recklessness; I admit that I am made of softer stuff, and fear dangers afar off. However, I would forbid him to raise disturbances between the States, for I think that the right course is for us ambassadors not to meddle with anything. Philip is marching to Thermopylae; I cover my face. No man will judge me because Philip takes up arms; I shall be judged for any unnecessary word that I utter, or for any action in which I exceed my instructions."'[58]

The failure of Demosthenes to rise to the occasion when he had the opportunity of delivering an impressive speech before Philip, during the first embassy, forms the groundwork for excellent comedy on the part of Aeschines. Demosthenes, by his rival's account, was usually so intolerable as a companion that his colleagues refused to stay in the same lodging with him whenever another was obtainable; but he had found opportunity to impress them with his own sense of his importance as an orator. These professions are well indicated in a few words. The account of his failure, of Philip's patronizing encouragement, of the fiasco in which the whole proceedings terminated, are sketched with a delicate malice that must have made any defence or explanation impossible; indeed Demosthenes seems to have attempted no reply:

'When these and other speeches had been made, it was Demosthenes' turn to play his part in the embassy, and everybody was most attentive, expecting to hear a speech of exceptional power; for, as we gathered later, even Philip and his companions had heard the report of his ambitious promises. When everybody was thus prepared to listen to him, the brute gave utterance to some sort of obscure exordium, half-dead with nervous-ness, and having made a little progress over the surface of the subject he suddenly halted and hesitated, and at last completely lost his way. Philip, seeing the state he was in, urged him to take courage, and not to think he had failed because, like an actor, he had forgotten his part; but to try quietly and little by little to recollect himself and make the speech as he intended it. But he, having once been flurried, and lost the thread of his written speech, could not recover himself again; he tried once more, and failed in the same way. A silence followed, after which the herald dismissed the embassy.'[59]

Aeschines not only excelled in this class of circumstantial caricature, but he could win a laugh by a single phrase. It is well known that Midias, after various discreditable quarrels, put the final touch to his insolence by a public assault on Demosthenes, whose face he slapped in the theatre. Demosthenes on many occasions made capital out of this assault; which fact inspires the remark of Aeschines, 'His face is his fortune.' Of his dexterity in repartee a single instance may be quoted: Demosthenes, in an outburst of indignation, had suggested that the court should refuse to be impressed by the oratory of a man who was notoriously corrupt, but should rather be prejudiced by it against him.[60] Aeschines, catching at the words, rather than the spirit, retorted, 'Though you, gentlemen, have taken a solemn oath to give an impartial hearing to both parties, he has dared to urge you not to listen to the voice of the defendant.'[61]

5. TREATMENT OF SUBJECTS: GENERAL ESTIMATE

During his tenure of the office of . . . clerk to the ecclesia—Aeschines must have gained a thorough knowledge of the procedure of that assembly, and of law. This comes out in his general treatment of his subjects, and particularly in his legal arguments, which are clear and convincing. In the speech against Ctesiphon, where the irregularities of the proceedings about Demosthenes' crown gave him a good subject for argument, he makes out a very strong case.

In the structure of his speeches he follows a chronological order. He realized well that the style of his eloquence lent itself naturally to bright and attractive narrative. His versatility saves him from becoming tedious; at one time he can speak with a noble solemnity which reminds M. Croiset of the eloquence of the pulpit,[62] at another, the lightness of his touch almost conceals the bitterness of his sentiments and the seriousness of his purpose.[63] He can speak of himself with dignity, of his family with true feeling; careful argument succeeds to lucid narrative; crisp interrogation, reinforced by powerful sarcasm, to masterly exposition. He can awaken his hearers' interest by an indication of the course which he intends to follow, and this interest is sustained by all the resources of an eloquence which, though at times sophistical, and though disfigured by occasional blemishes, has more of naturalness and shows less traces of scholastic elaboration, than that of any other great orator. He is abler than Andocides, more varied than Lysias, more alive than Isaeus.

His natural gifts place him above Lycurgus, though our insight into the latter's high character gives him a powerful claim to our consideration. Blass ranks him below Hyperides, but a study of the lighter passages in Aeschines leads us to believe that, had he turned his attention to private cases, he might have equalled or surpassed that polished orator on his own chosen ground. The unanimous judgment of ancient and modern times places him far below Demosthenes, who stands apart without a rival; but in one quality, at least, he surpasses the paragon. Demosthenes, according to the opinion of Longinus, is apt to make his hearers laugh not with him but at him;[64] Aeschines never turns the laugh against himself.

Aeschines is perhaps less read than he deserves; he has suffered from historical bias, and the prevalent contempt for his qualities as a statesman has led to an undue disregard of his virtues as an orator. There is nothing unfamiliar in this judgment; other orators have suffered in the same way at the hands of prejudiced historians.[65]

It is interesting to read the account of Aeschines in Blass' *Attische Beredsamkeit;* the gifted scholar apparently starts with a strong prejudice against his author, and is almost too ready to insist on his faults; but time after time he is obliged to admit the existence of positive merits, and in the end he seems, almost against his will, to have been forced to modify his judgment; while the care and impartiality with which he has detailed all points, good and bad alike, provides material for a more favourable estimate such as that of Croiset.

6. CONTENTS OF SPEECHES

A short account of the subject-matter of the three speeches may conclude this chapter.

1. AGAINST TIMARCHUS.

The speech begins (§§ 1-2) with a statement of the prosecutor's motives; § 3 states the position which he intends to assume—that Timarchus, by breaking the laws, has made the bringing of this action inevitable. Laws relating to the matter are read and fully discussed (§§ 4-36).

This preliminary legal statement, apart from the particular case, puts the prosecution on a sounder footing than if the speech had begun at once with the narrative.

§§ 37-76. *The first charge* (immorality). Narrative of the private life of Timarchus, interspersed with evidence and argument as to his political disabilities.

§§ 77-93. Examples of disability imposed on other grounds. Precedents for a verdict in accordance with general knowledge even when the evidence is defective.

§§ 94-105. *The second charge.* Timarchus is a spendthrift. Narrative and evidence about his prodigality.

§§ 106-115. *The third charge.* His corruptness in public life.

§ 116, recapitulation. §§ 117-176, anticipation of the defence.

§§ 177-195. Epilogue, announced beforehand (§ 117) as an 'exhortation to a virtuous life.' § 196, a short conclusion—'I have instructed you in the laws, I have examined the life of the defendant; I now retire, leaving the matter in your hands.'

2. ON THE EMBASSY.

Demosthenes had accused Aeschines of treason; his speech, it is to be noted, dealt really with the second embassy only, and the events in Athens subsequent to it, though he makes some reference to the third embassy, and implies that Aeschines was corrupt even before the second. He follows no chronological order, so that his story is hard to follow. Aeschines, on the other hand, has a great appearance of lucidity, treating all events in chronological order; but this is misleading, for, in order to divert attention from the period in which his conduct was questionable, he spends a disproportionate time in describing the first embassy, in connection with which no accusation is made by Demosthenes.

The exordium (§§ 1-11) contains a strong appeal for an impartial hearing. The events of the first embassy to Philip are the subject of an amusing narrative at the expense of Demosthenes (§§ 12-39); the return of the envoys and their reports, etc., occupy §§ 40-55. The same clearness does not appear in the rest of the speech. Aeschines has to make a defence on various charges brought against himself, so a plain narrative is not enough. The chief charges were that Aeschines was in the pay of Philip, and that he deceived the people as to Philip's intentions, thus leading them into actions which proved disastrous. The former charge could not be proved by Demosthenes, however strong his suspicions were; the facts relating to the peace of Philocrates and the delay in the ratification of the agreement with Philip were matters of common knowledge; it was only a question of intention. The defence of Aeschines is that he deceived the people because he was himself deceived—a confession of credulity and incompetence. The narrative is not continuous; details about the embassy to Philip, the embassy to the Arcadians, and the fate of Cersobleptes, are to some extent mixed together. Reference is also made to some specific charges, *e.g.* the case of the Olynthian woman, the speech before the Amphictyons, the singing of the paean, etc. In the two latter cases there is no defence, but an attempt at justification (§§ 55-170). The epilogue begins with an historical survey of Athenian affairs, which is stolen either from Andocides or from some popular commonplace book, and contains the usual appeal to the judges to save the speaker from his adversaries' malice.

He ends by calling on Eubulus and Phocion to speak for him. (§§ 171-178.)

Stress has been laid in these pages on the somewhat disjointed character of the sections dealing with the principal charges, and it cannot be denied that the defence is sometimes vague; that Aeschines seems to aim not at refuting but eluding the accusations. These imperfections come out on an analysis; but the speech taken as a whole is a very fine piece of advocacy, and makes the acquittal of the speaker quite intelligible.

3. AGAINST CTESIPHON.

The speech opens with an elaboration of a trite commonplace, modelled on the style of Andocides, about the vicious cleverness of the speaker's opponents and his own simple trust in the laws. Aeschines proposes to prove that the procedure of Ctesiphon was illegal, his statements false, and his action harmful. (§§ 1-8.)

First charge—'The proposal to grant a crown to Demosthenes was illegal, because Demosthenes was at the time liable to ευθυνα (§§ 9-12). All statements to the contrary notwithstanding, a consideration of the laws proves conclusively that Demosthenes was so liable.' (§§ 13-31.)

Second charge—'It was illegal for the proclamation of the crown to be made in the theatre.' (§§ 32-48.)

Third charge—'The statements on which the proposal was made, viz. that the public counsel and public actions of Demosthenes are for the best interests of the people, are false.' (§ 49.)

The first two charges are dealt with by means of legal argument, in which Aeschines, as usual, displays considerable ability. The third and longest section of the speech (§§ 49-176) is less satisfactory. The orator proposes to set aside the private life of his enemy, though he hints that many incidents might be adduced to prove its general worthlessness (§§ 51-53), and to deal only with his public policy. This he does, in chronological order and at great length. Numerous occasions are described on which the policy of Demosthenes was detrimental to Athens. The arguments with which the narrative is interspersed are often of a trivial nature, consisting sometimes of appeals to superstition, as when he tells us that troops were sent to Chaeronea, although the proper sacrifices had not been performed; and attempts to show that Demosthenes is an [àlitērios] for whose sin the whole city must suffer. Taken in detail, some of these passages are impressive; but the weakness of the whole is that Aeschines himself does not declare any serious or systematic policy. This section contains incidentally digressions, in the taste of the day, about the family and character of Demosthenes.[66]

§§ 177-190 contain some references to heroes of antiquity, by way of invidious comparison; §§ 191-202, the deterioration of procedure in the courts.[67]

§§ 203-205, recapitulation; §§ 206-212, further incrimination of Demosthenes, and §§ 213-214, of Ctesiphon. §§ 215-229, chiefly refutation of charges against Aeschines.

§§ 230-259, further general discussion of the illegality of the measure and the unworthiness of Demosthenes. The final appeal to the past—'Think you not that Themistocles and the heroes who fell at Marathon and Plataea, and the very graves of our ancestors, will groan aloud if a crown is to be granted to one who concerts with the barbarians for the ruin of Greece?' ends abruptly and grotesquely with an invocation to 'Earth and Sun and Virtue and Intelligence and Education, through which we distinguish between the noble and the base.'

It reminds us strangely of the invocations put into the mouth of Euripides by Aristophanes.[68]

Notes

1. See *Timarchus*, § 49, where Aeschines states, in 346 B.C., that he is rather over forty-five years old.

2. Aesch., *de Leg.*, § 147. Dem. (*de Cor.*, 129 *sqq.*) asserts that he was originally a slave named Tromes (*Coward*), but changed his name to Atrometus (*Dauntless*).

3. Dem., *de Cor.*, §§ 258-259. See further *infra*, p. 249.

4. However, his elder brother, Philocrates, was elected general three times in succession, and his younger brother, Aphobetus, was sent as an ambassador to the Great King.—Aesch., *de Leg.*, § 149.

5. *de Cor.*, § 262, *vide infra*, p. 249.

6. *de Leg.*, § 79; *vide infra*, p. 168.

7. See *de Pace* (*passim*) delivered in the same year.

8. Aesch., *Ctes.*, §§ 222-225. . . .

9. Hyper., *adv. Dem.*, xxiv.

10. *de Leg.*, § 79.

11. Dem., *de Falsa Leg.*, §§ 145, 166-177; *de Cor.*, § 41.

12. *Timarchus*, § 174; *Ctes.*, § 58.

13. *Supra*, p. 148.

14. *de Leg.*, § 163.

15. *Vide supra*, p. 166. . . .

16. *de Cor.*, §§ 129, 262, etc. Further, *de Falsa Leg.*, § 246. A tritagonist would ordinarily have to play the parts of kings and tyrants, who must as a rule be majestic characters. . . .

17. *Timarch.*, § 25.

18. Dem., *de Falsa Leg.*, § 252. . . .

19. *Supra*, pp. 167-170.

20. Dem., *de Cor.*, § 128. . . .

21. *Infra*, pp. 184, 187.

22. *Timarch.*, § 26. Aeschines adds a characteristically Greek touch—'his body was so horribly out of condi-

tion through his drunkenness and other excesses that decent people covered their eyes.' It was the neglect of the body, rather than the exposure of the arms and legs, which is exaggerated into 'nakedness,' that really shocked the spectators, in addition to the 'rough-and-tumble' gestures of the orator.

23. *Timarch.,* §§ 37-38.

24. *Timarch.,* § 39. [*Akuros*] is used in a double sense; the early actions of Timarchus are unratified in the sense of not proved; the actions of the Thirty are not ratified by the succeeding governments. It is a looseness of expression which does not spoil the general sense, and there is, perhaps, an implied reference to the *Amnesty,* declared after the expulsion of the Thirty. Similarly Aeschines declares an *amnesty* for all the offences of Timarchus before a certain date.

25. *Ibid.,* § 55. In § 70 there is a further apology. Cf. also § 76.

26. *Timarch.,* § 53.

27. Cf. *infra,* p. 191.

28. *Timarch.,* § 48.

29. Dem., *de Falsa Leg.,* §§ 2, 257.

30. [*Xenía*] expressing the mutual relations of host and guest, cannot be adequately translated into English.

31. *de Cor.,* § 51.

32. *Ibid.,* § 284.

33. Aesch., *de Leg.,* §§ 25-33.

34. *Ibid.,* §§ 75-78.

35. *Ibid.,* § 79.

36. *Ctes.,* §§ 119-121.

37. Aesch., *de Leg.,* § 153.

38. *E.g., de Leg.,* § 147. His esteem for his mother is expressed, *ibid.,* § 148.

39. *de Leg.,* § 152.

40. p. 178.

41. *Ctes.,* § 218. . . .

42. *E.g.* the fine passage about Thebes, *infra,* p. 186.

43. The speech of Lysias against Eratosthenes, for instance, conains many complicated sentences which are unnecessarily obscure. . . .

44. Cf. his frequent references to his speeches, *supra,* p. 177.

45. *E.g. de Leg.* . . . Blass, vol. iii. pt. 2, p. 232, notes that there is more consistent care on this point in the *de Legatione* than in the other two speeches.

46. *Ctes.,* § 99.

47. *Ibid.,* § 78.

48. *de Leg.,* § 81.

49. Cf. *Ctes.,* § 198. . . .

50. *E.g.* iambics, *Ctes.,* § 239. . . .

51. *Ctes.,* § 135.

52. *de Leg.,* §§ 110, 21.

53. *Ctes.,* §§ 192-193.

54. *Ctes.,* §§ 133-136.

55. *Ctes.,* §§ 99-100.

56. Dem., *de Cor.,* §§ 129, 259.

57. *Ctes.,* §§ 172-173.

58. *de Leg.,* §§ 106-107.

59. *de Leg.,* §§ 34-35. . . .

60. *de Falsa Leg.,* § 339.

61. Aesch., *de Leg.,* § 1.

62. *La Litt. Grecque,* iv. 643, with reference particularly to *Ctes.,* § 133 (quoted above, p. 186) and §§ 152 *sqq.*

63. *E.g.* on Demosthenes, quoted *supra,* pp. 187-188.

64. *de Sublim.,* ch. xxiv. . . .

65. Mommsen (Book v., ch. xii. pp. 609-610, Eng. ed. of 1887) could write of Cicero: 'Cicero had no conviction and no passion; he was nothing but an advocate, and not a good one.' . . . 'If there is anything wonderful in the case, it is in truth not the orations but the admiration which they excited.'

66. *E.g.,* in particular, §§ 171-176, partly quoted *supra,* p. 188.

67. Quoted *supra,* p. 185.

68. *Frogs,* 892. . . .

Charles Darwin Adams (essay date 1919)

SOURCE: An introduction to *The Speeches of Aeschines,* William Heinemann, 1919, pp. vii-xxiii.

[*In the following excerpt, Adams provides a biographical sketch of Aeschines, concentrating on his political career and his feud with Demosthenes.*]

THE LIFE OF AESCHINES

Our knowledge of the family and life of Aeschines comes from his own speeches and those of Demosthenes. The brief biographies which have come down to us are late and untrustworthy. At the time of the speech **On the Embassy** we hear of Aeschines' father as an old man of ninety-four years. He was in the court-room, and Demosthenes, speaking to a jury some of whom, at least, were likely to know something of the family, and speaking subject to contradiction by Aeschines, whose plea was to follow his, makes no serious charge against Aeschines' family. He speaks contemptuously of the poverty of the schoolmaster-father (xix. 249) and sarcastically of the mother's "harvest" from the property of the people who resorted to her "initiations and purifications" (xix. 199, 249, 281). But in the speech *On the Crown,* delivered thirteen years later, when the father was no longer alive and few of the hearers would remember the family, and when, moreover, Demosthenes, as the last speaker in the case, was not subject to contradiction by Aeschines, he gives free rein to a malignant imagination, and paints a picture of a slave-schoolmaster and a shameless harlot mother, which deserves no serious attention. From the uncontradicted statements of both orators in their speeches **On the Embassy** we gather the following facts.

Aeschines was born about 390 B.C. His father, Atrometus, had already lost his property in the Peloponnesian war, had been exiled with the rest of the democrats by the Thirty Tyrants, and had shared in the glorious enterprise of the democratic "return." The mother, Glaucothea, was sister of a successful general, Cleobulus. The children of such parents had a right to be proud both of the purity of their blood and the patriotic achievements of father and uncle. But the losses by war and exile forced the father to take up the little honoured profession of schoolmaster, while the mother, we may perhaps believe, contributed something to the support of the family by service as a priestess in some one of the secret religious cults.

We hear of three sons in the schoolmaster's family, all reaching positions of some honour in the public service. The eldest, Philochares, served under the famous Iphicrates, and was himself in 343 serving his third successive term as general. The third son, Aphobetus, had in the same year already made a record for himself as an ambassador to Persia, and had received the high honour of election as a special Commissioner of Finance.

Aeschines, the second son, was performing the regular services of an Athenian young man as cadet when the battle of Leuctra plunged Greece into the nine years' Theban wars. He won the praise of his commander in an expedition for the relief of Phlius in 366, and served in other Athenian expeditions, at last taking part in the battle of Mantinea. All this was in his early manhood. In subsequent years we find him serving in the successful expedition for the relief of Eretria in Euboea, hastily organized under the enthusiasm aroused by Timotheus (357 B.C.), and in the Euboean expedition of 348. In the latter, Aeschines' bravery at the battle of Tamynae was so distinguished that he received a wreath of honour from his commanding officers, and was appointed one of the two messengers to carry the news of the victory to Athens, where he was again crowned as the bringer of good news (Aeschines **On the Embassy,** §§ 167 ff.).

In the earlier years of his citizenship Aeschines was employed with his younger brother as a clerk in the civil service. But military service and clerical employment were only incidental or temporary occupations for the gifted young man. His early profession became that of tragic actor. The organization of the Athenian stage was such that a group of three men naturally formed a "company." Aeschines became the third member of a company of which the two most famous actors of the time, Theodorus and Aristodemus, were the chiefs. We conclude that as an actor he fell just short of the highest attainments. The sneers with which Demosthenes in his speech *On the Crown* refers to his efforts on the stage are in flat contradiction to Demosthenes' own testimony in the earlier speech that he was associated with actors of such rank. It appears from Demosthenes xix. 337 that by the year 343 Aeschines had left the stage.

We cannot trace the steps by which Aeschines made his way to political influence. We hear only of his holding an elective clerkship, probably that of reader of documents to senate and assembly, a position for which he was well fitted by his stage training in elocution. But when in 348 Philip of Macedon had destroyed Olynthus and seized the whole Chalcidic peninsula, Aeschines took an active part in arousing Athens to meet the danger which was threatening her interests. And when, on motion of Eubulus, it was voted to send ambassadors to the Greek states to invite them to a congress for concerted action toward Macedon—whether for war or peace—Aeschines was sent on one of the most important missions, that to Arcadia. Two facts are evident here: that Aeschines was now, at the age forty-two, already a man of influence in political affairs, and that he was a supporter of Eubulus, the great leader of the conservatives. When, shortly after this, Aeschines' former associate on the stage, Aristodemus, had unofficially opened the way for peace negotiations with Philip, it was natural that Aeschines, both as his personal friend and a man already active in anti-Macedonian preparations, should be made one of the ten ambassadors to treat with Philip. Here he came into intimate relations with Demosthenes, who had already come to the front, during Philip's movement against Olynthus, as the ablest of the radical leaders. The part which Aeschines and Demosthenes each played in this embassy to Macedonia, in the deliberations at Athens with the ambassadors whom Philip sent in his turn, in the negotiations of the second embassy (for the ratification of the peace of Philocrates, which Philip's ambassadors had negotiated at Athens), and in the final report at Athens, is discussed by both orators in great detail and with irreconcilable contradictions in the speeches **On the Embassy** and *On the Crown.* It seems to the writer probable that Aeschines worked honourably on the first embassy, though with less effect than his vanity led him to think; that he agreed with Demosthenes in at first opposing the terms proposed by Philocrates, but joined Demosthenes the next day in accepting them as the best to which Philip's ambassadors would consent; that he went on the second embassy believing that he could persuade Philip to interpret the peace in a way more favourable to

Athens than the literal terms of the treaty demanded, and that he returned to Athens convinced that he had succeeded and that Philip was about to humble Thebes. In all this he had been completely deceived by the astute Macedonian, and by his report to the people he prevented any attempt on the part of Athens to interfere before Philip could come down and take possession of Phocis. Of course in all this Demosthenes saw sheer bribery. He was probably honest in his conviction that Aeschines had, after the first embassy, gone over to the paid service of Philip. Of this there is no proof whatever; the conduct of Aeschines is entirely explicable as that of a man of only mediocre political ability, flattered by his success as a public speaker and his rapid advance as a diplomat, and shrewdly used by Philip, the master of diplomacy.

On receipt of the news of the surrender of the Phocians, ambassadors were appointed to go to Philip for the protection of Athenian interests. They found Philip and his Thessalian and Theban allies deliberating with the Amphictyonic Council (in a special session, to which Athens had refused to send delegates) as to the fate of the Phocians. Aeschines, though properly having no voice in the Council, appeared before them and pleaded successfully for a mitigation of the severe penalty that some of the delegates were urging.

After the decision of the Amphictyonic Council as to the fate of the Phocians, and the reorganization of the Council, Philip held a thanksgiving feast, in which Aeschines and the other Athenian ambassadors took part.

On his return to Athens Aeschines found himself under grave suspicion. The peace was now detested by the whole people, and all who had urged it were suspected of having acted as agents of Macedon. Meanwhile Demosthenes, whether from an honest conviction that Aeschines had been playing the traitor, or in order to turn the anger of the people from himself as one of the authors of the peace, made haste to bring indictment against Aeschines on the charge of treason in the second embassy. In this proceeding Demosthenes was joined by Timarchus, a prominent politician of the anti-Macedonian group, and an associate of Demosthenes in the senate the year before. Aeschines was in extreme peril. His first move was to secure delay until popular excitement should have time to abate, and to discredit the prosecution, by bringing a counter indictment against Timarchus. It was notorious that Timarchus had in his earlier life been a spendthrift and a libertine. Aeschines now attacked him in the courts under a law which excluded from the platform of the Athenian assembly any man found to have prostituted his person or squandered his patrimony. Aeschines won his case, thus ridding himself of one of his prosecutors, and prejudicing Demosthenes' suit.

Demosthenes nevertheless persisted in the prosecution, and in 343 the case against Aeschines came to trial. The speeches of both prosecutor and defendant are preserved. Both show how deadly the hatred between the two men had become. Demosthenes failed to secure conviction in

the court, but the effect of the attack must have been to shake the confidence of the people in Aeschines' loyalty, while it made Demosthenes still more prominent as the head of the anti-Macedonian movement.

In the following years it is evident that both men were constantly on the watch for opportunities for personal attack, but Aeschines seems to have taken no prominent part in public affairs. Demosthenes was steadily growing in influence, arousing the anti-Macedonian feeling in Athens, and building up an alliance with other states against Philip. He had finally succeeded in bringing Athens to an open break with Philip, and in checking his advance to the Euxine by the rescue of Perinthus and Byzantium, when in 339 his enemy Aeschines quite unexpectedly found himself in a position which seemed to promise the recovery of his own prestige and his return to influence in international affairs. The occasion was a meeting of the Amphictyonic Council at Delphi. Aeschines was one of the Athenian delegation, though not one of the two voting members. A sharp dispute having arisen between the representatives of the little state Amphissa and the Athenian representatives, Aeschines took the lead in proposing the proclamation of a holy war against the Amphissians, on the ground that they had transgressed ancient decrees setting aside certain territory close to Delphi as consecrated to Apollo. Returning to Athens, elated at the prominence that he had attained in the Amphictyonic proceedings, Aeschines tried to persuade the people to endorse his holy war. In this he met the determined opposition of Demosthenes, who succeeded in convincing the people that a war of this sort would, like the late Phocian war, give to Philip precisely the opportunity he was waiting for—to come down into central Greece as champion of one section against another, and so to gain control of both. The other Amphictyonic states voted for the war, but Athens and Thebes held aloof, and together stood against Philip when, under the opportunity offered by the war, he came down with his allies. (A full account of the whole affair is given in the speech of Aeschines *Against Ctesiphon,* §§ 106 ff., and that of Demosthenes *On the Crown,* §§ 145 ff.) In all this Amphictyonic proceeding Aeschines had shown himself zealous and eloquent, nor is there any reason for believing Demosthenes' charge that he had been hired by Philip to stir up an Amphictyonic war. The only criticism that can be made as to his motives is that perhaps he was actuated in part by ambition to secure personal and party advantage over Demosthenes. But he was fatally short-sighted. The one disaster against which any public man in Athens should have been on his guard at just that time was any disturbance among the Greek states that could give Philip a pretext for intervention.

After the defeat of Athens and her allies at Chaeronea in 338, Aeschines was one of the ambassadors sent by Athens to open negotiations for peace, a service to which he was naturally called both because of his cordial relations with Philip on the two earlier embassies, and because of his opposition to the war party of Demosthenes.

We have no further mention of definite political activity of Aeschines until the year 336, when Ctesiphon made his motion that the city should confer a golden crown on Demosthenes in recognition of his lifelong patriotic service. Aeschines now saw his opportunity for revenge for the savage attack that Demosthenes had made on him seven years before. He instituted suit against Ctesiphon as having made an illegal motion. For reasons that are wholly unknown to us the trial of the case was delayed for six years. When at last the trial came, Aeschines was overwhelmingly defeated. His humiliation was such that he left the city. He is said to have gone to Ephesus, thence to Rhodes, where he became a teacher of rhetoric, and finally to have removed to Samos, where he died at the age of seventy-five.

A review of Aeschines' political career shows that he was not, like Demosthenes, a great party leader, nor does he seem to have been constantly active in public affairs (*cp.* Demosthenes *On the Crown,* §§ 307 ff.). Only on special occasions did he come into prominence. He was a steady supporter of Eubulus and Phocion, the great conservatives, who after the establishment of Philip's power in the north believed in a policy of peace with him. There is no doubt that Aeschines was a friend of both Philip and Alexander, but there is no proof that he was ever in their pay; there was no need of bribery with a man whose limited understanding and unlimited vanity made him so easy a tool.

In the two speeches of Aeschines in which we should expect a review of the whole field of international relations during the critical period of the rise of the Macedonian power, we find nowhere any large grasp of the situation, no broad view of either Athenian or Hellenic interests, nothing statesman-like in the discussion of policies. This is the fundamental defect that places him on a plane entirely below that of Demosthenes. Both men indulge in all possible accusations and slanders, both carry personal attack beyond the bounds of decency; but in Demosthenes these personal features are subordinate; the final impression, in the case of Demosthenes' speech *On the Crown,* at least, is one of broad statesmanship. To this height Aeschines cannot rise.

We know nothing of Aeschines' training for public speaking. The brief biographies which have come down to us connect him with some of the rhetorical teachers of the time, but these accounts are late and untrustworthy. His training for the stage and his experience there gave him a refined literary taste, and a wide and excellent vocabulary, together with thorough discipline in elocution and gesture. Moreover the current rhetorical devices, the "figures" of speech and rhetoric, all the superficial tricks of the trade, were so generally "in the air" in the time of Aeschines' youth, that he required no special training of the schools to give him the mastery of them which his speeches show. He never, however, attained full command of the condensed, rounded rhetorical period, which is the consummate product of the art of rhetoric. He is at his best in

clear narrative and vivid description. Perhaps it was his early service in clerical offices which gave him his facility in expounding legal documents. In the higher forms of reasoning he is less successful. Personal feeling and prejudice are so constantly evident, and so often lead to exaggerated assertion and unfair inference, that he fails to carry conviction. His style passes readily from exposition and argument to the emotional, where he knows how to inspire the real tragic feeling of his earlier profession. Aeschines has the art of putting himself readily upon the most familiar terms with his audience; he likes to talk the matter over with them rather than to declaim to them; his only fault here is a tendency to assume something of the didactic tone of the schoolmaster. He has the pride in exhibiting his knowledge of history and in quotation of poetry that is apt to mark the self-made man, and his vanity in his influence as statesman and orator is unconcealed. He often assumes the high moral and patriotic tone, but somehow his moral indignation seldom rings true. This is perhaps in part due to the difficulty of his situation. Assuming that he was honourably convinced that the best interests of Athens demanded that she keep the friendship of Philip and Alexander, we can see how impossible it was for him to speak out candidly in defence of this conviction. Even after Philip's unexpectedly mild treatment of Athens when the battle of Chaeronea had left her helpless in his hands, the mass of the people looked upon the Macedonian as a deadly foe, and hated the position of dependence into which he had brought their city. Many modern students can and do argue persuasively for the benefits that came to Greece through the extension of the power of Macedon and her world conquest; perhaps Aeschines believed in them, but he could not say so in the Athenian assembly or before an Athenian jury. This fact made it impossible for him to reach the heights of impassioned eloquence that were open to Demosthenes, whose words expressed the deepest convictions of his soul.

Galen O. Rowe (essay date 1966)

SOURCE: "The Portrait of Aeschines in the *Oration on the Crown,*" in *Transactions and Proceedings of the American Philological Association,* Vol. 97, 1966, pp. 397-406.

[In the following essay, Rowe contends that Demosthenes succeeded in his major attack on Aeschines by representing him as a comic impostor.]

The separate techniques of character assassination employed by Demosthenes and Aeschines in their famous oratorical duel were distinguished by Ivo Bruns who, with obvious disapproval, noted that Demosthenes' portrait of his enemy had little factual basis; Aeschines, on the other hand, he praised for skilfully exploiting his opponent's weaknesses in such a way that his description, though unfavorable, was true in many respects to its object.[1] It is significant that this distinction of the two portraits harmonizes with the basic difference in tenor of the two orations. Aeschines' *Against Ctesiphon* makes telling use of strong factual evidence (e.g. the illegality of Ctesiphon's proposal, the disastrous consequences of Demosthenes' policies), while the *Oration on the Crown* skirts the facts and seeks to establish the issue on an abstract, moral plane. Lacking strong refutation for Aeschines' specific charges, Demosthenes was concerned that his defense transcend the finite situation and assume universal validity. From the standpoint of character portrayal, it was not his intention to represent the real Aeschines but to create an idealized, and therefore fictional, type who would play a well defined role among the other *dramatis personae* of his oration.

The terms of abuse referring to Aeschines are highly suggestive of the language of Greek comedy. Out of 47 instances of derogatory epithet in the *Oration on the Crown,* 39 can be found in the plays of Aristophanes and in the comic fragments.[2] These include pejoratives which, though frequently used in comedy, are also common in other kinds of Greek literature, so that comic usage does not necessarily imply that the epithets are comic *per se.* There are, however, convincing indications that Demosthenes' description of Aeschines is to have comic overtones. The language of comedy is characterized by its quest for the bizarre effect through neologisms and strange compounds. Demosthenes in his portrayal of Aeschines resorts to the same technique. . . . The diminutive is another type of comic expression in the speech. Aeschines is called a "manikin" (242 . . .); he fawns upon "petty officials" (261 . . .). The animal world was for Aristophanes a chief source for human caricature, as the titles *Wasps, Birds,* and *Frogs* will reveal. The epithet [*kínados*] (Sicilian word for "fox") is twice (162, 242) applied to Aeschines, and . . . "ape," is used once (242). Both words appear as epithets in comedy.[3] Aeschines' cowardice is underscored by the proverb, "you lived the life of a rabbit" (263). As a final species of comic language one may note words with unusual sounds. . . .[4]

In addition to epithets appearing only once or twice, there are comic descriptions and associations reiterated throughout the speech. Demosthenes seizes every opportunity to stress Aeschines' greed and the demeaning occupations to which it had led him. Aeschines and his kind are characterized as men "who measure happiness by their bellies and by their shame" (296).[5] Demosthenes depicts him as a young boy leading a procession of Bacchanals and receiving for his services "sops and rolls and cakes" (260). After becoming a citizen, Aeschines took the job of waiting on petty magistrates (261). Subsequently he hired himself out to a troupe of actors and played the smallest parts, taking for his pay "figs and grapes and olives" (262).[6] Aeschines is like a "balance verging to the side of monetary gain" (298). The Orator stresses the idea that his opponent has sold his loyalty to the enemy.[7] He refuses to grace Aeschines' association with Alexander and Philip by the name of friendship (52):

> I rebuke you for friendship with Alexander? When did you get it, or how did you rate it? I certainly wouldn't

call you the guest of Alexander or the friend of Philip— I'm not so daffy—unless one must call hired hands and wage-earners the friends and guests of their employers.

Like the other recurrent descriptions which will be examined, the picture of Aeschines as the hireling demonstrates Demosthenes' constant attempt to expose Aeschines as something less than he pretends to be.

A second recurring association is made of Aeschines with sickness and physical affliction. Demosthenes refers to his opponents as "polluted men, each of whom mutilated his own country" (296). Early in the speech he describes his efforts on Athens' behalf and attributes their lack of success to the fact that "the cities were diseased; their political leaders were corrupting themselves by taking bribes" (45). Against this background of sickness Aeschines is often inserted. In one instance he is regarded as a symptom (198):

> Suppose something is being done which supports Athenian interests; Aeschines is silent. Suppose there has been trouble, and something unexpected has occurred; Aeschines is to the fore, like ruptures and strains in the body when it is afflicted by some disease.

Aeschines, Demosthenes declares, has never tendered any "healthy" . . . advice (23). Instead, he is like a doctor who, while his patients are ill, refuses to prescribe a remedy, but, when their funeral rites are being observed, joins the procession explaining in detail what the victim should have done to escape death (243). Elsewhere Aeschines is regarded not as the doctor but as the victim of illness. When there is need for constructive counsel, Aeschines maintains a "festering" . . . silence (307). The particular malady from which he suffers is madness. Demosthenes calls him "thunderstruck" (243), a recurring comic epithet. His raving madness requires a dose of hellebore (121). The imagery of physical corruption reaches its climax in Demosthenes' concluding prayer (324):

> I pray to all the gods that they refuse assent to this desire but rather implant in these men a better mind and a better spirit; if they are beyond cure, may they and they alone be quickly and utterly destroyed.

Medical language is frequent in Greek comedy.[8] The quack-doctor, a character who pretends to be what he is not, appears regularly as a comic type.[9]

The greatest concentration of Demosthenes' invective is leveled at his opponent's career as an actor. "Third-rate actor" . . .[10] is an epithet applied to Aeschines five times. But there is strong indication that Demosthenes wanted to do more than disparage his opponent's ability; he wanted to place it in the realm of comedy. In the epithets one notices the incongruous joining of nouns and modifiers. Aeschines is called a "tragic Theocrines" (313), an allusion to an actor who belied the dignity of tragedy by turning sycophant and informer. Another incongruous epithet is "errant tragic ape" (242), where the coupling of the word "tragic" with a comic epithet not only vitiates the serious nature of tragedy but also establishes the bizarre aura of comedy.[11] "Rustic Oenomaus" (242) illustrates the same technique. The story was told that Aeschines, while playing the role of Sophocles' Oenomaus, stumbled on the stage and, encumbered by his costume, was unable to regain his feet.[12] The adjective "rustic" suggests two ideas: First, Demosthenes mentions that Aeschines "murdered miserably Oenomaus" (180) at the country Dionysia in Collytus—a slur on the quality of the acting. Not so well-defined, but nonetheless inherent, in the term "rustic" is the comic level to which Aeschines had reduced the tragic hero Oenomaus.[13] In addition to the epithets, which undermine Aeschines' stage career by throwing it into comic perspective, Demosthenes provides a humorous account of the performances (262):

> You hired yourself out to the actors Simucas and Socrates, known as "The Heavy Groaners"; and you played your third parts while collecting figs and grapes and olives, like a produce dealer from other people's gardens, getting more from this source than from your dramatic contests, in which you and your troupe contested for your lives. For there was a constant and truceless war between you and the spectators, from whom you received so many wounds that you naturally consider cowards those who have had no experience in these hazards.

Parody of tragedy is a favorite ploy of comedy. Not only tragic themes and characters but also tragic actors and playwrights are fed into its gristmill. One will recall that in the *Frogs* the tragedians Aeschylus and Euripides, by parodying each other's lines, are reduced to comic stature. Demosthenes likewise travesties some excerpts from Aeschines' performances (267). Aeschines' real forte, he implies, is comedy, not tragedy. In the present lawsuit "he is playing a stage part, piling up charges and jokes and abuse" (15). He screams all kinds of filthy names at Demosthenes, "like a comic reveler from a wagon" (122).

The three recurrent images of Aeschines as the political hireling, the quack-doctor, and the third-rate actor have both individual and combined significance. Separately they may be seen as emphasizing Aeschines' venality, corruption, and hypocrisy. But what all three have in common is indicative of a more subtle purpose than solely that of assailing an opponent in the usual manner. The three descriptions represent a specific type of comic character—the *alazôn*. Close parallels to Aeschines as the political hireling are found in some of the *alazones* of Aristophanes. The venal and name-dropping Commissioner in the *Birds* (1025-33) is one example. In the *Acharnians* (133-41) Theorus, who gave himself up to the luxuries of Sitacles' palace and neglected the business of his embassy, is identified as an *alazôn*.[14] The quack-doctor, though not prominent in any complete extant comedies, was a common *alazôn* type; and the disparagement of Aeschines' dramatic career is similar to that suffered by the *alazones* Euripides and Aeschylus in the *Frogs*.[15] Aristotle, to whom we are indebted for the technical application of the term, defines the *alazôn* as "one who pretends to have worthy qualities which he either does not possess or which he possesses in a lesser degree than he claims" (*EN* 1127A21). In the plays of Aristophanes the *alazôn* also may be seen as the intruder,[16] such as the *alazones* in the *Birds* (904-1057), who attempt to establish themselves in Cloudcuckooborough and are summarily exposed and expelled. It was Demosthenes' purpose to represent Aeschines as the comic impostor and, in so doing, to expose and alienate him.

Although comic elements often appear in the language of oratorical invective,[17] Demosthenes' exploitation of the comic idiom is unique because of its intensity and consistency. The portrait of Aeschines as the comic *alazôn* is too relentlessly held up to view not to be the result of deliberate design. From a tactical standpoint, however, such a portrait incurs serious disadvantages. There is the danger that it would be too fictitious and consequently incredible to the audience. A second danger lies in the nature of the *alazôn,* who tends to be an ineffectual bluff rather than a sinister threat. If he failed to present Aeschines as a dark adversary Demosthenes could not have expected his counteraccusations to carry much weight.[18] The reason overriding these disadvantages can be found in Demosthenes' defense of his own policies.

From 350 B.C. until the defeat at Chaeronea in 338, Demosthenes had constantly advocated armed resistance to Philip's growing domination. He had succeeded in creating an alliance of other Greek states under the leadership of Athens. Philip's victory was no foregone conclusion. It appeared that the alliance, having enjoyed initial successes, was a match for him in battle. But, in the words of Plutarch, "Some divine fate, as it seems, or some revolution of events put a period that day to the freedom of Greece."[19] After the battle the disquieting oracles, to which Demosthenes had refused credence, were remembered. It was not difficult to see him as an individual cursed by fate, who had involved his fellow citizens in tragic catastrophe—an idea which Aeschines had emphasized in his attacks.[20] In the *Oration on the Crown,* however, Demosthenes, while admitting the tragic significance of the defeat, emphatically denies that his misfortune had precipitated disaster for Athens; rather, he asserts, "how much more just and truthful is it to consider that a fate common to all men, as it seems, or a certain hard and unexpected burden of troubles has been responsible for these miseries" (271). Demosthenes' role during the crisis was the only one a loyal Athenian could have played. His policy had been determined by the glorious precedents established by Athenian statesmen in the past (66-69). Throughout the speech he employs the modest metaphor of the obedient soldier in referring to his services as a statesman.[21] Skilfully the orator changes the question from "Were Demosthenes' policies the cause of defeat?" to "Did Athens act properly in resisting Philip?" To the latter question he readily gives an affirmative answer (199-200):

> I wish to make a rather startling assertion. . . . If coming events were clear to all, and all had seen them ahead of time, . . . yet not even then ought the city to have abandoned her purposes, if indeed she had regard

for her reputation or her ancestors or for time to come. As it was, she simply seems to have failed to succeed, and that is the common lot of man, when Providence wills it.

(199-200)

Athens, not Demosthenes, is the main character in the conflict with Philip. But, more important, she is conceived as the tragic protagonist who can regret her fate but not her actions. In referring to the struggle with Philip, Demosthenes employs the imagery of tragedy. With Philip he associates natural elements to underscore his treachery and the swift, unexpected nature of his movements. Philip's capture of Elatea posed an immediate threat to Athens; and, had it not been for the resistance of the Thebans, he would have swept down upon the city "like a winter torrent."[22] Weather imagery is again employed when Demosthenes' policy made the danger of Philip's encroachments pass by "like a cloud" (188). Demosthenes hesitates to recall an incident before Philip's final and absolute victory, which has caused the past to vanish as though "obliterated . . . by a flood" (214). The association of Philip with natural elements reaches its high point in the following passage (194):

> If the fateful thunderstorm in all its fury was too much not only for us but for all the rest of the Greeks as well, what were we to do? It is just as if one were to hold responsible for the shipwreck the owner who has taken every precaution, has provided his ship with everything he believes will ensure its safety; but then the ship encounters a storm and its tackling falters or is completely shattered. 'But I was not the captain of the ship,' he might say (just as I was not a general), 'nor did I control fate; rather, fate controlled everything.'

Two ideas in this passage call for elaboration. The first is that Philip is portrayed in his role as the thunderstorm—an instrument of destiny over which human effort and wisdom have little control. Secondly, there is the unmistakable inclusion of the ship-of-state imagery, which figures prominently in Greek tragedy. Athens is depicted here as the ship; and Demosthenes, continuing the analogy, represents himself as the owner who had done everything to ensure the ship's safety. The ship-of-state imagery is echoed later in the oration, when Demosthenes declares that Aeschines by failing to demonstrate loyalty to Athens does not "ride at the same anchor with the people" (281). The portrayal of Athens as the ship and Philip as the storm vividly projects the struggle to cosmic proportions. Though Athens was destined to lose the war and her liberty, it remained within her power to preserve her dignity and to assert her moral choice—it is in the expression of this view that the language of Demosthenes reaches the heights of tragic poetry.[23]

The success of the *Oration on the Crown* is all the more notable when it is realized that there was every reason for its failure. Legally the case lay almost entirely in Aeschines' favor; the proposal of a crown for Demosthenes was clearly contrary to the laws. Moreover, Demosthenes'

policies, attacked relentlessly and vigorously by Aeschines, were extremely vulnerable primarily because they had led to defeat. Demosthenes overcame all of the difficulties by conveying to his fellow citizens his own tragic vision of Athens in her struggle with Philip. The ignominy was transformed into glory, the defeat became instead a moral triumph. Demosthenes caused his audience to see themselves as the heroes in the tragedy and therefore proudly to assume with him the responsibility for what had happened. It was for this reason that Aeschines was relegated to the realm of comedy. As one who opposed Demosthenes' policies, policies which Athens had adopted and pursued to the bitter end, Aeschines was alienated as the incongruous impostor, the *alazôn* of the comic stage.

Notes

1. *Das literarische Porträt der Griechen* (Berlin 1896) 572, 579. Admittedly, the distinction is not immediately obvious. In fact Bruns states in regard to Aeschines, "bewegt er sich ganz im Stil der demosthenischen Invektive" (578). However, he asserts, "für eine auf feinerer Beobachtung beruhende Herabwürdigung der Individualität des Gegners fehlte dem Demosthenes die Fähigkeit" and speaks of the "Zerrbilder seines Meidias und Aeschines" (572). Contrariwise, Aeschines "erweckt eine Vorstellung, an die man zu glauben vermag; dies ist kein Popanz wie die Gegner in den demosthenischen Reden, die alle aus Teufelei und Dummheit zu gleichen Theilen zusammengebraut sind" (579).

2. "Instances" include repeated occurrences of an epithet. Put in different, though less meaningful, terms, 27 out of 35 of the epithets are found in comedy. This tabulation includes words from comedy only if they are there used as epithets. In determining what is a pejorative epithet in comedy I consulted Albert Müller, "Die Schimpfwörter in der griechischen Komödie," *Philologus* 72 (1913) 321-37. . . .

3. For the former see *Clouds* 448 and *Birds* 429. Of the latter there are eight instances in Aristophanes alone.

4. Much of the foregoing material stems directly from Friedrich Blass, *Die attische Beredsamkeit* (Leipzig 1893) 3.92-93, whose acute observation of the comic words in the speech prompted me to investigate further.

5. The prominent role of the belly in comedy need not be elaborated here. However, there is a remarkable parallel to Aeschines in the character of Heracles, who, as a member of the gods' embassy, readily accepts the conditions of Peisthetacrus in exchange for a banquet (*Birds* 1591-1605).

6. Goodwin, *Demosthenes On the Crown* (Cambridge 1901) 184, explains, "the band of players subsisted chiefly on the fruit which Aeschines, as their hired servant, collected from the neighbouring farms by begging, stealing, or buying, as he found most convenient." If this interpretation is accepted, it is

possible to see Aeschines in the comic rôle of the fruit-stealer. See Pickard-Cambridge, *Dithyramb, Tragedy and Comedy* (Oxford 1927) 230.

7. See 38, 41, 47, 49, 50, 138.

8. See Harold W. Miller, "Aristophanes and Medical Language," *TAPA* 76 (1945) 74-84.

9. Pickard-Cambridge (above, note 7) 230. . . .

10. O. J. Todd, ". . . A Reconsideration," *CQ* 32 (1938) 37: "Of course, the word ["third-rate actor"] in Demosthenes is derogatory . . . not because in itself it means 'third-rate performer' but because it lays stress on inferiority in rank, on the man's being in the lowest grade in the normal theatrical troupe of the times (at least so far as concerns performances outside of Athens), entailing an unmistakable *implication* as to the actor's ability."

11. Implied in the term "ape" is the notion of pretense and unsuccessful imitation. See Aristophanes, *Acharnians* 120, and William C. McDermott, "The Ape in Greek Literature," *TAPA* 66 (1935) 165-176. Aeschines only succeeded in aping tragedy.

12. Anonymous *Life of Aeschines* 7. The story was told by Demochares, the nephew of Demosthenes.

13. Bruns (above, note 1) 576, explains, "wir würden etwa sagen: Komödiantenkönig vom Vorstadttheater."

14. Demosthenes lays heavy emphasis on the fact that Aeschines also had neglected his embassy. In return for Philip's bribes, Aeschines and his fellow ambassadors had delayed to administer the peace oaths for three months, although the matter required maximum promptness (30, 31). Otto Ribbeck, *Alazon* (Leipzig 1882) 6-7, notes that diplomats regularly are *alazôn* types in comedy.

15. See above, note 10, and Pickard-Cambridge (above, note 7) 270-71.

16. F. M. Cornford, *The Origin of Attic Comedy* (London 1914) 140-141, "He [*alazôn*] is essentially the unwelcome intruder who interrupts sacrifice, cooking, or feast, and claims an undeserved share in the fruits of victory."

17. T. B. L. Webster, *Art and Literature in Fourth Century Athens* (London 1956) 47, "Some of the violence of Aristophanic comedy seems to have spilled over into political eloquence; but comedy also could still be political and it is not always easy to decide whether a comic poet is borrowing from an orator or an orator from a comic poet."

18. This had in fact occurred in the trial concerning the embassy. Aeschines (2.9) pointed out that Demosthenes' description of him was self-contradictory. On the one hand, Demosthenes represented him as worthless and contemptible; on the other, he wished to have him considered as formidable a person as Al-

cibiades or Themistocles. In the *Oration on the Crown* Demosthenes himself seems to have been aware of the inconsistency (see 142).

19. *Life of Demosthenes* 29.1.

20. Aeschines 3.111, 114, 157, 158.

21. See 62, 173, 211, 300.

22. Similarly Philip's representative, Python, is described to the court as "rushing upon you with a flood of cloquence" (136).

23. Wilhelm Fox, *Die Kranzrede des Demosthenes* (Leipzig 1880) 53, compares the *Oration on the Crown* with heroic poetry: "Hier wie dort das Menschen und Völkerleben in seiner grossartigen Entwickelung mit hochinteressanten Conflicten und Kämpfen und tragischen Geschicken, aber alles im Zusammenhang mit dem Walten höherer Mächte, die nach unerforschlich Gesetzen das Schicksal bestimmen.

Cecil W. Wooten (essay date 1988)

SOURCE: "Clarity and Obscurity in the Speeches of Aeschines," in *American Journal of Philology*, Vol. 109, Spring, 1988, pp. 40-43.

[*In the following essay, Wooten analyzes Aeschines's varied uses of distinct, enumerated arguments to achieve advantage over his opponents.*]

One of the most striking features of the oratory of Aeschines is what Hermogenes calls *eukrineia* or distinctness.[1] In the system of Hermogenes this is one of the two sub-types of style that create *saphēneia* or clarity. Distinctness involves an approach whose function, according to Hermogenes, is "to determine what aspects of the case the judges should consider first and what they should consider second and to make that clear to them."[2] Of the techniques that Hermogenes recommends for producing distinctness Aeschines is most fond of the one that states clearly in advance what arguments he is going to use and in what order he is going to present them.[3] The arguments are usually numbered, and Aeschines often states a series of points in general terms and then returns to them, in the same order, but this time in reference to a specific example. This sort of responsion makes his approach very distinct.

For example, toward the end of the speech *Against Ctesiphon* Aeschines enumerates five characteristics that should be found in a democratic politician (169-170) and then, in the same order, examines Demosthenes' career (171-173) to see if he possesses these qualities. Likewise, earlier in this speech, Aeschines enumerates the four periods in Demosthenes' political career that he will treat (54-57) and then addresses himself to each one, dealing "first with the first period, and second with the second, and third with the next, and fourth with the present situation" (57).

Throughout the discussion that follows Aeschines adheres to this scheme and makes it clear to his audience at each stage which period he is going to treat next (cf. 57, 79, 106, 159).

What is striking about all of this is not the fact that Aeschines enumerates points that he will treat. That approach is not uncommon in Attic oratory. However, Aeschines uses it much more frequently than other orators, and his lists are often longer than one usually finds. Other orators, for example, will state two or possibly three arguments that they will discuss.[4] Aeschines sometimes states as many as four or five and follows the informing scheme that he has set up, which he often repeats, more strictly than most other orators.[5] This makes his oratory very patterned and quite easy to follow.

However, there is one well known instance where Aeschines uses this sort of elaborate structure and patterning, not so much to give clarity to his speech, which is its function according to Hermogenes, but to put his opponent in an awkward position. Toward the end of the speech **Against Ctesiphon** (203-204) Aeschines gives a résumé of how he has presented his case and asks that the jury demand that Demosthenes follow the same order in his own speech: "that he make his defence first in reference to the law of accountability, secondly in reference to the law concerning proclamations, and thirdly, and most importantly, that he show that he is not unworthy of the reward" (205). This procedure, however, would have forced Demosthenes into putting his weakest arguments at the beginning of his speech, which is certainly not a good idea from a rhetorical point of view. On the other hand, he could not afford to seem to be avoiding the first two charges in the indictment either. Demosthenes solves this rhetorical dilemma admirably, but a less adept orator would have been put in an almost untenable position.[6]

There is another instance, however, where Aeschines uses a very distinct, and seemingly quite reasonable, approach, not so much to inconvenience his opponent, as to "throw dust in the eyes of the jury."[7] Early in his speech **Against Timarchus,** in a section that functions as the partition, Aeschines says:

> And now in my speech before you I want to follow the same order that the lawgiver followed in his laws.[8] For first I shall describe to you the laws that concern the orderly conduct of your children, then, secondly, those that concern the youths, and thirdly, in order, those that concern the other ages, not only in reference to private citizens but also those who are in political life. For in this way I assume that my arguments will be most easily followed. And also at the same time I want to describe to you first what the laws of the city are like and then after this to examine the character of Timarchus. For you will find that he has lived contrary to all the laws.
>
> (8)

Aeschines then proceeds to discuss (9-36), in a very orderly way, the laws in Athens that regulated male prostitution and morality in general.

However, almost none of these laws have any bearing whatsoever on the case of Timarchus, and later in his speech Aeschines does not even attempt to show that they do. The laws regulating schools (9-12), penalizing guardians who prostitute their wards (13-14), and punishing those who use violence to attain their sexual ends (14-16) have absolutely no relevance to this case.[9] Moreover, of the laws that prohibit certain citizens from speaking in the assembly (28-36), only the third and fourth categories, those who have prostituted themselves and those who have squandered their inheritance, apply to Timarchus (29-30); and it is the charge of prostitution that Aeschines really dwells upon.

This whole first section of the speech, therefore, is nothing but an attempt to build up prejudice against Timarchus by implying that he is somehow guilty of transgressing all the laws that Aeschines cites. The purpose of this part of the speech, contrary to what Aeschines says (8), is not to make his arguments easier to follow but, by means of a lot of irrelevant legalism, to create an unfavorable impression of Timarchus early in the speech and to divert the jury's attention from what is really at issue in this case.[10]

Therefore, one sees in this speech that Aeschines sometimes uses enumeration, not to create clarity (*saphēneia*) but to produce obscurity (*asapheia*). Or rather there is a clarity on the surface of the speech that only obfuscates what is really at issue. And that can be a very effective rhetorical technique.

Notes

1. Cf. *Hermogenes' On Types of Style,* tr. by Cecil Wooten (Chapel Hill 1987) 14-18. It is quite striking, however, that the only ancient critic who attributes this quality to Aeschines is Photius; cf. J. F. Kindstrand, *The Stylistic Evaluation of Aeschines in Antiquity* (Uppsala 1982) 62.

2. *Hermogenes' On Types of Style,* 14.

3. Cf. 1.4, 8, 28-30, 153-154, 156-157; 2.11, 26, 64, 97, 109, 131-132, 180; 3.1, 2, 6, 54-55, 57, 64-65, 79, 91, 99, 106, 141, 145, 148, 159, 169-170, 197, 203-205, 208. Aeschines also uses the other techniques recommended by Hermogenes for producing distinctness: the use of *symplēroseis* or indications that one train of thought is being brought to a close and that another is being introduced (cf. 1.22); the use of rhetorical questions that he then answers himself (cf. 1.28-30, 154); the narration of events in the order in which they took place (cf. 2.96); and the use of background material (cf. 2.44). None of these approaches, however, is used nearly so frequently or so extensively as the enumeration of points to be made.

4. Hermogenes gives some examples from Demosthenes; cf. *Hermogenes's On Types of Style,* 14, 16.

5. Cf. 1.28-30; 2.64, 131-132; 3.54-55, 169-170.

6. Cf. George Kennedy, *The Art of Persuasion in Greece* (Princeton 1963) 230-231.

7. I am thinking of what Cicero is supposed to have said about his speech *Pro Cluentio* (Quintilian 2.17.21).

8. Aeschines has outlined this in the preceding section and repeats it here. See the comments about responsion above.

9. Cf. K. J. Dover, *Greek Homosexuality* (London 1978) 27-39.

10. Diversionary tactics and legalism are typical of Aeschines' speeches; see Kennedy, 238.

Edward M. Harris (essay date 1988)

SOURCE: "When Was Aeschines Born?" in *Classical Philology,* Vol. 83, No. 3, July, 1988, pp. 211-14.

[*In the following essay, Harris reveals a possible rhetorical deception on the part of Aeschines regarding the relative ages of Misgolas and Timarchus.*]

At first glance, the answer to this question appears to be rather simple, for Aeschines himself states quite plainly in his speech against Timarchus (l. 49) that he was then forty-five years old: since the speech was delivered in 346/45 B.C., he would have been born in 391/90 or 390/89.[1] But this is not all that Aeschines says in the passage. He goes on to remind the court that many men do not look as old as their years—Misgolas among them: his youthful appearance notwithstanding, Misgolas is actually the same age as Aeschines himself, who with his gray hair would seem to be much older. This observation leads him to warn the jurors that their impression that Misgolas and Timarchus are the same age is quite mistaken. The jurors are left to draw the obvious conclusion that Timarchus is in fact younger than Misgolas. As F. Blass pointed out, however, Timarchus was a member of the Council in 361/60 and therefore must have been at least thirty in that year.[2] This would date Timarchus' birth to 391/90 or 390/89 at the very latest—and so to the same time as, if not earlier than, the birth of Aeschines and his coeval, Misgolas. Yet this conclusion would seem to be impossible, since Aeschines unambiguously implies that Timarchus is younger than Misgolas.

Blass did not propose a solution to this problem, which did not receive further consideration until D. M. Lewis examined it afresh in 1958.[3] Lewis considered four ways of resolving the difficulty in the passage as it stands, but rejected all of them and concluded that the text must be corrupt. . . . In support of his emendation he pointed out that according to the *Life of Aeschines* attributed to a certain Apollonius, Aeschines died during Antipater's purge (i.e., in 322) at the age of seventy-five; on that chronology he would have been born in either 398/97 or 397/96. Yet this still does not coincide with the date of 399/98 (or 400/399) that would result from Lewis' emendation.

This lack of strict congruity is not the only weakness in Lewis' argument; more fundamentally, his use of the *Life of Aeschines* attributed to Apollonius is in itself questionable. Each of the ancient biographies of Aeschines gives a different account of his activities after the trial of Ctesiphon in 330 and of his death, and we cannot determine which (if any) offers the correct version.[4] That the biography attributed to Apollonius is the only one to carry an alternative form of the name of Aeschines' mother . . . is not remarkable and does not prove (*pace* Lewis) that the author had access to material about Aeschines' life beyond his extant speeches and those of Demosthenes. Another explanation of this alternative version of her name is more likely. It is clear that the earlier biographers whom Apollonius read noted Demosthenes' claim (18. 129-30) that Aeschines' father had originally been a slave, named . . . "Trembler", and that after he gained his freedom he altered his name . . . to hide his servile background. Taking his cue from Demosthenes, one of these earlier biographers must have assumed that the name of Aeschines' mother had been similarly transformed. . . .

Lewis was correct to assume that Aeschines probably was not lying about his own age; but nothing prevents us from thinking that he was being deceptive in another respect. To begin with, we should note how important Misgolas' age is to Aeschines' case against Timarchus. Aeschines is accusing Timarchus of prostitution and claims that Misgolas paid him for his favors. For the charge to be plausible, Timarchus must be younger than Misgolas, since it was customary in homosexual relationships in classical Athens for an older man to pursue a younger man.[6] Thus, Aeschines' charge that Timarchus sold his favors to Misgolas would not have appeared plausible if Timarchus was the same age as, or older than, Misgolas.

Let us suppose the following. Aeschines, Misgolas, and Timarchus were all the same age (Timarchus may have even been slightly older than the other two), but Aeschines was completely gray-haired, as he himself tells us. Aeschines wished to create the impression that Misgolas was older than Timarchus, so that his charge of prostitution against Timarchus would appear credible. He therefore said that although Misgolas seemed to be Timarchus' age, he was really his own (i.e., Aeschines') age. The jury, seeing Aeschines' gray hair, was to conclude that since Misgolas was the same age as Aeschines—who with his gray hair looked much older than Timarchus—Misgolas must also have been older than Timarchus.

One might object that this deception could easily have been exposed by the defense, who only needed to add what Aeschines had deliberately omitted—that Timarchus was in fact the same age as (or slightly older than) Misgolas. But such an objection forgets that prosecutors in classical Athens did not hesitate to assert or imply all manner of things about their opponents, even when the assertions could easily be refuted. We need only compare Demosthenes' charge (19. 150-64) that Aeschines had deliberately delayed the swearing of the oaths for the Peace of Philocrates in order to enable Philip to subdue Cersebleptes. To refute this charge, Aeschines only needed to have the clerk of the court read out the date of Cersebleptes' capitulation to Philip—as indeed he did (2. 91-92), thereby proving that the delay had had no effect on the fate of Cersebleptes.

The solution that I have proposed has an important advantage over an emendation that provides Aeschines with an earlier date of birth: it is more consistent with what we know about Aeschines' military service. Aeschines tells us (2. 168) that on his first military campaign he saw action with Alcibiades, who was leading Athenian troops to help the Phliasians. This campaign took place in 366.[7] If Aeschines was born in 391/90 or 390/89, he would have gone on his first campaign at the age of twenty-four, around four years after completing his service as ephebe, which began after his eighteenth birthday and lasted two years.[8] On the other hand, if he was born in 398 or earlier, he would have been thirty-two or older when he went on his first campaign. An interval of four or five years between the completion of his service as ephebe and his first military campaign is not surprising, but an interval of twelve or more years strains credibility, especially when we know that the period from 378 to 366 was by no means peaceful.[9] Such a long interval becomes even less credible when we recall that the younger age-classes were called up far more frequently than the older age-classes, which were summoned only in emergencies.[10] Had Aeschines managed to evade military service for such a long period by means of various excuses and schemes, Demosthenes would certainly have pounced on this dereliction of duty in his speeches against his rival;[11] and it is hard to believe that a general like Phocion would have come forward to testify for a draft-dodger.[12]

Our discussion has confirmed that there is no problem with the information about his age that Aeschines gives us in his speech against Timarchus; what we should not believe is his implication that Misgolas was older than Timarchus. As a result, we can accept Aeschines' statement that he was forty-five in 346/45 and infer that he was born in either 391/90 or 390/89. This conclusion also has implications for the career of Aeschines' fellow ephebe Nausicles, about whose date of birth we know nothing save that he was an exact contemporary of Aeschines:[13] his birth also should be dated to 391/90 or 390/89. But these are not the only things to be gained from an examination of the problem. I hope that the discussion of the difficulties surrounding the evidence for Aeschines' date of birth has had some value in illustrating the kind of rhetorical legerdemain an orator might employ to deceive his audience. It is precisely this sort of deception that should make us wary when we are dealing with the information provided by the Attic orators.[14]

Notes

1. For the date of the speech, see E. M. Harris, "The Date of the Trial of Timarchus," *Hermes* 113 (1985): 376-80; the trial probably took place early in the ar-chonship of Archias (= late summer 346). For the problem involved in determining a date of birth from information about a person's age in a given archon-year, see J. K. Davies, *Athenian Propertied Families, 600-300 B.C.* (Oxford, 1971), pp. 125-26.

2. *Die attische Beredsamkeit²*, vol. 3.2 (Leipzig, 1893), p. 170, drawing on Aeschin. 1. 109.

3. "When Was Aeschines Born?" *CR* 8 (1958): 108. Lewis' argument was accepted by J. K. Davies, *Athenian Propertied Families*, pp. 545-46.

4. For a collection of the evidence, see A. Schaefer, *Demosthenes und seine Zeit²*, vol. 3 (Leipzig, 1887), p. 292, nn. 1 and 2. On the information about Aeschines' death provided by Apollonius Schaefer commented: "die ganze Stelle ist so absurd, dass nichts daraus zu entnehmen ist."

5. Cf. Schaefer, ibid., 1:224 (who did not, however, specifically attribute the invention of the name to the ancient biographers). . . .

6. K. J. Dover, *Greek Homosexuality* (Cambridge, Mass., 1978), pp. 85-88; see also the useful collection of references to representations in vase-paintings compiled by M. Golden, "Slavery and Homosexuality at Athens," *Phoenix* 38 (1984): 321-24. That this custom also obtained in homosexual relationships involving prostitutes is indicated by Aeschin. 1. 95 (when Timarchus was past his prime, he had a difficult time finding clients).

7. Xen. *Hell.* 7. 2. 17-23; on this campaign, see W. E. Thompson, "Chares at Phlius," *Philologus* 127 (1983): 303-5.

8. A youth became an ephebe at the same time that he enrolled in the deme register (Lycurg. *Leoc.* 76); this occurred when he was eighteen years old: see Arist. *Ath. Pol.* 42. 1, with P. J. Rhodes, *A Commentary on the Aristotelian "Athenaion Politeia"* (Oxford, 1981), pp. 497-98.

9. Troops were sent to Thebes in 377 (Xen. *Hell.* 5. 4. 54), and in the same year a levy of 20,000 hoplites was voted (Diod. Sic. 15. 29. 7). In 377/76 Chabrias campaigned on Euboea and the islands (Diod. Sic. 15. 30. 5), and in the following year Timotheus led the fleet to Corcyra (Xen. *Hell.* 5. 4. 63-64). In 370/69 Iphicrates brought Athenian troops to aid Sparta (Diod. Sic. 15. 63, Xen. *Hell.* 6. 5. 49-52). In 368/67 Autocles took troops to aid Alexander of Pherae (Diod. Sic. 15. 71. 3), and from 368 to 364 Iphicrates attempted to retake Amphipolis (Aeschin. 2. 27, Dem. 23. 149, 151).

10. For the older men called up in emergencies, see Dem. 3. 4, Aeschin. 2. 133 (reading τετταράκοντα).

11. As he did in his speech against Meidias, 21. 163-67.

12. For Phocion testifying on behalf of Aeschines, see Aeschin. 2. 170.

13. Aeschin. 2. 184; Davies, *Athenian Propertied Families,* p. 396, is thus incorrect to place his birth "in the region of 398-6."

14. An earlier version of this note formed a part of chapter 2 of my dissertation, "The Political Career of Aeschines" (Harvard, 1983). I would like to thank Professor Badian, who directed my dissertation, for several helpful suggestions; thanks are also due to the Editor for his comments.

Edward M. Harris (essay date 1995)

SOURCE: "Family, Early Career, and Start in Politics," in *Aeschines and Athenian Politics,* Oxford University Press, 1995, pp. 17-40.

[*In the following excerpt, Harris examines Aeschines's family background and his careers as a public secretary and an actor, explaining how he overcame certain disadvantages to enter politics.*]

Even in the case of the most important figures in antiquity, the information we possess about their early lives is scant at best. We do not know the year of birth for many famous people, and little is told to us about their education and early activities. Occasionally we are fortunate enough to have a few anecdotes about the childhood and youth of a prominent figure, but these too must be treated with great caution. Anecdotes are often transmitted orally for several generations before being written down and are thus subject to all the changes that this kind of source works on its material. The ancient historians themselves took little or no interest in the early lives of great men and tended instead to direct their attention primarily to battles and political events, which they felt to be the true subject matter of history. Biographies were written about remarkable individuals, but these were almost invariably composed many years after the deaths of their subjects by writers who often had much the same sources as scholars today have. Consequently, these biographies rarely add much to our meager stock of information. When they do contain matter that is not found in other sources, it is unlikely to be the product of painstaking research. Rather, it is most probably a fiction invented by an imaginative biographer, who, frustrated by the paucity and dullness of the sources available to him, took the liberty of inventing sensational details.[1]

In the case of Aeschines we are relatively lucky to have a number of statements drawn from his own speeches and those of his opponent Demosthenes about his family background and his activities prior to his entry into politics. Although it is impossible to draw any conclusions about the formative influences on his personality from these few scraps of information, we can still look at his social background and consider how wealthy his family was and what advantages or liabilities this background gave him. This in turn will help us to understand why he

took the route he did to enter politics in Athens and also to explain why he entered politics relatively late in his life. Yet before we can discuss the position of Aeschines and his family in Athenian society, it is first necessary to examine briefly certain aspects of the social structure of that society. As with any community, the population of Athens could be divided into numerous sets of groups according to various criteria. Since we are concerned, however, primarily with the impact that wealth and social status had on the chances of an Athenian citizen for political success, the most important sets of groups for our purposes will be, first, the liturgical and military classes, and second, the status-groups designated by various labels, but best known by the terms *kaloi kagathoi* and *poneroi*.[2]

Although legal and political rights were for the most part shared equally by all citizens in the fourth century, military and financial burdens were still distributed according to wealth. The most affluent men in Athens formed the liturgical class, those who served in the cavalry as young men and when older acted as captains of the triremes of the Athenian fleet. These men were also called on to finance the approximately one hundred annual festival liturgies. Of these the most famous were those for the dramatic contests. Each man who volunteered or was selected by the archon for this task was assigned to produce the plays of one of the authors whose work had been selected for performance that year. Such a peson was called a *choregos* and paid the wages of the chorus and bought the costumes for the entire troupe. Prizes were awarded for the best plays at these festivals and as a result the *choregoi* could become quite competitive, spending as much as two thousand drachmai in their efforts to outdo each other. As trierarch, the member of the liturgical class would be assigned a trireme on which he would serve as captain for a year and be expected to make sure that his ship was fully equipped. The public treasury normally provided the equipment for the trireme, including sails, tackle, and oars, in addition to the funds needed to buy rations and to pay the crew; the trierarch himself was obligated to make some contribution toward the upkeep of the ship. This amount appears to have been somewhere between forty and sixty *mnai,* but those who wished to impress their fellow citizens with their devotion to the city might spend much more. About twelve hundred men formed the liturgical class in the fourth century. No set qualification existed for inclusion in this class, but it has been calculated that "during the fourth century men whose property was worth less than 3 *tal.* were free from liturgical obligations, while men whose property was worth over 4 *tal.* were very unlikely to escape such obligations in the long run."[3]

A slightly larger group than the twelve hundred called on to serve as trierarchs and to pay for the festival liturgies was made up of those who were required to pay the *eisphora,* an extraordinary levy on property for war purposes. In 378 those who were subject to this levy were grouped into one hundred symmories, and each one of the symmories was headed by three men who were called respectively the *hegemon* (leader), *deuteros* (second man), and *tritos* (third man). These men would advance to the fleet the entire sum to be contributed by the entire symmory and then collect this sum, minus what they themselves owed, from the other members of the symmory. The "Three Hundred" who acted as the leaders, second men, and third men of the symmories were the wealthiest men in Attica. They had to be; the payments they had to advance to the navy were quite substantial and must have created strains on even the very largest fortunes.[4]

Those who did not have enough money to perform liturgies might become hoplites in the army provided their property was above a certain minimum. Everyone who met this property qualification was enrolled as an ephebe as soon as he reached the age of eighteen and was registered as a citizen in his deme. All those ephebes who were enrolled in the same year formed an age class and had their names recorded together on a tablet placed in the archives. As ephebes, these young men received military training for two years in outposts scattered throughout the Attic countryside. Every hoplite who graduated from this training was liable for duty up to age sixty unless disabled for some reason, but the older men appear to have been called up only in emergencies. The number of Athenian hoplites reached a high of 18,000 to 25,000 in 431, then must have fallen sharply in the following decades as the losses from the plague and the Peloponnesian War took their toll. By 400 there may have been as few as 10,000, but their numbers rose throughout the fourth century and appear to have reached 14,500 by 322. Citizens who possessed less than the minimum needed for hoplite service were generally free from military duties and financial burdens, yet might row in the fleet for a wage if they wished to. These were the poorest citizens in Athens and were called thetes. We have no reliable figures for the number of thetes in any period, but it seems reasonable to infer that their total was roughly equivalent to that of the hoplites.[5]

When attempting to determine the financial resources of an Athenian citizen, it is obviously useful to know what duties he was asked to perform for the community. Even in the absence of any firm knowledge of a man's holdings, we can still get some idea of the relative size of his fortune if we can find out whether he served as a hoplite or as a trierarch. This is important information for, as we will see, a large income gave one a distinct advantage in Athenian politics. At the same time, we should bear in mind that the possession of wealth did not automatically win a man respect in Athenian society. Money and property may have been a necessary condition for social prestige, but they were not a sufficient condition. The Athenian who owned several farms and workshops staffed by slaves might still not be deemed worthy of the hand of a girl whose father prided himself on being one of the *kaloi kagathoi*. There is likewise no reason to think that someone who did not have quite enough property to perfrom liturgies would be ipso facto banned from polite society.[6]

This brings us to the topic of status-groups, the other aspect of Athenian social structure we need to examine.

Despite the fact that all Athenians were equal in most regards when it came to legal and political rights, they nonetheless tended to divide themselves roughly into two status-groups. In one of these groups were the *kaloi kagathoi* (gentlemen), *chrestoi* (good people), *gnorimoi* (well-known), *beltistoi* (best people), in short, those who were considered respectable. In the other group were the *poneroi* (wretched), *kakoi* (bad), and *banausoi* (laborers), those who were unable to meet the criteria for inclusion in respectable society. We should be careful to refrain from regarding the *kaloi kagathoi* as nobles or aristocrats since those words conjure up visions of a class whose members enjoy hereditary privileges, own large ancestral estates, and possess formal titles such as "duke," "marquis," and "earl." This kind of class never existed in Classical Athens. These status groups were purely informal—the *kaloi kagathoi* did not keep a list of those whom they thought socially acceptable. Anyone could claim to be a *kalos kagathos,* imitate their life-style, and try to join their company in the gymnasium. But the members of polite society were also free to shun anyone who in their opinion was déclassé.[7]

The *kaloi kagathoi* were united not so much by common material interests as by a common life-style. These gentlemen aspired to be both independent and generous. In daily life they pursued those activities that they considered to be conducive to moral and intellectual refinement. Independence meant economic self-sufficiency, freedom from the need to work for another man. One of the greatest misfortunes that could befall an Athenian citizen was the necessity of having to hire oneself out to someone else. This placed an Athenian in the position of a slave who had to take orders from his master. Aside from the humiliation, the physical work performed by hired hands was viewed as demeaning; it made one coarse and unfit for more dignified pursuits. The ideal was to have enough property to live off the income provided by farms or workshops staffed by slaves. This kind of arrangement gave one the leisure to participate in activities like exercise in the gymnasium, racing horses, attending fashionable symposia, and pursuing a career in politics. The *kalos kagathos* revealed his noble and generous nature by helping his friends and by performing liturgies for the community.[8]

The life of a *kalos kagathos* required a substantial amount of property. It is therefore no wonder that the *kaloi kagathoi* were often referred to as *hoi plousioi* (the rich). Those who served in the cavalry and performed liturgies surely had enough to afford the necessary life-style, but those further down the economic scale might also be able to qualify. In fact, several authors imply that many of the hoplites could be considered *kaloi kagathoi*. But it was not enough to be affluent and lead the life of a *kalos kagathos;* it was also necessary to have parents who were thought to be respectable. Hence the gentleman was often described as *eugenes* or *gennaios* (wellborn). One did not have to have a long line of ancestors stretching all the way back to Solon and beyond, but it could help. Certainly those who were so favored did not hesitate to remind others of their distinguished lineages and naturally expected respect and deference in return. And just as old wealth could be a source of prestige, nouveaux riches met with resentment. Aristotle, for example, advises the prospective orator that it is far more easy to stir up indignation against a man whose wealth has been recently acquired than one who has received his property through inheritance. Cratinus put the newly rich in the same category as slaves and other undesirables. The social prejudice against those whose parents did not make it into the ranks of the *kaloi kagathoi* can be seen in the case of Iphicrates. Despite his entry into the liturgical class and his election to the generalship, Iphicrates was nevertheless insulted for his humble origins. Phormion and Pasion were among the wealthiest men in Athens, yet they could still be taunted for their servile birth.[9]

If one was to aspire to the life-style of a *kalos kagathos,* one of the prerequisites was a good education. This meant the traditional schooling, which consisted of learning the works of the poets, especially Homer, exercise in the gymnasium, and training in music. All this gave one discipline, character, social grace, and a good physique. Knowledge of the poets and musical skill was a sine qua non for the gentleman who wished to make a good impression at a symposium. Exercise out of doors in the gymnasium made it possible to distinguish the bodies of the *kaloi kagathoi* from those of the *banausoi.* Gentlemen were well tanned with broad shoulders and muscular thighs and buttocks. The *banausos* had a pale complexion and a body deformed from toiling indoors all day and from bending over his work. The *banausos* had neither the time nor the money to spend on education; he would barely know how to read and write.[10]

Since many Athenians could fulfill some, but not all, of the criteria for inclusion among the *kaloi kagathoi,* there was no clear dividing line between the *kaloi kagathoi* and the *poneroi,* between the social elite and the mass of citizens. For example, the independent farmer who owned and worked his fields did not fit neatly into either group. Farming was more respectable than most of the manual trades, and it was not considered undignified for a gentleman to spend time in the country directing the work on his estate. But the farmer who was not wealthy enough to buy many slaves or hire free men to do most of his work and thus had to perform many of the tasks required in sowing and harvesting his crops could not imitate the life-style of the *kalos kagathos.* He would have little time to gain an education or exercise in the gymnasium. Although he could boast of a certain degree of self-sufficiency and did not have to work for another man, he lacked the leisure to acquire the refinement of a gentleman and remained rustic and unsophisticated, an *agroikos.* The independent farmer occupied a sort of middle ground between the two extremes represented by the *kaloi kagathoi* and the *poneroi.* This group was by no means insignificant, but probably made up a large proportion of the entire citizen population of Attica.[11]

FAMILY BACKGROUND

With these considerations in mind, we can now study the social position of Aeschines and his family. All the information we have about Aeschines' family is derived from two main sources, Aeschines himself and his opponent Demosthenes. Not surprisingly their respective portraits of his parents differ markedly. The difficulties of reconciling these two portraits are aggravated by the fact that neither orator provides any evidence to prove his claims. Yet although all of Demosthenes' wilder allegations can be dismissed as slander and many of Aeschines' inflated claims to respectability can easily be punctured, we will find there remains a small residue of fact on which both men tacitly agree. From these few facts significant conclusions about the social status of Aeschines' family can be drawn.[12]

When we scrutinize the statements of the two men, we need to look at each one in the context in which it was delivered. For instance, we should first consider the statements made by Demosthenes as prosecutor in 343 so that when we come to the information in the speech Aeschines delivered at the same trial, we will know what attacks he was responding to. As we turn to the comments made by Demosthenes at the trial of Ctesiphon in 330, we must likewise remember that on that occasion Aeschines had no chance to reply to anything his opponent said about his parents.

We begin therefore with the speech Demosthenes made as prosecutor in 343. In this speech Demosthenes makes only a few isolated remarks about Aeschines' parents. In one place he describes how Aeschines' mother made money carrying out religious purifications and how his father earned his living by teaching reading and writing. Elsewhere in the speech Demosthenes calls the father, Atrometus, a *grammatistes,* "schoolteacher," and relates how the mother, Glaucothea, gathered together bands of worshippers for some degenerate purpose. He does not specify what this scandalous activity was, but by assuring the court that another priestess was condemned to death for performing the same act, implies that it was very sacrilegious. After this abuse, he challenges his opponent to name any benefits he and his father have brought the city and suggests several possible answers, such as service in the cavalry or as a hoplite, performance of a trierarchy, financing a chorus or some other liturgy, or payment of the *eisphora.*[13]

It is difficult to evaluate any of these statements before we look at Aeschines' reply to them. We should however note his challenge to Aeschines to list any services he and his family have performed for the city. Numerous court speeches reveal that it was normal for the defendant to provide proof of his patriotism and good will toward the community by citing all the duties he had performed on its behalf. This was done not only with the intention of demonstrating one's good character, but also in hope that the members of the court would feel grateful for all the favors he had bestowed upon them. Yet, although it was customary for the defendant to remind the court of his generosity, it was unusual for the accuser to challenge him to do so, and the fact that Demosthenes invites Aeschines to list his services to the Athenians strongly suggests that he is confident that his opponent will have a hard time complying with his request.[14]

Aeschines begins the reply he delivered in 343 to Demosthenes' insults about his parents with an account of his father Atrometus, who was born in 437/36 or 436/35. It is perhaps significant that Aeschines never mentions here or elsewhere any ancestors before his father. There is no reason to go so far as to infer from his silence that they were slaves or freedmen, but we are safe in assuming that they were probably undistinguished and performed no memorable deeds. Aeschines attempts to give the impression that his father was associated with some of the older, more respectable families in Athens when he says that Atrometus belongs to the same phratry as the Eteobutadai, who held the priesthood of Athena Polias. This means very little, however, since many Athenians were enrolled in a phratry, many of which were headed by well-known *gene* such as the Eteobutadai. Aeschines then recounts how his father spent his youth competing in athletic contests. The aim of this should be obvious: Aeschines is trying to show that his father, at least as a young man, was free from the need to work for a living and pursed the life-style of a *kalos kagathos,* exercising regularly in the gymnasium.[15]

Aeschines continues by telling how Atrometus was prevented from practicing as an athlete by the loss of property during the Peloponnesian War. Aeschines is probably referring to the damage inflicted by the Spartans after they occupied Dekeleia in 413 and not to the incursions made by the Peloponnesian army in the early years of the war. The latter began in 431 when Atrometus was only six or seven years old, thus well before he could have begun his athletic career. Besides, it is unlikely that Atrometus and his family would have suffered very much from the early invasions even if the bulk of their property lay in or near their deme of Kothokidai, which happened to lie right in the path of the Peloponnesian army. Thucydides reports that these incursions were of short duration, did not cause much damage, and left the fields to be worked the rest of the year.[16]

Aeschines passes over what his father did between the time he lost his property and the time he was forced into exile by the Thirty, but he does say something about his activities during the reign of the Thirty. His motive for this should be transparent—he had no wish to dwell on his father's poverty in these years. Aeschines understandably prefers to say that Atrometus was banished by the Thirty and helped to restore the democracy. Aeschines' description of his father's heroic actions against the Thirty is clearly aimed at refuting Demosthenes' charge that his family had never rendered the city any major services.[17]

Aeschines' account of these events invites scrutiny. He tells us that his father was exiled, accompanied his wife to Corinth, then went to Asia where he served as a soldier and took part in some battles, and ultimately returned to Athens in time to aid in the overthrow of the oligarchy. The chronology of these actions presents difficulties. The precise date on which the Thirty came into power is unknown, but they seized control of Athens by the summer of 404 and were out of power by the late summer of 403. Aeschines nevertheless claims that his father traveled to Corinth, then went to Asia, fought in several battles there, and returned to Athens all within this space of time. Moreover, Atrometus could not have arrived in Asia until the late summer of 404 at the earliest, too late for the campaigning season of 404. And he must have left in the early spring of 403 to make it back to join Thrasybulus and the other exiles in restoring the democracy, and therefore too early to fight in the campaigning season of 403 in Asia. A scholium on this passage states that Atrometus was hired by a Persian satrap, but this is probably a guess, for the author of the scholium cites no authority and is apparently unable to name the satrap. We certainly do not hear of any band of Greek mercenaries serving in Asia in this year. The only mercenaries fighting in Asia during this period whom we hear about in our sources are those recruited by Clearchus in 403 to march with Cyrus in his campaign against the Persian king.[18]

Aeschines' brief account of Atrometus' activity during the reign of the Thirty clearly cannot be accepted as it stands. Aeschines may possibly have gone so far as to invent the story of his father's exile and participation in the restoration of the democracy. As we have already seen, Aeschines had a strong motive for doing this, but in the absence of conclusive proof all we can do is to express doubt. Yet Aeschines had no reason to invent the story of his father's military service in Asia since this was not especially praiseworthy. Everyone would have assumed that fighting in Asia meant service as a mercenary, and that was nothing to boast about since mercenary service was often the sign of poverty. Given these considerations, the safest conclusion is to move Atrometus' service as mercenary down to the 390s when our sources tell us many Greeks were hiring themselves out as soldiers to Persian satraps. Aeschines may then have placed his father's mercenary service after his exile under the Thirty to give the impression that Atrometus had been forced to take service in Asia for political reasons and not because of his poverty, as was in fact the case.[19]

In the same passage where he recounts the exploits of his father, Aeschines also mentions that Atrometus took his wife to Corinth before he set out for Asia. There she presumably remained until his return. Unlike Demosthenes, Aeschines does not refer to his mother by her name Glaucothea, but calls her "my mother." This is due to the Athenian sense of propriety which forbade a man to utter in public the name of a respectable woman and constrained him to refer to her only with a periphrasis such as "the wife of Atrometus." It is thanks only to the contempt of Demosthenes, who did not feel these scruples about his opponent's mother, that we possess our knowledge of her name. In the other passage from this speech where he refers to his mother, Aeschines uses another periphrasis, this time calling her the sister of Cleobulus, the son of Glaucus of Acharnai, who along with Demaenetus, a member of the *genos* of the Bouzygai, defeated Chilon, the commander of the Spartan fleet. It is curious how Aeschines slips in the name of the famous *genos* to which Demaenetus belongs. Unable to show that his own ancestors were members of the more celebrated *gene,* Aeschines tries to create the impression that his relatives were closely associated with men from these *gene,* just as he linked his father with the Eteobutadai. Unlike the case with his father, however, Aeschines names his mother's father and says that her brother achieved renown in a naval battle.[20]

Which naval battle was this? At first glance it might appear to be identical to an incident recounted in the *Hellenica Oxyrhynchia.* According to this work, a certain Demaenetus in the year 397/96 commandeered a trireme from the dockyard of the Athenian fleet in the Piraeus. With the consent of the Council, but without the approval of the Assembly, Demaenetus sailed away with the intention of joining Conon. As soon as word of Demaenetus' action got out, there was an uproar, and the leaders of the city were accused of dragging Athens into war with Sparta. The members of the Council then decided to convoke a meeting of the Assembly. At the meeting a decision was made to inform Milon, the Spartan harmost on Aegina, that Demaenetus had sailed without the permission of the Athenian people. Immediately after receiving the message, Milon sailed off in pursuit and caught up with Demaenetus off Thorikos on the east coast of Attica. Just as they story reaches its climax, the papyrus becomes very fragmentary, but the tattered remains seem to indicate the Demaenetus abandoned his ship and then was able to obtain another in which he resumed his journey to Conon. Milon seized the ship Demaenetus had abandoned, but did not pursue him further and returned to Aegina.[21]

There are of course discrepancies between this account and what Aeschines says about the battle his uncle took part in, but they may be the product of Aeschines' imperfect knowledge of events that had taken place before his birth. Aeschines is elsewhere rather careless about details of Athenian history and could easily have substituted the name "Chilon" for "Milon." Nor should we discount the possibility that Aeschines, who has a noticeable tendency to exaggerate his family's prestige, transformed what had been a small skirmish with the Spartan harmost on Aegina into a full-scale naval battle with the commander of the entire Spartan fleet. Thus if the naval battle alluded to by Aeschines is indeed identical with the incident involving Demaenetus described in the *Hellenica Oxyrhynchia,* we can see that fighting in this action could hardly have brought Cleobulus much renown. Alternatively, Aeschines may be referring to some other battle that was so insignificant that it failed to attract the notice of the historians whose narratives of this period survive.[22]

What Aeschines fails to say about his family in these passages from his speech of 343 is equally as significant as what he does say. In response to Demosthenes' challenge to list all his public services, Aeschines has very little to offer: his father was one of several hundred who helped restore the democracy in 403, and his uncle took part in some obscure naval engagement against the Spartans. One thing is quite clear: no one in his family could boast of having attained major public office, served as trierarch, or performed festival liturgies. Notable also is the fact that Aeschines does not deny that his father was a schoolteacher. He even admits Atrometus was not affluent, having lost his property during the Peloponnesian War and then being forced to earn money as a mercenary in Asia. For the moment we will leave aside the question of just how poor Atrometus was, but at this point we can safely conclude that he was not in the liturgical class. This probably held true for Glaucothea's family as well.

At the trial of Ctesiphon in 330 Demosthenes once more attacked Aeschines' parents. This time his insults grew more vicious. Demosthenes charges Atrometus was originally a slave named Tromes, "Trembler," and used to work for a certain Elpias, who taught school near the temple of Theseus. His mother was formerly a prostitute and was rescued from this "excellent profession" by the aid of the boatswain Phormio, the slave of Dion of Phrearroi. Her disgusting conduct earned her the nickname Empousa, "Hobgobblin." In another passage from the same speech, Demosthenes recounts with great sarcasm and unconcealed glee how Aeschines spent his youth doing chores for his parents. As a child, he ground ink and washed down the benches for the students at this father's school. When he was older, he assisted his mother while she performed initiations. He read to her from holy books, then at night donned a fawnskin, held the cup from which libations were poured, purified the initiates with mud and bran, and led them in a chant that went "I have escaped the bad, I have found the good." By day he marched bands of initiates crowned with fennel and white poplar through the streets of Athens, handled snakes, and carried ivy and the winnowing fan, all the while shouting "Hyes, attes! Attes, hyes!"[23]

We do not need to search far to find a reason for the higher degree of insult in this speech: at the trial of Ctesiphon, Demosthenes was speaking last and knew that his opponent would have no opportunity to reply to his slanders. The allegations about Atrometus being a slave and Glaucothea being a prostitute can be discarded. If there was any truth to these charges, Demosthenes ought to have uttered them in his earlier speech. In other respects, however, Demosthenes is rather consistent: he calls Atrometus a schoolteacher and says that Glaucothea was a priestess in both speeches. In the later speech he goes into far greater detail in his description of her priestly duties, but it is difficult to identify the rites that Demosthenes is talking about. Of the several candidates proposed, none has won general acceptance. The mysteries of Dionysus have been suggested, and so have those of Sabazius. Yet the reading of holy books and the emphasis on purification seem to point in the direction of Orphic practices. I doubt that Demosthenes is portraying these rites with clinical accuracy. The uncertainty about their precise identity is most likely due to the orator's indiscriminate jumbling of practices drawn from different types of exotic ceremonies, all thrown together for the sake of humorous effect by a process of comic syncretism. The most we can say with some certainty is that Glaucothea conducted some kind of private purification ritual for the benefit of anyone who wished to participate.[24]

What can we conclude about Aeschines' parents from this material? The statements of Aeschines and Demosthenes concur insofar as they both represent Atrometus as not belonging to the wealthier stratum of Athenian society. But if Atrometus, at least after his losses in the Peloponnesian War, was not wealthy, how poor was he? Something can be inferred from his profession as schoolteacher. The fact that he had to work for a living indicates that he is not likely to have had a large amount of property, but given the absence of any details about his assets it is impossible to tell whether he was a thete or not. The best evidence for Atrometus' economic position is the fact that his son Aeschines was able to serve as a hoplite. Service as a hoplite, though not one of the most expensive duties demanded of a citizen, did nevertheless require some expenditure. In fact, some who met the property qualification could not afford the expenses of a military campaign. Since it is unlikely that Aeschines and his brothers could have acquired enough money by themselves before reaching the age of majority at eighteen to afford the necessary equipment, it is safe to conclude that Atrometus must have had enough property to qualify as a hoplite. Atrometus was thus by no means poverty-stricken, although he may have appeared so to Demosthenes, whose fortune was one of the largest in Attica.[25]

As for social status, Atrometus was hardly a *kalos kagathos*. The need to work for a living robbed him of the leisure to pursue the life of a gentleman. Nor was the profession of schoolmaster highly respected. For instance, one of the many insults directed at Epicurus by his rivals was that his father taught school for a pitiful fee. Yet this profession must have been more respectable than the manual crafts. After all, the children whom Atrometus taught must have come from those families that could afford to give their sons a good education. This enabled Aeschines and his brothers to grow up in the company of the young *kaloi kagathoi* and thereby to become acquainted with those who would serve in the cavalry and become trierarchs in later life. Their familiarity with the young *kaloi kagathoi* made it easier for them to mingle with the members of respectable society in the gymnasia, where Aeschines claimed, not without plausibility, he and his brothers passed their leisure hours. Yet, despite these advantages, it was still an embarrassment for Aeschines to have had a father who had been a schoolteacher, a fact that Demosthenes never permitted him to forget.[26]

Before moving on to discuss the family of Aeschines' mother, there is an additional piece of evidence to consider, one not found in the speeches. This is the tombstone of Aeschines' maternal uncle Cleobulus. The tombstone consists of a stele, which carries an inscription in which Cleobulus is praised as a seer and as a soldier who was crowned for his valor in battle. Above the inscription is a sculpted relief depicting an eagle grasping a snake in its talons. The relief must represent the kind of portent that a seer was trained to interpret and thus symbolizes Cleobulus' profession. It is ill-advised to draw any conclusions about the social position of Cleobulus from the fact that he was honored with such a memorial. This type of stele could not have cost much more than thirty drachmai at the very most, not a large sum, one that was certainly within the reach of a man who had served as hoplite. And Cleobulus' tombstone is far less elaborate than many of the more lavish funeral monuments of the period. We also know that the custom of paying such honors to the dead was not confined to a small elite, but was fairly widespread. Yet his military service still indicates that Cleobulus like his brother-in-law Atrometus was of hoplite status.[27]

Nor should we conclude that Cleobulus' profession as seer and Glaucothea's priesthood reveal that they both came from an old priestly family and were thus far more respectable than the slanders of Demosthenes would permit us to believe. Such a conclusion would be mistaken for two reasons. First, it is clear that Glaucothea was not a priestess in one of the famous state cults that alone conferred a large measure of prestige. Far otherwise; she appears to have held private ceremonies for which she may have charged a fee, if we can believe Demosthenes. There was nothing especially dishonorable about such religious practices, however ridiculous Demosthenes tries to make them appear. Second, it is necessary to distinguish between a seer and a priest. The priest was one who performed sacrifices on behalf of a group of people who formed a religious association. These associations might be public or private. Priests and priestesses derived their prestige from the importance of the cults they administered. A cult like that of Athena Polias was obviously a source of great pride to the Eteobutadai, whose daughters held its priesthood. Yet if the cult were a minor one, it would bring little renown to those who conducted its rites. The priesthoods of public cults were official positions, and some were elective just like the magistracies. On the other hand, the magistrates of the city might themselves act as priests and perform sacrifices on behalf of the entire city.

The seer was very different from a priest. The seer did not inherit his position, nor was he appointed or elected to it. Instead he learned the skill of prophecy. Although this skill, like many others in Archaic and Classical Greece, was often passed down from father to son, it could theoretically be learned and practiced by anyone in the community. The skill of prophecy consisted of ascertaining the will of the gods by a variety of means, the most traditional one being the interpretation of omens such as the flight of birds. The seer was normally called on by individual clients to give advice about what sacrifices they should perform in order to assuage the anger of the gods or to improve their lot in life. The seer was generally consulted about sacrifices on private matters, but might also offer his advice from time to time at public meetings. Unlike the priest, the seer did nor perform sacrifices on behalf of others; rather he acted as a religious expert who used his knowledge to counsel his clients. Despite the fact that anyone who wished to could try to prophesy, not everyone was equally good at it. Some, such as the seer who correctly suggested to Xenophon that a sacrifice to Zeus Meilichios would put an end to his run of back luck, were very gifted. But others who were not so successful at producing positive results were often regarded as charlatans and quacks. In contrast to the priest, whose prestige derived from the renown of the cult he administered, the seer owed his prestige to the success and reliability of his prophecies. The best ones were naturally in high demand and might gain widespread fame. One thinks immediately of Lampon, who attained prominence in the fifth century and earned the friendship of Pericles. Sthorys, a seer from Thrace, was awarded citizenship by the Athenian people for his accurate prophecy of Conon's naval victory over the Spartans. Talented seers could command impressive fees. A seer named Thrasyllus retired to his native Aegina with a large fortune after a lucrative career making prophecies.[28]

We can now see there is no reason to believe that Glaucothea and Cleobulus belonged to a prominent priestly family. Cleobulus was not even a priest, and Glaucothea was only a priestess in a small private cult. Given our ignorance about Cleobulus' record as a seer, we have no way of knowing how much prestige he enjoyed. Indeed, Aeschines' complete silence about his uncle's profession suggests that Cleobulus never made any stunning prophecies and remained just an obscure seer, certainly not in the class of a Lampon or a Thrasyllus.

The picture that emerges from the information provided by Aeschines and Demosthenes is of a family that was not poor, but without the advantages of birth and wealth that would have enabled Aeschines and his brothers to gain easy acceptance into the circle of respectable society. Just the same, Atrometus was able to give his sons one social advantage: a traditional education. Among his claims to be included among the *kaloi kagathoi,* this certainly proved to be Aeschines' strong suit, and he put it to good use in his court speeches, where by his extensive quotations from the poets he portrays himself as a cultured gentleman. This helps to explain why of all the Attic orators Aeschines is the one who is most addicted to reciting long passages of poetry. Unable to point to any famous ancestors or to numerous public services performed by his family, Aeschines could only use what he had learned from his education to show that he merited the respect to which a *kalos kagathos* was entitled. His obvious pride in his education made him a bit of a snob. In all three of his speeches he often berates his enemies for their lack of knowledge and refinement.[29]

But Atrometus was not affluent enough to pay for the lessons given by the professional teachers of rhetoric such as Isocrates, who charged one thousand drachmai for his entire course. Yet the lack of this kind of training was not considered a social handicap; study with the professional teachers of rhetoric or the Sophists was not a prerequisite for becoming a *kalos kagathos.* If anything, their influence was often seen as pernicious. The hostility of Pheidippides toward Socrates and his ilk at the beginning of Aristophanes' *Clouds* was no doubt characteristic of the attitude held by many *kaloi kagathoi* toward the Sophists and teachers of rhetoric. When his father Strepsiades insists that Socrates and his associates in the Thinkery are *kaloi kagathoi,* Pheidippides strenuously denies his claim. They are *poneroi,* he asseverates, men who go barefoot and are as pale as *banausoi.* If he studies with them, he will lose his sun-tanned complexion gained while racing horses and exercising in the gymnasium. Once he has become as pale as these eggheads, he will never be able to show his face to the young men who serve with him in the cavalry. The attitude of Pheidippides is similar to that of several other *kaloi kagathoi* whom we meet in the dialogues of Plato. In the *Meno* Anytus says he has had his own son educated in the traditional manner, but has a horror of Sophists. Callicles, who figures so prominently in the *Gorgias,* calls them worthless fellows. And in the dialogue named after him, Laches declares that quibbling over words is suitable for a Sophist, but not for a man who wishes to lead the city. Cleon appealed to this widespread prejudice when he compared those who opposed his drastic measures for Mytilene to Sophists.[30]

Oddly enough, the social position of Atrometus' family is best characterized by no one other than Demosthenes. When speaking about the professions of Aeschines and his brothers, Demosthenes admits condescendingly that they were not entirely blameworthy, but goes on to assert that they are not deserving of the generalship either. Despite his hostility, Demosthenes does not place Atrometus and his family at the bottom of the Athenian social scale, but was equally certain that they did not belong to the upper crust, that segment of society that in his opinion was alone worthy of election to the generalship. His lack of social advantages did not ultimately prevent Aeschines and his brothers from entering politics and achieving a modest degree of success. Whatever Demosthenes may have thought about his family's social status, Aeschines' brother Philochares was elected general at least three times. Nonetheless, his modest means forced him to work for a living for several years before he was able to attract the attention of two powerful men who helped him to get started on a political career.[31]

Early Career

Aeschines has little to say about his life in the years before he entered politics. The only information he provides comes from his speech of 343 where he lists the military campaigns he has served on to demonstrate his patriotism. There he recounts that he fought at Nemea (366), at Mantinea (362), and in the two campaigns on Euboea (357 and 348). In the second campaign on Euboea his conduct was so valorous that he received two crowns, one at the battle site and another in the Assembly. His omission of his activities in this period is not a sign of embarrassment on his part; they were simply not relevant to his aim of proving to the court that he was a loyal Athenian citizen who had risked his life for his community and thus deserved their gratitude.[32]

Where Aeschines is silent, Demosthenes gleefully fills in. To be sure, we must scrutinize his evidence with care. Yet amid the torrent of reckless slander, Demosthenes provides us with some reliable information that sheds light on Aeschines' activities prior to his entry into politics. Aeschines had to work for a living during these years, but the jobs he took were good training for his public career. And despite the scorn heaped on them by Demosthenes, they did not cripple Aeschines with serious social handicaps.

In his speech of 343, Demosthenes relates that Aeschines and his brother Aphobetus first served as undersecretaries, earning two or three drachmas a day. In another passage from the same speech, he reminds Aeschines that he should not be ignorant of the curse pronounced by the herald since it was his duty when he served as assistant to the Council and Assembly to read the law about the curse to the herald. His comments in this speech are merely scornful, but his invective grows more bitter in the speech delivered for Ctesiphon. There he declares that Aeschines began to work for the community as a public secretary upon reaching the age of majority, but left that profession after having committed the kind of crimes he now charges others with. Demosthenes characteristically fails to specify his opponent's crimes, and we should also bear in mind that Aeschines had no chance to reply to these remarks since Demosthenes was speaking last on this occasion. Not that Aeschines would have bothered to rebut them, had he had the opportunity. This sort of vague abuse was all too common and easily ignored.[33]

To judge from Demosthenes' statements, Aeschines appears to have started out as an undersecretary to various magistrates. These secretaries were drawn from a pool and were prohibited from serving the same magistracy for two years in a row. The restriction was probably enacted to prevent them from becoming too powerful by learning more about the duties of the magistracies than those who held the positions each year. The office to which Demosthenes says Aeschines was later elected must be that of the secretary who read documents to the Council and Assembly. This office was always elective, unlike the Secretary for the Laws, which was always selected by lot, and the Secretary for the Council, which was elective at first, then after 368/67 selected by lot. Since Demosthenes implies that Aeschines spent several years serving as undersecretary before his election to the post of public secretary, it is unlikely he would have been able to stand for election to the post of Secretary for the Council before it ceased to be elective. Furthermore, the other two

secretaries appear to have been responsible only to the Council whereas Demosthenes reveals that Aeschines served both the Council and Assembly simultaneously. Finally, Demosthenes' statement that Aeschines read out the law about the curse to the herald certainly fits the office of the secretary who read documents to the Council and Assembly better than the other two posts.[34]

Aeschines was eminently well suited for the position because of his remarkable voice. His service in the post must have been a valuable education, for it appears to have given him a good knowledge of laws and decrees, one which he drew on heavily during his prosecutions of Timarchus and Ctesiphon. The position of undersecretary was not a dishonorable one, as even Demosthenes admits, but the fact that Aeschines had to accept a paid position indicates that he did not have enough wealth to support himself without working for a living. This was clearly something of an embarrassment for him later. On the other hand, it was an honor to win election to the post of public secretary and to take one's meals in the *tholos* along with the *prytanes*.[35]

Demosthenes says that after finishing his service as a public secretary, Aeschines became an actor. In his speech of 343 he describes how Aeschines was a member of a troupe that included Theodorus and Aristodemus. Unlike his more distinguished colleagues, who took the better parts, Aeschines always performed the third, or less important, roles. Demosthenes takes obvious pleasure in reminding the court how it was customary for the third actor (*tritagonistes*) to perform the part of tyrant, such as Creon in Sophocles' *Antigone*. Elsewhere in the same speech Demosthenes recounts how Aeschines, despite his remarkable voice, was driven from the stage by the jeers of the audience and forced to quit the profession. In his speech of 330 Demosthenes again refers to Aeschines as *tritagonistes,* but instead of making him an associate of the renowned Theodorus and Aristodemus, places him in the company of Simylus and Socrates, otherwise known as "The Growlers." As we noted before, Demosthenes' invective becomes more biting in the later speech. Here he says that it was not hisses and catcalls that drove Aeschines from the stage, but figs, olives, and grapes. Demosthenes adds sarcastically that these vegetables provided him with more sustenance than the meager fees he collected for his wretched acting. Since Demosthenes spoke at the trial of Ctesiphon without fear of rebuttal, we should accordingly place more weight on the remarks made in his earlier speech.[36]

It is important to note that Demosthenes taunts Aeschines not for having been an actor, but for being an incompetent actor. When insulting Aeschines, he never calls him *hypocrites* (actor), but *tritagonistes,* the one who is confined to lesser roles because of his mediocre skills. Aeschines alludes to these comments about his acting, but never attempts to refute them point by point. In accordance with the principles we have laid down, we should accept the essential point of Demosthenes' remarks, that is, that Aeschines was at one time an actor. Yet at the same time, we have a right to be skeptical about the details provided by Demosthenes, especially the more insulting ones found in his later speech.[37]

Was Aeschines ashamed of the fact that he had once been an actor? One might well come to that conclusion after reading a work entitled *Problems* attributed to Aristotle. There the question is raised "Why are the artists of Dionysus in the majority of cases bad men?" and the answer given is that they are depraved because they have no time to spend in pursuit of wisdom and are either profligate or in need all of the time. Yet this is only the opinion of a philosopher and not the only evidence available to us. A better indication of social attitudes toward actors are the activities of some contemporary actors. Neoptolemus, highly prized for his voice by Philip II of Macedon and several others, served as ambassador for the king on a mission to Athens and was instrumental in persuading the Athenians to begin negotiations with the king in 346. Another actor, Aristodemus, was elected by the Athenians to go as ambassador to Philip in 347 and later to Thessaly and Magnesia. According to Aeschines, Demosthenes himself proposed a crown for Aristodemus as a reward for his services on the last two missions. In short, there is no reason to believe that actors were generally despised. On the contrary, some of them enjoyed so much respect that they were entrusted with positions of honor and responsibility. Their ability to speak effectively was highly valued in a society where oratory was important in both politics and diplomacy and made them attractive candidates to act as ambassadors to speak on behalf of their cities abroad. This was certainly true for Aeschines, who soon after entering his political career put his trained voice to use on embassies to the Peloponnese, Macedon, and Delphi.[38]

If Aeschines failed to respond to Demosthenes' attacks on his acting, it was not because he was ashamed to have followed that profession at one time. As for his talent as an actor, we have no means of judging. Demosthenes, our principal informant on this matter, is not an impartial drama critic. The fact that Aeschines shared the stage with two of the most famous actors of his day would appear to indicate he had some talent, though not enough to place him in the first rank. Nor do we have any idea how much Aeschines would have earned as an actor. The most successful could reap impressive rewards for their performances, but Aeschines was probably not among their number.[39]

Demosthenes' claim that Aeschines left the stage because hostile audiences made it dangerous for him to remain there does not inspire confidence in its veracity. Aeschines is far more likely to have given up acting because he was able to better his position in society by means of marriage and thus no longer found it necessary to work for a living. The date of his marriage is not known, but in 343 he introduced his wife and three small children to beg the court for mercy at his trial. The very young age of his children appears to point to a recent marriage, probably around 348, just around the time he entered the political arena.[40]

The father of Aeschines' bride was a man named Philodemus. He seems to have been influential in his deme of Paiania, because Aeschines says that he was called upon to vouch for Demosthenes when the latter was enrolled on the list of citizens upon coming of age. Demosthenes' allegation made in 330 that Aeschines inherited five talents from Philodemus' son Philon also gives the impression that the family was rather wealthy. This impression is strengthened by the fact that Philodemus' uncle was a member of the Thousand, a group of property owners who were liable for the trierarchy and for liturgies. Whether we should believe Demosthenes' allegation, however, is another question. Demosthenes provides this information when accusing Aeschines of failing to perform liturgies despite his ability to do so. Since Demosthenes was speaking for the defendant when he made the charge, it is impossible to know how Aeschines would have responded to it. Demosthenes may have invented the legacy or inflated its value to make Aeschines' failure to perform liturgies appear to be the result of lack of public spirit and not his lack of means. Yet Philon's ability to bequeath such a large amount must have appeared plausible. Certainly Demosthenes could not have told this story unless Philon's wealth was common knowledge.[41]

Even if Aeschines never inherited any money from Philon, he must have received a sizable dowry from his father-in-law Philodemus. As a rich man, Philodemus may have presented his son-in-law with up to a talent. Whatever the exact sum, it seems to have been enough to allow Aeschines to stop working for a living. By the time Demosthenes prosecuted him in 343, Aeschines could no longer be ridiculed for having to labor for wages. But the dowry did not lift Aeschines into the liturgical class. If it had, the ambitious Aeschines ought to have undertaken one or more liturgies before his trial in 343 and to have boasted about them in the speech he delivered then as was traditional for a defendant to do. Yet if Aeschines had been in the liturgical class and had failed to perform any liturgies by 343, Demosthenes would definitely have made an issue of it in his speech of that year just as he did later in 330. Instead Demosthenes in 343 attributed the failure of Aeschines' family to undertake liturgies to poverty, not to lack of patriotism.[42]

Looking back over Aeschines' early career, one cannot help but be struck by the contrast it forms with that of Demosthenes. Demosthenes was fortunate enough to have a father whose property of almost fourteen talents made him one of the wealthiest men in Attica. He was less lucky in his father's choice of guardians, who embezzled most of the assets he inherited. Despite the dishonesty of his guardians, Demosthenes was able to recover much of his property and to acquire not only a traditional education, but also training with Isaeus. Before the age of thirty, Demosthenes had completed four trierarchies, either on his own or in conjunction with another. By age thirty-six he had acted as *choregos* for the Panathenaea and had voluntarily produced a dithyrambic performance at the Dionysia as well as provided a feast for his entire tribe. While still in his twenties, he may have prosecuted Cephisodotus, if we can trust Aeschines on this point. After this legal battle, he refrained from prosecuting others until Meidias' outrageous behavior prompted him to seek revenge in court. He did keep active in the courts indirectly, however, by writing speeches for other politicians. Demosthenes gave his first speech in the Assembly at around age thirty and spoke frequently thereafter.[43]

Demosthenes was not unique in getting such an early start. Timarchus, who was about the same age as Aeschines, was active as a member of the Council at roughly age thirty or shortly after; a few years later he served as a magistrate on Andros. By the time of his trial in 346 Timarchus had served on numerous embassies. Nausicles, another contemporary of Aeschines, had already been elected general at least once by the time he reached his late thirties in 353/52, the year in which he won acclaim for defending the pass at Thermopylai against Philip of Macedon. In comparison with these men, Aeschines was a later starter: he gave his maiden speech in the Assembly in 348 when he was about forty-two.[44]

When both men were elected to serve on the First Embassy to Philip in 346, Demosthenes, who was about six years younger than Aeschines, had far more experience in politics and had accomplished far greater services for the city. It is therefore not surprising to find him looking down on Aeschines as an upstart who was usurping honors and privileges to which his social background did not entitle him. Next we need to examine how Aeschines managed to rise so swiftly to prominence in the Assembly despite his lack of those advantages that had enabled Demosthenes to begin his public career at a much earlier age.

AESCHINES' ENTRY INTO POLITICS

To understand what it meant to be a politician and how one started on a political career in Classical Athens, a brief look at the political institutions of the city is necessary. The most powerful political institution in Athens was the Assembly, where all major decisions regarding important issues, both foreign and domestic, were voted on by the citizens of Athens. The Athenians of the Classical period did not elect officials to make crucial political decisions for them. They met at least forty times a year to listen to debates and make collective decisions directly. The Council of Five Hundred and the magistrates only reported to the Assembly and carried out its policies. Not only could every citizen vote in the Assembly; anyone who wished to could also make a proposal and submit it to the Athenian people for consideration. If the proposal gained a majority of the votes cast by the Assembly, it became official policy. One did not need to be elected to office to exert a decisive influence on the affairs of the city. All one had to do was to stand up at a meeting of the Assembly and speak one's mind.[45]

Although the Assembly was open to all Athenians who wished to address it, few actually took full advantage of the opportunity. Out of the thousands of Athenian citizens, only a handful appear to have regularly spoken on public issues and made proposals concerning foreign and domestic matters. The Athenians called these men *rhetores*—orators—and that is precisely what they were, men who exercised an influence in politics not by virtue of holding an office, but solely through their ability to speak persuasively to a large gathering of men. Although *rhetores* might be elected to minor offices or selected by lot to serve in the Council, these activities were secondary to their main role, which was to give advice to the Athenian people on public matters. They measured their success not so much by the importance of the positions they held as by the number of proposals they convinced the Assembly to ratify that brought benefits to the Athenian people. The highest honor a *rhetor* could aspire to was to be awarded a gold crown and to have a motion of praise for his accomplishments read out in the Assembly and the Theater of Dionysus.[46]

The most powerful official post a *rhetor* might hold was to serve as ambassador for his city during negotiations with a foreign state. Since the Athenians did not maintain a professional diplomatic corps, they elected those *rhetores* who advised them about foreign affairs as ambassadors and sent them abroad to negotiate treaties and alliances. But these appointments usually lasted just a short time, not longer than it took to travel abroad, conduct the negotiations, and return to Athens. After delivering their reports about their embassies, they relinquished their posts and returned to their customary role as *rhetores*.[47]

The only magistrates who held much power in Athens were the ten generals who were elected annually by the Assembly to lead the army and navy. Theirs was the most prestigious office an Athenian could aspire to. For the ambitious it afforded the chance to win lasting fame by winning victories over the enemies of Athens. Yet no matter how successful a general might be, he still had to submit to the will of the Assembly and carry out its orders. The prestige his office conferred on him made it easier for the general to gain a favorable hearing, but the office did not grant him any special privileges in the Assembly. If he wished to influence public decisions, the general had to submit a proposal to the Assembly in the same way as any other Athenian citizen.[48]

The traditional way to get started in politics was to demonstrate one's good will toward the Athenian people by a conspicuous display of generosity. This could be done in several ways, perhaps the most effective one being to spend lavishly on a chorus for one of the dramatic festivals. Such an effort not only helped to bring victory to one's tribe, but provided entertainment for all who attended the performance. Another way of winning favor was to provide a sumptuous meal for one's tribe when called to finance one of the official feasts that accompanied the City Dionysia and the Great Panathenaea. According to an anecdote recounted by Plutarch, Alcibiades made his debut in the Assembly by making a voluntary contribution (*epidosis*) when an appeal was made to the wealthy for financial assistance. The anecdote may be fictional, but it aptly illustrates how important such generosity was for establishing one's reputation. Nor did one have to distribute largesse only through public channels; it was equally possible to do private favors for one's fellow citizens. Cimon used his enormous wealth to make gifts of food and clothing to poor Athenians. Mantitheus boasted to a court that he had given thirty drachmai apiece to poor men of his deme to cover their personal expenses during a military campaign. Demosthenes donated money to pay the ransom of several Athenians held prisoner in Macedon. After his victory in the chariot races at the Pythian games, Chabrias invited many to celebrate his achievement at a feast at Colias.[49]

The gratitude and recognition gained from this generosity came in handy at meetings of the Assembly. The Athenians were not ones to forget a favor and often repaid their benefactors by casting votes for them when they were candidates for public office. Xenophon describes how a certain Nicomachides complained to Socrates about losing to the wealthy Antisthenes in his bid to be elected general. Antisthenes had fewer qualifications for the post than Nicomachides, but had courted popularity by winning first place at many dramatic competitions. It is perhaps no accident that the first public activity of Pericles we know about is his victory as *choregos* for Aeschylus' dramatic trilogy of 472. Nicias was able to maintain public favor by his unstinting generosity, most notably by his benefactions to the sanctuary of Apollo on Delos. The situation did not change in the fourth century: Demosthenes tells us how Meidias was in the habit of citing his many liturgies when speaking in the Assembly.[50]

Another way to start on a political career was through the courts. Since there was no public prosecutor in Athens, it was possible for anyone to prosecute someone whom he suspected of a public crime. Several ambitious men took advantage of this opportunity to accuse prominent politicians of various crimes against the community, such as treason or embezzlement. Because these cases were tried before courts staffed by hundreds of citizens and often drew large crowds of spectators, they might serve as a means of drawing attention to the aspiring politician intent on gaining a reputation for protecting the public interest. The first person to pursue this path with notable success was Cleon; all the other prominent politicians before him chose to make their way in politics by means of liturgies, private generosity, and military service. Several men in the fourth century, such as Hyperides, Aristogeiton, Aristophon, and Lycurgus, followed Cleon's example with varying degrees of success. This path, however, involved certain risks. A man who prosecuted too frequently might acquire a reputation for being a *sykophantes,* one who prosecuted for private gain or slandered the rich and powerful out of envy at their good fortune. Success in the courts might thrust one suddenly into the political

spotlight, but a humiliating defeat could plunge a man into permanent ignominy. Even success in court was not without danger. Every man whom a politician brought into court would become his sworn enemy. The more one prosecuted, the more numerous one's enemies became. Each one of these enemies, not to mention their many relatives and friends, would be eager to retaliate by launching prosecutions of their own. Nothing demonstrates this better than the example of Timarchus. Together with Demosthenes, Timarchus accused Aeschines of betraying Athenian interests as ambassador to Philip in 346. Before the case came to court, however, Aeschines struck back by accusing Timarchus of having violated the law that forbid male prostitutes to address the Assembly. Aeschines was able to bring his case to court first and obtained a conviction, which cost Timarchus his citizen rights.[51]

When embarking on a political career, it is always advantageous to have powerful friends and relatives. In democratic Athens, where all offices were filled by election or lot, it was not possible to gain appointment merely on the strength of one's connections. The Athenians still felt that they could tell a great deal about a man from his parents and from the company he kept. They were naturally more inclined to trust those who were descended from, or associated with, men who had proven to be reliable in the past. When it came to electing ambassadors, the Assembly often picked men whose ancestors had maintained ties with the community to which the embassy was being sent. In the fifth century, the political scene was dominated by men such as Miltiades, Cimon, Thucydides (the son of Melesias), Pericles, and Alcibiades, who belonged to old and well-established families. But the turmoil at the end of the fifth century decimated the ranks of these families. As a result, Athenian politics in the fourth century was full of politicians and generals whose family trees were quite barren when it came to illustrious ancestors. Some men, such as Callistratus, whose uncle Agyrrhius had been active in politics, and Timotheus, whose father Conon had won the battle of Cnidus over the Spartan fleet in 394, did not have to struggle up from obscurity, but they tended to be the exception to the rule of *novi homines*. Although the majority of those who served as generals or spoke in the Assembly did not have prestigious families to help them get started, they could still attach themselves to prominent figures and hope their endorsements would boost their chances for advancement. Phocion, for example, fought several campaigns with Chabrias and became his protégé. Chabrias in return promoted Phocion's career and assigned him to missions that helped to build his reputation.[52]

The path that Aeschines took when entering politics was partly dictated by circumstances and partly the result of personal choice. Given his limited resources, the possibility of gaining popularity by performing expensive liturgies was automatically ruled out. Yet the same could not be said for the possibility of making his mark as a prosecutor in the courts. Though not blessed with a large inheritance, Aeschines was endowed with an excellent voice and some talent as an actor. These qualities clearly stood him in good stead when he brought Timarchus to trial in 346, but by then Aeschines had already become prominent, having addressed the Assembly many times and having served on four important embassies. And when he prosecuted Timarchus, it was only in self-defense. Had Timarchus and Demosthenes not charged him at his *euthynai* with betraying Athenian interests, Aeschines would never have brought his suit at all. So reluctant was Aeschines to resort to the courts when attacking opponents that he did not bring charges against another person until ten years later when in 336 he accused Ctesiphon of proposing an illegal decree. He then waited another six years before he felt confident enough to allow the case to be heard. His unwillingness to use the courts to further his career is all the more surprising considering how well he did against Timarchus.[53]

One of the reasons why Aeschines did not choose to make his reputation in the court is that he was able to get his start by other means. As we will soon see, Aeschines was lucky enough to gain the friendship of two men whose opinions and abilities were highly esteemed in the Assembly. Their friendship helped him to achieve prominence without creating risks and incurring opprobrium. The Athenians regarded the courts as a place for sordid wrangling, not the sort of area the members of polite society spent much time in. In fact, one of the most effective ways of winning a court's favor was to claim that one had never before been involved in a legal dispute. Aeschines, like anyone who aspired to be a *kalos kagathos*, did not prosecute unless he absolutely had to. There may have been another consideration that deterred him. Prosecutions gained a man enemies who would seek to retaliate by bringing charges against him. That was less of a threat to a rich man, who, when accused of wrongdoing, could always cite his numerous benefactions and expect to win acquittal from a grateful court. But Aeschines could not rely on such a method of defense. Speaking on his own behalf in 343, Aeschines had little to boast about in terms of public service. The best he could do was to mention the campaigns he had fought and a crown won for bravery in battle. That was not very impressive when placed next to Demosthenes' list of liturgies and may in part account for the narrow margin by which he was acquitted of charges for which there was no solid evidence. Considering his vulnerability to judicial attack, it is not surprising Aeschines did not go out of his way to make enemies of prominent men by prosecuting them.[54]

The lack of a large fortune was not the only disadvantage Aeschines inherited from his family. Since his mother and father do not appear to have been related to any of the powerful families in Attica, Aeschines had no relatives who could have helped him launch his political career. His father had never participated in politics beyond performing his normal duties as citizen and had enjoyed no close friendship with any famous general or politician. Despite his father's membership in the phratry to which the Eteobutadai belonged, Aeschines never appears to have been connected with Lycurgus, the most distinguished member of that *genos* during his lifetime. Although his uncle Cleobulus won a crown for valor in battle, he may have been dead by the time his nephew was ready to speak in the Assembly. The only man to our knowledge associated with Cleobulus was Demaenetus, but no evidence indicates he ever lent Aeschines support. Aeschines' older brother Philochares was a general during the years 345/44, 344/43, and 343/42, but his tenure began after Aeschines had served on several embassies. If anything, Philochares may have owed his rise to his brother's success. Iphicrates, to whom Philochares had attached himself earlier in his career, was dead by 352. His son Menestheus, though married to the daughter of the renowned Timotheus, never appears to have come near to equaling his father's reputation and influence. Nor could Menetheus' father-in-law Timotheus have helped Aeschines: after his trial in 354/53 Timotheus went into exile. His son Conon remained in Athens, but never rose to prominence. Thus all the influential men whom Aeschines could have met through family connections were either dead or in no position to assist him getting started in politics.[55]

Aeschines made one valuable friend while training as an ephebe. This was Nausicles, who later nominated him for election as ambassador in 346. Nausicles also served on the same embassy and later testified on Aeschines' behalf at his trial in 343. Nausicles became a national hero when he commanded the Athenian expedition that prevented Philip from seizing Thermopylai in 352 and won a gold crown in recognition of his achievement. Yet despite his support at a crucial juncture, it was not Nausicles who was responsible for starting Aeschines on his political career.[56]

The political patron who launched Aeschines on his career in the Assembly appears to have been Phocion. Aeschines came to the attention of Phocion during the Athenian campaign on Euboea in 348. In that year, Plutarch of Eretria asked the Athenians to ward off the threat of his neighbor Callias of Chalcis. The Assembly granted his request and sent a force of hoplite and cavalry to Euboea under the command of Phocion. Aeschines joined the expedition, possibly as a volunteer. He was about forty-two at the time, and men thirty-five and older were usually called up only in emergencies. It was not Aeschines' first campaign. He had previously fought with distinction on an expedition to bring supplies to Phleious in 366, at the Battle of Mantinea in 362, and on an earlier campaign in Euboea in 357. After landing his troops on Euboea, Phocion led the force inland until he reached the territory around Tamynai, where he was ambushed and cut off by Callias' troops. During the ensuing battle, Aeschines fought as a member of a company of picked troops that played a decisive role in securing the Athenian victory. His bravery in action was so great that he was awarded a crown of honor on the battlefield. As a further honor, he was selected to accompany the taxiarch Temenides to announce the victory to the Assembly. During his report to the Assembly, Temenides spoke about Aeschines' valor with such enthusiasm that the Athenians rewarded him with another crown of honor.[57]

The campaign on Euboea was the beginning of a long friendship between Aeschines and Phocion. When Aeschines was charged with treason by Demosthenes, Phocion stepped forward in court to testify on his behalf. In 338 after the Athenian defeat at Chaeronea, the two men went as ambassadors to negotiate peace with Philip. It may have been through Phocion that Aeschines struck up an association with Eubulus. Shortly after his awards for bravery, Aeschines made his debut in the Assembly speaking in support of a proposal made by Eubulus. After the Assembly ratified the proposal, Aeschines was elected as one of the ambassadors sent to carry out Eubulus' decree. In subsequent years Aeschines continued to champion Eubulus' policies. In 346 the two men advocated peace with Philip in the Assembly during the meeting of Elaphebolion 18. When Aeschines was prosecuted by Demosthenes in 343 for his role in negotiating the peace, Aeschines claimed it was not himself, but the policy of Eubulus that was being attacked. Eubulus agreed with Aeschines' assessment of Demosthenes' motive for he appeared on his friend's behalf at the trial. Eubulus may have introduced Aeschines to several prominent men in his circle, who were later seen in his company. The most notorious of these was Meidias, who feuded with Demosthenes and punched him during the festival of Dionysus in 348. When Demosthenes brought Meidias to trial in 346, Eubulus declared he would testify for him presumably out of friendship. Meidias accompanied Aeschines to Delphi as *pylagoros* in 339 and died shortly after. The warmth with which Aeschines refers to Meidias in his speech against Ctesiphon strongly suggests they were close friends. The Stephanus who accompanied Aeschines on the Third Embassy to Philip in 346 may be identical with Stephanus of Eroiadai with whom Eubulus socialized. Aeschines and Stephanus may have had a common friend in Phaedrus, the son of Callias of Sphettos, which would lend some support to the identification.[58]

Phocion may have also assisted Aeschines in finding a wife. Philodemus, the father of Aeschines' bride, had two sons, one of whom, Philon, had served under Chabrias in Egypt. Phocion had been Chabrias' protégé, and after his mentor's death, looked after his incorrigible son Ctesippus. Since there are no other known links between the families of Aeschines and Philodemus, it is possible that Phocion, who may have made the acquaintance of Philon through their common friend Chabrias, may have introduced Aeschines to Philon and recommended him as a suitable candidate for the hand of his sister. Admittedly this is only speculation, but such a hypothesis would explain how Aeschines was able to marry a woman from a family which was socially above his own station.[59]

Eubulus and Phocion were very useful friends for a novice politician to have. Eubulus exercised great influence in public through his control of the Theoric Fund. This fund was ostensibly created for the inauspicious purpose of making small grants to citizens to enable them to attend major religious festivals. Sometime in the 350s, however, Eubulus and Diophantus persuaded the Athenians to have all the surplus revenues from the public budget paid into this fund, a move which gave those in control of the fund the power to initiate expensive construction projects. There was probably little money in the fund during the lean years after the Social War when Athenian revenues dropped to 130 talents a year. In the next decade the financial picture brightened, and revenues rose to 400 talents a year, enabling Eubulus to build dockyards, an arsenal, and roads. All of these projects must have greatly enhanced his prestige in the Assembly. The appointment of Aeschines' younger brother Aphobetus to a position supervising Athenian revenues may have been the result of Eubulus' recommendation.[60]

While Eubulus gained a reputation for financial expertise, Phocion won his laurels on the battlefield. Phocion first gained distinction at the Battle of Naxos in 376 where he commanded the left wing of the Athenian fleet and contributed to Chabrias' victory over the Spartans. We know nothing of his exploits in the next three decades aside from his command at Chios in 356 during the Social War and his victory at Tamynai in 348, but the silence of our sources should not lead us to conclude he was otherwise inactive during the period. The Athenians clearly trusted his ability and judgment for they elected him general forty-five times before his death in 318.[61]

What probably made Aeschines attractive to these men was his ability to speak. Neither Phocion nor Eubulus seems to have had much talent as an orator. According to Plutarch, Phocion attempted to serve Athens both as a general on the battlefield and as a speaker in the Assembly. His aspiration to excel in both arenas defied a contemporary trend. In Phocion's day, the *bema* or rostrum of the Assembly was monopolized by *rhetores,* not generals. Despite his unfashionable ambition, Phocion's accomplishments as a speaker never equaled those he achieved on campaign. In fact, none of our sources record an event when a speech of Phocion had a major impact on Athenian policy during Aeschines' years in the Assembly. His eloquence seems to have been more laconic than Attic: all he left behind was a set of blunt epigrams, which delighted Plutarch, but do not appear to have endeared him to his fellow citizens. Phocion and Eubulus therefore needed someone to express their views on the Assembly. Aeschines' strong voice and dramatic training made him eminently well qualified for the task.[62]

We must not make the mistake of viewing Aeschines as merely the mouthpiece of a political party headed by Phocion and Eubulus. Aeschines may have claimed in 343 that he was being prosecuted for the policies of Eubulus, but it would be unwise to rule out the possibility that Aeschines was incapable of exercising his own judgment or influencing his more experienced associates. Second, there never existed in Classical Athens the kind of political parties we are familiar with. The modern political party, with its elaborate organizational structure, elected and appointed officials, regular meetings, mass membership, ideological commitments, and access to mass media, was unknown in antiquity. Politics was on a much smaller scale. In place of parties, there were loose-knit groups of *rhetores* and generals, individuals joined by the bonds of friendship or expedience, who aided each other in pursuit of success in the courts and the Assembly. It would be misleading to label these groups "parties" for that would give the erroneous impression that they were more stable and organized than they actually were. Aeschines, Eubulus, Phocion, and their friends did not constitute a party. Rather, they saw eye to eye on important issues and cooperated to further their common goals and their individual careers.[63]

Despite his late start in politics, Aeschines rose to prominence relatively quickly. While Demosthenes was not elected to an important embassy until eight years after his first speech in the Assembly, Aeschines earned this honor almost immediately. Lack of wealth delayed his entry into politics, but it did not slow him down once he was started. Had he been born a thete, however, he might not have been able to get started at all: he would never have qualified to go on campaign as a hoplite, and his marriage to the daughter of Philodemus would have been out of the question. His father's modest amount of property made the difference between a late start and no start at all. Yet what is most interesting about Aeschines' early career is that it reveals that politics in Athens was not dominated by a privileged elite who had large incomes and illustrious ancestors and stood at a distance from the mass of citizens. When Pericles boasted that it was talent that counted when the Athenians selected men for positions of honor, not membership in a restricted group, he may have been exaggerating a bit. But he was not too far from the truth.[64]

Notes

1. Unreliability of anecdotes: Vansina (1985) 95-96, 106, 132-33, 165-66, 169-70, 172. Interests of ancient biographers: Momigliano (1971) 71ff. Information found in lives of poets derived from statements in their works and inferences therefrom: Lefkowitz (1981). Information in lives of Aeschines derived mostly from statements found in his speeches and those of Demosthenes: Blass (1887-98) 3.2.154. Kindstrand (1982) 68-84 has examined the evidence furnished by the lives of Aeschines about his teachers and his teaching on Rhodes. While he rejects the statements about the former as "historically false," he is inclined to trust in the information about his teaching on Rhodes. But see Harris (1988b).

2. I am thus not concerned with the Solonian orders, which had fallen into desuetude by the fourth century: *Ath. Pol.* 7.4; 47.1 with Rhodes (1981) 145-46, 551. For the term "status-group" see Weber (1946) 186-88.

Davies (1981) 13-14 mistakenly conflates the two kinds of groups when he states that "the selection of the men who perform liturgies to embody the Athenian propertied class is the selection, not of an amorphous arbitrarily defined group of men at the top of the economic scale, but that of a group which

with its special burdens, responsibilities and privileges formed a recognized social class." Davies bases his view primarily on [X.] *Ath.* 1.13, but ignores other passages in the work where the author stresses birth and education, rather than wealth, in the determination of social class (cf. 1.2, 5, 13; 2.15). To borrow the terminology of R. Centers (1949) 12-29, the liturgical class formed a "social stratum" in which membership was determined by one criterion, in this case wealth, and not a "social class" in which membership is determined by class consciousness. Cf. the distinction made by Cantril (1943) between "social class" and "economic class." For a useful set of criteria to establish the existence of a "social class," see Ossowski (1963) 135-36. Whereas the liturgical class could be termed a "social stratum" (Centers) or "economic class" (Cantril), it exhibited little evidence of class consciousness; the *kaloi kagathoi* did possess the requisite qualities of a "social class" by their strong sense of class consciousness and shared life-style. Because it was difficult to maintain the life-style of a *kalos kagathos* without a certain amount of property, many members of the liturgical class were considered to be *kaloi kagathoi* and vice versa, but the two groups were not identical in their membership, which was defined in different ways. These fundamental methodological issues are passed over by Ober (1989).

3. On the cavalry in general see Bugh (1988). Recruiting of the cavalry: X. *Hipparch.* 1.9, 12 (Hipparchs enroll); *Ath. Pol.* 49.2 (*katalogeis* enroll). For the date of the change, see Bugh (1982). (I find Bugh's explanation for the change unconvincing.) The community provided the recruit with a loan toward the purchase of a horse (see Lys. 16.6-7 with Kroll [1977] 97-100) and with fodder (*Ath. Pol.* 49.1; Meiggs and Lewis [1969] #84, line 4; *IG* ii^2 1264, lines 5-8; *scholia ad* Dem. 24.101), but the rest of the expenses were paid by the recruit and must have been substantial. For *hippotrophia* as a luxury affordable only by the wealthy, see Davies (1981) 97-105. It would thus have been natural for the Hipparchs or *katalogeis* to look for recruits in the houses of those who performed liturgies. Note that someone who served in the cavalry as a young man was expected to perform liturgies when older (Dem. 42.21-25) and that the size of the cavalry was roughly the same as that of the liturgical class (Ar. *Eq.* 225; X. *Hipparch.* 9.3 and Dem. 14.13 place it at 1,000; *Ath. Pol.* 24.3 and Th. 2.13 place it at 1,200).

Number of liturgies: Davies (1967). Selection of *choregoi*: *Ath. Pol.* 56.3 with Rhodes (1981) 622-23. Duties of *choregos*: Pickard-Cambridge (1968) 75-78, 86-93. Cost of putting on a performance: Lys. 21.1. Costs of liturgies: Amit (1965) 103-15. The trierarchical system was reformed about 357: MacDowell (1986). Size of the liturgical class in the fourth century: Rhodes (1982) 2-5. Property required for inclusion in the liturgical class: Davies (1971) xxiv.

4. On the *eisphora* symmories see MacDowell (1986). On the question of the *proeisphorontes* see Wallace (1989b).

5. On the ephebeia in general see Pélékidis (1962). Age-classes: *Ath. Pol.* 53.4. Service as ephebes: Aeschin. 2.167; *Ath. Pol.* 42.3-4. Calling up by age-class: *Ath. Pol.* 53.7. Service until age fifty-nine: *Ath. Pol.* 53.4. Older men called up only in emergencies: Dem. 3.4; Aeschin. 2.133.. . . There may have been an alternate method of calling up hoplites: Rhodes (1981) 327. For a summary of recent work on the population of Athens see Rhodes (1988) 271-77. For a different view see Hansen (1982), (1985), (1988).

6. For the distinction between the liturgical class and the *kaloi kagathoi* see note 2.

7. For the absence of an aristocracy of birth in Classical Greece see Veyne (1990) 120-22. This important work, which was originally published in French in 1976, is completely ignored by Ober (1989), whose own account of status places too much emphasis on birth and neglects other criteria. Finley (1985) 35-61 discusses social status, but his analysis is marred by his unwillingness to identify the specific criteria for social respectability. For an attempt to classify the various meanings of the term *kalos kagathos* see Wankel (1961). This work contains good discussions of individual passages, but the attempt to classify all uses of the term is too rigid. Nor am I convinced by his argument that the term changes its meaning during the fourth century.

8. "Being a *kalos kagathos* was a matter of what is nowadays called 'life-style'." (de Ste. Croix [1972] 372). Ideal of self-sufficiency: Aymard (1943). Misfortune of having to work for another: X. *Mem.* 2.1.8.3-4; Arist. *Rh.* 1.9.1367a27; *Pol.* 1.5.1260a36-b6. Manual work undertaken only under the constraint of poverty and considered slavish: [Dem.] 57.45; Aymard (1948). Attitudes to hired labor: de Ste. Croix (1981) 179-204. Physical work considered demeaning: X. *Oec.* 4.2-3; Pl. *R.* 2.371c. Importance of leisure: Arist. *Pol.* 2.5.1269a34-36; 4.4.1291b25-26; 7.8.1329a1-2; 7.13.1333a33-36; 7.13.1334a14-16. On the symposium in general see Murray (1983). Hunting and exercising in the gymnasium: Ar. *Eq.* 1383; *Nub.* 1,002-23; *Ran.* 727-29; Isoc. 7.45 (note how he surreptitiously slips in philosophy at the end of his list of respectable activities—one wonders if his opinion was shared by other *kaloi kagathoi*). Observe how Aeschines in response to Demosthenes' aspersions on the social standing of his brother Philochares asserts he frequented the gymnasia: Aeschin. 2.149.

9. *Kalos kagathos* as *plousios:* Pl. *R.* 8.569a; [X.] *Ath.* 1.2, 14; 2.15. Hoplites linked with *gennaioi* and *chrestoi:* [X.] *Ath.* 1.2; X. *Mem.* 3.5.19. Hoplites as *gnorimoi:* Arist. *Pol.* 5.2.1303a8-10. Cavalrymen as *kaloi kagathoi:* Ar. *Eq.* 225-27; Din. 3.12. The word *gennaioi* used to describe upper class: [X.] *Ath.* 1.2.4-5, 13-4; Isoc. 16.25, 31, 33; 19.7, 33. *Eugeneia* as the product of old wealth: Arist. *Pol.* 4.6.1294a21-22; 5.1.1301b3-4. Note that when the Sausage-Seller is questioned to see if he is really a *poneros,* he is asked about his parents (Ar. *Eq.* 185-86).

Although a few sophists began in the later fifth century to question the importance of good birth, it is clear from the remarks of Antiphon fr. 44B (Diels-Kranz) that the prejudice in favor of it was still widespread. For skepticism about its value, see Eur. *Dictys* fr. 336, *Alex.* fr. 52; *El.* 367-85 (life-style and the kind of company one keeps are better indications of respectability than wealth and birth).

Boasting about ancestors: Lys. 6.54; 10.27-28; Isoc. 16.25. Aristotle's advice: Arist. *Rh.* 2.9.1387a18-31. Cratinus on *nouveaux riches:* Cratin. fr. 201 (Kock). Taunt directed at Iphicrates: Plu. *Mor.* 187b; Arist. *Rh.* 1.9.1367b18. Compare the insult cast at Apollodorus for his father's servile birth: [Dem.] 50.26. Insults to Phormio and Pasion: [Dem.] 45.73-76, 81-82, 86. Other disparaging allusions to servile birth: Lys. 13.18, 64, 73, 76; 30.2, 5, 27; Dem. 21.149-50.

Davies (1981) 71 believes that expressions of hostility against parvenus were less frequent in the period after 386 and attributes this phenomenon to a change in social attitudes. But if attitudes had changed so much, why does Aristotle, writing after 386, advise those speaking in court to appeal to the prejudice against parvenus?

10. For an exposition of the content and ideals of the traditional education, see Pl. *Men.* 94b1-4; *Prt.* 325a8-326c1; Ar. *Nub.* 961-1023 (albeit with a satiric twist). Marrou (1967) 76-77 argues that there was a "démocratisation" of the traditional education in Athens during the fifth century, but still recognizes that it remained "more or less . . . the privilege of an elite" (*de fait, elle restera toujours plus ou moins, comme le souligne Platon, le privilège d'une élite, qui seule la poussera jusqu'au bout, étant plus à même de consentir les sacrifices qu'elle exige et mieux placé pour en apprécier les avantages*). Connection between education and social status: Isoc. 13.6; 15.220; 16.33; Lys. 20.11-12; Ar. *Eq.* 191-92; *Ran.* 728-29; [X.] *Ath.* 1.13; X. *Symp.* 3.4. Physical deformity of the *banausos:* X. *Oec.* 4.2-3. Note also that at Ar. *Ec.* 385-87 Chremes explains the paleness of the women disguised as men by assuming that they are cobblers. The physique of the thetes was also disfigured by rowing in the fleet (Ar. *Eq.* 1368). For the ignorance of the *poneros* see Ar. *Eq.* 188-89; [X.] *Ath.* 1.5, 7. Cf. lack of education as an insult: Aeschin. 1.166; 2.113; 3.130 (all directed at Demosthenes and all untrue); Eup. fr. 183 (Kock).

11. Praise of farming: X. *Oec. 5.* We must not think of Attic farmers as a homogeneous mass of poor peasants existing at the level of bare subsistence. Many served as hoplites, and a few like Strepsiades were successful enough to marry into older, more respectable families. Absence of leisure for farmers: Arist:

Pol. 6.2.1318b10-15; 7.8.1329a1-2. Farmers set apart from *demos:* [X.] *Ath.* 2.14. The social ambivalence toward farmers is reflected in Aristotle's *Politics.* In his eyes a democracy that includes farmers, but bars other members of the lower classes will be better governed than a state that does not thus discriminate (*Pol.* 6.2.1318b6-17; 4.5.1292b26-35). Yet when constructing his ideal state, Aristotle excludes farmers completely and assigns their tasks to slaves and *perioikoi* (*Pol.* 1329a1-2, 25-26). Vast majority of Athenian citizens hold land: Lys. 34 *hyp.* (If Phormisius' proposal to limit citizenship to those who held land had passed, only 5,000 would have been disenfranchised. I do not share the skepticism of Gomme (1933) 26-27 about the figure.)

12. The most thorough treatment of Aeschines' family background and early career is Schaefer (1885-87) 1:215-28. Although Schaefer has many useful observations about the sources, he is overly inclined to accept Demosthenes' slanders. Blass (1887-98) 3.2: 154-59 for the most part follows Schaefer, as does Thalheim (1894) 1050-51. Ramming (1965) 24-25 merely summarizes the statements found in the speeches without analyzing them.

13. Dem. 19.249, 281. Cf. 199.

14. Defendants boast of services to Athens: Davies (1971) xviii, notes 3 and 4. "Forensic *charis*": Davies (1981) 92-95. A challenge to list services to the city is not found in the following speeches made by prosecutors: Lys. 26, 27, 28, 29, 30; Aeschin. 1, 3. On the psychology of "euergetism" in the Classical Greek *polis* and later see Veyne (1990) 70-200.

15. Atrometus' year of birth: Aeschin. 2.147. Problem involved in determining year of birth from information about age in a given year: Davies (1971) 125-26. Atrometus spends his youth exercising in the gymnasium: Aeschin. 2.147. Atrometus' membership in the same phratry as the Eteobutadai insignificant: Blass (1887-98) 3.2: 156, note 3. Role of *gene* within phratries: Andrewes (1961); Lambert (1993) 59-74.

16. Spartan raids in early part of war: Th. 2.19; 3.1.26. Damage resulting from occupation of Dekeleia: Th. 7.27.5. While the occupation of Dekeleia caused much harm, it is unlikely to have done lasting damage to Athenian agriculture: Hanson (1983). Kothokidai as Aeschines' deme: Dem. 18.180. Location of Kothokidai: Traill (1975) 44.

17. Atrometus' service during the reign of the Thirty: Aeschin. 2.147.

18. Date of appointment of Thirty: Rhodes (1981) 436-37. Date of the restoration of the democracy: Rhodes (1981) 462-63. Suggestion that Aeschines fought for a satrap: *scholion ad* Aeschin. 2.147. Clearchus recruits mercenaries for Cyrus: D.S. 14.12.9.

19. Mercenary service as a sign of poverty: Is. 2.6. Cf. Demosthenes' statement that Aeschines' brother-in-law hired himself out to Chabrias, probably meant as an insult (Dem. 19.287). For the problem involved with the name of the brother-in-law, see Harris (1986a). Greek mercenaries in Asia during the 390s: D. S. 14.37.1; X. *HG* 3.2.15; Parke (1933) 43-48. Davies (1971) 545 does not discuss the chronological problems posed by Aeschines' account of his father's activities, but nevertheless places his mercenary service in the 390s.

Although Atrometus may have helped to overthrow the Thirty in 403, he was probably not one of the men of Phyle. These men received rewards for their actions (Aristophon of Azenia, for example, received *ateleia* [Dem. 20.148]) and had their names on a stele honoring their deeds. Fragments of this stele have been identified by Raubitschek (1941), but they are too few to allow us to determine whether Atrometus' name stood on it. Nonetheless, Aeschines was aware of the decree for he had it read out in court in 330 (Aeschin. 3.187-90). If Atrometus had in fact been one of those honored, we would expect Aeschines to have cited the fact or to have mentioned any award made to his father.

20. Aeschines' references to his mother: Aeschin. 2.78, 148. Athenian customs about using a woman's name: Schaps (1977).

21. Demaenetus' exploit: *Hell. Oxy.* 1.1-3; 3.1-2 with Bruce (1967) 50-51.

22. For Aeschines' carelessness about historical facts, see for example, Aeschin. 3.139 where he claims Pyrrhander of Anaphlystos never was able to convince the Thebans to conclude an alliance with Athens. In point of fact Pyrrhander was one of the ambassadors who helped to bring Thebes into the Second Athenian Confederacy (*IG* ii² 43, lines 76-77). Compare also the numerous errors in his account of fifth-century history: Aeschin. 2.172-76. A similar account is found in And. 3.3-12. It is generally believed that Aeschines drew upon Andocides (e.g. Thomas (1989) 119), but I find it difficult to believe Andocides would have made such egregious errors about events shortly before his birth. Is it not more likely that Aeschines made these mistakes, which were then copied by the person who composed the forgery *De Pace,* which was preserved alongside another forgery, *Against Alcibiades,* in the corpus of Andocides' works? This would make the theory of Thompson (1967) that Hellanicus was the ultimate source of both Andocides and Aeschines unnecessary.

23. Demosthenes' slanders in 330: Dem. 18.129-30, 258-60.

24. Glaucothea's rites as those of Dionysus Sabazius: Wankel (1976) 1133ff. Burkert (1987) 19, 33, 43, 70, 96-97. Dionysiac elements: Cole (1980). Orphic influence: Parker (1983) 303. Elements reminiscent of the Eleusinian Mysteries: Roussel (1930) 58-65 (*liknon*).

25. Aeschines' service as hoplite: Aeschin. 2.167-70. Cost of armor and weapons: Connor (1988) 10, note

30. Inability of hoplite to afford expenses of campaign: Lys. 16.14.

26. Epicurus insulted for being the son of a schoolteacher: D. L. 10.4. Although the source for this information is not contemporary, it probably derives ultimately from remarks made by Epicurus' rivals. Aeschines' brothers frequent the gymnasia: Aeschin. 2.149. Aeschines frequents the gymnasia: Aeschin. 1.135; 3.216. Cf. [Plu.] *Mor.* 840a.

27. Cleobulus' tombstone: Papademetriou (1957). Costs of stelai: *IG* ii² 133, lines 17-20 (twenty drachmai); 148, lines 6-10 (twenty drachmai); 212, lines 47-49 (thirty drachmai); 226, lines 21-26 (thirty drachmai). The fact that the stele made for Cleobulus contained a relief would not have made it more expensive. Compare the stele bearing the decree against tyranny (Meritt [1952] 355-59). This stele is adorned with a relief depicting Democracy placing a wreath on the head of a figure representing the People of Athens and is inscribed with a decree containing far more letters than the couplet on Cleobulus' tombstone, yet its cost was only twenty drachmai. For more lavish tombstones see Diepolder (1931) plates 23, 26, 27, 30, 31, 37, 40, 41, 46, 47, 54. Custom of honoring the dead not confined to a small elite: Humphreys (1980) 123.

28. Claim that Aeschines came from an old priestly family: Papademetriou (1957) 163. Priests classified as magistrates: Pl. *Lg.* 758e1-759e3; Arist. *Pol.* 4.12.1299a15-19. Priests undergo *euthynai* just as magistrates do: Aeschin. 3.18. Distinction made between priest and seer: Pl. *Plt.* 290c-d. On seers in general see Bouché-Leclerc (1879-82) 1-226. For a list of all known *manteis* in the Archaic and Classical periods see Kett (1966). *Loci classici* for the right of anyone to prophesy: Hom. *Il.* 12.200-50 (Hector challenges the interpretation made by Polydamas of the omen of the eagle); *Od.* 2.146-207 (Eurymachus challenges the interpretation made by Halitherses); Hdt. 7.143 (Themistocles offers different interpretation of Delphic oracle). Practice of divination: Halliday (1913). Importance of flight of birds in *mantike*: Aesch. *Pr.* 488-92; X. *Mem.* 1.1.3. Seers offer advice at public meetings: Th. 8.1.1; *Ath. Pol.* 54.6. Advice of seer given to Xenophon: X. *An.* 7.8.1-6. Certain seers regarded as quacks and charlatans: Pl. *R.* 364b-c; *Lg.* 909b-d; Ar. *Av.* 959-91; *Nub.* 332. By contrast the seers of tragedy, such as Teiresias in Sophocles' *Oedipus the King* and *Antigone* and in Euripides' *Bacchae* and Calchas in Sophocles' *Ajax,* are quite trustworthy and respectable. Lampon: Th. 5.19.2; 24.1; *IG* i² 76, line 47; Plu. *Per.* 6.2. Sthorys granted citizenship for accurate prophecy: Osborne (1970). Thrasyllus: Isoc. 19.5-7.

29. Aeschines recites poetry: Aeschin. 1.129-29, 144, 148-52; 2.158; 3.135, 184-85, 190. Role of poetry in training of orator: North (1952). Use of poetry in Attic oratory: Perlman (1964). Aeschines criticizes

enemies for lack of knowledge and refinement: Aeschin. 1.137, 166; 2.39, 151; 3.117, 130, 238, 241. Cf. Blass (1887-98) 2:181, note 5. Note his frequent use of words denoting lack of refinement: *apaideusia* (Aeschin. 1.132; 2.113, 153; 3.241), *apaideutos* (Aeschin. 1.45, 137, 166, 185; 3.130); *apaideutos* (adv.) (Aeschin. 3.238); *aschemoneo* (2.39, 151, 246); *aschemon* (2.152); *aschemosyne* (3.76). By contrast only two of these words are found in Demosthenes' entire oeuvre: *apaideutos* (20.119), *aschemoneo* (22.53). The words are not found at all in Andocides, Dinarchus, Lycurgus, Isaeus, Antiphon, and Lysias. On Aeschines' education in general, see Blass (1887-98) 2:181-85. Aeschines receives education from his father: Quint. *Inst.* 2.17.12.

30. Aeschines' lack of rhetorical training: Phld. *Rh.* 1.14; 2.97 (Sudhaus). Isocrates' fees: Dem. 35.42; Plu. *Dem.* 5.6; [Plu.] *Mor.* 873d; 838e. [Plu.] *Mor.* 838f claims Isocrates never asked for fees from Athenians. This is accepted by Davies (1971) 246, but the information found in Demosthenes disproves it. Hostility of Pheidippides: Ar. *Nub.* 100-25. Anytus' attitude toward Sophists: Pl. *Men.* 91c. Social status of Anytus: Lys. 13.78; Pl. *Men.* 90b; X. *Ap.* 29. Callicles' contempt: Pl. *Grg.* 520a. Laches' attitude: Pl. *La.* 197d. Other evidence of upper-class attitudes toward the Sophists: Pl. *Phdr.* 257d; *Prt.* 312a-b. One cannot claim that the statements made about the Sophists by the young *kaloi kagathoi* in the dialogues are the product of Platonic malice and cannot therefore be cited as evidence of upper-class attitudes, since Socrates, who acts to some extent as Plato's mouthpiece, is far more gentle in his criticisms. Xenophon appears to be more harsh (Guthrie [1971] 37). Cleon's appeal to prejudice against Sophists: Th. 3.38.7. Connor (1971) 163ff. fails to draw a distinction between attitudes toward the traditional education and toward the Sophists and as a result misinterprets Cleon's remarks. A similar mistake is made by Ober (1989) 156-91, who also fails to understand Aeschines' use of poetry.

31. Demosthenes on social status of Aeschines' family: Dem. 19.237.

32. Aeschines' military career: Aeschin. 2.168-70.

33. Aeschines and Aphobetus serve as undersecretaries: Dem. 19.237. Demosthenes reminds Aeschines of the herald's curse: Dem. 19.70. Cf. 200, 237, 314. Aeschines as secretary: Dem. 18.261. Aeschines' younger brother Aphobetus (Aeschin. 2.149) may have been Secretary of the Council in 319/18 if he is identical with the Aphobetus found in *IG* ii² 387, line 3. However, the inscription is fragmentary and the demotic is missing, making it risky to posit an identification on the basis of the name alone—see Thompson (1974). Furthermore, Aeschines held the post of secretary when he was younger and before moving on to the higher post of ambassador. It is thus unlikely that Aphobetus would have taken the

position of secretary when he was around sixty after having held more prestigious positions.

34. Public secretaries: *Ath. Pol.* 54.3-5 with Rhodes (1972) 135-41.

35. Aeschines' voice: Dem. 19.126, 199, 206, 337-40. Aeschines' familiarity with laws and decrees: Aeschin. 1.9-35; 3.9-48. Cf. [Plu.] *Mor.* 840f. Privileges of secretaries: *Ath. Pol.* 54.3-4 with Rhodes (1981) 520.

36. Aeschines becomes actor after public secretary: Dem. 18.261-62. Aeschines' acting career: Dem. 18.262; 19.246, 337. Meaning of the term *tritagonistes*: Pickard-Cambridge (1968) 133.

37. Aeschines alludes to Demosthenes' remarks about his acting: Aeschin. 2.157.

38. Low opinion of actors: [Arist.] *Pr.* 30.10. This evidence was accepted by Schaefer (1887-89) 1:251. Neoptolemus as Athenian ambassador: Dem. 5.6; 19.12, 315. Aristodemus as Athenian ambassador: Aeschin. 2.15-17, 52; 3.83; Dem. 19.315.

39. An anecdote of Critolaus reported by Aulus Gellius (11.9.2) records that Aristodemus received a talent for a performance. On actors in general, see Ghiron-Bistagne (1976).

40. Aeschines brings family into court: Aeschin. 2.152, 179. Custom of defendant using his family to arouse pity: Hyp. *Eux.* 41. X. *Mem.* 4.4.4 incorrectly implies the practice was illegal.

41. Aeschines marries daughter of Philodemus: Aeschin. 2.152. Aeschines inherits five talents from Philon: Dem. 18.312. Philodemus' uncle a member of the Thousand: *IG* ii^2 1929, line 18. Stemma of Aeschines' family: Davies (1971) 543, 546. Function of the Thousand: Rhodes (1982) 11-14.

42. Evidence for the size of dowries in Classical Athens: Casson (1976) 53-56. Defendants list services to state: note 14 above. It is perhaps no coincidence that none of the men known to have challenged to an *antidosis* procedure is known to have been active in politics at the time of the challenge. Isocrates is the only prominent person known to have been challenged, but he never aspired to public office (Isoc. 15). The unknown defendant of Lys. 3 was challenged and lost, but he does not appear to have been a politician. Nor were Phaenippus (Dem. 42) and Megacleides (D. H. *Din.* 13), who were also challenged to an *antidosis*. Pasicles, the son of Pasion, was involved in a suit concerning an *antidosis,* but he too never pursued a career in politics as far as we can tell (Hyp. fr. 134 [Kenyon] = Harpocration *s.v. symmoria*). Demosthenes charges that Meidias had to be challenged to an *antidosis* before he performed any liturgies (Dem. 21.156), but this is the testimony of a hostile source, who fails to specify the date, challenger, and circumstances. Even if the charge

were true, the incident might have occurred before Meidias entered politics. Demosthenes himself was challenged to an *antidosis* by Meidias' brother Thrasylochus (Dem. 21.78-9; 28.17). In this case, however, the circumstances were unusual, for the challenge was initiated not to force Demosthenes to undertake duties he was attempting to shirk, but as part of the legal maneuvers employed by his guardians. Despite the burden the liturgy placed on his troubled estate, Demosthenes responded by performing the duty.

43. Demosthenes as *hegemon* of his symmory: Dem. 21.157. Demosthenes' property: Davies (1971) 126-36 with the correction of Harris (1988c) 361-62. Demosthenes' troubles with his guardians: Dem. 27-31. Training with Isaeus: [Plu.] *Mor.* 839e; 844b-c. Demosthenes' liturgies: Davies (1971) 135-37. Prosecution of Cephisodotus: Aeschin. 3.51. Demosthenes as *logographos:* Chapter 1, note 17. Demosthenes delivers first speech in 354/53: D.H. *Amm.* 1.4. Date of Demosthenes' birth: Harris (1989b) 121-25.

44. Date of Timarchus' birth: Aeschin. 1.49 with Harris (1988a). Timarchus as member of Council and as magistrate on Andros: Aeschin. 1.107-8. Timarchus serves on embassies: Aeschin. 1. 120. Nausicles as contemporary of Aeschines: Aeschin. 2.184. Nausicles' victory at Thermopylai: D.S. 16.37.3. Aeschines' date of birth: Aeschin. 1.49 with Harris (1988a). Aeschines' first speech in the Assembly: Chapter 3.

45. On the powers of the Athenian Assembly see Hansen (1987) 94-124. For the right of anyone to address the Assembly see Aeschin. 1.27; Eur. *Suppl.* 438-41.

46. For the small number of citizens who regularly spoke see Perlman (1963) 328-30. Although the number of those who spoke frequently was small, the total number of those who spoke and moved decrees at least once must have been surprisingly large: Hansen (1989) 93-127. On the term *rhetores* see Hansen (1989) 1-24. For the offices held by Athenian politicians see Roberts (1982a).

47. On ambassadors in Athens and other Greek states see Mosley (1973).

48. Annual election of generals: *Ath. Pol.* 61.1 with Rhodes (1981) 677-78. Absence of special privileges for generals: Rhodes (1972) 43-46. It is possible that in the fifth century "convening the ecclesia and arranging its agenda at this time may have been the joint prerogative of the *prytanes* (acting on behalf of the *boule*) and the generals" (Rhodes), but otherwise the generals do not appear to have possessed privileged access to the Council.

49. Importance of spending money to win *charis*: Davies (1981) 91-101. Financing feast for tribe at festival: Dem. 21.156. Alcibiades' *epidosis*: Plu. *Alc.* 10. On

the *epidosis* in general see Migeotte (1992). Cimon's largesse: Plu. *Cim.* 10; *Ath. Pol.* 27.3. Mantitheus' boast: Lys. 16.14. Demosthenes ransoms prisoners: Dem. 19.166-71. Aeschin. 2.100; [Plu.] *Mor.* 851a. Chabrias celebrates victory at Colias: [Dem.] 59.33.

50. Nicomachides' complaint: X. *Mem.* 3.4.1-3. Pericles' victory as *choregos*: *IG* ii² 2318, lines 9-11. Nicias' generosity: Plu. *Nic.* 3. Meidias cites his liturgies: Dem. 21.153.

51. Size of courts: *Ath. Pol.* 68.1 with Rhodes (1981) 728-29. Audience at trials: Dem. 20.165; 54.41. Prosecutions by Lycurgus: D.S. 16.88.1; Lycurg. 1; frr. 75, 77, 91 (Sauppe). Prosecutions by Hyperides: Hyp. *Phil.; Dem.; Eux.* 29. Prosecutions by Aristophon: Din. 3.17; [Dem.] 51.9, 16. Prosecutions by Aristogeiton: Dem. 25.37-38, 87, 94. Trial of Timarchus: chapter 5.

It is significant that we never hear of Miltiades, Cimon, Themistocles, Aristides, Nicias, or Alcibiades acting as prosecutors on public charges. Pericles acted as prosecutor once, but that was only after he was elected to the position by the Assembly. According to Plutarch, he performed the task with conspicuous distaste (Plu. *Cim.* 14.3-5; *Per.* 10.6. But see also *Ath. Pol.* 27.1). The only one before Cleon to make a career of prosecuting public officials appears to have been Ephialtes (*Ath. Pol.* 25.1-2). His unusual career won him an unusual end: he was the only Athenian politician known to have been assassinated in the fifth century before the Revolution of 411. Did his fate deter others from following the same path for the next three decades?

52. Tendency to elect as ambassadors men who have ties to foreign city: Mosley (1973) 44. Family of Alcibiades: Davies (1971) 9-22. Family of Cimon and Miltiades: Davies (1971) 294-312. Family of Thucydides: Davies (1971) 230-37. Family of Pericles: Davies (1971) 455-60. Family of Callistratus: Davies (1971) 277-82. Family of Timotheus: Davies (1971) 506-12. For a complete list of all Athenians known to have been *rhetores* and generals in the years 403-322, see Hansen (1989) 25-72. Very few of these men had fathers or other ancestors who achieved renown in politics. This is true not only for the numerous obscure figures, but also for some of the most prominent politicians in the period including Demosthenes, Eubulus, Demades, Aristophon, Apollodorus, Iphicrates, Hyperides, and Chares. But see Davies (1981) 117-30. Phocion as Chabrias' *protégé*: Plu. *Phoc.* 6-7.

53. For the trial of Timarchus see chapter 5.

54. Habitual prosecutors as *poneroi*: Isoc. 15.99-100; Lys. 7.1. Term "sycophant" used as an insult: Aeschin. 3.172. Note that the most popular thing done by the Thirty Tyrants was the execution of the sycophants: X. *HG.* 2.3.12, 38; Lys. 25.19; *Ath. Pol.* 35.3. Osborne (1990) attempts to whitewash the sycophants, but his arguments are demolished by Harvey (1990). Harvey gives a complete list of *testimonia* for sycophants. Many of those who brought *graphai* against politicians tried to justify their prosecutions by claiming they were only pursuing a private feud (Aeschin. 1.1-3; [Dem.] 58.1-4; 59. 1-16). Courts unworthy of a *gennaios*: Ar. *V.* 503-7. Note also how speakers often tried to win the good will of a court by pleading inexperience in legal proceedings: Aeschin. 1.1; Pl. *Ap.* 17d; Lys. 7.1. Cf. Aeschin. 2.182.

55. Lycurgus as member of Eteobutadai: [Plu.] *Mor.* 842b. Philochares as general: Aeschin. 2.149. Iphicrates is referred to in the past tense in Dem. 23.129-36. This speech was delivered in 352/51 (D.H. *Amm.* 1.4). Marriage of Menestheus to Timotheus' daughter: [Dem.] 49.66. Exile of Timotheus: Nep. *Tim.* 3.5. Career of Conon: Davies (1971) 511-12.

56. Nausicles nominates Aeschines: Aeschin. 2.18. Nausicles as ambassador: Chapter 3. Nausicles testifies for Aeschines: Aeschin. 2.184. Nausicles gains fame at Thermopylai: D.S. 16.37.3; 38.2; Justin 8.2.8. Gold crown for Nausicles: *IG* ii² 1496, lines 49-51; Dem. 18.114; Davies (1971) 396. Importance of ties between contemporaries: Rhodes (1986) 135-36.

57. Aeschines' honors: Aeschin. 2.168-70. Phocion's campaign on Euboea: Plu. *Phoc.* 12-14; Aeschin. 3.86-88; Dem. 21.161-67; 39.16; [Dem.] 59.4 with Cawkwell (1962a) 127-30, Brunt (1969) 245-48, and Griffith (1979) 318, note 2. For the correct name of the taxiarch, see von Wilamowitz (1909). The speculative attempt of Knoepfler (1981) to reconstruct Phocion's strategy is flawed by his mistaken belief that the cavalry Demosthenes (21.163) states landed at Argura was part of the original expedition. But the words of Demosthenes make it clear that this force was sent much later to relieve . . . the cavalry that originally went with Phocion to Euboea. For a criticism of the analysis of the campaign made by Tritle (1988) 76-86 see Cartledge (1989) 79.

58. Phocion and Eubulus appear on behalf of Aeschines: Aeschin. 2.170, 184. Aeschines sent as ambassador under the decree of Eubulus: Dem. 19.304. Aeschines attacked for supporting policy of Eubulus: Aeschin. 2.8. Aeschines and Eubulus advocate peace with Philip in 346: Chapter 4. Aeschines and Phocion negotiate with Philip after Chaeronea: Aeschin. 3.227; Dem. 18.282; Nepos *Phocion* 1.3; Plu. *Phoc.* 17. Meidias as associate of Eubulus: Dem. 21.205-7. Aeschines' praise for Meidias: Aeschin. 3.115. Stephanus as an associate of Eubulus: [Dem.] 59.48. Stephanus and Aeschines on Third Embassy: Aeschin. 2.140. Phaedrus provides testimony for Aeschines: Aeschin. 1.43-50. Association of Stephanus and Phaedrus: *IG* ii² 213.

59. Philon serves with Chabrias in Egypt: Dem. 19.287. For the problem involved with Philon's name see Harris (1986a). Phocion and Chabrias: Plu. *Phoc.* 6-7.

60. Eubulus and the Theoric Fund: Cawkwell (1963a). Increase in Athenian revenues: Dem. 10.37-38. Eubulus' building projects: Aeschin. 3.25. Aeschines may exaggerate Eubulus' power—see de Ste. Croix (1964). Aphobetus' position: Aeschin. 2.149.

61. Phocion's role in battles near Naxos and Chios: Plu. *Phoc.* 6. Phocion elected general forty-five times: Plu. *Phoc.* 8.2 with Tritle (1992). Gehrke (1976) 5-17 analyzes Phocion's leadership at Tamynai and on Cyprus in 344 and concludes "er keineswegs ein Feldherr mit überragenden militärischen Fähigkeiten war" (*he was in no way a commander with outstanding military abilities*). He criticizes him for allowing part of his army to be drawn into battle too early and for failing to remain close to his troops while busy with the sacrifices at Tamynai. He does credit the general with "eine bemerkenswerte Tapferkeit im Gefecht" (*a noteworthy bravery in battle*) and with good judgment, but finds this latter virtue "eine politische, nicht eine militärische Qualität" (*a political, not a military quality*). This is unfair. It is unreasonable to blame Phocion for the lack of discipline among his troops, who may well have been trained by others. Furthermore, we should note that it was actually Plutarch who allowed his troops to be drawn into battle prematurely and that Phocion's infantry remained in position until he gave his order. And Phocion's attention to the sacrifices was part of his duty as a commanding officer (e.g., Hdt. 6.1121; 9.36-37). Indeed, had he not waited for a good omen, his haste might have had a disastrous effect on the morale of his troops. Gehrke also ignores Plutarch's attractive suggestion that Phocion's delay might have been deliberate, aimed at drawing the enemy closer to his camp before opening battle. Since his camp was located in a strong position atop a ridge, this tactic made good sense. Nor can Phocion's presence of mind in the face of an initial setback and good judgment be dismissed as merely "political qualities." Both are certainly the mark of a good field commander. Gehrke further takes Phocion to task for allowing his troops to plunder while on Cyprus. This criticism is also unfair; the soldiers were following the traditional practice of gathering supplies in enemy territory. Diodorus, for one, saw nothing untoward in their behavior. In fact, news of the rich plunder had one very beneficial effect: it attracted more mercenaries. For a more positive estimate of Phocion's military abilities, see Tritle (1988) 76-96.

62. Phocion as a speaker in the Assembly: Plu. *Phoc.* 7. Unpopularity as a speaker: Plu. *Phoc.* 3. Tritle (1988) 97-100 adduces evidence to show that Phocion advised the Assembly on several occasions, but his attested political activity is rather meager for someone whose career lasted as long as his did.

63. On the nature of political groups in Athens see the sensible summary in Hansen (1991) 277-87.

64. Pericles' boast: Th. 2.37.2 with the analysis of Harris (1992a). Lack of wealth as impediment to political career: Rhodes (1986) 144. Aeschines' career shows how simplistic it is to analyze Athenian politics in terms of a rigid divide between a privileged elite and a passive mass of citizens. For this mistaken approach, see Ober (1989) 112-18. Compare Aeschin. 1.27.

Davies (1971) 547 thinks there "is just enough information about Aeschines' property . . . to allow the suspicion that he could have joined his wife's family in the liturgical class, had he wished to do so," yet recognizes that most of the information is unreliable since it comes from Demosthenes. We have already discussed the alleged legacy from Philon; for the bribes from Philip (Dem. 19.167), see chapter 5.1; for the "loan" from the Three Hundred, see chapter 7. Demosthenes' charges about a farm at Pydna (Dem. 19.145, 312; cf. *scholia ad* Aeschin. 1.3) and a farm in Boeotia (Dem. 18.41; cf. Philodemus *Rh.* 2.172) are not supported by evidence. Davies attributes "his failure to contribute to *epidoseis* or to perform liturgies" to the fact that "the bulk of his property lay abroad and was therefore out of the reach of an *antidosis* challenge or of an *apographe* of unregistered property." Even if this property in foreign territory existed, why does Demosthenes nowhere furnish any evidence at all about it?

Works Cited

Amit, M. (1965). *Athens and the Sea: A Study in Athenian Sea-Power.* Brussels.

Andrewes, A. (1956). "Philochorus on Phratries." *JHS* 81: 1-15.

Aymard, A. (1948). "L'idée de travail dans la Grèce antique." *Journal de psychologie* 41: 29-41.

Blass, F. (1887-98). *Die attische Beredsamkeit,* 2nd ed. Leipzig.

Bouché-Leclercq, A. (1879-82). *Histoire de la divination dans l'antiquité.* 4 vols. Paris.

Bruce, I. A. F. (1967). *Commentary to the Hellenica Oxyrhynchia.* Cambridge.

Brunt, P. (1969). "Euboea in the Time of Philip II." *CQ* 19: 245-65.

Bugh, G. (1982). "Introduction of the *katalogeis* of the Athenian Cavalry." *TAPhA* 112: 23-32.

———. (1988). *The Horsemen of Athens.* Princeton.

Burkert, W. (1987). *Ancient Mystery Cults.* Cambridge, Mass.

Cantril, H. (1943). "Identification with Social and Economic Class." *Journal of Abnormal and Social Psychology* 38: 74-80.

Cartledge, P. A. (1989). Review of Tritle (1988). *CR* 39: 79-80.

Casson. L.———. (1976). "The Athenian Upper Class and New Comedy." *TAPhA* 106: 29-59.

Cawkwell, G. L. (1962a). "The Defence of Olynthus." *CQ* 12: 122-40.

———. (1963a). "Eubulus." *JHS* 83: 47-67.

Centers, R. (1949). *The Psychology of Social Class.* Princeton.

Cole, S. G. (1980). "New Evidence for the Mysteries of Dionysus." *GRBS* 21: 223-38.

Connor, W. R. (1971). *The New Politicians of Fifth-century Athens.* Princeton.

———. (1988). "Early Greek Land Warfare as Symbolic Expression." *Past and Present* 119: 3-29.

Davies, J. K. (1967). "Demosthenes on Liturgies: A Note." *JHS* 87: 33-40.

———. (1971). *Athenian Propertied Families 600-300* B.C. Oxford.

———. (1981). *Wealth and the Power of Wealth in Classical Athens.* New York.

Diepolder, H. (1931). *Die attischen Grabreliefs des 5. und 4. Jahrhunderts v. Chr.* Berlin.

Finley, M. I. (1985). *The Ancient Economy,* 2nd ed. Berkeley and Los Angeles.

Gehrke, H.-J. (1976). *Phocion: Studien zur Erfassung seiner historischen Gestalt.* Munich.

Ghiron-Bistagne, P. (1976). *Recherches sur les acteurs dans la Grèce antique.* Paris.

Gomme, A. W. (1933). *The Population of Athens in the Fifth and Fourth Centuries* B.C. Oxford.

Griffith, G. T. (1979). *A History of Macedonia.* Vol. 2: 203-735. Oxford.

Guthrie, W. K. C. (1971). *The Sophists.* Cambridge.

Halliday, W. R. (1913). *Greek Divination.* London.

Hansen, M. H. (1982). "Demographic Reflections on the Number of Athenian Citizens 451-309 B.C." *AJAH* 7: 172-89.

———. (1985). *Demography and Democracy. The Number of Athenian Citizens in the Fourth Century* B.C. Herning.

———. (1987). *The Athenian Assembly in the Age of Demosthenes.* Oxford.

———. (1988). *Three Studies in Athenian Demography.* Copenhagen.

———. (1989). *The Athenian Eccelesia: A Collection of Articles 1983-89.* Copenhagen.

Harris, E. M. (1986a). "The Names of Aeschines' Brothers-in-Law." *AJPh* 107: 99-102.

———. (1988a). "The Date of Apollodorus' Speech Against Timotheus and Its Implications for Athenian History and Legal Procedure." *AJPh* 109: 44-52.

———. (1988b). "The Date of Aeschines' Birth." *CPh* 83: 211-14.

———. (1988c). "When Is a Sale not a Sale? The Riddle of Athenian Terminology for Real Security Revisited." *CQ* 38: 351-81.

———. (1989b). "Demosthenes' Speech Against Meidias." *HSPh* 92: 117-36.

———. (1992a). "Pericles' Praise of Athenian Democracy." *HSPh* 94: 57-67.

Harvey, F. D. (1990). "The Sykophant and Sykophancy: Vexatious Redefinition?" In Cartledge, Millett, and Todd (1990): 103-21.

Humphreys, S. C. (1980). "Family Tombs and Tomb Cults in Ancient Athens: Tradition or Traditionalism?" *JHS* 100: 96-126.

Kett, P. (1966). "Prosopographie der historischen griechischen Manteis bis auf die Zeit Alexander des Grossen." Diss., Erlangen.

Kindstrand, J. F. (1982). *The Stylistic Evaluation of Aeschines in Antiquity.* Uppsala.

Knoepfler, D. (1981). "Argoura: Un toponyme eubéen dans la Midienne de Démosthène." *BCH* 105: 289-329.

Kroll, J. (1977). "An Archive of the Athenian Cavalry." *Hesperia* 46: 83-140.

Lambert, S. D. (1993). *The Phratries of Attica.* Ann Arbor.

Lefkowitz, M. R. (1981). *The Lives of the Greek Poets.* Baltimore.

MacDowell, D. M. (1986). "The Law of Periandros about Symmories." *CQ* 36: 438-49.

Marrou, H.-I. (1967). *Histoire de l'éducation dans l'antiquité.* Paris.

Meiggs, R. and D. M. Lewis. (1969). *A Selection of Greek Historical Inscriptions.* Oxford.

Meritt. B. D. (1952). "Greek Inscriptions." *Hesperia* 21: 340-410.

Migeotte, L. (1992). *Les souscriptions publiques dans les cités grecques.* Geneva and Quebec.

Momigliano, A. (1971). *The Development of Greek Biography.* Cambridge, Mass.

Mosley, D. J. (1973). *Envoys and Diplomacy in Ancient Greece.* Wiesbaden.

Murray, O. (1983). "The Greek Symposium in History." In E. Gabba, ed., *Tria Corda: scritti in onore di A. Momigliano.* Como.

North, H. (1952). "The Use of Poetry in the Training of the Ancient Orator." *Traditio* 8: 1-33.

Ober, J. (1989). *Mass and Elite in Democratic Athens.* Princeton.

Osborne, M. J. (1970). "Honours for Sthorys." *BSA* 65: 151-74.

Osborne, R. (1990). "Vexatious Litigation in Classical Athens: Sykophancy and the Sykophant." In Cartledge, Millett, and Todd (1990): 103-21.

Ossowski, S. (1963). *Class Structure in the Social Consciousness.* Trans. S. Patterson. New York.

Papedemetriou, G. (1957). "Aeschines" Uncle, Cleobulus the Seer (in Modern Greek)." *Platon* 9: 154-63.

Parke, H. W. (1933). *Greek Mercenary Soldiers.* Oxford.

Parker, R. (1983). *Miasma: Pollution and Purification in Early Greek Religion.* Oxford.

Pélékidis, Ch. (1962). *Histoire de l'éphébie attique dès origines à 31 avant J.C.* Paris.

Perlman, S.———. (1963). "The Politicians in the Athenian Democracy of the Fourth Century B.C." *Athenaeum* 41: 327-55.

———. (1964). "Quotations from Poetry in Attic Orators of the Fourth Century B.C." *AJPh* 85: 155-72.

Pickard-Cambridge, A. (1968). *The Dramatic Festival of Athens,* 2nd ed. Eds. J. Gould and D. M. Lewis. Oxford.

Ramming, G. (1965). "Die politischen Ziele und Wege des Aischines." Diss., Erlangen.

Raubitschek, A. E. (1941). "The Heroes of Phyle." *Hesperia* 10: 284-95.

Rhodes, P. J. (1972). *The Athenian Boule.* Oxford.

———. (1981). *A Commentary on the Aristotelian Athenaion Politeia.* Oxford.

———. (1982). "Problems in the Athenian *Eisphora* and Liturgies." *AJAH* 7: 1-19.

———. (1986). "Political Activity in Classical Athens." *JHS* 106: 132-44.

———. (1988). *Thucydides: History II.* Warminster.

Roberts, J. T. (1982a). "Athens' So-called Unofficial Politicians." *Hermes* 110: 354-62.

Roussel, P. (1930). "Initiation préalable et les symboles Eleusiniens." *BCH* 54: 58-65.

de Ste. Croix, G. E. M. (1964). Review of J. J. Buchanan, *Theorika. A Study of Monetary Distributions to the Athenian Citizenry during the Fifth and Fourth Centuries* B.C. *CR* 14: 190-92.

———. (1972). *The Origins of the Peloponnesian War.* London.

Schaefer, A. (1885-87). *Demosthenes und seine Zeit,* 2nd ed. 3 vols. Leipzig.

Schaps, D. (1977). "The Woman Least Mentioned." *CQ* 27: 323-30.

Thalheim, T. (1894). "Aischines (15)." *RE* 1: 1,050-52.

Thomas, R. (1989). *Oral Tradition and Written Record in Classical Athens.* Cambridge.

Thompson, W. E. (1967). "Andocides and Hellanicus." *TAPhA* 98: 483-90.

———. (1974). "Tot Atheniensibus idem nomen erat." In D. W. Bradeen and M. F. McGregor, eds., *Phoros, Tribute to Benjamin Dean Meritt.* Locust Valley, N.Y.: 144-49.

Traill, J. S. (1975). *The Political Organization of Attica.* Hesperia Suppl. 14. Princeton.

Tritle, L. A. (1988). *Phocion the Good.* New York and Sydney.

———. (1992). "Forty-five or What? The Generalships of Phocion." *LCM* 17: 19-23.

Vansina, J. (1985). *Oral Tradition as History.* Madison, Wisc.

Veyne, P. (1990). *Bread and Circuses: Historical Sociology and Political Pluralism.* Trans. B. Pearce. London.

Wallace, R. W. (1989b). "The Athenian *Proeispherontes.*" *Hesperia* 58: 473-90.

Wankel, H. (1961). *Kalos kai Agathos.* Frankfurt.

———. (1976). *Demosthenes: Rede für Ktesiphon über den Kranz.* 2 vols. Heidelberg.

Weber, M. (1946). *From Max Weber: Essays in Sociology.* Trans. and ed. H. H. Gerth and C. Wright Mills. New York.

Wilamowitz-Moellendorf, U. von. (1909). "Lesefrüchte." *Hermes* 44: 445-76.

FURTHER READING

Bibliography

Badian, E. and Julia Heskel. "Aeschines 2.12–18: A Study in Rhetoric and Chronology." *Phoenix* 41, No. 3 (Autumn, 1987): 264–71.
> Stress that Aeschines had particular motives for writing his account of the peace with Philip, and warn that historians should not be unduly swayed by his rhetorical skill.

Diller, Aubrey. "The Manuscript Tradition of Aeschines' Orations." *Illinois Classical Studies* 4 (1979): 34-64.
> Describes many different Aeschines manuscripts, most of which are from the fifteenth or sixteenth centuries.

Criticism

Cawkwell, G. L. "Aeschines and the Peace of Philocrates." *Revue des Etudes Grecques* 73, No. 347-48 (July-December 1960): 416-38.

Explains why Aeschines was forced to change his position regarding a peace decree with Philip.

————. "Aeschines and the Ruin of Phocis in 346." *Revue des Etudes Grecques* 75, No. 356-58 (July-December 1962): 453-59.

Argues that Demosthenes's account of Aeschines's role in the fall of Phocis is impossible to accept.

Dyck, Andrew R. "The Function and Persuasive Power of Demosthenes's Portrait of Aeschines in the Speech *On the Crown*." *Greece & Rome* 32, No. 1 (April 1985): 42-48.

Analyzes Demosthenes's attack on Aeschines and reveals elements that made it credible and effective to its intended audience.

Harris, Edward M. *"The Names of Aeschines' Brothers-in-Law." American Journal of Philology* 107, No. 1 (Spring 1986): 99-102.

Discusses the use of nicknames as insults, specifically as practiced by Demosthenes in attacking relatives of Aeschines.

Kindstrand, Jan Fredrik. *The Stylistic Evaluation of Aeschines in Antiquity.* Uppsala, Sweden: Almqvist & Wiksell International, 1982, 104p.

Surveys the assessment of Aeschines's writing by such critics as Cicero, Quintilian, and Philostratus.

Additional information on Aeschines's life and career is contained in the following source published by the Gale Group: *Dictionary of Literary Biography,* **Vol. 176.**

Democritus

c. 460 B.C.-c. 370 B.C.

Greek philosopher.

INTRODUCTION

Democritus is best known for the atomic or atomistic theory he co-developed with his teacher, Leucippus. Although a contemporary of Socrates, Democritus is considered among the last of the pre-Socratics. It is generally believed that Leucippus contributed more to atomism's founding than Democritus, but that Democritus was more responsible for the theory's refinement. Although their work was based on the earlier theories of the Milesians, the two made notable advancements, particularly in their explanation of density. The atomic theory is mechanistic: it holds that all matter is composed of an infinite number of indivisible and indestructible atoms of various shapes moving about in an infinite void, in an infinite universe, always and forever colliding with each other, and sometimes joining to form combinations. Nothing happens by chance, nor on purpose, and all can be explained in terms of mechanical principles, one thing causing another. Democritus's philosophy, including his belief that the soul itself is composed of atoms, angered some philosophers including Plato—who pointedly did not mention him—and Aristotle, who, in his writings, criticized Democritus and his theory. Most of the few hundred fragments that remain of Democritus's writings deal with ethics rather than atomism. His ethics stress moderation and the practice of that which is beneficial to society. Democritus also asserted that man's belief in divinities is due to his ignorance about nature, and his emphasis on cheerfulness as the goal for all individuals led to his nickname, the Laughing Philosopher.

BIOGRAPHICAL INFORMATION

Democritus was born on the northern shore of the Aegean Sea in Abdera, a city of ancient Thrace which was also home to the Sophist Protagoras. Little else is known about his life, except that he traveled on one occasion to talk with Anaxagoras, the leading scientist of Athens, but was rebuffed. It is believed that Democritus was fairly wealthy and that he traveled extensively in the East—to Egypt, Babylon, India, and Persia. He lived a long life, probably ninety years or more.

MAJOR WORKS

Democritus is said to have written many books (seventy, according to Diogenes Laertius), including one entitled *Little Cosmology* as a nod to Leucippus's *Great Cosmology*. The ancients report he was fascinated by all subjects, and wrote on music and on all aspects of science, including biology and astronomy. Only fragments of his work survive, however, and most of these are concerned with ethics. In these terse fragments, Democritus discusses laws and his belief that individuals will obey them because it is in their collective self-interest to do so. He explains the importance of maintaining a balance between too much and too little material wealth, and also promotes altruism.

CRITICAL RECEPTION

Democritus's ideas failed to please those who attempted to explain the nature of things by looking at their function, as well as those who tried to explain the world in terms of a divine power. Socrates, Plato, and Aristotle all disagreed with him. In modern times he is credited with starting on the correct path: without modern scientific tools, Democritus could do little more than practice atomism as a philosophy. Robert L. Oldershaw points out, though, that "he had a remarkably modern understanding of concepts like the conservation of mass/energy, the indirect nature of perception, the continual formation of and destruction of physical systems, the reality of empty space, the basic theory of colours and the fundamental principles of causality and determinism." Most scholars have acknowledged the impossibility of determining exactly where Leucippus's ideas end and Democritus's begin, but they continue to debate whether or not Democritus authored the ethical fragments often attributed to him. One group believes he was not the author since there is little similarity between the atomic theory writings and the ethical fragments, and further, they question why so many of these fairly unremarkable ethical pieces exist. The opposition maintains that Democritus was responsible for both sets of writings; that they lack similarity because they are concerned with vastly different topics; that they nonetheless do contain some similar elements; and that the Cynics may have preserved the ethical fragments, which would explain why so many of them are extant. Some scholars concentrate on Democritus's political theory, so far as it can be deduced. Eric A. Havelock investigates Democritus's views on laws intended to promote good behavior in society, while Michael Nill studies Democritus's views governing higher and lower forms of pleasure and their function in a well-run community. Jonathan Barnes explores the dilemma the atomists faced concerning belief and the imprecise nature of knowledge. There is disagreement on exactly what Democritus meant in certain instances—understandable given the dearth of surviving texts. Richard D. McKirahan takes a close look at the extant fragments of Democritus and places them alongside the work of contemporaneous and near-contemporaneous commentators in an attempt not only to explain atomism but to explain what the ancients thought it meant. C. C. W. Taylor contributes a similar effort in his study of Democritus's theological writings.

PRINCIPAL WORKS

Die Fragmente der Vorsokratiker (prose) 1952

Principal English Translations

Ancilla to the Pre-Socratic Philosophers: A Complete Translation of the Fragments in Diels, "Fragmente der Vorsokratiker" (translated by Kathleen Freeman) 1957
The Atomists: Leucippus and Democritus (translated by C. C. W. Taylor) 1999

* A German edition, edited by H. Diels, that includes the extant Greek fragments of Democritus, with mention of the *Little Cosmology.*

CRITICISM

Eric A. Havelock (essay date 1957)

SOURCE: "The Political Theory of Democritus," in *The Liberal Temper in Greek Politics,* 1957. Yale University Press, 1964, pp. 125-54.

[*In the following excerpt, Havelock examines Democritus's political statements and concludes that he was satisfied to leave some problems unsolved.*]

The political theory of Democritus has been preserved by antiquity in the form of some twenty-three aphorisms, or programmatic statements, attributed to his name. These are contained in a large 'chrestomathy' or anthology of useful statements compiled perhaps in the early fifth century of our era by John of Stobi [4.1 On Polity; 4.2 On Laws; 4.5 On Government]. The reader whose conception of Greek philosophy follows traditional lines will, when he looks at this allegedly Democritean material, be tempted to say to himself: 'Democritus was famous in antiquity for a materialist metaphysic. He taught the doctrine of a mechanical universe in which infinite atoms moving through infinite space perpetually collided to form combinations essentially fortuitous. Whatever be the precise meaning of these statements about man in society, their doctrine must derive from the general theory of his

system. Let us, therefore, in attempting to interpret the political theory of Democritus, first assume that it depends on his atomic principles and reflects the same mechanism and determinism.'

But when we consider the problem of how to connect his atomism with his politics, the testimonies fail us. Democritus clearly had precise views about many matters affecting society and the city state and law and justice. But no writer of antiquity reports where Democritus the atomist stood in relation to Democritus the political scientist. There were writers after him who claimed the Democritean tradition, and who did make the connection for themselves. One thinks, for example, of Lucretius, but this is not the same thing as reporting for Democritus, the man of Abdera. This adopted son of Athens was an intellectual of the Periclean Age. That a connection existed between his politics and his cosmology is virtually certain. Quotation from Democritus conveys the impression of a keen and a coherent mind, thinking structurally. The impression is reinforced by what tradition says of his metaphysics. If we say he was coherent and cogent rather than systematic, it is because the term systematic is better reserved to describe that mastery of the technique of exposition which was achieved in the ideologies of Plato and Aristotle. The style of Democritus is essentially pre-Platonic. It reflects those methods of organizing ideas which were characteristic of the age. We perceive in him an intuitive coherence which we can, if we choose, reformulate and reproduce as a system. But in the absence of any explicit report which defines the connection between his politics and his metaphysics, let us postpone this question. Let us first estimate his statements about man and society in their own right and determine whether they exhibit an inner direction. If they do, then a just estimate of their logic may put us on a road of connection between metaphysics and politics more reliable than any that might suggest itself if we used traditional assumptions about materialism and mechanism.

It is difficult to describe the sayings of Democritus as either aphorisms or proverbs or axioms or maxims. They overlap these categories. To understand them, one has to understand the role of the gnomic method in antiquity. Here it is pertinent to note a historical distinction. The rounded sentence began its career in the preliterate days of oral communication, when indoctrination depended on word of mouth and retention of doctrine depended on the memory. Democritus himself was a writer, but he wrote in a period when readers were still outnumbered by listeners. It is therefore not surprising that he compressed his ideas into gnomic formulations, for he can be pictured, like the poets who were his contemporaries, as composing under what we may call a form of audience-control. Collections of *gnomae,* therefore, stamped with the hallmark of individual thinkers were characteristic of the first stage of Greek prose writing. But the anthologies of such which were accumulated systematically in the Hellenistic Age and later, and which dominated so much thinking and writing in later antiquity and the Middle Ages, were devoted to the special task of preserving in an epoch of books and readers that kind of material which was still suitable for oral memorization. Fresh thinking was now done on paper in continuous exposition. Thus the province of the *gnome* (Latin *sententia*) ceased to be the creative and became the commonplace.

This tended subtly to alter the vocabulary, temper and tone of the ancient gnomic statements as they were preserved. It was as though the chemical thinking of pre-Platonic antiquity, a dynamic creative process, had now been precipitated in crystallized form at the bottom of the glass; and one collected, arranged and packaged the crystals in commonplace books. The historian, therefore, who examines the preserved statements of any pre-Platonic thinker has to fortify himself against two quite different sources of error, the one in the text, the other in himself. On the one hand, there are the ancient compiler and the compiler from whom he may have compiled; they may have edited the material subtly but inescapably out of its archaic and awkward originality, by changes in vocabulary or syntax, by omissions or eclectic additions of commonplaces of other thinkers. The historian, therefore, is all the more thankful when he deals with a philosopher who adhered to metre. But on the other hand, even when an original survives in its archaic stiffness and angularity, the modern mind approaches it half expecting that it will be, indeed, a commonplace, a proverb or maxim with recognizable relation to the accumulated truisms of Western culture. What is specific and original in terminology, what is surprising and significant in syntax, will tend to be glossed over and ignored. The sayings of Heraclitus are notorious for their concentration and obscurity, but are only an extreme example of a method of exposition which is still discernible in Anaxagoras. The sayings of Democritus are stylistically intermediate between these two thinkers. They are little universes in themselves, and yet also they can be said to be flung like the feathered phrases of the epic minstrel from a mind comprehensive in vision, yet intensely particular in formulation. In short, the political sayings of Democritus present themselves both as self-contained units and yet as items in a 'system'. They can be marshalled and deployed one by one in a sequence which gradually exposes the coherence of their inner logic. They are, so to speak, electrically charged, but the messages they deliver can be monitored because they are transmitting over a consistent wavelength.

1 [*FVS*[6] 68 B257]

As to animals in given cases
of killing and not killing the rule is as follows:
if an animal does wrong
or desires to do wrong
and if a man kill it
he shall be counted exempt from penalties.
To perform this promotes well-being
rather than the reverse.

2 [B259A]

According as has been written concerning wild things
    and

creeping things,
if they are 'enemy',
so also [such is my doctrine] is it needful to do in the
    case of
human beings.

3 [B258]

If a thing does injury contrary to right
it is needful to kill it.
This covers all cases.
If a man do so
he shall increase the portion in which he partakes of
    right
and security
in any [social] order.

4 [B259B]

According to the custom laws of the fathers
you kill the 'enemy' in every [social] order
where custom-law in that order does not prohibit;
for the several groups there are prohibitions
of local religious sanctions
of solemnized contracts
of oaths

5 [B256]

Right is to perform what is needful
and wrong is to fail to perform what is needful
and to decline to do so.

6 [B261]

If men have wrong done to them
there is need to avenge them so far as is feasible.
This should not be passed over.
This kind of thing is right and also good
and the other kind of thing is wrong and also bad.

This group of formulations has a long ancestry. In its curiously stiff archaic simplicity and its participial constructions, it recalls both the syntax and the subject-matter of the Code of Hammurabi, that cuneiform original of the legal systems of the Near East and the West. But the Greek thinker has cast his legalisms in a typically Hellenic and rational context. He is looking at the behaviour of man in a cosmic and historical setting. Why concentrate on such a trivial matter as the ethics of disposing of dangerous animals, the goring ox, the vicious dog? In primitive communities, such issues provoked disputes between neighbours over valuable property, and it is easy to see how their disposition required the aid of regularity in a code. But Democritus is not interested in the custom-laws of a rural economy, not, that is, for their own sake. He is looking at the usage of men toward animals in order to extract a criterion for the usage of men toward other men. He says so explicitly (No. 2). We might expect the reverse line of reasoning. Surely the disposition of hostile animals is an application of the laws of property among men. But this is not the historical genetic approach of Democritus. He is searching less for the principles than for the methods by which human communities have been able to found themselves. He finds the method in law enforcement. This in turn depends for its effectiveness on the application of sanctions, and the essential sanction is the right to kill, legally that is. The power to execute is primary, if societies are to exist at all. He finds the prototype of this power in the right to kill animals. Why? The only answer can be that his conception of human society is based upon an anthropology in which man, himself an animal species, proceeded to organize himself in social orders (*cosmoi*) in order to protect himself against other species. When Democritus first states the rule of killing and not killing, he speaks of animals as 'living things' (*zoa*). This word could include men; in the 'zoogonies', the origin of the animal and human species was described without distinction of kind. In the anthropologies constructed on this foundation, organized war against the animals had been recognized as a necessary stage in man's social advance. Such had been the *mythos,* the drama in which his early departure from primitivism had been imaginatively conceived. Democritus takes this drama and uses it genetically to establish basic criteria for right and wrong. In the same genetic spirit he cites ancestral usage, not to support some specific party programme in the present, as was often done by practical politicians, but in its most general sense as that pattern of behaviour historically devised and normatively sanctioned in the remote past.

What then do we mean by 'Right' and 'Unright' (*dike* and *adikia*)? This is the question he asks. And his mind (we can see the naturalist, the materialist at work here) argues that to understand them we have to understand the minimum parts, so to speak, out of which they are constructed. In a civilized society they may be symbols for complicated value-judgments or applications of value-judgments; but they had an historical origin. This was essentially simple; nor will they ever lose the quality of their origin. The origin lay in the sanction of protection to achieve security. The sanction itself in its simplest form was negative—the right to kill the 'enemy'. To forget this is to betray society (as he later argues). It is not verbal looseness on his part when he speaks of animals 'doing wrong'. He deliberately reduces wrong, and therefore right, to bare essentials by viewing animal as man and man as animal. To make this quite clear, he reformulates the rule in the most general terms possible:

> 'If a thing does injury contrary to right it is needful to kill it.'

> (3)

By 'contrary to right' he indicates the violation of another's security, and to make clear that this minimum condition of right and wrong is meant seriously as a definition of their essence, he makes the definition explicit—

> 'To do right is to do what you have to do,
> to do what there is *need* of . . .'

> (item 5)

—in the most simple and concrete sense.

If we have defined the repulse of injury as self-protection, however, we can begin to mistranslate the direction of his thought, which would seem an apology for modified anarchy, with atomized individuals repelling wrong but otherwise minding their own business. Strictly speaking, Democritus has no word for individual, that is, for individual self-subsistent personality, and he is incapable of thinking of the concept. His terminology baffles us because while viewing groups or aggregates as made up of simple parts he never seems to visualize the laws of behaviour of the parts without automatically visualizing that behaviour as social. He certainly considered the savage condition of man as pre-civic; but he almost certainly never imagined it as wholly atomized into individuals. Just as in the early anthropologies, the killing of 'enemies' was rationalized as that condition necessary for protecting organized society, so in Democritus as he warms to his theme and further defines the action taken against 'the enemy' the action is discovered to be social (item 4), sanctioned by the social order (*cosmos*) in which you are living. If you kill, you kill in the name of social security, and your act is sanctioned by this 'need'. Nay more, in those human groups which constitute social orders, the definition of 'right' (*dike*) now advances to a more complex level: the sanction of killing is regulated. It is qualified by religious provisions and exceptions. These, he observes keenly, are local (item 4). His empiricism here reinforces his historical method. The right of asylum, for example, the protection afforded by temples to wrong-doers, depends upon the validity of local cults. There is no standard pattern for these. But solemnized agreements accompanied by libations (his next example) reflect practices widespread and accepted, and so do the oaths by which host swears to protect guest, or friend defends friend, or tribes and cities ratify their agreements. These also cut down the freedom to kill the 'enemy'. Democritus in effect argues that no social group ever applies the simple law of self-protection in its total sense. There is a possibility of mitigation, of truce, of agreement in the unending effort to establish security. Is he in effect pointing to the regulation of intergroup relations as requiring a set of rules more complicated than mere outlawry? Is he hinting that societies, as they progress, learn other usages beside that of right and unright? He has not yet reached the *polis* but he is getting nearer to it.

Thus far, unright and right, respectively, could be described as symbols of aggression on the one hand and repulse or correction of aggression on the other. The first premisses of moral man, if such these be, are disappointingly negative. But when Democritus sums up the rule of the right to kill and states it as a general principle 'covering all cases', he significantly describes the wrong-doer not merely as the 'enemy' but as the 'injurer' (No. 3). He uses the participle of an epic verb. His style still falls short of the prosaic in the technical sense of that term. But, stylistic considerations apart, he adopts a word which in Homer indicated injury, damage, disaster, done in hostile relations between enemies (for example, by Greeks or Trojans). Injured feelings are not in question. He is advancing by implication a definition of unright as the infliction of material damage. This supplies a hint of the direction of his thought, a hint confirmed by his defence (No. 1) of killing the animal who is 'enemy'.

> 'To perform this promotes well-being
> rather than the reverse.'

Injury or damage on the one hand, well-being or prosperity on the other, are placed in antithesis. You have to prevent or decrease the former, and to assist or increase the latter. He is thinking perhaps in terms of some calculus, for he says:

> 'contribute to well-being rather than the reverse'

and it is also symptomatic that when he formulates the right to kill as a necessary law (items 2, 3), his verb of compulsion (*chre*) symbolizes the need arising out of the inherent situation, rather than that impersonal compulsion (*ananke*) imposed from some source external to the situation.

This calculus suggests that he is looking for an operational definition of right and unright. Across the intervening centuries we hear an echo of this, of course unpremeditated, in the accents of Jeremy Bentham. But the comparison with English Utilitarianism is no sooner made than it should be withdrawn. The greatest good of the greatest number is a formula built on the conception of units of personality which can be added up to form arithmetic aggregates. No fresh values enter in at the group level which are not present in its atomized parts. Democritus, to repeat what has already been said, shares with his age an inability to reach such a concept of the human ethos. He would have rejected it as an illusion, we suspect, had it been stated to him. His utilitarianism, then, if it be fair to use the term—and it probably is, for the symbols of utility, profit and interest had already been advanced by thinkers of the naturalist school before Plato united them strategically with the form of the good—his utilitarianism conceives of well-being versus ill-being, of profit versus damage, as indicating alternative conditions which affect the person and his community simultaneously, for a person's 'way of life' is life in a community. The group and its component parts have a double-acting relationship. The group is a dynamic context. This is not spelled out for us in Democritus' statements. It is reflected, however, in the ambiguity of his terminology. For example, when he surrounds the right to kill with qualifications (No. 4), he says:

> 'For the several groups there are prohibitions.'

Here the phrase 'several groups' seeks to translate an untranslatable ambivalence. More strikingly, he says of the man who carries out the need for killing the injurer (No. 3):

> 'He shall increase the portion in which he partakes of
> right and
> security
> in any society.'

Democritus means that such a man in the first instance increases the security of the community. But to this security he has himself contributed by his act. He therefore feels good because of his service and also deserves well of the community which he has served. His 'portion' is not a fraction of the whole, but amounts to a degree of participation.

So far the Democritean theory of right has presented itself in these legalisms as resting on narrow and negative premises. To argue that human society could only start its ascent toward civilization by strict enforcement of the most primitive laws of security is no doubt true and valuable; but it does not express the hallmark of civilization itself. Seized as he was of the value of security as a positive thing, Democritus was bound to enlarge and advance his conception until it could comprehend action not only narrowly defensive but also helpful and co-operative. This he begins to do by propounding axiom No. 6; that if you repulse injury and punish it, you do not do this for yourself alone. In a community, you do this in the interests of others who are wronged.

> 'If men have wrong done to them there is need to
> avenge
> them so far as is feasible.
> This kind of thing is right and also good.'

This carries us beyond narrowly selfish considerations. Such action is therefore always in danger of being ignored or 'passed over.' But (if we may fill in his thought for him) a community comes into existence not as a mere sum of private interests, each protecting their own security, but as a complex in which the need of avenging all who are wronged becomes a matter of 'principle', we would say. It has to be recognized, regardless of whether or not the particular victims are strong enough to protect themselves without help. He uses the verb 'avenge' perhaps to locate the rule far back in primitive society as he has already located the right of self-preservation. It is the prototype of those methods of legal redress which an advanced society makes available as a substitute for direct succour. But the point is that at least some vengeance must always be taken, whoever is wronged, in order to guarantee that a collective system of mutual security will work for all members. If he asks for it 'so far as is feasible', he may mean to hint that group protection by members for other members has always had limited efficacy as contrasted with direct action. But when he vigorously defends this vicarious rule as 'right and also good', and the opposite as 'wrong and also bad', the second adjective in each pair points up the utility and strength which accrue to the community as a whole.

Two-thirds of Democritus' social and political axioms still remain to be considered. They deal with matters of increasing complexity—law and custom, faction and consensus, the *polis,* its ethos and administration. His thinking in politics seems to have proceeded along organic lines, viewing the human group as founded on a very few simple principles but discovering and then solving more complicated issues in later stages of development. This kind of progress means that the problems formulated for solution cease to be negative and become positive. They advance from mere security to the creative values and enjoyments of a *polis* type of community.

7 [B249]

Faction within the clan is a bad thing for both sides.
Those who win and those who lose share impartially in
common disaster.

8 [B245в]

Envious malice between men constitutes the genesis
of faction.

9 [B245a]

The custom laws would not prevent each of us from
living
his life in accordance with those powers and opportunities
which are his own
if it were not true that A inflicted injury on B.

10 [B248]

It is the desire of custom law to do good to the way of
life
of men
but it is able to do this only when men also desire to
have
good done to them.
If men hearken to it
the custom law demonstrates to them that excellence
which
is its own.

To establish the basis of sociality, human beings must initially recognize sanctions which protect the group from without. This is a simpler matter than maintaining its cohesion within. If right is a value-symbol to be placed on action taken against the anti-social 'enemy', then the objective of reconciling tensions within will call into play other terms and different formulae.

These four political axioms focus their attention on the provenance of custom-law. In Greek tradition, Greek law (*nomos*) came to be viewed as the specific creation of the city-state. The virtual identification of nomos and polis was already implicit in the theory (or the myth) of law-givers who had established 'polities', that is, civic institutions. The idealism of Plato and the teleology of Aristotle only confirmed the identification and made it an article of faith. But Democritus true to his genetic method sees law generated as a solution to problems which were already crystallizing in pre-civic conditions. The factional quarrel which threatens to split the civic group and end its existence can be seen already at work in the clan of blood-kindred. Long before Democritus, Solon had phrased it in this way, and his successor in the democratic experiment, Cleisthenes, had set out to solve the problem practically, by breaking up the ancient clans and distributing their

members among *demes*. Perhaps both men confronted an ancient inheritance, handed down from more primitive days, in the form of blood-feud, which dividing a clan of kindred families can decimate its members. Herodotus saw the same danger in a Pan-Hellenic setting: the quarrel over the command of the united forces against Persia at Salamis; and he applied the same phrase to describe it. These examples show that the clan (*phyle*) did not describe a kin-group of any defined size. Depending on context, it might refer to the consanguinity of a kin-group within a *polis,* or to all members of a *polis* as for example Athenians, or to all Greeks as a 'race'. Democritus, then, in presenting the factions of the clan as a problem in politics, takes advantage of the ambiguity. He wants a term as general as possible in order to view faction historically as a process endemic in the social order at all stages of its evolution. Upon this perennial and now proverbial danger he places a reflective interpretation. Historically, the way of settling a feud had been a conflict which ended in victory and subjugation. This solution is illusory, says Democritus. The victors and vanquished have suffered a common destruction. Of what, we may ask? In any immediate sense, the vanquished lose definite things like life or status or property; and the victors gain corresponding and equally definite benefits. Democritus cannot be defining loss in these terms. Something has been destroyed which was the common property of the two factions before the fighting began.

That common property could be defined as the group's over-all security, or its law. But Democritus does not at once jump, as a more traditional and superficial thinker might, to the necessity of supporting law at all costs—*eunomia*, the Greeks called it—as a preventive of faction. The enemy from without the group had been simply 'the enemy', externally viewed. You do not have to deal with his ethos or motives. You establish the rule of right (*dike*) on purely positivist lines. Punishment by expulsion or elimination or execution is the first law of group survival. But it is only the first law. For an in-group problem, you are forced to consider the inner ethos and motives of human beings. Thus, still looking at the cause of feud genetically, you discover it in the propensity of the human animal to compete and to conceive and nurse a grudge against his competitor, to make envious comparisons. These connotations are all packed into the Greek noun *phthonos* and its more ancient verb *phthoneo*. Competition, primarily envious, secondarily emulative, between fellow-craftsmen had become a proverb before Hesiod. Envious malice describes an emotion not self-generated in isolation but one which *ab initio* exists between two or more people. The curse of Adam is the way Adam handles his primary relationships with other Adams. Adam the single man never existed. The 'grudge' is almost the condition of being a human being so far as our manhood depends on some relationship to other men. Hence Democritus, viewing the growth of morals and politics from an anthropological standpoint, at least implies that within this growth are comprehended two warring principles: an inherent grudge of man against man; and a compulsion nevertheless to live in groups which can co-operate because the grudge is somehow controlled or sublimated. Hebraic analogies even when helpful can often mislead. Did 'malice' express the Greek equivalent for original sin? Or was it not more characteristic of Greek realism combined with Greek rationalism to assume that if two men or groups could advance in prosperity at mathematically equal rates, grudge and envy would not arise; but that chance and fortune see to it that they almost never do; and so the envy on one side and the fear on the other that result are reactions of the human material to an emotional strain imposed upon it by the non-mathematical operation of circumstances. This might have been Democritus' complete doctrine. We cannot be sure. In what we have of him, we start with the fact of the competitive grudge as an originating force (*arche*) which sets in motion divisive and destructive faction.

For this endemic danger the remedy is law, and the initial operation of law has to be viewed negatively as a restraint on the use of one's own elbow-room (no. 9). Up to this point, the mind and method of Democritus have sought to understand and to solve political problems simply by describing them. Is he here, at the introduction of law, at last forced to take refuge in a solution conceived *a priori*: a *deus ex machina*, some force, moral or theological, exercising a power over the historical process which is independent of that process? In making law the personal subject of verbs like 'prevent' and 'do good,' it might almost seem that he does, indeed, resort to that kind of syntax in which the structures of idealists are built. But the Greek *nomos*, when he used the word, had not yet acquired the *a priori* or 'geometric' significance with which Plato's later thinking endowed it and which passed over into the natural law of the Stoics, of St. Thomas, and of the rationalists of the seventeenth century. *Nomos* is not translatable by a single word. It had an ambivalence in the Greek mind, and yet the shape of this ambivalence was incisive and powerful. When Pindar sang that 'custom-law was lord of all men', Herodotus in effect added, 'Yes indeed: the lawful customs of the races of men are various; but each evokes its own fierce loyalty from its own devotees'. These two citations give the polarity of the Greek term better than anything else that could be said about it. It is untranslatable because it comprehends two concepts later split apart in the Western tradition: custom, usage or habit on the one hand, created by man locally and fortuitously, but also controlling man in attitude and act; law on the other hand, passionless, wise, universal, above and beyond men, but requiring their obedience and reverence as to a god. *Nomos* in fact in the fifth century was 'usage-which-is-solemn'.

Thus Democritus in effect is arguing that one positive and inherent force in men, that of competitive suspicion, can be balanced or controlled by another and often is: the preference for conformity to collective habits which we might call a sort of force of inertia. *Nomos* gathers momentum in society and controls its acts and relations by virtue, perhaps, of an inherent laziness, a conservatism in the human raw material which while aggressive and envious is also prone to prefer the familiar and the consistent. The 'right way' of behaving in a thousand matters of daily decision is just the accepted way. All this Democritus does not say: but his term *nomos* speaks for itself if we keep it in the context of the vocabulary of the fifth century and do not transfer it to the late fourth. There is a theoretic capacity plus opportunity (*exousia*) at the disposal of every man personally (item 9), but it is only theoretical. Man is normally too given to familiar standardized usages to exercise it outside of or against the group, except he have the support of a group within the group. Hence it is factionalism (*stasis*) of group within group that is really dangerous (item 7) much more so than the anarchism of the lawless man. With him society can and does deal. He does not have any *nomos*-support whatever. But in a sense every member of a faction or a class does have support: he has that minimum portion of law which can be used as group loyalty, though it is not the fully formed law of a society.

'Envy' and 'custom', then, have always been competing forces, genetically speaking. But Democritus makes a value-judgment here: he expresses a preference, the Hellenic preference. Custom law is good and useful. It can indeed be viewed as having a desire or purpose to 'do good to man's way of life' (No 10). Democritus is still speaking historically. The way of life is not mine or yours personally. It is the life lived in a society, as the anthropologists had spoken of it. The restraint of common custom is not merely negative, then: it paves the way for a more positive possibility. Wherever Democritus speaks of 'good', he is looking to the future, to the further utility of man in society. What benefits of custom law he has in mind will appear in due course. But in the present stated axiom, what preoccupies him is the paradox that while custom-law has a power to benefit this power is not automatic. It depends for its validity upon the equally valid acquiescence given by the members of society. The reasoning is in a closed circle. It has to be, to accord with the complete facts of life. Perhaps he means too that custom-law is a total thing. It either works, is accepted and loved and finds its own justification in the smooth functioning of harmony between men, men's obedience and their sense of benefit: or it disintegrates wholly, collapses into lawlessness (*anomia*); the group ceases to function as a group. And automatically the members thereof are deprived of their power to understand or imagine the virtue of that condition which is now not theirs. For their very anarchy controls their judgment. *Nomos* is not like a piece of property which you could abandon or pick up again at will. It is painfully acquired; it makes total sense when you have it; but when you lose it, it becomes indeed a lost cause.

What else Democritus has to say about politics—and there is a good deal—moves us into more familiar ground, familiar, that is, from the point of view of Plato and Aristotle. The city-state, its character and peculiar problems, come into plain view. Hitherto they have not been in the foreground. Whether Democritus was prepared to construct a series of ascending social integrations from savagery to the city and, if so, what these were, is uncertain. It would seem that Aristotle's simple and elegant sequence of household, village and city is in that form the creation of his own teleological needs, rather than a faithful reproduction of the Greek anthropological view. Democritus certainly conceived of society before the city-state. But the evidence for this lies mainly in the kind of terminology he uses, rather than in explicit historical statements. He must have refused to posit the *polis* as the one definitive social order. For example, he uses the two words 'order' and 'shape' (*cosmos* and *rhuthmos*) to describe a given stage or type of social organization. But his method is not typological, nor is his approach constitutional, in the manner of the idealists who followed him. His mind moves in genetic relations, not in *a priori* forms. Thus he speaks (in a statement still to be presented) of the Athenian democracy as the 'presently constituted shape of things'. This is not quite the same thing as saying 'under this political constitution'; and the temporal qualification suggests that there have been and will be other shapes. Indeed, both *cosmos* and *rhuthmos* are dynamic terms describing an animated order and a moving shape. They were so used also in his atomic metaphysics.

A citation of Plutarch's reports a reference in Democritus to

'governments or polities and friendships of kings'

as the source of

'great and glorious benefits for our way of life'.

This sounds like a recollection of some genetic account of the rise of government with authority to organize society, a stage which Democritus may have superimposed upon his validation of right and custom-law. That is, he may first have looked at those fundamental sanctions which support the existence of any society, primitive or advanced, and then proceeded to consider the problems of constitutional authority and to indicate some of the solutions achieved historically in tribal oligarchy or in monarchy or in democracy alike. But this reconstruction of his thought is speculative. That his premises were historical is revealed in the preserved vocabulary of his axiomatic statements about the city-state. A group of three of these can now be presented.

11 [B260]

If a man kill any highwayman or pirate
he shall be counted exempt from penalty
whether [he kill] by direct action
or by orders
or by vote.

12 [B262a]

In the case of those who commit acts that deserve
  expulsion
or imprisonment
and in the case of [all] who deserve penalty
the vote must condemn them

and not absolve them.

13 [B262b]

If a man in violation of custom law
absolve [another]
using [motives of] gain or pleasure to formulate [the
  issue]
he does wrong
and inevitably this will be on his heart.

On the face of it, these three axioms repeat the primary proposition already fully covered that the very existence of any society depends in the first instance upon the enforcement of sanctions against the social 'enemy'. Justice, genetically validated by the measures taken by the human species against other species, originates at this elementary and negative level. But in axiom No. 11, which heads this group of three, Democritus classifies three kinds of sanctions, and the distinctions are significant. In the first, penalty is imposed by direct action; this identifies the condition of primitive society. In the second, it is done by orders given; this, we suggest, identifies a more organized community in which responsibility for social security is wielded by a king; in this authority the original right of direct action, always close to anarchy, is now vested. Any seventeenth-century believer in the divine right of kings would have understood at once what Democritus meant here. But there is a third possibility: action can be taken through vote. Democritus would not limit this procedure to what would be styled in a technical sense democracy. He could have in mind any society in which legal sanctions can be taken by collective decision. Under certain circumstances this could be true even of Homeric society and certainly of any city-state unless governed by a despot. But the order of precedence in these alternatives is not accidental; it suggests the thought that organs of collective responsibility tend to displace earlier and simpler devices of government. The anthropological method of Democritus, proceeding from savage to civilized condition, has reached the voting society, as we might call it. The language of No. 12, the next axiom, is the language of Athenian democracy. The area of application for sanctions which protect society is no longer confined within the simplicities of robbery or piracy, and the penalty of liquidation through killing is also far too simple for use in such a complex organism as a city-state. But the principle remains that sanctions must be implemented: that is our first duty to the society in which we live, for only this can guarantee the initial stability and authority of what is becoming (Democritus does not say so) a legal system responsible to popular control. Statement No. 13 makes it even clearer that Democritus is now addressing himself to the Athenian judge and jury (no distinction was drawn between them) whose primary function is not mercy or leniency but the decision to convict where conviction is deserved. In this way is the stern logic maintained by which a society stands or falls. The citizen in a voting society will be tempted to deviate from this, because in a voting society the voter's immediate interest and the long-range social interest can come into conflict. So political theory has at this point to take note of gain and pleasure (item 13) as twin motivations which complicate the process of judicial decision. Democritus did not oppose either provided they coincided with public utility, or at least did not conflict with it. But the latter must predominate, and this requires a correct 'formulation' of the issue in the voter's mind. Democritus has here involved his political with his psychological theory, which no complete account of his philosophy can afford to ignore. However, the political thread of his thinking is separable and the final unwinding of it is near at hand.

14 [B255]

At that time when the powerful [classes] confronting the have-
nots take it on themselves to pay toll to them and to do
things for them and to please them:
This is the [situation] in which you get [the phenomenon of]
compassion and the end of isolation and the creation of
comradeship and mutual defence
and then civic consensus
and then other goods beyond the capacity of anyone to
catalogue in full.

15 [B250]

It is consensus that makes possible for cities the [execution of]
mighty works
enabling them to execute and carry through wars.

16 [B252b]

A city managed prosperously means complete stability-and-
success for everybody.
In this [condition] is comprehended all.
If this [condition] is secured, this means general security; if
this [condition] is dissolved, this means general demoralization.

17 [B252a]

It is needful that greater importance be placed upon the
[area of] the civic than on any other,
and upon its good management:
avoiding any competition
that goes beyond reason
and any access of private power
that may cut across the utility of the common [wealth].

18 [B251]

Poverty under a democracy is as much to be preferred above
what men of power call prosperity
as is liberty above bondage.

The first of this group of statements constitutes the most remarkable single utterance of a political theorist of Hel-

las. Considering its epoch, it is as remarkable as anything in the whole history of political theory. Neither in content nor in temper has it a parallel in the better-known classic thinkers. Ethically speaking, it seems to carry the colour of certain values which are defined in the New Testament; politically, with its stress on what looks like a social conscience, it reads like a formula suitable to the liberalism of the age of Mill or T. H. Green. It is true that the objective towards which the statement is directed was becoming a commonplace: unanimity of the citizen body had been viewed as a political ideal long before Plato cemented the conception into an almost mathematical unity of the state. It is equally true that this condition of consensus adds little to Democritus' previous principle that the cohesion and the stability of the group are the first objective of politics. It does however describe this as a mood, so to speak, of a citizen body which is facing up to this condition consciously and deliberately.

But what is the originating cause of such a mood? A less subtle thinker would reply: obedience to the laws; an idealist would substantiate this answer by the proposition that the laws represent eternal forms of Good and Right which give them independent validity and influence over the minds of men. For Democritus causes are always genetic not teleological. He looks to processes rather than to patterns for the explanation of politics. Law, as we have seen, is for him the sum of a system of habits, which places a brake on human wilfulness. But this can never of itself evoke the co-operation of a harmonious community. So Democritus is forced once more to get behind custom to ethos, that complex of behaviour patterns out of which standardized practice grows. Is there some element here which historically becomes the means of calling social consensus into being? He finds it in a human propensity, under given conditions, to altruism and compassion.

It is often said that Greek rationalism could not find room for pity as such, and might even deplore it as a sentimental violation of a good man's integrity. This does not misrepresent the main tradition as defined by the classic writers and thinkers, to the end of the fourth century. There were however exceptions. Even in the fifth century, Aeschylus in his portrayal of Prometheus chose to dramatize not only the hero's gifts of technology to man but his compassion for man, and in the same spirit the Chorus are invited to have compassion on him. The tragedy conveys to its audience the strong impression that somehow, in the unfolding history of civilization, the cause of technology and the cause of compassion are bound up together. The remarkable thing about compassion in Democritus is that it is presented in conjunction with altruism as a political principle of the first importance, a kind of human energy comparable to other energies of the human ethos, and one which can have structural effect upon the condition of the body politic. In this respect, the thought of Democritus is tougher and more systematic than that of Rousseau. Compassion is not to be viewed as an intuitive recoil from suffering in others, a vague but powerful sentiment rooted in the untutored primitive. It is a phenomenon which presents itself at an advanced stage of human culture, and it is the specific property of the stronger and more successful elements in that culture.

But why should it arise at all? Democritus, without breaking the sequence of his genetic method, could have argued that the necessary concessions which may be made by the strong toward the weak, by the rich towards the poor, are simply exacted from them by the demand for over-all group security. Instead of that, he proposes an addition to the ethos of human beings, a fresh ingredient in their make-up. Does he here then take leave of his method, abandoning history in favour of an unsupported aspiration? Does his picture of altruism mean that he is tempted into the fantasy of wish-fulfilment?

A Marxist, schooled in the doctrine of class-struggle as fundamental, would say he did. Democritus, be it noted, goes half-way towards such realism. He does not pretend like Plato that class divisions in the city-state can be treated by the theorist as abnormalities. They, as much as right and law, are part of the historical process of politics. But where does his discovery of altruism—which at this point mitigates the class division so decisively—come from?

The riddle can be read and the method of Democritus placed in consistent perspective once it is assumed that he is looking at a famous crisis in the history of the city-state. His working model is the Athens of Solon, when a programme of political reform was adopted by consent. The crisis was in its overt aspects economic, and was alleviated by a famous financial arrangement later known as the Great Disburdening. But the underlying problems were those of political conciliation and they were solved in some body of legislation in which the competing interests of rich and poor, hill, plain and coast, landowner, merchant and craftsman were reconciled. The most conspicuous of these reforms made office-holders responsible to audit, political and pecuniary, after their terms of office; and the right of audit was vested in the commons. This feature had impressed itself upon the mind of Democritus, as we shall see.

Tradition in retrospect always likes to dramatize political policies as personal at the expense of the social forces which made policy possible. But Democritus goes behind the sanctification of Solon and asks what made possible his choice as umpire and what made his solutions acceptable. He finds the only possible answer to lie in some ethos of consent on the part of the privileged classes of that period. For change was effected by voluntary reform, not enforced by revolution. Nor, presumably, in the philosopher's view, could any revolution have been successful; or rather, if it were, the community as Democritus viewed it would have been destroyed. Had he not said that in a collision of factions victors and vanquished suffer a common destruction (axiom 7)? At any rate, discord in Solonian Athens did not come to the breaking point: it proved negotiable. He might have pointed to simple fear as the ethos causative of prudence; however, knowing some of

the recorded facts perhaps better than we do, he discerned as the causative factor some mood of altruism and compassion latent in the governing classes, a mood which he describes as self-generated. For 'they took it on themselves'.

This historical frame of reference suggests a vivid context for the succeeding statements. Solon led to Cleisthenes, and to the formal establishment through further constitutional reform of 'The Democracy'. Cleisthenes was followed by Marathon and Salamis. Victory over the Persians was followed by the Delian League and the rise of the Athenian empire, culminating in the Age of Pericles with its supreme confidence and its brilliant achievements. Democritus views the entire story and frames an explanation for it. It is a single political process set in motion when liberal political principles were originally applied. Once those precious ingredients were released, the vital dynamic consensus of a city came into being, not as a single mood but as a continuing and evolving energy. So were made possible the 'mighty works', 'the execution and carrying through of great wars' (item 15). The mechanism of civic strength and achievement lay not in individual leadership but in a happy race of men: when the city-state is managed prosperously, this means stability and success for all its members (item 16). He is looking now at the Periclean age in which he lived.

However, Democritus does not allow these historical glories to carry him over into some Hegelian vision of the corporate community. His analysis remains complex: consensus had been achieved in a competitive situation by the addition of non-competitive forces. Once achieved, it therefore cannot be viewed as becoming a static condition or even an ideal formula into which individual energies become absorbed. Itself produced by process, it releases further process; thus competition between individuals and groups continues, but now it does not go 'beyond reason' (item 17): men continue to seek power for themselves but within a formula set, not by custom law so much as the 'utility of the commonwealth'. This is a rational criterion of civic good. Presumably therefore men had a capacity to envisage it and calculate it and in his psychology Democritus elsewhere explains that they have.

What is the total character of such a society? Has it a name? He names it himself in his summing up. 'Poverty under democracy is better than any prosperity among the powerful (item 18). This reads like the sentiment of some man of Athens, say between 440 and 420. He was not a native son but he had come to Athens to live there. And like Herodotus in the same period he fell under Athens' spell. May this not help to illuminate the obscure chronology of his life? He was surely a spiritual son of the age of Pericles. It is also hard to avoid the conclusion that when Thucydides penned the Funeral Speech of Pericles he was expressing an intellectual debt to Democritus.

If the philosopher turns to the age of Solon and after to explain the origin and behaviour of a liberal society, can his methodology as a theorist be defended as genetic and as consistent? To a modern mind, equipped with distinctions between sciences to which he was a stranger, it might seem that while he laid his foundations in anthropology and argued then deductively from a few principles, his superstructure is empirically derived from a quite recent and limited historical experience. This would recall a similar split in the thinking of Hobbes, where a deductive psychology is allied with Hobbes's present sense of the need to support absolute monarchy under given historical conditions. But for a thinker of the mid-fifth century B.C., the distinction between anthropology and history scarcely existed. The ancient times were in perspective foreshortened and their vast story of previous social development was telescoped into traditions of recent memory. Had not human history for Hesiod begun with the heroes of the Trojan war? Thus it is reasonable to assume that when Democritus says of compassion and the end of isolation that these arose 'at that time when the powerful took upon themselves to pay toll', etc., he is fitting the phenomena of the Solonic epoch into their genetic place in the anthropological story: here was a crucial stage in the advance from primitivism towards civilization. A science of man better equipped than his can afford to smile at the naïvety of such a foreshortening, but can it afford to dismiss his premiss that altruism has a historical basis?

19 [B254]

If inferior [citizens] proceed to the prerogatives of office
the more unfit they are when they proceed
the more negligible they become
and are filled with witlessness and overconfidence.

20 [B267]

The exercise of authority is by nature proper to the superior.

21 [B265a]

Men have better memories for errors than for successful
performance.

22 [B265b]

If [a trustee] restores a deposit
he need not expect to be [morally] approved.
If he default,
he can expect to have bad things said about him and done
to him.
It is just [to treat] anyone in authority in the same manner.

23 [B265c]

A man in authority is expected to perform well and not badly.
This is the [formal] assumption on which he was elected.

The political vision of Democritus is complex—more complex, as far as we know, than that of any of his successors. Perhaps it was because he kept his eye closer than any other did to all the factors of the historical process which had generated politics, and not just to some of them. Having recognized the quality of the Athenian democracy and the Athenian democratic process from Solon to Pericles as a supreme achievement, he raises at once the problem of effective authority in such a society, and gives an explicit answer: it can be solved only by recognizing the aristocratic principle: society divides itself into the superior and inferior; to entrust government to the latter is folly (items 19, 20).

The first thing to realize is what he means by superior. In this word, *kreitton,* the meanings of stronger and better crossed each other. The ambivalence produced a great deal of semantic confusion in Democritus' successors, a confusion compounded by Plato's polemics against them. What Democritus means by superior is sufficiently indicated by the terms in which he describes the behaviour of its opposite number, the inferior: negligence, stupidity, overconfidence. If the last is a partly moral defect, the first two are certainly intellectual. The first criterion of distinction is brains. So far, then, Democritus seems to anticipate the principle of Plato, that men are disparate in terms of intellectual ability. Therefore his argument for natural superiority comes to no more than the proposition that democracy must somehow get men of quality and ability to assume authority, and that, if it does not, the common estate suffers. He calls such types the 'effective citizens' (in No. 24 below). Yet he assumes that they are 'elected' and not self-appointed (No. 23). It is perhaps symptomatic of his position as a social theorist that he seems to suggest that the defects of the inferior are compounded by inappropriate responsibilities (item 19). That is, the social context available to a man's ethos can determine what becomes of the potentialities of that ethos. Plato after him made a similar point when, in insisting on specialization of function appropriate to each type, he argued that round pegs in square holes exhibit dangerous effects which would otherwise not arise.

Government, then, as distinct from society, is by nature proper to the superior. Does Democritus see the problem of reconciling this with the presuppositions of democracy? It is to his lasting credit that he does. The dilemma is very real: if political responsibility is to be distributed widely over society, this implies a degree of popular control over the state apparatus. Yet if office should be restricted to the superior, how can you have popular control of the superior, and how justify it? The answer given, with striking originality, anticipates the theory of government propounded by Hobbes, yet in a version subtler than Hobbes's political circumstances allowed him to envisage. Authority is a deposit which the community is capable of vesting in the holder of authority as in a trustee (item 22): that is, a virtual contract is entered into whereby we surrender the right to rule to those best able to exercise it. But when Democritus says a deposit, which the trustee is expected to return and get no thanks for it, he envisages a contract with a time-limit. He is obviously inspired here by the audit system instituted by Solon and further developed in the Cleisthenic constitution. Office-holders are elected for a term. Then they surrender their deposit and are examined on the use they have made of it. Conceivably the metaphor, borrowed from elementary commercial practice, was used in Solon's day to justify the arrangement; or perhaps Democritus invented it. At any rate, it reconciles Hobbes's perception that for effective government you have to assume the existence of some kind of contract with the requirement of an Athenian democrat that sovereignty be never absolute—a requirement which for historical reasons did not trouble Hobbes. The theory, or more correctly the analogy in which the theory is implicit, also has the effect of viewing political power (*arche*) as executive authority rather than as legislative sovereignty. It would have been better for Plato's political theory had he more plainly seen the distinction himself. Democritus, still keeping the audit system in view, argues that no form of political authority can ever be explained as privilege or prerogative. It comes into existence by definition only as a vehicle of good government (item 23). Plato would agree in the abstract, but Democritus applies this to the actual man who governs, not an ideal philosopher, but a fallible official subject to recall.

The contract theory thus stated had in various versions a long history after Democritus' day. It may be doubted whether it was ever stated so succinctly or with such satisfaction to the competing claims of authority and liberty. Positing as it does an arrangement between citizens and their rulers, it is to be distinguished from a parallel but different concept of compact (*syntheke*), an agreement between the citizens themselves. This was advanced in the generation after Democritus to justify the existence of custom-law within the body politic, as against the executive authority that rules over it. In Democritus' own day, the urgent need was to devise a theory supporting the practice of annual elections which could command intellectual respect. He earned the eternal credit of supplying it.

24 [B253a]

For the effective [citizens] expediency does not lie in omitting
their own business
in order to handle affairs.
Their own business gets into a bad way.

25 [B253b]

However if there is some error or omission in public business
the cry of disapproval goes up
even though no dishonest or wrongful act is involved.

26 [B253c]

Omission and wrong-doing alike incur the peril of criticism

and indeed punishment as well.

27 [B253d]

Error is inevitable,
but for men to sympathize with it does not come easy.

28 [B266a]

The shape [of society] presently prevailing has no device
against wrong being done to men in authority
even though they be perfect . . .

29 [B266c]

Somehow, the [shape of] things should be so ordered
as to cover the following problem also:
if a man does no wrong himself,
no matter how thoroughly he censure wrong-doers,
he should never find himself in their power.
If his acts are right,
some defence, of ordinance or otherwise,
should be there to protect him.

For Democritus, there were some problems that remained unresolved. As his rationale of man in society nears its conclusion, he casts his eye upon a stubborn fact: a democratic society cannot yet be a just society in any Platonic sense of that word. Better the Solonian democracy than any other polity, far better. But a question remains. He is still looking at the audit of office-holders and the way it is carried out. It is an operation of the multitude, relying not on judicial precision, not even on their collective will to achieve a common good. It may be doubted whether Democritus could ever have accepted the conception of such a will had it been proposed to him. No, the audit relies on certain factors in the human ethos: here again he turns to his psychology of that motivation in men which, as we have seen, is for him so complicated:

Men have better memories for errors than for successful performance

(No. 21).

This is what creates the possibility of the audit system and makes it effective. Men can always summon zeal for it. But, equally, the audit can therefore be undiscriminating. There are forms of error which are pardonable, as distinguished from crimes which are punishable. But the human ethos, with its proclivity to remember vice and forget virtue, can alter the focus of the facts; forgetting the virtues that mitigate errors, it can convert errors into crimes. How then do you combine the audit with complete justice to the executive? He notes that in Athenian democracy at its best, the effective citizen who had his own business to manage makes sacrifices if he takes on governmental responsibility (item 24). He does not actually say he should be paid, compensated by a salary for it: yet his intent may be to justify this Periclean policy. It also follows, because of the motivations upon which the machinery of the audit relies, that in addition to the sacrifice the citizen exposes himself to a genuine risk:

honest administration need not be perfect; a man can err and yet be guiltless of crime or peculation (item 25). The end result for him is, however, the same as if he had committed crimes (item 26). He

> 'has wrong done to him'

(item 28).

This violates the rule of moral logic. The just should not be exposed to injustice. There should be some mechanism or device, legal or otherwise, both to prevent an irrationality and to defend the security of the just (item 28). Thus at the end Democritus returns to the problem of security against wrong with which his story of civilization had begun. But it is now viewed at an advanced level of culture in a context of great complexity.

It would be interesting to reflect upon later solutions to this question thus posed by Democritus for western society. In effect, no absolute solution has been found. After Aristotle, political theory was for a long time formulated in mainly teleological or authoritarian terms. Since the problem is specific to the democratic process, it could not agitate the attention of thinkers very closely until after Cromwell. Since the eighteenth century, western democracy in effect has formulated a double solution. On the one hand, it has distinguished judicial and executive functions from legislative, and on the whole (with exceptions, to be sure) has made the former a matter of 'civil service' not subject to audit and reprisal. The acts of the legislative power, on the other hand, are in fact subject to audit through the party system, by which a government is 'voted down' and 'thrown out of office' for what are judged to be errors or crimes according to the voter's prejudices, and very often for errors which it did not commit. The solution, in fact, has been to separate the concepts of criminal guilt and political error, and to assume that guilt, under normal circumstances, does not arise in the processes of government. As to error, it is penalized unfairly, but the penalty consists merely in the deprivation of opportunity for the further exercise of power. A thinker of ancient Athens would be no more capable of drawing these distinctions achieved by modern democracy than he would be of rationalizing and accepting the party system as a genuine method of government.

This takes us far afield from Democritus. But that the problem he posed had to await the long passage of time for even partial solution is a tribute to the greatness of the man who could face and state the problem; who could realize that the triumphant democratic polity of Athens was not the last word in politics, without making that an excuse for rejecting it in the lofty manner of Plato. It may be said: did not Plato face the question? He did, but he solved it only by erasing it, for the problem turned on the complexities of the relationship between democracy and authority; and he would not admit that the relationship had any right to exist. Having educated the superior to be superior, he proposed to put them in power and give them machinery for self-perpetuation. So far as the issue of

sovereignty was concerned, this was a simple regression to the mythical centuries before Solon. Part of Plato's weakness, as of Aristotle's, was the conviction that in politics all problems, as they may be soluble theoretically, must therefore be solved now.

Democritus was content to leave something unsolved, and his readiness in this respect reveals the measure of his stature as a political thinker, for it grows from his conception of politics as a continuing process which, as it began far back in the past, in the savage, will still continue beyond the present. That is why the words *cosmos* and *rhuthmos* recur in these axiomatic statements. The anthropological story is one of the invention of successive tools and devices which in politics are addressed to solving political problems. We are waiting just now, he says, for a fresh addition to these devices. For the presently constituted society, no such device yet exists.

The same anthropological story describes how human beings have become successively shaped into societies none of which have teleological finality. The present shaping now asks for a piece of ordering, a new addition to the accumulating patterns of human relations.

This conclusion to his politics makes it feasible to suggest the basic relationship of his political theory to his physics or meta-physics. It would have been dangerous to suggest it at the beginning of our study. Do not all historians repeat the tale of his neat mechanical universe of oscillating or rotating atoms blindly throwing themselves through a limitless void and blindly engaging, among other things, in the accidental creation of the human species, which with equal accident is then moved by mechanical impulsion of pleasure and pain upon its amoral course?

This nightmare is a figment of text-books, even if the text-books go back as far as antiquity. What we do perceive is a naturalism, rather than a materialism, which insists (1) that the world is a physical 'order', as its Greek label *cosmos* implies, successively integrated out of chaos and successively replacing simple patterns by more complex ones, though without benefit of an ordering mind, since the tendency to organization is inherent in atomic behaviour; (2) that human society equally forms itself from the dust into increasingly complex patterns describable in terms not of mechanical but of political behaviour, patterns not produced in response to eternal verities nor directed by an all-powerful providence, but rather themselves producing for solution a series of problems with which atomic man has to wrestle, for they are problems of pleasure and pain, profit and loss, right and wrong, good and bad; and these have always been of major importance to the human species since it was first formed.

Appendix

While the floruit of Democritus as established by Apollodorus (420 B.C.) seems to be based on an unreliable computation (forty years after Anaxagoras) critics have continued to assume that Democ. was younger than Protagoras. Whether or not this be true—and the style of Democritus at least bespeaks his reliance on oral methods of publication—the difference cannot have been great, and I feel personally convinced that the structural and systematic analysis of the human condition carried out by the atomist must have supplied the intellectual foundation for the sophistic communications-theory. Hence the order of treatment in chapters VI, VII and VIII.

That group of statements treated in this chapter seem to have been largely by-passed by historians; a clue to indifference may lie in the myopic statement of Burnet, *Thales to Plato,* p. 201: 'What we have of him has been preserved mainly because he was a great coiner of telling phrases, and these have found their way into anthologies. That is not the sort of material we require for the interpretation of a philosophical system, and it is very doubtful whether we have some of his deepest thoughts at all.'

Reluctance to accept Democritean material in Stobaeus (*FVS* 169-297) as authentic (cf. Sinclair, *op. cit.,* p. 65, n. i, where however the cross-reference to the admittedly spurious Pythagorean material appears scarcely relevant) seems to derive mainly from failure to understand it. I hope my explication may help to settle the matter, on grounds of (*a*) vocabulary: e.g. could any post-Platonic writer have described a given social grouping as *cosmos* or *rhuthmos,* rather than, say, *sustema*? (*b*) continuity with pre-Socratic anthropology; (*c*) close attachment to political events in Athens from Solon to Pericles. This Stobaeus material (in contrast to the 'Democrates' material) is free from that kind of moralizing characteristic of Peripatetic and Stoic editors; cf. the very different fate that befell 'Antiphon' (below, appendix to cap. X).

Items nos. 1 and 3 in my series (*FVS* 68B257, 258), which seem crucial for establishing the continuity, in Dem.'s thought, between the defence of the human species against its rivals and the development of the primary social sanctions, are unluckily omitted in the useful collection of W. Kranz, *Vorsok. Denker* (1949), pp. 204-208.

Items 4, 9, 10, and 13: *nomos* in these contexts, as generally elsewhere when used in pre-Platonic authors (Sophocles, Archelaus, Antiphon), I have sought to render by linking the ideas of 'custom' and 'usage' with that of 'law'; *nomos* is admittedly usage which is 'solemn', but on the other hand is never wholly hypostatized as 'law' in the absolute, until enclosed in the context of the Socratic search for universals. Lines 450-457 of the *Antigone* are often translated as if they did describe Kantian universal imperatives (cf., e.g., Sinclair, *op. cit.,* pp. 49-50 and 89), but they refer, as both the Greek text and the dramatic context reveal, specifically to the solemn usages surrounding the treatment of the dead, especially when they are blood-kin. Similarly, *Oed. T.* lines 863-872 refer to the equally solemn usages (also familial) which forbid patricide and incest, crimes which the chorus forebode may be in the offing, though not yet revealed. Both passages could in fact provide text for Democritus' own approach to *nomos* as social usage, which, because it

represents stages of historical growth responsive to social need, is not thereby any less essential or sacred. Aristotle's interpretation (*Rhet.* 1.13.2.) is unhistorical.

Items 2, 4, 8, 9, 12, 13, 16, 17, 21-29) correspond to only 7 distinct entries in Stobaeus, which I have sub-divided into the separate aphorisms of which they seem to be composed. Such combinations, often formed with scant attention to the logic of the original, are characteristic of editors of *florilegia;* sometimes a connective . . . is inserted, sometimes not. . . .

Robert S. Brumbaugh (essay date 1964)

SOURCE: "Democritus and the Atomic Theory: Materialism," in *The Philosophers of Greece,* Thomas Y. Crowell Company, 1964, pp. 78-92.

[*In the following excerpt, Brumbaugh summarizes Democritus's atomist philosophy, considers some criticisms of it, and relates it to the development of Greek mechanical devices.*]

> There is no chance, but all is from necessity.
>
> LEUCIPUS

> Nothing exists but atoms and the void.
>
> DEMOCRITUS

Applying the logic developed in the Eleatic school by Parmenides and Zeno to the ideas of matter that had been formulated by the Milesians, Leucippus and Democritus produced a new philosophy—materialism. Their thesis was that all reality consists of hard indivisible particles, moving and colliding in empty space. This was the first philosophical or scientific statement of the atomic theory. But in this Greek form, the theory is somewhat different from later versions. And it is important not to confuse it with later philosophical ideas or with the theories of twentieth-century atomic physics.

When Democritus of Abdera was a young man, he journeyed to Athens, hoping to talk with Anaxagoras, the leading scientist and philosopher of the circle of artists and intelligentsia that Pericles, the Athenian statesman, had gathered around him. But the eminent older man had no time for a bright young theorist from a foreign city and did not see him. Disappointed, Democritus wrote, "I came to Athens, and no one knew me."[1] How different he would find the trip today, where the main approach to the city from the northeast runs past the impressive "DEMOCRITUS NUCLEAR RESEARCH LABORATORY." The name is a reminder that ancient Greece was the original home of the "atomic theory," and that Democritus was its first great developer. It is to variations on the theme of Democritus' ideas that modern science and technology owe much of their spectacular development; and it was atomism that provided the final concepts needed for materialism to appear as a powerful and coherent system of philosophy.[2]

Credit for the invention of this theory is given to a philosopher named Leucippus, but we know almost nothing about him, and it was in the systematic explanation and applications of Democritus that the theory became stabilized and influential.[3]

Democritus of Abdera lived about 400 B.C. He lived at the same time as Socrates, and we are therefore ignoring chronological order when we follow the accustomed practice of discussing him as a pre-Socratic philosopher. But in a way it is entirely reasonable to do so, for Democritus represents the final synthesis of ideas that brought to systematic completion the Milesian effort to understand the underlying material components and mechanisms of nature. Socrates began a revolution in thought by rejecting the claim that science can answer all questions of ethics, human life, and philosophy.

There is something not unlike William James's division of philosophers into "tough- and tender-minded," in the ancient world's contrast of Heraclitus and Democritus as the weeping and laughing philosophers: "Heraclitus weeps, and Democritus laughs, at all things."

Of the events of Democritus' life we know little; the one personal item is his remark quoted above: "I came to Athens and no one knew me"—a clear record of unappreciated genius that has been sympathized with by many a later scholar. Of his thought, we know a good deal, for his atomic theory was criticized extensively by Aristotle and quoted approvingly by Epicurus (whose extensive philosophic "Letter to Herodotus" has been preserved in the medley of lives and opinions in Diogenes Laërtius' book).[4]

The atomic theory as Democritus developed it was a combination of the Milesian science, Eleatic logic, and probably the development of technology that preceded it.[5] Long before Leucippus or Democritus developed the notion of atoms, others had suggested that the physical world is made up of small particles. Empedocles had suggested that each of "the elements" comes in small particles of definite size and shape. This idea in turn traces back to the Pythagorean notion of small "regular solids" as the "molecular parts" of nature. Earlier, the Pythagorean attempt to bring mathematics and physics together by building a physical world out of points led in this same direction. Most important in the background of this theory, however, must have been the use of mechanical models to study natural process, which was introduced by Anaximander. In the model, a natural phenomenon is duplicated by the mechanical interaction of small, separate "parts." Therefore, it is tempting, when one wonders *why* model-building works, to test the hypothesis that the model is like nature because nature, too, is a complex combination of small parts that interact mechanically. This notion gains plausibility when technology shows that mechanisms can perform functions of a much more complex kind than earlier thinkers had imagined.

The essential ideas of Greek atomism as a physical theory are four: first, that matter comes in separate, smallest particles which are "uncuttable" (*atoma-* "unable to be cut"); second, that an empty space exists, in which these particles move; third, that the atoms differ only in shape and volume; fourth, that all change is the result of transfer of momentum by the moving atoms and such transfer can occur only by contact—there is, of course, no "action at a distance" in this scheme.[6]

The atoms of this theory are small, hard chunks of being (which, like the One Being of Parmenides, are indivisible, because there are no inner veins of not-being along which they could be "cut"). They have none of the "secondary" qualities—color, flavor, and so on—that we experience, but only shape and extension. (The idea of a qualitatively neutral matter is finally clearly formulated here.)

The atoms differ from each other, singly and in their combinations, "in shape, position, and order." Thus, A differs from B in shape; N from Z in position; AZ from ZA in order.[7] These particles come in all sorts of shapes, for, as Democritus argues, "There is no reason why they should have one shape rather than another." They have always been in motion, and as they move about they collide; sometimes they "interlock" and hold together; sometimes they "rebound" from a collision.[8] (The Roman poet Lucretius, trying to present a popular, imaginative picture of atomism, pictures "hooks" on the atoms that fasten them together.) All change is ultimately, therefore, change of place and transfer of momentum among these hard particles, and all objects are aggregates packed together in more and less stable patterns.

This notion of all change as a transfer of motion or change of "packing" among differently shaped, hard particles offered an immediate and satisfying explanation of many phenomena that physics wanted to explain.

First of all, consider condensation and rarefaction, changes that have continued to play a central part in physics ever since Anaximenes. If density depends on the relative amount of empty space between the particles of a substance, it is easy to see how pressure leads to condensation, while bombardment by small "fire" particles will spread the atoms apart, leading to rarefaction. And, in principle at least, science has found no more satisfying explanation of differences and changes in density.

The Ionian accounts of the formation of the world by a "spinning vortex," in which different elements collect in different levels because of their respective mass, worked excellently when the vortex was reinterpreted as made up of many fine particles. It could be argued, with close analogies to experience, that collisions would tend to make the smaller atoms "rebound" further, gradually forcing them to the outside. Empedocles' analysis of "pores and effluences" could be taken over, and was much more satisfactory when the pores were genuinely "empty spaces" in latticeworks of atoms. Anaximander's "models" were, of course, the strongest argument in favor of this new approach to physical reality; for the atomic theory could explain the fact that nature behaved like a machine because it really was a complex mechanism.

So far, the new theory could synthesize and improve on all of the developments of physics up to its inception. There seemed no sharp limit to the phenomena it could explain. In principle, the atomic theorists believed that physics was identical with philosophy; that to the question, What is being?, science had finally found the answer, "In reality, nothing exists but atoms and the void."

The logical and philosophical background of this new theory played a crucial part in the emergence of atomism as a systematic materialistic philosophy, rather than a specialized physical theory. The scientists of Ionia and the logicians of Elea were almost equally responsible for this. Tracing the line back to Parmenides, the reasoning leads directly to atomism, in the following way:

1. Parmenides had shown to the satisfaction of the atomic theorists that the existence of change, or even the appearance of change, required that being be many, not one; and, if many, divided by not-being into its separate parts;

2. But common sense and Ionian science made it clear that "nature" does change, if not really, in some abstract sense, at least apparently;

3. Therefore, reality must be divided into many parts; and not-being must exist as their separator.

(As a matter of fact, this line of argument, which Democritus accepts, had already been outlined by Melissus of Samos, a philosopher who followed the ideas and methods of Zeno and Parmenides, but Melissus had gone on to reject the conclusion as absurd. since it asserted the existence of not-being. Leucippus and Democritus, on the other hand, accepted the conclusion as actually true, since it was a necessary condition for the appearance of change.)

This Eleatic ancestry also shows in the clear, rigorous logic by which the characteristics of atoms and space are deduced. The atoms are in fact small chunks of Parmenidean "being," and each one has the properties of *indivisibility, homogeneity, qualitative neutrality* that Parmenides had ascribed to his One Being. If they were otherwise, the atoms would necessarily have some not-being within them, and so would be, not single particles of matter, but collections of several parts. Empty space is Eleatic not-being: it is defined as having no resistance, density, or cohesion: it cannot, therefore, *do* or *transmit* anything, since "nothing comes from nothing." Any interaction must be the result of two units of being coming together.

The theory thus synthesizes earlier traditions into a new philosophy that has methods and logical rules of its own. The way to understand a subject matter, it assures us, is to analyze every subject matter into its least parts and to find their pattern of combination. If the theory is right, there

will always be such parts, and phenomena can always be explained and duplicated by study of their mechanical interaction.

The proponents of the atomic theory further claimed that it could be used to explain medicine, psychology, ethics, and the theory of knowledge, as well as physics and chemistry. In these extensions it sometimes ran into difficulties—for example, in ethics its idea of absolute determinism was hard to adapt to the notion of freedom of choice. But it also had some remarkable successes. For example, in medicine, the doctors and surgeons of that day found that the atomists' idea of treating the body as a complex machine fitted their own practical knowledge of the body's mechanics. It was clear that the workings of the muscular and skeletal system, the ebb and flow of blood (they did not, of course, know of its circulation), the effects of damage to the brain could all be mechanically explained. The processes and functions involving an interaction of the mind and body were obviously more complex. For example, there were patients who complained of pain, though physically there was nothing wrong with them; their trouble had a psychological origin. It was not clear then—and still is not clear today—how such phenomena as these could be reduced to mechanical explanation. But that they could, somehow, be so reduced the atomists were certain.

The old indecisions about *psyche,* reflected in attempts to make the soul *pneuma* or *aer*—but still to hold religious views that would make it immortal—or to make *psyche* a part of the regular order of the physical world—but still have it initiate motion by a kind of "free decision" to act—had found a decisive resolution. The self was no exception to the total structure of reality; it was corporeal and part of nature, and only illusion and wishful thinking had led mankind to believe in its freedom or immortality. The soul, because of its sensitivity and activity, was supposed to be made up of particularly small, mobile atoms (probably spherical to account for their mobility), which responded by inner movement to the impacts of sensation from the outer world.[9] When, after a disturbance, the soul moved back into equilibrium, its motion was amplified and transmitted to the body, and also was transmuted into consciousness and thought.

The theory provided a new tool for exploring the mechanism of sensation. Since all "action" is the result of contact, sense perception was explained as the impression made on the senses by atoms from outside. Visible surfaces, for example, radiated atomic films that moved through the air and struck the eye. The clarity of vision depended both on the strength of this constant radiation and on the state of the medium. If the air atoms between the observer and the object were moving violently, the image would be distorted. Even if it were not moving violently, there would be some friction. The corners of the film traveling from a square tower would be knocked off: the eye would receive the impression of a round tower. For transmission and distortion of visual images and sound, for an analysis of touch and taste, the theory gave new precision to accounts of sensation and illusion. Philosophers have never forgotten the new sharpness which this application gave to accounts of the work of the senses, and of the different "perspectives" that objects present to us under different conditions of observation.[10]

Consistent with their philosophical position, the atomic theorists treated so-called secondary qualities (warmth, weight, color, taste), not as objective properties of things, but as a subjective contribution by the observer. All of these exist only "by convention," writes Democritus. "By convention"—here is the opposite of existing "in reality" or "by nature." The phrase extends the notion of social custom and law—distinctively human constructions—to the senses of the observer who clothes the neutral outer world, which consists of "nothing but atoms and the void," with its apparent qualities. There are some early and rather unsatisfactory suggestions in Democritus' fragments of the way in which different "colorless" or "black-and-white" configurations of atoms are perceived as having color.

In the field of ethics, the price of consistency seems rather high. Since all events are the mechanical result of physical chains of causality (one of the two surviving fragments of Leucippus says, "Nothing occurs by chance, but all is from necessity"), there is no place for human freedom in this scheme. Neither is there any way for a purpose to be explained, and there is no assurance, on the basis of this theory, that observations from the past will have any relevance in the future: the theory will accept only direct observation as evidence, and the future can never be directly observed. On the other hand, the theory is an excellent antidote to the superstitious component of the then current religious notions.

Various sayings, attributed to Democritus, show how atomism was able logically to connect itself with ethical recommendations. According to these, the soul will either be disturbed, so that its motion affects the body in a violent way, or it will be at rest, in which case it regulates thoughts and actions harmoniously. Freedom from disturbance is the condition that causes human happiness, and this is the ethical goal. A society in which individual men meet and associate like atoms will be stabilized when collisions are kept to a minimum.

It may seem strange to find, in the ethical fragments of Democritus, statements about what we *ought* to choose or to do, for the theory leaves no place for human freedom of choice. Sometimes this problem is met by saying that because of our ignorance, we seem to have freedom, since we do not know all of the small contributing causes that made a given decision inevitable. In the light of our illusion, we make moral judgments, administer justice, and feel responsible for our own destinies. (To dismiss human freedom, in order to keep the explanation of reality simple and precise, is not satisfying to those for whom ethics is the most important part of philosophy. Later, Epicurus and his school added the notion that the atoms sometimes

"swerve" unpredictably, in an attempt to give freedom and chance some foundation in natural science.)

Ethics and politics based on an atomist philosophy are clear and realistic; it is tempting to develop them in this way. Nevertheless, throughout the history of Western thought, no one has satisfactorily reconciled his notion of human nature with rigorous physical necessity. Materialism as a philosophy, based on atomism as its scientific application, has remained ever since Greek times an important and attractive speculative synthesis. There was a period of eclipse during the Middle Ages, because materialism so evidently went contrary to the Christian religion, but there have been three different versions of the theory: the Greek original, the later Roman adaptation of Epicurus and his school, and our contemporary interpretation. . . . What is particularly interesting about these three variations on a philosophic theme is the different excellences of each version: Democritus' atomism is, of the three, the most clear and rigorous in its logic and its deductions; Epicurus' atomism is less interested in logical elegance than in the *ethical* implications of atomism, and the theory is reconstructed around these ethical applications; our contemporary concern is less with the logical rigor, or the moral impact of our theory, than with the *physical* applications for description and control. We may now be moving toward a theory that will combine the excellences of each of these three.[11] . . .

Four more specific criticisms might also be noted here as suggesting limits to the theory—and criticisms continue to be made.[12]

First, there is the criticism that in an atomist's universe, there can be *no theory* at all.[13] For to claim that a theory is generally true and that people should believe it, presupposes a theorist who has examined the evidence and chosen the best explanation from among alternatives. But if "all is from necessity," including all psychological processes, what any man thinks is simply a necessary, mechanical outcome of previous conditioning. The objection, notice, is, not that someone who believes the atomic theory is *wrong,* but only that he is inconsistent in holding that this belief can represent more than a personal reflection of his past experience and that he, therefore, has no right to say that anyone else ought to agree with him.

Second, there is the question of whether the so-called secondary qualities can really be relegated to existence "by convention."[14] To explain how a black-and-white world can appear colored, for example, scientists have devised excellent laboratory experiments in which patterns built from colorless elements show how the observer perceives color. But it is sheer Milesian absentmindedness to think that this explains how I perceive color. The scientist, treating his experiment as a model of the brain, forgets his own part in it. He can show, granted, that a pattern of colorless impulses can look colored, but he has not shown how the observer knows it has this color. What, in the model of the brain, corresponds to the experimenter in the laboratory, who "sees" the color emerge from the neutral pattern?

Third, there is the question of whether "empty space" is an intelligible scientific concept at all.[15] If like Democritus we treat it as pure not-being, then can we say that it "separates" the atoms that move about in it? This third objection does not apply, as the first two do, so directly to our modern theory as to the two older versions.

Fourth, there is the objection that there is our own awareness of our freedom, responsibility, and sensitivity to value and purpose. Here the atomic theory may be in the same position that Eleatic philosophy confronted with its denial of motion. Even if ultimately these things are an illusion, isn't it necessary for an adequate theory to show how it is possible for the illusion to appear? And can this be done by any theory that supposes at the outset that there is no place in reality for freedom or value?

Perhaps the first atomic theorists were too optimistic in thinking that their ideas could answer all of the questions of philosophy. In the following chapters, we will see how a new attention to the human observer led to the different speculative synthesis of Platonic idealism and the final attempt of Aristotle to combine Platonism and materialism, which ends the Hellenic epoch of Greek thought.

As a final comment on the relation of technology to the atomic theory, I should like to note that the atomic theory has always been useful when applied to experience. It is a particularly useful view for the inventor or engineer who wants to get a set of mechanical parts to work together automatically and perform some useful function. Would the theory have seemed plausible and remained so intellectually important in a culture with no technology to give it imaginative plausibility and concrete illustration? One would certainly think not, and the fact that in ancient India atomism was thought of as a theoretical position but discarded as implausible matches this expectation.[16] But until recently we had no notion of the true ancient Greek attitude toward technological gadgetry. Classical literature offered several references deprecating arts and crafts and almost no passages describing inventions or equipment. On the basis of this evidence, we would have had to picture the classical atomist as a very strange human being, able to be as fascinated by abstract mechanical design as we are but without any concrete experience with mechanisms.

New archeological evidence shows, however, that by the time of Leucippus and Democritus there was enough use of mechanism to make the analogy of ancient and modern atomic theorists plausible. Factors partly of custom, regulating what themes were or were not the sort of thing to put in book form, partly of supply and demand, determining what available written works would be best sellers and hence recopied and preserved, operated to cause a gap in the older picture. For a clear, demonstrated tradition of scientific apparatus, we are still about fifty years short of closing the gap between Hellenistic and Hellenic periods. But for the discovery of a number of more modest devices that show exactly what we want to know, 1957 in the Athenian Agora proved a decisive year.[17]

Aristotle in his *Constitution of Athens,* itself not recovered until the turn of the present century, describes the equipment and procedure used in impaneling jurors and deciding cases in court. His description has overtones of a Rube Goldberg dream. In 1957, archeologists first discovered ancient equipment that confirms Aristotle's statements. Let us look at one or two of these applications of mechanical ingenuity to insure legal impartiality. The American voting machine will be seen to have an interesting Athenian ancestor, both in the problem necessitating its invention and the lever-gear-and-wheel solutions.

A secret ballot was essential, if jurors were not to be criticized, intimidated, or assassinated for voting the wrong way. And a single ballot for each juror was similarly essential if someone with a dozen extra ballots up his sleeve was to be prevented from dropping them all in the box. The Greeks devised voting tokens to meet the first requirement. Identical in appearance—round wheels, with short shafts sticking out at each side—were these "pebbles" (a name preserved from a simpler time) used in voting. They differed only in that the shaft of one was solid, that of the other hollow: the juror was required to hold his tokens with thumb and finger over the shafts, so that no one else could see the difference. (A further refinement is still not wholly understood: the clerk was required to put the two ballots "on a lampstand" from which they were picked up, in the manner just described, by the juror.) Second, to insure that only a single vote be cast, the voting cask had a top with a slot exactly designed to admit only one disk-and-shaft token. The essential principle of the coin-operated slot-machine or the modern telephone has thus an ancient Athenian ancestry. A special tally board was used to count the ballots, and a courtroom water clock officially measured pleading time.[18]

The Greeks took it as a practical axiom that, if anyone knew who the specific jurors would be, no case would be impartially decided. To rule out the possibility of coercion a splendid selection-by-lot mechanism had been invented and mass-produced; twenty were required in preparing for a day in court. So far as I know, no actual traces of the other courtroom devices have been found: a hundred hoppers holding acorns, each lettered from A to L; colored staves used to route jurymen to the courtroom where they were allocated; tokens entitling jurors to payment on surrender to the court; some way of standardizing fractions of a day that allowed for case presentation as between the day-lengths of December and July. But even without these, the documents and finds to date confirm the philosophically interesting hint: that the Greek world, at the time of the atomic theory, had enough mechanical ingenuity and gadgetry to give some concrete content to the vision of reality as a large congeries of small indivisible wheels, slots, and shafts in some magnificent machine.

Notes

1. DK A9; B116.

2. The tremendous historical importance of the atomic theory hardly needs documentation; see, for example,

Sambursky, *op. cit.,* pp. 105 ff. (where however the Greek and Roman versions are combined; they are distinguished and summarized on pp. 128 ff.).

3. For Leucippus, see Kirk and Raven, *op. cit.,* p. 403; C. Bailey, *The Greek Atomists and Epicurus,* Oxford, 1928; Leucippus in DK B1, B1a, B2.

4. Book X, on Epicurus, was copied by Diogenes Laërtius from contemporary primary source material; his treatments of the Epicureans and the Stoics are reliable and important. Epicurus' "Letter to Herodotus," which Diogenes Laërtius quotes, is an excellent summary of Epicurus' doctrine.

5. Here again we have difficulty in judging the exact balance between pure theory and experiment, or at least observation, that went into the makeup of this theory. See above pp. 88 ff. and the divergent views of Sambursky and Claggett. Also see the end of the present chapter, below, for some evidence that the technology of the time would have made close interaction of the theory and immediate observation possible.

6. DK B9. Cf. M. Jammer, *Concepts of Space,* with a Foreword by A. Einstein, Cambridge, Mass., 1954. On the reasons why atoms (pieces of pure "being") can't be "cut," compare with Parmenides' rejection of plurality, above.

7. Aristotle, *Met.* 985b13; DK, Leucippus, A10.

8. All shapes, endless motion: Aristotle, *loc. cit.*

9. Soul atoms finest: Aristotle: *De Anima.*

10. Emanation theory of perception; compare the "pores and particles" of Empedocles, above, Ch. VIII.

11. In the following table, the Greek atomic theory is reconstructed from fragments and reports of Democritus; the Roman version from Epicurus' *Letter,* in Diogenes Laërtius; the contemporary is a composite based on a consensus of a number of sources, and on some discussions with colleagues in physics at Yale.

12. Two of the four criticisms that follow are cited in modern formulation, where they are clearer and stronger than in their classical occurrences.

13. For the "no theory" objection, see N. P. Stallknecht's presentation of this point in "Descartes," Stallknecht and Brumbaugh, *Spirit,* pp. 252-54.

14. For the "no secondary qualities" objection, see Whitehead's statement, *SMW,* chap. v.

15. Aristotle is already clear on the "empty space" objection; see his proof that there is no "void," to which he devotes *Physics* IV, 213A12 ff.

16. For atomism in India, see the account of the Charvaka school in Radhakrishnan, *op. cit.*

17. For the excavations and finds, see the *Guide to the Agora,* 2nd edition, published by the American School of Classical Studies in Athens, Athens, 1963.

18. Aristotle, *Aristotle's Constitution of Athens,* trans. with notes by K. von Fritz and E. Kapp, New York, 1950, paragraphs 63-69, with notes.

Edward Hussey (essay date 1972)

SOURCE: "Cosmology from Parmenides to Democritus," in *The Presocratics,* Duckworth, 1972, pp. 127-48.

[*In the following excerpt, Hussey summarizes the atomistic theory and explains in what ways it was revolutionary.*]

THE ATOMISTS: LEUCIPPUS AND DEMOCRITUS

Of the life of Leucippus we know next to nothing, and there is little trustworthy information about that of Democritus. Both were citizens of Abdera, a small city on the northern shores of the Aegean, which like Elea had been founded by refugees from old Ionia. Democritus was perhaps the younger and, born like Socrates around 470, he lived on well into the fourth century.

Leucippus and Democritus were responsible for the Atomistic theory. Even though they were contemporaries of Socrates, their speculations are traditionally and reasonably grouped under the heading 'Presocratic', for the Atomistic theory is the last and greatest original effort in that kind of physical speculation which originated with the Milesians. The respective shares of Leucippus and Democritus in its creation cannot be certainly defined, but it seems likely that the leading ideas of the theory were due to Leucippus, and that Democritus, a more prolific and many-sided but less original thinker, worked out the applications in greater detail. There are a few inessential points on which the opinions of the two are said to have differed, but it is not possible to prove disagreement on any fundamental question.

The starting-point for the Atomists, as for Anaxagoras, was the effort to find a way of reconciling the Eleatic arguments, so far as they were taken to be valid, with the construction of a cosmology that accounted for the perceptible world. But while Anaxagoras tried to create a multiplicity without definite units, the Atomists took very seriously the need for indisputable and absolute units of whatever existed, and therefore collided with Parmenides and Zeno at a different set of points.

Zeno had argued that two things that are can be distinguished into two units only by means of some third thing 'between' them, that must itself be; and thence arises an infinite progression. For this reason, Leucippus, according to Aristotle (*de Gen. et Corr.* 325^a 23-9; *Metaphysics* 985^b 4-10), took a drastic step: he proposed to introduce 'that which is not' (*to mē on*) as a factor in the explanation of the world, and so to assert (it would seem) that it somehow *was.* As Aristotle puts it, the proposal of Leucippus is unintelligible because it is so blatantly self-contradictory; but there are good reasons for thinking that Aristotle is mistaken. For another remark, by Democritus, says, not that 'the non-existent exists just as much as the existent', but that 'the "nothing" exists just as much as the "thing"'. Here the words translated by 'the "nothing"' are '*to mēden*', 'that which is nothing', and the words translated by 'the "thing"' are '*to den*', where '*den*' is a nonce-word, formed from '*mēden*' by the removal of the negative prefix '*mē-*'. The point of this linguistic joke must be that '*to mēden*' is *not* to be taken, as Aristotle wrongly takes it, as equivalent to 'the non-existent', since what is not *to mēden* is not *to on* but *to den*. The point that Democritus seems to be indicating is that 'nothingness' is just as real as any 'thing', but differs in not being a 'thing', or, as one might say, not being an individual or a primary object of reference, though to say this is to import a higher level of sophistication than was available at the time. How does this distinction help to answer Zeno? If 'things' are separated by 'the nothing', what separates or distinguishes 'the nothing' from any 'thing'? There are no reports on what the Atomists replied or would have replied to this question, but it seems that consistently with their position they had just one convincing answer. Qualitatively, 'the nothing' is distinguished from any 'thing' simply by lack of 'thingness', by not being an individual with all that that implies. Spatially, there is no further entity required to divide 'nothing' from any 'thing'. For though there must be a *boundary,* this can perfectly well be *part* of the 'thing'. This kind of question about the topology of space was later treated elaborately by Aristotle, but it must be admitted that he gives no hint that the Atomists had contributed anything to the debate. Some indication that Democritus was interested in these questions is given by a puzzle of his preserved by a later writer (DK 68 B 155). The substance of it is this: suppose on a line there can be two points 'next to' one another with no intervening point. Then let a right cone be intersected by a plane parallel to its base and passing through the point on its axis which is 'next above' the point where the axis meets the base. Will the circle of intersection be smaller than or equal to the base? Clearly either answer leads to absurd results, which shows that two points on a line cannot be 'next to' one another in this way. It is interesting that Democritus should be arguing like this since the density of points on a line is crucial for the suggested answer to Zeno. If points on a line were not dense, then one could ask what separated the last point in a 'thing' from the first point in 'the nothing', and there would be no plausible answer.

Once 'the nothing' was admitted, it could perform two functions: it separated 'things' from one another, and so made a plurality possible, and it allowed change of place by things, so making possible all change which could be reduced to rearrangements of unit 'things'. 'The nothing' therefore functioned as 'empty space', or 'void', and the sources usually call it 'the void' (*to kenon*). It was the first time that a well-thought out concept of a purely passive and empty space had been propounded, though it may well be that the mysterious 'Pythagoreans', of whose opinions Aristotle tells (see Chapter Four) had hit upon the idea of a unit-separating void before the Atomists did. Though condemned in ancient times by the high authority of Aristotle, and in modern times by many influential thinkers, the notion of a purely passive space has a way of persisting and of making itself indispensable to physics; so its introduction by the Atomists is a noteworthy landmark.

The 'things', the units that moved about in, and were separated by, 'the nothing', were to be indisputably *units;* so each of them was uncreated and imperishable, and could not be divided, whence the name *atomon,* 'indivisible thing'. Each atom was in fact the heir to many properties of Parmenides' 'that which is'. But not to all; most obviously, the atoms were in space, and might be of any shape.

Some confusion has existed ever since the time of Aristotle over the question whether the atoms were 'mathematically' or 'theoretically' as well as physically indivisible. The problem arises in this way: it is clear from many pieces of evidence that the atoms were thought of as spatially extended and as having various shapes, which could (for instance) cause them to interlock, and as possessing weight in proportion to their volume. They could vary in size, and according to one (late) witness Democritus imposed no upper limit of size on his atoms. Not all of the evidence available is totally reliable; there are some contradictions, and a suspicion that the doxographic tradition has been infected by the misrepresentations of an Epicurean writer. Nevertheless, it is clear that the atoms were spatially extended, three-dimensional objects. Any such object can be said to be 'theoretically' divisible, in the sense that one can always distinguish, at least in thought, as Zeno had pointed out, two or more distinct and spatially separate three-dimensional regions within it—that is to say, this is possible if one accepts ordinary ideas about the local topological structure of space, and in particular those assumptions about that structure which are enshrined in Euclidean geometry.

The Atomists, then, were in a dilemma. Either they had to deny that atoms were 'theoretically' divisible, which in turn meant either overturning ordinary notions of space or refusing size and shape to atoms; or they had to allow 'theoretical' divisibility and thereby to fall foul of the arguments of Zeno, that what was even 'theoretically' divisible had ceased to be a true unit and contained infinitely many sub-units. Since it is clear that atoms did have size, and almost certain that no innovations were made in ordinary notions of space by the Atomists, it would seem to follow that atoms must have been 'theoretically' divisible. The difficulty is that Aristotle, who would be expected to be the most competent witness, speaks in a way that seems to mean that the atoms were not 'theoretically' divisible. Aristotle, however, had his own theory about the relationship between 'theoretical' and 'physical' divisibility, and it is likely that he did not prevent his private assumptions from colouring the account he gave of the Atomists. The doxographical evidence is self-contradictory and of doubtful value.

It is necessary, therefore, to suppose that the Atomists acknowledged the 'theoretical' divisibility of the atoms while denying their physical divisibility. The problems discovered by Zeno about space and change would still, of course, remain, and how the Atomists proposed to deal with them is not known.

The atoms, then, were spatially extended and physically indivisible. They were also unlimited in number, unchanging in shape, size and internal structure, and they moved for ever in a limitless void. The Atomists now had the task of accounting for the observed structure of the world and the contents of personal experience on these economical foundations.

It is natural to begin by asking about the ways in which the atoms moved. The evidence is conflicting and there may have been deliberate distortion by Epicurean sources. Aristotle, so far as he goes, is the most reliable witness. His testimony (DK 68 A 37) seems to show that the atoms had no inherent tendency to move, and that there was not (as there was in Epicurus' universe) an absolute 'upwards' or 'downwards'—the void was symmetrical in every respect. Accordingly, atoms moved only because impelled by the impact of other atoms. They were said to have weight in proportion to their size, and weight could be explained in terms of resistance to impact. Whether an atom, if undisturbed, was thought to continue in its state of motion indefinitely or gradually to come to rest, is not clear.

Within a *kosmos* other dynamical principles were thought to apply, of which the justification in terms of collisions of atoms is not obvious. Heavier atoms were more drawn towards the centre than light atoms, and there was also a tendency for atoms of like size and shape to congregate together. Democritus appealed (fr. 164), in support of this principle, to the analogy provided by the arrangements of pebbles of various configurations on a sea-shore. It is likely that this kind of analogy was the most that could be offered by the Atomists to make plausible some of the steps postulated in the creation of *kosmoi* from atoms and void. There is no sign that they made any real advance towards a systematic treatment of dynamics, much less a mathematical one.

For this reason, the cosmological devices used by the Atomists to explain the creation and working of *kosmoi* do not differ much from those well-established in the Presocratic tradition. They give the impression of being artificially pasted on to the new metaphysical foundations. The formation of a *kosmos* was roughly as follows. A chance and sudden congregation of atoms of the same order of size in a relatively crowded space caused a rotatory movement to occur. This may have been supported by analogies in observed facts: vortices are observed to form in water when it runs out of a large vessel through a narrow passage. What was further required, then, was a way of shutting atoms in from the rest of the universe. This was done by supposing the formation by random movements of a 'fence' of interlocked atoms. In favour of this step, it can at least be said that there would be a kind of 'natural

selection' at work; atoms once interlocked would stay interlocked unless subject to exceptionally strong and well-directed blows from outside. The principle of 'like to like' would guarantee that 'fences', once in existence, would tend to extend themselves, and that the atoms shut into any *kosmos* were all of more or the less the same size, a point important for the theory of perception.

Once the rotation had begun, the cosmogony proceeded on familiar lines. By a process of segration by weight, the four elements—which were explained by four particularly natural and stable kinds of 'molecule'—are created and sorted into the usual arrangement, and function thereafter in traditional fashion. Traditional also was the possibility of the existence of an unlimited number of *kosmoi* simultaneously in different parts of the void; possibly new was the idea that the collapse of a *kosmos,* which occurred eventually upon excessive pressure from outside, left 'ruins' which often furnished material for a new *kosmos.*

In one respect the system of the Atomists was revolutionary. All their predecessors had asserted, either explicitly or implicitly, that the intelligibility and rationality of the universe depended ultimately upon its subjection to a divine power which in some sense was conscious and intelligent. The earliest thinkers had no doubt said rather little about the nature and purposes of the deity. Heraclitus and Anaxagoras had said more. Even in Parmenides, 'that which is' is a timeless unified thought; and the same is true, with some qualification, for the 'Sphere of Love' in Empedocles. It is true that the Sphere comes to be only intermittently; yet because 'everything has thought and a share of intelligence', it is always potentially present in the scattered thoughts of the various particles of matter. The Atomists went counter to the whole tradition by removing everything 'mental' from the list of ultimate constituents, a noteworthy act which must be examined more closely.

The reduction of everything to atoms and 'void' did not by itself entail the denial of an ultimate 'mental' constituent, for it would have been possible to suppose that each atom was a mind—again, a suggestion of Leibniz's monads. But such minds would have had to be timeless, since the internal structure of atoms could not be allowed to change in time; and therefore would not have been able to play any part, as minds, in the determination of events in the universe. The inner logic of the Atomist theory, therefore, led straight to the conclusion that consciousness and perception, as they are known in ordinary experiences, are epiphenomena, determined and accounted for completely by the states and rearrangements of components not themselves capable of consciousness or perception. (It is for this reason that Democritus has to say that perceptible qualities exist 'by courtesy' only (see Chapter Six).) It followed that the whole history of the universe was determined, if at all, by a 'meaningless' necessity inherent in the laws governing the collision and rebound of atoms, a force which was devoid of any inherent tendency to the better, or of any regard for the wishes and requirements of such accidental by-products as conscious beings. Democritus conceded, indeed, that 'gods' might exist; but by 'gods' he meant only conscious beings which were created and perishable, though noticeably superior to human beings in size, beauty, strength, intelligence and moral qualities.

The last and greatest representative of the Milesian tradition, therefore, was the first explicit materialist. It would be wrong to conclude from this that materialism had been 'in' the tradition all along. Anaxagoras' system represents another equally possible line of development. Neither of these lines was to be taken any further, however, for a long time. The sophistic age had undermined the whole tradition of cosmology, and when in the fourth century cosmological ideas began again to be discussed, the dominant minds, shaped in the fire of philosophical debate, gave them a different turn and subordinated them to other considerations.

Works Cited

The Atomists: C. Bailey, *The Greek Atomists and Epicurus* (Oxford, 1928); V. E. Alfieri, *Atomos Idea* (Florence, 1953).

Jonathan Barnes (essay date 1979)

SOURCE: "The Bounds of Knowledge," in *The Presocratic Philosophers: Volume 2: Empedocles to Democritus,* Routledge & Kegan Paul, 1979, pp. 234-62.

[*In the following excerpt, Barnes discusses Democritus's skepticism regarding humankind's ability to know anything with certainty.*]

Democritean Scepticism

Metrodorus of Chios, a pupil of Democritus (e.g., Clement, 70 A 1) who held solidly to the main tenets of atomism (e.g., Theophrastus, A 3), purveys an extreme scepticism which foreshadows, in its ingenious comprehensiveness, the most extravagant claims of Pyrrho: at the beginning of his book *Concerning Nature* Metrodorus said:

> None of us knows anything, not even that very fact whether we know or do not know; nor do we know what not to know and to know are, nor, in general, whether anything is or is not.

> (505: B 1)[1]

Of Metrodorus' book little else survives and nothing tells us what his scepticism rested upon, or why he wrote *Concerning Nature* at all. His scepticism, however, like his atomism, was inherited. For according to Democritus,

> In reality (*eteêi*) we know nothing; for truth is in a pit.

> (506: 68 B 117)

Our main source for Democritus' scepticism is Sextus; and I quote the chief Democritean fragments in their Sextan setting:

> Democritus sometimes does away with what appears to the senses. . . . In the *Cratunteria*, though he had promised to ascribe the power of conviction to the senses, he is none the less found condemning them; for he says:

> We in actuality grasp nothing firm, but what changes (*metapipton*) in accordance with the contact (*diathigên**)[2] between our body and the things which enter into it and the things which strike against it [= B 9].

> And again he says:

> Now that in reality (*eteêi*) we do not grasp of what sort each thing is or is not, has been made clear in many ways [= B 10].

> And in *Concerning Forms* he says:

> A man must know by this rule that he is separated from reality (*eteê*) [= B 6].

> And again:

> This argument too makes it clear that in reality (*eteêi*) we know nothing about anything; but belief (*doxis*) for each group of men is a reshaping (*epirhusmiê*) [= B 7].

> And again:

> Yet it will be clear that to know what sort each thing is in reality (*eteêi*) is inaccessible [= B 8].

> In those passages he pretty well destroys apprehension in its entirety, even if he explicitly attacks only the senses. But in the *Canons* he says that there are two kinds of knowing (*gnôseis*), one via the senses, one via the intellect (*dianoia*); he calls the one via the intellect 'legitimate (*gnêsiê*)', ascribing to it reliability for the judgment of truth, and he names that via the senses 'bastard (*skotiê*)', denying it inerrancy in the discrimination of what is true. These are his words:

> Of knowledge (*gnômê*) there are two forms, the one legitimate, the other bastard; and to the bastard belong all these: sight, hearing, smell, taste, touch. And the other is legitimate, and separated from that.

> Then, preferring the legitimate to the bastard, he continues:

> When the bastard can no longer see anything smaller, or hear, or smell, or taste, or perceive by touch, † but more fine † [= B 11].

> Thus according to him too, reason, which he calls legitimate knowledge, is a criterion.

> (507: *adv Math* VII. 135-9)

Fragments B 7 and B 10 show that Democritus' scepticism was not merely a glum asseveration of intellectual impotence, but the melancholy conclusion of a set of arguments. Two of Democritus' arguments can, I think, be reconstructed.

First, there is *doxis epirhusmiê* of B 7. I suppose that '*doxis epirhusmiê*' means 'belief is a rearrangement of our constituent atoms', i.e. 'coming to believe that *P* is having certain parts (e.g., cerebral parts) of one's atomic substructure rearranged' (cf. Theophrastus, *Sens* §58 = A 135).[3] Belief, then, cannot ever amount to knowledge, because it is never anything more than an atomic rearrangement. I guess that Democritus is supposing, if only tacitly, that knowledge is essentially reasoned belief: opinion not arrived at by rational considerations cannot qualify as knowledge. But if every belief is simply a cerebral alteration (caused, no doubt, by our changing relation with other atomic conglomerates), then no belief can be rational. To put it crudely, causally determined cerebral mutations cannot be identical with rationally accepted beliefs.

The argument has connexions with Xenophanes (vol. 1, p. 142); but it is less subtle and less persuasive than Xenophanes' argument. According to Xenophanes, certain types of causal chain prevent a caused belief from counting as knowledge; according to Democritus, any belief, being the physical result of a causal chain, is disqualified from knowledge. Democritus, I think, is simply wrong: my belief that *P* may constitute knowledge even if it is itself a physical state (a state of my nervous system) and even if it stands at the end of a causal chain (as surely it does). Roughly speaking, the belief is knowledge if the physical state which embodies it was caused, mediately or immediately by the fact that *P* (i.e., if it is true that because *P* I believe that *P*); and the belief is rational if the physical state which embodies it was caused by certain other beliefs (i.e., if because I believe that *Q* I believe that *P*, where *Q* in fact gives good grounds for *P*). If a causal theory of knowledge can be worked out in detail, then Democritus' argument for scepticism in B 7 must be rejected.

Second, there is B 9. Sextus evidently thinks that Democritus means 'perceive' by 'grasp (*sunienai*)'; and he may be right. But Democritus is not simply 'condemning' the senses: he is offering an argument. The point, I think, is this: cognitive processes are interactions between observers and objects of observation; the processes, atomically construed, consist in the impingement of atoms from the object on the body of the observer. Now any such process involves a change in the object; for it loses at least those atoms which impinge upon the observer. Consequently, we can never know the state of any object; for any attempt to discover it thereby changes it. We grasp nothing 'firm'; for our very grip disturbs. Knowledge alters the known; and therefore knowledge is impossible.

According to modern physical theory, we discover the position and characteristics of an object by way of some physical interaction with it: in the simplest case, I see where the cat is by shining a torch on it and receiving the reflected rays. What goes for cats goes for sub-atomic particles; to tell where a particle is I must fire a ray at it and receive it on the rebound. But sub-atomic particles are delicate things, and when a ray hits them they are shaken;

thus the reflected ray will not give me the information I want. It cannot tell me where the particle is and how it is travelling; for the impact, without which I can know nothing of the particle, will change the particle's trajectory. (That is meant as a kindergarten version of the reasoning behind Heisenberg's Indeterminacy Principle; science for the infant is usually bad science, but I hope that the point of my parallel is not wholly blunted by my puerile exposition.)

Atomic structures cannot be known; for the process of acquiring knowledge necessarily distorts those structures. The quest for knowledge is like the search for the end of the rainbow: we can never discover the pot of gold; for our journey towards the rainbow's end in itself moves the rainbow to a different and ever distant location.

The argument that I have dredged from B 9 is not *a priori*: it depends on Democritean physics and psychology. I guess that it may present a plausible deduction from those Atomist theories, though I doubt if there is enough evidence for us to test its validity. In any case, there is no philosophical way of attacking it: it fails if the physics and psychology are false (and I assume that they are).

> Metrodorus of Chios said that no one knows anything: the things we believe we know we do not strictly (*akribôs*) know; nor should we attend to our senses. For everything is by belief.
>
> (508: Epiphanius, 70 A 23)

Leucippus insists that we have belief, but no more (Epiphanius, 67 A 33); and in many of the fragments I have quoted, Democritus denies that we have genuine knowledge. Many sceptical philosophers seem to be making what is little more than a verbal point: we do not, strictly speaking, *know* anything, but we can, of course, have reasonable beliefs. Such thinkers set the canons of knowledge artificially high: knowledge must be certain, or infallible, or necessary, or indubitable, or whatever. If the canons are set high, then knowledge is indeed beyond us; but ordinary men are quite happy with relaxed canons, and those sceptics who allow reasonable belief in fact allow precisely the thing that ordinary men call knowledge.

The Atomists, however, do not even allow reasonable belief: their arguments against knowledge, in so far as we know them, are equally arguments against reasonable belief. We have beliefs: that is an incontestable empirical fact. Our beliefs do not amount to knowledge: that is the argument of the Abderites. Yet our beliefs are not even reasonable: being atomically caused, they are not founded on reason; and the physics of the cognitive processes assures us that no impressions of external reality are accurate. If there is no room for knowledge, by the same token there is no room for reasoned belief: 'everything is by belief'—but that, far from being a consolation, is only a cause for despair. The urbane scepticism of Locke allows a decent wattage to the human candle: our light extends as far as we need, but not as far as we like to boast. Abderite scepticism is Pyrrhonian: the light of the mind is an *ignis fatuus*.

That conclusion did not please Democritus; indeed, as Sextus observes, his fragments do not exhibit consistency. Fragment B 11 tails off into corruption; but the general sense of Democritus' remarks is clear enough: 'the bastard way of knowing (*skotiê gnôsis*)' will not carry us to the finest or ultimate constituents of stuff; for that, 'the legitimate way of knowing (*gnêsiê gnôsis*)' is needed. That coheres with Democritus' approval of the Anaxagorean slogan: *opsis tôn adêlôn ta phainomena*—what the senses cannot apprehend must be grasped by the intellect. There seems, then, to be an empiricist Democritus rising in revolt against the sceptic.

And perhaps the sceptical fragments have been misread: the Heisenbergian argument, after all, at most shows that we cannot directly apprehend the atomic elements of things; it does not show that we may make no inferences from perceptible things to their elemental structure. B 9 and B 10 consistently say that we cannot 'grasp' things in their reality; but that only means that atoms are not open to perceptual knowledge.[4] Thus we may find a positive epistemology for Democritus: 'All knowledge rests on perception: and perception will not, directly, yield knowledge of what exists *eteêi*. But by perception we may come to know about what is *nomôi*, and intellectual attention to those sensual pronouncements will enable us to procure an inferential knowledge of genuine reality.'

Alas, that happy picture is mistaken. The *doxis epirhusmiê* argument is resolutely sceptical; and B 6, B 7, B 8, and B 117 leave no room for any knowledge at all. Moreover, Democritus recognized that the empiricist intimations of B 11 were misleading:

> Having slandered the phenomena . . . he makes the senses address the intellect thus: 'Wretched mind! Do you take your evidence from us and then overthrow us? Our overthrow is your downfall.'
>
> (509: B 125)

In a puckish mood, Russell once observed that naive realism leads us to accept the assertions of modern science; and that modern science then proves realism false. Realism is false if it is true; hence it is false. And if science rests on realism, then it is built upon sand. The parallel with Democritus is plain: the observations of the senses give us a set of facts upon which an atomistic science is reared; the science then proves the irrationality of all belief and the unreliability of the senses. If the senses are to be trusted, they are not to be trusted; hence they are not to be trusted. And if atomism rests upon the senses, then atomism is ill founded.

Did the mind answer the senses? Had Democritus any solution to the problem which 509 candidly poses? There is no evidence that he had; and I am inclined to think that he had not. It is, I suppose, a tribute to Democritus'

honesty that he acknowledged his plight; but it derogates somewhat from his philosophical reputation that he made no move to escape from the *impasse* he found himself in.

Notes

1. Cf. Sextus, 70 A 25; Philodemus, A 25; Epiphanius, A 23; Diogenes Laertius, IX.58 = 72 A 1. The text of 505 is reconstructed in part from Cicero's translation, and the details are far from certain.

2. The MSS. read *diathêkên* ('disposition'). . . .

3. The word '*epirhusmiê*' itself has foxed the scholars; de Ley plausibly suggests *ameipsirhusmiê* (cf. B 139), which would have the sense I give to *epirhusmiê*.

4. And some translate *idmen* in 506 as 'know by experience' (see especially Cleve, 428-31). Compare Fränkel's version of Xenophanes' sceptical fragment (vol. 1, p. 138). But *idmen* means no more than 'know'; and B 7 and B 8 are more than enough to impose a scepticism on Democritus.

Appendix A: Sources

Our knowledge of the Presocratic philosophers is almost entirely indirect; for even where we possess their actual words, those words are preserved, fragmentarily, as quotations in the works of later authors. The sources we rely upon for *testimonia* and fragments span two millennia: they differ widely, one from another, in their literary aims, their historical competence, and their philosophical interests.

This appendix lists *in chronological order* the ancient authors I have quoted from or alluded to in the text and the notes. Some of the authors are (from a Presocratic point of view) of minor or minimal importance. A single asterisk is prefixed to the names of the more freely flowing sources; and those few gushing streams are marked by a pair of stars. Each name is followed by a date, often roundly given, and the briefest of biographical sentences. When a 'principal work' is named, that is not necessarily the author's major *opus,* but rather the book which holds most interest for students of the Presocratics.

Where no edition of the ancient text is mentioned, the reader may assume that I have used only the excerpts printed in Diels-Kranz. In citing editions I use these abbreviations:

CIAG: *Commentaria in Aristotelem Graeca* (Berlin, 1881-1909)

OCT: Oxford Classical Texts

SdA :*Die Schule des Aristoteles,* ed. F. Wehrli (Basel, 1967-9²)

THEOPHRASTUS: 371-287; Aristotle's greatest pupil and his successor. Only fragments survive. Abbreviation: *Sens de Sensu* Edition: Diels [4].

PHILODEMUS: *c*.80-*c*.35 BC; Epicurean philosopher, fragments of whose works were discovered in the lava of Vesuvius.

DIOGENES LAERTIUS:? third century; scissors and paste historian of philosophy. Work: *Lives of the Philosophers.* Edition: OCT, Long.

SEXTUS EMPIRICUS: fl. 180-200, massive compiler of sceptical *topoi* and our main source for ancient scepticism. Abbreviations and Editions:

adv Math: Against the Mathematicians (Teubner, Mau)

Pyrr Hyp: Outlines of Pyrrhonism (Teubner, Mau).

EPIPHANIUS: *c*.315-403, bishop of Salamis. Edition: Diels [4].

F. M. Cleve: *The Giants of Pre-Sophistic Greek Philosophy* (The Hague, 1965)

H. Fränkel: *Early Greek Poetry and Philosophy,* trans. M. Hadas and J. Willis (Oxford, 1975)

H. de Ley: '. . . critical note on Democritus Fr. 7', *H* 97, 1969, 497-8

Charles H. Kahn (essay date 1985)

SOURCE: "Democritus and the Origins of Moral Psychology," in *American Journal of Philology,* Vol. 106, No. 1, 1985, pp. 1-31.

[*In the following essay, Kahn explores Democritus's texts as a source for moral psychology and ethics in the time of Socrates.*]

The fragments of Democritus constitute the most important body of material for the history of philosophical ethics and psychology before the dialogues of Plato. This fact has not received the attention it deserves, largely because interest in Democritus has focused on his physical doctrines. The physical theory is known to us from Aristotle and the doxography, but the fragments themselves speak primarily about matters of conduct, moral psychology, and the conditions of happiness. Now of pre-Platonic philosophers whose written work has reached us, only Heraclitus and Democritus deal with such themes. We have every reason to believe that Socrates did so too, but there is no pre-Platonic documentation for his views. Of course, we also have ethical and psychological comments in the works of fifth century orators, poets, and historians and in the occasional words of a sophist such as Antiphon arguing that justice is not advantageous. But before the dialogues of Plato, the only substantial texts dealing with ethics and psychology from a speculative or philosophical point of view, and hence the oldest documents in the history of moral philosophy properly speaking, are the fragments of Heraclitus and Democritus.

The utterances of the dark Ephesian are unquestionably superb, but they are brief, enigmatic, and chronologically remote. Democritus is a contemporary of Socrates, and his literary remains are considerably more abundant than those of any other fifth century philosopher. They provide us with our best evidence for the level that had been reached by moral reflection in the lifetime of Socrates. They permit us to imagine the kind of thing Socrates himself might have said; hence their study will be useful for reconstructing the background for Plato's own work. Even if Plato had not read the books from which these quotations are taken (which seems to me most unlikely), they faithfully reflect, in a way the dialogues cannot do, the climate of opinion within which Plato's ideas took shape and which he could take for granted as the starting point for his own work.

What I propose, then, is to exploit these texts as a documentary source for moral psychology in the age of Socrates. In order to keep the issue of documentation in sharp focus, I must largely ignore the figure of Socrates himself. We can study connections between Heraclitus and Democritus, between Democritus and Plato, and even between Democritus and Epicurus on the firm basis of a comparison between texts written by the philosopher himself. But in the case of Socrates, we have neither his own words nor any reliable fifth century report. Once we begin to use fourth century texts (i.e., Plato, Xenophon, Aristotle) as the the basis for a comparison between Socrates and Democritus, we take our stand on slippery ground. For we must then somehow settle by conjecture the question how far our fourth century source is literally faithful to his fifth century subject, and there is no way to check such a conjecture. So I will leave untouched the issue of whether Socrates influenced Democritus, or conversely. I am inclined to believe that they are quite independent of one another, but I would not know how to argue this point.

Before we consider the texts, there is a word to be said about the nature of the evidence. The documentation concerning Democritus is unlike that for any other early thinker. Plato never mentions his name.[1] Aristotle and Theophrastus discuss his physical doctrines at length but are silent concerning his moral philosophy.[2] Only the Hellenistic doxography, reflected in Cicero, Arius Didymus, Diogenes, and Clement (DK A 169, 167, 1.45, B4), offers a brief summary of what is there construed as his theory of the *telos* or ultimate goal of human life. On the other hand, very few of the nearly 300 surviving fragments deal with physical theory at all; the vast majority discuss topics in ethics and moral psychology. This anomalous situation is further complicated by the fact that 86 brief quotations are preserved in a collection attributed not to Democritus but to "Demokrates." More than one-third of these quotations are found also in Stobaeus, where they are cited under the name of Democritus. Stobaeus is our only source for another 100 fragments on moral psychology, including some that are recognized as inauthentic.[3] All this gives grounds for suspicion, and some scholars (most recently

Guthrie[4]) have expressed doubts about both collections. The problem is too complex for a full discussion here, and I can only briefly state my conclusions.

1. The bulk of the Stobaeus fragments, including all of the longer quotations (with the possible exception of B 297, on which I suspend judgment), seem to me clearly genuine. This judgment is based in the first instance on a sense for Democritus' style after many re-readings of the fragments, together with a feeling for what fits into the conceptual climate of the late fifth century. Although this judgment is inevitably subjective, it seems to be shared by most (not all) of the scholars who have spent much time with the fragments. And the stylistic judgment can be confirmed by two more objective criteria: (a) the use made of Heraclitean phrases in B 171 and B 236, the significance of which will be discussed below, and (b) the echoes of Democritus in the writings of Epicurus. It turns out that in his ethics Epicurus is scarcely less dependent on Democritus than in his physics. In at least one case there is a striking verbal parallel: . . . Epicurus *Kyria Doxa* 16 is directly modeled on . . . Democritus B 119.[5] And in many cases there is a close coincidence of thought.[6] These parallels have been much discussed, and it is generally agreed that they are to be explained by the influence of Democritus' work on Epicurus.[7] In this respect we have excellent evidence for the authenticity of about a dozen fragments from the Stobaeus collection.

2. The situation is not the same for the shorter maxims, including most of those in the "Demokrates" collection. These are on the whole less convincing, both in style and content, and some of them seem clearly to be alien intrusions. Thus, B 45 ("He who does injustice is more miserable than he who suffers it"), B 49 ("It is hard to be ruled by one's inferior"), and B 73 ("Righteous eros desires the beautiful without hybris") strike me as too specifically Platonic to be authentic: one would have to suppose that Democritus had read not only the *Gorgias* but also the *Republic* and the *Symposium* or *Phaedrus*.[8] There seem to be no clear parallels to the "Demokrates" fragments in Epicurus, and the two Heraclitean echoes in these maxims have a mechanical quality that is quite unlike those in the Stobaeus collection.[9]

3. Since the suspicious Demokrates aphorisms B 49 and B 73 are among those which are also cited by Stobaeus, it seems clear that both collections are contaminated. On the other hand, many of the shorter maxims in both sets are simply summary statements of views more fully expressed in the longer quotations.[10] To this extent even the Demokrates collection contains authentic material. But it testifies to a process of simplification and adulteration that had already begun in the generally superior collection we find reflected in Stobaeus.[11]

4. It is normally only the longer fragments that permit us to recognize with some confidence the style and viewpoint of a fifth century author. Hence, with rare exceptions,[12] I shall use the shorter quotations only to support or clarify

views that can be documented from the longer texts. Any interpretation that relies primarily or exclusively on brief maxims of the "Demokrates" type is bound to rest on shaky ground.[13]

Turning now to the fragments, I begin with a survey of the principal themes to be illustrated here:

1. Soul and body as a pair, with soul as superior.

2. The soul using the body as its instrument.

3. The soul as seat of happiness and suffering, reason and emotion, character and intelligence.

4. Psychic combat against pleasure or strong emotion, with action and decision determined by the factor that prevails.

5. Desire and pleasure as reciprocals. Desire itself conceived as a lack or need.

6. Reason and sense perception as distinct modes of cognition.

7. Rational thought and emotion or desire as distinct principles of motivation.

8. Democritus' conception of virtue and the good life.

Except in connection with the last theme, I shall not be primarily concerned with Democritus' originality as a thinker, though I will touch on this point. My aim is to exploit the fragments as evidence for the general level reached by moral psychology in the age of Socrates. The issue of originality could be adequately dealt with only on the basis of a much fuller comparison with contemporary authors.

1. SOUL AND BODY AS A PAIR, WITH SOUL AS SUPERIOR

Here there is no doubt that both the parallel and the contrast between body and soul are part of the common conceptual equipment of Democritus' generation: the evidence from Antiphon the orator, Lysias, and Gorgias is unambiguous.[14] And the view of the soul as in some sense superior is also common to other authors; after all, *psychē* connotes life, while *sōma* designates the corpse. What is more striking is the peculiar twist that Democritus gives to this superiority.

> B 187. It is fitting for men to take more account of the soul than of the body. For the perfection of soul corrects the inferior condition of the body. But strength of body without calculation (*logismos*) makes the soul no better.

Note the suggestion here that the excellence of the psyche lies in reasoning or prudence—in other words, that virtue is knowledge. But we are even more directly reminded of Socrates' insistence in the *Apology* that one should be concerned "neither for bodies nor for wealth before or to the same degree as making one's *psychē* as good as possible," since "excellence (*aretē*) is not produced from wealth, but from excellence men acquire wealth and all other goods."[15] The two texts are sufficiently different for neither to count as a verbal echo of the other, but they agree in defending the greater importance of psychic excellence in terms of its causal priority: the soul is the source of other goods.

We have a much closer parallel to B 187 in *Republic* III, as Natorp noticed long ago. At the beginning of the discussion of gymnastics Socrates remarks: "It does not seem to me the case that, when a body is in good shape (*chrēston*), it will by its own excellence make the soul good; but on the contrary, a good soul renders by its excellence the body as good as possible" (403D). Here we have precisely the thought of B 187, and the resemblance is too close to be a chance coincidence. It is just possible that both authors are following a common source; the notion that intelligent living can preserve or restore health is a familiar enough idea in this period.[16] But the exact parallelism of negative and affirmative clauses is most naturally explained by the assumption that one author is echoing another, perhaps unconsciously. If B 187 is authentic, Plato must be the debtor here, and everything points in that direction. For B 187 expresses a crucial Democritean doctrine, the conception of the psyche as agent or guiding principle of the body. (See B 159, cited in the next section.) For Plato, on the other hand, the passage quoted from *Republic* III is a casual remark introduced solely to justify the more extensive treatment of music as training for the psyche. Plato will end this discussion by rejecting this contrast and insisting instead that gymnastics too aims to train the soul (410C-411E).

The notion that the soul rules or controls the body is always taken for granted by Plato and never argued for. (See, e.g., *Phaedo* 94B4-6.) One might suppose that it is an idea he got from Socrates; I want to suggest that he got it from Democritus: this is an idea Democritus had developed so systematically that Plato can take it for granted.[17] If it had been a specifically Socratic claim, he would have been *less* inclined to take it for granted. For his general practice is to argue for Socratic conclusions from premises which his interlocutor is prepared to accept. I think that Democritus must be, behind the scenes, one of Plato's principal interlocutors in the early dialogues. As the major philosopher of the previous generation, he is in some respects an opponent against whom Socratic theses must be defended. But in other respects Democritus has decisively prepared the way for Plato's own restatement of the Socratic notion of soul tendance.

2. THE SOUL USING THE BODY AS ITS INSTRUMENT

This is the moral equivalent of Democritus' physical doctrine, reported by Aristotle, that the psyche is the cause of motion in the body.[18] The fragments express this view only in moral terms.

> B 159 [from Plutarch]. If the body takes the soul to court, accusing it of all the pain and suffering of a

lifetime, and he [sc. Democritus] is to be judge of the case, he would gladly find the soul guilty for having ruined the body with neglect and dissolved it with drunkenness, for having debauched and distracted it with sensual indulgence; just as the user of a tool (*organon*) or equipment in bad condition is held responsible for its reckless misuse.

The trial of the *psychē*, accused by the body of criminal neglect, is one of Democritus' more picturesque inventions, comparable to the dialogue between the senses and the mind (*phrēn*), from which we have the memorable line: "Poor mind, you overthrow us but you take your convictions from us: our overthrow is your fall" (B 125). The imagery of the lawcourt in B 159 parallels that of the wrestling match in B 125. The surprising note in the contrast between body and soul is that the psyche figures here as source of vice and corruption for the very same reason that it is the source of virtue and health in B 187: the soul is in charge of the body and must be held responsible. The causal relation here is precisely that expressed in Plato's doctrine that the soul rules the body, but by emphasizing the harm that the soul may cause, Democritus turns the point of this doctrine against the rather different view that we know from the *Phaedo* and elsewhere—that the body is (in Vlastos' phrase) a moral nuisance, the source of sensual indulgence and psychic pollution.[19] Now if B 159 preserves an authentic statement of Democritus, which seems to me certain, it cannot be directed against the *Phaedo*. Is it directed against the historical Socrates? Or, more plausibly, is it directed against some older, quasi-Orphic view of the body as tomb or prison of the soul?[20] We do not know. What we can recognize in B 159 is a negative attitude to the psyche which would be antipathetic to Plato. But we also recognize a view of the body as *organon*, the tool or instrument of the soul, which Plato and Aristotle can take for granted.[21] In Plato and Aristotle, the metaphor of the "tool" is faded or fading; in Democritus it is vivid and probably original.

The negative and (to speak anachronistically) anti-Platonic tendency is conspicuous in another fragment that focuses on a mind-body contrast.

> B 223. What the body (*skēnos*, habitation) requires is available to all without toil and trouble. What requires toil and trouble and makes life painful is not what the body longs for (*himeiretai*) but what (is desired by) the bad grasp[22] of the mind (*gnōmē*).

The personification of the body here as subject of desires is not strictly compatible with its role as passive instrument of the psyche. We will see that such inconsistency is typical for Democritus' references to desire. The term *gnōmē* here (for "mind," "thought," or "cognition") occurs where B 187 and 159 would lead us to expect *psychē*. I think it would be a mistake to regard the two terms as synonymous, though they may have been competitors in this period as expressions for the emerging notion of a psychic center, "the core and carrier of the personality."[23]

It was probably the Socratic-Platonic choice of *psyche* for this role that determined the terminology that remains standard to this day. But that choice was itself favored by the wide range of meanings for *psyche* in earlier usage, including manly spirit, subject of sensual gratification, and the principle of silent thought and prudent counsel.[24] The term *gnōmē* (from *gignōskō,* to recognize or know) was limited by its primarily cognitive or deliberative connotations. Democritus' usage is fluctuating, however, and in B 223 *gnōmē* seems to be a candidate for the same role that *psyche* plays in B 187 and 159. The issue is more than terminological. The precise relationship between the *psyche* as such and rational thought and planning (as designated by *gnōmē*) is one of the unresolved problems of Democritean psychology, and more generally of psychological thought before Plato. Aristotle says Democritus identified soul (*psyche*) and intellect (*nous*),[25] but that is misleading. It would be more accurate to say that he did not clearly distinguish the two, because he had no entirely consistent terminology for designating either one. (See further under topic 7.)

What Plato would find *most* antipathetic in Democritus is, of course, his materialism—that is, his view of the psyche as a purely corporeal constituent that is destroyed or dissipated with the death of the body. This view is abundantly documented in the testimonia but not directly expressed in the fragments (unless B 297 is authentic). It presumably underlies the statements about cognition that emphasize the extent to which our thought is dependent on corporeal factors.

> B 9. In truth, we know nothing exactly, but <what we know is> what changes about according to the disposition of the body and the things which enter <the body> and the things which press against it.

Here again we may wonder how this passivity of our cognition in regard to bodily changes is compatible with the causal initiative of the psyche in B 187 and 159. We do not know whether Democritus tried to reconcile these views or simply treated the psyche as active in decisions but passive in cognition. It seems to be the same physiological psychology as in B 9 that underlies one of the most fascinating brief quotations.

> B 158 [from Plutarch]. As Democritus says, human beings think new thoughts every day (*nea eph' hēmerēi phroneontes*).

Here we have an unmistakable verbal echo of Heraclitus fr. 6 (Diels) "the sun is new every day"; and the context in Plutarch confirms some reference to the sun. But Democritus has combined this allusion with two other Heraclitean thoughts: (1) the river of restless change (Heraclitus frs. 12 and 91), and (2) the conception of our mental state as a reflection of our physical condition. Heraclitus had joined the mental with the physical in his statements that it is a "wet soul" that causes the drunken man to stumble (fr. 117), whereas the "dry soul is wisest and best" (fr. 118). Democritus' psychophysics is more complex: "our

opinions are shaped by the formative flow from outside" (B7). Hence the novelty of our thinking (*phronein*) is both a strength and a weakness. It keeps us in touch with the outside world, providing us with information and also (like Heraclitus' sun) with renewal and persistence; but it reveals the hopelessly partial and ephemeral character of our cognitive grasp. B 158 makes clear that the Heraclitean echoes in Democritus are no mere ornament of style but involve profound rethinking of Heraclitean ideas. This will be illustrated for the next two topics as well.

The discussion of B 9, 7, and 158 has led us from the theme of the soul's causal responsibility for the body to the rather different notion that mental phenomena depend on bodily processes. There need be no doctrinal inconsistency, since the psyche itself is a corporeal principle, composed like fire of spherical atoms (A 104). But in the absence of any detailed account of the mechanics of perceptual judgment and decision making, we must simply leave it an open question how far (or whether) Democritus tried to link up the psychophysiology of his theory of cognition with his discussion of moral psychology and action.

3. The Soul as Seat of Happiness and Suffering, Reason and Emotion, Character and Intelligence

> B 171. Fortune (*eudaimoniē*) dwells not in flocks nor in gold; the psyche is the dwelling of the *daimōn*.

As the body is the habitation (*skēnos*) of the soul, so the soul in turn is the home of the *daimōn,* the divine power of happiness and misfortune. The last three words . . . are almost as richly suggestive as the formula of Heraclitus, which they are designed to recall . . . (fr. 119), "man's character is his *daimōn*," his fortune for good or for evil. This echo of Heraclitus implies that for Democritus too the soul is the seat not only of happiness but also of character.[26] For both philosophers, this will be so because happiness and misery are themselves directly dependent on moral character and cognitive insight or the lack thereof.

Democritus' general doctrine is clear enough on this point, but to see how it is articulated in his conception of the psyche, we must pay close attention to the fragments. Again, his depiction of the role of the psyche is not wholly consistent. On the one hand, according to B 187 (p. 6) the excellence or perfection (*teleotēs*) of the soul will correct the defects of the body by reasoning or calculation—that is, by control of the vital motions in accordance with a rational understanding of what contributes to health and "cheerfulness" (*euthymiē*). The function of Democritus' moral aphorisms is precisely to provide such an understanding. They teach us that an excess or deficiency in pleasure or other intense experiences "will impose great movements upon the *psyche*," which is incompatible with its stability and cheerfulness (B 191). If one misdirects his mind (*gnōmē*) and thought (*dianoia*), he will fall prey to *pleonexia,* excessive desire, and "suffer harm in his soul" (*kakopathein tēi psychēi*, ibid.). Thus, in B 191 the psyche is the passive victim of emotion,[27] whereas in B 187 it was the active agent of control. This systematic inconsistency at the level of verbal imagery will be most naturally explained if we assume that Democritus (like Gorgias and other authors of the late fifth century) conceives the soul rather vaguely as the field or locus of what we recognize as distinct psychic factors, so that it can in different contexts be identified in turn with rational thought and guidance or with passive perception, with emotional experience, feeling, and one's overall "state of mind," or with the person himself as the subject of these states.[28]

I assume, then, that the daimon of B 171 which dwells in the psyche is the mental state of happiness or misery as this depends on one's character and rational understanding. But the language of the fragments does not suggest the notion of the psyche as a unified subject of experience, nor do we get any coherent picture of how the various psychic factors are related to one another. In this domain Democritus' language is expressive rather than analytical or explanatory. This is best illustrated by the long text of B 191, from which I have already quoted some phrases:

> Human beings acquire cheerfulness (*euthymiē*) by moderation in enjoyment and measured balance in their life. But deficiencies and excesses tend to change about <into their opposites> and to cause great movements in the soul. Souls that move over great intervals are neither stable nor cheerful. So one should keep one's mind (*gnōmē*) on what is possible and be satisfied with what is present and available, taking little heed of people who are envied and admired and not fixing one's attention (*dianoia*) upon them, but observe the lives of those who suffer and notice what they endure, so that what you presently have will appear great and enviable and you will no longer suffer evil in your soul by desiring more than you have. . . . <One should> compare one's life to those who are less fortunate and count oneself happy by considering what they suffer and how much better your own life is. If you hold fast to this frame of mind (*gnōmē*) you will live more cheerfully and drive not a few plagues (*kēres*) from your life: envy and jealousy and ill-will.

Besides anticipating a famous passage in Lucretius (II. 1-6) on beholding the misfortunes of others, this text illustrates the practical acuteness of Democritus as a psychological observer and the lack of any theoretical fixity or precision in his conception of the psyche. At one point he speaks of the soul as if it were the subject of the mental state: it is the psyche itself which is "neither stable nor cheerful." This phrase treats the psyche as simply equivalent to the human being, who is the proper subject of cheerfulness. But in the very same sentence the soul is also said to be "moved over great intervals," and these motions are "imposed" or "inflicted" on the soul by excesses or deficiencies of pleasure and desire.[29] It is obviously not the human being as such who is moved over great intervals by strong emotion. Thus, the psyche is also conceived as the passive or affective aspect of one's personality, one's mood or state of mind, where this is

thought of as *acted upon* by the forces of pleasure and desire, themselves weakly personified as distinct agents acting as it were from outside. Similarly, in the last sentence of B 191, the emotions of envy, jealousy, and ill-will (*phthonos, zēlos, dysmeniē*) are represented as evil powers or *kēres* to be driven from one's life. In this almost Homeric personification of psychic powers, the soul figures as a passive plaything, victimized or rescued by forces beyond its control.[30] So in B 290: "Expell by reason (*logismōi*) uncontrolled grief from <your> paralyzed psyche." Here the soul is numbed by sorrow, salvaged by reflection,[31] and both of these factors, as well as the psyche itself, are at least verbally distinct from the person to whom the command is addressed.

What these expressions show is not that Democritus has an inconsistent concept of the soul, but rather that his treatment of the psyche is not fully conceptualized. His description of mental phenomena has not reached the level of a psychological *theory;* he relies entirely on the shifting metaphors of quasi-poetic speech. Hence, in some contexts the psyche (or its excellence) can be identified with the person either as a rational agent, using his reason (*logismos*) to improve the body (B 187), or as an irresponsible agent, damaging the body by his neglect (B 159). In other contexts, as we have just seen, the psyche is not the agent or person himself but his emotional nature, which is moved by pleasure or numbed by grief (B 191, 290). Probably no thinker who attempts to describe our mental and emotional life can avoid such inconsistency in expression. But in Democritus there is no trace of any *attempt* to escape the limitations of this idiomatic phraseology, no effort to frame a coherent model for psychological description and explanation. This task remained for Plato to undertake. We can see the first step toward such a model in the passage of the *Gorgias* which speaks of "that part of the soul where the desires are located" (493A); but a full-scale model comes only with the tripartite psychology of the *Republic*. It is the merest beginnings of such an effort that can be recognized in Democritus' treatment of the next theme.

4. PSYCHIC COMBAT AGAINST PLEASURE OR STRONG EMOTION, WHERE ACTION AND DECISION ARE DETERMINED BY THE FACTOR THAT PREVAILS

Agonistic imagery runs all through the fragments, as in the wrestling match between mind and the senses (B 125) and the lawsuit between body and soul (B 159).[32] But for psychic conflict Democritus again takes his cue from Heraclitus.

> B 236. To fight against anger (*thymos*) is hard. But it is a man's task to conquer (*krateein*) if he has good sense (*eulogistos*).

Heraclitus had depicted *thymos* as a formidable opponent, "hard to fight against, for it buys what it wants at the expense of the psyche" (fr. 85 Diels). Whatever Heraclitus may have meant by *psychē* here, Democritus takes up the notion of courage or manliness (*andros de* . . .), which is one of the idiomatic connotations of *psychē,* reinforced here by the metaphor of combat. In his own version of the unity of the virtues, Democritus points out that courage depends not only on *thymos* (as in Plato's tripartite psychology) but also on prudence and good judgment.[33] Implicitly, then, we have a combat between reason and passion. In B 236, passion is conceived, however, not in general but specifically as anger,[34] and reason is not articulated as a separate factor but included in the adjectival characterization of the man who acts (*anēr eulogistos*). (Contrast the appearance of *logismos* in substantival form in B 187 and 290.) So although Democritus has pursued the imagery of psychic conflict further than Heraclitus by referring to the victory of the stronger party, it is still a combat between the man and his emotion as a quasi-external opponent, not between two rival factors in the soul. The same holds for B 214:

> The brave man is he who prevails (*kreissōn*) not only over enemies but also over pleasures. There are some who are masters of cities but slaves to women.[35]

Here, instead of the manly force of anger, we have as psychic opponent the effeminate power of sensuality. This idea of being dominated by sensual pleasure brings us close to the classic notion of *akrasia,* lack of mastery over the impulse of pleasure and desire. This notion is made explicit in B 234:

> Men in their prayers ask for health from the gods; they do not know that they have the power for this in themselves. But because of a lack of mastery (*akrasiē*) they act on the enemy's side and themselves betray the cause of health to their desires (*epithymiai*).

In this case, the enemy is not pleasure as such but desires whose gratification will ruin one's health. (For the close conceptual tie between pleasure and desire see the next topic.) *Akrasia* consists precisely in being defeated by such desires, when it is in one's power to prevail. Democritus' point is that such a defeat occurs because the agent goes over to his opponent's side, by identifying himself with his desires.

Democritus' reference to *akrasia* reminds us of the vulgar account of "being defeated by pleasures" which Plato rejects in *Protagoras* 352D ff., but it differs from that account in two respects: (1) Democritus emphasizes the responsibility of the agent as an accomplice in his own defeat, and (2) he does not mention the point that is essential to Socrates: that the agent "knows what is best" but acts otherwise. On the contrary, says Democritus, such men "do not know that they have this power <for health, i.e., for what is best> in themselves." So Democritus does not actually describe the phenomenon that Socrates wishes to deny. On the contrary, he implies that such loss of mastery depends on a failure of understanding: wisdom should be able to rid the soul of its destructive passions (B 31). Thus, Democritus defends a position that is close to that of Socrates at the end of the *Protagoras,* although the role of reason is understood in quite different terms. (The

fragments show no trace of a hedonistic calculus such as we find in the *Protagoras.* See under topic 8 below.)

In each of the three texts just discussed (B 236, 214, 234), the conflict is not between reason and passion but between the human agent and powers that assail him as it were from outside. Given these descriptions, it seems but a small step to recast the combat as a contest between rational and nonrational factors *within the psyche.* But that is precisely the step that will transform these vivid metaphors into a coherent psychological model. And I see no evidence of anyone's having taken this step before Plato.[36] Certainly Democritus did not.

5. DESIRE AND PLEASURE AS RECIPROCAL CONCEPTS; DESIRE ITSELF UNDERSTOOD AS A LACK OR NEED

As noted, the combat with pleasures in B 214 is paralleled by the combat with desires in 234. This is characteristic of Democritus' use: desire is desire for pleasure; pleasure is (typically, if not exclusively) the gratification of desire. I assume that Democritus is not so much innovating here as reflecting the ordinary sense attached to these terms.[37] We recognize the conjunction or equivalence of *epithymia* and *hēdonē* that is taken for granted in the debate with Callicles in the *Gorgias*[38] and in Aristotle's definition of *epithymia* as "desire for pleasure." This connection between the concepts of pleasure and desire may seem to us the merest common sense. But common sense needs to be articulated before it can be incorporated into a psychological theory. Here again we find Democritus providing the articulation from which Plato and Aristotle will construct their theory.

This connection is illustrated in the longest discussion of sensual appetite, which also introduces the notion of desire as a lack.

> B 235. Those who derive their pleasures from the belly by exceeding a due measure in food or drink or sex, all these get pleasures that are brief and temporary, lasting only as long as they are eating and drinking; but the griefs they get are many. For this kind of desire is ever present for the same things; and when they get what they desire, the pleasure is quickly past and there is no good in these things except for the brief enjoyment. And then they feel the same needs again.

What Democritus classifies as "pleasures of the belly" are just what Plato and Aristotle will recognize as the basic appetites (*epithymiai*): hunger, thirst, and sex. Democritus' point is the grave disproportion between these desires and their gratification. Whereas the desires are permanent and recurrent, the corresponding pleasures are momentary and fleeting. So the pursuit of this kind of pleasure is doomed to frustration; we will have to satisfy the same desires again and again. Hence, moderation (*kairos*) is the only rational course. Democritus may be some sort of hedonist, since he recognizes joy and joylessness, *terpsis* and *aterpeia,* as marking the boundary between what is advantageous and disadvantageous (B 4 and 188). But he is no

Callicles, avid for the maximal experience of desire and gratification. On the contrary, his insistence on the insatiable character of these appetites prefigures Socrates' allegory of filling the leaky jar with water from a sieve (*Gorgias* 493B).

Another fragment extends this analysis to the lust for riches, with a striking echo of Heraclitus.

> B 219. The desire (*orexis*) for wealth, unless it is limited by satisfaction (*koros*), is much harder to bear than extreme poverty. For greater desires produce greater needs.

The last five words reinstantiate the phonetic-syntactic pattern of a mysterious five-word aphorism of Heraclitus (fr. 25): "Greater dooms are allotted greater destinies" (with the same juxtaposition of *mezonas . . . mezones* in the center of the clause). Whether there is any contact with the thought of the Heraclitean aphorism is uncertain, since that fragment is one of the darkest. But the characteristic use of Heraclitean phrasing in B 219 seems to guarantee its authenticity, which is important for two reasons: (1) this is the first attested occurrence of the noun *orexis*,[39] which is never used by Plato but which provides Aristotle with his generic term for desire; and (2) by correlating desire with lack or need (*endeia*), B 219 suggests the conception of desire as deficiency, with the corresponding notion of pleasure as the "fulfillment" of this lack. Democritus himself does not *have* a deficiency theory of pleasure and desire: desires are said here to produce needs, not to be produced by them. And satisfaction (*koros*) is not schematized as a filling up but allegorized as a kind of mythical person, marking off the boundary that sets limits to desire.

For completeness, I list in the Appendix all Democritean fragments dealing with the notion of desire. In these texts the general level of conceptualization is that of weak personification, as with the treatment of other psychic factors examined so far. Thus, intense desires are said to "blind the psyche" for other interests (B 72, in the Demokrates collection). Note that if this metaphor is taken literally, desires and psyche are conceived of as independent agents.

6. REASON AND SENSE PERCEPTION AS DISTINCT MODES OF COGNITION

Democritus' theory of knowledge lies beyond the scope of this paper, but some general grasp of his concept of the mind is required for understanding his moral psychology. B 11 (from Sextus), which draws the distinction between genuine (*gnēsiē*) and dark or spurious cognition (*skotiē gnōmē*), enumerates the dark kinds as "sight, hearing, smell, taste, touch." The nobler sort is "separate from this." Thus, Democritus recognizes the five special senses and a sixth, more refined mode of apprehension which is quite different and which we might call "thinking."[40] The fragments offer no general term for sense perception (other than "obscure *gnōmē*"); but the verb *aisthanesthai* does

occur in the reference to touch in B 11, and the corresponding noun (*aisthēsis*) could well have been used by Democritus in the great mass of his writing that has been lost.[41] Another quotation (from Galen) has the senses as a group addressing themselves to the mind or *phrēn*, presumably the organ of genuine *gnōmē;* "Poor *phrēn*, you overthrow us . . ." (B 125).[42] Galen paraphrases *phrēn* by *dianoia* "thought," a word that occurs elsewhere in the fragments as an equivalent of *gnōmē* (B 191; cf. *dianoeisthai* for mathematical thinking in B 155). Democritus thus anticipates, probably for the first time,[43] the classic distinction between sense perception and rational or nonsensory thought which both Plato and Aristotle can take for granted. It is, I suggest, the work of Democritus which permits Plato to refer without a word of explanation to "seeing and hearing and the other senses" (*Phaedo* 75A-B) and to contrast this with a kind of knowledge that is radically different, whose object is accessible "only to the reasoning of thought" (*ho tēs dianoias logismos*, 79A3).[44] Plato and Democritus are both heirs to the epistemic dualism of Parmenides, but in different ways. Democritus can draw a rigorous distinction between two kinds of cognition because he has succeeded in separating the sense qualities as such, which exist only by custom (*nomos*), from the objects of genuine knowledge: atoms and the void, which exist in reality (B 9 = B 125). The identification of the sense qualities and the recognition of the senses as such go hand in hand, and in both cases Democritus seems to have been a pioneer.

7. RATIONAL THOUGHT AND EMOTION OR DESIRE AS DISTINCT PRINCIPLES OF MOTIVATION?

We might expect to find Democritus drawing a distinction between reason and passion corresponding to his antithesis between reason and sense. Unfortunately, the conceptual development is not that straightforward, and the fact that it is not may itself be the most important insight that we can derive from a close study of the fragments. Like all later authors, Democritus uses the same terms for reason or intellect in its practical-prudential as in its theoretical-scientific application: for reason as the principle of intelligent behavior and for reason as the principle for knowing the truth about the world.[45] It is, of course, the practical sense of rationality—acting intelligently rather than foolishly, thoughtfully rather than recklessly—which is the older, more familiar notion and more abundantly attested in the fragments. The other, properly epistemic notion of reason is essentially a creation of the new science and a correlate of the philosophic distinctions between appearance and reality, between traditional errors and true insight into the nature of things. It is, as we have seen, Democritus (following Parmenides and others) who first defines the epistemic concept of reason in a rigorous way by a sharp contrast with sense perception. But he still has no precise terminology for the new notion; he simply uses the terms that have traditionally been associated with rationality in the practical sphere: *phrēn, gnōmē, dianoeisthai*. The use of this vocabulary reflects an important but unrecognized assumption that has rarely been questioned, then or since: that prudential and epistemic[46] rationality, practical and theoretical reason, are the exercises of a single principle or at least spring from a common source.

The conceptual development of the notion of reason is closely tied to the history of its terminology, but the two do not coincide. Although Democritus has no unambiguous term for "reason" as a mode of cognition, he has defined the concept unambiguously by a negative feature, its contrast to sense perception. Given the global notion of cognition as information and belief about the world, rational knowledge is identified as that kind of cognition that is not directly dependent on the anatomy of the sense organs. It is important to note here that, because of their natural basis in the human body, the enumeration of the five senses reports a plain matter of fact, like the shape of the earth or the explanation of a solar eclipse. Hence, when the senses are enumerated, whether by Democritus or by some unknown predecessor, the job is done once and for all: the five senses are the same for us as for Democritus. And insofar as the notion of rational cognition is defined negatively, by its distinction from sense perception as in Democritus B 11 and 125, the reference of this concept is fixed with equal definiteness, even though the terminology for it is still fluctuating.

When we turn from cognition to motivation and look for a neat contrast between reason and passion to match that between reason and sense perception, we find nothing of the sort. For here there is no natural or secure basis for marking off the domain of emotion, feeling, and affect, nothing that can correspond to the anatomical delineation of the senses.[47] The ordinary, pre-theoretical notion of reason is not defined by a contrast with emotion at all but by the opposition between acting reasonably or foolishly, with foresight or without. This practical notion of rationality is then given an entirely new content by the philosophers (beginning with Heraclitus and Parmenides) who develop a notion of mind or intelligence as a theoretical capacity to understand the nature of things. It is this notion which Democritus has identified by the contrast with sense perception. And once he has done so, the concept of mind or reason is in a state of creative fermentation and confusion. It will have to be clarified by a systematic account of the parts or faculties of the psyche, in which the epistemic and prudential roles of reason are somehow distinguished and reconciled. That will be the work of Plato and Aristotle. But until this work is done, there is no basis for any clear contrast between reason and emotion. The general concept of emotion (or passion or affect) remains to be identified, and from the beginning its definition will be heavily theory-laden in a way that the identifying definition of sense-perception need not be. The classification of the emotions, and even the choice of a term for "emotion," will reflect some theory or model for conceptualizing the psyche. Hence, the absence of a combat between reason and passion in Democritus, to parallel the oppositions between reason and sense, body and soul, is more than an incidental fact about the use of metaphor in the fragments. Before Plato no one can describe such a conflict because no one has the conceptual

equipment needed to refer to feeling, emotion, and affect in general terms, so as to set them over against the principle of reason. That is what we see emerging for the first time in the passage of the *Gorgias* where Plato speaks of "the part (or region) of the psyche where the desires are found" (493A3-B1).

It is the concept of desire with (as has been pointed out) the intimately connected concept of pleasure that plays the central role in what *we* may describe as Democritus' theory of the emotions. But this role reflects not so much a theoretical view as simply the facts of the case in our mental life. It is desire (and particularly the animal appetites) together with pleasure and pain as positive and negative states of feeling that come closest to providing a natural or objective point of reference for the realm of emotion and affect. Hence, Aristotle will on the one hand attempt to classify all sorts of motivational impulse under the heading of "desire" (*orexis*), while on the other hand he offers a characterization of *pathos* ("affect") as "appetite, anger, fear, confidence, envy, joy, affection (*philia*), hatred, yearning, jealousy, pity, and generally whatever is accompanied by pleasure or pain" (*NE* II. 6, 1105^{b}21 ff.). In Democritus we find no comparable attempt at generalization.[48] Various emotions are mentioned, but there is little or nothing in the way of classification or conceptual unification. Aside from cheerfulness (*euthymiē*), pleasure and joy, pain and grief, and desire (see the Appendix), all of which occur frequently, the fragments refer separately to:

fear (*phobos* B 268; cf. 41, 297; *deima* 199, 215; *dedoika* 174, 205, 206; cf. *hyperdedoika* 278)

confidence, fearlessness (*tharsos, athambiē* 215, 216, 258)

boldness (in bad sense: *thrasos* 254)

hope (*elpis* 185, 221, 287, 292; cf. 58)

shame or respect (*aidōs, aideisthai, aischynesthai* 179, 244, 264; cf. 84)

admiration (*thaumazein* 191)

envy (*phthonos* 191, 245; cf. 88)

jealousy (*zēlos* 191)

ill-will (*dysmeniē* 191)

goodwill (*eunoia* 268)

friendship, affection (*philia* 186; cf. 103, etc.)

hatred (*stygeein* 199)

contentiousness (*philonikia* 237, 252)

It is probably an accident that sexual desire (*erōs*), greed (*pleonexia*), and regret (*metameleia*) are attested only in the Demokrates collection.[49]

Except for the allegorical reference to three negative emotions as "plagues" (*kēres*) in B 191, the fragments show no trace of any larger grouping or classification. As noted, there is at best a first glimmer of the notion of a combat between reason and emotion in B 236 and 290.

8. DEMOCRITUS' CONCEPTION OF THE GOOD LIFE

This discussion has not focused on Democritus' originality as a thinker but rather on the evidence of the fragments for the stage that psychological reflection had reached in the generation before Plato's dialogues. In many respects, Democritus has appeared here simply as the spokesman for his age: in the parallelism of body and soul, in the depiction of psychic conflict, in the conception of the psyche as locus for happiness and misery, character and emotion, and in making use of a notion of rationality that is both prudential and epistemic. In other respects, he seems to have achieved greater clarity in the formulation of ideas that other authors must have prepared: in the conception of the psyche as master and user of the body, in the intimate link between pleasure and desire, above all in the sharp distinction between sense perception and some more adequate type of cognition. A full account of Democritus' original contribution to moral psychology would have to include his conception of happiness as *euthymiē* and his use of pleasure as a criterion. However, my understanding of Democritus' treatment of pleasure differs so greatly from the usual view that I can only offer here a few grounds for dissent.

An extreme version of the standard view was recently formulated by Gosling and Taylor:

> He (Democritus) attempted to ground his moralizing in a systematic ethical theory. . . . He explicitly laid down a test or criterion to be applied in deciding questions of conduct, that criterion being fixed by consideration of an ultimate aim or purpose in human life. The achievement of that aim was the supreme good, and human conduct and things which human beings use were to be judged good or bad in so far as they tended to help or hinder the achievement of it. . . . Democritus saw the aim of life as the achievement of a state of tranquillity rather than as a life of pleasure as it would commonly be recognized, and thus anticipated the central doctrine of Epicurean ethics . . . [but, like the Epicureans, he thought] that the life of tranquillity is the pleasantest life.[50]

To assign to Democritus an ethical theory of this kind is to take for granted the notion of a *telos* or supreme good, the unifying goal of human life "for the sake of which everything else is chosen," a notion gradually elaborated by Plato in the dialogues and systematized by Aristotle in his *Ethics*. Now this notion is explicitly presupposed by the Hellenistic doxography that we find reflected in Cicero, Arius Didymus, Diogenes Laertius, and Clement, where Democritus' view is assimilated to the *telos* theories of post-Aristotelian moral philosophy.[51] But we need not follow the doxographers in attributing the Hellenistic concept of *telos* to a pre-Platonic moralist.[52] An unprejudiced reading of the fragments does not support the view that Democritus' ethical thought is dominated by the pursuit of any single goal. And insofar as one principal

preoccupation can be discerned throughout the fragments, it is a concern for the role of reason in human life—that is, for the extent to which thoughtful judgment and careful reflection can protect us against the uncertainties of fortune on the one hand and self-inflicted grief on the other. Here moral philosophy is a guide to life not by telling us how to decide what is right or what is expedient but by increasing the share of reason and hence of autonomy in our experience of good and evil, joy and grief. The term *autarkeia*, "independence, self-sufficiency," is as conspicuous in the fragments as is *euthymiē*,[53] and Democritus might almost be regarded as a precursor of the Stoics rather than of the Epicureans.

Seen in his own time, however, the natural point of comparison is with Socrates. Like Socrates, Democritus has an "inner" conception of happiness, located in the psyche rather than in possessions or in the esteem shown to you by others. And as for Socrates, this inner peace and comfort rests for Democritus too upon the consciousness of a life lived according to *aretē* or moral excellence. Again, as with Socrates, Democritus' conception of excellence is a unified one in which the "quiet" or cooperative virtues of justice and temperance occupy center stage and determine the content of more "competitive" excellences like courage (see, e.g., B 214). More than Socrates, however, Democritus is prepared to recommend the virtues for their role in making one's life agreeable: "*sōphrosynē* increases one's delights and makes pleasure greater" (B 211). Pleasure and grief, joy and joylessness, may thus be invoked as "the boundary mark (*ouros*) of what is advantageous and disadvantageous" (B 4, 188). Here Democritus reminds us of Socrates' unexpected hedonism at the end of the *Protagoras*.[54] But other texts are difficult to reconcile with hedonism, even with the measured hedonism of the *Protagoras*: "one should not choose all pleasure but pleasure in what is noble (*to kalon*)" (B 207); the brave man must "prevail over pleasures" (B 214); the soul debauches the body "by indulgence in pleasure" (*philēdoniai*, B 159); it is from such pleasures that wickedness is produced (*kakotēs*, B 178). Democritus' attitude to pleasure seems rather like that of Aristotle: "our whole study and pursuit of virtue must be concerned with pleasures and pains; for someone who deals with these well will be a good man, but he who deals with them badly will himself be bad" (*NE* II.3, 1105^{a}10). And just as Aristotle holds the life of virtue and *eudaimonia* to be the most pleasant life, so does Democritus insist on the positive experience of joy or "cheerfulness" which marks success in living a rational life and which can serve as a guide in the choice of particular pleasures: "the best thing for a man will be to live his life with as much joy (*euthymeisthai*) as possible and as little grief. And this will be, if he does not take his pleasures in things mortal" (*ta thnēta*, B 189)[55]—for example, in the fleeting pleasures of the belly (B 235).

As Vlastos has pointed out, the hedonism of B 189—that is, the pursuit of cheerfulness and the avoidance of grief—is not so much a new philosophical doctrine as the expression of a widespread view, shared by the poets and by the medical writers, that joy is the natural feeling of health and vitality whereas joylessness, grief, and pain are the marks of death and disease.[56] Here again, Democritus is performing the pre-theoretical role of articulating in general terms a popular view of pleasure, which Plato will then develop as a systematic theory in the *Protagoras*. The hedonism that Socrates expounds in the *Protagoras* is not Democritus' view, and it is not the view of "the many" either, since they do not formulate philosophical theories. But it would not be inaccurate to see Democritus here as the intermediate stage between the inarticulate hedonism of common sense and popular literature, on the one hand, and the philosophical hedonism of the *Protagoras* on the other.

That pleasure as such cannot be the final consideration for Democritus is best seen in what is probably the most original feature of his ethical doctrine, his remarks about shame and self-respect. Whereas Socrates' appeal is ultimately to reason or cognition, to the judgment of "one who has knowledge" and to "the *logos* which seems best upon reflection" (*Crito* 47D ff., 46B), Democritus' appeal is to an inner standard that is less principled and more personal: "Do not feel more shame before men than before yourself; be no more willing to do evil if no one is to find out than if all men are to know. But show respect above all before yourself and establish this law for your soul, so as to do no unseemly act" (B 264). The phrase *heōuton aideisthai* means both to show yourself respect and to be ashamed in your own eyes.[57] The force of this expression can only be understood in the light of the traditional shame standard of Greek morality, which is here stood on its head. In place of the hero's code, which identifies his self-respect with his status in the eyes of others, Democritus proposes an inner "law for the psyche" that is an almost literal anticipation of Kant's notion of the moral law as autonomy or self-legislation. The Democritean sage is a free spirit, traditionalist in many respects, dissident in others (for example, on begetting children and on concern for the afterlife). For morality as for happiness, his standard is internal: "the psyche is the dwelling place of the *daimōn*." The *daimōn* is, traditionally, the divine power that assigns good or bad fortune; for Democritus, the human being is himself largely responsible for this outcome. In the notion of the indwelling *daimōn* as in the notion of self-respect (rather than in his looser, less coherent notion of the psyche), Democritus might claim to have made the first attempt at a philosophical formulation of the concept of the self.[58]

Notes

1. Some scholars have concluded that Plato's silence bespeaks ignorance. Diogenes Laertius (IX.40 = DK 68.A 1) assumes that it is deliberate, and I think he must be right.

2. The silence of Theophrastus is easy to understand, since his doxography deals only with natural philosophy. Aristotle's attitude is more puzzling, given his

great interest in Democritus' physical theory. Apparently he found the ethical writings not to his taste, perhaps because they seemed so wholly superseded by Plato's dialogues.

3. See Stobaeus IV.41, 59 (cited in DK after B 288) and IV.50, 80-81 (after B 296).

4. W. K. C. Guthrie, *A History of Greek Philosophy*, II (Cambridge 1965) 489-92. Guthrie's skepticism has not been generally followed. See recently David B. Claus, *Toward the Soul* (Yale 1981) 142-48, and J. C. B. Gosling and C. C. W. Taylor, *The Greeks on Pleasure* (Oxford 1982) 27 f. For an early expression of more moderate skepticism, see H. von Arnim's review of Natorp's *Die Ethika des Demokritos* in *Göttingische gelehrte Anzeigen* (1894) 881-90, who is rightly suspicious of the Demokrates collection (p. 887), but recognizes that the Stobaeus collection contains some material whose authenticity is much better established (pp. 884, 886). For a full review of the scholarship on authenticity down to 1948, see W. Schmid and O. Stählin, *Geschichte der griechischen Literatur* VII, I.5, pp. 251-53.

5. This was seen long ago by Usener in his *Epicurea* (1881) 396; cf. Diels' citation of B 119. Note that B 119 is quoted not only by Dionysios but also by Stobaeus; Stobeaus' text is fuller and more accurate.

6. For examples compare B 174 and B 215 with Epicurus *K.D.* 17 and 34; B 176 with *Epist.* III.134; B 199 and 203 with fr. 496 Usener; B 223 with *Ep.* III.130, *K.D.* 15, 21 etc.; B 224 (and 202) with *Sent. Vat.* 35, fr. 204 Usener; B 234 with *S.V.* 65; B 246 with *Ep.* III.131, fr. 602 Usener, etc.; B 283 with fr. 202 Usener; B 284 with *S.V.* 68.

7. See R. Philippson, "Demokrits Sittensprüche," *Hermes* 59 (1924) 367-419; P. von der Mühll, "Epikurs Κύριαι δόξαι und Demokrit," in *Ausgewählte Kleine Schriften* (= *Schweiz. Beiträge zur Altertumswissenschaft* Heft 12, Basel 1975) 371-77; Diskin Clay, "Epicurus' . . . ," *GRBS* 13 (1972) 60 f. I am grateful to Diskin Clay for calling my attention to these parallels.

8. Of course, one might try to defend B 45, 49, and 73 by claiming that Democritus and Plato are independently preserving an opinion of the historical Socrates. But to embark on this kind of pseudohistorical conjecture is precisely to abandon the documentary approach that I am advocating here. In the case of Demokrates B 83, "The cause of wrongdoing (*hamartia*) is ignorance of what is better," the Socratic-Platonic influence is obvious; and the doctrine seems to contradict Democritus' own account of *akrasia* in B 234 (see below, p. 16).

9. Demokrates B 64 . . . and B 65 . . . represent feeble imitations of Heraclitus fr. 40 DK.

10. Thus Demokrates B 84 is an abridgment of the important statements on self-respect, B 244 and 264.

The clearest case of authentic material in "Demokrates" is B 36, which consists of two out of the three sentences that form B 187, one of Democritus' most distinctive comments on body and soul. Another plausible Demokrates text is B 98. . . . where a Heraclitean thought is expressed in Heraclitean language. But in this case the thought is not original enough to guarantee its authenticity.

11. Diskin Clay points out that the relationship of Epicurus' *Vatican Sayings* to his *Kyriai Doxai* shows a similar process: the Vatican collection gives shorter, more diverse material, which in at least one case (*S. V.* 36) cannot be a quotation. How did the Democritean collections originate? We do not know. P. von der Mühll was inclined to believe that Democritus himself composed a book of maxims (*hypothēkai*): see von der Mühll (note 7 above, p. 374), following Friedländer in *Hermes* 48 (1913) 603-16. Philippson (note 7 above, p. 409) thought of a disciple. More recently Zeph Stewart has suggested that the Cynics helped preserve and transform these collections. See "Democritus and the Cynics" in *HSPh* 63 (1958) 179-91. But Stewart also recognizes that some of Stobaeus' material has come to him "through another and better protected excerpting tradition" (p. 191, n. 44). For a different view of the tradition, see S. Luria, "Zur Frage der materialistischen Begründung der Ethik bei Demokrit," *Deutsche Akademie Berlin, Altertumswissenschaft* 44 (1964) 4.

12. E.g., B 188 is confirmed by the quotation in Clement (B 4); B 171 and 236 are authenticated by their use of Heraclitus. B 158 is in an entirely different category, since it is not an anthology maxim but a blended quotation in Plutarch; and here again we have a Heraclitean echo.

13. This seems to me to undermine some of the principal conclusions in Vlastos' brilliant reconstruction in "Ethics and Physics in Democritus," *PhR* 54 (1945) 578-92, and 55 (1946) 53-64. See, for example, his heavy reliance there (1945, pp. 587-92) on B 74 ("Accept nothing pleasant, unless it is beneficial") and B 69 ("For human beings what is good and true is the same for all; what is pleasant is different for different people"), both from the Demokrates collection and unparalleled in the longer fragments. Similar scruples arise for the use of these maxims by C. C. W. Taylor, "Pleasure, Knowledge and Sensation in Democritus," *Phronesis* 12 (1967) 16 f. and 25 f.; and likewise in Gosling and Taylor (note 4 above, pp. 31 f. and 34 f.). In what follows, these works by Vlastos, Taylor, and Gosling and Taylor will be cited by the author's name alone. Similarly for Claus, *Toward the Soul* (cited in note 4 above).

14. See, e.g., Gorgias *Helen* 1: "the adornment of body is beauty, of soul it is wisdom." Full documentation in Claus, ch. 4 (pp. 141 ff.). How old is this body-soul parallelism? With a different terminology it can be traced back as far as Xenophanes fr. 23: "one god

. . . not similar to mortals in shape (*demas*) nor in thought (*noēma*)."

15. *Ap.* 20B. Cf. Vlastos (1945) 580, with n. 16. Note that *aretē* (of the soul) in the *Apology* corresponds neatly to *teleotēs* and *ameinōn* (*psychē*), contrasted with *mochthēriē,* in B 187. For the general thought, see also *Protagoras* 313A ff., esp. 313A: "the psyche, on which all your affairs depend for turning out well or ill." There is a more rigorous development of the thought of B 187 in *Republic* X: "The evil (*ponēria*) of the body will not produce psychic evil in the soul" (610A5), where a Democritean premise is used in the proof of immortality!

16. See Antiphon fr. 2 (cited below in note 17) and the medical literature on regimen.

17. Democritus is developing a common view: "For all human beings the mind (*gnōmē*) leads the body both to health and disease and to all other things" (Antiphon fr. 2). But note that Antiphon does not mention the *psychē* here. I can find no pre-Platonic parallel to Democritus' systematic emphasis on the causal responsibility of the *psychē*. Where the soul is mentioned in connection with medical regimen, it tends to be the object, not the subject, of therapy. See Claus, pp. 150-53.

It is often assumed that Plato was ignorant of Democritus' work. As far as I can see, this assumption is based largely on an over-interpretation of B 116 (= D.L. IX.36): "I went to Athens, and no one knew me." (What Diogenes claims in this connection is that Democritus was unknown *to Socrates,* not to Plato!) I think the parallel between B 187 and *Rep.* III, 403D is enough by itself to prove this assumption false.

18. *DA* 405^{a}6-9, 405^{a}10, 406^{b}16, 20-22, etc. See DK A.101 and 104. As Vlastos points out (1945, p. 579, n. 9), Plato later adopts this view in his own definition of the soul as self-mover and source of motion (*Phaedrus* 245E). Unfortunately, I can find no clear trace of the physical doctrine in the fragments. B 191, which speaks of the *kinēseis* of soul, describes it only as moved (by extreme experiences), not as cause of motion.

19. Vlastos (1945, p. 579), with references to Plato in n. 13. Note that this view is potentially inconsistent with the doctrine that the soul controls the body. In the *Republic*, Plato eliminates the inconsistency by transferring sensual appetite from the body to a distinct part of the psyche. The *Timaeus* attempts to reconcile both views by explaining the "mortal" aspects of the psyche as a consequence of its presence in the body (42A ff., 43A, etc.).

20. Compare Democritus' designation of the body as *skēnos,* the tent or habitation (of the psyche). Whether or not this terminology is original with him, it is in any case justified by his physical doctrine. It also seems to be directed *against* any view of the

body as tomb, prison, or place of exile. For Democritus, only in the body can the soul be at home.

21. *Rep.* VI, 508B3: the eye as the most sun-like among "the *organa* for the senses"; so also *Theaet.* 184D4, 185A5, etc. Cf. Aristotle *DA* 412ᵃ28-ᵇ6 and Bonitz *Index* 521ᵇ31 ff.

22. . . . "bad touch" or "contact"? Text and interpretation are uncertain.

23. Arthur W. H. Adkins, *From the Many to the One* (London 1970) 65, referring to *psychē*. In Antiphon fr. 2 (note 12 above), *gnōmē* designates the mind as source of planning and control, but in B 223 it is apparently responsible for desire as well.

24. See Claus, ch. 2 passim.

25. *DA* 404ᵃ28 (= DK A 101). As H. Langerbeck points out (. . . [Berlin 1935] = *Neue Philologische Untersuchungen* 10) 80, this is interpretation rather than report on Aristotle's part.

26. For *ēthos* in the fragments, see B 192 and (in the Demokrates collection) B 57, 61, and 100. None of these texts is above suspicion, but the general conception is borne out by the longer fragments.

27. Compare our passivity in cognition in B 9 (where there is no reference to the psyche): "In reality we know nothing certain, but only what changes according to the disposition of the body and what enters and what presses against (the body)."

28. The use of *psychē* in fifth century poetry also permits the word to mean (according to context) sexual passion, courage, or simply "life"; see Claus (pp. 69-91). It is presumably this bewildering flexibility and not some unattested and inexplicable decline in ordinary usage that accounts for the avoidance of the term *psychē* by an austere author like Thucydides. (Contra Claus [p. 91], who speaks of the term's "being eliminated from common prose usage" in Herodotus and Thucydides. But in the first place we have no substantial evidence for *any* prose usage before Herodotus; and furthermore the evidence from Antiphon, Lysias, and Gorgias, as well as from Democritus [all cited by Claus (pp. 141 ff.)], shows that the term was freely used by some early prose authors.)

29. I do not mean to rule out the possibility (urged by von Fritz and Vlastos) that the *kinēseis* of the soul are ultimately to be interpreted in terms of its atomic constitution. But there is nothing in the fragments on *psychē* that directly suggests or supports such an interpretation. The "stability" of one's life and character may be a reflection of the relative immobility of one's soul-atoms, but that is surely not the primary meaning of *eustathees* in B 191: the natural reading is in terms of lived experience, not psychophysics. We do not even know whether *kinēsis* is the term Democritus would have used for the motion of

atoms (though he does use it for the movement of the waves in B 164).

30. Compare B 285: human life is "feeble and brief and beset by many plagues (*kēres*) and difficulties."

31. So in B 31: as medicine cures the body of disease, so wisdom frees the soul from passions (*pathē*), where the thought is Democritean, even if the language is not. (See note 49 below).

32. Cf. B 176: Nature, as the weaker but more reliable factor, prevails (*nikai*) over fortune.

33. For the interdependence of courage, knowledge, and justice (*orthoprageein, euthygnōmos*), see B 181; for the connection of courage and temperance, see B 214, cited in the text. In B 179 *aretē* is said to be "held together" or supported (*synechein*) by a due sense of shame (*aideisthai*).

34. For this interpretation of *thymos*, see *The Art and Thought of Heraclitus*, p. 242, with n. 334 on p. 331.

35. See the remark attributed to Sophocles in old age (Plato *Rep.* I, 329C): when someone asked him if he could still have intercourse with a woman, Sophocles replied, "Peace, man! I am glad to have escaped that, like someone who has run away from an insane and cruel master" (*despotēs*: cf. *despozousi, douleuousin* in Dem. B 214).

36. The *appearance* of such a step can be given by the quasi-allegorical suggestion of a combat between good sense (*noos*) and anger or passion (*thymos*), as in Theognis 631. . . . But here there is no reference to the psyche and hence no psychological model at all: *noos* and *thymos* are conceived simply as possessions or as intimate companions of the person in question.

37. Compare the saying ascribed to Thales, "the sweetest thing is to get what you desire (*epithymeis*)," DK I, p. 64, n. 10, with parallels cited in *The Art and Thought of Heraclitus*, p. 182.

38. See *Gorgias* 484D5; 491D12, E9-492A3, A7; 494A7, C2, etc.

39. With B 72 and 284, B 219 represents the only occurrence of the term *orexis* before Aristotle.

40. I see no point in speculating (with Guthrie [note 4 above] 449-51) on what might lie behind the obscure doxographical report that Democritus recognized *more* than five senses "for irrational animals, wise men, and gods" (DK A 116). Aetius is too confused a source for us to have any hope of reconstructing the basis of such a report.

41. Langerbeck . . . (note 25 above, p. 114) emphasizes that there is no generic term for sense perception in B 11, and wishes to deny that Democritus has made the epistemic distinction between perception and thought (p. 115). But he offers no alternative explana-

tion either for the two kinds of *gnōmē* in B 11 or for the opposition between *phren* and "we others" in B 125.

42. *Phrēn* is the term for a cognitive faculty or organ in B 125 and also in B 129. . . . Its cognates signify practical wisdom: *phronēsis* in B 2, 119, 193; *phronein* in B 183. (Similarly in the Demokrates aphorisms B 42 and 58.) Because of the nature of the texts selected by the anthologers, most cognitive terms are attested primarily or exclusively in this practical sense, e.g., *nous* in B 175 and 282, *logismos* in B 187 and 290, *dianoia* in B 191. But the same vocabulary would presumably serve for theoretical reason when the occasion arose. Thus, *gnōmē* ("thought," "judgment," "mind," "state of mind") generally occurs in the fragments in connection with an emotional state or practical intent, but it also designates the two types of cognition in B 11. Similarly for *dianoia, dianoeisthai,* which is practical in B 191, theoretical in B 155. In B 129 *noeisthai* apparently refers to nonsensory cognition.

43. The distinction may have been drawn by Leucippus, but we have no evidence for this. The roots go back to Parmenides, of course, who urges his reader to "behold beings with the mind (*noos*)" in fr. 4 and "to judge my proof by rational argument" (*logos*) in fr. 7.5. But the text of Parmenides' poem does not sharply distinguish the senses as Democritus does in B 11 and 125. Thus, in Parmenides fr. 7.5, the tongue stands not for taste but for talk, and *noos/noēma* applies indifferently to perception and thought (fr. 16). Anaxagoras (fr. 12) and Diogenes (fr. 5) explicitly assign *nous/noēsis* to animals as well as to humans; in effect, they identify sensation, cognition, and animal vitality. Empedocles is even more generous: for him "*all* things have a share in *phronēsis* and *nōma* (= *noēma*)" (fr. 110.10). It is not in such a context that we can expect a sharp differentiation between sensory and nonsensory cognition.

If Walter Burkert were correct in including Philolaus B 13 with the genuine fragments (B 1-7), we would have a clear anticipation of the Platonic distinction between *nous* and *aisthēsis* prior to Democritus, and with a terminological precision that has no parallel even in Democritus. See his *Lore and Science in Ancient Pythagoreanism* (= *Weisheit und Wissenschaft,* transl. E. L. Minar, Jr.) 269-71. In view of the other pre-Socratic evidence just cited, this terminological isolation should cast some doubt on the authenticity of Philolaus B 13. And in my opinion the anatomical distribution of psychic functions in this text smacks suspiciously of the *Timaeus.*

44. For *logismos* and *dianoia* in Democritus, see note 44 above. The parallel between vision and the eye of the mind (*gnōmē*) is common in late fifth century texts. See Antiphon B 1 with the Hippocratic passage cited by Diels ad loc. (*de arte* 2), where *gnōmēi noēsai* stands next to *ophthalmoisin idein.*

45. See note 44 above on *gnōmē, dianoia,* and *logismos.* The fact that *logismos* is attested only in a practical sense is probably an accident of our documentation. It is interesting that *nous (anoia, anoēmōn,* etc.) also occurs in the fragments only for practical intelligence, whereas Plato and Aristotle will establish this as the standard term for the cognitive faculty, thus consecrating the union of the two concepts of reason.

46. Note that *epistasthai,* the verb from which we have the term *epistēmē* for (scientific) knowledge, originally indicated the practical mastery of a subject matter, the knowhow that is characteristic of an overseer or supervisor (*epistatēs*) who "stands over" the task to be performed by virtue of his skill (*epistamenos*).

47. As Amelie Rorty has put it, "emotions do not form a natural class" (in "Aristotle on the Metaphysical Status of the Passions," forthcoming in *RMeta*).

48. There is only an apparent exception in B 31 (from Clement): "according to Democritus, medicine cures diseases of the body, but wisdom rids the soul of passions (*pathē*)." Although this probably does reflect something Democritus said, the phraseology is certainly Clement's. (The idea of rhetoric or philosophy as medicine for the soul is a common one, echoed for example by Socrates in the *Hippias Minor* 372 E7 ff.: "you will do me much greater good by ridding my soul of ignorance than by ridding my body of disease"; and compare the *technē alypias* in Antiphon A 6 with Guthrie's comment, *History* III, 290.) *Pathos* in the sense of "emotion, affect" is introduced by Aristotle as a technical term (*NE* 1105^{b}21, cited above; cf. Bonitz, *Index* 557^{a}41 ff.); in Plato and earlier writers it simply means "experience" or "what happens to one." Clement's formula actually presupposes the Stoic definition of *pathos* as an excessive or harmful affect that reason should eliminate. Democritus cannot have meant that wisdom should eliminate *emotions,* since the desirable condition of cheerfulness (*euthymiē*) is itself an emotional state.

49. B 73, 86, 43 (cf. *metanoein* in B 66).

50. Gosling and Taylor, pp. 29-31.

51. DK A 169, 167, 1.45, and B 4. Note the appropriate caveat of Bailey: the end (*telos*) "is the conception of a later age and implies a far more logically worked-out system of ethics" (*The Greek Atomists and Epicurus,* pp. 190 f.).

52. For a justified protest against this misreading of Democritus, see Langerbeck (note 25 above) 56-75: Democritus' thought is focused on the notion of security (*asphaleia*) and stability (*mēketi metapiptein*); but "nothing points to *euthymiē* as systematic center for a scientific ethics" (p. 60). We may add that even Epicurean theory was probably not as rigorously con-

sequentialist as Gosling and Taylor would suggest for Democritus, with all judgments of good and bad based solely on the contribution to the final goal as in Utilitarian theory. Certainly Aristotle's own ethics is not "teleological" in this sense.

53. For *autarkēs,* see B 176, 210; the thought without the word is there in 119 and 146. Cf. B 234 (the power of health is in ourselves). Hence the importance of *ponos* and *mathēsis.* And see below on *aidōs:* the standard for conduct is also in ourselves, not in the eyes of others.

54. The parallel to the *Protagoras* in often drawn, e.g., by Guthrie (note 4 above) 494.

55. The authenticity of B 189 has been doubted by Claus (p. 148n) on insufficient grounds. (B 235 on the brevity and futility of sensual pleasure can show what Democritus meant by *ta thnēta.*) The language here seems to me much more convincingly Democritean than in the Demokrates aphorism B 37, which describes the goods of the psyche as "more divine" than those of the body.

56. See Vlastos (pp. 586 f.).

57. For a parallel comment on self-shame and self-respect, see B 244 with B 84. B 179 emphasizes the role of shame in moral education: *to aideisthai,* "the greatest support of *aretē.*" Shame before others is the training and propaedeutic for the final stage of shame before onself. The importance of *aidōs* for Democritus again reminds us of Plato's *Protagoras,* where *aidōs* and *dikē* are presented (in the Prometheus myth) as the basis of social morality.

58. For some pre-Democritean reflection on the self, see Heraclitus frs. 101 and 116 (Diels) with my comment, *The Art and Thought of Heraclitus,* p. 116.

Appendix:

DEMOCRITUS' REFERENCES TO DESIRE

The fragments make regular use of two terms for desire: *orexis, oregomai* (six occurrences) and *epithymiē, epithymeein* (five occurrences). Other verbs occur more rarely.

I. *Orexis, oregomai*

B 72 (Demokrates): Violent *orexeis* for one thing blind the soul for other things.

201. Fools desire (*oregontai*) long life without enjoying the length of their life.

202. Fools desire (*oregontai*) what is absent, but they waste what is present, which is more profitable than things which are past.

205. Fools desire (*oregontai*) life in fearing death.

219. Desire (*orexis*) for money, if it is not limited by satiety, is much harder to bear than extreme poverty. For greater desires (*orexeis*) produce greater needs.

284. If you do not desire (*epithymeis*) many things, a few things will seem many to you. For small desire (*orexis*) makes poverty as strong as wealth.

II. *Epithymia, epithymeein*

70. (Demokrates): Immoderate desire (*epithymein*) is the mark of the child, not of a man.

191. Human beings achieve cheerfulness by moderation in enjoyment (*metriotēti terpsios*) and a measured balance (*symmetria*) in their life. . . . You should observe the lives of those who are in distress . . . so that you will no longer suffer evil in your soul by desiring (*epithymeonti*) more than you have. . . . <The person who admires those who are more fortunate> is obliged always to try for something new from the desire (*epithymia*) to do something irremediable and against the law.

224. The desire (*epithymia*) for more spoils what one has, like the dog in Aesop's fable (who dropped its bone reaching for its reflection).

234. By failure of self-mastery (*akrasiē*) they betray the cause of health to their desires (*epithymiai*). (For full text, see above, p. 16.)

235. [The pleasures of the belly are brief. . . .] For this kind of desire (*epithymein*) is always present for the same things, and when they get what they desire (*epithymeousi*), the pleasure is quickly past. . . . (For full text, see above, p. 16.)

284. See above, under *orexis.*

III. *Other expressions for desire or preference*

A. *Ephiesthai* B 73 (Demokrates, and unusually suspicious): Legitimate eros is striving after (*ephiesthai*) handsome objects (boys?) without doing them violence.

B. *Himeiresthai* B 223. The body does not long for (*himeiretai*) things that require toil and trouble and make life painful. (See fuller text below under *chrēizein.*)

C. *Ethelein*

199. Fools who hate life want (*ethelousi*) to live from fear of Hades.

206. Fools want (*ethelousin*) to grow old because they fear death.

(Note: The formula in 199 and 206 is parallel to that in B 201, 202, 205, where we have *oregontai* instead of *ethelousin.*)

D. *Chrēizein*

223. What the body requires (*chrēizei*) is easily available to all without toil and trouble; as for those things that require (*chrēizei*) toil and trouble and make life painful, it is not the body that longs for these but the ill grasp of the mind.

E. *Diōkein*

203. Human beings pursue (*diōkousin*) death in fleeing from it. (Note: The formula parallels that with *oregontai* and *ethelousin:* see above on B 206.)

The various verbs seem almost interchangeable and require no comment. However, the nominalizations (*orexis* and *epithymia*) become subjects in turn for a different verb and thus take on the literary color of a slight personification: desires make the soul blind (B 72) or produce needs (B 219); moderate desire strengthens poverty (284), as desire for more ruins what one has (224). This personification of desire follows the normal pattern in Democritus and other authors for abstract terms formed by nominalization of the corresponding verb.

Note that *orexis* is desire for wealth in 219 and 284; *epithymein* refers to sensual desires ("the belly") in 235 and probably in 234. Since both nouns occur in the same context in 284, Democritus is not likely to have intended any substantial difference between the two terms. The verbs are slightly more vivid and perhaps more individual: there probably persists an etymological connotation of "reaching out for" in *oregomai* and "having one's heart (*thymos*) set upon" in *epithymeein*.

Michael Nill (essay date 1985)

SOURCE: "Democritus," in *Morality and Self-Interest in Protagoras, Antiphon and Democritus*, E. J. Brill, 1985, pp. 75-91.

[*In the following excerpt, Nill examines Democritus's moral theory, particularly concerning pleasure and the ability of an individual to attain an ideal state.*]

Democritus (c. 460-396 B.C.) was a younger contemporary of Protagoras; both were born in Abdera.[1] Although he had encyclopedic interests and was the author of many works, the 298 fragments ascribed to him in Diels-Kranz are at most all that has survived of his writings.[2] Almost all of these fragments concern ethical matters. But despite this, Democritus has generally not been known for his moral theory. He has always, and rightly, been considered an important figure in the history of natural philosophy for his theory of atomism.

Commentators on the ethical fragments have often found them to be of little or no philosophical importance[3] and have sometimes questioned their authenticity. The issue of whether these fragments are authentic is not important in the context of the present study, which is only interested in these fragments insofar as they represent the views of an early Greek moral theorist concerned with the issue of the compatibility of self-interest and morality. Thus, it would make little difference here whether the fragments be attributed to Democritus or one of his contemporaries, although my own view is that they probably should be assigned to Democritus.[4] On the other hand, it is a crucial question in the present context whether the fragments have philosophical importance. It is true, of course, that the ethical fragments are written in a style closer to the philosophically unrigorous fragments of Antiphon's *On Concord* than to those from *On Truth*. But it cannot be

concluded from this fact that they are trivial. On the contrary, the fragments strongly imply that Democritus held moral views which he rigorously argued for. They not only reflect the concerns of the other theorists so far discussed in this study, but also mark an important advance.

A brief glance at several of the fragments provides a useful, preliminary indication of both the focus of Democritus' moral theory and the relationship between his views and those of Protagoras and Antiphon. The following fragment, for example, shows that Democritus shared with Protagoras certain beliefs about the value of *nomoi*:

> Law (*nomos*) wishes to benefit the life of men. It is able (to do this) whenever men themselves wish to receive benefit. For it shows to men (agents) who obey it, their own particular excellence (*idie arete*).
>
> (fr. 248)

In this fragment Democritus endorses the view that *nomoi* are of benefit to men. Indeed, an harmonious political community provides goods which "no one would be able to enumerate" (fr. 255). *Nomoi* are necessary for harmony in the city (fr. 245); and in fr. 252 he remarks that "the well-run polis is the greatest source of safety and contains all in itself; when this is safe, all is safe, when it is destroyed, all is destroyed." Democritus thus adopts the Protagorean view that *nomoi* are a necessary condition for political communities and human survival. In addition, he follows Protagoras in linking *nomima kai dikaia* (fr. 174) and thus thinks of *nomoi* in terms of moral requirements.

These views are traditional and Protagorean; but his following remarks suggest that he went well beyond traditional defenses of *nomoi*:

> The one employing exhortation and persuasion of reason (*peitho logou*) appears stronger in respect to *arete* than one employing *nomos* and constraint (*ananke*). For it is probable that the one who is prevented from injustice by *nomos* would commit wrong in secret, but it is not likely that the man who is led to what is necessary (*deon*) by persuasion would do anything discordant (*plemmeles*). And thus, a man acting rightly through intelligence (*synesis*) and knowledge becomes at the same time courageous and a man of upright thought.
>
> (fr. 181)

Democritus suggests he has an answer to the escaping-notice problem. There is, he says, some *logos* which will convince men to act morally on all occasions. Further, to act in this way is to act with intelligence (*synesis*), that is, with prudence and practical wisdom.[5] Thus Democritus is claiming that agents have self-interested reasons for acting morally even when they can escape notice in acting. Of course, neither Protagoras nor any other traditional defender of *nomoi* made such a strong claim. And needless to say, Democritus would not have tried to defend this claim on the basis of Protagorean arguments. In this fragment Democritus implicitly acknowledges the validity of Antiphon's critique of Protagorean views. But insofar as he claims that there is some *logos* which will convince agents not to do wrong in secret, he rejects Antiphon's conclusion that agents do not always have reasons to act morally.

Fr. 248 (already quoted) gives some indication of how Democritus went about rejecting Antiphon's conclusion. He remarks that *nomos* shows to agents who obey it their own particular excellence (*arete*).[6] That Democritus is thinking of this good (*arete*) as prudential is made clear by the fact that he mentions it in the context of arguing that observing *nomoi* is beneficial for agents. In obeying *nomoi*, agents are shown (promote) their own good. His argument suggests that he responded to Antiphon's claim that moral requirements ought not always be obeyed by arguing that there is some prudential good for persons which is promoted by acting morally.[7] It appears, then, that the focus of Democritus' moral theory is on the individual and the good for persons. His focus is the same as Antiphon's, but it is a focus which is quite different from Protagoras'.

The fragments and ancient testimony indicate that Democritus saw the good for persons in terms of the attainment of an ideal state or condition. He used a number of different terms to characterize this state. Stobaeus[8] notes that Democritus characterized this state as *eudaimonia, euthymia, euesto, harmonia, symmetria,* and *ataraxia.* Diogenes Laertius[9] remarks that Democritus gave many names to *euthymia,* including *euesto;* and Clement[10] notes the same thing, but adds that Democritus also used the word '*athambia*' to designate man's end (*telos*) or ideal state. That most of these words were used by Democritus is confirmed by the extant fragments. '*Euthymia*' (or cognates) is found, for example, in frr. 3, 174, 189, 191, and 286; '*symmetria*' in fr. 191; '*euesto*' (well-being) in fr. 257; '*eudaimonia*' (happiness) in frr. 170 and 171. *Ataraxia* is an Epicurean word, and probably should not be attributed to Democritus; however, *athambia* (imperturbability), a word roughly equivalent to *ataraxia* in meaning, is found in frr. 215 and 216.

Since the emphasis in the extant fragments is on *euthymia,* I shall generally confine my discussion to this term. It is, however, a word which is not easy to translate, Traditionally it has meant cheerfulness and this is perhaps the English word which comes closest to Democritus' meaning. But he packs so much into his notion of *euthymia* that no one-word translation is adequate or particularly helpful. Probably all the terms which Democritus uses for the ideal state refer to different aspects of that state or characterize it from different perspectives.[11] But in any case, all of these terms decribe a certain state or condition of the soul (*psyche*).[12]

Fr. 191 provides a convenient and important overview of Democritus' conception of human good:

> *Euthymia* arises for men from moderation (*metriotes*) of pleasure and harmoniousness (*symmetria*) of life.

Things in excess or deficiency are apt to change and create disturbances (movements) in the soul. But souls moved by great divergences (*diastemata*) are not stable, nor do they have *euthymia.* Accordingly it is necessary to keep one's mind on things possible and find satisfaction in things that are present. . . . If you no longer desire more [than you have], you cease to suffer in your soul. . . . Thinking thus, one will expel the not little sources of destruction in life: jealousy, envy, and spite.

This fragment touches on central features of *euthymia.* One of these is the notion that *euthymia* requires moderation of pleasure; and there are two components to this notion. First, moderation of pleasure involves the maintenance of overall pleasure in the soul, that is, a proper balance among the various pleasures one accepts.[13] No pleasure should be admitted into one's soul if it would conflict with one's maintaining a due balance of pleasures (fr. 74). In fr. 72, for example, Democritus remarks that a very strong desire for any one thing blinds the soul to all others, so that the pursuit of any pleasure (or at least the pursuit of certain kinds of pleasure) to the exclusion of others is detrimental to one's well-being. Second, moderation of pleasure involves observing the limits of any given pleasure. These limits are fixed by nature; beyond them lie excess and pain: if anyone exceeds due measure, the most pleasant things become most unpleasant (fr. 233). The two senses of moderation of pleasure are related insofar as the pursuit of any given pleasure beyond its proper limit will be incompatible with maintaining a proper balance of pleasures in one's soul.

If one is to maintain *euthymia,* certain pleasures, according to Democritus, must be pursued with much caution. Among such pleasures are bodily pleasures or pleasures of sensation. In fr. 235 he says,

> All who derive their pleasures from the stomach, exceeding what is fitting in eating, drinking, or sexual activity have pleasures that are brief and short-lived; [they have pleasures] only while they are eating and drinking, but pains that are many. For this desire is always present for the same things, and when people get what they desire, the pleasure passes quickly, and they have nothing good for themselves except a brief enjoyment; and then again the need for the same things returns.

One important question to be asked here is why Democritus thinks those who derive pleasures from the senses exceed what is fitting. 'Exceeding (*hyperballein*) what is fitting' recalls Democritus' claim in fr. 191 that things in excess (*hyperballonta*) create disturbances in the soul. Fr. 235 should be interpreted in light of this claim. Thus, those who derive their pleasures from the senses are those who are constantly confronted by that excess (or deficiency) which causes disturbances in one's soul, for they are constantly desiring more (excess) by virtue of the fact that they are always perceiving themselves to be in a state of deficiency and lack—except for those brief periods when they are actually indulging in pleasures of sensation (or perhaps also for a brief period thereafter). Such persons do not lead lives which are compatible with *euthymia*. Democritus *might* be making the point that such persons eat or drink too much on occasions when they eat or drink, but his major point is that they have souls which are (virtually) never at rest, balanced, or in equilibrium. It is primarily in this sense that he thinks of them as exceeding what is fitting. His argument is directed against those who derived pleasure *exclusively* from sensations.[14] It should be noted that no fragment gives any indication that he thought finding (some) satisfaction in pleasures of sensation is incompatible with the maintenance of *euthymia*.

In addition to pleasures of sensation, pleasures of external goods like wealth or possessions must also be pursued with much caution. In fr. 219, Democritus notes that

> striving after possessions/wealth, if not limited by sufficiency, is far more painful than extreme poverty; for greater desires make for greater needs (*endeiai*).

There is, of course, virtually no limit to the amount of wealth a person might desire. If a person puts no limit on this desire, then he will forever feel himself in a state of deficiency and pain. His soul will constantly be in a disturbed state; and he will always be desiring more (excess). His situation would be analogous to that of those who restrict their pleasure to bodily sensations; and he is perhaps worse off because he will not even have brief moments of pleasure and satisfaction. As with sensuous pleasure, neither the desire of unlimited wealth nor the exclusive pursuit of it is compatible with *euthymia*.

This initial discussion makes clear that *euthymia* requires that one be properly disposed to pleasures. Indeed, the relationship between *euthymia* and pleasure is a central component of Democritus' theory of human good. This relationship is a complex one and needs to spelled out in considerable detail.

In fr. 188 (= fr. 4), Democritus says the following about pleasure:

> Pleasure (*terpsis*) or the lack of pleasure is the criterion (*horos;* landmark, sign) for what is advantageous (*symphoron*) and disadvantageous.

In other words, pleasure is the criterion for *euthymia* or the ideal state for man. On the other hand, Democritus prescribes the following in fr. 74:

> Accept nothing which is pleasant (*hedu*) unless it is advantageous.

As has often been noted, there is an apparent discrepancy between the two fragments; for if some pleasures are not advantageous (fr. 74), then pleasure cannot be the criterion for advantage (fr. 188). Some commentators have argued that Democritus distinguished between higher and lower pleasures and that he saw the good for persons primarily in terms of higher pleasures.[15] Higher pleasures are intellectual and spiritual pleasures; lower pleasures include bodily pleasures and pleasures derived from external goods. This interpretation provides one way in which the apparent discrepancy in the above two fragments can be reconciled. Higher pleasures alone are the criterion for advantage (fr. 188), while there are lower pleasures which are not (or may not be) advantageous (fr. 74).[16]

Support for this interpretation has been seen in those fragments which are thought to indicate a negative view of so-called lower pleasures. For example, in fr. 40 he remarks that men find happiness (*eudaimonia*) neither through the body nor through possessions (cf. frr. 171, 214, 235). In addition, Democritus claims that things of the soul are superior to the body (e.g., frr. 37, 187, 189); and he sometimes speaks of this superiority in terms of the superiority of the divine over the human (mortal) (e.g., fr. 37; cf. fr. 189).[17] Hence, it might he thought that for Democritus true pleasure, that pleasure which is the criterion for advantage, is exclusively intellectual and spiritual.

This interpretation would make Democritus' theory quite advanced: his conception of the good for persons would be completely internalized; that is, not only would *euthymia* itself be an inner good, but also the pleasures which promote it would be essentially inner, spiritual ones. On this interpretation, bodily and external goods would be valuable only insofar as they make possible the attainment of *euthymia and* the pursuit of, say, intellectual pleasures.

However, I do not think Democritus held any such view.[18] No ancient source attributes this view to him, and the extant fragments hardly even mention intellectual pleasures.[19] More importantly, there are claims in the fragments which indicate that Democritus did not think of intellectual pleasures as the criterion for advantage. To begin with, I would suggest that his notion that *euthymia* is brought about by moderation of pleasure indicates that in large part he saw the proper acceptance of bodily pleasures and pleasures derived from external goods as that what brings *euthymia* about. It is, after all, these pleasures which are normally and rightly thought to require moderation. It would simply not be relevant or appropriate to talk about *euthymia* as a state brought about by moderation of pleasure, if the pleasure in question is intellectual. Intellectual pleasures are such that one does not need to be advised to pursue them moderately except, of course, when one is pursuing them to such an extent that one is neglecting survival needs.[20]

Of course, it might be thought that moderation of pleasure means that one must be moderate when indulging in the lower pleasures in order to make *euthymia and* the successful pursuit of higher pleasures possible. No fragment, however, implies that Democritus held such a view. And there are strong reasons for not attributing this view to him. For one thing, lower pleasures would then be a mere means to other, higher ones. This would be difficult to reconcile with Democritus' obvious interest in lower pleasures as such and with his obvious concern for showing how they can be maximized. As he says in fr. 211, moderation increases pleasures (see also fr. 233).[21]

Indeed, to attribute to Democritus this view is to miss a prominent feature of his theory. He is emphatic in his belief that all the things in the world are good and that the goods of the world are only turned into evils as a result of an improper disposition to them. In fr. 175 he says:

> The gods are the givers of all good things, both in the past and now. They are not, however, the givers of things which are bad, harmful or non-beneficial, either in the past or now, but men fall into these through blindness of mind and lack of sense.

And in fr. 173 he remarks that evil comes out of good if one does not know how to 'guide' and 'drive' correctly. Surely the goods in question would include bodily and external goods, as Democritus makes clear in fr. 77: "Fame and wealth without intelligence are dangerous possessions." This implies, of course, that fame and wealth, if made use of with intelligence, would be goods. The wealth which is at issue in fr. 77 is clearly substantial and well above that level which could be described as 'moderate'.[22] Frr. 229, 279, 280, 285, 286 all assert or imply that at least a moderate amount of wealth is a good for persons.

Democritus' emphatic belief that the things of the world are good strongly suggests that (1) he did not see the goods of the world as a mere means to higher, intellectual pleasures and (2) he saw the good for persons to lie in the proper acceptance of all pleasures and goods without distinction as to whether they are higher or lower ones.[23] It is not certain kinds of pleasures that are to be shunned, but the improper acceptance or pursuit of any given pleasure. For example, excessive eating or exclusive attention to eating would turn the good of eating into an evil. Indeed, it is Democritus' view that any good can be turned into an evil if one's use of it or desire for it is at odds with *euthymia*.

Thus, when he claims in fr. 74 that one should not accept any pleasure which is not advantageous, he is claiming that a person should not accept any given pleasure (1) if it is incompatible with the maintenance of an overall balance of pleasures in his soul, (2) if he already has his fill of that pleasure and further indulgence would involve excess, or (3) if the pursuit of that pleasure would create disturbances in the soul. Accepting or pursuing any given pleasure under any of these conditions would result in more pain than pleasure. On this interpretation, fr. 74 would be entirely consistent with fr. 188 where pleasure is viewed as the criterion for advantage.[24] Those fragments which appear to take a negative view of so-called lower pleasures are best interpreted as a warning that such pleasures are to be pursued with caution if one is to attain *euthymia*. And those fragments which assert the superiority of the soul over the body and external goods should be understood as expressions of the view that what makes for the good life is not bodily or external goods in *themselves,* but a proper pattern of pleasures in the soul, a soul that has a proper disposition to pleasures, and a soul which has properly controlled desires.

Democritus did not completely internalize the good for persons. Although he internalized it to a great extent

inasmuch as *euthymia* is an inner good, the properly accepted pleasures which produce this inner good would be, at least for most men, primarily non-inner ones. In addition, *euthymia* involves the *active,* albeit proper, acceptance of pleasures. As Taylor correctly argues, *euthymia* is not to be understood as mere tranquility or freedom from fear and anxiety.[25] "They are fools," claims Democritus, "who live without enjoyment of life" (fr. 200); "life without festival is like a long road without an inn" (fr. 230).

However, this interpretation of *euthymia* as the active, proper acceptance of pleasures raises the crucial question of whether the good life depends, in any important sense, on the quantity of the particular pleasures one accepts, whether, for example, the good life depends on having more, rather than less pleasure-producing goods like wealth. An answer to this question is crucial for determining Democritus' conception of human good; for if the good life depends in any important sense on the quantity of pleasures properly accepted, one is going to lead a quite different life than one would lead otherwise. However, to answer this question, it will first be necessary to spell out two notions found in Democritus' important sketch of *euthymia* in fr. 191 (quoted above on p. 77): (1) *euthymia* involves attending to and finding satisfaction in things which are possible and (2) *euthymia* involves finding satisfaction with things that are present and at hand. Democritus does not appear to acknowledge the distinction between these two notions; but as we shall see, they do not come to the same thing.

Democritus' first notion that one ought to restrict one's desires to things which are possible is not an expression of the truism that one ought not to pursue things that are impossible to obtain.[26] This point is made clear in fr. 3 where he contrasts things that are possible with (good) fortune (*tyche,* chance) which leads men on to more (*es to pleon,* excess) by (false) seeming. He remarks that one ought to discount or rate low the presence of good fortune and not reach for more than is possible since fullness is safer than "overfullness." In part, Democritus is pointing out that good fortune (abundant wealth, for example) has a tendency to cause one to be overconfident and attempt things beyond one's reach. But more importantly, he is drawing attention to the problematic nature of (good) *tyche.* Whether or not one attains good fortune is a matter of chance and does not, in an important sense, depend on one's own actions. "*Tyche* is a giver of great gifts, but it is unreliable; on the other hand, *physis* is self-sufficient and it thus conquers by its smaller power the greater promise of hope" (fr. 176; cf. fr. 210). "Fools," says Democritus, "are shaped by the gifts of *tyche* . . ." (fr. 197).

Democritus' position is not that one ought to reject good fortune or that abundant wealth is necessarily incompatible with *euthymia,* but rather that it is incompatible with *euthymia* to pursue good fortune or to rely on retaining it. Attempting to pursue it would involve having great desires, that is, desires for a great amount of external goods (frr.

284, 219). Given the realities of life, the desire for good fortune will more likely than not be frustrated and will create disturbances in one's soul. But the wise man who acts in accord with the first notion of *euthymia* restricts his desires to goods which are normally obtainable by his own efforts and not a matter of chance. Such a man would, for example, desire and pursue the attainment of a 'moderate' amount of wealth (fr. 285).[27]

However, Democritus' second notion, the notion that a man with *euthymia* finds satisfaction in things which are present (fr. 191), would seem to involve a stronger claim. That is, he would seem to be claiming that *euthymia* involves the absence of any desire to increase one's goods (that is, any or all goods which produce pleasures that *can* be components of a proper balance of pleasures in a man with *euthymia*). In fr. 191, he specifically cautions against thinking about things which are envied and admired; rather, one should think of those in distress; for by doing so, one's own condition seems great and enviable. In fr. 224, he argues that the desire for more than one has destroys the good that one has at present. And in fr. 231, he claims that the right-minded man is one who is not grieved by what he does not have, but enjoys what he has (cf. fr. 202). This view of *euthymia* would be most accurately described as contentment: *euthymia* would consist of finding satisfaction in what one has, regardless of what that might be. In such a state one would experience no deficiency or excess; one's soul would be without disturbances or even movements. Democritus seems to think that (virtually) no one needs to desire and pursue more than he has: "The things needed by the body are available to all without toil and trouble; but the things which require toil and trouble and which make life disagreeable are not desired by the body, but by the ill-constitution of the mind" (fr. 223). In other words, the bodily and external goods necessary for a pleasant and good life are (normally) present to everyone. It would seem, then, that *euthymia* is compatible with a minimal level of goods and wealth. Indeed, Democritus suggests that living one's life with only minimal goods is not necessarily to live in a condition of poverty. Whether one lives in poverty or not is, in large part, a product of one's outlook and desires; as he notes in fr. 284, small appetite makes poverty equivalent to wealth. Poverty and wealth are terms for lack and sufficiency (fr. 283); one lives in poverty when one thinks one has insufficient wealth.

The above discussion suggests that there is a tension in Democritus' view of *euthymia*. On the one hand, when *euthymia* is seen as involving satisfaction with things that one has at present, it involves contentment and the complete absence of desire to increase one's goods. A person with this kind of *euthymia* would always experience fullness, regardless of what possessions or level of wealth he happens to have. On the other hand, when *euthymia* is seen in terms of pursuing and finding satisfaction in things which are possible to obtain by one's own efforts, it is compatible with some dissatisfaction with one's current good. And thus on this view, *euthymia* would

be (sometimes) compatible with desiring and pursuing an increase of goods. This tension has serious implications for the earlier-posed question of whether the good life ever depends, in any important sense, on the quantity of pleasures one accepts or on the quantity of pleasure-producing goods one has.

The first thing to be noted is that the good life cannot depend solely on the quantity of pleasures since a balance of pleasures in the soul would not necessarily be produced by maximizing the quantity of any particular pleasure or by maximizing the number of one's pleasures. However, quantity of pleasures does affect, to some extent, the degree to which one possesses the good life.

This is best seen by looking again at Democritus' view of wealth. On the one hand, he argues that poverty is compatible with *euthymia* or human good on grounds that one can find satisfaction in things at hand and that small appetite makes poverty the equivalent of wealth. But on the other hand, he remarks in fr. 291, for example, that it is a mark of a man with *sophrosyne* to *bear* poverty well. The clear implication of this fragment is that poverty is not a desirable condition to be in although, of course, it is compatible with *euthymia*. And given, as we have seen, that levels of wealth above or perhaps even substantially above the poverty level are compatible with *euthymia*, it would appear that Democritus would agree with the following: X, a man who has *euthymia* and a level of wealth above the level of poverty is objectively better off than Y, a man who has *euthymia* and who lives in poverty. And thus either (1) X has realized a higher degree of *euthymia* (human good) than Y or (2) X and Y possess an equal amount of *euthymia*, but X possesses a greater amount of human good. On the second view, *euthymia* would be a necessary, but not sufficient condition for (maximum) human good. But on either view, the degree to which X and Y possess human good is partly dependent on the quantity of pleasure-producing goods they have.

The upshot of this discussion is that Democritus is committed to the view that those who find the pleasures of wealth and possessions important would ordinarily be objectively better off if they had more wealth than they currently possess provided the possession of it be compatible with *euthymia*. But the fact that Democritus is committed to this view does not mean that he is committed to the view that these people would be subjectively better off if they had more wealth or that they would be better off in any sense if they pursued it. Whether he is committed to this further consequence depends on which view of *euthymia* is adopted. On the view of *euthymia* as complete satisfaction with things one has presently, one would not be subjectively better off with more wealth since one's level of wealth—whatever it may be—should be experienced as fullness. Nor would one be better off in any sense desiring and pursuing more wealth. However, on the view of *euthymia* as satisfaction with things possible to obtain by one's own efforts, people who find the pleasures of wealth important would, at least in some cases, be subjectively better off with more wealth. If *euthymia* is compatible with some dissatisfaction with their current goods, such people would be subjectively better off possessing the increase of goods they desire so long as the pursuit of it is compatible with maintaining *euthymia*. In fr. 243 Democritus endorses the desires and pursuits of these people when he remarks that toil is more pleasant than rest when men attain that for which they labor or know that they will attain it.

In discussing Democritus' conception of the good for persons, I have focused on his attitude toward wealth (possessions) because it is a traditional good which many people pursue and because the way one spells out the relationship between wealth and the good for persons has direct bearing on the question of whether morality and self-interest are compatible. The tension in Democritus' view of wealth is, at bottom, caused by the fact that he did not *completely* internalize man's good: while *euthymia,* the good for persons, is an inner good, the pleasures which bring it about are for most men largely non-inner. That Democritus *largely* internalized man's good marks a significant advance over Antiphon and Protagoras; and thus when viewed from an historical perspective, the kind of tension which exists in Democritus' view of wealth is readily explicable and understandable. Less understandable, however, is the tension in his notion of *euthymia;* but we can perhaps account for it in the following way: On the one hand, his view of *euthymia* as complete satisfaction would seem to be prompted by (1) his belief that dissatisfaction is at the heart of much individual unhappiness and social unrest and (2) his interest in showing that poverty does not preclude happiness. On the other hand, his view of *euthymia* as compatible with some dissatisfaction would seem to be prompted by his belief that the goods of the world are a good for persons and hence worthwhile pursuing.

My analysis thus far has been concerned with the self-regarding actions an agent must perform if he is to attain *euthymia.* What remains to be done now is (1) to confirm the thesis that on Democritus's view, self-interest is compatible with and promoted by the other-regarding behavior required by morality and (2) to determine how Democritus justified that view.

As for (1), the fragments clearly show that Democritus believed morality and self-interest compatible. In fr. 174, for example, he remarks that

> the cheerful man (*euthymos*), impelled to acts that are just and lawful (*dikaia kai nomima*), rejoices day and night and is strong and free from troubles. But the one who is neglectful of justice and does not do what he ought to do, all such things are distressful to him whenever he remembers them, and he is fearful and reproaches himself.

The man with *euthymia,* then, is happy (partly) because he obeys *nomima kai dikaia;* disregard for *nomoi,* on the other hand, leads to pain and, presumably, the loss of *eu-* *thymia.* Thus Democritus is claiming not only that moral requirements and self-interest (*euthymia*) are compatible, but also that acting morally is a necessary condition for *euthymia* and happiness.

Further, in fr. 181 (quoted above on p. 76) he argues that men will (likely) act morally—even when they can act in secret—if they have been persuaded by reason (*logos*), that is, if they have knowledge and understanding or intelligence (*synesis*). Conversely, "the cause of wrongdoing (*hamartia*) is ignorance of what is better" (fr. 83).[28] The fragments as a whole emphasize the importance of intelligence and understanding for determining how to maximize one's self-interest. For example, he remarks in fr. 77 that fame and wealth are not safe possessions without intelligence (*synesis,* the same word as used in fr. 181).[29] That is, they are dangerous possessions if one does not have the practical wisdom and prudential good sense to use them properly in promoting self-interest. Thus when Democritus says that one will (likely) act morally when one has knowledge and intelligence (fr. 181), he is claiming that those who know what is in their true self-interest will (likely) act morally even when they can act in secret.

However, it is in fr. 45 where he indicates just how strongly he is committed to the view that moral action is in one's self-interest: "The one who commits an injustice is more unhappy than the one who suffers an injustice." Democritus claims here that committing an injustice does more harm to one's soul and is more at odds with one's self-interest than suffering an injustice. This claim strongly endorses the view that acting justly benefits agents. Indeed, Democritus may have been the first to make this claim in Ancient Greece although, of course, he may have been preceded by Socrates. Moreover, given that the question of compatibility of morality and self-interest was such a controversial issue among Democritus' contemporaries, the fact that he makes such a strong claim suggests that he thought he could provide a substantive defense for it.[30]

Scholars generally have not addressed the issue of the compatibility of morality and *euthymia* although Colvin and Irwin have recently given it some attention. Colvin correctly sees that Democritus needs an argument to refute the view that it is beneficial to act unjustly in secret, and he also correctly sees that the best argument would show that a wrongdoer is more harmed than the wronged (fr. 45).[31] However, he finds no evidence of such an argument in the fragments and concludes that Democritus made his claim in fr. 45 without the Socratic elenchus to back it up. Irwin, on the other hand, does think that Democritus presented an argument and that it is very close to the one employed by Socrates; but he adds that Democritus' and Socrates' arguments are open to the same objections.[32] In essence, he thinks Democritus argued in the following way: (1) The best condition of the soul is undisturbed harmony (fr. 191); (2) harmony requires (practical) wisdom to prevent disturbances in the soul (fr. 31); (3) wisdom requires temperance (*sophrosyne*) in order to avoid the distress caused by greedy and intemperate desires; (4)

justice and temperance prohibit acting upon greedy and intemperate desires; and thus (5) it is advantageous for agents to observe the requirements of morality.

Irwin is on the right track, I think, in suggesting that Democritus, like Socrates/Plato, attempted to justify acting justly on grounds of the intrinsic benefits of just action, that is, on grounds that acting justly in itself benefits an agent's soul. And it is certainly plausible to hold that Democritus could have argued in a way similar to the one Irwin has suggested. Democritus did believe that one's true interest lies in maintaining a harmonious condition of the soul and that this condition can only be attained by practicing temperance and by placing strict control on one's desires and one's pursuit of pleasure. And it is obvious that in many cases the temperance necessary for *euthymia* will require one to regard the interests of others.

But as Irwin points out, there is an obvious and serious shortcoming in the argument he attributes to Democritus; that is, the argument does not show why the moral *arete* of temperance which prescribes temperate behavior towards others and regard for their interests is always compatible with the prudential *arete* of temperance by which an agent controls his desires in order to pursue successfully his rational aims and attain harmony in his soul. Say, for example, that someone has the rational aim of attending college, an aim that is compatible with *euthymia*. And say further that in attempting to procure the money to attend college, he practices the self-regarding *arete* of temperance so that his desires do not conflict with his pursuit of procuring the money he needs. The argument Irwin attributes to Democritus would not show that this person would necessarily be acting contrary to the self-regarding temperance required for *euthymia* if he stole the money which he needed. This, of course, is the very issue raised by Socrates when he asks Protagoras whether it is possible to exercise (self-regarding) temperance in committing an injustice (*Protagoras* 333b-c).[33] On the basis of the argument Irwin attributes to Democritus, Democritus would not be able to provide a negative answer to Socrates' question. However, if Democritus did use this argument, it would only have been one of the arguments he used. And it seems to me that Irwin is mistaken to model Democritus' defense of acting justly so closely on the one used by Socrates.[34] Democritus' defense is both stronger and more complex than Irwin maintains.

Democritus' strongest argument for the intrinsic benefits of acting justly focuses more on the need to avoid jealousy and envy than on the need to practice temperance. In fr. 245 he argues as follows:

> *Nomoi* would not prevent each individual from living according to his own inclination (*exousia;* power, authority) if individuals did not harm each other; for jealousy (*phthonos*) creates the beginning of strife (*stasis*).

I take this fragment to mean that *nomoi* would not be established to prevent men from acting on their own inclination if men were not inclined to harm each other. On Democritus' view then, men harm each other if left to their own devices because they act from reasons of jealousy. *Nomoi* are created and designed to prevent this; in other words, *nomoi* embody prescriptions prohibiting jealous behavior.

Clearly the views of Democritus about the role of *nomoi* differ significantly from those of Protagoras. The latter had argued that justice and *nomoi* are good and necessary insofar as they prevent injury and secure the existence of political communities. Although, of course, Democritus would agree with Protagoras' position, he primarily sees the good of *nomoi* in terms of human psychology and the good for persons (agents). It is this shift in focus which allows Democritus to argue for the view—as Protagoras could not—that agents have sufficient reasons to obey the laws in all circumstances.

The crux of Democritus' argument lies in his appeal to the notion that jealousy is incompatible with *euthymia*. In fr. 88, he remarks that the jealous or envious man grieves (torments) himself as if an enemy. In other words, being jealous of the goods and happiness of others makes one hate oneself and be dissatisfied with one's present goods. Jealousy, as it were, makes one an enemy to oneself. And just as jealousy creates strife in a political community (fr. 245), so it creates strife in one's soul. In fr. 191, Democritus says that if one dwells on goods that are present to oneself, one promotes *euthymia* and expels destructive elements in life like envy, jealousy, and spite. He also makes the point in this fragment that dwelling on the goods of others incites one to act contrary to the laws. Democritus' argument, then, for the view that acting justly in itself benefits agents is as follows:

(1) *Nomoi* embody prescriptions prohibiting jealous action

(2) Acting jealously is contrary to one's self-interest

(3) Therefore, it is disadvantageous for agents to disobey *nomoi* and disregard the interests of others.

Conversely, it will be advantageous for agents to regard moral requirements because such action promotes non-jealous action and satisfaction with oneself and one's condition.

Democritus' argument has considerable strengths, and certainly it is stronger than the one Irwin attributes to him. However, it rests on the assumption that all unjust actions are ultimately motivated by jealousy; and it will be necessary to determine how adequately Democritus could justify this assumption in order to evaluate the effectiveness of his argument.

It seems to me that the only way he could support his assumption would be to argue as follows: (1) All acts of disregarding the rights of others (as those rights are defined by the *nomima kai dikaia*) involve attemps to increase one's goods; (2) one would not attempt to do this unless one were dissatisfied with one's goods; (3) dissatisfaction with one's goods is always motivated, at bottom, by feeling envious and jealous of the goods of others, goods which one does not currently have, but would like to have; and hence (4) all unjust actions are motivated by feelings of jealousy.

There is one notable and striking feature of this argument: It would commit Democritus to the view that acts of pursuing an increase of one's goods are always motivated by jealousy even where such action does not involve committing an injustice. Given that jealousy is contrary to self-interest, it would follow that an agent never has self-interested reasons to desire an increase of goods. This consequence squares with that notion of *euthymia* which counsels complete satisfaction with goods that are present, for in that case an agent never has self-interested reasons to increase his goods. On this view of *euthymia,* it seems plausible to hold that all desire for increasing one's goods is motivated by jealousy.[35] Given this, the above defense of Democritus' assumption works; and he thus has a very strong argument to show that acting unjustly is intrinsically disadvantageous since he establishes a necessary correlation between morality and self-interest.

There are, however, two further problems to be considered. First, although the ultimate success of Democritus' argument depends on how convincingly he could defend the notion that complete satisfaction with goods at hand is the good for persons, he is not in a position to do so; for as we have seen, he has another notion of *euthymia,* one that is compatible with increasing one's goods. On this second notion of *euthymia,* he could no longer argue that *all* pursuit of an increase of goods is necessarily motivated by jealousy, given that jealousy and self-interest (*euthymia*) are incompatible. Rather, he would have to argue that jealousy is the motivating force for those actions which specifically involve increasing one's goods by immoral means. But this would not be a plausible position. To use a previous example, if it is compatible with a certain person's *euthymia* to desire and pursue the goal of bettering himself by attending college, there would be no reason to assert that he would necessarily be acting jealously if he stole the money which he needed for pursuing his goal. Rather, his action could merely be motivated by his desire to better himself—a desire which is compatible with *euthymia.*

The problem is strikingly brought to the fore in fr. 78: "To make money is not without use; but if it comes from wrongdoing, nothing is worse." Here Democritus presupposes that it is sometimes compatible with *euthymia* to better one's condition; but then he cannot show why nothing is worse than wrongdoing or why acts of wrongdoing are necessarily motivated by jealousy. Of course, Democritus might well have mistakenly assumed that anytime someone disregards the interests of others he is acting with jealousy (or spite) toward the persons he wrongs. Given that it would have been an easy enough assumption to make, it is possible that he did not try to argue for it

and did not see that his argument for the compatibility of self-interest and morality is flawed when *euthymia* is seen as being compatible with some pursuit of an increase of goods.

The second problem in Democritus' argument is that certain prescriptions of justice cannot plausibly be said to be prescriptions prohibiting jealous action. For example, in frr. 258-262 Democritus argues that justice requires one to do his best to ensure the punishment of wrongdoers. And in fr. 38, he may be thinking that justice requires one to prevent another from doing a wrong if it is possible to do so. These requirements have nothing to do with matters of jealousy, nor would disregard of them ordinarily be motivated by feelings of jealousy. Thus Democritus could not argue that observing these requirements benefits agents because it is not advantageous to act on feelings of jealousy. He could, however, readily defend them on the basis of Protagorean arguments. Maintaining a well-functioning political community requires that wrongdoers be punished or 're-educated'; and in a well-run state, the person who acts in accord with these requirements can reasonably expect his actions to be reciprocated when he himself has been wronged by someone. But, of course, Protagoras could not justify the claim that it is never in one's interest to disregard these requirements—and neither could Democritus, given what we have seen of his views thus far.

However, this second problem in Democritus' argument is not serious insofar as the problem concerns relatively few requirements of justice. On the other hand, it is a serious problem that his argument is not very effective when *euthymia* is viewed as satisfaction with and pursuit of goods which are obtainable by one's own efforts. The problem is particularly serious since the pursuit of wealth is not necessarily incompatible with *euthymia* and it is not Democritus' view that wealth is a good only insofar as it makes possible the pursuit of intellectual, higher pleasures. Much wrongdoing is committed in pursuing external goods like wealth. What Democritus clearly needs is an argument to support the view that acting justly in itself necessarily promotes *euthymia*—when *euthymia* is viewed as a state which can be compatible with some dissatisfaction with one's goods. In other words, he needs an argument to show that it is intrinsically disadvantageous for an agent to increase his goods by unjust means, even though increasing one's goods by just means can be in an agent's interest.

Although I do not believe Democritus could provide such an argument, he does restrict significantly the circumstances in which it would be in an agent's interest to act unjustly. He does this by putting strict restrictions on the conditions under which it would be compatible with *euthymia* to desire and pursue an increase of goods. To begin with, *euthymia* requires that one desire and pursue only those goods which are possible to obtain by one's own efforts; it would create disadvantageous disturbances in the soul to desire things which one does not have reasonable expectation of attaining on one's own. As Democritus notes in fr. 243, toil is pleasant (only) when men attain or know that they will attain that for which they labor. Furthermore, *euthymia* requires that a person's desires not blind his soul to other goods and that the attainment of his desires be compatible with the maintenance of overall pleasure in his soul. And finally, desire cannot be motivated by jealousy: the presence of jealousy indicates that a person desires something primarily because he perceives that someone else has a good which he does not have, and not because he has carefully considered whether it would really be in his own interest to possess that good.

In many circumstances, then, it will not be advantageous for a person to seek an increase of goods; but clearly there would still be occasions on which it would be beneficial. And thus it might well be that stealing, for example, would be in person's interest if he can act in accord with all the requirements of *euthymia,* maintaining a balance of pleasures in his soul and so forth, and if he can expect to escape notice in acting.[36]

There are two ways Democritus could attempt to overcome this deficiency in his theory. First, he could try to argue that acting unjustly is always disadvantageous for agents because of disadvantages which are *extrinsic* to such action. He does seem to argue for this view in fr. 215: "The reward of justice is confidence of mind and imperturbability (*athambia*), but the result of injustice is fear of disaster." And in fr. 174, he claims that the *euthymos* man who obeys the *nomima kai dikaia* is free from worry, but that those who disregard justice live in fear. Such fear, of course, would create disadvantageous disturbances in the soul; and hence acting unjustly would not be in an agent's interest. This argument has some force; but it is not strong enough to show that it would never be in an agent's interest to act unjustly: it is empirically implausible that every agent would suffer from fear as a result of every immoral act he commits. In any case, even though Democritus does appear to employ this argument, he did not consider it an important one; for he expressly states in fr. 41 that one should not refrain from wrongdoing because of fear.[37]

The second way Democritus could attempt to overcome the deficiency in his defense of the compatibility of morality and a person's good would be to try to argue that promoting the good of others is an *end* which is a component of one's own good. Thus far I have only discussed the compatibility of morality and a person's good in terms of moral action benefiting agents because such action would be an instrumental *means* by which one can further one's own good. Defending the good of moral action in these terms can make no appeal to the notion that altruistic action or the promotion of the good of others *for its own sake* is a good for persons (agents).[38] If Democritus did, in fact, appeal to this notion, he would be, as far as I can tell, the first Greek moral theorist to do so. According to Irwin, this notion is found in Plato and Aristotle.[39]

There is some indication in the fragments that Democritus might actually have appealed to this notion. I would call

attention here to the fact that Democritus speaks approvingly of the following three kinds of action: (1) showing generosity without expecting (any?) return (fr. 96); (2) having pity for those who suffer misfortune or who are worse off than oneself (frr. 255, 107a); and (3) giving aid, if one is wealthy and powerful, to the people in one's political community (fr. 255; cf. fr. 282). It is possible, of course, that he defended the action in (3) as being in accord with self-interest on grounds that such action secures social peace and harmony. It is also possible that he defended the actions in (2) and *perhaps* (1) as being in accord with self-interest on grounds of reciprocity: Life is such that good fortune is fleeting (fr. 285); and so when someone has good fortune, he ought to help others when possible and reasonable to do so because it is quite possible that at some time in the future he himself might need such help. If Democritus did, in fact, argue in this way in defense of these actions, his arguments would have been quite weak.

It seems to me, however, that his approval of these actions could be better accounted for on grounds that he held the view that promoting the good of others is a component of one's own good. If he held such a view and if he could successfully defend it, he would be able to show that agents have self-regarding reasons not only to perform these actions, but also to regard always the interests of others.

Although I do think the fragments provide *some* indication that Democritus held the view that altruism is a component of one's good, it is not clear that he actually argued for it. On the other hand, the fragments do supply the raw material out of which an argument can be constructed. His probable approach would have been to argue that altruism is a necessary consequence of having *euthymia;* and his argument, roughly speaking, would have been as follows:[40] The attainment of *euthymia* is the good for persons. The attainment of this requires, among other things, the knowledge that life is beset with problems and that good fortune cannot be pursued or relied upon (frr. 176, 285). This knowledge comes from observing one's own life and the lives of others and involves recognition of the fact that misfortunes are common to all human beings (fr. 293). Recognition of this fact establishes for the man with *euthymia* a bond between himself and others. When the *euthymos* man sees the misfortunes of others, he not only mourns for and pities his own (actual and potential) misfortunes, but also mourns for and pities the misfortunes of others because he recognizes that men have misfortunes in common: "It is proper, since we are human beings, not to laugh at the misfortunes of others, but to mourn" (fr. 107a; cf. fr. 293).[41] The *euthymos* man expresses this pity for others by promoting their good (as implied by frr. 96, 255, 282). Thus, altruism is a component of one's own good because it is a consequence of having *euthymia.*

However interesting this argument may be, it is, at bottom, unsuccessful; for it illegitimately moves from the fact that the man with *euthymia* sees misfortune as the common lot of humanity to the claim that the man with *euthymia* desires to benefit others. The fact that this argument is not successful is not surprising: it is extremely difficult to provide compelling reasons to pursue altruism as a part of one's own good. If Democritus did hold this view, it is far from certain that he would have argued for it; and I think it unlikely that he would actually have laid out an argument as elaborate as the one I suggested. But even granting that he argued rigorously for the view in question, it is virtually certain that he would not have been able to argue successfully for it. And thus, he would still be without a conclusive argument to demonstrate that acting morally is congruent with an agent's good or *euthymia,* when *euthymia* is understood as satisfaction with goods obtainable by one's own efforts. And as far as I can tell, there are no further claims or arguments in the fragments which give any indication that he had such a conclusive argument.

Although in the course of my discussion I have been insistent in pointing out the weaknesses in Democritus' defense of the compatibility of morality and self-interest, these weaknesses should not be allowed to obscure the strength of that defense. The difficulty of arguing for the view that one's morality promotes one's self-interest should not be underestimated; in fact, it may be impossible to provide a successful argument. Democritus' attempt seems particularly remarkable when viewed from an historical perspective. The evidence suggests that no early Greek moral theorist—except perhaps Socrates—could provide a defense of moral requirements that approached the cogency of the one provided by Democritus. The other defenses which have come down to us are traditional and Protagorean.

As I suggested in the last chapter, a close examination of Antiphon's theory could indicate to a perceptive theorist that there is a crucial relationship between one's conception of the good for persons and one's answer to the question of whether acting morally is compatible with self-interest. Antiphon himself does not appear to have been aware of that relationship. Democritus was, and he may have been the first. But of course, one is not likely to be aware of this relationship unless one is aware of the possibility that the good for persons might be an inner good. Democritus was aware of this possibility. Indeed, he (largely) internalized man's good; and again, he may have been the first Greek moralist to do so. It was precisely because he had a largely inner conception of human good that he was able to provide a strong case for the benefits of acting morally—in particular, that he was able to argue for the view that acting justly benefits agents because of advantages which are intrinsic to such action. He appears to have been the first Greek moral theorist to argue for such a view. In doing so, he anticipated Plato. And as we have seen, he may have even taken groping steps toward the view that promoting the good of others is a component of one's own good.

On the other hand, there are certain important areas in which his moral theory did not mark any advance. There is, for example, no evidence that he took an interest in defining the various moral *aretai.* And insofar as he saw moral requirements in terms of the customs and laws of existing political communities, he grounded the content of morality in the same unsatisfactory way as Protagoras. Not only is the legal conception of morality, in itself, a clearly deficient one, but it also makes even more difficult the task of demonstrating the compatibility of self-interest and moral action. But despite these shortcomings, his accomplishments are remarkable, and his importance in the development of Greek moral theory is indisputable.

My discussion of Democritus' views brings to a fitting close this study of early Greek moral theory. The next advances in the defense of acting morally are those made by Plato. But Plato clearly owed much to the work of his predecessors. Indeed, my analysis of Protagoras, Antiphon, and Democritus has shown that they laid out all the central issues and many of the arguments which are relevant to the question of the relationship between morality and a person's egoistic good.

Notes

1. Commentators are in general agreement that Democritus was born around 460 B.C. The date of his death, however, is a more controversial issue. In suggesting that he died around 396 B.C., I am following Davison (pp. 38-39). For a general discussion of Democritus' dates and life, see Guthrie, II, 386-387.

2. For a discussion of the various writings of Democritus, see Freeman, *The Pre-Socratic Philosophers,* pp. 293-299.

3. It is a rather commonly held view that Democritus was not a systematic moral theorist. Bailey, for example, remarks that "Democritus' 'ethic' hardly amounts to a moral theory: there is no effort to set the picture of the 'cheerful' man on a firm philosophical basis . . ." (*The Greek Atomists and Epicurus* (New York: Russell & Russell, 1964), p. 522). For a selective bibliography of others who share Bailey's view, see Guthrie, II, 492, n.1. In general, those commentators who disagree with Bailey's assessment do so on grounds that there is a systematic connection between Democritus' ethical and physical theories. However, my analysis in this chapter will show that Democritus' moral views are philosophical, systematic, and perfectly intelligible apart from any consideration of their connection to his physical views. And, in fact, I shall not discuss this issue. On my view there is simply not enough evidence to establish the connection in question. Vlastos' attempt to establish it is the most elaborate, impressive, and ambitious one to date ("Ethics and Physics in Democritus," *Philosophical Review* 54 (1945), 578-592 and 55 (1946), 53-64). Taylor, however, has convincingly shown that Vlastos' arguments are open to very serious doubts ("Pleasure, Knowledge and Sensation in Democritus," *Phronesis* 12 (1967), 6-27, esp. 8-16). Barnes (II, 231-232) briefly evaluates the vari-

ous theories of those who argue for a systematic connection between Democritus' ethical and physical views and concludes, rightly I think, that the fragments do not support their theories. Indeed, the very attempt to establish the connection may be questionable. As Barnes remarks, "Ethics and physics, so far as I can see, have no systematic interconnexion at all; in many boring little ways a man's natural philosophy will rub off on his moralizing, but no general or systematic influence is even conceivable. The long scholarly discussion of the possible 'materialistic foundation' of Democritus' ethics is empty. . . ." On the other hand, ethics and physics can, as Barnes notes, be inconsistent. And they appear to be in Democritus: his physical theory is deterministic, while the ethical fragments take it as given that man has free will. On this point, see Bailey, p. 188.

4. Essentially two arguments are employed to cast doubt on the authenticity of the ethical fragments, specifically those fragments preserved in the Stobaeus anthology (frr. 169-297) and the fragments in the Democrates (*sic*) collection (frr. 35-115). First, no ancient source, including Plato and Aristotle, even mentions that Democritus had any interest in moral theory until Seneca in the first century A.D. remarks that Democritus wrote an excellent book about *euthymia* (*De tranquilitate animi* II.3); if Democritus had been the author of ethical writings, surely the ancient sources would have mentioned this and discussed his views. And even if one could explain how the ancient sources could have been silent about Democritus' moral theory for over four hundred years, one could not give a reasonable account of how his ethical writings would have been preserved and transmitted. This first argument has been plausibly countered by both Stewart ("Democritus and the Cynics," *Harvard Studies in Classical Philology* 63 (1958), 179-191) and Voros ("The Ethical Fragments of Democritus: The Problem of the Authenticity," *Hellenica* 26 (1973), 193-206). In brief, Stewart argues that (1) the Cynics were interested in various aspects of Democritus' moral views and thus preserved his ethical writings and (2) for a variety of reasons, the other ancient philosophical schools were not interested in his views or were actually hostile to them. Voros agrees that it was the Cynics who were originally interested in Democritus' moral theory, but additionally argues that Democritus' ethical writings became available at the Ptolemaic Library in Alexandria and that Seneca, Clement, and perhaps even Diogenes Laertius actually read Democritus' book on *euthymia,* a book which could have been available later to Stobaeus. The second argument against the authenticity of the ethical fragments is that they are trivial and hence could not have been written by a first-rate thinker like Democritus. Guthrie relies heavily on this argument (II, 489-492). It is my view, however, that they

are not trivial; and I trust that my analysis of them in this chapter will convince the reader of that view. Given that the ethical fragments reflect concerns which were current in Democritus' lifetime and given the lack of force of the two arguments against the authenticity of the ethical fragments, I see no reason not to attribute these fragments to Democritus. Of course, the case for the authenticity of the fragments would be secured if it could be established that there is a connection between Democritus' views in the ethical fragments and his physical theory; but as suggested in n. 3 above, such a connection cannot be established

5. On p. 84, I defend the view that the intelligence and knowledge referred to in fr. 181 are to be understood as (self-regarding) practical wisdom or prudence.

6. The Greek reads: *toisi gar peithomenoisi ten idien areten endeiknytai. 'Idien areten'* could mean either (1) the excellence (*arete*) which belongs to *nomos* or (2) the excellence which belongs to men (if they obey *nomos*). Colvin notes that translators have wavered in their interpretation of this passage; but he concludes, rightly I think, that *'idien areten'* is best interpreted in sense (2) ("A New Look at the Ethics of Democritus," Diss. Indiana Univ. 1974, pp. 104-105).

7. It needs to be kept in mind throughout that I am not claiming that Democritus was necessarily directly attempting to refute Antiphon, but rather that he was attempting to refute those who held views similar to Antiphon's.

8. Diels-Kranz, 68.A167.

9. *Lives of the Philosophers* IX.45.

10. Diels-Kranz, 68.B4.

11. McGibbon suggests the different terms Democritus used for the ideal state were related as follows: "*Euthymia, euesto* and *eudaimonia* are wider terms than the others, the last two perhaps describing the ideal state in an overall way from an outside viewpoint, while *euthymia* gives emphasis to the subject as actually feeling. *Harmonia* and *symmetria* refer to the balance in the ideal state, the former perhaps emphasizing the difference of the ingredients which go to make it, the latter stressing the correct proportion in which these different ingredients are mixed. Finally, *ataraxia* and *athambia* indicate that the ideal state is not subject to disturbance" ("Pleasure as the 'Criterion' in Democritus," *Phronesis* 5 (1960), 75-77, esp. 76-77).

12. In my discussion of Democritus' conception of the good for persons, I shall not attempt to give a complete characterization of the man who possesses *euthymia.* I restrict my analysis to what will be relevant to the issue of the compatibility of morality and self-interest.

13. Taylor sees overall pleasure as *the* central feature of Democritus' notion of *euthymia* ("Pleasure," pp. 16-19). I generally agree with his view.

14. Indeed, his argument would not be valid if it were not directed against those who derive their pleasure exclusively from sensations. If the people Democritus is discussing in this fragment derived their pleasures from sensations *and* other things, it would not necessarily be true that their souls would always be in a constant state of unrest. Whether or not their souls would be in such a state would depend on what additional pleasures they pursued and how they pursued them.

15. For example, Natorp, *Die Ethika des Demokritos: Text und Untersuchung* (Marburg, 1893) and Voros, "The Ethical Theory of Democritus: What is the 'Criterion'?, *Platon* 27 (1975), 20-25.

16. As far as I can tell, absolutely nothing can be made of the fact that the word for pleasure in fr. 188 is '*terpsis*' while in fr. 74 the word used is '*hedu*'. Voros thinks differently: for him, *terpsis* is Democritus' term for intellectual pleasures, while *hedu* is a term used for any pleasure ("The Ethical Theory of Democritus: What Is the 'Criterion'?", pp. 22-24). But it seems to me that these two terms (or cognates) are used synonymously in frr. 211 and 235. Indeed, the *terpsis* in question in fr. 235, far from being intellectual pleasure, is that short pleasure derived from sensations immediately after, say, eating or drinking. See also n. 20 below.

17. As Vlastos argues, talk of the divine and the gods (e.g., fr. 175) is not to be taken literally ("Ethics and Physics," pp. 580-582). The existence of life after death is denied in fr. 297.

18. My analysis of Democritus' conception of human good so far in this chapter suggests, but does not actually establish that he did not hold such a theory. What I have said about his views could be spelled out in such a way as to be made compatible with the view that intellectual pleasure is the criterion for advantage.

19. Taylor nicely shows that some of the fragments thought to refer to intellectual pleasures (e.g., frr. 194, 112) are best interpreted in a different way ("Pleasure," pp. 6-8).

20. This circumstance is simply too uncommon for Democritus to have emphasized the need to moderate intellectual pleasure. And the fact that it is ordinarily inappropriate to talk about moderating intellectual pleasure is another indication that *terpsis* is not Democritus' word for intellectual pleasure; for in frr. 191 and 211, he specifically mentions the need to moderate *terpsis* (fr. 191) and *ta terpna* (fr. 211).

21. Again, since Democritus is talking about moderation in pursuit of pleasure, he would not be talking about intellectual pleasures in these two fragments (211 and 233). Fr. 211 merely claims that moderation increases pleasure; and it would be implausible to suggest that this claim involves the view that moderation of lower pleasures increases intellectual pleasures.

22. Democritus would not be claiming wealth is a potentially dangerous possession if he had moderate wealth in mind, given that he thinks moderate wealth is safe (fr. 285). Further, the fact that wealth is juxtaposed with fame (*doxa*) also indicates that the level of wealth in question is substantial.

23. I am not, of course, implying that Democritus thought any given person should pursue all available pleasures. Besides, Democritus remarks in fr. 69 that what is good and true is the same for all men, but that this is not the case for what is pleasant. Thus, what pleasures a particular person actually pursues will depend on his temperament although it is in each person's interest to balance the pleasures in his soul so as to promote *euthymia*. A person's temperament might be such that he finds his pleasure in intellectual pursuits and finds no pleasure in wealth and possessions beyond the barest minimum needed for survival. But, of course, most people do not have such a temperament; and as I have been, in effect, arguing in the text, Democritus does not suggest that it is each person's true good to have or work towards having such a temperament or to measure advantage by the standard of what promotes intellectual pleasure.

24. My resolution of the apparent discrepancy between frr. 188 and 74 comes closest to Taylor's ("Pleasure," pp. 16-19). For other attempts to resolve the apparent discrepancy, see Vlastos ("Ethics and Physics," pp. 586-590) and McGibbon ("Pleasure," pp. 75-76).

25. "Pleasure," pp. 7, 17-18.

26. Democritus would agree with this truism on grounds that desire and pursuit of the impossible would create constant disturbances in one's soul and because one would always be feeling deficient and desiring more (than one has).

27. Traditionally the Greeks were of the view that one important component of good fortune was abundant wealth. In fr. 286 Democritus counters this view to some extent: "The man of good fortune is one who is happy with moderate means; the man of ill-fortune is one who is unhappy with great possessions."

28. Fr. 83 is almost certainly referring to immoral action. Democritus regularly uses '*hamartia*' (and cognates) to designate actions which involve disregard for the interests of others. See frr. 41, 181, 253, and 265; but cf. fr. 228.

29. Many of the fragments mention or imply that one needs to act with intelligence in order to promote one's self-interest. See also frr. 52, 54, 58, 119, 236, 292.

30. Guthrie (II, 490) notes that fr. 45 is "astonishingly Socratic or Platonic" and thinks it is one of the fragments that indicates that the ethical fragments are not authentic. It could also be noted here that fr. 45 is one of the fragments from the Democrates collection, fragments whose authenticity is more open to doubt than those found in Stobaeus. However, my interpretation of Democritus does not depend on fr. 45 being authentic. It would still be clear from other fragments that (1) he held the view that acting morally promotes one's self-interest and (2) he thought he could provide a substantive defense of that view.

31. pp. 59-60 and n. 23.

32. p. 32. Irwin's remarks about Democritus are brief, and I have added some details to the argument he attributes to Democritus.

33. I discussed this passage from the *Protagoras* on p. 44.

34. The arguments of Socrates which Irwin seems to have in mind are found in the *Gorgias, Republic* I, and perhaps even *Republic* IV, as well as those partial arguments found in various early dialogues. Irwin provides a thorough and excellent critique of these arguments throughout his book; but see especially pp. 52-53, 57-60, 125-127, 177-189, and 212-217.

35. The issue here is complicated. On the one hand, the notion of *euthymia* as complete satisfaction involves the view that it is not in one's self-interest to act immorally—on the assumption that such action only occurs when one attempts to increase one's goods. On the other hand, it does not in any obvious sense involve the further view that increasing one's goods is not in one's self-interest *because such action is motivated by jealousy*. But in the present context, it is precisely this further view which needs to be defended. Democritus would be able to present the following plausible argument: (Virtually) everyone's good is sufficient for the good life; and everyone can and should experience his good as fullness. Dissatisfaction arises when someone compares his own goods with the goods others have and, as a result, finds his own goods deficient. This is the source of jealousy. The jealousy in question, however, would not necessarily involve ill-will towards others or the desire to increase one's good at their expense.

36. To determine how many different circumstances there would be in which acting unjustly might be beneficial, one would need to spell out in detail all the restrictions Democritus placed on pursuing an increase of goods. I have not tried to spell out either of these things in detail. To do so would not be productive—or even fair to Democritus—unless we had more of his writings.

37. Democritus probably did not consider his argument from fear an important one because he recognized its weakness and because he, like Socrates/Plato, wanted to defend just action on grounds of its intrinsic advantages. The complete text of fr. 41 is as follows: "Do not refrain from wrongdoing because of fear, but because of what is necessary/needful (*to deon*)." Voros takes *'to deon'* to mean moral duty and calls this fragment "the noblest moment" of Democritus' moral theory ("The Ethical Theory of Democritus: "On Duty," *Platon* 26 (1974), 113-122, esp. 119). I do not think *'to deon'* means moral duty, but the issue here is complex and concerns the question of whether Democritus had a notion of conscience and adopted the moral point of view as his criterion for action (in circumstances where the interests of others are at issue). If he did adopt this criterion, then it would be his view that agents should act morally whether or not such action is in their self-interest. Inasmuch as Democritus thought moral action congruent with self-interest, practically speaking, nothing is at stake in the question of whether or not he adopted the moral point of view as his criterion for action (in appropriate circumstances). My own view is that he did not adopt this criterion, but I do not have room to discuss this issue here. I hope to do so in a future paper.

38. In the claim that altruism is a component of one's own good, the good in question cannot be (exclusively) egoistic or self-interested. The good of altruism cannot be defended on grounds of self-interest: to act altruistically is precisely *not* to act from reasons of self-interest. One could only argue that agents have *self-regarding* reasons to act altruistically. For the distinction between self-regarding and self-interested reasons, see n. 2 in Chapter One.

39. pp. 254-259. The notion of altruism as a component of one's own good is not a prominent feature of Plato's and Aristotle's moral theory. In fact, I am not entirely convinced that Plato even had this notion.

40. I realize that I am being rather speculative in constructing an argument which the evidence suggests Democritus might have used if he argued for a view which I think he might have held. However, it is for the purpose of exploring all possibilities that I construct the argument.

41. Two things need to be noted here. First, the mourning in question (*olophyresthai*) obviously cannot be such that it is incompatible with *euthymia*. And second, the text of the fragment does not actually specify who should be the object of mourning: oneself or the others who have met misfortune. The argument requires that the man with *euthymia* mourn for others, and not just for himself; but, of course, this step in the argument is the crucial and controversial one.

Works Cited

Bailey, Cyril. *The Greek Atomists and Epicurus: A Study.* Oxford, 1928; rpt. New York: Russell and Russell, 1964.

Barnes, Jonathan. *The Pre-Socratic Philosophers.* Vol. II. London: Routledge & Kegan Paul, 1979.

Colvin, Michael G. "A New Look at the Ethics of Democritus." Diss. Indiana Univ. 1974.

Davison, J.A. "Protagoras, Democritus, and Anaxagoras." *Classical Quarterly,* NS 3 (1953), 33-45.

Diels, Hermann, and Walther Kranz. *Die Fragmente der Vorsokratiker.* 6th ed. 3 vols. Berlin: Weidmannsche Verlagsbuchhandlung, 1951-1952.

Freeman, Kathleen. *The Pre-Socratic Philosophers: A Companion to Diels, 'Fragmente der Vorsokratiker'.* 2nd ed. Cambridge, Mass.: Harvard Univ. Press, 1959.

Guthrie, W.K.C. *A History of Greek Philosophy.* Vols. II and III. Cambridge: Cambridge Univ. Press, 1965 and 1969.

Irwin, Terry. *Plato's Moral Theory: The Early and Middle Dialogues.* Oxford: Clarendon Press, 1977.

McGibbon, Donal. "Pleasure as the 'Criterion' in Democritus." *Phronesis* 5 (1960), 75-77.

Natorp, Paul. *Die Ethika des Demokritos: Text und Untersuchung.* Marburg, 1893.

Stewart, Zeph. "Democritus and the Cynics." *Harvard Studies in Classical Philology* 63 (1958), 179-191.

Taylor, C.C.W. "Pleasure, Knowledge and Sensation in Democritus." *Phronesis* 12 (1967), 6-27.

Vlastos, Gregory. "Ethics and Physics in Democritus." *Philosophical Review* 54 (1945), 578-592 and 55 (1946), 53-64.

Voros, F.K. "The Ethical Fragments of Democritus: The Problem of the Authenticity." *Hellenica* 26 (1973), 193-206.

———. "The Ethical Theory of Democritus: What Is the 'Criterion'?" *Platon* 27 (1975), 20-25.

Raymond Godfrey (essay date 1990)

SOURCE: "Democritus and the Impossibility of Collision," in *Philosophy,* Vol. 65, No. 252, April, 1990, pp. 212-17.

[*In the following essay, Godfrey explains a modern argument concerning the mathematical indivisibility of atoms and compares it to Greek thought on the subject.*]

The Abderite philosophers Leucippus and Democritus sought to solve many of the problems facing Greek thought in the fifth century B.C. by taking all things to be made up of atoms of matter moving in a void. One of the major controversies surrounding their work is whether their atomism was logical or merely physical. Did they consider their atoms to be mathematically indivisible?

An important cause of difficulty here is that Democritus seems to have been fully involved in the mathematics of his day[1] and to have been aware of the discussion of infinite divisibility and points with no magnitude, found, for example, in the paradoxes of Zeno.[2] It seems unlikely that such a man would cheerfully hold that his atoms could have shape without having parts and without having magnitude. The different shapes of atoms was a major part of his physical theory, which makes it difficult to see how he could have held that they were partless and thus mathematically indivisible.

On the face of it, the Abderites would have done more towards solving the logical problems of the day if the indivisibility of their atoms had been more than merely physical. It would, therefore, be convenient to have a mathematical interpretation of indivisibility which did not involve complete lack of magnitude and shape.

I hope to show that A. David Kline and Carl A. Matheson[3] provide a modern and revitalized version of something very close to the very arguments which Leucippus and Democritus advanced.

THE KLINE-MATHESON ARGUMENT

Kline and Matheson argue plausibly against the naive attractions of what they call completely mechanistic physics, by attempting to show that within such a theoretical framework there would be no possibility of collision. The completely mechanistic physics would thus lack the single mechanism claimed by it, in preference to any form of action at a distance.

Their argument is simply stated in seven succinct sentences. The bulk of their article attempts to identify all logically possible responses to the simple argument and to point out reasons why these are unattractive. What matters, however, is not whether they can make these responses unattractive to those of us who are sufficiently sophisticated to take various field theories in our stride, but whether they can make them appear unattractive in terms of criteria acceptable to those naive enough to espouse a completely mechanistic physics.

If Kline and Matheson are correct and if they had presented their arguments to Leucippus and Democritus, the Abderites would have accepted the impossibility of collision and deserted their completely mechanistic physics.

THREE MEANINGS OF 'TOUCHING'

The most contentious of the seven lines in Kline and Matheson's argument against the possibility of collision is:

'(2) If two bodies are touching, then they either occupy adjacent points in space or they overlap.'

This omits a third possibility (which they later admit) that two bodies are touching when the distance between them is zero. It is not fair on the Abderites to omit this here because it is quite likely that they would offer this interpretation of touching in preference to the other two.

That bodies should occupy adjacent points in space is impossible for anyone who accepts Kline and Matheson's statement:

'(3) Space is continuous'

But, although this employs the language and conceptual paraphernalia of modern mathematics, its acceptance does not require a modern mathematical training in the techniques and theory of analysis. Anyone familiar with the arguments of Zeno would have to be offered powerful counter-arguments before they would start thinking in terms of adjacent points. Only the modern codification was lacking in the fifth century understanding of these issues.[4]

Kline and Matheson argue that an adherent of a completely mechanistic physics could not defend the possibility of collision by allowing material bodies to overlap at a point since this would render completely mysterious the fact that the same bodies could not overlap further and thus pass through each other rather than collide and rebound in the manner required for a completely mechanistic physics. In connection with the Abderites this argument is unnecessary since the idea of physical objects overlapping is unacceptable to naive modern ears and we have no reason to suspect that it was less so to the Greeks.

There is no reason to think that the Abderites would have rejected the third interpretation. There was an argument current at that time that two things could not be separate without something to separate them.[5] If two adjacent atoms were to touch and yet remain two, they would need something to keep them separate. If they were adjacent then what was between them would have to be nothing. The Abderites held that the void was nothing.[6] There was also an idea in circulation that a geometrical point of zero magnitude was nothing.[7] A void of zero magnitude separating the atoms would meet all requirements and explain the Abderite view that the reason why two touching atoms can be separated is that there is void between them.[8] Thus when two atoms were 'touching' the distance between them would be zero.

The Topological Response

Kline and Matheson pick out, as the most interesting response to their argument, the topological response. This is the view that physical objects are topologically open and do not include their own boundaries. Thus, when two such bodies are in contact along a boundary, the boundary is not occupied by either of them. They take this response to be most interesting because, if anybody wished to make it, it would invalidate the argument against the possibility of collision. They offer three objections to this response.

The First Objection

Kline and Matheson 'find the assertion that a physical object does not include its boundary to be completely mysterious'. This claim, if seen as more than an introspective account of their personal experience, is not reasonable.

As the topological boundary of an object has zero width it is not open to inspection by the senses; so other considerations must determine what is the most attractive way to deal with this boundary. Since an atom in empty space must be surrounded by space, i.e. surrounded by nothing, and since what has zero width and zero volume is (in practical physical terms) nothing, it actually seems quite sensible to assign the boundary to empty space rather than to the atom itself.

This view obviously rests on an assumption that empty space is fairly freely interchangeable with nothing and this assumption could lead to arguments about whether a vacuum is something or about whether nothing is something which exists. In this sort of argument it would be difficult not to confuse grammar with insight and perhaps even more difficult not to feel pressed into certain statements merely to avoid appearing to confuse grammar with insight.[9]

In their completely mechanistic physics the Abderites clearly found it attractive to hold that the universe is made up of particles of matter in a void. It was also attractive (and, in a sense, correct) to see the particles of matter as being something and the void as being nothing.[10]

It is even possible to see that attraction in speaking of matter as that which is and the void as that which is not.[11] This is not the place, however, for a full discussion of that issue.

Now a material particle is surrounded by the void, i.e. surrounded by nothing. It is, therefore, quite natural to think of the object being bounded by nothing and thus having a boundary which is void.

These remarks clearly do not constitute an argument in favour of holding physical objects to be topologically open but they show that this view is not 'completely mysterious'. If some proponent of a completely mechanistic physics were to offer this as an argument, then people disposed to reject his views would be able no doubt to regard this as not much more than equivocation and confusion. It is no more so, however, than the view apparently assumed by Kline and Matheson, that it is natural to regard the boundary of a physical object as being part of that object.

The Second Objection

Kline and Matheson claim that an explanation must be provided of why all physical objects are open, why no physical objects include their boundaries. However, once someone accepts the attractiveness of the idea that a physical object should not include its boundaries (e.g. in the light of the comments above) it seems fruitless to try to distinguish between those objects which are open and those which are not. There would be nothing in their appearance to distinguish them. People would want to say pretty much the same sorts of things about them. The only way of detecting which objects were not open would be their inability to collide with other closed objects. Someone whose metaphysical leanings favoured the openness of physical objects would therefore find that the evidence of his senses, in so far as it was relevant, favoured the openness of all physical objects.[12] This would support his inclination to see objects in this way. There is nothing more objectionable in this than in any of the broad assumptions about the properties of all entities of a certain type which particle physics is bound to involve.

There would be no observable difference between a topologically open physical object and one which was exactly similar except that it was topologically closed. The topological boundary of the object has no volume and could not hold anything which could intervene in our perception of the open physical object or the closed object less its boundary.

An open physical object is not necessarily fuzzy in the way that a ball of wool is fuzzy. It could be smoother than a polished crystal ball. The object could extend exactly equally in all directions from a central point exactly as far as the boundary. Direct observation of an individual physical object would give us no cause for thinking either that it was open or that it was closed. Other considerations would have to help us decide. One such consideration might be the fact that collision and contact between physical objects is observed and from this we can deduce (by the arguments of Kline and Matheson) that for each part of the common boundary at least one of the objects in contact or collision fails to include it.

It would be rather more mysterious if rules were produced to tell us which object failed to include which parts of its boundary rather than simply accept that all physical objects are completely open in topological terms.

THE THIRD OBJECTION

Finally they state that a continuous open object split into two parts would not produce two open objects. The boundary between the two parts, having contained matter before the split, must contain matter after the split and thus one of the new physical objects would include at least part of its boundary. The consequent need for material particles to be seen as indivisible atoms is taken as making this position unattractive.

It is, in fact, difficult to see why an event which was grave enough to cause the particle to split (without moving) should not be grave enough to cause the matter (of zero mass and volume) in the boundary to move away (through zero distance).

The Greeks did take this sort of problem seriously.[13] If, however, Leucippus and Democritus held a view similar to that pilloried by Kline and Matheson, they would have no

need to consider the gravity of the events involved in atomic fission. They would have a sense in which their atoms could be mathematically indivisible whilst having shape and magnitude. Thus they would avoid most of the logical problems besetting the physics of their day and at the same time offer the only account of contact between extended material bodies which is acceptable when translated into standard modern topology.

Notes

1. When Thrasyllos arranged the works of Democritus in thirteen tetralogies, three of these were concerned with mathematics.

2. Ancient commentators were sufficiently impressed with the importance of the links between Democritus, Leucippus and Zeno that they report that Leucippus 'heard' Zeno.

3. 'The Logical Impossibility of Collision', *Philosophy* 62, No. 242 (October 1987), 509-15.

4. Strictly speaking there is no evidence that anyone before Aristotle hit upon the idea of the finite sum of an infinite series. If this element of our modern conceptual toolkit was absent from the fifth century, it seems to have been the only one.

5. Aristotle, *De Generatione et Corruptione* I.8.324b mentions this doctrine as part of the background against which the Abderite philosophy developed.

6. Cf., e.g., Aristotle, *Metaphysics* I.4.985b.

7. Simplicius, *Physics* 139, includes this as part of a long argument of Zeno.

8. Simplicius, *De Caelo* 242.

9. Cf. C. J. F. Williams, 'The Ontological Disproof of the Vacuum', *Philosophy*, 59, No. 229 (July 1984), 382-4.

10. Simplicius, *De Caelo* 294, cites Aristotle for this.

11. Cf. Aristotle *Metaphysics* I.4.985b.

12. Aristotle, *De Generatione et Corruptione* I.2.316a suggests that Democritus would have been interested in this sort of consideration.

13. Cf. the argument of Zeno already mentioned in note 7, which is concerned with the effect or lack of effect of adding a single point to an extended body and of removing a single point.

Reid Barbour (essay date 1992)

SOURCE: "Remarkable Ingratitude: Bacon, Prometheus, Democritus," in *Studies in English Literature, 1500-1900*, Vol. 32, No. 1, Winter, 1992, pp. 79-90.

[*In the following essay, Barbour explores the influence of Democritus on Francis Bacon's essay on Prometheus.*]

Despite Robert Kargon's argument that Bacon abandoned atomism, the seventeenth-century reformer never got Epicureanism off his mind.[1] More carefully than any of his contemporaries, Bacon explored the relations between the atomism, hedonism, and theology of Democritus, Epicurus, and Lucretius, which appear in a wide arrange of contexts and with an array of values in Bacon's works. At times Bacon praises the sect for their close observations of nature, or for their refusal of Aristotle; but he also scolds them for their anthropomorphisms or for their dogmatism. They succeed, Bacon believes, in looking beyond the formal bogeys of Plato and Aristotle into the particles and motions of nature, but err in idolizing the private blessings of their masters. Unlike his contemporaries, Bacon was capable of culling out the various strands of the philosophy; and though he sometimes confused the three major atomists, the reformer of science privileged Democritus as the father unspoiled by the prodigal errors of his Epicureanized sons.[2] But no matter what his preferences, the Greek philosophy of atomism and pleasure forced Bacon to clarify the place of his own science in a cosmos designed and controlled by divine providence. In its complex lineage and notorious heritage, Epicureanism represented to Bacon a provocative model of everything that was at once productive and dangerous about his own program of reform.

In several key texts, Bacon attempts to articulate the superior insights of Epicureanism, even as he distances his new learning from the Greek philosophy and its transgressions against God, order, and virtue. Several of the essays included among the interpretations of myth in *De Sapientia Veterum* have been read in the context of Greek atomism. I want to add another myth to this list already featuring Cupid and Coelum. Bacon's essay on Prometheus epitomizes his long and hard struggle with the Epicureans in the advancement of learning. In Bacon's reading of the myth, Democritus is at first applauded for opposing a Prometheus who stands against pleasure but for providence. Now Bacon knows that Democritus precedes the Epicureans per se. But given the infamous legacy of the sons of Democritus, the mythographer at last gives science back to Prometheus in an about face. Science appears to reside, then, somewhere between the myth and the philosophy, yet on no halcyon middle ground: for Prometheus and Democritus, the demigod and the atomist, can trade places in the most disconcerting fashion.

I

The trouble with Prometheus begins when Bacon glosses the thief of fire as "providence." According to Charles W. Lemmi, there was nothing new about this. Prometheus was often considered to represent "human forethought" and therefore "an enlightened leader and reformer who, so to speak, invented civilization."[3] Whatever the traditions behind Bacon's reading of the myth, this prudent and inventive Prometheus serves the new advancement of learning for clear and specific reasons:

> *Prometheus* doth cleerely and elegantly signifie *Prouidence*: For in the vniuersality of nature, the fab-

ricque and constitution of Man onely was by the Ancients pict out and chosen, and attributed vnto *Prouidence,* as a peculiar worke. The reason of it seemes to bee, not onely in that the nature of man is capable of a minde and vnderstanding, which is the seate of *Prouidence,* and therefore it would seeme strange and incredible that the reason and minde should so proceed and flowe from dumbe and deafe principles, as that it should necessarily be concluded, the soule of man to be indued with prouidence, not without the example, intention, and stampe of a greater prouidence.

> (124-25)

There are two providences with which Prometheus is allied: the one heavenly, the other human. Bacon insists here that the two are really one: human foresight is the seat of God's providence, which has designed and implanted that faculty in the human soul "as a peculiar worke." Never mind that Prometheus makes a career out of vexing Jupiter, who himself wants nothing more than to see the demigod punished. Prometheus represents for Bacon the perfect correspondence between a beneficent heaven and the world that it creates from "example, intention, and stampe." More than this, Prometheus proves that human beings center the universe and prevent it from lapsing into mere fortuity where "all things would seeme to stray and wander without purpose" (125). Everything in the cosmos serves humankind, for this is the great creator's plan.

There are obvious reasons why the harmony between heaven and humanity supports the advancement of learning. If the sciences demand of their human agents a clarity of vision with which to revise the past and to investigate nature anew, it certainly helps to know that God is behind the whole enterprise. One can imagine some problems: human providence may find itself disagreeing with the divine, or divine providence may find its human counterpart presuming just a little too much in the correspondence. Indeed, Bacon often worries about such conflicts and idols. In the essay on Prometheus, however, the correspondence between one providence and another begins to fail when Bacon glosses the mythical theft of fire and its aftermath. With his first transgression, Prometheus violates his providential stature on both counts: he challenges the prerogatives of a Jupiter whose vigilance is both more and less awake to the trickery; but he also fails to foresee the consequences of his own act, which according to Bacon are very strange indeed.

Legend has it that the human beneficiaries of Prometheus's crimes proved ungrateful, complaining to Jupiter who gave them perpetual youth for their efforts. That this gift was soon and carelessly squandered might lead a reader to think that humankind was punished for its lack of foresight, that is, its opposition to Prometheus. But Bacon turns the tables in the most astonishing fashion. Opposition to Prometheus was, Bacon claims, a first step in the advancement of learning:

> Seemes it not strange, that ingratitude towards the author of a benefit . . . should find such approbation

and reward? No, it seemes to be otherwise: for the meaning of the Allegory is this, That mens outcries vpon the defects of nature and Arte, proceed from an excellent disposition of the minde, and turne to their good, whereas the silencing of them is hatefull to the Gods, and redounds not so much to their profit.

(129)

In this analysis, Prometheus stands for the tyranny of tradition over science, for the slavery of the human mind to authorities (like Aristotle) or to unexamined paradigms of nature. If Prometheus has occluded the progress of exploration and discovery, then it follows that providence itself is culpable. But Bacon has given us two kinds of providence. "Foresight" might deserve some blame if its premature assumptions block the ongoing experience of natural phenomena. That is, foresight might depend on the belief that there will be no surprises in nature or throughout history. But God's providence, or rather human reconstructions of its divine schemes, can obstruct the advancement of learning too. Nature goes wanting as men and women look to the heavens for all their answers. Once supportive of the sciences but now stagnant, both heavenly and human providences lock the new learning in a stranglehold that some alternative hero must break. That hero proves to be Democritus.

II

The argument that human submission to divine providence impedes the reform of life on earth was, as Bacon knew well, Epicurean. As if on cue, Democritus enters the essay on Prometheus, opposing the stasis that the mythic hero represents. Throughout his works, Bacon admires Democritus more than the successive atomists who added hedonism, heightened fortuity, and emphasized the theological superstructure of Epicurus's intermundane gods. Sometimes this admiration goes so far as to argue that Democritus affirms providence.[4] In "Of Atheism," he is but one of the atomists who proves the providence of God no matter what tradition holds. In Bacon's reading of the myth of Coelum, however, Democritus is singled out for his proximity to scripture: "This Fable seemes enigmatically to shew from whence all things tooke their beginning, not much differing from that opinion of philosophers, which *Democritus* afterwards laboured to mainteine, attributing eternity to the first Matter and not to the world. In which he comes somwhat neere the truth of diuine writ, telling vs of a huge deformed Masse, before the beginning of the six daies worke" (62). In the same essay, Bacon cites Lucretius's hope that the *gubernans fortuna* will see fit to defer the collapse of the world; Bacon's translator, Gorges, renders the Latin phrase as "guiding prouidence" (64-65).

Bacon seems intent, then, on aligning Democritus with providence of both kinds; the Greek was among the first to approach nature with a care like that which Bacon wants for his moderns, and his atomism proves God's designs on the world, no matter what the intentions of the atomist himself. But Bacon knew well that Democritus's atomism

stood emphatically against providence. For Bacon, as for many seventeenth-century authors, the "dumbe and deafe principles" opposing providence were, more often than not, the atoms that Democritus and Epicurus imagined as the basis of all things.[5] In his reading of Cupid, as in other texts, Bacon leaves no trace of a doubt that he associated Epicurus with Democritus as two theorists of the atom, and that he exerted great effort in rethinking the atom whose qualities he likens to Cupid's blindness, nakedness, archery, and age. Both Cupid and the atom are beyond the scope of the senses—hence Democritus's contention that truth lies hidden in a dark well. The atom is, moreover, the "*principium*" that both rivals providence as the first cause, and erases providence altogether. Only a providential God could build "order and beautie" out of atoms, but those same atoms, the "principall law of Nature," are "things emptie and destitute of prouidence, and as it were blinde" (82). Atoms may be pure and indivisible—they may indeed prove that God exists—but the legacy of atomism unsettles any complacent belief in the harmony of the two providences.

For Bacon, Democritus questions more than just Promethean providence; the atomist also challenges the hegemony of Aristotle for which Prometheus stands. But Democritus is not really an extremist whose place it is to gravitate as far away from fixity as possible. Rather, Bacon credits the father of atomism with a productive reconciliation between exploratory skepticism and a conclusive dogmatism: the Greek philosopher "with great moderation complained how that all things were inuolued in a mist . . . that wee know nothing, that wee discerned nothing, that trueth was drowned in the depthes of obscuritie, and that false things were wonderfully ioynd and intermixt with true" (130-31). As Montaigne knew, Epicureans can be read as committed dogmatists or inquisitive skeptics: their belief in the atoms and void aspires to certainty, yet their challenge to formal metaphysics and traditional ethics encourages a distrust of received ideas.[6] In his essay on Prometheus, however, Bacon sees Democritus as a moderate skeptic, poised between the extreme skepticism of the New Academy and the blind confidence of the Peripatetics. Indeed, not long after his praise for the atomist, the mythographer applauds the marriage of the "*Dogmaticall* and *Empiricall*," which entails a methodized experience of nature, "the conduct of experience, as by a certaine rule and method" (133).

Midway through the reading of Prometheus, then, Democritus emerges as a harbinger of induction, opposing a providence that can paralyze the advancement of learning. But in other works by Bacon, Democritus proves Promethean in two ways, affirming God's providence but also casting the shadow of authority over Epicurus and his followers. Conversely, Prometheus can turn Democritean in his reformation of the human sciences. In *De Augmentis Scientiarum,* for instance, Prometheus's discovery of fire is celebrated for its fortuity—for its elevation of experience and chance over logic.[7] At the end of Bacon's reading of Promethean myth, moreover, the games held in honor of the mythic hero are said to represent human cooperation in the promotion of science. In the heritage of these games, Prometheus stands as the first demigod to challenge the few idolized authorities preventing the reformation of the organon.

Even if the Promethean games fail to promote the idealized providence with which Bacon begins, his Prometheus returns nonetheless to supplant the Democritus who has figured so centrally in the explanation of human ingratitude. Yet Bacon goes even further in undercutting the legacy of Democritus. Between Bacon's reading of human ingratitude and his interpretation of the Promethean games lies Pandora, whom Bacon, like Comes, aligns with pleasure.[8] No matter that Democritus is not directly responsible for the hedonism of Epicurus: even so, Pandora introduces the most controversial and potentially embarrassing creed of Democritus's followers. Although Bacon separates the philosophical aspects of the myth from its religious and moral facets, he was too careful a student of Epicureanism not to know that atomism and hedonism are linked in that philosophy.[9] Joining the atom and desire, his Cupid is but one instance of the growing Renaissance awareness that the Epicureans were at once atomists and hedonists. Pandora, who falls under the moral rubric of the gloss, threatens with pleasure the Prometheus whose allegiance to the fatalism and pleasure-hating of the Stoics is written large toward the end of the essay.

As a stand-in for Epicurus, whose name he partly bears, Epimetheus betrays providence at the moment when he embraces pleasure: in their love of "voluptuousnes," "they that are of *Epimetheus* his sect, are improuident, not foreseeing what may come to passe hereafter, esteeming that best which seemes most sweete for the present" (137). Despite Bacon's remark in another text that the Epicureans were always good citizens, this combination of anti-providentialism and hedonism is said to wreak havoc on kingdoms and commonwealths.[10] Prometheus's games, we have seen, reclaim him for the cause of new learning. But no matter what Prometheus's failures in the advancement of learning, his foresight is partly redeemed by the imprudence of his brother in the moral section of the mythography.

But not wholly. The "schollers" who follow Prometheus "are men endued with prudence," but they err insofar as "they depriue themselues, and defraud their *Genius* of many lawfull pleasures, and diuers recreations" (138). From Erasmus and Valla to Robert Burton, Renaissance writers attempt to dispel misguided notions of Epicurean hedonism, and to show that by "pleasure," Epicurus meant a tranquillity of mind and soundness of body enabled by a life of virtue.[11] In the early decades of the seventeenth century, English authors have a vested interest in the debate over hedonism insofar as the court and its church take such an emphatic position in approving the festive or sacred uses of pleasure. When Bacon tells us that the eagle gnawing at Prometheus's liver is the very emblem of "fresh anxieties and feares," his defense of innocent pleasure is

even more clearly Epicurean. Just such anxieties could be cleared by the "lawful pleasures" advanced from Epicurus to the Book of Sport. Although Bacon does not acknowledge it, his citation of Virgil's well-known lines describes the Lucretian Epicurus as well as anyone: "Happie is hee that knowes the cause of things, / And that with dauntlesse courage treads vpon / All feare and Fates" (140). With a knowledge "de rerum natura," Epicurus tempers fatalism and its discontents just as surely as he challenges the authority of Aristotle and Plato.

For Bacon, then, Prometheus represents the failure of a culture not just to advance the new science, but also to mitigate the anxiety of fatalism with pleasure. These failures can spell trouble for the commonwealth. In his essay on sedition, Bacon remarks that Epimetheus is perhaps better equipped than his brother to handle discontent in the state because the improvident brother gives vent to calamity yet keeps hope alive for the people.[12] It is, after all, Prometheus, not his brother, who suffers for his transgressions. And it is the thief of fire whose booty leads a commonwealth into voluptuous laxity in the first place:

> And it is a common, but apt, interpretation, by *Pandora* to be meant pleasure & voluptuousnes, which (when the ciuill life is pampered with too much Arte, and culture, and superfluitie) is ingendred, as it were, by the efficacy of fire, and therefore the worke of voluptuousnes is attributed vnto Vulcan, who also himselfe doth represent fire.
>
> (136)

Given the dangers of pleasure, Bacon makes the case that the "commodities of prouidence" depend on Stoicism and Christianity: in rescuing Prometheus, Hercules embodies both the fortitude of Seneca and the incarnation of Christ. But the value of these commodities is unstable in the advancement of learning against providence; pleasures—both "pampered" and "lawfull"—only add to the instability of the myth.

At the end of his reading of Prometheus, Bacon places his own allegory—and his own program—in a Promethean position. The author admits his likeness to Prometheus when he stops short of a full-scale interpretation of the myth's religious import, remarking that he has "interdicted [his] penne all liberty in this kinde, lest [he] should vse strange fire at the altar of the Lord" (144). Prometheus, we recall, not only stole fire but offered a mocksacrifice to Jupiter. Bacon's offering of religious allegory seems to return fire as a mock-offering, to repeat the kind of "strange" ingratitude that humanity showed their providential maker. But the erasure of the religious import of the myth imitates the Epicureans in removing providence altogether, leaving Bacon to search the recesses of nature for atoms, not for the handwriting of God.

If the Epicureans encourage the isolation of the gods from human science, Prometheus tries to collapse the two in his attempted rape of Minerva. Bacon mentions the transgression as an afterthought, but his reading of the episode is crucial for science:

> which is nothing els but to shewe, that when we are puft vp with much learning and science, they goe about oftentimes, to make euen diuine Oracles subject to sense and reason, whence most certainly followes a continual distraction, & restlesse griping of the mind.
>
> (141)

As innocent pleasures pacify the soul and heal the body, so the humble division of oracles and sense cures the "restlesse griping of the mind." There are problems with this advice too. A dichotomy between nature and grace can segregate the human sciences so that they become utterly profane—this Charles notes in his copy of Bacon's *Advancement.*[13] At the very least, the barrier between human providence and divine might serve as a cover for the Epicurean tendency to elevate a few privileged mortals to the level of the gods. Indeed more than once Bacon comments on "the opinion of Epicurus . . . who supposed the gods to be of human shape" (*Advancement,* 119). But no matter what the hidden dangers of separating divinity and science, Prometheus's rape is openly blasphemous or at best inhibitive, figuring the "continual distraction" of the scientist by theology. As Bacon's reading of the myth proceeds, the ideal conjunction of human and divine providences is replaced either by extreme divisions or by impious conflations of the two.

III

Between divinity and fortuity, Bacon's program for the advancement of learning models itself on two rivals, Prometheus and Democritus. But the two keep changing places. Prometheus is at once rebel and authority; Democritus, at once skeptic and dogmatist. Both have their theological perils. Democritus denies (but also proves) providence, while Prometheus, always irksome to Jupiter, represents providence in its two senses. One fathers a sect of hedonists, while the other is punished for his flagrant disregard for Jupiter's feelings. Neither the hero nor the philosopher is quite right for the advancement of learning. In his preface to *The Wisdom of the Ancients,* Bacon proposes that myth hides philosophy—as nature hides both atoms and providence—from the vulgar eye. Yet the dynamic between myth and philosophy is much more vexed than hide-and-seek. Bacon's science must navigate an ever changing field of discourse; it must seek a productive and secure position between a centered vision (that may prove myopic) and a radical materialism (that may turn blind). One critic, John C. Briggs, has shown the considerable effort that Bacon devoted to articulating the religious analogues of his great instauration. In the manner of the essay on Prometheus, these negotiations between the sacred and profane are altogether paradoxical.[14]

For all his advancement of science and humanity, Prometheus represents for Bacon the fixed and traditional, the divine and mortal providence that anticipates what it already knows, that locates humanity in the center of a cosmos whose structure is deduced from the assumption of providence. Prometheus transgresses on the side of stasis, of what humankind has always imagined itself to be. But Democritus and Epicurus herald a reform whose dangers include an anti-providential materialism and troublesome hedonism, and whose discoveries can topple over into a dispersive skepticism or, more likely, a new dogmatism. Locked in an embrace between the myth and the philosophy, Baconian science labors for its own space, method, and agenda. Perhaps, with all the perils of discovering fire or envisioning atoms, the ancients were wise to hide the dangers of science in a myth. Or maybe the delays in the advancement of learning have been fortuitous: time, Bacon declares, submerged the truths of the atomist. Whatever the impediments of the past, the myths of *De Sapientia Veterum* are among Bacon's most provocative recognitions that the deepest commitments of seventeenth-century culture, including its investments in providence, might prove some strange ingratitude to God, "equalizing, in a manner, their owne defects with Gods perfection" (129). Without warning, Prometheus might change into Democritus, and vice versa.

With his program of reform, then, Bacon presents strange fire to the gods controlling his world. Like Prometheus, he offers two bulls, one by which science promises to obey the gods, the other by which science mocks their providential designs. As one critic has said, Bacon's Prometheus and Epimetheus are more than brothers; they are almost interchangeable.[15] With Epicurus in the role of the improvident brother, Bacon's essay on the "state of man" makes gestures toward the wider Stuart contexts of science and its dilemmas. It is true that Bacon wavers in the value that he assigns the atomists; their account of physical causes may prove excellent—"more real and better enquired than that of Aristotle and Plato" (*Advancement,* 96)—or "ignorant"—"a meere toy" (*De Sapientia Veterum,* 81). But it is equally true that Bacon promotes the same ambivalence about another Stuart discourse—one also caught between mechanism and the gods—This discourse is the masque, which epitomizes the Stuart uncertainty about how to justify a godlike power when so many rival factions are vying for the authority of God's providence. It would not have surprised Bacon, had he lived to see it, that the masquers of the 1630s were asked to envision their monarchs and nobles as so many refined atoms. Nor would it have surprised him that the masque-makers spent more and more time on the machines by which these atomic gods could make their grand entrances. That the metaphoric power of the atom would make its way into defenses of political authority is an event that Bacon recommends.[16]

In his reading of the Promethean myth, Bacon may "interdict" his pen from crossing the line dividing science from the rest of culture; but myth, Bacon knows, does not respect these lines, converting one signification into another without gratitude for the intentions of the myth-maker. "Neither am I ignorant how fickle and inconstant a thing fiction is," he writes in the preface to *De Sapientia*

Veterum, by way of apology for his usurpation of the very myths that might defy Bacon's own designs on nature. Like fortuitous atoms, so myth: the interpreter hopes for an internal fixity—of particle, of meaning—that might get lost in transmission. But myth is not alone in its slippages: philosophy, too, especially that spawned by Bacon's favorite, Democritus, is virtually fictive in eluding the grasp of its glossator.

Notes

1. Robert Hugh Kargon, *Atomism in England from Hariot to Newton* (Oxford: Clarendon Press, 1966), pp. 43-53. For Bacon's "consistent . . . interest" in atomism, see Graham Rees, "Atomism and 'Subtlety' in Francis Bacon's Philosophy," *Annals of Science* 37, 5 (September 1980): 549-71; and Lisa Jardine, *Francis Bacon: Discovery and the Art of Discourse* (Cambridge: Cambridge Univ. Press, 1974), p. 114. I cite the *De Sapientia Veterum* from its 1619 translation by Arthur Gorges (New York: Garland, 1976); the text for all other works by Bacon is *The Philosophical Works of Francis Bacon,* ed. John M. Robertson (New York: Dutton, 1905). All citations will appear in the text.

2. For Bacon's revival of atomism, see Fulton Henry Anderson, *The Philosophy of Francis Bacon* (Chicago: Univ. of Chicago Press, 1948).

3. Charles W. Lemmi, *The Classic Deities in Bacon: A Study in Mythological Symbolism* (Baltimore: Johns Hopkins Univ. Press, 1933), pp. 128-40, 129, 128. For the importance of providence in Bacon's program, see Sidney Warhaft, "The Providential Order in Bacon's New Philosophy," in *Francis Bacon's Legacy of Texts: "The Art of Discovery,"* ed. William A. Sessions (New York: AMS Press, 1990), pp. 151-67.

4. Cf. *Of the Advancement of Learning,* pp. 96-97 on Democritus's division of science from theology: "Neither doth this call in question or derogate from divine providence, but highly confirm and exalt it." Bacon isn't the only one in the seventeenth century to argue that atomism confirms the mysterious workings of God better than does plenism; and the idea extends to the praise of a monarch who creates a masque as though out of atoms (in *The King and Queenes Entertainement at Richmond,* 1636).

5. Lucretius's is the seminal text in the use of *principium* for the atom, but the usage is common in the seventeenth century; for example, in Nicholas Hill's *Philosophia Epicurea* (1601, 1619). Again from Lucretius, atoms are "blind" in two senses, fortuitous and invisible. In his essay on Cupid, Bacon differentiates between Epicurus and Democritus regarding their theories of atomic motion; but he knows that whatever their differences, the two agree on the basic constituents of the universe.

6. Montaigne's interest in the Epicureans is visible on almost every page of his essays. But he writes in the tradition of humanists (Valla, More, Erasmus, and others) who revitalized the hedonism of the Greek sect.

7. "And if you like better, according to the tradition of the Greeks, to ascribe the first inventions to men; yet you would not say that Prometheus was led by speculation to the discovery of fire, or that when he first struck the flint he expected the spark; but rather that he lighted on it by accident, and (as they say) stole it from Jupiter" (*De Augmentis,* p. 501).

8. See Lemmi, *The Classic Deities in Bacon,* p. 130. In 1621 Richard Brathwaite explicitly connects Pandora to Epicurus; see *Natures Embassie* (Boston: Robert Roberts, 1877), p. 128.

9. Diskin Clay comments on growing scholarly care in the Renaissance over the relation between the atomists. See *Lucretius and Epicurus* (Ithaca: Cornell Univ. Press, 1983), p. 54.

10. See *De Augmentis,* p. 549: "It was not the Epicureans but the Stoics that troubled the ancient states."

11. For one example of early seventeenth-century authors revaluing Epicurean pleasure, see Robert Burton, *The Anatomy of Melancholy,* ed. Holbrook Jackson (New York: Vintage, 1977), 2:102: "A quiet mind is that *voluptas,* or *summum bonum,* of Epicurus . . . not to grieve, but to want cares and have a quiet soul, is the only pleasure of the world, as Seneca truly recites his opinion, not that of eating and drinking, which injurious Aristotle maliciously puts upon him, and for which he is mistaken . . . slandered without a cause, and lashed by all posterity."

12. See Jerry Weinberger, *Science, Faith, and Politics: Francis Bacon and the Utopian Roots of the Modern Age: A Commentary on Bacon's "Advancement of Learning"* (Ithaca: Cornell Univ. Press, 1985), pp. 158-61.

13. Charles's copy of *Advancement* is in the British Library; his response that the Epicurean reaction against superstition leads to profanity is written in answer to the aphorism recorded in note 10 above.

14. John C. Briggs, *Francis Bacon and the Rhetoric of Nature* (Cambridge, MA and London: Harvard University Press, 1989).

15. See Weinberger, *Science, Faith, and Politics,* pp. 159-60, on Bacon's statement in Essay 15 that "the part of Epimetheus ought well become Prometheus."

16. In the *Advancement,* Bacon compares atoms in physics to the family unit in society as proof of the prime philosophy. One of the accounts of the masque involving atoms is Carew's "In Answer of an Elegiacall Letter upon the Death of the King of Sweden from Aurelian Townsend, Inviting Me to Write on that Subject." See also Walter Charleton, *Physiologia Epicuro-Gassendo-Charltoniana* (New York and

London: Johnson Reprint Corporation, 1966), p. 344; and the entertainment recorded in note 4 above. The debate over mystery and mechanism in the masque is well known, but the investments of the court culture in science have not been fully studied. For a start, see R. Malcolm Smuts, *Court Culture and the Origins of a Royalist Tradition in Early Stuart England* (Philadelphia: Univ. of Pennsylvania Press, 1987), pp. 154-59; and Stephen Orgel and Roy Strong, *Inigo Jones: The Theatre of the Stuart Court*, 2 vols. (Berkeley and Los Angeles: Univ. of California Press; London: Sotheby Parke Bernet, 1973), 1:13.

Richard D. McKirahan, Jr. (essay date 1994)

SOURCE: "Fifth-Century Atomism: Leucippus and Democritus," in *Philosophy before Socrates: An Introduction with Texts and Commentary,* Hackett Publishing Company, Inc., 1994, pp. 303-43.

[*In the following excerpt, McKirahan explicates passages concerning atomic theory by Democritus and ancient Greek commentators.*]

The third and most ambitious response to the Eleatic challenge was the atomic theory, invented by Leucippus and developed by Democritus. Leucippus is a shadowy character[1] who we are told was from (a) Miletus, (b) Elea, and (c) Abdera[2], though these claims could simply reflect the facts that (a) his philosophy was strongly of the Ionian type, (b) he was keenly aware of the Eleatic challenge, and (c) his pupil Democritus was from Abdera. Of his dates we are equally in the dark. Democritus, born c. 460, was his student. It is likely that Leucippus proposed the atomic theory in the decade 440-430. He wrote works called *The Great World System* and *On Mind*.

Democritus' birthdate is inferred from his own statement[3] that he was young in the old age of Anaxagoras (born c. 500). Diogenes Laertius reports that Anaxagoras was forty years older than Democritus.[4] Since this makes Democritus ten years younger than Socrates, the title "Presocratic" is not quite correct. He lived to a ripe old age (perhaps over 100), therefore well into Plato's career and into the time when Aristotle had begun his philosophical work. Born on the Thracian mainland in the remote Greek city of Abdera, which also produced the Sophist Protagoras, Democritus traveled widely in non-Greek lands for study and research. He is unique among the philosophers treated in this book in the large number of his writings. We know the titles of about seventy works, on a wide variety of subjects. The main headings are ethics, natural philosophy, mathematics, "music" (in the broad Greek sense which includes language and literature[5]), technical subjects (including medical writings and works on farming, painting, and military strategy), and writings based on his travels. He was later known as the laughing philosopher, allegedly because of his reaction to human follies.

More fragments survive from Democritus than from any other presocratic philosopher, but the great majority are on ethics, and their authenticity and their exact relation to the atomic theory are in many cases doubtful. Our knowledge of atomism depends on testimonia (as opposed to actual fragments) to a greater degree than is the case for our knowledge of the theories of Empedocles and Anaxagoras; unfortunately, the Aristotelian tradition that preserves most of the information is hostile to atomism.

Attempts have been made to distinguish between Leucippus' and Democritus' contributions to the atomic theory.[6] In general, it appears that Leucippus, like Empedocles and Anaxagoras, sketched out a physical theory in response to the Eleatics, as well as a cosmogony and cosmology that treated additional problems. Democritus then did what had not been done before, and his contribution is a turning point in the history of thought. He accepted the theory essentially as stated by Leucippus, but went on to explain in detail a wide range of natural phenomena, working out elaborate (though not always very clear) accounts of how the five senses function and also how thought and other cognitive activities take place. He also saw (possibly) the need for developing a mathematical basis for his physical theory and (certainly) the need for an appropriate theory of knowledge. To a greater extent than his predecessors seem to have done with their theories, Democritus aimed to establish a thoroughgoing atomistic account of all aspects of the world and of humanity. It is a great shame that not one of his works has survived complete—the price, perhaps, of doing his work in Abdera instead of Athens, and also of championing a theory that was on the one hand apparently despised by Plato (who never mentions Democritus), Aristotle (who argues powerfully against the atomic theory), and the Stoics (who constituted the dominant philosophical movement of the Hellenistic age), and which on the other was taken over and adapted by Epicurus, whose pride and influence were such that his followers revered him as The Master and paid no attention to the sources to which he owed almost all his ideas about the natural world. In what follows, little effort will be made to distinguish the contributions of Leucippus from those of Democritus, and I shall speak in general of the Atomists.

PRINCIPLES OF THE ATOMIC THEORY

16.1 Leucippus and his associate Democritus declare the full and the empty [void] to be the elements, calling the former "what is" (TO ON) and the other "what is not" (TO ME ON). Of these the one, "what is," is full and solid, the other, "what is not," is empty [void] and rare. (This is why they say that what is is no more than what is not, because the void is no less than body is.) These are the material causes of existing things. . . . They declare that the differences <among these> are the causes of the rest. Moreover, they say that the differences are three: shape, arrangement, and position. For they say that what is differs only in "rhythm," "touching," and "turning"—and of these "rhythm" is shape, "touching" is arrangement, and "turning" is position.

For *A* differs from *N* in shape, *AN* from *NA* in arrangement, and *Z* from *N* in position.

(Aristotle, *Metaphysics* 1.4 985b4-19 = DK 67A6)

16.2 After making the shapes, Democritus and Leucippus make alteration and coming to be out of them: coming to be and destruction by means of separation and combination, alteration by means of arrangement and position. Since they held that the truth is in the appearance, and appearances are opposite and unlimited, they made the shapes unlimited,[7] so that by reason of changes of the composite, the same thing seems opposite to different people, and it shifts position when a small amount is mixed in, and it appears completely different when one thing shifts position. For tragedy and comedy come to be out of the same letters.

(Aristotle, *On Generation and Corruption* 1.1 315b6-15 = DK 67A97)

16.3 Democritus believes that the nature of the eternal things is small substances (OUSAI[8]) unlimited in multitude. As a place for these he hypothesizes something else, unlimited in size, and he calls the place by the names "void," "nothing" (OUDEN) and "unlimited" [or, "infinite"] and he calls each of the substances "hing" (DEN) and "compact" and "what is." He holds that the substances are so small that they escape our senses. They have all kinds of forms and shapes and differences in size. Out of these as elements he generates and combines visible and perceptible bodies. <These substances> contend with one another and move in the void on account of their dissimilarity and the other differences I have mentioned, and as they move they strike against one another and become entangled in a way that makes them be in contact and close to one another, but does not make any thing out of them that is truly one, for it is quite foolish <to think> that two or more things could ever come to be one. The grounds he gives for why the substances stay together up to a point are that the bodies fit together and hold each other fast. For some of them are rough, some are hooked, others concave and others convex, while yet others have innumerable other differences. So he thinks that they cling to each other and stay together until some stronger necessity comes along from the environment and shakes them and scatters them apart. He describes the generation and its contrary, separation, not only for animals but also for plants, KOSMOI, and altogether for all perceptible bodies.

(Aristotle, *On Democritus,* quoted by Simplicius, *Commentary on Aristotle's On the Heaven* 295.1-22 = DK 68A37)

16.4 Leucippus . . . did not follow the same path as Parmenides and Xenophanes concerning things that are, but seemingly the opposite one. For while they made the universe one, immovable, ungenerated, and limited, and did not even permit the investigation of what is not, he posited the atoms as unlimited and ever moving elements, and an unlimited multitude of shapes among them on the grounds that they are no more like this than like that, since he observed that coming to be and change are unceasing in things that are. Further, he posited that what is is no more than what is not, and both are equally causes of what comes to be. For supposing the substance of the atoms to be compact and

full, he said it is "being" and that it moves in the void, which he called "not-being" and which he declares is no less than what is. His associate, Democritus of Abdera, likewise posited the full and the void as principles, of which he calls the former "being" and the latter "not-being." For positing the atoms as matter for the things that are they generate the rest by means of their differences. These are three: rhythm, turning, and touching, i.e., shape, position, and arrangement. For like is by nature moved by like, and things of the same kind move towards one another, and each of the shapes produces a different composition when arranged in a different compound. Thus, since the principles are unlimited, they reasonably promised to account for all attributes and substances—how and through what cause anything comes to be. This is why they say that only those who make the elements unlimited account for everything reasonably. They say that the multitude of the shapes among the atoms is unlimited on the grounds that they are no more like this than like that. For they themselves assign this as a cause of the unlimitedness.

(Simplicius, *Commentary on Aristotle's Physics* 28.4-26 = DK 67A8 68A38)

16.5 Leucippus and Democritus have accounted for all things very systematically and in a single theory, taking the natural starting point as their own. For some of the early philosophers held that what is, is necessarily one and immovable. For the void is not, and motion is impossible without a separate void, nor can there be many things without something to keep them apart. . . . Leucippus thought he had arguments that agreed with perception in not abolishing coming to be, destruction, motion, or plurality. Agreeing on these matters with the phenomena and agreeing with those who support the one [i.e., the Eleatics] that there could be no motion without void, he asserts that void is not-being and nothing of what is is not-being, since what strictly is, is completely full. But this is not one, but they are unlimited in multitude and invisible because of the minuteness of their size. These move in the void (for there is void) and they produce coming to be by coming together, and destruction by coming apart, and they act and are acted upon wherever they happen to be in contact (for in this way they are not one), and they generate <compounds> by becoming combined and entangled. A plurality could not come to be from what is in reality one, nor one from what is really many, but this is impossible.

(Aristotle, *On Generation and Corruption* 1.8 324b35-325a36 = DK 67A7)

There are two types of elements: atoms and void. Atoms are indivisible (the word ATOMOS means "uncuttable," "unsplittable") building blocks too small to be seen, which move in the void and combine to form compounds, some of which are large enough to be perceived. Atoms are called "full," "solid," "compact," "what is," "being," and "hing," while void is empty (KENON, the word translated "void" means "empty"), "rare," "unlimited" or "infinite," "what is not," "not-being," and "nothing." Among these descriptions of atoms and void, which emphasize their strongly contrasting natures, "hing" contrasts with "nothing" as "nothing" minus the negative "not." This translation reflects the Greek, in which OUDEN ("nothing") minus OU ("not") gives DEN, a word which neatly makes the Atomists' point.[9]

ATOMS

Atoms are eternal (16.3), and, as the following passages show, uniform in substance, without perceptible qualities, and differing only in their spatial properties—size and shape, the latter illustrated by the letters of the alphabet (16.1).

> 16.6 They declare that their nature is one, as if each were a separate piece of gold.
>
> (Aristotle, *On the Heaven* 1.7 275b32-276a1 = DK 67A19)

> 16.7 Plato and Democritus supposed that only the intelligible things are true; Democritus <held this view> because there is by nature no perceptible substrate, whereas the atoms, which combine to form all things, have a nature deprived of every perceptible quality.
>
> (Sextus Empiricus, *Against the Mathematicians* 8.6 = DK 68A59)

> 16.8 Democritus specified two <basic properties of atoms>: size and shape; and Epicurus added weight as a third.
>
> (Aetius 1.3.18 = DK 68A47)

Moreover, there are an unlimited number of atoms, with an unlimited number of shapes moving in unlimited void. The Atomists offered arguments for the view that the number of shapes is unlimited. (A) Truth is in the appearance; appearances are unlimited; therefore the shapes are unlimited (16.2, 16.4). (B) They are no more like this than like that; therefore there is an unlimited multitude of shapes (16.4)—an argument that evidently depends on the Principle of Sufficient Reason, encountered previously in Anaximander and Parmenides.[10]

The unlimited number of shapes entails an unlimited number of atoms.

> 16.9 Since the bodies differ in shape, and the shapes are unlimited, they declare the simple bodies too to be unlimited. But they did not determine further what is the shape of each of the elements, only assigning a spherical shape to fire. They distinguished air and water and the others by largeness and smallness.
>
> (Aristotle, *On the Heaven* 3.4 303a11-15 = DK 67A15)

This property in turn, presumably, was thought to entail an unlimited amount of void for them to move in (although we do not have any record of arguments that the void is unlimited).

Parallel reasoning to (B) would conclude that there are atoms of all possible sizes ("all kinds of . . . differences in size" [16.3]). Indeed, one source declares that Democritus believed there can be an atom the size of the KOSMOS

(16.22). But since there is strong evidence (16.3, 16.5, 16.11) that both Leucippus and Democritus held that the atoms are very small, indeed "invisible because of the minuteness of their size," it is best to hold that Democritus believed that atoms could in principle be any size (which could have led to the interpretation that he held that some atoms are in fact huge), and yet he, like Leucippus, believed that in fact they are all too small to be seen.[11] This question aside, however, it seems that size as well as shape governs the sorts of compounds in which an atom can be found (16.9).

All atoms are made of the same stuff. Moreover, this stuff, and consequently the atoms themselves, have no perceptible qualities. They are not hard or soft, hot or cold, wet or dry. These are properties of macroscopic perceptible compounds of atoms and depend on the atomic structure of the compounds rather than the nature of the individual component atoms.

It is not certain why the Atomists supposed that atoms have no perceptible qualities, but their theory lends itself to some speculations. First, with such atoms it is easier to account for a wider range of changes in quality at the macroscopic level. For example, iron, which is gray, becomes red when heated. If it were composed of gray atoms this change would be hard to explain. But if color depends on atomic structure and movement, we may suppose that heat alters the structure and movement of the atoms in the iron. Second, individual atoms cannot be perceived,[12] hence they cannot have perceptible qualities. Third, since an atom lacks such qualities it can form part of many different compounds with different qualities, as a spherical atom can in one context be a soul atom and in another a fire atom. Fourth, the atomic theory is a beautifully simple theory that rests on a small number of principles. Part of its simplicity resides in the fact that atoms have so few inherent properties.

The atoms are impassive, incapable of being affected or acted upon.

> 16.10 These men [Leucippus, Democritus, and Epicurus] said that the principles are unlimited in multitude, and they believed them to be atoms and indivisible and incapable of being acted upon because they are compact and have no share of void. (For they claimed that division occurs where there is void in bodies.)
>
> (Simplicius, *Commentary on Aristotle's On the Heaven* 242.18-21 = DK 67A14)

Also, "on account of their hardness the atoms are not acted upon and do not change" (16.34). Since they are quality-less, they cannot change in quality. Nor can they change in quantity by becoming either more or fewer (which would involve generation or destruction) or by growing or shrinking. The only sort of change an atom could suffer would be change in its spatial properties (size and shape), which is prevented by the absence of internal void (so that it cannot bend or break). The unique statement that the atoms are also incapable of acting (16.34) must be understood in this context: they cannot cause changes in other atoms. The contrary claim that "they act and are acted upon whenever they happen to be in contact" (16.5) will refer to their behavior not as individual atoms, but as components of compounds.

The atoms' indivisible nature was the subject of a lively debate. The following passage records some of the Atomists' arguments on the point.

> 16.11 Those who abandoned division to infinity on the grounds that we cannot divide to infinity and as a result cannot guarantee that the division cannot end, declared that bodies are composed of indivisible things and are divided into indivisibles. Except that Leucippus and Democritus hold that the cause of the primary bodies' indivisibility is not only their inability to be affected but also their minute size and lack of parts.
>
> (Simplicius, *Commentary on Aristotle's Physics* 925.10-15 = DK 67A13)

The atoms are indivisible because (A) they cannot be affected, (B) they are so small, and (C) they have no parts. But all three of these considerations beg the question. For example, we cannot know that they have no parts unless we already know that they are indivisible (assuming that "parts" is meant in the only way that makes sense in the context: parts into which a thing can be divided).

The first part of 16.11, however, puts these arguments in a different light (if the reasoning can be attributed to the Atomists). Zeno had shown (Argument 2, pp. 183-85, above) that unacceptable consequences follow on the assumption that a finite-sized object is infinitely divisible. Complete the division and either the resulting least parts have no size or they have some positive size. But either way, the parts cannot be reassembled to form the original object. If they have no size, when put together they result in something with no size. If they have a positive size, no matter how small, when an infinite number of them are put together, the result is something of infinite, not finite size. The Atomists avoided this argument.[13] In the absence of a guarantee that bodies are infinitely divisible, they simply declared that they are not: i.e., that bodies are ultimately composed of indivisibles. This amounts to hypothesizing the existence of atoms in the absence of a conclusive reason not to do so. The next step would be to describe the atoms so as to corroborate their indivisibility and also explain why we fail to perceive them directly—and the properties mentioned above contribute to this enterprise.

Another passage goes further, arguing that bodies cannot be "everywhere divisible."

> 16.12 Democritus would appear to have been persuaded by arguments that are relevant and appropriate to the science of nature. The point will be clear as we proceed. For there is a difficulty in supposing that there is some body, a magnitude, that is everywhere divisible and that this [the complete division] is possible. For what will there be that escapes the division? . . . Now since

such a body is everywhere divisible, let it be divided. What, then, will be left? A magnitude? But this cannot be. For there will be something that has not been divided, whereas we supposed that it was everywhere divisible. But if there will be no body or magnitude left and yet the division will take place, either <the original body> will consist of points and its components will be without magnitude, or it will be nothing at all, so that it could come to be out of nothing and be composed of nothing, and the whole thing would then be nothing but an appearance. Likewise, if it is composed of points, it will not be a quantity. For when they were in contact and there was a single magnitude and they coincided, they made the whole thing none the larger. For when it is divided into two or more, the whole is no smaller or larger than before. And so, even if all the points are put together they will not make any magnitude. . . . These problems result from supposing that any body whatever of any size is everywhere divisible. . . . And so, since magnitudes cannot be composed of contacts or points, it is necessary for there to be indivisible bodies and magnitudes.

> (Aristotle, *On Generation and Corruption* 1.2 316a13-b16 = DK 68A48b)

Now "everywhere divisible" is different from "infinitely divisible." Dividing a magnitude one meter long in half and then dividing one of these halves in half, etc., is an infinite division that leaves pieces of positive size: one piece half a meter long, one piece a quarter of a meter long, etc. Dividing the magnitude everywhere, perhaps by dividing it into two pieces half a meter long and then dividing both of these pieces into halves and continuing to subdivide each of the products of the previous division, leaves pieces of no positive size. But even though being everywhere divisible is a stronger condition than being infinitely divisible, it, rather than infinite divisibility, is the antithesis of atomism and hence a view the Atomists need to reject. Thus, 16.12's argument is appropriate. If the argument succeeds there is good reason to adopt some kind of atomic theory. However, the argument rests on the assumption not just that a magnitude is everywhere divisible, but that division can be carried out in such a way that the magnitude is actually divided at every place, which is quite a different claim, and one that proponents of the former need not accept.

As far as the evidence goes, then, the Atomists did not prove that there are atoms. A body can be everywhere divisible even if not actually divided everywhere. But they did succeed in avoiding the Scylla and Charybdis of Zeno's Argument 2. This is sufficient to show that physically indivisible bodies are possible, though not enough to escape all of Zeno's arguments. For physical indivisibility does not guarantee geometrical or theoretical indivisibility.[14] Atoms have sizes and shapes, and shapes involve spatial extension. For example, Democritus speaks of fire as composed of spherical atoms. A spherical atom may be a very small sphere, but in thought even if not with a knife, we can distinguish one part of the sphere from the other. And once we can do this much, others of Zeno's paradoxes take hold—the Dichotomy and the Achilles (see pp. 187-89). We cannot traverse an atom because we would first have to cross half[15] of it, then half the remainder, etc.

It is a matter of current controversy whether the fifth-century Atomists believed that atoms are geometrically or theoretically as well as physically indivisible.[16] The philosophically correct move would be to distinguish between kinds of indivisibility and hold that atoms are theoretically divisible, but not physically so. Alternatively and plausibly, the Atomists may not have explicitly distinguished among different kinds of indivisibility. (Such distinctions are more at home in Aristotle than in the fifth century.) They may have conceived of divisibility and indivisibility solely as physical properties and felt free to distinguish parts of atoms in thought, without supposing that doing so requires atoms to be divisible in any way. They would then be in a position to admit that atoms are theoretically and geometrically divisible once the relevant distinctions were made.[17] In fact, as we saw in discussing Zeno, theoretical divisibility to infinity is an illusory problem. There is no need to take any step to oppose it (let alone a philosophically unsound step) because the option Zeno offers between final parts of no size and final parts of some size is misleading: neither of these results will obtain.

The Atomists were aware of the positive Eleatic doctrines of Parmenides and Melissus as well as Zeno's attacks on plurality, and there is no doubt that atomism is a response to the Eleatic challenge. It preserves the world of experience with its change, coming into being, destruction, etc., by saying that these features are due to unchanging atoms that have many of the properties of Parmenides' one being. Melissus said "if there were many, they would have to be such as I say the one is" (15.10 sec. 2), and some say that the Atomists responded by endowing each of their atoms with the attributes of the one. This is true to an extent. Like the Eleatic one, each atom is uncreated and indestructible, therefore eternal. It is continuous and indivisible. It is unchanging in quality; in fact, like the Eleatic one, it has no qualities. Moreover, relatively to itself it does not move: its logically distinguishable parts always have the same positions relative to one another. Each atom is, of course, finite in size (like Parmenides' but unlike Melissus' one).[18] Contrary to Parmenides' demand, an atom is not spatially invariant: different parts do have different locations relative to one another. But still, at the level of the individual atom, not considered in its relations to other atoms, there is temporal invariance. Since there is no change or internal motion, an atom is identical with itself throughout its eternal existence.

VOID

The void fulfills two main functions. It enables the atoms to move, and it makes possible and preserves their uniqueness and identity: "motion is impossible without a separate void, nor can there be many things without something to keep them apart" (16.5). Regarding the latter point, they held that if there were no void to separate atoms, all there

is would consist of a single infinitely large indivisible mass of matter. "Division occurs where there is void in bodies" (16.10). Strictly speaking, atoms are never in contact with one another.

> 16.13 When Democritus said that the atoms are in contact with each other, he did not mean contact strictly speaking . . . but the condition in which the atoms are near one another and not far apart is what he called contact. For no matter what, they are separated by the void.
>
> (Philoponus, *Commentary on Aristotle's On Generation and Corruption* 158.27-159.3 = DK 67A7)

Even in a compound, where they are very close to one another, they are separated by void, so that a compound is not like a jigsaw puzzle with no gaps between the pieces. Why not? Because atoms are identified only by their spatial extension, and if two atoms fit together perfectly with no gaps, so that the resulting thing is uniformly dense, compact, etc., they would no longer be two, but would have become one. And the Atomists, echoing Eleatic sentiments, insist that compounds are not true unities: "it is quite foolish <to think> that two or more things could ever come to be one" (16.3), "a plurality could not come to be from what is in reality one, nor one from what is really many" (16.5).

According to some sources, the Atomists posited that void exists (16.3, 16.4, and 16.5[19]). However, they did offer arguments. One, which is another application of the Principle of Sufficient Reason, goes as follows.

> 16.14 There is no more reason for the thing to be than the nothing.
>
> (Democritus, DK 68B156)

The following passage presents four of their reasons for believing in the void, all of which are inconclusive.[20]

> 16.15 People mean by void an interval in which there is no perceptible body. Since they believe that everything that is is body, they say that void is that in which there is nothing at all. . . . So it is necessary to prove[21] . . . that there is no interval different from bodies . . . which breaks up the whole body so that it is not continuous, as Democritus and Leucippus say, and many other natural philosophers, or anything outside the whole body, which is continuous. They say that (1) there would be no change in place (i.e., motion and growth), since motion would not seem to exist if there were no void, since what is full cannot admit anything. . . . (2) Some things are seen to contract and be compressed; for example, they say that the jars hold the wine along with the wineskins, since the compressed body contracts into the voids that are in it. Further (3) all believe that growth takes place through void, since the nourishment is a body and two bodies cannot be together. (4) They also use as evidence what happens with ash, which receives as much water as the empty vessel.
>
> (Aristotle, *Physics* 4.6 213a27-b22 = DK 67A19)

Void is to be distinguished from air, whose corporeal nature had been hinted at as far back as Anaximenes and was assumed in Empedocles' clepsydra analogy (14.105). Nor is it the same thing as space. Consider a fish in a body of water, such as the water in a fishbowl. The water and the fish both occupy space and have locations; they occupy different regions of space and have different locations. Similarly, atoms and void both occupy space and have location. Where there is void there are no atoms, and where there are atoms there is no void. The atoms move through the void in the same sense as that in which the fish swims through the water. Thus, the water and the void are both *in* space and neither is to be confused with the space in which the fish or atoms move.[22] I disagree with Aristotle's interpretation that void is the space or place in which the atoms move (16.3).[23]

The Atomists emphasized void's existence and nature with a paradox: Leucippus "asserts that void is not-being, and nothing of what is is not-being, since what strictly is is completely full" (16.5); "what is is no more than what is not, because the void is no less than body is" (16.1); "both [what is and what is not] are equally causes of what comes to be" (16.4). Further, Democritus calls the void "nothing" (16.3), so that nothing exists.

These assertions do more than pose riddles; they fly in the face of the Eleatic challenge. Parmenides had declared that "it is not possible for nothing to be" (11.6 l. 2), and that what is not cannot be known or declared (11.2 lines 7-8), and he had forbidden inquiry along that path (11.2 lines 5-6). Moreover, he had ruled out plurality on the grounds that there are no stretches of what is not to separate bits of what is (11.8 lines 44-49),[24] and Melissus had disproved the possibility of motion on similar grounds (13.9 sec. 9). In this intellectual context it is simply unsatisfactory to assert baldly that "nothing" is one of the physical principles and to declare that nothing exists just as much as "hing."

Some think that calling the void "nothing" is a move to avoid Zeno's Argument 3 (pp. 185-86), which would entail an infinite number of atoms in a finite area. Zeno argued "if there are many . . . there are always others between the things that are, and again others between these, and so the things that are are unlimited" (12.5). The Atomists can respond that in between the things that are (atoms) is nothing (void), so Zeno's regress fails to take hold.

However, the existence of what is not represents a major departure from Eleatic doctrine. The anti-Parmenidean declaration "what is not is" was considered previously. But further, the existence of void goes against Melissus' argument "Nor is any of it empty. For what is empty is nothing, and of course what is nothing would not be" (15.9 sec. 7). As we have seen, the Atomists, while agreeing with the premise that what is empty is nothing, deny the last assertion of the argument, and claim that what is nothing (the void) is.

The void also runs afoul of Parmenides' more abstract reasoning. "Nor is it any more in any way . . . or any less" (11.8 lines 23-24) and "It is right for what is to be not incomplete; for it is not lacking; if it were (lacking), it would lack everything" (11.8 lines 32-33); "For it must be not at all greater or at all smaller here than there" (11.8 l. 44); "Nor (is it the case that) what is is in such a way that there could be more of what is here and less there" (11.8 lines 47-48). The Atomists' claim, that void is just as much as atoms are, is sufficient to meet some of these claims. Although in a sense there is less where there is void than where there are atoms, still, void is on a par with atoms in the relevant respect, being. But the argument at 11.8 lines 32-33, which Parmenides uses to establish that what is has all coherently conceivable and describable attributes, cannot be met in this way. Void obviously lacks most of the attributes of the atoms, and so would not be. The Atomists might counter this argument either by denying the premise on which it turns, "it must either fully be or not" (11.8 l. 11), or by distinguishing between the existential interpretation of that principle, which they accept at the atomic level (void and atoms both exist fully), and the predicative interpretation, which they could deny (an existing thing can fail to have all possible predicates).

Still, the assertion that "nothing" exists is badly defended. The argument that there is no less reason for "nothing" than for "hing" to be would not have impressed Parmenides, who believed there to be a good reason why "nothing" could not be: it cannot be thought or spoken of. But this is a consequence of an argument of which one premise is that it is not possible for nothing to be (11.6 lines 1-2). This premise is undefended and need not be accepted if there is no reason to. Democritus argued that in the absence of a reason to accept the premise, there is no reason not to hold that "nothing" is just as much as "hing," and he could give as a positive reason for believing in its existence the role it plays in his system.

The assertion that what is not is just as much as what is, thus may not simply be a paradox for paradox's sake. It succinctly brings out the fundamental conflict with Parmenides and invites us to consider the role "what is not" plays in the atomic theory, so that we can judge by reference to the success of the theory the merits of the claim that what is not is.

Can the void be spoken and thought of? In a sense it can, quite obviously. It can be characterized in terms of its rules of occupying space, making possible the motions of atoms, etc. But the Atomists tend to describe it negatively, by contrast with the atoms. It is "empty" as opposed to "full," and is "rare" only in an extended use of that word. Although the presence of void is needed to account for certain qualities of compounds, it is more natural to describe those compounds as consisting of atoms more or less separated, or atoms arranged in a certain way. If atoms are quality-less, so is the void, and the void per se lacks even the spatial properties of atoms. It has no shape or size of its own (aside from its infinite amount). Thus, the Atomists can hold that the void is per se virtually unthinkable and indescribable, and except for the various ways it can be described by contrast with and in relation to the atoms, the only feature it has of its own is infinite extension.

ATOMIC MOTION

The infinitely many atoms are all in motion in the infinite void. As an atom moves it may meet with other atoms of the same kind or of different kinds. Such collisions can result in the atoms rebounding away from one another or in their coming together to form compounds. Before discussing compounds, it will be useful to discuss the atoms' motion.

Aristotle makes several complaints against the Atomists' accounts of atomic motion.

16.16 This is why Leucippus and Democritus, who say that the primary bodies are always moving in the void (i.e., the unlimited) must specify what motion they have and what is their natural motion.

(Aristotle, *On the Heaven* 3.2 300b8-11 = DK 67A16)

16.17 Concerning the origin and manner of motion in existing things, these men too, like the rest, lazily neglected to give an account.

(Aristotle, *Metaphysics* 1.4 985b19-20 = DK 67A6)
(continuation of 16.1)

16.18 For they say that there is always motion. But they do not say why or what motion it is, nor, if it is of one sort or another, do they state the cause.

(Aristotle, *Metaphysics* 12.6 1071b33-35 = DK 67A18)

It seems certain that they did not specify the nature or cause of the atoms' original motion. Thus, the isolated statement

16.19 They say that motion occurs on account of the void. For they too say that nature undergoes motion in respect of place.

(Aristotle, *Physics* 8.9 265b24-25 = DK 68A58)

must mean merely that the void is a necessary condition for motion, not that it is a cause in the sense of the source of the motion.

However, Aristotle's objections are misconceived. Since atoms and void are eternal and eternally in motion, there was no initial state corresponding to the period in Anaxagoras' cosmogony in which "all things were together" (16.1). The Atomists therefore avoid Parmenides' question "what necessity would have stirred it up to grow later rather than earlier" (11.8 l. 10). There is no need to posit a cause of the beginning of motion, since motion has always existed.

Likewise there is no need to talk of an original form of motion. An atom's motion now is determined by its most recent history of contact with other atoms, like the motion of billiard balls after they have collided. If we have perfectly elastic billiard balls and a billiard table with perfectly elastic cushions, and the balls roll on the table without friction or wind resistance, then if the balls are in motion, they will never stop moving unless affected from the outside in the future, and likewise, unless they have been affected from outside in the past, they have always been moving. There is no initial static condition and no first movement, but at any moment—past, present, or future—their motion is determined by their immediately previous history.

There is good evidence that this was the Atomists' view of atomic motion.

16.20 Leucippus and Democritus said that their primary bodies, the atoms, are always moving in the unlimited void by compulsion.

(Simplicius, *Commentary on Aristotle's On the Heaven* 583.18-20 = DK 67A16)

16.21 Democritus, saying that the atoms are naturally motionless, declares that they move "by a blow."

(Simplicius, *Commentary on Aristotle's Physics* 42.10-11 = DK 68A47)

16.22 Democritus says that the primary bodies (these are the compact things) do not possess weight but move by knocking against one another in the unlimited, and there can be an atom the size of the KOSMOS.

(Aetius 1.12.6 = DK 68A47)

16.23 These men [Leucippus and Democritus] say that the atoms move by hitting and knocking against each other, but they do not specify the source of their natural motion. For the motion of knocking each other is compelled and not natural, and compelled motion is posterior to natural motion.

(Alexander, *Commentary on Aristotle's Metaphysics* 36.21-25 = DK 67A6)

These passages agree that the atoms move as the result of striking one another. As 16.20 asserts, this is always the case: an atom is always moving, at all times its movements are due to previous collisions, and there was no first collision. In Aristotelian terminology, such motion is "compelled" as opposed to "natural." Aristotle's belief in natural motion, a body's motion toward its natural place,[25] and its priority to compelled motion affects several of the sources. The atoms do not have an inherent tendency either to be at rest or to move in any particular direction or towards any particular location, and so they do not have any "natural" motion.[26]

16.24 They said that moving in virtue of the weight in them, <the atoms> move[27] in respect of place through the void, which yields and does not resist. For they said that they "are hurled all about." And they attribute this motion to the elements as not only their primary but their only motion, whereas things composed of the elements have the other kinds of motion. For they grow and decrease, change, come to be and are destroyed as the primary bodies combine and separate.

(Simplicius, *Commentary on Aristotle's Physics* 1318.35-1319.5 = DK 68A58)

16.25 Democritus indicated a single type of motion, that due to vibration.

(Aetius 1.23.3 = DK 68A47)

The words translated "are hurled all about" and "vibration"[28] are etymologically related and presumably refer to the same kind of movement, the bouncing back and forth of the atoms between collisions.

Our discussion of the atoms' original and natural motion leads directly to the vexed question whether they have weight. The evidence is conflicting and problematic: in addition to 16.8 there is also the following.

16.26 Democritus and later Epicurus said that all the atoms have the same nature and possess weight, but since some are heavier, when these settle down the lighter ones are squeezed out and move upwards, and in this way they say that some things appear light and others heavy.

(Simplicius, *Commentary on Aristotle's On the Heaven* 569.5-9 = DK 68A61)

16.27 Democritus says that each of the indivisibles is heavier according as its quantity is greater.

(Aristotle, *On Generation and Corruption* 1.8 326a9-10 = DK 68A60)

16.28 Those <who call the primary bodies> solid can rather say that the larger is heavier. But since compounds do not appear to behave in this way, but we see many that are smaller in bulk but heavier, as bronze is heavier than wood, some think and say that the cause is different—that the void enclosed within makes the bodies light and sometimes makes larger things lighter, since they contain more void. . . . But those who make these distinctions must add not only that something contains more void if it is lighter, but also that it contains less solid.

(Aristotle, *On the Heaven* 4.2 309a1-14 = DK 68A60)

Also 16.22.

It will help to draw two distinctions. First, atoms may have weight and yet not have it as one of their primary properties (16.8). Since atoms are all made of the same uniform stuff, their size and shape will determine how much of that stuff is in them, which will in turn determine their weight (16.27). Second, weight can be understood in different ways, including (A) as a tendency to move or otherwise be affected by a certain force (for example, gravity), or alternatively (B) as a tendency to move in a certain direction (for Aristotle, this direction is towards the center of the KOSMOS; for Epicurus, it is downwards), or (C) as a tendency to move in certain ways under certain conditions, differently in different conditions, with no universal tendency to move in any particular direction. As our treatment of atomic motion has shown, the Atomists are committed to view (C). An atom's motion at any moment is determined solely by its previous collision with other atoms. No appeal need be made to any immaterial force like gravity, which has no place in ancient atomism.

However, in certain contexts, such as the KOSMOS we live in, matter does have a tendency to move in a certain direction and in general to display the characteristics we associate with weight: for example, that heavier bodies sink and lighter ones rise, and that there is no necessary relation between a body's size and its weight. Some of these phenomena are explained in 16.26 and 16.28. Others are due to the effects of the cosmogonic vortex, in which like atoms move toward like and the heavier ones toward the center (see pp. 324-26). If this account is correct, the Atomists succeed in accounting for many phenomena of gravity and weight within the confines of their materialistic and mechanistic theory.

If all events are due to the mechanical motion and interaction of atoms in the void, atomism seems to entail a rigid determinism. Perhaps surprisingly, the problems determinism raises for understanding human actions and for central concepts in ethics were not explored until later in the Greek philosophical tradition. Nevertheless, the Atomists and those who discussed their theory did recognize some of its implications for causality. The single surviving sentence of Leucippus bears on this aspect of the atomic theory.

16.29 No thing happens at random but all things as a result of a reason and by necessity.

(Leucippus, DK 67B2)

At first sight this appears to deny the mechanistic picture of the atomistic universe presented previously. "Nothing at random" gives the impression that all things happen for a purpose, and "all things as a result of a reason" suggests that the universe is governed by a purposeful intelligence, much like Heraclitus' rational LOGOS. But these impressions are misleading. The key to the fragment is the notion of necessity. Leucippus holds that everything that happens—all movements and interactions of atoms in the void—happens of necessity in that, given the nature of atoms and void, and given the positions and motions of the atoms, things cannot happen otherwise. This necessity is blind necessity, as opposed to conscious or unconscious plan and purpose. It follows immediately that nothing happens by chance or at random. Moreover, there is a reason why everything takes place—not because there is a governing mind, but in the sense that every event has an explanation.[29]

Democritus followed Leucippus in this view.

16.30 Democritus leaves aside purpose, but refers all things which nature employs to necessity.

(Aristotle, *Generation of Animals* 5.8 789b2-4 = DK 68A66)

16.31 <Concerning necessity> Democritus <speaks of> knocking against <each other> and motion and "blow" of matter.

(Aetius 1.26.2 = DK 68A66)

16.32 <Democritus> seemed to employ chance in his

cosmogony, but in his detailed discussions he declares that chance is the cause of nothing, and he refers to other causes.

(Simplicius, *Commentary on Aristotle's Physics* 330.14-17 = DK 68A68)

All events are the necessary consequences of the interaction of atoms, so that chance and purpose form no part of a correct explanation of anything that happens.

COMPOUNDS

"They declare that the differences (among these) are the causes of the rest. Moreover, they say that the differences are three: shape, arrangement, and position. . . . For *A* differs from *N* in shape, *AN* from *NA* in arrangement, and *Z* from *N* in position" (from 16.1). It is possible that the use of letters to illustrate properties of the atoms goes back to the Atomists themselves. This analogy is carried further in 16.2: tragedies and comedies are written with the same letters.[30] These three kinds of differences are of different types. Whereas the first kind (*A* and *N*) illustrates differences in shapes of individual atoms, the second explicitly and the third implicitly have to do with the roles of atoms in compounds. The second shows how the same atoms can form different compounds (here think of the syllables 'an' and 'na'), and the third shows how a single atom can play different roles depending on its immediate context. Both fire and souls are composed of spherical atoms, but that is not to say that souls are fiery or that fire has the attributes of soul. A single spherical atom out of context cannot be identified as either a soul atom or a fire atom, and in fact by itself it is neither, though in the appropriate context it can be either.[31]

Compounds arise when atoms moving through the void come into contact with one another and instead of rebounding become enmeshed.

16.33 These atoms, which are separate from one another in the unlimited void and differ in shape and size and position, and arrangement, move in the void, and when they overtake one another they collide, and some rebound in whatever direction they may happen to, but others become entangled in virtue of the relation of their shapes, sizes, positions, and arrangements, and stay together, and this is how compounds are produced.

(Simplicius, *Commentary on Aristotle's On the Heaven* 242.21-26 = DK 67A14) (continuation of 16.10)

16.34 What does Democritus say? That substances unlimited in multitude, atomic and not different in kind, and moreover incapable of acting or being acted upon, are in motion, scattered in the void. When they approach one another or collide or become entangled, the compounds appear as water or fire or as a plant or a human, but all things are atoms, which he calls forms; there is nothing else. For from what is not there is no coming to be, and nothing could come to be from things that are because on account of their hardness the atoms are not acted upon and do not change.

(Plutarch, *Against Colotes* 8 1110F-1111A = DK 68A57)

Compounds, though composed of eternal atoms, are not permanent. They last until struck from outside in the right place by other atoms of sufficient size and appropriate shape, moving with appropriate speed (16.3).

Perceptible qualities of compounds are due to the shape, size, arrangement, and position, and possibly the motions, of the quality-less atoms that compose them. Democritus attempted to apply this general principle to specific cases, as the following passages show.

16.35 Leucippus and Democritus, calling the smallest and primary bodies atoms, <say> that in virtue of differences in their shapes and position and order, some bodies come to be hot and fiery—those composed of rather sharp and minute primary bodies situated in a similar position, while others come to be cold and watery—those composed of the opposite kinds of bodies. And some come to be bright and shining while others come to be dim and dark.

(Simplicius, *Commentary on Aristotle's Physics* 36.1-7 = DK 67A14)

16.36 He makes sweet that which is round and good-sized; astringent that which is large, rough, polygonal, and not rounded; sharp tasting, as its name indicates, that which is sharp in body, and angular, bent and not rounded; pungent that which is round and small and angular and bent; salty that which is angular and good-sized and crooked and equal sided; bitter that which is round and smooth, crooked and small sized; oily that which is fine and round and small.

(Theophrastus, *Causes of Plants* 6.1.6 = DK 68A129)

The naiveté of these accounts is less important than Democritus' recognition of the need to show how the theory could be put to use to explain specific phenomena.

Void is also invoked to account for certain qualities. In heavy things the atoms are closely packed, leaving little room for void, and in light things there is more void (16.28). A similar account is given of hard and soft, and an attempt was made to distinguish the heavy from the hard and the light from the soft in terms of the position of the atoms.

16.37 Iron is harder and lead is heavier, since iron has its atoms arranged unevenly and has large quantities of void in many places . . . while lead has less void but its atoms are arranged evenly throughout. This is why it is heavier, but softer than iron.

(Theophrastus, *On Sensation* 62 = DK 68A135)

Equally important, changes in compounds are explained in terms of changes in the spatial relations of atoms: compounds are generated and grow when atoms combine in appropriate ways; they decrease and are destroyed when the atoms separate; they alter (change in quality) when the component atoms change their arrangements and relative positions (16.2, 16.3, 16.24). The same explanation also goes for phase changes.

16.38 We see that the same continuous body is sometimes liquid and sometimes solid—not suffering this change by means of separation and combination or by turning and touching as Democritus says; for it did not become solid from liquid by being transposed or changing its nature.

(Aristotle, *On Generation and Corruption* 1.9
327a16-20 = DK 68A38)

The Atomists' aim is clear: to account for the macroscopic phenomenal world in terms of the behavior of the microscopic atoms. They present a two-world theory in which the phenomena in one world are reduced to entities and events in the other. The two worlds are strikingly different: the complex phenomenal world with its many different kinds of things, which behave in many ways, is contrasted with the simple world of atoms which are made of but a single type of material, which differ only in size and shape, and whose only behavior is to move in place. The claim that all qualities, events, and changes in the phenomenal world can be reduced to changes in the relative positions of eternal, unchanging, quality-less atoms is remarkably ambitious even in the presocratic tradition, and Democritus' efforts to show how the theory works in detail are unique among the Presocratics.

COSMOGONY

The origin of the KOSMOS is described in the following passage.

16.39 [Leucippus] declares the universe to be unlimited. . . . Of this, some is full and some is empty [void], and he declares these [full and void] to be elements. An unlimited number of KOSMOI arise out of these and are destroyed into these. The KOSMOI come into being in the following way. Many bodies of all sorts of shapes by virtue of being cut off from the unlimited move into a great void. They collect together and form a single vortex. In it they knock against one another and move around in all different ways, and they separate apart, like moving towards like. When they are no longer able to rotate in equilibrium, the fine ones depart into the void outside as if sifted. The rest remain together, become entangled, and hurry on their way together, and form a first spherical complex. This stands apart like a membrane, enclosing all kinds of bodies in it. As these whirl around by virtue of the resistance of the center, the surrounding membrane becomes thin, since the adjacent atoms are always joining the fluid motion when they come into contact with the vortex. And the earth came into being in this way when the atoms moving to the center remained together. And again the surrounding membrane-like thing itself grows because bodies strike it from outside. Moving in a vortex it acquires whatever it comes into contact with. Some of these become intertwined and form a complex, at first damp and muddy, but when they have dried out and rotate with the vortex of the whole, they catch fire and form the nature of the stars.

(Diogenes Laertius, *Lives of the Philosophers* 9.31-32
= DK 67A1)

This passage begins by distinguishing the universe (literally, "the whole") from a KOSMOS: the former is the totality consisting of all the atoms and all the void; the latter is a world system that is limited both spatially and temporally. There are an infinite number of KOSMOI scattered randomly through the universe, and they come to be and suffer destruction at different times. Though each KOSMOS has its own unique history, since 16.39 is a general account of the origin of KOSMOI, it follows that KOSMOI significantly resemble one another.

Many details of the cosmogony are muddy, but the general picture is clear. (a) Atomic collisions and motions sometimes bring a vast number of atoms of different shapes into a region of the universe where they are relatively isolated from other atoms. (b) The motions and interactions of these atoms create a vortex in which (c) similar atoms move toward one another. The mechanical nature of this sorting is described in the following fragment, which illustrates again[32] Democritus' tendency to employ arguments by analogy—in this case, a correspondence in the behavior of animate and inanimate things.

16.40 Animals flock together with animals of the same kind—doves with doves, cranes with cranes, and likewise for the other irrational kinds. It is also thus for inanimate things, as can be seen easily in the case of seeds being sifted and pebbles on the shore. For through the swirling motion of the sieve lentils are placed separately with lentils, wheat with wheat, and barley with barley, and through the motion of the waves, long pebbles are cast to the same place as long ones and round ones to the same place as round ones, as if the similarity in these had some mutually attractive force for things.

(Democritus, DK 68B164)

To return to 16.39, (d) the rotation of the vortex drives the smaller (therefore lighter) atoms to the periphery, and finally (e) out of the system altogether, while (f) the remaining atoms form a spherical structure ("like a membrane"—a spherical shell, not a solid sphere), which continues to revolve. (g) In the continued rotation, like-to-like separation continues, with the larger, heavier atoms coming together toward the center to form the earth, and the outer shell becoming increasingly thinner. But then (h) the outer shell is increased when other atoms in the vicinity are caught up in the whirl. (i) Some of the atoms in the shell form a system that (curiously) is at first moist but later (j) ignited and thus forms the visible stars.

It is worth adding that there is nothing inevitable in this sequence of events. We may imagine that for every time a KOSMOS is formed, there are many times when a sufficiently large number of atoms come together (stage a) but fail to form a vortex (stage b), just hovering in the same area until their interactions cause them to disperse.

The crucial features of this cosmogony are that it results from mechanical atomic movements without purpose or divine agency, and that our KOSMOS is not special, only one of an infinite number of similar KOSMOI with similar histories. That our world is not unique or located at the center of the universe, and that we are insignificant from a cosmic point of view, are strikingly modern ideas and drastic departures from common sense and from what sense experience would lead us to believe. The Atomists' readiness to embrace these counterintuitive consequences of their physical system is a measure of their boldness.

A system that posits an infinite number of worlds naturally invites speculation about their nature. The small amount of information on the ancient Atomists' views on this matter is contained in the following testimonium, which leaves it unclear whether they described the other worlds in detail.

> 16.41 There are an infinite number of KOSMOI of different sizes. In some there is no sun or moon. In some the sun and moon are larger than ours and in others there are more. The distances between the KOSMOI are unequal and in one region there are more, in another fewer. Some are growing, some are at their peak, and some are declining, and here one is coming into being, there one is ceasing to be. They are destroyed when they collide with one another. Some KOSMOI have no animals, plants or any moisture. . . . A KOSMOS is at its peak until it is no longer able to take anything in from outside.
>
> (Hippolytus, *Refutation* 1.13.2-4 = DK 68A40) (the omitted words are translated in 16.43)

16.41 states that a KOSMOS is destroyed when it collides with another—apparently a cosmic vortex can move through the void the way whirlwinds move through the air. But the mention of KOSMOI that are declining and failing suggests that they can also be destroyed from within, as it were. The final sentence explains the circumstances in which a KOSMOS declines without explaining why those conditions occur. This theory may reflect ancient theories that the bodies of animals deteriorate in old age through loss of the ability to absorb nutrition. If so, the "death" of a KOSMOS could be understood as the final stage in such decline, where its atoms are dispersed—again, through the mechanical motions of its constituent atoms. There is no set lifespan for a KOSMOS, but the mechanical necessity of atomic interactions guarantees that KOSMOI must come to an end.

COSMOLOGY

The Atomists paid more attention than many of their predecessors to astronomy. Their views stemmed from a variety of sources as far back as Anaximenes, and they do not seem to have made a consistent effort to explain heavenly phenomena in terms of the behavior of atoms and void. The following theories are representative.

> 16.42 The orbit of the sun is furthest out, that of the moon is nearest to the earth, and the others are in between these. All the stars are on fire because of the speed of their motion, but the sun is also on fire because of the stars. The moon has only a small share of fire. The sun and moon eclipse . . . [something is missing from the text] because the earth is tilted toward the south. The regions to the north are always covered with

snow and very cold and frozen. The sun eclipses rarely, but the moon does so continuously because their orbits are unequal.

> (Diogenes Laertius, *Lives of the Philosophers* 9.33 = DK 67A1) (continuation of 16.39)

> 16.43 In our own KOSMOS the earth came into being before the stars. The moon is lowest, then the sun, then the fixed stars. The planets themselves have different heights.

> (Hippolytus, *Refutation* 1.13.4 = DK 68A40)

Leucippus placed the sun furthest from the earth (16.42), Democritus the stars (16.43). The Pythagoreans may have previously paid attention to the orbits of the planets,[33] but Democritus had a special interest in them (perhaps a result of his travels in the East where he could have gained knowledge of Babylonian astronomy) and wrote a treatise on them. Democritus also agreed with Anaxagoras on the nature of the Milky Way and of comets.[34] Both Atomists place the earth at the center of our KOSMOS, and they agree that it is supported by air beneath it.[35] For Leucippus it is flat; for Democritus, concave.[36] Democritus departs from tradition by making the earth not round but oval or oblong, with its length one and one-half times its width.[37] Leucippus, interestingly, believed that the earth, still under the influence of the vortex, "revolves about the center,"[38] but (again because of the role of the vortex) he failed to go on to make the heavenly bodies stationary and explain their apparent movements as due to the earth's rotation. Democritus explained the angle between the celestial north pole and the zenith as due to the earth's having tilted.[39]

> 16.44 Because the southerly part of the surrounding <and supporting air> is weaker, the earth, as it was growing, tilted in this direction. For the northern parts are intemperate, but the southern parts are temperate. This is why it tilted in this direction, where it is above average in fruits and growth.

> (Aetius 3.12.2 = DK 68A96)

Apparently, the extra weight of vegetation tended to push the southern part down, while the air there, thinner because of the excessive heat in that region, was less able to support it.

In meteorological matters, Democritus was more consistent in offering atomistic explanations.

> 16.45 Democritus stated that thunder results from an uneven union <of atoms> compelling the cloud which surrounds it to move downwards. Lightning is the collision of clouds, as a result of which the atoms which give rise to fire move together through empty places with much void to the same place by means of their jostling alongside one another. A thunderbolt occurs when there is a violent motion of purer and finer fire-producing atoms which are more even and "close-fitted" (the word Democritus himself uses). A waterspout occurs when collections of fire containing much void are held back in regions with a lot of void and in wrappings of special membranes, and form bodies because of this rich mixture and make a rush toward the depth.

> (Aetius 3.3.11 = DK 68A93)

THE MICROCOSM

In a famous fragment, Democritus calls a human being "a small (MIKROS) KOSMOS".[40] The idea that humans function on the principles that govern the world is hardly new with the Atomists. Earlier Presocratics at least as far back as Anaximenes had exploited it, explaining cosmic phenomena in terms of human phenomena and vice versa. The roots of the idea extend far back into prephilosophical animistic thought. Although the conception was not new with the Atomists, it had particular force for them since they set out to account for all aspects of the KOSMOS, including animals and human beings, on atomic principles. Their task, then, was to explain how life can arise out of the movement of atoms and how all life's activities can be reduced to atomic behavior. To account for these aspects of the world was perhaps the severest challenge the Atomists faced, and it may be that "microcosm" was their battle cry.

For the origin of life, including human life, Democritus follows Anaximander and other Presocratics in saying that living beings arose from water and mud, a "moisture which gives rise to life."[41] This is all we are told. Living things differ from the inanimate by the presence of soul. For the Atomists, the soul consists of spherical atoms, because of their mobility. Change and movement are therefore seen to be the key features of living things. The fact that spherical atoms are also the constituents of fire has already been remarked. If there is any connection between these two functions of such atoms, it will be that most animals are warm while alive and cold after death. The soul is a material entity. The soul's atoms are not destroyed at death, but disperse from the dead body. They disperse gradually, an idea that makes sense in terms of the likely physical behavior of the atoms and which also accounts for the fact that some vital functions, such as the growth of hair and fingernails, continue for a time after death.[42] Democritus informs us that there were no certain criteria that doctors trusted for determining the end of life.[43]

The soul atoms are scattered throughout the body. Their small size and their shape make them most able to move among other atoms without getting entangled into compounds. In what seems a hopelessly naive way, the Atomists believed that the motions of an animal's body are produced by contact of the easily moving soul atoms with other atoms in the body. Aristotle's criticism is appropriate.

16.46 Some say that the soul moves the body in which it is found in the same way as it moves itself, Democritus, for example, whose view is similar to what we find in Philippos the comic poet. He says that Daedalus made the wooden statue of Aphrodite move by pouring quicksilver into it. Democritus speaks similarly, since he says that moving spherical atoms, whose nature is never to stay still, draw the entire body along with them and move it. But we will ask if these same things also produce rest. How they will do so is difficult or impossible to state. In general, the soul does not appear

to move the body in this way, but through choice of some kind and through thought.

(Aristotle, *On the Soul* 1.3 406b16-25; part = DK 68A104)

SENSATION AND THOUGHT

The other principal functions of soul are sensation and thought, and Democritus probably believed that the soul atoms that perform these functions are concentrated in the head.[44] The Atomists had much to say about sensation in general and the five senses individually. Leucippus proposed a clear but crude theory, which Democritus elaborated. Theophrastus' long and critical discussion of Democritus' doctrines[45] provides most of our information. In general, all sensation results from the contact of atoms. Atoms of the perceived object strike atoms in the sense organ, which transmit the sense impressions to the soul atoms. In effect, all five senses are reduced to the sense of touch. Thus, Democritus makes all sensory objects objects of touch.[46] Since sensation depends on the interaction of the sensed object and the sensing animal, the condition of the sensor affects the sensations: sensations are relative to the observer. On the other hand, they are not purely relative since they also depend on the sensed object, which exists objectively, and whose atoms have objective attributes of size, shape, and position. This tension between subjectivism and objectivism is crucial in understanding the epistemology of the Atomists.[47]

Two of the senses, touch and taste, involve direct contact of the sensed object with the body of the sensor. With the remaining three, sight, hearing, and smell, where the object does not normally touch the sense organ, the Atomists need to explain in atomic terms how the object can affect our senses at a distance.

We saw previously how Democritus associates different tastes with different atomic shapes (16.36) and different tactile qualities with different atomic arrangements (16.35, 16.37). No more need be said here about these senses, except to point out an objection Theophrastus makes to the doctrine of taste and which he says applies to the atomist account of all five senses.[48] Atomic shape is an objective property, and if different tastes are defined in terms of different atomic shapes, taste is objective too. But this view contradicts the relativity of sensations to the sensor. The same thing may taste sweet to some and bitter to others, but an atom cannot be spherical to some and otherwise to others. (Cf. 16.50.)

Democritus' account of sight is the most interesting account of a sense that takes place at a distance. The Atomists adapted Empedocles' doctrine that physical objects give off films or effluences which enter our body through pores.[49] For the Atomists, the effluences are thin films of atoms that form an image of the object and move through the space between the object and the eye. Leucippus offered a simple theory: these films, which have the shape of the sense object, strike the eye, where they form a reflection of the object in the pupil. In this way vision occurs.[50] Democritus modified this theory.

> 16.47 The visual impression does not come to be in the pupil right away, but the air between the eye and the object is contracted and stamped by the object and by the seeing thing. For there is a continual effluence from everything. Then this [air], which is solid and changed in color, forms an impression in the eyes which are moist.
>
> (Theophrastus, *On Sensation* 50 = DK 68A135)

Good vision requires the parts of the eye to be in good condition. For instance, the "veins" must be straight and dry, to conform in shape to the images or impressions and to transmit them accurately to the soul atoms in the body.[51] The mechanics of vision are hard to understand. The nature of the interaction between the film of atoms from the object and the atoms emitted by the eye is especially obscure. The account as we have it leaves many questions open. Why do physical objects not decrease in size as the result of continually losing films of atoms? When we see the Parthenon, how can a film the size of the Parthenon fit into an eye? (Is this why Democritus modified Leucippus' theory and spoke of contraction in the intervening air?) This account explains how a visual impression has the same shape as the object, but does not explain how we see colors, and although Democritus says a good deal about color, it is unclear how to fit what he says into his account of vision.

Democritus recognizes four primary colors: white, black, red, and yellow.[52] He associates each of these with certain atomic shapes and arrangements of atoms on the surface of objects. For example, in things with hard surfaces, which are bright, conspicuous, and without shadows, white is associated with smooth atoms; and in friable things with easily crushed surfaces, it is associated with round atoms set slantwise to one another and in pairs, with the entire arrangement as even as possible. The other colors arise from mixtures of the primaries, and Democritus goes into some detail about how particular blends yield particular colors.[53]

Thought resembles sensation. Both sensations and thoughts are "alterations of the body" and both "take place when images enter from outside."[54] "He makes thought dependent on bodily condition as is appropriate, since he makes the soul a body."[55] Further, thinking arises from the same sort of process as sensations do, especially sight. Apparently the films of atoms that activate thought are not in all cases the same as those that activate the sense organs, though those too affect thought after the sense organs transmit them to the soul. But since not all thinking is reflection on present sensations, some of the films entering from outside affect the soul directly, not through the mediation of the senses. The atoms in these films may be too fine to be noticed by the senses.[56] A similar account is offered of dreams.[57]

The naiveté of these attempts to explain the phenomena of sensation and thought does not need to be stressed. They raise many questions that they seem unable to answer, and they are open to many obvious objections. From our information about these theories,[58] it appears that the Atomists failed to face three issues in particular. First, they reduce all thought and sensation to movements of the soul atoms, but do not say why some movements are perceived as sounds, others as tastes, and others as thoughts. Second, they do not clearly distinguish between mental events and the concomitant bodily states. Third, they do not account for the voluntary and apparently undetermined nature of some thought, but seem to think that our thoughts are determined by the atomic films striking us at a given moment. Cicero makes fun of this flaw: "If I begin to think of the island of Britain, will its film of atoms fly to my breast?"[59]

Although these theories are easy to criticize, we must recall that Leucippus and Democritus were the first philosophers to attempt so detailed an account of thought and perception. They performed an important service by exploring how far a purely materialist theory of cognition can go. The questions their accounts left open and the objections others made to their views stimulated further thought on the subject and pointed out to later investigators (notably their harsh critics Aristotle and Theophrastus) many important problems that needed to be tackled.

KNOWLEDGE

The philosophies of Anaxagoras, Empedocles, and the Atomists save the phenomenal world from the Eleatic challenge by postulating a more fundamental level of reality that conforms in some degree to the demands of the Eleatics and which also accounts for the sensible phenomena that the Eleatics rejected. These accounts raise important questions not only about the nature of reality but also about our knowledge of reality. For if one goal of the exercise is to rescue the senses and the sensible world, and doing so requires explaining them as mere epiphenomena of a realm of reality that is inaccessible to the senses, does it not follow that the senses and the world they reveal are unredeemed? And if another goal is the empiricists' aim to ground knowledge in the reports of sense perception, is it not fatal if the basic entities prove to be in principle imperceptible? For the system will rest upon things whose existence and behavior are not known through the principal avenue of knowledge.

These issues are more pressing for the Atomists than for Empedocles or Anaxagoras, whose basic things are in some sense perceptible. Democritus paid them due attention. He wrote a work called *Canon*, or *Canons*,[60] which opposed scientific demonstration and contrasted the senses unfavorably with the mind as sources of knowledge,[61] and one called the *Confirmations* (*Kratunteria*)"[62]

It is deeply frustrating that little remains of Democritus' work on this subject. Even the descriptions of the works just mentioned seem to conflict with one another, and the situation is no better with the other material we possess.

The problem is partly due to the nature of our sources. Sextus Empiricus (second century A.D.), to whom we owe much of our information, tries to make Democritus into a fellow sceptic, but does so by quoting him out of context. Immediately after the sentence quoted at the end of the previous paragraph, he goes on to say that Democritus' theory of perception does not provide a basis for certain knowledge. For perception depends on interaction between our body and atoms from the perceived object, and since the atomic composition of both our body and the object is subject to change from time to time, our perceptions are not sufficiently stable for exact understanding.

> 16.48 None the less he is found condemning them [the senses]. For he says, "We in fact understand nothing exactly [or, exact], but what changes according to the disposition both of the body and of the things that enter it and offer resistance to it."
>
> (Democritus, DK 68B9, part, and context from Sextus Empiricus, *Against the Mathematicians* 7.136 = DK 68B9)

Further, some of Democritus' epistemological discussion was cast in the form of a dialogue between mind and the senses (see below, 16.56), which makes it extremely difficult to assess isolated excerpts.

In general, the atomic theory provides a variety of viewpoints from which to approach epistemological issues, and our severely limited sources may simply not add up to a coherent theory just because their contexts have been lost. In what follows I attempt to make sense of the extant information by fitting it into the framework of the atomic theory developed earlier in this chapter. Two principal distinctions govern the following discussion: that between the objective and subjective components of sensation (see pp. 330-31), and that between judgment of perceptible qualities, based on the senses, and judgment of atoms and the void, based on the mind.

> 16.49 There are two kinds of judgment, one legitimate and the other bastard. All the following belong to the bastard: sight, hearing, smell, taste, touch. The other is legitimate and is separated from this. When the bastard one is unable to see or hear or smell or taste or grasp by touch any further in the direction of smallness, but <we need to go still further> towards what is fine, <then the legitimate one enables us to carry on>.[63]
>
> (Democritus, DK 68B11)

> 16.50 By convention [or, custom], sweet; by convention bitter; by convention, hot; by convention, cold; by convention, color; but in reality, atoms and void.[64]
>
> (Democritus, DK 68B9, part)

Knowledge of atoms and void is legitimate because it is objective and based on what exists in reality. The senses yield bastard judgment because they reveal perceptible qualities, which are properties not of atoms but of compounds. Worse, these qualities are not even objective properties that compounds have in their own right, but result from interaction between the perceived object and the observer's sense organs. How an object appears differs from perceiver to perceiver and in the same perceiver from time to time, depending on the condition of the sense organ, so that there is no objective reason to attribute any particular quality to a given object. Such attributions are only "by convention." Thus, the senses fail to produce legitimate judgment for three separate reasons: they have a subjective component, their objects are compounds, not the primary entities atoms and void, and the qualities they perceive are not the basic atomic properties of shape, order, and position.

Some of Democritus' remarks so emphasize the difficulty of going beyond appearances to reality that he has seemed to some a thorough sceptic about the possibility of knowledge:[65] in addition to 16.48, also the following.

> 16.51 A person must know by this rule [KANON: measuring stick, standard] that he is separated from reality.
>
> (Democritus, DK 68B6)

> 16.52 In fact it will be clear that to know in reality what each thing is like is a matter of perplexity [or, . . . that people are at a loss to know in reality what each thing is like]
>
> (Democritus, DK 68B8)

> 16.53 In reality we know nothing about anything, but for each person opinion is a reshaping [of the soul atoms by the atoms entering from without].
>
> (Democritus, DK 68B7)

> 16.54 Either nothing is true, or at least to us it is unclear [or, hidden].
>
> (Aristotle, *Metaphysics* 4.5 1009b11-12 = DK 68A112)

On the other hand, there is good evidence that Democritus was far from a sceptic, as in reports like the following.

> 16.55 It is because these thinkers suppose knowledge to be sensation, and this to be a physical alteration, that they say that what appears to our senses must be true.
>
> (Aristotle, *Metaphysics* 4.5 1009b12-15 = DK 68A112) (continuation of 16.54)

Also "truth is in the appearance" (16.2).[66] The apparent contradiction[67] between these claims and the previously quoted fragments makes for severe difficulties in understanding the Atomists' epistemology. I suggest that 16.2 and 16.55 reflect Democritus' view that sensations do have an objective basis in reality (being caused by the atoms of the perceived object) and are not simply arbitrary fictions of our mind. Sensations, which are the effects of atomic interactions, really exist. "True" here may mean "based in reality" as opposed to fictional.

Democritus also recognizes a genuine form of judgment alongside the obscure judgments due to the senses. And although atoms and void are imperceptible, the Atomists claim to have grasped the truth. How this can happen is suggested by the report[68] that Democritus approved of Anaxagoras' assertion (16.21) "Appearances are a sight of the unseen." Perception of macroscopic phenomena constitutes the first step in acquiring knowledge of the microscopic truth.

In what appears to be a moment of self-awareness, Democritus portrays the senses as addressing the mind in a dialogue or legal suit, as follows.

> 16.56 Wretched mind, after taking your evidence from us do you throw us down? Throwing us down is a fall[69] for you!
>
> (Democritus, DK 68B125)

Mind's reply should be that the senses provide the necessary starting point for inquiry. Even though the resulting theory reveals the shortcomings of the senses, it could not have been reached without their help. Moreover, sensible attributes include shape, size, position, and arrangement (conspicuously absent from 16.50), the primary qualities of the atoms. And even though we cannot perceive atoms and void, still, our sensations have an objective basis in compounds of atoms, which, although not basic entities, certainly exist. As 16.2 explains, the behavior and appearance of sensible compounds are grounds for inferences to the nature and behavior of their constituent atoms. Again, "appearances are a sight of the unseen." Thus, sensible reality constitutes the data that the atomic theory is to account for. Finally, far from simply discrediting the senses, the atomic theory explains how and why they go wrong, and how they are related to truth and reality.

We have no information on how the atomists believed it is possible to move from the level of sense experience, in which we are separated from reality and believe in qualities that have no real existence, to the level of reason, in which we possess secure, objective knowledge of the truth of things. Thought, like the senses, depends on films of atoms and on the condition of the atoms in the thinking soul. It has been suggested that the mind has direct awareness of atoms by virtue of their striking its atoms, but this does not explain how the senses provide the evidence the mind uses in grasping the truth of things. Some process of reasoning is needed to get from the one kind of grasp to the other, and it is doubtful that so crude a materialist theory as fifth-century atomism could come close to accounting for such a mental process.

The Gods

Since all sensation and thought result from our contact with atoms from outside us, and since we have conceptions of gods, there must be a basis in reality for these conceptions. Democritus therefore recognized the existence of gods, but the sources leave his actual views on this subject unclear. The most interesting information is the following statement.

> 16.57 Democritus says that certain images of atoms approach humans, and of them some cause good and others evil, and as a result he prayed "to meet with propitious images." These are large and immense, and

difficult to destroy though not indestructible. They indicate the future in advance to people when they are seen and emit voices. As a result people of ancient times, upon perceiving the appearances of these things, supposed that they are a god, though there is no other god aside from these having an indestructible nature.

> (Sextus Empiricus, *Against the Mathematicians* 9.19 = DK 68B166)

This passage makes it seem that the images themselves are gods, but other sources[70] say that Democritus also said that the gods are things that are the source of these images in the same way that other physical objects emit films of atoms that affect our mind and senses. The ability of these images to predict the future must be a concession to ordinary superstitious belief, since it is hard to square with the atomic theory. The extremely long-lasting but not eternal nature of these gods seems to show that Democritus was willing to accommodate his theology to common belief only within limits. No atomic compound is completely indestructible.

Ethics

The vast majority of Democritus' fragments are on ethical matters, though the authenticity of many of the ethical fragments is disputable. Democritus seems to have thought that the atomic theory provided a physical basis for ethics.

> 16.58 Cheerfulness arises in people through moderation of enjoyment and due proportion in life. Deficiencies and excesses tend to change suddenly and give rise to large movements in the soul. Souls which undergo motions involving large intervals are neither steady nor cheerful. . . .
>
> (Democritus, DK 68B191)

This fragment must be taken in connection with the statement that

> 16.59 The goal of life is cheerfulness, which is not the same as pleasure . . . but the state in which the soul continues calmly and stably, disturbed by no fear or superstition or any other emotion. He also calls it well-being and many other names.
>
> (Diogenes Laertius, *Lives of the Philosophers* 9.45 = DK 68A1)

The references in 16.58 to movements in the soul and large intervals seem to refer to the atoms that constitute the soul. Not that all movement of the spherical soul atoms is bad: they remain the most mobile atoms of all, and the functioning of the soul depends on their movements.

16.58 and 16.59 identify a particular physical condition of soul as the goal of life and give us an indication (cheerfulness) by which we can recognize whether our soul is in this state. The remainder of the fragment (not quoted here) specifies certain ways of thinking and behaving (avoid envy, consider yourself fortunate in comparison with the truly wretched, etc.) that will contribute to a life aimed at this goal. The identification of the objective physical basis of cheerfulness or well-being as the goal of life accords with Democritus' distinction between cheerfulness and pleasure. Not all pleasures are to be pursued.

> 16.60 Accept nothing pleasant unless it is beneficial.
>
> (Democritus, DK 68B74)

> 16.61 To all humans the same thing is good and true, but different people find different things pleasant.
>
> (Democritus, DK 68B69)

What is beneficial is what helps attain or maintain a state of well-being, the one thing that is good for all. Still, pleasure is not altogether divorced from cheerfulness. Some pleasures are beneficial and we should pursue them. As for the rest, it is within our power to master them.

> 16.62 Brave is not only he who masters the enemy but also he who masters pleasures. Some are lords of cities but slaves of women.
>
> (Democritus, DK 68B214)

We even have the capacity to reform ourselves so as to take pleasure in beneficial things.

> 16.63 Nature and teaching are closely related. For teaching reshapes the person, and by reshaping makes <his> nature.
>
> (Democritus, DK 68B33)

In this fragment, METARUSMEIN, translated "reshape," must designate an alteration in the RUSMOS or "rhythm" (the Atomists' technical term for shape)[71] of the soul's atoms. When these atoms are rearranged, the soul undergoes a significant alteration: its very nature (its atomic structure) is affected. The word PHYSIOPOIEIN, translated "makes <his> nature," is found only here. Doubtless an invention of Democritus, the word boldly puts his point that we can be affected at the most fundamental level by our experiences, and contributes as well to the interpretation of this point in terms of the atomic theory. In this way what we find pleasant depends on our soul's state, and since we can affect this, we can also determine our pleasures.

> 16.64 Best for a person is to live his life being as cheerful and as little distressed as possible. This will occur if he does not make his pleasures in mortal things.
>
> (Democritus, DK 68B189)

> 16.65 All those who make their pleasures from the belly, exceeding the right time for food, drink, or sex, have short-lived pleasures—only for as long as they eat or drink—but many pains.
>
> (Democritus, DK 68B235)

We are to "make our pleasures" from the things that promote and preserve the objective, lasting state of true cheerfulness. Thus, Democritus the laughing philosopher is no simple hedonist, but the proponent of a naturalistic ethics based on his physical theory and also on both the real condition and the potentialities of human nature.

Many of the ethical fragments can be read in the light of this connection between physical theory and ethics. It is easy to relate Democritus' counsels of moderation, prudence, doing right rather than wrong, and obeying rather than disobeying the laws to this view of the goal of life. However, it is not clear that he worked out a detailed ethical system, as some have claimed.[72]

HOW FAR ATOMISM?

The atomic theory is a theory about the nature of physical reality. however, it is possible to develop atomistic philosophical interpretations of other phenomena as well. Some later Greek philosophers held that time is not continuous, but composed of indivisible least instants, and likewise for spatial extension ("place") and motion.[73] I have alluded to the controversy of whether the fifth-century Atomists believed that atoms are theoretically as well as physically indivisible, and it is quite possible that Epicurus was following Democritus in his atomistic view of time.

One interesting fragment survies that is relevant to the question of indivisible spatial magnitudes.

> 16.66 If a cone is cut by a plane parallel to the base, what should we think about the surfaces of the segments? Do they prove to be equal or unequal? For if they are unequal, they will make the cone uneven, but with many steplike notches and roughnesses, but if they are equal <the surfaces of> the segments will be equal, and the cone will appear to have the property of a cylinder, being composed of equal, not unequal circles, which is most absurd.
>
> (Democritus, DK 68B155)

The difficulty is that the fragment states the dilemma but does not indicate Democritus' solution. Clearly enough, an atomistic view of space would compel him to say that the apparently smooth surface of a cone is really (i.e., at the atomic level) jagged, but in that case there is no real dilemma at all. In the end it must be admitted that the fragment as it stands is compatible with spatial atomism but cannot be used as evidence that Democritus advocated that view.

It is reasonable to press on to ask what the subject matter of geometry is for Democritus. For he was a mathematician of note. He is credited with stating, though not proving, the theorems that the volume of a cone is one-third that of a cylinder with the same base and height and that the volume of a pyramid is one-third that of a prism with the same base and height.[74] Is geometry somehow related to the atomic theory or is it a separate subject, not intended to describe physical reality at all, whether compounds, atoms, or the void?[75] Given Democritus' interest in the shapes of atoms, it seems to me very likely that geometry, viewed as the analysis of magnitudes, which include shapes, was not meant to be without application in the physical world in general or to atoms in particular. That geometry applies to the atoms themselves becomes almost inescapable on the interpretation of atoms as geometrically divisible though physically divisible (see p. 312).[76]

THE FATE OF THE ATOMIC THEORY

The view that matter is composed of atoms did not, of course, die with Democritus. In fact, there is a historical link between fifth-century atomism and today's atomic theory. But it is far from true either that once discovered, the atomic theory gained universal acceptance or that twentieth-century atomic theory closely resembles the atomism of Leucippus and Democritus. In what follows I shall briefly sketch a few of the most important stages in the history of responses to and developments in the atomic theory, both in antiquity and in modern times.

PLATO. Although Plato mentions many of his philosophical predecessors and contemporaries, he never refers to Democritus by name. Nevertheless, some points of contact have been found between the Atomists' cosmogony and that given in Plato's *Timaeus,* and the "geometrical atomism" of that dialogue may owe some of its inspiration to Democritus. Still, the differences between the two thinkers are profound. Plato's idealism makes beauty, goodness, and order the foundations of a grand teleological scheme that is the antithesis of Democritus' non-moral, mechanical materialism.

THE ARISTOTELIAN TRADITION. Aristotle, his commentators, and Theophrastus knew of fifth-century atomism and frequently discussed it. Their attitude is in general hostile and their discussions mostly consist of unsympathetic criticisms based on their own system, which is incompatible with atomism.

EPICURUS (341-271). Democritus had a number of followers during his lifetime and after his death. The most important was Epicurus, who founded a school of philosophy in Athens. Like other philosophers of the Hellenistic period, Epicurus' chief interests were in ethics, but the physical theory on which his entire philosophical system rested was Leucippus' and Democritus' atomic theory with a few modifications. There are only a finite number of atomic shapes; atoms are physically but not theoretically indivisible, though they have theoretical parts which are indivisible; weight is a fundamental property of atoms; atoms had an original motion in which they were falling at equal velocities in paralle downward trajectories through the void; the initial collisions resulted from occasional uncaused "swerves." In the area of human action, the swerve, as the only kind of atomic movement not caused mechanically (and therefore, in theory, predictably) by interaction with other atoms, becomes the key to account for free will. The gods are located in the tracts of the universe between KOSMOI—remote and unconcerned with human events, and therefore wrongly considered as figures of awe and dread. As with Democritus, the soul is composed of atoms and disperses at death; Epicurus inferred from this thesis that there is no afterlife to fear. This is not the place to go further into Epicurean philosophy, but from what has been said it is clear that atomism remained a vital part of the Greek intellectual tradition long after the end of the presocratic period. In this respect it is unique among the presocratic systems.

MODERN ATOMIC THEORY. Epicurus' atomism was revived in the seventeenth century by Descartes' opponent Gassendi, and in the eighteenth century it was common ground that matter was composed of ultimate units that are hard, unchanging, and endowed with shape and weight. The classical chemical theory of the nineteenth century continued to envisage atoms as the smallest units of matter, and the distinction between atoms and molecules is a recognizable development of the ancient distinction between atoms and compounds. The idea that atoms have physically separable parts (electrons, protons, etc.) is anathema to the ancient atomic theory, but the obvious response is that what corresponds to Democritus' unsplittable atoms are what we (incorrectly) call subatomic particles. The most important differences between ancient and modern atomic theory therefore are not in the splittability of the modern (so-called) atom. Rather they are to be found in the nonmaterialistic aspects of the modern atom. Nothing in the ancient theory corresponds to the forces that bind the atom together or that bind atoms together into molecules, and the thought that in some sense matter and energy (a concept absent in the ancients) are equivalent is incomprehensible to the thought of Democritus.

In addition, the atomic theory is accepted for different reasons now. In the fifth century it was presented as one response among others to the Eleatic challenge. Those few who accepted it will have done so for philosophical reasons or because they found the theory satisfactory, or at least preferable to its rivals, as a device for explaining many aspects of the world. But the theory was supported by a priori reasoning rather than empirical evidence. In this, ancient atomic theory was no worse than other ancient theories of the ultimate nature of reality. There is no need to do more than state that, by contrast, modern atomic theory is based on empirical evidence and has gradually emerged as the hypothesis that has best withstood experimental and theoretical challenges. It is subject to further extension and modifications, and even to wholesale revision on the basis of further theoretical and experimental work. Thus, ancient and modern atomic theory, while historically related, are different not only in detail but also in approach, but here as elsewhere much of the philosophical ground covered by the modern theory was first explored and seen to be fertile by the keensighted ancients.

Notes

1. Virtually nothing is known about his life. Epicurus (341-271), the most famous Atomist of antiquity, is reported to have denied Leucippus' existence (Diogenes Laertius, *Lives of the Philosophers* 10.13 = DK 67A2).

2. Diogenes Laertius, *Lives of the Philosophers* 9.30 (= DK 67A1).

3. Democritus, DK 68B5.

4. Diogenes Laertius, *Lives of the Philosophers* 9.41 (= DK 68B5).

5. The term "music" was originally used of any art governed by a Muse, such as singing, playing instruments, dancing, and poetry.

6. Most notably by C. Bailey, *The Greek Atomists and Epicurus* (Oxford, 1928).

7. APEIRON. For the sake of consistency with earlier chapters I continue to translate this word "unlimited," but in many of the passages on the Atomists it is appropriately taken as "infinite."

8. OUSIA, "substance," is a noun derived from the verb EINAI, "to be." There is a connection in language and meaning between OUSIA and ON (16.1).

9. The Atomists did not invent this word, which was used by the sixth-century lyric poet Alcaeus (fr. 23 [Diehl]).

10. See 5.13, 11.8 lines 9-11.

11. For further discussion of this point, see Guthrie, *HGP,* vol. 2, pp. 394-95.

12. For the Atomists' account of vision, which depends on atoms being emitted from the perceived object (hence a single atom, which cannot emit other atoms, is invisible), see pp. 331-32.

13. Aristotle says that "some gave in to (Zeno's arguments) by positing atomic magnitudes" (Aristotle, *Physics* 1.3 187a1-3 = DK 29A22). They "gave in" in the sense that they admitted their logical force, and avoided them by denying the hypothesis on which they depend, that what is is infinitely divisible.

14. As I use these terms, an atom is geometrically indivisible if we cannot distinguish (even without physical division) the sides from the corners, the center from the edges, the right half from the left half (given its position), etc. An atom is theoretically indivisible if it lacks geometrically or otherwise distinguishable parts. For a different account of kinds of divisibility, see Barnes, *The Presocratic Philosophers,* pp. 356-57.

15. Half on the Dichotomy paradox, some larger fraction on the Achilles.

16. Champions of theoretical indivisibility include Guthrie, *HGP,* vol. 2, pp. 396, 503-7, and Furley, *The Greek Cosmologists,* pp. 124-31; among the opponents are Barnes, *The Presocratic Philosophers,* pp. 352-60. Epicurus seems to have believed that atoms are theoretically divisible into theoretically indivisible parts.

17. H. Mendell argues ably for this view ("Democritus on Mathematical and Physical Shapes and the Emergence of Fifth Century Geometry," unpublished essay).

18. See pp. 172-73, 297.

19. 16.4 and 16.5 put the Atomists' hypothesis of the existence of void in an anti-Eleatic context.

20. Aristotle points out their shortcomings in *Physics* 4.7.

21. This passage forms part of Aristotle's treatment of void in which he presents the arguments offered in favor of the thesis that void exists, and shows why they fail.

22. For further discussion of these issues in Melissus as well as the Atomists, see D. Sedley, "Two Conceptions of Vacuum," *Phronesis* 27 (1982): 175-93.

23. Aristotle declares that proponents of the existence of void conceive of it as "place in which there is no body" (*Physics* 4.7 213b33, not in DK). Since Aristotle defines the place of something as "the innermost motionless boundary of what contains it" (*Physics* 4.4 212a20-21, not in DK), or, less precisely, as "what contains the thing whose place it is, and is no part of that thing" (*Physics* 4.4 210b34-211a1, not in DK), he takes void to be, in some sense, a potential container of body.

24. On the interpretation offered in chap. 11, these lines contain Parmenides' argument for spatial invariance, while 11.8 lines 22-25 argue for temporal invariance: there are no spatial or temporal stretches of what is not separating bits of what is.

25. The four Aristotelian elements have natural places. For example, earth's is at the center of the KOSMOS, and the natural motion of earth is toward the center. See Aristotle, *On the Heaven* 1.8.

26. I take it that this fact is behind the first clause of 16.21 and the second clause of 16.23.

27. KINEISTHAI. For Aristotle this word covers motion in place and also other changes, such as the "motions" listed at the end of this passage.

28. The words are PERIPALASSESTHAI and PALMOS, both derived from the root PAL-, "to shake."

29. The word translated "reason" is LOGOS. This word need not imply the existence of a reasoning agent, only that a reason could in principle be given if one were sought.

30. It is likely that the analogy in 16.2 comes from an atomist text, though it could be Aristotle's.

31. Aristotle's unsympathetic report that "Democritus declares the soul to be some kind of fire and hot, for the shapes and atoms being infinite, he says the spherical ones are fire and soul" (*On the Soul* 1.2 403b31-404a2 = DK 67A28), is therefore unfair. Moreover, for all the sources tell us, the atoms which make up souls could be spheres of different sizes from those that make up fire.

32. See 16.1.

33. See 9.31, 9.32, and discussion pp. 105-107.

34. The Milky Way is the light of stars from which the earth blocks the rays of the sun (Aristotle, *Meteorologica* 1.8 345a25-31 = DK 59A80); comets are a conjunction of planets so near as to be in apparent contact (Aristotle, *Meteorologica* 1.6 342b27-29 = DK 59A81).

35. This view goes back to Anaximenes (see 6.8).

36. Diogenes Laertius, *Lives of the Philosophers* 9.30 (= DK 67A1), Aetius 3.10.5 (= DK 68A94).

37. Democritus, DK 68B15.

38. Diogenes Laertius, *Lives of the Philosophers* 9.30 (= DK 67A1).

39. Here he disagrees with Empedocles and Anaxagoras, who held that the heavens tilted (Aetius 2.8.2 = DK 31A58 for Empedocles, Aetius 2.8.1 = DK 59A67 for Anaxagoras).

40. Democritus, DK 68B34.

41. Aetius 5.19.6 (= DK 68A139).

42. Tertullian, *On the Soul* 51 (= DK 68A160).

43. Celsus 2.6 (= DK 68A160).

44. Aetius 4.5.1 (= DK 68A105).

45. Theophrastus, *On Sensation* 49-83 (= DK 68A135).

46. This is Aristotle's observation (Aristotle, *On Sensation* 4 442a29-b1 = DK 68A119).

47. See pp. 334-335.

48. Theophrastus, *On Sensation* 69 (= DK 68A135).

49. See p. 282-283.

50. Alexander, *Commentary on Aristotle's On Sensation* 24.14-22 (= DK 67A29).

51. Theophrastus, *On Sensation* 50 (= DK 68A135)

52. These were the four basic colors used by Greek painters.

53. Theophrastus, *On Sensation* 73-82 (= DK 68A135).

54. Aetius 4.8.5, 4.8.10 (= DK 67A30).

55. Theophrastus, *On Sensation* 58 (= DK 68A135).

56. This interpretation follows Guthrie, *HGP*, vol. 2, pp. 452-53.

57. Plutarch, *Table Talk* 8.10 p. 735A-B (= DK 68A77).

58. Our information depends almost entirely on the hostile Aristotelian-Theophrastean tradition and may not always be fair to the Atomists.

59. Cicero, *Letters to his Friends* 15.16.1 (= DK 68A118).

60. Epicurus' work on epistemology had the same title.

61. Sextus Empiricus, *Against the Mathematicians* 8.327 (= DK 68B10b), 7.138 (= DK 68B11).

62. Sextus Empiricus, *Against the Mathematicians* 7.136 (= DK 68B9).

63. This fragment trails off into corruption, but there is general agreement about the sense of what is missing.

64. The contrast between "by convention" (NOMOS) and "in reality" recalls that between NOMOS and PHYSIS which was prominent in other intellectual contexts in the late fifth century. See chap. 22.

65. Notably Barnes, *The Presocratic Philosophers,* pp. 559-64. Asmis, *Epicurus' Scientific Method,* pp. 337-50, casts him as a sceptic about humans' capacity to attain knowledge since we must employ the senses, but as possibly holding a rationalist belief in the ability of reason to attain truth without the use of sense perception. Guthrie, *HGP,* vol. 2, pp. 454-65, does a good job of posing the problems and setting out the evidence.

66. Another passage attesting this view is Aristotle, *On the Soul* 1.2 404a28-29 (= DK 68A101).

67. The fact that 16.55 occurs in Aristotle just after 16.54 has been taken to prove that Aristotle did not think that the two statements are contradictory (Guthrie, *HGP*, vol. 2, p. 460), but it is quite likely that Aristotle took them out of different contexts in Democritus.

68. Sextus Empiricus, *Against the Mathematicians* 7.140 (= DK 59B21a).

69. The word is a technical term in wrestling for a fall. It is sometimes translated here more colorlessly as "downfall."

70. Cicero, *On the Nature of the Gods* 1.12.29 (= DK 68A74); Clement, *Stromata* 5.88 (= DK 68A79).

71. See 16.1.

72. For an interesting attempt to construct an ethical theory out of the fragments and relate it to the atomic theory and to fifth-century medical doctrines, see G. Vlastos, "Ethics and Physics in Democritus," *Philosophical Review* 54 (1945): 578-92, and 55 (1946): 53-64; reprinted in *Studies in Presocratic Philosophy,* vol. 2, pp. 381-408.

73. Simplicius says that the Epicureans believed in atomic units of all these types (*Commentary on Aristotle's Physics* 934.23-30, not in DK). See discussion in A. Long and D. Sedley, *The Hellenistic Philosophers,* vol. 1, pp. 51-52.

74. Archimedes, *Method* 430.2-9 in vol. 2 of Heiberg's edition (Leipzig, 1913), printed in a note at DK, vol. 2, p. 174.

75. This latter view is held by Furley, *The Greek Cosmologists,* vol. 1, pp. 129-31. It accords with and is

to some extent dependent on Furley's belief that Democritean atoms are theoretically indivisible.

76. In this interpretation I agree with H. Mendell (op. cit. [p. 312 n. 17]), who discusses the issues more fully.

Abbreviations

DK: H. Diels and W. Kranz, *Die Fragmente der Vorsokratiker,* 6th ed., Berlin, 1951 and later editions. The standard edition of the Presocratic Philosophers. Each Presocratic is assigned a number. The fragments of each Presocratic are also assigned numbers preceded by the letter "B." Thus, the number for Heraclitus is 22, and Heraclitus' fragment 101 is referred to as DK 22B101. Testimonia are likewise identified by numbers preceded by the letter "A." The DK references are used very widely in books and articles on the Presocratics.

HGP: W. K. C. Guthrie, *A History of Greek Philosophy,* 6 vols., Cambridge, 1962-1981. The first three volumes are relevant to the period treated in the present work.

KR: G. S. Kirk and J. E. Raven, *The Presocratic Philosophers,* Cambridge, 1957.

KRS: G. S. Kirk, J. E. Raven and M. Schofield, *The Presocratic Philosophers,* 2nd ed., Cambridge, 1983.

Alan Chalmers (essay date 1997)

SOURCE: "Did Democritus Ascribe Weight to Atoms?" in *Australasian Journal of Philosophy,* Vol. 75, No. 3, September, 1997, pp 279-87.

[*In the following essay, Chalmers attempts to eliminate contradictions concerning the weight of atoms in Democritus's theory by making fine distinctions in particular definitions.*]

I. INTRODUCTION

The problems concerning the question of whether or not Democritus ascribed weight to atoms are twofold. First, if we take their words at face value, it would appear that the ancient Greek commentators on Democritus disagreed on the matter. Aristotle and his pupil Theophrastus both made statements that can readily be taken as attributing weight or heaviness to Democritean atoms, as did Simplicius, who had access to a work by Aristotle on Democritus which is now lost. Aetius, by contrast, claimed the contrary. Second, modern commentators are in disagreement concerning how this difficulty is to be resolved.

Kirk, Raven and Schofield [9, p. 141] have identified and translated the key passages from the Greek commentators. According to Aristotle, Democritus claimed that 'each of the indivisibles is heavier in proportion to its excess'. The remark of Theophrastus that 'Democritus distinguishes heavy and light by size' can be taken as claiming the same

thing, whilst the claim of Simplicius that 'Democritus' school thinks that everything possesses weight' can certainly be read as claiming that atoms do. By contrast, according to Aetius, writing in the second century A.D., 'Democritus says that primary bodies (that is, the solid atoms) do not possess weight'. In each of these instances, the Greek for 'heavy' or 'weight' is ['*baros*'] or a derivative. Kirk, Raven and Schofield, noting the threat of contradiction here, suggest two possible responses. The first relies on the distinction between atoms moving freely in the void, on the one hand, and atoms caught in the vortex corresponding to our world or cosmos, on the other. If it is assumed that atoms do not possess weight of themselves but only come to have weight as the result of collisions they experience in vortices that constitute worlds such as ours, and if, further, we interpret those claims attributing weight to atoms as referring to atoms in a world and those denying weight to atoms as referring to atoms in the void, then the apparently conflicting claims can be reconciled. Versions of this position have been defended by Burnett [2, pp. 341-347] and Guthrie [6, pp. 400-404]. The second response suggested by Kirk, Raven and Schofield is to dismiss Aetius' claim as mistaken. This, of course, leaves open the question of the precise sense in which Democritean atoms do possess weight.

In the following I suggest that neither response is the correct one. Several meanings attached to the term ['*baros*'] in ancient Greek talk which, indeed, have their correlates in modern, everyday usage of the terms 'heavy' and 'weight'. Once these meanings are identified and distinguished, it can be appreciated that Democritean atoms can be said both to possess and not to possess weight or heaviness, depending on which meaning of those terms is intended. This opens the way for a reading of the quotations cited above as each correctly recording a feature of Democritean atomism, with no contradiction involved.

II. ARISTOTLE, THEOPHRASTUS AND SIMPLICIUS

The first option of Kirk, Raven and Schofield, which requires us to read Aristotle, Theophrastus and Simplicius as attributing weight to atoms only when they are situated in a world, is not viable. This has been argued forcefully and in detail by O'Brien [13]. Once the three quotations in question are taken in context, it is clear that weight is being attributed to atoms in themselves, whether they are in a world or not.

Aristotle's remark appears in a passage (*On Generation and Corruption,* i, 8, 326a, 1-19) in which he considers, and criticises, the Democritean view that atoms are one and changeless. He groups together three pairs of qualities, hot and cold, heavy and light, and hard and soft and suggests that if one of these pairs can be attributed to individual atoms then there is no good reason why we should not attribute all three to them. He claims that, as a matter of fact, Democritus does attribute hotness to round atoms (and infers that coldness must be attributed to some other shape of atom) and he also claims that Democritus attributes heaviness and lightness to atoms. (It is here that Aristotle cites Democritus' claim that 'each of the individuals is heavier in proportion to its excess'.) Thus, Aristotle argues, we have some mutually supporting evidence for attributing a degree of hotness, heaviness and hardness to atoms. However, this, in Aristotle's view, undermines the Democritean view that atoms are changeless, for a hot atom can be expected to cool in contact with a cold one and a soft atom will be subject to compression. Leaving aside the question of the cogency of Aristotle's argument and the 'questionable character of his implication that Democritus attributed a degree of heat to atoms, it should be noted that the whole discussion concerns individual atoms as such, and whether or not they are changeless in the strong sense claimed by Democritus. Aristotle invokes Democritus' attribution of weight to atoms to assist him in an argument to the effect that they must be subject to change. The nature of the vortex that constitutes our world and the effect this has on atoms in it is completely irrelevant to the argument. The passage therefore gives no support to Kirk, Raven and Schofield's first option. O'Brien [13, pp. 115-131, 154-161] has argued in detail that the same can be said for the quotations from Theophrastus and Simplicius, once they are taken in context.

III. THE DENIAL OF WEIGHT TO DEMOCRITEAN ATOMS BY AETIUS

According to Aristotle, naturally occurring things, as opposed to artifacts, have a natural motion distinctive of the kind of natural thing that they are (*Physics,* II. 192b). The growth of plants and animals is natural as is the motion of material objects, either up or down depending on the relative proportions of the four elements air, earth, fire and water, that they contain. Nature is the cause of natural motions. 'All natural bodies and magnitudes we hold to be, as such, capable of locomotion; for nature, we say, is their principle of movement' (*De Caelo,* I, 2, 15-17). Motions that are not natural are forced, and require a non-natural cause, that is, a cause other than nature. If material objects are to have natural motions then there must be absolute directions to which those motions are referred. Aristotle's finite, earth-centred cosmos provides those directions, down, towards the centre and up, away from the centre. 'Let us then apply the term "heavy" to that which moves naturally towards the centre and "light" to that which moves naturally away from the centre' (*De Caelo,* I, 3, 269b, 22-24).

From this perspective it is not difficult to see the objections that an Aristotelian would have to Democritean atomism, objections that may well have led Epicurus to modify it in the way that he did. Democritean atoms constantly collide, are 'scattered around' and move away 'in any chance direction' [9, pp. 424, 426]. Consequently, there is no motion that is natural to them, nor are there any special directions in an infinite void to which such natural motions might be referred. Whilst collisions can change the motion of atoms, it is difficult to see how they could ever

have a motion to *be* changed in the absence of natural motion. For it is virtually a tautology for an Aristotelian to note that there can be no motion in nature in the absence of natural motion. The disorderly motions of atoms in Democritus' theory are incompatible with an orderly, natural world since, as Aristotle observes in *Physics,* VIII, 1, 11-12 'that which is produced or directed by nature can never be anything disorderly: for nature is everywhere the cause of order'. In *Metaphysics,* 1, 4, 985b, 18-19 and 12, 6, 1071b, 32-37 and *On The Heavens,* 3, 1, 300b, 8-16, Aristotle argues that Leucippus and Democritus failed to specify the cause of atomic motions and failed to identify what motion of atoms was natural to them as opposed to forced. As a matter of observable fact, heavy objects do fall downwards naturally and light objects do rise upwards naturally, whilst some objects fall down in some media and rise in others. The Democritean theory cannot accommodate these observations, according to Aristotle. Epicurus, for instance in his *Letter to Herodotus,* 60, was, by contrast, able to confront and attempt to meet these kinds of criticism, at least in part, by introducing a direction into the void, downwards, and attributing weight to atoms, which served as the natural cause of their downwards motion.

Aetius, writing in the second century AD, was aware of the Aristotelian criticism of Democritean atomism and of the Epicurean attempt to meet it. He was able to recognise the introduction of weight, interpreted as a tendency to move 'downwards' as an Epicurean innovation within the atomic theory. In this context, the denial by Aetius that Democritus attributed weight to atoms should be interpreted as the denial that Democritus attributed to them a tendency to move downwards.

This interpretation is borne out once Aetius' remarks are taken in their context. Let us consider first the explicit denial by Aetius (1, 12, 6) that Democritus attributed weight to atoms. 'Democritus says that the primary bodies (that, is, the solid atoms) do not possess weight but move in the infinite as the result of striking one another' [9, p. 421]. This remark comes in a context where Aetius has been discussing the atomism of Epicurus (1, 12, 5). He notes that in the latter theory there are three causes of the motion of atoms—weight, the cause of downwards motion, swerves—that are necessary to initiate collisions amongst the downward rain of atoms, and the collisions themselves. Then comes the contrast with Democritus, cited above. For Democritus there is only one cause of motion, collisions. Democritean atoms do not possess weight, as a cause of motion. This had already been implicit in an earlier passage (1, 3, 18) in which Aetius asserted that Epicurus added weight as a property of atoms to the properties of shape and size that Democritus attributed to them. Consequently, provided we are clear about the sense in which 'weight' is being used, there seem to be scant grounds for adopting the second option suggested by Kirk, Raven and Schofield for reconciling the various claims concerning weight attributed to Democritus. It seems inappropriate, and unnecessary, to reject

Aetius' claims as a misrepresentation of Democritus' view, and I am puzzled by the fact that O'Brien [13, p. 301] opts for a version of that view, as does Jonathan Barnes [1, pp. 365-367].

The claim by Aetius that Democritus did not attribute weight to atoms is clear and unproblematic. By it, Aetius indicated that Democritean atoms did not possess a natural tendency to move downwards, and so differed in precisely this respect from the atoms of Epicurus. Whether Democritean atoms might be said to possess weight in some other sense is a question to which we now turn.

IV. THE SENSE IN WHICH DEMOCRITEAN ATOMS HAVE WEIGHT

There are usages of the terms 'heavy' and 'weight' in modern everyday talk that can be identified in, or plausibly attributed to, the Presocratics as well, and which are distinct from their association with a tendency to move downwards. One such usage relates to what is more accurately described as density. So the claim that gold is heavier than lead is a careless way of saying that it is more dense. Whilst this notion has necessary associations with weight understood as a tendency to move downwards, so that a cubic centimetre of gold will have a greater such tendency than an equal volume of lead, the notion of density can be understood independently of this sense of weight. It can be understood in terms of thickness and thinness, so that air or a heap of feathers are understood to become more dense when they are compressed. Talk of dense crowds illustrates this usage, as does Anaximenes' understanding of how a diversity of substances can be formed from a single primary substance, air, by 'thickening and thinning out' [9, p. 45]. The Democriteans had a novel way of giving an account of density, independently of any implications this might have for weight understood as a tendency to move downwards. The density of a substance is determined by the amount of its volume that is filled by atoms as opposed to void. Insofar as 'heavy' and 'weight' can be used to denote 'dense' and 'density' respectively, we have here a sense of those former terms that is not tied necessarily to a tendency to move downwards. However, this second sense of 'weight' does not offer a solution to our problem of the sense that can be made of attributing weight to Democritean atoms. Strictly speaking, the definition of density in terms of the ratio of space filled by atoms to space empty of atoms does not apply to individual atoms and, insofar as it does, leads to the conclusion that all atoms have the same density. Identifying weight with density makes nonsense of the Democritean claim that atoms are heavy in proportion to their size.

There is a further common sense of 'heavy' and 'weight' which is more promising for our purpose. I suggest that the following assertions make common sense. 'A heavy object, once set in motion, is difficult to stop, and, for a given speed, the greater its weight the more difficult it is to stop. The heavier an object the more difficult it is to

move. One might be able to effectively kick a ball, but a similar effort executed on a round boulder may result in a painful foot and a stationary stone. If two objects moving with similar speeds collide, the motion of the heavier is affected less than the motion of the lighter.' The modern reader familiar with Newtonian physics will note that this usage of 'heaviness' and 'weight' refers to what is more accurately designated as 'inertial mass'. But my argument does not require that degree of sophistication. Rather I wish to establish merely that there is a sense of 'heaviness' and 'weight' at work in everyday talk and exemplified in everyday experience which is distinct from the conception of weight understood as a tendency to fall. What is more, that conception is ideally suited for dealing with colliding atoms as they figure in Democritean atomism. Further, I suggest that the examples I have chosen to illustrate my point, and many others like them, would have made as much sense to the Presocratics as they do to us. To avoid using 'mass', and the possible charge of anachronism, I coin the word 'unwieldiness' to refer to that property of a heavy object that determines the degree of difficulty involved in moving or stopping it. This is distinct from the tendency objects have to fall.

There are usages of [*baros*] around the time of Democritus that call for a translation in terms of unwieldiness rather than gravitational weight. For example, a usage of [*baros*] common in the writings of Hippocrates is in the context of heavy limbs, where it seems that difficulty of movement, rather than gravitational weight, is being referred to. In one place, at least, the association of [*baros*] with difficulty of movement is made explicit.[1] Another source of appropriate examples is the pseudo-Aristotelian text *On Mechanics*. In that text we find discussions of how the movement of a heavy object is facilitated by levers where the motions involved are not simply those of lifting an object vertically against gravity but also horizontal and other motions. We find [*baros*] used to express the view that 'the smaller and the lighter is more easily moved than the larger and heavier' and that heavy objects collect at the centre of an eddy of water because they are better able to resist the motion [8, pp. 357, 361].

We know from the Greek commentators on Democritus that, according to him, the atoms 'struggle and move in the void', that they experience 'mutual collisions and blows' and that 'they have effects and are affected whenever they are in contact' [9, pp. 423, 424, 407]. What is more, the view attributed to Democritus by Diogenes Laertius and by Aetius that everything happens by necessity strongly suggests that the motions of atoms after a collision are in some way determined by their motions before the collision. This is almost explicit in the extract from Aetius that reads: 'On the nature of necessity / Democritus means by it the resistance and movement and blows of matter' [9, p. 419]. It does not seem too much to presume that unwieldiness, in the sense that I have construed it in the previous paragraph, was seen by Democritus as one of the determinants of the effect of a collision, along with the speeds, directions and shapes of the colliding atoms. If we adopt this suggestion, then the sentence 'each of the individuals is heavy in proportion to its excess' makes immediate sense if we write 'unwieldy' for 'heavy'. For unwieldiness can be presumed to depend on the amount of matter, which for a single atom depends only on its size.

My claim that it is not anachronistic to attribute weight, understood as unwieldiness, to Democritean atoms is borne out to some extent by the fact that that notion can be found at work in the atomism of Epicurus and Lucretius also. Here we need to distinguish weight understood as unwieldiness from weight understood as a tendency to move downwards, for, as we have noted, the latter notion is ascribed to atoms by Epicurus and Lucretius, although not by Democritus.

The argument that the attribution of unwieldiness to atoms was a conceptual necessity for Democritus, insofar as it was needed as a factor determining the result of collisions, would seem to apply to Epicurus also. However, the matter is not entirely straightforward. Indeed, if the interpretation of David Konstan is correct [10, pp. 395-398] atoms do not collide at all, but merely change course once their mutual approach leaves no unit of space remaining between them. Nevertheless, there is at least one passage in which Epicurus talks of atomic collisions in a way that seems to involve [*baros*] interpreted as unwieldiness. In that passage, Epicurus insists that atoms move always at the same speed in whatever direction they might be moving: 'For however far along either kind of trajectory it gets, for that distance it will move as fast as thought, until it is in collision, either through an external cause or through its own weight in relation to the force of the impacting body' [12, p. 48]. Both O'Brien and Furley, for example, read into this passage the idea that the effect of a collision on an atom will depend on its weight in relation to the atom with which it collides, and I agree provided weight is interpreted as unwieldiness. Furley, for example, claims that 'the passage permits us to say that in computing the result of a collision between two atoms (if it were possible to do so), the weight of the atoms would enter into the calculation'. Furley explains that in claiming that, in collisions, atoms offer resistance by virtue of their weight, he is not 'attributing to Epicurus an anachronistic theory of inertia', adding that 'it is a matter of pure common sense, and one which cannot have escaped his [Epicurus'] observation, that heavier bodies are harder to budge than lighter ones' [3, p. 230]. Part of my point, of course, is that it cannot have escaped Democritus' observation either. I am certainly not alone, then, in reading into Epicurus the sense of heaviness, interpreted as unwieldiness, that I have attributed to Democritean atoms.

Weight, in the sense of unwieldiness, can also be discerned, quite unambiguously, in Lucretius' version of Epicureanism. It is at least implicit in his claim that 'it must often happen that two of them [atoms] in their course knock together and immediately bounce apart in opposite directions, a natural consequence of their hardness and solidity

and the absence of anything behind to stop them' [11, p. 62]. Indeed, it is explicit if the Latin *ponderibus solidis* is taken to imply heaviness, as Sisson [15, p. 46] and Long and Sedley [12, p. 46] have done. Another aspect of what I have presented as the common sense notion of unwieldiness is present in Lucretius' discussion of sensation, which in his view arises when films emanating from objects impinge on the senses. One reason that Lucretius gives for the rapid speed at which he supposes these films to travel is that, being light, a high speed is imparted to them by a small impulse, with one translator at least finding in the Latin the notion that, for a given impulse, speed is proportional to lightness.[2]

Those commentators that attributed weight to Democritean atoms can be taken as correctly asserting that he attributed unwieldiness to them. The denial by Aetius that Democritean atoms had weight can be interpreted, equally correctly, as denying that they had a natural tendency to move downwards.

V. COMPARISON WITH OTHER AUTHORS

My solution to the problem posed by the apparently contradictory positions attributed to Democritus' stance on the question of whether atoms have weight can be compared to others that have recently been proposed. David Hahm [7] has defended a version of the first option of Kirk, Raven and Schofield. I have argued above that there is no support in the texts for the view that Democritus attributed weight to atoms as a result of their participation in a cosmos.

Furley notes that the position that corresponds to the first option of Kirk, Raven and Schofield has received 'general agreement', but describes it as 'very dubious' [4, p. 86]. In this we concur. However, the position he adopts as an alternative is to attribute to Democritus the view that atoms possess weight in much the same way as they possess weight for Epicurus, namely as a natural tendency to move downwards. A key reason he gives for this concerns the difficulty Democritus would have faced explaining the common fact that heavy objects fall to the ground. Furley is right about the implausibility of attempts to explain weight by appeal to vortices that constitute our world. As an alternative, he suggests that Democritus solved the problem of free fall by attributing weight to atoms in the same way that Epicurus did. Furley [4, p. 97] suggests that this move was simply 'inferred from sense experience' by Democritus.

I am dissatisfied with Furley's position for two reasons. First, whilst it seems likely that Democritus did not succeed in spelling out an adequate explanation of gravity, it seems to me unreasonable to expect him to have done so. Democritean atomism is best seen as a general solution to the problem posed by Parmenides, and shows in a notional way how the phenomena, such as sense perception, astronomy, gravity, biological and chemical change and so on might conceivably be explained in a mechanical, non-teleological way. None of the actual explanations of such phenomena ventured by Democritus stand close inspection. Very few interpretations of Democritus would withstand the demand that they should. Consequently, it does not seem to me to be a strong argument against an interpretation of Democritus that it does not entail an adequate account of gravity. It can also be noted that, to the extent that Furley's line of argument has force, it tells against all the mechanical philosophies of the seventeenth century. The mechanical philosophers acknowledged that gravity needed to be explained in some way by the motion of matter, but, in the main, freely admitted the inadequacy of their attempts to do so.

My second dissatisfaction with Furley's position is that it itself is not immune to his own line of argument. Furley's reason for attributing an inherent tendency to fall downwards to atoms is that this step removes the problem of explaining gravity. But things are not nearly so straightforward. The reason for this is that the step from falling atoms to observable falling objects is by no means direct. That this is so is clear from Epicurean atomism, where an inherent tendency to fall is indeed attributed to atoms. In Epicurean atomism the speed at which atoms move is much faster than observable speeds, the latter being the complex result of intertwining and colliding atoms. Indeed, the atoms themselves are assumed to move 'as fast as thought'. The speeds of observable objects are to the speeds of atoms as the speed at which a swarm of bees moves is to the speed of individual bees. The Epicurean explanation of why observable objects fall with relatively small, observable speeds, and catch the earth up, thus falling 'towards' the earth, is quite complex, and, one might add, quite contrived and implausible. I do not know what detailed account Furley wishes to attribute to Democritus, but my point is that merely attributing to atoms a tendency to fall downwards in the void does not of itself explain why objects such as stones fall to the earth. If a stone and the earth are alike made up of atoms that possess a tendency to fall, then some explanation is required of why stones fall to the earth, catching up the earth, in the way that they are observed to do. Furley's position does not have the advantage over the more standard accounts of Democritean atomism that he claims it to have. It does not offer a ready explanation of gravity. What is more, because of the indirect and complicated connection between the motion of individual atoms and of macroscopic objects, a tendency for atoms to fall cannot be straightforwardly 'inferred from sense experience'.

Some elements of the view I advocate here are at least implicit in O'Brien's work [13], whilst Jonathan Barnes [1, p. 365] has interpreted Democritus as attributing 'mass' to atoms, although without elaborating on or justifying his stance. Konstan [10, p. 410] has also suggested that both Democritus and Epicurus attributed weight to atoms in a sense distinct from gravity drawing on the notion of [ekthlipsi], the term used by the Ancients to refer to a theory of displacement or extrusion 'according to which heavier or denser objects had the capacity to drive lighter ones out

and upward'. I can agree with Konstan that this notion is distinct from, though connected with, gravity. However, putting stress on it does not get to the heart of the matter, because [ekthlipsi] is an effect that, for Democritus, is in need of an atomic explanation. Konstan does propose an atomic explanation on behalf of Democritus. I am not sure that his suggestion is adequate in all respects, but, whether it is or not, Konstan appeals, in his proposal, to the 'power of atoms to jostle their lighter neighbours out of the way'. This, of course, is just one aspect of the unwieldiness that I am suggesting Democritus ascribed to atoms.

VI. Conclusion

It seems to me that there is much to be said for taking Aetius at his word, and accepting that Epicurus added to Democritean atoms the inherent tendency to move downwards, and that he did this to meet what he saw as valid in Aristotle's critique of Democritus. Democritean atoms possessed weight as an inherent property, but one that corresponded to unwieldiness, rather than a tendency to fall downwards. The fact that both gravity and unwieldiness were referred to by the single Greek word, [baros], accounts for the fact that various claims of commentators concerning the nature of weight in Democritean atomism appear on the surface to be contradictory. Careful attention to the distinction enables these difficulties to be straightforwardly removed.

It was left to Newton to make explicit and precise the distinction between gravitational and inertial mass. However, an anticipation of the distinction was already implicit in common parlance at the time of Democritus, as has been demonstrated by a little philological analysis. I have coined the word 'unwieldiness' to refer to the common sense precursor of inertial mass, and have argued that Democritus attributed that property to atoms, using the term 'weight' [baros] to do so.

Notes

1. Potter [14, p. 17] translates Hippocrates, *De Morbis,* 3, 7, 6 as 'his chest seems to sigh and to contain a heaviness that prevents it from moving'. See also *De Morbis,* 2, 40, 59 (heaviness in loins and legs), *De Affectionibus,* 14, 18 (heaviness of the body) and *Aphorisms,* 4, 20, 2 (heaviness of the knees).

2. The relevant passage in *De rerum natura,* 4, 192-194 is translated by Lathan [11, p. 136] as 'a very slight initial impetus far away from their rear sufficed to launch them and they continue on their course at a velocity proportional to their lightness'.

References

1. J. Barnes, *The Presocratic Philosophers* (London: Routledge, 1993).

2. J. Burnett, *Early Greek Philosophy,* 4th edn. (London: A. and C. Black, 1930).

3. D. J. Furley, *Two Studies in the Greek Atomists* (Princeton: Princeton University Press, 1967).

4. ———.'Aristotle and the Atomists on Motion in the Void' in P. K. Machamer and R. G. Turnbull (eds.), *Interrelations in the History and Philosophy of Science* (Columbus: Ohio State University Press, 1976) pp. 83–100.

5. ———. 'Weight and Motion in Democritus's Theory', *Oxford Studies in Ancient Philosophy* 1 (1983) pp. 193–209.

6. W. Guthrie, *A History of Greek Philosophy*, vol. 2 (Cambridge: Cambridge University Press, 1965).

7. D. E. Hahm, 'Weight and Lightness in Aristotle and His Predecessors,' in P. Machamer and R. G. Turnbull (eds.) *Interrelations in the History and Philosophy of Science* (Columbus: Ohio State University Press, 1976) pp. 56–82.

8. W. S. Hett, *Aristotle: Minor Works* (London: Heinemann, 1936).

9. G. S. Kirk, J. E. Raven and M. Schofield, *The Presocratic Philosophers* (Cambridge: Cambridge University Press, 1983).

10. D. Konstan, 'Problems in Epicurean Physics', *Isis* 70 (1979) pp. 394–418.

11. R. Latham, *On the Nature of Things* (Harmondsworth: Penguin, 1951).

12. A. Long and D. N. Sedley, *The Hellenistic Philosophers* (Cambridge: Cambridge University Press, 1987).

13. D. O'Brien, *Democritus, Weight and Size: An Exercise in the Reconstruction of Greek Philosophy* (Paris: Les Belles Lettres, 1981).

14. P. Potter, *Hippocrates* (Cambridge, MA: Harvard University Press, 1988).

15. C. H. Sisson, *De rerum natura* (Manchester: Carcanet Press, 1976).

Robert L. Oldershaw (essay date 1998)

SOURCE: "Democritus—Scientific Wizard of the 5th Century B.C.," in *Speculations in Science and Technology*, Vol. 21, No. 1, March, 1998, pp. 37-44.

[*In the following essay, Oldershaw explains the methodology that enabled Democritus to achieve extraordinary results considering the unavailability of all but the most rudimentary form of mathematics.*]

LAUGHTER IN THE GARDEN

An elderly man sat in a beautiful garden on the outskirts of Abdera, Greece, staring fixedly at various parts of his natural surroundings. He often chuckled to himself and occasionally burst out laughing to the heavens. At first his neighbours just winked at each other and smiled, but as this odd behaviour persisted they became concerned for the old man's well-being. Eventually the authorities were summoned and the man in the garden was politely questioned about his eccentricities. The report of the investigation concluded that the man had some very strange ideas, including more than a few heretical ones. However, he was judged to be friendly, remarkably sharp in debate, and no threat to himself or his neighbours. Little did they know that he would one day be regarded as one of the greatest intellects of ancient Greece.

The man in the garden was Democritus, the "laughing philosopher" of Abdera, whose life encompassed roughly 458 to 368 BC. He led a small school of natural philosophers, now known as the Atomists, who believed that our macroscopic world could best be understood in terms of indivisible microscopic building blocks called atoms (*a* meaning "not" and *tomos* meaning "cut"). Democritus also had a remarkably modern understanding of concepts like the conservation of mass/energy, the indirect nature of perception, the continual formation and destruction of physical systems, the reality of empty space, the basic theory of colours and the fundamental principles of causality and determinism. He hypothesized that light consists of corporeal emanations from the surfaces of objects, that the Sun is immense and very distant, and that the Milky Way is the light of countless unresolved stars like the Sun. This record is far too good to be chalked up to lucky guesses. Such consistently successful results show that Democritus and his followers had developed a powerful new system for gaining knowledge—they had begun to explore empirical science, and its methods, thousands of years before it rose up again from the ashes of Medieval mysticism.

The great 17th century physicist Sir Issac Newton once commented that: 'If I have seen a bit farther than my contemporaries, it is because I have stood on the shoulders of giants.' Copernicus, Galileo and Kepler would have figured prominently among those "giants," since their revolutionary works set the stage for Newton's grand unification of physics. Rather than a solitary genius like Einstein, who independently discovered radical new ideas, Democritus was more like Newton in that he wove the separate threads of his predecessors into a coherent whole; that is, he combined and extended their ideas to create a more unified and more accurate world view, i.e. the atomic paradigm.

It is a shame that so little of Democritus' writing is available to us today. Of the approximately 73 books that he wrote, covering a surprisingly diverse range of topics, we only have a few fragments of original text left to study. Throughout the centuries there have been powerful forces that have been opposed to the "unorthodox" ideas of Democritus. Plato, for one, is reported to have argued for burning Democritus' books. Aristotle seemed less hostile, but still quite ambivalent. For the most part we must rely on the works of other philosophers and chroniclers to learn of the ideas of Democritus and the Atomists [1]. The tale that unfolds reveals the power of scientific reasoning to illuminate the darkness.

OF ATOMS, COLOURS, LIGHT AND STARS

For all the homage paid to well-known ancient Greek philosophers, one must remember that the 5th century B.C. was a time when logic was quite plastic, and obscurant explanations often were favoured. Albert Einstein's reactions to some of the ancient texts, experienced while reading them to his convalescing sister, underscore this situation:

> They were actually deceptive. If they had not been so obscure and so confusing, this kind of philosophy would not have held its own for very long. But most men revere words that they cannot understand and consider a writer whom they can to be superficial.

Consider Zeno's paradox in which Achilles tries to run a 100 yard dash. Zeno argued that he must first run one half of the distance (50 yards). Then he would have to transit one half of the remaining distance (25 yards), and then one half of the remaining distance (12.5 yards), and so on forever. Zeno concluded therefore that, *mathematically speaking,* Achilles could never reach the finish line, and ultimately that motion is impossible. This sounds like a really sharp argument for about 2 seconds and then reality sets in. Runners do reach finish lines; it's just that the ancient Greeks had not mastered the concepts of velocity and infinity. Basically, the paradox arose because their rudimentary analysis said one thing and nature said quite another. The amazing thing is that many philosophers after Zeno have had more faith (or interest) in the "logical" nonsense than in the observational evidence staring them in the face.

Even more telling is the ancient Greek model of the universe wherein Atlas is holding the World on his shoulders and kneeling on elephants, who stand on the back of a big turtle, or some such bizarre arrangement. Could they possibly have meant this literally, or was it merely a dubious metaphor?

Legend has it that one day Democritus smelled bread baking in another room, and concluded that something small enough to be invisible left the bread and wafted through the air to him. Having an insatiable curiosity, he was determined to pursue this idea, and fortunately an Atomist school had already been founded by Leucippus. Democritus enthusiastically joined this group, eventually taking over the leadership role and developing the atomic doctrine into a far more detailed and self-consistent body of knowledge. He reasoned that atoms were incomprehensibly small and numerous, that they were in constant motion and that they could have differing sizes, shapes and masses. Different substances were postulated to be the result of differing atomic constituents (e.g. salt and quartz) and/or their motions (e.g. ice and water). Nowadays we are so used to the idea of the atomic structure of matter that it is difficult for us to imagine anything else. Yet for over 2000 years the exquisite paradigm of atomism was considered little more than a crank theory. Even as late as the final decade of the 1800s, when indirect evidence for the atomic basis of nature was quite strong, famous scientists like the chemist Ostwald and the physicist Mach still rejected atomism as mere speculation. Most Greek philosophers preferred the idea that a wooden table was made of wood, without microscopic substructure, or the idea that all things were combinations of earth, air, fire and water.

The key to the enlightenment of Democritus' investigations, as opposed to the less successful attempts of other philosophers, was that Democritus would not fall back on "tooth fairies" when the theoretical going got rough. Democritus viewed nature as an orderly system, and believed that all phenomena had simple mechanical explanations. When sea water dried and left crystals behind, it was not a gift from Poseidon. Rather, the atoms of the sea water had changed their motions, with some escaping and some forming crystals. One wonders how a theory like atomism, which explained so many phenomena sensibly and self-consistently, could have been regarded with varying degrees of scorn. But so it was, and perhaps it would be best to refrain from attempting to answer that question until the end of our story.

Another major advance by Democritus was the concept of empty space, or the "void" as it was named. This concept, and the insightful corollary that there is no intrinsic up or down in space, was absent from most ancient Greek philosophies. Atomism, on the other hand, inherently postulates the reality of space since the basic idea of that theory is discrete atoms moving through regions of emptiness. This concept is more important than it might first appear. It is hard to imagine the development of modern physics without the concept of space and the analysis of motion within spatial reference frames.

When you have macroscopic objects that are built up from atoms and are usually zipping around at fairly large velocities, you can expect some impressive collisions and pyrotechnics. Democritus clearly stated that although atoms were indivisible (well, after all, he did not have an accelerator), composite objects like loaves of bread or stars would be broken down and built up in a continual dance of destruction and creation. The beauty of this concept is in part due to its implication of the conservation of mass/energy, which is another cornerstone of modern physics. This is truly remarkable; at a time when many were talking about gods throwing thunderbolts from the clouds, Democritus was working out the fundamental laws of nature.

To most of us, ancient Greek theorizing in the realm of astronomy sounds almost childish. For example, stars were interpreted as pin pricks in a dark shell surrounding the Earth, and the Sun was thought to be only slightly larger than the Goodyear blimp. In defence of those early philosophers it can be said that the ideas of ancient Greek astronomy make some sense if you look at them as naive literal interpretations of outward appearances. Stars do look a bit like pin pricks in a dark shell. So it took a penetrating mind to go beyond mere appearances using logic, careful observations and pattern recognition to lift the veils of nature. Democritus argued that the Sun was a colossal object lying at an astronomical distance from Earth. He also recognized that the "fixed" stars were other suns unimaginably farther away and moving about in space like gigantic atoms through the void. Thousands of years before Galileo proved it, the Atomists argued correctly that the glowing Milky Way, which arches across the night sky, was composed of countless suns too distant to be seen individually. Democritus reasoned that the "moving stars" (planets) were relatively nearby Earth-like objects, and that other solar systems might have two suns, or no planets, or planets without water and life. The Atomists also knew that the Moon was relatively nearby and that the mottled image of this orb was due to mountains and valleys. It hardly seems possible that this wonderful understanding of nature could have been attained when civilization was still in the Iron Age, nearly 2000 years before the discovery of the telescope.

Today we are quite used to the idea that sense perceptions are indirect; it is hard for us to imagine an alternative. When we see a person, there is a string of events leading to that perception. Light is sent from a source to the person, is re-radiated and reflected from the person, travels to the observer's eye and is processed as a three-dimensional image by the eye/brain system. When we touch an object we actually do not even come into solid contact with it. Rather, as decreed by the laws of atomic physics, the outer electron clouds of atoms in the fingers repulse those in the object with increasing strength as they are forced closer together. While most of his contemporaries had trouble with these ideas, Democritus had a very modern conception of the indirectness of our sensory contact with our surroundings. Using the atomic theory he made subtle distinctions between intrinsic properties such as hardness, and more subjective qualities like sweetness. Moreover, the Atomists had a good working understanding of basic colour theory: that there are three primary colours which can be combined in different proportions to form the other colours. To be sure, Democritus was not always right. He devised reasonable, but incorrect, theories for earthquakes and magnets. Yet the overall record of Democritus and his colleagues is truly amazing.

Physics without Mathematics?

One of the more intriguing aspects of the successes chalked up by the Atomists is that they were achieved virtually in the absence of mathematics, as we know it. In the 5th century BC only the most rudimentary arithmetic and geometry were available. The Pythagoreans were just beginning to discover the mysteries of geometry and numbers, Euclid's geometry was nearly 100 years off in the future, and calculus would not be born for more than 20 centuries. In spite of this limitation, Democritus and his colleagues were able to develop a highly advanced understanding of nature and the fundamental principles of physics. It is natural to wonder how they succeeded against seemingly formidable odds. Since the 1500s mathematics has played an increasingly important role in the development of physics/astronomy. As Galileo put it in his book, *The Assayer:*

> Philosophy is written in this grand book, the universe which stands continually open to our gaze. But the book cannot be understood unless one first learns to comprehend the language and read the letters in which it is composed. It is written in the language of mathematics, and its characters are triangles, circles, and other geometric figures. Without a knowledge of them, it is humanly impossible to understand a single word of it. Without these, one wanders about in a dark and obscure labyrinth.

If this is true then how could Democritus and the Atomists have achieved such a clear reading of "the book?"

A resolution of this apparent paradox can be perhaps be found in the development of electromagnetic theory by Faraday and Maxwell. Faraday described himself, quite sincerely, as "non-mathematical," but it was he who first grasped the basic concepts of electromagnetism: the fundamental reciprocity wherein electric currents generate magnetic fields, while changing magnetic fields generate electric currents, and the powerful new concept of an electromagnetic *field*. Pondering these seminal ideas, Maxwell, who was an excellent and insightful mathematician, translated Faraday's qualitative ideas into a rigorous mathematical theory. Perhaps we can learn from this example that science requires both conceptual and mathematical approaches. There is certainly no need to defend the importance of mathematical thinking, as eloquently advocated by Galileo, but there is perhaps a need to appreciate the power of the empirical/conceptual approach, which sifts through observational data, searching for basic relationships and patterns.

When you have modern scientists refer to Galileo and say, in so many words, 'no math, no science,' or when influential scientists such as Dirac say, 'Don't confuse me with observations and heuristic patterns; let me concentrate on creating elegant equations,' then you have only half of the story of science. Science works best when there is a mutual respect for, and interplay between, the theoretical/mathematical approach and the empirical/conceptual approach to knowledge. Democritus was a prime example of someone with the latter talent, and his achievements, like those of Faraday, bear witness to the power of the empirical/conceptual approach. The true genius of Einstein lay largely in the fact that he could, with some crucial mathematical help from his former teacher Karl Schwarzschild and his friend Marcel Grossmann, wield the powers of both approaches: the empirical/conceptual approach to generate bold new ideas and the more abstract theoretical/mathematical approach to formulate and extend those ideas.

The Basic Method of Democritus

The following strategies that Democritus and the Atomists (and many adherents of the Ionian School) used to acquire knowledge were simple but effective.

(1) The Atomists believed that if you wanted to understand nature, then you needed to study *nature,* not abstract ideals, or mysticism, or past authority. Observations are the crucial starting point for all studies.

(2) From many careful observations the student of nature hopes to find an idea or pattern that ties seemingly disparate facts into a coherent theory. For Democratus it was the baking bread puzzle that catalysed the creation of a unifying atomic paradigm from a multitude of independent observations.

(3) The Atomists believed that nature could be approximated as a simple mechanical system, and that all events are linked in a causal chain. Explanations that invoke supernatural forces or violate causality were not acceptable.

(4) Ideas could be tested by seeing whether they could explain other *known* phenomena, i.e. beyond those phenomena used to develop the general paradigm. These would be regarded as retrodictions, rather than true predictions. One could also test whether inferences and logical consequences derived from the theory are consistent with *new* discoveries. Such tests involve rudimentary predictions.

(5) The Atomists were also sophisticated enough to distrust absolute statements and claims of final knowledge. Human knowledge was recognized to be inherently limited and involved varying degrees of uncertainty. The best one could hope for was to approach nature's inner workings by successively better approximations. Like Galileo, they believed that "the authority of a thousand is not worth the humble reasoning of a single individual."

This approach—accumulate empirical knowledge; search the data for simple ideas that are rational, mechanical and causal; and develop inferences and deductions that can be tested—might seem too simple to have led to such success, but it is essentially the scientific method.

The foundation that underlies the phenomenal success of the Atomist school is their paradigm that nature is built up from atoms in continual motion. Their empirical approach led them to this powerful world view and from there it only required hard work, logic and pattern recognition to pick the fruit from their tree of knowledge. Through no fault of their own, Democritus and his school of Atomists could not utilize the full scientific method, which relies heavily on generating definitive predictions and testing them empirically. The experimental capabilities at that time were simply too crude for advanced prediction and testing, and the modern ideas of experimentation were not well-formulated yet. However, they made use of "thought experiments" where theoretical conclusions are deduced from the paradigm and compared with the real world. This is still a valued scientific tool whereby a theory's consistency with nature can be checked.

Responses to Atomism

Unfortunately, the Atomists' teachings were often treated with indifference or scorn. The most common complaint with their atomic paradigm was that the continual creation and destruction of *composite* objects seemed to imply that chance played a major role in natural phenomena. This appeared to conflict with the experience and belief systems of the critics. However, the critics failed to recognize that Atomism is the antithesis of chance: the paradigm is strictly causal and deterministic. The *apparent* randomness stems from limits to our powers of observation and data processing. Other criticism emphasized that Democritus could not offer a "first cause" for how the chain of causality got started. However, it is not the business of science to talk of a "first cause," and in the case of an infinite universe there is no "first cause." Another serious "problem" was the Atomists' rejection of a final "purpose" towards which the universe is evolving. An "undirected" universe was unacceptable to the majority of ancient Greeks.

Democritus believed in what the majority of contemporary scientists now believe in: that the universe has not been, and is not being, manipulated by a transcendental force towards some final goal. Rather, the universe is thought to unfold in a manner similar to the evolution of life. Fundamental forces and laws drive and constrain all phenomena, but not towards some prearranged end state. Readers of Stephen Jay Gould's wonderful books on evolution, such as *The Panda's Thumb,* have heard eloquent arguments for this view of life and the universe. And even if there were a "final purpose," it would no more be the business of science than a "first cause."

There also was the largely unspoken criticism that the Atomist paradigm lacked excitement; it was simply not sensational enough. How could it compete with gods throwing lightning bolts from thunderheads or the unrestricted possibilities of pure thought? Unfortunately, many ancients preferred mysticism or abstract theoretical methods over simple empiricism. Without adequate grounding in empirical knowledge of nature they could not appreciate the power and beauty of Atomism.

Quite probably the more bizarre ideas resulting from revelation and "pure thought" methods were a main source of humour for the laughing philosopher. He taught that passion can interfere with the search for knowledge. Strong emotions like hate and fear are forms of stress that cause the brain to bypass its higher functions and concentrate on lower survival functions such as fight/flight, good/bad, and us/them. Flexibility, sophistication and objectivity, which are crucial to higher learning, if not immediate survival, are decreased by emotion.

Democritus argued that anger, hatred and other forms of debilitating emotion were to be avoided, while cheerfulness and peace of mind were to be cultivated. These attributes were not to be gained through self-indulgence, the accumulation of wealth, or the endless battle for power and attention, but rather through moderation and contemplation of the harmony of nature. This emphasis on achieving well-being through insight and self-control is especially applicable to our times, when we are relentlessly encouraged to indulge ourselves. As his name suggests, he was a lover of democracy, commenting:

> Poverty in a democracy is as much to be preferred to what is called prosperity under despots as freedom is to slavery.

Democritus was a person of encyclopaedic knowledge and a first rate scientist who recommended hard work, serious study and service to others. When he knew that death was near, he stopped taking sustenance so as to spare himself, his family and his friends the futile agony of a prolonged terminal illness. He lived with dignity and he died with dignity.

WHAT IF?

Most people who pursue knowledge to the college level or beyond will have heard of Plato and Aristotle. Of that group, a sizable fraction will know something of their contributions to human civilization. But how many people have heard of Democritus, and more importantly, have some familiarity with his work? Probably not that many. What if the reverse were true: that Democritus was better known than Plato or Aristotle because, from 400 B.C. to the present, his work had been considered profound and useful? What if democracy had taken root and flourished 20 centuries earlier? What would our civilization be like now if the empiricism of the Atomists' science had won the day in 400 B.C. and thrived like it has in the last four centuries? Of one thing we can be reasonably sure: the technological advance of civilization would have been sped up to a remarkable degree. Consider that in 400 years we have gone from hammer-and-leech "medicine" to organ transplants, from moveable type to the Internet, from donkey carts to the Space Shuttle. We have gone from Galileo's discovery of mountains on the Moon to astronauts bouncing around on the lunar surface. It staggers the imagination. But if we are amazed at the rapid change of the past 400 years, consider starting our scientific civilization 2000 years earlier.

No one would suggest that science alone could drive and sustain human civilization. Productive forms of the mystic world view provide encouragement and solace; they act as a well-spring for art, music and drama. Likewise, abstract idealism has been a continual fount of valuable contributions to human knowledge and culture. Yet I would argue that humanity would have been better off if the path of science, which is the path of reason, empiricism and experimental testing, had been the dominant path for the last 2400 years instead of the last 400 years.

Some view science as having a dark side that would have made the human condition far worse, pointing to nuclear weapons, pollution and population-related problems. But this argument stems from a misunderstanding of what science really is. The science advocated by Democritus, Galileo, Newton and Einstein, who led countless others, requires humility, honesty and freedom from bias. It strives for integrity, dedication and wonder. There is no dark side to *this* science. Dangers that are mistakenly attributed to science can usually be traced back to a dark side of human nature: insecurities that foster greed and paranoia. It is human greed for power that rationalizes cruel and selfish human activities, ignores the desecration of our environment, and leads to counterproductive technologies. In 400 years, we still have not fully learned the spiritual and humane lessons of science, falling short of the example set by Democritus. Sometimes it seems as if humanity has acted like a child ripping open a new present and playing with it before reading the instructions. But given the choice of living in Mediaeval times or the nuclear era, most of us would choose the latter. Nearly all of those who chose otherwise would probably regret their decision in a matter of days, if not hours. Perhaps if we had been granted an additional 2000 years to work at it, starting in a pre-technological era, we would have learned to control our dark side. Perhaps by now we would have more fully embraced the light of reason, and our understanding of the beauty and balance of nature would have become deeper and more widespread.

Democritus, whose students nicknamed him "Wisdom," was a very special person. Like Galileo, Newton and Einstein he showed what the human mind can accomplish with integrity and sustained concentration. I like to think of him sitting in his garden admiring a dewy spider web, laughing about the Atlas myth (What does the turtle stand on?), and contemplating travel to other star systems or what humans would be thinking about three millennia hence.

Norman F. Hall (essay date 1999)

SOURCE: "Ode to a Grecian Atomist," in *The Humanist*, Vol. 59, No. 1, January-February, 1999, pp. 34-35.

[*In the following essay, Hall answers moral arguments against modern science that parallel objections made against atomism in the time of Democritus.*]

The ancient Greek atomism of Democritis and Leucippus was an attempt to reconcile observations of the physical world with the existing philosophical wisdom concerning change in the world. Although the methods of reasoning they used were not those of the modern scientific method, it is remarkable how close many of the properties of their atoms come to matching those of the atoms of modern science. At the very least, it seems from a modern viewpoint that atomism should have prevailed, if only as a good working hypothesis. Why was it so thoroughly rejected?

One of the most telling arguments used against the claims of the ancient Greek atomists is almost identical to that leveled against materialist, reductive science, and naturalism today: if the world is only atoms and the void, then why tell the truth and why fight for Athens? If there is no component of divine intention to be found in an atomist understanding of physical change, then how can there be any morality?

The answer to this "moral argument" against a godless scientific understanding of the universe has always been clear, but today it is seldom given voice: we tell the truth because it is only by trying to tell the truth as we see it that we came to even suspect that the world might be made of atoms; and we fight for Athens because, if we fail to defend the city-state that has allowed us the freedom of thought to consider such questions, where will we do our thinking in the future? If we value the scientific or philosophical finding, we must value the process that made that finding possible.

Today, it is to the modern process of science—and to our hopes for its continuation—that we must look for the beginnings of a humanist and scientific ethic. Too often science is seen as devoid of ethical content—a list of what "is" with no ability to provide any guidance as to what "ought" to be. But science is not just a looseleaf notebook of facts and experimental findings; it is a method of approaching questions about the world based on a personal commitment to a strict ethic. Those who value the knowledge to be revealed by the application of the scientific method—and who wish to understand the world through science—must agree to tell the truth, not only to each other but to themselves.

The ethical dimension of science was not always so obscure. It was forcefully stated forty years ago by Jacob Bronowski in his book *Science and Human Values.* Bronowski identified the spark that began the scientific revolution as the "habit of truth," which makes science not a search for concepts beyond challenge but a never-ending search for the mutual respect that can make us human. As he put it: "Theory and experiment alike become meaningless unless the scientist brings to them, and his fellows can assume in him, the respect of a lucid honesty with himself."

Now, at the end of the twentieth century, what was so clear at mid-century is forgotten, and the myth that science has nothing to tell us about moral values is so deeply entrenched that it goes almost completely unchallenged—so pervasive that even scientists and humanists unthinkingly promote it. In March 1998, it was the theme of an essay entitled "Oppressed by Evolution" by Matt Cartmill in the popular American science magazine *Discover.* Two issues later, not one dissenting opinion had been published by the magazine.

Bronowski recognized the signs of the popular distrust of science (the attitude that "scientists should be on tap, not on top," as Winston Churchill plainly put it) and identified its root cause. A decade after he had participated in the scientific inspection of the ruins of Nagasaki, Japan, Bronowski wrote:

> The dilemma of today is not that the human values cannot control a mechanical science. It is the other way about: the scientific spirit is more human than the machinery of governments. . . . The body of technical science burdens us because we are trying to employ the body without the spirit; we are trying to buy the corpse of science.

Science is misperceived by the public as being identical to its current "findings" and, even when its "method" is taught, that becomes a cold and meaningless algorithm rather than a commitment to an ethic. In today's market, the findings of science are strictly separated from the ethic that gave rise to them, which is buried as unwanted offal. The corpse—the raw meat of scientific discovery—is available in every store, and the skin is stuffed and on display in the museums and schools for our entertainment or poor education.

Those who benefit from the sale of the corpse do not value the knowledge to be revealed by the application of the scientific method and do not wish to understand the world through science. Science has become, at the same time, a cornucopia of high-tech toys and a part of the entertainment industry. Its role is to provide first the inspiration for dinosaur and meteor movies, then the special effects to carry them out.

Humanism has done no better. At the turn of the century and of the millennium, the greatest failing of organized humanism is that it has articulated no compelling answer to the moral challenge laid down millennia ago: if the world is only atoms and the void, then why tell the truth and why fight for Athens? Still mired in controversies between foundationalism and anti-foundationalism, still looking on the one hand for the absolute answers of religion and on the other for an evolutionary excuse for acting out of our pre-rational convictions of "intrinsic horror," humanism has missed the boat—both figuratively and literally.

Humanist morality isn't, and shouldn't be, bound either to unmoving foundations in logic or revelation or to the emotive flotsam of the last few million years of evolution. If we are to avoid drowning, we must recognize that we are all in the same ethical boat and that boat is constantly under construction. This is today as it has always been.

What is different today is what tools and materials we have available to aid the moral shipwrights in redesigning the craft to sail the rough seas ahead. Neither the stones of unquestioned revelation from a mythical God nor the iron-mongery of an unworkable exact moral calculus have proved seaworthy by themselves. Nor will we survive by lashing ourselves to the broken masts and planking, the tree roots and seaweed we find floating up from our past evolution and culture.

The future of humanity is ours to shape. We must use all the materials at hand, after careful inspection. The recently broken planking, along with the evolved and gnarled roots, can be smoothed and made to serve. The iron nails of logic can help to hold it all together—provided we remember that iron rusts! Even the dead weight of religion, if taken in moderation, can serve as ballast.

But the effort will all be in vain without a workable notion of how and what to build. Today science provides the best hope we have for devising a plan for a vessel that—constructed with honest labor—may see us through at least some of the coming storms before it must again be rebuilt under us.

In his article "Faith, Science, and the Soul: On the Pragmatic Virtues of Naturalism" in the May/June 1993 *Humanist,* Thomas Clark asks:

> If it were suddenly discovered that the whole edifice of science was fraudulent or misguided, would that significantly change what we want in life? Would we cease being humanistic in our approach to the problems that currently beset us? I strongly doubt it.

I strongly disagree with Clark in this. Such a discovery would and should profoundly change humanism's approach to life. If telling the truth cannot help us, then all we have left are lies and illusions. And anyone who thinks otherwise is simply out of touch with the lessons of the twentieth century. That such nonsense is still being entertained as humanist philosophy in 1998 is a shameful sign that organized humanism is woefully unready for the challenges of the twenty-first century.

C. C. W. Taylor (essay date 1999)

SOURCE: "Commentary," in *The Atomists: Leucippus and Democritus,* University of Toronto Press, 1999, pp. 157-234.

[*In the following excerpt, Taylor examines Democritus's ideas on the gods and religion.*]

THEOLOGY

Democritus' theology is naturalistic, in its accounts both of the nature of the gods and of the origins and grounds of belief in their existence. Despite obscurity over some details (see below), it is clear that he believed that there are gods, which are living, intelligent, material beings (of a peculiar sort), playing a significant role in human affairs. They are atomic compounds, and like all such compounds they come to be and perish. They did not, of course, create the physical world (of which they are part), nor, though they are intelligent, do they organize or control it. (For discussion of the atomists' denial of providence, see above on Chance and Necessity.) They are as firmly part of the natural order as any other living beings.

What kind of beings, then, are they? The answer to this question connects with the discussion of the previous section, since there is clear evidence that Democritus believed the gods to be living *eidōla,* probably of gigantic size, possessing intelligence, moral character, and interest in human affairs.[1] Diogenes of Oenoanda (211) criticizes this theory from an Epicurean standpoint; perception, intelligence, and the use of language require a solid subject, and cannot therefore be attributes of mere atomic films.[2] This criticism presumably relies on the Epicurean doctrine that the mind is an internal organ situated in the chest; given that doctrine, films of atoms flowing off the surfaces of bodies cannot themselves possess mentality. But we saw in the previous section that, per contra, the Democritean picture of the mind as suffused throughout the entire body, including its surface, entails the possession of mentality by the *eidōla* emitted by a mentally endowed being. The account of the gods as *eidōla* is clearly attested by Cicero (172a-c), Augustine (172d), Plutarch (175a), and Sextus (173b, 175b); the latter passage is especially significant in containing, among other detail, the explicit statement that *eidōla* were the only kind of divine beings which Democritus recognized.

That presents a prima facie difficulty, both because the theory might seem to require that living divine *eidōla* must be emitted by living divine beings, of which they are *eidōla,* and because passage 172a contains some suggestion that as well as the *eidōla* Democritus postulated gods of other kinds. The first difficulty is illusory; every *eidōlon* must be emitted by some atomic aggregate or aggregates,[3] but there is no requirement that an *eidōlon* of a thing of a certain kind should have been emitted by an actual thing of that kind. An *eidōlon* of a centaur need not have flowed from the surface of an actual centaur, but could have arisen from the chance collision of *eidōla* flowing from the surfaces of a horse and of a man (see above). Since according to Sextus (173b) Democritus' gods were in human form, the theory need have no difficulty in identifying their source as actual humans. But what about the detail that they are of enormous size, or even, as stated by Cicero's Cotta 'of such an enormous size as to enfold the entire world' (172c)?

It is important to be clear on whether Democritus' doctrine was (i) that the gods are *eidōla,* of enormous size, of living beings in human form, or (ii) that the gods are *eidōla* of living beings of human form and of enormous size. Doctrine i requires that the *eidōla* are themselves enormous, ii does not.[4] If Democritus' doctrine was ii, there is no difficulty in accounting for the origin of such images. They originate from ordinary humans, and there is no question as to how they have attained their enormous size, because they do not have enormous size. There is of course the question of how they come to represent things as of enormous size; this is essentially a question about Democritus' theory of mental representation, which prompts fascinating speculation with, unfortunately, little or no textual foundation. Did Democritus believe that we can somehow alter the relative dimensions of the *eidōla* of a human being and of a mountain to produce the image of a human being the size of a mountain? Describing Epicurus' theory, Sextus says (*Against the Mathematicians* IX.45) that we form the conception of a Cyclops by 'magnifying the ordinary man in fantasy'; this might refer to first imagining a man of ordinary size and then simply imagining a much bigger man (which is relatively unproblematic), or to the more problematic activity of first forming the mental image of a man of ordinary size and then somehow magnifying that image to generate the image of a man of much greater size. Given Democritus' account of thought as stimulation by *eidōla* (see previous section), if he held anything like the view which Sextus attributes to Epicurus, it must have been more like the latter, problematic version. But the attribution to the mind of powers to operate on its *eidōla* is something of which there is no trace in the textual evidence; moreover, given the physical nature of *eidōla*, the mind would presumably have to enlarge them physically, and it is hard even to envisage how it might be supposed to do that.

Given these problems, it might be easier to suppose that Democritus' theory was i, viz. that the divine *eidōla* actually are of enormous size. In that event, where do they come from? Various possibilities suggest themselves. One is that their source was actual gigantic humans, perhaps living in the remote past. (We know that the divine *eidōla* were especially long-lasting (175b).) Another is that, though originating from humans of normal size, they became enormously enlarged through accretion of extraneous atoms in the course of their long life. A third is that they emanate from gigantic humanoid inhabitants of another world than ours.[5] In any of these events the theory is spared the problem of explaining how the mind enlarges its *eidōla*, but at the cost of having instead to explain how *eidōla* larger than a human body could be physically registered by that body; clearly the simple model of a seal impressed on wax is inadequate, but the sources suggest no alternative.

According to Cicero (172c), Plutarch (175a), and Sextus (175b), some of these *eidōla* are harmful and some beneficial, while Sextus adds that they foretell the future by speaking to humans. The wording of the Cicero and Sextus passages leaves it open whether the good and harm done to humans are conceived as mere natural effects of the encounters with the *eidōla*, or effects intentionally brought about by them; Plutarch, on the other hand, clearly interprets Democritus as holding the latter view, since he credits him with thinking that some *eidōla* are malicious, and with praying to meet only those which are 'propitious' (i.e., those which are well disposed, by contrast with the wicked). Sextus' testimony of the prophetic activity of the *eidōla* confirms that they act intentionally, which in turn confirms Plutarch's testimony of their beneficence or malevolence. (Prophecy is presumably an instance of

beneficence, on the assumption that prophecies are normally intended to benefit those to whom they are delivered.)

Most of our other evidence is consistent with the above doctrine, though in some cases suggestive of misunderstanding on the part of the authors who transmit it. Thus the report of Stobaeus (171a) that god is mind in spherical fire, the suggestion of Cicero's Cotta that the gods are the basic principles of mind in the universe (172c), and even St Cyril's extravagant-sounding assertion that according to Democritus god is the soul of the world (171a) are all best read as versions, garbled according to the preconceptions of each author, of the authentic Democritean doctrine that the divine *eidōla*, as living beings, contain a high proportion of soul-atoms, which we know to be spherical and therefore fiery (cf. 106). The statement of the elder Pliny (174) that Democritus believed in just two gods, Punishment and Reward (or perhaps 'Good and Harm' ['Poenam et Beneficium']), is presumably an echo of his doctrine that the divine *eidōla* are either beneficent or hostile. Rather more worrying is the suggestion of Cicero's Velleius (172a), echoed by Augustine (172d), that in addition to the *eidōla* themselves Democritus believed that the beings which emit the *eidōla* are also divine. This, if accurate, would ascribe to Democritus a hybrid theory incorporating both the belief in living *eidōla* and the theory of later Epicurean sources (and perhaps, though disputed by Long and Sedley (see n. 46 above) of Epicurus himself) that the gods are living beings apprehended via *eidōla*. Lactantius (172e) goes to the length of denying that the gods were composed of atoms, since it was impossible for atomic compounds to exist eternally. We can be certain that this misrepresents Democritus. Even if, like some of his successors, he believed in gods over and above the divine *eidōla*, he is as firmly committed as they to the doctrine that those beings are apprehended by humans via *eidōla*. But only atomic compounds can emit *eidōla*; hence the gods must be atomic compounds, and like all compounds must eventually be dissolved. The version of the hybrid theory suggested by the texts of Cicero and Augustine, which does not include the thesis of the eternity of the gods, cannot be set aside so easily. It is, however, explicitly contradicted by Sextus (175b), which suggests that we should look for some way of understanding this testimony as a distortion of some aspect of the *eidōla* theory. We might tentatively suggest that Democritus described the sources of his divine *eidōla* as themselves gods in a reductive spirit; we encounter (in dreams etc.) *eidōla* of gods, and what those 'gods' (i.e., the things that produce those *eidōla*) really are are nothing but men of old.[6]

We should consider whether any light is thrown on this question by the evidence of Democritus' views on the origins of religion. The sources identify two types of phenomena as having given rise to religious belief, firstly the occurrence of *eidōla* themselves (175b), and secondly celestial phenomena such as thunder, lightning, and eclipses (173a). The latter testimony is supported by the quotation recorded by Clement (D14), which describes a few learned people raising their hands to the sky and saying that Zeus ordains all things, i.e., ascribing all celestial phenomena to divine agency. It is likely that these accounts were seen by Democritus as in one way or another complementary. He may simply have thought of them as mutually reinforcing kinds of evidence. Or perhaps, in a more sophisticated manner, he appealed to *eidōla* to explain how humans acquired the concept of gods, and to celestial phenomena to explain why they believed that gods exist. The fragment may be taken to give some support to the reductive interpretation suggested in the preceding paragraph. Certainly it can itself be read reductively; what we now call (i.e., what really is) air the learned men of the past called Zeus, i.e., Zeus really is nothing but air.

Democritus' theology thus contrives to incorporate some of the most characteristic features of the gods of traditional belief, notably their anthropomorphism, power, longevity (though not, crucially, immortality), personal interaction with humans, and interest (for good or ill) in human affairs, within the framework of a naturalistic and materialistic theory. It is thus, despite the bold originality of its account of the divine nature, notably more conservative than some of its predecessors (especially the non-anthropomorphic theology of Xenophanes) and than its Epicurean successor, whose main concern is to exclude the gods from all concern with human affairs.

Notes

1. Barnes ch. 21 (*c*) agrees with Cicero's Balbus (172b) in interpreting Democritus' theory of the gods as amounting to atheism, since in holding the gods to be *eidōla* he takes them to be nothing more than the contents of human fantasy, particularly in the form of dreams. (Similarly Vlastos n. 24 'consider[s] the *eidola* as an aetiological explanation of the popular belief in the gods, and nothing more.') But for Democritus *eidōla* are not intrinsically psychological; they are not contents of psychological states, but part of the objective world, causing psychological states through their impact on physical minds.

2. In the light of this criticism, it is particularly interesting that Long and Sedley vol. 1, pp. 144-9 attribute the Democritean theory to Epicurus himself, and come very close to accepting Barnes' characterization of it as amounting to atheism.

3. This assumes that all *eidōla* are of the same kind, viz. the kind described in our sources for the atomists' theories of perception and thought. Eisenberger pp. 147-8 appears to envisage that the divine *eidōla* are of a distinct kind, viz. free-standing atomic films in human form, which have no source other than the atoms which constitute them and the forces which form those atoms into aggregates. (Bicknell has a similar view.) Considerations of economy count against this multiplication of kinds of *eidōla;* 'conventional' *eidōla* can explain the phenomena just as well as the special sort postulated by the authors mentioned.

4. It appears that Epicurus held that an *eidōlon* representing its source as F (e.g., a visual impression of a distant tower as small and round) was itself F (see Taylor), but there is no evidence to justify the ascription of that doctrine to Democritus.

5. This might explain 'of such an enormous size as to enfold the entire world' (172c). If the atomists believed that there are remote worlds composed of atoms of enormous size (see above, 'Differentiating Properties of Atoms'), then the *eidōla* emitted by inhabitants of those worlds might be big enough to enfold the whole of our world.

6. The hybrid theory is defended by McGibbon, and criticized (to my mind effectively) by Eisenberger.

Notes on Sources

AUGUSTINE (St.) Theologian; 4th-5th c. AD. *Academica* ed. W.M. Green, Utrecht and Antwerp, 1956. *Letters* ed. *CSEL* vol. 24.

CICERO Roman statesman and philosopher; 1st c. BC (L).

CLEMENT Bishop of Alexandria; 3rd c. AD. Ed. O. Stählin, Leipzig, 1905-36. *Miscellanies* rev. L. Früchtel, Berlin, 1960. *Protrepticus* and *Paedagogus* rev. U. Treu. Berlin, 1972).

DIOGENES OF OENOANDA 2nd c. AD. Author of inscription setting out fundamentals of Epicureanism. Ed. M.F. Smith, *Diogenes of Oenoanda; The Epicurean Inscription* (with trans.), Naples, 1993.

PLINY (the Elder) Roman encyclopedist; 1st c. AD (L).

PLUTARCH Philosopher, historian, and essayist; 1st-2nd c. AD (L).

SEXTUS (Empiricus) Sceptical philosopher; 2nd c. AD (L).

STOBAEUS (John of Stobi) Anthologist; 5th c. AD. Ed. C. Wachsmuth and O. Hense, Berlin, 1884-1912.

Works Cited

Barnes, J. (1982) *The Presocratic Philosophers*, 2nd ed., London and New York, chs. 17, 19 (*b*), 20, 21 (*c*), 23 (*d*), 24(*e*).

Bicknell, P. (1969) 'Democritus' Theory of Precognition,' *Revue des Etudes Grecques* 82, 318-26.

Eisenberger, H. (1970) 'Demokrits Vorstellung vom Sein und Wirken der Götter,' *Rheinisches Museum* 113, 141-58.

McGibbon, D. (1965) 'The Religious Thought of Democritus,' *Hermes* 93, 385-97.

Taylor, C. C. W. (1980) '"All Perceptions Are True,"' in M. Schofield, M. Burnyeat, and J. Barnes, eds., *Doubt and Dogmatism*, Oxford, 105-24.

Vlastos, G. (1945 and 1946) 'Ethics and Physics in Democritus,' *Philosophical Review* 54, 578-92 and 55, 53-

64, repr. in R.E. Allen and D.J. Furley, eds. (1975) *Studies in Presocratic Philosophy,* London, vol. 2, 381-408, and in G. Vlastos, (1995) *Studies in Greek Philosophy,* ed. D.W Graham, Princeton, vol. 1, 328-50.

FURTHER READING

Criticism

Ganson, Todd Stuart. "Democritus against Reducing Sensible Qualities." *Ancient Philosophy* 19, No.1 (1999): 201-15.

> Examines Democritus's views regarding sensory awareness and contends that they are not those of a reductionist.

Hahm, David E. "Chrysippus' Solution to the Democritean Dilemma of the Cone." *Isis* 63, No. 217 (June 1972): 205-20.

> Explains how Chrysippus solved a problem posed by Democritus by reformulating it.

McGibbon, Donald. "Pleasure as the 'Criterion' in Democritus." *Phronesis* 5, No. 2 (1960): 75-77.

> Attempts to demonstrate that two statements made by Democritus concerning pleasure are not in conflict with each other.

O'Keefe, Timothy. "The Ontological Status of Sensible Qualities for Democritus and Epicurus." *Ancient Philosophy* 17, No. 1 (Spring 1997): 119-34.

> Investigates the reasons for Democritus's skepticism and explains how Epicurus modified and improved Democritus's ontology.

Procopé, J. F. "Democritus on Politics and the Care of the Soul." *Classical Quarterly* 39, No. 2 (July-December 1989): 307-31.

> Examines Democritus's views on government, democracy, the public good, and justice.

Ring, Merrill. "Redoing Science." In *Beginning with the Pre-Socratics,* pp. 134-57. Mountain View, Calif.: Mayfield Publishing Company, 1987.

> Explains three significant scientific responses, one of which is atomism, to Parmenides's notion concerning the impossibility of change.

Stewart, Zeph. "Democritus and the Cynics." *Harvard Studies in Classical Philology* 63 (1958): 179-91.

> Contends that the fragments of Democritus's writings concerning ethics were preserved by the Cynics and their allies.

Taylor, C. C. W. "Pleasure, Knowledge and Sensation in Democritus." *Phronesis* 12, No. 1 (1967): 6-27.

> Makes a connection in methodology between Democritus's atomism and his ethical writings.

Vlastos, Gregory. "Ethics and Physics in Democritus." *Philosophical Review* 54 (1945): 578-92 and 55 (1946): 53-64.

> Examines aspects of Democritus's ethical writings which can be linked to his physics.

Whyte, Lancelot Law. "Atomism." In *Essay on Atomism: From Democritus to 1960,* pp. 12-30. Middletown, Conn.: Wesleyan University Press, 1961.

> Provides an overview of the history of atomism.

Julius Caesar
100 B.C.-44 B.C.

(Full name Gaius Julius Caesar) Roman prose writer, general, and dictator.

INTRODUCTION

Widely acknowledged as a military genius, Caesar extended Rome's boundary to the Atlantic by conquering Gaul, prevailed in the Roman civil war, and in 44 B.C. declared himself dictator for life. His war chronicles, hybrids of commentary and history, are classics in military thought: *De Bello Gallico* (before 46 B.C.; *On the Gallic War*) and *De Bello Civili* (c. 44 B.C.; *On the Civil War*) are praised by critics for their clarity and precision, and are important historically as the only extant record of many significant events. His exactness and economy in his use of words is best known through his description of vanquishing Zela in Asia Minor: "Veni, vidi, vici," which translates to "I came, I saw, I conquered." His oratorical skills were superb; it has been said that only Cicero was his superior. Caesar, Rome's most famous general, has also been immortalized through William Shakespeare's tragedy *Julius Caesar*. In the play Shakespeare has Cassius say of Caesar: "Why, man, he doth bestride the narrow world / Like a Colossus, and we petty men / Walk under his huge legs and peep about / To find ourselves dishonorable graves."

BIOGRAPHICAL INFORMATION

Caesar was born in Rome to Gaius Caesar and Aurelia. Although his family were aristocrats, the power of the patricians was no longer an important factor in politics. In 86 B.C. Caesar was appointed to a position of little importance by Gaius Marius, an important member of the popular party with anti-senatorial views. A couple of years later Caesar married Cornelia, the daughter of Lucius Cornelius Cinna, an associate of Marius. Caesar served with the army in Asia from 81 to 78 B.C. before returning to Rome. He unsuccessfully prosecuted two cases, which nevertheless brought him considerable public attention, and then left for Rhodes to study rhetoric with Cicero's teacher. Pirates interfered with his trip to Rhodes and kidnaped Caesar; later, Caesar hunted the pirates down and crucified them. He returned to Rome in 73 B.C., was elected a priest, and then became a senator in 70 B.C. Caesar served as governor of Farther Spain for the year 61 B.C. and then formed the first triumvirate with Crassus and the general Pompey. He was elected consul in 59 B.C., followed by governship of Roman Gaul. From 58 to 51 B.C.

Caesar conquered Gallic Gaul, now part of France. Crassus had died in 53 B.C. and Caesar's good relationship with Pompey ended when Pompey was appointed sole consul in 52 B.C. by the senate. Outright civil war began in 49 B.C. when Caesar crossed the Rubicon river, which separated Gaul and Italy. Caesar conquered Italy, then Spain, and chased Pompey to Egypt, where Pompey had already been murdered by the time of Caesar's arrival. Caesar lived with Cleopatra in Alexandria and fought more campaigns against Pompey's supporters. He became elevated to a godlike level by the citizens of Rome and relished his absolute power; he had a broad vision for reform of Rome, but little time to carry out his plans. Shortly after Caesar declared himself emperor for life in 44 B.C., a group of some sixty senators (out of a total of nine hundred) who believed that Caesar was a threat to the republic, conspired to assassinate him. Caesar was attacked while sitting in his chair at the senate. Although he fended off the first attempt to kill him, a group too powerful for one man to fight rushed him and stabbed him twenty-three times. His death did not strengthen the republic, but rather plunged Rome into a civil war that lasted thirteen years and from which it never fully recovered.

MAJOR WORKS

Caesar's commentaries on his campaigns are typically divided into two distinct works. Part one comprises *De Bello Gallico,* which describes Caesar's battles against Gaul, Britain, and Germany. Its first seven books, covering the period from 58 to 52 B.C., one volume per year, were written by Caesar, but the eighth book was written by Hirtius. The second work is *De Bello Civili,* which describes the war against Pompey. Its three books, covering the years 49 to 48 B.C., were also written by Caesar. The final commentaries on Caesar are composed by others: they include *Bellum Alexandrium, Bellum Africum,* and *Bellum Hispaniense.* The last three works leave off at 45 B.C.. Caesar also wrote a book on grammar, a collection of witty sayings and jokes, and some poems. Except for a few lines quoted in the writings of others, these works are no longer extant.

CRITICAL RECEPTION

Considerable controversy exists concerning exactly when Caesar wrote *De Bello Gallico* and when it was first published. If it was written during the years 52 to 51 B.C., as many historians believe, Caesar's motives for writing it would have been vastly different than if had written it years later. As C. E. Stevens and others have indicated, Caesar intended to run for office in 50 B.C.. The work was definitely published by 46 B.C.; if it was published nearer to that date than to 51 B.C., Caesar would have had less reason to distort his record, as scholars point out. This leads to another area of controversy, that of deciding what audience Caesar addressed in his writings. Another matter of interest to critics is one of genre. There has been much debate concerning how best to describe Caesar's work: notes, *commentarii,* annals, or *historia*? F. E. Adcock explains how Caesar incorporated elements from all of these genres to create a composite form. Scholars also vigorously discuss the question of how honest Caesar is in the way he describes events. While all agree that no one can be totally objective in describing events in which he himself prominently figures, some critics believe that some of Caesar's interpretations are deliberately misleading. C. E. Stevens accuses Caesar of juggling facts. John H. Collins is inclined to believe Caesar; he thinks some of the problem comes from readers reading too much into Caesar's words. Andreola Rossi, however, points out that Caesar intends his readers to reach the stretched interpretations they sometimes reach. J. P. V. D. Balsdon concludes his study of the problem of Caesar's veracity with no firm conclusion except that extremists on either side of the

question are likely wrong. Caesar's lucid writing style has been criticized as being too plain, monotonous, and pedestrian, but this view is now largely being eclipsed. H. C. Gotoff, for example, credits Caesar with employing some interesting variations of Latin grammar. Military historians praise Caesar's study of the large picture of war and are fascinated by his explanation of tactics. Adcock writes regarding the way Caesar describes battles, "it is hard to imagine how better it could be done."

PRINCIPAL WORKS

De Bello Gallico (history) before 46 B.C.
De Bello Civili (history) c. 44 B.C.

Principal English Translations

Caesar: The Conquest of Gaul (translated by S. A. Handford) 1951
Caesar's Gallic War (translated by Joseph Pearl) 1962
Caesar: The Civil War (translated by Jane F. Mitchell) 1967
The Battle for Gaul (translated by Anne and Peter Wiseman) 1980
Seven Commentaries on the Gallic War (translated by Carolyn Hammond) 1996
The Civil War (translated by J. M. Carter) 1997

CRITICISM

C. E. Stevens (lecture date 1951)

SOURCE: "The *Bellum Gallicum* as a Work of Propaganda," in *Latomus,* Vol. 11, 1952, pp. 2-18.

[*In the following essay, originally delivered as a lecture in 1951, Stevens examines instances in* De Bello Gallico *in which Caesar conceals the truth or interprets events self-servingly.*]

It is not possible to consider the **Bellum Gallicum** as a work of propaganda unless a position can be taken up on the date of its composition. We know from external evidence only that it was published not later than 46 B. C.,[1] but the fact that the story of the campaign of 51 B. C. is written by another hand would lead us to suspect that Caesars's own books of the *commentaries* were written, as has long been the general belief of scholars[2], in the winter of 52-51 B. C. The campaign of 52 B. C., though not the end (and realised by Caesar, as his legionary dispositions and his determination to winter in Gaul prove[3], as not the end of the war), marked nevertheless the end of the national resistance, with the *supplicatio* of twenty days to crown it[4]. If Caesar had left the writing of the *commentaries* to 50 B. C., as Holmes, for instance, was inclined to believe[5], we may ask why he did not complete them; book VIII, even with the post-war politics from Hirtius' more prolix pen, is not a long book. I accept then the date of 52-51 B. C. for publication. I accept also the inference drawn by Nipperdey and accepted by Holmes[6] and others of the simultaneous composition and publication of all seven books[7].

Nevertheless there is a point to be made. Though it should be true that the seven books of our *commentaries* were published simultaneously, it was Caesar's duty to send regular despatches to the senate[8], and on more than one occasion in the *commentaries* he mentions these *litterae*[9]. They would remain on the senatorial files, indeed a summary, if not the full text, could presumably be read by the public in the *acta diurna*. It would be impossible grossly to garble facts which were already on the record, though the point of view in presenting them could be altered (and I hope to show on one occasion that it was). Salomon Reinach[10] has done good service in calling attention to these despatches, *ephemerides,* as they seem to have been called, with special reference to the circumstances of Caesar's first campaign, that of 58 B. C. Indeed I am not sure that the quotation of Servius (*ad Aen.,* XI, 743)[11] and perhaps the anecdote of Plutarch (*Caes.,* XXVI, 4) which seems to go with it, may not be truly from the *ephemeris* behind our book VII, introduced by Caesar as rather a good joke but not thought worthy of inclusion in the commentaries[12].

If we accept the simultaneous publication and the date of 52-51 B. C., an interesting point emerges. Balsdon and I have argued that Caesar intended to stand at the consular elections of 50 B. C.[13]. If this is so, then on the analogy of Cicero's canvass[14], Caesar's should have begun in 51 B. C. He himself used to send home from Gaul commendatory documents for candidates that he favoured[15]. The *commentaries* then should be a kind of immense self-commendation to take the place of the *prensatio* of Caesar, absent during the canvass and to be absent by the Law of the Ten Tribunes during the election itself. It may even have overshot the mark. One would like to think that M. Marcellus' motion of recall, first broached in May 51 B. C.[16],—*quoniam bello confecto pax esset ac dimitti deberet victor exercitus*[17]—was motivated precisely by the publication of the *commentaries.*

These circumstances of publication will perhaps bring into even clearer relief certain passages well known to scholars. In 52 B. C. Pompey, whom public opinion had expected to be consul in that year with Caesar himself as colleague[18], had sold himself to the *optimates,* but the bargain was far from sealed. In 51 B. C. Pompey, we remember, was responsible for quashing the motion, hostile to Caesar, of M. Marcellus[19]; with Pompey, again if Balsdon and myself are right, Caesar was to make the *negotium* in the autumn of that year[20]. It is natural, therefore, in *commentaries* published in 52-51 B. C. to find Pompey complimented on

the *virtus* with which he has restored order in 52 B. C.[21], even though the restoration was accompanied by an assault against enemies of the optimate party[22]. Pompey is thanked for the legion which he had put at Caesar's disposal in 54-53 B. C.; his continued residence close to the city is declared to be in the public interest, and the transfer of the legion is due to private friendship and sense of the public weal[23]. The sense of public duty attributed to Pompey is given point by the frequent mentions of the *populus Romanus,* whose interests are always before Caesar as he fights[24]. And here it is surely the *popularis,* the heir of Marius who speaks. It is *populus Romanus* always, *senatus populusque Romanus* never[25]. Caesar avenges the honour of the *populus Romanus* and is pleased to note that he is at the same time avenging the honour of his wife's family, the Calpurnii Pisones[26]. Even his *dignitas,* dearer to him than life itself, as he was later to assert[27], demands that the Rhine be crossed not on ships but by a bridge; but is it not his own *dignitas,* it is not less the *dignitas* of the *populus Romanus*[28]. Thus we can easily believe that, while Caesar and Pompey are both actuated by patriotism, "it is the *optimates* who are prepared to sacrifice their country's good for political ends. As Ariovistus is made to tell Caesar[29], if he killed Caesar, he would gratify many leaders of the Roman people: this he knew for certain by messengers from them". We are not to forget the contrast between these *principes populi Romani* (who have so styled themselves in correspondence with a barbarian) and Caesar, who is fighting its battles.

Not that these battles, after the difficulties of the first year have been got round, are felt to need justification. Victory, as Cicero could remind even an audience of optimate *pontifices,* justifies any means that the victor uses to gain for himself the position to win it[30]. "En deux ans", as Camille Jullian[31] well describes the campaigns of 58 and 57 B. C., "il avait combattu tour à tour pour garantir sa province, pour protéger ses alliés, pour contenir ses adversaires et pour soumettre les indifférents". After all, the senate had in a manner ratified those actions of his, which enabled him to say *pacata Gallia* in 57 B. C., by an unparalleled *supplicatio*[32], and who was he to contradict this or such jingoism as Cicero's in the senate next year[33]? In point of fact, the words of Cicero find no echo in Caesar's narrative. It may pay materially to be on Caesar's side, as it paid the Remi and the Aeudi[34], but there is no clap-trap of an imperial mission. Dumnorix proclaims with his last breath that he is a free man and citizen of a free community[35], and Vercingetorix, as he goes into captivity, proclaims (and Caesar says no word to impugn the claim) that he has taken up arms for the liberty of all[36]. Though we may wish to suspect that the massacre of the Usipetes and Tencteri was not really justified by the treachery of their cavalry[37], the story which so horrified Cato is told straight[38]. Perhaps all that one can say is that an ambiguity is allowed to be present in the reader's mind on the precise signification of *Gallia.* While in book I and the beginning of book II it normally means the restricted, Celtican region[39], its meaning slides later into that of the whole area[40], as provincialised in 51 B.C.[41]. Indeed we are introduced to this ambiguity in the famous first chapter of book I[42].

Justification after 58 B. C. then is not attempted, though points which would lead a reader to congratulate himself that Gaul was conquered are given their weight. He is not to forget the Cimbri and Teutones who are mentioned wherever relevant[43] and even dragged into a rather taste-less speech in *oratio recta* put into the mouth of an Arver-nian shut up in Alesia[44]. Caesar has saved Rome—Cicero had made that clear[45]—from repetitions of that alarm. And a trick can be picked up in praise not only of Marius, the family connexion, but of Marius' army[46]. Caesar is the political heir of Marius, his army the military heirs of the military machine that Marius made.

But while justification of the campaigns need not be at-tempted, nothing must be written which will sell Caesar short. Minor checks may be admitted, but Caesar must be seen to have the initiative throughout, and the *felicitas*[47] which inspires his directing mind must inform all. Even the great Labienus, who realises in a crisis that in the absence of his *imperator* the strength of character on which he must rely is his own[48], twice advises his troops (he is the only *legatus* who is allowed a reported speech) to fight as though the *imperator* were at hand[49]. Legions will not fight, the Gauls are made to assert, unless the *imperator* is back in the province[50]. It is the good *legatus,* Cotta, together with most of the tribunes and centurions, who urges that winter-quarters must not be shifted without Caesar's express permission[51]; and the contrary decision leads to a disaster. A slight disregard of formal instructions by Q. Cicero nearly leads to another and is gently repri-manded[52]. When real calamities occur, they are due to the foolishness of a *legatus*—Aduatuca[53] or the over-confidence of soldiers—Gergovia[54]. Nevertheless I hope to show that on two important occasions in the Gallic war Caesar did not have the initiative. On one his plan went completely astray and he has not told us. On the other his moves conformed to those of his adversary and he has written as far as possible to show that his adversary's moves conformed to his.

The former is the Invasion of Britain. We learn from Strabo[55] that the motive for the revolt of the Veneti was to stop Caesar from invading Britain and ruining their trade. According to Caesar its motive was the taking of hostages from the Veneti and their attempt to blackmail Crassus into returning them by detaining his commissaries[56]. It may be true to say *ut sunt Gallorum subita et repentina consilia*[57], but it needs more than that to explain why the revolt of the Veneti was joined by precisely those states which are likely to have been interested in British trade (including the far-distant Morini and Menapii[58]) and why the Veneti obtained help from Britain itself[59]. And there may be more. Caesar tells us that he had a fleet built for this campaign. Nevertheless he attempted to subdue the Veneti by land operations without using it at all[60]. Of course it is true, as Caesar reminds us[61], that the Romans

did not like trusting themselves to the sea. Nevertheless we can see that when it became necessary to decide the campaign by naval operations, Caesar's fleet was found to be not at all satisfactory for a battle in Atlantic waters. The suspicion must surely arise that the ships that fought it were intended for a different purpose.

The suspicion is deepened when we notice that Caesar seems to be juggling with the facts about the fleet in more than one way. In one passage[62] he states that he gave orders to build galleys—*naves longae*—on the Loire immediately on the news of the revolt. A little later, however, he tells us that he put D. Brutus in command not only of the "fleet" but of "the Gallic vessels which he had ordered to concentrate from the territories of the Pictones, the San-toni and the *other pacified regions*[63]". But where are these regions from which ships were requisitioned which appear to be distinguished from those of the "fleet", and what sort of ships are they likely to have been? To take the first question, we cannot place them to the south of the Ga-ronne, for that is Aquitania, which Caesar is preparing to "pacify" at this very moment. Dio Cassius, whose narra-tive at this point may be independent[64], seems to imply that they were constructed higher up the Loire—and this, though Caesar's narrative implies requisition rather than construction, might seem possible and has an analogy[65]. Nevertheless it would surely be strange if Caesar, intend-ing a distinction between shipyards on the lower and up-per reaches of the Loire, should express this distinction by the Loire *simpliciter* in one passage and "the other paci-fied regions" in the other. Moreover it would appear that Dio's remarks on the fleet are really nothing more than misreadings and misinterpretations of Caesar[66]. In truth it is difficult to seek these "pacified regions" except on the north coast, from which, as any yachtsman knows, it would be no attractive matter to sail them through the Four and the Raz into Venetic waters. To take the second point, Caesar makes clear that the ships of the Veneti were superior to his own in every respect save in speed and oarsmanship[67]. In other words is is clear that he fought the battle with the *naves longae* that had been built for him on the Loire. Then were the requisitioned ships *naves longae* too? This is surely improbable, for he tells us that *naves longae* were unfamiliar to the Britons whom he invaded next year[68]. For this invasion he embarked his troops all on 98 *naves onerariae*[69]. It is true that this fleet was partly requisitioned *ex finitimis regionibus,* nevertheless we must not forget that it was also composed of the fleet that he had ordered to concentrate for the compaign against the Veneti[70]. Remembering again the difficulty of taking ships round Finistère, we may find it likely that Caesar has been deceiving his readers. He had been requisitioning ocean going vessels some time in 56 B.C. from tribes along the Channel coast for a purpose which was not a "campaign against the Veneti" at all.

But when in 56 B. C.? Here we find Caesar juggling with the times. The purpose of my argument is to show that the Veneti had revolted because a naval force had been ordered, not that a naval force had been ordered because the Veneti had revolted; in other words that Caesar did intend to invade Britain in 56 B. C. and the Veneti knew it. Caesar could rebut that quick enough if he showed that the requisitioning of ships, which we have shown to be probably ocean going vessels from Channel ports, occurred late in 56 B. C.—too late for an invasion of Britain and thus too late to inspire a revolt of the Veneti. And one may suspect that his mind was working in that way when in book IV he dates the requisitioning to the *summer* of 56 B. C.[71]. But this will not fit his narrative of book III. Here the chronology dates the outbreak of the revolt to the winter of 57-56 B. C.[72], and the order for the construction of the *naves longae* in the Loire while he was still away, but about to return as soon "as the season allowed"[73]. The order for requisitioning is not timed, but it had already been, given[74] before the appointment of D. Brutus as naval commander which was among the measures taken by Caesar on his way to Brittany[75]. This appointment preceded the abortive land campaign which occupied him for "the great part of the summer"[76]. Thus by this narrative the naval concentration is not in the summer of 56 B. C. but much earlier; but the revolt is early too and so is Caesar's arrival in Gaul in response to it. This narrative is self-consistent and also avoids the suspicion of a British project in 56 B. C.; but it is not consistent with external chronology. This was the year of Luca and we can check Caesar's movements from Cicero's letters. He did not leave for Gaul "as soon as the season allowed"; he was still in Italy at least as late as the first week in April[77].

Now perhaps we may be allowed to throw another small point into the scales. In his account of the winter-quarters of 57 B. C.[78], Caesar states that the legions were sent to the territories of Carnutes, Andes, Turoni, "and the states which were near the areas where he had made war". There is by no means necessarily here evidence of intent to deceive. Nevertheless we can remind ourselves that Caesar's readers had no maps[79]; and in fact the states must be located among the Belgae, for it is clear that here Labienus himself was posted[80]. Caesar has, to say the least, not helped his readers to discover that a body of his troops under his chief subordinate was not far from those Morini who joined the Veneti in revolt, who needed a campaign later in 56 B. C.[81] and from whose territory there was the shortest crossing to Britain[82].

Perhaps it may be permissible to attempt a reconstruction of the plan. It is possible that both the eastern and the western controllers of British trade routes, the Morini and Menapii on the one hand, the inhabitants of the Breton peninsula on the other, were simultaneously nervous because they were simultaneously affected[83], that Caesar planned a double invasion, not only by the route of 55 and 54 B. C., but by the age-old prehistoric sea-route to southwest Britain[84], and that the ocean-going vessels of the Veneti would have transported the western force, had not their revolt compelled Caesar to sink them. It might be plausible to suggest that the voyage of a certain P. Crassus, reported by Strabo[85], was undertaken by Caesar's quaestor as a reconnaissance for it.

It may be possible to indicate the relation of this projected invasion to the political manoeuvres at Rome. In passages which will be examined below, Cicero speaks of a proposal to despatch *decem legati* to Gaul. A commission of ten *legates* is virtually invariably the precursor to the conversion of a conquered area into a province of the Roman Empire; and it would be natural to refer such a proposal to the projected provincialisation of "pacified" Gaul[86]. Scholars refuse it, however, and refer the words to the appointment of ten subordinate generals to work under Caesar for further Gallic campaigns[87], because they cannot see how Caesar could seem to welcome the provincialisation of Gaul on the one hand and to press for an extension of command on the other. It looks, however, as though this difficulty will disappear if we are allowed the plan for an invasion of Britain in 56 B. C. The news of the pacification of Gaul, which reached Rome in the autumn of 57 B. C.[88], indeed inspired on Cicero's proposal and with Pompey's approval the grant of a *supplicatio,* the longest ever known[89]; nevertheless it is unlikely that a senate whom Caesar had so flouted as consul was thus honouring him entirely for his *beaux yeux.* The news of pacification would lead politicians, especially hostile politicians, to think of provincialisation connoted by the despatch of these *decem legati,* for this could enable them to claim, at least on grounds of equity, that Caesar should come home and disband his army[90]. Domitius Ahenobarbus seems to have been taking this line early in 56 B. C.[91] and it even seems to have received the support of Pompey, jealous of Caesar's success[92]. Caesar's reply, if we have interpreted events rightly, was to make plans for an invasion of Britain in 56 B.C., a plan involving orders for the construction of galleys, recruitment of their crews and requisitioning of ocean-going craft. If he could show that an invasion of Britain was necessary to secure peace in his pacified Gaul (and he could use the sort of arguments that he uses in the *commentaries* to justify the later invasions[93]), then he could well submit to the despatch of *decem legati* to provincialise what he had already conquered, for he would be making new conquests further away, and would submit the more cheerfully if the decision to send them was accompanied by that approval for his plan of new conquests connoted by a grant of pay for the troops and by legal action which implied the prolongation of his command certainly until the end of 54 B. C., which would seem time enough to make the new conquests, if they proceeded with the speed of the old[94]. Discussions on this point would seem to have been proceding during March 56 B. C., in the shadow of the Luca agreement[95], and it is to that date and surely to that motivation that we should attribute the outbreak of the revolt among the Veneti and their allies. But the revolt meant that Gaul was not pacified, ready for provincialisation and the despatch of *decem legati* yet. The grant of pay and the prolonged command must now be used for mopping-up operations inside Gaul, and when Cicero was put up to speak for Caesar in Gaul, this is what he said[96]. Not a word of an expedition to Britain from him—nor, in this year, from Caesar. He has concealed a British scheme that went astray.

And not the only time. Before ever he sailed for Britain in 54 B. C., Caesar is careful to prepare the reader for the necessity of its return by proclaiming that he feared trouble in Gaul during his absence[97]. Nevertheless he took more than half his legions—five out of eight—and half his cavalry[98], and lets slip that he intended to winter in the island but was prevented by Gallic disturbances[99]. Clearly then Britain was meant to produce better results than he was able actually to report. I suspect indeed, as the late Martin Charlesworth used to say to me, that he intended to conquer not only the whole of Britain but Ireland as well in the five campaigning seasons put at his disposal by the *Lex Pompeia Licinia* passed the year before[100], Ireland that he, like others, believed to be quite close to Spain[101], close in fact to that promontory which he had visited himself[102], where a lighthouse was to be erected from which, it was alleged, Britain could be seen[103]. And it all ended in a treaty patched up for him by his own henchman, Commius, and the uncertain prospects of tribute from Kent and Hertfordshire[104].

The failure of the great expedition of 54 B. C. made it necessary to modify the account of that of the year before. This was intended, as I have argued elsewhere[105], as a reconnaissance of Roman public opinion no less than of Britain, possibly to show to all the necessity and the justification of the further years of command which his triumviral colleagues were to grant him by the *Lex Pompeia Licinia*[106]. And it was a treasure hunt into the bargain (as we learn from Cicero, naturally not from Caesar)[107]—which, of course, would increase its propaganda value. As propaganda, therefore, for the proposed conquest, it was loudly trumpeted as the triumph over Oceanus itself, the same triumph that struck the imagination of Claudius a century later[108]. Caesar indeed triumphs over Oceanus in his despatches of 55 B. C., as we shall demonstrate; in the *commentaries* it needs a sharp eye to discover that Oceanus exists[109]. But when Lucan put into the mouth of Pompey in reproach of Caesar the words— *Oceanumque vocans incerti stagna profundi / territa quaesitis ostendit terga Britannis*[110], he cannot be criticising the treatment of Oceanus in the *commentaries*. Authorities such as Plutarch[111] place Lucan's jibe in its context. "Caesar was the first to launch a fleet upon the western ocean and to sail through the Atlantic sea carrying an army to wage war. The island . . . furnished matter of dispute to multitudes of writers, some of whom averred that it never had existed and did not then exist." And Dio Cassius, using similar language[112], tells us outright that this verification of the unknown was the reason why Caesar was awarded the longest *supplicatio* that the or any man in Roman history had ever had. Caesar stated himself that he received a *supplicatio of* twenty days[113], but the reasons for the longest ever—he does not tell us so, but we can work it out—he does not give (nor any hint of its connexion with the *Lex Pompeia Licinia*), because, if I am right, it was given on receipt of despatches written as propaganda for a great conquest—which did not come off.

In the other case it is a question of Caesar's operations at Gergovia and Alesia. Caesar's account can be summarised as follows. He was besieging Vercingetorix in Gergovia and the siege was proceding with success when a mutiny of the Aeduan cavalry engineered by Litaviccus was followed by a rising of the Aedui against the Roman citizens quartered among them. He then realised that a more extended Gallic rebellion was probable and hoped accordingly to obtain some prestige success at Gergovia which would give him an excuse for raising the siege[114]. He would have obtained such a success, which consisted in capturing camps outside the city wall, had it not been for the indiscipline of his own soldiers. After quitting Gergovia he saves himself by extraordinary marches, defeats Vercingetorix in a cavalry battle, coops him up in Alesia, defeats the relieving force—and then it is the end. Thus Caesar, though obstructed by his own soldiers at Gergovia and by Vercingetorix and the relieving army at Alesia, in essence retains the initiative throughout.

But the picture does not fit the facts. According to Caesar an essential factor in his attempt not on Gergovia, we remember, but to obtain a prestige success at Gergovia, was the employment of 10.000 Aedui on his right flank[115]. Can we believe that if the state had been in open revolt, murdering Roman citizens wherever they could be found (which is what Caesar says[116]), he would have used so many troops whose temper must have become so unreliable simply in the hope of a prestige success? He would have risked the annihilation of his legions. And that is not all. After he had failed to obtain this prestige success, he was told by Eporedorix that the mutineer Litaviccus has gone off *ad sollicitandos Haeduos,* and Eporedorix asked if he could go to stop him. *Etsi multis iam rebus perfidiam Haeduorum perspectam habebat atque horum discessu admaturari defectionem civitatis existimabat,* says Caesar, he let him go. But *admaturari defectionem civitatis* is sheer nonsense. The *defectio* had already happened; according to Caesar himself, while the siege of Gergovia was going on, the chief magistrate of the Aedui, the Vergobret, was leading the massacre of Roman citizens[117].

The truth must be that Caesar was not in the least satisfied, as he asks us to believe[118], with the capture of three empty camps outside the town-wall. He did not want a prestige success; he wanted to capture Gergovia. He failed and his failure was the cause of the general rebellion of the Aedui. Caesar has magnified a mutiny of certain patriotic units among the Aedui during the siege into such a general rebellion as made it necessary to look for a prestige success; and then he blames his soldiers for overconfidence (blame which soldiers would be proud to take), because he did not get it. He has used the mutiny of certain patriots to antedate the general rebellion of the tribe which was caused in fact simply because he had suffered a serious reverse. Indeed it is possible that Dio Cassius, though his narrative is somewhat confused, has seen the truth[119].

Moreover Caesar, to keep the initiative, must defeat Vercingetorix in the cavalry battle and force him to take refuge in Alesia. But Caesar's own narrative makes clear that

Vercingetorix had already made preparations to stand a siege[120]; indeed it seems likely that the whole plan of a pan-Gallic relief force had already been conceived[121]. The fact is that strategically Vercingetorix had the initiative. His strategy was conceived, I submit, on simple lines. The original plan was to force the Romans out of free Gaul by a policy of scorched earth[122]. But this might be difficult to impose on other tribes, and his experience outside Avaricum led him to give this plan a second member. He had enticed Ceasar's troops to appear before his own—in his own absence—on unfavourable ground from which they had been forced to make an ignominious withdrawal[123]. I think that Vercingetorix, who had thus duped Caesar more probably than not by accident, drew a deduction. To encourage and reinforce the policy of scorched earth, Caesar should be induced to make fruitless moves against Gauls in impregnable hill-forts. With this plan he succeeded brilliantly at Gergovia and intended to try the same at Alesia, where he had made preparations accordingly. His cavalry skirmish was thus an attempt, as it were, to pick up a trick on the way, which Caesar has magnified into a decisive battle, compelling Vercingetorix to stand a siege. In fact, it is not Caesar who has trapped Vercingetorix in Alesia, but Vercingetorix who has trapped Caesar between himself in Alesia and the relieving army. And what a place Alesia was! We learn from Diodorus (not from Caesar!) that it was "honoured by the Gauls as the hearth and metropolis of the whole of Gaul"[124]. Vercingetorix meant to trap Caesar at the holy centre of Gaul—and he had done it. When we remember the speech put into Vercingetorix' mouth, that he "would make one council of Gaul against which the world would not prevail[125]", we may be allowed to conjecture that he intended after victory to proclaim himself in Gaul's metropolis the king of Gaul. As a king who had lost, he rode grandly caparisoned (we do not hear this from Caesar) around the tribunal of Caesar, the "imperator", who had won[126]. It was one of the tragic moments of the world's history if I have interpreted the story aright. How titanic then appears Caesar who could conceal it all for the stern duty of impressing his own continual *felicitas* and mastery of events upon the electors at the consular *comitia* of 50 B. C.!

Notes

1. CICERO, *Brutus*, 75, 262.

2. HOLMES, *Caesar's Conquest of Gaul* (cited as *Gaul*), 202.

3. *B. G.*, VII, 90, 8 (All references are to the *Bellum Gallicum* unless otherwise specified).

4. VII, 90, 8.

5. *Gaul*, 209.

6. *Gaul*, 203.

7. The view of HALKIN (*Mélanges Paul Thomas*, 407-416), that the *commentaries* were published in three instalments, books I and II, III and IV, V-VII, though accepted by Carcopino (*César*, 762, n. 66) is not seriously argued, and I have refuted it by implication in the text.

8. CICERO, *De Prov. Cons.*, 6, 14; *In Pisonem*, 16, 38.

9. II, 35, 4; IV, 38, 5; VII, 90, 8.

10. *Revue de Philologie*, XXXIX, 29-49.

11. *C. Julius Caesar, cum dimicaret in Gallia et ab hoste raptus equo eius portaretur armatus, occurrit cuidam ex hostibus, qui eum nosset, et insultans ait: 'cecos ac cesar'* (*v. l.* '*caesar caesar*'), *quod Gallorum lingua 'dimitte' significat: et ita actum est ut dimitteretur; hoc autem ipse Caesar in ephemeride sua dicit, ubi propriam commemorat felicitatem.* . . .

12. Reinach assumes that these stories were fraudulently attributed to *ephemerides* by anti-Caesarian authors such as Tanusius Geminus; this seems to me neither necessary nor likely.

13. *A. J. P.*, LIX, 178; *J. R. S.*, XXIX, 176.

14. CICERO, *Att.*, I, 1, 1.

15. SUETONIUS, *Divus Iulius*, 23, 2.

16. CAELIUS *ap.* CICERON., *Fam.*, VIII, 1, 2.

17. SUETONIUS, *Divus Iulius*, 28, 2.

18. SUETONIUS, *Divus Iulius*, 26, 1; DIO, XL, 50,3 - 51,1.

19. CICERO, *Att.*, VIII, 3, 3; APPIAN, *B. C.*, II, 26.

20. *A. J. P.*, LIX, 178; *J. R. S.*, XXIX, 176.

21. VII, 6, 1.

22. ASCONIUS (Clark), p. 56, ll. 3-5.

23. VI, 1, 2, 3.

24. But not always as he writes! For the *populus Romanus* ceases to appear in book VII after 17, 3 (Avaricum). It looks as though the approach to a climax of the thrilling narrative caused Caesar to forget his propaganda.

25. The contrast with Cicero, who, after early coquetting with the cause of *populares*, never left *senatus* out, is piquant—and instructive. See Mommsen's elucidation of his practice, *Staatsrecht*, III, 1257, 1258.

26. I, 12, 7.

27. *B. C.*, I, 9, 2.

28. IV, 17, 1.

29. I, 44, 12.

30. *De Domo*, 8, 18.

31. *Hist. Gaule*, III, 276.

32. II, 35, 1, 4.

33. *De Prov. Cons.*, 13, 33.

34. VI, 12, 6-9; VII, 54, 3.

35. V, 7, 8.

36. VII, 89, 1.

37. IV, 7-15.

38. SUETONIUS, *Divus Iulius,* 24, 3; PLUTARCH, *Caes.,* XXII, 3; *Cato minor,* LI, 1; APPIAN, *Celtica,* XVIII.

39. *Gallia* means Celtican Gaul always in book I (except in the geographical introduction, I, 1) and in II, 1, 2 and II, 2, 3 (but not II, 1, 1); exceptionally, describing the Celtican empire of Celtillus, VII, 4, 1.

40. *Gallia* is clearly Gaul in the wide sense (best seen perhaps in VI, 5, 4) onwards from II, 4, 2—which may, however, still exclude the Aquitani, until they have been subdued (II, 35, 1; III, 11, 3—but compare III, 20, 1).

41. *Fasti Cuprenses* (*Inscr. Italiae,* XIII, 1, p. 244); SALLUST, *Hist.,* I, 11; SUETONIUS, *Divus Iulius,* 25, 1; EUTROPIUS, VI, 17, 3.

42. I, 1, 1, 2, 4-6 (I see no good reason for condemning sections 5-7).

43. I, 33, 4; II, 4, 2; 29, 4.

44. VII, 77, 12.

45. *De prov. cons.,* 13, 32.

46. I, 40, 5. Holmes, following Meusel, is surely wrong in expelling the capital propaganda point about the army.

47. I, 40, 13. Is there a slight hint that he must be regarded as not inferior to Pompey (compare CICERO, *De Imp. Cn. Pompei,* 10, 28; 16, 47)?

48. VII, 59, 6.

49. VI, 8, 4; VII, 62, 2.

50. VII, 1, 7.

51. V, 28, 3.

52. VI, 42, 1; possibly more strongly in a letter to Marcus (CHARISIUS, I, 126, 9—Keil; Tyrrell and Purser, VI, 295).

53. V, 52, 6.

54. VII, 52.

55. IV, 4, 1, p. 194. . . .

56. III, 8, 2. Moreover Caesar strains truth by calling these *praefecti tribunique militum* (III, 7, 3) in later passages *legati* (III, 16, 4 and 9. 3—the latter passage again wrongly ejected by Meusel and Holmes).

57. III, 8, 3.

58. On the evidence of coins for trade with south-east Britain see BROOKE, *Antiquity,* VII, 269-274; *Num. Chron.,* XIII, 99-107, who warns us, however, that the ascription of a type widely diffused in Britain to the Morini may be incorrect.

59. III, 9, 10.

60. III, 12.

61. III, 12, 5.

62. III, 9, 1.

63. III, 11, 5.

64. Jullian thinks so (*Hist. Gaule,* III, 297, n. 4).

65. XXXIX, 40, 3; compare v. 5, 2.

66. The bringing of 'swift ships' (? *naves longae*) round from the Mediterranean (XXXIX, 40, 5) looks like simple careless copying of III, 9, 1.

67. III, 13, 7.

68. IV, 25, 1.

69. IV, 22, 3, 4. We are not told the number of galleys (*naves longae*) used in 55 B. C. In the next year he had about 600 transports and 28 *naves longae* (v. 2, 2).

70. IV, 21, 4; 22, 3, 4.

71. IV, 21, 4; *quam superiore aestate ad Veneticum bellum fecerat classem.*

72. III, 7, 1.

73. III, 9, 2 *cum primum per anni tempus potuit.*

74. III, 11, 5 *D. Brutum . . . classi Gallicisque navibus, quas ex Pictonibus et Santonis reliquisque pacatis regionibus convenire iusserat praefecit.*

75. III, 11, 5.

76. III, 12, 5.

77. Carcopino, *César,* 776; HOLMES, *Roman Republic,* II, 295. The exact date with reference to the seasons of the year depends on the adjustment of the traditional to the Julian calendar. I choose Holmes's forensically as less favourable to my argument; Carcopino's would bring it fairly to the middle of April.

78. II, 35, 3.

79. Compare CICERO, *Qu. fr.,* III, 8, 2; *ubi enim isti Nervii et quam longe absint nescio.*

80. III, 11, 1, 2.

81. III, 28.

82. IV, 21, 3.

83. Ireland may already have been in Caesar's mind, in which case the evidence cited below would be relevant now, and see *Appendix.*

84. See most recently, WHEELER, *Maiden Castle,* 386. A third line of attack, to Southampton Water, as subsequently achieved in the 'Second Belgic Invasion' of *c.* 50 B. C. (on which see Hawkes, *Hants*

Field Club, XIII, 160) is also possible, though there is no actual evidence for it.

85. III, 5, 11, p. 176. Save that he does not make the point of reconnaissance for a projected invasion, this is more or less how Holmes (*Ancient Britain,* 497) looks at Strabo's account.

86. See on this notably BALSDON, *J. R. S.,* XXIX, 171.

87. *E. g.* HOLMES, *Roman Republic,* II, 294; CARCOPINO, *César,* 781.

88. The time is established by the chronological series of events as CICERO gives them, *Fam.,* I, 9, 14.

89. II, 35, 4; CICERO, *De Prov. Cons.,* 10, 25; 11, 27; *Pro Balbo,* 27, 61.

90. Compare SUETONIUS, *Divus Iulius,* 24, 3. But I am very doubtful whether the *senatus consultum* really contained a clause *donec debellatum foret,* as Balsdon believes (*J. R. S.,* XXIX, 170).

91. SUETONIUS, *Divus Iulius,* 24, 1.

92. DIO, XXXIX, 25, 2.

93. IV, 20, 1; V, 12, 2.

94. CICERO, *Fam.,* I, 7, 10: *nam et stipendium Caesari decretum est et decem legati et ne lege Sempronia succederetur facile perfectum est.* Compare CICERO, *De prov. Cons.,* 11, 28; *Pro Balbo* 27, 61; PLUTARCH, *Caesar,* XXI, 3-4 (misdated) and see *Appendix.*

95. It is with these discussions, still conducted, as I believe, in the context of a projected invasion of Britain in 56 B. C. that I would connect Cicero, *ad Qu. fr.,* II, 4, 5.

96. *De Prov. Cons.,* 12, 29. The speech would have been very different if the Veneti had not revolted!

97. V, 5, 4.

98. V, 5, 3; 8, 2.

99. V, 22, 4.

100. He comes near saying it in *The Lost Province,* 5.

101. V, 13, 2. I believe that chapters 12-14 were copied out rapidly by Caesar from an authority (like the chapters on Druidism), but I do not think that they are spurious. Compare TACITUS, *Agricola,* 24, 1.

102. Dio, XXXVII, 53, 4.

103. OROSIUS, I, 2, 71, 81; compare the Irish traditions based on Orosius which MACNEILL examines, *Phases of Irish History,* 93. O'RAHILLY, it may be worth noting (*Early Irish History,* 208), is convinced of an invasion of Ireland by refugees from Caesar's Gallic campaigns. This might well make Ireland interesting to Caesar.

104. V, 22, 3-5.

105. *Antiquity,* XXI, 3-9.

106. This novel point needs more than a footnote; I argue it in *Appendix.*

107. *Att.,* IV, 16, 7.

108. *I. L. S.,* 212: *iactationem gloriae prolati imperi ultra Oceanum;* compare *Anth. Lat.,* 419-426.

109. IV, 29, 1.

110. *Pharsalia,* II, 571, 572. Moreover when the panegyrist of *Pan. Lat.,* VIII, 11, 3 states—for what he is worth—of Caesar: *alium se orbem terrarum scripsit repperisse,* he is attributing to Caesar what is not in the *commentaries.* I assume that both derive from the despatches by way of Livy, who should be the source of Eutropius' statement—contradicted implicitly by Caesar (II, 14, 4; III, 9, 10; IV, 20, 1)—that the Britons had never heard of Rome before (VI, 17, 3).

111. *Caesar,* XXIII, 2.

112. XXXIX, 53. Compare the language of the Proscription edict of 43 B. C. (not genuine, but probably an early invention) as given by Appian, B. C., IV, 8.

113. IV, 38, 5.

114. VII, 43, 5.

115. VII, 34, 1; 50, 1.

116. VII, 42, 4-6.

117. VII, 54, 2.

118. VII, 47, 1: *consecutus id quod animo proposuerat.*

119. XL, 38, 1.

120. VII, 69, 5; 71, 7.

121. As CARCOPINO, *César,* 824 supports, with plausible arguments. LATOMUS XI. - 2.

122. VII, 14, 4-10.

123. VII, 19. HOLMES, *Gaul,* 744, following Paul Menge, thinks that Vercingetorix planned to deceive Caesar. I feel doubtful.

124. IV, 19, 2.

125. VII, 29, 6.

126. FLORUS, I, 45 (III, 11), 26; PLUTARCH, *Caesar,* XXVII, 5; DIO, XL, 41.

F. E. Adcock (essay date 1956)

SOURCE: "The Literary Form," "The Purpose and Content of Caesar's *Commentaries,*" and "Style and Personality," in *Caesar as Man of Letters,* Cambridge University Press, 1956, pp. 6-49, 63-76.

[*In the following excerpt, Adcock explains how Caesar enlarged the genre of* commentarii, *examines his motivations for writing, and asserts that his plain and precise writing style accurately reflects his personality.*]

The extant continuous writings of Caesar were entitled *C. Iuli Caesaris commentarii rerum gestarum.* After the researches of F. W. Kelsey,[1] this seems to be beyond doubt, and it has not been seriously doubted. What we possess must have been contained in nine rolls—the first seven books of the *Gallic War,* covering the years 58-52 B.C. being rolls I-VII; then roll IX—the first two books of the *Civil War* covering the year 49; and roll X the third book of the *Civil War* describing the events of 48 B.C. until the narrative breaks off late in that year. Between roll VII and roll IX there lay the eighth book of the *Gallic War,* written by Hirtius, and the series of commentaries in the Caesarian Corpus was completed by the addition of three rolls containing the *Bellum Alexandrinum,* the *Bellum Africum* or *Africanum,* and *Bellum Hispaniense.* The whole series thus describes the military achievements of Caesar from the moment he arrived in Gaul in 58 B.C. to his victory over the younger Cn. Pompeius in 45 B.C. and its immediate consequences. Caesar's authorship of rolls I-VII, IX and X was no secret in his own times and it is hard to believe that it was ever concealed. They reveal at first hand the mind of the man whose exploits they describe, and it must have been at once plain that no one else can have written them. The theme of Caesar's commentaries is his *res gestae* whether in Gaul or in the theatres of war of that part of the *Bellum Civile*—or, as Caesar called it, the *civilis dissensio*—of which he himself wrote. By the time of Suetonius a distinction was made between Caesar's account of events in Gaul and his account of the Civil War, but, primarily, the simple description of the theme was *res gestae.*

A *commentarius* was a form of composition that already had a long history. The word corresponds in Latin to the Greek word *hypomnema,* which may be translated *aide-mémoire,* and the Greek word and its Latin equivalent are used of written matter that serves the purpose of an *aide-mémoire.* The origin of such writings is, primarily, official or private, and it is found in the times of Alexander the Great and his successors, an inheritance from the practice of Oriental monarchies so far as it was not the natural product of administrative convenience. On the military side, *hypomnemata* might be the wardiaries of generals, dispatches and reports such as have been found in a papyrus of the reign of Ptolemy VIII. In civil administration they may be memoranda or bureaucratic records. They may be Court journals in the Hellenistic kingdoms and so on. They are not, to begin with, intended for publication. In private life they may be written material for speeches—at least the word 'commentarius' is used in Cicero of the notes for a speech—or they may be private papers and memoranda. Thus Caelius[2] sends to Cicero, then governing Cilicia, a 'commentarius rerum urbanarum' which contains a catalogue of events at Rome for Cicero's information. Not all of it, Caelius implies, is worth Cice-

ro's attention: 'ex quo tu quae digna sunt selige'. So far, it may be said that *hypomnemata* or *commentarii* are, in general, statements of facts for their own sake, so far as they are not just helps to memory; though, inevitably, they may contain the facts as they are discerned by their authors. Such are *commentarii* in their origin. Literary merit is not their concern. They should be precise and clear, or they would defeat their own purpose, and that is all.

In contrast to these there is *historia.* To the Romans, of Caesar's day and afterwards, *historia* was, above all, an achievement of literary art. It is to Quintilian 'proxima poetis et quodammodo carmen solutum'.[3] The author of a work of *historia* was, above all, a stylist: what he regarded as fine writing was his chief aim, and not the discovery of truth. This does not mean that his work should not be credible or sincere—Livy is sincere even when he cannot be judged credible—but the merit of *historia* and the merit of establishing truth of fact are not one merit but two. The 'brevitas' of Sallust, 'primus Romana Crispus in historia',[4] is unlike enough to the 'lactea ubertas' of Livy, but what they are both concerned with, above all, is the same thing, a literary achievement.

Between *commentarius* of the original type and *historia* there is room for something which is not quite either the one or the other, something more than the first in content and less than the second in style. It is a development of the *commentarius,* and it is, as has been well observed,[5] something more Roman than Greek. This intermediate stage had been attained before the time of Caesar. Commentaries of this kind may be the material which the writer of *historia* can take and transmute by the alchemy of his literary art. This had been realized as will be seen presently, and it finds a place in Lucian's essay *Quomodo historia scribenda est.*[6] Such a *commentarius* of the intermediate stage may have absorbed or digested *commentarii* of the original type, or worked them together into a narrative which is not yet *historia* but has attained that synoptic view of events which Polybius claimed to have achieved. It is a natural process, and it is natural that it should be applied by the person most concerned with the events it describes. But it remains a *commentarius* until the man of letters converts it into *historia.* Though the author of the *commentarius* may describe things from his own standpoint, it still purports to be a statement of the facts for their own sake.

The development of the commentary to be the material of *historia* may conveniently be illustrated from a letter written by Lucius Verus to his tutor, Fronto.[7] The letter was written in A.D. 165, but the practical and psychological processes are near enough to those of the last decades of the Republic. Verus had been the nominal architect of a victory over the Parthians, though the strategical plan had been devised by Marcus Aurelius and had been executed by two able generals, Avidius Cassius and Martius Verus. Lucius Verus, a prince in search of a panegyrist, writes to Fronto to say he is forwarding the dispatches of his subordinates and has directed the two generals to draw up *commentarii* describing their operations for Fronto's use. He then offers to prepare a *commentarius* of his own in whatever form his tutor suggests. 'I am ready', he says, 'to fall in with your suggestions, provided my exploits are put by you in a bright light. Of course you will not overlook my *orationes* to the Senate and *adlocutiones* to my army.' Thus Fronto will have material for the speeches that were an adornment of *historia*. 'My *res gestae*', Verus concludes, 'whatever their character, are of course no greater than they actually are, but they will appear to be as great as you wish them to appear to be.' Fronto did not refuse this naïve request, and there have survived some fragmentary specimens of the preamble to the *historia*, which he probably did not live to complete. The *commentarius* material placed at Fronto's disposal thus ranges from matter of the original type to the more advanced form. It awaits conversion into the full-dress literary form of the *historia*, which, to judge from the fragments of the preamble, would have been full-dress indeed.

What Lucius Verus had done, Cicero had done before him, if with less *naïveté*. In June 60 B.C. he wrote in Greek a *commentarius consulatus sui* and sent it to Poseidonius, the leading Greek man of letters of the day, with the request that he would treat of these events 'ornatius'. Poseidonius neatly replied that when he read the *commentarius* he did not feel bold enough to attempt the theme.[8] Four years later Cicero tried again. He encouraged the Roman man of letters, L. Lucceius, to write a *historia* which would include the Catilinarian conspiracy and promised to send the *commentarii* for it.[9] Lucceius agreed, the *commentarii* were sent, but the *historia* was not written.[10] Cicero's *commentarius consulatus sui* was, indeed, no ordinary *commentarius*. He writes thus to Atticus, who also had written a *commentarius* on the same theme:

> On the first of June I met your servant. . . . He handed to me your letter and a *commentarius* on my consulship written in Greek. I am very glad that some time ago I gave to L. Cossinius to bring to you the book I had written on the same theme also in Greek, for if I had read yours first you would say I had plagiarized from you. Though yours—while I enjoyed reading it—seemed to me a trifle rough and unkempt ('horridula atque incompta'), yet its neglect of adornment seemed an adornment in itself, and it was like women who were thought to have the best scent because they used none; whereas my book has used up all the unguents of Isocrates, all the perfumes of his pupils and a trace of Aristotelian cosmetics.

Cicero writes to his friend with a kind of apologetic self-irony. But he could not refrain from fine writing about what appeared to him, more clearly than to others, a fine subject, *consulatus suus*. And he was not deprived of free will by the convention of a literary form. But the traditional form for a *commentarius*, however far it had gone on the way to *historia*, was simple and matter-of-fact.

In 46 B.C. when Cicero wrote his *Brutus*, having read those at least of Caesar's **Commentaries** which treated of his exploits in Gaul, he said they were written 'that others might have material to their hand if they composed a *historia*'.[11] So far he is placing them in the category of commentaries that await transmutation into *historia*, but he adds a significant phrase 'so that Caesar may have seemed a benefactor to the foolish who wished to take the curling-tongs to them, but that sensible men were frightened off writing on the basis of them'. Cicero may have remembered the answer of Poseidonius, and have laid a little flattering unction to his soul. So, too, Hirtius, in the preface to the Eighth Book of the **Gallic War,** says that Caesar's **Commentaries** have been published 'that *writers* might not lack knowledge of these great events', but he adds 'and they are so approved by all men's judgement'—'ut praerepta, non praebita facultas scriptoribus videatur'. Cicero's verdict, echoed, we may suppose, by Hirtius, is that Caesar's writings have a quality which precludes attempts by others to do better what Caesar has done so well. His **Commentaries,** while they remain commentaries, have a literary eminence in their own right. When Cicero wrote the *Brutus* he was in a rare mood of hope of Caesar as a statesman, and the all-powerful dictator would read what he had written, but Cicero was an honest critic, a dictator himself in his own field, the field of letters, and it need not be doubted that he said what he thought. To him the **Commentaries** approach the literary finality appropriate to the finished product of *historia*. When he praises them—'nudi enim sunt, recti et venusti, omni ornatu orationis tamquam veste detracta', he adds 'nihil est enim in *historia* pura et inlustri brevitate dulcius'. It would seem that this sensitive and instructed critic of letters believed, if only for a moment, that Caesar's **Commentaries** challenged *historia* on its own ground with comparable, if not identical, qualities.

When Caesar set out for Gaul he was not yet in the first rank of generals, but he was an orator of an acknowledged eminence at a time when oratorical power was one hallmark of literary distinction. Hortensius, the older rival of Cicero, had lost ground. Now, if Cicero was the first orator of Rome, Caesar was advancing to the second place until he found other things to do than to be an orator. Quintilian, who was fortunate enough to be able to read Caesar's speeches, says of his oratory 'si foro tantum vacasset, non alius ex nostris contra Ciceronem nominaretur', and adds, to justify his judgement, 'tanta in eo vis est, id acumen, ea concitatio, ut illum eodem animo dixisse quo bellavit appareat; exornat tamen haec omnia mira sermonis, cuius proprie studiosus fuit, elegantia'.[12] Caesar's force and vehemence, especially in his younger days, are well attested. For these qualities the manner of a *commentarius* offered little scope, though, as will be seen, they are at times discernible. But what Cicero praises as his 'pura et inlustris brevitas' could be attained by his 'mira sermonis elegantia'. The simplicity appropriate to the *commentarius* appealed to Caesar's literary predilections. As between the florid style of the Asianic school and the austere plain style of the Atticists Caesar was inclined to the Atticists, if not slavishly or to excess. His mentor in oratory had been Apollonius Molon of Rhodes, who set himself against the redundant Asianic style. It would be rash to assume that Caesar was not capable of going his own way, but, granted that, Molon's teaching may well have been to his mind.

Another of his teachers was the grammarian Antonius Gnipho, who carried further a systematic purism inspired by the study of language and its forms that the Stoics had inaugurated, and aroused in Caesar an interest in linguistic niceties, especially in the forms of words. In 55 B.C. Cicero in his *De Oratore*[13] had taken these doctrines lightly and had claimed for an orator a freedom to follow general use without requiring the justification of what was called analogy which would dictate the forms of words by a kind of orthographical orthodoxy. It is a reasonable conjecture[14] that Caesar was moved to spend some leisure in the winter of 55/54 in writing his two books *De Analogia,* incidentally refuting Cicero's concessions to popular usage.

Whether or not in his commentaries Caesar insisted upon the orthographical forms of his analogistic theory it is hard to say. The MS. tradition, on the whole, suggests that he did not,[15] but MS. tradition is not a certain guide. He may, however, very well have supposed that a work like his **Commentaries** was not the place for theoretical niceties. His famous injunction to keep clear of 'inauditum atque insolens verbum' was doubtless directed against neologisms, but it may have haunted him when it came to grammatical forms that had only theoretical justification. As Eduard Norden in his *Antike Kunstprosa* has shown, Latin had been becoming more systematic in structure and, at the same time, less luxuriant in vocabulary. To give Norden's illustration: in the second-century *de Bacchanalibus* of 186 B.C. four different words are used to mean 'conspiring together'—'coniurare, convovere, conspondere, compromittere'. Of these four, only the first 'coniurare' remained in use with this meaning in the Ciceronian period. It is well known how Caesar seemed at times to have decided that a particular thing is most properly described by a particular word. For him a river is always 'flumen' and never 'fluvius' or 'amnis'. The economy of his style is in the new tradition of Latin—in Newman's phrase, 'always the right word for the right idea and never a word too much'. The simple brevity appropriate to the *commentarius* form did not preclude the exercise of Caesar's 'mira sermonis elegantia, cuius proprie studiosus fuit'.

The theme of Caesar's **Commentaries** is his *res gestae* and this fact brings in another element which is less objective than the older *commentarius*. It is autobiographical, or, if not that, descriptive of the events in which some eminent man had played a leading part. Great men had begun to write about their own doings in self-justification or to claim the form of immortality which Roman aristocrats prized, the memory of their services to the State. Like the ecclesiastic who set up his epitaph in anticipation of his demise, they thought it well to be their own chroniclers. When Cicero wrote the *Brutus* he cited two such works. One is that of M. Aemilius Scaurus *de vita sua;*[16] the other,

a book by C. Lutatius Catulus the elder, *de consulatu suo et de rebus gestis suis,*[17] written 'molli et Xenophontio genere sermonis'. Aemilius Scaurus had enjoyed more continuous good fortune than good repute, and his work may have been in part an 'apologia pro vita sua'. Catulus's campaign in north Italy had been the high light of his military career, though it was overshadowed by the exploits of his colleague Marius. He dedicated his book to the poet A. Furius, and it has been plausibly conjectured[18] that he hoped his friend would write an epic on the Cimbrian War in which his merits would be immortalized. Cicero says that the works of Scaurus and Catulus were no longer read in his day, but this is not to be taken *au pied de la lettre*. The elder Pliny, Tacitus and Valerius Maximus knew of Scaurus's autobiography, and a reference in Frontinus is probably ultimately derived from the same work. Two centuries later Fronto speaks of certain *Epistulae* of Catulus which are probably his dispatches to the Senate and material for his book. More relevant were Sulla's twenty-two books which, to judge from the ancient references, probably bore the title *L. Cornelii Sullae commentarii rerum gestarum*. It is plain from Plutarch's *Lives* of Marius and of Sulla that, as the dictator contemplated his rivals and enemies, he did not write 'sine ira et studio' and that when he wrote of himself he wrote *con amore*. It would be idle to suppose that in such works the author did not give himself the benefit of any doubt, or that when members of the high aristocracy of Rome read Caesar's *commentarii rerum gestarum* they imagined that their author had a disinterested desire to tell the truth, the whole truth, and nothing but the truth. This is a matter to be discussed later (pp. 22ff.). It is enough to say at this point that the *res gestae* element has to be remembered in evaluating the composite literary character of Caesar's writings.

Finally, there is an ingredient in the composition of Caesar's works which affects alike their content and their style, and that is the personality of the author. Granted that Caesar was *omnium consensu* a skilful man of letters, he was more than that—he was a man endowed with a 'vivida vis animi', of singular determination and resource, ruefully admitted to be 'a portent of terrible vigilance, speed and application'.[19] Whatever the literary form which he employed, and however well he preserved its conventions, it was not possible that his personality should not be at times visible, so that his commentaries are a plain texture shot with genius.

It is often said that Caesar had a purpose in writing his **Commentaries** and it is sometimes said, and more often implied, that his purpose was political or, at least, directly concerned with his own advancement. In an age in which publicity is the servant of policy and ambition it is natural for us to suppose that this would be so, and that Caesar would not neglect any means that helped found his own interests and the interests of whatever cause he wished to serve. If he has little to say about Roman politics except in self-justification at the outbreak of the Civil War, this may be regarded as the art that conceals art. Mr T. E. Page is credited with the dictum 'Caesar's **Gallic War** indeed—a subtle political pamphlet beginning with the words "All Gaul is divided into three parts'". It is a hard saying, but it is not all the truth. There is in Caesar's writings an element of propaganda, but it is not predominant, and it is not what matters most.

Propaganda does not exist in a vacuum, and it is worth while to consider to whom the propaganda, what there is of it, was addressed. When Mommsen declared that Caesar's *Commentaries* were the report of the democratic general to the People, he is expressing his view that Caesar was the democratic champion of the People against a blind or unworthy aristocracy. But this view does Caesar less or more than justice. He was ready to invoke the sovereignty of the People at need to overcome opposition if he could not achieve his ends, whether of personal ambition or of statesmanship, otherwise. But the voice of the People was to be an echo of his own. Like most Romans whose position made them stand for Rome, he sought the greatness of Rome against all comers. But he must have been aware that, for most of the time and in most matters, Rome was the Senate first and the People afterwards, if at all. The Senate was guided by consuls and consulars and might be hampered by tribunes. At elections all kinds of influences, reputable and disreputable, played upon the part of the electorate that voted. It was possible for tribunes to bring proposals before the Concilium Plebis, but what one tribune proposed another tribune could veto. And the Senate, by convention, settled many questions, especially the kind of questions that mattered most to a proconsul. The courts which might sit in judgement on his actions when he returned to Rome were manned by members of the upper classes, and from the decision of these courts there was no appeal. In the absence of an adequate police force, the progress of public affairs might at times be hampered or deflected by the riff-raff of the city. But the riff-raff of the city did not read books. The goodwill of the towns of Italy might be of value at elections or when some proposal was strengthened by the manifestation of a wide public opinion in its favour. But here too it was probably the local notables that counted, if they took the trouble to bring themselves and their clients to Rome. But, for most purposes at most times, public opinion was made by what senators said in the Senate or in private or wrote to their friends. Caesar was at pains to conduct a correspondence with men like Cicero, who in turn could influence this public opinion. He had a patronage that could help his friends and the friends of his friends. The wealth of rich men of the senatorial or equestrian order might be used for political ends, for votes in elections or in the courts might be bought. The governor of a province had to take account of financial interests established there so as not to offend rich men whose influence could do him harm. Caesar, in Gaul outside the old Province, had no old financial interests to consider but could help or hinder new ones. There were scattered over Italy men who had served under this general or that, though Caesar had not commanded large armies before he went to Gaul, and most of those who had served under him served with him still.

When all these things are borne in mind, and when it is remembered how small and slow would be the circulation of an ancient book, even granted that secondary circulation that comes from the diffusion of opinion by speech or private correspondence, Caesar must have known that, both for his present interests and his future reputation, he must write, primarily, for men of his own class and, above all, for the aristocracy of Rome which rated military skill and success more highly than anything else. Within his own army his influence, so far as it was not secured by the high military tradition and discipline of the legions, rested on success and the effect of his personality on his officers, from the *legati* downwards to the centurions in their hierarchical precedence of rank, and then on the legionaries themselves. The men of the Tenth Legion did not need to await the publication of a *commentarius* to know what Caesar thought of them and trusted them to achieve.

The moment when the most widespread effect was most needed was before an election to high office, and so the publication of the *Commentaries* may have preceded by several months the earliest moment at which Caesar may have contemplated becoming a candidate for his second consulship. But apart from any possible choice of the moment for publication, the writing of the *Commentaries,* if the view that this proceeded year by year is accepted, would have, in the main, the purpose of describing what happened as Caesar saw it, in part to satisfy a kind of intellectual appreciation of his own doings and that of others, in part to satisfy an interest in military technique which he shared with most men of his own class, the technique including a mastery over men as well as over things, and, finally, the promotion of his own *dignitas,* which is the acceptance of his claim to high office and public consideration and honours, to the opportunity to guide policy and be master of the event, and to the recognition of what he, and those who fought with him, had done to serve the greatness of Rome. He did not deny to the enemies of Rome the right to fight against her, and he did not seek to belittle or condemn them, if only because he would have done the same in their place. But he had inherited a tradition that taught him to maintain and extend the power of Rome, and he was ready to be judged by the extent to which he fulfilled that purpose. He did not need to convince himself of his own greatness; he sought to make it impossible for others to deny it, to underrate it or leave it unrewarded. This is, in a sense, propaganda, but to call Caesar's writings nothing else is to underrate alike their purpose and their quality.

It is to be remembered that, quite apart from any ulterior purpose that Caesar may have had, his *Commentaries* were bound to be subjective in the sense that they reveal events as Caesar saw them. The literary form, the content, the arrangement, the tradition of the *Commentaries,* cannot prevent their being so. Had Labienus written *Commentaries on the Gallic War* or Pompey *Commentaries on the Civil War,* they would have been different from Caesar's writings in emphasis and interpretation. No man, however sincere, however content to let the facts speak for themselves, can describe great events in which he took a leading part with perfect objectivity. They become part of himself and are seen as he sees himself in his mirror, not as others may see them or as they may see him in action. And when a great man judges the action of his helpers or his antagonists he is bound to measure them by his own standards and to see them in relation to his own fortunes and purposes. Clear-sighted as Caesar was, in order to see things as they are, it is plain that they must be seen, as it were, *de haut en bas* from his self-confident intellectual eminence. The acts of other men, the way things turned out, are bound to be the raw material of his *res gestae*.

Caesar was above 'peacock tail-spreading vanity' as he was above 'hissing gander-like pride', but he had no doubt of his own greatness, and of his inborn right to it. He is not only adroit but wholly sincere when he writes to Cicero of himself and of his enemies: 'I desire nothing more than that I should be like myself—and they like themselves.' This does not mean that Caesar might not be high-handed with the factual truth, which was to him a good servant but a bad master. In the justification of his acts, to himself as to others, he may give himself the benefit of the doubt, and he was not scrupulous to his own hurt. If, for example, he sent a dispatch to the Senate which would make it hard for his enemies to cavil at his actions or condemn his purposes, what he aimed at writing then need not be the truth, the whole truth and nothing but the truth. And in his **Commentaries** he was not concerned to refute his dispatches.

1. THE FIRST BOOK OF THE *GALLIC WAR*

With this in mind, we may turn to the **Commentaries** to see what they contain which assists an understanding of how things looked to Caesar, and how, with his help, they look to others, and to ourselves. The effect of the *commentarius* form is perhaps most clearly to be discerned in the First Book of the **Gallic War.** The traditional form of the *commentarius* was concerned with events in isolation, each event being recorded, as it were, for its own sake. The more nearly a narrative approaches this traditional form the more it is a statement of acts and the less it is concerned with the interrelation of acts. Herein there may lie an economy of the truth, conscious or unconscious. The main theme of the First Book of the **Gallic War** is twofold: first the operations of Caesar against the Helvetii, which lead to their defeat, second the operations of Caesar against the German Ariovistus, which lead to his defeat. Each of these is a war in its own right, in each of these Caesar is the prime agent, and thus the *res gestae* or autobiographical element in the **Commentaries** finds expression. The story of each series of operations is told with matter-of-fact brevity, with an unadorned precision of phrasing that suited Caesar's literary predilections, as it suited the traditional manner of a *commentarius*.

Many scholars have been critical of the First Book as a witness of truth. They have no other comparable ancient account to use as a control; Cicero's letters give no help.

The military events were known to Caesar's officers, and must have been, if only briefly, reported to the Senate in accordance with the standard practice of proconsuls. There was, it is true, a tradition which declared that the defeat of the Tigurini, who were caught on the wrong side of the river Arar, was the exploit not of Caesar but of Labienus.[20] This tradition, however, appears to go back to Labienus himself, who is not an impartial witness. It is not difficult to suppose that Labienus, who often led the cavalry, began the attack on Caesar's instructions, and that Caesar with three legions came up and finished it. He may have omitted to mention Labienus's share in what he represents as, in fact, a kind of family revenge for the killing by the Tigurini of his father-in-law's grandfather, L. Piso, half a century before.[21] Caesar does not fail to give due credit to his *legati* where they are acting as independent commanders, and the incident does not make his account of military events suspect. Like most generals, Caesar, consciously or not, exaggerated the numbers of the enemy or their losses; he may have concealed mistakes, but he does not conceal the fact that the final battle with the Helvetii might well have gone the other way—'ita ancipiti proelio diu atque acriter pugnatum est'[22]—or that the battle against Ariovistus was restored by the timely action of the young P. Crassus.[23] He does not allege that when he turned away from following the Helvetii he hoped that they would be induced to give him the opportunity of fighting them on favourable ground, as they did.

There is no doubt that Caesar took considerable risks and that he could have protected the Roman province without attacking the Helvetii, and that the immediate interests of Rome did not require Caesar to take so strong a line with Ariovistus. The *commentarius* form makes it natural to keep Caesar's dealings with the Helvetii and Ariovistus separate and, as *res gestae,* they are just two successive exploits. But is that, or need that be, all the truth? For example, when Caesar had denied to the Helvetii a passage through the province, could he not have arranged with Ariovistus, whom he had caused to be recognized as the Friend of the Roman People, that the Sequani should be told not to open to the emigrants the pass through their territory, which Caesar says was easily defensible? The Sequani would not have dared to disobey. The Helvetii might have abandoned their project, or if they took, as they might, a more northerly route, they would pass through territory towards which Rome had no obligations. The Gauls, reinforced by the immigration of the Helvetii and their allies, might perhaps make head against the Germans, and Roman interests would, for the present at least, be secure without any exertions on Rome's part. That would be a quite traditional process of Roman statecraft. In any event, an alliance between Gauls and Germans might seem highly improbable. There are, in fact, various policies which Caesar might have adopted if his object had been limited to preserving existing Roman interests and showing some consideration for the friends and allies of Rome including 'their brothers, the Aedui'.

How far Caesar was conscious of these possibilities it is hard to say: the *commentarius* form does not at least bring them to the notice of his readers. It suits Caesar's drastic methods to act as he did. Another proconsul might have acted otherwise, though when there had been an alarm at Rome in March 60 B.C. and the consul Metellus Celer had been marked out to be the next proconsul in Transalpine Gaul, Cicero says that he was disappointed when the alarm came to nothing, for he was dreaming of a triumph.[24] It may be that war with the Helvetii was certain because it was the first war in Gaul which Caesar could find ready to his hand. Caesar does not need to say this, if we may assume it to be true. What he does say is that Rome did not allow barbarians to cross one of their provinces. He reminds his future readers of the last immigration, with the dangers it brought, fifty years before, and he says: 'Caesar non exspectandum sibi statuit, dum omnibus fortunis sociorum consumptis in Santonos Helvetii pervenirent.'[25] He passed beyond the province and attacked. In the end he defeats the Helvetii and compels (and allows) the major part of them and their allies to return to their homes so as not to produce a vacuum into which Germans might be drawn and so come dangerously near to the Roman province.

The communities of Central Gaul were impressed by Caesar's victory. They had suffered, or they feared to suffer, from Ariovistus with his growing power reinforced by relays of Germans from across the Rhine. There is no reason to doubt that the proRoman leader of the Aedui, Diviciacus, who had sought the help of the Senate two years before, now sought the help of Caesar. The formulation of his hopes—Caesarem vel auctoritate sua atque exercitus [vel] recenti victoria vel nomine populi Romani deterrere posse ne maior multitudo Germanorum Rhenum traducatur, Galliamque omnem ab Ariovisti iniuria posse defendere'[26]—may been have prearranged. It was the springboard for Caesar's next leap. Caesar assured the Gallic notables 'magnam se habere spem, et beneficio suo et auctoritate adductum Ariovistum finem iniuriis facturum'.[27] He then sets out a series of considerations which, he says, moved him 'ad eam rem cogitandam et suscipiendam'. They are in terms suited to Roman interests, pride and fears, the old fears that had haunted Rome since the days of the Cimbri and Teutoni and even longer—'quibus rebus quam maturrime occurrendum putabat'. They may, indeed, reflect the kind of thing Caesar wrote when he reported to the Senate the inception of this enterprise after it had succeeded. He adds the revealing sentence: 'Ipse autem Ariovistus tantos sibi spiritus, tantam adrogantiam sumpserat, ut ferendus non videretur.' This reflects his belief that, in fact, the only settlement would be by war. He believed he knew his Ariovistus and he was sure he knew himself. With a firm hand he guided the negotiations that followed to their destined end.

At this point, as in his account of the incipient mutiny at Vesontio and his handling of it, his personality becomes dominant. He appears to believe that Ariovistus may come to a peaceful settlement, though he has good grounds for confidence if he does not. 'Denique hos esse eosdem quibuscum saepe numero Helvetii congressi non solum in suis sed etiam in illorum finibus plerumque superarint, qui tamen pares esse nostro exercitui non potuerint.'[28] So Napoleon, in a Caesarian moment: 'ces mêmes Prussiens qui sont aujourd'hui si vantards étaient à 3 contre 1 à Jéna et à 9 contre 1 à Montmirail'. In what follows Caesar displays his eminent understanding of the art of being a soldier's general, an art that never deserted him. There is no reason to doubt the essential truth of his report of his speech,[29] least of all of its famous close: 'Quod si praeterea nemo sequatur, tamen se cum sola decima legione iturum, de qua non dubitet, sibique eam praetoriam cohortem futuram.' All this shows how in Caesar's hands the *commentarius* form could be made to convey the revelation of his own personality in the easy mastery of men. There is no rhetoric, and the note is not forced. Caesar was speaking to his aristocratic officers, and all his centurions, not only those seniors who normally attended his *consilium,* and to a larger audience, those Romans who had an ingrained instinct for war and an ingrained respect for those who understood the lessons of that hard teacher. And he knew what the men of the Tenth Legion would say when their centurions passed the word round. His army fought well when it came to fighting, and Ariovistus was decisively defeated. A remnant of his forces escaped across the Rhine, and the Suebi who had gathered on the river began to return to their homes.

Much has been made of the fact that the same Caesar who as consul had caused Ariovistus to be declared the Friend of the Roman People, as proconsul marched against him. It is not known when in his consulship the title was conferred, whether before or after Caesar had Transalpine Gaul added to his *provincia* as proconsul. If it was before, and perhaps even if it was after, that event, Caesar may have been bribed, and that was all. He needed money and Rome needed friends—for so long as it needed them. If Ariovistus was not a subservient friend he was no friend at all: *amicus* was as *amicus* did. Orators existed to cloak this fact by fine words. Had Caesar been defeated by Ariovistus he might have been prosecuted for a blunder transmuted into a crime. What mattered was success. Success meant innocence, unless he was arraigned before a court to whom guilt or innocence was of no moment. Or the naming of Ariovistus as *amicus* was an indication of policy—to put him on an equality with the Aedui, the long-established 'brothers' of Rome, to be on with the new love before being off with the old. Whichever was the reason, the *amicitia* of Ariovistus was a debating point in debate (as Caesar made it)[30] and to the Romans a standard of conduct for Ariovistus: to Ariovistus a standard of conduct for Rome, but Caesar had not to satisfy Ariovistus but Rome, and late Republican Rome judged Romans by success, if it judged by any standard at all. How greatly the Senate was concerned about the German peril is a matter of conjecture, but its elimination, if only temporary, meant one complication the less in a world that had been becoming inconveniently more complicated for more than a generation. Whenever Caesar wrote his account of the year 58, the events of that year, taken by themselves, were an asset and not a liability in his balance sheet as it stood when that year closed—'una aestate duobus maximis bellis confectis.'[31]

2. THE SECOND BOOK

Even before the autumn of 58 B.C. had ended, Caesar put his legions into winter quarters in the territory of the Sequani, most probably in and around the *place d'armes* of Vesontio (Besançon). He retired to his other province of Cisalpine Gaul, to the peaceful jurisdiction of a Roman governor. What reasons he gave to the Senate, if he gave any, for stationing his army outside his own province, he does not reveal. The effect was to produce a hostile reaction among the great confederacy of the Belgae, whom he had described as the most warlike people of Gaul.[32] The news of this was sent to him, and he raised two more legions this side the Alps and returned to his army when the season was far enough advanced to ease his supplies of food and the Belgae had time to prepare to take the field. The disunions that afflicted the national movement brought to the side of Rome the Remi, 'qui dicerent se suaque omnia in fidem atque potestatem populi Romani permittere neque se cum Belgis reliquis consensisse neque contra populum Romanum coniurasse'.[33] All was in order: there was a *coniuratio* of enemies of Rome; Germans this side the Rhine had joined the Belgae; and there were new subjects to protect. By wariness alternating with vigour Caesar caused the enemy concentration to break up and attacked the tribes piecemeal. For a time all went according to plan, but he was surprised by the Nervii and only just won one of the hardest battles of his career. 'That day he overcame the Nervii.' His account will be analysed in a later chapter (pp. 69f.). He claimed the almost complete destruction of the Nervii, and went on to deal with the Atuatuci, whose chief town was taken after they had broken the terms of a capitulation. More than fifty thousand inhabitants were sold into slavery. The campaign was a typically Roman combination of diplomatic reasonableness and military ruthlessness, which to Romans justified itself by its success. Caesar had sent the young Publius Crassus with a legion to south-west Gaul and news came that the tribes of the Atlantic seaboard had submitted to Roman power. The report proved, in the end, optimistic, but it served Caesar's purpose. Tribes beyond the Rhine, so he says, sent envoys promising to give hostages and to obey his commands, and he bade them send again at the beginning of the next summer, as he was in a hurry to go to northern Italy and Illyricum.[34] He sent a dispatch to the Senate whereupon 'a public thanks-giving of fifteen days was decreed for his achievements—a greater honour than had previously been granted to anyone'.[35]

3. THE THIRD BOOK

So ends the Second Book with a fanfare of triumph. Events were to show that Caesar was making a large overdraft on his military credit. He may have included in his letter to the Senate that he was sending Servius Galba with a legion and some cavalry to open up the route across the Alps, wintering in the mountains if he thought it needful. Galba

failed to achieve this object, and after a hard-won defensive battle withdrew to the Roman province.[36]

How far Caesar may have deceived himself about the position in Gaul it is hard to say. It was perhaps reasonable for him to suppose, as he says, that Gaul was pacified, at least in the sense that it contained no people who were in arms against Rome, so that the Roman province beyond the Alps was secure. He was responsible for Illyricum, and set out to acquaint himself with that region when news came that the Roman peace was broken. The maritime Veneti on the west coast of Gaul had started a strong reaction, and had taken Roman officers to exchange against the hostages they had given to Publius Crassus. Whatever Caesar may have thought before, he realized that the Gauls feared to be reduced to subjection: 'they were easily provoked to war, and all men naturally love freedom and hate servitude'.[37] The Veneti were ringed round with armies, and Caesar himself marched against them. A fleet was built, and a victory at sea ended the hopes of the Veneti, who surrendered at discretion. They had loved freedom beyond their means. Their councillors were executed and the rest of the population were sold as slaves. Even so, not all Gaul was 'pacified', for the coastal tribes of the Morini and Menapii between the Somme and the Rhine remained in arms. There was only enough summer left for a short campaign, and Caesar was not able to solve the military problems presented by the forests and marshes into which the enemy could retire and take refuge.

Caesar had no doubt reported to the Senate his action against the Veneti and his own success and that of his lieutenants. But, at the most, he had only made truer the claim of the previous year that Gaul was pacified and he has nothing to say of a thanksgiving granted to him. It is possible that he was beginning to believe that the Gallic problem did not end with Gaul. During the year 56 his political position had been secured by a renewed agreement with Pompey and Crassus, and his command in Gaul had been prolonged to last until 50 B.C. if not later. Thus Caesar could pursue long plans as proconsul if he wished to do so, and bring Germany and Britain within his calculations. The next year was in fact to contain three events: the sharp repulse of a German invasion, and two reconnaissances, the one across the Rhine, the other across the English Channel.

4. THE FOURTH BOOK

In 58 B.C. Caesar had driven the German Ariovistus out of Gaul. During the winter of 56/55 he became aware that a new invasion of Gaul was happening and that behind the invasion, and indeed the cause of it, there was the dangerous power of the Suebi, 'the most numerous and most warlike of the German peoples'.[38] He explains that they had driven from their homes two tribes, the Usipetes and Tencteri, who in the end had crossed the lower Rhine into Gallic territory to find lands to settle. He took the field earlier than usual, marched against them and destroyed them by trickery and the merciless use of force. He then decided to bridge the Rhine and enter Germany. He explains his motives: he wished to deter further German aggression by showing that the Romans were able and ready to cross the river, to impress this fact on the Sugambri on the right bank, and to encourage the Ubii, who had sought Roman protection, to believe that, with Roman help at need, they could maintain themselves against the Suebi.[39] In the course of eighteen days he ravaged the country of the Sugambri, displayed his legions to the Ubii, and returned to Gaul, destroying the bridge behind him. But he did not venture to advance far enough to give battle to the Suebi, who had concentrated far back in their territory and left to him an empty country to march across. Caesar declared that he had achieved all his objects.

Then, though summer was near its end, Caesar carried out a brief invasion of Britain. He says that in almost all the campaigns in Gaul the Britons had sent help to his enemies, and that it would be an advantage to become acquainted with the land, harbours and landing-places, for of all these the Gauls knew hardly anything.[40] The British help to the Gauls and the Gallic ignorance of Britain are not beyond doubt. That Caesar wished to see what could be done about a serious invasion of Britain is probable enough. There may have been another reason, to make an effect on Roman society. Cicero in his speech on the consular provinces, delivered in 56, had proclaimed not only the conquest of the old enemies of Rome but the opening of new regions of the earth.[41] The admirers of Pompey had dilated on his achievements in the East in like terms a decade before. Germany was still *terra incognita,* and Britain was near the world's end, and stretched into mystery. The Romans, so far as they were explorers, had explored sword in hand, and if Caesar's main purposes were military rather than tinged with the spirit of inquiry that had been a part of Alexander's expedition to India, he might well have in mind the impression his enterprises might produce. Neither the demonstration into Germany nor the reconnaissance into Britain meant any significant extension of Roman power, but they had their effect, and on the news of them the Senate decreed a further thanksgiving of twenty days. And during the winter great preparations were made to carry a larger army to Britain in the next year (54 B.C.).

5. THE FIFTH BOOK

In Gaul itself Caesar had sought to increase the influence of the Aedui, the old allies of Rome, and to advance the local power of chieftains whom he believed he could trust. In doing so he had incurred the hostility of Indutiomarus, an able and determined chief among the Treveri. Gallic notables were to accompany the Roman army to Britain as hostages for the good behaviour of their communities, and when the Aeduan chief Dumnorix tried to escape he was pursued and killed. It was becoming plain that the best the Gallic leaders could expect was to be the clients of Rome. Although an army of three legions under Labienus watched Roman interests in Gaul, Caesar campaigned in Britain with the knowledge that he must not stay too long. The

south-eastern Britons had found an able leader in Cassivelaunus, who led the national resistance until Caesar was content to admit him to a surrender which was complete enough to protect Roman prestige. And that was all. Caesar returned to the continent.

The enterprise, for all the skill and fighting power displayed in the campaign, had proved a doubtful investment of Caesar's military strength. For when Caesar returned and held a council of Gallic leaders at Samarobriva he had cause for anxiety. He distributed his legions in a wide arc in north-eastern Gaul. The reason he gave for this distribution was that there had been a poor harvest and this was the best way of securing his supplies of corn for the winter. But when he says that no two legions were more than a hundred miles apart except one that was in a perfectly peaceful district he gives a hint of danger, and he determined to stay at hand until all the legions had fortified their appointed positions. Whatever his fears, they were justified. A widespread revolt had been planned by Indutiomarus and the first blow was struck by the Eburones under an able and relentless leader, Ambiorix. A Roman army of a legion and five cohorts under his lieutenants Sabinus and Cotta was lured out of its camp and destroyed almost to a man. The Nervii, in numbers that refute Caesar's claim that he almost destroyed them three years before, attacked the camp of Quintus Cicero. He was invited to march out into safety. But he was not to be tricked and held out stoutly. How dangerous the situation was may be seen from the fact that no word had reached Caesar until a slave sent by Cicero got through to him with an appeal for help. His chief lieutenant, Labienus, was pinned down by the Treveri. Acting with great speed and resource Caesar marched to the relief of Cicero just in time. It had been a near run thing and, all that winter, Caesar stayed in Gaul beset with anxieties. Only the Aedui and the Remi could be trusted. The general readiness to revolt was, Caesar says, not so surprising: among many other reasons, it was natural that tribes, considered the bravest and most warlike of mankind, should resent bitterly the complete loss of this reputation which submission to the rule of Rome entailed.[42]

Whereas in the third and fourth years of his governorship of Gaul Caesar appears to have the initiative, with the winter of the fourth to fifth year he is really on the defensive. Rome had two formidable and enterprising enemies, Indutiomarus and Ambiorix, and Labienus skilfully drew Indutiomarus within his reach and killed him— 'Fortune justified the plan that human foresight had devised.'[43] This success made Gaul somewhat quieter for the time being. Three legions were raised to do more than replace the loss of the army of Sabinus and Cotta. 'This large and rapid reinforcement showed what Rome's organization and resources could accomplish.'[44]

6. THE SIXTH BOOK

In 53 B.C. Caesar himself took the field before the normal campaigning season began, and re-established Rome's control of central Gaul. Labienus reduced the Treveri to submission, and set up a loyal chieftain to rule over them. There remained Ambiorix, and Caesar was concerned to prevent his receiving help from the Menapii, who had so far shown no signs of submitting to Rome, and from Germans beyond the Rhine. He swept through the country of the Menapii and then decided to cross the Rhine for a second time. But, once more, he did not feel able to advance so far as to bring the Suebi to battle, and once more he retired, though he left part of the bridge standing to show that he might return to the German side of the river.

Then came the systematic devastation of the country of Ambiorix, the attempt to make a solitude so as to call it peace. A general invitation to all comers to plunder the territory of the Eburones was accepted by 200 horsemen of the Sugambri, who then were tempted to try their luck in a surprise attack on Q. Cicero at Atuatuca, where he guarded the *impedimenta* of Caesar's army. The surprise was all but successful; Cicero had become careless and the recruits he had with him were seized with panic: indeed, only the bravery of the centurions and some veterans prevented a serious disaster. Caesar complained that fortune played hhim false,[45] and all the efforts he made to capture Ambiorix just missed success. He executed a Gallic chief who had plotted a revolt and outlawed others who had not waited to be tried. Two legions were posted among the Treveri, two others among the Lingones, and the remaining six were left concentrated in central Gaul. It is clear from the dispositions that Caesar was ill at ease, but he returned to Italy for the winter 'as he had planned to do'.[46]

7. THE SEVENTH BOOK

The book which follows is the climax of Caesar's own *Commentaries on the Gallic War.* It begins with the words 'Quieta Gallia', and goes on to present a chronicle of dangers which taxed Caesar's skill and courage as never before. So far as the first two words justify his absence south of the Alps 'as he had determined', the justification is submerged by a vivid account of the widespread resentment at the loss of Gallic freedom, of the hopes aroused by his presumed preoccupation with a political crisis at Rome, of the progress made by the national movement under a new leader before the news reached Caesar, of his perplexities and the risks he had to run to rejoin the army, so that with all his speed and resource it was hard to brave winter and his enemies with success. The striking compliment which he was to pay to his lieutenant Labienus, 'tantis subito difficultatibus obiectis ab animi virtute auxilium petendum videbat',[47] gives the essence of his own reaction to these perplexities.

While the fighting strength of his army was at its zenith, Gaul had become a sea of enemies; the friends of Rome were few, and their loyalty was precarious. The faithful Commius[48] even deserted his fidelity, the disunion of the Gauls was transmuted into a good measure of unity under Vercingetorix, the leader of the Arverni; a people who, a

generation before, had held the primacy of Gaul, a general able to organize for victory and to rise superior to reverses. Caesar had pursued the traditional Roman policy of promoting friends of Rome and trusting to client princes and above all to the power of the Aedui: in this crisis the policy became a liability rather than an asset. The season did not admit of the rapid movements that might have daunted the insurgents, the siege of Avaricum succeeded but at the cost of twenty-seven precious days. The siege of Gergovia was ended by a reverse which Caesar comes short of dissembling by saying that his troops overran his own discretion, if even that is true. For all the vigour of Caesar and Labienus, it seemed impossible to grasp and retain the initiative, to bring about a decisive battle under favourable conditions.

The narrative moves with urgent, almost anxious speed. The defensive system which rested on hostages kept in the territory of the Aedui breaks down when they take the field against the Romans, and it looks as though the great adventure of the conquest of Gaul might end in failure. The Roman province has to be rapidly organized for defence and Caesar, surrounded by enemies, has to put out all his skill to find a way of restoring the military situation. Vercingetorix suffers a reverse and retires on Alesia, and Caesar risks all on the hazard of besieging him, while the Gauls raise a great army which might hope to destroy the legions. For if Caesar's defence against them failed, it was the end of him and his whole army. Had this happened it is hard to see how the province could have weathered the storm, and how nearly it happened is plain from his narrative. The climax of the battle is reached; the fighting qualities of the legions, the vigour and courage of Caesar himself achieve victory. Vercingetorix surrenders, and the campaign ends with the Roman forces disposed to make good the control of central Gaul. The last of Caesar's own *Commentaries* on Gaul ends with the news reaching the Senate and the voting of a final *supplicatio*. Caesar himself winters at Bibracte for he knows that he is needed. His lieutenant Hirtius, who describes the events of the next two years in the Eighth Book of the *Commentaries* begins his book with the words 'Omni Gallia devicta'. The rest of that book shows how much has still to be done to make those words wholly true. But for whatever reason, Caesar is content to end his own story of his achievements in Gaul with the crowning mercy of Alesia.

8. THE *CIVIL WAR*

When we turn to the *Civil War,* it is noticeable that it begins with the first day of a Roman year by the current calendar. For that is the day on which the first event mentioned occurred. The first two books cover roughly the events of the year 49 and between them made up one *Commentarius.* But some scattered operations which happened in this year are brought into the Third Book, so that the strict division of *commentarii* by years is not preserved any more than between the second and third books of the *Gallic War* (p. 35). In the earlier chapters of Book I Caesar presents his case as regards the political and constitutional aspect of the outbreak of the war. Caesar is an advocate for himself, not wholly scrupulous, but wholly sincere. It is plain that he believed that he had not received the treatment which his exploits and his *dignitas* deserved, and that his army shared his belief. He did not seek to overthrow the Republican constitution, but only to have it work for his interests and not against them. He was prepared to meet his enemies at least part of the way provided he did not forfeit his career, to come to terms with Pompey in a new coalition in which, however, he would be at an advantage over his former ally. The *civilis dissensio* need not be a *bellum civile;* it was not by his choosing that his enemies made it one. As he said at Pharsalus, 'they would have it so'—'hoc voluerunt'.[49] The exposition is subtly contrived so as to be built up partly of what he said and did and what his opponents said and did, but it does not attain an objectivity in which no one could believe.

The military operations are militarily discussed with a cool evaluation of the application of *ratio belli* by both sides. It is taken for granted that Caesar would not sacrifice any military advantage to assist negotiations, and that his enemies would take the same line. But Caesar was anxious to show clemency where he could safely do so, to avoid bloodshed if he could advance his ends without it. The folly of Domitius Ahenobarbus at Corfinium, the pessimism of Afranius, the brutal violence of Petreius, the vacillation of Varro, the bad faith of the Massiliotes, the timidity of Varus, are revealed, but so far there is nothing that would embitter the conflict past reconciliation. There is no triumph over Pompey at his withdrawal from Italy, which Caesar no doubt judged more justly than Cicero, who complained of it, as though he understood war. There is not even a reference to the desertion of Labienus, though the fact that he was now in the opposite camp might be deduced from an incidental remark.[50] The support given by Juba of Numidia to his enemies in Africa is, in a way, justified.[51]

The Third Book strikes a sharper note. Metellus, Scipio, Labienus, Bibulus are attacked, the thwarting of Caesar's efforts to find a way to peace by the violence of Labienus, the egotistical ambition, the partisan hatreds, the unreasoning self-confidence of the nobles are portrayed. The skill of Pompey is not denied, but the break-down of his spirit when his plan miscarried at Pharsalus is revealed—'summae rei diffidens et tamen eventum exspectans'.[52] The death of Pompey is recorded curtly after a phrase in which some critics have seen a touch of irony.[53] The book seems to reflect the anxieties that beset Caesar, the strain on his troops and the courage which both needed until the victory at Pharsalus and then the reaction to triumphant self-confidence 'confisus fama rerum gestarum' which made him believe everywhere was safe for him.[54] The anger of Caesar at finding himself in danger from the *soldateska* of Achillas and from the intrigues of Pothinus glows in the closing chapters of the book, which ends abruptly. If Caesar wrote the last words 'This was the beginning of the war of Alexandria' they seem to dismiss a topic beneath the level of Caesar's attention. It has been suggested[55] that the statement of the preceding sentence that he put Pothinus to death is a kind of dramatic ending with the avenging of Pompey, but that is an over-subtlety and to the matter-of-fact Romans Pompey would not be avenged while his assassins, Achillas and Septimius, lived. The *Commentarius* does not contain all the history of the year's operations, and it remains, for whatever reason, formally incomplete.

.　.　.　.　.

What has appeared in the preceding three chapters, the plain unadorned matter-of-fact character of a *commentarius,* the content of which is so predominantly a narration of military events militarily viewed by a military man, would make a reader expect to find the style of the *Commentaries* uniform almost to the point of monotony. It would be very much the same story told in very much the same way, for it need not, or should not, be told otherwise. But there is more than this: Caesar had the habit, it would seem, of deciding what was the best word for this and that, and then never admitting any other. As is pointed out in the first chapter (p. 16) Latin had been a rather luxuriant language with several words meaning very much the same thing, but since the second century B.C. it had been pruned. This process was carried further by Caesar, so that when the same thing happens it is natural and proper to find the same words or phrases used about it. The precision of his mind works in with his interest in words and language, tends to reflect the recurrence of an idea or of an action in a repetition of words and phrases, and this helps to produce a uniformity of diction.

Granted that this is so, the intensive study by so many scholars of Caesar's vocabulary and phraseology has not been in vain. It has shown how little ambiguity or vagueness has slipped past the guard of Caesar's sharp clear mind to cloud the *elegantia* of his style.[56] Apart from faults in the manuscript tradition of the text, there may be passages in which some report or the like by another hand has not been fully converted by Caesar into his own diction. This may be so more often in the *Civil War* than in the *Gallic War,* if, as is probable, Caesar produced parts of the *Bellum Civile* under pressure of haste. But when account is taken of these possibilities, the major part of the *Commentaries* shows the special qualities of the Caesarian style.

The precision in the use of words, the *pura et inlustris brevitas* which Cicero praises in Caesar's writing is a constant phenomenon. But as the *Commentaries* proceed, they exhibit some difference of style. It has often been observed how the First Book of the *Gallic War* is more formal in the *commentarius* manner than the Second, and that after the Second the style becomes slightly more informal in the next four books. The Seventh Book has more movement still and, as it were, flows faster, and the same is true of the books of the *Civil War.* The constructions and run of sentences become freer, and there are changes of a kind which suggest a change of habit rather than a reasoned change of preference in the search for the right word. Such a change of habit is hard to understand if Caesar composed the first seven books of the **Gallic War** in one continuous literary activity within a short space of time. It is in fact a strong, perhaps the most cogent, argument for the view that the **Gallic War** was written in stages over a number of years. If this is so, it may have been quite natural for Caesar to become less concerned to preserve the stylistic effect that belongs to the *commentarius* form. There appears, indeed, in the First Book of the **Gallic War** to be deliberate avoidance of literary polish. Thus in the third chapter two successive sentences begin with the phrase 'ad eas res conficiendas'. In neither sentence can the phrase be merely struck out as an interpolation without harming the sense, and it is hard to suppose that the repetition is due to hasty writing. It appears rather to be a deliberate roughening of the style. So too there are instances in which the antecedent to a relative is repeated in the relative clause, with something of the cumbrousness which is characteristic of Roman formal documents. This kind of thing disappears in the later books of the **Gallic War.** In the first six books we do not find speeches in *oratio recta*. It is necessary to give the gist of what was said on occasion, but this is done in *oratio obliqua*, thus avoiding the dramatic literary effect of a fictitious speech in direct speech which is the ornament appropriate to the literary character of *historia*. In the Seventh Book there is one complete speech in *oratio recta,* that of the Gallic chief Critognatus during the siege of Alesia.[57] Critognatus urges his compatriots to do as they once did when the Cimbri and Teutoni invaded them and feed upon those who are unfit for war. The striking character of this suggestion is used by Caesar to justify the insertion of the speech—'non praetereunda videtur oratio Critognati propter eius singularem et nefariam crudelitatem'. But when one reads the speech one finds that the singular and nefarious cruelty plays a small part in it, and what one remembers is what Caesar may have meant his readers to remember—the difference between the transient raid of the Cimbri and Teutoni and the eternal yoke of iron which Rome and Caesar are placing on the necks of the Gauls.

A somewhat subtler use of the same device is to be found in the speech in the same book,[58] in which Vercingetorix defends himself before his countrymen when they accuse him of treachery. The speech is in *oratio obliqua* except that in two places with peculiar dramatic force there is a sudden turn to *oratio recta*. The first is '"Haec ut intellegatis" inquit "a me sincere pronuntiari, audite Romanos milites"', and the second is as dramatic—'"Haec" inquit "a me" Vercingetorix "beneficia habetis, quem proditionis insimulatis; cuius opera sine vestro sanguine tantum exercitum victorem fame paene consumptum videtis; quem turpiter se ex hac fuga recipientem, ne qua civitas suis finibus recipiat, a me provisum est."' A good critic has well observed the skill with which the first 'a me' in this passage is thrown into relief by its position between 'inquit' and 'Vercingetorix',[59] and the same device is used again to underline the self-sacrifice of the centurion Mar-

cus Petronius,[60] or the fatal plea of Sabinus at the council of war that preceded the destruction of his army.[61]

In the **Civil War** there is one speech, or rather a pair of speeches, in *oratio recta*—those of Curio before the disaster which befell him in Africa;[62] and here Caesar violates his general rule to give an impression of the fiery spirit of his friend. Caesar plainly cared much for Curio, and the speeches are an epitaph. They are fictitious in the sense that the phrasing is Caesar's—with the brilliant ending 'Equidem me Caesaris militem dici volui, vos me imperatoris nomine appellavistis. cuius si vos paenitet, vestrum vobis beneficium remitto, mihi meum restituite nomen, ne ad contumeliam honorem dedisse videamini.' And there is another exception in the short speeches of Pompey and of Labienus before the battle of Pharsalus—the fanfare of pride before the cold narrative of the battle itself.[63]

The plainness of the narrative style, combined with the brevity in which Latin surpasses other great languages, can produce a singularly striking effect without any use of rhetorical ornament. For example, at the crisis before Alesia when the relieving army is making its final effort from without, and Vercingetorix is making a desperate sortie from within, Caesar chooses a place where he can see what is happening and dispatches help, now here, now there, to his lieutenants; until at last, when almost all seems lost, there comes the simple undramatic sentence—'accelerat Caesar, ut proelio intersit',[64] then the one vivid touch—'eius adventu colore vestitus cognito'. This is not for picturesque effect, it is that the colour shows the *imperator* himself is there in his battle-cloak. The battle reaches its climax, until in a sharp *staccato* come the brief sentences, like blows that hammer defeat into victory:[65] 'Nostri omissis pilis gladiis rem gerunt. repente post tergum equitatus cernitur; cohortes illae adpropinquant. hostes terga vertunt; fugientibus equites occurrunt. fit magna caedes.' There is hardly a word that is not pure prose, but the effect is epic. Whether the effect is deliberate artistry or whether Caesar wrote down or dictated straight after the battle exactly what happened and then saw that it was good, no one can say. What is certain is that it is hard to imagine how better it could be done, and it was done within the economy of the *commentarius*.

The battle pieces of Caesar, indeed, stand by themselves in ancient history-writing if we except the highest efforts of Thucydides in his Seventh Book. The best worth examination is the battle with the Nervii, a desperate encounter battle.[66] How concrete is the picture of the place where the Romans halt, how skilful is the suggestion that Caesar had after all done what a good general could do (despite Napoleon's strictures) in his first disposition, how sudden the attack comes; then the phrases which show what the moment needed—'Caesari omnia uno tempore erant agenda'; then follow three chapters in which the growing confusion of the battle, the quickening of its tempo are reflected in the rhythm and in the grammatical construction of the sentences until the climax is reached when

Caesar's Gallic cavalry rides for home bearing the news: 'Romanos pulsos superatosque, castris impedimentisque eorum hostes potitos.' In these chapters there is no word of Caesar. The battle is for the moment out of hand. And then the next chapter begins with the word 'Caesar', and there follows the brilliant little description of his own intervention, how he snatches a shield and rallies his troops. The tide of battle halts and then turns, and the rhythm makes it audible to the ear—first the spondees of the halt and then the movement again—'Cuius adventu spe illata militibus ac redintegrato animo' and so on. (It is to be remembered that ancient narrative was written, or dictated, to be read aloud.) And then Caesar again, but this time not the fighting soldier but the disposing commander—'Caesar, cum septimam legionem, quae iuxta constiterat, item urgeri ab hoste vidisset, tribunos militum monuit.' Then the steady advance to victory and with victory the phrases that praise the enemy—how after all they had performed what was almost a military miracle: 'Hard it was what they had done but their high spirit had made it easy.' The battle had been a desperate affair: it is described as no other battle in Roman literature. Pharsalus is another story: there we do not find the concreteness of the setting, still less the part that Caesar himself played in the actual engagement; instead the perfect formal description of a battle as a work of military art—almost a game of military chess, the unconscious hint of the fact that by then Caesar had become a virtuoso in the art of war, almost an impersonal directing intelligence.

Thus it may be seen that Caesar's **Commentaries,** whether of his set purpose or not, reflect the personality of the writer, and his mind. It is to be remembered that Caesar is not content to do no more than set down simply a string of events. By now the Romans had come to expect more than that. Hirtius had praised Caesar's 'verissima scientia suorum consiliorum explicandorum'.[67] Caesar is concerned not only with actions but with the springs and motives of actions. There had, in fact, been a reaction against the mere annalistic record of events. Fifty years before Caesar, Sempronius Asellio had written: 'nobis non modo satis esse video, quod factum esset, id pronuntiare, sed etiam, quo consilio quaque ratione gesta essent, demonstrate.'[68]

While Caesar's style is in general not ornamented with rhetorical devices, the **Commentaries** contain passages in which there is a formal composition which might be due to the desire to produce an artistic effect. For example, it has been observed that in the opening chapter of the first book of the **Civil War** the personages who take part in the debate in the Senate are so enumerated as to produce a definite effect. But this may be due rather to Caesar's orderly mind than to the employment of a rhetorical arrangement for effect. If we may suppose that the stylistic effectiveness of the account of the battles against the Nervii and before Alesia is due not to conscious art but to the vividness of the events in Caesar's mind as he wrote, we may suppose that a dramatic quality in Caesar's narrative, where it is found, is the direct unartificial effect of the *vivida vis animi* with which he remembered as well as

acted. It is the strong impact of Caesar's mind, rather than conscious art, that creates his style, where it rises to distinctiveness. It may march along, orderly as a legion, setting out intelligibly and with intelligence the course of action or the *ratio belli* and practical calculations that are the springs of action. Most of what happens seems to be inevitable, almost remote, without emotion. Thus, when Caesar has described the surprise attack on the Usipetes and Tencteri, he continues: 'at reliqua multitudo puerorum mulierumque—nam cum omnibus suis domo excesserant Rhenumque transierant—passim fugere coepit, ad quos consectandos Caesar equitatum misit'.[69] This is not a device to leave his readers to imagine the scene for themselves; nor is it the conscious hardening of his heart; it is that his heart is not awake. But when, at Dyrrhachium, his own army breaks so that it is out of hand, then 'eodem quo venerant receptu sibi consulebant *omniaque erant tumultus timoris fugae plena,* adeo ut, cum Caesar signa fugientium manu prenderet et consistere iuberet, alii dimissis equis eundem cursum confugerent, alii ex metu etiam signa dimitterent, neque quisquam omnino consisteret'.[70] Here, as Caesar lives again through this crisis in his fortunes, the plain style is for a moment infused with the vividness of his recollection. When the army of Curio is routed in Africa the climax is reached with almost the same phrase: 'plena erant omnia timoris et luctus'.[71] Here Caesar is stirred by the thought of that disaster which broke the victorious course of the war and by his sympathy for his troops, but above all he records the death of his friend in expiation of his fault—'at Curio numquam se amisso exercitu, quem a Caesare <suae> fidei commissum acceperit, in eius conspectum reversurum confirmat atque ita proelians interficitur'.[72]

As in Caesar's account the swift achievement of victory before Alesia once the tide of battle has turned is reflected in a rapid *staccato,* so the urgency of speed in a supreme effort may be reflected by a use of the historic present to a degree rarely found elsewhere in the **Commentaries.** Once Caesar has crossed the Rubicon it is for him all-important to sweep down Italy and above all, if possible, to intercept the retreat of Pompey across the Adriatic. In the chapters which describe this effort there are found at least as many historic presents as in all the rest of his writings put together. This is to be explained not so much by the desire to impress the reader by a kind of rhetorical device as by the subconscious revelation of Caesar's own vehement desire to finish the war at a stroke. The reader would know that Caesar did not in fact achieve this purpose; what mattered was not what the reader would think but what Caesar felt and hoped and strove to attain.

Thus the study of Caesar's style may be revealing for the study of Caesar's mind and will, especially at moments of crisis. When he is describing the doings of his lieutenants the style is, in general, less emphatic, less vigorous, though even in these, as in the account of Curio's campaign or, again, in that of the disaster to the army of Sabinus and Cotta and the events that led to it, there is a more dramatic treatment of the situation. It becomes more personal as

Caesar's imagination of what must have happened is engaged. On the whole, though, the operations of the *legati* are described so that the military quality of their actions, their *consilia,* so far as these are their own and not Caesar's at one remove, can be appraised, but that is all.

None the less, a close study of those parts of Caesar's narrative which rest on the reports of his lieutenants may reveal stylistic touches which are taken over in a kind of submerged quotation. Thus in the account of the siege of Massilia the texture of the narrative appears to show three strands, the matter-of-fact technical siegecraft of Trebonius, a livelier tone in the report of naval operations which would be supplied by the admiral Decimus Brutus, and the occasional comment of Caesar himself.

There is a habit of Caesar which may reflect more than one stylistic motive. When he is describing actions or the springs of action he invariably refers to himself in the third person by his name Caesar. This may in part be due to his adoption of the **Commentarius** form, though that form is found elsewhere to admit the use of the first person by a narrator. It is true that the use of the third person has an air of objectivity, almost of detachment, which may subtly win the reader's assent; though it may seem to be monotonous, it serves the clarity of the narrative: it perhaps needs no other explanation. But it may, at least in part, be a revealing mannerism. Here and there, outside the **Commentaries,** what seems to be good tradition shows Caesar referring to himself by his name, where the first person would seem more natural. The famous words 'You carry Caesar and Caesar's fortune' is hardly an example, for his boatman needed to be told who his passenger was. But the equally famous dictum that Caesar's wife must be above suspicion might have run 'my wife' or 'the wife of a Pontifex Maximus'. To say 'Caesar's wife' has something that is in a way more than either, something that has a sharper impact. The effect may be illustrated, though it is no more than an illustration, by the high-riding words that Shakespeare makes Caesar use in his decision to go to the Senate House on the Ides of March, when the omens give their warning of danger:

> The gods do this in shame of cowardice:
> Caesar should be a beast without a heart
> If he should stay at home to-day—for fear.
> No, Caesar shall not: danger knows full well
> That Caesar is more dangerous than he:
> We are two lions litter'd in one day
> And I the elder and more terrible,
> And Caesar shall go forth.

To return to what is evidence. When at Pharsalus Caesar saw his enemies broken he spoke words that may well have been truly recorded by Asinius Pollio, who stood at his side. 'Hoc voluerunt'—they would have it so; and then—'tantis rebus gestis Gaius Caesar condemnatus essem, nisi ab exercitu auxilium petissem'.[73] Here, in this *cri du cœur,* his name springs to his lips, it adds something, it throws into the scale his belief in his own greatness. It is thus possible that the constant use of his name in the **Com-** *mentaries* is not only a convention or a mask of objectiveness, but includes, as it were, the natural, almost automatic, expression of his conscious preeminence.

Notes

1. 'The title of Caesar's Work', *Trans. Amer. Phil. Assoc.* XXXVI (1905), pp. 211-38.

2. *ad Fam.* VIII, 11, 4.

3. *Inst. Or.* X, 1, 31.

4. Martial, XIV, 191, 2.

5. By F. Jacoby, *Die Fragm. der griech. Historiker,* II D, pp. 639 f.

6. 48 ff.

7. In *ad Verum Imp.* II, 3.

8. *ad Attic.* II, 1, 1-2.

9. *ad Fam.* V, 12, 10.

10. *ad Attic.* IV, 6, 4; IV, 11, 2.

11. 75, 262.

12. *Inst. Or.* X, 1, 114.

13. III, 37, 150-38, 154.

14. See G. L. Hendrickson in *Class. Philology,* I (1906), pp. 97 ff.

15. See W. A. Oldfather and G. Bloom in *Class. Journ.* XXII (1927), pp. 584-602.

16. *Brutus,* 29, 112; Pliny, *N.H.* XXXIII, 21; Tacitus, *Agric.* I, 3; Val. Max. IV, 4, 11; Frontinus, *Start.* IV, 3, 13.

17. *Brutus,* 35, 132.

18. H. Peter, *Hist. Rom. Rel.,* I, p. cclxv.

19. *ad Attic.* VIII, 9, 4.

20. Plutarch, *Caesar,* 18, 1; Appian, *Celt.* 1, 3, and XV; Dio Cassius XXXVIII, 32, 4; Caesar and Dio Cassius do not mention Labienus.

21. *B.G.* 1, 12, 7.

22. *B.G.* 1, 26, 1.

23. *B.G.* 1, 52, 7.

24. *ad Attic.* 1, 20, 5.

25. *B.G.* 1, 11, 6.

26. *B.G.* 1, 31, 16.

27. *B.G.* 1, 33, 1.

28. *B.G.* 1, 40, 7.

29. Its truth is not challenged by Plutarch, *Caesar,* 19, or by the long harangue composed by Dio Cassius, XXXVIII, 36-46.

30. *B.G.* I, 43.

31. *B.G.* I, 54, 2.

32. *B.G.* I, 1, 2.

33. *B.G.* II, 3, 2.

34. *B.G.* II, 35, 1-2.

35. *B.G.* II, 35, 4.

36. *B.G.* III, 1-6.

37. *B.G.* III, 10, 3.

38. *B.G.* IV, 1, 3.

39. *B.G.* IV, 16.

40. *B.G.* IV, 20, 1-2.

41. 13, 33; see also Catullus, II, 9-12.

42. *B.G.* V, 54, 5.

43. *B.G.* V, 58, 6.

44. *B.G.* VI, 1, 3.

45. *B.G.* VI, 43, 4.

46. *B.G.* VI, 44, 3.

47. *B.G.* VII, 59, 6.

48. See below, p. 79.

49. Suetonius, *Divus Iulius,* 30, 4.

50. *B.C.* I, 15, 2.

51. *B.C.* II, 25, 4.

52. *B.C.* III, 94, 6.

53. *B.C.* III, 104, 3: 'naviculam parvulam conscendit cum paucis suis; ibi ab Achilla et Septimio interficitur.'

54. *B.C.* III, 106, 3.

55. By K. Barwick in *Philologus, Suppl.* XXXII, 2, p. 133f.

56. 'Elegantia' imports the choice of the right word, rather than any elaboration or elevation of style. See E. E. Sikes in *Camb. Anc. Hist.* IX, p. 764.

57. *B.G.* VII, 77, 3-16.

58. *B.G.* VII, 20.

59. H. Oppermann, *Caesar, der Schriftsteller und sein Werk,* p. 82.

60. *B.G.* VII, 50, 4-6.

61. *B.G.* V, 30.

62. *B.C.* II, 31-2.

63. *B.C.* III, 86-7.

64. *B.G.* VII, 87, 3.

65. *B.G.* VII, 88, 2-3.

66. *B.G.* II, 18ff.; this analysis owes much to the insight of Oppermann, *op. cit.,* pp. 56ff.

67. *B.G.* VIII, *Praef.* 7.

68. H. Peter, *Hist. Rom. Rel.* I, p. 179.

69. *B.G.* IV, 14, 5.

70. *B.C.* III, 69, 4.

71. *B.C.* II, 41, 8.

72. *B.C.* II, 42, 4.

73. Suetonius, *Divus Iulius,* 30, 4.

John H. Collins (essay date 1959)

SOURCE: "On the Date and Interpretation of the *Bellum Civile,*" in *American Journal of Philology,* Vol. LXXX, No. 2, April, 1959, pp. 113-32.

[*In the following essay, Collins argues that Caesar was a moderate rather than a revolutionary, and that most of his writings should be accepted as truth, not propaganda.*]

I.

In a fundamental article in *Rheinisches Museum* nearly fifty years ago, A. Klotz,[1] summing up the evidence and earlier discussion and adding solid arguments of his own, showed with great probability that the **Bellum Civile** was not published in the lifetime of Caesar, nor from any finally revised copy, but was superficially edited and published shortly after his death by Aulus Hirtius, who had as his text the unfinished and unpolished manuscript from Caesar's literary remains. The view thus nailed down by Klotz, though attacked in the following decades by E. Kalinka[2] and others, may be considered the received doctrine on the matter down to 1938, when K. Barwick published his elaborate study, *Caesars Commentarii und das Corpus Caesarianum.*[3] In 1951 Barwick again took up the problem in his *Caesars Bellum Civile. Tendenz, Abfassungszeit und Stil,* and with further argument based on intensive linguistic analysis and historical reconstruction, attempted to make good the thesis that the **B. C.** [**Bellum Civile**] was written and published as part of Caesar's propaganda campaign during the war, and that it appeared in two parts, Books 1-2 as a unit at the end of the year 49, and Book 3 at the end of 48 or early in 47. Klotz had in the meantime published his *Editio altera* of the **B. C.,**[4] and in his *Praefatio* had answered Barwick's 1938 arguments and further fortified his own earlier position. Although Barwick has convinced some scholars,[5] I believe the general view of Klotz still commands a majority agreement.[6]

The main arguments for Klotz' theory may be briefly summarized: (1) the "rough-draft" or "skizzenhafter Zustand" of the work as a whole, especially as compared with the balanced organization and artistic finish of the **Bellum**

Gallicum; (2) the abrupt break-off at the end, indicating that it is unfinished; (3) the silence of Cicero, who never alludes to the *B. C.;*[7] (4) the criticism of Asinius Pollio cited by Suetonius (*Caes.,* 56, 4): *parum diligenter parumque integra veritate compositos putat, cum Caesar pleraque et quae per alios erant gesta temere crediderit et quae per se, vel consulto vel etiam memoria lapsus peram ediderit; existimatque rescripturum et correcturum fuisse,* which is apparently to be completed by the thought, "if he had lived to do it";[8] (5) the express words of Hirtius (*B. G. [Bellum Gallicum],* VIII, *Praef.* 2): *novissimumque imperfectum ab rebus gestis Alexandriae confeci,* since *novissimum imperfectum* apparently refers to *B. C.,* III.[9] It should perhaps be added that the older arguments, based on the phrases *bello confecto* (*B. C.,* III, 57, 5; 60, 4) and *bello perfecto* (*B. C.,* III, 18, 5) have long been discounted as of no weight.

The cumulative force of this evidence is overwhelming, nor have the counter arguments of Kalinka and Barwick been able to weaken it significantly. Barwick's case is built mainly upon his concept of the *B. C.* as timely propaganda requiring immediate publication for its effectiveness, but his strongest arguments indicate only that the *B. C.* was *written* during the progress of the war, or directly after Pharsalus, and prove nothing regarding the time of publication.[10] Kalinka was even driven to the astonishing theory of an *unauthorized* or pirated publication in his attempt to meet Klotz' arguments based on the unevenness of the text.

In 1952 I reasoned[11] that it was incredible that Caesar should have written the *B. C.* in, say, 48 or 47, and then let it lie for years without completing or publishing it. Believing further that posthumous publication had been proved by Klotz, I concluded that the work was written in the last months of Caesar's life, after the return from Spain in the late summer of 45, and was left incomplete at his death. Further reflection on the whole problem in the last few years has convinced me that this view is incorrect, and I now believe with P. Fabre[12] that the *B. C.* was written in late 48 or early 47 in Egypt at odd intervals during the so-called Alexandrian War, that it was laid aside incomplete for reasons which are speculative but which I hope to make plausible, and that it was found among Caesar's papers after his death in approximately the condition in which we now have it. In other words, I believe that Barwick is correct in fixing an early date of composition, and that Klotz is correct in fixing a posthumous date of publication. I wish here to set this view forth with such evidence as I can bring, and to indicate certain wider consequences bearing on the historical interpretation and credibility of the work itself.

II.

What ultimate plans for the organization of the Roman *Imperium* Caesar may have formed or entertained in his last months will doubtless always be discussed and can never be satisfactorily settled.[13] But there can be no doubt about one thing—he had no intention of imitating Sulla by resigning the dictatorship. His own words as reported by Titus Ampius in Suetonius' account (*Caes.,* 77): *nihil esse rem publicam, appellationem modo sine corpore ac specie. Sullam nescisse litteras, qui dictaturam deposuerit* fit together with his acts and omissions to act, and leave no doubt of his determination to maintain his despotic position. That he consciously intended to found a Hellenistic God-kingdom on the model of Alexander has been powerfully argued by Meyer and others;[14] that he had the slightest intention of "re-establishing the republic" as Cicero publicly called upon him to do (*Pro Marc.,* 26-7), and as Sallust also urged (*Ep. ad Caes.,* I, 6, 3), or even of re-establishing some sort of shadow republic as Augustus later found expedient, is believed, as far as I am aware, by no one. His government after Thapsus was a humane but quite naked absolutism, conducted with conspicuous contempt for the *mos maiorum,*[15] and the assumption of the lifetime dictatorship in early 44, against the whole weight of constitutional tradition, was an open declaration that he had done, finally and deliberately, with the old republican ideology.

With this post-Thapsus, monarchial Caesar clearly in mind (it matters little whether he laid great stress on the title *Rex;* his regal bearing and arrogation of royal power made mere titles of minor importance), let us turn to the *B. C.,* and ask how well it fits the character of its author as that character reveals itself in its last phase. We shall find, I think, that the *B. C.* does not fit at all; that it is a work *republican* through and through; that it neither contains the spirit nor the foreshadowing of the "monarchial" or "imperial" idea; that even interpreted as propaganda, it is not propaganda for monarchy nor for any projected reform or re-organization of the Roman governmental system. As a product of the mind of the "late" Caesar, known to us from Suetonius, from Cicero's correspondence of the years 45-44, and from the miscellaneous anecdotes in Plutarch, Dio Cassius, Appian, and other writers, of the Caesar driving for the possession of absolute power, and in visible ways corrupted by power in the sense of Lord Acton's aphorism, the republican *Gedankenwelt* of the *B. C.* is hardly thinkable.

Since the above statements will appear radical to many, and have indeed been specifically denied,[16] it is necessary to support them here by a somewhat detailed collection of the evidence.

That the *B. C.* does not contain any clear political "slogan" or announcement of the "imperial idea" has often been noted. U. Knoche writes:[17] "Sieht man Caesars Schriften durch . . . so ist es bemerkenswert, wie häufig von der *Fortuna* die Rede ist und wie der Gedanke an ein römisches Schicksal ganz zurücktritt. Geradezu erstaunlich und erschreckened ist es aber, eine wie geringe Rolle dort überhaupt in Wirklichkeit der Reichsgedanke spielt; und es ist sonderbar, dass Caesar, der Meister der Propaganda, sich diese Parole hat entgehn lassen." The sole instance in the *B. C.* of an expression that may be thought in some sense to announce a "program" or overall political plan is a phrase in a letter to Metellus Scipio urging as objectives to be sought, *quietem Italiae, pacem provinciarum, salutem imperi* (*B. C.,* III, 57, 4). These words do sum up, with remarkable accuracy and insight, the great needs of the Roman world, and Gelzer[18] has repeatedly cited them to show Caesar's statesmanly grasp of the problems before him, and his vision beyond the limited horizon of the old *res publica* incorporating merely the city-state of Rome, or at most, the citizen body of Italy. But these words in their actual context cannot be taken as a program or even as a slogan, whatever may be their value as proof of Caesar's understanding and statesman's concern. The message in which they occur is an offer of peace on the principle of return to the *status quo ante bellum,* that is, re-establishment of the senatorial oligarchy and the rest of the legal and customary *res publica.*

At no time in the *B. C.* does Caesar indicate a desire or intention of altering or reforming, to say nothing of revolutionizing, the old constitution. The propaganda of the work has, in fact, the exactly opposite tendency of emphasizing Caesar's defense of the old constitution. His expressed reasons for invading Italy are (1) to support the rights of the tribunes (*B. C.,* I, 5, 1-2; 22, 5; 32, 6); (2) to free the Roman people from the *factio paucorum* (I, 22, 5; 85, 4); (3) to preserve his personal *dignitas* against the *iniuriae* and *contumeliae* of his *inimici* (I, 7, 1; 7-8; 22, 5; 32, 2; cf. Cic., *Att.,* VII, 11, 1). His conditions of peace, as stated in the *B. C.,* never require any constitutional change, but stress on the contrary his constant desire and willingness to submit to the republican laws. He is prepared to suffer all for the good of the state (I, 9, 3; 5). He asks only free elections and personal security (I, 9, 5; 85, 11; III, 10, 8-10). This picture of his demands and intentions is supplemented but not altered by the strictly contemporary evidence of the Ciceronian correspondence (note especially, *Att.,* VIII, 9, 4: *aiebat* (Balbus the Younger) *nihil malle Caesarem quam ut Pompeium adsequeretur . . . et rediret in gratiam; . . . Balbus quidem maior ad me scribit nihil malle Caesarem quam principe Pompeio sine metu vivere*). It is the Pompeians who are accused of innovation: *novum in rem publicam introductum exemplum* (*B. C.,* I, 7, 2); *in se* (i. e., Caesar) *novi generis imperia constitui* (I, 85, 8). Still more specifically the Pompeians are charged with contemptuous disregard for law and custom: *Consules, quod ante id tempus accidit numquam, ex urbe proficiscuntur . . . contra omnia vetustatis exempla . . . omnia divina humanaque iura permiscentur* (I, 6, 7-8).

The question of the sincerity or truth of this presentation is at the moment irrelevant; the point to be noted is that Caesar is at pains to appear as the loyal son of the republic, forced to take arms in the republic's defense, and wishing nothing as reward but the restoration of the old state of things, *otium* (I, 5, 5), and peace. There is not a sentence in the *B. C.* the *political tendency* of which could not be approved by Cicero, or for that matter, by Cato; there is no threat of innovation (those of Caesar's followers who entertained radical hopes of confiscation and *novae tabulae*

were quickly disillusioned; cf. Caelius Rufus, *Fam.,* VIII, 17, 2; *hic nunc praeter faeneratores paucos nec homo nec ordo quisquam est nisi Pompeianus*), and no expression of dissatisfaction with the former condition of the *res publica* except that the selfishness and ambition of a few men, of the *factio paucorum,* was preventing the system from functioning. Caesar reduces the whole political question to the level of a personal quarrel in which Pompey, supported and egged on by Caesar's *inimici,* preferred to throw the state into a turmoil rather than permit Caesar his well-earned place of equal *dignitas* (*B. C.,* I, 4, 4. Lucan's well-known *nec quemquam iam ferre potest Caesarve priorem / Pompeiusve parem* does not misrepresent Caesar's own statement). The modern idea that there was a general crisis, economic and political, in the Mediterranean world that could be resolved only by a fundamental change in the governmental organization, with one-man rule replacing the old rivalry of the *potentes*[19] for money and *honores,* is not remotely suggested, not even darkly hinted by Caesar.

We find this so hard to believe that we read into Caesar what we cannot find explicit in his work. L. Wickert writes of the peace propaganda of the *B. C.* thus:[20] "Caesars Absicht war, nachzuweisen, nicht nur, dass er den Frieden gewollt habe, sondern auch, dass er im Kampfe mit den Pompeianern und im Gegensatz zu ihnen alles getan habe, um die alte *res publica* zu retten" (a correct and excellent statement); "dass aber das Verhalten der Gegner und die Ereignisse selbst es ihm unmöglich gemacht hätten, diese Plan durchzuführen" (partly correct, but one sees here the beginning of subjective addition); "dass er Schritt für Schritt gegen seinen ursprünglichen Willen mit zwingender Notwendigkeit dazu geführt worden sei, die Verfassung in der Weise umzugestalten, dass die Monarchie und—können wir hinzufügen—der Reichsstaat das Ergebnis sein mussten" (for this last view there is in the *B. C.* no trace; it is a modern and wholly subjective interpretation based on knowledge of the actual later imperial development). The only passage in the *B. C.* that gives the slightest color to the last part of Wickert's sentence is that of Caesar's speech to his rump senate of 1 April 49 (*B. C.,* I, 32, 7): *Pro quibus rebus hortatur ac postulat, ut rem publicam suscipiant atque una secum administrent. Sin timore defugiant, illis se oneri non futurum et per se rem publicam administraturum.* There is no announcement here of a coming Reichsstaat, or of any general constitutional reform; there is, as Gelzer[21] has pointed out, a threat to act independently, and thus an attempt to force co-operation by the reluctant senate, but again there is nothing that a Cicero or a Cato could not have approved in principle. The idea of a *temporary* dictatorship to deal with a public emergency, whether formally tendered by a vote of the senate or taken in hand *de facto* by a strong consul, was one of the oldest traditions of the Roman constitution. In Caesar's words there is no break with the *res publica,* but rather the use of the *res publica* as a slogan.

In conformity with his striving to appear as the *bonus civis, rei publicae natus,* Caesar continually implies that his march into Italy in 49 (the touchiest point of his case: note Mommsen's struggle to justify it in the *Rechtsfrage*) was supported by almost universal consent. Towns and soldiers are again and again represented as eager to yield themselves, and as submitting with great impatience to control by Pompeians. A monotonous parade of surrenderers and collaborationists is set forth in *B. C.,* I, 12-18. At Iguvium, *Caesar certior factus . . . omnium esse . . . optimam erga se voluntatem.* Thermus, who was holding the town for the Pompeians, flees, and *milites in itinere ab eo discedunt . . . Curio summa omnium voluntate Iguvium recipit* (I, 12, 1-3; note the tendentious *recipit* for *capit* or *occupat*). Practically the same formula describes the seizure of Auximum, with the addition of an honorary citation: *neque se neque reliquos municipes pati posse C. Caesarem imperatorem, bene de re publica meritum, tantis rebus gestis oppido moenibusque prohiberi* (I, 13, 1). In Picenum, Pompey's special stronghold, *cunctae earum regionum praefecturae libentissimis animis eum recipiunt exercitumque eius omnibus rebus iuvant* (I, 15, 1; a cynic may wonder how many peremptory requisitions helped the help); *Etiam Cingulo, quod oppidum Labienus constituerat . . . ad eum legati veniunt quaeque imperaverit se cupidissime facturos pollicentur* (I, 15, 2). Never was conquering army so enthusiastically greeted. If there was a sullen citizen or two who with Cicero was wondering *utrum de imperatore populi Romani an de Hannibale loquimur (Att.,* VII, 11, 1), we should never learn the fact from Caesar.

This "bandwagon propaganda" is extended and emphasized throughout the *B. C.*[22] In some passages it is given a definite political, even legal connotation. At Oricum *L. Torquatus . . . conatus portis clausis oppidum defendere cum Graecos murum ascendere atque arma capere iuberet, illi autem se contra imperium populi Romani pugnaturos esse negarent (B. C.,* III, 11, 3-4). Again at Apollonia, where L. Staberius attempted like Torquatus to defend the town and secure hostages from the inhabitants, *illi vero daturos se negare, neque portas consuli praeclusuros, neque sibi iudicium sumpturos contra atque omnis Italia populusque Romanus iudicavisset* (III, 12, 2). In Syria the soldiers of Metellus Scipio threatened mutiny, *ac non nullae militum voces . . . sese contra civem et consulem arma non laturos* (III, 31, 4). Caesar urged the Massilians: *debere eos Italiae totius auctoritatem sequi potius quam unius hominis voluntati obtemperare* (I, 35, 1). As factual reports of words actually spoken these passages are obviously strongly colored and "stylized," but they prove beyond cavil Caesar's keen wish to *legitimate* his victory in conformity with republican principles. Of similar tendency is the ostentatious deference to the *comitia* advertised in III, 1, 5: *Statuerat enim prius hos* (those exiled during Pompey's domination) *iudicio populi debere restitui quam suo beneficio videri receptos, ne aut ingratus in referenda gratia aut arrogans in praeripiendo populi beneficio videretur.* In his last months Caesar treated the *comitia* with sovereign contempt, ordering mock elections at his personal pleasure, and outraging republican feelings: *Incredibile est quam turpiter mihi facere videar, qui his rebus intersim,* wrote Cicero to Curius. *Ille autem* (i. e.,

Caesar), *qui comitiis tributis esset auspicatus, centuriata habuit, consulem hora septima renuntiavit, qui usque ad K. Ian. esset quae erant futurae mane postridie. Ita Caninio consule scito neminem prandisse (Fam.,* VII, 30, 1, January 44).[23]

Caesar's anxiety to placate republican opinion is shown less conspicuously, but none the less significantly, in his omissions. Rambaud[24] has with great plausibility suggested that the reason the name of Cicero does not appear in the *B. C.* is that it was precisely Caesar's failure to win Cicero to his side that made his claim to represent the old republic look thin. "D'un côté, elle [i. e., the unsuccessful sollicitation of Cicero] aide à comprendre que le *Bellum Civile* n'ait pas nommé Cicéron à qui César accordait tant d'importance en 49; l'abstention prudente de ce politique, son absence au sénat le premier avril, démentaient l'argumentation césarienne." Cicero's defiance of Caesar at the interview of 28 March 49 (*Att.,* IX, 18) was unquestionably a serious setback for Caesar's policy, and all the more painful that it was unexpected. "Menschlich gesehn ist es vielleicht die erstaunlichste Niederlage, die Caesar erlitten hat."[25] Caesar passed it over in silence in the *B. C.* not only because it was a psychological defeat, but because it damaged the picture of republicanism he was striving to paint. There was perhaps not another man in Italy whose judgment of the political rightness of his conduct Caesar so much valued, or whose approval would in fact have been more valuable to him.

No phase of Caesar's conduct in the civil war impressed his contemporaries (and indeed posterity) more strongly than his *clementia.* In the *B. C.* this policy is given a very prominent place and is unquestionably one of the major strands of the Caesarian propaganda. But it has often been noted that Caesar, though he rings the changes on the idea so tirelessly that a modern scholar has facetiously suggested that the book should be titled *Bellum Civile, sive de Caesaris clementia,*[26] deliberately avoids the word; he speaks instead of *lenitas,* and of *incolumes dimittere* or *incolumes conservare;* his supporters speak of *temperantia* and *humanitas* (Caelius, *Fam.,* VIII, 15, 1; Dolabella, *Fam.,* IX, 9, 3). The reason is not far to seek. *Clementia* is the virtue of the legitimate monarch, not of the *primus inter pares.*[27] It was exactly because he was unwilling to accept Caesar's *clementia,* unwilling to recognize any right of Caesar to exercise *clementia,* that Cato preferred death, and Caesar's avoidance of the word shows in striking fashion his care to stay inside the republican tradition of equality. He similarly avoids the word in his famous letter on the capitulation of Corfinium (*Att.,* IX, 7-c), but speaks of *misericordia* and *liberalitas,* and it is his opponent Cicero who writes bitterly of *insidiosa clementia (Att.,* VIII, 16, 2).[28]

All this conspicuous, not to say ostentatious republicanism of the *B. C.* is incompatible with the Caesar of 46-44, "the crony of Quirinus stepping down from his place among the gods" (*Quid? tu hunc de pompa Quirini contubernalem his nostris moderatis epistulis laetaturum putas?*

Cic., *Att.,* XIII, 28, 2). It is equally discordant and unfitting whether read as apologetic or as preparatory propaganda. As apologetic, it is too grossly contradicted by the events of 46-44, too easily turned to ridicule, to be effective; as preparatory propaganda, it prepares for the wrong thing. When one considers the deep-cutting change that took place in Caesar's character and outlook in his last phase,[29] the conclusion is strongly suggested that the *B. C.* is a product of his earlier period.

The argument of Barwick, based on considerations of the timely character of the propaganda and *tendance,* and on the time-conditioned judgments of men (note especially the rather severe criticism of M. Varro, *B. C.,* II, 17-20), reinforces the above line of thought, and points to late 48 or early 47 as the date of composition. To Barwick's evidence may be added the remarks of P. Fabre,[30] who cites the fine saying of Louis XII: "Le roi de France ne venge pas les injures du duc d'Orléans," and asks whether Caesar would have carried on his quarrel with the dead: "Après la guerre d'Espagne, et déjà même après la guerre d'Afrique, quel intérêt eût trouvé le maître absolu de Rome, le tout-puissant dicateur . . . à dessiner en traits satiriques et mordants des ennemis que la mort ou la soumission avait réduits à l'impuissance?" We know, indeed, that he did pursue Cato beyond the grave, but this is to be explained by Cato's special position as a symbol of continuing resistance. Is it not more likely that the persiflage with Metellus Scipio (*His temporibus Scipio detrimentis quibusdam circa montem Amanum acceptis imperatorem se appellaverat,* **B. C.,** III, 31, 1) was written while this contemptible Pompeian leader was still in active opposition? The disparaging observations on Afranius (*B. C.,* I, 84, 4; 85, 1) and Petreius (I, 75, 2) are also more fitting if written before Thapsus and the deaths of these men.

One of the remarks of Caesar quoted earlier, *omnia divina humanaque iura permiscentur* (**B. C.,** I, 6, 8), inspired a comment by Eduard Meyer:[31] "Caesar hat sich die schöne Schlussphrase nicht entgehen lassen" (he used it again, *B. C.,* I, 32, 5!) "die er ebensogut auf seine eignen, ganz gleichartigen Massregeln als Monarch hätte anwenden können." Meyer might have added that Cicero actually did apply virtually this formula to Caesar's conduct: *omnia iura divina et humana pervertit propter eum quem sibi ipse opinionis errore finxerat principatum* (*De Off.,* I, 26). I suggest that what was obvious to Cicero and Meyer was probably obvious also to Caesar, and that it is unlikely that he would have allowed "die schöne Schlussphrase" to appear had he been writing at a date when it could so easily and effectively be turned to scorn.

None of these indications of the time of writing of the *B. C.* is decisive, but the ease with which they may be individually discounted must not be permitted to obscure the fact that they are parallel, not linked indications, so that their cumulative force is not to be despised. But it may well be asked why, if Caesar wrote the *B. C.* in 48-47 for political ends, did he not publish it at once? This question seemed to me unanswerable when I first considered the problem, and led me to suppose that the work could only have been written toward the end of Caesar's life, at the earliest after Thapsus. But if it can be shown that events interrupted the writing and made the original purpose obsolete, the natural objection to a widely separated date of writing and publication disappears, and the arguments of Barwick and Klotz are no longer opposed, but point together to the same conclusion: *writing in 48-47; publication in 44-43.*

III.

When Caesar arrived at Alexandria some seven weeks after Pharsalus, and was shown the head of Pompey, who had been murdered a few days before, he very probably believed, with that sanguine temperament that had led him to write of the condition of Gaul at the end of 56, *omnibus de causis Caesar pacatam Galliam existimaret* (*B. G.,* III, 7, 1), that the civil war was virtually over, and that he needed but show himself in Italy to find all opposition broken: *Caesar confisus fama rerum gestarum infirmis auxiliis proficisci non dubitaverat aeque omnem sibi locum tutum fore existimans* (**B. C.,** III, 106, 3). The objects for which he had fought the civil war were attained; he had recovered his *dignitas,* and his soldiers might now expect to recover their *libertas* (**B. C.,** III, 91, 2). In this spirit of optimistic self-satisfaction he had marched around the Aegean to the Hellespont, and had sailed thence to Ephesus and Rhodes, hearing and recording, with harmless pride, the stories of prodigies that circulated through the East in the wake of his victory (**B. C.,** III, 105). From Rhodes he had crossed the Mediterranean to Alexandria. It is quite possible that he dictated part if not most of the *B. C.* at intervals of this journey, as we know was his custom in traveling (cf. the *De Analogia* and the *Iter,* Sueton., *Caes.,* 56, 5). He was nominally in pursuit of Pompey, but he did not press the matter with Caesarian *celeritas.* For a Pompeius Magnus was hardly a fit subject for *liberalitas sive misericordia.*

Immediately after his arrival at Alexandria on approximately 2 October 48 (27 July by the corrected calendar), two unforeseen developments combined to turn his adventurous life to a new course: he met Cleopatra and he became involved in the dangerous struggle for the control of Egypt known as the Alexandrian war.

Our firm knowledge of the events at Alexandria rests mainly on the account of Hirtius, who was not, however, present himself, but put together his narrative from Caesar's private conversations (*quae bella . . . ex parte nobis Caesaris sermone sunt nota,* **B. G.,** VIII, *Praef.* 8) supplemented no doubt by other reports written or oral. He tells us nothing of Caesar's personal life, prudently suppressing, in deference to Roman "Victorianism" and xenophobia, what he knew of Caesar's liaison with the woman he had recognized as the legitimate Egyptian queen. To eke out the purely military history of Hirtius we have some 500 lines of the tenth book of Lucan's *Pharsalia,* based in all probability on Livy, but of course heavily loaded with poetical invention, exaggeration, and bitter anti-Caesar partisanship. At a hardly higher level of reliability stand the brief and contradictory notices in Suetonius, Plutarch, Dio Cassius, and Appian. In the nature of the case, rumor and speculation must have embroidered the known facts. Yet there can be no question whatever that Cleopatra gained a powerful influence over Caesar, or that she continued for the rest of Caesar's life to hold a place of major importance in his plans. The failure of our main source to discuss the psychological and moral background of the Alexandrian war must not lead us to ignore, or treat as trivial gossip, the decisive importance of the Egyptian period in Caesar's personal development. With good reason has Cleopatra been called "die genialste Frau der Weltgeschichte,"[32] and with good reason did the Romans fear her "as they had feared no other but Hannibal."[33]

Caesar remained in Egypt some eight months, the last two of which were spent in a pleasure-trip up the Nile with Cleopatra.[34] He then departed to take up again the affairs of empire, which had assumed a seriously threatening form during his period of neglect. But a year later we find Cleopatra in Rome, living in Caesar's own sumptuous residence across the Tiber, where she remained until after the murder of the dictator, caring for Caesar's son Caesarion and "playing the queen" to the rage of republican Romans (Cicero, *Att.*, XV, 15, 2). Caesar had her statue publicly set up next to that of Venus Victrix (Genetrix), his own patron goddess, and much of the intrigue and scheming of the last months of his life—the plan to assume the title *Rex* outside Italy, the rumor that he intended to remove the seat of government to Alexandria, and the astonishing law which Helvius Cinna was charged with introducing to enable Caesar to marry *uxores liberorum quaerendorum causa quas et quot vellet* (Suet., *Caes.*, 52, 3)—is unquestionably closely connected with his serious involvement with the Egyptian enchantress.[35]

It is of course impossible to know the precise manner in which the fabulous luxury and display, the excesses of power and pleasure that Caesar found at the Alexandrian court worked upon his mind, but there are many proofs that the post-Alexandrian, post-Cleopatra Caesar is a very different man from the Caesar of Corfinium and Ilerda.[36] The imagination of Lucan has painted the scene in florid rhetoric, and a greater than Lucan was inspired by his description[37] to write:

> High on a throne of royal state, which far
> Outshone the wealth of Ormus and of Ind,
> Or where the gorgeous East, with richest hand,
> Showers on her kings barbaric pearl and gold,
> Satan exalted sat.

All circumstances united to turn the Roman *Imperator* into the oriental *Rex*, to harden his contempt for the stupid oligarchy that had rejected him, and to fill his soul with that *superbia* and delusion of grandeur which three years later made him so hateful that his old friends and camp comrades combined to murder him.

If, as has been suggested, Caesar wrote the **B. C.** in the period immediately following Pharsalus, partly during his leisurely journey to Egypt and partly during intervals in the palace at Alexandria (when one considers that the so-called "Alexandrian war" lasted some six months, but that the actual fighting took up only a few days, it is clear that many free intervals must have been available), it is easy to understand both the republican tone and ideology of the work and its propaganda of self-justification. It is Caesar's *apologia* for his conduct of the civil war, addressed to Romans; to Romans first of all of the aristocracy that had fought against him (other than the irreconcilable leaders). Its *tendance* is open and straightforward: to clear Caesar of any charge of attacking the republic, to set forth his deeds in the best light, to destroy the moral credit of his adversaries, to be admired, to triumph. One may see in it not unjustly a certain spirit of self-satisfied exuberance, a tempered repetition of the *fiducia* of 59: *Quo gaudio elatus non temperavit, quin paucos post dies frequenti curia iactaret, invitis et gementibus adversariis adeptum se quae concupisset, proinde ex eo insultaturum omnium capitibus* (Suet., *Caes.*, 22, 2). It contains no subtle double-talk looking toward monarchy; the ideals and standards of conduct to which it appeals are the ideals and standards of the old republic, of Cicero and of Cato. It contains no "Caesarism" in the sense which that word has assumed in modern times, but is throughout the work of a Roman republican aristocrat, successful in the lawful game that the Roman aristocracy played, the game of competition for honors and position. Having swept the board in this game, Caesar might well say *Satis diu vel naturae vixi vel gloriae.*

In Egypt, however, falling increasingly under the influence of Cleopatra and of the atmosphere of oriental despotism and oriental luxury, Caesar gradually lost interest in the Roman ideal of aristocratic *libertas,* and became convinced that Sulla had been a simpleton when he resigned the dictatorship. When he finally returned to Italy from the East at the end of 47, he came determined to hold power in perpetuity, and to increase the pomp and splendor of his position in ways that would have seemed frivolous to the Caesar who had given his bed to Oppius and had slept on the ground.

But it was not alone the corrupting influence of refined and exotic luxury that worked upon Caesar's character during the Egyptian interlude. He visited the tomb of the great Macedonian conqueror, whose career had stimulated his imagination since his youth, and he saw in active operation the most complex and developed administrative bureaucracy of the ancient world. "Ganz gewiss hat Caesar seinen Aufenthalt in Ägypten nach der glücklichen Beendigung des Alexandrinischen Krieges nicht bloss zum Tändeln mit Kleopatra benutzt, sondern ausser anderm auch zum Studium einer Verwaltung, von der die römische unendlich viel lernen konnte."[38] A new Caesar developed in Egypt, perhaps for both better and worse, for it was in Egypt that Caesar decided not only on personal monarchy, but on many of those schemes of reform and reorganization to which his modern admirers have appealed as evidence of his statesmanship. We *know* that the calendar reform came from Egypt, and we may guess that many another project (one thinks of the dream of piercing the Isthmus of Corinth with a canal in imitation of the great Pharaoh) was likewise the product of the fertile Nile and its ripe civilization.

In Dio Cassius' history (XLIII, 15-18) stands a speech allegedly delivered *ad Quirites* on the occasion of Caesar's victorious return from Africa (and his visit to his Sardinian "farm," *Fam.,* IX, 7, 2). Dio's habit of manufacturing rhetorical speeches is too well known to permit anyone to accept this piece as representing with accuracy an original documentary source, but it is not probable that it is fabricated out of hand. In it Caesar announces a program of general reform under the principle that the eighteenth century called "enlightened despotism." For what it may be worth, this doubtless garbled speech may be taken as the herald of the new Caesar, the Caesar who has given his name to "Caesarism."

By this time the manuscript of the **Bellum Civile** was a forgotten paper of the past. It no longer corresponded to the psychology of its author. It remained untouched in Caesar's archives until the summer of 44, when it was resurrected by Hirtius and given over to the copyists.[39] Thus the arguments of both Barwick and Klotz have their respective validity. We need assume neither that Caesar published a work in a "skizzenhafter Zustand," nor that he pursued propaganda objectives that were long obsolete.[40]

IV.

If the foregoing discussion is correct in its main outlines and conclusion, consequences of no small importance to the understanding of the events of 50-49 must be reckoned with. First of all, we must not attribute to Caesar the fixed intention at the beginning of the civil war, or even after the struggle at Dyrrachium and the victory of Pharasalus, of destroying the republic and establishing a personal *regnum.* We must take more seriously than recent scholarship has done his comparatively modest professions of objectives as stated in the conditions given to L. Roscius and L. Caesar (**B. C.,** I, 9, 5-6).[41] We must not give a Machiavellian or even a Hitlerian twist to his claims of peaceful intentions, or to his announcement of a *nova ratio vincendi, ut misericordia et liberalitate nos muniamus* (*Att.,* IX, 7-c, 1).[42] His letters in the Ciceronian collection (*Att.,* IX, 6-a; 7-c; 16, 2), and the letters of his agents Balbus and Oppius (*Att.,* VIII, 15-a; IX, 7-a; 13-a) must be taken as more sincere and more "republican" than they have frequently been judged. We must not re-interpret the plain words of our sources with modern diplomatic subtlety, or in the light of modern knowledge of an imperial development that no man could foresee in 49 B.C. When Caesar held his famous interview with Cicero at Formiae on 28 March 49, he really meant what he said: *Veni igitur et age de pace* (*Att.,* IX, 18, 1). He wanted civil peace, *dignitas* and *otium,* and he did not demand dictatorial powers for himself as their price.

The large-scale plans of reform (*lex Iulia municipalis*), of colonization, of vast engineering projects, and of personal government, with the striving for excessive honors and semi-divine titles, are all products of the later Caesar, and cannot be safely appealed to as evidence for his purposes in 49, to say nothing of his purposes in 59 or 60.[43] One may guess that had he been granted his second consulship for the year 48, he would not have attempted to revolutionize the state, but would have been content with a proconsulship thereafter to take vengeance on the Parthian for Carrhae.

It was the stubbornness, suspiciousness, and vindictiveness of the Pompeian-Catonian opposition—Marcus Bibulus, Lucius Domitius, Metellus Scipio, Faustus Sulla, Lentulus Crus, and their *amici*—unwilling and temperamentally unable to believe in a moderate Caesar, a Caesar *bonus civis*—that drove matters to civil war, and brought to naught the peace efforts of Cicero and other reasonable men. Pompey himself, as Cicero expressly says (*Victa est auctoritas mea non tam a Pompeio* [*nam is movebatur*] *quam ab iis qui duce Pompeio freti peropportunam et rebus domesticis et cupiditatibus suis illius belli victoriam fore putabant,* to A. Caecina, *Fam.,* VI, 6, 6), and as Caesar implies (*Ipse Pompeius, ab inimicis Caesaris incitatus,* **B. C.,** I, 4, 4), could probably have been brought to a second Luca agreement, which would by no means necessarily have involved a despotic or "unrepublican" rule by Caesar. There was room within the constitution for orderly reform, and it is a tragedy of world history that Rome could not use for orderly reform the services of her greatest son. Through civil war the way led to military dictatorship and totalitarianism. It was the way chosen by a stiff-necked aristocracy unable to forget and unable to learn. As Caesar truly said as he gazed at the desolation of Pharsalus: *Hoc voluerunt; tantis rebus gestis Gaius Caesar condemnatus essem, nisi ab exercitu auxilium petissem* (Suet., *Caes.,* 30, 4). Perhaps after all, if we could really look into the wheels and levers of history, we should find that it was not Caesar, but Cato and Cleopatra, who founded the Roman empire!

Notes

Addendum: After this article was submitted, there came into my hands an article by Karlhans Abel, "Zur Datierung von Cäsars Bellum Civile," *Museum Helveticum,* XV (1958), pp. 56-74, who argues sharply that the so-called "Legalitätstendenz" of the *B. C.* cannot be used as evidence of the date of composition. His entire article should be read in connection with the line of argument offered in section II above.

1. "Zu Caesars Bellum Civile," *Rh. M.,* 1911, pp. 80 ff. Cf. *R.-E.,* X, col. 270.

2. "Die Herausgabe des Bellum Civile," *Wien. Stud.,* 1912, pp. 203 ff. Cf. Bursian *Jahresberichte,* CCXXIV (1927); CCLXIV (1939), with citation of additional literature.

3. *Philol., Suppl.,* XXXI, 2 (1938).

4. Teubner edition, Leipzig, 1950.

5. Lloyd W. Daly, *A. J. P.,* 1953, p. 195; F. E. Adcock, *Caesar as Man of Letters* (Cambridge, 1956), is doubtful; see note 40 below.

6. U. Knoche, "Caesars Commentarii, ihr Gegenstand und ihre Absicht," *Gymnasium,* 1951, Heft 2; P. Fabre, *Bellum Civile* (3rd Budé edition, Paris, 1947), pp. xxiii-xxiv; M. Rambaud, *L'art de la déformation historique dans les Commentaires de César* (Paris, 1953). I have myself tried to show the insufficiency of some of Barwick's arguments in an appendix to my Frankfurt dissertation, *Propaganda, Ethics, and Psychological Assumptions in Caesar's Writings* (1952).

7. The passage of *Brut.,* 262 has since Nipperdey been generally recognized as applying only to the *B. G.,* and Barwick has not shaken this *res iudicata;* the attempt to find echoes of the *B. C.* in Cicero's *Pro Ligario,* 18 is also unsuccessful, in that the catchwords (*dignitas, contumelia*) and arguments by which Caesar justified his war-making were in common circulation long before the *B. C.* Cicero was already complaining of Caesar's sensitive *dignitas* in January 49 (*Att.,* VII, 11, 1).

8. Cf. Knoche, *op. cit.* (note 6 above), p. 155, n. 30: "Das stärkste Argument für die postume Edition des BC sind m. E. die worte des Asinius Pollio."

9. Cf. Klotz, *Cäsarstudien* (Leipzig, 1910), pp. 155-6; Rice Holmes, *Caesar de Bello Gallico* (Oxford, 1914), p. 362, n. 2.

10. F. Lossmann, "Zur literarischen Kritik Suetons," *Hermes,* LXXXV (1957), pp. 47-58, analyzes the meaning of Suetonius' version of Pollio's criticism (it is important to note that we do not have Pollio's exact words), and its bearing on the problem of date, with great sharpness and detail. His final conclusion supports Klotz' theory of posthumous publication. See also his careful review of Barwick, *Gnomon,* 1956, pp. 355-62.

11. *Op. cit.* (note 6), pp. 55-6.

12. Budé edition, p. xxi. Fabre believes the *B. C.* was written before Thapsus. See citation at note 30 below.

13. Cf. R. Syme, *The Roman Revolution* (Oxford, 1939), p. 53.

14. Ed. Meyer, *Caesars Monarchie und das Principat des Pompeius* (Stuttgart-Berlin, 1918); W. Steidle, *Sueton und die antike Biographie, Zetemata,* Heft 1 (Munich, 1951), pp. 60 ff.

15. In "Caesar and the Corruption of Power," *Historia,* 1955, pp. 445-65, I have tried to show this contempt in some detail; here I may summarily refer to chapters 76-80 of Suetonius' *Caesar,* recalling their importance as a Roman moral judgment recently stressed by Steidle, *op. cit.* (note 14).

16. Among better company, by me, who thought I could find evidence in the *B. C.* of Caesar's desire to appear as the *patronus* of the Roman state, *op. cit.* (note 6), p. 76; cf. citation from L. Wickert, note 20 below.

17. "Die geistige Vorbereitung der augusteischen Epoche," in *Das neue Bild der Antike,* ed. H. Berve (Leipzig, 1942), II, p. 213.

18. *Caesar, der Politiker und Staatsmann* (4th ed., Munich, 1942), p. 262; *Vom römischen Staat* (Leipzig, 1943), I, p. 137; II, p. 178.

19. *certamina potentium,* Tacitus, *Ann.,* I, 2.

20. "Zu Caesars Reichspolitik," *Klio,* 1937, pp. 232 ff.

21. "Caesar," in *Das neue Bild der Antike,* II, p. 188 = *Vom römischen Staat,* I, p. 126.

22. A full citation of passages with sharply critical discussion is given by Rambaud, *op. cit.* (note 6), pp. 277-83.

23. Cf. further discussion of the "Legalitätstendenz" in Barwick, *Caesars Bellum Civile,* pp. 109-114. The preceding two paragraphs have been adapted with minor revision from my dissertation, *op. cit.* (note 6), pp. 78-80.

24. *Op. cit.* (note 6), p. 151.

25. O. Seel, *Cicero* (Stuttgart, 1953), p. 199.

26. P. Fabre, Budé edition, p. xxx.

27. Seneca, *De Clem.,* II, 3, 1: *Clementia est temperantia animi in potestate ulciscendi vel lenitas superioris adversus inferiorem in constituendis poenis.* Cf. Rambaud, *op. cit.* (note 6), pp. 289-93.

28. M. Treu, "Zur Clementia Caesaris," *M. H.,* 1948, pp. 197 ff., and Rambaud, *op. cit.* (note 6), pp. 289 ff., have strongly attacked the sincerity of Caesar's professions, and have developed the view given contemporary expression by young Curio: *ipsum autem non voluntate aut natura non esse crudelem, sed quod popularem putaret esse clementiam* (*Att.,* X, 4, 8). It would require a second article to give in detail my reasons for disagreeing with this view; briefly, I may remark that Cicero, although he wrote of *insidiosa clementia* at the time, did not later doubt its genuineness, despite the hatred he felt for Caesar. But the question of sincerity is quite secondary here to the estimate of Caesar's "republicanism" in the *B. C.* Sincere or Machiavellian, Caesar presents his *clementia* or *liberalitas* as the good will of a republican *nobilis,* not as the condescension of a monarch.

29. Cf. my "Caesar and the Corruption of Power."

30. Budé edition, 1947, p. xxi. Fabre, however, agrees with Klotz in assigning a posthumous date of publication.

31. *Op. cit.* (note 14), p. 289, n. 1.

32. Title of book by Otto van Wertheimer (1930). Cf. also Th. Birt, *Frauen der Antike* (Leipzig, 1932), and F. Stähelin's *R.-E.* article (1921).

33. W. W. Tarn, *Oxford Classical Dictionary* (1949), article "Cleopatra."

34. Louis E. Lord, "The Date of Julius Caesar's Departure from Alexandria," *J. R. S.,* 1938, pp. 19-40, discredits, perhaps correctly, the alleged pleasure-trip. The point is not essential to the matter of this article.

35. Full citation of sources and of the most important modern literature in Stähelin, *R. E.,* XI, col. 755. F. E. Adcock, *C. A. H.,* IX, p. 724, n. 1, rejects, without good reason, the account of the proposed law to permit polygamy. Correct view in Meyer, *op. cit.* (note 14), p. 518. From an obscure reference in Cicero (*Att.,* XIV, 20, 3) it may reasonably be inferred that Cleopatra was pregnant with Caesar's second child at the date of the assassination. Cf. J. Carcopino, *Cicero: the Secrets of his Correspondence* (London, 1951), II, pp. 314-17, who believes, however, that the reference is to the birth of Caesarion. No one else that I know doubts that Caesarion was born in 47.

36. Cf. my "Caesar and the Corruption of Power."

37. Of course I do not *know* this; let Milton scholars speak.

38. H. Willrich, "Caligula," *Klio,* 1903, p. 89.

39. Rambaud, *op. cit.* (note 6), p. 367, supposes that the *B. C.* was published after Caesar's death by Antony and Faberius.

40. F. E. Adcock, *Caesar as Man of Letters,* declines to commit himself definitely, but follows Barwick's general argument. His most interesting remark in connection with this paper is his suggestion that, after Pharsalus, "though Caesar did not cease to be a man of letters, he had come to care less for self-justification once he had the supreme justification of success. He seems to have become willing to leave to others the narratives of his victories. And the less he came to care for the conventions of the republic, the less he was anxious to maintain that he had preserved them."

41. K. von Fritz, "The Mission of L. Caesar and Roscius," *T. A. P. A.,* 1941, pp. 125 ff., refuses to take these proposals as offering a serious basis of peaceful compromise.

42. As M. Treu, *op. cit.* (note 28).

43. As is well known, Mommsen's brilliant portrait attributes to Caesar a conscious aiming, from his earliest youth, at the goal of statesmanly reform through the establishment of monarchy. Cicero, *Phil.,* II, 116, says of Caesar *multos annos regnare meditatus,* but this, and similar attributions by opponents, need not be taken too seriously.

Zwi Yavetz (essay date 1979)

SOURCE: "Caesar and Caesarism in the Historical Writing of the Nineteenth and Twentieth Centuries," in *Julius Caesar and His Public Image,* Cornell University Press, 1983, pp. 10-57.

[*In the following excerpt, originally published in German in 1979, Yavetz surveys modern interpretations of Caesar, focusing on the question of whether he should be considered a dictator.*]

THE PROBLEM[1]

In 1953 Hermann Strasburger startled a group of German teachers when he stated briefly and persuasively,[2] that Julius Caesar, despite his image of great popularity,[3] was nothing more than a lonely dictator: not a single Roman senator supported his fateful decision to cross the Rubicon.

Before he took this risk, Caesar addressed his companions, 'My friends, if I do not cross this stream, there will be manifold distress for me; if I do cross it, it will be for all mankind.'[4] This warning left his friends unmoved. Some of them, including Calpurnius Piso (his father-in-law), Publius Dolabella, Scribonius Curio, Sulpicius Rufus and Trebatius Testa, absolutely refused to cross the Rubicon; others, like Oppius, Balbus and Matius (who were reckoned in Rome to be Caesar's most trusted associates), had their own views about it. According to Strasburger, one factor was crucial: at no point did Caesar command the total devotion of his followers.

Strasburger did not concern himself with Caesar's plans, his final aims, or his place in history. He agreed with Jakob Burckhardt that, 'so far-reaching a view, implying that Caesar's plans were on a world-wide scale, must, since it is based on false assumptions, lead to wrong conclusions.'

At the beginning of his career Caesar was merely a Roman senator,[5] and it is highly debatable whether he was at that time capable of thinking of himself as an absolute monarch. Most modern historians[6] reject as unhistorical Suetonius' assertion in the name of Cicero,[7] 'Caesar in his consulship established the despotism which he had already in mind when he was aedile.'

It was only after the conquest of Gaul that Caesar decided on war as the means of raising his own *dignitas* to a level with that of Pompey.[8] Viewed from this angle, Caesar was not for one moment planning for monarchy in the year 49 BC, he was not attempting to undermine the Republic, and he was not yet thinking of transforming it into an empire by means of a 'new order'. Caesar declared that his aims in waging war were 'the tranquillity of Italy, the peace of the provinces, the safety of the Empire',[9] but Strasburger dismissed these as words of propaganda, and having nothing in common with the pronouncements of a manifesto. Actually, Caesar was anything but a revolutionary; it was he who suggested a spirit of co-operation in the Senate, and challenged senators to share with him the burden of leading the state.[10]

In assessing Caesar, Strasburger asserted that Caesar was no Augustus, no Trajan and no Hadrian: he was the last patrician of the old school.

Caesar's isolation grew from day to day. While his soldiers and the masses worshipped him like an idol, his peers, and even his closest friends, accused him of tyranny. His murderers had no alternative plans of any kind. They wanted quite simply nothing more than to be rid of the hated dictator. The fact that some of Caesar's laws remained in force even after his death proves only that there was a practical necessity for them. In the last analysis no one regretted his murder.

Thus far Strasburger.

The German teachers were shocked.[11] In their view, Strasburger had 'assassinated' one of their great heroes, and some of them even wondered whether they were justified in continuing to teach the works of Caesar in their schools. In their perplexity, they sought advice from the great Matthias Gelzer,[12] so that they could bolster their belief in the view expressed in all the editions of his book[13] that Caesar was, in fact, a great statesman.

Gelzer (rightly) praised Strasburger's article as brilliant. He agreed that Caesar was, perhaps, unloved by his contemporaries, but categorically disputed the conclusion that he was nothing but an average Roman politician. To wage war on a well-established oligarchy—and a victorious one—was the act of a great statesman. In contrast to Augustus, whose motto was *festina lente,* Caesar was a great improviser. In his latter days he acted like a monarch, but that is not the decisive factor for an assessment of his achievement. Caesar had a plan. Tranquillity for Italy, peace for the provinces and safety for the Empire, was more than a mere slogan. It constituted a programme, 'in so far as one should expect a programme from Roman statesmen at all'.[14] Finally, Caesar's legislation was proof of his statesmanlike insight and energy.

It is to be hoped that Gelzer succeeded in allaying the fears of those teachers who felt deprived of an heroic figure. Yet, even if the 'Gallic War' is again being taught in those high schools that have not so far totally abolished the teaching of Latin, the controversy over Caesar has nevertheless not reached a conclusion—and never will.[15]

In the sixth edition of his biography of Caesar (1960),[16] Gelzer was more sceptical in his assessments of the aims of the dictator than in his earlier writings. Two decades previously he had argued against Eduard Meyer, who emphasized Caesar's personal power rather than his political intentions. 'Living ourselves at a time when the political order is in a state of evolution, we are better able to comprehend some aspects of Caesar than former genera-

tions . . . Caesar founded the Roman *Kaisertum* designated by his name,' he wrote in 1942.[17]

After the war, Gelzer changed his mind,

> He published no programme; a practical politician through and through, he recognized the problems in every situation and set about mastering them with a will. Our sources . . . give us an insight into individual cases but no certain information about his innermost thoughts. We may go so far as to assert that eventually the dictatorship for life corresponded to his wishes. But it remains obscure when . . . he decided on this form for his principatus. For it is not possible to determine how far the extravagant senatorial decrees which granted him this vast power were inspired by himself. We must guard against ascribing to him actions, plans and motives for which there is no authority.[18]

We do not know what provoked the change in Gelzer's point of view. Possibly the impact of Syme's research drove him closer to Strasburger's argument. It is also possible that his experiences under a dictatorship in World War II moved the scholar, who never overlooked a source, to take more seriously the judgment of Cicero, who remarked after Caesar's murder, 'So great was his passion for wrong-doing that the very doing of wrong was a joy to him for its own sake even when there was no motive for it.'[19] Finally, it is also possible that he was influenced by a seldom-quoted passage of Pliny, who not only praised Caesar's intellectual vitality, the extent of his benefactions and his military genius, but also pointed out that his wars cost 1,192,000 lives, which is why Caesar neglected to mention the casualty figures in his writings.[20] In the last edition of the most comprehensive and important biography of Caesar written in the twentieth century, Gelzer stated that Caesar did not shrink from corruption or acts of violence to further his purposes, and that he was a man who simply had no moral scruples where politics were concerned.

Although Gelzer never questioned Caesar's greatness as a statesman, his hesitation in making a total assessment of the man was criticized by Otto Seel,[21] who risked a more acute formulation of the question, namely whether Caesar was merely a successful scoundrel, or whether he should be regarded with awe, respect, enthusiasm and affection—a prototype worthy of imitation. To dismiss this question would be to debase history itself. One can understand Seel's aversion to scholars parading patient wisdom, ironic scepticism and cheerful resignation in their books, yet this appears to be caused by the fact that the days are long since gone when Theodor Mommsen could believe that Caesar's personality might be sketched either superficially or more profoundly, but not differently.[22] (See also p. 37.)

Cicero was of a different opinion. In 46 BC he addressed Caesar,

> Among those yet unborn there shall arise, as there has arisen among us, sharp division; some shall laud your achievements to the skies, and others shall ignore them.
>
> (Cic., *pro Marc.,* 29)

The problem was clearly recognized by Tacitus, 'the killing of the dictator Caesar had seemed to some the worst, and to others the fairest, of high exploits (*Ann.* I, 8, 6). And Seneca found it difficult to answer Livy's question, whether it would have been better for the Republic or not if Caesar had not been born at all (Sen., *Nat. Quaest.* V, 18, 4).[23]

Historiography followed the same path. It was not enough to describe Caesar as a man with 'two souls in but one breast'. He was no Jekyll and Hyde, but rather a phenomenon of many facets which are confirmed in iconographic studies. Likenesses of Caesar show every possible character trait: majesty, pride, disdain, audacity, reflectiveness, elegance, wit, corruption and affection.[24] For two thousand years Caesar's personality has intrigued the heart of Europe.[25] In time, a 'Caesar myth' developed, and eventually an 'ism' was attached to his name. This last complication makes it necessary to define this controversial concept before returning to the investigation of Caesar the man.

CAESARISM

Historians and political scientists of the nineteenth century made more frequent use of the expression 'Caesarism' than their twentieth-century counterparts. W. Roscher provides a good example.[26] He knew, as did numerous political scientists before him, that democracy can degenerate into military despotism. The two Napoleons come to mind: Caesarism was frequently used as a synonym for Bonapartism. What expression would Roscher have used, had he written his book after World War I can only be guessed. Fascism, perhaps. His interest lay not so much in the personality of the ruler as in his attitude to the various groupings and strata of society. Everything was promised to everyone, and only the leader's genius could preserve a certain unity. No rational acts could bridge the contradictions in his programme; it depended simply and solely on blind belief in the superhuman capabilities of the ruler.

When Napoleon created his new nobility, he said to some, 'I guarantee revolution; this caste is highly democratic, for all the time everyone is being summoned to it.' To the great proprietors he said, 'It will secure the throne'; to the friends of moderate monarchy, 'It will be opposed to the abuse of absolute power, for it is becoming influential in the country'; to the Jacobins, 'Exult, for, the ancient nobility is completely destroyed', and to the old aristocracy, 'In decking yourselves with fresh honours you are reviving your own again.'[27]

Roscher was, in fact, talking about Napoleon I, but a similar account could easily be given of Napoleon III. Did not the latter promise, 'l'Empire c'est la paix', only to entangle France a few months later in the hopeless Crimean War? Did he not promise the Italian nationalists and likewise the Pope his support, only to disappoint both ultimately? Did he not promise free trade and protective tariffs, but when his position shifted was he not obliged to vindicate French prestige by a Mexican adventure? A. J. P. Taylor expresses it admirably,

> The more we strip off the disguises, the more the disguises appear. Such was Louis Napoleon, the man of mystery: conspirator and statesman, dreamer and realist, despot and democrat, maker of wars and peace, creator and muddler. You can go on indefinitely.[28]

Was Caesar's fate any different? Did he not also enter into fateful connections with a very mixed collection of advisers, then being compelled to satisfy the desires of a motley group of dependants (see pp. 168 ff.)?[29]

Pompey, his great adversary, was not so clever. Cicero assessed one of Pompey's speeches as being 'of no comfort to the poor or interest to the rascals; the rich were not pleased and the honest men were not edified' (Cic., *ad Att.* I, 14). Caesar would not have let such an opportunity slip away. He would have obliged everyone, at least for a short time. And it was precisely this gift that led some political scientists to regard him as the father of modern Caesarism.

Gleichschaltung is the dictator's ideal and goal—or, in Heinrich von Treitschke's words, 'Before the Emperor's divine blood all subjects are fundamentally alike.'[30] So must Roman Caesarism have also appeared: slaves ruled their owners, freedmen their *patroni,* the upper classes succumbed to the strictest control and the masses were entertained with sport and the circus. One of the emperors is alleged to have said to his people, 'Devote your leisure to games and to the races in the circus. Let me be concerned with the needs of the state, and busy yourselves with your pleasures' (*SHA, Firmus* 5).[31] In a letter ascribed to Sallust, we read his advice to Caesar that the common people (corrupted by the corn dole and other hand-outs) must be occupied with their own concerns, to prevent them from causing any political damage.

That was Caesarism, a form of rule, which, under the cloak of a legitimate monarchy, was in reality based on military power. The old institutions remained unchanged. The magistracies kept their former names, and the real situation was concealed under a camouflage of artful legal fictions. Government was based on an association of heterogeneous groups, often opposed to one another, from which the key position of the leader necessarily emerged, for only he could oblige everyone. Tacitus described the situation clearly: Augustus 'conciliated the army by gratuities, the populace by cheapened corn, the world by the amenities of peace' (*Ann.* I, 2).

The concept of Caesarism, however, was not yet known to Tacitus. It was used for the first time in 1850 (!) by an enthusiastic Bonapartist, Frannçois Auguste Romieu (in *Ere des Césars*). Burckhardt did not take exception to this usage. In his opinion, Caesarism, as a concept, was nonetheless very well defined.[32] Mommsen, too, made use of the concept of Caesarism in his *History of Rome,* although, in contrast to Romieu, he loathed Bonapartism. His readers misunderstood him, however, in so far as they believed he (Mommsen) supported absolute monarchy even in his own day. In the second edition of his book the celebrated historian then clarified his view by being sharply critical of autocracy. He made clear his distinction between Julius Caesar the man, on the one hand, and Caesarism as a form of government on the other.[33] Some of his arguments are worth quoting:

At this point, however, it is proper expressly once and for all to postulate what the historian everywhere tacitly presumes, and to protest against the custom—common to simplicity and perfidy—of using historical praise and historical censure, dissociated from the given circumstances, as phrases of general application, and in the present case of construing the judgment respecting Caesar into a judgment concerning what is called Caesarism.

It is true that the history of past centuries ought to be the teacher of the present; but not in the vulgar sense, as if one could simply by turning over the leaves discover the conjunctures for the present from in records of the past, and collect from these the symptoms for a political diagnosis and the specifics for a prescription;[34] it is instructive only in so far as the observation of older forms of culture reveals the organic conditions of civilization generally—the fundamental forces everywhere alike, and the manner of their combination everywhere different—and leads and encourages men, not to unreflecting imitation, but to independent reproduction. *In this sense the history of Caesar and of Roman Imperialism, with all the unsurpassed greatness of the master-worker, with all the historical necessity of the work, is in truth a more bitter censure of modern autocracy than could be written by the hand of man* (my italics, Z.Y.).

According to the same law of nature, in virtue of which the smallest organism infinitely surpasses the most artistic machine, every constitution, however defective, which gives play to the free self-determination of a majority of citizens infinitely surpasses the most brilliant and humane absolutism; for the former is capable of development and therefore living, the latter is what it is and therefore dead. This law of nature has been verified in the Roman absolute military monarchy and all the more completely verified, that, under the impulse of its creator's genius and in the absence of all extraneous material complications, that monarchy developed itself more purely and freely than any similar state.

From Caesar's time, as the sequel will show and Gibbon showed long ago, the Roman system had only an external coherence and received only a mechanical extension, while internally it became even with him utterly withered and dead. If, in the early stages of the autocracy and, above all, in Caesar's own soul, the hopeful dream of a combination of free popular development and absolute rule was still cherished, the government of the highly gifted emperors of the Julian house soon taught men in a terrible way how far it was possible to hold fire and water in the same vessel.

Caesar's work was necessary and salutary, not because it was or could be fraught with blessing in itself, but because—with the national organization of antiquity, which was based on slavery and was an utter stranger to republican-constitutional representation, and in presence of the legitimate civic constitution which in the course of five hundred years had ripened into oligarchic absolutism—absolute military monarchy was the copestone logically necessary and the least of evils.

When once the slave-holding aristocracy in Virginia and the Carolinas shall have carried matters as far as their counterparts in Sullan Rome, Caesarism will there too be legitimized at the bar of history; where it appears under other conditions of development, it is at once a caricature and a usurpation. But history will not submit to curtail the true Caesar of his due honour, because the verdict may lead simplicity astray in the presence of bad Caesars, and may give to roguery occasion for lying and fraud. She too is a Bible, and if she cannot any more than the Bible hinder the fool from misunderstanding and the devil from quoting her, she too will be able to bear with, and to requite, them both.[35]

After Mommsen only a few historians made use of the concept of Caesarism, although political scientists still refer to it. Roscher has already been mentioned, F. Ruestow constitutes a further example,[36] as does Robert von Pöhlmann: the latter applied concepts such as communism and socialism to the classical world, and also used the concept of Caesarism where appropriate. In fact, in 1895 Pöhlmann published *Die Entstehung des Caesarismus*,[37] which added something to the contribution of his predecessors. He was not satisfied with Roscher's statement that it is possible to find prototypes of Caesarism in Roman history (such as, for example, Scipio, Marius, Sulla and Pompey). In his view Roman Caesarism had its origin in the late Greek tyrannies. Dionysius of Syracuse, Agathocles, Euphron of Sicyon, Chaeron of Pellene, Clearchus of Heraclea and Nabis of Sparta were the models for Caesarism. As far as these rulers were concerned, Pöhlmann maintained, they were indifferent to the concepts of morality, justice and law. Therefore, it was not difficult for them to be two-faced by appearing to be absolute monarchs to some and extreme democrats to others.

In general, nineteenth-century scholars were agreed that Caesarism was the outcome of a degenerate democracy, and that the rise of a dictator is usually facilitated by unavoidable conflict between the love of freedom—characteristic of the wealthy and educated classes—and the desire for equality among the masses. These objectives are mutually exclusive, and incompatible in the long run. The appetite of the mob may be contained for a while, but in the course of time its greed grows, for, as Pöhlmann said, 'the communist idea of sharing one another's victuals for these proletarians has become second nature'.

In these circumstances, the most able withdraw from state service and leave the field to professional politicians, the gulf between the social classes deepens and the demagogues intensify their efforts. Unrest breaks out, and eventually people begin to yearn for the benefactor as sole ruler. Of course, they desire a prudent and moderate ruler, but that does not always turn out to be the case. Usually they put up with one who is not so good, for 'in the last resort they prefer to permit person and property to be consumed by a single lion rather than by a hundred jackals or even a thousand rats' (Roscher).

Pöhlmann identified this type of Caesarism as being already present in fourth-century Greece, and thought that the beginnings of a Sultanism can even be traced in Alexander of Macedon and in Julius Caesar (p. 105). Therefore, Roscher's complaint in 1888 that the word Caesarism was used in an unscholarly fashion is readily understandable, as was his unwillingness to accept a definition such as that of Littré, 'Princes brought to government by democracy, but clad with absolute power.'

And yet, the concept of Caesarism still appears in the literature of the twentieth century. Spengler believed that democracy was doomed and predicted the approach of Caesarism with firm and measured steps. Antonio Gramsci[38] made use of the concepts of progressive and regressive Caesarism, and maintained that 'Caesar and Napoleon are examples of progressive Caesarism' because, under their regimes, the revolutionary element put the conservative in the shade.

Even if we grant that the elements sketched above are common to all Caesarisms, that every 'Caesar' seeks to attach himself to his predecessors, and that every sole ruler must declare, like Napoleon 'I must remain great, glorious, and admired'; does that bring us any closer to a better understanding of this specific phenomenon?

The use of the word Caesarism, however, does not lead to a real understanding of the problem. Karl Marx had no doubt about that. In his essay, 'Der 18. Brumaire des Louis Bonaparte', he characterized Caesarism as a schoolboy expression and its use as a superficial analogizing of history. N. A. Maškin, one of the Soviet Union's most important historians, agrees with Marx in this respect, because he finds that an analogy between Fascism, Bonapartism, and a proletarian regime has no historical value of any kind. For all that, Maškin is unable to dismiss the question of Caesarism easily, for the expression 'Roman Caesarism' (whatever its worth) occurs in the works of Lenin, an authority with whom a Soviet historian will not lightly venture to argue.[39]

A. Momigliano could not be restrained by such inhibitions. He based his criticism of those contemporary historians who employed the concept of Caesarism on the proposition that this kind of terminology was utterly unintelligible to the man of antiquity, while at the same time it is too inexact for the modern man.[40]

Caesarism is a typically nineteenth-century concept, which was necessary to help explain the emotional and demagogic factors in the government of the two Napoleons. In the twentieth century, however, Caesarism is of as little use as Fascism in helping us understand Caesar.

Detailed elaborations of the differences between the world of antiquity and the modern world are superfluous. Roman equites were not capitalists and the plebs were not proletarians. The Senate was no parliament, and the Roman popular assemblies have no counterpart in the modern world. Caesar was first and foremost a Roman senator, and to be able to understand him properly he must be placed within the context of his own time, that of Rome in the last century BC. But even then, many problems remain unsolved. The fact that the concept of Caesarism has developed a diversity of meanings in modern historical writing only proves once again that 'all history is contemporary history' (Croce). The truth of this statement finds its expression in the assessment of Caesar as a man and a ruler.

CAESAR

Mention has already been made of Mommsen's Caesarism as an anti-autocratic manifesto. He did not shed a single tear over the destruction of the old corrupt republican form of government, to which Caesar dealt the *coup de grâce*. Mommsen, the liberal revolutionary of 1848 and arch-enemy of the Prussian aristocrats, wrote history that offered the educated reader as much pleasure as it provided provocative reflection for the scholar. To familiarize the German reader with the Roman personalities, the author of the *Römisches Staatsrecht* even described a Roman magistrate as Burgomaster, and compared Cato with Don Quixote, Sulla with Don Juan and the great Pompey with a sergeant-major. His view of the Roman Republic was to,

> Try to imagine London with the slave population of New Orleans, the police of Constantinople, the lack of industry of present-day Rome, and agitated by politics like the Paris of 1848, and an approximate picture will be attained of the grandeur of the Republic whose decline is deplored by Cicero and his friends in their glum letters.[41]

Such a regime could not long endure. Yet, as luck would have it, the man responsible for its downfall was 'a king anointed with the oil of democracy'.[42] Caesar was a monarch, not a deluded dictator. His personality was flawless, he was sincere, adaptable and fair, and appears to have wanted to be nothing other than *primus inter pares*. He understood how to avoid the error of so many who brought the abrupt tone of military command into politics. Caesar was a great statesman and a great realist. Each of his steps was prudently planned. None of his successes should be regarded as an isolated incident because there were none. The outstanding characteristic of his life's work was its complete harmony. Caesar was the last creative genius of the ancient world and the sole one that Rome produced.

Mommsen's view found followers not only in the nineteenth century, but also in the twentieth, who carried it further with minor variations. Many of them agreed that Caesar was a great statesman, a benevolent ruler, of noble distinction, and that it was he who laid the foundation for the Roman Empire.[43] Some condemned the conspiracy against him as the act of mean and envious persons.[44] Others enthusiastically praised his deep understanding of his times and his clear vision of the future.[45] But Hegel, himself a great admirer of Caesar, would not have accepted these paeans for one moment. In his lectures on the history of philosophy, he described him as a man,

> who may be cited as a paragon of Roman adaptation of means to ends—who formed his resolves with the most unerring perspicuity, and executed them with the greatest vigor and practical skill, without passion. Caesar, in terms of history, did right, since he furnished a mediating element, and that kind of political bond which men's condition required. Caesar effected two objects; he deterred domestic strife, and at the same time developed a new struggle beyond the limits of the empire. For the conquest of the world had reached hitherto only to the circle of the Alps, but Caesar opened up a new scene of achievement: he founded the theatre which was on the point of becoming the centre of History. He then achieved universal sovereignty by a struggle which was decided not in Rome itself, but by his conquest of the whole Roman World. His position was indeed hostile to the Republic, but, properly speaking, only to its shadow; for all that remained of that Republic was entirely powerless.[46]

But Hegel, too, knew that Caesar, fighting for his honour and esteem, reacted instinctively to the historical constraints of the moment. Not every one of his successes was based on prudent foresight. Hegel, like Mommsen, deplored Caesar's murder and bitterly criticized that small band who did away with the great man from pure envy. For all that, Hegel would probably scarcely approve of Mommsen's view of Caesar as the last great personality of the ancient world. Later scholars too are opposed to Mommsen's view, but unfortunately a complete survey of all the disagreements is impossible in a short work. Instead, there follows a roughly schematized examination of five main theories, organized to show the principal tendencies of each. We must also add the *caveat* that this investigation is restricted to so-called 'professional historians'—and cannot extend to philosophers and littérateurs, although they have made many contributions towards a more penetrating discussion of Caesar. This is why Hegel is alluded to only briefly, and not because we belittle his influence, quite the contrary.

A considerable number of historians have resisted Hegel's philosophy of history. They preferred to concern themselves with Caesar the historic figure as sketched by the sources, and not with a Caesar who served Hegel merely as an example for a paragon of Roman adaptation of means to ends.

F. Gundolf, in considering the views of Caesar from Petrarch to Nietzsche and Wagner, maintained in one of his brilliant synopses (to say it is inexact is pointless, for he had no intention of being exact) that with regard to Caesar 'the French were best at assessing his person, the English his work, and the Germans his mind'. Yet, by means of an excursus that guides his readers from Petrarch and Dante, Montaigne and Voltaire, Klopstock and Goethe, to Mom-

msen and Burckhardt, Nietzsche and Wagner (to mention only the most important), he proves that European men of letters never intended to tabulate Julius Caesar in a short and narrow column.

They all went back to Petrarch, who again relied on Cicero. A man of letters himself, Cicero understood Caesar's multifaceted character, but was continually tormented by the discord between Caesar's greatness and his wantonness. Just as Petrarch could grasp that Caesar was Cupid's slave and Glory's fellow-traveller, it was unnecessary for Herder to hate Caesar in order to love Brutus; and, just as Byron tormented himself with the Caesar who wrecked the Republic, Lamartine, too, was torn between his admiration for Caesar's rich gifts and his aversion to their pernicious application.

The theme has been treated exhaustively by Gundolf in two well-known books, and although some topics could be added to the content, or alternative opinions discussed, in their genre they will remain unsurpassed for many years to come.[47] Professional historians, however, were not as sophisticated.

In 1901 G. Ferrero published *Grandezza e Decadenza di Roma*. Caesar was, for him, a great general and a gifted writer, but never developed into a great statesman. Ferrero admired Caesar's practical thinking, well-balanced intelligence, untiring facility for achievement and quick power of decision. On the other hand, he saw in Caesar a spirit of destruction whose mission was principally one of annihilation, and who brought about the decline and break-up of the ancient world. According to Ferrero, Caesar's contemporaries could expect nothing from him, and to succeeding generations in Europe his greatest act was the conquest of Gaul, an achievement to which he himself attached very little importance.[48] After Munda his dictatorship dissolved into an aimless, degenerate opportunism that recalled the fanciful intrigues of the old Republic. Ferrero maintained that Caesar had neither a political nor a legislative programme; he was an adventurer, whose only coherent plan was for the war in the east and the annexation of Parthia. Ferrero concluded, from a bust in the Louvre, that the dictator's face expressed deep physical suffering. In 44 BC Caesar was tired and exhausted.

In 1933 Ferrero wrote a preface to the English translation of his book.[49] Banished from Fascist Italy, he was teaching history at the University of Geneva. He did not alter his views. Rather, he saw his book as an anti-Fascist, or, should the reader prefer it, an anti-Bolshevist history of Julius Caesar. He sharply criticized historians of the nineteenth century who appeared to be swept by waves of enthusiasm for the gifted dictator, and who were not prepared to be satisfied with a single slice of historical greatness at the beginning of the nineteenth century (Napoleon).

After 1830, when the horrors of Napoleon had been forgotten, Caesar found favour in all circles. Conservatives considered him a bulwark against the liberal and democratic tendencies of the middle and lower classes, while liberals thought of him as a weapon against traditional monarchy, the principle of dynasticism and respect for the old classes. Thus, in the historical writing of the nineteenth century, there took shape one who resembled a quasi-elder brother of Napoleon rather than the historic Caesar.

At the beginning of the twentieth century a gradual disengagement from the romanticism of the nineteenth century became apparent, and historians, too, began to see Caesar in another light. However, World War I intervened, and these ideas went awry. Revolution and changes of regime in various European countries permitted the revival once more of the old romantic illusion of the dictator as saviour. Ferrero fits in at this point. He made no secret of his opinion, and is unequivocal,

> If the West fails to put an end to the fairy-tale and to introduce some clarity into the confusion of facts, it (the West) will fall victim to usurpers who are swaggering about all over Europe, Asia, and America. The West has nothing to hope for from usurpers, and should be on its guard against bombastic promises, made by people who believe they can alter the course of history.[50]

His hatred of all dictators won Ferrero many followers. In 1942 L. R. Taylor compared Caesar with Mussolini, and in 1948 F. R. Cowell compared him with Hitler, remarking *inter alia,*

> Useful and important as were some of his ideas [Caesar's], they did not amount to a New Deal, still less did they offer any hope of enlarging the lives of the masses and so of filling the vacuum of Roman social life with a new moral spirit. We have seen dictators fail in our own day—despite their tremendous propaganda machines—which for a time seemed likely to wield an influence over the minds of their victims. Caesar did not form a political party. He did no more than recruit a gang. He was supported by some respectable figures—but all in all—apart from the solid ranks of his legions—he was supported only by a few personal friends. Most of his supporters came from the disaffected classes, needy debtors, failures and misfits.[51]

Notwithstanding the vast gulf between Mommsen and Ferrero, they do have something in common: both admitted to their political conviction either in the preface or in the body of the work. Thus, their *Zeitgeist* is easily detectable. In any case, it would be unjust to criticize only those who openly acknowledge their prejudice. Every historian of the past is also a man of his age, and nobody is free from bias.

Historians who wrote after World War I disclosed their personal views only rarely. Accordingly, it is not easy to judge their political motivation. Conjecture is possible, not certainty. Tacitus might have maliciously put it: the one who conceals his ways is no better than the others—'occultior non melior' (*Hist.* II, 38).

Communist and Fascist interpretations of history are the exception. They leave nothing to the reader's imagination. To Fascist historians, Caesar was the great magician of antiquity, who attempted to improve the social position of the provincials in order to achieve a supra-national or imperial homogeneous organism.

A. Ferrabino, in *Cesare* (Turin, 1941) was not as simpleminded. He believed not only in the indestructibility of Romanity and its universality, but also depicted Caesar as an instrument of divine will. In his view Caesar founded a new order, based on the concepts of *clementia, aequitas* and *voluntas* of the nations.

It is not surprising that a reaction set in after World War II. Italian scholars seem to have lost all interest in studying Julius Caesar, the statesman and conqueror, and concentrated instead on a thorough investigation of Caesar's writings and the *Corpus Caesarianum,* as well as on an analysis of his personality as it emerged from the literary stance of the *commentarii.* In this respect, they made a decisive contribution and yet, although there is a wealth of allusions to political and social questions to be found, we cannot concern ourselves more closely with their writings in the present context.[52]

Soviet researchers, on the other hand, stressed Caesar's position as the representative of the slave owners who supported his dictatorship in the hope that through it the old regime, which was being destroyed by slave uprisings and the unrest of the plebs, might be rescued. This kind of historiography is worth a special study.[53]

THE HELLENISTIC MONARCHY

Towards the end of World War I Eduard Meyer published *Caesars Monarchie und das Principat des Pompeius,* one of the most authoritative works written in the first half of the twentieth century. In the first edition he did not even mention Ferrero, but in the third edition (1922) he conceded that Ferrero's work was certainly interesting and even stimulating. However, 'if the author intended to offer us a picture true to history, he [Ferrero] failed in his aim' (p. 330). Even Mommsen, who was Meyer's predecessor as Professor of Ancient History at the University of Berlin, was not spared. A Caesar as sketched by Mommsen had, in Meyer's view, never existed. It is no coincidence that Mommsen never wrote a fourth volume of his Roman history to embrace the foundation of the Principate. After the third volume he published a fifth, on the Roman provinces. The reason, in Meyer's view, was very simple: after Mommsen's Caesar there was no room left for Augustus.[54]

Meyer rejected the theory that Caesar occupied himself with plans for monarchy from the beginning of his career. He also repudiated the Shakespearean Caesar: 'the vain, pompous, cantankerous, ageing egotist surrounded by sycophants, swayed by flatterers, suffering from a fever in Spain and from a falling sickness'.[55] Meyer's Caesar had no ideals of any sort. He was fighting for a position of power (p. 468), and one who intends to achieve it must overcome opposition. After his victory over Pompey, he could not let power slip from his grasp. The conferment of royal dignity, therefore, was an attempt to legitimize usurpation and establish it on a legal basis. 'Caesar's *intentions* and the steps he took *to achieve the final aim* are as clearly displayed as anything else in his history' (p. 504), and no inconsistencies or Sultanic whims can be traced in his conduct (as, for example, Pöhlmann thought (p. 18)). In his latter days, it was his intention to turn himself into an absolute monarch in the oriental style and attain once more the world monarchy of Alexander. The conquest of Dacia and Parthia, the transfer of the capital from Rome to Alexandria, and the foundation of a dynasty—all were integral components of the grand master's plan. Meyer accepted Caesar's plans as described in Plutarch, *Caes.* 58, as authentic and concludes that Caesar consciously strove for divine honours, as reported in Suetonius (*Div. Jul.* 76),

> For not only did he accept excessive honours, such as an uninterrupted consulship, the dictatorship for life, and the censorship of public morals, as well as the forenamed Imperator, the surname of Father of his country, a statue among those of the kings, and a raised couch in the orchestra; but he also allowed honours to be bestowed on him which were too great for mortal man: a gold throne in the House and on the judgment seat; a chariot and litter in the procession at the circus; temples, altars and statues beside those of the gods; a special priest, an additional college of the Luperci and the calling of one of the months by his name.

This passage has been arbitrarily selected to illustrate and sum up a series of honours. A full account of all such honours might suggest that Caesar's aim was for royal dignity and deification but would overload this chapter. Countless books and treatises have been written on this subject, and the abundance of material is, in truth, vast, but one striking fact emerges: the reports concerning Caesar's aim of royal dignity and deification have their origin in texts of the imperial period (the few indications in contemporary sources do not suffice to give a comprehensive picture). One cannot fail, however, to be impressed by the persistence with which these stories continue to recur. Meyer fully documented Caesar's presumption and stubborn purpose in order to emphasize the signs of kingship and divinity (p. 447).

Meyer stressed that such conduct could not be considered fortuitous, and that Mommsen was wrong in assuming that the royal title was of secondary importance to Caesar. It is precisely in the case of monarchy that the title is absolutely inseparable from the power.[56] That Julius Caesar valued it highly is mentioned by Plutarch, Dio, Suetonius and Appian, and is emphasized by the historians who preceded Meyer.[57] But Meyer was the first to produce a fully-fledged theory that envisaged as the final aim of Caesar's work a Hellenistic monarchy, and this signifies a state structured with an absolute ruler at its head, who enjoys divine worship.

Is it at all possible to find an explanation for this theory in *Zeitgeist?* Certainty is impossible; we may only hazard conjectures. Meyer, more than any other ancient historian, went to great pains to integrate the history of Greece and Rome with that of other Mediterranean and Near Eastern peoples of the time. In his view the picture of the history of the ancient world is necessarily distorted when the fate of individual nations is examined independently. His *Geschichte des Altertums* was intended to make good such an omission. At the same time, concerned with interpretations of historical methodology, he published various articles on the subject.[58] World War I, however, prevented a visit to the East, and his universal history was never completed. Instead, he published a series of monographs, including the one on Caesar and Pompey. At that time (1918) Oswald Spengler's *Untergang des Abendlandes* fascinated many of the readers who identified Germany's collapse in 1918 with the decline of the West. Only a few historians agreed with Spengler. Meyer, however, while critical of details, sympathized with Spengler more than any other professional historian.[59] Meyer may have been tormented for some time by the weakening of the West. Therefore, Caesar's attempt to unite West and East, to wipe out the dividing line between victors and vanquished, and to found a new regime in Rome might have impressed Meyer so forcefully that he allowed himself to accept without hesitation sources which, under other circumstances, he would have subjected to thorough-going criticism. Thus Meyer made some far-reaching generalizations that he could not document, and expressly mentioned Caesar's tendency to put citizens and non-citizens on an equal plane and to 'subject the empire to a process of levelling down. Before the absolute ruler legal differences between subjects disappear in a subjection that affects all alike' (p. 483).

It is, therefore, quite remarkable that Meyer, a scholar whose knowledge of the sources was unrivalled, made not a single reference to evidence that pointed out that Pompey (who, according to Meyer, was the precursor of the 'Western' Principate) also attempted to imitate Alexander of Macedon. Let an extract from a contemporary text (Sall., *Hist.* III, 88) testify, 'Sed Pompeius a prima adulescentia sermone fautorum similem fore se credens Alexandro regi facta consultaque eius quidem aemulus erat'. Did Meyer perhaps think a 'western' statesman like Pompey was incapable of such an idea?[60]

By and large, Meyer's work was positively received, with only a few objectors to his main ideas.[61] However, under the influence of recent studies of a more fundamental nature such as those of P. A. Brunt and E. Badian, C. Nicolet and C. Meier, there was a retreat from Meyer's obsolete terminology. For example, after Nicolet's monumental work *L'Ordre equestre,* no one would write, like Meyer, 'Brutus belonged to the democratic party, i.e. the party of the equites' (p. 450). The oriental (= Hellenistic, absolute) monarchy, on the other hand, became in Meyer's day one of the accepted 'facts', although with many variants.

J. Carcopino is a case in point. His work[62] is too important and too original to be treated as a parenthesis to that of Meyer, yet in a schematic survey such as this it is not possible to give everyone his due. On the one hand, Carcopino was sharply critical of Meyer, and wrote that his book was 'badly structured, badly written, but illuminated throughout by a splendid intelligence' (p. 592). He decisively rejected the difference between Caesar and Augustus put forward by Meyer, and saw in Caesar the true founder of the Roman Empire, 'Caesar created the fertile elements of this "Empire", to which the ancients owed several centuries of beneficent peace.' On the other hand, Carcopino was in no doubt about Caesar's intention to exercise dominion over Rome as monarch. Caesar isolated himself from the city population so that he could better rule over it; he did not stumble into monarchy, but planned it carefully. Yet Roman monarchy of the eighth to sixth centuries BC was essentially different from Caesar's monarchy. The earlier monarchy was transitory, fortuitous, elective, secular and moderate, in contrast to Caesar's monarchy, which was solidly planned, divine, absolute and based on a plebiscite.

E. Pais, in *Richerche sulla Storia e sul Diritto Romano* (vol. I, 1918), came to similar conclusions independently, and spoke of 'Caesar's aspiration to the throne', but he stressed, more strongly than Meyer, the role of Cleopatra. H. Volkmann maintained that Caesar wished to elevate himself to king and god, and described his relationship with Cleopatra as a union in which affection and political considerations were inseparably amalgamated (*Kleopatra,* 1953, p. 61 and 77). In *Divinity of the Roman Emperor* (1931) L. R. Taylor never doubted Caesar's political intentions. L. Cerfaux and J. Tondriau emphasized that Caesar strove for a 'kingship, oriental and divine in its tendency',[63] and L. Homo, too, in *Les institutions politiques Romaines,* accepted Meyer's thesis completely.

The Soviet scholar N. A. Maškin followed Meyer's arguments and updated them by using Marxist terminology. C. N. Cochrane, the Canadian scholar, insisted that the sources left no room for any doubt that in the latter months of his life Caesar conclusively set his sights on the Alexandrine monarchy,[64] and in 1948 E. Kornemann returned to his view, developed at the end of the nineteenth century, that Caesar's dreams of empire expressed themselves in the grandiose plan to destroy the Parthian kingdom, push forward through the Caucasus to Dacia, and, by a concentrated attack from the east and west, stab the Germans in the back.[65]

These few examples prove only that the attempt to classify views about Caesar according to national points of view must fail. There is no English, German, Italian or American interpretation. Anatole France and C. Jullian attached themselves to Mommsen. The views of J. Carcopino and L. Homo were closer to those of Meyer, who, for his part, was criticized by his countrymen M. Gelzer and P. Strack.[66] Some English scholars, including F. E. Adcock, R. Syme and J. P. V. D. Balsdon, roundly rejected Meyer's

interpretation, which leads one to refer to an 'English view'. But the Italian, L. Pareti (just like the English) does not believe that Caesar wanted to make himself a king or god.[67] The important fact is that the English scholars used different arguments from each other. In the matter of method Syme, from Oxford, was closer to the German F. Münzer than to Adcock, his Cambridge colleague.

THE MINIMALISTS

A further wave of criticism—that opposed Mommsen's view—arose in Britain. This school ought to be designated 'Minimalist' rather than 'British', since W. W. Fowler and C. Merivale cannot be considered among its members. On the one hand, we have seen that Meyer was not prepared to concede Caesar's greatness as portrayed by Mommsen. On the other, for all the energy Meyer expended in advancing his theory of the Hellenistic monarchy, he nevertheless considered Caesar an interlude. The real precursor of Augustus' principate was Pompey, and the future state theory was already sketched in Cicero's *De Republica* and in his speech on behalf of Marcellus. By and large, Caesar had no grasp of the historic moment, and historical development took a path different from the one he had previously delineated.[68]

H. F. Pelham had quite different objections. He suggested, however, an open admission: that we have no key of any kind to the understanding of Caesar's future plans, even if we assume that he had the fundamental capability of such foresight.[69] Adcock did not consider it necessary to imagine a Hellenistic monarchy, in order to explain the participation of several honourable men in the conspiracy against the dictator.[70] Caesar was murdered for what he was and not for what he might perhaps have been. Meyer's Caesar was, for Syme, a mythical Caesar, conceived intellectually.[71] (Actually, Meyer encountered precisely the same objection that he had levelled against Mommsen's Caesar.) If one must judge Caesar, that judgment must be based on facts and not on alleged intentions. One need not believe that Caesar planned a Hellenistic monarchy, irrespective of how one defines this concept. The simple charge of dictatorship suffices. For Syme, Caesar's final aims are uninteresting. He excluded statements about intentions from the realm of proof and counterproof:[72] Caesar should be left as he is in his time and generation, and one should neither laud him for superhuman vision, nor damn him for his blind haste to pluck unripe fruit.

Syme's *Roman Revolution* is not a book about Caesar and Augustus. It is a study of the metamorphosis of the regime and the administrative hierarchy. Caesar set in motion a process which was to last long after his time. Many of the measures he hit upon were temporary and of limited purpose, which left behind the impression of superficial action. On the other hand, the elevation of the non-political classes[73] had an effect long after his death. Syme is convinced that the history of the end of the Republic and the beginning of the Principate was that of the ruling classes. The fact that he does not mention the lower classes lies not in lack of interest but in lack of evidence. We know more about the upper classes because they had more freedom of action.[74] Rome was always ruled by an oligarchy, open or concealed,[75] and it is precisely this oligarchy which Syme presents to his readers. Caesar's new party is better portrayed by sketching men and their personal connections, hopes and ambitions, than by an investigation of political programmes and ideologies. Thus prosopography is a necessary instrument in Syme's hands, but it never impedes the account of events.

Syme offers technical matter for the specialist in special sections, but the more general reader has no difficulty in understanding the manifold adumbrations of the new Caesarian party. To contrast reviled good-for-nothings on the one hand and noble patriots on the other is schematic and leads to the wrong conclusions. Caesar's party was an amalgam of senators, knights, centurions, businessmen, bankers from the *municipia* and provinces, kings and princes. Caesar's connections with the representatives of business interests were as good as his connections with the landowners. He never preached a radical division of property. The heterogeneousness of his followers was the dictator's strength and made him independent of individual factions. Syme believed that Caesar, without benevolence, would have been a second Sulla or a Gaius Gracchus, had he not lacked a revolutionary programme. He was a true Roman, more than any other. The sources of his plans for a Hellenistic monarchy are either hostile or posthumous. Concerning his plans for the future, there is room for opinion, but no certainty. No evidence for such plans is to be found in his dictatorship, and, lastly, 'a fabricated concatenation of unrealized intentions may be logical, artistic and persuasive—but it is not history' (p. 271).

On this point Syme agrees with Adcock, who also argues that there is insufficient evidence to prove Caesar's official deification in his lifetime. All the honours he enjoyed can be explained as an exaggerated expression of recognition of what he had achieved.[76]

It is true that contemporary sources are often more valuable than posthumous ones. Nevertheless, one can scarcely imagine that Suetonius, of all people, should have invented the story of the honours offered to Caesar.

At any rate, with reference to Tiberius, he makes it abundantly clear that the princeps refused divine honours,

> Of many high honours he accepted only a few of the more modest. He barely consented to allow his birthday . . . to be recognized by the addition of a single two-horse chariot. He forbade the voting of temples, flamens and priests without his permission; and this he gave only with the understanding that they were not to be placed among the likenesses of the gods but among the adornments of the temples. He would not allow an oath to be taken ratifying his acts, nor the name Tiberius to be given to the month of September.
>
> (Suet., *Tib.* 26)[77]

There is no basis for the assumption that Suetonius was particularly hostile to Caesar;[78] in any case there is room for serious doubt that he is indulging in his own opinions. Had Caesar refused the honours (as Tiberius did) the fact would have been recorded. Indeed, Cassius Dio and Appian frequently reported his refusal to accept certain honours. And yet Suetonius' account is rejected because he was not Caesar's contemporary. But Cicero was.

In a letter of June 45 (*ad Att.* XII, 45), Cicero talked about Caesar as 'Synnaos/contubernalis Quirini'. This letter could be interpreted as a bad joke, had not Cicero's statements in the *Philippics* been even more pointed (II, 110). He listed certain divine honours in particular, and added, 'As Jupiter, as Mars, as Quirinus has a flamen, so the flamen to divine Julius is Marcus Antonius'. Turning to Antony, he castigated him, 'O detestable man, whether as priest of Caesar or of a dead man!'. This passage, weighty even in Syme's view,[79] caused scholars of the 1950s and 1960s to take up a novel position on Cicero's argument. That brings us to the fourth theory, which may be termed Revisionist.

THE REVISIONISTS

These scholars are all more sharply critical of Syme than of Meyer, and not one of them is prepared to come to terms with any diminution in Caesar's greatness. At first glance, it might be supposed that the Minimalists, who were British, would necessarily have been less enthusiastic about Caesar because they were reared on Shakespeare. They were probably undecided even in their youth whether the great hero of the drama was Caesar or Brutus.

However, that is not the case. Shakespeare modelled his tragedy on Plutarch, and accepted the latter's notion that Caesar was an ambitious man (Plut., *Caes.* 69). But Shakespeare was equally impressed by the tragedy of the conspirators, in that their work came to nothing even before it came to pass. Yet he did not despise Caesar, and it is no coincidence that these words were given to Antony, 'Caesar was the noblest man that ever lived in the tide of times'. And, as Prince Edward says in Richard III,

> This Julius Caesar was a famous man:
> With what his valour did enrich his wit,
> His wit set down to make his valour live;
> Death makes no conquest of this conqueror,
> For now he lives in fame, though not in life.

W. W. Fowler[80] is right when he stresses that Shakespeare's Brutus never censures Caesar the man. Only lesser intellects refuse to understand clearly Caesar's eruptions of *superbia,* and when Antony's slave, speaking on behalf of his master, says to Brutus, 'Caesar was mighty, bold, royal, and loving', the reader is alerted to the fact that this is not merely Antony's opinion. Shakespeare himself probably leaned toward this view, and, as we now turn to a description of the historians we designate Revisionists, we must count among them all those who, in rejecting Meyer's idea of a Hellenistic monarchy, are nevertheless not prepared to subscribe to the statement that Caesar was no more than a regular Roman dictator and the last Roman patrician, and that his similarities to Sulla were more striking than the differences (Adcock).

In 1953 J. Vogt published a new interpretation of the passage from Cicero's *Philippics*[81] cited above (pp. 32 f.), and came to the conclusion that Caesar really had enjoyed divine honours, and that, although the Romans would not have opposed the idea of such honours for a genius like Caesar, they would have shuddered at the title of king. V. Ehrenberg[82] took Vogt's reflections a stage further. In his opinion it was not the constitutional honours and the trappings to which Caesar owed his position—so much higher than that of a regular dictator—but to his personal power which grew from day to day. Ehrenberg accepted Vogt's explanation of the significance of 'bases for sacred statues, an enormous god-like statue in his house and his own priest', and came to the conclusion that, in regard to Caesar's general and religious policy, Roman and non-Roman elements alike characterized his regime. As a result he was the first of the Caesars and not the last of the patricians.

K. Kraft contributed extremely detailed investigations of the coins of that period which led him to recognize that Caesar's aim was to reintroduce the old pattern of Roman kingship and not the Hellenistic—oriental—form.[83] Kraft examined the wreath worn by Caesar on portrait coins and concluded that this was not the triumphator's laurel wreath, which he was permitted to wear continuously after his victory in Spain (Dio XLIII, 43, 1), but was a gold one as represented in Etruscan paintings and on coins and vases. By the time of the Lupercalia (February 15), Caesar is portrayed as wearing this wreath (*coronatus*) for the purpose of making clear to all present that he had in mind a 'royal symbol in the Roman national tradition' (p. 60). Therefore he indignantly refused the diadem offered by Antony, since gold wreath and diadem were incompatible.

Here we have the actual essence of the Revisionist school, which began to flourish after World War II. Yet even in historical research, 'there is nothing new under the sun'. References to kingship of an old Italian style are to be found earlier in Mommsen, and also, many years later, in A. Ferrabino. As far as the history of ideas is concerned 'Revisionism' goes back to A. Bachofen, but he had no influence of any sort on any historian. He believed in Rome's mission to subdue the sensual materialism of the East, and, by the establishment of the patriarchal state, to replace it by the virile spirit of the West. For him, Caesar was a western hero whose building of Rome was not after a foreign pattern. The argument had come full circle, 'from the son of the oriental Aphrodite had emerged the creator of the Western Empire'.[84] But, as pointed out, Bachofen made no impression on twentieth-century historians, and the immense influence of Meyer's work allowed the theory of a Roman type of kingship to sink into oblivion. Vogt, Ehrenberg and Kraft gave it fresh impetus, and many followed in their footsteps.

L. Wickert[85] positioned himself between the two camps. In his inaugural lecture in the Chair of Ancient History at Cologne, he essentially attached himself to Meyer's school. He remarked that Caesar, for all his greatness, could be considered as an interlude, 'Yielding to a playful impulse, one might, in theory, remove from history the monarchy of the strongest master Rome had ever produced, but never the principate of Augustus.' Likewise, he did not exclude Hellenistic influences on Caesar. But in the last resort Caesar's actual achievement is not to be derived from Hellenism. It is Caesarian and simultaneously Roman. Caesar was the first to embrace the idea of empire in an inspired fashion—he also decided to put it into practice. His most important achievement was the extension of the citizenship of Rome to citizenship of the empire. Rome, formerly head of a commonwealth, expanded to become head of an empire. The process of representation for the empire's population begins with the appointment of provincials to the Senate—in spite of the angry opposition of conservative Roman senators.

F. Vittinghoff[86] proceeded in this direction. In fact, he was concerned only with Caesar's colonization and policy on citizenship, but *inter alia* put forward the view that for Caesar, Italy and Rome signified the fulcrum of the empire. In Strabo (V, 216) we read, 'And at the present time . . . they (sc. the Italians) are all Romans', and in Vellius Pat. (II, 15, 2) they are already 'men of the same race and blood'. That was Caesar's idea of empire. In this respect, it is unproductive to look to the Hellenistic kings as prototypes. Caesar's work was so completely orientated towards the future that his contemporaries could not appraise it (p. 95).

In 1958 H. Oppermann, who had already proved to be a distinguished Caesarian scholar by his earlier work on Caesar as a man of letters, stated that Meyer's evidence for the Hellenistic monarchy did not always stand up to meticulous examination.[87] In his opinion, a sharp distinction should be drawn between Caesar's titulature in Rome and in the Empire. The decision on Caesar's title in the area designated *domi* was postponed until the end of the projected Parthian war. Until 44 BC he was satisfied with the dictatorship, an entirely Roman office, which Sulla had also held. Kingship should apply only in the realm of *militiae*: it would appear natural to the eastern regions. Oppermann pointed out that this new form of world dominion, unlike divine kingship, was not based on the mysterious incarnation of a god in human form—a mystery that man cannot grasp, but before which he can only bend the knee—but on the greatness and majesty of the man in question. That is not a Hellenistic idea but a European one, and Caesar had fought for the leadership of the European part of the empire. His victory over Pompey signified the victory of the West in the historic struggle between Europe and Asia.

Charisma,[88] F. Taeger's two-volume work, appeared two years later. Taeger had no doubts about Caesar's steadfast determination to translate his power into the form of a kingdom to be held by his house in perpetuity and of his equally firm belief in the providential nature of his undertaking. Incarnation was indispensable to his political position, and the connection of the cult of *clementia* with the cult of Caesar presupposed deification as an established component of the new ruling ideology. On the one hand the great Julius resembled Alexander (Taeger remained convinced that Caesar was already *divus* in his lifetime), yet Meyer's view that Caesar intended to introduce a Hellenistic monarchy to Rome is but a half-truth. In an attempt to demonstrate that Caesar's efforts in this direction were a product of the Roman environment rather than an import from the Orient, Taeger remarked, 'Caesar's position aroused in his opponents and adherents attitudes that promoted him to the realm of charisma. This emotion was genuine and had its roots in Roman religion.'

R. Klein also attempted to describe a Caesar whose thought took root from the irrational and the metaphysical.[89] As a pupil of Seel, he also believed that history cannot be realized without a tincture of the irrational, the tragic and the transcendental. Klein rejected Meyer's notion of a Hellenistic monarchy as well as his observation that Caesar considered religion merely as a tool to be used for political ends.[90] He tended to follow B. E. Giovanetti, who stressed Caesar's attachment to the irrational.[91] Romulus was not a mere model for Caesar, and in this respect the chapters in Book II of Dionysius of Halicarnassus, recognized many years previously by M. Pohlenz as a piece of political pamphleteering of the Caesarian period, served as a useful source for Klein.[92] As *Basileus,* alongside supreme command in war, Caesar was obliged to exercise the supreme religious functions in the state. His *Regnum* was not an office but a sacred duty, and the people were obliged to suffer his performance of it as the rule of a deity.

Finally, J. Dobesch[93] also scrutinized yet once more Caesar's deification in his lifetime and campaign for the royal title. His analysis showed that Caesar did desire royal dignity and divine status. But, in spite of his well-ordered source material and his clear and logical style, Dobesch could not produce any new evidence because it simply does not exist. Thus many readers continued to harbour doubts. As one conservative scholar opposed to the theory of divine kingship put it, 'You cannot build a king out of a golden crown and a pair of red shoes' (Balsdon).[94]

Those who reject Caesar's aims to achieve kingship prove less extreme than the exponents of such a view. It is perhaps interesting to note that the opponents of the kingship theory make use of the same arguments as those employed by Napoleon I when he composed *Précis des Guerres de Jules César* in exile on St Helena. Napoleon concluded that the accounts of Caesar's efforts to become king were a shameless slander on the part of his assassins, 'To justify after the event a murder that was slipshod in its execution and ill-advised, the conspirators and their partisans alleged that Caesar wanted to make himself king,

a statement obviously constituting an absurdity and calumny . . .' The French emperor could hardly imagine that Caesar could be capable of seeking 'stability and grandeur' in the crown of a Philip, Perseus, Attalus, Mithridates, Pharnaces or Ptolemy.[95]

A more detailed scrutiny of the 'revisionist' view would unnecessarily inflate this chapter. This brief survey may satisfy the non-specialist and professional historians will turn to the sources anyway. But the exception proves the rule, for the indefatigable studies of two great scholars—A. Alföldi and S. Weinstock, who devoted virtually their whole lives to the subject—can scarcely receive their due in a few lines. They ought to be treated in somewhat greater detail.

The essential significance of Alföldi's contribution lies in the fact that he was not content to evaluate once more the literary and epigraphic material, but took pains to analyse afresh and reinterpret the evidence of the coins. He was the leading exponent in our time of the view that, even if the sole rule of an autocrat had its origins in the Greek east, 'in the last resort this foreign element too became fused with Rome, and was eventually submerged in the political arena as on the battlefields'.

In his work on Caesar's monarchy published in 1952,[96] Alföldi attempted to evaluate the complex evidence of the coinage in relation to the events of the first months of the year 44 BC. He came to the clear conclusion that Caesar did, in fact, want the title of king, but the Senate begrudged it him. All attempts to achieve it also foundered in that year, and Caesar was eventually obliged to be content with the compromise solution that he could employ the title only in the provinces but had to be satisfied with *dictator perpetuo* (never *perpetuus!*) in Rome and Italy. This compromise solution was to be announced at the meeting of the Senate on March 15 on the basis of a Sibylline oracle. This step of Caesar's did away with his obligation to abdicate.

On the basis of his work on the coinage Alföldi established an exact chronology for the events of February and March of 44 BC. Until then it was generally accepted, and, in fact, based on an express assertion in Cicero (*Phil.* II, 87), that Caesar was already dictator for life at the time of the Lupercalia on February 15. Alföldi rejected Cicero's statement. In his assessment of an issue of M. Mettius (with the legend CAES. DICT. QVART.), he found that instead of the *lituus,* which normally appears on the *denarii* of Mettius, there is clearly recognizable the diadem, which Caesar refused at the Lupercalia, and dedicated to Jupiter on the Capitol. Alföldi spotted on the coins a diadem hanging on a hook (Alföldi, *loc. cit.* pls 2, 5, 6), and concluded that Mettius wished to perpetuate this gesture of Caesar's, for he could have struck these coins only immediately after February 15. In fact, Caesar does not appear on these coins as DICT. PERP. (dictator for life), but as DICT. QVART. (dictator for the fourth time).

Consequently, if Alföldi is right with his interpretation of the 'diadem', the exact chronology—with its far-reaching historical implications that literary sources cannot provide—appears to be:

1 January 44: *denarii* of the old style with 'Sulla's dream'

2 Beginning of February until shortly after February 15: issues with Caesar's portrait and legend CAES. DICT. QVART.

3 March I CAES. IMP.

4 After March I CAESAR DICTATOR PERPETVO

5 All the coins struck by Macer and Maridianus with the legend CAES. DICT. PERPETVO and CAESAR PARENS PATRIAE, portraying Caesar with veiled head, are to be attributed, at the earliest, to the period after the Ides of March

Up to April 10, the coins with DICT. PERP. remained in circulation but after the abolition of the dictatorship the coins with *parens patriae* appeared. At that point Antony needed to show Caesar in priestly garb, to demonstrate to the Roman people that its Pontifex Maximus had been murdered. He himself appears as consul on the denarius struck by Macer, with head covered and beard unshaven as a sign of mourning. No one can still harbour doubts about Caesar's final plans, for 'he assigned the charge of the mint and of the public revenues to his own slaves' (Suet., *Div. Jul.* 76, 3), and that, too, was one of the reasons that led to his murder.

Alföldi pursued the subject further in a series of articles in *Museum Helveticum,* the *Schweizer Münzblätter* and the *Schweizer Numismatische Rundschau,* etc.,[97] and later presented his discoveries to his followers and critics in two impressive volumes (only one of which has been published), entitled *Caesar im Jahre 44.*[98] He remained, apparently, largely true to his former opinions, although he modified certain points in matters of detail.

Alföldi was convinced of Caesar's endeavours towards monarchy, although he attempted to prove that they were not the sudden whim of a confident autocrat. Quite the contrary. In the time of Scipio Africanus a vague vision of a saviour was awakened in the Roman people (*Phoenix* XXIV (1970), p. 166), while since Sulla's time monarchy had been knocking at the gates of Rome. From the turn of the last century of the Republic the saviour theory was proclaimed on the annual issues of *denarii.* The belief in the return of a 'Golden Age' became fused with the yearning of the masses for a new Romulus. Alföldi pointed out that even those in the highest circles in Rome attempted to work out the imminent return of the ideal king of antiquity through the arithmetical tricks of astrology. Prominent politicians from Sulla to Augustus wanted to be considered the new Romulus. The misgivings of lesser persons concerning a rule by a king—so dreaded by the Senate—disappeared over the years. For them the dream come true would be the return of a king, and the hated symbols of sovereignty, such as diadem, sceptre and the ruler's wreath, are concealed by the apparently guiltless garb of a king of

remote antiquity. Thus a predisposition for a king's actual return is facilitated by fantasy.

In 67 BC, Pompey was reviled as Romulus by a consul, yet five years later Romulus appeared on the issues of *denarii* struck by M. Plaetorius Cestianus. Pompey's exaltation at the end of the Republic—an alternative to his glorification as saviour—had to be enveloped in the Romulus Allegory.[99] Foundation and establishment of a new order were prized even by Cicero as acts of the highest virtue, and the concepts *conditor, servator, parens* and *deus* are inseparable from the concept of the new Romulus.

The virtues of Romulus as depicted by Dionysius of Halicarnassus are intelligible only through their adaptation to Caesar's political programme. Caesar was reviled as Romulus by Catullus (29, 5; 28, 15; 49, 1), yet Alföldi had no doubt that in the last phase of his life Caesar strove to be compared with Romulus. He wanted to derive his claim to renew Romulus' virtues as ruler from his family tradition: the red shoes, the garb of the former kings, the purple gown and white diadem[100] were symbols of the Caesarian-Romulean monarchy that Caesar so fervently desired. But, since he also knew how much the appellation 'king' in Rome was held in odium, his real aim had to be camouflaged by the catchword *parens patriae.*

The old father-symbol penetrated political life in the first century BC. Even before this it was a stereotyped honour accorded to many, and thus provided an established title for one. The expression *pater patriae* has a different significance with reference to Cicero than with reference to Caesar, who was continuously *parens* but never *pater,* and the Brundisium inscription, 'C. Julio Caesari pont. max. patri patriae' (*ILS* 71), is, in Alföldi's opinion, a scholarly forgery. Further, Cicero was hailed as *pater patriae* for giving the order for the execution of the Catilinarians, and his *severitas* was accordingly represented as the virtue of a saviour. Caesar, on the other hand, was called *parens patriae* on account of his *clementia.* The gentle, fatherly quality of the benevolent prince is antithesized with the tyrant's anger and the *mitissimus parens* with the *crudelis tyrannus* (*de dom.* 94). As domestic slaves swore by the *genius* of the head of the household, men must now swear by Caesar's *genius;* and, as, according to tradition, it was a worse offence to kill a *parens patriae* than to kill one's own father ('est atrocius patriae parentem quam suum occidere'). Caesar was foolish enough to discharge his bodyguard in the hope that he could rely on his legally established *sacrosanctitas.* That was his undoing, and Rome lost a man of unheard-of tolerance and magnanimous *clementia.*

Alföldi, it must be granted, never obscured his views in hazy phraseology. On the contrary, he ruthlessly judged the republican regime as 'a collective monarchy of the nobles who were sucking the blood from the Empire like leeches'.[101] It did not occur to him that Caesar broke the law by crossing the Rubicon, and he posed the question whether the frenzy of the gangs in Rome before Caesar's rise to power had been in any sense constitutional. 'One might describe the event in terms of an analogy, as the act of conceiving outside the mother's body, in the case of the Republic—a conception outside the constitution. The emergence of the child into the world spelt certain death for the mother.'

Likewise, Caesar should not be blamed for trying to become king. The idea occurred to him only after the Senate had showered him with honours—initially against his will—which eventually led him to overstep the limits of the permissible 'only after the chorus of time-servers had led the way'.[102] In an article, 'La divinisation de César', Alföldi also remarked that 'a slavish Senate' had pronounced Caesar a god.[103] In his general eulogy of Caesar he recalls the emotional style of nineteenth-century scholars, 'He (Caesar) wanted to rule as sovereign, but preferred to expose his body to his murderers' daggers rather than go on wasting his life away like a tyrant reliant on a bodyguard for safety. The *nobile letum Catonis* has its counterpart: the *nobile letum Caesaris*'.[104]

Despite the impressive collection of sources and numismatic evidence Alföldi used to support his thesis, his work attracted little attention in the English-speaking West. In E. S. Gruen's highly interesting and stimulating book, which concludes with an extensive bibliography, Alföldi is not mentioned[105]—whether accidentally or intentionally can only be surmised. Yet it must surely be recognized that Gruen totally disagrees with Alföldi, and rejects as 'hindsight' the theory that, since the time of Sulla, the idea of monarchy hovered like a bird of prey over the gates of Rome. Actually, in speaking of the Romans' longing for a great man, Alföldi reflected to some extent the remarks of Gundolf, written before Hitler's rise to power, 'Today, since the need for a strong man is voiced, since men, weary of critics and carpers, make do with sergeants instead of generals, since, particularly in Germany, the government of the people is entrusted to any especially noteworthy talent displayed by soldiers, economists, civil servants or writers . . .'

Alföldi himself admitted, 'My researches on the year 44 have been rejected without serious argument and have remained ignored.'[106] There are some important reasons why this is so. In the first place, there is no agreement about the significance of *pater patriae*. In Alföldi's view the expression *pater* constitutes a superior concept, embracing the whole essence of the *princeps*. This title, in his opinion, is the immediate prerequisite for one man's rule; it is not merely an honorary title; it puts the whole community under an obligation to the one in power.

Most scholars reject Alföldi's position. It was Mommsen's opinion that the title *pater* was not essential to the emperor's position, and that no rights were associated with it.[107] A. von Premerstein took it simply as an honorary title; for A. H. M. Jones it was 'a harmless and ornamental title and office', and even S. Weinstock attributed no decisive importance to it.[108] We cannot attempt a more detailed discussion of all the different opinions on this question, but it is sufficient to say that there is no agreement on the significance of the distinction between *parens* and *pater,* nor, indeed, on the significance of the title *imperator,* which Caesar, in Alföldi's view, adopted after his failure to be proclaimed king on 15 February 44, since only this title remained acceptable to the republicans.[109]

Despite their readiness to make use of Dio, Appian, Suetonius and Plutarch as important sources for Caesar's history, modern scholars are not prepared, without further discussion, to take as gospel every statement of later sources. Alföldi, in turn, was not prepared to recognize this problem, and introduced the coinage as conclusive proof for his fundamental statements about Caesar's honours. But it is precisely here that he encountered the most decisive opposition from his fellow numismatists. Although impressed by his acuteness and originality, they did not agree that the Roman mint-masters would have worked into their coins 'shrewdly conceived combinations of types'.[110] A numismatist as remarkable as M. H. Crawford is strongly critical of Alföldi's work.[111] The latter's basic argument, that it was possible to discover on the coinage of the first century BC the desire for a new Romulus, is rejected as 'obsessed with supposed prophecies of a golden age and full of surprising assertions'.[112]

In a short footnote (n. 108), Weinstock, who was ideologically not far removed from Alföldi, observed that although the latter had devoted a hundred pages to an examination of the concept *pater patriae* only a few of them touch on the problem. Alföldi continued the argument with Weinstock—after the latter's death—and replied in a long article (*Gnomon* XII 1975, 154-79). Non-specialists should steer clear of such debates. Yet, the most important objections raised by experts such as C. M. Kraay and R. A. G. Carson in England, and, independently, by H. Volkmann in Germany, must be briefly mentioned.[113]

All scholars are united in their recognition of Alföldi's pains to work out a precise chronological table of the issues and a detailed sequence of the dictator's intentions. Kraay, however, maintained that most of Alföldi's conclusions were untenable, and that they yielded no key to Caesar's policy. Alföldi was convinced that he could prove which coins were struck before February 15, which were struck in the second half of February, and which were struck at the beginning of March. But on this point there is no agreement. These are weighty questions not to be ignored.

Carson rejected the conclusion that Caesar, convinced of the failure of his attempt to become king on February 15, allowed coins to be struck in the second half of February merely with the legend IMP., and only at the beginning of March issued those with DICT. PERP. It is, however, expressly reported in a contemporary source such as Cicero (*Phil.* II, 34; 87) that Caesar was already *dictator perpetuus* on February 15. Why, then, throw away a reliable literary source in favour of a baseless numismatic theory? Why should the assumption of the title *imperator* be seen as surrender to the republicans? Was even a ten-year dictatorship so acceptable to these republicans?

Furthermore, on what ground should it be supposed that the series with CAES. DICT. (later replaced by PATER PATRIAE) and those with the legend CAES. IMP. were not struck simultaneously (1) as a normal state issue, which Caesar employed to demonstrate the offices on the basis of which he governed, or (2) to supply coinage for the Parthian wars, designed by the commander-in-chief?

Finally, even if it is generally recognized that the discovery of the Mettius *denarius* in the Königliches Munzkabinett at The Hague (unknown until 1952), and its description, was a brilliant stroke by Alföldi, it remains hazardous to draw very far-reaching inferences when only a single specimen is available for study. Alföldi's own analysis arouses serious doubt. Kraay is not convinced that the *denarius* shows Caesar's diadem hanging up in the temple, and takes it as unproven that a *lituus* is not here quite simply in question. Indeed, it is true that on the rest of the Mettius *denarii* with the legend CAES. DICT. QVART. a *lituus* inclined to the right instead of the left appears. But a *lituus* inclined to the left appears on Mettius *denarii* with the legend CAES. IMP., so it is not unusual.

The most important argument in opposition to Alföldi's views appeared in a long monograph by D. Felber.[114] Naturally, he follows the views of Kraay and Carson relating to the chronology of the coins. However, he returns to the conclusion that Caesar became dictator for life on February 15, and rejects Alföldi's interpretation derived from 'Sulla's Dream', that coins with different legends are to be put in chronological order and that all the issues with the *caput velatum* are posthumous.

We shall return to Felber in another connection; at this point it need only be remarked that his devastating criticism could lead to the conclusion that one should not attribute an exaggerated significance to coins. It would be worth while to ponder on Jones' sensible advice, 'If numismatists wish . . . to assist historians, I would suggest that they should pay less attention to the political interpretation of the coins . . . Latterly the value of numismatic evidence has tended to be overstrained and its interpretation has become over-subtle'.[115]

To sum up, it must be said that Alföldi's opponents have not actually proven any new theory, but have demolished his argument by their sceptical observations and thereby pointed in a new direction.

If one studies Alföldi's thorough criticism of Weinstock's book,[116] one might be surprised that the critic and the subject of his criticism belong to the same school, here termed the Revisionist. But in fact Alföldi's criticism was not fundamental. His attack on Weinstock's numismatic analysis was the more acute, mainly because the latter had taken scarcely any notice of the results of his own research.

In numerous details, *inter alia* in matters of ancient Roman religion, he also stands apart from Weinstock.

By and large, however, there are no differences of opinion between the two scholars, as Alföldi dealt with the question of kingship, and Weinstock concerned himself with the deification. They agree that Caesar strove for both in his lifetime, even if Weinstock's precise wording was the more cautious and reserved. His enormous knowledge was steeped in German and Italian scholarship, but in the course of a long life in the atmosphere of an Oxford college he adapted to English style and English ways of thought. Using expressions like 'may' and 'might' he frequently softened the pointedness of an argument that would doubtless have aroused antagonism in another language.

Weinstock guarded against speaking of Caesar's far-reaching schemes, but likewise did not sketch him as a child of fortune or superman. Yet he, too, agreed with the view, as did Alföldi, that it was Caesar's first task to set up a monarchy (p. 281), and that at a certain point of time he was not satisfied with it, 'While fighting in Parthia, his rule was to be strengthened by religious means and his divinity was to be established gradually' (p. 286). Both Alföldi and Weinstock agreed that religious honours at this point became a constitutional necessity, since actual power was transferred from the annual magistrates to the one and only ruler.[117]

Weinstock's position on deification mirrored Alföldi's criticism of Meyer's idea of a Hellenistic monarchy and his substitution of the idea of a western monarchy, 'Caesar's new position in Rome was to be prepared in a Roman fashion: the influence of Greek Soteres, Gods, and kings can be felt, but what was made of it was due to the influence of an old Roman tradition' (p. 167), and, further, '[Caesar] did not want to appear as an innovator, nor to spread a new philosophy of life, but to be guided by tradition—yet one who at the end radically broke with it' (p. 411). This is the fundamental view that made Weinstock a representative of the Revisionist school. It is also the main theme of his book *Divus Julius*, which is not only a work on the deification of Caesar but a history of ideas, with the object of explaining how a particular atmosphere facilitated such deification. Since a mechanical incorporation of oriental rites into Rome appeared to him logically unacceptable, Weinstock described the development of the 'cults of personified values', *concordia, salus, pietas, victoria, honos, virtus, iustitia,* and finally, of course, *clementia,* in all their details,—one of the finest chapters in the book. The connection of these virtues with a statesman forms the core of the whole work.

In Weinstock's 450 closely-printed pages Caesar appears before us, not as the acute, tireless politician and army commander or the dictator driven by ambition, but 'as an imaginative and daring religious reformer who created and planned new cults, accepted extraordinary honours and died when he was about to become a divine ruler' (*ibid.*).

In contrast to this view Alföldi particularly stressed the enthusiasm with which the Senate compelled Caesar to accept all possible honours. But Weinstock forcefully maintained, 'Caesar was not a passive recipient. The decrees often fulfilled his expectations' (p. 412). 'He was involved in detailed planning of his cult and moved first towards an accumulation of priesthoods.' It was no accident that Caesar made every effort so that his adoptive son should inherit the office of Pontifex Maximus from him (p. 33). 'Varro dedicated to him his *Antiquitates Rerum divinarum* and Granius Flaccus *De indigitamentis* which was probably another antiquarian survey of prayer and ritual' (p. 32). Finally Caesar emerges as one who strove after a 'sacred kingship' (p. 323).

In Weinstock's favour it must be said that he warned his readers that some of his assertions were nothing more than learned conjectures, often emerging from evidence of doubtful reliability. His greatest service was to promote general public awareness of an elementary fact: that one ought not to judge Caesar without taking into account the religious background of the time (p. 260), and in this respect his work is preferable to that of B. E. Giovanetti published in 1937.

But even after a thorough study of his comprehensive work some questions remain, of which a single example may suffice. At one point Weinstock described in detail the religious tradition of the Julian family, a tradition that had its origins in Bovillae. He analysed a small incident related by Cassius Dio (XLI, 39, 2), of how Caesar set about sacrificing a bull to Fortuna, before putting to sea in pursuit of Pompey, and of how the bull eluded him. Weinstock arrived at a far-fetched interpretation—again taking assistance from the little word 'may', 'He may have intended to make the bull of Bovillae as popular as the she-wolf of Rome' (p. 7). The Julii had for years been responsible for local rites in Bovillae—and probably also in Alba. The ritual of the Feriae Latinae was celebrated on the Alban Mount by a *rex,* which explains why, in 45 BC, Caesar began to dress in the garb of the Alban kings.

But with the help of the word 'may' a different conjecture is also possible: the bull was also the ensign of the Italians, and if Vell. Pat. II, 27, 2 reports that Italian freedom was ravaged by the Roman wolves, so the Roman she-wolf's subjection by the Italian bull may be symbolically portrayed on the coinage (Hill, *Hist. Roman Coins* (1909), pl. XI, 49). Perhaps one should be permitted the conjecture that Caesar did not have his family emblem in mind at all, but was rather attempting to drop a hint to the Italians that their support in the war against Pompey could turn out to be profitable for them. And the question mark remains.

In addition, it is hard to be convinced that Caesar was a religious man, for Weinstock himself expressed astonishment that Caesar did not take the trouble in any of his writings to stress that he was a citizen who continually observed his religious duty (p. 26). It must also be added that Caesar—like every influential Roman—had a very good understanding indeed of how the masses could be manipulated with the aid of religion (Polyb. VI, 56), but he never allowed himself to be deterred from his purpose by religious scruples (Suet., *Div. Jul.* 59, 1; 81, 4).

Weinstock's assumption that Caesar treated Apollo as his ancestral god remains only a conjecture based on a passage of Dio concerning the statement of Atia to the effect that Apollo begat her son. Likewise, no one allows himself to be convinced that Caesar became Jupiter Julius in his lifetime. None of the stories that appear in Dio (such as p. 264, n. 6, on Dio XLI, 15, 4; 16, 4), can be regarded as solid fact beyond all doubt.[118] All scholars from Mommsen to Adcock read these same sources, and the majority formed the conclusion that it was only after his death that Caesar legally became *divus.*[119] But the Revisionists stubbornly stick to their view, and eventually Balsdon desisted from further discussion: 'The truth is that in this sharp division of opinion scholars on either side preach to the converted.'[120]

In our view, Vogt's briefer and more penetrating article would have sufficed to present us with the insoluble problem. Some may have presumed that further discussion was futile. And yet it is not surprising that by way of reaction another group of scholars surfaced whom we term the Sceptics.

THE SCEPTICS

This section does not permit as simple a systematization as the earlier ones. There is no lack of common ground, yet most of the adherents of this school go their own ways. In general, it may be said that the Sceptics are usually prepared to accept the fact that even with the evidence that is available today it is impossible to penetrate to the full truth. At the outset they abandoned research into intentions and questions such as 'Did Caesar strive after honours, or was it the Senate that showered him with honours?', because satisfactory answers are not possible.

One has the impression that the consequences of World War II are readily discernible in the historical research of the last thirty years. Not only has Germany taken enormous strides towards the Anglo-Saxon democracies, but disapproving remarks about German historical research have disappeared from English works; on some issues an exchange of roles seems to have taken place. In fact, an extremely sceptical view on the divinity of humans might have been expected in the British Isles. Yet we read in Jocelyn Toynbee, a most distinguished archaeologist, that 'to the Greeks and Romans men and gods were not on two completely separated differential levels, and that a mortal could move godward by ascending degrees until he reached virtual identification with an immortal god'. She thinks that, with the aid of detailed research, 'the case of transition from man to god can be observed'.[121]

Precisely the opposite can be read in Carl Joachim Classen's article 'Gottmenschen in der römischen Republik'.[122]

He comes to the conclusion that no individual Roman was honoured in a way that brought him nearer to the gods either in his lifetime or after his death. Contrary to the Greek conception, a deep gulf separated man and god. *Genii* are not divine, for there are as many *genii* as there are living men. Sacrifices are a way of offering honour and respect: they are also owed to gods, but not only to gods. They are a kind of thanksgiving for a particular achievement brought to fulfilment. Classen is prepared to admit that Caesar's measures were more audacious than those of all his predecessors, but no more than that.

Of course, everything cannot be blamed on World War II. E. J. Bickermann's warning, voiced in 1930, must not be forgotten, especially with regard to research into the emperor cult.[123] In his opinion it was not permissible 'to confuse ideology with the sacral law which alone determines worship, and nobody should confuse divinity and association with the divine'.[124]

A new view can be traced in the research of C. Habicht,[125] which was also mirrored in studies of Caesar and his desire for deification. R. Cohen remarked that the ruler cult is 'the most delicate question in the organization of monarchy',[126] and in L. Cerfaux and J. Tondriau we read, 'A cult is a matter of feeling, and the intentions that dictate it almost always escape us. Nothing is more dangerous than to try to reconstruct, above all in matters of religion, the mentality and reasoning of a man of the ancient world.'[127] These warnings were eventually heeded.

M. Liberanome, who was concerned with Caesar's aims for kingship, was much more cautious than Weinstock, although he admits the religious vitality of the people.[128] Elsewhere we noted Felber's decisive objections to Alföldi's chronology derived from the coinage, but he should again be mentioned in the present context, since he can serve as a prototype for the 'Sceptics'. Not content merely with a fresh examination of the numismatic material, Felber also reassessed the literary sources from which conclusions concerning Caesar's aim for kingship and deification may suitably be drawn, 'It is to be doubted that Caesar, in the attire in which he showed himself to the public at the Lupercalia, was unmistakably distinguished as the new Romulus and old Roman king.'[129] And, 'the assertion that Caesar had already introduced the title *imperator* as a personal name and mark of the ruler in the sense of the *praenomen imperatoris* of the empire, is untenable' (pp. 231 ff.).[130] And, 'the view that the dictator intended to acquire the title of king with the aid of a sibylline oracle does not hold water' (pp. 254 ff.). And finally (from the sources at our disposal), '. . . one can get no answer to the question whether Caesar, in fact, wanted to establish a kingdom' (p. 273).

Gustav Haber,[131] a pupil of Vogt, is also doubtful about Caesar's aims regarding kingship, and in 1968 Helga Gesche, a pupil of K. Kraft, published a brief, clear, and impressive book, which provides a fundamental analysis of all the literary, epigraphic and numismatic material connected with the deification of Caesar.[132] Her critics must be impressed by the meticulousness of her investigations, even if they do not agree with her conclusions.[133] Frau Gesche particularly stresses the difference between the concepts *Vergötterung* and *Vergottung,* and comes to the clear conclusion that on the coins struck before Caesar's death epithets such as *Deus* or *Divus Caesar* are missing, and that the dictator was never represented as a god (p. 16, especially n. 26).

Nevertheless, Helga Gesche, for all her caution, also believes that Caesar not only strove for deification, but also planned in advance for the time after his death. Of course, there is no evidence for such a view as yet, and, therefore, it is pointless to start the discussion afresh. As the source material at our disposal does not allow for a decision, it would be preferable to abandon the question for the time being, rather than hazard further guesses. As a sceptical English scholar put it, 'The foot of Hercules may be a sufficient clue to his stature, but we shall scarcely succeed in reconstructing him from the parings of his toenails.'[134]

The real protagonist of sober judgment in Caesar's case is Hermann Strasburger. As far back as 1937, in his review of H. Rudolph's *Stadt und Staat im römischen Italien* (Leipzig 1935), he warned against treating Caesar as a superman, and attempted to put him into measured perspective.[135] The proper perspective, however, was achieved in his brilliant essay 'Caesar im Urteil der Zeitgenossen', with which we introduced this historiographic section.

W. Schmitthenner, too, in a thorough analysis of all the events preceding the assassination of Caesar, had to take into account the doubts of numerous scholars, *viz.* that with regard to Caesar's final plans there can be only opinion, but no certainty, despite the pains and discoveries of the numismatists. Schmitthenner's sceptical view contained a warning, 'If we allow ourselves to be led by the search for truth, positions that are compulsorily established suddenly become open and inexact.'[136]

Strasburger's influence was felt as much in England as in Germany. Thus R. E. Smith, for instance, was not interested in whether Caesar really aimed at kingship, 'Whether Caesar ever had in mind to take the name of king we cannot know, nor does it greatly matter.'[137] Smith, like Strasburger, was mainly concerned with what Caesar's contemporaries thought about him, and assumed that they considered him a tyrant who put himself at the head of a Republic that stood for annual magistrates.

One finds similar conclusions, although based on a different theoretical foundation, in Christian Meier's brief remarks about Caesar.[138] In his opinion, the basic reason for Caesar's failure lay in the fundamental circumstances of the world in which he lived, not in this or that mistake or attribute of the dictator. Meier finds little value in posing the question of whether Caesar intended to found a monarchy. We simply do not know that. We know only

that he reigned as a monarch and possessed the full powers of a monarch. 'He could command, dispose, forbid, establish institutions, do away with them, alter them, give laws, circumvent them, break them, elect and suspend magistrates as he willed.'

We know, too, that Caesar was given exaggerated honours, partly associated with royalty and partly with divinity, without being admittedly marked out as a king or god. Meier supposes that Caesar either had not given any thought to instituting a monarchy in Rome, or at least saw no viable way of approaching this aim. He was, above all, a pragmatist and improviser, and convinced himself that he could improve everything.

Meier stated that to Caesar and his followers the question of *regnum* and *respublica* was one and the same. His considerations were those of a typical Roman aristocrat who conceived no new constitutional ideas. 'Had the commonwealth been a piece of clay, politics a matter of manufacture, and not a vital process of manoeuvring, then Caesar would have been quite happy.' In truth, things appeared to be quite different. Meier pointed out that the omnipotent victor and dictator Caesar was actually powerless (*ohnmächtig*). That everything depended on him

disturbed him no less than it vexed Cicero. Too many demands were made upon him; he felt oppressed, and as a result of *ennui* planned a Parthian war instead of restructuring the state and society. This was not due to Caesar's personality or character. Within Roman society there was no touchpoint which might have sparked off a direct conflict, in the course of which it might have been possible to work towards a new structure. To do this, there would have to have been some sort of articulated social group or class involved in a kind of emergency, surmountable only through a fundamental and comprehensive reform (or revolution). In the 50s and 40s of the first century BC the principle of the commonwealth was only extended, not supplanted, and Caesar's personality can be understood in the context of a crisis without an alternative.

Meier's view is contained in a popular work that until now has provoked only an insignificant response. Yet, a thorough investigation in the direction taken by this book would be desirable, although Meier himself doubted the interests of his professional colleagues in themes of this kind.

This survey would not be complete without a reference to J. H. Collins, a scholar who is not easily classified although he wrote many important works including an excellent article, 'Caesar and the Corruption of Power'.[139] An American who worked under Gelzer in Germany, he brought his critical examination of the sources to a high level, but did not hesitate to make use of the social sciences such as sociology and psychology in his research.[140] Collins believed that contemporary researchers shrink from generalizations, which are reserved for chatter in the corridors and the faculty commonrooms. He was convinced that there is one Caesar for the years between 60 and 48 BC and another for the years between 46 and 44 BC. The turning-point is thus the year 47 BC, the year that brought him into contact with the East and Cleopatra. She was more than a mistress. She was, as Horace put it, 'no ordinary woman'.

Collins maintained that Caesar's contemporaries also noticed changes in his nature and conduct. Initially they believed in him, but in the final analysis they were bitterly disappointed. Between 50 and 46 BC Sallust was still expecting Caesar to reform the Republic. Collins supported this view by reference to the *Letters of Sallust,* in which the writer addressed these words to Caesar,

> But if you have in you the spirit which has from the very beginning dismayed the faction of the nobles, which restored the Roman commons to freedom after a grievous slavery, which in your praetorship routed your armed enemies without resort to arms, which has achieved so many and such glorious deeds at home and abroad that not even your enemies dare to make any complaint except of your greatness; if you have that spirit, pray give ear to what I shall say about our country's welfare.
>
> (*Letter to Caesar* I, 2, 4)

Sallust suggested a series of ideas for reform, but later lost all hope. Caesar changed into a tyrant and was murdered.

The serious doubts of H. Last, R. Syme and E. Fraenkel as to the authenticity of the letters did not prevent Collins from recognizing Sallust as the author. But Collins could have invoked the doubtless authentic work of Sallust, *The Jugurthine War* (3, 2), written after Caesar's death, 'For to rule one's country or subjects by force, although you both have the power to correct abuses, and do correct them, is nevertheless tyrannical . . .'

Cicero's relationship with Caesar (according to Collins) was similar. In the years between 55 and 53 BC they were intimate friends. Even after the civil wars Cicero continued to hope that Caesar would restore the Republic (his speech *Pro Marcello*). Later came disappointment, and then the irrevocable breach.[141] Cicero's mixed feelings towards Caesar were made abundantly clear in a letter of May 4, 44 (*ad Att.* XIV, 17). Cicero recalled that Caesar's behaviour towards him was moderate enough but otherwise unbending (*de div.* II, 23). Collins rightly emphasized that to Cicero Caesar was an enigma because he did not fit into any of the categories of his moral philosophy.

To sum up, in Collins' view there was sufficient evidence to suggest that Caesar's deepest political conviction was based on the old *republica.* Only when he began to despair of it did he feel that despotism was the only other way open to him. But his arrogance, illusions of grandeur, aggressiveness towards the Senate and respect for *nobilitas* of great distinction was not purely arbitrary. The view that the Republic deserted Caesar and not Caesar the Republic is the truer of the two; and, if that is right, Balsdon also deserves credit for his statement (*Historia* VII (1958), 86, 94) that Caesar was not murdered because he had changed, but because he had not changed.

To add further notion or surmise to this medley of opinions would be a real presumption, but I would like to suggest some thoughts that might be worthy of further study.

Caesar is one of the phenomena that appear upon the stage of history in times of crisis and hope. His rule drew support from a heterogeneous social group, a fact impressively proved by Syme's research. Yet it does not clearly emerge from all the studies we have mentioned that each of these groups expected a different solution to the acute problems of the day from Caesar. Each group saw him in a distinct way: some saw him as a man of clemency, others as the harsh ruler. Some expected a land distribution, others the cancellation of debts. Some hoped he would restore the Republic to its former greatness, others wanted its abolition once and for all. Each individual was convinced that his picture of Caesar was the right one.

Collins drew a distinction between the Caesar of the years before 46 BC and the Caesar of later years, which does not solve the problem, however, since there were 'several Caesars' before 46 BC as well as after it. In 49 BC Caesar crossed the Rubicon, apparently to plead for the tribunes' rights, but in the same year he himself infringed on the rights of Metellus when he tried to make himself master of the treasury in the temple of Saturn.

In 49 BC a cancellation of debts was generally expected, but towards the end of that year the money-lenders, bankers and wholesale merchants were among Caesar's most loyal followers. After the crossing of the Rubicon, there was some expectation that Caesar would reach an understanding with all the members of the *nobilitas;* indeed, he made extraordinary efforts to reach such an understanding with them. Many were receptive to his canvassing, and the list of consuls for the years between 49 and 44 BC proves that the firmly entrenched *nobilitas* understood how necessary it was to preserve their influence in the state.

Who and what, then, was Caesar? Strasburger and Balsdon, Béranger and others proved that Caesar was a tyrant.[142] But that was only in the eyes of a limited group of senators in the latter days of Caesar's life. Did the people think so too? In another book[143] I have attempted to explore the masses' image of Caesar. It is not easy to free oneself of the picture of Caesar as portrayed, above all, in the writings of Cicero and Sallust because the common man wrote no literary works and it is difficult to say with certainty what the masses thought. But the attempt is worth while. From close consideration of his conduct, however, there is no doubt about how Caesar wanted to appear in the eyes of the people, and that he held himself up to the plebs as the popular father-figure freed from the shackles of the Senate.

There are historians who maintain that the similarities between Caesar and Pompey are greater than the differences. Even if that is true, and the difference is much less than we suppose, the Roman plebs were not of this opinion. When Julius Caesar organized games and festivals, on a generous scale, the people were jubilant. Yet, when Pompey permitted eighteen elephants and five hundred lions to be brought into the arena, sympathy was shown for the animals and he was met with angry abuse.[144] Why? How did the ideal figure of a leader appear in the eyes of the people? It is apparent that concern for the physical well-being of the masses was only one factor. All Roman rulers bribed the people with bread and circuses, and yet the one was popular and the other hated. Seneca provided us with the answer: the giving is not the decisive factor but the manner of the giving.[145] 'Idem est quod datur, sed interest quomodo detur'. The people were more easily swayed by how a ruler did than by what he did, and respected the one who at least took the trouble to appear popular.[146] When Caesar decided to live in the poor quarter (before the elections!), the people saw no false altruism in the action.[147] They preferred him to Pompey, who made not the slightest effort 'to climb down to the people'. Therefore, it is not surprising that after Ilerda all 'civil war games' played by Roman children ended with the victory of the 'Caesarians'.[148] The vast mass of the people loathed the members of the *nobilitas,* but were powerless against them. The most popular political leaders (all aristocrats in origin) were those who criticized and debased the existing 'establishment' of senators in public and *coram publico* made much of the fact that they—'although senators themselves'—were not the slaves of their class.[149] The common people are not always as capricious as the sources make out. Perhaps Goethe was quite right when he wrote,

> Tell me, are we doing the right thing? We must deceive the rabble, See just how inept, how boorish, and
> how transparently stupid it is! It appears inept and stupid, just
> because you are deceiving it, Only be honest, and it, believe me,
> is human and shrewd.

(Venetian Epigrams).

Caesar grasped every opportunity and spared no efforts to appear to be the people's friend, a man whose chief concern was the well-being of the common man.

Is that the true Caesar? I have never maintained so. I suppose there will be those who will say that my position is influenced by the conduct of those politicians in our age of mass media who are primarily interested in burnishing their personal image before the television cameras and the press.

Such criticism would be justified. Each generation writes history anew and adds its own ingredient to existing knowledge. I cannot quarrel with Friedrich Frhr. von Wieser's observation that the present is the teacher of the knowledge of the past. I have not discovered the quest for the 'image'. It does exist in the sources, but it seems to me that insufficient attention has been paid to it. In any case, this is not the last word on Caesar's place in history, and I am far from solving the enigma of Caesar the man.

If we tried to discover how the Gauls,[150] the Jews, the *municipales* in Italy or the merchants in Spain saw Caesar, it would become clear that there are still several 'Caesars'. But, even if we could not know which of them is the 'true' Caesar, we would better understand why he remains such an enigma to the present day. 'Maxima quaeque ambigua sunt'—it is precisely the most important state of affairs that remain ambiguous (Tac., *Ann.* III, 19, 2).[151]

However, nothing is achieved by extreme scepticism. A Cambridge modern historian explains, 'The historian who tries to reject everything that is unproven will be rejecting much that is true. His talent lies neither in a corrosive and tiresome scepticism about everything, nor in absolute positivism, but in discernment and discrimination, best called historical understanding'.[152]

If we knew exactly what Caesar's intentions were, our subject would become wholly factual. But since we do not know them, we must be content with the English maxim, 'People should be judged by facts, not by alleged intentions'. What, then, are these facts? Thirty-eight laws and measures are supposedly associated with Caesar's name. It ought to be possible, by a thorough investigation of these laws and measures, to understand how Caesar was assessed by different sections of the public? It is worth

making the attempt. Moreover, can something be learned about Caesar's aims and personality from his laws?

Notes

1. This chapter is in no way designed to be exhaustive. It is intended as a general survey for the educated reader, not for the specialist. In addition, the interested reader might like to read further in G. Walter, *César,* Paris 1947; M. Rambaud, *L'art de déformation historique dans les commentaries de César,* Paris 1966; *id.,* 'Rapport sur César', Ass. G. Budé, *Actes Congr. Lyons* 1958, Paris 1960, pp. 205-38; J. H. Collins, 'A Selective Survey of Caesar Scholarship since 1935', *Class. World* 57 (1963/64), pp. 46-51 and pp. 81-88; H. Opperman, 'Probleme und heutiger Stand der Caesarforschung', ed. D. Rasmussen, *Caesar, WdF.* XLIII, Darmstadt 1976, pp. 485-522.

   While the present book was in preparation it was too late for me to take into account Helga Gesche, *Caesar, Erträge, der Forschung,* vol. LI, Darmstadt 1976. In this work Helga Gesche has collected and arranged chronologically and by subject some 2,000 titles selected from the academic literature published between 1918 and 1972-73. More important is the fact that she succeeded in overcoming an almost insurmountable task in producing not merely a survey of the literature but an accompanying critique of outstanding quality that immediately makes all other surveys of research seem out of date. In the not too distant future her work will rank as an essential component of every Caesarian scholar's library, and in the course of time the comprehensive bibliography can be cited, quite simply, by a brief reference, 'see Gesche, No. 620' etc. Nor was E. Wistrand's excellent study, *Caesar and contemporary Roman society.* Göteborg 1978, taken into account.

2. H. Stasburger, 'Caesar im Urteil der Zeitgenossen', *Hist. Zeitschrift* 175 (1953), pp. 225-64, Darmstadt 1968.

3. On the concept of 'image' in classical antiquity, see Appendix, p. 214.

4. Plut., *Caes.* 32; App., *BC* II, 35.

5. H. Strasburger, *Caesars Eintritt in die Geschichte,* Munich 1938; L. R. Taylor, 'The Rise of Julius Caesar', *Greece and Rome* IV (1957), pp. 10-18; 'Caesar's Early Career', *Classical Philology* XXXVI (1941), pp. 421 ff.

6. Suet., *Div. Jul.* 9, 2.

7. R. Syme, *The Roman Revolution,* Oxford 1939, p. 47, cf. J. Carcopino, *Les Etapes de l'impérialisme Romain,* Paris 1961, pp. 118 ff.; *id., Julius César,* Paris 1968.

8. See the recently published study of Kurt Raaflaub, 'Dignitatis contentio', *Vestigia,* vol. 20, Munich 1974.

9. Caes., *BC.* III, 57, 4. Similarly, too, U. Knoche in his article 'Die geistige Vorbereitung der augustäischen Epoche', in *Das neue Bild der Antike* (1942), p. 213: 'But actually it is astonishing and shocking (*sic!*) how small a role the idea of empire plays at all here. And it is extraordinary that Caesar, the master of propaganda, allowed this role to escape him.' Naturally Knoche particularly underlines Caesar's notions of leadership and following. This volume appeared at the time of the Nazi regime in Germany, and was edited by H. Berve.

10. *BC.* I, 32, 7. It is noteworthy that Strasburger does not quote the second part of Caesar's suggestion, I, 32, 7, 'But if they shrink through fear he will not burden them, and will administer the state himself.' That is simultaneously an invitation and a threat, and it is scarcely to be supposed that the Senate was overjoyed about it. See J. H. Collins, 'Caesar and the Corruption of Power', *Historia* IV (1955), p. 445.

11. W. den Boer, 'Caesar zweitausend Jahre nach seinem Tod', *WdF* XLIII, p. 436.

12. M. Gelzer, 'War Caesar ein Staatsmann?', *Hist. Zeitschrift* 178 (1954), pp. 449-70 (= *Kleine Schriften*, Wiesbaden 1963, vol. II, pp. 286 ff.).

13. *Id., Kleine Schriften,* vol. III, p. 190.

14. *Ibid.* vol. II, p. 301.

15. A. Heuss, *HZ CLXXXII* (1956), p. 28 (see also A. Heuss, 'Matius als Zeuge von Caesar's staatsmännischer Größe', *Historia* XI (1962), p. 118.

16. M. Gelzer, *Caesar*, Stuttgart 1921. See also his article, 'Caesars weltgeschichtliche Leistung', *Vorträge und Schriften, Preuss. Akademie d. Wiss.*, Heft 6, Berlin 1941 (= *Vom römischen Staat* II, pp. 147 ff.).

17. *Das neue Bild der Antike,* vol. II, p. 199. But otherwise Gelzer preserved his academic integrity during the Nazi period. Only in a lecture 'Caesars weltgeschichtliche Leistung', Berlin 1941 (De Gruyter), p. 4, was there the hint that it was not easy for him in every respect. He compared Caesar with Frederick the Great, with Napoleon, Richelieu and Bismarck, 'not to mention those who are still alive'. Is this irony or evasion? Yet there is no doubt about his general attitude. In 1928 he took up a critical position towards F. Münzer's *Entstehung des römischen Prinzipats,* Münster 1927, and made comments against the enthusiasm for the rule of the individual, 'Because we have conceived of a period of history as necessary, must we also hail it as salutary?'

18. M. Gelzer, *Caesar: Politician and Statesman,* tr. P. Needham, Oxford 1968, pp. 329-30 (= *Caesar*, Wiesbaden 1960, p. 306).

19. Cic., *de off.* II, 84.

20. Plin., *NH* VII, 91-2.

21. O. Seel, 'Zur Problematik der Grösse', *Caesarstudien,* Stuttgart 1967, pp. 43-92, especially p. 57.

22. Th. Mommsen, *Römische Geschichte,* vol. III, Berlin 1909 edition, p. 479 (*History of Rome,* vol. IV, tr. W. Dickson, London 1894 edition, p. 440.

23. J. Geiger, 'Zum Bild Caesars in der römischen Kaiserzeit', *Historia* XXIV (1975), p. 444.

24. R. Herbig, 'Neue Studien zur Ikonographie des Julius Caesar', *Kölner Jahrbücher für Vor und Frühgeschichte* IV (1959), p. 7 = *Gymnasium* LXXII (1965), p. 161 = *WdF* XLIII (1967), p. 69. Cf. also J. M. C. Toynbee, 'Portraits of Julius Caesar', *Greece and Rome* IV (1957), p. 2; Erika Simon, 'Neue Literatur zum Caesarporträt', *Gymnasium* XXVI (1954), p. 527.

25. J. H. Collins, *Gnomon* XXVI (1954), p. 527.

26. W. Roscher, *Politik, Geschichtliche Naturlehre der Monarchie, Aristokratie,* Stuttgart 1893, p. 588.

27. *Mémoires de Mme de Remusat* III, p. 349.

28. A. J. P. Taylor, *From Napoleon to Lenin. Historical Essays,* New York 1966, pp, 12-20.

29. Two additional passages of Cicero are worth mentioning in this connection, *ad fam.* XII, 18, 2, 'for the issues of civil war are invariably such that it is not only the victor's wishes that are carried out, but those also have to be humoured by whose assistance the victory was won', and *ibid.* 4, 9, 3, 'For there are many things a victor is obliged to do even against his will at the caprice of those who helped him to victory.'

30. L. Wickert, 'Zu Caesars Reichspolitik', *Klio* XXX (1937), pp. 232-53.

31. Presumably in 1895 Roscher was not yet aware of the then sensational articles of Dessau in *Hermes* XXIV (1889), pp. 337-92; XXVII (1892), pp. 561-605, on the historical value of the *SHA*. In any case the passage cited above can serve only by way of illustration.

32. Cf. A. Momigliano, 'Per un riesame della storia dell' idea di Cesarismo', *RSI* LXVIII (1956), p. 220-29, and 'Burckhardt e la parola Cesarismo', *ibid.* LXXIV (1962), pp. 369-71, and, in Hebrew, C. Wirszubski, 'The domination of Julius Caesar', *Molad* (Sept. 1957), pp. 348 ff., with similar conclusions.

33. L. Hartmann, *Theodor Mommsen,* Gotha 1908, pp. 66-77. Napoleon III himself wrote a book about Caesar, but his German tutor (Froehner) was under no illusions about Napoleon's philological and historical knowledge. In his memoirs he remarked that Napoleon muddled *Grammatici* with *Gromatici,* and was absolutely convinced that he had read Livy Book XI (!).

34. I assume that, in speaking of the vulgar sense, Mommsen would have had in mind such sentences as 'Ro-

man history in general, viewed in the proper light, is and remains the most trustworthy guide, not only for our time, but for all times'. This sentence comes from Hitler's *Mein Kampf* (1939), p. 470.

35. Th. Mommsen, *Römische Geschichte,* vol. III, p. 477 f. (= Eng. tr. in Everyman's Lib., Vol. IV, pp. 439-440.

36. W. Roscher, 'Umrisse zur Naturlehre des Caesarismus', *Abh. der Sächs. Gesellschaft der Wissenschaften,* vol. X (1888), p. 641; F. Ruestow, *Der Caesarismus, sein Wesen and Schaffen,* Zürich 1879.

37. R. v. Pöhlmann, 'Entstehung des Caesarismus', *Altertum und Gegenwart,* Munich 1895, p. 245.

38. A. Gramsci, 'Note sul Machiavelli, sulla politica e sullo stato moderno', Einaudi-Jovino (1949), pp. 58-60 especially stresses the 'conciliatory character of Caesarism'.

39. N. A. Maškin, *Printsipat Avgusta,* Moscow 1949 (pp. 47 ff. German edition).

40. Momigliano, see n. 32.

41. Th. Mommsen, *loc. cit.* p. 513.

42. It is perhaps noteworthy that Caesar's power appeared legitimate to Napoleon, 'because it was the result . . . of the people's wish' (whether Napoleon was familiar with App., *BC* I, 4, 16 is debatable).

43. C. Merivale, *The Fall of the Roman Republic,* London 1874; W. W. Fowler, *Julius Caesar and the Foundation of the Roman Imperial System,* London 1892, to mention but two English examples. L. Wickert (*loc. cit.* p. 232) believed that an idea of empire always develops when the territory of the state grows beyond a certain limit. Caesar's plan was to reshape the Imperium Romanum, replacing the Republican state that was head of a community by a state ruled by a monarch that was head of an empire. A necessary factor in the fulfilment of this task is the absolute rule of the individual, for only the monarch who is superior to all his subjects can gain the requisite support, impossible for collegiate government in the Roman style, involving several principals.

44. E. G. Brandes, *Caesar,* 2 vols, Copenhagen 1918-21; or, E. Kornemann, *Weltgeschichte des Mittelmeerraumes,* Munich 1948, 'The crime of March 15th effaced forever the empire planned by the powerful Julius.'

45. E.g. G. A. v. Mess, *Caesar,* Leipzig 1913, pp. 162-66, 'His aim was legalized monarchy. He was not only an innovator, but stirred into growth and strengthened what remained strong and healthy in the old roots; he was above party politics, and was the man to put new content into the old form.' Mess considered that Caesar's election as Pontifex Maximus ('head of the state church'), was a 'preparation for popular monarchy' (p. 41).

46. G. W. F. Hegel, *Vorlesungen über die Philosophie der Geschichte* (ed. Brunstäd), Leipzig 1907 (Reclam Verlag), pp. 400-1 (= English translation by J. Sibree, New York 1944, pp. 312-13). Many nineteenth-century scholars who were not Hegelians shared this view, e.g. Droysen, who in 1834 wrote to Welcker that he had always preferred Alexander to Demosthenes and Caesar to Cato (G. Droysen, *Briefwechsel* (ed. R. Hübner), 1929, vol. I, p. 66.

47. F. Gundolf, *Caesar, Geschichte seines Ruhmes,* Berlin 1924, and *Caesar in 19. Jahrhundert,* Berlin 1926.

48. So, too, Jose Ortega y Gasset, *The Revolt of the Masses,* New York 1950, p. 118.

49. G. Ferrero, *The Life of Caesar,* London 1933, the second volume of his work *Grandezza edecadenza di Roma,* Turin 1904.

50. At first glance it may seem that there were no real anti-Caesarians before Ferrero, while devotees of Julius Caesar were to be found even among the founders of American democracy. Dumas Malone, *Jefferson and his Time,* Boston 1951, vol. II, p. 286, maintained that Hamilton was a great admirer of Caesar. In an article that has appeared recently Thomas P. Govan has proved precisely the opposite and has convincingly demonstrated that Hamilton, in fact, championed Ferrero's ideas even during the American Revolution. In his view, Caesar was not only an efficient general and despotic autocrat, he was also a Catiline—a demagogic conspirator—who flattered the people and destroyed their freedom. To warn Washington against people of this kind, Hamilton wrote, 'When a man unprincipled in private life, desperate in his fortune, . . . possessed of considerable talents, having the advantage of military habits, despotic in his ordinary demeanour . . . is seen to mount the hobby horse of popularity . . . it may justly be suspected that his object is to throw things into confusion, that he may 'ride the storm and direct the whirlwind.'

Hamilton hated those who fostered the folly and prejudices of the people and who played on their ambitions and fears. His comparison of Jefferson with Caesar in 1792 was no compliment. (Thomas P. Govan, 'Alexander Hamilton and Julius Caesar', *The William and Mary Quarterly,* July 1975, p. 477. I am grateful to my friend Prof. T. Draper for the reference to this article).

51. L. R. Taylor, 'Caesar and the Roman Nobility', *TAPA* LXXIII (1942), pp. 10-27; F. R. Cowell, *Cicero and the Roman Republic,* London 1948, pp. 203-4. This anti-Caesarian attitude is also not a new one. Since the time of Machiavelli and up to the French Revolution, conspirators whose declared aim was to free their enslaved country were highly regarded. The argument has become more intense since the time of Napoleon.

52. The new direction of Italian research on Caesar after World War II was instituted by G. Perotta with the

article 'Cesare scrittore', *Maia* I (1948), pp. 5-32. Cf. also G. Funaioli, 'Giulio Cesare scrittore', *Studi Romani* V (1957), p. 136; E. Paratore, 'Cesare scrittore', *Cesare nel bimillianario della morte* (ed. Radio Italiana), Rome 1956, p. 23; A. La Penna, *Cesare—La guerra civile—Introduzione,* Turin 1954.

See also the important works of G. Pacucci, G. Funaioli, E. Paratore, A. La Penna, L. Canali (*Personalità e stile di Cesare,* Rome 1963); F. Semi (*Il sentimento di Cesare,* Padua 1966), and the extremely useful synopsis by E. Paratore, 'Das Caesarbild des 20. Jahrhunderts in Italien', *Caesar, WdF.,* see n. 24. I have unfortunately been unable to obtain G. Costa, *Giulio Cesare,* Rome 1934. See now J. Kroymann, 'Caesar und das Corpus Caesarianum in der neueren Forschung, *ANRW* I, 3, 457.

53. As an example of Soviet literature see Maskin (n. 39). Western Marxists did not follow the path of their Soviet colleagues, and works of the Italian left (cf. n. 52) such as those of Canali and La Penna are stimulating and refreshing.

54. See also U. v. Wilamowitz, 'Th. Mommsen. Warum hat er den vierten Band der Römischen Geschichte nicht geschrieben?', *International Monatschrift* XII (1918), p. 205, and especially the fine article by A. Wucher, 'Mommsens unvolendete Römische Geschichte', *Saeculum* IV (1953), pp. 414 ff.

55. J. H. Collins, *loc. cit.* (p. 12, n. 10).

56. This was also the view of E. Herzog, *Geschichte und System der römischen Staatsverfassung,* Leipzig 1884-91, II. 1, p. 44 (1887). He did not doubt that Caesar strove for sole rulership as a regular, permanent form of government, and in this connection the title never bothered him.

57. E.g., E. Kornemann, 'Ägyptische Einflüsse im römischen Kaiserreich', *N. Jahrb. f.d. kl. Altertumswissenschaft* 1889, p. 118; J. Kaerst, *Studien zur Entwicklung und theoretischen Begründung der Monarchie im Altertum,* Munich 1898, especially pp. 80 ff.; H. Willrich, 'Caligula', *Klio* III (1902), p. 89. A. V. Domaszewski, 'Kleine Beiträge zur Kaisergeschichte', *Philologus* XXI (1908), p. 1.

58. See his *Kleine Schriften.*

59. E. Meyer, *Spenglers Untergang des Abendlandes,* Berlin 1925.

60. O. Weippert, *Alexander Imitatio und römische Geschichte in republikanischer Zeit,* Augsburg 1972, pp. 56 ff.

61. Cf., however, Gelzer's review of the year 1918, reprinted in *Kleine Schriften,* vol. III, p. 190.

62. J. Carcopino, *César,* Paris 1935; cf. 'La Royauté de César et de l'Empire universel', *Les Etapes de l'impérialisme Romain,* Paris 1961, pp. 118 ff., with the important review of T. Gagé, 'De César à Auguste', *RH* CLXXVII (1936), pp. 279-342. Also R. Etienne, *Les Ides de Mars,* Paris 1973, whose interpretation is similar to Carcopino's.

63. L. Cerfaux and J. Tondriau, *Le culte des souverains,* Tournay 1957.

64. C. N. Cochrane, *Christianity and Classical Culture,* Oxford 1940.

65. E. Kornemann, *Weltgeschichte des Mittelmeerraumes,* Munich 1948, vol. I, p. 478.

66. P. Strack, 'Zum Gottkönigtum Caesars, Probleme der augustäischen Erneuerung', *Gymnasium* IV (1938), p. 21; also C. Koch, *Gottheit und Mensch im Wandel der römischen Staatsform* (1942), now in 'Religio. Studien zu Kult und Glauben der Römer', *Erlanger Beiträge zur Sprache und Kunstwissenschaft,* vol. VII, Nuremberg 1960, p. 94.

67. L. Pareti, *Storia di Roma e del impero Romano,* 6 vols. Turin 1952-61.

68. Cf. E. Meyer, 'Kaiser Augustus', *Kl. Schriften,* and E. Burck, 'Staat, Volk und Dichtung im republikanischen Rom', *Hermes* LXXI (1936), p. 307. Burck maintained that Augustus retreated from Caesar's notion of the Hellenistic state, embraced the old Roman tradition, and made way for a blood (*blutmässig*) reformation. The expression *blutmässig* was apparently better conceived in 1936.

69. H. F. Pelham, *Essays in Roman History.* Oxford 1911, p. 27.

70. *CAH* IX, p. 724.

71. R. Syme, *The Roman Revolution,* Oxford 1939, p. 54.

72. R. Syme, 'Caesar, the Senate and Italy', *PBSR* XIV (1938), p. 2.

73. When Syme spoke of non-political classes he meant tax farmers, wealthy merchants and great landowners who had no political ambitions and supported any regime that could guarantee them economic returns.

74. Cf., the outstanding small volume, unfortunately all too seldom cited, *Colonial Elites,* Oxford 1958, pp. 27, 52.

75. R. Syme, *The Roman Revolution* p. 346.

76. F. E. Adcock, *CAH* IX, p. 271, and also the important article by J. P. V. D. Balsdon, 'The Ides of March', *Historia* XII (1953), pp. 80-94. The most important review of Syme's work, long since recognized as 'classic', comes from A. Momigliano (*JRS* XXX (1940), p. 75). Momigliano applauded Syme's work as a masterpiece, but was critical of the one-sidedness of its prosopography, ('prosopography is not history'), and regretted that 'spiritual interests of people are considered much less than their marriages'. Numerous scholars have since associated

themselves with Momigliano, including A. W. Sherwin-White (*JRS* LIX (1969), p. 287), whom Lintott praised 'for considering ideas and actions of contestants rather than their matrimonial bulletins'. Momigliano also regretted that Syme had not attached enough importance to Roman law, and in another place he pointed out that it would have been desirable to enquire '. . . how the Romans knew and used law and constitutional practices as the tool for building an empire. The Romans did not rule the world by nepotism' (*Contributo alla storia degli Studi classici* I, Rome 1955, p. 399). From another marginal comment it might be concluded that Momigliano was haunted by the question of whether Syme had in mind the rise of Fascism when he wrote the *Roman Revolution,* 'A candid admission of the purpose of one's own study, a clear analysis of the implications of one's own bias helps to define the limits of one's own historical research' (*Contributo* I, p. 374). In fact, it is not altogether easy to discover the *Zeitgeist* from Syme's text. It was easier in the case of Niebuhr. But one thing is clear: Syme learned more from Münzer than from Namier, and there is no reason for supposing that he had eighteenth-century England in mind when he wrote his *Roman Revolution.* He believed in the role of Dynamis and Tyche in history rather than in established trends that can be predicted, and in a period such as that before World War II, when political ideology was awash in a wave of slogans, he was more interested in the actors on the stage of history than in their warnings, 'Bonum publicum simulantes pro sua quisque potentia certabant'.

77. The Spartan Agesilaus likewise most vigorously refused divine honours (Plut., *Mor.* 210 D). Thus he once enquired of the inhabitants of Thasus whether they were in a position to change a mortal into a god. When they assented, he suggested they first make themselves into gods, then he would believe that they could also deify him (Plut., *Agesilaus* 21, 5; *Mor.* 213 A).

78. W. Steidle, *Sueton und die antike Biographie,* Munich 1963, pp. 13 ff.

79. Cf., Syme, *Roman Revolution,* p. 54, 'Cic. Phil. II, 110, however, is a difficult passage'.

80. W. W. Fowler, *Roman Essays,* Oxford 1920, p. 268.

81. J. Vogt, 'Zum Herrscherkult bei Julius Caesar', *Studies presented to D. M. Robinson,* vol. II, St Louis 1953, p. 1138.

82. V. Ehrenberg, 'Caesar's Final Aims', *HSCP* LXVIII (1969), p. 149 = *Man, State and Diety* 1974, 127.

83. K. Kraft, 'Der goldene Kranz Caesars und der Kampf um die Entlarvung des Tyrannen', *Jahrbücher für Numismatik und Geldgeschichte* IV (1952), p. 7. Cf., also the critical article of D. Felber, 'Caesars Streben nach der Königswürde', *Untersuchungen zur*

römischen Geschichte (ed. F. Altheim), vol. I, Frankfurt/M 1961, pp. 211 ff.

84. F. Gundolf, *Caesar im 19 Jahrhundert,* Berlin 1926, p. 79.

85. L. Wickert, 'Caesars Monarchie und der Prinzipat des Augustus', *NJAB* IV (1941), pp. 12-23.

86. F. Vittinghoff, *Römische Kolonisation und Bürgerrechtspolitik,* Mainz 1951.

87. H. Opperman, *Caesar—Wegbereiter Europas,* Göttingen 1958, especially pp. 96-97; 106-7.

88. F. Taeger, *Charisma,* Stuttgart 1960, vol. II, pp. 50 ff., 65, 68, 70, 72.

89. R. Klein, *Königtum und Königzeit bei Cicero* (diss.), Erlangen 1962, especially pp. 57-59, 67.

90. E. Meyer, *Caesars Monarchie,* p. 401. Cf. F. Altheim, *Römische Religionsgeschichte* II, Baden-Baden 1953, p. 63.

91. B. E. Giovanetti, *La religione di Cesare,* Milan 1937.

92. M. Pohlenz, 'Eine politische Tendenzschrift aus Caesars Zeit', *Hermes* LIX (1924), p. 157. Pohlenz's view was not shared by all scholars. Some attributed the passage of Dionysius to the Augustan period (e.g. Premerstein), others to the time of Sulla (e.g. E. Gabba, 'Studi su Dionigi da Alecarnasso', *Athenaeum* XXXVIII (1960), pp. 175 ff.

93. J. Dobesch, *Caesars Apotheose zu Lebzeiten und sein Ringen um den Königstitel,* Vienna 1966, reviewed in *JRS* VII (1967), pp. 247-48 and E. Rawson, *JRS* LXV (1975), p. 148.

94. The review by J. P. V. D. Balsdon, *Gnomon* XXXIX (1967), pp. 150 ff. is important. See also K. W. Welwei, 'Das Angebot des Diadems an Caesar und das Luperkalienfest', *Historia* XVI (1967), p. 44.

95. *Correspondance de Napoléon I,* vol. 32, p. 86, cited by Alföldi in 'Der neue Romulus', *MH* VIII (1951), p. 208.

96. *Ibid.*

97. See the bibliography of A. Alföldi, *Antiquitas,* series 4, vol. III, 1966, XIII.

98. At the time of writing only vol. 2 of *Das Zeugnis der Münzen,* Bonn 1974 (*Antiquitas,* vol. XVII), was available to me.

99. *MH* VII (1950), pp. 1-13.

100. On the diadem as employed by the Persians and Alexander, see Hans-Werner Ritter, *Diadem und Königsherrschaft,* Munich 1965 (*Vestigia* 7).

101. *Phoenix* XXIV (1970), p. 166.

102. *Gnom.* XII (1975), p. 12.

103. *RN* XV, 1973, p. 126.

104. *Phoenix* XXIV (1970), p. 176.

105. E. Gruen, *The Last Generation of the Roman Republic,* Berkeley-Los Angeles-London 1974, p. 544.

106. Alföldi, *loc. cit.* p. 105.

107. *Staatsrecht* II, p. 780.

108. S. Weinstock, *Divus Julius,* Oxford 1971, p. 200, n. 4. A. H. M. Jones, *JRS* XLI (1951), pp. 117, 119, contra, A. Alföldi, *Vater des Vaterlandes,* Darmstadt 1971.

109. E.g., R. Syme, 'Imperator Caesar. A Study in Nomenclature', *Historia* VII (1958), pp. 172-88. R. Combes, *Imperator,* Paris 1966. J. Deininger, 'Von der Republik zur Monarchi', *Aufstieg und Niedergang der römischen Welt* (ed. Temporini), vol. I (1972), p. 982, with the conclusion that neither the coins nor the epigraphic evidence offers any clear proof that Imperator was more than a title to Caesar.

110. A. Alföldi, 'Der machtverheissende Traum des Sulla', *Jahrb. d. bernischen Hist. Museums in Bern* XLI-XLII (1961), p. 284.

111. Michael H. Crawford, *Roman Republican Coinage,* 2 vols, Cambridge 1974. To cite only a few examples: p. 83, n. 5: 'The arrangement proposed by A. Alföldi, *JNR* 1954 may safely be ignored'. Or p. 89, n. 2: 'The attempt of Alföldi to date this issue must be regarded as a failure'. Or, '. . . the unacceptable view of Alföldi', p. 488, n. 1.

112. *Ibid.* p. 601, n. 3; p. 733, n. 2.

113. C. M. Kraay, 'Caesar's Quattuorviri of 44 BC: The Arrangement of their Issue', *NC* XIV, Ser. 6 (1954), p. 18; R. A. G. Carson, *Gnomon* XXVIII (1956), pp. 181-86 and *Greece and Rome* IV (1957), pp. 46-53. H. Volkmann, 'Caesars letzte Pläne im Spiegel der Münzen', *Gymnasium* LXIV (1957), p. 299.

114. D. Felber, 'Caesars Streben nach der Königswürde' in *Untersuchungen zur römischen Geschichte* (ed. F. Altheim), Frankfurt/M. 1961, vol. I, pp. 211-84.

115. A. H. M. Jones, 'Numismatics and History', *Essays in Roman Coinage presented to H. Mattingly* (ed. R. A. G. Carson and C. H. V. Sutherland), Oxford 1956, p. 32.

116. S. Weinstock, *Divus Julius loc. cit.,* reviewed by A. Alföldi, *Gnomon* XII (1975), pp. 154-79; R. E. Palmer, *Athenaeum* LI (1973), p. 201, and J. A. North, *JRS* LXV (1975), p. 171.

117. Weinstock, *loc. cit.* p. 3; Alföldi, *Gnomon, loc. cit.* p. 158.

118. E.g. R. Syme, 'Livy and Augustus', *HSCP* LXIV (1959), 80, no. 85: 'Dio's passage (LXIV, 4, 3) is a patent anachronism'.

119. *Staatsrecht* II, p. 756, n. 1. Adcock. *CAHM* IX, 721.

120. *Gnomon* XXXIX (1967), p. 155.

121. *NC* VI, Ser. 6 (1947), pp. 127 ff.

122. *Gymnasium* LXX (1963), pp. 312 ff. especially p. 333.

123. E. J. Bickerman, 'Die römische Kaiserapotheose', *Archiv für Religionswissenschaft* XXVII (1930), p. 1.

124. *Id.,* 'Consecratio, Culte des Souverains', *Fondation Hardt, Entretiens* XIX, Geneva 1973, pp. 3-37, especially p. 7.

125. C. Habicht, *Gottmenschtum und griechische Städte,* Munich 1957 (Zetemata, no. 14) (cf. n. 121), pp. 41 ff. and most recently in 'Consecratio'.

126. R. Cohen, *La Grèce et l'Hellenisation du monde antique,* Paris 1939, p. 614.

127. Cerfaux and Tondriau, *loc. cit.* p. 77.

128. M. Liberanome, 'Alcune osservazioni su Cesare e Antonio', *RFIC* XVI (1968), pp. 407 ff.

129. Felber, *loc. cit.* p. 226.

130. Cf. n. 106. and n. 111.

131. G. Haber, *Untersuchungen zu Caesars Pontifikat,* Tübingen 1971.

132. H. Gesche, *Die Vergottung Caesars,* Frankfurt/M. 1968.

133. A. Alföldi, *Phoenix* XXIV (1970), p. 169.

134. M. Cary, 'The Municipal Legislation of Julius Caesar', *JRS* XXVII (1937), p. 49.

135. *Gnomon* XIII (1937), p. 191.

136. W. Schmitthenner, 'Das Attentat auf Caesar', *Gesch. i. Wiss. u. Unterr.* XIII (1962), pp. 685 ff., especially p. 694.

137. R. E. Smith, 'Conspiracy and the Conspirators', *Greece and Rome* IV (1957), p. 62.

138. C. Meier, *Entstehung des Begriffs 'Demokratie', vier Prolegomena zu einer historischen Theorie,* Frankfurt/M. 1970, pp. 131-35.

139. J. H. Collins, *Historia* IV (1955), p. 445.

140. In his thesis, unfortunately unpublished, *Propaganda, Ethics and Psychological Assumptions in Caesar's Writings* (diss.), Frankfurt/M. 1952.

141. Collins assumed that Cicero would have happily seen Caesar dead (*ad Att.* XII, 4; XIII, 40). Other scholars do not take these passages seriously.

142. J. Béranger, 'Tyrannus: Notes sur la notion de Tyrannie chez les Romains particulièrement à l'époque de César et de Cicéron', *REL* XIII (1935), p. 85; 'Cicéron précurseur politique', *Hermes* LXXXVII (1959), p. 103. W. Allen, 'Caesar's Regnum', *TAPA* LXXXIV (1953), p. 227.

143. Z. Yavetz, *Plebs and Princeps,* Oxford 1969, p. 38.

144. For the evidence, *ibid.* p. 50.

145. *Ibid.* p. 101. Idem est quod datur sed interest quomodo detur.

146. *Ibid.* p. 53.

147. *Ibid.* p. 99.

148. *Ibid.* p. 50, n. 7.

149. *Ibid.* pp. 114-16.

150. G. Schulte-Holtey, *Untersuchung zum Gallischen Widerstand gegen Caesar* (diss.), Münster 1968. Others are inclined to stress the interests of Gallic merchants under Roman occupation, e.g. N. J. De Witt, 'Toward Misunderstanding Caesar', *Studies in Honor of Ullman,* St Louis 1960, p. 137; and C. Jullian, *Vercingetorix,* Paris, 1911, who deplores Caesar's conquest of Gaul as a conquest that arrested the development of Celtic civilization:

151. This sceptical view has deep roots. The question had already been posed by Livy: whether it would have been better for the state for Caesar to be born or for him not to have been born ('in incerto esse utrum illum magis nasci an non nasci rei publicae profuerit', Sen. *Nat. Quaest.* 5, 18, 4). Seneca had no clear answer to this question.

152. D. Thompson, *The Aims of History,* London 1969.

Abbreviations

Abbot-Johnson: F. F. Abbot - A. Ch. Johnson, *Municipal Administration in the Roman Empire,* Princeton 1926.

A. N. R. W.: *Aufstieg und Niedergang der römischen Welt* (Hrsg. H. Temporini), Berlin-New York 1972.

A. R. S. P.: *Annali della R. Scuola Normale Superiore di Pisa*

C. A. H.: *Cambridge Ancient History*

C. I. L.: *Corpus Inscriptionum Latinarum*

E. S. A. R.: T. Frank (ed.), *An Economic Survey of Ancient Rome,* Paterson, N. J. 1959.

F. A. S.: *Frankfurter althistorische Studien*

F. G. H.: F. Jacoby (Hrsg.), *Fragmente der griechischen Historiker*

FIRA (Riccobono): S. Riccobono, *Fontes Iuris Romani Antejustiniani*

G. W. U.: *Geschichte in Wissenschaft und Unterricht*

I. G. R. R.: *Inscriptiones Graecae ad res Romanas pertinentes*

I. L. S.: *Inscriptiones Latinae Selectae*

M. G. W. J.: *Monatsschrift für Geschichte und Wissenschaft des Judentums*

M. R. R.: T. R. S. Broughton, *The Magistrates of the Roman Republic,* New York 1951.

N. J. A. B.: *Neue Jahrbücher für Antike und deutsche Bildung.*

R. E.: *Paulys Realencyclopädie der classischen Altertumswissenschaft*

R. G.: Th. Mommsen, *Römische Geschichte.*

Rotondi: G. Rotondi, *Leges Publicae Populi Romani.*

R. R. (Syme): Sir Ronald Syme, *The Roman Revolution,* Oxford 1939.

R. R. (Varro): M. Terentius Varro, *de re rustica.*

S. I. G.: W. Dittenberger (Hrsg.), *Sylloge Inscriptionum Graecarum.*

WdF: *Wege der Forschung,* (Wissenschaftliche Buchgesellschaft, Darmstadt).

All other abbreviations (names of series, periodicals etc.) correspond to the ones used in *l'Année Philolgique.*

C. B. R. Pelling (essay date 1981)

SOURCE: "Caesar's Battle-Descriptions and the Defeat of Ariovistus," in *Latomus,* Vol. 40, No. 4, October-December, 1981, pp. 741-66.

[*In the following essay, Pelling argues that many of Caesar's battles and maneuvers were too complex to be understood by his intended readers, so that he simplified his accounts accordingly.*]

Caesar's military descriptions mark him out among ancient writers. He paints them in the firmest lines; he is uniquely able to communicate to his audience the important strands in the strategy of a campaign, or the tactics of a battle. This tends to inspire modern scholars with an unfortunate confidence. We have a clear and definite picture of the course of events: we expect it to be an easy matter to fit Caesar's narrative to the terrain, and to determine the exact theatre of the campaigns and battles which he describes. Most of the modern topographical discussions of his campaigns are confident and precise. And yet our expectations have proved delusive. Archaeology alone has been genuinely successful in deciding topographical issues, as (it may be argued) at Gergovia and Alesia. Where archaeological evidence is not to hand, scarcely one of Caesar's battlefields has been determined in such a manner as to quell dispute.

It is time to stop considering topographical questions in isolation, and to adopt a new approach. Caesar painted his pictures firmly; but how concerned was he to give accurate and precise detail? He was writing for an audience at Rome. That audience had no more than the vaguest notion of the geography of Gaul, and that audience had no useful maps. 'Every day', Caesar's successes brought new names of races, tribes, locations to Roman ears[1]; 'no writing, report, or rumour' had ever celebrated the regions which Caesar now conquered for Rome[2]. Who really knew anything of the Nervii, where their country lay, how far removed from Italy and Rome[3]? Such an audience would find it extraordinarily difficult to grasp the complexities of terrain, or of fortification, or of strategic manœuvre; it would soon grow impatient with the effort. It would be very odd, if Caesar had not sought to ease their path. A flood of complexities might too easily obscure the important points of the narrative. Caesar would naturally suppress many of the details of terrain or of military movements, and present his audience with *a very simplified model*.

The first part of this paper will illustrate this point from three of Caesar's more routine battle-descriptions. The second will turn to the most difficult and controversial of all his topographical accounts, that of the war with Ariovistus.

Caesar's Narrative Technique

We may begin with the battle of the Aisne, fought against the *Belgae* in 57 (**B.G.** [*De Bello Gallico*], 2.1-11)[4]. After his arrival at the Belgic frontier, Caesar remained for some days in the territory of the *Remi;* he was probably based on *Durocortorum,* the main town of the *Remi,* for that period[5]. When news arrived that the *Belgae* were marching against him, he hurried to cross the Aisne, and encamped close to the river's right bank. *Quae res . . . latus unum castrorum ripis fluminis muniebat* (2. 5. 5). Nearby there was a bridge over the Aisne, presumably the bridge by which Caesar had crossed. He defended this with a *praesidium* on the right bank and a camp of six cohorts, commanded by Titurius Sabinus, on the left. The approaching *Belgae* meanwhile attacked the *oppidum Bibrax,* some eight miles away from Caesar's main camp; but Caesar sent a light-armed detachment to its defence, and the town was saved. The *Belgae* then arrived before Caesar's main camp, and occupied a position less than two miles distant. Their camp was more than eight miles in width.

Caesar at first restricted his troops to cavalry skirmishes: *Vbi nostros non esse inferiores intellexit, loco pro castris ad aciem instruendam natura opportuno atque idoneo, quod is collis ubi castra posita erant paululum ex planitie editus tantum aduersus in latitudinem patebat quantum loci acies instructa occupare poterat, atque ex utraque parte lateris deiectus habebat et in frontem leniter fastigatus paulatim ad planitiem redibat, ab utroque latere eius collis transuersam fossam obduxit circiter passuum quadringentorum, et ad extremas fossas castella constituit ibique tormenta collocauit ne, cum aciem instruxisset, hostes, quod tantum multitudine poterant, ab lateribus pugnantes suos circumuenire possent* (2. 8. 2-4). Both sides then drew up the bulk of their forces in front of their camps: a marsh then separated the two armies. Still no pitched battle was fought, and, after an indecisive cavalry

engagement, Caesar led his men back to their camp. The *Belgae* next found a ford and tried to cross the Aisne, hoping to attack the smaller Roman camp. Titurius informed Caesar of the danger, and Caesar vigorously attacked the enemy army, wreaking such slaughter that the entire enemy force decided to withdraw. Caesar pursued on the following day with devastating effect.

This battlefield ought to be identifiable: we could scarcely hope for more detailed information. It must be very close to the right bank of the Aisne (2. 5. 5); and, if Caesar started from Reims, the battlefield should not be far from there. It probably lies close to an ancient road, for the *Belgae* were marching on Caesar and would naturally have taken the easiest route[6]. We have perhaps the most explicit natural description in the **Commentaries** to help us locate Caesar's camp. Two miles further from the river there should be sufficient room for the Belgic position, eight miles wide. Between the two there should be a marsh, but there should also be ground firm enough to permit cavalry manœuvres. There should be a ford close to the battlefield. Even if *Bibrax* cannot be securely identified[7], we should surely have enough material to fix the site.

But we do not. We can certainly narrow the possibilities to just two candidates, Berry-au-Bac (Mauchamp) and Chaudardes. . . .[8] The main road from Reims to the north seems to have passed through Berry-au-Bac[9], sufficiently close to both possible sites. Whether the site be fixed as Berry or Chaudardes, a very plausible ford can be found at Gernicourt[10]. Both locations have plausible marshes. Both can afford eight-mile tracts suitable for the Belgic camp. But both sites also have difficulties, and the merits of the two cases are still very evenly balanced.

(1) Napoléon thought that his excavations had constituted decisive proof for Berry-au-Bac: he discovered remains of a camp and two entrenchments (see Figure 1). But his discoveries do not really meet the demands of Caesar's description[11]. The Roman army was drawn up *pro castris* and faced the enemy: we naturally assume that the Romans stood between their camp (behind them) and the Belgic army (before them). Yet Napoléon's reconstruction implies that the entire *acies* stood to the left of the Roman camp[12]. Caesar certainly leads us to expect fortifications at both sides of the hill and the battle-line (*ab utroque latere eius collis*), and suggests that both flanks needed protection from attack (*ne ab lateribus*—note the plural—*pugnantes suos circumuenire possent*); Napoléon leaves the left quite denuded[13]. It is perhaps possible that a further earthwork remains undiscovered in the region of Gernicourt, at the west of the proposed line; but Napoléon's fortifications are much too complex simply to be the right-wing construction[14]. Nor does the nature of the terrain correspond to Caesar's description: *lateris deiectus* probably implies that the west and east of the hill are marked by fairly steep slopes. It has long been noticed that the western slope is much too gentle[15], and in fact the eastern slope is little better. The plateau itself seems rather too wide for Caesar's line of six legions. All this is hardly satisfactory.

(2) Chaudardes would be a more obvious site to fortify, and certainly has much to recommend it. Its descents to west and east are much steeper than the equivalents at Berry, and (*pace* Holmes) the plateau is almost exactly the right size to accommodate the line of six legions. That line should naturally occupy a little more than two kilometres[16]; Chaudardes plateau is approximately 2.5 km wide. But it too has its disadvantages. The plain to the north is today heavily forested, and it is hard to believe that it was ever good cavalry country. Nor does Caesar's *in frontem leniter fastigatus paulatim ad planitiem redibat* accurately reflect the complexities of the terrain. The ground immediately north of the 'plateau' slopes noticeably upwards from east to west. At the east the plateau *frons* is rather too steep, while at the west it is in parts lower than the ground immediately to the north.

It is impossible to decide between these two locations, but that is not our present concern. The important point is that, on either account, Caesar has given us a simplified model. If the battle was fought at Berry, he has disguised the position of his camp, and exaggerated the slope at the east and west ends; he has misrepresented the nature of his dispositions, which must have left gaps between both flanks and the edges of the plateau; and he has simplified the detail of his fortifications. If the battle was fought at Chaudardes, he has obscured the complexities of the *frons* and its relation to the adjacent terrain; and there is something odd about the description of the cavalry fighting. There is nothing surprising or sinister in this. Caesar was simply trying to help his readers. Wherever the battle was fought, the true complexities would be extraordinarily difficult and distracting to explain. Caesar preferred to concentrate on the main points of the battle, and to simplify his natural description in a manner which would make these points easier to grasp.

The next example is the battle *ad Sabim,* fought later in 57, where Caesar defeated the *Neruii* (*B.G.,* 2. 16-28). Most discussions of this battle have started from the assumption that the *Sabis* should be the Sambre, but none of these reconstructions could give a plausible strategic pattern to the campaign[17]. It now seems likely that the equation *Sabis = Sambre* is no more than a fourteenth-century conjecture, and possesses no authority[18].

It seems most likely that Caesar, after receiving the submission of the *Ambiani* (2. 15. 2), was marching along the road from Amiens through Cambrai to Bavay, the Nervian capital[19]. The site should presumably be sought on or near this road. The choice lies between a position on the Escaut (near Cambrai) or a position on the Selle (near Saulzoir). The Escaut site would probably be the stronger point of defence[20]. But it is hard to find topographical details which answer at all plausibly to Caesar's description, and the Escaut identification would imply that Caesar here confused *Sabis* and *Scaldis*[21]. The elaborate discussion of P. Turquin marks out a very plausible site in the environs of Saulzoir, and swings the balance of probability heavily in the Selle's favour[22]. If so, Caesar's description

of *latissimum flumen* and *altissimae ripae* would be hyperbolic (2. 27. 5); but that, perhaps, would be no surprise.

The main difficulty for both the Escaut and the Selle identifications is presented by 2. 16. 1: *cum per eorum finis triduum iter fecisset, inueniebat ex captiuis Sabim flumen ab castris suis non amplius milia passuum decem abesse.* As Schmittlein insists, *eorum* there should certainly = *Neruiorum*[23]. The western boundary of the *Neruii* was probably not far west of Cambrai[24]. This does not make any sense at all if *Sabis* refers to the Escaut: Caesar could barely have crossed the frontier before he received his information, and a 'three-day march' is quite ridiculous. Even Saulzoir is only 16 km from Cambrai. Turquin's site can hardly have been more than 36 km from the Nervian frontier, and it should follow that three days' march had taken the Roman army only twenty kilometres. It is true that they were marching through hostile territory, and that their progress was impeded by the Nervian barriers (2. 17. 4-5); but this still seems far too short a distance. It is more likely that Caesar is again giving a simplified version, as he seeks to keep his reader's mind on essentials. He had been marching for three days against the *Neruii;* that was what mattered. His audience would not know or care where the Nervian frontier lay[25]. Caesar may not have known himself. He certainly did not want to introduce stray complications, and preferred to obscure the fact that a considerable part of that three-day march had been outside Nervian territory, before he reached the frontier. *Per eorum fines* was a pardonable simplification, which would at the same time emphasise the dangers of the march. He had presumably started at Amiens, or perhaps a little to the east of that city[26].

The final example is Caesar's battle against the *Vsipetes* and *Tencteri.* Much of the discussion must be concerned with the manuscript text of *B.G.,* 4. 15. 2: the defeated Germans fled *ad confluentem Mosae et Rheni.* Can those words mean what they say? Or must we assume that Caesar wrote (or at least should have written) *Mosellae?* If the text can be defended, the battlefield will presumably be near to Kleve or Goch[27]—though the featureless nature of the country and the variations in the course of the Meuse exclude any great precision. If Caesar means the Moselle, the battle will have to be transferred to the vicinity of Koblenz[28].

This is no place for a full discussion. The point is that, on either account, Caesar has left a very great amount unsaid. The last topographical indication of the German position was 4. 6. 4: *Germani latius uagabantur et in finis Eburonum et Condrusorum . . . peruenerant.* Even that is not very clear: it is uncertain whether Caesar is there referring to the whole German army, or simply to a few wandering detachments. But it is anyway a great surprise for us to find ourselves near either Koblenz or Kleve. If the battle was near Koblenz, Caesar has left it quite obscure why the Germans chose to go there. Their detachment among the *Ambiuariti* (4. 9. 3) will find it difficult to rejoin them; and the natural strategy would surely be to retreat northwards, drawing Caesar as far as possible away from his reliable allies, lengthening his lines of communication. If it was the main force of the Germans which had reached the *Eburones* and *Condrusi,* we should expect them to retreat; if the main force was still near Kleve, we should expect them to stay there. Instead, we are asked to assume that they struck off south-eastwards, deep into the country of the *Treueri.* If they did, it is eloquent that Caesar did not think it worth explaining—or even mentioning.

But, of course, there are severe difficulties in the way of defending the manuscript text. The notion of a 'confluence of the Meuse and the Rhine' may itself be something of a nonsense, for 4. 10. 1 seems to make it clear that the stream of the Rhine which met the Meuse was called the *Vacalus* (i.e. the Waal)[29]. We might also be concerned by Caesar's silence about the German retreat from the *Eburones* and *Condrusi;* or by the fact that he tells us nothing of a long Roman march up the Rhine to make their bridge, which seems to have been near Andernach; or by the uncomfortably large distance of the return journey to the *Vbii,* which the German envoys promise to cover in just three days (4. 11. 2-3)[30]. These problems are just as real as those which face the Moselle identification, but in both cases the problems are of the same kind[31]. They rest on Caesar's silence; they rest on topographical difficulties which we, with the aid of autopsy and detailed maps, can expose. That is surely the wrong approach. Caesar's immediate audience would find no difficulty in these silences. They would not know where the *Eburones* and the *Condrusi* were to be found; they would not know how far it was to the *Vbii;* they would not be able to tell exactly where Caesar built his bridge. Caesar could again safely simplify his account, and omit marches and movements which would complicate his narrative and confuse the reader. Whichever location we choose, it is clear that this is what he has done.

The choice must be made on other grounds. All Caesar's narrative has suggested a site close to the Meuse. The introduction of the river's name (4. 9. 3) is immediately explained at 4. 10. 1. That explanation has its obscurities and its inaccuracies, but, given Caesar's penchant for geographical vagueness and simplification, it need not follow that it is seriously corrupt. 4. 10. 1-5 has directed our attention to the Meuse and the Rhine. If *Mosellae* is read at 4. 15. 2, the sudden transfer of the reader to the area of the Moselle, with the unheralded and unexplained introduction of so important a river, would be as artistically inelegant as it is strategically obscure. The inelegance is the more important point, for it is a roughness which Caesar's audience would have noticed in his narrative, and therefore a roughness which he would have taken pains to avoid. He would not have made so much of the Meuse, or he would at least have introduced a similar excursus on the Moselle itself. It seems likely that the manuscript reading at 4. 15. 2 must stand, and Caesar's silences must simply be accepted. It would follow that the battle was fought near Goch or Kleve.

The moral of all this is clear enough. As we turn to Ariovistus, examining the topography of a new campaign and a new battle, we must be prepared to find a far more complex and irregular terrain than Caesar's language would imply. We must not always expect an explanation of difficulties which are only discernible to those who know the country, or who can consult a detailed map. We may expect Caesar to have sketched the main lines, but no more, of the strategic background or of the course of the battle. We are entitled to look for a theatre which fits those main lines—but we may never be sure that Caesar has told us the whole story, and we must be particularly chary of resting any argument on Caesar's *silences*. It is evident that the investigation will be a difficult and delicate one, and that many questions may only be decided with a greater or smaller degree of probability.

CAESAR AND ARIOVISTUS

(A) THE NARRATIVE.

These features of Caesar's technique evidently complicate topographical inquiry, and many cases will be quite hopeless. But, within limits, progress may still be made. The Ariovistus campaign has provoked more discussion and less agreement than any other[32]; but even here the possibilities may at least be narrowed.

Immediately after the army's panic at *Vesontio*, Caesar set out to march against Ariovistus: *et itinere exquisito per Diuiciacum, quod ex aliis ei maximam fidem habebat, ut milium amplius quinquaginta circuitu locis apertis exercitum duceret, de quarta uigilia, ut dixerat, profectus est. septimo die, cum iter non intermitteret, ab exploratoribus certior factus est Ariouisti copias a nostris milibus passuum quattuor et uiginti abesse* (1. 41. 4-5). Ariovistus then invited Caesar to parly, and this meeting was held at a place where *planities erat magna et in ea tumulus terrenus satis grandis* (1. 43. 1). No agreement was reached. A few days later Ariovistus treacherously arrested two envoys of Caesar (1. 47), and *eodem die castra promouit et milibus passuum sex a Caesaris castris sub monte consedit* (1. 48. 1). There is good reason to think that Caesar, too, had by now moved closer to Ariovistus[33].

Postridie eius diei (Ariovistus) *praeter castra Caesaris suas copias traduxit et milibus passuum duobus ultra eum castra fecit, eo consilio uti frumento commeatuque qui ex Sequanis et Aeduis supportaretur Caesarem intercluderet* (1. 48. 2). For the following five days Caesar offered battle, but Ariovistus declined, restricting himself to cavalry skirmishes. *Vbi eum castris se tenere Caesar intellexit, ne diutius commeatu prohiberetur, ultra eum locum, quo in loco Germani consederant, circiter passus sescentos ab his, castris idoneum locum delegit acieque triplici instructa ad eum locum uenit* (1. 49. 1). Ariovistus attacked, but the camp was successfully fortified. Caesar left two legions there with some of the auxiliaries; the other four legions returned to the larger camp. On the following day Caesar tried again to provoke a battle, but did not succeed. He returned to camp around noon. Ariovistus then attacked the smaller camp with vigour, and fighting continued until evening.

The next day saw the decisive battle. Caesar drew up all his *alarii* in front of the smaller camp, *quod minus multitudine militum legionariorum pro hostium numero ualebat, ut ad speciem alariis uteretur* (1. 51. 1). He himself, *triplici instructa acie,* advanced to the enemy camp. This time the Germans were compelled to accept the challenge. Caesar himself *a dextro cornu, quod eam partem minime firmam hostium esse animaduerterat, proelium commisit* (1. 52. 2); in the sequel, *cum hostium acies a sinistro cornu pulsa atque in fugam conuersa esset, a dextro cornu uehementer multitudine suorum nostram aciem premebant* (1. 52. 6). These two items seem to give a coherent picture. *Dextro cornu* in 52. 2 seems clearly to refer to the *Roman* right, while *sinistro* and *dextro* in 52. 6 should naturally describe events from the *German* viewpoint. If so, the battle followed a characteristic pattern, and both right wings succeeded in forcing their enemy to retreat.

Roman cavalry reinforcements led by P. Crassus saved the day, and the Germans were driven into flight. The distance of their flight is important and problematic. The manuscripts of the *B.G.* give five miles: *atque omnes hostes terga conuerterant neque prius fugere destiterunt quam ad flumen Rhenum milia passuum ex eo loco circiter quinque peruenerunt* (1. 53. 1). But Plutarch (*Caes.,* 19. 11) and Orosius (6. 7. 10) both give figures which indicate a distance of *fifty* miles for this flight to the Rhine. . . . Both writers ultimately derive much of their material from Caesar's account[34]. It is a natural possibility that they here reflect an early reading *quinquaginta* in Caesar's text. Equally, it is possible that the figure of fifty represents an error made by an intermediate source (perhaps Pollio), and inherited by Plutarch and Orosius; or the two later authors may even have suffered an identical easy corruption. Either 'five' or 'fifty' should remain possibilities, and only the identification of the battlefield itself can decide between the two.

Caesar thus gives only two place-names, Besançon at the beginning and the Rhine at the end. It is not surprising that a multitude of sites have been suggested. . . . The five most favoured candidates [include]: (1) a site just south of Ribeauvillé (Stoffel, with many followers); (2) a site some fifteen kilometres east of this, near Ohnenheim (Jordan); (3) a series of sites around Cernay (many scholars since Napoléon III, especially Jullian, Hatt: the most plausible reconstruction is that of Jullian); (4) a site between Mulhouse and Basel (Bazouin, Miltner, Morgan); (5) a site in the environs of Belfort, as suggested by Napoléon I and elaborately argued by Schmittlein.

(B) THE INDICATIONS OF THE SITE.

The evidence is very tenuous, and it may be helpful to list the principal pointers to the battle's location.

(1) The time taken to march from *Vesontio:* on the seventh day of his march, Caesar was twenty-four miles from Ario-

vistus' first camp. When pressed, an army could doubtless move at 15 miles a day or more; but the most likely average figure for a day's march is perhaps 10-13 Roman miles[35]. Caesar's speed on this occasion was probably close to the average. He was marching cautiously: he did not know of Ariovistus' precise location until the news arrived on the seventh day[36], and he was sufficiently apprehensive of ambush to follow his *circuitus* rather than the direct route. But, equally, he would not want to dawdle. He did not grant his troops their customary rest-day (*cum iter non intermitteret*), doubtless hoping to reach open country as soon as possible[37]. We might expect him to cover something like sixty to eighty miles on the first six days; the length of the seventh march is unknown.

(2) The general probabilities of the line of march. It seems likely that Ariovistus is starting from Upper Alsace; Caesar is setting out from *Vesontio*. This *prima facie* makes a site as far north as Ribeauvillé, or as far south-east as Mulhouse-Basel, hard to explain[38]. Of course, here we must be careful. Any number of strategic considerations may have intervened to draw the armies away from their natural route, and we cannot be sure that Caesar would have told us about them. But this remains a factor which favours Cernay or Belfort, both of which would be natural positions for Ariovistus to reach and occupy.

(3) *Sub monte* at 1. 48. 1. There must be at least one mountain or hill in the region, and this should overlook the site of Ariovistus' second camp.

(4) Ariovistus' manœuvre of 1. 48. 2. This is rather odd: Caesar allows the German horde to march past his flank and cut his communications. Caesar of course had *exploratores,* who had been active a few days earlier (1. 41. 5), and he surely knew that Ariovistus had been on the move the day before. He must have been unusually negligent to allow this manœuvre to succeed unmolested—unless the Germans were in some way protected by the lie of the land[39]. Again, not a decisive point. There may have been more to this march than Caesar's language would suggest; Caesar may even have been negligent; or he may simply have suppressed mention of an unsuccessful cavalry engagement. But it would be reassuring to find a site which provided a natural explanation.

(5) *Quinque* or *quinquaginta*. This is the most specific indication, and discussion must start from here. At first sight *nec prius fugere destiterunt* seems to favour *quinque* in Caesar's text: it is hardly possible that the exhausted Germans could literally have fled without respite for fifty miles. But is it not equally unlikely that Caesar would adopt so emphatic a tone, if the Rhine were a mere five miles distant[40]? *Fuga* need not have all the breathless and hectic connotations of the English 'flight' or the German 'Flucht'; *fuga* can be a fairly measured and prolonged affair[41]. Caesar quite possibly means that the Germans made no attempt to regroup, and did not stop for any length of time, before reaching the Rhine. The 'flight' does not in fact seem to have been too hectic: the Germans have time

to look for boats (1. 53. 2-3), and it is likely that the cavalry pursuit was somewhat delayed (1. 53. 3, cf. perhaps Frontin. *Strat.*, 2. 1. 16). The picture of 'the Germans diving into the Rhine like lemmings'[42] should anyway be abandoned. It may be that this flight was similar to that of the *Heluetii* (1. 26. 5), who fled day and night for four days, covering over 50 miles. *Quinquaginta* at 1. 53. 1 should certainly remain a possibility.

Whether 'five' or 'fifty', we should not be too confident of its accuracy. Caesar would not have known the exact distance: he would hardly instruct his legionaries to count their paces as they pursued, and the cavalry would have little idea of how far they had ridden. The figure is likely to be impressionistic guesswork, probably too low rather than too high: Caesar had no interest in minimising this *fuga*. Brackets of 3. 5-5. 5 miles, or 35-55 miles, might be realistic. Nor should we assume that the Germans withdrew in a single body; nor that they all took the most direct route to the Rhine.

Discussion should be based on these five points. But, before proceeding further, we should dismiss some other factors which do *not* provide reliable indications.

(1) In his elaborate argument for Belfort, Schmittlein rested much of his case on *milium amplius quinquaginta circuitu* (1. 41. 4). Following Stolle, he thought that this 'detour of more than fifty miles' should represent the whole length of Caesar's march[43]. Caesar certainly does not mean this. The clause *ut . . . duceret* defines and explains *itinere exquisito*: it specifies the length of detour which Diviciacus' informants recommended to Caesar when he was still at *Vesontio*[44]. A detour through open country was needed to avoid the dangerous road mentioned at 1. 39. 6, and Caesar duly informed himself of this alternative route. But he certainly would not envisage halting as soon as this detour was complete. He would stop when he received news that Ariovistus was close at hand, and this news eventually arrived on the seventh day. He could not know how far he would march *while he was still at Vesontio,* and could merely concern himself with avoiding the difficult early part of the route. Diviciacus' recommendations provide no pointer to the total distance which Caesar eventually marched, and Caesar's language leaves it quite possible that, once the detour was complete, his troops marched on a considerable way.

The distance by the direct route from *Vesontio* to Belfort is about 57 Roman miles; to Montbéliard, about 54. This *circuitus* would naturally add to that figure, but, as the reconstruction of Caesar's route can only be guesswork, the distance from *Vesontio* to either Belfort or Montbéliard by this route cannot be known.

(2) Another favourite argument has rested on the *planities magna* of 1. 43. 1: most have thought that this should be the plain of Alsace, in one sense the only 'great plain' of the region. This need not follow. '"Gross" ist ein sehr dehnbarer Begriff' (Stolle), and takes its colouring from its context. A plain such as that proposed by Schmittlein, on the site of the present Belfort-Chaux airport, would certainly be possible: in the foothills of the Vosges, *any* plain large enough to accommodate two cavalry forces and leave room for a gap of 400 paces (1. 43. 2-3) could be described as *magna*[45].

(3) Many searchers have started from the *tumulus terrenus* of 1. 43. 1, and assumed that this should still be visible. The oddity of the phrase was noticed by Holmes[46]: why should Caesar bother to specify *terrenus*? Holmes suggested that this might be an earthen barrow or mound, an artificial construction which might easily have now disappeared. This is surely possible, though equally Caesar may be constrasting this *tumulus* with nearby rocky eminences (cf. Livy, 38. 20. 4). Most of the suggested sites can in fact provide a *tumulus,* but we cannot demand this as a *sine qua non.*

(c) THE THEORIES.

We should start from *quinque* and *quinquaginta*. The site may be either five or fifty miles from the Rhine, and we should certainly allow a margin for erratic guesswork. Yet the traditional favourites, Ribeauvillé and Cernay, are well outside these margins, and wilfully ignore the only numbers we have: both sites are about fifteen miles from the Rhine[47]. This in itself is enough to exclude them. And, in both cases, the river Ill presents a second problem. Both sites are west of the Ill, and the fugitives would have to negotiate that considerable river before reaching the Rhine. It would be the Ill which occasioned the greater slaughter, the Ill which, once crossed, gave the Germans safety and respite. The only solution is to suppose that Caesar described the Ill as the *Rhenus:* a very unlikely 'simplification'.

Both Ribeauvillé and Cernay have further difficulties of their own:

(1) Ribeauvillé is a long way north. It is hard to see why the armies should have gone there in the first place, and even harder to believe that Caesar could march so far in seven days. Stoffel's site is 189 km (over 120 Roman miles) from Besannçon; we earlier gave limits of sixty to eighty miles for the first six days, then the seventh day's march. Moreover, Stoffel's reconstruction makes little strategic sense. He makes Caesar encamp on the left bank of the Fecht, between Ostheim and Gemar; Ariovistus' flank march is conducted along the heights of Zellenberg. Caesar, we must remember, was the first to encamp. Stoffel leaves it hard to understand why he should thus occupy the featureless territory towards the Ill, allowing Ariovistus to pitch camp in the foothills of the Vosges. Caesar stood in fear of Ariovistus' cavalry: it would be much more sensible, and characteristic, for Caesar himself to occupy a camp in the foothills.

(2) There is little to recommend Cernay. The arguments in its favour are largely *a priori,* for it was a junction of

major roads. It is difficult to formulate a reconstruction which explains Ariovistus' unimpeded flank march: indeed, the only attempt which squarely faces this problem is that of Jullian. He places Caesar's *castra maiora* some two kilometres south-west of Cernay, and thinks that Ariovistus marched along the foothills of the Vosges from Cernay to Thann. Autopsy suggests that this is not possible. The hillocks rise sharply and steeply from the plain to form individual mounds, giving no continuous ridge. The individual hillocks would be difficult enough to negotiate, and such a march would be physically impossible. Ariovistus could not have attempted to climb these hills; he would have no choice but to conduct his march along the plain at their foot. But then nothing is explained, for his army is as exposed as ever. More recently, Hatt has claimed that archaeological evidence indicates a site slightly further east: Caesar's *castra maiora* should be just west of Wittelsheim, and Ariovistus' flank march should have led him to a camp 3 km south-west of this. Caesar's *castra minora* are placed between Aspach-le-Haut and Aspach-le-Bas[48]. A fuller presentation of this evidence may make a reconsideration necessary, but, as reported, the finds do not make the solution attractive. They seem to be quite undated. The resulting reconstruction is unsatisfactory in detail, for it leaves the German flank march exposed, and gives an implausible strategic importance to the *castra minora* in the battle itself.

The choice lies between *quinque* and *quinquaginta* at 1. 53. 1. If we accept *quinque,* we must place the battle in the plain between the Ill and the Rhine. There is not much to be said for putting it as far north as Ohnenheim (Jordan). That makes Caesar march a very long way north; and it is hard to find a plausible *mons* for Ariovistus' second camp. (If Caesar means one of the Vosges hills, it is difficult to understand how Ariovistus' flank march could have been allowed to cross the Ill). And, once again, Caesar would be unwise to assume such an exposed position in the plain; he would much more naturally keep to the safer hills.

These arguments may be generalised, for there are no plausible *montes* between the Rhine and the Ill north of Mulhouse. The *quinque* figure would thus lead irresistibly to the suggestions of Miltner, and, with a different orientation, Bazouin and Morgan, preferring sites between Mulhouse and Basel[49]. But here, too, there are difficulties. The region is fairly flat, and the German flank march would probably be exposed; and it is still hard to find a *mons* which convinces[50]. The region is good for cavalry, and Caesar would be unwise to allow himself to be drawn to it. And the greatest problem is clearly seen by Miltner and Morgan themselves, as they try to explain how the armies came to be so far to the south-east. (a) Miltner thinks that Ariovistus was anxious to link with the *Heluetii,* now returned to their native land after their abortive migration: that is why Miltner places the Germans to the south of Caesar. This does not ring true. The *Heluetii* must now have been extraordinarily weakened, and their relations with Ariovistus had never been good[51]. It is not credible that he should think their help more reliable, or potentially

more valuable, than the Suebian reinforcements to the north (1. 37. 3). (b) Miltner also recognises the importance of those *Suebi,* and suggests that Caesar had an interest in drawing Ariovistus away from them to the south[52]. This is more plausible; but it still hard to see why Ariovistus should allow himself to be drawn. He would have done better to adopt the waiting game which had been so successful at *Magetobriga*[53], remaining in Upper Alsace and giving the *Suebi* a chance to join him. That would leave two options, either to wait for the *Suebi,* or to strike at Caesar's elongated and exposed communications. (c) Finally, Morgan points to the advantages to Caesar of avoiding the plain of Alsace, since he feared the German cavalry; and he suggests that Caesar may have wished to keep the option of retreating southward to the *Rauraci* or *Heluetii,* both of whom he had just subdued. But the Roman lines of communication led not to the *Rauraci* or the *Heluetii,* but to the *Aedui,* the *Sequani,* and perhaps the *Leuci* and *Lingones*[54]. Those would be the lines Caesar would wish to protect; those lands, not those of his recent enemies, would be his favoured directions of retreat. The Mulhouse-Basel location must leave these lines very vulnerable, especially if Caesar did not know the exact position of the Germans as he marched.

All these arguments are of course dangerous. Generals do not always read events correctly; and the preliminary manœuvres may anyway have been more complex than Caesar's words would suggest, and there may have been other factors to draw the armies to the south-east. If this solution is correct, we should have to assume that the narrative was very bare and simplified, and that vital features of the campaign were unexplained; but, by now, that would be no surprise. The Mulhouse-Basel location remains improbable: credible topographical details are hard to find, and it is difficult even to conjecture a plausible strategic background. But, given the characteristics of Caesar's narrative technique, this solution is not quite impossible.

Still, the difficulties of this reconstruction strengthen the case for *quinquaginta* at 1. 53. 1. That leads naturally to the solution of Schmittlein, a site in the neighbourhood of Belfort. That is the natural place for Ariovistus, coming from upper Alsace, and Caesar, coming from *Vesontio,* to meet; and the land to the north is far too mountainous to admit any alternative sites fifty miles from the Rhine. Schmittlein places Caesar's first camp near Montbéliard, and assumes that he moved nearer Ariovistus in the course of the negotiations. The first German camp will be near Rougemont-Lauw, the second close to Vescemont. For the final positions, see Figure 3: he places the main Roman camp on the heights of Cravanche, which have a commanding view northwards (the direction from which Ariovistus would approach); the final German camp is located on le Vallon and la Miotte; and he suggests Les Barres for Caesar's second camp, south-east of the first camp and south-west of Ariovistus.

It is not hard to find difficulties in this account. Belfort is not even fifty miles from the Rhine; the distance is about thirty-five miles. We should have to assume that the Germans took an indirect route, some perhaps fleeing north-east rather than east; or that Caesar allowed himself a generous rounding; or that he simply guessed too high. None of these assumptions is impossible, but the distance is still uncomfortably near to the lower limit which we earlier allowed. Again, some critics have thought the distance from *Vesontio* intolerably small—about fifty-four miles by the direct route from *Vesontio* to Montbéliard, where Schmittlein puts Caesar's first camp[55]. But here Schmittlein can be defended. Our estimate for Caesar's march gave sixty to eighty miles during the first six days, then an unknown amount on the seventh[56]. We cannot know what route Caesar took[57]; but it certainly involved the long *circuitus,* and might well be considerably longer than the direct road. Our estimate fits the Montbéliard identification well enough.

Graver difficulties are presented by Schmittlein's detailed suggestions. The final German camp should cut Caesar's communications (1. 48. 2). These communications stretched south-west, west, and perhaps north, to *Vesontio,* to the *Sequani* and *Aedui,* and perhaps to the *Leuci* and *Lingones.* A German camp on la Miotte does little to impede these. The Rougemont-Lauw and Vescemont identifications are no more than guesses. And the worst difficulties are presented by the position he suggests for the Roman *castra minora,* not much more than one kilometre south-east of the main camp. First, both Roman positions now lie on the same side of Ariovistus' camp: that is impossible to reconcile with *ultra eum locum* at 1. 49. 1. Secondly, we have seen that the items of 1. 52. 2 and 1. 52. 6 present a coherent picture, with Caesar commanding from the Roman right, and both right wings forcing their enemy to retreat. It is also likely that the detail of 1. 51. 1 (the force from the second camp *minus multitudine militum legionariorum pro hostium numero ualebat*) is picked up and echoed at 1. 52. 6 (in the battle the Germans *a dextro cornu uehementer multitudine suorum nostram aciem premebant*). If so, the German right wing seems to stand opposite the force from the Roman *castra minora:* it is implied that the Roman line in front of both camps is continuous, and the *alarii,* coming from the smaller camp, stand on the left of the main Roman force. Schmittlein finds it hard to account for this. With the two Roman camps as close as he suggests, the line will certainly be continuous, but the *alarii* will now be on the right of the main force. He has therefore to give a forced interpretation of 1. 52. 2 and 1. 52. 6: *dextro cornu* at 52. 2 now has to give the detail from the German viewpoint, so that Caesar can command from the Roman left; and the indications of 52. 6 have to be given from the Roman point of view, so that both left wings can be successful. This reverses the natural reading of both items, and Schmittlein's suggestion has not won favour[58].

Yet perhaps the Belfort model can be saved. Either of two approaches might be rewarding:

(1) We might assume that Schmittlein has rightly identified the battlefield, but reversed the camps of the two

sides. If Caesar had occupied la Miotte, it is quite likely that Ariovistus would occupy Cravanche, and such a camp would now genuinely hinder Caesar's communications. The Les Barres location may be retained for the *castra minora,* and this answers quite well to *sescentos passus* at 1. 49. 1. The battle would now be fought a short distance south-west of Schmittlein's proposed position.

(2) Even so, the battlefield remains cramped, and it is hard to believe that both sides could operate as if the Savoureuse did not exist. Both Cravanche and (especially) la Miotte are higher and steeper than the camps Caesar usually favoured in such circumstances[59], though this is compensated by the impressive northern view which both hills command. But it is more likely that the whole battle should be transferred some way south-east, to the rather larger plain south-east and east of Danjoutin. A suitable location for Caesar's first camp would be offered by the hill on which the Fort de Vézelois now stands, some four kilometres south-east of Belfort. Its gently rising slope corresponds to the type of camp which Caesar usually preferred, and the hill has commanding views north and east-south-east. From it a strong army might easily control the Savoureuse valley. Ariovistus' second camp, six miles away and *sub monte,* causes no difficulty: a precise identification is impossible, but there are a number of possible sites below the Forêt de Roppe, between Valdoie and Rougemont-le-Château. Ariovistus' final camp should be two miles from Fort de Vézelois, and able to control Caesar's communications. The most likely possibility is the hillock overlooking Andelnans, some 1.5 kilometres west of Meroux, just east of the modern Belfort-Montbéliard road. The Roman *castra minora* might be placed on the hill a little to the south, close to Sevenans.

No especial importance need be attached to these detailed proposals: they merely illustrate that there are locations near Belfort which are not vulnerable to the objections which face Schmittlein. His general thesis remains quite plausible, and it does seem that the environs of Belfort have more to recommend them than any other proposed site. The Belfort region is the most plausible point for the two armies to meet, and the hills surrounding Belfort a natural position for Caesar to choose to occupy. The Belfort-Chaux airport presents a plausible *planities.* The precise route of Ariovistus' flank march cannot be recovered—but, in this land of hills, ridges, and forests, it would be odd if he could not find a route which was naturally protected against a Roman attack.

The status of this conclusion must again be stressed. We are not dealing with certainties: Caesar's narrative technique does not permit it. The strategy of the campaign, the course of the fighting, the nature of the terrain may all have been more complex than Caesar's language would suggest; and these complications may have led both generals to act, or to allow their enemy to act, in ways which we find hard to understand. It may still be that the Mulhouse-Basel solution is correct, however difficult it is to explain how the armies reached that region. Even on the Belfort identification, the figure of fifty miles is not wholly satisfactory, though it can be explained. And, on any account, the narrative remains bare and terse: note, for instance, the extreme economy of Caesar's description of the German flank march (48. 2). Given these qualifications, Belfort presents the fewest difficulties. Plutarch's [*tetrakosíous*] and Orosius' *quinquaginta* are vindicated, and *quinquaginta* should be read at ***B.G.***, 1. 53. 1.

Notes

1. CIC., *Prov. Cons.*, 22.

2. *Ib.*, 33; cf. his similar remark concerning Cilicia, *Att.*, 5. 20. 1.

3. CIC., *Q. fr.*, 3. 6 (8). 2.

4. The most important modern discussions are: NAPOLÉON III, *Hist de Jules César*, ii (1866), 85-94 and pl. 8; K. LEHMANN, *N. Jb.*, 7 (1901), 506-9, and *Klio*, 6 (1906), 237-48; C. JULLIAN, *Histoire de la Gaule*, iii (1909), 251, n. 5 and 253, n. 2; T. RICE HOLMES, *Caesar's Conquest of Gaul*, 2nd ed. (1911), 658-68, with full references to the earlier literature; J. N. HOUGH, *CJ*, 36 (1941), 337-45; G. STÉGEN *LEC*, 19 (1951), 209-16, and *LEC*, 26 (1958), 240-2; R. SCHMITTLEIN, *Avec César en Gaule*, i (1970), 298-304; Chr. PEYRE, *REL*, 56 (1978), 175-215.

5. HOLMES, 660; cf. *B.G.*, 6. 44. *Durocortorum* seems to be the modern Reims: see HOLMES, 354, and JULLIAN, iii. 408.

6. Though it is not clear where the *Belgae* started from: perhaps La Fère or further north (HOLMES, 658-9), rather than Soissons (JULLIAN, iii. 251, n. 5).

7. Perhaps Bièvres (LEHMANN, *Klio*, art. cit., 247-8), perhaps Vieux-Laon (NAPOLÉON, ii. 101, n. 1; HOLMES, 398-400; M. RAMBAUD, comm. on *B.G.*, ii-iii [Paris, 1965], 55). Beaurieux (JULLIAN, iii. 253, n. 2 and 254, n. 2) is not plausible: see HOLMES, *ib.*, WHEELER and RICHARDSON, *Hill Forts of Northern France* [1957], 13 and n. 2, followed by SCHMITTLEIN, 299-300, identify *Bibrax* with Vieux-Reims, close to the modern Condé-sur-Suippe. This is hardly plausible in view of Caesar's *ex itinere* (2. 6. 1), suggesting strongly that *Bibrax* was close to the Belgic line of march, and surely excluding the possibility that the *Belgae* crossed the Aisne to attack *Bibrax*, then re-crossed to face Caesar. Once the *Belgae* had crossed the river, why should they not have moved instead on the unprotected lands of the *Remi*, about which Caesar was so anxious (2. 5. 5)?

8. See the judicious discussion of HOLMES, 659-66.

9. Cf. LEHMANN, *N. Jb.*, art. cit., 507; HOLMES, 665, n. 5, 666-7, and *The Roman Republic*, ii (1923), 337.

10. HOLMES, 667-8.

11. Cf. esp. LEHMANN, *N. Jb.*, art. cit.; HOLMES, 660-4; STÉGEN, *lec*, 19 (1951), 209-16 (on the implications of

Caesar's language). HOUGH, *CJ*, 36 (1941), 337-45, and, more elaborately, PEYRE, *REL*, 56 (1978), 175-215, argue that Caesar's language can be reconciled with Napoléon's discoveries, but both are forced into strained and unconvincing interpretations of the Latin: see following notes. Rambaud therefore speculates that Napoléon's fortification may represent *hiberna* of 52-1 B.C., and prefers the Chaudardes site (Comm. on *B.G.*, ii-iii, 52-3). Napoléon's discoveries have recently been confirmed by aerial photographs (cf. e.g. PEYRE, 188-93 with Plates 4-5), but these do not prove that this was Caesar's camp in 57.

12. Unless we assume that the Roman battle-line faced west, rather than north (JULLIAN, iii. 255, n. 1): this is not plausible (HOLMES, 661-2). If the main gate of the Roman camp faced S.W. rather than N.W., there is perhaps a certain sense in which the *acies* was drawn up *pro castris* (so Hough and Peyre). Yet no-one would have guessed from Caesar's account that the line was drawn up in this way, and (as HOUGH, 340, admits) Caesar has certainly written in a misleading and simplified way.

13. Mr. Morgan reminds me that the curve of the Aisne would give some protection to the left, and suggests that fortification would have been unnecessary; cf. HOUGH, 343. But (1) any advance of the Roman army *would* leave the left unprotected, and extremely vulnerable to the overlapping Belgic right; and (2)—the important point here—Caesar's language (*ab utroque latere, lateribus*) would anyway remain simplified and misleading. Most implausibly, Hough and Peyre take *ab utroque latere eius collis* to be the N.W. and S.E. sides of the hill: Hough adds that the *frons* would not be the 'front' which faced the enemy, but the S.W. side of the hill. If they were right, Caesar's account would again be extremely obscure and misleading: without knowledge of the country, none of his audience would have guessed that both these *latera* lay to the right of his *acies* (as Peyre insists), or that the *frons* did not face the enemy and the plain (so Hough). But in fact we surely take the *latitudo* of the hill facing the enemy (8. 2) to be the distance between the two *latera*; if so, the *latera* can only be the 'sides' to the N.E. and S.W.

14. Nor do the distances seem to correspond to Caesar's *passuum quadringentorum* (HOLMES, 663; PEYRE, 206). But Mr. Morgan, referring to CASSINI, *Nouvelle carte . . . de la France* (1744), observes that the Aisne changed its course between then and 1866, when Napoléon wrote. Cf. also PEYRE, 192-3. This change may have obliterated the furthest extremity of the southern trench; *passuum quadringentorum* may thus be an accurate description.

15. HOLMES, 662-3. The attempts of Hough and Peyre to refer the *deiectus* to the steeper N.W. and S.E. slopes are misconceived: cf. n. 13 above.

16. HOLMES, 665-6; cf. J. STOFFEL, *Guerre civile* (1887), ii. 327-8. RAMBAUD, Comm. on *B.G.,* ii-iii, 59-60, seems to over-estimate.

17. Esp. JULLIAN, iii. 261, n. 2; HOLMES, 671-7; G. BOULMONT, *RBPh,* 3 (1924), 19-34; M. LIZIN, *LEC,* 22 (1954), 401-6; cf. the list of P. TURQUIN, *LEC,* 23 (1955), 115. SCHMITTLEIN, *Avec César en Gaule,* i. 311-30, retains the Sambre identification (cf. *RIO,* 15 (1963), 133-49 and 161-8), but he is no more convincing than his predecessors.

18. M. ARNOULD, *RBPh,* 20 (1941), 29-106, esp. 84-5, 91-5. The objections of SCHMITTLEIN, *RIO,* 15 (1963), 142-49, are inconclusive. However, Arnould's further attempt to connect phonetically *Sabis* and *Selle* is less cogent: cf. SCHMITTLEIN, art. cit., 138-42.

19. Cf. SCHMITTLEIN, art.cit., 134-6. For the line of this road, see A. LEDUQUE, *Esquisse de topographie historique sur l'Ambiane* (1972), 134-6; TURQUIN, *LEC,* 23 (1955), 138-9.

20. Cf. M. FRAIKIN, *LEC,* 22 (1954), 287-90; R. VERDIÈRE, *RBPh,* 32 (1954), 302-3, and *RBPh,* 53 (1975), 52.

21. Cf. *B.G.,* 6. 33. 3 (though that is itself confused) and the discussion of VERDIÈRE, *RBPh,* 53 (1975), 48-51.

22. *LEC,* 23 (1955), 113-56.

23. *Pace* TURQUIN, 125-6. Cf. SCHMITTLEIN, *RIO,* 15 (1963), 164-5; *Avec César en Gaule,* i. 313-5. Rambaud's discussion of the passage is unnecessarily non-committal (comm. on *B.G.,* ii-iii, 79-80).

24. Cf. A. LEDUQUE, *Recherches topo-historiques sur l'Atrébatie* (1966), 31-3; G. FAIDER-FEYTMANS, *LEC,* 21 (1952), 338-58, at 347, 357-8. The diocesan evidence for the Nervian boundary is not entirely reliable, but this section of its seems firm enough: cf. J. DUNLAP, *CP,* 26 (1931), 321.

25. Cf. CIC, *Q. fr.,* 3. 6(8). 2.

26. TURQUIN, 125-6 makes Caesar start from Amiens itself, which would certainly be the natural place to receive the submission of the *Ambiani.* But, if the Selle identification is right, this would imply a march of 76 km in three days, with the last day's route leading through hostile terrain. We should not underestimate Caesar's *celeritas,* but, even leaving the Nervian obstacles out of account, 76 km seems too much. See works cited at n. 36 below. If the Escaut identification is preferred, Amiens would be a more plausible starting-point.

27. So NAPOLÉON, ii. 138-9; cf. esp. A. T. WALKER, *CJ,* 17 (1921-2), 77-86; R. DION, *REL,* 41 (1963), 186-209, who at 194, n. 1 has some good remarks about Caesar's technique; A. GRISART, *LEC,* 28 (1960), 169-70, n. 87.

28. So e.g. Cluver, Long, von Göler, Holmes.

29. Caution is here necessary. The paradosis seems to be *Mosa profluit ex monte Vosego, qui est in finibus Lin-gonum, et parte quadam ex Rheno recepta, quae appellatur Vacalus insulamque efficit Batavorum, in Oceanum influit, neque longius ab Oceano milibus passuum LXXX in Rhenum influit.* This is evidently corrupt. The traditional healing is the deletion of *-que* after *insulam,* and of *in Oceanum influit.* But T. BERRES, *Hermes,* 98 (1970), 154-63, argues that Caesar wrote *Mosa . . . Lingonum, neque longius ab Oceano milibus passuum LXXX in Rhenum influit,* and that the alternative conception and formulation *et parte quadam . . . in Oceanum influit* is owed to an early recension, not to Caesar himself. Cf. RAMBAUD, *ad loc.* Berres' argument is not cogent in detail (cf. e.g. n. 31, below), but this is not the place for a full discussion.

30. See the detailed discussion of HOLMES, 691-706, esp. 698-702. GRISART, *l.c.,* rates these silences as decisive in favour of the Moselle.

31. Except for the surprise of Caesar's calling the Waal the *Rhenus.* That is a looseness, but no more: it is clear from the paradosis of 4. 10. 1 itself that the Waal was envisaged as a part, or a continuation, of the Rhine. Cf. TAC., *Ann.,* 2. 6. 4, *uerso cognomine Vahalem accolae dicunt,* with Furneaux's note. BERRES, art. cit., exaggerates the difficulties presented by Caesar's formulation.

32. The modern bibliography is vast. The most important items are: STOFFEL, *Guerre de César et d'Arioviste* (1890); F. STOLLE, *Wo schlug Cäsar den Ariovist?* (1899); JULLIAN, iii. 221-41, esp. 231, n. 4; HOLMES, 57-68 and 636-57; A. BAZOUIN, *REL,* 14 (1936), 28-9, with a necessary correction by A. DAIN, *REL,* 15 (1937), 269-72; F. MILTNER, *Klio,* 34 (1941), 181-95; Ch. JORDAN, *Arioviste et les Germains chassés d'Alsace en 58 av. J.-C.* (1951); R. SCHMITTLEIN, *La première campagne de César contre les Germains* (1956), with extensive bibliography but omitting Miltner's important article; J. H. COLLINS' review of Schmittlein, *Gnomon,* 30 (1958), 300-305; J.-J. HATT, *REL,* 49 (1971), 20-1; J. D. MORGAN, *Caesar's defeat of Ariovistus,* to appear.

33. It is hard to believe that there would be time in one day for Caesar's legates to ride twenty-four miles to Ariovistus' camp; for Ariovistus ostentatiously to arrest them; for the Germans to break camp; for the full body of their force (apparently including women and children, 1. 50. 4-5, 51. 3, 53. 4) to march eighteen miles; and for them finally to pitch a new camp. Shorter distances must be involved, and it is easiest to assume that Caesar had moved nearer the enemy. Cf. esp. MILTNER, art. cit., 189-92.

34. Plutarch probably found Caesar's account transmitted in Pollio: cf. my article in *JHS,* 99 (1979), 74-96, esp. 84-91 with nn. 77, 108. Orosius presumably derives from Livy, who himself based parts of his account on Pollio: cf. art. cit., nn. 73, 124. . . .

35. This is no place for a full discussion of this complicated problem. SCHMITTLEIN, *La première cam-*

pagne, 105-24, overstates the case for a short daily march of less than 20 km (cf. esp RAMBAUD, *REL,* 35 [1957], 400, and *REL,* 50 [1972], 58); but some of his arguments are difficult to dismiss. Cf. STOLLE, art. cit., 27-40.

36. This is the natural inference from 1. 41. 5. Note that Caesar had earlier feared that Ariovistus might reach *Vesontio* before the Romans (1. 38). As he eventually marched over fifty miles beyond *Vesontio* before establishing Ariovistus' position, it is clear that his intelligence of the German movements was limited.

37. I owe this point to Mr. Morgan. Roman troops were normally rested every fifth day.

38. Cf. with regard to Ribeauvillé, WALKER, *CJ,* 1 (1905-6), 213-20.

39. This point is well made by STOFFEL, 94.

40. Cf. STOLLE, art. cit., 10-11. Particularly after the massive Helvetian flight of 1. 26. 5, five miles does seem too small a distance to be remarked.

41. E.g. *B.G.,* 1. 27. 4; *B.C.,* 3. 94. 4, with my article in *Hist.,* 22 (1973), 259, n. 67.

42. The phrase of COLLINS, art. cit., 305.

43. *La première campagne,* 143-8, cf. 105-24; STOLLE, art. cit., 3-10.

44. *Itinere exquisito per Diuiciacum* suggests that Diviciacus did not know the route himself, but was asked to make inquiries on Caesar's behalf. *Pace* STOLLE, art. cit., 6-7, there is no difficulty there.

45. Cf STOLLE, art. cit., 12-14; F. KROON, *Mnem.,* 3. 5 (1937), 143; SCHMITTLEIN, *La première campagne,* 150-1; COLLINS, art. cit., 301-2. Mr. Morgan objects that at *B.G.,* 3. 1. 5, *non magna planitie* is used of a nearby plain which extends for several square miles, and is larger than Schmittlein's site. At that point of his narrative, Caesar is preparing the scene for the assault on Galba's camp: when he is thinking of vulnerability to such an attack, a plain of this size might well seem cramped. It need not follow that Caesar would apply the same standards when describing a plain chosen for a *conference.*

46. HOLMES, 639-40.

47. Hence HOLMES, 657, proposed *quindecim milia* at 1. 53. 1; justly stigmatised by MILTNER, art. cit., 183, n. 1, as 'jeder methodischen Grundlage entbehrende Willkür'. In his edition of 1914, Holmes more cautiously read *quinquaginta.*

48. Résumé in *REL,* 49 (1971), 20-1.

49. Bazouin places Caesar's camp in the reign of Rantz-willer and Magstatt, and Ariovistus to the north of this (first in the forest of Harth, then at the foot of the 'Signal d'Illfurt'). Miltner places Caesar's first camp close to Habsheim, and Ariovistus south of

this; the first German camp is placed in the region of Basel, and their flank march on the heights west of Habsheim. Morgan puts the Roman *castra maiora* on the Hittenberg, 1 km west of Hésingue, and the *castra minora* between Attenschwiller and Folgens-bourg; the German camp is located at Attenschwiller. (Morgan's reconstruction is the most plausible and closely argued, with good criticisms of his two predecessors).

50. The Signal d'Illfurt does not really 'dominate the area', as Bazouin claimed. Morgan places the *castra sub monte* at Sierentz, but here too there is no very plausible *mons.*

51. Cf. 1. 1. 4, 1. 40. 7.

52. MILTNER, art. cit., 186-7. This is hard to reconcile with his own thesis, placing Ariovistus south of Caesar in an unexplained manner; but it might provide a strategic explanation of the reverse reconstructions of Bazouin and Morgan.

53. Cf. 1. 40. 8-9, 1. 44. 3.

54. Cf. 1. 48. 2 (*Aedui* and *Sequani*), 1. 40. 11 (*Leuci* and *Lingones*). By *Sequani* we should of course understand that part of their country which they had retained from the encroachments of Ariovistus. Cf. HOLMES, 652, n. 1.

55. The criticism is made by COLLINS, art. cit., 304-5, and esp. by RAMBAUD (reviews cited in n. 36); so also MORGAN, in his paper to appear. Schmittlein's own defence, assuming that the Romans marched a *total* of fifty miles, is not satisfactory: above, p. 757-758.

56. Above, p. 754.

57. Schmittlein's conjectural route (*La première campagne,* 145-8) is based on his misunderstanding of *circuitu,* and is not plausible.

58. Cf. the sceptical remarks of COLLINS, art. cit., 305; J. P. V. D. BALDSON, *History,* 43 (1958), 44-5.

59. Cf. JULLIAN, iii. 179, n. 3.

Christian Meier (essay date 1982)

SOURCE: "Caesar and the War as Reflected in His Commentaries," in *Caesar,* translated by David McLintock, BasicBooks, 1995, pp. 254-64.

[*In the following excerpt, originally published in German in 1982, Meier explains how in* De Bello Gallico *Caesar triumphs by taking the offensive, presenting himself in total control, and purposely avoiding self-justification.*]

Caesar's book on the Gallic War was in the tradition of reports by Roman military commanders, but at the same time quite novel in that it was composed in a style that matched the highest literary standards. Though ostensibly a campaign report, it is also a highly idiosyncratic expression of the author's personality.

Such a self-portrait naturally has an apologetic purpose. Hence, Caesar's memoir—as well as the conscious and unconscious wishes that guided it—misrepresents certain matters, passes over others in silence or treats them only cursorily, and gives a somewhat partial account of the whole. This is often hard to check, since for the most part Caesar's report is our only source. Where it is possible to check it, Caesar himself usually provides clues that help in unmasking him. For he leaves many contradictions unresolved, unlike a petty deceiver, who would have been consistent. And he reports many things that today seem discreditable—and probably did at the time. In view of Caesar's evident skill in trimming the facts to his own advantage, it seems all the more remarkable that in many cases he refrained from doing so—even where he was vulnerable on ethical grounds. This does not seem fortuitous. Strasburger speaks of a certain 'immoralism' in Caesar's writings.

Apart from its propagandist tendency, the work has a documentary purpose. Caesar records his deeds for posterity. For the Roman nobility, and for Caesar more than others, fame was a great spur. He sought to pit himself against transience. And while they had to enlist others to write about them, he could write about himself. Nor did he wish to draw a false picture of himself, since he was certain that he need not fear the judgement of posterity.

Caesar's account gives an impression of total objectivity. He always speaks of himself in the third person, using the first only in his authorial capacity, when admitting to ignorance or proffering a judgement. His language earned the admiration of Cicero, the most competent of his contemporaries, which is all the more noteworthy as Cicero favoured a quite different style. He found Caesar's commentaries 'unadorned, straightforward and graceful; any oratorical devices are laid aside like a garment. But, wishing to provide only the material on which others might draw for their historical accounts, he perhaps did the foolish a favour by giving them something on which to practise their hair-waving arts, while deterring the wise from writing at all. For in historical writing nothing is more pleasing than pure, lucid brevity.' Caesar's supporter Aulus Hirtius, who later wrote the eighth book of the **Bellum Gallicum,** refers to this judgement and then adds, 'Our admiration is of course even greater than others'; for they know only how well and faultlessly he wrote, while we know with what ease and rapidity.'

The perfection of these reports may lie in their directness, their art in their artlessness, but, as Otto Seel observed, simplicity combines with subtlety of diction, cool detachment with vibrant intensity, elegance with a dryness that does not shun repetition, smooth transitions with abrupt breaks. No Latin author adheres as precisely as Caesar to the rules of grammar. 'And yet, in spite of this, hardly any Latin style is so personal, so charged with individuality.'

Caesar's language is extremely economical. He uses less than thirteen hundred words, occasional technical terms apart. His vocabulary belongs to the language of everyday speech. As Fränkel put it, 'an ordinary, almost spare language is used to capture extraordinary deeds, whose greatness lies not in any kind of originality, but in an instinctive grasp of what is right, in the intrepidity of total commitment, swift execution, and unflagging perseverance'.

What really interests us is Caesar's way of describing events and conditions and at the same time presenting himself. The skilful, yet at the same time artless character of Caesar's narrative argues a degree of stylization, to which of course he subjected himself too. For what we feel to be his greatness presumably has something to do with the fact that he was his own man—that his personality was shaped by his own will and that he found the sphere in which he could realize it. Will and destiny combined in him in a special way, and the former seems to have been the more potent of the two.

He shaped not only himself and his deeds, but also his account of them, in a manner at once so personal and so masterful that this account contains a special truth. To put it briefly: in the **Bellum Gallicum** Caesar presents himself in all innocence as a Roman governor who performs his multifarious tasks in a traditional fashion, conscientiously and circumspectly, as duty requires. He does not appear to be defending himself. Quite the contrary.

Naturally there is no mention of the fact that Caesar, as Sallust writes, 'longed for a major command, an army, and a new war in which his energy could be brilliantly proven'. Nor do we read anything of the principle that Cicero found so laudable, even though it was quite at variance with previous practice—the principle of not merely reacting to attacks and defending the Roman province, but of bringing the whole of Gaul under Roman rule in the interest of a lasting peace. True, Caesar now and then allows us glimpses of a wider context, embracing the whole of Gaul, but he refrains from saying that he ever conceived such a grand design.

Rather, he at first lets it appear as if he proceeded step by step, adopting a fundamentally defensive stance, consonant with the principles of Rome's foreign policy. Allies must be protected and dangerous neighbours opposed. He protected Rome's allies selectively, as his interests required. And in taking preventive measures against the Helvetii he counted on the reader's lack of geographical knowledge, for the territory the Helvetii wished to conquer was nowhere contiguous with the Roman province. At first sight, then, it seems as though he moved from pure defence in isolated cases to the conquest of the whole territory—which, according to Cicero, was how things usually happened in the Roman empire. It might be said that Caesar concealed his intention to conquer. It would be more correct to say that he did not expressly state it.

For he makes no secret of it. Whatever the truth with regard to the Helvetii and Ariovistus, his intentions became clear by the first winter at the latest, when the legions took up quarters in conquered territory. According to his own account, the Belgae recognized this too. Moreover, there was no reason whatever for the conquest of Brittany and Normandy. In 56 his intention becomes quite obvious. In one of his typical sentences, in which the verb is delayed to the end, he writes: 'At about the same time, although summer was almost spent, Caesar, seeing that after the whole of Gaul had been pacified the Morini and Menapii were still under arms and had sent no envoy to talk peace, and believing that he could quickly end this war, dispatched his army there.' It is typical of Caesar's presentation that circumstances are introduced as motives and incorporated into the dynamic of the action, that the syntactic build-up draws the reader into the movement and that the tension is released only when the action begins. Yet this is a stylistic observation. Neither the Morini nor the Menapii had been involved in the fighting. The fact that they were 'still under arms' meant no more than that they were still free and had not yet surrendered to him.

Caesar's account makes it clear that he expected all the Gauls to submit. He gave them orders that they were expected to obey. Every tribe he encountered, with the exception of Rome's long-standing friends, had to submit. They all had to give hostages. If they did, Caesar usually treated them leniently. This was evidence of his clemency. Any prince or tribe who refused to submit was in the wrong and so gave Caesar a pretext for war.

All this was at odds with the Roman principle that only just wars might be waged. And a war was just only if its purpose was to right a wrong. Yet it could hardly be wrong for a foreign power to fail to do what Caesar demanded. And there was a good reason for Rome's defensive policy. After all, the Senate had instructed the governor to help the Haedui 'if this is not detrimental to the interest of Rome'.

It is true that demands of the kind made by Caesar were sometimes addressed to Rome's neighbours, but they were not common—except in the course of a major war—and gave rise at most to minor wars. No one operated on a grand scale outside his own province as Caesar did, demanding universal obedience and submission.

Yet it is not only this demand that Caesar makes clear. More than once he reports that the Gauls wished to be free. On one occasion he states that 'human nature is universally imbued with the desire for liberty and detests servitude.' He understands the pride that caused brave tribes, accustomed to victory, to resist defeat. His description is generally fair and arouses the reader's sympathy for the Gauls—or at least the modern reader's. Yet it is clear that their pride and their desire for liberty were just one more reason for treating them with severity. Caesar proceeded from the premise that they must be subjugated, even if the Senate wished the Gauls to remain free.

As he makes his intention clear without declaring it, he cannot advance any reasons for it. At most he can hint at a few. Occasionally he gives the reader to understand that there was much disorder in Gaul before he intervened. He also speaks of the danger posed by the Helvetii and the Germans, which he dutifully forestalled or contained. Yet he does not go beyond hints.

Naturally one must beware of viewing Caesar's desire for conquest with modern eyes. Thoroughly Roman and unused to being challenged, he was not plagued by doubts or the need to justify Roman expansion. To this extent he did not differ from his contemporaries. Yet he was not bound by the attitudes that had constantly inhibited such expansion or made it dependent on special circumstances. Above all, even if there was no need to justify oneself for the sake of the peoples involved, it was not self-evident that one might flout the rules enjoined upon a Roman governor.

Hence, what Caesar's book reveals, with little attempt at dissimulation, was an enormity even by contemporary standards: one man decided, without authority, to conquer the whole of Gaul, simply because he felt it ought to be conquered, employing an army of eight legions, only four of which were provided by the Roman Senate and people, the other four being raised by himself and supplemented later by two more.

Yet what was he to do? Was he to admit that all this was the outcome of his own arbitrary decision and give his reasons for deeming it right? Would that not have meant severing all his links with the Senate and people? He probably thought it best neither to acknowledge nor to deny his intention, but to imply that it was self-evident—at least after his battles against the Helvetii and Ariovistus, when he found himself more deeply involved in the affairs of Gaul. Anyone who demanded further justification could be indirectly likened to the officers at Vesontio: they had no reason to question the prudence and circumspection of their commander, so why should anyone else doubt his devotion to duty or the propriety of his conduct?

Against any questions and objections Caesar sets himself and his actions. It is through these that he hopes to convince. It is these that are at issue, and ultimately the subject of his book. And by speaking of them in his own way he imposes his own perspective. He never thought to convince his opponents. He addressed himself to those senators and knights who were still undecided, relatively open-minded and impressionable.

He thus defends himself not by justifying his actions, but by rehearsing them. In other words, he adopts an offensive stance. He shows how a responsible, prudent governor must conduct himself: he must not be constrained by petty restrictions, by the need to muddle through, tolerating much, turning a blind eye, and intervening only occasionally; he must not be bound by an attitude that was utterly unimpressive, but in keeping with the current mood. Having no governmental apparatus or sizeable military forces, and therefore unable to achieve much by coercion, Rome usually had to rely on numerous contacts, showing consideration to various parties and adopting a piecemeal approach to problems, though this often went with an excessive degree of carelessness and self-interest. This is what made Caesar so different: he set out to perform his tasks comprehensively and energetically. While seeming to act step by step, as the situation evolved, and to concentrate wholly on the present, he was not content merely to react to events, but took preventive action and never lost sight of the wider context. Aware of every problem and prepared for action whenever it was called for, he set new standards, and by matching up to these standards he was able to demonstrate his superiority.

This he regarded as the proper way to act; to show no consideration, to aim for total success, to behave with generosity and forbearance when necessary, but also with appalling severity and cruelty, as he did in the later campaigns. Yet even the later severity must have seemed to him consistent with his duty. In extreme situations any means was justified. Caesar certainly could not imagine that the way in which he discharged his office would strike any fair-minded Roman as improper. Otherwise he would have been bound to have doubts about himself. His high standards would have been wrong. Time and again he proudly asserts that this or that was intolerable to him and the Roman people and contrary to Roman custom. No compromises are made, no mitigation allowed: the demands of honour are paramount. According to a Greek historian, Caesar once said that this was how the ancestors had acted—boldly, making audacious plans and risking all in their execution. To them fortune meant nothing other than doing what was necessary; inactivity would have been regarded as misfortune.

By performing his duties in this way—which was alarmingly at variance with many well-founded rules, but contrasted agreeably with the negligence and indolence that were prevalent in Rome—Caesar justified himself in a way that could hardly fail to put any would-be critic to shame. Once again, as in so many of his speeches, but this time in a form that has come down to us, he demonstrated his superiority.

In his reports, moreover, he always seems to be fully in control, circumspect and well organized. We repeatedly hear of his arranging for supplies to arrive at the right moment. Nothing disconcerts him; he always knows what is to be done. Admittedly there is much that he cannot foresee, yet he is aware of this and envisages various possibilities. He is therefore cautious, armed against contingency, able to react to any eventuality. Naturally he also has to rely on his junior commanders and his soldiers, whom he praises for doing their duty in exemplary fashion and sometimes fighting battles on their own initiative. Caesar and his soldiers—these are the special assets on Rome's balance sheet. Caesar does not obtrude his own part in military events.

It is certainly not wrong to discern, in his manner of presenting himself, the implication that, because Rome's

governors normally acted differently, she needed a buffer against the Germans, her nearest and most dangerous opponents to the north.

The political isolation that forced him into his career of conquest corresponded to his dissatisfaction with the normal Roman tempo. Underlying both was Caesar's exceptional will to assert himself. His dissatisfaction gave an objective content to his determination to conquer. His weakness became his strength.

．．．．．

It may be presumed that Caesar's way of describing events—which was no doubt essentially how he understood them—accorded with his conception of how political and military events arise. In an extremely concentrated—and restricted—manner he writes almost solely of the actions of various subjects and ignores the wide intermediate area that normally extends between the actors and conditions their actions. Caesar rarely gives an appreciation of the overall situation, of the tasks, the opportunities and the difficulties it entails, before turning to the actions of the subjects. Conditions and situations are usually presented as circumstances determining the action: Caesar sees that such and such is the case and does this or that. Even his descriptions of the landscape are bound up with the action: one follows Caesar's gaze as he surveys the terrain before deciding on the appropriate measures: the landscape is thus drawn into the action. Difficulties are presented as tasks. The less the actors are absorbed in the conditions, the greater they appear. So clearly and sharply are they projected on the screen that they seem to occupy it completely; everything in the background is blurred and unrecognizable. What he depicts is not a total configuration to which many factors contribute, but a limited number of interacting subjects.

Every sentence is trained on a target, an action conditioned by all the foregoing circumstances. There are scarcely any periods of rest. Everything is movement. The immense dynamism of Caesar's rapid, audacious and wide-ranging campaigns is directly mirrored in his narrative. Yet although the action is described baldly, with little plasticity or graphic detail, it is easy to take in. In all essentials the configurations are presented clearly, with the special 'vividness that a game of chess has for the inner eye of an expert and that a clearly appreciated problem or an elegant method has for the mathematician' (Klingner). One is not aware of the observer, only of the doer, proceeding step by step from situation to situation. The opponents too are drawn in Caesar's own likeness; they have reasonable, comprehensible motives and are credited with the most intelligent intentions. The actions of individuals on the opposing side are taken into account and seen to play a large part in determining the events.

Moreover, the régime that Caesar builds up is no more than the sum of interpersonal relations. How persons relate to one another is what counts. There is no talk of institutions, of attempts at persuasion or reconciliation, of administrative problems, of establishing a system of government. The state of affairs that his conquests were aimed at is described broadly as *imperium in Gallia* ('command in Gaul'). General tendencies—processes at work under the surface, as it were—find no mention. The soldiers march, camps are built, demands are issued, battles fought and conquests made. Caesar gives orders; even security and food supplies are ensured by giving orders to those who are to provide them.

Klingner speaks of a 'ruthlessly simplified approach to things, carried to extreme lengths. Whatever does not pertain to the planning and action of the commander and the politician is excluded.' This accounts for the exceptional clarity and perspicuity of Caesar's account. 'No half-distinct background elements obtrude. We see nothing but the matter Caesar had in hand at any given time.'

Everything is concentrated on action and consists in action; consequently, the fact that Caesar was never entrusted with the task that he mastered so consummately is consigned to the background. Caesar directly involved his readers, like his soldiers, in the accomplishment of an enterprise upon which he himself had resolved.

Only at one point does he break out of the narrow narrative confines. This is in the sixth book, where he gives a comparative ethnology of the Gauls and the Germans. At first sight these chapters seem to have no function. By implication, however, they explain why Caesar broke off his campaign against the Germans without subjugating them: for here one reads that Germany, contrary to current opinion, is quite unlike Gaul. To conquer it would be both difficult and unrewarding. Again Caesar refrains from going beyond implication. Yet should he have said in so many words that he really wanted to conquer Germany too? He neither admits it nor denies it.

A special feature of Caesar's account is the almost total exclusion of emotion. Only the soldiers are allowed to feel fear. Caesar is seemingly immune to it. It has been said that Caesar's commentaries owe their formal assurance to the same strength that produced his actions. There is certainly much truth in this, even if this strength is unlikely to have been as effective in reality as it appears in his account. He cannot have possessed the superhuman superiority that his writings suggest.

Historians familiar with the sources can point to a difficult situation in the civil war for which we have a parallel account, probably based on a report by a member of Caesar's staff. We learn that after suffering a defeat, Caesar spent a sleepless night, tormented by dark thoughts and by the realization that his planning had been wrong. At first he believed the situation hopeless, but after much mental turmoil he finally arrived at a decision. Caesar's own account states: 'Caesar gave up his previous plans, believing that he must change his whole strategy.' This suggests that he was merely adapting himself to a new situation. Similarly, we learn of the doubts and scruples that assailed

him before he crossed the Rubicon, but these find no place in his own account.

Yet it runs counter to all human experience to take such a self-presentation, with all its abbreviations, at face value. That such doubts are justified, even with regard to the great figures of history, is amply demonstrated by what we know of various situations in which Frederick the Great or Napoleon found themselves.

We may presume that Caesar enveloped himself in a cloak of outward serenity and superiority. One of his officers tells how on one occasion, in an almost hopeless situation, the soldiers found encouragement 'in the expression of their commander's face, in his freshness and wonderful cheerfulness. For he appeared full of assurance and confidence.' And this was certainly the rule rather than the exception. Caesar's superiority and serenity fascinated simple spirits, but to others they made him inscrutable and sinister, especially as they went with immense concentration. And the outward image he displayed may in large measure have determined his inner attitude. His essentially playful temperament, his wilfulness, and his faith in the fortune conferred by Venus, may have played a part too.

Yet behind this there was doubtless a degree of sensitivity, insecurity, doubt and vacillation; there must have been times when all seemed hopeless and he found himself staring spellbound at disaster. In the seventh book, which describes the great crisis of the Gallic war, he even hints that on occasion he came close to abandoning everything, lest even the old Roman province should fall victim to the Gallic onslaught. Indeed, towards the end of his book he reveals a good deal more of himself and writes with rather more freedom.

There was one question that he could hardly suppress entirely: What was the point of his unremitting activity, his subjugation of Gaul, and perhaps of the sacrifices his soldiers had to make in order to achieve it?

However, it could hardly prevail over the joy he felt at so conspicuously proving his worth: ultimately his strength and the possibilities open to him were equal to the immense task he had set himself. Overcoming all the complexities in his character, he always reverted to action, in which he found concentration and attained an effectiveness that increasingly built up a real world of his own, in which he could enjoy a multitude of opportunities and accomplish great feats, even though they might eventually cut him off from other worlds, especially the one inhabited by his peers, Rome's ruling class, including Pompey. But he would have to wait and see what happened. In 57 the real test still lay ahead, both politically and militarily.

'I often marvel,' wrote Stifter, 'when I come to ponder whether to award the prize to Caesar's deeds or to his writings, how much I vacillate and how impossible I find it to decide. Both are so clear, so powerful, so assured, that we probably have little to compare with them.' And both are presented to us in the commentaries with a naturalness that, on closer inspection, seems positively unreal, yet in a style that suggests the ultimate in objectivity.

Cynthia Damon (essay date 1994)

SOURCE: "Caesar's Practical Prose," in *Classical Journal,* Vol. 89, No. 2, December-January, 1994, pp. 183-95.

[*In the following essay, Damon explains that, in reading* De Bello Civili, *it is important to recognize the character traits of the individuals discussed, to understand Caesar's narrative as a Roman would have, to notice repeated events, and to realize that recurrent events can lead to different outcomes.*]

Thirty years ago, when Matthias Gelzer had the opportunity of addressing an audience of teachers of Latin and ancient history, he chose for his topic "Caesar as an historian."[1] He argued that Caesar was not an historian in the modern sense of the word—not objective, not dependent on inadequate sources, not university trained—but that his *commentarii* were, given ancient criteria for the genre, historiographical texts, something to set beside Sallust for the history of the late Republic, something to put in front of Appian and Cassius Dio. In making this claim Gelzer was attempting to quell a flood of scholarship which had fastened limpet-like on the chronological problems in the **Bellum Civile** and on Asinius Pollio's assertion that Caesar himself would have changed many things in the commentaries if he had lived long enough to do so, scholarship that was trying to reduce the *commentarii* to the category of propaganda.[2] Now propaganda is a highly inflammatory label to apply to a text, and one with the worst possible associations in the events of this century. The fact that Caesar produced in the *Anticato* an extended piece of invective against the republican martyr lends a sort of plausibility to the label. Anyone who can tell the sort of stories about Cato that Caesar seems to have told—besides the standard remarks about drunkenness and incest there were some more creative touches, too, such as the description of Cato's sifting through the ashes of his brother's pyre to find bits of melted gold—anyone who would say this, it is felt, or who would claim divine and regal ancestry for his aunt Julia, would not shrink from tinting the account of his own *res gestae* rose.[3] And anyone who handles such a text without the precautions needed for other forms of radioactive material is liable to be viewed as contaminated. Yet we don't have to accept the alternatives proposed so far, Gelzer's black on white "history" label or the flashing red "propaganda" label; we can open the text and sample it for ourselves.

Now much of the history of Latin pedagogy is founded upon the premise that when we open our texts we will find Latin that is clear and, what is better, pure. On the one hand no sentences which weave together a seemingly infinite number of subordinate clauses which answer the listener's qualms before he has any, which concede some points, explain away other ones, which set out the conditions for the truth of what is being said, which characterize the speaker as an eminently reliable sort and his cause as a worthy one, which make use of structural elements such as anaphora, correlatives, or lists, and which use all these devices in order to achieve their goal, getting the listener to do something that the speaker assumes he is reluctant to do. Sentences like the previous one, in fact, are not present to make the students groan. On the other hand, so the style books say, the language of Caesar is pure, no atrocities of form or vocabulary allowed. When Caesar has occasion to describe a hill, for example, he doesn't do what Cato the Elder did in his *Origines* and call it "a wart," a *verruca.* Many criteria by which to measure the clarity and purity of Caesar's Latin have been found, for scholars have taken the fact that Caesar produced a grammatical treatise, the *de Analogia,* as a mandate for almost unlimited attention to matters of diction and style.[4] But I want to argue that, despite the clarity, despite the purity, Caesar is one of the most challenging Latin authors, particularly in the **Bellum Civile,** the text on which I focus here.

Now there are really two different ways of reading the **Bellum Civile**—one can read the text sentence by sentence and follow Caesar and his legates from Italy to Spain to Africa to Greece to Asia to Alexandria. This is as dull and as inconsequential as my string of prepositional phrases is. Caesar's narrative has none of the dramatic tension that Herodotus achieves in Books 7-8 when he describes Xerxes' forces moving slowly but inexorably towards Athens, drinking rivers dry as they pass. This first method of reading is rather like following Ariadne's thread through a labyrinth—it is gratifying to reach the end, of course, but one retains no lasting impression of the places one has been. The other method of reading the **Bellum Civile** aims at fashioning a net of memory and understanding by tying the knots which link episodes and characters that are found on the long strand of narrative. This method is a good deal more arduous than the first, because Caesar, writing for readers who wanted to understand and judge recent events and the actors in them, leaves a great deal of the responsibility for interpretation to his readers. In this paper I will examine four areas of reader responsibility that I find particularly fruitful, four tasks that, if exercised diligently, make the text so much more than a repository of clear sentences and pure vocabulary.

The first responsibility is to flesh out the names. Caesar's account of the first 19 months of the civil war is far richer in names than any of the histories of the parallel tradition, and each of these names was, for Caesar, a convenient abbreviation for the personality, the goals, the achievements and the connections of an individual well known to his audience. He doesn't provide character sketches, but that is not to say that Caesar refrains from characterization—not at all. His technique is rather to report his characters' words and deeds quite fully, then to rely on his readers to judge them. (By "quite fully" I mean with considerably more detail than, say, Appian or Dio or even Plutarch do in their accounts of the same events.) A glance at Caesar's treatment of Labienus in the *Bellum Civile* makes the point quite clear.

If you remember your *Bellum Gallicum,* you will know that Labienus was Caesar's most trusted *legatus* in Gaul, the one with responsibility for the largest number of legions and the greatest freedom for independent action. The association between the two men went back to before Caesar's tenure in Gaul, too, for they were both involved in the trial of poor old Rabirius Postumus in 63, Labienus as the prosecutor, Caesar as a *iudex*.[5] And from Hirtius' book 8 of the *Bellum Gallicum* we know that Caesar had taken careful thought for Labienus' post-*bellum* career as well—he wanted a consulship for Labienus in 48.[6] Now 48 was a year in which Caesar himself intended to be consul—he may have hoped that Labienus would prove more cooperative than his colleague in 59, the inimitable Marcus Bibulus. Labienus was an associate of long standing, then. Yet early on in the *Bellum Civile* his name is mentioned in a context which shows that he is on Pompey's side.

The topic of *BC* [*Bellum Civile*] 1.15 is the open-armed reception that Caesar says his forces received in parts of Italy where one might not have expected them to be welcome. First mentioned is the territory around Picenum, that is to say, Pompey's home ground. Next he says that "even Cingulum offered support and obedience." Why the "even"? Because, he explains, Cingulum was a town that Labienus had founded and built with his own money.[7] Nothing could be less demonstrative, less emotional, but the information is there for those who care to follow Labienus through the civil war. And Labienus' desertion must have cost Caesar something or the Pompeian Cicero would not have expressed himself so enthusiastically upon hearing of it: "I call Labienus a hero," he says on 23 January 49, "it is the finest political action we have seen for a long while. If he has achieved nothing else, he has made Caesar smart."[8] Smarting or not, Caesar made no comment; Dio, on the other hand, chooses to guide his readers' interpretation of Labienus' desertion, saying: "The reason was that when he had acquired wealth and fame he began to conduct himself more haughtily than his rank warranted, and Caesar, seeing that he put himself on the same level with his superior, ceased to be so fond of him. And so, as Labienus could not endure this change and was at the same time afraid of coming to some harm, he transferred his allegiance" (41.4.3-4). I cite this passage not so much because the explanation is convincing, but to show that the desertion cries out for interpretation, and that Caesar provides none. Caesar's reticence is not, I think, to be ascribed to indifference, or to a fixed policy of suppressing events that revealed dissatisfaction in his own camp, however; Dio, having given his set piece on *perfidia*, evinces almost no further interest in Labienus, but Caesar brings him front and center repeatedly.[9] And at each of his appearances Labienus is behaving atrociously.

"Atrociously," of course, is my word, not Caesar's—he reports events without labelling them. Which is not to say that Caesar reports the truth and the whole truth, of course not. Selective reporting is just as powerful a device of persuasion as colorful packaging. And when Caesar has Labienus make his entrance into the *Bellum Civile* swearing that he will not desert Pompey and will suffer whatever fate the future has in store for Pompey (*BC* 3.13), he may reasonably expect his readers to question the reliability of Labienus' oath.[10] We will come back to the role of oaths in the *Bellum Civile,* but we are not finished with Labienus yet.

He next appears on the banks of the river Apsus, which flowed between the rival camps in Greece (3.19). The soldiers on the two sides had gotten in the habit of discussing ways and means of ending the war, making, Caesar says, limited non-aggression agreements—*pactiones*—to facilitate their conversations. Labienus bursts in rudely upon one such colloquium and all of a sudden there are weapons flying everywhere. Since all of the wounded are Caesarians whereas Labienus is shielded by his soldiers, there is a certain amount of pressure to conclude that it was the Pompeians who had violated the current *pactio*. It is Labienus, at any rate, who has the final word: "there will be no peace," he says, "until we have Caesar's head." End of scene.

But it is not long before the unnecessary cruelty to which Labienus—that is to say, Caesar's version of Labienus—gives expression here is shown in action again. In *BC* 3.71 Caesar describes the aftermath of Pompey's victory at Dyrrachium, allotting four sentences, and only four sentences, to the task. In the first two he reports the casualties to his side. In the third we learn that Pompey, the victor, was saluted as imperator by his troops, and that with uncharacteristic modesty he did not publicize the fact. Again, the word "uncharacteristic" is mine, not Caesar's. Caesar's reader, however, can supply the adjective, for Caesar has mentioned three times already the boasting reports spread about by Pompey and his legates after each even minor success.[11] We will come back to this point, too, but we can't leave 3.71 just yet. The fourth and longest sentence here belongs to Labienus: "with Pompey's permission Labienus ordered that the captives be turned over to him. When they were brought out into view, he called them his 'comrades in arms' and asked, most insultingly, whether veterans were in the habit of turning tail. Then he killed them."[12] Labienus' brutality towards the very men that he had led to such heady successes in Gaul is startling, the more so because of the "explanation" Caesar gives for it: "the turncoat," he says, "was trying to persuade the Pompeians of his good faith—*quo maior perfugae fides haberetur.* This quiet oxymoron is as close as Caesar gets to an explicit statement about character traits in the *Bellum Civile.*

Labienus leaves this text just before the battle of Pharsalus, departing with a boast and yet another oath: he will return to camp a victor, he swears, or not at all (3.87.5).

But although neither he nor any of the other Pompeian officers who echo his oath returns to camp, they don't they die on the field, either. Some escape only to be killed by their own men (this is how Lucius Domitius meets his end [3.99.5]), others (Brutus among them) capitulate, and still others, like Labienus, escape successfully to carry on the war in new theatres.

Cruel and unreliable, that is the way Caesar characterizes Labienus, though without using either one of those adjectives. This is not the writing of an indifferent or impartial reporter, but an eminently practical selection and arrangement of incidents to achieve an utterly damning whole.

The next reader responsibility that I'd like to illustrate for you is perhaps the most burdensome for us, though the original audience would have experienced no difficulty in filling it: it is simply to read as a Roman. To be alert, for example, to contraventions of *mores* that Caesar doesn't trouble to footnote for you. Help on some small points is available in Plutarch and in Appian and Dio, who were writing for audiences to whom reading as Romans did not come much more easily than it does to us. Thus when Pompey, as we saw earlier, was saluted as imperator after the battle of Dyrrachium, and yet refrained from broadcasting the title, Dio explains to his 3rd-century Greek-speaking audience that "Pompey was unwilling to show exultation over the downfall of citizens" (41.52.1). Appian, an historian of the 2nd century, helps us put two other salutations in context. When the Caesarian Curio first landed his two legions in Africa, he arrived near Utica before the country dwellers had finished conveying their goods into the walled city. The commander of the Pompeian forces inside the city sent some 600 Numidian horsemen and 400 footsoldiers to the defense of these hapless folk. But Curio's men forced the Pompeians to withdraw leaving some 120 dead on the field. As a result of this engagement Curio was saluted as imperator *universi exercitus conclamatione*. Caesar leaves the account at that, but Appian supplies his readers with a cultural context: "The title of imperator is an honor conferred upon generals by their soldiers, who thus testify that they consider them worthy to be their commanders. It used to be that the general accepted this honor only for the greatest exploits. At present I understand that the distinction is limited to cases where at least 10,000 of the enemy have been killed" (2.7.44). Appian's figure of 10,000 may be too high, but it is abundantly clear that Curio's forces are overenthusiastic about this rather minor scuffle. The event does not reflect poorly on Curio, since Caesar does not suggest that he elicited the salutation, but it is an oddity that a Roman reader would have queried. Why were these troops so eager to show their approval of Curio? Our examination of Labienus' activities allows us to suggest an explanation, for it emerges later in the narrative of Curio's African debacle that the 2 legions he had with him were troops that Caesar had taken from Domitius at Corfinium. Perhaps these ex-Pompeians, like the ex-Caesarian Labienus, were under some pressure to give public and irrevocable proof of their enthusiasm for their new "friends." Readers who

had just lived through a civil war would have been alert to the difficulty of their situation. But I said that Appian helps us with two salutations, so let us move on to the other.

Paragraph 31 of Book 3 begins with the name Scipio. Caesar does not tell us that the man's full name was Quintus Caecilius Metellus Pius Scipio, or that he was Pompey's father-in-law and a remarkably arrogant individual, but we are expected to know these facts and apply them to our reading of the event. Caesar reports that Scipio suffered some losses in his province of Syria, and had himself saluted as imperator. He doesn't expostulate here the way Cicero does at some of Verres' more innovative extortions, but then Caesar was not writing for an audience that would have to pronounce judgment within hours after hearing the narrative of events, but rather for readers who wanted to inform themselves about the origins of the Civil war and about Caesar as a participant therein. Caesar's audience had time to savor the irony palpable in the modest little sentence which begins with the ablative absolute *detrimentis . . . acceptis* and ends with the main clause *imperatorem se appellaverat*.

Now in fleshing out the names of Caesar's characters and in reading with Roman eyes the modern reader has to work much harder than the Roman reader, and with less hope of fully understanding the narrative. Reader responsibilities numbers 3 and 4, on the other hand, require the same effort from both types of reader and produce the same rewards for them.

Let me try to give you a taste of some of those rewards. Responsibility #3 is paying attention to recurrent events. This is where we come back to those oaths. We have already seen Labienus attempting to strengthen Pompeian resolve by instigating extraordinary oaths of loyalty on two occasions. (By extraordinary I mean something other than the soldier's regular *sacramentum* pledging obedience to his general.) It turns out that Caesar shows similar oath-takings on other occasions, too, and that the oath-takers are always Pompeian.[13] One might suppose that Caesar's supporters never needed such artificial aids to loyalty. And one certainly should suppose that Caesar is creating this impression deliberately, for neither Dio nor Appian nor Plutarch nor Suetonius mentions any of the oaths.[14]

Other recurrent events that Caesar uses in aid of his characterization without adjectives are refusals to send help when one's own supporters are in difficulties—this is naturally another Pompeian trait—as are the arming of slaves, boastful reports, cruelty to captives and plundering temples. By contrast Caesar is repeatedly shown guaranteeing the safety of those of the enemy who come into his hands, winning races for strategic points, weighing alternatives rationally, and so on. Each reading of the **Bellum Civile** brings more to light.

Paying attention to these recurrent events greatly facilitates the exercise of reader responsibility number 4, noticing when similar situations give rise to different outcomes. This is perhaps the richest source of those connecting knots that make the **Bellum Civile** into such an effective fabric of representation. I said earlier that the arming of slaves was one of the recurrent events which contributed to the negative characterization of the Pompeians. Yet Caesar reports that his own supporters, the citizens of the Greek city of Salonae, did the same thing, once (3.9.3). Why would he make such a damaging admission? Precisely, I think, to give his reader a standard by which to judge Pompeian actions. The people of Salonae resort to this *extremum auxilium* only in the direst of straits, under siege. Too few even at the outset to defend their walls properly, they saw their situation deteriorate as the continued fighting reduced the number of effective defenders. The freeing and arming of slaves of military age was as much an index of their peril as was the fact that the only material available for the manufacture of the rope they needed was their wives' hair. Among Caesar's supporters, then, desperate straits give rise to desperate measures such as the arming of ex-slaves. Yet the Pompeians, according to Caesar anyway, armed slaves even as a precautionary measure: in January of 49, when Lentulus and Pompey, consul and proconsul respectively, that is to say officials with an almost unlimited authority for legitimate conscriptions, are holding a *dilectus* of all Italy, they also arm slaves.[15] Of Pompey's involvement Caesar allows himself the wry remark: "He armed slaves and herdsmen and gave them horses. In this way he created some 300 cavalrymen."[16] Caesar doesn't draw attention to the contrast in situations, but it is there for the reader to see.

Book 2 of the **Bellum Civile** provides a contrast on a larger scale, a contrast between Pompeian and Caesarian *legati*. As we saw in the case of Labienus, some of Caesar's most effective writing is devoted to character portrayal. His interest in giving the reader the materials with which to judge the various actions and actors of Rome's civil war is not shared by Appian and Dio, who devote much of their narratives to standard civil war topoi—the powerful emotions aroused in combatants and non-combatants alike, the paradoxical situations that occur in civil wars, and so on. Dio's interest in Labienus, you remember, was almost exclusively in his capacity as an illustration of *perfidia*. Appian mentions Labienus just once. A similar disparity is to be found in the attention devoted to Marcus Terentius Varro.

Varro, the polymath author of nearly 500 books of Latin prose, the friend of Cicero and Atticus, subsequently the author of plans for Caesar's enormous new libraries, is an important figure in Roman literary history. He was less important in the history of the civil war, for all that he was Pompey's legate in further Spain, and Dio accordingly allots him a scant half-sentence reference, reporting that some of the troops that Caesar won over in Spain were from Varro's legions (41.23.2). Neither Appian nor Plutarch has any interest in the fellow whatsoever. The campaign in further Spain was a very minor affair which

was won without a single battle and which delayed Caesar for only a short time before he set out for Marseilles. Caesar, however, lavishes on Varro the attention that his literary merits deserve, although, as we shall see, Varro was probably not particularly grateful for the favor.

For 5 long chapters near the beginning of Book 2 Caesar focuses on Varro's timorous tergiversations—though he doesn't call them tergiversations, nor label them timorous (2.17-21). There was not in this case, as there had been in the depiction of Labienus, any prior wrong to avenge, so one may well wonder, why the fuss? By the end of Book 2 the reader has the answer, for Varro's drifting loyalties serve as foil for the steadfastness with which Caesar endows his character Curio, the story of whose end is told in living color in the final panel of the book. And this contrasting pair itself provides a background against which to measure the behavior of Marcus Bibulus in Book 3.

Varro's position as Pompey's legate in further Spain is mentioned briefly at 1.38.1, but he has no part to play in Caesar's rather detailed account of his own struggles against the legates of hither Spain, Afranius and Petreius. It is not until 2.17 that Varro moves into the limelight. When he does, he is revealed disheartened by Pompey's withdrawal from Italy, and is speaking *amicissime* about Caesar. On every possible occasion and to anyone who cared to listen, says Caesar, Varro states that, though as legate he has a duty to Pompey, his personal ties with Caesar are no less strong. He claims, too, that his responsibilities as legate, which he calls a *fiduciaria opera*, oblige him to know the temper of his province, and this, he says, is altogether favorable to Caesar. However, when the future looks more promising for the Pompeians, Varro reacts by strengthening his military position with new levies, new stockpiles of grain, new ships, new monetary requisitions. He commits himself further by putting a dependent of the Pompeian Lucius Domitius in charge of Cadiz, where Varro is concentrating his forces. (This, incidentally, is another case where reader responsibility number two is fruitful—the new commander, Gaius Gallonius, had come to Spain to watch over Domitius' interest in the execution of a will—with legal expertise and equestrian status he was in no way qualified to command six cohorts and to have the charge of *arma omnia publica ac privata* which Varro gives him.) Varro makes his choice of sides the clearer by arranging assemblies in which he announces that he has heard from the best authorities that Caesar has suffered numerous reverses. Here, Caesar's readers are inclined to suppose that Varro is either credulous or mendacious, for Caesar has just said that the reports on which Varro relied were letters from Afranius about his meagre successes in hither Spain, letters whose tone was *elatius atque inflatius* (2.17.4). The balance turns in favor of judging the man credulous when we read that Varro—whose provincial administration is exceedingly harsh—reserves particularly harsh treatment for cities and individuals who favor Caesar. Varro is at his most Pompeian (in both loyalty and behavior) when he compels the entire province to swear an oath *in sua et Pompei verba*

(2.18.5). However, things get sticky when Caesar turns his attention to further Spain. The provincials respond with the enthusiasm that Varro himself had noticed earlier. As had happened in Italy before and would be happening soon in Greece (at least as Caesar tells the story), town after town closed its gates to the Pompeians in order to welcome Caesar the better. Not only that, but troops, too, including half of those under the out-of-place Gallonius, declare for Caesar. Humiliation of humiliations, one of Varro's own legions offers its services to Caesar while its commander looks on, helpless to stop the desertion.[17] Whereupon Varro, for all his talk about the province being a *fiduciaria opera,* promptly hands his other legion over to Caesar and informs him of the whereabouts of the grain, ships and money that he had amassed. All in all, it is not a flattering portrait. And it becomes even less so when set beside that of Curio.

The Curio episode is a fascinating and much studied narrative, filled with enticing incidents—sneaky Pompeian commanders urging Curio's troops to change allegiance, an assassination attempt by a courageous man from the ranks—and endowed with considerable stylistic variety, too—long speeches reported in *oratio recta,* for example. But for now I will ignore all of these distracting riches and focus on one sentence, the one in which Caesar reports Curio's final words. When his last tactical manoeuvre fails, Curio is urged by a staff officer to save himself. But Curio, says Caesar, insisted that, having lost the army which Caesar had entrusted to his keeping, he would never face Caesar again.[18] He then plunges into the battle and dies fighting. As do his men: *milites ad unum omnes interficiuntur.* The contrast with Varro's easy abandonment of the army and province entrusted to him is unavoidable. (And one may assume that Varro did not share Curio's scruples about facing the commander he had failed, since we know that he proceeded from Spain to Pompey's camp at Dyrrachium.[19]) There is also a contrast to draw here between Curio and Lucius Domitius, the Pompeian commander who had abandoned troops and whole regions that were under his care not once but twice, at Corfinium and at Marseilles, but I have stressed the contrast with Varro because his story was so patently told for its thematic rather than its historical importance.

However, I don't want to leave you with the false impression that steadfastness was unknown in the Pompeian camp. Caesar's narrative does not cover the period of Cato's defense of Utica, but he does allow Marcus Bibulus a loyal death. Given the history of bad relations between the men who had been colleagues in the consulship of 59, however, the reader might expect to find plenty of hidden barbs.[20] Again, I'll mention just one. It is a barb whose sharpness is better perceived by readers who keep in mind the contrasting behaviors of Varro and Curio. In 49, Bibulus' charge was oversight of all the ships that Pompey had mustered for the defense of Greece. Things did not go well: not only did Caesar thumb his nose at Bibulus' 110 ships and bring a good portion of his army over to Greece successfully, but once there he proceeded to keep the

Pompeian ships from coming to land to resupply. Bibulus himself falls sick on board ship, where there is no medical attention to be had. Loath to give up the task he had undertaken, he stays put, and dies. Even from this brief paraphrase of the passage, you can see that Caesar makes Bibulus' behavior look less like loyalty to a cause or fidelity to Pompey and more like the same misguided and ultimately ineffective stubbornness that characterized his opposition to Caesar in 59.

Varro, Curio, Bibulus—they are offered by Caesar to the reader for judgment, as, ultimately, are the rivals about whom these lesser planets orbit.

Well, I hope I have given you a sense of why I keep coming back to the **Bellum Civile.** When I said that what I wanted to do was show how difficult, really, it is to read Caesar, I meant that not as a deterrent, but as a challenge, and even as lure. It is precisely because the text is difficult that it is always fresh, always yields something new to the reader. The more one knows about things Roman, the more exciting a text the **Bellum Civile** becomes, so although the practical-minded Caesar abandoned his commentary because he despaired of its achieving the effect he intended it to have, we can make Caesar's practical prose work for us as a cord which will raise a curtain on the spectacle of Rome at the end the Republic. The reason it is such a good text to teach is that it allows the students the satisfaction of reading the Latin with a fair degree of success, and allows class time to be spent on the fun stuff, on helping the students read the text as a story, as political rhetoric, as autobiography, as a social document, as history.[21]

Notes

1. . . . The talk was given on 16 November 1961. It was published in Gelzer's *Kleine Schriften* (Wiesbaden 1963) 2.307-35, and again in D. Rasmussen, ed. *Caesar. Wege der Forschung* 43 (Darmstadt 1974), 438-73.

2. *Pollio Asinius parum diligenter parumque integra veritate compositos putat, cum Caesar pleraque et quae per alios erant gesta temere crediderit et quae per se, vel consulto vel etiam memoria lapsus perperam ediderit; existimatque rescripturum et correcturum fuisse* (Suetonius *Divus Julius* 56.4). This statement may have contributed to Pollio's justification for writing a history of the period himself.

3. The extant fragments are conveniently collected in the 3rd volume of A. Klotz' Teubner edition of Caesar.

4. The *de Analogia* was written in either 55/54 or 53/52 (while Caesar was administering assizes in Cisalpina) and was dedicated to Cicero. Cicero says that its topic was *de ratione Latine loquendi,* and quotes a dictum from the first book: *verborum dilectum originem esse eloquentiae* (*Brutus* 253). According to Fronto Caesar wrote *de nominibus declinandis, de verborum aspirationibus et rationibus* (p. 210.1-2 van

den Hout). The extant fragments deal with the usage of words such as *arma, comitia, inimicitiae* (always plural in form) and with the proper forms of 3rd declension words. One might summarize the message of the treatise as we know it as "choose the right word and use it in the proper form."

5. Dio 37.26ff., Suetonius *Divus Julius* 12.

6. *T. Labienum praefecit togatae, quo maiore commendatione conciliaretur ad consulatus petitionem, BG* 8.52. There are grave textual difficulties here, however. See M. Gelzer, *Caesar, Politician and Statesman,* tr. P. Needham (Cambridge, MA 1968) 186 note 3.

7. *BC* 1.15.2: *etiam Cingulo, quod oppidum Labienus constituerat suaque pecunia exaedificaverat, ad eum legati veniunt, quaeque imperaverit, se cupidissime facturos pollicentur.*

8. *Att.* 7.13.1: *Labienum* ηρωα *iudico. facinus iam diu nullum civile praeclarius qui, ut aliud nihil, hoc tamen profecit, dedit illi dolorem.* Cf. *Att.* 7.12.5, where Cicero maintains that if Labienus had deserted before Pompey left Rome *damnasse . . . sceleris hominem amicum rei publicae causa videretur.*

9. Dio has four passing references which show Labienus' whereabouts but little else (42.10.3, 43.2.1, 43.4.5, 43.30.4). Labienus' final appearance in Dio's text is more interesting, since it shows how Labienus was felt to be a feather in the wind. When during a battle in Spain he used a tactic which looked like a retreat, the whole Pompeian army lost heart and collapsed (43.38.2-3).

10. *princeps Labienus procedit iuratque se eum non deserturum eundemque casum subiturum quemcumque ei fortuna tribuisset* (3.13.3).

11. 2.17.4, 3.23, 3.45, cf. 3.72.

12. *at Labienus cum ab eo impetravisset, ut sibi captivos tradi iuberet, omnis productos ostentationis, ut videbatur, causa, quo maior perfugae fides haberetur, commilitones appellans et magna verborum contumelia interrogans, solerentne veterani milites fugere, in omnium conspectu interfecit* (3.71.4).

13. 1.76.2-3, 2.18.5.

14. And even the prevention of oath-taking can illustrate the different levels of partisan enthusiasm on the two sides: Caesar requires as one of the conditions for peace in Spain that no one be made to take an oath against his will: *nequis invitus sacramentum dicere cogetur a Caesare cavetur* (1.86.3).

15. 1.14, 1.24.

16. 1.24: *servos pastores armat atque iis equos attribuit. ex his circiter CCC equites confecit.*

17. This legion, incidentally, was called the *legio vernacula,* as having been based on the Pompeian muster of slaves.

18. 2.42.4: *at Curio numquam se amisso exercitu quem a Caesar suae fidei commissum acceperit in eius conspectum reversurum confirmat.*

19. Cic. *Div.* 1.68, 2.114.

20. In Book 3 Caesar makes numerous references to Bibulus's activities: 5.4, 7.1-2, 8.3, 14.2, 15-18, 31.3.

21. Teaching the *Bellum Civile* is more attractive than ever now, in view of the publication of a new commentary on Books 1-2: J. M. Carter, *Julius Caesar, The Civil War Books I & II* (Warminster 1991). A companion volume on Book 3 is promised.

John Henderson (essay date 1996)

SOURCE: "XPDNC / Writing Caesar," in *Classical Antiquity,* Vol. 15, No. 2, October, 1996, pp. 261-88.

[*In the following essay, Henderson explores how the act of writing helped to create the image of Caesar that he wanted to project of himself.*]

Whereupon Henderson rose, in his place, to speak his motion (*surrexit sententiae suae loco dicendae*). And moved (*pro sententia sua hoc censuit*):[1]

> that: Caesar's *Caesar* tells, undecidably, of a peace-keeping war[2] which didn't have to be, yet had to be, fought over the "self-regard" the world owed him and his Caesar self (*dignitas*)—"not status for Caesar but something approaching self-respect" (his apologist might aver) "and knowledge of his actual worth and the offices it entitled him to seek, meaning more to him than life itself."[3] From the horse's mouth, what a Caesar is worth, *is.*

> —that: the monological, even monomaniacal, myth of Caesar's writing puts **De Bello Ciuili** in denial, where fiercely dialogical contestation powers and motivates every turn of the rhetoric through its repression. The text plays host to the welter of writings occasioned by the dispute between Caesar and his world; parasitic on them, Caesar hides his parade of self.

> —that: Caesar's *Commentarii* run, and should be read, together: notwithstanding that they are all divided into three parts.

> —that: Caesar, "whose every word denied the inevitability of such an outcome,"[4] wrote all over the *imperium.* Caesar wrote his self, *Caesar,* onto the world, until the world, and all the writing in it, was his. The writing that won and lost a world war.

> —that: *Bellum Ciuile* reinforces Caesar's thinking over Caesar's thinking. In the protestation of a Roman identity, the masking/marking of iconoclasm with conformity.

1. CROSSING OUT THE RUBICON (*FAC ET EXCUSA*)[5]

The Man who is born to be a dictator is not compelled; he wills it. He is not driven forward, but drives himself. There is nothing immodest about this.[6]

Litteris Caesaris . . . "The letter from Caesar was successfully delivered to the consuls and the utmost exertions of the tribunes just about got it read out to the Senate; but nothing could get a motion arising from the letter put to the Senate. Instead, the consuls put to them the national interest." (*BC* [*Bellum Ciuile*] 1.1.1f.) *Not,* then, the letter of *Caesar,* the letters written by Caesar, Caesar's writing; but the *res publica.* So begins the text of Caesar's **Bellum Ciuile,** at once opening the rift that would tear down *SPQR* and write up *Caesares.*

Readers are never to have this letter from Caesar to the Senate read out to them. One had to be there. Some editors cannot believe this is not the chance injustice of scribal accident.[7] They cannot believe how unlucky Caesar's **Bellum Ciuile** has been, to be deprived of its opening paragraph, or so.[8] "The contents of Caesar's letter were very important and however hastily Caesar may have written the **BC** it is almost inconceivable that he did not spell out the offer he was making: that either he should be allowed to retain his command, or that all holders of commands should lay them down."[9] The majority view, however, has been to accept this abrupt opening as Caesar's, to the letter.

The abruptness of the denial of debate on the matter of the letter from Caesar stands, in any event, as the symptomatic gesture that inaugurates the **Bellum Ciuile,** just as it initiates the civil war.[10] The consuls of Rome refuse to comply with Caesar's written will. In so doing, they treat his letter as the report of a magistrate to the government; chivvied by the tribunes, they give the despatch an official hearing, despite pressing crisis; but insofar as Caesar's writing required to be handled as a proposal from afar, an *in absentia* representation to the Senate seeking to determine a vote, it is disallowed. Instead, a procession of senior figures produces an array of *sententiae,* from which the presiding consul selected the motion "that Caesar disband his army before a certain date, on pain of being seen to act against the national interest" (1.2.6). The veto from two tribunes on this successfully carried proposal was a week later dealt with by passage of the emergency decree *(illud extremum atque ultimum senatus consultum),* according to which the magistrates should "protect the national interest from damage" *(dent operam . . . ne quid res publica detrimenti capiat),* and the "inscription" of this declaration of martial law *(perscribuntur)* issued instantly in the "flight of tribunes <i.e. as if "*the* tribunes"> to Caesar" at Ravenna *(profugiunt,* 1.2.7, 5.3). The consul who blocked Caesar's written will was Lentulus Crus. He is to die a short way from the end of Caesar's text, "arrested by a king," the Pharaoh of Egypt, "and executed in confinement" (3.104.3).[11] The proposer of the motion against Caesar was Metellus Scipio, joined in his resistance by Cato, through discussions convened by Pompey in an after-dusk unofficial meeting of senators (1.4.1-3). Both of these survive Caesar's text, though not before Cato has been humiliated when he flees Sicily before a shot was fired, complaining of being "abandoned and betrayed" by Pompey (1.30.5),[12] and Scipio satirized as first a "self-

proclaimed *imperator*" after some setbacks in Syria, then the would-be despoiler of Ephesian Diana, and finally hubristic contender for Caesar's priesthood, counting chickens before Pharsalus (3.31.1, 33.1f., 83.1f.).[13] Caesar's text is to cease—abruptly—with Pompey's killer, Pothinus the Pharaoh's eunuch guardian, himself "put to death by Caesar" (the last words of *BC,* 3.112.12, . . . *a Caesare est interfectus;* Pompey killed at 3.104.3). Yes, up to a point, the **Civil War** hangs together. Caesar picks off both the villains he stigmatized to begin with and the villains he picked out along the way.

All Caesar's writing in the **BC** constitutes a commentary on that first, slighted, text of his, suppressed from the historical (i.e. written) record by the enemies of Caesar in the Senate. This is indeed Caesar's own claim, regularly and insistently reiterated throughout the three books. His text bears witness to his keenness to propose a cessation of hostilities, until this becomes the theme of his prebattle speech to his army before do-or-die Pharsalus (3.90). Much of the text's business is taken up with supplying terms for that missing, and/or suppressed, opening letter from Caesar, from the paraphrase he gives to intermediaries to take to Pompey at the outset, "when he sent a letter to the Senate 'that all should leave their armies,' he couldn't even get that" (1.9.3, *ut omnes ab exercitibus discederent).*[14] The lists and précis lengthen and shift, asserting, or betraying, a range of self-estimations: ". . . asserting the right to freedom of himself and the Roman People from oppression by a minority wedge" (. . . *ut se et populum Romanum factione paucorum oppressum in libertatem uindicaret,* 1.22.5), for example; or ". . . the senators should prosecute the national interest and govern together with himself; but if they ducked it for fear, he wouldn't shirk the burden and would govern the nation on his own account" (. . . *ut rem publicam suscipiant atque una secum administrent. sin timore defugiant illi, se oneri non defuturum et per se rem publicam administraturum,* 32.7).[15] Caesar himself sails close to the wind at Massilia: "You should follow the authority of all Italy rather than defer to the will of a single person" (. . . *debere eos Italiae totius auctoritatem sequi potius quam unius hominis uoluntati obtemperare,* 35.1). And the game is all but up in Greece, when Caesar tries to give his final warning through Vibullius and his message shows Pompey his *alter ego* as would-be cosmocrat: "if fortune gives just a bit to one of the two rivals, the one who seemed superior would not abide by the peace terms and the one who was confident that he was going to be master of the universe would not be content with even shares" (. . . *neque aequa parte contentum qui se omnia habiturum uideretur,* 3.10.7).[16] As shall be seen, the telegraphing of terms comes to founder on talks about talks, the slippery, "practical," business of framing the exchange of terms. But terms *are* formulated, throughout this process of deferral, terms that set Caesar's self *before* the Roman state.

If every action in the text is a shot in the word war, each ascription of a view, position, or identity also colors its representation dialectically. The writing of *Bellum Ciuile* is strung, like all discourse, between (i) the selection of actional terms that determine reality and its mutation, and (ii) the supply of relational terms which establish a modal set toward the contest of wills:[17] thus (i) Caesar, of course, plainly polarizes (his own) "set-back" against (their) "disaster," "elimination" against "massacre"; (Pompeian) "flight" against (Caesarian) "withdrawal," "boast" vs. "pledge," & c.; but (ii) he also implants *attitude*, by dramatizing acts of judgment, reactions and responses: his account of his adversaries shows them to think, speak and write in self-seeking hatefulness. *They* brutalize themselves, they drag everyone they can down with them, they monger war from nothing; whereas *Caesar* wants no enemy, reinstates order and ideals, stays warm, human and social. All the solidary sentiments are his, the violence and tyranny theirs. This work of euphemism and denigration is passed off as description, while Caesar creates a profile for his Caesar from negative ventriloquist representation of his opponents. His Caesar thus depends dialogically on the projection of unattractive images of power and knowledge onto the othered. Not Caesar but Cornelius Lentulus, for a start, lets the biggest cat out of the bag: "hyping himself to his cronies as a/the second Sulla, for imperial mastery to revisit" (*seque alterum fore Sullam inter suos gloriatur ad quem summa imperii redeat*, 1.4.2).[18]

In the course of the narrative, it becomes clear how writing has, if it has, a role to play in <the> ***Bellum Ciuile***. On the one hand, letters are centrally important, and the letters that compose them carry the brunt of the campaign; for this war is, before all, a war of words, where the prize at stake in the *Kriegschuldfrage* is, more than diplomatic victory in psychological warfare, the very stairway to world supremacy.[19] The stated, proclaimed, bandied platforms formulated by the combatants would win, accredit or dispute, and would set the seal on, interpret and calibrate, the victory. Moreover, Caesar's own text is itself nothing other than the most lengthy version of the case he put forward before the Senate, before the descent into hostilities, before the text could start. The vindication of the "truth" of Caesar's glaringly missing, or (let it be plainly said) *purloined*, letter is the work set for the narration at the outset.

The writing of letters plays a shaping role in the fighting, as the war accumulates archival substance for the eventual writing: this *dictator* could dictate four letters to four different scribes at once—something of a strategic advantage, the smart weapon of smartness.[20] In this world, commanders report to base, just as proconsul Caesar had written his despatches from Gaul to the Senate through the 50s bce. They communicate and share knowledge—to provide for detailed calculations of movements and counter-moves, and (counter-)intelligence on both sides. But most typically they bear orders, or requests for orders, and are themselves borne by messengers as the most authentic versions of the will of the generalissimos. Letters are written and conveyed by messengers; the messengers carry *mandata*, whether in writing or for oral delivery is often unclear, and perhaps still more often an immaterial triviality; crucially, most of the messages are in the imperative, and, harbingers of an imperial future of *fiat* and decree, they make things happen—if only their delivery. But, even so, in this world writing is also, paradoxically, at a discount. This is a world of action and of reactions, where the *œuvre* of Caesar displays not the literate orator and man of writing-culture, but his giant maneuvers athwart the empire. A chief-of-staff's ciphers must deliver on this, or be dead letters.

Yet, since the *Iliad*, the business of war-correspondence has always inescapably *moralized* culture through the blockage of communication, through the blockade on colloquy. Thus, a certain L. Caesar began the invasion (so to say)[21] by arriving at Ariminum with business to discuss (1.8.2-11.3): "he finished the conversation that was the reason why he had come, then indicated he was instructed by Pompey to speak to Caesar on private business (*mandata priuati officii*). Pompey wanted to be clean in Caesar's eyes, in case he took for an insult what Pompey had done for the nation (*rei publicae causa*): he had *always held* public interest above private ties" (*rei publicae commoda priuatis necessitudinibus potiora*). Further assurances of the same kind were added by praetor Roscius. Caesar's response is a paradigmatic display of acuity wrapped in statesmanlike courtesy, marked by his characteristic concessionary gesture,[22] despite his own better judgment: "although these doings seemed without relevance for easing the wrongs done Caesar, nevertheless he took the opportunity of these suitable people to be intermediaries for delivering his will to Pompey. He asked the pair of them, since they had brought Pompey's message to him (*mandata*), not to shirk taking his demands back to Pompey too (*postulata*), in case with an ounce of effort they might be able to get rid of a vast quarrel and so free all Italy from terror. . . . So that all this might come about more easily and on settled terms, and be sworn on oath, either Pompey should come closer himself or allow Caesar to come; it would turn out that all the quarrel would be settled by talking with each other." No cloak-and-dagger shabbiness from *Caesar*, but all the graces, and, congruently, the offer to short-circuit hostility and hostilities with face-to-face companionability. The ethos at the other end of this mission earns writing Caesar's ire: "taking the instructions, Roscius with <L.> Caesar reached Capua and there found the consuls and Pompey; he announced Caesar's demands. They pondered the issue, replied and sent back through them a written message to Caesar (*scripta . . . mandata*), summarized as follows: Caesar return to Gaul, quit Ariminum, dismiss troops; if he did this, Pompey go to Spain. Meantime, till pledge were received that Caesar would do what he promised, consuls and Pompey not to desist from levying." Where Caesar self-deprecates his fraternal greetings as *postulata* but dignifies the terse insults that returned as *mandata*, the generosity of his fulsome self-declaration to the go-betweens damns the cold inhumanity of his adversaries' intransigence not least by the modality encoded in the contrast in syntax. As the *Commentarius* comments, "An unequal exchange, these demands . . ." (*erat iniqua condi-*

cio postulare . . .). Dutifully rebutting the proposal point-by-point, Caesar saw the strangled message screaming through the laconic formality: "Not to find time for talking together and not to promise to come brought it across that there was serious giving up on peace." With the famous pendent "therefore" at this juncture (*itaque*, 1.11.4), the drive is on, and will not stop before Suez. So see how it all started here, when Pompey traded on the separation of young L. Caesar from his father, Caesar's legate, and their need to talk, but himself failed to meet even the basic etiquette of agreeing to meet with his old partner.

At the end of the road, Pompey will find himself obliged to "send a request to be received in the name of guest-friendship and friendship with the host's father. . . . The people sent by Pompey did their diplomatic job, but then started chatting all too freely with the guards." The result: "those who were sent by Pompey were given a generous up-front reply (*palam*) and were told to tell him to come. But the same people began a plot and sent on the quiet (*clam*)—a pair of heavies to kill Pompey" (3.103.3-104.2). Messages bring finality.

Between these moments, letters and instructions divide the sides in antipathy, even as they both pull their separate business together. "Domitius sent to Pompey in Apulia people who knew the area, for a large bonus, plus a letter to beg and pray for help. . . . When the town was mostly enveloped, those sent to Pompey returned. After reading the letter, Domitius started acting. . . . Pompey had written back that . . . if there was any chance, Domitius should come to him with all his resources.—Not that he could . . ." (1.17-19). The letter gets through, but only to draw a blank, or worse, and decipher as betrayal.

Later, the grand pattern of hubris is marked by "the letter and messengers that brought word to Rome" (*litteris nuntiisque*), "written out by Afranius and Petreius and friends in anything but the plain and dry style" (*pleniora etiam atque uberiora . . . perscribebant*). This started a dash of runners to Pompey in Greece, "some bent on being first to bring such news, others worried they might seem to have waited on the out-turn of the war, or to have come at the end of the queue" (1.53).

The same communiqué, "written out really expansively and windily by Afranius," set Varro in further Spain "to dance to fortune's dance" into self-deflating mockery of resistance to Caesar. His downfall is sealed by a letter from the people of Gades to say that they were joining Caesar, which prompted him to "send to Caesar that he was ready to hand his remaining legion over to anyone he told him to" (2.17.4-20.7). Script for a farce.[23]

The tragic equivalent: "Caesar's messengers and letter announcing (genuine) victory in Spain," which inspired his lieutenant Curio to fatal over-confidence in Africa—disregarding the messages that reached Curio and his opponent at the same moment, to the effect that Juba's vast hordes were at hand (2.37.1f.).

Readers regain the narrative track when "Caesar's letter arrived, informing Calenus that the ports and shorelines were all occupied by the other side's fleet," just as he put out to sea with the reinforcements embarked, "in accordance with Caesar's orders." One private vessel under its own steam went ahead: every last human on board was executed, to the very last one (3.14). This was, truly, a red letter day.

Polarized parallelism between the principals goes on through the contrasts between their correspondence: "Pompey's admirals were torn off a strip (*castigabantur*) by a volley of letters for failing to stop Caesar's crossing"; "troubled by developments, Caesar wrote pretty strictly to his men in Brundisium" (3.25.2f.). In his bureau as in all else, Pompey is an outmaneuvered but considerable opposite number—worth writing a war with, a decent way to write Caesar, the best of a bad job.[24]

Through all the deadlock and circling, the consul Caesar parlays unilaterally, for the duration. Two matching episodes tell of perfidy within the business of negotiation: first Caesar picks twice-pardoned Vibullius "to send with instructions to Pompey, summarized as: both men to bring their obstinacy to an end, walk away from war and risk fortune no further. . . . Vibullius heard the account and thought it no less necessary for Pompey to be informed of Caesar's sudden approach (*aduentu Caesaris*), so that he could take counsel for that, before any dealings began on the instructions" (3.10.2-11.1). Then, "informed by letter about the demands of Libo and Bibulus," Caesar calls them "for talks." Caesar had to excuse Bibulus, "whose reason for shunning the talks was in case a matter of the greatest hope and greatest expediency might be hog-tied by his wrath." They said they wanted "to learn Caesar's demands and send to C.-in-C. Pompey," but Caesar sussed them out by requiring personally supervised "safe-conduct for representatives to Pompey"; Libo "would not receive Caesar's representatives nor assure their safety, but referred the whole matter to Pompey." So "Caesar realized that Libo had started up the whole scheme in view of the danger he was in . . . and was coming across with no hope or term for peace" (3.16.2-17.6). *Waffungstillstandsunterredung* was only a pretext for playing for time.

Furthermore, when Scipio entered the frame, Caesar "didn't forget his original strategy," but sent him a mutual friend, Clodius, "handing him a letter and giving him instructions for Scipio, which summarizes as: Caesar had tried everything for peace, and reckoned that the zero progress was the fault of the people he had wanted to take responsibility for the business, because they were afraid to carry his instructions to Pompey at a bad moment. . . . Clodius delivered these instructions to Scipio," but "he wasn't allowed to join any talks . . . and went back to Caesar in failure" (3.57). The breakdown in communication has now itself broken down. And, this time, Caesar's message is a masquerade—really a string of bare insults.

But the mail will get through, eventually: though Pompey "never got used to writing-in his acclamation as *imperator* as his letter-head" (3.71.3), the victory he won it for was quite wrongly diagnosed by his officers, who therefore turned it into defeat (in analysis)[25] and the occasion of their own fatal and final hubris: "just as if they had won by their own courage and as if no change of fortune could occur, they celebrated that day's victory all through planet earth, by word of mouth and by letter" (*fama ac litteris*, 72.4). Now this climax to Caesar's chain of dramatic tales of reversal[26] makes big big waves: "Pompey had sent out letters through every province and township about the battle at Dyrrhachium, and rumor had hustled far more extensively and windily than what had actually happened: Caesar repelled and on the run, most all his forces lost" (79.4). This hype, the telltale miscommunication that betokens a fake sociality, the Pompeians' spurious bid to speak to and for their country, and *not* the actual battle at Dyrrhachium, threatened to break the inexorable pattern of the narrative. Caesar was obliged to force it back into shape, encouraging a fresh spate of loyalty to himself by sensational but (he has said) "controlled" aggression. As Henderson will have demonstrated, they *must* have brought it on themselves, when Caesar must take out a people's town: regrets, he had a few, but then again, almost too few to mention.

So Caesar writes his instructions, demands, letters. They invite readers to come to talk, if only about talks. His *Commentarii* do not pretend to be other than documentary drafts, a condensed saturation of documentation, intermediate between the utilitarian pragmatics of the performative world of reports to GCHQ and orders to units, and the elaborated synthesis of a historian's finished text.

The *Commentarii,* that is to say, pretend to be no other than rough drafts, a provisional string of raw documents, indeterminate between the signals telegraphed from generals to soldiers and back and the clamorous prosecution of a raft of conditions for a new political order.

"In a real sense, as long as Caesar could write this narrative, the Republic still existed. For such writing would show it was still possible to know the public interest rather than simply to idealize it."[27] Or, rather, as any less partisan view would have it, writing Caesar turns on disavowed will to power.

2. Write Every Wrong

As when <Shakespeare> said in the person of Caesar, one speaking to him, "Caesar, thou dost me wrong"—he replied: "Caesar did never wrong but with just cause."[28]

Like many who believe their own propaganda, <he> often used the Caesarean third person.[29]

The most obvious place to look for Caesar's missing letter is *not* in the putative preliminary lacuna, where the reader was not privileged or entitled to hear its wording before the senatorial meeting despatched it to the rapidly filling wastebasket of Republican history's might-have-beens, but rather in every letter he goes on to write as commentary

on his claimed attempt to stave off the need to fight, write and right the Civil War. Caesar has hidden the letter of his law where it is most easily overlooked, on display through the pages of his public record.[30]

His account might easily read as, exactly, confirmation that his initial representation of the sending of this first-ditch letter as an attempt to pull everyone back from the brink to safety was itself the prototype for all his subsequent barrage of *déformations* of the historical record.[31] In any event—and this is the point, certainly the predicament readers are in—every re-formulation of Caesar's terms in the course of the three books is put across as a raise on the same stakes he began with. Readers begin with the question of his sincerity, the authorial sincerity embodied in the promissory terms of the pledges he vouches for. As the opening episode means to suggest or impose, this intersects with the question whether sincerity from Caesar *could* affect the reception it was possible to give him, once the Senate conspired to cross its Rubicon and quarantine contacts from him. This compounded question will never be left behind: it extends, unfolds and articulates to become the question of the **BC.**

So can be read the first displacement operated by this project of writing Caesar in that opening blockage of any motion based on Caesar's letter. According to Caesar, even those who blocked serious consideration of the missive, Lentulus and Scipio, told the house they and Pompey might or might not do a deal of some sort with Caesar, take it or leave it; and a series of senators nevertheless ventured proposals pacific or appeasing (1.1.2-2.4). The text indeed wades straight into efforts by the players to interpret Caesar's will and read Caesar—while the attendant events were being shaped to exclude effective moves to meet him half-way. By the time Caesar supplies readers with that first, foregrounded, summary of his letter's drift (1.9.3), he has shown how irretrievable a situation had (been) developed, and has obliged his reader to reflect on the momentum endemic to the escalation from entrenched antagonism to all-out war.

The letter of Caesar had been a text and an affidavit: could he be held to it, or did the spirit which prompted its sentiments belong strictly to that determinate instant of history? Could letters hold on to what they meant in a context of slide and slippage into crisis—or could no one dare credit them with meaning what they <would have> said?[32] A letter belongs to its moment, even if that moment never arrived. However, *this* absent letter presences the eternal moment of Caesar's text.

Now the momentaneous *Caesar* the Romans of the time were "reading," and the *Caesar* that he was and is writing, were not invented from scratch. That is, at least, first base or bivouac in Caesar's self-presentation. Rather, this is the proconsul of Rome, victor over Gaul and Germany, proved in a series of wars and ordeals against the age-old barbarian threat to Roman Italy, the unprecedentedly acclaimed *imperator.* This is the hero of a thousand despatches, written up as the mastermind of the sevenfold *Gallic Wars,* equally apt to write as to fight. This same exemplary citizen and would-be servant of Rome is now the victim of his own success. Writing just one more epistle back home, he is feared and cold-shouldered. As if he leads a Gallic tumult, or as if the Roman government were tribal chieftains intimidated by the approach of the Roman Caesar they had learned to know and (rightly) fear. Yes, the trace of Gaul will persist in *De Bello Ciuili.*

In time, Caesar's lieutenant and amanuensis Hirtius would ape the *hupomnêmata* of Alexander's marshals, plug the gap in his leader's story, in his text and in his rhetoric. But when he did that, with *De Bello Gallico* VIII, the Caesar he would be writing for would have moved on many a mile. The project had become to complete the record of Caesar's progress to full "rationalization" of the Republican system of a bouleutic Senate supervising its temporary and inducted magisterial representatives—and the eventual nemesis of assassination by former associates and adversaries in coalition. The loyal Caesarian Hirtius' mimetic project of marching behind Caesar in filling out the record of his campaigns,[33] provisionally working up the most suitable primary despatches he could solder together into a supplementary *Commentarius,* may have been completed under the aegis of the dictator, as he seems to claim. Or the project may have been finished after Caesar's example, by the compilation of the remaining episodes in the *corpus Caesarianum,* up to and including, or down to, Caesar's ultimate battle of Munda, at the world's edge (**BG** [*De Bello Gallico*] 8 *Praef.*). Something an administrator *could* delegate, perhaps. The effect, at any rate, is to complete the soldierly biography of the soldier Caesar, as if the completion of his world conquest remained primarily a military matter, the progressive consolidation of exploits from *prouincia* to *prouincia.* But, it is patent to all, the geopolitics of Caesar's career invaginate any such portrait.

At any rate, the story Caesar made true by fighting, then writing, the Civil War down to his victory over, and vengeance for, Pompey made Caesar himself into an over-achieving *imperator* who could scarcely—and this on the most optimistic reckoning—take one more step without confirming the fears he has rejected so firmly from the outset.[34]

By the end of *Book III,* the fame of *Caesar* meant the world was his oyster. As he (correctly as ever) reckoned, "all space shall be indifferently secure for Caesar" (3.106.3, *aeque omnem sibi locum tutum fore*), even if he does contrive to camouflage this new omnipotence adequately behind his cliffhanger of a finale: Caesar's back to the wall in Egypt. Romans must see that *he* is the new Savior: Pompeius—never *Magnus* in **BC**—has (it could seem) been cut down to size in the city that is the necropolis of Alexander, whose degenerate Ptolemaic wardens must be punished for the hubris they dare commit on the person of the great Roman Pompey, and then on the majesty of the serving consul of the *populus Romanus,* Caesar. (The Alexandrians killed Pompey "because the *fa-*

sces paraded before Caesar . . . This was treason against the <*videlicet* Egyptian> crown," 3.106.4: *quod fasces anteferrentur . . . maiestatem regiam minui.*) At this juncture, Caesar, come from the other end of the earth and its untamed barbarians of Britain all the way to the corrupt hyperculture of Egypt's eunuchs, queens and boy-kings, stands forth as beacon to all those in peril on the political main: he takes charge of the Pharus (112)—though, ironically, he could not himself sail out of Alexandria against the prevailing winds (107.1), the political winds that had blown him clean across the map, blowing with him until the end-point where *he* had prevailed over his Roman adversaries.

On the one hand, the victory at Pharsalus turned Caesar into the (double) savior of Ephesian Diana (105.1-3), blessed by annunciation across the Hellenistic East of the Macedonian diadochoi—from Olympia to Antioch to Ptolemais to Pergamum to Tralles—blessed, that is, with the charisma of a new super-Alexander (105.3-6). On the other, Caesar finds himself, for the first and last time in the text but, fatally, not for the last time in his life, as over-confident as any of his Roman adversaries had proved, and by "trusting in *fama*" gets outnumbered and bottled up "with troops no way numerous enough to trust in" (106.3, 109.2). For all the world, if one knew no better, like some second-rate Pompey. Like some Hector caught by his swift-footed Achill*as*?

As Caesar plays the perfect Roman magistrate in Alexandria, he gets the chance to re-play, his way, the Lentulus scene where he and writing Caesar came in. In Egypt there is, naturally, civil war, fought between kin. First, brother and sister; then another sister joins in, but soon disputes break out *de principatu,* and the united front needed to face the alien Roman teeters on the edge of collapse—just as the text gives out. *These* disputants *were* all *reges*—whereas Julius would continue, less and less plausibly from this moment on, to repeat to his subjects *Caesaremse, non regem, esse.*[35] Caesar thought the quarrel "involved the national interest and his own, as invested in his office" (*ad populum Romanum et ad se, quod esset consul, pertinere*). He also had a personal stake of honor, in the shape of past connections with the disputants (107.2)—just as in that opening chapter of *BC* Lentulus had, he said, had with Caesar (1.1.3). Caesar knew the solution: "Our recommendation is that Ptolemy R. and Cleopatra his sister dismiss the armies they have, and negotiate their differences before himself at law rather than between themselves at arms" (107.2, *sibi placere regem Ptolemaeum atque eius sororem Cleopatram exercitus quos haberent dimittere et de controuersiis iure apud se potius quam inter se armis disceptare;* cf. *Bell. Gall.* 8.55, *ad fin., quoad sibi spes aliqua relinqueretur iure potius disceptandi quam belli gerendi,* and 1.9.3-5, *omnes ab exercitibus discederent . . . ipsi exercitus dimittant . . . ,* etc.). In the text, the threatened fusion of *se* with *se* here surely tells tales on the repressed investment in this work of boundarying the self against the disowned selves that are scheduled for abjection. Caesar cannot quite rise above his own rhetoric. Meantime, in the action, the solution doesn't work, for *this* state is indeed truly rotten, and needs saving from itself.

Caesar in Egypt faces the classic impurity of molten civil war: a rabble of Gabinius' former troops now married to natives, spawning hybrids as they unlearned "the name and norms of the Roman people" *(nomen disciplinamque populi Romani)* and turned to Alexandrian ways of license. Add a heap of bandits and robbers from all over, rootless flux. Stir in lots of criminals with a price on their heads, chuck-out exiles. Every runaway Roman slave made a bee-line for the foreign legion at Alex. Long decadence had made civil war a way of life: in the anti-politics of chaos, these forces stuck together, settling the hash of courtiers, extorting bonuses from the palace and even king-making.

These experienced mercenary muckers made of Caesar what civil war threatens to make of any commander, or disputant: a street-fighter, Caesar must descend to messy working from house to house, must turn the apparatus of orderly civic life into so many sordid fortifications and foxholes—theater, palace, harbor, docks, lighthouse. Egypt ultimately makes of Caesar <a parody of> the Sulla he had always absolutely abjured to become—for all the world like some Clodius, a bit-part Catiline.[36]

But this, the start of the *Bellum Alexandrinum,* was not a *Roman* civil war.[37] Here, Caesar could insist, was Caesar the servant of Rome still, carrying on where he left off in the wastes of the north, down in the post-civilized pit of the south, standard-bearer for the ethical center of the Roman world, upholding the order of Republican institutions. Best if the writer Caesar desists here. Rather than take his readers and his notes up the Nile, to serve Clio by living it up and writing it up on Cleo's barge!

Besides, the wars to come, in Africa and Spain, were both easy and impossible to tell as un*Civil Wars,* with too many eminent Roman deaths, among them the suicides of the greatest Republican names alive, the aristocrat in spades, Metellus Scipio, and the walking legend Cato the martyr; and worse to come, with the unglamorous chore of mopping up Pompey's litter. No doubt it could be done, by Caesar, rather than botched as it is by his loyal lieutenants. But whatever the causation, the question should be asked, just *what* flows from the fact that Caesar's text stops where it does, delegating the task of completing the campaign report to adjutant acolytes in the secretariat?[38]

Henderson's story had to be that the débâcle in Alexandria caps Caesar's denial that he has fought a civil war. He may have been dragged involuntarily into circumstances that look mighty like civil war, but anyone who should take the trouble and take up the challenge to write up these drafted *Commentarii* will find that Caesar has consistently and resolutely engaged (us) in, at most, an involuntary series of *bella minus quam ciuilia* ("Wars this side of civil").

There *is* Civil War in the *Bellum Ciuile.* But it appears just where Caesar doesn't. Inside the walls of Corfinium, under Caesar's blockade (1.20.3); in the mutual destruction of ships bent on battering the enemy in Massilian naumachy (2.6.4); and in Thessaly, where the Pompeian leader must be a *ueteris homo potentiae,* and his Caesarian rival a *summae nobilitatis adulescens* (3.35.2). The pattern where fraternization threatens to dissolve hostility into integration, but is foiled by desperate officers, *does* threaten to bring the horror too close to Caesar: in Spain, "civil war," a sedition within the opponents' camp, has the troops "look out and call for anyone in Caesar's camp they knew or who came from the same town . . . complaining of bearing arms against people who were close to them and related by blood." "Two camps were just looking like one," when the Pompeian generals returned, to turn it round with savage war-crimes and cursed oaths (1.74-6). In return, as was noticed, Curio off in Africa had to scotch Varus' efforts to seduce the former Pompeian soldiers he once messed with at Corfinium (2.28). And in Greece, "between the two camps of Pompey and of Caesar, there was one river alone." The soldiers kept talking to each other. Caesar sent Vatinius to the bank to yell out awkward questions about "why citizens couldn't send representatives to citizens . . . especially when the object was to stop citizens fighting a decisive war with citizens . . ." *(ciuibus ad ciues . . . ciues cum ciuibus).* Talks got as far as fixing venue and time, hopes ran high, but *BC*'s villain, Labienus, pounced, as mysterious missiles hailed down, and told them off: "Stop talking about a settlement; for there can be no peace for us without fetching Caesar's head back with us" (3.19: *capite relato).* This "near thing" is twinned with Pompey's immediately preceding declaration, in response to proposals to discuss Caesar's instructions: "he interrupted him in full flow and barred him from another word, saying, 'What use do I have for life or citizen status if I seem to have them by Caesar's favor? That opinion of the matter will be ineradicable, when . . . I'm thought to have been brought back to Italy [. . .]'" (3.18.4f., *reductus).* So Civil War is waged in *Pompey*'s camp; and Caesar is involved only as disputant trying (so Caesar writes) to end the dispute.

Otherwise, so Henderson observed, civil war in *BC* abides where it should—in downtown Alexandria. And Caesar searches only for "a farewell to arms on equal terms" *(aequis condicionibus ab armis discedatur,* 1.26.4), as he is led west to "learn the lie of the land / his opponents' position" *(cognita locorum natura . . . ubi cognouit per Afranium stare quominus proelio dimicaretur)* and offer battle in Spain "on equal ground" *(aequo loco,* 1.41.2f.), then as consul establishes "evenness" in the civil administration *(aequitate decreti,* 3.20.2), pleads for an armistice while the balance between the two sides was still "even" *(aequa parte,* 10.7), and still, at the death, offers battle "on even ground" against Pompey in Greece *(aequum in locum,* 55.1): although Pompey "kept drawing up his line at the roots of his hill, waiting to see if Caesar would subject himself to uneven ground" *(iniquis locis),* "one fine day Pompey's line advanced a little further beyond its daily routine, so it seemed possible for the fight to be on ground that was not uneven" (*non iniquo loco,* 85.1, 3). Pompey had all along "refused to let anyone get even with him in dignity" (*neminem dignitate secum exaequari uolebat,* 1.4.4). The rest, the text leaves to be gathered, is history.

3. LE PORTRAIT DE CÉSAR, C'EST CÉSAR[39]

Soy esa torpe intensidad que es un alma[40]

. . . . ut de suis homines laudibus libenter praedicant . . .[41]

In <his> truth, Caesar stoutly avoided invading his country; and neither has he left it, at the death. He was no Gallic barbarian; he is no Oriental Sultan. Instead, his orders have consistently preserved Roman order, in the lines of his regimental formations,[42] the precision of his circumvallations, the organization of supply, engineering, logistics.[43] And performatively his writing gives the order to relate his orders to the national interest. This, Caesar's message runs, is how these three books of *writing-talk* come to exist.

The author Caesar does not tell all that Caesar the actor did or was. In particular, his Caesar is not sighted composing the two books *De Analogia* on crossing the Alps between winter quarters and the front (Spring 54 BCE). Here *Caesar the* purist *Man of Letters* once told Cicero's Empire how to speak Latin, in no uncertain terms.[44] He could make words stick to the world, close up description and prescription so tight that *nomen* and *nominatum* must bond in unique propriety.[45] *Commentarii* in this stylistics could slough or veil their definitionally subjective particularity as a species of memoirs, for their narration blanks out marks of personality, limiting the narrative to an ascetic régime of reportage paradedly shorn of palpable *mentalité.* What was done, not what was being thought of; tactics not strategy; a world of detail, observation, specification, not overview, impression, valorization.

The proconsul in this field is but *primus inter pares* among the characters, an agent with the same strong exteriority of an officer-administrator's accounts; the narrator with the omniscience of retrospect writes a Caesar strictly intent on his business, dividing and ruling tribes and chiefs in the time-honored manner of the Roman commander.[46] *Any* officer might be compiling these reports from the frontier? Almost.[47] But the writing Caesar twins with the written *Caesar* in their shared manner,[48] of swift, forceful, precise, pointed application to the matter in hand, customized rhetoric indistinguishable from impassive dash—"il velo dell'impassibilità, dietro il quale lo scrittore si nasconde."[49] One signifier per signified. And in the *BC,* the dyad will shoot the moon.

That tenacious construction, the conqueror of Gaul, must become the reserve of credit that the *Bellum Ciuile* draws on. One complete set of *Commentarii,* one narrated *Bellum,* one Caesar. By analogical theory, *BG* and *BC* must bear the same referentiality, formal and actual, across the textual wound that is to be sutured by Hirtius. In this poetics, there will be no holding the boundary between Gaul and Italy, which Caesar and his texts must cross and recross as they progress their work.[50] The seven hundred and seventy five occurrences of "the letters of C-æ-s-a-r" (the letters of Caesar's name) that line up through *BG* and *BC* are one, in seamlessness.[51]

The narrative works hard to make the theory bite: features of *BG* litter the stages of *BC.* Guerrilla warfare in Spain has rubbed off on the legions "because they have got used to fighting Lusitanians and other barbarians in a barbarian-style of battle: this is something that generally happens, that soldiers are greatly affected by the habit of the regions in which soldiers have matured" (1.44.2). Lusitanian and local troops found it "easy to swim a river, because the habit of all of them is not to go on campaign without skins <for floats>"(48.7), while "Caesar ordered his soldiers to make boats <—coracles—> of a kind that experience of Britain had taught him in earlier years" (54.1). To aid Caesar, a huge convoy of Gauls treks over the mountains—"cavalry with long wagon-trains and heavy baggage, as the Gallic way has it. . . . All sorts of men, plus slaves and children; complete lack of order and discipline, with each person doing his thing and all of them traveling along without a worry in their heads—still practicing the anarchy of earlier times and migrations" (51.1f.). Shades of the Helvetii: even at Phocaean Massilia, rough mountain tribesmen from the hinterland, called the Albici, put up a fine fight (34.4, 56.2, 58.4, 2.2.6, 6.3). In Africa, Curio faced more othered "natives": "the Numidians bivouacked all over the place, no shape at all—that certain way with barbarians" (2.38.4), and the *déjà vu* feeling is completed when Juba deploys the "two thousand Spanish and Gallic horse" of his bodyguard, who did the traditional maneuver of fake retreat, before the sucker-punch (40f.). Greece had "barbarians" of its own, of course, as at Salonae (3.9.1), but wherever Caesar, or indeed Pompey, go, still the familiar old braves who have stayed the whole distance in writing Caesar ride in from the pages of the *BG:* most memorably the two Allobrog troopers, "men of unmatched courage, on whose top-quality services, best of warriors, Caesar had capitalized in all his *Gallic Wars*" (3.59.1f.; cf. 63.5, 79.6, 84.5). With the assistance of these old totems, Caesar's old wars are reinscribed to make up the *Bellum <quam minime> Ciuile* ("The War *non*-Civil").

4. MEIN BUMPF

In short, you can beat personality tests.[52]

Crude, violent, barbarous, the enemy has been cleanly divided from Rome; the mission of the *imperium,* a secure future behind pacified borders, has been celebrated for *Latinitas;* the moral center has repelled extremism far away to the Atlantic margins, rectified by Roman order: such are the grand mythologizations of the "realist" story of proconsular *res gestae*—the *Caesaris . . . monimenta magni.*[53] Now the *Bellum Gallicum*'s greatest accomplishment, *Caesar,* must make himself count in a world bent on othering *him,* with ritual, with ridicule, and with righteousness. Caesar is The One, the same, in the field and on the page. His meanings must prevail, as before.

The authorities at Rome determined to prevent Caesar from articulating his case. They ruled out his criteria for making an intervention, effectively banishing him from the *res publica:* "they no longer lived in the same worlds, even though the words they spoke, barely now more than a convention, sounded the same."[54] Like Coriolanus, Caesar must invent a one-man collectivity where he may retort in defiance, "I banish you." If this was to respond to elimination outside the state by setting himself in its place,[55] he must transform the basis of his claim to serve the Republic still, the proconsul's solidarity with his legions, into a revisionary dispensation where Rome was retrieved from inimical déformation and distorting *Tendenz.* Caesar's victories will say what goes, what is what, and straighten out the rules for wor(l)d-dealing in Rome.[56] It wasn't Caesar's fault. It wasn't Rome's. Just a misguided cabal of losers.

So the arrogation of power for a Caesarian logonomy must amount to a complete bouleversement, tearing up the codes of his defeated enemies, reversing their verdicts, and yet, finally, dissolving the claim that any revolution has occurred. No, Caesar was never enemy to Rome; his vindication of the *res publica* brought no *nouae tabulae;* rather, he brought restoration, repair and renewal to the city. Those lost ones had done "what had never happened before" and gone "against all parallels from Antiquity," "introduced the political novelty of armed quashing of tribunician veto," "uttered new-fangled orders" (1.6.7f., 7.2, 85.8). All over Italy, "funds were extracted from the townships, lifted from consecrated shrines—throwing the divine and human rulebooks into confusion" (1.6.8).[57] Contrast Caesar, who saved that "holy of holies, the Roman treasury" (1.14.1), as he will restore his bullion and dedications to Hercules of Gades (2.21.3); later, a letter's opportune arrival from Pompey, urgent because of Caesar's lightning approach, "saved Diana of Ephesus' ancient vaults" from Scipio—shortly before another timely letter, from Favonius, turned Scipio's course, and "so Domitius' energy saved Cassius, Scipio's velocity saved Favonius" (3.33, *. . . haec res Ephesiae pecuniae salutem attulit,* 36.6f., *. . . ita Cassio industria Domiti, Fauonio Scipionis celeritas salutem adtulit*). Finally, as was remarked, "Caesar saved Ephesus' treasures a second time" (105.2, *ita duobus temporibus Ephesiae pecuniae Caesar auxilium tulit*). The one-and-only, true, Caesar.

That "Caesar's arrival caused panic flight" of his opponent as he violated every code ("arrival," or "epiphany": *interpellatum aduentu Caesaris profugisse,* 105.1) is the refrain established from the very start, where Caesar's adversaries are swept away in flight by his very proximity (1.13.1-3, *aduentu Caesaris cognito . . . Varus . . . profugit,* 15.3, *Lentulus Spinther . . . Caesaris aduentu cognito profugit,* 3.12.1-3, *[Caesaris] aduentu audito L. Staberius . . . profugit*).[58] So all fund-raising opportunities come not from

Caesar, who only rewards his troops' efforts above and beyond the call of duty, but are, without exception, desecration: illegal expropriations meant to bribe the world's population to face Caesar.[59]

Caesar's sanctity (he *was,* since 63, *pontifex maximus*) is further entrusted to narrative in military dress through the medium of the military oath of loyalty, named *religio* (1.67.3): his opponents stopped fraternization between the two camps dead by exacting "an oath not to desert or betray the army and generals, and not to plan their own individual salvation"; combined with their terroristic reprisals, the "unprecedented sanction of the oath" prevented progress to peace (*iusiurandum; crudelitas in supplicio, noua religio iuris iurandi,* 1.76.2-5). On the other hand, when their old commander Varus talks over the former Pompeian troops by recalling their "first memory of taking the oath," the failed Caesar-clone Curio bucks up his panicky squad by discrediting "the oath dissolved by their surrender" in favor of the "fresh oath" sworn to serve Caesar; in the teeth of disaster, he himself refused to come back without the army entrusted him by Caesar and went down fighting (*primam sacramenti . . . memoriam; sacramentum; noua religio,* 2.28.2, 32.9f.; 42.5).[60] To stop his panicking army in Greece bolting from Caesar's approach, "Labienus swore he would not desert Pompey and would take his chances with him, and the rest then followed suit" (3.13.3f.). But when crews surrendered on receipt of Otacilius' "oath not to harm them, they were all led out and executed before his very eyes, in violation of the oath's sanction" (*iureiurando; contra religionem iurisiurandi,* 3.28.4): when his town came out for Caesar, Otacilius at once took to his heels (*fugit,* 29.1). For the climax of Pharsalus, Labienus again dashingly "took an oath that he would not return to camp unless victorious," and got the rest, including Pompey himself, to follow suit (*iurauit,* 3.87.5f.). Pompey precisely fled back to camp, in the "rout" (*fuga*) that ensued, whereas the Caesarian hero Crastinus showed how it should be done, with the simplicity of a promise—minus the histrionics of oath-taking—"I shall see today, my general, that you thank me alive or dead" (91.3). In the event, Crastinus (*Tomorrow's man* of the present moment: *cras,* cf. *hodie*), "was killed in combat, when a sword stabbed his face/mouth: and so it came true, all he'd said on his way to the fight . . ." (99.2f., *gladio in os aduersum coniecto*). Here the savage justice of slaughter through the mouth seals the "truth" of his appeal to his ole buddies: "Follow me, . . . and give your general the service you pledged" (*uestro imperatori quam constituistis operam date,* 91.2). Self-reflexively, the character books his place in Caesar's heart, and record: an exemplum to be mentioned in despatches: *BC* is, not least, figured as Caesar's homage to his army, written *fides.*

Finally, "the edict signed by Pompey, which told all males of serviceable age to enlist, whether Greeks or Roman citizens," failed, as Pompey was shooed onwards by Caesar's relentless approach and his "flight" (*fuga*) continued past shut city-gates as "the word of Caesar's approach spread through city on city" (*iurandi causa; cog-*

nito Caesarisque aduentu ex eo loco discessit, iamque de Caesaris aduentu fama ad ciuitates perferebatur, 102.2, 4, 8). The only place on earth which would take Pompey in, perverse Egypt, duly did take him in, and treacherously executed him, too, at the hands of the Egyptian minion and of Pompey's former aide "against the pirates," now turned pirate, not on the high seas but in a "toy dinghy"— the state that Pompey's ship had shrunk to (*bello praedonum; nauiculam paruulam,* 104.3). The ultimate poetic irony, then, is when (it has already been observed) Caesar's "approach" behind his *consular* fasces stirs this one township's population against Caesar, while he is kept from flight by the winds and, more than taken in by treacherous Alexandria's open door, he is holed up there at journey's end!

Now all this combination of sacrality and finance, words and bonds, that Henderson has rehearsed, goes to prove this was never a tale of civil war. Caesar did not engage in any such abomination, however it may have threatened to engulf and stain his majestic state procession bringing peace on earth. Those self-dramatizing oaths always figured in tragical narrative structures as prelude to nemesis, after fortune has oppressed Caesar, then capsized to punish his rivals for hubristic over-confidence on a Herodotean scale.[61]

Caesar made his righteousness plain to doubters among his readers when he assumed the *fasces* at Rome to inaugurate, bless, and commandeer **BC** Book III. As who did not know?, debt cancellation "habitually follows wars and civil fallout" (*fere bella et ciuiles dissensiones sequi consueuit);* the unjustly condemned victims of Pompey's law Caesar "put back into one piece again" (*in integrum restituit),* by due process of magisterial legislation *ad populum.* When these unfortunates offered him their services *initio belli ciuilis* (3.1.4)—one of the very few concessions Caesar ever makes to the stakes of his title and his predicament[62]—*he did no such thing.* Rather, he acted *as if* he had taken up their offer, though he had never fought dirty from the beginning of the troubles onwards. "He had decided they should be restored by the verdict of the Roman People rather than rescued by favor of Caesar" (3.1.3-5).[63]

This from Caesar as legitimate and acknowledged *dictator* of Rome, and duly elected consul designate, to boot. Now for a negative proof, if proof could be needed. While he religiously held the elections and the Latin festival before duly abdicating the temporary crisis post of dictator and setting off to campaign abroad, his own aide, Caelius Rufus, tried to stir up, as praetor, resentment against Caesar's new equity; failing to find cracks here, Caelius turned to legislative intervention but was suppressed and suspended from office by consul and Senate; resorting to an unholy alliance with Pompey's discredited and banished former aide, Milo, he tried to stir up rebellion in Italy, while pretending to join Caesar. Their gladiators and *pastores,* debtors and armed slaves, and attempts to bribe Caesar's Gallic and Spanish cavalry, were scotched by local

citizenry and a legion. Milo was killed by a rock flung from a town-wall; Caelius by Caesar's troopers. "So it was that this overture to world-shaking events . . . had a lightning and effortless finale" (3.20-22, *Ita magnarum initia rerum . . . celerem et facilem exitum habuerunt).* Here, in microcosm, is the turmoil and contamination of civil war—what *could have* filled the pages of the **Bellum Ciuile.** A caricature because a miniature, a storm in a might-have-been teacup; but, for all that, an exemplary lesson in the temperate abstention of the Pompey-Caesar dissension from the anticipated brew of social anarchy, opportunistic terrorism and cataclysmic mischief.

Above all, Caesar uses the Caelius-Milo sideshow to displace from himself the mindset of devilment. The minions ape the comradely conduct of war which the leaders manage to preserve between them through the narrative, as if by concerted arrangement. And Caesar begins his show-down campaign against Pompey as the moderate and balanced representative of legitimate Roman authority, impossible to confuse with any traitorous trouble-maker such as the *hostis* renegade Caelius (3.21.5). The "secret messages" from Caelius to Milo (*clam nuntiis,* 21.4) Caelius dissimulated virtually at once; Milo's "letter," circulated to claim he acted under Pompey's "orders" as the commission brought to him by an intermediary (*litteris . . . mandata,* 22.1), cut no ice, so he dropped the idea on the instant. Contrast these botched perversions with Caesar's crusade of honest negotiation and sincere self-positioning . . .

Well on the way to becoming *Caesar,* the consul installs the "representational economy" of his self, plotting self-action in relation to his progressive escape from the bind of his framing as invader of his country, toward transcendence of the parameters within which civic identities should abide.[64] When writing Caesar prepares to leave him ice-cold in Alex, he has, for the first time, been disjoined from his armies. No longer the soldiers' soldier, he has not yet the autarky of the autonomous imperial ruler; but, now that there is no need to defeat Pompey, he must float upstream, and get ready to re-negotiate the terms of his interactive sociality with the rest of his world's *ciues Romani.* Readers know how far he is to travel toward arrogating the Pharaonic preeminence that commands official history in any autocracy. Caesar will dispense and *own* justice, his will to power coincident with the political will. For a short pancratic while, before the first Ides of March in Julian temporality initiated his ascension to divinity as *Diuus Iulius,* Caesar could try out less deprecatory selves for size. It would be left for Lucan to read/write back into the *Civil War* zone the prefiguration of every monarch of the West by "Julius Caesar (the *memorable* Roman Emperor)."[65]

Yet in the anathematic Caesarian third person narration,[66] there already lurks the logic of a subservience of the world of writing Caesar to the writing *of* Caesar. The narrator's devotion to first-hand "I"-witness depiction of the generalissimo in the ascendant threatens to model already the exclusive focusing of history on a Sun-King's au-tofellatory self-orbiting.[67]

5. L'État c'est Moi

Empires do not suffer emptiness of purpose at the time of their creation. It is when they have become estab-lished that aims are lost and replaced by vague ritual.[68]

All latin masters hav one joke.

Caesar ad sum jam forte.[69]

Writing Caesar necessarily paints himself into a complex and contradictory corner between conflicting discourses. On the one hand, the armies he led were "incomparably superior to any forces at the disposal of his adversaries."[70] The celerity which gave him a bloodless occupation of Italy was not simply a genius' trademark;[71] it also labels the expediency of his cause: "[H]e would not yield the advantage that the rapidity of his offensive gave him . . . , never prepared to lose the momentum of his offensive."[72] Military superiority must be veiled: this is *not* why Caesar would march on his country. Not that he ever did any such thing, nor does it in (that misnomer) the **De Bello Ciuili.**

No. Caesar has nothing to hide. Just not his style. As Hend-erson has noted and Caesar told, he nailed his colors to the mast, catalogues the Italian communities that spontane-ously, enthusiastically, convincedly came over. Call it "bandwagon propaganda,"[73] but these peoples of Italy were won over by the justice of his case, his forbearance, sensitivity, authenticity. The (discredited) government representatives disqualified themselves: they turned tail, ditched their men, abandoned their vaunts, saved their skins because they were found out, cowardly, inept, hypocritical. *None* of this was the result of the imminent approach of the largest fighting force on the planet (= *Caesar*), veterans of no holds barred massacre and all-out scourging of the Hun and the Gaul, not at all.[74]

Nothing to fear from their rapacity, not with this proconsul disciplinarian at the reins (actually, Caesar admits it once, "urgently instructing Trebonius *per litteras* not to let the town be forcibly stormed, in case the soldiers . . . killed all the adults, which they were threatening to do, and were with difficulty held from bursting into the town," 2.13.3f.).[75] Nothing to fear, for those who learned the dual lesson of the twin Thessalian towns of (1) Gomphi, where the ap-proaching Caesar's response to being misunderstood and refused entry was exemplary terrorism *pour encourager les autres,* as "he yielded the township to the troops for plunder" (*reliquis ciuitatibus huius urbis exemplo inferre terrorem . . . ad diripiendum militibus concessit,* 3.80.6f.); and (2) Metropolis, which was indeed encouraged by the chomping and gnashing of Gomphoi to admit Caesar, escape the same fate and provide the rest of Thessaly, and indeed the Roman and every *soi-disant* metropolis, with the moral (3.81). So: Caesar's men only behaved like those who crushed Gaul so they did not need to crush anyone (else). And, to read those who write *on* Caesar, it need never be known that this was a one-man superpower that

tells the world it (he) was. That is not what the row of flag waving townsfolk lined their streets to say when they volunteered "to do the things he ordered" (*quaeque imper-auerat se cupidissime facturos,* 1.15.2, *sese paratos esse . . . quaeque imperauerat facere,* 20.5, *quae imperaret facturos, seseque imperata facturos,* 60.1, 3.12.4, *ciuitates imperata facturas,* 34.2)—for all that this <abject, if momentary, submission>[76] is what it (and they?) meant: sc. (1) what the losers of Gomphi wanted to tell Caesar when they thought him beaten and shut their gates on him (3.80.); (2) the correlative of what the people of Antioch and its Roman citizens told the Pompeian fugitives, once beaten: "If you approach, it will gravely endanger your necks" (3.102.6, *ne Antiochiam adirent; id si fecissent, magno eorum capitis periculo futurum*); (3) *denique* (writes Caesar) what Alexandria did to fallen Pompey: "just the way disaster regularly turns friends to enemies" (*ut plerumque in calamitate ex amicis inimici exsistunt,* 104.1).

It was *not* that Caesar's lightning trajectory promised all the world in his path that an open arms welcome would help speed him on his way, the low-cost wait-and-see policy of prudence. Why, no one in the **Bellum Ciuile** supposes that this renegade Alexander controlled *only* his next host, while those in his wake hoped (erroneously) that Caesar could not be everywhere at once. The regroup-ing of government troops in the West behind Caesar's lines awaits Hirtius' sequel, after the initial sortie to hunt Pompey down is brought to a satisfactory conclusion. Nor had Caesar, in pursuit of the soonest cessation of the troubles, left the new provincial front-line unforgivably bereft of legions—as he would accuse irresponsible Scipio of doing when he left the Parthians rampant in his rear, and *his* men muttered, "We'll go if we're led at the enemy, but we ain't gonna shoot no citizen, nor no consul, neither" (*sese, contra hostem si ducerentur, ituros, contra ciuem et consulem arma non laturos,* 3.31.3f.).

For dutiful Caesar took care to leave regiments behind in Gaul, and had fresh outfits raised among the tribesmen. Not—not only—to block any assault from Spain (2.37, 39). Caesar's prompt siege also took Massilia out of the war, have mercy, as the obvious port and springboard for any counter-invasion of Italy from the West. That this plan, the plan to save Italy, continued seamlessly from the campaigns against the barbarians, except that success in Gaul had brought Caesar enormous fresh reserves of recruits and levies to use *against* Rome, was a fact that must both be obscured and yet also, for other consider-ations, paraded.[77]

Caesar's command of his men rested on the mutual solidar-ity of loyal Roman vets. who had been through hell and high water together on an unconscionably prolonged tour of duty—"Nine long years,"[78] "something that had never ever happened in the army of Caesar,"[79] "Alesia and Avari-cum—conquerors of most mighty nations,"[80] "just like Gergovia"[81]—they had seen many a close-run scrap. He was one of the boys, engrossing them within his own name-and-fame (e.g. *frumentum . . . reliqui si quid fuerat, Caesar superioribus diebus consumpserat,* 1.48.5, as if Caesar wolfed the lot), and never once tagging them *Caesariani,* but always *nostri,* in flagrant violation of his self-denying third-person autodiegetic narrative form.[82] His proconsular dignity *did* at the outset repose on this guaranteed domain of mass approval: "a victorious general who had served the state well," as the counselors of Auximum <are supposed to> put it, "with what great achievements" (*imperatorem bene de re publica meritum tantis rebus gestis,* 1.13.1). One day's march was doubtless much the same as another, whether it took the standards into forbidden Italy or anywhere else. But this shower were not simply Caesar's might; this 'orrible lot (must somehow) model also his right.[83] Not just because they were bonded by transgression, as full of mercy as anyone with a price on their head. Not just—

Well. The same general who had (this must be so) mobilized and summoned his crack units from their original encampments to join him at the double, on the worst-case scenario, or the long-prepared plan,[84] of immediately overrunning all Italy, to wage his non-war of non-aggression, also made a virtue of his military ethos: straight talking and no taking needless risks or treating men as expendable cannon-fodder. This became and becomes the kernel of his pitch that *he* would avoid loss of life *on both sides.*[85]

Far from setting a fearful horde on the civilians back home, Caesar would fight the good fight, *no* fight. Not unless it was picked with him. Far from prosecuting energetic *Blitzkrieg,* Caesar was not even at war—let alone civil war. Instead, the diplomatic mission to secure fair treatment for himself and his band of triumphant heroes rested on a solid bedrock of orderly communications, a word that was his bond, orders that kept his myriads in order. Streets rumbling with tanks? What tanks? What rapid reaction force? What peace-keepers?

Written Caesar stands on his dignity, from unopposed pacifier of Gaul to consul cornered in the suburbs of Egypt. His writer sees to that any which way, somehow. Rhyming writer-reader relations with officer-men rapport, until none can either discern the last proconsular conqueror of the Republic or discriminate the first writer and mythographer of the Empire. Only (the titular) "LETTER[S] OF CAESAR."

imagine that a general electroencephalocardioso-matopsychogram were possible.[86]

Notes

1. The sections of Henderson's essay articulate terms for this initial motion, cursively and cursorily as Caesar. Explicit recapitulation is as foreign to this pleading as capitulation.

2. Caesar "fights for peace," Collins (1972) 957. For the liveliest introduction to *BC,* see Richter 166-79.

On the opening chapters, cf. H. Oppermann, "Aufbau. Anfang des Bellum Civile," in Rasmussen 138-64.

3. Raditsa 450f.

4. Ibid. 448.

5. "First do, and then justify." For Caesar's "ben calcolata reticenza" on the Rubicon, cf. Pascucci 519f.

6. A. Hitler, *Der Hitler-Prozess,* in A. Bullock, *Hitler, A Study in Tyranny* (Harmondsworth, 1962) 117.

7. To start with *consules* is the Roman way; but *unnamed* consuls are an odd way to begin—as adrift as the Republican calendar, which Caesar would soon reform: the timing of the *Bellum Ciuile* would then require re-scheduling, commandeered by Julian temporality from 46 BCE.

8. Esp. Carter 28, "All surviving manuscripts . . . lack the beginning of the work"; cf. 153f. for "strong reasons for believing that at least several sentences have been lost from the start of the book." M. Gelzer, *Caesar. Politician and Statesman* (Oxford, 1969) 190 n. 5, "Unfortunately the beginning of Caesar's *bellum civile* as preserved in our manuscripts is defective, and the end of Hirtius' b.G. 8 is also missing." Brunt 18, "The end of Hirtius' narrative and the beginning of Caesar's are both lost." Raditsa 439, "The mutilated state of the end of bG 8 and the beginning of bc 1 make it difficult to assert with full confidence that Caesar omitted the contents of his letter to the Senate." The MSS have the irritating intrusion *a Fabio C.* between the opening . . . *litteris* and *Caesaris* (= *a Curione?* Cf. Richter 175).

9. Carter 153.

10. Barwick 17f. argues that Caesar withholds the contents of his letter because, or lest, they might seem tantamount to menacing arrogance.

11. This event is marked out by *necare,* a solitarium in *BC* (I. Opelt, "'Töten' und 'Sterben' in Caesars Sprache," *Glotta* 58 (1980) 103-119, at 112.

12. Cf. LaPenna 194.

13. Cf. Eden 115f.

14. *ne id quidem impetrauisse* here amounts to a back reference to the opening sentence of *BC.* Cf. the version in Suet. *Div. Iul.* 29.2, *ne sibi beneficium populi adimeretur, aut ut ceteri quoque imperatores ab exercitibus discederent.* Appian *Bell. Ciu.* 2.32.128 claims the letter "included a proud account of all Caesar had done from the start, plus a challenge to Pompey to resign simultaneously"; cf. Dio 41.1.3f. (See F. Kraner, F. Hofmann, H. Meusel, H. Oppermann, *C. Iulii Caesaris Commentarii De Bello Ciuli* [Berlin, 1959] 12f.)

15. "Half way between a threat and a promise," comments Collins (1972) 957. That is, a threat; all the way (*docet,* wrote Caesar, 32.2).

16. For the terms stipulated by Caesar, cf. LaPenna 196-98, Barwick 47-70. Suet. *Iul.* 86 underscores Caesar's New Order: *non tam sua quam rei publicae interesse uti saluus esset; se iam pridem potentiae gloriaeque abunde adeptum, rem publicam si quid sibi eueniret, neque quietam fore et aliquanto deteriore condicione ciuilia bella subituram.*

17. See R. Hodge and G. Kress, *Language as Ideology* (London, 1993) 162-64.

18. On the Sullan typology, cf. Collins (1972) 961f. Prejudice for "the One" over "the Many" is coterminous with Caesar*ism,* surfacing again e.g. at 3.18.2, where the *summa imperii* went to no one admiral after the death of butcher Bibulus. Prelude to the squabbling marshals counting *their* chickens before Pharsalus (3.83).

19. Cf. Collins (1972) 945f.

20. Plin *Nat. Hist.* 7.91. Cf. Rambaud 23.

21. For close reading of 1.8.1, cf. Pascucci 517-19.

22. See the important paper of W. W. Batstone, *"Etsi:* A Tendentious Hypotaxis in Caesar's Plain Style," *AJPh* 111 (1990) 348-60.

23. For the farcical treatment of Varro, cf. A. Haury, "Ce brave Varron . . . (César, *Ciu.,* II, 17-21)," in *Mélanges d'archéologie, d'épigraphie et d'histoire offerts à Jérome Carcopino* (Paris, 1966) 507-513; LaPenna 194; Eden 116. See Rowe for the articulation between the dramas in nearer and further Spain.

24. "Tear off a strip" is colloquial for "rebuke" (as sergeant-major to ordinary soldiers). Respect for Pompey: Collins (1972) 954; irony: Perrotta 20f.; satire: LaPenna 193f. In *BC III,* Caesar writes the pair Caesar and Pompey into all but parodic parallelism, e.g. 45.1f., 76.1f.

25. Explained well by Eden 108.

26. Rowe.

27. Raditsa 434.

28. B. Jonson, *Discoveries,* in J. D. Wilson, "Ben Jonson and 'Julius Caesar,'" in P. Ure, *Shakespeare, Julius Caesar: A Selection of Critical Essays* (London, 1969) 241-52, at 245.

29. S. Sebag Montefiore, *King's Parade* (Harmondsworth, 1992) 67.

30. The modeling of the transference, the repetition compulsion, within reading staged in Poe's *The Purloined Letter,* the "figure in the text, something hidden in full view as one reads," is summarized effectively in E. Wright, *Psychoanalytic Criticism: Theory in Practice* (London, 1984) 66f., 113, 114-16; cf. J. Henderson, "Becoming a Heroine (IST): Penelope's Ovid," *LCM* 11 (1986) 7-10, 21-24, 37-40, 67-70, 81-85, 114-20, on epistoliterarity.

31. The classic prosecution of the guilt of Caesar *scriptor* compounding that of Caesar *imperator* is Rambaud.

32. Raditsa 439f. shows brilliantly, as Caesarian partisan, how the narrative mimes the impact of the events on interpretation of those events.

33. Cf. J. Tatum, *Xenophon's Imperial Fiction: On the Education of Cyrus* (Princeton, 1989) 208 for the compulsive drive of the bioscript primer: at the end, "The text of the *Cyropaedia* dissolves in mimetic replication of Cyrus, with his lieutenants and satraps doing what Xenophon's readers may now do in turn: imitate Cyrus."

34. Contrast Collins (1959) 117, "BC is a work *republican* through and through; . . . it neither contains the spirit nor the foreshadowing of the 'monarchial' or 'imperial' idea" (discussed by Mutschler 198f.).

35. Suet. *Diu. Iul.* 79.2: "Caesar," that is, "—not some dime-a-dozen king."

36. Anarchic confusion in arming slaves formulaically tars the opposition with making war on the *ciuitas,* e.g. 1.24.1, 3.22.2, 3.103.1, Rambaud 339, Collins (1972) 953.

37. Cf. F. Ahl, *Lucan: An Introduction* (Cornell, 1976) 307. R. M. Ogilvie, "Caesar," in E. J. Kenney and W. V. Clausen, eds., *The Cambridge History of Classical Literature,* Vol. II (Cambridge, 1982) 281-85, at 284f. accepts the incomplete state and status of *BC* III. Barwick 93-106 argues cogently (if only the uncanny or poetic be banished from our order of history) that *BC* is a finished, not an uncompleted, work. J. M. Carter, *Julius Caesar, The Civil War Book III* (Warminster, 1993) 233 notes laconically, "Caesar's narrative stops here, in mid-course."

38. The argument that Caesar's greatest reader and interpreter, Lucan, makes much of the point of termination of Caesar's *BC* in his own *bella plus quam ciuilia* is more than presentably set out in J. Masters, *Poetry and Civil War in Lucan's "Bellum Civile"* (Cambridge, 1992) 216-59, "The Endlessness of the Civil War."

39. See Marin 206-214, esp. 213, "to paint the king's portrait is to make the portrait of all possible future kings."

40. "I am this groping intensity that is a soul," J. L. Borges, *Selected Poems 1923-1967* (Harmondsworth, 1962) 54: *"Mi Vida Entera"* (= "My Whole Life").

41. "<These things were extra windily recounted by them—> the way people do speak out freely in their own praise," 2.39.4: displaced away from (= onto) Caesar, as reflection on Curio's cavalry.

42. *suos ordines seruare,* e.g. 1.44.3 and *passim*—military morality.

43. Caesar writes of engineering feats, instead of Caesar fighting, from Corfinium (1.21.4f., 19.5) and Brundi-

sium (25.5), to Spanish ditch *without* rampart (41.4: a ruse), multi-channel ford (61), or the staple *uallo fossaque* (81.6; cf. Rambaud 248-50, "Travaux et Flottes"). War at Massilia, when out of the shipyards, consists in fanatically devoted description of fiendish towers and ramps (2.8-13.1, 15f.). In Greece, the war is a sapper's paradise: *erat noua et inusitata belli ratio . . . in nouo genere belli nouae ab utrisque bellandi rationes reperiebantur* (3.47.1, 50.1, cf. 39f., 43.2, 44.3, 46.1, 54, 58, 63.1). Beats civil war (like other ways in which mass killing can be recharged in telling of derring-do: for example, the race for the pass in Spain, 1.70, and the cross-country dash, 1.79).

44. Cf. E. Rawson, *Intellectual Life in the Late Republic* (London, 1985) 122, G. L. Hendrickson, "The *De Analogia* of Julius Caesar: Its Occasion, Nature, and Date, with additional Fragments," *CPh* 1 (1906) 97-120, W. A. Oldfather and G. Bloom, "Caesar's Grammatical Theories and his own Practise," *CJ* 22 (1926-1927) 584-602; for political grammar, cf. P. Sinclair, "Political Declensions in Latin Grammar and Oratory, 55 BCE-CE 39," in A. J. Boyle, ed., *Roman Literature and Ideology: Essays for J. P. Sullivan* (Victoria, 1995 = *Ramus* 24.1) 92-109, at 93.

45. E.g. Eden 86, "the same words for the same situations." The Caesar of the Classical canon models (a) cultural politics where normative logocentrism is worn as the badge of semiotic power: "Caesar seems to have viewed the anarchic growth of language with disfavor, and in trying to bring order out of chaos to have applied almost a logician's insistence on having only one symbol for one concept or relationship" (ibid. 97; cf. Pascucci 493, 501). Readers need not imagine a cosmos of Caesarian Newspeak, but should rather trace the Caesarian texts' trading on the legend of their monologism from continual and cardinal violation to violation. The old style of scientist study of Caesarian purism (e.g. J.J. Schlicher, "The Development of Caesar's Narrative Style," *CPh* 31 (1936) 212-24: "the low percentage of dominant verbs preceded by two or more subordinate clauses or phrases in Books i and ii is probably due to the greater brevity and simplicity of the sentences, which average 30.3 per 100 lines") has yielded to a more recent quest to tease out the self-disguised art of a plain stylist (H. C. Gotoff, "Towards a Practical Criticism of Caesar's Prose Style," *ICS* 9 (1984) 1-18: "Obviously the Commentaries are a form of self-advertisement; what form of self-advertisement is less obvious. . . . It may be that Caesar has succeeded all too well in disguising his art; that centuries of readers . . . have failed to notice his diversity, his deceptiveness, and his power" (5f.). "Caesarian prose style," that is to say, still gathers formalist panegyric (cf. M. F. Williams, "Caesar's Bibracte Narrative and the Aims of Caesarian Style," *ICS* 10 (1985) 215-26) that is dead set against invasion by the politics of discourse. But what got written in 1942 as N. J. de-Witt, "The Non-Political Nature of Caesar's Com-

mentaries," *TAPA* 73 (1942) 341-52? And what in 1948, as Perrotta 29, "Egli è il più grande Romano di tutti i tempi e riassume in sè tutta la gloria di Roma: ha l'impeto guerriero di Mario e il senno politico di Silla, l'audacia riformatrice dei Gracchi e l'aristocratica saggezza degli Scipioni"?

46. Cf. R. R. Dyer, "Rhetoric and Intention in Cicero's *Pro Marcello*," *JRS* 80 (1990) 17-30, at 18 for the idea that Caesar's treatment of pacified Rome was on a continuum with the way he had earlier treated Gaul.

47. See Bérard esp. 93, "Il ne s'agit donc pas d'une autobiographie . . . mais d'un autoportrait."

48. For the classic account of Caesar's style as mimetic of his generalship, see H. Fränkel, "Über philologische Interpretation am Beispiel von Caesars Gallischem Krieg," Rasmussen, 165-88, esp. 182ff.

49. Perrotta 27. Cf. Bérard 94, "deux personnages, l'auteur-narrateur et le proconsul-protagoniste, qui se cachent mutuellement." F. E. Adcock, *Caesar as a Man of Letters* (Cambridge, 1956) 76, manages to speak of written Caesar as "the natural, almost automatic, expression of his conscious pre-eminence." Raditsa, who took the notion that there must have been a *Machtsfrage* behind the Caesarian *Rechtsfrage* seriously: "Such statements have consequences. One sees them in the faces of one's students" (440 n. 68)—admired Caesar because he "distinguished thought from feeling but did not suffer their opposition," adding in a footnote, "Hans Oppermann (Berlin, 1933: repeated in "Probleme und heutiger Stand der Caesarforschung," in Rasmussen 485-522, at 497) has beautifully put this . . . : '*Der wichtigste* (reason for the resistance to and murder of Caesar) *ist vielleicht die Einheit von Caesars Persönlichkeit . . . ist Caesar die letzte Verkörperung der Lebensganzheit in der Antike*'" (442 and n. 74).

50. Esp. Collins (1972) 932f., 942, puts notable effort into severing the limbs of the *Caesarian corpus*.

51. The often-repeated count was made by Rambaud 196f.; *Caesar* is normatively salient in its sense-units, cf. M. Rambaud, "Essai sur le style du *Bellum Ciuile*," *IL* 14 (1962) 60-69, 108-113, at 67f. . . .

52. D. Huff, *Score: The Strategy of Taking Tests* (Harmondsworth, 1964) 110.

53. Catull. 11.10, "Caesar the Great's legacy."

54. Raditsa 449.

55. Cf. S. Petrey, *Speech Acts and Literary Theory* (London, 1990) 95f., 98f., S. Cavell, *Disowning Knowledge: In Six Plays of Shakespeare* (Cambridge, 1987) 143-77, "*Coriolanus* and Interpretations of Politics ('Who does the wolf love?')." Raditsa 439 bites the bullet, to show it isn't one: "the Senate grew incapable of negotiations with Caesar, and took unilateral steps toward war. It collapsed completely

when it passed the *senatus ultimum consultum.* In its threat, it forced Caesar, who did not take threats lightly, to act."

56. Caesar stresses he is the very model of the military *passim,* but esp. with his tactical play with the Roman reveille: *"uasa" militari more conclamari* (1.66.1: a ruse), *ne conclamatis quidem "uasis"* vs. *"uasis" que militari more conclamatis* (3.37.5 vs. 38.1: bungle vs. ruse). Disgrace at Dyrrhachium hurt, *quod ante in exercitu Caesaris non accidit, ut rei militaris dedecus admittatur* (3.64.4), but Caesar's "Up and at 'em" speech before Pharsalus was perfect: *exercitum cum militari more ad pugnam cohortaretur . . .* (3.90.1).

57. Cf. 1.32.5, *omnia permisceri mallent . . .*

58. See the powerful blueprint of W. W. Batstone, "A Narrative Gestalt and the Force of Caesar's Style," *Mnemosyne* 44 (1991) 126-36, esp. 128f.; Rambaud 254f. saw how the formula encompassed the entire narrative.

59. See M. McDonnell, "Borrowing to Bribe Soldiers: Caesar's *De Bello Civili* 1.39," *Hermes* 118 (1990) 55-66.

60. Seeing Caesar's Curio as "ein jungeres Abbild seiner selbst," H. Oppermann, "Curio—Miles Caesaris?" *Hermes* 105 (1977) 351-68, at 352, cf. Gärtner 122-25.

61. See Rowe 404 (but cf. the critique in Mutschler 222 and n. 1).

62. The *Bellum Ciuile,* first called *bellum* at 1.25.3 (Pompey), 26.6 (Caesar; cf. 35.1, etc.). As throughout Latinity (V. Rosenberger, *Bella et Expeditiones. Die antike Terminologie der Kriege Roms* [Stuttgart, 1992] 150-60, esp. 158), euphemisms predominate, e.g. *conficiendi negotii, initio dissensionis* (1.29.1, 3.88.2; cf. Rambaud 66). At times Caesar talks as a military expert of "War," *simpliciter,* for all the world as if circumstances don't alter cases (1.21.1, *quod saepe in bello paruis momentis magni casus interciderent,* 3.32.5, *quod in bello plerumque accidere consueuit,* 92.4f., *est quaedam animi incitatio atque alacritas naturaliter innata omnibus, quae studio pugnae incenditur . . . neque frustra antiquitus institutum est . . .*). Very rarely, Caesar steels himself to slip in pontification that does belong in a *Bellum Ciuile: quod perterritus miles in ciuili dissensione timori magis quam religioni consulere consuerit* (1.67.3), and *qui fere bella et ciuiles dissensiones sequi consueuit* (3.1.3). In the latter outrage, one can't even tell whether to read in *ciuilia* with *bella.*

63. On Caesar's financial moderation, mimetically captured in the apt syntax of *et ad timorem nouarum tabularum tollendum minuendumue . . . et ad debitorum tuendam existimationem esse aptissimum existimauit* (3.1.2), cf. LaPenna 198-200.

64. Cf. D. Battaglia, ed., *Rhetorics of Self-Making* (Berkeley, 1995), "Problematizing the Self: A Thematic Introduction," 2-4 for interesting (anthropological) rehearsal of this critique/jargon.

65. W. C. Sellar and R. J. Yeatman, *1066 and All That* (Harmondsworth, 1960) 9.

66. "We thought him too cold or—shall we say?—'icily regular'. We cursed his eternal third person." (H. P. Cooke, *In the Days of our Youth* (London, 1925) 12, *cit.* C. Stray, "The Smell of Latin Grammar: Contrary Imaginings in English Classrooms," *Bulletin of the John Rylands Library of Manchester* 76 (1994) 201-220, at 204). This is all about power and the normative didaxis figured in this sadodispassionate "set book": "The first author read is Caesar—particularly adapted to disgust a twelve-year-old boy with Latin." (E. R. Curtius, *European Literature and the Latin Middle Ages* [London, 1953] 51 n. Cf. E. Owen, "Caesar in American Schools Prior to 1860," *CJ* 31 [1935-1936] 212-22.) Writing out of Berkeley, R. T. Lakoff, *Talking Power: The Politics of Language* (New York, 1990) 239-53, "Winning Hearts and Minds: Pragmatic Homonymy and Beyond" compares and contrasts Caesar's third person with that of Lieutenant Colonel Oliver North: North "uses it to create emotional identification," Caesar "detachment. But the positive impact of intimacy in a liteness style precisely parallels that of aloofness for a *gravitas* culture. The impact of each on its intended audience is similar. Both engender trust: *this is a good person.* . . . The plots are the same for both, and both shows are smash hits."

67. Cf. Marin 39-88, "The King's Narrative, or How to Write History."

68. F. Herbert, *Dune Messiah* (London, 1969) 47: "*Words of Muad'dib by Princess Irulan.*"

69. G. Willans and R. Searle, *Down with Skool!* (London, 1973) 47.

70. Brunt 13, citing Cic. *Ad Fam.* 8.14.3.

71. For Caesar's mastery of the time-space-sociopolitical continuum, cf. H. Fugier, "Un thème de la propagande Césarienne dans le *De Bello Ciuili:* César, Maître du Temps," *Bulletin de la Faculté de Lettres à Strasbourg* 47 (1968) 127-33.

72. Brunt 21, 22.

73. Collins (1959) 120f., (1972) 958f.

74. See Collins (1972) 933f., for Caesar's atrocities and "ethnic cleansing" in Gaul, esp. *BG* 4.11.5. Caesar would hold the world record for scalps in battle: 1,192,000 (Plin. *Nat. Hist.* 7.92).

75. This was Massilia, symbolic home of the free, as Caesar indicates, when "he preserved them more for their name and fame in Ancient History than the way they'd treated him," 2.22.6; for Caesarian troops bent on plunder, cf. 1.21.2, 3.97.1.

76. The terms belong in the minds if not the mouths of Caesar's soldiers, cf. 3.6.1, *imperaret quod uellet, quodcumque imperauisset, se aequo animo esse facturos.*

77. E.g. the brace of Gallic chieftains who desert Caesar, 3.59; who later tip off Domitius, 80.7, cf. 84.4. Turncoat Labienus is wrong as ever, "Do not think, Pompey, that this is the army that flattened Gaul and Germany . . . ," 87.1.

78. As Caesar told his troops, who roar approval, 1.7.7f. Cf. 1.39.2.

79. 3.64.4.

80. 3.47.5.

81. 3.73.6: an intertextual signal, cf. Gärtner 127.

82. Cf. Perrotta 14f.

83. These expressions are more army slang, from sarge to privates.

84. This suspicion is unsuccessfully neutralized by displacement onto Pompey: Caesar tells his troops the Spanish armies were "fostered against him for full many a year. . . . The whole shooting-match was readied against Caesar" (1.85.5, 8).

85. E.g. LaPenna 200 and Collins (1972) 960f. examine Caesar's abjuration of bloodshed (1.72, 74, 76, 3.90, 98 . . .), but without (I think) getting *the* point: linkage.

86. J. Derrida, "Dialanguages," in *Points* (Stanford, 1995) 144.

Bibliography

Barwick, K. 1951. *Cæsars Bellum Civile: Tendenz, Aufbau, Abfassungszeit und Stil.* Berlin.

Bérard, F. 1993. "Les *Commentaires* de César: Autobiographie, Mémoires ou Histoire?" In M.-F. Baslez, P. Hoffmann, L. Pernot, eds., *L'Invention de l'Autobiographie d'Hésiode à Saint Augustin.* Paris. (= *Études de Littérature Ancienne* 5: 85-95.)

Brunt, P. A. 1986. "Cicero's *Officium* in the Civil War." *JRS* 76: 12-32.

Carter, J. M. 1991. *Julius Cæsar, The Civil War Books I & II.* Warminster.

Collins, J. H. 1959. "On the Date and Interpretation of the *Bellum Civile.*" *AJPh* 60: 113-32.

———. 1972. "Cæsar as Political Propagandist." *ANRW* I.1: 922-66.

Eden, P. T. 1962. "Cæsar's Style: Inheritance versus Intelligence." *Glotta* 40: 74- 117.

Gärtner, H. A. 1975. *Beobachtungen zu Bauelementen in der antiken Historiographie, besonders bei Livius und Cæsar.* Historia Einzelschriften 25.

LaPenna, A. 1952. "Tendenze e arte del Bellum civile di Cesare." *Maia* 5: 191-233.

Marin, L. 1988. *Portrait of the King.* Basingstoke.

Mutschler, F.-H. 1975. *Erzählstil und Propaganda in Cæsars Kommentarien.* Heidelberg.

Pascucci, G. 1973. "Interpretazione linguistica e stilistica del Cesare autentico." *ANRW* I.3: 488-522.

Perrotta, G. 1948. "Cesare Scrittore." *Maia* 1: 5-32.

Raditsa, L. 1973. "Julius Cæsar and his Writings." *ANRW* I.3: 417-56.

Rambaud, M. 1953 (1966). *L'Art de la Déformation Historique dans les Commentaires de César.* Paris.

Rasmussen, D. 1967. *Caesar.* Darmstadt. (= *Wege der Forschung,* Bd. 43)

Richter, W. 1977. *Cæsar als Darsteller seiner Taten.* Heidelberg.

Rowe, G. O. 1967. "Dramatic Structures in Cæsar's *Bellum Civile.*" *TAPA* 98: 399-414.

J. E. Lendon (essay date 1999)

SOURCE: "The Rhetoric of Combat: Greek Military Theory and Roman Culture in Julius Caesar's Battle Descriptions," in *Classical Antiquity,* Vol. 18, No. 2, October, 1999, pp. 273-329.

[In the following essay, Lendon explains how Caesar adapted Greek theories of warfare to better reflect Roman values and culture, particularly the Roman emphasis on courage.]

War eclipses all other subjects in the classical historians: not without reason did the Cretan in Plato's *Laws* (625e) describe war as the permanent condition of mankind. Battle descriptions in ancient authors are legion; Xenophon's *Hellenica* alone describes or mentions over one hundred and fifty military engagements.[1] So too is modern interest in old battles perennial. A gigantic scholarly literature seeks to locate ancient battlefields, to reconstruct the movements of armies upon them, and to divine the strategies of the great captains. Methods improve with time: the floppy sun-hat of today's wanderer over ancient fields shelters modern instruments of source-comparison far more sensitive than the clumsy engines cooled by the trim kepi of his nineteenth-century predecessor. Yet the intellectual underpinnings (to say nothing of the motivations) of this project remain firmly rooted in the nineteenth century. "How very much superior to Caesar's is Thucydides' style of battle narrative," writes the military historian John Keegan, exemplifying the easy assumption that there is a timeless ideal towards which military history tends, and that each ancient writer, and each battle description in that writer, can be evaluated in terms of how closely that ideal is approached.[2] But that timeless ideal is a mirage: nothing more, in fact, than our own conception of how battles work, a historically contingent vision not necessarily any less freighted with the arbitrary than the vision of any generation before. For battle descriptions are by nature highly artificial, ours no less than theirs, and both our and ancient conventions of battle description are products as much of culture as of observation.

No one is born able to describe what happens in a battle, and the experience of battle does not in itself supply the necessary language. "What was Iwo Jima like? It was . . . it was . . . it was fucking rough, man! I know that, but what was it like? Really . . . really . . . really tough!"[3] Yet since earliest times men have talked about battles even more than they have fought them, and so in every land an idiom has grown up to abet such talk, a treasury of images and metaphors, the creation and resource of soldiers— armed or armchair—and historians, of epic poets and drunks in bars. This inherited way of talking and writing about battle, this rhetoric of combat, seems perfectly natural to those who use it, a polished mirror held up to reality. Yet in fact it has many arbitrary and fanciful elements: where (nowadays) is the pushing when troops push forward? Where is the pulling when they pull back? More than a half-awareness of this artificiality, is, of course, impossible because this rhetoric is not merely a machine to convert experience into words, but the very armature upon which that experience is organized and made sense of. For the soldier the raw experience of battle is one of sights, noises, terrors, and alimentary misadventures. But when he mentally files those experiences under "the decisive flank-battle near Ypres during the retirement to Dunkirk" he is already ensorcelled by the inherited rhetoric of battle description.[4]

Noticing the differences between our own ways of describing battle and those of other lands and the past should make us notice the unreality of both. Yet these differences are easy to miss, since they are not instantly shocking and revolting, like pulling in a three-eyed trout. Modern readers can read and understand battle descriptions in Greek or Latin authors quite without the baffled frustration with which they greet ancient technical descriptions of music, or classical poetry's ubiquitous weaving metaphors. The mind does not like to be confused, and so insensibly shunts the minecarts of alien concepts onto familiar tracks. The abiding similarity of the experience described, as well as cultural influence over many centuries, have ensured a high degree of likeness over time and borders in the way battles are thought about in the Western tradition. And the universalizing claims of the modern theory of war discourage notice of cultural eccentricity: if military science is a science indeed, its algebra can hardly be different in different lands.

The first purpose of this paper is to convey a sense of the alienness of battle description in an alien culture. At its heart lies a detailed exposition of the mechanics of battle description in Julius Caesar's accounts of his Gallic and Civil Wars. From the broad use made of Caesar in sixteenth- through nineteenth-century military thinking, one might imagine him the classical author whose conceptions of battle translated most easily into modern terms.[5] But this expectation is confounded: analysis of Caesar's way of understanding battles reveals that his conceptions are further from our own than are those of his Greek predecessors. What is described in a battle description depends on unconscious cultural and conscious intellectual decisions about what it is important to describe, and Greek decisions were closer to ours than were Caesar's.

If battle description reflects culture, moreover, the study of Roman battle description promises insight into Roman culture. Traditional military history, where the exact details of battle are the object of inquiry, can be turned on its head: the way ancient authors describe the details of battle can tell us about the mental rigging of the societies in which they lived.

Understanding the mechanics of battle in ancient authors also offers a corrective to traditional methods of reconstructing ancient battles. Very rarely have the battle pieces of ancient historians been studied as a group within the work of an author, or as a group compared to those of other authors. Scholarship in ancient military history has traditionally proceeded battle by battle, and often with a tone of austere fault-finding, carping about the incompleteness and topographical inexactness of ancient authors' accounts. Modern authors become grumpy because ancient authors often do not write in accord with modern conventions of battle description. But comparison of many ancient battle descriptions reveals that ancient authors have their own conventions with which to accord: not merely obvious large-scale stylistic models like the invented paired harangues with which some classical historians adorn their battles, but deep-seated inherited convictions about what factors were decisive in battle, what details ought to be related, and how the narrative of events should be structured. These grand intellectual heirlooms are assembled from small-scale hand-me-down metaphorical schemata, like the "push" of the Greek phalanx, which guide authors' understanding of battles unawares. No one now would study speeches in the classical historians without a knowledge of their conventions, and few would judge such speeches except within the bounds of those conventions. No one should study or judge ancient battle descriptions—in the very same historians—as unproblematic attempts to depict reality, independent of convention and ideology. For the reader who does so may mistake for observed fact what convention shrilly demands, and accept as absent what convention blindly excludes. Study of ancient convention may, at the same time, offer insight into ancient realities which the arrogant imposition of modern convention hides: Caesar offers a broader set of explanations for victory in battle than our modern convention allows.

Caesar's battle descriptions are interesting also because he stands at the end of a tradition of soldier-authors: Thucydides, Xenophon, Polybius, and Caesar had all witnessed battles, and all had a professional interest in how they worked. The tradition of battle descriptions flows on after Caesar, indeed rises to a torrent in Livy, but often as a purely literary tradition, historians learning how to describe battles from reading other historians.[6] The tradition from Thucydides to Caesar, on the other hand, is far richer. These writers may have read and directly influenced each other, or read other lost accounts of battles (it makes little difference), but, more important, they also borrowed naturally from the talk of the camp, and, from Xenophon's day on, consciously or unconsciously from the thinking and writing of professional Greek military experts. This paper also attempts to trace the many-skeined intellectual tradition of ancient military thinking, to follow its progress over the boundary from Greece to Rome, and to investigate how it was received in a foreign land. This is done by contrasting Caesar's battle descriptions with those of Greek predecessors, especially Xenophon and Polybius. The success of Greek military thinking at Rome is a particularly interesting case of Hellenization: war was hardly an area—like bucolic poetry, for example—where the Romans had no tradition of their own. And Caesar is uniquely suited to be the subject of such a study: at once a bilingual Hellenistic intellectual with broad cultural interests[7] (in this, super-typical of his age), and at the same time a Roman marshal who reports, by and large, on events he himself has seen, ensuring that the mix of Roman and Greek ideas that appears in his work also existed in his head, and was not the incidental result of a patchwork composition from Greek and Roman sources.

Finally, Caesar's conquest of Gaul—so many nations and millions subdued with so modest a force in so few years—is an astonishing military achievement. A close examination of how Caesar describes battle may reveal how he understands battle, and how Caesar understands battle may offer a path towards understanding his military genius and the success of Roman arms in the late Republic.

I. Caesar and Military Theory

Clausewitz had little patience for those who larded their military treatises with classical examples. "Vanity and charlatanism" were at the bottom of it, he suspected, and classical allusions were usually "embellishments to cover up holes and errors."[8] Yet it might have eased his dyspepsia somewhat to realize that the author of a favorite treasury of such classical persiflage, Julius Caesar, wrestled in his own writings with problems similar to those of Clausewitz. For Clausewitz was a Romantic, a Schiller with cannon, a thinker who violently rejected the materialist military theories of Enlightenment military sages. Away with von Bölow's doctrine of the base, and his fallacious reduction of warfare to geometry! Away with Jomini's doctrine of interior lines! Such theories "direct their attention only to physical quantities, while all of military action is shot through with psychological forces and effects." Yet the very fact of their unquantifiability makes the incorporation of such non-material elements into theory problematic:

Clausewitz's solution was to view military theory not as an arid set of rules to be applied but as a body of historical knowledge upon which the commander might draw.[9] To both Clausewitz's Romanticism and his method Caesar would have been sympathetic: despite his debt to inherited ways of making sense of combat, the Roman stood in opposition to contemporary materialist strains of military thinking and offered a narrative of his campaigns which, *en passant,* armed its reader with a more powerful set of intellectual tools with which to understand the complex and ever-changing phenomena of battle.[10]

Although one of the classical historians' most typical enterprises, describing battles was hardly the easiest.[11] Remarking on the confusion of a night engagement, Thucydides observes that battles by day are hard enough to reconstruct, since each witness only knows what goes on in his own vicinity (7.44.1). And however conscientious the classical historian is in gathering information, he must still structure his account: select the events to describe, and both order and rank his material, deciding which of many incidents were important to the outcome of the battle and which were worth telling for their own sake, perhaps imposing an armature of cause and effect, perhaps creating a linear account out of simultaneous events. Thus, however accurately the historian represents a battle, and however mundane the results of his effort may be, all battle descriptions are works of artistry. Caesar's battle descriptions are not works of fiction, but attempts to reduce the chaos of reality to understandable narrative, perhaps favorable to himself and his men. For this he necessarily relies upon preconceived models for interpreting his and his army's experience of combat. He makes use of preexisting schemes, however implicit, about how battles work.[12] In a dismissive context Sallust reveals the intellectual tradition upon which Caesar—or any other late-Republican Roman writer—could draw for such theories: "the records of our ancestors and the military precepts of the Greeks" (*acta maiorum et Graecorum militaria praecepta, Jug.* 85.12).[13] But Roman records that might have influenced Caesar—Latin battle descriptions written before Caesar's day—have almost entirely perished.[14] And vanished without a trace as well is the rough wisdom of the generations of centurions that would have formed the basis of the military knowledge of those who, like Sallust's Marius, learned about battle from fighting rather than reading (*Jug.* 85.7-14; cf. Pliny *Ep.* 8.14.4-5).[15] No firm conclusions, therefore, can be drawn about Caesar's originality in the Latin tradition.[16] Yet Sallust says that Romans relied also on Greek military writers, and it was to them that a correspondent of Cicero's turned when writing to the orator with advice about his command in Cilicia (*ad Fam.* 9.25.1).[17] Indeed, any late-Republican Roman seeking theoretical works on warfare necessarily resorted to Greek authors, since technical Latin military writing seems to have dwindled after its founding in Cato the Elder's (lost) second-century BC *de Re Militari,* and only revives under the empire.[18] And about this Greek tradition we know a great deal, both because works in it survive and because of its influence on Greek historians, especially

Polybius. Yet in the end, although profoundly indebted to the Greek tradition of military theory,[19] Caesar went far beyond it, creating in his battle descriptions an artistic unity that blended Greek theory with aspects of traditional Roman military thinking and his own experience. If Caesar's battles are often frustrating to the modern military historian to reconstruct, it is because his conceptions about what was important in battle are so very different from ours, and so different too from those of his Greek predecessors.[20]

II. The Problem of Pharsalus

Caesar's method of battle description, and some of the problems it poses, are vividly on display in his depiction of the battle of Pharsalus (C [*Bellum Civile*] 3.85-95).[21] Caesar is quite clear about the reason for his victory, but much of Caesar's narrative seems implicitly to contradict his explicit statement about why he won the battle.

As Caesar tells it, when he realizes that Pompey is willing to offer battle, he addresses a few remarks to his troops: they are to make themselves ready in *animus,* in spirit, or morale, for the fray. Next, Caesar's brief harangue is balanced by a report of a council of the Pompeian leaders some days earlier. Pompey there discussed tactics—he preened over the prospect of a flanking move by his much superior cavalry that would win the battle before the legions engaged. His stated motivation for explaining his plan was to encourage his officers, in order that they might go into battle with a stouter *animus;* he too urged them to make themselves ready in *animus* for the struggle. Labienus' remarks that followed were on the same theme. He explained that Caesar's army was—because of casualties and wastage—much inferior to that which conquered Gaul. The conference broke up "in great hopefulness and universal high spirits." Now Caesar leaves the *animus* theme and describes in detail the dispositions of both armies on the field, noting that he, Caesar, arranged a special reserve—a fourth line in addition to the usual three of a legionary deployment—to face the flanking Pompeian cavalry, exhorting this force in particular that victory would depend on their *virtus,* their bravery. He also gives strict instructions that his third line especially should not engage without specific orders from himself. Then he returns to the *animus* theme, exhorting the rest of the army, so that his troops are "burning with enthusiasm for the fight" (*studio pugnae ardentibus*), and then gives the signal for the attack. An *excursus* then follows, describing the boasting of C. Crastinus, formerly first centurion of Caesar's Tenth Legion, a man of unique *virtus* (*vir singulari virtute*). "Today, imperator, I will give you reason to thank me, whether I am living or dead," says he, and bravely charges the enemy with one hundred and twenty volunteers. The high *virtus* of Caesar's soldiers is confirmed.

We learn next, however, that Pompey has made a terrible mistake. On the advice of C. Triarius, Pompey ordered his legionaries to receive the charge of Caesar's legions at a stand, in order to face with undisrupted formation an enemy whose ranks had become disordered by their rapid advance. Pompey reasoned that his own infantry would also be better protected against Caesar's javelins in close formation, and Caesar's troops would be tired out by the run. Caesar singles out this plan for criticism, editorializing—with a rare reference to himself in the first person—that

> it seems to me that in this Pompey acted against the dictates of reason, for there is a certain excitement of *animus* and enthusiasm [*alacritas*] naturally innate to all men, which is kindled by eagerness for the fight. Commanders ought to increase this, rather than repress it. It was not in vain that the ancients ordained that signals ring out in every direction and that the whole army raise a cry, thinking that the foe would thereby be terrified [*terreri*] and their own men inspired [*incitari*].
>
> (*C* 3.92)

Caesar, in short, thinks Pompey took a tactically blinkered view of the situation and failed to consider the psychological dimension of his orders. The reader expects this striking homily, the climax of extensive attention to morale in this battle description, to bring on the climax of the battle as well: the inspired Caesarians should charge the deflated Pompeians and victory should be theirs. But nothing of the sort happens. The Caesarians do charge (because of their great experience they deftly stop to rest halfway to the enemy, so as not to arrive exhausted), but the Pompeians receive their attack and resist, fighting at close quarters. Caesar's account now shifts to the flank. Here Pompey's cavalry begin to surround Caesar's army and meets the fourth line, the reserve that Caesar had provided against them, which charges the cavalry with such force (*tanta vi*) that they are driven from the field. This reserve then begins to surround Pompey's army in turn and attack it in the rear. Now Caesar releases the third line of his legionaries into the stalemate of the legionary battle, replacing exhausted (*defessi*) men with those he had carefully kept fresh (*integri*). Finally the Pompeians, attacked both front and rear, break. Caesar remarks with some complacency that he "had not erred in thinking that victory would originate from those cohorts which he had posted opposite the cavalry in the fourth line, as he had said when he was exhorting the troops."

Why Caesar thinks he won—the encirclement of Pompey's legions by Caesar's deftly deployed fourth line at the same time that they were being attacked from the front by fresh troops—seems clear. Caesar concluded that he had won because of his superior tactics, a judgment confirmed by the expert Frontinus (*Strat.* 2.3.22). Yet there is much in Caesar's account which seems to tell in other directions. First there is Caesar's remarkable finger-wagging at the moral consequences of Pompey's not letting his troops charge. What is the relationship of that passage to the actual outcome of the battle? Why, more generally, in a battle that Caesar depicts as turning on his tactical expertise, is he so careful to describe at length the measures of both sides to ensure the morale, *animus,* of their soldiers? Why, finally, do we hear so much about the courage—*virtus*—of Crastinus, to whom Caesar returns after his account of the surrender of Pompey's army in the wake of the battle proper, to offer an epitaph. "Caesar judged that Crastinus had shown the highest *virtus* in that battle, and judged that he had received a very great favor from him" (*C* 3.99). All this talk of *virtus* recalls Caesar's exhortation to his fourth line, that victory would depend on their *virtus,* courage.

It is attractive to attribute this seemingly irrelevant material—sallies against Pompey's stupidity and arrogance and praise for the courage of Caesar's soldiers—to propagandistic aims in Caesar's narrative.[22] To do so accords with the widest skein of twentieth-century scholarship on Caesar's writing, the relentless quest to show that Caesar's accounts are deeply tendentious, the truth ingeniously concealed and transformed for political ends.[23] Nor will the myriad snufflers after this succulent truffle be put off the scent by the objection that attacks on Pompey's generalship might actually detract from Caesar's achievement in defeating him, or that Caesar's praise of his soldiers might plant in his reader's mind the unwelcome suspicion that their excellence, rather than their marshal's, was decisive. Yet even assuming a devious and thorough-going *Tendenz* on Caesar's part, that exhausted conclusion demands an answer to a more interesting prior question. Why, given the infinity of possible ways of deforming or falsifying the narrative of a battle, does Caesar choose to emphasize morale and courage in addition to tactics? Perhaps Caesar's battle descriptions are tendentious, but to tell lies Caesar must have a grammar of battle description from which to build the lies, a grammar which exists before the lies. How does that grammar work and where does it come from? To understand why Caesar describes battles as he does it is necessary to trace through his writings the three themes that articulate his account of the battle of Pharsalus—tactics, *animus,* and *virtus*—while investigating Caesar's relationship to older traditions of military thinking; and finally to consider how he uses those three themes to assemble battle descriptions that reflect his vision of generalship.

III. THEORIES OF TACTICS

Understanding the detailed mechanics of battle and how to describe those mechanics in writing is learned, not natural. The Greeks had evolved a metaphorical system to understand and depict the ordering, movement, and clash of troops on the field of battle. Julius Caesar uses a similar system, probably adapted from the Greeks, but with significant differences based on Roman experience.

POLYBIUS AND THE GREEK TRADITION OF TACTICS

Caesar's criticism of the immobility of Pompey's legions at Pharsalus leaps out at the modern reader, just as it leapt out at Caesar's ancient readers, Plutarch (*Caes.* 44.4, *Pomp.* 69.5) and Appian (*BC* 2.79), so many centuries ago. Caesar notes that this foolish plan was pressed upon Pompey by

one C. Triarius.[24] But where did C. Triarius, that "very serious and learned young man" (Cic. *Fin.* 1.5.13), get it? Plutarch attributes the decision to fear that Pompey's inexperienced legions would fall into disorder (*Pomp.* 69.4), while Appian observes that "some persons praise this stratagem as the best thing to do when encircled." Plutarch's concern with disorder and Appian's allusion to an erudite "some" guide us into a stream of Greek military science that emphasized proper deployment and formation, . . . and the maintenance of good order, . . . as the keys to victory. The seeds of this outlook can be detected in Herodotus. Although his descriptions of battle by land and sea often make the reader feel he has wandered into the heroic world of the *Iliad,* nevertheless the historian puts down Greek survival at Artemisium to the confusion into which the Persian fleet fell (8.16) and attributes the Greek victory at Salamis to the same cause, "since the Greeks fought with proper discipline and in ordered ranks, and the barbarians with no order" (8.86 . . .). The Persian loss at Plataea should not be set down to inferiority in courage or strength, he notes, but to inferior equipment, skill, and tactics, since they hurled themselves against the Spartan line in small groups (9.62-63). To Thucydides falling into disorder is the most common cause of defeat in battle (5.10.6-8, 7.23.3, 7.36.6, 7.43.7-44.1, 8.105.2-3),[25] a fate that especially befalls those inferior in practice and military experience, a favorite theme of Thucydides (2.84.3, 2.91.4-92.1 [with 2.87-89], 6.72). Seeing his forces fall into disorder, the wise general withdraws his army before the onset (7.3.3). To Xenophon too disorder is disastrous (*Anab.* 3.4.19, 6.5.9, *Cyr.* 1.6.35).[26]

These historians' analyses are based on an understanding of the realities of sea and land battle in their time—in engagements between tight lines of oared galleys or heavy infantry closely arrayed in the phalanx, keeping proper order was essential. But perhaps to be associated with the rise of professional experts in tactics in the late fifth century BC[27] was the transformation of such observations into doctrine and the elevation of such doctrines of deployment and formation—tactics narrowly conceived—to be queen of the intellectual battlefield. The earliest Greek tactical manual that survives, the first-century BC treatise of Asclepiodotus, stands in a tradition old by its day.[28] He teaches the proper order and formation of an army based on the Macedonian phalanx, conceived in highly abstract mathematical and geometrical terms.[29]

The historian Polybius—also the author of a lost manual on tactics (9.20.4)[30]—is an inheritor of this same tradition, albeit a less doctrinaire one, and when he asks himself in his *Histories* "why it has occurred that the Romans have prevailed and borne away first place in the contests of war" (18.28.4), it is to questions of formation and armament—the phalanx against the deployment of the Roman legion—that he naturally turns. Nose to nose on a flat battlefield the phalanx is irresistible, he says; but its tight formation is easily broken up by irregular terrain or enemy action, and the phalanx becomes ineffective in confusion. That is why the Romans win (18.29-32). Just as in Thucydides and Xenophon, the disorder of one side or the other in a battle is often decisive in Polybius (1.19.10, 1.40.13-14, 10.39.6-8).[31] Indeed, order's pivotal role is so natural that its consequences can simply be assumed. "As he [the Carthaginian admiral] was rounding the Cape of Italy he came upon the enemy sailing in good order and formation, and he lost most of his ships" . . . 1.21.11; cf. 1.25.1-4; Thuc. 4.129.4, 6.97.4; Xen. *Hell.* 1.5.14, 4.8.18-19), writes Polybius, confident that the causal connection between order and victory, disorder and defeat, will be understood. So Philopoemen's careful training of the Achaean cavalry to ride in formation and keep station meets with Polybian approval, with his hero naturally "taking it for granted that there is nothing more dangerous or useless, than for cavalry who have broken their formation . . . in squadrons to essay to engage in combat" (10.23.8).[32]

To prevent (potentially decisive) disorder in his own army, and inflict it upon the foe, the Polybian general must attend particularly to his deployment. When Hannibal arranges a perfect deployment at Zama, but loses anyway, Polybius must appeal to fortune for an explanation (15.15-16). Different formations and armaments work differently on different terrain, and the general who fails to deploy in a fashion appropriate to the terrain will lose. Aratus foolishly decided to face the Aetolians on rough ground, with gloomy consequences: "the result of the battle was that which follows naturally on such an outset" (4.11.7-9 with 4.14.6; cf. 1.30, 2.68). Thus "in most battles by land and sea in a war differences of position cause defeat," and it is the duty of the historian to report knowledgeably about topography (5.21.3-9). Indeed to Polybius the essential duty of an historian when describing a battle is to lay out the physical deployment—the formations and evolutions (. . . 12.25[f].3)—of the forces on the field. The wretched Callisthenes (12.17-22), Ephorus (12.25[f]), and Zeno (16.18-19), all too ignorant to get such descriptions right, are severely castigated. The expert Polybius sometimes offers criticism of the deployments he describes: Regulus did well to deploy a deep infantry line against elephants, but against the numerous Carthaginian cavalry his arrangements were hopeless (1.33.10; cf. 1.26.16, 2.28.6, 2.33). This Greek conception of tactics—generalship conceived as a matter of order, deployment, formation, and terrain—is a deep structure which undergirds Polybius' battle descriptions.

Polybius' account of the battle of Cynoscephalae, which is followed (and implicitly explained) by his contrast between the legion and phalanx, illustrates Polybius' tactical conception of battle, and offers a tour of the analytical concepts and terminology the Greeks had developed to understand battle conceived in this light (18.21-26).[33] The Macedonian army of Philip V and the Roman army of T. Flamininus were groping for one another in the fog. Advance parties of both armies met unexpectedly and were briefly "thrown into confusion." . . . Recovering, they fought, but "in the close struggle (. . . [also embrace or intertwining]), the Romans were over-weighed . . . and suffered badly." But Flamininus sent help, and the Mace-

donians "were pressed . . . in their turn and over-weighed . . ." and fled to the heights, sending to Philip for aid. He sent reinforcements, and having added to their number a "heavy band" (. . . a homericism), the Macedonians "pressed upon" . . . the Romans and drove them from the high ground. Flamininus then arrayed his whole force in line of battle, and Philip, despite his well-grounded concern about the unsuitability of the terrain for his phalanx, was lured into a general engagement by the sanguine reports of messengers. The Roman legionaries now supported their light-armed troops, and the latter, "taking advantage of the additional help thrown into the scale, as it were . . . , and pressing the enemy heavily . . . , they killed many of them." To recover the situation Philip charges with his phalanx, although all his heavy troops have yet to come over the hill. "His right wing acquitted itself brilliantly in the fight, making its onset from an advantageous position . . . , being superior in the weight of their formation (. . . cf. 2.3.5-6, 2.68.9), and excelling greatly because of the difference in armament (theirs being suited to the occasion)" (cf. 2.30.7-8, 2.33; Xen. *Hell.* 3.4.14). So the Roman left was "squeezed back". . . . But on the other flank the Macedonians were still crossing the hill and there Flamininus attacked with his elephants leading the Roman troops. "The Macedonians, having no-one to give them orders, were unable to form up and assume the formation suitable for the phalanx both because of the difficulty of the ground and because, busy making an approach to those fighting, they were in marching order rather than in line of battle . . . , and so they did not even receive the Romans into hand-to-hand combat, but gave way terrified and broken up by the elephants alone." Now the Roman left—which the Macedonian phalanx was "pressing with its weight" . . .—was rescued. Romans from the victorious right took the phalanx in the rear with terrible slaughter: a phalanx cannot turn about, nor can its members fight individually, Polybius notes. This unanswerable attack put the victorious phalanx to flight, and the day belonged to the Romans.

This selective summary of Polybius' account of Cynoscephalae highlights his focus on formation and order, the dangers of disorder, and the physical metaphors—weight and pressing—that he uses to describe combat. These metaphors are not fanciful in their origins, but drawn from Greek experience. For battles which pitted phalanx against phalanx often involved a good deal of actual pushing of one side against another.[34] And thus to conceive the action of bodies of troops upon one another in terms of weight, as here, or mass or power . . . , was natural.[35] But in Polybius' mental world not only phalanxes push and weigh, at Cynoscephalae light troops and Romans with their more open formations do as well, as elsewhere do ships (1.51.5, 1.51.8; cf. Xen. *Hell.* 4.6.8, 5.4.42-43). A set of metaphors drawn from experience has been elaborated into a physical theory of battle.[36] And that theory of order and physical forces produces highly geometrical battle descriptions, like those of Cannae by land (3.113-16) and Ecnomus by sea (1.26-8).

CAESAR

The tactical mechanics of Caesar's battle descriptions betray a debt to Greek theories of tactics, but Caesar bases his metaphorical system on Roman rather than Greek methods of fighting. This Roman scheme is elaborated to cover the same phenomena as Greek tactical science—disorder, deployment, formation, maneuver, terrain—but its elements fit in Caesar's mechanical system differently and receive different emphasis.

Like that of the Greeks, Caesar's conception of combat depends upon physical metaphors. An attack exerts *vis,* force (*C* 3.93; cf. *B.Afr.* 69-70)[37] . . . The pressing metaphor, so common in Greek battle descriptions, is prominent as well.[38] Caesar's bilingual education allowed him to draw upon Greek thinking and theory for a metaphorical arsenal to describe the mechanics of combat.[39] But Caesar adapts Greek conceptions to his experience of Roman reality: unlike the Greeks, Caesar tends to envisage the fundamental mechanics of battle not as the pushing of a weight but as the crash of one moving force, an *impetus,* against a stationary one, which must sustain (*sustinere, G* [*De Bello Gallico*] 1.24, 26, 4.37) or bear (*ferre, G* 5.21, *C* 2.25) that force.[40] Battle is envisaged as a bare-knuckle boxing match, where fast fists crash into immobile jaws, until one jaw or the other breaks. "Caesar's horsemen made an *impetus* against the cohorts, and men with small shields could not long sustain (*sustinere*) the *vis* of the cavalry. They were all surrounded by the cavalry . . . and slain" (*C* 1.70). This structure manifests itself by sea as well as by land (*C* 2.6, 3.101). So dominating, indeed, is this metaphor that Caesar relies on it even when *both* armies are in rapid motion towards each other, as at the battle against Ariovistus when

> our men made their *impetus* upon the enemy so fiercely . . . and the enemy ran to the attack (*procurrerunt*) so suddenly and fast, that there was no space to throw javelins at the enemy. With javelins cast aside the fighting was with swords at close quarters. But in accord with their custom the Germans quickly formed a tight formation (*phalange facta*) and successfully sustained the *impetus* of the swords.
>
> (*G* 1.52)

Caesar assigns the *impetus* to the Romans; yet it would have been equally true, in this collision of mutually charging soldiers, to imagine the Romans as sustaining the German *impetus.*

Into this basic physical model of battle Caesar integrates the events and phenomena of combat. A hail of missiles exerts a *vis* (*C* 2.6; cf. *G* 5.43; *B.Alex.* 20), and numbers push: "on the right wing they pressed our battle line forcefully by virtue of the multitude of them" (*vehementer multitudine suorum nostram aciem premebant, G* 1.52; cf. *C* 1.46, *G* 7.80; *vim multitudinis, B.Afr.* 66, 52). Cavalry can push as well (*C* 1.70, *premeretur*). The physical strength, *vires,* of soldiers tends to be conflated in Caesar's mind with the metaphorical *vis* of the *impetus* or of resistance to

it. When the Seduni and Veragri attack Galba's camp in the Alps, they imagine that the Romans "could not even sustain their first *impetus*" (*G* 3.2). They charge the camp (*G* 3.4-5; cf. 7.48; *B.Afr.* 78), but "at first our men resisted strongly with their strength intact" (*integris viribus fortiter repugnare*), and "whatever part of the camp, denuded of defenders, seemed pressed (*premi*), they rushed there and bore aid." Yet as the day advanced the alpine tribesmen could replace their wounded and tired with fresh men, which, because of their scanty numbers, the Romans could not. "Now the fighting had gone on continually for more than six hours, and not only our *vires* but our missiles were running out, and the enemy pressed more violently (*instarent acrius*), and began to break down the rampart and fill the trenches as our men became more tired" (*languidioribusque nostris*). The Romans are going to lose this imagined pushing match, and a change of tactics is needed to win the day. Caesar tends to conflate wounds and exhaustion (thus *vulneribus defessi,* "worn out by wounds," *G* 1.25) since their result, the reduction of *vires,* and thus pressure to the front, is the same. "The soldiers of the Ninth and Tenth Legions . . . cast their javelins and at the charge from high ground quickly drove the Atrebates . . . fatigued with tiredness and exhausted by wounds, into the river" (*lassitudine exanimatos vulneribusque confectos, G* 2.23).

Other factors that might weaken an *impetus,* or the resistance to it, Caesar classifies in two broad overlapping categories: forces are *impediti,* encumbered, or *perturbati,* in confusion (*C* 2.26 for the pair). Two enemy ships have rammed each other: "the ships . . . close by . . . made an *impetus* against those ships that were *impediti,* and quickly sank them" (*C* 2.6). By land an army in line of march with its baggage is encumbered (*G* 6.8, 7.66, *C* 3.75), as are soldiers carrying stuff to fill up Roman trenches (*G* 3.19) or bearing shields pierced by javelins (*G* 1.25). Confusion consists of inability to maintain formation or follow the correct standards (*G* 4.26), and it may result from receiving an *impetus* (*G* 5.37), a hail of missiles (*G* 1.25; cf. Polyb. 11.12.5), and especially from being attacked unexpectedly (*G* 4.12, 4.32, *C* 3.101 at sea). It is partially to benefit from the hoped-for confusion of Caesar's ranks that Pompey commands that his legions should hold their ground at Pharsalus, "to allow the [Caesarian] line to break up" during their long charge, "in order that the first onslaught and *vis* be broken and the line of battle spread out, and for Pompey's men, properly arranged in their ranks, to assail scattered troops" (*C* 3.92). Close formation, like that of Ariovistus' Germans, makes it easier to sustain an *impetus* (cf. *G* 1.24). But for soldiers to be pressed so close together that they cannot ply their weapons is a form of confusion (*G* 4.32) and encumberment (*G* 2.25); it makes it impossible to avoid missiles cast at them (*G* 5.35).

Integrated too into Caesar's physics of battle is terrain, whether natural or man-made.[41] At Alesia during the final Gallic assault "neither earthworks nor trenches could sustain the force (*vim*) of the enemies" (*G* 7.87). But at

Massilia later Caesar's besieging soldiers built a brick tower near the walls of the city. "It was to here they used to retire, and it was from here, if a greater *vis* crushed against them (*oppresserat*), they fought back" (*C* 2.8). On the opposite side of the Thames ford stands an army of Britons; they have fortified the bank with stakes and hidden others under the water. Caesar orders the attack. "The soldiers moved with such speed (*celeritate*) and momentum (*impetu*), even though only their heads were above water, that the enemy could not sustain the *impetus* of the legions and the cavalry, quitted the bank, and fled" (*G* 5.18). Water, then, is expected to soften an *impetus*. Those fighting from a river (*G* 2.10) or the sea (*G* 4.26) or a swamp (*G* 2.9) against those on dry land fight *impediti,* encumbered. Terrain which produces this effect—forest (*G* 3.28, 5.19), or swamp (*G* 6.34, 7.19), or river banks (*C* 3.75, 3.88)—is itself by projection an encumbered place, an *impeditus locus.*[42]

Caesar's simplifying physical conception of battle allows him to reduce most considerations of terrain to the category of *locus iniquus,* where the lay of the land places one side at a disadvantage.[43] A place can simply be described thus, with no indication of exactly in what the *iniquitas* consists (*C* 1.81). A place offering only a narrow approach against the enemy, where only a few men can fight, and where relief of the exhausted will be difficult, is a *locus iniquus* (*C* 1.45). But the most common form of *locus iniquus* is a lower position on a slope (e.g. *G* 2.23, *C* 3.51). A charge up a hill is exhausting (*G* 3.19), and the higher army can cast its javelins with greater force and accuracy (*C* 1.45, *G* 3.4; cf. Xen. *Hell.* 2.4.15-16). At the battle against the Helvetti the Gauls advance in close formation (*phalange*) against Caesar's army on a hillside. But the Romans' javelins were thrown from the higher ground and thus easily broke the Gallic mass; indeed some with such force that they pierced two Gallic shields, encumbering their bearers when the Romans made their *impetus* against the disordered Helvetii (*G* 1.25). The same advantage with missiles is gained by casting them from sea-side cliffs (*G* 4.23), entrenchments (*G* 3.4, 3.25; Hirt. *BG* 8.9), a wagon laager (*G* 1.26), high ships (*G* 3.14), or a pile of bodies (*G* 2.27). If it is easy to throw downwards, it is hard to throw upwards (*G* 3.14). In general, an *impetus* made downhill is expected to be very hard for the enemy to sustain (*G* 3.2); those higher press (*premere*) on those lower (*C* 1.45).

In a battle conceived according to this tactical schema the business of the general is cerebral management of physical realities. As the Gauls probe Caesar's great double ring of defenses at Alesia for weak points, as they shift their points of attack, Caesar secures a position with a broad outlook and from there artfully doles out reinforcements to wherever the Romans are hard-pressed (*G* 7.85-87). Where his troops are outnumbered the tactical general sends up reinforcements (*G* 1.52); he takes measures to prevent the units of his army from being outflanked (*G* 2.8, 3.28, *C* 1.40; cf. *B.Afr.* 15, 17, 58) especially on the right, shieldless, "open" side, where the soldiers are especially vulnerable to missiles (*G* 4.26, 5.35), and contrives to outflank

and surround his enemy (*G* 3.26, *C* 3.86; cf. *B.Afr.* 59; Xen. *Hell.* 4.2.22) and cast missiles upon their open side (*G* 4.25). He attends to the *vires* of his troops—replacing the wounded and the tired (*C* 1.45), avoiding battle when his army is exhausted (*C* 1.65; cf. *B.Afr.* 42), and striving to tire out his enemy (*C* 3.85; cf. *B.Afr.* 75). Since the *vires* of soldiers lessen when they run short of food (*G* 7.20, *C* 1.52), Caesar attends carefully to the supplies of his army (*C* 3.42, 3.85), maneuvering to ensure that they are not disrupted, and maneuvers as well to cut off the supplies of his enemy (*G* 3.23: this tactic is the *consuetudo populi Romani; G* 6.10, *C* 3.41, 3.58). Plotting and maneuvering to place the enemy in a *locus iniquus* and to avoid one himself, the tactical general is acutely sensitive to the lay of the land, and must "take counsel from the nature of the place" (*C* 3.43; cf. *G* 7.74), as Caesar puts it.

It seems highly likely (although it cannot, of course, be proved) that Caesar's sophisticated tactical physics was an adaptation (by him or lost Latin predecessors) of the Greek conception of battle to Roman experience. Caesar depends on the Greeks for the fundamental metaphors, that of pressing, and the conception of the clash of arms in terms of force. . . . It is on the nature of the force exerted that Caesar diverges from the Greek tradition. For the ruling Greek weight metaphor did not describe the impact of the Roman legion, more loosely deployed than the massive Greek phalanx.[44] Thus Caesar's physical conception of battle is naturally less one of weighing than of crashing. Caesar's metaphorical system ramifies from the *impetus* of the legionary charge. . . . Caesar's physics is based on moving forces, the Greek conception, in essence, on stationary, pushing forces. Differences in the basic conceptual model, moreover, create differences of emphasis in battle description. Polybius mentions terrain which might cause disorder (the nemesis of pushing weight) to the easily disordered phalanx. His fastidiousness about topographical reporting—however congenial to us—is the result of tactical thinking that arises from a certain method of fighting. Disorder is less dangerous to Caesar's legions, and the lay of the land simply less important to him: terrain is primarily interesting to Caesar if it slows (or speeds up) the *impetus* of troops moving across it. Caesar's model of the physics of battle does not demand Polybius' topographical precision.

Drawing on the Greeks, we too use metaphors drawn from physics to think about battle. The Greek theory of battle elaborated from the push of the phalanx still influences our conceptions: military forces push, press, weigh, and give way in our minds much as once they did in Greek minds. Yet the comfortable familiarity of such metaphorical weapons to the modern hand must not conceal the fact that they, like spears and rifles, had to be invented, and once invented adapted to the experience of their users. Julius Caesar offers one such adaptation; comparing his mechanics of battle with Polybius' and our own produces a vivid sense of the artificiality of all of them.

IV. *Animus*

To receive Caesar's charge at a stand was against the dictates of reason, wrote Caesar in his criticism of Pompey at Pharsalus, for that was to ignore the psychological dimension of the *impetus*. He attacks the elevation of formation over psychology elsewhere too: in 54 BC a detachment of Caesar's army under Sabinus and Cotta was ambushed on the road by the Gauls (*G* 5.32-37), and Cotta made the decision to abandon the baggage and form a defensive circle (*orbis*). "This plan, which is hardly to be scorned in such a situation, nevertheless turned out badly. For it reduced the hope of our troops and made the enemy more eager for the fight (*ad pugnam alacriores effecit*), since it could not be done without creating the appearance of the greatest fear and desperation" (*G* 5.33; cf. 2.17 on the moral effect of loss of the baggage). This was the beginning of disaster, and Caesar uses the occasion to editorialize on the inadequacy of command conceived as too narrowly tactical—command which might approve the abandonment of the baggage regardless of the psychological consequences—and to call for a kind of generalship that gave due attention to the relative morale of the armies in contention, to the *animus* of the troops.[45]

XENOPHON AND THE GREEK TRADITION OF MILITARY PSYCHOLOGY

In insisting upon the salience of psychological factors in battle, Caesar enters on one side of an old Greek argument. "He taught me drawing up soldiers . . .—and nothing else," complains a character in Xenophon about an early military sophist (*Mem.* 3.1.5), and then has Socrates dilate on other aspects of military knowledge the professional failed to teach. Xenophon expands his attack on this narrowly tactical conception of military education in the *Cyropaedia*, when he imagines Cyrus asking his father to pay a similar expert who had promised to teach him generalship (*Cyr.* 1.6.12-14).[46] Was his training any use? asked his father. Had the professional taught him about supplies, or health, and "had he taught me so that I would be able to instill enthusiasm . . . in an army, noting that in every undertaking enthusiasm or discouragement . . . made a tremendous difference?" (cf. *Cyr.* 1.6.19). The hired expert had not, and it was left to Cyrus' father to make clear to the young conqueror "that formations . . . were only a small part of generalship" (cf. *Cyr.* 8.5.15).

Xenophon was attacking a strain of Greek military thinking which survives to us in the tradition of the Greek tactical manuals, and, to a lesser degree, in Polybius.[47] For battle conceived strictly as a matter of forms and forces was covertly reductionist and totalizing. "These, in short, are the principles of the tactician," writes Asclepiodotus in conclusion to his tactical work, "they bring safety to those who employ them, and danger to those who do not" (12.11). So, he implies, victory is simply a matter of drawing up troops, since that is all he discusses.

Xenophon, by contrast, thought that "neither numbers nor physical strength make for victory in war, but whichever side—with the gods' help—advances upon the enemy stouter in spirit . . . , their foes usually do not stand against them" (Xen. *Anab.* 3.1.42; cf. *Cyr.* 3.3.19). Xenophon's stated opinion was that psychology was the most important factor in winning battles. A survey of his writings suggests that he has overstated his case in the passion of controversy. For Xenophon was no scorner of tactics: he often stops his narrative for detailed dissertations on formation and drill in the spirit of the later tactical manuals (*Anab.* 3.4.19-23, 4.3.26-29, 4.8.10-13, *Cyr.* 2.3.21-22, 2.4.2-4, *Lac. Pol.* 11.5-10).[48] And a great many of his battle descriptions are austerely tactical, or have psychology sprinkled here and there as decoration like the confectioner's sugar of a stingy pastry chef (e.g. *Hell.* 1.6.29-34, 2.4.32-34, 4.2.13-23, 6.4.9-14, *Cyr.* 6.3.18-7.1.40). But there are plenty of battle descriptions in Xenophon—both of historical battles (*Hell.* 4.4.9-12, 4.5.13-17, 5.4.42-45, 7.1.31, 7.2.22-23) and an imagined battle in the *Cyropaedia* (3.3.25-67)—where psychological factors are decisive.

Just as schemata the Greeks used for describing battle in physical terms are visible in Polybius, so Xenophon offers a tour of the simplifying assumptions with which Greeks made a science of the psychology of soldiers in battle. Xenophon's machinery of military psychology . . . is founded on a dichotomy between . . . confidence, boldness, martial enthusiasm, and . . . fear or panic (*Anab.* 3.2.16, *Cyr.* 3.3.19, 5.2.33, 5.3.47, *Eq. Mag.* 5.3). Almost synonymous is the polarity between . . . high spirits and . . . low spirits (*Anab.* 3.1.39-41, *Hell.* 7.4.24, *Cyr.* 1.6.13). . . . Reciprocity operates between the opposite ends of the axis: the extreme high spirits of one army can be enough alone to produce panic in the other army (*Cyr.* 3.3.59-63, *Hell.* 7.2.21-23; cf. *Cyr.* 3.3.30), while signs of fear raise the spirits of the enemy (*Hell.* 3.5.22, *Anab.* 4.6.9). Soldiers' very high spirits shade in Xenophon's mind into the insolent aggressiveness of *hybris* (*Hell.* 3.5.22-24): contempt . . . for the enemy is valuable because it makes soldiers fight more boldly in battle (*Hell.* 3.4.19, *Cyr.* 3.3.31), but it can be dangerous because contemptuous soldiers are careless (*Hell.* 4.1.17, 5.3.1).

The Greeks had an old, deep-rooted respect for the terrifying irrationality of the moods of soldiers in battle, a respect manifested in cults to Pan, the god of panic, and sacrifices to Artemis.[49] Drawing upon this tradition, Xenophon knows that states of high and low spirits can be wholly irrational.[50] The gods may bring high spirits (*Hell.* 7.1.31, 7.2.21, *Anab.* 3.1.42), and panic may crash down like a thunderbolt from a clear sky (*Anab.* 2.2.19-21).[51] Panics are contagious (*Hell.* 5.2.41, 5.4.45, 7.5.24; cf. Thuc. 4.96), and psychological effects . . . are exaggerated in large bodies of men (*Cyr.* 5.2.33-34). . . .

Thus casualties inspire the side inflicting them (*Hell.* 4.5.16) and demoralize the side suffering them, especially if the fallen are generals or men of distinction (*Hell.* 7.4.24, 7.5.25). Situations dangerous in the battle conceived tactically cause fear in the battle viewed psychologically: seeing one's battle line fall into disorder (*Anab.* 4.8.10), being surrounded (*Cyr.* 7.1.24), or having enemies behind (*Anab.* 3.4.20, *Hell.* 4.4.11-12, 7.5.24), thinking one is being ambushed or that the enemy is receiving reinforcements (*Eq. Mag.* 5.8, 8.20).

Xenophon has an interlocutor of Cyrus urge him to raise the spirits of his army before battle with a speech, but Xenophon has Cyrus reply that careful training beforehand is much more significant to the psychology of soldiers in battle than oratory on the field (*Cyr.* 3.3.49-55). By the way Xenophon treats the subject, the utility of the pre-battle harangue was evidently controversial in his day, and Xenophon takes a pessimistic view.[52] Oratory is more useful for reviving the spirits of a discouraged army (*Anab.* 3.1.39-42; cf. Onasander 1.13-14), an end which can also be accomplished by rest or victory (*Cyr.* 5.2.32, 5.2.34, *Hell.* 7.1.19, *Anab.* 6.5.30).

More than giving speeches, Xenophon's general is most often found devising and employing psychological tricks and stratagems.[53] In this, Xenophon was carried along by powerful Greek intellectual currents: besides tactics, the second great stream of Greek military thinking was the collection of cunning stratagems, the systematic application of *metis* to warfare.[54] Herodotus hastens to point out warlike tricks (e.g. 1.21-22, 8.22, 8.75) and a systematic interest in stratagem can be detected in Thucydides.[55] In the Hellenistic period stratagem collections began to be compiled and two Roman-era collections of ancient military stratagems survive.[56] Appian describes the immobility of Pompey's infantry at Pharsalus as a stratagem, and many Greek stratagems were tactical in nature, but Greek collections of stratagems represented an anecdotal tradition independent of Greek tactical science that comprehended, indeed emphasized, the psychological aspects of warfare.[57] It is to a great extent through Greek interest in military trickery that psychology makes its way onto the Greek mental battlefield.[58]

Xenophon's description of the battle of Mantinea in 362 BC (*Hell.* 7.5.20-25) is an excellent instance of the integration of psychological factors into battle description through the medium of stratagem. Epaminondas' first trick is to form his army into line of battle—to give the impression that he intended to fight that day—but then to move away and pretend to make camp. "By doing this he caused a relaxation in the enemy's psychological readiness for the fight . . . , and a relaxation of their formation. . . ." And indeed when Epaminondas ordered the attack he fell upon an enemy unprepared both in order and spirit: "all were like men about to suffer, rather than accomplish, something" (cf. *Cyr.* 7.5.21, *Hell.* 4.8.38). Before the onset Epaminondas deepened the left wing of his phalanx, replicating his famous tactic at Leuctra (Xen. *Hell.* 6.4.12; cf. *Cyr.* 7.5.3), and drew his weaker right wing back to protect it from early engagement. But the rationale Xenophon attributes to Epaminondas for this arrangement at Mantinea is psychological: the moral consequences of the first clash of arms, he thought, were contagious, and if his

weak right wing were put to flight, it would discourage the rest of his army and strengthen the enemy. The same logic dictated the stratagem of strengthening his cavalry with a leavening of infantry. It was essential to win the first encounter, he thought, "for it is hard to find men willing to hold their positions, when they see any of their own side fleeing." Finally, to prevent the enemy troops opposed to his lagging right from assisting those attacked by his powerful left, Epaminondas posted froops on hills overlooking them, to place them in fear . . . of being attacked from the rear if they went to help their allies. And Epaminondas was correct in all his psychological strategizing. "By gaining mastery where he struck, he made the whole of the enemy flee."

The salience of psychological factors in this battle description is striking, but no less striking is the nexus between those factors and stratagem. Xenophon's interest in military psychology is greatest where he is not just reporting panics and the like, but pointing out the stratagems that gave rise to them. One of the two great imaginary battles in the *Cyropaedia* is conceived as a tutorial in psychological stratagems (*Cyr.* 3.3.12-67; the other, 6.3.18-7.1.40, is a tutorial on tactics): among the topics covered are the terror inspired by the offensive (3.3.18-19), by revealing one's strength all at once (3.3.28), the need to conceal one's small numbers lest the enemy have contempt for one's army and be reassured (3.3.31), as well as the futility of oratory before battle in contrast to training (3.3.49-55), already mentioned. So utter is Cyrus' psychological mastery that the enemy flees without a blow (3.3.63).

In contrast to Xenophon's enthusiasm for military psychology, the austere Polybius looks first to tactics and only second to psychology to understand battles: his is a middle position between Xenophon and the tactical writers, who tend to ignore psychology. Polybius may have the widest general interest in human psychology of all the surviving classical historians,[59] but the prominence of psychology in his battle descriptions is not proportionate to his expansiveness on psychology in general. On the eve of Pharsalus, Brutus sat making an epitome of Polybius (Plut. *Brutus* 4.4). If C. Triarius had been reading Polybius' description of Cynoscephalae over Brutus' shoulder that would certainly explain the advice he gave to Pompey about the primacy of formation over psychology to oppose Caesar's charge. Where psychology does feature in Polybius' descriptions of battles, it is often poorly integrated into the chain of causation that leads to victory: in Polybius' account of Drepanum, for example, Adherbal's encouragement of the Carthaginians is depicted, as well as the resulting lather of martial enthusiasm (1.49.10-11), but Carthaginian high spirits have no role in Polybius' careful analysis of the reasons the Carthaginians win (1.51), all of them tactical (cf. 1.32-34). The nexus between military psychology and stratagem, moreover, is even more marked in Polybius than in Xenophon (e.g. 3.116.8, 11.16, 11.22.1-4, and 24.6); in Polybius, for the most part, psychological events occur because generals plan for them.

Polybius describes how the stratagems of Hamilcar Barca produced panic in his foes during the Carthaginian war against their mercenaries (1.84.8; cf. 1.75-76).[60] At the siege of New Carthage, just as Scipio sounded the attack, Mago cunningly launched a sortie to astound . . . the Romans. But Scipio had foreseen this stratagem and countered with one of his own: he planned to lure the enemy troops far from the walls, so that, destroying them, he would demoralize . . . the defenders of the town and ensure that they would never sortie again (10.12.4-7). Scipio encouraged his troops by his presence, arousing their enthusiasm . . . , and thus contributed greatly to the victory (cf. 5.85.8). Yet this too is conceived as a stratagem: he had arranged to be protected by three men bearing large shields (10.13.1-5). To Xenophon stratagem is a useful avenue to military psychology, but Polybius finds it hard to turn off that road. The science of stratagem could be a constraint on Greek understanding of soldiers' psychology, because it encouraged Greeks to look for psychology only where stratagem could also be found. Experts who thought along Polybius' lines were confident that their science of stratagem offered the general mastery of human emotion.

The ironic end of Xenophon's Mantinea might be conceived as Xenophon's answer to Polybius: Epaminondas' death at the moment of triumph deprived his side of a decisive victory, because the fall of the master of psychological stratagem threw his army into an unplanned-for panic. The victorious hoplites of Epaminondas' left simply stopped where they were, and his victorious cavalry "escaped through the fleeing enemy like beaten and terrified men." The end result was that although everyone predicted a decisive battle, and a clear decision as to who should be master of Greece, "the god so arranged it that both sides should set up a trophy as victors . . . and in Greece there was even more confusion and chaos after the battle than before" (*Hell.* 7.5.25-27). So Xenophon reasserts the essential irrationality of military psychology. Although interested in stratagem, Xenophon is not prepared to confine his understanding of soldiers' moods in battle to the inherited structures of that science.

CAESAR

Caesar's strictures on Pompey's plan at Pharsalus signify his participation in the Greek debate on the importance of psychology in battle and signal that on this question he sailed the same intellectual currents as Xenophon.[61] To Caesar morale was not to be ignored, nor was it a sporadic, occasional concern (as conceiving it narrowly in terms of stratagem implicitly made it): to Caesar morale was a constant preoccupation.[62] The outlines of Caesar's understanding of *animus* . . . are very similar to, and probably borrowed from, the Greeks. Both gather all forms of low morale—from quiet discouragement, to defeatism, to fear, to desperate irrational panic—into one broad functional category. . . . Similarly both gather high morale, god-sent inspiration, the thrill of victory, and the mad joy of the attack into another omnibus category. There

is nothing inevitable about either grouping: the similarity suggests Greek influence. In describing morale Caesar and Xenophon are often describing the same or similar real phenomena. But even allowing for the consequent natural similarity of their depictions, Caesar's treatment of morale, and his intermittent editorial remarks upon it, are strikingly similar to Xenophon's.

Caesar gives even greater prominence to the theme of morale than Xenophon: no ancient writer who had actually seen a battle gives psychology a larger role in his battle descriptions than Caesar,[63] and no ancient writer offers as extensive or elaborated a treatment of the phenomena.[64] Thus in Caesar we can see how many themes which are treated tersely in Greek authors play out in detail. . . . Like Xenophon, Caesar too has much to say about the internal logic of panic (*C* 2.29, *G* 1.39, 6.37, 7.84) and its disastrous consequences. At the announcement of the defeat of Curio the remnant of his army in Africa, snug and for the moment unthreatened in their well-fortified camp, fell into a panic. "So great was everyone's fear (*terror*), that some said that Juba's forces were approaching, others that Varus' legions were pressing upon them, and that they could see the dust from their approach, when nothing of the kind was happening. Yet others feared that the enemy fleet would quickly fall upon them" (*C* 2.43). The Caesarian warships flee, the cargo ships with them, soldiers rush aboard the few remaining vessels and, overloading them, sink some. The army surrenders (*C* 2.43-44). One of Caesar's continuators refers to "combat and shouting (*congressus . . . et clamor*), the two chief ways an enemy becomes terrified" (*B.Hisp.* 31). But soldiers in Caesar are easily alarmed by any surprise (*G* 6.39, 7.28; cf. *B.Afr.* 29) or anything unfamiliar, by British chariots (*G* 4.33; cf. Polyb. 2.29.5-9); by the catch-as-catch-can tactics of the Pompeians in Spain, learned from the Lusitanians (*C* 1.44-45); by having to fight half-submerged in the English Channel (*G* 4.24), a crisis which Caesar reverses by sending Roman warships, bristling with artillery, against the Britons on the shore, which frighten them as unfamiliar in turn (*G* 4.25). Green troops are especially vulnerable to such panic (*G* 6.39), while long experience provides some protection against it (*C* 3.84).

Just as in Xenophon, the aspects of battle conceived tactically cast reflections in the world of morale, because they may inspire terror. The prospect of being outnumbered may inspire fear (*C* 1.56, 3.84), while fighting encumbered with baggage is expected to reduce the *animus* of the soldiers (*G* 3.24). But these are the huge, misshapen, and terrifying reflections of fun-house mirrors, for soldiers' reactions are often far out of proportion to the real danger, the consequences of their panic sometimes much more dangerous than what they feared. Having seen some of their light-armed troops surrounded and exterminated by Curio's cavalry, the whole Pompeian army near Utica abandons its advantageous position: "the *animus* of Attius' soldiers, seized by fear (*timor*) and flight and the slaughter of their comrades, gave no thought to resistance. All thought they were even now being surrounded by cavalry" (*C* 2.34; cf. *B.Alex.* 18). They take to flight before Curio's men can land a blow. Vercingetorix's Gauls are also given to such exaggerated panics at the prospect of being surrounded (*G* 7.67, 7.82). Similarly, soldiers are extremely nervous about being outflanked on their open side. During the civil war in Spain the rushes of small numbers of Pompeian troops play to this fear, which in turn infects much of Caesar's line of battle (*C* 1.44-45). Before Gergovia friendly Gauls appearing on the *latus apertum* are transformed into enemies by the Roman soldiers' dread (*G* 7.50).

Like the strategmatic Greek general, Caesar's general must attend to the *animus* of his troops before, during, and after the battle. When deciding whether to offer battle, a general always must attend closely to the relative *animus* of his own and the enemy's army, since it governs their fighting quality. In Spain Caesar's cavalry have ridden down some Pompeian skirmishers.

> There was an opportunity for success. It did not escape Caesar that an army terrified (*perterritum*) by such a loss in full sight could not resist (*sustinere*), especially when surrounded on all sides by cavalry, if the conflict was in a flat and open place. Battle was begged of him from every quarter. The *legati*, centurions and military tribunes ran up: he should not hesitate to commit to battle. The *animi* of all the soldiers were ready as could be. But Afranius' troops gave many indications of fear (*timor*): they had not helped their own men, they would not come down from the hill, they were hardly sustaining the attacks of the cavalry and they were crammed together with all the standards collected in one place, observing neither their ranks nor their standards.
>
> (*C* 1.71; cf. *C* 2.34; Polyb. 1.33.5, 1.45.1-2)

Caesar refuses battle, not because he discountenances the psychological analysis provided by his officers, but because he hopes that the psychological dominance of his army is so great that the enemy will surrender without bloodshed.

In the opposite case, if the enemy has the advantage in *animus*—if they are elated (*G* 1.15) or Caesar's own troops are cast down—battle is avoided until the balance is restored or a moral advantage can be gained (cf. Front. *Strat.* 2.1.3). Very great decisions, like Caesar's withdrawal from Dyrrachium, are properly made on this basis—Caesar judges his army terrified and retreats (*C* 3.74), and is not prepared to seek a general engagement with Pompey until he is confident that the passage of time has restored his soldiers' spirits (*C* 3.84). The general uses skirmishing before a battle to test the *animus* of his soldiers (*G* 7.36) and, if successful, to increase it (*C* 3.84).[65] For just as in Xenophon, the low spirits of one army exhilarate the other (*C* 2.31; cf. *B.Alex.* 31). Rattled units are kept in the rear (*G* 4.13). A rattled enemy, on the other hand, is an invitation to attack (*G* 2.12; cf. *B.Afr.* 82), and when soldiers become aware of the enemy's timidity they also become more eager to fight, an enthusiasm of which advantage can be taken (*G* 3.24).

Just as he is alert to theirs, so too Caesar's enemies are alert to the *animus* of his army and make their decisions on the same basis (*G* 1.23). For this reason bad morale may need to be hidden (*C* 2.31) and a bold front maintained (*C* 3.48). But the enemy's eagerness to take advantage of superiority in *animus* can offer the general opportunities for stratagems, since low spirits can be feigned and the enemy induced to attack at a disadvantage. The general pretends that his army is terrified—keeping within his camp, ordering the rampart to be built higher, the gates to be barricaded, confusion and fear to be simulated in the process. This lures the enemy to cross a river and to advance up a hill under the walls of Caesar's camp—lures them into a *locus iniquus* where a sally from the camp destroys them (*G* 5.50-51; cf. 5.57-58).

When battle looms, *animus* prescribes duties to the general. In the Gallic ambush of 54 Caesar thinks Cotta's decision to abandon the baggage (cf. Xen. *Anab.* 7.8.16) and form a circle was lamentable. But Caesar does praise Cotta, not for his tactics, but for his oratory: it is chiefly in encouraging the soldiers that Cotta "does his duty as a commander" (*G* 5.33). To Caesar, harangues to his soldiers before battle are an indispensable part of generalship, a conventional "military custom" (*militari more*, *C* 3.90).[66] At the battle of the Sambre the Romans were caught by the rapidity of the Gauls' attack. "Caesar had to do everything in a moment: hoist the standard for the call to arms, sound the trumpet, recall the soldiers from entrenching . . . form the line of battle, encourage the soldiers, give the signal" (*G* 2.20). The signals given, encouragement is his next priority, and he harangues the Tenth Legion upon which he happened in the confusion (*G* 2.21, 2.25). Given its importance to the *animus* of the troops, the harangue is not sacrificed even when time is most critical. Xenophon discountenances the speech before battle, while Caesar approves of it. They are both participants in a comfortable old Greek controversy.

Just like Xenophon's Epaminondas, Caesar deploys and maneuvers for psychological reasons, to hurt the *animus* of his foes and to increase that of his own soldiers. When the enemy is trying to fortify a camp, a general might send forth cavalry to attempt to throw them into a state of terror (*C* 1.42; cf. *B.Alex.* 14; *B.Afr.* 70), and the opposing general might dig a trench to prevent just that (*C* 1.41). If an army seems to cower in its camp, cavalry are sent around it to terrify them further (*G* 5.57). So that Vercingetorix's cavalry will fight *maiore animo*, the Gallic captain deploys all his forces in front of the enemy camp to strike terror into the Romans (*G* 7.66). To counter him Caesar draws up his line, to reassure his cavalry (*G* 7.67). At Alesia Caesar draws up his legions behind the horse, with the result that "the *animus* of our men was increased" (*G* 7.70, *nostris animus augetur*). As battle progresses, when the *animus* general recognizes that his opponents have fallen into a state of panic, he knows to press his advantage. "You see the foe panic-stricken, Curio! Why do you hesitate to take advantage of the opportunity?" (*C* 2.34; cf. 3.95; *B.Alex.* 30; Xen. *Cyr.* 5.2.32, *Anab.* 6.5.30). And so Curio leads his men to the charge and the foe flees.

Finally, in the event of defeat, the general—just like Xenophon's general—turns immediately to restoring the crushed *animus* of his soldiers. He calls an assembly and explains it away, telling them not to take it to heart—attributes it to fortune or over-boldness, and recalls their previous victories (*C* 3.73, *G* 7.52-53). Caesar understands that skirmishes between small forces, especially if witnessed by the whole army, can have a great effect on *animus*. And so before withdrawing from the field after his failure at Gergovia Caesar arranges cavalry skirmishes, which the Romans win. "When he judged that the Gauls' boasting had been diminished and the *animi* of his soldiers firmed up (*confirmandos*), he moved his camp into the territory of the Aedui" (*G* 7.53).

Caesar's depiction of military psychology is fuller than that provided by surviving Greek authors, but for the most part similar to, and very probably derivative from, the strain of Greek military thinking that survives to us in Xenophon. Yet as with Caesar's adaptation of Greek tactical models, his Roman experience led him to modify and elaborate what he inherited from the Greeks, and those modifications have ramifications for the way he describes battles.

Polybius describes—in some surprise—the qualities the Romans looked for in a centurion. "They do not want centurions to be bold and danger-loving . . . as much as authoritative and steady and wise of spirit" (. . . 6.24.9). Plutarch allows us to interpret this passage when he expands upon the very similar ethos of the Spartans, which he thinks equally unusual (*Lyc.* 22.3). The Spartans advance to battle "marching in step to the rhythm of the flute with no confusion in their spirits . . . , but going calmly . . . and cheerfully into danger to the music of their hymn. Nor is it likely that excessive fear or passion . . . will befall men so disposed, but rather stability of mind. . . ." This military ethic—which Greek authors saw in both Spartans and Romans—tried to avoid both positive and negative excesses of morale. A strand of Greek military thinking, traces of which survive in Onasander's first-century AD Greek work on generalship (14.1), advocated this position. But among Greeks it remained controversial: Onasander must assure his reader that working to frighten overconfident soldiers will not make them terrified, but merely steady. . . . His view stood against the broader Greek preference for high morale: one of the qualities a Greek like Polybius looks for in an effective officer is "Hellenic ardor" . . . which permits a leader to whip up his soldiers into a froth of enthusiasm (5.64.5-7).

In the Roman case, by contrast, Polybius alludes to a military culture which had a deep strain of admiration for steadiness and calm in battle at the expense of extravagant emotion. This strain of thinking hardly dominated. Roman armies did not enter battle with Quaker solemnity, and Caesar is perfectly aware that elevated spirits made their possessors hard to resist in battle, and criticizes Pompey for ignoring that fact (*C* 3.92; cf. *G* 5.47). But this ethos of calm was prominent enough in the Roman context to

manifest itself in the deep structure of the way Caesar thinks about morale. Xenophon's schema is a very Greek polarity: two categories, high spirits and low, which are good and bad respectively. Caesar, free from the Greek cultural prison of polarities, works with a three-level model: between high spirits, "elated (*elati*) by hope of a speedy victory, the flight of the enemy, and by successful engagements previously" (*G* 7.47), and low, panic (*terror, timor*), there is an intermediate state of calm, *animus aequus* (*C* 1.58; cf. 3.6, 3.41). When troops recover from a panic in Caesar they are "firmed up" in spirit (*firmare* or *confirmare;* esp. *C* 3.65), returned to the middle state of calm. . . . For the most part, in Caesar, it is this intermediate state of calm that is desirable: "it is the universal vice of human nature," Caesar editorializes, "that in unusual and unfamiliar circumstances we are too confident or too violently terrified" (*C* 2.4; cf. Hirt. *BG* 8.13). Caesar agreed all too well with Xenophon on the dangers presented by high and low spirits: high spirits can produce bad judgment and lead their possessors into dangerous places (*G* 7.47, *C* 3.72; cf. *B.Afr.* 82-83); panic or low spirits pose the same hazards of flight and defeat they do in Greek authors.

The impact of Caesar's three-level scheme of morale on battle description is especially well illustrated by his account of the climactic engagement at Dyrrachium (*C* 3.62-71). Caesar loses at Dyrrachium and eventually has to withdraw from the field to restore the morale of his shaken army. His account of the battle may therefore be apologetic: Caesar blames fortune for disasters for which fortune might well reproach Caesar (*C* 3.68). But apologetic or not, his is not an account which could easily have been constructed by a Greek on the basis of Xenophon's conception of military psychology.

At Dyrrachium Caesar has a double set of entrenchments running down to the sea, but the envisioned cross-wall is not finished. Using ships to move his soldiers, Pompey attacks both faces of both walls and puts their defenders to flight. Now Caesar's lieutenant Marcellinus sends up some cohorts in support.

> But these, seeing the fleeing men, could not firm them up (*confirmare*) by their coming nor themselves bear the *impetus* of the enemies. Whatever additional help was sent was corrupted by the terror (*timor*) of those fleeing and added to the fear (*terror*) and the peril. . . . Now the Pompeians were approaching the camp of Marcellinus with great slaughter, and no slight *terror* rushed upon our remaining cohorts. But M. Antonius, who held the closest position among the guard posts when he heard the news, was seen descending from higher ground with twelve cohorts. His arrival stopped the Pompeians and firmed up (*firmavit*) our men, so that they recovered themselves from the extremity of fear (*timor*).

> (*C* 3.64-65)

Just as in Xenophon, terror is extremely contagious and leaps from unit to unit as terrified men infect those they meet (cf. *G* 6.40, 7.47, *C* 1.45; Hirt. *BG* 8.13). But factors are at work to restore a state of calm, which eventually prevails. The situation is bad: there is, of course, no question of elation among the Caesarians, merely of liberation from panic. Caesar uses his three-level model of morale to depict a limited movement between panic fear and the intermediate state of *aequus animus*. Caesar's scheme notices smaller changes in morale than Xenophon's scheme.

Attention to smaller changes, in turn, requires attention to smaller causes for those changes. Most of the large-scale reasons for improvement in morale in Caesar can be paralleled in Greek authors. In Caesar a respite from fighting can "firm up" (*G* 6.38, *C* 3.84) the terrified, just like a rest can improve morale in Xenophon. In Caesar as in Polybius the arrival of a commander (*G* 2.25, 4.34, 6.41; cf. Polyb. 5.85.8) or (as here) the prospect of reinforcement (cf. *C* 3.69; *B.A.fr.* 18, 52; Polyb. 1.28.8, 3.105.6) can also be cheering. But what is striking in Caesar's description of Dyrrachium is not the conventional fact of the reassuring effect of reinforcements, but the topographical detail that accompanies them—the reinforcements firm up Caesar's soldiers because they are seen approaching on the high ground. In Caesar landscape is described not only because of its significance to a battle described tactically, which is why Greek authors usually include it in battle descriptions, but because of its psychological significance.

Caesar's account of Dyracchium continues with an extended topographical description of an abandoned camp on the battlefield, of a smaller camp within that camp, and of an earthwork running from that camp down to the river (*C* 3.66). This passage is unusual in Caesar for its length and detail. Pompeian troops have occupied the camp: some of the topographical detail is needed to understand Caesar's tactical description of his attack on them. But the major importance of the topographical description is to explain the psychological events that ruin his attack. Taking the Pompeians by surprise, Caesar's troops break into the camp. The cohorts of Caesar's right wing and his cavalry break a narrow passage through the earthwork extending to the river (*C* 3.67-68). But now Pompey arrives with five legions.

> At the same moment his cavalry approached our horse, and his formed line of battle came into sight of our troops who were occupying the camp. Suddenly everything was changed. The Pompeian legion [in the camp], firmed up (*confirmata*) by hope that it would soon be helped, attempted to resist at the decuman gate, and on its own made an *impetus* at our men. Caesar's horse, because it had ascended the earthwork by a narrow path, feared for its retreat and began to flee. The right wing, because it was cut off from the left, having noticed the terror of the cavalry, began to withdraw over that part of the earthwork it had thrown down, in order not to be overwhelmed within the fortifications. And many of them, lest they get caught up in the narrow spaces, jumped from the ten-foot parapet into the trenches. When these first men fell the others tried to gain safety and escape over their bodies.

> The soldiers of the left wing, when they saw from the rampart the approach of Pompey and the flight of our men, feared lest they get caught up in narrow spaces, with an enemy both inside and outside the camp, and took their own counsel for retreat by the way they had entered. Everything was full of tumult, fear (*timor*), and flight, to the extent that when Caesar seized the standards of those in flight and ordered them to halt, some gave their horses their head and fled right on, some released the standards in fear, and not one of them stopped.

(*C* 3.69)

There is almost no actual fighting here. Caesar's troops fall into a snowballing terror at the thought of what might happen if they are caught in a *locus iniquus*, and disaster ensues. We understand the origin of their fear from Caesar's careful topographical introduction to his narrative of the catastrophe. Landscape viewed through the lens of *animus* is a monstrously exaggerated version of the tactical landscape, the terrifying high and leaping shadows cast by a fire into a dark wood by night (cf. *G* 1.39). Mixed with those terrible features of terrain are the points of vantage—hilltops and ridge lines—where objects of fear or reassurance come into view or from where they can be seen (cf. Hirt. *BG* 8.29; *B.Afr.* 40). The *animus* landscape is a place of hauntings too. The panic of Roman soldiers when attacked unexpectedly by Germans is added to by the memory that Sabinus and Cotta marched to disaster from that very fort in which the Romans cower (*G* 6.37). In his systematic attribution of psychological consequences to topographical features, and in his description of topographical features because of their psychological—rather than strictly tactical—significance, Caesar goes beyond his Greek models. He does so because his Roman experience suggested a different model of soldiers' psychology, which demanded in turn a more nuanced understanding of exactly how psychological events in battle come about.

Among Greek military experts, there was an old controversy about the role of psychology in battle, and about how that psychology ought to be understood and managed. At one dismissive extreme stood the tactical purists, confident that their science of formations and deployment, their physics of battle, was the key to victory. More open to psychology were those officers—like Polybius—who collected stratagems to get the better of their enemies. Since many stratagems were psychological in nature, psychology was part of their military art. Yet stratagem also constrained their conception of psychology, tending to reduce psychology to a function of stratagem. At the other Greek extreme Xenophon represents to us a tradition of thinking that elevated psychology to parity with tactics, even to superiority over tactics in the heat of argument. Such thinking was interested in stratagem, psychological and otherwise, but was also keenly aware of the importance of unplanned psychological events, of psychology as it existed outside the box of stratagem, not bound to the agency of a specific individual.

It was from the Greek position on military psychology that survives to us in Xenophon that Julius Caesar set out. There are striking similarities between Caesar's conception of morale and Xenophon's: as with Caesar's conception of tactics, the fundamental intellectual machinery Caesar uses to imagine military psychology is probably borrowed—by Caesar or his Roman predecessors—from the Greeks. Caesar's position as a military intellectual in the Greek tradition is suggested also by his systematic interest in stratagem: his continuator Hirtius notes that Caesar wrote so as to highlight his cunning planning (*consilia, BG 8. pr*),[67] associating him with the Greek stratagem tradition, and the pages of Caesar are filled with tricks and deceptions.[68] The familiar Greek nexus between stratagem and psychology is also plainly evident in Caesar (*G* 4.25, 7.66-67, *C* 1.41-42). But, like Xenophon, Caesar refused to view psychology strictly as a function of stratagem. With his comments about Pompey at Pharsalus, Caesar takes sides in a Greek debate about the importance of morale in battle, and he situates his writing in a Greek tradition which emphasized morale as a perennial factor to be managed rather than an exceptional factor which came into play when the opportunity for a stratagem presented itself. The most striking quality about Caesar's treatment of morale is simply how extensive it is, and how much more important morale is in Caesar's battle descriptions than in the battle descriptions of earlier Greek writers, even Xenophon.

Yet just as Roman experience with the legion suggested a metaphorical system ramifying from the crash rather than the push of the phalanx, Roman military culture suggested modifications to inherited Greek schemes for understanding military psychology. Although fully aware of the advantages of elation in battle, Roman soldiers esteemed also a calm state of mind situated between the Greek categories of high and low morale. The consequence of this outlook, in Caesar's hands, is a different model of soldiers' psychology than that of the Greeks, which results in turn in a more subtle understanding of the causes of psychological phenomena and the significance of terrain. In Caesar's battle description this psychological vision of battle mixes and mingles with his tactical vision, to produce battle descriptions that would have pleased Clausewitz as "shot through with psychological forces and effects."

V. *VIRTUS*

The third theme in Caesar's description of Pharsalus is that of courage, *virtus*. In a post-psychoanalytic age we are not very comfortable with a distinction between courage, an abiding—perhaps inborn—aspect of character, and flighty morale, a subdivision of psychology. But ancient psychology was less imperialistic than modern. And ancient men were happier than modern to think that their contemporaries acted thus and so because it was their singular nature to do so: ancient men thought in terms of permanent character, we in terms of fungible personality. In a military context, Greeks and Romans saw no dif-

ficulty drawing a sharp categorical line between morale, . . . or *animus*, and courage, . . . or *virtus*. But on the significance of courage in battle Caesar parted company with the Greeks. The two main traditions of Greek military thinking, tactics and stratagem, were dismissive of courage as a decisive factor in battle. Caesar's Roman tradition, by contrast, was conflicted, admiring both victory by guile and victory by sheer bravery. In describing the role of bravery in battle, and in his analysis of that role, Caesar reaches furthest beyond the tradition of Greek military thinking to which he is otherwise so indebted.

THE GREEK TRADITION

Drawing upon their epic past, Greek historians felt that one of the functions of a battle description was to relate . . . individuals' glorious deeds of courage. This is especially striking in Herodotus, where, for example, the historian lists those who conducted themselves most bravely at the battle of Plataea (9.71-74; cf. 6.114, 7.181, 7.226-27, 8.17, 8.93, 9.105),[69] but the custom is still very much alive in Xenophon (*Hell.* 1.2.10, 1.6.32, 4.3.19, 4.8.32, 7.5.16) and Polybius (10.49.14, 11.2.1, 11.18.1-4, 16.5; cf. 16.30.3).[70] Caesar follows in this tradition with his tale of Crastinus at Pharsalus, and with other *aristeai*, most strikingly that of the centurions Vorenus and Pullo (*G* 5.44; cf. *G* 7.25, 7.47, 7.50).[71] But to conceive of battle in terms of physical tactics, or in terms of stratagems, did not encourage Greek military thinkers to root victory or defeat in the bravery of individuals or the differences in bravery between military units, armies, or peoples. From Herodotus' depictions of Salamis and Plataea on, Greek military thinking manifested itself in a strain of Greek historical writing that tended to wall off bravery—although usually worth recording in its own right—from the outcome of battles.[72] This is especially the lesson of Thucydides' account of Phormio's second victory in the gulf of Corinth. The Peloponnesian commander gives a speech urging his men to rely on their superior courage (. . . 2.87) and discounting the Athenian advantage in experience in fighting at sea; but in his speech the Athenian commander Phormio assails the Peloponnesian thinking, stressing instead Athenian experience in naval tactics; indeed bravery, he argues, is merely a function of experience (2.89).[73] The Athenians win the battle against great odds, settling the controversy for the reader (2.90-92; cf. 6.69.1). Viewing bravery as a function of knowledge seems to have been a Socratic position (Arist. *NE* 3.8.6 [=116b]; cf. Xen. *Mem.* 3.9.2; Plato *Laches* 193-99, *Prot.* 349-51, 359-60),[74] and Xenophon offers a variation on it when he has Cyrus argue that it is chiefly training that distinguishes the brave man . . . from the coward . . . (*Cyr.* 3.3.50, 3.3.55, 7.5.75).[75]

This strain of hostility to the agency of bravery is especially striking if one compares the battle descriptions of Xenophon and Polybius to those of Caesar's Greek contemporary Diodorus Siculus, participant in and heir to a more rhetorical historical tradition. Diodorus diverges from the experts Xenophon and Polybius in his regular attribution of a pivotal role in battle to sheer courage (18.15.2-3, 18.45.2, 19.30.5, 20.38.5, . . .). "In fights on land," he writes, "courage . . . becomes evident, because it can gain the upper hand if no accidents intrude" (20.51.5). In Polybius, much closer to the tradition of theoretical Greek military thinking, bravery is sometimes used as a shorthand to explain a victory upon which the author does not then choose to dwell (2.9.5, 2.55.4), or to explain, in general terms, the overall outcome of wars (5.76.11; cf. Xen. *Hell.* 2.4.40-41), like Rome's victories over Carthage. In that context Polybius argues that Italians are by nature stronger and braver than Phoenicians and Libyans; that citizens are braver than mercenaries and become even braver in defeat; and that the customs of the Romans (such as the great aristocratic funerals, which he then describes) make them braver still (6.52; cf. 1.64.6).[76] But as Polybius' descriptions of warfare move from the distant and general to the closer and specific—to detailed depictions of individual battles—bravery tends to find itself outside the chain of causation that leads to victory, displaced by the tactical conception of battle and discountenanced by the strategmatic outlook, which set victory by art above victory by brute courage. Of the Punic wars, Polybius writes, "in naval matters the Romans are much inferior in experience . . . but win on the whole because of the bravery of their men . . . ; for although nautical skill contributes largely to battles on the sea, nevertheless the bravery of the marines . . . weighs most in the scales of victory" (6.52.8-9). Yet this general diagnosis is hardly consistent with his highly tactical depictions of the sea battles of the First Punic War (1.23, 1.25, 1.26-28, 1.50-51), where the superior bravery of the Roman marines merits only a passing mention (1.61.3).[77] Standing close to the military tradition, Polybius' battles generally turn on tactics and stratagems rather than bravery.[78] His, instead, is a world where "at first the mercenaries prevailed by virtue of their skill and courage . . . , and wounded many of the Romans, but relying on the exactness of their formation and their armament . . . the Romans kept advancing" (15.13.1-2). In Polybian battle descriptions bravery is more often than not the desperate resort of those who are going to lose (1.30.11-12, 1.84.5, 3.115.4-5, 5.100.1-2, 18.21.8; cf. Herod. 1.176, 5.2).

There is even less discussion of bravery in Xenophon's battles than in Polybius'. Bravery makes its appearance in harangues before battle (*Anab.* 1.7.3, 3.2.15, 6.5.24), but in one such context Xenophon alludes to the artificiality and conventionality of such rhetoric (*Cyr.* 7.1.17-18). Otherwise, bravery appears in paradoxical contexts, as when the traditionally despised Eleans overcome the Arcadians, Argives, and Athenians (*Hell.* 7.4.30), or when Athenian horse overcomes the celebrated Thessalian cavalry (*Hell.* 7.5.16-17). It is almost as if Xenophon is mocking traditional Greek concepts of bravery.

The tenor of Greek military thinking was, thus, to render differences in bravery beside the point. In this tradition the bravery of his army is the involuntary refuge of the inept general, the general who had been bettered in tactics or

stratagem. In Thucydides' description of Mantinea, the Spartans, cast into confusion by the imbecile orders of their king, and "utterly worsted in skill" . . . , nevertheless won by bravery (. . . 5.72.2). The Roman deployment against the Insubres was deeply foolish, Polybius complains, but nevertheless the Romans won by their bravery (. . . 2.33.9).

CAESAR

There are distinct echoes of this dismissive Greek attitude to courage in Caesar. Servius Galba's Twelfth Legion sorties from its camp, "placing all hope of safety in *virtus*" (*G* 3.5), and routs the enemy. But this desperate sortie was needed because Galba's idiocy had left the legion cut off in the Alps, wintering in an incomplete, badly placed camp. Attacked by Alpine tribesmen, outnumbered, exhausted, wounded, and out of missiles, the Romans are saved by bravery—in pointed contrast to the preparations of their general (cf. Livy 6.30.5-6, 35.6.9-10). And when bravery takes the place of proper planning or good order, in Caesar, it is more usually futile: when the foolishness of Titurius Sabinus has led the Romans into a Gallic ambush, "our soldiers, deserted by their leader and by fortune, nevertheless placed all hope for their safety in *virtus*" (*G* 5.34). Yet by the cunning of the ambush the Romans were surrounded in a valley and crammed together in a small area. "There was no room left for *virtus*" (*nec virtuti locus relinquebatur, G* 5.35), and the Romans were destroyed. Having foolishly led an outnumbered and exhausted army into battle against impossible odds, Caesar's marshal Curio "encourages his men to repose all hope in *virtus*." "Nor was *virtus* lacking for the fight," notes Caesar, despite the troops' scantiness and exhaustion, and they drove back the Numidians, until, surrounded, exhausted, and hopeless, their spirit broke, and they took to "bewailing their own deaths, and commending their parents to those whom fortune might preserve from danger. Everything was fear and wailing" (*C* 2.41). They were slaughtered.

Caesar uses his description of his defeat at the battle of Gergovia (*G* 7.45-52) as an opportunity for a homily on the danger of foolish reliance on unreasoning *virtus*. Having contrived by stratagem to draw the Gauls away from their camps on the slope beneath the town, he ordered a limited attack, carefully instructing his legates to hold back the troops—if they advanced too far they would proceed on to disadvantageous ground and be at the mercy of the Gauls. Catching the Gauls by surprise, the Romans rapidly occupy their appointed objectives, but ignoring the recall and the efforts of Caesar's legates and the military tribunes to call them back, they continue to advance "elated by hope of a speedy victory, the flight of the enemy and by successful engagements previously, and thought nothing so difficult that it could not be done by courage (*virtus*)." The centurion Lucius Fabius mounts the wall, and the demoralization of the Gauls is stressed by a warm description of the hysterical terror of their women. But now the Gauls, overcoming their initial panic, begin to wax in number. "For the Romans the contest was equal in neither ground nor number. Men tired out by the run and the length of the battle could not easily resist men who were fresh and sound." "The battle was fought most ferociously at close quarters, the enemy trusting to the ground and their numbers, our men to courage (*virtus*)." And the ground and numbers overcame *virtus,* especially when the Romans fell into an alarm because of the approach of the Aedui, allies mistaken for enemies. The Romans are pushed back with losses, and the disaster is rendered vivid by notices of the death of Lucius Fabius and another brave, foolish centurion. The next day Caesar calls his army to assembly, and lectures them (and us). "Although he greatly admired the greatness of spirit (*animi magnitudinem,* used more or less synonymously with *virtus*)[79] of those whom no camp fortifications, no height of hill, no town wall could slow . . . he wanted obedience and self-control (*modestiam et continentiam*) no less than *virtus* and greatness of spirit" (*C* 7.52).

So far Caesar seems loyal to the Greek military tradition, esteeming artful generalship and sparing of men. Urged to battle by his army, he thinks, "why should he try fortune? Especially when it was no less the role of the *imperator* to overcome by planning than by the sword" (*consilio superare quam gladio, C* 1.72; cf. *G* 7.19; *B.Afr.* 14). But this Greek conception stands in striking contrast—in contradiction—to another, more Roman, understanding of the role of *virtus* in battle, which is no less prominent in Caesar's writings. This manifests itself in Caesar's account of the sea fight in 49 BC between his commander Decimus Brutus and the Pompeian L. Domitius Ahenobarbus, commanding Massilian ships (*C* 1.56-58; cf. *B.Alex.* 15-16). Caesar describes the disadvantages under which his side labored: the Massilian fleet was much larger and manned by better seamen, while the Caesarian ships were badly built and slow. The Massilians naturally attempted the sophisticated naval tactics by which a skilled fleet of galleys could press its advantage against an unskilled. But liberal provision of grappling hooks on the Caesarian side created a land battle by sea. For this too the Pompeians were hardly unprepared, having shipped savage warriors of the Albici, barbarians from the hills around Massilia, as marines. "When [the Pompeians] by necessity came closer, instead of the science and tricks of their steersmen they had resort to the *virtus* of the mountaineers." But Caesar had manned his ships with picked centurions and legionaries, the bravest (*fortissimi*) men in his army. "The fighting was carried on with the greatest bravery and intensity (*fortissime atque acerrime*) on both sides, nor did the Albici—harsh mountaineers, practiced in arms—yield much to our men in *virtus*." Not much, perhaps, but enough. And the Caesarians calmly (*animo aequo*) boarded and captured ship after ship.

To Caesar what decided this battle was the difference in *virtus* between his men and the Albici. Nor was this because his officer Decimus Brutus had failed in his duty: the deft maneuvers of the skilled Massilian steersmen (analogous to Caesar's own maneuvers on so many occasions) are sneered at as "tricks," *artificia,* obscurely il-

legitimate. They are distractions from the crux of the matter, the hand-to-hand combat in which *virtus* reveals itself. The most systematic presentation of this way of conceiving warfare can be found in remarks Caesar attributes to Divico, leader of the Helvetii, warning the Roman general against fighting that tribe.

> He ought to remember the old disaster of the Romans [at the hands of the Helvetii, in 107 BC] and the unblemished *virtus* of the Helvetii. He [Caesar, in a recent victory] had set upon one canton unexpectedly when those who had crossed the river could not help them; thus he should not merely on that account rate his own *virtus* highly nor despise them. They had learned from their fathers and ancestors to fight on the basis of *virtus,* rather than tricks and ambushes (*magis virtute quam dolo contenderent aut insidiis niterentur*).

> (*G* 1.13; cf. *B.Afr.* 73)

Virtus is expected to be decisive, and everything that gets in the way of *virtus*—tricks and ambushes—is sordid (cf. *B.Alex.* 29). Caesar has Vercingetorix reecho this sentiment, telling his army after Avaricum not to be disheartened. "The Romans had not won by *virtus* or in a pitched battle, but by trickery and knowledge of siegecraft" (*G* 7.29, *sed artificio quodam et scientia oppugnationis*).

This is no barbarian gasconade, but the traditional code of the Romans.[80] Sallust presents Metellus, fighting Jugurtha in Africa, as badly outmaneuvered. "On Metellus' side was the *virtus* of his soldiers, but the ground was against him; Jugurtha had all advantages except in soldiers" (*Jug.* 52.2). Metellus' eventual victory is received with special satisfaction at Rome, "because he had led his army in the ancestral manner: although in a bad position he had been victorious by *virtus* nonetheless" (*Jug.* 55.1). "Our ancestors did not wage war by ambushes or night battles, nor by pretended flight and unforeseen return to an enemy off his guard, that they might glory in cunning rather than real *virtus,*" Livy has old senators grumble, about the dubious diplomacy of Marcius Philippus and Aulus Attius in Greece in 171 BC (42.47.5; cf. Tac. *Ann.* 2.88). And Polybius contrasts the Greek enthusiasm for military trickery with a lingering Roman distaste for it, and notes the Roman preference for hard fighting at close quarters (Polyb. 13.3.7; cf. 36.9.9). Despite a venerable Roman tradition of admiration for cunning in battle,[81] there survived a strong sense that Romans ought to prevail by bravery unadorned, that the truest victory was by *virtus,* and that only a defeat by *virtus* was a true defeat.

Caesar picks up this strand after his own defeat at Gergovia, telling his troops not to be downhearted, since they were defeated by the *locus iniquus* rather than the Gauls' *virtus* (*G* 7.53). Similarly, Caesar notes that the Pompeians should not have become overconfident after his setback at Dyrrachium. They were acting as if they had been victorious by *virtus* rather than by the fortuitous panic of Caesar's men (*C* 3.72). In the sea battle against the Massilians Caesar betrays a certain satisfaction when the extraneous particularities of battle—of number, of position, of *ani-*

mus—are swept away, and courage wrestles undistracted against courage. Like Romans in general,[82] at some level Caesar thinks that battles are supposed to be fought by *virtus*. Like Romans in general, he does not resolve the contradiction between conceptions of battle dependent on *virtus* and on stratagem. Indeed, as an author Caesar may rely upon that contradiction in the minds of his Roman reader: he and his army can appear in a good light both in battles won by craft and in battles won by hard fighting. If a battle be lost, he can portray his men fighting admirably in one realm, in *virtus*, even if they are defeated in strategy.

In thinking about battle in terms of *virtus*, Caesar draws upon a very old stratum of Roman thinking about warfare.[83] Usually translated "bravery," *virtus* comes close to "masculinity": it denotes the competitive male excellence of traditional Mediterranean societies. As such it must be constantly proved and reasserted, and the old custom of the Romans was to do so not in small-scale internal violence (as many feuding peoples do), but instead primarily in war.[84] As well as being conceived as a matter of physical realities and the vertiginous see-sawing of *animus*, battle in Caesar manifests itself as a contest for masculine dominance, a battle of roosters or of drunkards in a bar, a Florentine duel or a Sicilian vendetta.

The *virtus* battle tests masculine excellence in the eyes of a real or imagined public. In the realm of *virtus* the constant preoccupation of the soldier is with what people will think. "Since the fighting occurred in view of everyone, and nothing done well or shamefully could be concealed, lust for praise and fear of ignominy drove both sides to *virtus*" (*G* 7.80, *laudis cupiditas et timor ignominiae ad virtutem excitabant;* cf. Hirt. *BG* 8.42; Xen. *Hell.* 7.1.30). The display of *virtus* over time earns a reputation, a reputation of which soldiers are fiercely protective. Attacked by surprise by Germans, Caesar's green legionaries fall apart. Not so their centurions. Promoted to their positions because of their *virtus*, they die fighting bravely, "lest they lose the renown for military accomplishment which they had won in the past" (*G* 6.40, *rei militaris laudem;* cf. *C* 3.28, 3.101; Thuc. 2.11.2; Xen. *Hell.* 7.5.16; Polyb. 15.11.12). At the siege of Avaricum, Caesar tells his soldiers that he will withdraw if the scarcity of food becomes too severe. "All of them begged him not to: they had served many years under his command without incurring any disgrace (*ignominia*), never abandoning anything unachieved. And they would deem it a disgrace if they gave up a siege they had begun" (*G* 7.17). Having established a standard of conduct by their previous performance, soldiers cannot bear to imagine what the world will think of them if they fall away from it (cf. *B.Alex.* 16). Caesar notes with approval that, when starving, his soldiers "say nothing unworthy of the majesty of the Roman people and their own previous victories" (*G* 7.17; cf. 5.35).

Warfare is a contest of masculinity. If an individual like the Pompeian Antistius Turpio jeers that no Caesarian is equal to him, a Caesarian, Q. Pompeius Niger, will accept his challenge to single combat (*B.Hisp.* 25).[85] So similarly for a commander to offer battle—frequently by coming out of camp or down from a hill to a space where battle will occur on equal terms—is a challenge to the masculinity of the enemy commander and his army.

> Sabinus kept himself in camp. . . . Viridovix camped against him two miles away and every day led out his forces to give him the opportunity to fight, so that Sabinus not only fell into contempt among the enemy, but even was somewhat jeered at by our own soldiers.
>
> (*G* 3.17; cf. *C* 3.37; Livy 3.60.8; Thuc. 8.27)

To fail to respond to challenges to masculinity of this type is to fall into contempt, to surrender before the watching world one's claim to be a man. Just like a brawler picking a fight thrusts his intended foe back with light nudges, so the challenging army moves closer and closer (*C* 3.84; cf. *B.Afr.* 30-32). If those in camp do not come out, their humiliation is redoubled by the jeers of their enemies (*G* 5.58, *magna cum contumelia verborum;* cf. *B.Afr.* 31; Plut. *Marius* 16.3; Front. *Strat.* 1.11.1).[86] "The foe mocks us with every kind of insult (*omnibus contumeliis*), just as if we were women hiding behind the rampart," says a centurion in Livy (7.13.6), drawing an explicit connection between keeping in camp, enemy mockery, and deficiency in masculinity. And so generals do come out, even against their better judgment.

> Every day thereafter [Caesar] drew up his army in line of battle on a flat/fair place (*aequum locum*), in case Pompey should desire to fight a battle. He brought up his legions almost to Pompey's camp, so that his first line was only so far from the rampart that it could not be hit by a bolt from an artillery piece. Pompey, in order to maintain his fame and repute in the eyes of men (*famam opinionemque hominum teneret*), deployed his army in front of his camp so that the third line abutted the rampart, and so that the whole drawn-up formation could be protected by missiles cast from the rampart.
>
> (*C* 3.55; cf. 1.82; Tac. *Ann.* 3.20)

Pompey comes out as little as his concern for his reputation for *virtus* will allow him to. At Ruspina, Caesar (badly outnumbered and leading inexperienced troops) did not take the field against the taunting Scipio. His continuator felt he had to explain away this passivity: it is not that Caesar was not confident of victory (he asserts loyally), but that Caesar felt his reputation demanded *big* victories (*B.Afr.* 31). The continuator's evident discomfort reflects the strength of the expectation that under the code of *virtus* challenges to battle had to be met.

The fierce competition for primacy in masculinity makes soldiers yearn to expunge any taint. The besieged Massilians, having sued for a truce, take up arms again and surprise the Caesarian soldiers, burning their siegeworks. But Caesar's men erect replacements in record time, "for it grieved them that with the truce broken by a crime their *virtus* would be a subject of ridicule" (*C* 2.15, *suam virt-*

utem irrisui fore). By resisting at all, the Massilians had shown contempt (*contemptione sui*) for Caesar's legions, and this was one of the reasons that a massacre was to be expected if the town fell (*C* 2.13). "For them to go on boasting so long in our sight is very disgraceful and painful for us," growls a Rhodian ship-captain (but no feeble Greek—"to be compared to our men rather than the Greeks in greatness of spirit and *virtus*") in one of Caesar's continuators; "leave it in our hands, we'll keep up our side" (*B.Alex.* 15; cf. Front. *Strat.* 1.11.1).

In the wake of a lost battle soldiers are overwhelmed with a desire to try their luck again "to repair the disgrace" (*C* 3.74; cf. Xen. *Hell.* 6.4.14) with *virtus* (*C* 3.73) or to depart from the scene of their shame (*C* 3.24; cf. 3.100; Hirt. *BG* 8.13). In battle itself, flight (*C* 3.24; cf. *B.Afr.* 66, 75; Xen. *Hell.* 1.6.32; Polyb. 5.96.3), or the loss of a standard (*G* 4.25, *C* 3.64) or ships (*C* 3.100; cf. *B.Alex.* 11), is conceived as a disgrace. Since retreating is shameful (*C* 1.44) a commander might order a retreat to proceed "as honorably as possible" (*B.Afr.* 31, *quam honestissime;* cf. Xen. *Hell.* 7.4.13). At the Sambre the cavalry, having recovered their nerve, fight bravely "to wipe out the disgrace of their flight with *virtus*" (*G* 2.27, *turpitudinem fugae virtute delerent*). An enemy's advance in battle can be conceived of as insolent (*insolenter, C* 3.46; cf. *B.Alex.* 8, 27; Xen. *Hell.* 5.3.3), which drives their opponents to counter-attack. They charge unwisely into a *locus iniquus* (*C* 1.45). After battle both sides total up their claims to *virtus,* to establish who is best. After Ilerda,

> each side thought it had parted as superior. Afranius' men based their claim on the fact that, although they were by general consent thought inferior, they had held their ground for so long in hand-to-hand combat, resisted our men's *impetus,* that at the beginning they captured the place and hill which was the cause of the fighting and at the first clash made our men turn their backs in flight. Our men grounded their claim on the fact that they had sustained a battle for five hours in a *locus iniquus* and outnumbered, that they had ascended the hill with drawn swords and put their adversaries (who were fighting from a higher position) to flight and driven them into the town.
>
> (*C* 1.47)

The more difficult and challenging the circumstances in which they fought, the greater the soldiers' claim to *virtus.* In Caesar's continuators booty stands witness to such claims (*B.Alex.* 42), as do grisly trophies like the severed heads of enemies, insignia of *virtus* when impaled on sword points, and set to regard a besieged town (*B.Hisp.* 32).[87]

The code of *virtus* was not a strange archaic element of soldierly motivation, merely to be understood and accommodated by sophisticated commanders: *virtus* was a day-to-day practical concern of Caesar as general. One of the first duties of generalship is to establish the relative *virtus* of his army, and that of the enemy, for it is a factor in deciding whether he should offer battle (*G* 2.8, 3.24, *C*

2.16, 3.24). He knows from experience that the units of his own army have different *virtus* (*G* 1.40; cf. Hirt. *BG* 8.8), and each of the mass of tribes in Gaul has a particular martial reputation (*opinio virtutis, G* 7.59, 7.83; *gloria belli, G* 1.2), which can be found out by asking other Gauls (*G* 2.15). But such reputations are hardly infallible (*G* 2.24), and some—like that of Ariovistus' Germans, who so terrified Caesar's officers—were highly inflated. So Caesar also reckons *virtus* by logic, on the basis of Roman experience. "Is it of your own *virtus* or my zeal that you despair?" Caesar asks his panicked officers before marching against the Germans, and then proceeds to mobilize historical arguments to prove the Romans' superiority in *virtus:* Marius' army beat Germans—the Cimbri and Teutones—in the past; the Romans defeated the forces of Spartacus (many of them of German origin, we are expected to know); his own army beat the Helvetii, who had regularly defeated the Germans in their turn. True, Ariovistus' Germans had established an ascendancy over other Gauls, but they had taken them by surprise, "defeated them more by planning and craft than by *virtus*" (*magis ratione et consilio quam virtute vicisse, G* 1.40). Finally, if inquiry and logic fail to reveal the relative *virtus* of Romans and tribesmen, experiment is resorted to:

> Caesar at first decided to abstain from battle because of the multitude of the enemy and their reputation for *virtus* (*opinionem virtutis*). But by cavalry skirmishes every day he tried out what the enemy could accomplish by *virtus* and what our men could dare. When he had come to understand that ours were not inferior he chose a place in front of his camp opportune and suitable for drawing up a line of battle.
>
> (*G* 2.8; cf. 7.36)

All possible measures, in short, are undertaken to form an estimate of the *virtus* of the enemy.

When the relative *virtus* of friend and foe have been assessed, and the decision to join battle has been made, the general does what he can to call upon the *virtus* of his troops. The unchanging martial quality of his soldiers, *virtus* cannot be whipped up like *animus,* the volatile morale of the moment (cf. Sal. *Cat.* 58.1-2; *Jug.* 85.50). In his speech before battle the general urges upon his troops "to remember their *virtus* in the past (*suae pristinae virtutis*) and their very successful battles" (*G* 7.62; cf. 2.21; Sal. *Cat.* 58.12). That is, he reminds them of the reputation they have earned, so that they will strive harder not to lose it. With this done, the general's main duty (viewed from a *virtus* point of view) is to watch the battle—for *virtus* is public excellence, and is brought to the fore by an audience (*G* 7.80).[88] Thus in the Romans' sea battle against the Veneti of Brittany, once Roman machinery had mangled the rigging of the Gauls' prodigious sailing ships, "the rest of the contest lay in *virtus;* in which our soldiers easily excelled, the more so since the e events transpired in sight of Caesar and the whole army, so that no deed braver than others could lie hidden" (*G* 3.14; cf. Polyb. 2.69.4). For the same reason, before the battle with Ariovistus, Caesar "placed each of his legates and his quaestor in charge of an individual legion, so that each man might have them as witnesses to his *virtus*" (*G* 1.52; cf. Diod. 19.83.5). When Caesar is not present at a battle, his lieutenants urge his soldiers to imagine that he was there, watching them. "Display under my command that same *virtus* that you have so often shown to our *imperator,* and imagine that he is present and watching with his own eyes" (*G* 6.8; cf. 7.62).

In Caesar's universe, the *virtus* outlook is shared by his army and by his enemies. Foes display predictable *virtus* behavior, which can be ruthlessly exploited by the cunning stratagem-minded general. Indeed, the unresolved contradiction between Caesar's conceptions of the role of *virtus* and stratagem in warfare yawns widest when he proudly reports stratagems which take advantage of his opponents' preoccupation with *virtus*. Outnumbered by the Treveri across a deep river from his camp, and fearing an accession to them of German reinforcements, Labienus pretends terror and orders his camp struck amidst noise and confusion so that his departure will resemble flight. "It was intolerable to their [the Treveri's] dignity (*dignitas*) if they did not dare to attack with such great forces so small a force, especially when fleeing and encumbered. And they did not hesitate to cross the river and commit to battle in a *locus iniquus*" (*G* 6.8). Naturally Labienus thrashes them.

To take advantage of the enemy's *virtus* outlook does not always require such guile. Having decided that the *virtus* of the Belgae is not invincible, Caesar draws up his army to offer them battle, but only if they are willing to fight in an appalling *locus iniquus*. To get to him the Gauls will have to cross a marsh and advance up a hill against a Roman army with its flanks protected by entrenchments (*G* 2.8-9). Why does Caesar think they might attack nonetheless despite the disadvantages? What Caesar expects is that the Belgae will react just as his own soldiers did when facing Vercingetorix's host occupying a hill behind a swamp, when to attack them would have been to fight in a similar *locus iniquus*.

> Whoever saw how close they were together might have thought them prepared to fight a battle on equal terms (*aequo Marte*), but whoever considered the inequality of the situation realized that this was a display of empty pretense. The soldiers of Caesar considered it an offense to their dignity (*indignantes*) that the enemy could endure the sight of them with such a small space in between, and begged for the signal for battle.
>
>   (*G* 7.19; cf. *B.Alex.* 29)

Naturally Caesar refuses to give the signal, refusing to sacrifice the men that an assault on such unequal conditions would require. But, as Caesar tells it, the Gauls nevertheless claimed this as indicative of their superiority in *virtus,* with Vercingetorix crowing that "this enables them to despise the *virtus* of those who did not dare to engage and shamefully retreated to their camp" (*G* 7.20). Thus Caesar had every reason to think that a people with an *opinio virtutis* like that of the Belgae would find the challenge of battle irresistible, and contemplation of their

humiliation from failing to attack intolerable to their pride. Indeed, to the *virtus*-minded warrior, a *locus iniquus* might appear to make an attack more attractive, not less. For the worse the circumstances, the greater the display of *virtus*. At the siege of the stronghold of the Aduatuci the Gauls make a desperate night attack on the Roman siegeworks. "The enemy fought fiercely (*acriter*), as was meet (*debuit*) for brave men (*viris fortibus*) in the last extremity of hope fighting in a *locus iniquus* against men who threw missiles from rampart and towers, when all hope of safety was lodged in *virtus* alone" (*G* 2.33). It is the very difficulty of the situation, including the impossible lay of the ground, that demands the exercise of *virtus,* and that allows its display. It is the fact of their attack uphill in a restricted space, their fighting in a *locus iniquus,* that gives Caesar's soldiers the right to claim that they came off better in *virtus* at Ilerda (*C* 1.47, and see above). To the soldier bent on displaying *virtus* the terrain of the battlefield looks exactly like that of the battlefield of the tactical general—the slopes which help missiles fall heavy and true, the sucking swamps, the impeding rivers—but its significance is inverted. The more the tactical general would shy away from a *locus iniquus,* the more the soldier eager to display *virtus* yearns to assail it. For conceived in terms of *virtus* landscape takes on a memorial function. Caesar arrives at the camp where Q. Cicero was besieged. "He marveled at the towers erected, the mantlets, and the fortifications of the enemy"; only one Roman in ten is unwounded. "From all these things he judged how great the danger was and with how great *virtus* the affair had been carried on" (*G* 5.52). Or, alarmingly, the Helvetian Divico warns Caesar, "do not let this place, where they were meeting, take a famous name from or perpetuate the memory of a disaster of the Roman people and the destruction of an army" (*G* 1.13; cf. *B.Alex.* 72). Do not, he is saying, let the place become a monument to our *virtus* at your expense.

Greek battle descriptions were filled with accounts of the brave deeds of individuals and groups. Many of the roles bravery plays in Caesar's battles can be paralleled in scattered references in Greek authors. To a historian near the mainstream of Hellenistic history-writing, like Diodorus Siculus, the pivotal role of courage in battle was an easy assumption. But bravery fell uneasily into the categories in which Greek military experts—like Xenophon and Polybius—thought about how battles were won, and despite a strain of Greek political thinking which sought the origins of high bravery in civic customs and institutions (esp. Xen. *Lac. Pol.;* Polyb. 6.52-55; cf. Arist. *NE* 3.8 [=1116a-b]), the Greek military tradition never entirely succeeded in integrating courage into its conception of battle.

Wistful Greek longing for an honest day before the triumph of stratagem (Polyb. 13.3.2-3)[89] re-echoed thunderously at Rome. For there, reliance on stratagem—although old and respectable—crashed into a powerful contemporary sentiment that proper battles were won by *virtus* and that victory was greater in proportion to how out-generaled the Romans had been. In his failure to reconcile his reliance on stratagem with his conception of the importance of *vir-*

tus, Caesar simply reproduces the wider conflict of his society. But the conflict betrays the fact that bravery was much more central to the Roman conception of battle than it was in Greek theory, and Caesar fully integrates *virtus* into his battle descriptions. To Caesar bravery is not just something to be admired in passing, or a convenient generalizing short-hand; it is not decoration or *deus ex machina.* It is an essential—potentially decisive—cog in the mechanics of battle, important from minute to minute as a motivation of the troops and commanders, and carefully thought about by generals, who use it as the basis of stratagems. Like tactics and *animus, virtus* imposes its own significance upon the topography of the battlefield. It is in his understanding of the workings of bravery that Caesar reaches furthest beyond the Greek military tradition.

To a student of *Tendenz* in Caesar the marshal's attention to the bravery of his soldiers smacks of being a political project: it was upon the loyalty of his soldiers, after all, that Caesar's political predominance rested. Yet a Polybian treatment of bravery in battle—praising it in passing in the course of battle descriptions which hinge on other factors—would have been perfectly adequate for any strictly political end. Caesar may well use his understanding of *virtus* for devious purposes, to make himself and his army appear in a good light, to deflect attention from his mistakes, to deceive his reader. But he can do so because he and his prospective Roman reader share a pre-existing expectation that sheer courage is an important factor at every stage of battle. That shared expectation—an aspect of Roman culture—ramifies into Caesar's understanding of *virtus* on the battlefield. Caesar departs from the Greek understanding of courage not because he is Caesar the politician, but because he is Caesar the Roman.

VI. READING CAESAR'S BATTLE DESCRIPTIONS

Greek historians, heavily influenced by a tactical conception of combat, usually used that model as the structuring armature of their accounts of battles: the formation, deployment, and movement of forces tend to form the backbone of the narrative, with other material—stratagems, the brave deeds of individuals, remarkable occurrences like panics, paradoxes, and touching stories—included intermittently along the way. Caesar has similar descriptions—Alesia is conceived in this way—but he struggles against the domination of tactical schemata, and strives to give *animus* and *virtus* their proper prominence as well. Thus, as is true of Caesar's description of Pharsalus, the building blocks of his battle descriptions tend to be segments of narrative hanging upon all three of these themes; his depictions therefore often lack the firm tactical girdering of so many of Polybius' battles. This shifting of the camera between these different points of view, combined with the rushing speed of Caesar's narrative, produces accounts of battle that are highly artistic and impressionistic, series of self-contained vignettes, rapid slide-shows rather than movies, where the causal relationship between vignettes is often implied rather than stated.[90]

Caesar's conception of the relationship between tactics, *animus,* and *virtus* is fundamentally paratactic. To Caesar, these factors ideally combine to produce victory. This is nowhere more evident, and Caesar's method of describing a battle is nowhere more vividly displayed, than in his highly elaborated account of the battle of the Sambre against the Nervii.[91] Caesar begins with a description of the battlefield. The Roman route of approach, we learn first, was hampered by the formidable hedges characteristic of the country of the Nervii (*G* 2.17).

> This was the nature of the place which our men chose for the camp: a hill sloped down to the edge of the River Sabis . . . the angle of the slope consistent from the summit. Opposite and over against it a hill of equal slope arose from the river, the lower part open for two hundred paces, the upper part wooded, so that it could not easily be seen into. In those woods the enemy held themselves in hiding; next to the river on the open ground a few posts of cavalry were to be seen. The river was about three feet in depth.
>
> (*G* 2.18)

The opening of the battle is conceived primarily in tactical terms, and the tactical significance of each of the topographical details Caesar has provided quickly becomes evident. Caesar's cavalry and light troops cross the river and attack the enemy horse, but the trees on the enemy hill limit their pursuit to the open hillside and permit the enemy infantry, already in formation, to attack the whole Roman army simultaneously at the moment the first of the Roman baggage crests the hill. Now Caesar emphasizes the twin tactical themes of the speed of the enemy and the disorder of the Romans. "Suddenly they flew forth with all their forces and made an *impetus* upon our cavalry. Having easily repulsed and disordered (*pulsis ac proturbatis*) these they ran down to the river with incredible quickness, so that almost at the same moment the foe were seen at the tree line, in the river, at close quarters. And with the same speed they hastened up hill at our camp and those busy entrenching it" (*G* 2.19). Caesar, assisted by his legates and the experience of the troops, tries to create order out of chaos, but there is great confusion (*G* 2.20-21). The "nature of the ground and the slope of the hill" (which we learned about in the description of the field), as well as the speed of the enemy attack, divide the legions, which fight independently. The hedges (also previously advertised) block the view to the front and make it hard to deploy reinforcements and command the various elements of the Roman army. The situation is critical (*G* 2.22, *in tanta rerum iniquitate*).

Events now occur simultaneously at various places on the battlefield, and Caesar must put aside his roughly chronological narrative structure for a topographical one. He begins on the left, where the Ninth and Tenth Legions take advantage of the higher ground to drive back the exhausted and wounded Atrebates into the river, slaughter them while they are *impediti* in the water, and pursue them up the opposite hill (*in locum iniquum*). Caesar's eyes then sweep to the center where the Eleventh and Eighth Legions similarly advance downhill to the edge of the water, driving those opposed to them before them. But in so doing the legions uncover the flank of the Twelfth and Seventh Legions on the right (to which Caesar now directs his attention) and break a hole in the Roman line, uncovering the Roman camp. Packed in close formation the Nervii exploit this hole, occupy the Roman camp, and take the Twelfth and Seventh Legions in the flank (*G* 2.23).

Now suddenly the focus, and the significance of the description of the battlefield, shifts from tactics—order and disorder, charges down hills, formations—to *animus*. Since the Roman camp was on the crest of a hill, those in it could see and be seen by all. Observing the Romans advancing across the river in victory, the Roman camp-servants (the *calones,* a stern and pragmatic body of men, expected to defend the camp in a crisis) left the camp to plunder. When the Nervii became visible in the denuded camp they inspired desperate panic in the camp-servants, the retreating auxiliaries, and in the baggage train. A great snowballing terror seizes all except the legionaries (*G* 2.24). But suddenly the fortunes of battle turn. Caesar's focus now shifts back to the right wing where his personal intervention delivers from fear, and firms up the *animi* of, the Twelfth and Seventh Legions (*G* 2.25-26). When Caesar arrived at the Twelfth the legion had taken heavy casualties among its centurions, and lost a standard. Caesar saw that the situation was at a crisis—but diagnosed the crisis as one of spirit. "The rest of the men were becoming slower, and some from the rearmost ranks were deserting the battle, retiring to avoid the missiles." The men were closely packed together, hampering each other's fighting, and had gathered all the standards in a mass. We know from elsewhere (*C* 1.71; Hirt. *BG* 8.18) that these were well-understood signs of fear. Caesar's solution was to seize a shield and plunge into the front line, shouting encouragement to the troops. "His arrival inspired hope in the soldiers and revived their *animus*. Each man, even in extremity, wanted of his own accord to do his duty under the eyes of the *imperator*. The *impetus* of the enemy was slowed a bit."

The Gauls were still lapping around the edges of the legions, and so Caesar ordered the Seventh, neighbor to the Twelfth, to wheel behind the Twelfth Legion and stand back to back with it. "This done, each bore aid to the other, and not fearing that they would be surrounded by the enemy from the rear, they began to resist more bravely and fight more strongly." Again the danger Caesar diagnosed in encirclement was psychological, and he ordered a maneuver to bring psychological relief.

Meanwhile the two legions guarding the baggage crest the hill and come into sight, and from the opposite hill Titus Labienus, having taken the Gallic camp, and seeing what was going on from his own high ground, sends the Tenth Legion back to assist. This effects a revolution in the morale of the Roman forces. "Even our men who were lying down worn out by wounds renewed the fight propped on their shields; the camp-servants, seeing the enemy terrified (*perterritos*), attacked the armed foe even unarmed; and the cavalry fought at all points in rivalry with the legionaries, in order to obliterate the disgrace of their flight by *virtus*" (*G* 2.27).

And so to close the battle the focus—and with it the significance of the terrain—shifts once again, this time from *animus* to *virtus*. The reader already knows that the Nervii are men of outstanding *virtus*: shortly before he begins his account of the battle Caesar drives this point home by mentioning their scorn for civilized luxuries and their contempt for those who had surrendered to the Romans and thereby "cast away their ancestral *virtus*" (*G* 2.15). Now Caesar turns from the revival of the *animus* of the Romans to describe the last stand of the Nervii.

> The enemy, even with hope of safety gone, showed so great a *virtus,* that when the first rank fell, those behind them stood upon their lying bodies and fought from them, and when they fell, and the corpses were piled up, those who survived threw missiles at us and threw back our javelins as if from a mound. It is not without reason, therefore, that they must be judged to have been men of gigantic *virtus,* since they dared to cross a wide river, climb high banks, and ascend a *locus iniquus*. Greatness of soul (*magnitudo animi* [=*virtus*]) made the most difficult tasks easy.
>
> (*G* 2.27)

Such is Caesar's epitaph upon the Roman victory "which brought the race and name of the Nervii nearly to utter extermination" (*G* 2.28). The landscape, important at the beginning of the account to understanding the physics of the battle, then to the see-sawing morale of the sides, finally becomes a monument to the *virtus* of the Nervii.

Caesar's account takes the reader directly from the revival of the spirits of the Romans to the heroic last stand of the Nervii. But when exactly did the Nervii lose the battle so as to require a last stand? Where, indeed, was the last stand? Against which Roman units? The latest indication had the Nervii in the Roman camp, but if they were defending the camp (as Cassius Dio [39.3.2] interpreted Caesar's account) they would hardly need to fight on a mound of their own dead. Where too are the Eleventh and Eighth Legions, which pushed their way to the river? Combatants in the part of the battle described tactically, they simply vanish when Caesar's attention turns to *animus*. Such questions torment military historians trying to reconstruct the tactical progress of Caesar's battles. But so strictly tactical—so Polybian—a conception of battle is what Caesar is trying to avoid, because it would paint a false picture of the events. By describing the battle as he does, Caesar is trying to convey the deeper truth that there came a point in the battle where the location of troops—conceived tactically—was no longer very important; that suddenly what mattered was who could see what from where, and the psychological consequences of it. Then, as topographical indicators fall away altogether from his account, Caesar wants his reader to understand that what is important now is the action of *virtus* upon *virtus;* now he uses the terrain to illustrate that point. The story Caesar is telling is not just that of military movements, blunders, flank attacks, tactics. The story Caesar *is* telling is signaled early in the battle by his exhortation to his troops "that they should maintain a memory of their ancient *virtus,* that they should not be perturbed in *animus,* and that they should bravely sustain the *impetus* of the enemies (*impetum fortiter sustinerent*)" (*G* 2.21; cf. 3.19). To Caesar tactics (*impetus*), *animus,* and *virtus* share the battle equally, and by dividing the battle description into tactical, *animus,* and *virtus* segments, the very structure of the Roman general's account elegantly reflects that fact. To Caesar the best victory is victory in tactics, *animus,* and *virtus* all at once.

If Caesar's description of the battle of the Sambre illustrates his distance from the Greek tradition, his depiction of Pharsalus shows his proximity to it. Caesar explicitly describes Pharsalus as a tactical victory, and the diversions to tell the tale of the *virtus* of Crastinus, not clearly related to the outcome of the battle, would be at home in a Greek narrative. The main problem the narrative presents is the attention Caesar gives to *animus,* culminating in his denunciation of Pompey for his failure to understand the psychology of the charge. This passage interrupts the movement towards a tactical victory, but after it the battle description proceeds to its tactical conclusion. *Animus* is exalted, and then abandoned.

Perhaps Caesar's discussion of *animus* has a political motive, as discreditable to Pompey. But Caesar was also tempted to turn aside from his tactical narrative to comment on military psychology for intellectual reasons. For Caesar's tactical victory at Pharsalus placed him in the ironic danger of becoming a prominent *exemplum* for a view of generalship he did not share. The natural lesson of Pharsalus was that what matters most in battle is tactics and deployment. That is certainly the lesson Frontinus took away from the battle (*Strat.* 2.3.22), offering up Caesar's deployment to be admired and emulated. But Caesar was not prepared to become the hollow-cheeked poster-child of that narrow doctrine. Caesar was a general who took Xenophon's view of battle: to Caesar psychology was as important as tactics. The importance of considering the psychological consequences of one's orders was a polemical point which Caesar intended to make regardless of whether it confused the narrative of the battle.

And confuse the narrative it did: Caesar's criticism of Pompey had singular consequences for later Greek descriptions of the battle of Pharsalus. The criticism attracted notice: given Caesar's emphasis upon it, Pompey's failure cried out to be an important factor in his defeat. But Caesar had not made this connection, so those who followed him would have to do so themselves. Appian—who specifically mentions that he had read Caesar's account (*BC* 2.79)—tries to bridge the logical gap between Caesar's reproach of Pompey and the tactical conclusion to the battle. In his version Caesar's fourth line drives away Pompey's cavalry, thus uncovering the flank of Pompey's

legions. Next Appian elaborates Caesar's criticism of Pompey for not letting his legionaries charge, and the bad consequences of such a policy. "And so it fell out on that occasion," Appian writes, when the Tenth Legion, inspired by being allowed to charge, took Pompey's legions, deflated by their immobility and with flank uncovered, from the flank. This threw them into confusion, routed them, "and began the victory" (*BC* 2.79). The charge of the inspired Tenth Legion against the Pompeians' uncovered flank elegantly connects the morale of the charge to Caesar's eventual victory. But the flank charge of the Tenth is an event of which neither Caesar—in whom the fourth line makes the attack on flank and rear—nor any other surviving author knows. Appian has had to go a long way from Caesar's narrative to make sense of it.

Even stranger than Appian's reconciliation of Caesar's tactical and *animus* themes is the tradition that takes center stage in Plutarch's account. Here again the intervention of Caesar's fourth line is decisive. Its attack on Pompey's cavalry turns them to flight, and their flight "destroys everything" (*Caes.* 45.1-5). But Pompey's cavalry flee because of a psychological stratagem of Caesar's: according to this well-attested tale Caesar had told the legionaries facing the cavalry not to throw their javelins, but to thrust them into the faces of the young and beautiful cavalrymen, who would flee rather than face disfigurement (*Caes.* 45.2-3, *Pomp.* 69.3, 71.4-5; cf. Appian *BC* 2.76, 2.78; [Front.] *Strat.* 4.7.32; Polyaenus 8.23.25). The exact origin of this odd story can hardly be known: perhaps it arises from some dismissive remark Caesar actually made about Pompey's cavalry, reported in an independent tradition. But the elevation of the tale to the battle's decisive psychological stratagem may well be another solution to Appian's *aporia:* having read Caesar's passionate defense of psychological generalship in his criticism of Pompey—as Plutarch, for one, had (*Caes.* 44.8, *Pomp.* 69.5)—the reader looks around for a clear psychological decision to the battle, and what Caesar failed to supply, ingenuity did.

It was Julius Caesar who, by turning aside from his narrative to enter a Greek theoretical controversy, introduced psychology into the deepest stratum of the tradition of describing the battle of Pharsalus. The striking quality of this detour caused his narrative to be thoroughly misunderstood by Greek authors who came to describe the battle after him. Caesar's editorial comment prevailed over his tactical narrative: in the Greek tradition Pharsalus was remembered as a psychological victory. Appian refers to tactical thinkers who defended Pompey's plan on tactical grounds (*BC* 2.79). But in the face of that knowledge Appian preferred to follow—and try to repair—what he took to be Caesar's account. As a recorder of events Caesar failed, if success be defined as imposing his version on future generations. But as a military thinker in the Greek tradition who advocated a controversial point of view about the importance of psychology in battle, he won his point with posterity.

VII. Conclusion

$$dN^a/dt = -N^{ddPd}(r)$$

Model of Infantry Attack on Well Defended Position[92]

From the fifth century BC there can be detected in descriptions of battles in the Greek historians a substratum of shared assumptions about the factors that were decisive in combat. Soon those shared assumptions were elaborated into a tradition of written theory that stressed above all the importance of tactics—formation and deployment—and also the use of cunning stratagems to confound the enemy. Historical battle descriptions influenced by this tradition carefully described the tactics and stratagems of both sides and traced their consequences through to the outcome of the battle. The domination of this theory over Greek battle descriptions was, however, never complete. Other currents, artistic and rhetorical, were always influential, and authors near the mainstream of Hellenistic history writing often strove for extreme emotional effects, describing, for example, the expressions on the faces of severed heads (Diod. 17.58.5). Even sober authors close to the military tradition—Thucydides, himself a general, and Polybius, the author of a treatise on tactics—were not immune. The *locus classicus* of rhetorical battle description is Thucydides' much-imitated account of the climactic battle in the harbor at Syracuse (7.60-72), with its splendid paired speeches of encouragement, its pathetic depiction of the terrors of those watching the battle from the shore, and its absolute failure to reveal why the Syracusans won. Polybius' account of the battle of Chios (16.2-7), with only the sketchiest indication of the deployment, a mass of strange paradoxes, and much about the great deeds of the contending kings, can rank as a characteristically tumid Hellenistic effort (cf. 3.84.8-10, 5.48.9, 16.30-34).[93]

Julius Caesar was a participant in this lively tradition of Greek battle description. In his account of the battle of Tauroeis (*C* 2.4), the Massilians pathetically besiege their temples to implore the gods for victory, their desperation suspiciously similar to that of the watchers on the shore at Thucydides' Syracuse; and the Massilians' wailing when they hear of their loss (*C* 2.7) may nod at that of the Athenians in Xenophon hearing of the disaster at Aegospotami (*Hell.* 2.2.3-4).[94] But Caesar was not an uncritical heir to any part of this legacy. The core of the Greek tradition was a physical theory of battle elaborated from centuries of experience with the phalanx. This theory insensibly downplayed the significance of other factors in battle, with the paradoxical consequence that bravery was more prominent in the battle descriptions of less well-informed Greek historians (like Diodorus and some of his sources) than in those of military experts (like Xenophon and Polybius). Caesar's Roman background was less dismissive of courage than Greek military theory was. Greek interest in stratagem—the second great stream of Greek military thinking—offered an *entrée* for other factors, like military psychology, into Greek thinking about battle. But it could also restrict that thinking, and always threatened to reduce military psychology to a special case,

only occasionally important. Caesar allied himself with Greek military thinkers who gave psychology pride of place when thinking about battle: Caesar's command of Roman armies made him deem the management of morale (although conceived somewhat differently than by the Greeks) as important as tactics, evidently a polemical position given the stress he places upon it. Finally, Caesar's (or his lost Latin predecessors') experience of battle encouraged him to elaborate a tactical theory from the crash of the legionary charge, rather than the weighty push of the phalanx, and elaborate a psychological theory which incorporated the Roman military ethos of steadiness. Caesar, in short, adapts a Greek model of tactics, chooses (and adapts) a Greek position on psychology, and rejects the Greek dismissal of bravery. Caesar's conception of the mechanics of battle is a mixture of Greek and Roman, an adaptation rather than outright translation of Greek concepts, closer in spirit to the use of Greek models by Plautus than by Terence. Greek theory yields to Roman reality and Roman cultural expectations.

To the cultural historian, it is Caesar's split with the Greeks on the subject of bravery that stands out. Wondering about the significance of gladiatorial combat to Roman identity, Thomas Wiedemann points to the gladiator as the personification of the fundamental Roman value of *virtus*.[95] But as well as admiring *virtus* from their seats, many Romans of Caesar's day lived according to its stern code. Caesar's full integration of *virtus* into the mechanics of battle shows that *virtus* was not merely an adornment to please readers with a purely literary taste for Roman pluck, and not just a mechanism for flattering his soldiers. *Virtus* was a real part of the motivation of Roman soldiers and their élite officers. So Caesar's treatment of *virtus,* and its ramifications, helps us understand Roman behavior in arenas other than the battlefield. Roman competitiveness, stiff-necked pride, and vengefulness—the offspring of *virtus*—are evident both in the Roman forum and in the forum of Roman foreign relations.

The differences between Caesar's and Greek conceptions of how battles work, moreover, and the differences among Greek authors as well, let us look back at all ancient battle descriptions with a wiser eye. Behind a Greek battle description involving pushing and weight there may indeed lie a bloody squash on an historical battlefield. But it will always be hard to know, since the Greek rhetoric of battle was rich with pushing metaphors and might impose them regardless of physical reality. In Polybius' Cynoscephalae tactics are decisive. But Polybius had decided that tactics were, in general, the decisive factor in battles long before he came to describe Cynoscephalae. Xenophon identified a tactical stratagem as decisive at Leuctra (*Hell.* 6.4.12-14), while Diodorus attributes the ultimate victory to . . . the bravery . . . of the Theban picked men (Diod. 15.56.2). No doubt Xenophon is right, but it is unsettling that he (like other Greek military experts) was inclined to exclude bravery from the results of battles long before he came to write about Leuctra. . . . All ancient battle descriptions, in short, reflect a series of decisions made beforehand—many of them highly controversial in their own time—about how battles worked, decisions which guided how battle was depicted. When reconstructing an ancient battle, the first necessity is to ascertain the set of conventions the sources are using, to find out what they may be predisposed to see, and to determine what they may be predisposed to ignore. The reconstruction of an ancient battle must be attended with a sense both of how ancient conventions of battle description channel ancient narrative, and with a humble sense of how modern conventions of battle description channel our own evaluation of that narrative.

For if it is hard to reconstruct Caesar's battles, that is because our conception of battle is more like that of a Greek tactical thinker—a Polybius—than a Caesar. Despite Clausewitz and Ardant du Picq, the tenor of modern conceptions of battle is ardently materialist. At the natural end of modern thinking lies the project of conceiving battle in terms of mathematical equations,[96] and such an understanding necessarily guides the eyes of the reporter on battle to what can be quantified. Even in less arid modern conceptions, the vertiginous psychology of soldiers in battle is sanitized and scientized as "morale," and modern students of war have even less use than the Greeks for Caesar's category of *virtus*, tending—as the Greeks sometimes did—to confound it with psychology.[97] To Polybius, or us, exact topography is an essential part of an historian's description of a battle conceived primarily in physical, geometrical terms. But Caesar's divergence from this Greek tradition liberated him from Greek expectations about topographical exactitude. To Caesar the movement of troops over terrain was not necessarily the most important aspect of battle, the description of those movements and that terrain not necessarily the most useful way of getting at the heart of what happened in battle. Caesar's understanding of warfare suggested to him alternative topographies—those that psychology and bravery inscribe upon the land. If we have difficulty finding Caesar's battlefields on modern maps it is because he saw battlefields differently than we do, and sometimes many battlefields where we see only one.

Finally, an understanding of the way Caesar understood battle presents historical questions. The excellence of the Roman army has traditionally been explained in terms of its organization, discipline, and professionalism, the army imagined in mechanical terms, as a thundering turbine agleam with oil or as a more perfect *Wehrmacht*. The Roman army of late Republic and Empire conquered as the only modern institution in a primitive, *ad hoc*, world.[98] Recently, Adrian Goldsworthy has argued that the Roman army's success must be viewed less in tactical, mechanical terms and more in psychological terms.[99] As usual, ancient history is behind the times: stress on psychological as well as organizational factors in the excellence of Hitler's *Wehrmacht* is years old.[100] Caesar might chuckle at our debate about the Romans, so similar to the Greek debate he was familiar with about the primacy of tactics or morale. Comparing Caesar's conception of battle to that of the Greeks does confirm the need for attention to morale, but

it is Caesar's theory of *virtus* that draws the eye as unfamiliar. Perhaps, then, an understanding of the excellence of the Roman army may require attention not only to Roman drill, not only to the wild psychology of the battlefield, but also to the abiding militarism of Roman culture, to the Roman ability to preserve in the camp and display on later battlefields the drunken atavistic bravery of Rome's early, terrible, centuries. If the Roman army excelled as the only modern institution in a savage world, could it be that it excelled also by preserving the culture of a savage tribe in an increasingly modern world? So too the victories of a great Roman marshal, of a Julius Caesar, may not find their full explanation in terms of strategy, tactics, or morale, but also in cultural terms, in deep habits of thought and structures of emotion. Caesar stands between cultures, or was a member of a culture which itself stood between. He looks with a native Roman gleam upon the fiery-eyed world of *virtus*, the world of primitive masculine competition which his soldiers and his enemies share. But at the same time he views that world distantly and dispassionately, as Polybius blandly regards the mechanical evolutions of troops. Perhaps Caesar's Greek education not only equipped him with intellectual means to understand tactics and morale, but encouraged him to devise his own means to understand *virtus* in the same systematic terms. Perhaps Caesar's conquest of barbarians in Gaul depended in part on his ability to fathom what was barbarous in his own army, and the barbarian in himself.

Notes

1. Tuplin 1986: 37.

2. Keegan 1976: 68.

3. Frankel and Smith 1978: 74.

4. Cf. Keegan 1976: 36 and Fussell 1975: 169-90.

5. On Caesar's later influence, references gathered by Loreto 1993[1990]: n. 6. See also Keegan 1976: 63-66.

6. Velleius Paterculus, Josephus, Arrian, and Ammianus Marcellinus are, of course, exceptions.

7. On Caesar's education and interests, conveniently, Zecchini 1990: 449-53.

8. *Vom Kriege* bk. 2 ch. 6.

9. *Vom Kriege* bk. 2 ch. 2. On Clausewitz and the tradition he was reacting against, Gat 1989.

10. For speculation on the didactic purpose of Caesar's work and esp. his battle descriptions, Rüpke 1992: 209; cf. Adcock 1956: 22-23 and Loreto 1993[1990]: 311, 333-35; and for the didactic purpose of another kind of *commentarii* (pontifical), Linderski 1985: 215-22.

11. See Polybius' strictures on his predecessors, Polyb. 12.17-22, 12.25[f], 16.18-20; and cf. Whatley 1964: 120-23.

12. As any writer describing a battle must, Keegan 1976: 36-46, and esp. 63 (of later European use of Caesar): "[b]attles are extremely confusing; and confronted with the need to make sense of something he does not understand, even the cleverest, indeed pre-eminently the cleverest man, realizing his need for a language and metaphor he does not possess, will turn to look at what someone else has made of a similar set of events to guide his own pen."

13. For speculations on Caesar's military reading, Loreto 1993[1990]: 243-44.

14. With a few exceptions (extended passages are Cato fr. 83 [Peter] = Aul. Gell. 3.7; Claudius Quadrigarius fr. 10b [Peter] = Aul. Gell. 9.13.6-19; fr. 12 [Peter; authorship uncertain] = Aul. Gell. 9.11; and see the parody in Plaut. *Amph.* 188-261). In writing *commentarii* (the genre is much discussed, Gesche 1976: 70 gathers references), Caesar was preceded by great men like M. Aemilius Scaurus and Sulla, whose works fail to survive. Livy describes many early battles, often drawing on Latin predecessors, but his style in such descriptions depends heavily on Caesar (Walsh 1961: 43), and so renders deduction about the pre-Caesarian Latin tradition problematic.

15. For the military tenor of aristocratic education during the Republic, Harris 1979: 14-15.

16. Thus for "Caesar" below it may often be necessary to read, "the lost Latin tradition that Caesar inherited." Some insight into that Latin tradition may be possible by triangulating between Caesar and his contemporaries, Sallust, Hirtius (=Hirt. *BG*), and the anonymous chroniclers of Caesar's Alexandrian (=*B.Alex.*), African (=*B.Afr.*), and Spanish wars (=*B.Hisp.*); but it is impossible to establish the independence from Caesarian influence of these battle descriptions written by Caesar's friends. Best, then, to use these works as *comparanda* only.

17. More generally on the late-Republican use of military handbooks, Campbell 1987: 21.

18. For the fragments of Cato's *de Re Militari* (on which see Astin 1978: 184-85, 204-205), Jordan 1860: 80-82. Note also the (inconclusive) attempts of Schenk 1930 to distill some Cato from Vegetius. Some have detected signs of other early Roman works: it has been suggested that Polybius' description of the Roman army (6.19-42) may draw upon a Roman handbook for military tribunes (Rawson 1971: 14-15) and that Val. Max. 2.3.2 may allude to a military handbook of the Marian period (Neumann 1956: col. 356).

19. As he was to many other Greek models: for Caesar's debt to the conventions of Hellenistic history writing, see Feller 1929 and Gärtner 1975: 63-134. For tragic motifs, Rowe 1967 and Mutschler 1975; and for his ethnography, references are gathered in Mensching 1988: 39.

20. Caesarian battles have called forth a vast topographical literature, dedicated to locating the battlefields and explaining the military movements of the armies engaged. Gesche 1976: 247-57, 269-73, 277-79, 286-87 gathers many references. To gauge the difficulties see (e.g.) Béquignon 1970: cols. 1073-74 for eight proposed locations for the battle of Pharsalus, or Pelling 1981: 754 for five candidates for the location of the defeat of Ariovistus. For other interpretations of Caesar's topographical vagueness, Rambaud 1966: 40-43, 63-64 (a result of the official reports Caesar drew upon in his writing); Rambaud 1954/1955: 347-50 (purposefully vague from *Tendenz*); Rambaud 1967: 193 (simplified for aesthetic reasons); Pelling 1981: 741-42 (simplified for an impatient Roman audience ignorant of topography); Rüpke 1992: 209 (simplified for didactic purposes). All may well be right.

21. On this battle description see Rasmussen 1963: 119-29, Gärtner 1975: 130-33, and Rambaud 1954/1955 (to be used with care).

22. E.g. Rambaud 1954/1955: 353 for Crastinus and Rambaud 1966: 356-57 for Pompey.

23. See Richter 1977: 96 n. 3 and Gesche 1976: 71-78 with 257-58 and 124-25 with 279-80 for catalogues of the vast literature. Most recently, see the papers collected in Welch and Powell 1998.

24. *RE* 8A/1: col. 234 s.v. Valerius nr. 365.

25. Cf. de Romilly 1956: 168-72.

26. Cf. Dillery 1995: 28-29.

27. On professors of tactics, and their lessons, Anderson 1970: 94-110, Wheeler 1983, and Whitehead 1990: 34-35.

28. Bauer 1893 and Wheeler 1983: nn. 30-31 collect references to Hellenistic theorists. And despite his late date Asclepiodotus did not stand at the end of the tradition. The Roman imperial tactical works of Aelian and Arrian draw heavily (although perhaps indirectly) upon Asclepiodotus' own source, probably Poseidonius (see Dain 1946: 26-40 and Stadter 1978: 118; but *contra* Wheeler 1978: n. 9), although they wrote at an even greater remove from the world of Hellenistic warfare that was a fading memory even in Asclepiodotus' day.

29. Some Greek philosophers—and the Peripatetics were especially interested in tactics—considered tactics a branch of mathematics, and treated it as such: see Wheeler 1988a: 179.

30. For thoughts on the relationship between Polybius' tactical work and his *Histories,* Sacks 1981: 125-32. Polybius' *Tactica* has also been proposed as the root source of the later Greek tactical manuals, Devine 1995.

31. Poznanski 1994: 33-34.

32. Cf. Eckstein 1995: 161-93 for the (164) "Polybian ideology of command in war as the imposition of order and control—upon oneself, upon others, upon battle."

33. Generally on the Greek vocabulary of battle, Pritchett 1985: 44-93.

34. Hanson 1989: 171-84 and Pritchett 1985: 65-68, who notes (29) that the push image can be traced back to Homer, and Homer will have influenced later accounts. How much *actual* pushing occurred in the usual hoplite battle is controversial (see the literature collected in Goldsworthy 1997), but irrelevant to this argument.

35. Pritchett 1985: 67-68.

36. Cf. Krentz 1985: 55-56.

37. See the lexicons, Merguet 1886, Menge and Preuss 1890, and Meusel 1887-93 s.v. *vis* for more references.

38. Many instances *infra,* and see the lexicons (*supra,* n. 37) s. v. *insto* and *premo.*

39. There is no direct evidence that Caesar had read Polybius, but see Loreto 1993[1990]: 243-44 for speculations on some Polybian echoes.

40. See the lexicons (*supra,* n. 37) s.v. *impetus.* Contrast the range of words—with various connotations—that Greeks used to describe the onset, Lindauer 1889: 10-11.

41. For a more general treatment of Caesar's conception of the physical space of his battlefields, Rambaud 1974.

42. Cf. Rambaud 1954/1955: 361.

43. The opposite, the *locus aequus,* is sometimes a fair field, where neither side has an advantage, *C* 1.41, but often where the enemy is in a *locus iniquus, G* 3.17, *C* 2.33-34. On the *locus iniquus* in Caesar cf. Loreto 1993[1990]: n. 203. By contrast the Greek tradition elaborated a doctrine of the position of advantage, . . . usually a higher position on a slope; see Pritchett 1985: 76-81.

44. Cf. Goldsworthy 1996: 207-208. Which is not to say that Romans did not sometimes fight in very close order, Wheeler 1979: 303-18.

45. For morale in the Roman army, see R. MacMullen 1984[1990], Goldsworthy 1996 *passim,* and Lee 1996.

46. The *Cyropaedia* is a didactic work posing as an historical account of the life of Cyrus: Due 1989: 10-12, Gera 1993: 2, and esp. for the similarity of military material in the *Cyropaedia* to Spartan practice, see Anderson 1970: 11-12, 43-44, 75-78, 84-85, 96-104, and 165-91.

47. Cf. Delatte 1933: 23-24.

48. Cf. Breitenbach 1967: 1722, 1732-37 and Anderson 1970: 96-110, 165-91.

49. Pan, Borgeaud 1988: 133-37; Artemis, Vernant 1991.

50. See Eckstein 1995: 168-71 for similar observations in Polybius.

51. On Greek conceptions of military panic, Wheeler 1988a: 172-81; see esp. Thuc. 7.80; Aeneas Tacticus 27; Polyaenus 1.2.

52. That Xenophon (an expert) discountenances the speech before battle is ample proof that such speeches were regularly given (*pace* Hansen 1993), whatever the historicity of the actual speeches which appear in the historians. For why criticize something that people did not do?

53. On Xenophon and stratagem, Wheeler 1988b: 11. See especially Xenophon's *Hipparchicus;* and cf. the contemporary work of Aeneas Tacticus (with Whitehead 1990: 36-37 on the similarity of his outlook to Xenophon's).

54. For the tradition see Lammert 1931, Wheeler 1988c, 1988b: 11-13, and for their importance, esp. Xen. *Cyr.* 1.6.27, 1.6.37-41, *Hell.* 5.1.4, 6.1.15; Polyb. 9.12.2.

55. Herodotus, Krentz 1997: 58-59; Thucydides, Heza 1974 and Krentz 1997: 57-58.

56. The *Strategica* of Polyaenus and the *Strategemata* of Frontinus. On both, conveniently, Wheeler 1988b: 12-13 and Campbell 1987: 14-16.

57. Emphasizing the contrast between tactics and stratagem in the Greek mind, Polybius depicts Aratus as a genius at stratagems but hopeless in pitched battles (4.8.3-5).

58. For the psychological dimension of stratagem, Wheeler 1988a: 174-76.

59. Wunderer 1905, Pédech 1964: 210-53, and Davidson 1991.

60. On the inculcation of fear in Polybius, Guelfucci 1986: 232-33.

61. For what it is worth, Suetonius (*Jul.* 87) says that Caesar knew the *Cyropaedia;* it was much read in his generation (Cic. *Brutus* 112), and Cicero used it as a guide during his campaign in Cilicia (*ad Fam.* 9.25.1). See Münscher 1920: 74-83.

62. On Caesar's military psychology, cf. Loreto 1993[1990]: 297-98.

63. Cf. Goldsworthy 1996: 245.

64. Cf. Collins 1952: 107-25.

65. Cf. Goldsworthy 1996: 145.

66. Soldiers also encourage each other (*G* 6.40, 7.80; cf. Polyb. 1.76.2). Gauls and Germans share the custom

of relying upon their weeping women to inspire the men (*G* 1.51, 7.48); when their city is under siege, the old men and women of the Massilians serve the same function (*C* 2.4).

67. On *consilium* as a stratagem word, see Wheeler 1988c: 52-55.

68. On Caesar and stratagems, Feller 1929: 21-24.

69. de Romilly 1956: 113-15, Pritchett 1974: 283-86.

70. On Polybius' admiration for courage, Eckstein 1995: 28-55. But the austere Thucydides did not systematically describe deeds of valor.

71. On *aristeai* in Caesar, Feller 1929: 38-41, and Rasmussen 1963 collects instances where they are made more vivid with passages of direct discourse. *Aristeai* are prominent in the pre-Caesarian Roman tradition from what we can see of it (*supra*, n. 14), and there is no reason to think Caesar is directly following Greek models.

72. Cf. Wheeler 1991: 137-38.

73. de Romilly 1956: 142-43 and Crane 1998: 225-29.

74. de Romilly 1980: 309-15 compares the speech of Phormio in Thucydides to Plato's *Laches* and *Protagoras*.

75. For the mixture of birth and education in Xenophon's conception of [courage], Due 1989: 181, 184.

76. Cf. Pédech 1964: 424-25.

77. And sometimes seems to be denied, Polyb. 1.31.1, 1.51.3.

78. There are, of course, exceptions where bravery is important, e.g. Polyb. 5.23.9-10, 10.39.2. For Polybius' lexicon of bravery, Lindauer 1889: 19-20.

79. Cf. Knoche 1962[1935]: 39 and Hellegouarc'h 1963: 291.

80. On *virtus,* Eisenhut 1973 (with 44-46 on Caesar), but see the strictures of Harris 1979: 20 n. 3. On the role of *virtus* in Roman military thinking, Rosenstein 1990: 94. For *virtus* in Caesar cf. Rawlings 1998: 177-80.

81. Wheeler 1988d. Wheeler argues (193) that the Roman suspicion of cunning came late.

82. Perhaps the keen attention to *virtus* of the (rather unimaginative) author of the *B.Hisp.* reflects conventional soldierly views (7, 14, 16, 17, 19, 23-25, 31, 32).

83. Cf. Eisenhut 1973: 40-43. *Virtus* is much emphasized in the handful of surviving pre-Caesarian Latin battle descriptions, see *supra* n. 14.

84. Such competition characterized the Greeks as well, of course, but while a Greek like Xenophon emphasized competition in φιλ τιμία between individual soldiers on the same side (*Cyr.* 3.3.10, 7.1.18, *Anab.* 4.7.12, 5.2.11), Caesar stresses that between generals, armies, and units (but see *G.* 5.44, 7.47, 7.50 for individuals), so its consequences are much greater in Caesar.

85. On the wriggling necessary to refuse a challenge to single combat without loss of face, [Front.] *Strat.* 4.7.5.

86. Pritchett 1974: 153 gathers examples of taunting in the Greek tradition.

87. On Roman taking of heads, Goldsworthy 1996: 271-73.

88. Cf. Goldsworthy 1996: 153-54 for generals watching battles.

89. Pritchett 1974: 148, 174-76 gathers references to distaste for trickery in the Greek tradition.

90. Keegan 1976: 65 terms Caesar's style "disjunctive."

91. Discussion of the literary construction of this battle description begins with Oppermann 1933: 37-41, 56-64, 85-89. Later writing is collected by Görler 1980: n. 7. The "Battle of the Sambre" is a conventional name; the actual location of the battle is disputed: Gesche 1976: 249-51 gathers references.

92. Weiss 1983: 83.

93. On literary devices in Polybius' battle descriptions, D'Huys 1990.

94. Rambaud 1966: 230.

95. Wiedemann 1992: 35-38 and 1996.

96. Grounded (in Anglo-Saxon lands) on the equations of F. W. Lanchester, accessible in Lanchester 1916; used in many technical military publications, and subject to continual refinement: e.g. Dupuy 1979 and 1987.

97. See van Creveld's (1982: 11-17) dismissive treatment of "national character."

98. For summary of this view, Goldsworthy 1996: 1-2, 8-9, 283-84.

99. Goldsworthy 1996: 10, 244-46, 285-86.

100. E.g. van Creveld 1982 *passim.*

Bibliography

Adcock, F. E. 1956. *Caesar as Man of Letters*. Cambridge.

Anderson, J. K. 1970. *Military Theory and Practice in the Age of Xenophon*. Berkeley.

Astin, A. E. 1978. *Cato the Censor.* Oxford.

Bauer, A. 1893. "Die kriegswissenschaftliche Litteratur der Hellenen." In I. von Müller and A. Bauer, *Die griechischen Privat- und Kriegsaltertümer = Handbuch der klassischen Altertumswissenschaft* 4.1.2: 273-83. Munich.

Béquignon, Y. 1970. "Pharsalus." *RE* suppl. 12: cols. 1038-84.

Borgeaud, P. 1988. *The Cult of Pan in Ancient Greece.* Chicago.

Breitenbach, H. R. 1967. "Xenophon von Athen." *RE* 9A/2: cols. 1569-2052.

Campbell, B. 1987. "Teach Yourself How to be a General." *JRS* 77: 13-29.

Collins, J. H. 1952. *Propagands, Ethics, and Psychological Assumptions in Caesar's Writings.* Diss. Frankfurt.

Crane, G. 1998. *Thucydides and the Ancient Simplicity: The Limits of Political Realism.* Berkeley.

Creveld, M. van. 1982. *Fighting Power.* Westport.

Dain, A. 1946. *Histoire du texte d'Élien le tacticien.* Paris.

Davidson, J. 1991. "The Gaze in Polybius' *Histories.*" *JRS* 81: 10-24.

Delatte, A. 1933. *Le Troisième livre des souvenirs socratiques de Xénophon.* Liège.

Devine, A. M. 1995. "Polybius' Lost *Tactica*: The Ultimate Source for the Tactical Manuals of Asclepiodotus, Aelian, and Arrian?" *AHB* 9: 40-44.

D'Huys, V. 1990. "ΧΡΗΣΙΜΟΝ ΚΑΙ ΤΕΡΠΝΟΝ in Polybios' Schlachtschilderungen. Einige literarische Topoi in seiner Darstellung der Schlacht bei Zama (XV 9-16)." In H. Verdin et al., eds., *Purposes of History. Studies in Greek Historiography from the Fourth to the Second Centuries* BC, 267-88. Louvain.

Dillery, J. 1995. *Xenophon and the History of his Times.* London.

Due, B. 1989. *The Cyropaedia. Xenophon's Aims and Methods.* Aarhus and Copenhagen.

Dupuy, T. N. 1979. *Numbers, Predictions and War: Using History to Evaluate Combat Factors and Predict the Outcome of Battles.* Indianapolis and New York.

———. 1987. *Understanding War.* New York.

Eckstein, A. M. 1995. *Moral Vision in the Histories of Polybius.* Berkeley.

Eisenhut, W. 1973. *Virtus Romana: ihre Stellung im römischen Wertsystem.* Munich.

Feller, Th. 1929. *Caesars Kommentarien über den Gallischen Krieg und die kunstmässige Geschichtschreibung.* Diss. Breslau. Leipzig.

Frankel, N., and L. Smith. 1978. *Patton's Best: An Informal History of the 4th Armored Division.* New York.

Fussell, P. 1975. *The Great War and Modern Memory.* New York.

Gärtner, H. A. 1975. *Beobachtungen zu Bauelementen in der antiken Historiographie besonders bei Livius und Caesar = Historia* Einzelschriften 25. Wiesbaden.

Gat, A. 1989. *The Origins of Military Thought: From the Enlightenment to Clausewitz.* Oxford.

Gera, D. L. 1993. *Xenophon's Cyropaedia: Style, Genre, and Literary Technique.* Oxford.

Gesche, H. 1976. *Caesar* = Erträge der Forschung 51. Darmstadt.

Goldsworthy, A. K. 1996. The Roman Army at War: 100 BC - AD 200. Oxford.

———. 1997. "The *Othismos,* Myths and Heresies: The Nature of Hoplite Battle." *War in History* 4: 1-26.

Görler, W. 1980. "Caesar als Erzähler (am Beispiel von BG II 15-27)." *Der altsprachliche Unterricht* 23: 18-31.

Guelfucci, M. R. 1986. "La Peur dans l'oeuvre de Polybe." *Revue de Philologie* 60: 227-37.

Hansen, M. H. 1993. "The Battle Exhortation in Ancient Historiography. Fact or Fiction?" *Historia* 42: 161-80.

Hanson, V. D. 1989. *The Western Way of War.* New York.

Harris, W. V. 1979. War and Imperialism in Republican Rome. 327-70 BC. Oxford.

Hellegouarc'h, J. 1963. *Le Vocabulaire latin des relations et des partis politiques sous la République.* Paris.

Heza, E. 1974. "Ruse de guerre—trait caractéristique d'une tactique nouvelle dans l'oeuvre de Thucydide." *Eos* 62: 227-44.

Jordan, H. 1860. *M. Catonis praeter librum de re rustica quae extant.* Leipzig.

Keegan, J. 1976. *The Face of Battle.* New York.

Knoche, U. 1962[1935]. "*Magnitudo Animi.*" In id. *Vom Selbstverständnis der Römer = Gymnasium* Beihefte 2: 31-97. Heidelberg, 1962 = *Philologus* Suppl. 27.3 (1935): 1-88.

Krentz, P. 1985. "The Nature of Hoplite Battle." *ClAnt* 4: 50-61.

———. 1997. "The Strategic Culture of Periclean Athens." In C. D. Hamilton and id., eds., *Polis and Polemos. Essays on Politics, War and History in Ancient Greece, in Honor of Donald Kagan,* 55-72. Claremont.

Lammert, F. 1931. "Στρατηγηματα." *RE* 4A/1: cols. 174-81.

Lanchester, F. W. 1916. *Aircraft in Warfare: The Dawn of the Fourth Arm.* London.

Lee, A. D. 1996. "Morale and the Roman Experience of Battle." In A. B. Lloyd, ed., *Battle in Antiquity,* 199-217. London.

Lindauer, J. 1889. *De Polybii vocabulis militaribus* = Programm des kgl. Ludwigs-Gymnasiums, 1888/1889. Munich.

Linderski, J. 1985. "The *Libri Reconditi.*" *HSCP* 89: 207-34.

Loreto, L. 1993 [1990]. "Pensare la guerra in Cesare. Teoria e prassi." In D. Poli, ed., *La Cultura in Cesare*. Rome, 1993 = *Quaderni Linguistici e Filologici* 5 (1990): 239-343.

MacMullen, R. 1984[1990]. "The Legion as a Society." *Historia* 33 (1984): 440-56 = id. *Changes in the Roman Empire: Essays in the Ordinary*, 225-35. Princeton, 1990.

Menge, R., and S. Preuss. 1890. *Lexicon Caesarianum*. Leipzig.

Mensching, E. 1988. *Caesars Bellum Gallicum: Eine Einführung*. Frankfurt.

Merguet, H. 1886. *Lexikon zu den Schriften Cäsars und seiner Fortsetzer*. Jena.

Meusel, H. 1887-1893. *Lexicon Caesarianum*, vols. 1-2. Berlin.

Münscher, K. 1920. *Xenophon in der griechisch-römischen Literatur* = *Philologus* suppl. 13. Leipzig.

Mutschler, F.-H. 1975. *Erzählstil und Propaganda in Caesars Kommentarien* = Heidelberger Forschungen 15. Heidelberg.

Neumann, A. 1956. "Römisches Militärhandbuch." *RE* Suppl. 8: cols. 356-58.

Oppermann, H. 1933. *Caesar. Der Schriftsteller und sein Werk*. Leipzig.

Pédech, P. 1964. *La Méthode historique de Polybe*. Paris.

Pelling, C. 1981. "Caesar's Battle-Descriptions and the Defeat of Ariovistus." *Latomus* 40: 741-66.

Poznanski, L. 1994. "La Polémologie pragmatique de Polybe." *Journal des Savants*: 19-74.

Pritchett, W. K. 1974. *The Greek State at War*. Vol. 2. Berkeley.

———. 1985. *The Greek State at War*. Vol. 4. Berkeley.

Rambaud, M. 1954/1955. "Le Soleil de Pharsale." *Historia* 3: 346-78.

———. 1966. *L'Art de la déformation historique dans les commentaires de César*. Paris.

———. 1967. "L'Armée de César pendant la conquête de la Gaule." *L'Information historique* 29: 193-203.

———. 1974. "L'Espace dans le récit césarien." In R. Chevallier, ed., *Littérature gréco-romaine et géographie historique: Mélanges offerts à Roger Dion*, 111-29. Paris.

Rasmussen, D. 1963. *Caesars Commentarii: Stil und Stilwandel am Beispiel der direkten Rede*. Göttingen.

Rawlings, L. 1998. "Caesar's Portrayal of Gauls as Warriors." In Welch and Powell 1998: 171-92.

Rawson, E. 1971. "The Literary Sources for the Pre-Marian Army." *PBSR* 39: 13-31.

Richter, W. 1977. *Caesar als Darsteller seiner Taten: Eine Einführung*. Heidelberg.

Romilly, J. de. 1956. *Histoire et raison chez Thucydide*. Paris.

———. 1980. "Réflexions sur le courage chez Thucydide et chez Platon." *REG* 93: 307-23.

Rosenstein, N. 1990. *Imperatores Victi: Military Defeat and Aristocratic Competition in the Middle and Late Republic*. Berkeley.

Rowe, G. O. 1967. "Dramatic Structures in Caesar's *Bellum Civile*." *TAPA* 98: 399-414.

Rüpke, J. 1992. "Wer las Caesars *bella* als *commentarii*?" *Gymnasium* 99: 201-26.

Sacks, K. 1981. *Polybius on the Writing of History*. Berkeley.

Schenk, D. 1930. *Flavius Vegetius Renatus. Die Quellen der Epitoma Rei Militaris* = *Klio* Beiheft 22. Leipzig.

Stadter, P. A. 1978. "The *Ars Tactica* of Arrian: Tradition and Originality." *CP* 73: 117-28.

Tuplin, C. J. 1986. "Military Engagements in Xenophon's *Hellenica*." In I. S. Moxon et al., eds., *Past Perspectives: Studies in Greek and Roman Historical Writing*, 37-66. Cambridge.

Vernant, J.-P. 1991. "Artemis and Preliminary Sacrifice in Combat." In id., *Mortals and Immortals: Collected Essays*, F. I. Zeitlin, ed., 244-57. Princeton.

Walsh, P. G. 1961. *Livy: His Historical Aims and Methods*. Cambridge.

Weiss, H. K. 1983. "Requirements for the Theory of Combat." In M. Shubik, ed., *Mathematics of Conflict* = North-Holland Systems and Control Series 6: 73-88. Amsterdam and New York.

Welch, K., and A. Powell. 1998. *Julius Caesar as Artful Reporter: The War Commentaries as Political Instruments*. London.

Whatley, N. 1964. "On the Possibility of Reconstructing Marathon and Other Ancient Battles." *JHS* 84: 119-39.

Wheeler, E. L. 1978. "The Occasion of Arrian's *Tactica*." *GRBS* 19: 51-65.

———. 1979. "The Legion as Phalanx." *Chiron* 9: 303-18.

———. 1983. "The *Hoplomachoi* and Vegetius' Spartan Drillmasters." *Chiron* 13: 1-20.

———. 1988a. ". . . The History of a Greek Proverb." *GRBS* 29: 153-84.

———. 1988b. "The Modern Legality of Frontinus' Stratagems." *Militärgeschichtliche Mitteilungen* 44: 7-29.

———. 1988c. *Stratagem and the Vocabulary of Military Trickery* = *Mnemosyne* Suppl. 108. Leiden.

————. 1988d. "*Sapiens* and Stratagems: The Neglected Meaning of a *Cognomen.*" *Historia* 37: 166-95.

————. 1991. "The General as Hoplite." In V. D. Hanson, ed., *Hoplites: The Classical Greek Battle Experience,* 121-70. London.

Whitehead, D. 1990. *How to Survive under Siege. Aineias the Tactician.* Oxford.

Wiedemann, T. 1992. *Emperors and Gladiators.* London.

————. 1996. "Single Combat and Being Roman." *Ancient Society* 27: 91-103.

Wunderer, C. 1905. *Die psychologischen Anschauungen des Historikers Polybios* = Programm des kgl. humanistischen Gymnasiums zu Erlangen, 1904/1905. Erlangen.

Zecchini, G. 1990. "Cesare." In F. Della Corte, ed., *Dizionario degli scrittori greci e latini,* vol. 1.443-62. Milan.

Andreola Rossi (essay date 2000)

SOURCE: "The Camp of Pompey: Strategy of Representation in Caesar's *Bellum Ciuile,*" in *Classical Journal,* Vol. 95, No. 3, February-March, 2000, pp. 239-56.

[*In the following essay, Rossi contends that Caesar used established rhetorical models and types as a way of leading his readers towards the conclusions he wished them to reach.*]

Asinius' Pollio damaging judgment on the historical inaccuracy of Caesar's ***Commentarii***[1] has for a long time led many scholars to dismiss Caesar's historical works as an almost free-composed historical fiction, where events are, at best, systematically distorted, or even fabricated altogether.[2] It is only in recent years that scholars have begun a slow process of rehabilitation. On the one hand, they have called attention to the limited presence of large scale historical falsification in the ***Commentarii;*** and on the other, they have started to highlight the sophisticated nature of the narrative structure,[3] hidden behind a prose that Cicero had praised for its elegant clarity and directness of style.[4] It is what we may call Caesar's strategy of representation of events, not their falsification, which forces upon the reader the desired reading and interpretation. In a recent article, Damon[5] has studied one of these narrative strategies adopted by Caesar. She points out how in ***BC*** [*De Bellum Civili*] Caesar presents events and characters in a way that "aims at fashioning in the reader a net of memory and understanding by tying the knots which link episodes and characters that are found on the long strand of narrative."[6] It is this method, she argues, that leaves a great deal of the responsibility for interpretation to the readers.

Following this line of interpretation, I explore how this "net of memory," which Caesar aims at fashioning in his readers' mind, extends beyond the limits of his own text.

As an example I analyze Caesar's description of Pompey's camp after the battle of Pharsalus. Employing a type scene, a *topos,* familiar in the historiographic tradition, Caesar builds a network of correspondences with other events, thereby broadening and universalizing the significance of the narrated episode. It is through this device that he weaves efficaciously into his narrative an important ideological and political subtext that informs the narrative of ***BC.***

After the historical debacle of Pharsalus, the Pompeians are dispersed and, while a panic-stricken Pompey abandons the region in flight, Caesar, with his usual rapidity of action, strikes the Pompeians a final blow. He attacks their camp and, after a short skirmish with the Thracians and other barbarians who had been left in charge of it, Caesar and his soldiers finally get the better of their enemy.[7] What follows in the narration is a detailed description of the camp, in which a spectacle of lavishness is offered to the gaze of Caesar and his men (***BC*** 3.96.1-2):

> In castris Pompei uidere licuit trichilas structas, magnum argenti pondus expositum, recentibus caespiti- bus tabernacula constrata, L. etiam Lentuli et non nullorum tabernacula protecta hedera, multaque prae- eterea quae nimiam luxuriam et uictoriae fiduciam des- ignarent, ut facile existimari posset nihil eos de euentu eius diei timuisse, qui non necessarias conquirerent uo- luptates. At hi miserrimo ac patientissimo exercitui Caesaris luxuriem obiciebant, cui semper omnia ad necessarium usum defuissent.[8]

> "In Pompey's camp could be viewed artificial bowers, great quantities of silver laid out, tents floored with freshly cut turf, the tents of Lucius Lentulus and some others wreathed with ivy, and much else to indicate excessive luxury and confidence of victory. It was easy to deduce from their pursuit of inessential pleasures that they had no misgivings about the outcome of the day. Yet these were men who accused Caesar's wretched and long-suffering army of luxury, when it had never enjoyed sufficiency in its everyday needs."[9]

Significantly all the other historians who describe the aftermath of the battle of Pharsalus do not seem to follow Caesar in this description. Dio (41.61-63) and Velleius (2.52), although both reporting Caesar's acts of *clementia* following the battle of Pharsalus, omit altogether the description of Pompey's camp. Appian (***BC*** 2.81) reports briefly its capture, but does not make any mention of its lavishness. He only reports that Caesar and his men ate the supper which had been prepared to celebrate the upcoming victory (2.69) and that the entire army feasted at the enemy's expenses. A similar description is found in Plutarch (*Pomp.*72.4) where again the emphasis is not on *luxuria;* the Pompeians are rather charged with vanity . . . and folly . . . , for the adornments found in the camp were those of men who had sacrificed and were holding festivals rather than that of men who were arming themselves for battle.

What were Caesar's reasons to describe the camp of Pompey in such a fashion?

This passage, *prima facie,* could be compared to others of *BC,* where Caesar emphasizes the moral and military shortcomings of his enemy, for Pompey's camp, as Caesar himself points out, is a perfect reflection of the *nimia luxuria* and the excessive confidence in victory of the Pompeians.[10] We may cite one other such example. In *BC* 3.31-33 Caesar describes the Pompeians' mobilization of the resources of Syria and Asia under the authority of the then governor of Syria, Metellus Scipio, who in 52 had become both Pompey's consular colleague and his father-in-law.[11] The harsh and unfair exacting of such contributions, which Caesar describes in detail in *BC* 3.32, is labeled as a perfect *exemplum* of another important moral flaw of Pompey and his associates: *auaritia.*[12] The terminology employed here and in the previous passage is not fortuitous. Even a brief glimpse at contemporary authors shows how these two terms were loaded with moral and social significance in Roman political debate of the time. Sallust in his *Bellum Catilinae* presents Catiline, the enemy of the State, as a man spurred on by the corruption of public morals, which were ruined, according to Sallust, by two great evils, precisely *luxuria* and *auaritia.*[13] Likewise, Livy, a generation later, in the preface of his work accounts for the moral degeneration of Rome in similar terms. The reasons for Roman decline are "the immigration" of avarice and luxury in the Republic.[14]

Hence in Rome's contemporary political context, these two episodes may be interpreted as two paradigmatic *exempla.* They serve not only to highlight Pompeians' moral flaws and shortcomings, but they also cast them as the real menace for that Roman Republic that they supposedly embody in the war against Caesar. A reading of the episode along these lines fits perfectly the political and ideological program that many scholars have seen as the foundation of *BC,* namely to represent Caesar as the savior of the Republic, while the Pompeians are convicted of contemptuous disregard for Roman laws and customs.[15] Yet by employing a type scene familiar in the historiographic tradition Caesar is also able to build a network of correspondences with other events, thus directing the reader towards an even more damaging interpretation of the un-Republican behavior of the Pompeians.

Descriptions of conquered camps were not an unusual topic in historical accounts. Nonetheless Caesar's account here seems to follow a particular tradition, whose archetype may in meaningful ways be traced back to the famous description of Mardonius' camp after the Greek victory at Plataea, "the most glorious of victories ever known to men," as Herodotus hailed it.[16] In Herodotus' account, as the battle draws finally to a close and the Persians are put to flight, the Greeks, led by Pausanias, arrive in the Persian camp. Here they are greeted by a spectacle of opulence: the tents are adorned with gold and silver, the couches are gilded and silver-plated; everywhere there are golden bowls, cups and other drinking vessels and sacks with cauldrons of gold and silver.[17] The famous anecdote that follows, where the lavish Persian meal served with all the magnificence of a banquet is compared to the frugal Spartan diet, builds an even stronger antithesis between the Greeks and the *barbaroi* and so stresses the polarity of their behavior.[18] The former is fashioned on *parsimonia,* the latter on immoderate luxury. . . .[19] Though the story may be exquisitely Herodotean, surely the characterization of the Persians is not, for it finds precise parallels in contemporary Athenian representation of the Persians. As Hall rightly suggests in her study on the representation of the barbarian in Greek tragedy, *luxuria* had become one of the traits that shaped the ethnicity of the Persians in antithesis to the Greeks' own sense of identity. Various terms used in the *Persae* of Aeschylus to evoke the luxury of the Persian court were to become closely associated with the barbarian ethos,[20] especially . . . "luxury" and the concept of αβρ ϛύνη or αβρότηζ, an untranslatable term combining the senses of softness, delicacy and lack of restraint. It is for this reason that the Herodotean description of the Persian camp acquires deeper meaning: such a description becomes in Herodotus an important sign of Persian ethnicity. It is in this capacity that this representation becomes an important literary model, a sort of *topos,* dynamically re-employed and re-adapted by other historians to characterize the Asiatic East in antithesis to its Western opponents. This representation becomes, to use Hinds' terminology, a *topos*-code within which endlessly active (and endlessly interpretable) allusive variations can be contained.[21]

A case in point. As Alexander the Great moves against the Persian empire and wins a crucial victory at Issus against Darius,[22] soon to be the last monarch of the Persian Empire, a similar description follows. The description, although varying slightly from one historian to the other, shares all the principal Herodotean features. As Alexander and his men enter the camp, the wealth of the Persian camp is described in rich detail.[23] But in addition to the abundance of wealth, the Persian camp also betrays a more damaging flaw of Persian national character: their luxurious way of living. This concept is clearly expressed in Diodorus, for whom the camp and its wealth become a reflection of Persian *luxuria,*[24] τρυφη. Likewise Curtius defines the wealth in the Persian camp as an instrument of luxury, not of war. (*Ingens auri argentique pondus, non belli, sed luxuriae apparatum*).[25]

The same theme, although not explicitly expressed, is reiterated by Plutarch. In his account, as soon as Alexander and his men enter Darius' tent, they are met by a spectacle of lavishness: again we find basins and pitchers and tubs and caskets, all of gold, and expertly fashioned, while the apartment was fragrant with spices and unguents. Plutarch also reports that as soon as Alexander passed from this tent into another one amazing for size, height, and the furniture it contained, he looked to his companions and exclaimed: "This, as it would seem, is to be a king."[26] As noted by Hamilton,[27] the anecdote, in Herodotean fashion, is so constructed to highlight the polarity of behavior and attitude between Alexander and the Asian king, a polarity soon reinforced in the following narrative by various examples of the . . . frugality, of Alexander.[28]

Alexander, when asked by a woman named Ada to hire her bakers and cooks, is said by Plutarch, to have replied that he had been given better cooks by his tutor, Leonidas; namely for his breakfast a night march, and for his supper, a light breakfast. Alexander adds that Leonidas "used to come and open my chests of bedding and clothing, to see that my mother did not hide there for me some luxury and superfluity. . . ."[29]

We may now return to Caesar. From the examples cited above, it seems quite obvious that the description of Pompey's camp in Caesar's narrative follows a set of models, employed largely by Greek writers to characterize Persian ethnicity.[30] Thus, by fashioning his description of Pompey's camp in such a manner, Caesar implicitly assimilates Pompey's camp to that of an Oriental king.

But Pompey and his men are not merely likened to Orientals. As Caesar clearly states, they have inherited the most important trait of Oriental ethnicity: *nimia luxuria*. The un-Roman moral and political shortcomings of the Pompeians therefore assume a different nuance as they are directly assimilated to a foreign ethnicity. Accordingly Caesar's crucial refusal to plunder Pompey's camp[31] and the emphasis on the hardships to which his men are accustomed (*miserrimo ac patientissimo exercitui . . . omnia a d necessarium usum defuissent*) becomes emblematic of the polarity of behavior between the Caesarians and the now orientalized Pompeians.[32] New protagonists have been cast into old roles as they reflect the polarity of behavior between Easterners and Westerners distinctive of the *topos*.[33]

What was Caesar's aim in fashioning the episode in such a manner? The bitter irony of assimilating Pompey, the great conqueror of the East, to a defeated Oriental king is self-evident, especially since Romans would still have a sharp recollection of Pompey's magnificent third triumph at the end of the long wars in the East, celebrated in Rome just a few years earlier, in 61 BCE. The triumph, we are told by our ancient sources, exceeded in brilliancy any that had gone before and lasted for two full days.[34] Many nations were represented, but the most significant feature of the triumph was the imposing statue of Mithridates Eupator, the scion of the Royal house of Persia, which was eight cubits high and made of solid gold. With it came Mithridates' throne and scepter and, to stress the comparison between Pompey and Alexander the Great, the couch of King Darius I, the greater ancestor of the Persian monarch, whose empire had been conquered by Alexander. At the head of the procession, before Pompey himself, were led the five sons of Mithridates bearing the evocative names of Artaphernes, Cyrus, Oxathres, Darius and Xerxes as living representatives of the conquered East.[35] Thanks to this representation, Pompey the Great, who had likened his *res gestae* to those of Alexander, is implicitly cast in the role of these Oriental monarchs, as he is now defeated by a new Alexander: Caesar.[36]

But Caesar's representation of Pompey's camp has probably a more subtle propagandistic purpose and it is this description that may help us to unravel the important ideological and political message that permeates the work in its entirety.

The opening words of Lucan's *Pharsalia* defined the civil wars between Caesar and Pompey as *bella plus quam civilia*,[37] wars worse than civil wars, and time and again Lucan's epic borrows terminology and images from human anatomy to represent the *res publica* as a metaphorical body which has been torn apart as a result of internecine conflicts.[38] Lucan's emphasis in representing the civil war between Caesar and Pompey lies exactly on its status as a *bellum internum*. Because of it the ties that link the most sacrosanct relationships in a society are suddenly shattered: son kills father,[39] *socer* wages war against *gener*,[40] brother kills brother as Lucan's imagery brings to full circle the history of the city of Rome whose foundation is linked inextricably to Remus' death at the hands of his brother Romulus.[41]

As Latin poetry[42] articulates its description of the civil war between Pompey and Caesar as a fratricide, Caesar's political discourse in *BC* moves in the opposite direction: it tends towards a process of de-familiarization of the enemy, of de-romanization. It is through this strategy that the description of Pompey's camp and of his behavior assumes crucial ideological significance. Via this representation, the Pompeians are stripped altogether of their national identity as Romans, for their behavior becomes specifically linked to a foreign and, more specifically, to Oriental ethnicity.

To verify our interpretation of the passage we may now observe the ways in which this process of de-romanization and Orientalization of the Pompeians is operative in another section of *BC*.

Early in book 3 of *BC,* as Caesar is about to cross the Adriatic for a final confrontation with Pompey, he lists Pompey's forces at great length for three consecutive chapters.[43] He attempts no analysis of his own, nor does he make any explicit statement about his enemy's strength and weakness. As noted by Carter,[44] one of his aims, by presenting the majestic proportion of Pompey's army, is that of portraying Pompey as a Goliath and himself as a David. But Caesar's listing of Pompey's force has probably also another more important purpose. While there is no need to doubt the accuracy of Caesar's statistics, a comparison with our other sources shows how Caesar's list gives an exaggerated impression of the non-Italian preponderance in Pompey's army. A case in point. After listing Pompey's fleet assembled from Asia, the Cycladic islands, Corcyra, Athens, Pontus, Bithynia, Syria, Cilicia, Phoenicia, and Egypt,[45] Caesar moves on to list Pompey's legions, his archers, and finally his cavalry which is said to have amounted to 7000 men comprising the following contingents: Deiotarus had brought 600 Gauls, Ariobarzanes 500 from Cappadocia; Cotys 500 from Thrace; from Macedonia there were 200 under Rhascypolis, from Alexandria Pompey's son had brought 500 Gauls and

Germans; Pompey himself had conscribed 800 from his slaves and shepherds; 300 had been given by Tarcondarius from Galatia, 200 mounted archers had been sent from Syria by Antiochus of Commagene. To these Pompey had added Dardani and Bessi, likewise Macedonians, Thessalians and men belonging to other tribes and states, and so he had reached the number mentioned above.[46]

As the contributions from foreign nations total 3600, the rest is just dismissed as Dardani, Bessi, Macedonians, Thessalians and "men of other nations and states" (*ac reliquarum gentium et ciuitatum adiecerat*). No mention is made that among the other nations and states the largest contributor was Rome itself, as is clearly reported by Appian,[47] Dio,[48] and Plutarch. Plutarch actually goes as far as to say that Pompey's cavalry was "the flower of Rome and Italy, preeminent in lineage, wealth, and courage."[49] Caesar's inclusion of the Italian and Roman contingent under the heading "men of other nations and states" is pointedly evasive.

As Pompey had been made the embodiment of an Oriental king, similarly, as part of the same strategic design of representation, the war against him assumes the connotation no longer of a civil war, but it is represented as *bellum externum* against a foreign enemy.[50] In a narrative once again highly evocative of Herodotus' description of the Persian forces, in Caesar's *BC,* Pompey, the new King of Kings as he was called by some of his detractors,[51] threatens the West and what the West embodied now by Rome represents, at the head of a huge and heterogeneous barbarian army, in the fashion of a *nouvelle* Xerxes.[52]

What was the effectiveness of such a representation in Rome's political climate of the time? Surely Caesar's *BC* exploits some of the criticisms leveled against Pompey at the time. Pliny views the extravagant triumph of Pompey in 61 BCE over Asia as a victory of luxury over austerity (Pliny, *NH* 37.14 *seueritate uicta et ueriore luxuriae triumpho*) and he could be reechoing some of the complaints of Pompey's contemporaries. Already in 61, Pompey was spending his fortune on the building of a great palace, inspired by the *paradeisoi* of Oriental palaces and Plutarch (*Pomp.* 67.3), as we have seen previously, reports that Domitius Ahenobarbus called Pompey derisively King of Kings, a reference presumably to the Great King of Persia.[53] And also the army assembled by Pompey had raised the suspicions of the Romans. Some of Cicero's letters express his uneasiness about the foreign army assembled by Pompey and perceived as a threat to Rome. Although on the whole Cicero views Pompey as the champion of the Republican cause, and will eventually side with him, in his correspondence he nevertheless expresses his concerns. In his letter to Atticus dated Feb. 27, 49, written from Formiae, while Cicero was still deciding which course of action to follow, he voices his own doubts on Pompey's intention. He argues that Pompey has not abandoned Rome because it was impossible to defend it. It was Pompey's idea from the first to plunge the world into war, to stir up barbarous princes (*reges barbaros*) and

to bring savage tribes (*gentes feras*) under arms into Italy.[54] In a letter of the following month (March 18, 49), addressed again to Atticus from Formiae, a similar concern reemerges. Siding with Pompey would mean bringing hordes of Getae, Armenians and Colchians against Rome.[55] A letter from Brundisium on November 27, 48, after the battle of Pharsalus, expresses a similar dislike for the too close alliance that he had witnessed in Pompey's camp between the Pompeians and the barbarians.[56]

More specifically, though, it is the presentation of the Pompeians as embodiment of oriental *luxuria* that exploits current Roman fears about the East and the threat it poses to Rome's national identity. We had seen at the beginning of this study how the term *luxuria* had important political and ideological overtones in the writings of Livy and Sallust. *Luxuria* was perceived by these authors as the moral flaw responsible for endangering that social and moral stamina on which Rome had flourished and because of which it had been successful for so many centuries. This *luxuria,* viewed as foreign to Roman national identity, had begun to insinuate itself corrosively into the fabric of the Roman State as Rome had begun to come into close contact with the East. Roman contemporary political discourse viewed *luxuria* therefore as conjoined to Eastern ethnicity and recognized in Rome's interaction with the East the main reason for the present decline of Roman *mores.*

For Sallust, *luxuria* is a comparatively late development in the process of decline of Rome and in the *Bellum Catilinae* he voices the idea that the agent of the first importation of *luxuria* was precisely an army from Asia. The army was that of Sulla, who, in order to secure the loyalty of the army that he had led into Asia, had allowed it a luxury and license foreign to the manners of Roman forefathers. It was there that a Roman army had first learned to indulge in a luxurious way of living (*huc accedebat quod L. Sulla exercitum quem in Asia ductauerat, quo sibi fidum faceret, contra morem maiorum luxuriose nimisque liberaliter habuerat. Loca amoena, uoluptaria facile in otio ferocis militum animos molliuerant*).[57] But the idea may claim an even older tradition. In Livy, Cato's speech against the repeal of the *lex Oppia* argues notably the same idea, though Greece, too, is now charged by Cato with sharing that same ethos, that for Hellenic culture, had been a characterizing trait of Oriental ethnicity, in antithesis to their own.[58]

Apart from the speech of Cato, Livy himself, following most likely an earlier annalistic tradition, agrees with Sallust: the agent of the first importation of *luxuria* was an army from Asia.[59] In Livy and in the annalistic tradition that he represents, though, the army was that of Manlius Vulso. Livy exploits the theme in the opening chapter of book 39, creating a juxtaposition between the Roman military campaigns against the Ligurians on the one hand, and the military campaign against Asia on the other. The former had the effect of making the troops keener to show their valor (*nec alia prouincia militem ad uirtutem acuebat*).[60] The military campaign against Asia had achieved the opposite effect. As a result of the attractive nature of its cities, the abundance of provisions from land and sea, the effeminacy of its people, and the royal wealth, it had made Roman armies richer, rather than more courageous (*ditiores quam fortiores exercitus faciebat*).[61] This military decline, was soon followed by a moral one as Vulso's troops, returning in Rome to celebrate their triumph, introduced in the city for the first time Asian luxury (Livy, 39.6.6-9):[62]

> Neque ea sola infamiae erant quae in prouincia procul ab oculis facta narrabantur, sed ea etiam magis quae in militibus eius cotidie conspiciebantur. Luxuriae enim peregrinae origo ab exercitu Asiatico inuecta in urbem est. Ii primum lectos aeratos, uesfem stragulam pretiosam, plagulas et alia textilia, et quae tum magnificae supellectilis habebantur, monopodia et abacos Romam aduexerunt . . . epulae quoque ipsae et cura et sumptu maiore apparari coeptae. Tum coquus, uilissimum antiquis mancipium et aestimatione et usu, in pretio esse, et quod ministerium fuerat ars haberi coepta.

"Contributing to this notoriety were not merely the events reported as having taken place in his province far from Roman eyes, but even more the daily evidences among the soldiers, for the beginnings of foreign luxury were introduced into the city by the army from Asia. These soldiers were the first to bring to Rome bronze couches, costly coverlets, counterpanes and other woven cloths, as well as what was regarded at the time as sumptuous furniture—tables supported on a single pedestal, and sideboards . . . and the feasts themselves also began to be prepared with greater care and expense. Thereafter the cook, regarded by men of old as the paltriest of slaves both in monetary worth and in employment, began to be highly valued; what had been considered drudgery began to be accounted an art."

After listing these accessories of *luxuria,* introduced then for the first time in Rome, Livy concludes in a rather somber tone stating that the signs then appearing were merely the seeds of the *luxuria* to follow (*uix tamen illa quae tum conspiciebantur semina erant futurae luxuriae*).[63]

It is in this political context, when Rome was questioning itself seriously about the nature and the reasons of its moral decadence, that we may better understand the effectiveness of Pompey's representation in *BC*.[64] Taking advantage and exploiting Roman fears about the East and the threat that the corruptive influence of Oriental *luxuria* poses to Rome's national and moral identity, Caesar in *BC* casts a portrait of Pompey in such a like fashion. By describing Pompey's camp, according to a well-recognizable typology of representation of the Orientals, Pompey himself in *BC* becomes the embodiment of this Eastern threat. The great conqueror of the East has been conquered by the corruptive influence of the East and, in turn, has become the living embodiment of oriental *luxuria.* The fear expressed by Cato the Elder that Asia would sooner conquer Rome, than Rome Asia, finds its realization in Caesar's characterization of the Pompeians.[65] Conquered by Oriental *luxuria,* Pompey, with his heteroge-

neous and huge army, not only threatens the security of the state, but, at a deeper level, represents also a menace for the national and moral identity of the country which Caesar is now called to defend: Rome. Hence the battle of Pharsalus becomes, in Caesar's representation, not only a victory over Pompey but a great victory of the West over the East, exactly like Plataea 400 hundred years earlier.

Yet things were soon to change and the tables were soon turned. Caesar himself in the years following the battle of Pharsalus will become the target of a similar propaganda by his enemy. Un-Roman honors were bestowed upon him soon after his return to Rome and he began to enjoy a semi divine status in the fashion of an Oriental monarch.[66] And he was not discouraging such an assimilation. As pointed out by Weinstock it may well be that Caesar drove into Rome in his triumph chariot with white horses precisely because that was how the Persian kings used to appear. Later, he wore, or planned to wear, the Eastern tunic and wanted to wear a diadem, which, together with the tiara, was the principal attribute of the Persian kings.[67] Suetonius even reports the rumour, most likely unfounded and spread by his detractors, that Caesar had the intention of moving the capital of the empire from Rome to Alexandria.[68] Soon after the battle of Pharsalus, Rome and its political and cultural tradition was again threatened by the East, but this time, the threat was not Pompey, but Caesar himself.

Collins, following Barwick, fixed the date of *BC* in late 48 or early in 47[69] for the "legalitätstendenz" and the Republican tones of the work do not suit Caesar's later policy. The representation of Pompey's camp may further support their hypothesis. Even if *BC* was indeed published after Caesar's death, as many scholars suggest, most likely the work was written and completed by Caesar by the end of 47. After the year 47, a representation of Pompey as the incarnation of the Oriental threat would have just reminded the audience and the readers all too well of the threat that the now orientalized Caesar posed to the Roman system.

Artful reporter Caesar in his *BC* exploited the fears of a society who more and more saw the East as a potential threat to its own security and identity and he skillfully casts his enemy as the embodiment of this threat. At the end he himself will become victim of his own game but the representation of Pompey in *BC,* as an Eastern monarch, will have important consequences for it lays the foundation of the political propaganda of a generation later. As civil wars break out again in Rome, Augustus, during the war against Antony, will follow precisely in the footsteps of his predecessor. This time though, if not more skillful, Augustus will prove more successful than his adoptive father.

Notes

1. Suet. *Jul.* 56.4 *Pollio Asinius parum diligenter parumque integra ueritate compositos putat, cum Caesar pleraque et quae per alios erant gesta temere crediderit et quae per se, uel consulto uel etiam me-*

moria lapsus perperam ediderit; existimatque rescripturum et correcturum fuisse.

2. The most extreme statement of this view is that propounded by Rambaud. For a more moderate position see Balsdon 19-28; Stevens 3-18; 165-79.

3. This type of approach for *BG* is particularly evident in Welch and Powell. For *BC*, cf. La Penna 191-233; Rowe 399-414; Gotoff 1-18; Williams 215-226; Carter (1991) 16-27.

4. Cic. *Brut.* 262 *nudi enim sunt, recti et uenusti, omni ornatu orationis tamquam ueste detracta.* But on this passage see also Eden 74-75 who argues for the possibility that Cicero is here referring ruefully to the reception accorded his own *Commentarii*. Gotoff 2 raises instead the possibility that Cicero may be "groveling" in the *Brutus* passage. On the passage see also Williams 215. Whether Cicero is being disingenuous in this passage remains debatable, but Cicero's view, as it stands, was not shared by some modern scholars. Cf. for example Nettleship 47 who judges Caesar's *Commentarii* carelessly written. For a similar view cf. also Schlicher 212.

5. Damon 183-195.

6. Damon 185.

7. *BC* 95.

8. On this passage see Kraner, Hofmann, Meusel ad loc. Cf also Carter (1993) ad loc. Cf. also Rowe 411 who interprets Caesar's description of the camp's luxurious appearance and overconfidence of the enemy as a useful narrative device to underscore the reversal of fortunes of the Pompeians.

9. In poetry Lucan will describe the episode in 7.728-760 but in his account the emphasis will be on the plunder of the camp as a reflection of the *cupiditas* of the Caesarians. See especially 757-760 *ut rapiant, paruo scelus hoc uenisse putabunt. / cum sibi Tarpeias uictor desponderit arces, / cum spe Romanae promiserit omnia praedae / decipitur quod castra rapit.*

10. As noted by one of the referees, the term *avaritia* does not appear anywhere else in *BC*, making its double presence in 3.96 all the more relevant.

11. It is not clear whether the exactions detailed in *BC* 3.32 took place in Syria or in Asia or in both and, if in Asia, on whose authority. On the topic see Carter (1993) ad. loc. For a portrait of Scipio in Caesar see also *BC* 1.4.3, where he is accused of *ostentatio* and *adulatio*.

12. *BC* 3.32.1 *interim acerbissime imperatae pecuniae tota prouincia exigebantur. multa praeterea generatim ad auaritiam excogitabantur.*

13. Sal. *Cat.* 5.8 *incitabant praeterea corrupti ciuitatis mores, quos pessuma ac diuorsa inter se mala, luxu-*

ria atque auaritia, uexabant. For a similar idea cf. Sal. *Cat.* 12.2. On this passage see McGushin ad loc.

14. Livy, *Praef.* 11-12 *Ceterum aut me amor negotii suscepti fallit, aut nulla unquam res publica nec maior nec sanctior nec bonis exemplis ditior fuit, nec in quam ciuitatem tam serae auaritia luxuriaque immigrauerint, nec ubi tantus ac tam diu paupertati ac parsimoniae honos fuerit. Adeo quanto rerum minus, tanto minus cupiditatis erat: nuper diuitiae auaritiam et abundantes uoluptates desiderium per luxum atque libidinem pereundi perdendique omnia inuexere.* On Roman concern about *luxuria* and *auaritia* see Edwards 176ff. The backgrounds to this idea are traced by Earl 44ff. and Luce 271-275. See also Feldherr 37-50.

15. For a detailed discussion see Collins 113-132 who stresses how Caesar in *BC* strives to appear as a *bonus civis, rei publicae natus.* For a similar interpretation see Carter (1991) 18 and La Penna 195 ff.

16. Hdt. 9.64.1.

17. Hdt. 9.80 1ff. . . . For a similar description of the Persian camp see also 7.119 and 7. 190.

18. Hdt. 9.82. On this passage cf. also. How - Wells ad loc. and more in general on the representation of the Persians in Herodotus see Flory 81-119. See also Briant 69-105.

19. Hdt. 9.82.

20. Hall 80 ff. . . .

21. Hinds 42.

22. On the importance of the battle of Issus and its renown in antiquity see Polyb. 12.17.1.

23. Diod. 17.35.1-4; Curtius 3.11.20; Plut. *Alex.* 20.6-8. Among our ancient sources Arrian is the only one who reports that Alexander found only three thousand talents in the camp, but he adds that all the money and everything else a great king takes with him even on campaign for his extravagant way of living . . . he had already sent to Damascus (Arr. *An.* 2.11.10).

24. Diod. 35.4.

25. Curt. 3.11.20.

26. Plut. *Alex.* 20. 7-8.

27. Hamilton ad loc., who rightly points out that Alexander is here expressing pity for Darius for thinking that royalty consisted in mere wealth.

28. Plut. *Alex.* 22.4-5.

29. Plut. *Alex.* 22.5.

30. A similar account is found significantly in Livy (36.11.1-5), in his description of the winter quarters of Antiochus the Great, when Romans came for the

first time in close contact with Asia. Again, the description of the camp of the Oriental king is seen as a reflection of Oriental luxury (*cepit luxuria*). Cf. also Diod. 29.2. On Livy's passage and his sources see Briscoe ad loc.

31. *BC* 3.97.1 *Caesar castris potitus a militibus contendit ne in praeda occupati reliqui negotii gerendi facultatem dimitterent. qua re impetrata montem opere circummunire instituit.* On this passage see Carter (1993) ad loc. who rightly notes that one can only guess what the relation of this idealized picture may be to what actually happened when Caesar insisted on pursuing the Pompeians. For a different account of Caesar's usual behavior in battle and after victory see Suet. *Jul.* 67 *Ac non numquam post magnam pugnam atque victoriam, remisso officiorum munere, licentiam omnem passim lasciuiendi permittebat, iactare solitus milites suos etiam unguentatos bene pugnare posse . . . habebatque tam cultos, ut argento et auro politis armis ornaret, simul et ad speciem, et quo tenaciores eorum in proelio essent metu damni.*

32. *BC* 96.2.

33. As noted by one of the referees, Caesar will adopt a different strategy of representation in *BG*, where he will be at pains to portray his own most important foreign opponents, the Germans and the Belgians, as far removed from the softening effects of luxury. On the topic see also Rambaud 334-339.

34. On the magnificence of the triumph, all ancient sources seem to agree Cf. Plut. *Pomp.* 45.1-46.1; App. *Mith.* 116-117; Dio, 37.21; Vell. 2.40.3; Pliny, *NH* 7.97-99 and 37.11ff.

35. See Greenhalgh 168ff., who believes that the theme of the whole display was to compare Pompey and Alexander.

36. On Caesar as a new Alexander see Weinstock 83-90; 186-8.

37. Lucan, 1. See also Getty ad loc.

38. On this aspect of Lucan's poetry cf. Bartsch 10-12; 15-17; 20-22.

39. Cf. for example Lucan's description of the battle of Pharsalus 7.625-630 *quis cruor emissis perruperit aëra uenis / inque hostis cadat arma sui, quis pectora fratris / caedat et, ut notum possit spoliare cadaver, / abscisum longe mittat caput, ora parentis / quis laceret nimiaque probet spectantibus ira / quem iugulat, non esse patrem.*

40. Lucan, 1.111-20. On the passage and its meaning see Bartsch 15.

41. The link between the civil war and the foundation of Rome is made explicit by Lucan at 1. 94-97.

42. Lucan is not the first one to describe civil wars in such a fashion. In Catullus, Virgil and Lucretius the image of a brother who kills a brother becomes a convenient paradigm for civil wars. See for example Lucr. 3.70-72 *sanguine ciuili rem conflant . . . / crudeles gaudent in tristi funere fratris;* Cat. 64.399 *perfudere manus fraterno sanguine fratres;* Verg. *G.* 2.496 *infidos agitans discordia fratres;* 510 *gaudent perfusi sanguine fratrum.* On these two passages see Thomas ad loc. On the topic see also Hardie 29-32; 53-56; 67-68.

43. *BC* 3.3-5.

44. Carter ad loc.

45. *BC* 3.3.1-2.

46. *BC* 3.4.3-6.

47. App. *BC* 2.49. We may also notice that Appian specifies that Pompey intended to use auxiliaries mainly in garrison duty, in building fortifications, and in other services for the Italian soldiers, so that no one of the latter was kept away from the battles.

48. Dio, 41.55.2.

49. Plut. *Pomp.* 64.1 . . .

50. On the important difference between *Bellum Civile* and *Bellum Externum* in Roman culture see Jal 19-27. For other passages where Caesar stresses the heterogeneity and non-Roman nature of Pompey's army see Rambaud 340.

51. Plut. *Pomp.* 67.3 reports that this nickname, given to him by Ahenobarbus, made Pompey odious.

52. For a similar representation of Xerxes' and Darius' army with an emphasis on their majestic proportions and heterogeneity see respectively Hdt. 7.61-96 and Arr. *An.* 2.8.5-8.

53. On the topic see Van Ooteghem 317ff.; Bowie 470-481.

54. Cic. *Att.* 8.11.2. On the passage cf. Shackleton Bailey ad loc.

55. Cic. *Att.* 9.10.3 *me, quem non nulli conseruatorem istius urbis, parentemque esse dixerunt, Getarum et Armeniorum et Colchorum copias ad eam adducere?* See also Shackleton Bailey ad loc.

56. Cic. *Att.* 11.6.2 *me discessisse ab armis numquam paenituit; tanta erat in illis crudelitas, tanta cum barbaris gentibus coniunctio . . .* Cf. also *Fam.* 7.3.2 for similar ideas. Cf. also *Att.* 11.7.3 for Cicero's judgment on the alliance with Juba in the African war (*non esse barbaris auxiliis fallacissimae gentis rem publicam defendendam*).

57. Sal. *Cat.* 11.5. See also P. McGushin ad loc.

58. Livy, 34.4.3 *Haec ego, quo melior laetiorque in dies fortuna rei publicae est, quo magis imperium crescit—et iam in Graeciam Asiamque transcendimus omnibus libidinum inlecebris repletas et regias*

etiam adtrectamus gazas—, eo plus horreo, ne illae magis res nos ceperint, quam nos illas. On this passage and on Livy's sources for the speech see Briscoe ad loc.

59. On the relation between Sallust's account and Livy's see Earl 46ff. Earl notices the similarities between the two accounts both in their descriptions of the lax discipline of the armies and in listing articles of luxury. He then explains Sallust's postdating the various stages of moral decline as an effort on Sallust's part to be consistent, since his over-concentration on *concordia* has led him to reject the tradition of the growth of *luxuria* in the earlier second century. For a similar idea in Sallust see *Jug.* 41-42.

60. Livy, 39.1.3.

61. Livy, 39.1.4.

62. Walsh ad loc. rightly points out that this allegation already goes back to the annalist L. Piso. According to the Elder Pliny (*NH* 34.14=Piso fr. 34 P) he specifically mentioned the bronze couches, one-legged tables and sideboards imported into Rome to grace Vulso's triumph. For a full treatment of the idea of *luxuria* in Livy as a corrupting element that contributed to Rome's decline, see Luce 250-275. For other examples of the same theme linking *luxuria* to Oriental ethnicity see Cic. *ad Q. Frat.* 1.1.19; Tac. *Agr.* 6.2. Pliny, *NH* 34. 34.

63. Livy, 39.6.9.

64. On the seriousness of Roman concern about their moral decadence see Edwards 176.

65. Livy, 34. 4.3 *eo plus horreo, ne illae magis res nos ceperint quam nos illas.*

66. For a detailed list of all the honors bestowed on Caesar from 47 to 44 and the origins of such honors see Weinstock who rightly suggests that it was probably on his Eastern campaigns that Caesar conceived the plan of a Roman version of the ruler cult (413): "There it was a political and religious necessity to claim for himself what had been due to kings of the East . . . These preparations were intensified when the Parthian campaign became imminent. In Parthia Caesar meant to appear as a legitimate king, the heir to all its political and religious traditions, and he wished to be honored accordingly." On the topic see also Collins 127-28.

67. Weinstock 333 with relevant bibliography

68. Suet. *Jul.* 79 *Quin etiam uaria fama percrebuit migraturum Alexandream uel Ilium* . . . Cf also 52.3 where Elvius Cinna was charged with introducing an astonishing law which would enable Caesar to marry *uxores liberorum quaerendorum causa quas et quot uellet.*

69. The date of *BC* has always been controversial. Klotz showed with great probability that *BC* was not published in the lifetime of Caesar but was edited and published shortly after his death by Aulus Hirtius. The view was attacked by Kalinka and Barwick who believed that *BC* was written and published as part of Caesar's propaganda campaign during the war, and that it appeared in two parts, books 1-2 as a unit at the end of 49, and book 3 at the end of 48 or early in 47. Collins 130 adopts instead a middle ground position: the work was indeed written earlier (48) but, since, soon after it was written it no longer fit the new propaganda objectives of Caesar, it remained untouched in Caesar's archives until the summer of 44 when it was resurrected by Hirtius and given over to the copyists. Cf. also La Penna 231, who believes that *BC* was published by Caesar in 47-46, but that the later chapters (3.101 to the end) were probably written at a later date, for in those later chapters La Penna notices signs of a changed policy, especially in chapter 3.105 where: "Cesare . . . prepara il terreno nell'opinione pubblica per un potere assoluto di carattere orientale e teocratico."

Bibliography

Balsdon, J. P. V. D. 1957. "The Veracity of Caesar." *G&R* 4: 19-28.

Bartsch, S. 1997. *Ideology in Cold Blood. A Reading of Lucan's Civil War.* Cambridge MA: Harvard University Press.

Barwick, K. 1951. *Caesars Bellum Civile: Tendenz, Abfassungszeit und Stil.* Leipzig: Akademie Verlag.

Bowie, A. M. 1990. "The Death of Priam: Allegory and History in the *Aeneid.*" *CQ* 40:470-481.

Briant, P. 1988. *Hérodote et la Société Perse* in *FH* 35: 69-105.

Briscoe, J. 1981. *A Commentary on Livy. Books XXXIV-XXXVII.* Oxford: Clarendon Press.

Carter, J. M. 1991. *Julius Caesar. The Civil War. Books I-II.* Warminster: Aris & Phillips.

———. 1993. *Julius Caesar. The Civil War. Book III.* Warmister: Aris & Phillips.

Collins, J. H. 1959. "On the Date and Interpretation of the *Bellum Civile*" *AJP* 80: 113-132.

Damon, C. 1994. "Caesar's Practical Prose." *CJ* 89: 183-195.

Earl, D. C. 1961. *The Political Thought of Sallust.* Cambridge: Cambridge University Press.

Eden, P. T. 1962. "Caesar's Style: Inheritance versus Intelligence." *Glotta* 40: 74-117.

Edwards, C. 1993. *The Politics of Immorality in Ancient Rome.* Cambridge: Cambridge University Press.

Feldherr, A. 1998. *Spectacle and Society in Livy's History.* Berkeley: University of California Press.

Flory, S. 1987. *The Archaic Smile of Herodotus.* Detroit: Wayne State University Press.

Getty, R. J. 1940. *M. Annaei Lucani. De Bello Civili Liber I.* Cambridge: Cambridge University Press.

Gotoff, H. C. 1984. "Towards a Practical Criticism of Caesar's Prose Style." *Ill. Class. Studies* 9: 1-18.

Greenhalgh, P. 1981. *Pompey, the Roman Alexander.* Columbia: University of Missouri Press.

Hall, E. 1989. *Inventing the Barbarian. Greek Self-Definition through Tragedy.* Oxford: Clarendon Press.

Hamilton, J. R. 1969. *Plutarch. A commentary.* Oxford: Clarendon Press.

Hardie, P. 1993. *The Epic Successors of Virgil. A Study in the Dynamics of a Tradition.* Cambridge: Cambridge University Press.

Hinds, S. 1998. *Allusion and Intertext. Dynamics of Appropriation in Roman Poetry.* Cambridge: Cambridge University Press.

How, W. W. - Wells, J. 1928. *A Commentary o n Herodotus II.* Oxford: Clarendon Press.

Jal, P. 1963. *La guerre Civile a Rome, Étude Littéraire et Morale.* Paris: Presses Universitaires de France.

Kalinka, E. 1912. "Die Herausgabe des *Bellum Civile.*" *WS* 34:203-7.

Klotz, A. 1911. "Zu Caesars *Bellum Civile.*" *RhM* 66:81-93.

Kraner, F., Hofmann, F., Meusel, H. 1959. *C. Iulii Caesaris Commentarii De Bello Civili.* (12th ed. with textual and bibliographical addenda by H. Oppermann) Berlin: Weidmannsche Verlagsbuchhandlung.

Kurke, L. 1991. "The politics of αβρ ςύνη in Archaic Greece." *ClAnt* 10:91-120.

La Penna, A. 1952. "Tendenze e Arte del *Bellum civile* di Cesare." *Maia* 5: 191-233.

Luce, T. J. 1977. *Livy: The Composition of His History.* Princeton: Princeton University Press.

McGushin, P. 1977. *C. Sallustius Crispus, Bellum Catilinae. A Commentary.* Leiden: Mnemosyne, Bibliotheca Classica Batava. Supplementum 45.

Miles, G. B. 1986. "The Cycle of Roman History in Livy's First Pentad." *AJP* 107: 1-33.

Nettleship, H. 1886. "The Historical Development of Classical Latin Prose." *JPh* 15: 35-56.

Rambaud, M. 1953. *L' Art de la Déformation historique dans les Commentaires de César.* Paris: Les Belles Lettres.

Rowe, G. O. 1967. "Dramatic Structures in Caesar's *Bellum Civile.*" *TAPA* 98: 399-414.

Schlicher, J. J. 1936. "The Development of Caesar's Narrative Style." *CP* 21: 211-224.

Shackleton Bailey, D. R. 1968. *Cicero's Letters to Atticus IV.* Cambridge: Cambridge University Press.

Stevens, C. E. 1952. "The *Bellum Gallicum* as a Work of Propaganda." *Latomus* 11: 3-18; 165-79.

Thomas, R. 1988. *Virgil. Georgics* I. Cambridge: Cambridge University Press.

Van Ooteghem, J. 1954. *Pompée le Grand. Bâtisseur d'Empire.* Bruxelles: Mem. Acad. de Belgique 49.

Walsh, P. G. 1994. *Livy. Book 39.* Warminster: Aris & Phillips.

Weinstock, S. 1971. *Divus Julius.* Oxford: Clarendon Press.

Welch, K. and Powell, A. 1998. *Julius Caesar as Artful Reporter. The War Commentaries as Political Instruments.* London: Duckworth.

Williams, M. F. 1985. "Caesar's Bibracte Narrative and the Aims of Caesarian Style." *ICS* 10:215-226.

FURTHER READING

Bibliography

Brown, Virginia. *The Textual Transmission of Caesar's "Civil War."* Leiden, The Netherlands: E. J. Brill, 1972, 96p.

> Examines and describes assorted manuscripts of *De Bello Civili.*

Biographies

Fuller, J. F. C. *Julius Caesar: Man, Soldier, Tyrant.* London: Eyre & Spottiswoode, 1965, 114 p.

> Uses classical sources in assessing Caesar's career as a general as sometimes brilliant, but sometimes blundering.

Gelzer, Matthias, *Caesar: Politician and Statesman.* Translated by Peter Needham, 1921. Reprint. Harvard University Press, 1985, 368 p.

> Standard biography originally published in German.

Kahn, Arthur D. *The Education of Julius Caesar: A Biography, A Reconstruction.* New York: Schocken Books, 1986, 514 p.

> Explores the life of Caesar in the context of his times.

Criticism

Balsdon, J. P. V. D. "The Veracity of Caesar." *Greece and Rome* 4 (1957): 19-28.

> Explores problems that arise in determining the truthfulness of Caesar's writings.

Eden, P. T. "Caesar's Style: Inheritance versus Intelligence. *Glotta* 40 (1962): 74-117.

> Examines how and why Caesar developed his chronicles from the traditional *annales*.

Gotoff, H. C. "Towards a Practical Criticism of Caesar's Prose Style." *Illinois Classical Studies* 9 (Spring, 1984): 1-18.

> Argues that Caesar's sentence structure and overall writing style are not so plain as many critics believe.

Schlicher, J. J. "The Development of Caesar's Narrative Style." *Classical Philology* 21, No. 3 (July 1936): 212-24.

> Traces the evolution of Caesar's style from its early conservativeness to its following of contemporaneous rhetorical trends.

Wardle, D. "'The Sainted Julius': Valerius Maximus and the Dictator." *Classical Philology* 92, No. 4 (October 1997): 323-45.

> Assesses the importance of Valerius Maximus's portrayal of Caesar.

White, Peter. "Julius Caesar in Augustan Rome." *Phoenix* 42 (Winter 1988): 334-56.

> Examines Augustus's treatment of Caesar by way of monuments, ceremonies, and writing.

Williams, Mark F. "Caesar's Bibracte Narrative and the Aims of Caesarian Style." *Illinois Classical Studies* 10 (Fall, 1985): 215-26.

> Contends that scholars perform a disservice to Caesar's writings when they judge them according to standards of Ciceronian style.

Oedipus Tyrannus

Sophocles

c. 425 B.C.

(Also translated as *Oedipus Rex*) Greek play.

The following entry presents criticism on Sophocles's *Oedipus Tyrannus*. For more information on Sophocles's life and career, see *CMLC* Volume 2.

INTRODUCTION

Oedipus Tyrannus is considered Sophocles's masterpiece and is probably the most famous of all the Greek tragedies. Aristotle deemed it a perfect play. First performed about 425 B.C., not long after a plague had ravaged Athens, *Oedipus Tyrannus* is set in Thebes, a city falling to ruin from a similar calamity. King Oedipus is told that the city will continue to suffer until the murderer of the previous king is brought to justice. Oedipus vows to discover the evildoer's identity and to punish him. Unaware that he himself is the killer, Oedipus relentlessly pursues the truth until he discovers his own guilt and blinds himself so that he may never see his father in the afterworld. Sophocles took a well-known legend and intensified it for his Athenian audience by emphasizing qualities they held dear: courage, self-assuredness, and love for their city. In this play of man versus inexorable fate, Sophocles used dramatic irony to further develop audience interest: they know how the play will end, relishing the irony of the words spoken by the characters, who do not know. In his *Poetics,* Aristotle used *Oedipus Tyrannus* as a model tragedy, analyzing Sophocles's masterful use of reversal, discovery, and character. *Oedipus Tyrannus* has received considerable attention in modern times partly due to Sigmund Freud, who, tremendously moved by the play, popularized the notion of the Oedipus Complex. The play continues to engage audiences and scholars to this day.

PLOT AND MAJOR CHARACTERS

Oedipus Tyrannus opens with the people of Thebes praying for King Oedipus to save their dying city. Creon, the brother of Oedipus's wife, Jocasta, returns from a visit to the oracle of Apollo. He reports the oracle's message: the plague on Thebes is the result of the unpunished murder of the previous king, Laius. Oedipus vows to discover the murderer's identity and avenge Laius's death. He calls for Tiresias, an old blind seer, to reveal what he knows. The

seer refuses and Oedipus is enraged at his disobedience. Tiresias, also angered, then tells the King that it is Oedipus himself who, as the murderer, has defiled the city, and further, that he is unknowingly living with his closest kin in a shameful manner. Oedipus accuses the seer of conspiring with Creon to overthrow him. Tiresias replies that Oedipus will soon be horrified when he learns the truth of his parentage and of his marriage. Oedipus considers executing Creon but Jocasta intercedes, and Creon is exiled instead. Jocasta tries to reassure her husband by insisting that no one, not even oracles, can divine the future. As an example, she tells him that she and Laius were once told that their son would kill his father, and that this did not happen since their son died on a mountain, where he was abandoned as an infant, and Laius was killed by thieves—

there was a witness to the murder. This information does anything but calm Oedipus. He tells his wife that he had believed his parents to be Polybus of Corinth and Merope, a Dorian, until a drunken reveler at a banquet announced that Oedipus was someone else's son. Polybus and Merope, when questioned, were angry and upset, but neither confirmed nor denied the charge. Oedipus further recalls that he traveled to Delphi, to ask the oracle of Apollo the truth about his parentage. He was not given the answer he sought, but was instead told that he would slay his father and have children with his mother. In horror, he fled in the opposite direction of Corinth, until he came to a place where three roads intersected. He met a small party of men who rudely tried to shove him out of their way. Oedipus struck the driver and in return was struck by the man being drawn in the wagon; in the fight that followed, Oedipus slew them all—or so he thought. After Oedipus finishes his story, a messenger brings news that Polybus has died and Oedipus must return to rule Corinth as their king. He refuses, fearing that Apollo's oracle of fathering children by his mother might come true. The messenger tells Oedipus not to worry, that he was not really Polybus's son nor was Merope his mother. In reality a herdsman who worked for Laius gave Oedipus to the messenger, who in turn gave him to Polybus to raise as his own. Jocasta begs Oedipus to stop his search for the truth, but to no avail. The herdsman, who was also the witness to Laius's death, arrives. He admits that Laius had instructed him to kill the infant Oedipus but that he had given the child to the messenger instead. At last Oedipus realizes that he indeed has killed his father and sired four children with his mother. He rushes to find Jocasta and learns that she has locked herself in her room. He breaks the bolts of the doors and finds her hanged by her own hair. He rips out the brooches from the shoulders of her dress and gouges his eyes with them. Creon returns, now king, and Oedipus begs that he be exiled. Creon answers that the matter must be decided by the gods.

MAJOR THEMES

Sophocles includes several themes in his play: he explores the potential dangers of pursuing self-knowledge, the question of guilt and innocence, and the nature of fate. Perhaps no play has better demonstrated the maxim that a man's character is his fate, for it is in fulfilling his personal characteristics—his relentless pursuit of knowledge, his absolute confidence in himself, and his quickness to anger—that Oedipus meets his destiny, and the prophecies are realized.

CRITICAL RECEPTION

Sophocles, Aeschylus, and Euripides were recognized in their own time as masters of drama, and *Oedipus Tyrannus* was hailed as Sophocles's masterpiece. Since its brilliance is indisputable, critics concentrate on other matters, including formulating their own interpretations of the play and

discussing its themes, Sophocles's use of irony, and the function of the chorus. Francis Fergusson explores audience expectations and perceptions. Eric A. Havelock contends that signs of oral composition can be found in the play and that *Oedipus Tyrannus* was written during a major shift in composition styles. R. Drew Griffith explains that the ancient Greeks had a different view of what constituted guilt than modern man—that even though Oedipus was unaware of his father's identity when he killed him, he was nevertheless guilty of patricide. Some critics insist there are problems with understanding what actually transpired in the play's recalled events due to unresolved contradictions, for example the report that there were many men, not just one, who attacked and killed Laius. Erich Fromm considers Freud's interpretation of the play and the nature of patriarchal and matriarchal psychological principles. Critics agree that *Oedipus Tyrannus* is a gripping exploration of the role of the gods in man's life and a warning to mankind to avoid becoming too proud, too godlike. The numerous modern translations of the play, its continuing performance, and unwavering critical interest in it all attest to the magnitude of its popularity.

PRINCIPAL WORKS

Aias [*Ajax*] (drama) 450 B.C.
Antigonē [*Antigone*] (drama) 442? B.C.
Ichneutai [*The Trackers*] drama 440? B.C.
Trakhiniai [*The Trachiniae*] (drama) c. 440–30 B.C.
Oedipus Tyrannus (drama) 425? B.C.
Ēlektra [*Electra*] (drama) c. 425–10 B.C.
Philoktētēs [*Philoctetes*] (drama) 409 B.C.
Oedipus at Colonus (drama) 401 B.C.

Principal English Translations

Oedipus Tyrannus (translated by Luci Berkowitz) 1970
Oedipus the King (translated by Stephen Berg and Diskin Clay) 1990
Oedipus Rex (translated by E. H. Plumptre) 1993
Oedipus the King (translated by Bernard Knox) 1994
The Theban Plays (translated by David Grene) 1994
Oedipus Plays of Sophocles (translated by Paul Roche) 1996
Oedipus the King (translated by Nicholas Rudall) 2000
Oedipus Tyrannus (translated by Paul Woodruff) 2000

*Date indicated designates first performance.

CRITICISM

Erich Fromm (essay date 1949)

SOURCE: "The Oedipus Complex and the Oedipus Myth," in *The Family: Its Function and Destiny*, edited by Ruth Nanda Anshen, Harper & Brothers, 1949, pp. 420-48.

[*In the following excerpt, Fromm contends that* Oedipus Tyrannus *must be examined in conjunction with* Oedipus at Colonus *and* Antigone *in order for its theme of the son rebelling against patriarchal control to be fully explicated.*]

If the Oedipus Rex is capable of moving a modern reader or playgoer no less powerfully than it moved the contemporary Greeks, the only possible explanation is that the effect of the Greek tragedy does not depend upon the conflict between fate and human will, but upon the peculiar nature of the material by which this conflict is revealed. There must be a voice within us which is prepared to acknowledge the compelling power of fate in the Oedipus, while we are able to condemn the situations occurring in Die Ahnfrau or other tragedies of fate as arbitrary inventions. And there actually is a motive in the story of King Oedipus which explains the verdict of this inner voice. His fate moves us only because it might have been our own, because the oracle laid upon us before our birth the very curse which rested upon him. It may be that we are all destined to direct our first sexual impulses toward our mothers, and our first impulses of hatred and violence toward our fathers; our dreams convince us that we are. King Oedipus, who slew his father Laius and wedded his mother Jocasta, is nothing more or less than a wish-fulfillment—the fulfillment of the wish of our childhood. But we, more fortunate than he, in so far as we have not become psychoneurotics, have since our childhood succeeded in withdrawing our sexual impulses from our mothers, and in forgetting our jealousy of our fathers. We recoil from the person for whom this primitive wish of our childhood has been fulfilled with all the force of the repression which these wishes have undergone in our minds since childhood. As the poet brings the guilt of Oedipus to light by his investigation, he forces us to become aware of our own inner selves, in which the same impulses are still extant, even though they are suppressed. The antithesis with which the chorus departs:—

". . . Behold, this is Oedipus
who unravelled the great riddle, and was first in power,
Whose fortune all the townsmen praised and envied;
See in what dread adversity he sank!"

—this admonition touches us and our own pride, us who since the years of our childhood have grown so wise and so powerful in our own estimation. Like Oedipus, we live in ignorance of the desires that offend morality, the desires that nature has forced upon us and after their unveiling we may well prefer to avert our gaze from the scenes of our childhood.[1]

The concept of the Oedipus complex, which Freud so beautifully presents in the passage just quoted, became one of the cornerstones of his psychological system. He believed that this concept was the key to an understanding of history and of the evolution of religion and morality. His conviction was that this very complex constituted the fundamental mechanism in the development of the child, and he maintained that the Oedipus complex was the cause for psychopathological development and the "kernel of neurosis."

Here we shall limit ourselves to a brief description of the Oedipus complex with regard to the little boy.

Freud assumed that the little boy at the age of 4 or 5 is sexually attracted to his mother; hence he is jealous of his father, who appears to him as a superior, threatening rival; hence he becomes intensely afraid of his father and specifically afraid of being castrated. Since this fear becomes too intense for comfort and security, the boy changes his aim. He gives up the mother as an object of his sexual strivings and identifies himself with the father. In doing so he overcomes his fear, and at the same time his own masculine development is strengthened by the fact that he now wants to be like his father. Freud assumed that a particular identification takes place—namely, with the father's conscience, his commands, and his prohibitions—and that thus the bases for the development of conscience in the boy are laid.

In normal development, the Oedipus complex results in the strengthening of masculine development and in the growth of conscience. The boy's attachment to the mother is transferred later on to girls of his own age, although his choice of a love object may remain determined to some extent by the image of the mother. In the neurotic development the tie with the mother is not severed. She herself, or women who resemble her, remains the exclusive love object. In the latter case, the relationship to the mother surrogate retains the qualities which were characteristic of the little boy's attachment to his mother—those of dependency, lack of responsibility, and the need to be taken care of. Simultaneously, rivalry with the father or father surrogates and the hate and fear of them remain active too.

Freud assumed that the Oedipus complex determines also the development of the little girl, who is attached to the father and competes with the mother. Some theoretical difficulties, however, arise in the concept of the girl's Oedipus complex, a discussion of which would lead us too far into the intricacies of Freud's system and is at the same time not necessary here. For the same reason we shall omit a discussion of the passive attachment of the boy to the father, rooted in the boy's feminine component.

Freud's concept was a result of clinical observations and theoretical speculation, and it must have been very gratifying to him to discover that one of the classic Greek myths, that of Oedipus, seemed not only to be a symbolic expression but also a confirmation of his theory and that the fact of the incestuous tie to the mother and the resulting rivalry with the father was revealed by the myth to be one of the most profound, though unconscious, strivings in man.

Freud referred to the Oedipus myth in the version of Sophocles' tragedy **King Oedipus.** This tragedy tells us that an oracle has told Laius, the King of Thebes, and his wife, Jocasta, that if they would have a son this son would kill his father and marry his own mother. When a son, *Oedipus,* is born to them, Jocasta decides to escape the fate predicted by the oracle by killing the infant. She gives Oedipus to a shepherd who is to abandon the child in the woods with his feet bound so that he would die. But the shepherd, taking pity on the child, gives the infant to a man in the service of the King of Corinth, who in turn brings him to his master. The king adopts the boy as his own son, and the young prince grows up in Corinth not knowing that he is not the true son of the King of Corinth. He is told by the oracle in Delphi that it is his fate to kill his father and to marry his mother. He decides to avoid this fate by never going back to his alleged parents. On his way back from Delphi he engages in a violent argument with an old man riding in a carriage, loses his temper, and slays the man and his servant without knowing that he has slain his father, the King of Thebes.

His wanderings lead him to Thebes. There the Sphinx is devouring the young men and women of the city, and she will cease doing so only if someone will find the right answer to a riddle she asks. The riddle is this: "What is it which first goes on four, then on two, and eventually on three?" The city of Thebes has promised that anyone who can solve the riddle and thus free the city from the Sphinx will be made king and will be given the king's widow for a wife. Oedipus undertakes the venture. He finds the answer to the riddle—which is *man*, who as a child walks on all four, as an adult on two, and in his old age on three (with a cane). The Sphinx throws herself into the ocean, the city is saved from calamity, and Oedipus becomes king and marries Jocasta, his mother.

After Oedipus has reigned happily for some time, the city is ravaged by a plague which kills many of its citizens. The seer, Theiresias, reveals that the plague is the punishment for the twofold crime which Oedipus has committed, that of patricide and incest. Oedipus, after having tried desperately not to see this truth, blinds himself when he is compelled to see it, and Jocasta commits suicide. The tragedy ends at the point where Oedipus has suffered punishment for a crime which he committed unknowingly and in spite of his conscious effort to avoid committing it.

Was Freud justified in concluding that this myth confirms his view that unconscious incestuous drives and the resulting hate against the father-rival are to be found in any male child? Indeed, it does seem as if the myth confirmed Freud's theory that the Oedipus complex justifiably bears its name.

If we examine the myth more closely, however, questions arise which cast some doubts on the correctness of this view. The most pertinent question is this: If Freud's interpretation is right, we should expect the myth to tell us that Oedipus met Jocasta without knowing that she was his mother, fell in love with her, and then killed his father, again unknowingly. But there is no indication whatsoever in the myth that Oedipus is attracted by or falls in love with Jocasta. The only reason we are given for Oedipus' marriage to Jocasta is that she, as it were, goes with the throne. Should we believe that a myth the central theme of

which constitutes an incestuous relationship between mother and son would entirely omit the element of attraction between the two? This question is all the more weighty in view of the fact that, in the older versions of the oracle, the prediction of the marriage to the mother is mentioned only once in Nikolaus of Damascus' description, which according to Carl Roberts goes back to a relatively new source.[2]

Furthermore, Oedipus is described as the courageous and wise hero who becomes the benefactor of Thebes. How can we understand that the same Oedipus is described as having committed the crime most horrible in the eyes of his contemporaries? This question has sometimes been answered by pointing to the fact that it is the very essence of the Greek concept of tragedy that it is the powerful and strong who are suddenly struck by disaster. Whether such an answer is sufficient or whether another view can give us a more satisfactory answer remains to be seen.

The foregoing questions arise from a consideration of **King Oedipus.** If we examine only this tragedy, without taking into account the two other parts of the trilogy, **Oedipus at Colonus** and **Antigone,** no definite answer can be given. But we are at least in the position of formulating a hypothesis, namely *that the myth can be understood as a symbol not of the incestuous love between mother and son but of the rebellion of the son against the authority of the father in the patriarchal family; that the marriage of Oedipus and Jocasta is only a secondary element, only one of the symbols of the son's victory who takes his father's place and with it all his privileges.*

The validity of this hypothesis can be tested by examining the whole Oedipus myth, particularly in the form presented by Sophocles in the two other parts of his trilogy, **Oedipus at Colonus** and **Antigone.**[3]

In **Oedipus at Colonus** we find Oedipus near Athens at the grove of the Eumenides shortly before he dies. After having blinded himself, Oedipus had remained in Thebes, which was ruled by Creon, his uncle, who after some time exiled him. Oedipus' two daughters, Antigone and Ismene, accompanied him into exile; but his two sons, Eteocles and Polyneices, refused to help their blind father. After his departure, the two brothers strove for possession of the throne. Eteocles won; but Polyneices, refusing to yield, sought to conquer the city with outside help and to wrest the power from his brother. In **Oedipus at Colonus** we see him approach his father, begging his forgiveness and asking his assistance. But Oedipus is relentless in his hate against his sons. In spite of the passionate pleading of Polyneices, supported by Antigone's plea, he refuses forgiveness. His last words to his son are:

> And thou—begone, abhorred of me, and unfathered!— begone, thou vilest of the vile, and with thee take these my curses which I call down on thee—never to vanquish the land of thy race, no, nor ever return to hill-girt Argos, but by a kindred hand to die, and slay him by whom thou hast been driven out. Such is my

prayer; and I call the paternal darkness of dread Tartarus to take thee unto another home,—I call the spirits of this place,—I call the Destroying God, who hath set that dreadful hatred in you twain. Go, with these words in thine ears—go, and publish it to the Cadmeans all, yea, and to thine own staunch allies, that Oedipus hath divided such honours to his sons.[4]

In *Antigone* we find another father-son conflict as one of the central themes of the tragedy. Here Creon, the representative of the authoritarian principle in state and family, is opposed by his son, Haemon, who reproaches him for his ruthless despotism and his cruelty against Antigone. Haemon tries to kill his father and, failing to do so, kills himself.

We find that the theme which runs through the three tragedies is the conflict between father and son. In *King Oedipus*, Oedipus kills his father Laius who intended to take the infant's life. In *Oedipus at Colonus* Oedipus gives vent to his intense hate against his sons, and in *Antigone* we find the same hate again between Creon and Haemon. The problem of incest exists neither in the relationship between Oedipus' sons to their mother nor in the relationship between Haemon and his mother, Eurydice. If we interpret *King Oedipus* in the light of the whole trilogy, the assumption seems plausible that the real issue in *King Oedipus*, too, is the conflict between father and son and not the problem of incest.

Freud had interpreted the antagonism between Oedipus and his father as the unconscious rivalry caused by Oedipus' incestuous strivings. If we do not accept this explanation, the question arises as how otherwise to explain the conflict between father and son which we find in all the three tragedies. One clue is given in *Antigone*. The rebellion of Haemon against Creon is rooted in the particular structure of Creon's relationship to Haemon. Creon represents the strictly authoritarian principle both in the family and in the state, and it is against this type of authority that Haemon rebels. An analysis of the whole Oedipus trilogy will show that the struggle against paternal authority is its main theme and that the roots of this struggle go far back into the ancient fight between the patriarchal and matriarchal systems of society. Oedipus as well as Haemon and Antigone are representatives of the matriarchal principle; they attack a social and religious order based on the powers and privileges of the father, represented by Laius and Creon.

Since this interpretation is based on Bachofen's analysis of Greek mythology, it is necessary to acquaint the reader briefly with the principles of Bachofen's theory.

In his "Mutterrecht" (mother right), published in 1861, Bachofen suggested that in the beginning of human history sexual relations were promiscuous; that therefore only the mother's parenthood was unquestionable, to her alone consanguinity could be traced, and she was the authority and law giver—the ruler both in the family group and in society. On the basis of his analysis of religious docu-ments of Greek and Roman antiquity, Bachofen came to the conclusion that the supremacy of women had found its expression not only in the sphere of social and family organization but also in religion. He found evidence that the religion of the Olympian gods was preceded by a religion in which goddesses, mother-like figures, were the supreme deities.

Bachofen assumed that in a long-drawn-out historical process men defeated women, subdued them, and succeeded in making themselves the rulers in a social hierarchy. The patriarchal system which was thus established is characterized by monogamy (at least so far as women were concerned), by the authority of the father in the family, and by the dominant role of men in a hierarchically organized society. The religion of this patriarchal culture corresponded to its social organization. Instead of the mother-goddesses, male gods became supreme rulers over man, as the father was in the family.

One of the most striking and brilliant illustrations of Bachofen's interpretation of Greek myths is his analysis of Aeschylus' *Oresteia,* which according to Bachofen is a symbolic representation of a last fight between the maternal goddesses and the victorious paternal gods. Clytemnestra had killed her husband, Agamemnon, in order not to give up her lover, Aegisthus. Orestes, her son by Agamemnon, avenges his father's death by killing his mother and her lover. The Erinyes, representatives of the old mother-goddesses and the matriarchal principal, persecute Orestes and demand his punishment, while Apollo and Athene (the latter not born from woman but sprung from the head of Zeus), the representatives of the new patriarchal religion, are on Orestes' side. The argument is centered around the principles of patriarchal and matriarchal religion, respectively. For the matriarchal world there is only one sacred tie, that of mother and child, and consequently matricide is the ultimate and unforgivable crime. From the patriarchal point of view, the son's love and respect for the father is his paramount duty and therefore patricide is the paramount crime. Clytemnestra's killing of her husband, from the patriarchal standpoint a major crime because of the supreme position of the husband, is considered differently from the matriarchal standpoint, since "she was not related by blood to the man whom she killed." The murder of a husband does not concern the Erinyes, since to them only ties of blood and the sanctity of the mother count. To the Olympian gods, on the other hand, the murder of the mother is no crime if it is carried out as revenge for the father's death. In Aeschylus' *Oresteia,* Orestes is acquitted, but this victory of the patriarchal principle is somewhat mitigated by a compromise with the defeated goddesses. They agree to accept the new order and to be satisfied with a minor role as protectors of the earth and as goddesses of agricultural fertility.

Bachofen showed that the difference between the matriarchal and patriarchal order went far beyond the social supremacy of men and women respectively, but was one of social and moral principles. Matriarchal culture is characterized by an emphasis on ties of blood, ties to the soil, and a passive acceptance of all natural phenomena. Patriarchal society, in contrast, is characterized by respect for man-made law, by a predominance of rational thought, and by an effort to change natural phenomena by man. Insofar as these principles are concerned, the patriarchal culture constitutes a definite progress over the matriarchal world. In other respects, however, the matriarchal principles were superior to the victorious patriarchal ones. In the matriarchal concept all men are equal, since they are all the children of mothers and each one a child of Mother Earth. A mother loves her children all alike and without conditions, since her love is based on the fact that they are her children and not on any particular merit or achievement; the aim of life is the happiness of men, and there is nothing more important or dignified than human existence and life. The patriarchal system, on the other hand, considers obedience to authority to be the main virtue. Instead of the principle of equality we find the concept of the favorite son and a hierarchical order in society.

> The relationship [Bachofen says] through which mankind has first grown into civilization which is the beginning of the development of every virtue and of the formation of the nobler aspects of human existence is the matriarchal principle, which becomes effective as the principle of love, unity, and peace. The woman sooner than the man learns in caring for the infant to extend her love beyond her own self to other human beings and to direct all her gifts and imagination to the aim of preserving and beautifying the existence of another being. All development of civilization, devotion, care, and the mourning for the dead are rooted in her.[5]

> The motherly love is not only more tender but also more general and universal. . . . Its principle is that of universality, whereas the patriarchal principle is that of restrictions. . . . The idea of the universal brotherhood of man is rooted in the principle of motherhood, and this very idea vanishes with the development of patriarchal society. The patriarchal family is a closed and restricted organism. The matriarchal family, on the other hand, has that universal character with which all evolution begins and which is characteristic of maternal life in contrast to the spiritual, the image of Mother Earth, Demeter. Each woman's womb will give brothers and sisters to every human being until, with the development of the patriarchal principle, this unity is dissolved and superseded by the principle of hierarchy. In matriarchal societies, this principle has found frequent and even legally formulated expressions. It is the basis of the principle of universal freedom and equality which we find as one of the basic traits in matriarchal cultures. . . . Absence of inner disharmony, a longing for peace . . . a tender humaneness which one can still see in the facial expression of Egyptian statues penetrates the matriarchal world. . . .[6]

Bachofen's discovery found confirmation by an American scholar, L. H. Morgan, who entirely independently came to the conclusion[7] that the kinship system of the American Indians—similar to that found in Asia, Africa, and Australia—was based on the matriarchal principle and that the most significant institution in such cultures, the gens, was organized in conformity with the matriarchal principle. Morgan's conclusions about principles of value in a matriarchal society were quite similar to Bachofen's. He proposed that the higher form of civilization "will be a repetition—but on a higher level—of the principles of liberty, equality, and fraternity which characterized the ancient gens." Both Bachofen's and Morgan's theories of matriarchy were, if not entirely ignored, disputed by most anthropologists. This was also the case in the work of Robert Briffault, who in *The Mothers*[8] continued Bachofen's research and confirmed it by a brilliant analysis of new anthropological data. The violence of the antagonism against the theory of matriarchy arouses the suspicion that the criticism was not entirely free from an emotionally founded prejudice against an assumption so foreign to the thinking and feeling of our patriarchal culture. There is little doubt that many single objections to the matriarchal theory are justified. Nevertheless, Bachofen's main thesis that we find an older layer of matriarchal religion underneath the more recent patriarchal religion of Greece seems to me to be established by him beyond any doubt.

After this brief survey of Bachofen's theory we are in a better position to take up the discussion of our hypothesis that the hostility between father and son which is the theme running through Sophocles' trilogy is to be understood as an attack against the victorious patriarchal order by the representatives of the defeated matriarchal system.

King Oedipus offers little direct evidence except in some points which will be mentioned presently. But the original Oedipus myth in the various versions which existed in Greece and upon which Sophocles built his tragedy gives an important clue. In the various formulations of the myth, the figure of Oedipus was always connected with the cult of the earth goddesses, the representatives of matriarchal religion, according to Bachofen. In almost all versions of the Oedipus myth, from parts which deal with his exposure as an infant to those which are centered around his death, traces of this connection can be found.[9] Thus, for instance, Eteonos, the only Boeotian city which had a cult shrine of Oedipus and where the whole myth probably originated, also has the shrine of the earth goddess, Demeter.[10] At Colonus (near Athens), where Oedipus finds his last resting place, was an old shrine of Demeter and the Erinyes which has probably existed prior to the Oedipus myth.[11] As we shall see later on, Sophocles has emphasized this connection between Oedipus and the chthonic goddesses in *Oedipus at Colonus.*

Another aspect of the Oedipus myth—Oedipus' connection with the Sphinx—seems also to point to the connection between Oedipus and the matriarchal principle as described by Bachofen. The Sphinx had announced that the one who could solve her riddle would save the city from her wrath. Oedipus succeeds, where everyone else before him had failed, and thus becomes the saviour of

Thebes. But if we look at the riddle more closely we are struck by the insignificance of the riddle in comparison with the reward for its solution. Any clever boy of 12 might guess that that which goes first on four, then on two, and eventually on three is man. Why should the right guess be proof of such extraordinary powers as to make their possessor the saviour of the city? The answer to this question lies in an analysis of the real meaning of the riddle, an analysis which must follow the principles of interpretation of myths and dreams as they were developed by Bachofen and Freud.[12] They have shown that often the most important element in the real content of a dream or myth appears as a much less important or even insignificant part of the manifest formulation, whereas that part of the manifest formulation which has the main accent is only a minor part in the real content.[13]

Applying this principle to the Sphinx myth, it would seem that the important element in the riddle is not the part which is stressed in the manifest formulation of the myth, namely, the riddle itself, but the answer to the riddle, *man.* If we translate the Sphinx's words from symbolic into overt language we hear her say: He who knows that the most important answer man can give to the most difficult question with which he is confronted is man himself can save mankind. The riddle itself, the answer to which required nothing but cleverness, serves only as a veil for the latent meaning of the question, the importance of man. This very emphasis on the importance of man is part of the principle of the matriarchal world as Bachofen described it. Sophocles in *Antigone* made this principle the center of Antigone's as against Creon's position. What matters for Creon and the patriarchal order he represents is the state, man-made laws, and obedience to them. What matters to Antigone is man himself, the natural law, and love. Oedipus becomes the saviour of Thebes, proving by his very answer to the Sphinx that he belongs to the same world which is represented by Antigone and expressive of the matriarchal order.

One element in the myth and in Sophocles' *King Oedipus* seems to contradict our hypothesis—the figure of Jocasta. On the assumption that she symbolizes the motherly principle, the question arises why the mother is destroyed instead of being victorious, provided the explanation suggested here is correct. The answer to this question will show that the role of Jocasta not only does not contradict our hypothesis but tends to confirm it. Jocasta's crime is that of not having fulfilled her duty as a mother; she had wanted to kill her child in order to save her husband. This, from the standpoint of patriarchal society, is a legitimate decision, but from the standpoint of matriarchal society and matriarchal ethics it is the unforgivable crime. It is she who by committing this crime starts the chain of events which eventually lead to her own and to her husband's and son's destruction. In order to understand this point we must not lose sight of the fact that the myth as it was known to Sophocles had already been changed according to the patriarchal pattern, that the manifest and conscious frame of reference is that of patriarchy, and that the latent

and older meaning appears only in a veiled and often distorted form. The patriarchal system had been victorious, and the myth explains the reasons for the downfall of matriarchy. It proposes that the mother by violating her paramount duty brought about her own destruction. The final judgment, however, whether this interpretation of Jocasta's role and of *King Oedipus* is correct must wait until we have analyzed *Oedipus at Colonus* and *Antigone.*

In *Oedipus at Colonus* we see the blind Oedipus accompanied by his two daughters arriving near Athens, close to the grove of the goddesses of the earth. The oracle has prophesied that if Oedipus would be buried in this grove he would protect Athens from invasion by her enemies. In the course of the tragedy Oedipus makes known to Theseus the word of the oracle. Theseus gladly accepts the offer that he become the posthumous benefactor of Athens. Oedipus retreats into the grove of the goddesses and dies in a mysterious way not known to anybody but Theseus.

Who are these goddesses? Why do they offer a sanctuary to Oedipus? What does the oracle mean by telling us that Oedipus in finding his last home in this grove reverts to his role of saviour and benefactor?

In *Oedipus at Colonus* Oedipus implores the goddesses, saying:

> *Queens of dread aspect,* since your seat is the first in this land whereat I have bent the knee, show not yourselves ungracious to Phoebus or to myself; who, when he proclaimed that doom of many woes, spake of this as a rest for me after long years—on reaching my goal in a land where I should find a seat of the *Awful Goddesses,* and a hospitable shelter—even that there I should close my weary life, with benefits, through my having dwelt therein, for mine hosts, but ruin for those who sent me forth—who drove me away.[14]

Oedipus calls the goddesses "Queens of dread aspect" and "Awful Goddesses." Why are they "dreadful" and "awful," since to him they are the goddesses of his last resting place and those who will give him peace eventually? Why does the chorus say:

> A wanderer that old man must have been—a wanderer, not a dweller in the land; else never would he have advanced into this untrodden *grove of the maidens* with whom none may strive, *whose name we tremble to speak,* by whom we pass with eyes turned away, moving our lips, without sound or word, in still devotion.[15]

The answer to this question can be found only in that principle of interpretation, valid both for myths and dreams, which has been recognized by Bachofen and Freud. If an element appearing in a myth or in a dream belongs to a much earlier phase of development and is not part of the conscious frame of reference at the time of the final formulation of the myth, this element often carries with it the quality of dread and awfulness. Touching upon something hidden and taboo, the conscious mind is affected by a fear of a particular kind—the fear of the unknown and the mystifying.

Goethe, in one of the least understood passages of *Faust,* has treated the problem of the dread of the mysterious mothers in a spirit very similar to that in Sophocles' *Oedipus at Colonus.* Mephistopheles says:

> Unwilling I reveal a loftier mystery—
> In solitude are throned the *Goddesses,*
> No space around them, Place and Time still less;
> *Only to speak of them embarrasses;*
> *They are the Mothers!*
> FAUST *(terrified):* Mothers!
> MEPHISTOPHELES: *Hast thou dread?*
> FAUST: The Mothers! Mothers!—a strange word is said.
> MEPHISTOPHELES:
> It is so. Goddesses, unknown to ye,
> The Mothers, named by us unwillingly.
> Delve in the deepest depth must thou,
> to reach them:
> It is thine own fault that we for
> help beseech them.

Here too, as in Sophocles' tragedy, the feeling of dread and terror is bound up with the mere mentioning of the goddesses, who belong to an ancient world which now is banned from the light of day, from consciousness.

As we see from this short passage, Goethe anticipated Bachofen's theory; according to Eckermann's diary (January 10, 1830) Goethe mentioned that in reading Plutarch he found "that in Grecian antiquity the Mothers are spoken of as Goddesses." This passage in *Faust* has appeared enigmatic to most commentators who tried to explain the mothers as a symbol of Platonic ideas, the formless realm of the inner world of spirit, and so forth. Indeed, it must remain an enigma unless one understands it in the light of Bachofen's findings.

It is in the grove of these "awful" goddesses where Oedipus, the wanderer, at last comes to rest and finds his real home. Oedipus, although himself a man, belongs to the world of these matriarchal goddesses, and his strength lies in his connection with them.

Oedipus' return to the grove of the goddesses, though the most important, is not the only clue to the understanding of his position as representative of the matriarchal order. Sophocles makes another and very plain allusion to matriarchy by having Oedipus refer to Egyptian matriarchy[16] when he tells about his two daughters. This is the way he praises them:

> O true image of the *ways of Egypt that they show in their spirit and their life! For there the men sit weaving in the house, but the wives go forth to win the daily bread.* And in your case, my daughters, those to whom these toils belonged keep the house at home like girls, while ye, in their stead, bear your hapless father's burden.[17]

The same trend of thought is continued by Oedipus when he compares his daughters with his sons. Of Antigone and Ismene he says:

> Now, these girls preserve me, these my nurses, *these who are men not women,* in true service: but ye are aliens, and no sons of mine.[18]

We have raised the question whether, if incest was the essence of Oedipus' crime, the drama should have told us that he had fallen in love with Jocasta unwittingly. In *Oedipus at Colonus* Sophocles has Oedipus himself answer this question. The marriage to her was not the outcome of his own desire and decision; instead, she was one of the rewards for the city's saviour.

> Thebes bound me, all unknowingly, to the bride that was my curse.[19]

We have already pointed to the fact that the main theme of the trilogy, the conflict between father and son, finds its full expression in *Oedipus at Colonus;* here the hate between father and son is not, as in *King Oedipus,* unconscious; indeed, here Oedipus is very much aware of his hate against his sons, whom he accuses of having violated the eternal law of nature. He claims that his curse is stronger than the sons' prayer to Poseidon, "if indeed Justice (Dike, the *Goddess* of Justice who protects the eternal law of natural bonds and not the man-made rights of the first-born son), revealed of old, sits with Zeus in the might of eternal laws."[20] Simultaneously he gives expression to his hate against his own parents, accusing them of their intention to sacrifice his life. There is no indication in *Oedipus at Colonus* that the hostility of Oedipus' sons against their father has any connection with the incest motif. The only motivation which we can find in the tragedy is their wish for power and the rivalry with their father.

The end of *Oedipus at Colonus* clarifies still further the meaning of Oedipus' connection with the goddesses of the earth.

After the chorus has prayed to the "Unseen Goddesses," "the Goddess Infernal," the messenger reports how Oedipus died. He had taken leave of his daughters and—accompanied only, though not guided, by Theseus—walks to the holy place of the goddesses. He seems to need no guidance, since here at last he is at home and knows his way. The messenger sees Theseus

> . . . holding his hand before his face to screen his eyes, as if *some dread sight had been seen,* and such as none might endure to behold.[21]

We find here again the emphasis on something awful and terrifying which was already mentioned at the beginning of *Antigone;* it is the same awe of the unknown, of the mystery of the goddesses. The line following the ones just quoted makes it very clear how the remnants of the forgotten matriarchal religion as blended with the ruling patriarchal system. The messenger reports that he saw Theseus

> . . . *salute the earth and the home of the gods above, both at once, in one prayer.*[22]

But by what doom Oedipus perished, no man can tell, save Theseus alone. No fiery thunderbolt of the god removed him in that hour, nor any rising of storm from the sea; but either a messenger from the gods, *or the world of the dead, the nether adamant, riven for him in love,* without pain; for the passing of the man was not with lamentation, or in sickness and suffering, but, above mortals, wonderful. And if to any I seem to speak folly, I would not woo their belief, who count me foolish.[23]

The messenger is puzzled; he does not know whether Oedipus was removed from the earth by the gods above or by the gods below, by the world of the fathers or that of the mothers. But there seems to be little doubt that, in a formulation written centuries after the mother goddesses had been conquered by the Olympian gods, this doubt can only be the expression of a secret conviction that Oedipus was brought back to the place where he belongs, to the mothers.

How different is the end of *Oedipus at Colonus* from that of *King Oedipus.* In the latter his fate seemed to be sealed as that of the tragic criminal whose crime removes him forever from his family and from his fellow men, destined to be an outcast, abhorred though perhaps pitied by everyone. In the former he dies as a man surrounded by two loving daughters and by new friends whose benefactor he has become, not with a feeling of guilt but with a conviction of his right, not as an outcast but as one who has eventually found his home—with the earth and the goddesses who rule there. The tragic guilt which had pervaded *King Oedipus* has now been removed, and only one conflict has remained as bitter and unsolved as ever—that between father and son.

The conflict between the patriarchal and matriarchal principles is the theme of the third part of the trilogy, *Antigone.* Here the figure of Creon, which has been somewhat indistinct in the two former tragedies, becomes colorful and definite. He has become the tyrant of Thebes after Oedipus' two sons have been killed—one by attacking the city in order to gain power, the other defending his throne. Creon has ordered that the legitimate king should be buried and that the challenger's body should be left unburied— the greatest humiliation and dishonor to be done to a man, according to Greek custom. The principle which Creon represents is that of the supremacy of the law of the state over ties of blood, of obedience to authority over allegiance to the natural law of humanity. Antigone refuses to violate the laws of blood and of the solidarity of all human beings for the sake of an authoritarian hierarchical principle.

The two principles for which Creon and Antigone stand are exactly those which Bachofen characterized as the patriarchal as against the matriarchal principles. The matriarchal principle is that of blood relationship as the most fundamental and indestructible tie, of the equality of all men, of the respect for human life and of love. The patriarchal principle is that the ties between man and wife, between ruler and ruled, take precedence over ties of blood. It is the principle of order and authority, of obedience and hierarchy.

Antigone represents the matriarchal principle and thus is the uncompromising adversary of the representative of patriarchal authority, Creon. Ismene, in contrast, has accepted the defeat and given in to the victorious patriarchal order; she is a symbol of women under patriarchal domination. Sophocles makes her role very clear by having her say to Antigone, who has decided to defy Creon's command:

> And now *we* in turn—we two left all alone—think how we shall perish, more miserably than all the rest, if, in defiance of the law, we brave a king's decree or his powers. Nay, we must remember, first, *that we were born women, as who should not strive with men;* next, that we are ruled of the stronger, so that we must obey in these things, and in things yet sorer. I, therefore, asking the *Spirits Infernal* to pardon, seeing that force is put on me herein, will hearken to our rulers; for 'tis witless to be over busy.[24]

Ismene has accepted male authority as her ultimate norm; she has accepted the defeat of women "who should not strive with men." Her loyalty to the goddesses is only expressed in begging them to forgive her who has to yield to the force of the ruler.

The humanistic principle of the matriarchal world, with its emphasis on man's greatness and dignity, finds a beautiful and forceful expression in the chorus' praise of the power of man.

> Wonders are many, *and none is more wonderful than man;* the power that crosses the white sea, driven by the stormy south-wind, making a path under surges that threaten to engulf him; and *Earth, the eldest of the gods,* the immortal, the unwearied, doth he wear, turning the soil with the offspring of horses, as the ploughs go to and fro from year to year.[25]

The conflict between the two principles unfolds in the further development of the play. Antigone insists that the law she obeys is not that of the Olympian gods. Her law "is not of today or yesterday, but from all time, and no man knows when they were first put forth";[26] and, we may add, the law of burial, of returning the body to mother earth, is rooted in the very principles of matriarchal religion. Antigone stands for the solidarity of man and the principle of the all-embracing motherly love. "'Tis not my nature to join in hating but in loving."[27]

For Creon obedience to authority is the supreme value; human solidarity and love, if in conflict with obedience, have to yield. He has to defeat Antigone in order to uphold patriarchal authority and with it his virility.

> *Now verily I am no man, she is the man,* if this victory shall rest with her, and bring no penalty.[28]

Creon lays down the authoritarian, patriarchal principle in unequivocal language:

Yea, this, my son, should be thy heart's fixed law—in all things to *obey thy father's will.* 'Tis for this that men pray to see *dutiful children* grow up around them in their homes—that such may requite their father's foe with evil, and honour, as their father doth, his friend. But he who *begets unprofitable children*—what shall we say that he hath sown, but trouble for himself, and much triumph for his foes? Then do not thou, my son, at pleasure's back, dethrone thy reason for a woman's sake; knowing that this is a joy that soon grows cold in clasping arms—an evil woman to share thy bed and thy home. For what wound could strike deeper than a false friend? Nay, with loathing, and as if she were thine enemy, let this girl go to find a husband in the house of Hades. For since I have taken her, alone of all the city, in open disobedience, I will not make myself a liar to my people—I will slay her.

So let her appeal as she will to the majesty of kindred blood. If I am to nurture mine own kindred in naughtiness, needs must I bear with it in aliens. *He who does his duty in his own household will be found righteous in the State also. But if any one transgresses and does violence to the laws, or thinks to dictate to his rulers, such a one can win no praise from me. No, whomsoever the city may appoint, that man must be obeyed, in little things and great, in just things and unjust; and I should feel sure that one who thus obeys would be a good ruler no less than a good subject,* and in the storm of spears would stand his ground where he was set, loyal and dauntless at his comrade's side.

But disobedience is the worst of evils. This it is that ruins cities; this makes home desolate; by this, the ranks of allies are broken into headlong rout; but, of the lives whose course is fair, the greater part owes safety to obedience. *Therefore we must support the cause of order, and in no wise suffer a woman to worst us. Better to fall from power, if we must, by a man's hand; than we should be called weaker than a woman.*[29]

Authority in the family and authority in the state are the two interrelated supreme values for which Creon stands. Sons are the property of their fathers and their function is to be "serviceable" to the father. "Pater potestas" in the family is the basis for the ruler's power in the state. Citizens are the property of the state and its ruler, and "disobedience is the worst of evils."

Haemon, Creon's son, represents the principles for which Antigone fights. Although he tries at first to appease and persuade his father, he declares his opposition openly when he sees that his father will not yield. He relies on reason, "the highest of all things that we call our own," and on the will of the people. When Creon accuses Antigone of being tainted with the "malady of disobedience," Haemon's rebellious answer is:

Our Theban folk, with one voice, denies it.[30]

When Creon argues:

Am I to rule this land by other judgment than mine own?

Haemon's answer is:

That is no city which belongs to one man . . .
Thou wouldst make a good monarch of a desert.[31]

Creon brings the argument again to the crucial point by saying:

This boy, it seems, is the *woman's* champion.

And Haemon points to the matriarchal goddesses by answering:

And for thee, and for me, and for *the gods below.*[32]

The two principles have now been stated with full clarity, and the end of the tragedy only carries the action to the point of final decision. Creon has Antigone buried alive in a cave—again a symbolic expression of her connection with the goddesses of the earth. The seer, Teiresias, who in **King Oedipus** was instrumental in making Oedipus aware of his crime, appears again, this time to make Creon aware of his. Striken by panic, Creon gives in and tries to save Antigone. He rushes to the cave where she is entombed, but Antigone is already dead. Haemon tries to kill his father; when he fails, he takes his own life. Creon's wife, Eurydice, upon hearing the fate of her son, kills herself, cursing her husband as the murderer of her children. Creon recognizes the complete collapse of his world and the defeat of his principles. He admits his own moral bankruptcy, and the play ends with his confession:

Ah me, this guilt can never be fixed on any other mortal kind, for my acquittal! I, even I, was thy slayer, wretched that I am—I own the truth. Lead me away, O my servants, lead me hence with all speed, whose life is but as death! . . .

Lead me away, I pray you; a rash, foolish man; who have slain thee, ah, my son, unwittingly, and thee, too, my wife—unhappy that I am! I know not which way I should bend my gaze, or where I should seek support; for all is amiss with that which is in my hands,—and yonder again, a crushing fate hath leapt upon my head.[33]

We are now in a position to answer the questions which we raised at the beginning. Is the Oedipus myth as presented in Sophocles' trilogy centered around the crime of incest? Is the murder of the father the symbolic expression of a hate resulting from jealousy? Though the answer is doubtful at the end of **King Oedipus,** it is hardly doubtful any more at the end of **Antigone.** Not Oedipus but Creon is defeated in the end, and with him the principle of authoritarianism, of man's domination over men, the father's domination over his son, and the dictator's domination over the people. If we accept the theory of matriarchal forms of society and religion, then, indeed, there seems to be little doubt that Oedipus, Haemon, and Antigone are representatives of the old principles of matriarchy, those of equality and democracy, in contrast to Creon, who represents patriarchal domination and obedience.[34]

Our interpretation, however, needs to be supplemented by another consideration. Although the conflict between Oedipus, Antigone, and Haemon on the one side against Creon on the other contains a memory of the conflict between patriarchal and matriarchal principles, and particularly of its mythical elements, it must also be understood in terms of the specific political and cultural situation in Sophocles' time and of his reactions to that situation.

The Peloponnesian War, the threat to the political independence of Athens, and the plague which ravaged the city at the beginning of the war had helped to uproot the old religious and philosophical traditions. Indeed, attacks against religion were not new, but they reached a climax in the teachings of Sophocles' Sophist adversaries. He was opposed particularly to those Sophists who not only proclaimed despotism exercised by an intellectual elite but also unheld unrestricted self-ishness as a moral principle. The ethics of egotistical supermen proclaimed by this wing of the Sophists and their amoral opportunism were the very opposite of Sophocles' philosophy. In Creon Sophocles created a figure representing this school of sophism, and Creon's speeches resembled the Sophist pattern even in style and expression.[35]

In his argument against the Sophists, Sophocles gave new expression to the old religious traditions of the people with their emphasis on love, equality, and justice. "The religious attitude of Sophocles . . . is primarily concerned not with the official religion of the state but with those helpful secondary powers which always were closer to the faith of the masses than the aristocratic Olympians and to whom the people turned again in the dangers of the Peloponnesian War."[36] These "secondary powers," which were different from the "aristocratic Olympian" gods, are easily identified as the goddesses of the matriarchal world.

We see, then, that Sophocles' views expressed in the Oedipus trilogy are to be understood as a blend of his opposition to contemporary sophism and of his sympathy for the old, non-Olympian religious ideas.[37] In the name of both he proclaimed the principle that the dignity of man and the sanctity of human bonds must never be subordinated to inhuman and authoritarian claims of the state or to opportunistic considerations.[38]

Thus far we have been concerned only with the interpretation of the Oedipus myth and not with Freud's clinical description of the Oedipus complex. Quite regardless of the question of whether or not Freud's clinical description is correct, we arrive at the result that the complex centered around the boy's incestuous strivings toward his mother and his resulting hostility against the father is wrongly called an Oedipus complex. There is a complex, however, which fully deserves to be called an Oedipus complex, the rebellion of the son against the pressure of the father's authority—an authority rooted in the patriarchal, authoritarian structure of society.

The child does not meet society directly at first; he meets it through the medium of his parents, who in their character structure and methods of education represent the social structure and are the psychological agency of society, as it were. What, then, happens to the child in relationship to his parents? He meets through them the kind of authority which prevails in a patriarchal society, and this kind of authority tends to break his will, his spontaneity, his independence. But, since man is not born to be broken, the child fights against the authority represented by his parents; he fights not only for his freedom from pressure but also for his freedom to be himself, a full-fledged human being and not an automaton.

In this struggle some children are more successful than others; most of them are defeated to some extent in their fight for freedom. The ways in which the defeat is brought about are manifold, but, whatever they are, the scars left in the child's unsuccessful fight against irrational authority are to be found at the bottom of every neurosis. Such a scar is represented in a syndrome the most important features of which are: a weakening or paralysis of the individual's originality and spontaneity; a weakening of the self and the substitution of a pseudoself in which the feeling of "I am" is dulled and replaced by the experience of self as the sum total of expectations others have about the self; a substitution of heteronomy for autonomy; a fogginess, or, to use Dr. Sullivan's term, a parataxic quality in all interpersonal experiences.

It is the child's rebellion against proprietary paternal authority in all its various forms which can be properly called the Oedipus complex.

Does our interpretation of the Oedipus myth and of the Oedipus complex imply that Freud's theory was without foundation?

The history of thought is a history of continuous revision and reinterpretation of previous theoretical statements which at a later period appear to have expressed the optimum of truth attainable in a given historical period. With regard to Freud's theories the same holds true; there is hardly any theoretical statement of Freud's which does not contain at least a true kernel from which one can proceed to a more correct insight into the facts. Freud's theory of the Oedipus complex is a case in point.

Freud observed three facts, and each of these observations was valid. We now propose to show that the unified theoretical interpretation which he gave to his three observations was fallacious and that the progress of psychological theory lies in the direction of seeing the observed phenomena afresh and of interpreting them differently. The facts which Freud observed were the following: First, he noted the presence of sexual strivings in children. Although this phenomenon has found wide recognition today, at the beginning of the century it was a revolutionary and significant discovery which furthered our knowledge of child psychology tremendously. Second, Freud observed that the ties by which children are bound to their parents are often not severed at a time when in the normal development they should be severed and the child should become independent. He saw that this irrational "fixation" of children to their parents is to be found in all neuroses and is one of the causes for the development of neurotic symptoms and neurotic character traits. The significance of this discovery can hardly be overestimated. The more data we collect, the more it becomes apparent that the peculiar lack of maturity and self-assertion and the emotional and intellectual distortions which are so characteristic of every neurosis result from this fixation, which paralyzes the person's free use of his own emotional and intellectual powers. Third, Freud recognized the significance and frequency of conflicts between father and son, and he showed how an unsuccessful rebellion against the father's authority and the fears resulting from the defeat form the basis for a neurotic development.

The observation of these three phenomena led Freud to the formulation of a brilliant theory. He assumed that the second phenomenon, the attachment to the mother, was rooted in the first phenomenon, the sexual strivings of the child, and that the third phenomenon, the conflict with the father, was a result of this sexual rivalry. This theory is very appealing, indeed, because it has the advantage of explaining three different phenomena by one assumption and thus to require the least amount of theoretical construction. Individual and anthropological data[39] gathered since Freud formulated his theory, however, have shaken our conviction as to its validity. These data have shown that the Oedipus complex in Freud's sense is not a universal human phenomenon and that the child's rivalry with the father does not occur in cultures without strong patriarchal authority. Furthermore, it has become evident that the tie to the mother is not essentially a sexual tie—in fact, that infantile sexuality when not suppressed has as its normal aim autoerotic satisfactions and sexual contact with other children. Moreover, it has become evident that pathological dependence on the mother is caused by nonsexual factors—particularly by the dominating attitude of the mother, which makes the child helpless and frightened thus intensifying the need for the mother's protection and affection.

Freud's concept of the Oedipus complex is part of a broader concept in which neurosis is explained as the result of a conflict between the irrational passions of the child and the reality represented by the parents and by society. It is the child who is the "sinner," and neurosis is the punishment, as it were. The concept of the Oedipus complex presented here is also part of a larger concept of neurosis. The cause of neurosis is seen primarily not in the conflict between man's irrational passions and the justified demands of society but in man's legitimate striving for freedom and independence and in those social arrangements which thwart it and thus create destructive passion which in turn must be suppressed by external or internal force.[40]

While Freud assumes that the conflict arising from the child's incestuous strivings is rooted in his nature and thus

unavoidable, we believe that in a cultural situation in which respect for the integrity of every individual—hence of every child—is realized the Oedipus complex will belong to the past.

Notes

1. Sigmund Freud, "The Interpretation of Dreams," in *The Basic Writings of Sigmund Freud,* translated by Dr. A. A. Brill, New York, The Modern Library, Random House, Inc., 1938, p. 308.

2. Cf. Carl Roberts, *Oedipus,* Berlin, Weidmannsche Buchhandlung, 1915.

3. While it is true that the trilogy was not written in this order and while some scholars may be right in their assumption that Sophocles did not plan the three tragedies as a trilogy, the three must nevertheless be interpreted as a whole. It makes little sense to assume that Sophocles described the fate of Oedipus and his children in three tragedies without having in mind an inner coherence of the whole.

4. "Oedipus at Colonus," in Whitney J. Oates and Eugene O'Neill, Jr. (eds.), *The Complete Greek Drama,* vol. I, New York, Random House, 1938, pp. 1383 ff.

5. J. J. Bachofen, "*Der Mythus von Orient und Okzident,* edited by Manfred Schroeder, Munich, Ch. Becksche Buchhandlung, 1926, pp. 14 f.

6. *Ibid.,* pp. 15, 16.

7. Tentatively in his *Systems of Consanguinity and Affinity,* 1871, and more definitely in *Ancient Society,* Chicago, Charles H. Kerr & Company, 1877.

8. New York, The Macmillan Company, 1927.

9. Cf. Schneidewin, "Die Sage von Oedipus," in *Abhandlung der Gesenichte der W. z. Gott.,* 5 (1852), 192.

10. Cf. Carl Roberts, *op. cit.,* pp. 1 ff.

11. *Ibid.,* p. 21.

12. Their interpretation of the Sphinx myth, however, differs from the one which follows here. Bachofen emphasized the nature of the question and stated that the Sphinx defines man in terms of his telluric, material existence, that is, in matriarchal terms. Freud assumed that the riddle is the symbolic expression of the child's sexual curiosity.

13. For those readers who are not familiar with Freud's dream interpretation, one brief explanatory remark is in order. What I have called here the real thought of the dream or myth is what Freud calls the *latent* dream in contrast to the *manifest* content, which is the dream as remembered. Freud assumed that symbolic language was a secret code the main function of which was to distort and veil the latent thought. While in my opinion the main function of

symbolic language is not that of hiding but of giving fuller expression to inner experiences than conventional language permits, it remains nevertheless true that both dreams and myths also frequently tend to hide and distort the real meaning of the thought expressed. In dreams this is the case if the dreamer is not aware in waking life of the thoughts which he expresses in a dream and does not want to be fully aware of them even in his sleep. In myths the latent content is censored and changed if it deals with elements which are rooted in older historical periods forgotten, feared, or despised at the time the myth is formulated.

14. Translation by R. C. Webb, *op. cit.*, pp. 80 ff.

15. Translation by R. C. Webb, *ibid.*, pp. 130 ff.

16. Sophocles probably refers here to a passage from *Herodotus*, vol. II, p. 35.

17. *Ibid.*, pp. 338 f.

18. *Ibid.*, pp. 1367 f.

19. *Ibid.*, pp. 525 f.

20. *Ibid.*, pp. 1380 f.

21. *Ibid.*, pp. 1650 f.

22. *Ibid.*, pp. 1656 f.

23. *Ibid.*, pp. 1660 f.

24. *Ibid.*, pp. 50 f.

25. *Ibid.*, pp. 332 f.

26. *Ibid.*, pp. 455 f.

27. *Ibid.*, pp. 523 f.

28. *Ibid.*, p. 483.

29. *Ibid.*, pp. 640 f.

30. *Ibid.*, pp. 730 f.

31. *Ibid.*, pp. 740 f.

32. *Ibid.*, pp. 745 f.

33. *Ibid.*, pp. 1320 f.

34. No less a thinker than Hegel saw the conflict represented in Antigone in the same light many years prior to Bachofen. He says of Antigone: "The gods, however, which she worships are the gods below, the gods of Hades, the inner gods of emotion, of love, of blood, and not the gods of the day, of the free and self-conscious life, of the nation, and the state." (Hegel, *Aesthetik*, vol. II, p. 2, Absch., chap. 1; compare also *Philosophy of Religion*, vol. XVI, p. 133.) Hegel in this statement is so much on the side of the state and its laws that he defines Creon's principle as that of "the free life of the people and the state" in spite of the undeniable evidence that Creon does not represent freedom but dictatorship. In view of this one-sided sympathy of Hegel's, it is all the more significant that he states so clearly that Antigone stands for the principles of love, of blood and emotion, which later on Bachofen found to be the characteristic principles of the matriarchal world. While Hegel's sympathy for the patriarchal principles is not surprising, one does not expect to find it in Bachofen's writings. And yet Bachofen's own attitude to matriarchal society has been quite ambivalent. It seems that he loved matriarchal and hated patriarchal principles, but inasmuch as he was also a religious Protestant and a believer in the progress of reason he believed in the supremacy of the patriarchal principle over the matriarchate. In a great part of his writings his sympathy with the matriarchal principle finds expression. In other parts, and this holds true of his brief interpretation of the Oedipus myth (Bachofen's "Mutterrecht" in *Der Mythos vom Orient und Okzident, op. cit.*, pp. 259 f.), he, like Hegel, sides with the victorious Olympian gods. To him Oedipus stands on the frontier between the matriarchal and the patriarchal world. The fact that he does not know his father points to a matriarchal origin in which only the mother but not the father is certain. But the fact that he discovers eventually who his real father is, according to Bachofen, marks the beginning of the patriarchal family in which the true father is known. "Oedipus," he says, "is connected with the progress to a higher level of existence. He is one of those great figures whose suffering and pain lead to a more beautiful form of human civilization; one of those still rooted in the old order of things who are at the same time sacrificed and thus become the founders of a new epoch" (p. 266). Bachofen stresses the fact that the dreaded mother-goddesses, the Erinyes, have subordinated themselves to the Apollonian world and that the connection between Oedipus and them marks the victory of the patriarchal principle. It seems to me that Bachofen's interpretation does not do justice to the fact that Creon, although he is the only one who survives physically, symbolizing the victory of the patriarchal world, is the one who is morally defeated. It may be assumed that Sophocles intended to convey the idea that the patriarchal world was triumphant but that it would be defeated unless it adopted the humanistic principles of the older matriarchal order.

35. Cf. Callicles in Plato's *Georgias* and Thrasymachus in his *Republic*.

36. Wilhelm Schmid, "Geschichte der Griechischen Literatur," 1. Teil, in *Handbuch der Altertumswissenschaften*, edited by Walter Otto, 7. Abt., 1. Teil, 2. Band, Muenchen, 1934.

37. It is interesting to note that the same blend between progressive political ideas and a sympathy with mythical matriarchal principles is to be found again in the nineteenth century in Bachofen's, Engels', and Morgan's work. (Compare my paper on "Zur Rezep-

tion der Mutterrechtstheorie" in *Zeitschrift fuer So-zialforschung,* III (1934).

38. Cf. also Wilhelm Nestle, "Sophokles und die Sophistik," *Classical Philology,* Chicago, University of Chicago Press, 1910, vol. 5, II, pp. 129 ff.

    The problem of hostility between father and son was also of great personal significance in the life of the poet. His son Jophon sued the aged father and wanted the court to deprive him of the right to manage his own business affairs, a suit from which Sophocles emerged victoriously.

39. Cf. particularly Malinowski's work.

40. Cf. E. Fromm, *Man for Himself,* New York, Rinehart & Co., 1947.

Francis Fergusson (essay date 1949)

SOURCE: "*Oedipus*: Ritual and Play," in *Twentieth Century Interpretations of "Oedipus Rex,"* edited by Michael J. O'Brien, Prentice-Hall, Inc., 1968, pp. 57-62.

[*In the following essay, originally published in 1949, Fergusson describes the ritual involved in the audience's reception of* Oedipus Tyrannus *and the importance and function of the chorus.*]

The Cambridge School of Classical Anthropologists has shown in great detail that the form of Greek tragedy follows the form of a very ancient ritual, that of the *Eniautos-Daimon,* or seasonal god.[1] This was one of the most influential discoveries of the last few generations, and it gives us new insights into *Oedipus* which I think are not yet completely explored. The clue to Sophocles' dramatizing of the myth of Oedipus is to be found in this ancient ritual, which had a similar form and meaning—that is, it also moved in the "tragic rhythm."[2]

Experts in classical anthropology, like experts in other fields, dispute innumerable questions of fact and of interpretation which the layman can only pass over in respectful silence. One of the thornier questions seems to be whether myth or ritual came first. Is the ancient ceremony merely an enactment of the Ur-Myth of the year-god—Attis, or Adonis, or Osiris, or the "Fisher-King"—in any case that Hero-King-Father-High-Priest who fights with his rival, is slain and dismembered, then rises anew with the spring season? Or did the innumerable myths of this kind arise to "explain" a ritual which was perhaps mimed or danced or sung to celebrate the annual change of season?

For the purpose of understanding the form and meaning of *Oedipus,* it is not necessary to worry about the answer to this question of historic fact. The figure of Oedipus himself fulfills all the requirements of the scapegoat, the dismembered king or god-figure. The situation in which Thebes is presented at the beginning of the play—in peril of its life; its crops, its herds, its women mysteriously infertile, signs of a mortal disease of the City, and the disfavor of the gods—is like the withering which winter brings, and calls, in the same way, for struggle, dismemberment, death, and renewal. And this tragic sequence is the substance of the play. It is enough to know that myth and ritual are close together in their genesis, two direct imitations of the perennial experience of the race.

But when one considers *Oedipus* as a ritual one understands it in ways which one cannot by thinking of it merely as a dramatization of a story, even that story. Harrison has shown that the Festival of Dionysos, based ultimately upon the yearly vegetation ceremonies, included *rites de passage,* like that celebrating the assumption of adulthood—celebrations of the mystery of individual growth and development. At the same time, it was a prayer for the welfare of the whole City; and this welfare was understood not only as material prosperity, but also as the natural order of the family, the ancestors, the present members, and the generations still to come, and, by the same token, obedience to the gods who were jealous, each in his own province, of this natural and divinely sanctioned order and proportion.

We must suppose that Sophocles' audience (the whole population of the City) came early, prepared to spend the day in the bleachers. At their feet was the semicircular dancing-ground for the chorus, and the thrones for the priests, and the altar. Behind that was the raised platform for the principal actors, backed by the all-purpose, emblematic façade, which would presently be taken to represent Oedipus' palace in Thebes. The actors were not professionals in our sense, but citizens selected for a religious office, and Sophocles himself had trained them and the chorus.

This crowd must have had as much appetite for thrills and diversion as the crowds who assemble in our day for football games and musical comedies, and Sophocles certainly holds the attention with an exciting show. At the same time his audience must have been alert for the fine points of poetry and dramaturgy, for *Oedipus* is being offered in competition with other plays on the same bill. But the element which distinguishes this theater, giving it its unique directness and depth, is the *ritual expectancy* which Sophocles assumed in his audience. The nearest thing we have to this ritual sense of theater is, I suppose, to be found at an Easter performance of the *Mattias Passion.* We also can observe something similar in the dances and ritual mummery of the Pueblo Indians. Sophocles' audience must have been prepared, like the Indians standing around their plaza, to consider the playing, the make-believe it was about to see—the choral invocations, with dancing and chanting; the reasoned discourses and the terrible combats of the protagonists; the mourning, the rejoicing, and the contemplation of the final stage-picture or epiphany—as imitating and celebrating the mystery of human nature and destiny. And this mystery was at once that of individual growth and development, and that of the precarious life of the human City.

I have indicated how Sophocles presents the life of the mythic Oedipus in the tragic rhythm, the mysterious quest of life. Oedipus is shown seeking his own true being; but at the same time and by the same token, the welfare of the City. When one considers the ritual form of the whole play, it becomes evident that it presents the tragic but perennial, even normal, quest of the whole City for its well-being. In this larger action, Oedipus is only the protagonist, the first and most important champion. This tragic quest is realized by all the characters in their various ways; but in the development of the action as a whole it is the chorus alone that plays a part as important as that of Oedipus; its counterpart, in fact. The chorus holds the balance between Oedipus and his antagonists, marks the progress of their struggles, and restates the main theme, and its new variation, after each dialogue or agon. The ancient ritual was probably performed by a chorus alone without individual developments and variations, and the chorus, in **Oedipus,** is still the element that throws most light on the ritual form of the play as a whole.

The chorus consists of twelve or fifteen "Elders of Thebes." This group is not intended to represent literally all the citizens either of Thebes or of Athens. The play opens with a large delegation of Theban citizens before Oedipus' palace, and the chorus proper does not enter until after the prologue. Nor does the chorus speak directly for the Athenian audience; we are asked throughout to make-believe that the theater is the agora at Thebes; and at the same time Sophocles' audience is witnessing a ritual. It would, I think, be more accurate to say that the chorus represents the point of view and the faith of Thebes as a whole, and, by analogy, of the Athenian audience. Their errand before Oedipus' palace is like that of Sophocles' audience in the theater: they are watching a sacred combat, in the issue of which they have an all-important and official stake. Thus they represent the audience and the citizens in a particular way—not as a mob formed in response to some momentary feeling, but rather as an organ of a highly self-conscious community: something closer to the "conscience of the race" than to the overheated affectivity of a mob.

According to Aristotle, a Sophoclean chorus is a character that takes an important role in the action of the play, instead of merely making incidental music between the scenes, as in the plays of Euripides. The chorus may be described as a group personality, like an old Parliament. It has its own traditions, habits of thought and feeling, and mode of being. It exists, in a sense, as a living entity, but not with the sharp actuality of an individual. It perceives; but its perception is at once wider and vaguer than that of a single man. It shares, in its way, the seeking action of the play as a whole; but it cannot act in all the modes; it depends upon the chief agonists to invent and try out the detail of policy, just as a rather helpless but critical Parliament depends upon the Prime Minister to act but, in its less specific form of life, survives his destruction.

When the chorus enters after the prologue, with its questions, its invocation of the various gods, and its focus upon the hidden and jeopardized welfare of the City—Athens or Thebes—the list of essential *dramatis personae,* as well as the elements needed to celebrate the ritual, is complete, and the main action can begin. It is the function of the chorus to mark the stages of this action, and to perform the suffering and perceiving part of the tragic rhythm. The protagonist and his antagonists develop the "purpose" with which the tragic sequence begins; the chorus, with its less than individual being, broods over the agons, marks their stages with a word (like that of the chorus leader in the middle of the Tiresias scene), and (expressing its emotions and visions in song and dance) suffers the results, and the new perception at the end of the fight.

The choral odes are lyrics but they are not to be understood as poetry, the art of words, only, for they are intended also to be danced and sung. And though each chorus has its own shape, like that of a discrete lyric—its beginning, middle, and end—it represents also one passion or pathos in the changing action of the whole. This passion, like the other moments in the tragic rhythm, is felt at so general or, rather, so deep a level that it seems to contain both the mob ferocity that Nietzsche felt in it and, at the other extreme, the patience of prayer. It is informed by faith in the unseen order of nature and the gods, and moves through a sequence of modes of suffering. This may be illustrated from the chorus I have quoted at the end of the Tiresias scene.

It begins (close to the savage emotion of the end of the fight) with images suggesting that cruel "Bacchic frenzy" which is supposed to be the common root of tragedy and of the "old" comedy: "In panoply of fire and lightning / The son of Zeus now springs upon him." In the first antistrophe these images come together more clearly as we relish the chase; and the fleeing culprit, as we imagine him, begins to resemble Oedipus, who is lame, and always associated with the rough wilderness of Kithairon. But in the second strophe, as though appalled by its ambivalent feelings and the imagined possibilities, the chorus sinks back into a more dark and patient posture of suffering, "in awe," "hovering in hope." In the second antistrophe this is developed into something like the orthodox Christian attitude of prayer, based on faith, and assuming the possibility of a hitherto unimaginable truth and answer: "Zeus and Apollo are wise," etc. The whole chorus then ends with a new vision of Oedipus, of the culprit, and of the direction in which the welfare of the City is to be sought. This vision is still colored by the chorus's human love of Oedipus as Hero, for the chorus has still its own purgation to complete, cannot as yet accept completely either the suffering in store for it, or Oedipus as scapegoat. But it marks the end of the first complete "purpose-passion-perception" unit, and lays the basis for the new purpose which will begin the next unit.

It is also to be noted that the chorus changes the scene which we, as audience, are to imagine. During the agon between Oedipus and Tiresias, our attention is fixed upon their clash, and the scene is literal, close, and immediate: before Oedipus' palace. When the fighters depart and the choral music starts, the focus suddenly widens, as though we had been removed to a distance. We become aware of the interested City around the bright arena; and beyond that, still more dimly, of Nature, sacred to the hidden gods. Mr. Burke has expounded the fertile notion that human action may be understood in terms of the scene in which it occurs, and vice versa: the scene is defined by the mode of action. The chorus's action is not limited by the sharp, rationalized purposes of the protagonist; its mode of action, more patient, less sharply realized, is cognate with a wider, if less accurate, awareness of the scene of human life. But the chorus's action, as I have remarked, is not that of passion itself (Nietzsche's cosmic void of night) but suffering informed by the faith of the tribe in a human and a divinely sanctioned natural order: "If such deeds as these are honored," the chorus asks after Jocasta's impiety, "why should I dance and sing?" (lines 894, 895). Thus it is one of the most important functions of the chorus to reveal, in its widest and most mysterious extent, the theater of human life which the play, and indeed the whole Festival of Dionysos, assumed. Even when the chorus does not speak, but only watches, it maintains this theme and this perspective—ready to take the whole stage when the fighters depart.

If one thinks of the movement of the play, it appears that the tragic rhythm analyzes human action temporally into successive modes, as a crystal analyzes a white beam of light spatially into the colored bands of the spectrum. The chorus, always present, represents one of these modes, and at the recurrent moments when reasoned purpose is gone, it takes the stage with its faith-informed passion, moving through an ordered succession of modes of suffering, to a new perception of the immediate situation.

Notes

1. See especially Jane Ellen Harrison's *Ancient Art and Ritual,* and her *Themis* which contains an "Excursus on the ritual forms preserved in Greek Tragedy" by Professor Gilbert Murray.

2. In an earlier passage in his book (p. 18), Fergusson has explained "tragic rhythm" as the movement which constitutes the shape of the whole play and of each episode in the play. He adds: "Mr. Kenneth Burke has studied the tragic rhythm in his *Philosophy of Literary Form,* and also in *A Grammar of Motives,* where he gives the three moments traditional designations which are very suggestive: *Poiema, Pathema, Mathema.* They may also be called, for convenience, Purpose, Passion (or Suffering) and Perception. It is this tragic rhythm of action which is the substance or spiritual content of the play, and the clue to its extraordinarily comprehensive form" [*Editor's note*].

Philip Wheelwright (essay date 1954)

SOURCE: "The Guilt of Oedipus," in *Sophocles:"Oedipus Tyrannus,"* translated and edited by Luci Berkowitz and Theodore F. Brunner, W. W. Norton & Company, Inc., 1970, pp. 250-59.

[*In the following essay, originally published in 1954, Wheelwright argues that a key to understanding the meaning of* Oedipus Tyrannus *is found in its Greek title, which the critic renders as* Oedipus the Usurper.]

If we compare the best Hellenic studies of the last two or three decades with those of the half-century preceding, three new emphases become apparent: anthropological, psychological, and semantic. The change has been gradual, of course; and it might be objected that anthropology, in particular, is no new arrival, having been a factor in the critical consciousness of western Europe almost since the founding of the Royal Anthropological Institute in the early 1870's. But although that is true, and although scattered anthropological references can be found in the books and textual annotations of the older classicists, there are two reasons, I think, why the influence of anthropology did not become a substantial factor in classical scholarship until somewhat recently. One reason was the natural intellectual lag between any large discovery and the full realization of its pertinence. Partly the ingrained conservatism of many (by no means all) classical scholars, and partly the magnitude of the field newly opened up, made the process of reinterpretation a gradual one. The other reason lay in the uncertainty and lively disagreement among anthropologists themselves regarding the theoretical substructure of their researches. Until the turn of the century the animism of Tylor and Spencer exercised strong influence, especially in England; and such theories offered little to classical scholars that would change the tenor of their thinking or the direction of their researches. Belief in ghosts, in dreams, and in magic had always been a popular disposition, exploited by every teller of tales, without need of gloss.

But another anthropological theory began to find expression in the first decade of our century, which was to affect classical procedures a great deal. This was the theory variously called animatism, pre-animatism, and theory of mana—*protopsychism* might denote it best—associated particularly with the names of T. K. Preuss in Germany, R. R. Marett in England, and (as has been mentioned in another context), Lucien Lévy-Bruhl in France: that the primary religious phenomenon, the primordial stage in religious evolution (if we choose to think chronologically), is something vaguer and more fluid than either gods or human or ancestral souls; that it is an undefined sense of *presence,* stirring awe and perhaps dread in the beholder, capable on the one hand of developing at length into an object of reverence, and on the other of inviting attempts at magical control. Such is declared to have been the primitive belief-matrix from which religion, myth, and magic gradually, and sometimes divergently, evolved. The clearest indication of the power of the new theory to affect classical scholarship appears in Gilbert Murray's emphasis on the "error of treating Homer as primitive, and more generally in our unconscious insistence on starting with the notion of 'gods.'" Although Murray's specific evidences were drawn from within his own field of study, the new anthropological emphasis on intangibles was creating a climate of opinion and an openness of intellectual sensibility most favorable to his view.

The psychological element in classical modernism owes most, I suspect, to Nietzsche. The Nietzschean symbols of Apollo and Dionysus, although they oversimplified the many-sided phenomena of the Greek mind, provided a schema of interpretation which, so far as it went, was relevant. Moreover it set limits to the over-intellectualization of the Greek achievement of which traditional scholarship has often been guilty; and in doing so it invited attention to a rich field of evidence and allusion which the older scholars had not adequately explored. The effective presence of dark, vague chthonic forces, lacking the clear bright outlines and specious personality of the Olympian gods, was an aspect of the Greek thinkers' world which in the heyday of classical scholarship could be, if not quite neglected, at least explained away as atavisms. The Nietzschean rehabilitation of Dionysus, backed by such related German theories as Schopenhauer's philosophy of the will and von Hartmann's of the unconscious, and subsequently by the experimental approach to unconscious phenomena associated largely with the name of Freud, encouraged a disposition to look for nonrational mental factors in the interpretation of human phenomena. When this trend of psychological voluntarism (largely German, since the analogous work of de Biran, Ravaisson, and Fouillée in France exercised no comparable influence) began to unite early in the present century with the new protopsychic anthropology emanating largely from England, the result was to provoke the more forward-looking classicists—Jane Harrison and Gilbert Murray, for instance—to reëxamine their postulates of method and interpretation. Sometimes enthusiasm pushed them too far, as in Miss Harrison's celebrated cry, "There, I *knew* Zeus was only that old snake!" But a revised equilibrium was sought, and, in such admirable scholars as Werner Jaeger, Georges Méautis, and the late Francis M. Cornford, eventually found.

Of course the outstanding, or at any rate the most vociferated example of psychological method applied to classical problems has been Freud's Oedipus theory. Whatever the clinical uses of that provocative idea (and I suspect they have been overplayed) its interpretive value for an understanding either of the ancient legend or of Sophocles' two plays is sharply limited. For it is a commonplace among classical scholars that Oedipus himself never exhibits the well-known complex that bears his name. His marriage to Jocasta was a matter of civic duty: having rid the Thebans of the baleful Sphinx by answering her riddle

correctly, he received the throne of Thebes and the widowed queen to wife as his due reward. There is no indication in Sophocles' play or in any of the surviving records of the ancient myth, that Oedipus and Jocasta were drawn to each other erotically. But clearly Freud's interpretation of the Oedipus pattern could hold good of the ancient story only if there were an erotic attraction, whether conscious or repressed, between Oedipus and Jocasta, and moreover only if they felt, or if at least one of them felt, some conflict, however dimly, between the two relationships of son-mother and husband-wife.

Freud, to be sure, foresaw and met the objection after a fashion. The fact that Oedipus performed both acts, the slaying of his father and the bedding of his mother, without suspecting the true relationships, is in Freud's view "a deviation from the analytical subject matter which is easily intelligible and indeed inevitable." Inevitable, he explains, because of the need for "a poetic handling of the material"; for Freud's idea of poetry and the poetic seems to be pretty much limited to its alleged psychic function as a ritualized substitution for ideas which in their native form are suppressed. Intelligible, he goes on to explain, because "the ignorance of Oedipus is a legitimate representation of the unconsciousness into which, for adults, the whole experience has fallen; and the doom of the oracle, which makes or should make the hero innocent, is a recognition of the inevitability of the fate which has condemned every son to live through the Oedipus complex." Thus in interpreting the Greek myth of Oedipus as an embodiment of that psychotic pattern which he has named the Oedipus complex Freud is not insisting on the motivations of the characters in Sophocles' play but on the general unconscious acceptance of that pattern, by reason of which the myth took strong hold of the Greek popular imagination, finally causing Sophocles to recognize its unparalleled dramatic possibilities.

The first palpable expression of incestuous and patricidal elements in Oedipus' own psyche occurs, so far as I know, in Dryden and Lee's late seventeenth century version of the tragedy. In the opening scene of their *Oedipus*, Jocasta addresses her husband as though haunted by some dark intuition of her true relationship with him:

> When you chid, methought
> A mother's love start [*sic*] up in your defence,
> And bad me not be angry. Be not you;
> For I love Laius still, as wives should love,
> But you more tenderly, as part of me.

So much was Dryden's work. Nathaniel Lee, who wrote the second act, becomes tediously explicit:

> . . . This horrid sleep
> Dash'd my sick fancy with an act of incest:
> I dreamt, Jocasta, that thou wert my mother;
> Which, though impossible, so damps my spirits,
> That I could do a mischief on myself,
> Lest I should sleep, and dream the like again.

And Dryden, back on the job again in Act III, has Oedipus tell of an omen which struck him like "a pestilential blast":

A young stork
That bore his aged parent on his back;
Till weary with the weight, he shook him off,
And peck'd out both his eyes.

It would seem to have been Dryden and his collaborator then, not Sophocles, who introduced the Oedipus complex into literature. But the Dryden-Lee *Oedipus* is an inferior play, and the Oedipus story as they develop it is a hothouse growth, so artificial as to have lost most of its properly *mythic* character. Let us therefore look back to Sophocles' great play, the **Oedipus Tyrannus,** and inquire what its depth-meaning really is. For if we are to understand an archetype rightly, we must study it in its mature and artistically finished expressions even more painstakingly than in its cruder psychological and anthropological embodiments.

Erich Fromm, in *The Forgotten Language,* raises just this question of the depth-meaning of the play. Rejecting Freud's interpretation as inconsistent with the play's premises, he offers an alternative hypothesis of his own: namely that the Oedipus myth is "a symbol not of the incestuous love between mother and son but the rebellion of the son against the authority of the father in the patriarchal family; that the marriage of Oedipus and Jocasta is only a secondary element, only one of the symbols of the victory of the son, who takes his father's place and with it all his privileges." The dramatic conflict presented by Sophocles recapitulates, in Fromm's view, the prehistoric struggle between the matriarchal and the patriarchal forms of social organization. To substantiate this interpretation he appeals to Bachofen's theory that the earliest human sexual relations were promiscuous, and therefore, since only the mother's parenthood could be known, the inheritance of blood and hence of authority had to descend through her. Woman, therefore, Bachofen deduces, must have been the earliest lawgiver, and since the character of divinity in any period tends to reflect certain basic characteristics of human society, he draws the corollary that the religion of the Olympian gods was predated by a religion in which mother archetypes, dire and awful goddesses of which the Furies are the best known classical survival, were the supreme powers. Then in subsequent history (so the theory runs) man revolted against his servile role, and gradually succeeded in subduing woman, in establishing a patriarchal order on earth and the dynasty of the Olympian gods in heaven.

On the basis of Bachofen's provocative but tenuous theory Fromm amplifies his hypothesis, suggesting "that the hostility between father and son, which is the theme running through Sophocles' trilogy, is to be understood as an attack against the victorious patriarchal order by the representatives of the defeated matriarchal system." Notice his word "attack." Fromm interprets Sophocles as taking sides, as presenting a thesis. He sees the Theban dramas as intended to put across an idea—"the idea that the patriarchal world was triumphant, but that it would be defeated unless it adopted the humanistic principles of the older matriarchal order." The dramas, in short, (if we accept this interpretation) are didactic in intent; they are not primarily dramas, but dramatic vehicles for Sophocles' attack on the too brittle and too authoritarian principles of patriarchal rule, dramatic extrapolations of his nostalgia for the good old days of matriarchy.

In all interpretations let's keep our focus clear. The primary evidence of what a work of art means is always the work itself. Hints and clues may legitimately be sought outside, but their relevance and validity must always be appraised internally. Even if the theory of a primitive matriarchy should happen to be true, it does not follow that every ancient play must serve as a record of the prehistoric struggle. The *Oresteia* may indeed do so; the conflict between Apollo's command to Orestes to slay his mother and the wrath of the Furies as avengers of Clytemnestra's maternal rights lends a good deal of color to that view. But if we make any such judgment of the depth-meaning of the *Oresteia,* or for that matter if we dispute such a judgment, it must be primarily on the basis of evidence found within the play, rather than by undue reliance on sociological or psychological hypotheses. Can we find, then, in the **Oedipus Tyrannus,** any internal evidence of a conflict between the matriarchal and patriarchal principles?

The answer is plainly no, as any reader can see for himself; and even Mr. Fromm does not claim otherwise. He bases his interpretation of **Oedipus Tyrannus** partly upon the sociological theory just cited and partly upon an incident in each of Sophocles' other two Theban plays. In **Oedipus at Colonus** the now aged Oedipus expresses hatred and resentment against his two sons Polyneices and Eteocles. In the **Antigone,** where the dramatic action takes place after Oedipus' death, there is a violent flare-up of antipathy between Creon and his son Haemon. Fromm concludes: "If we interpret **King Oedipus** in the light of the whole trilogy, the assumption seems plausible that the real issue in **King Oedipus,** too, is the conflict between father and son . . ." Note the three main assumptions of his argument: (1) that the father-son antagonism in the other two Theban plays is of primary, not incidental, dramatic importance; (2) that the three Theban plays are closely enough related to justify a deduction of the meaning of one of them from the supposed meaning of the others; (3) that granted the legitimacy of such a deduction in general, it is reasonable to argue a father-son antagonism between Laius and Oedipus (for which there is no independent evidence) from the acknowledged father-son antagonism between Oedipus and his sons, and even from the existence of such a relationship between Creon and Haemon. The last assumption is so inherently weak as a principle of dramatic interpretation, and moreover is so logically dependent upon the validity of Assumption 2, that I shall not do more than cite it as a curious sample of circumambulatory reasoning. What, then, of the two remaining assumptions?

The **Antigone** is the one Theban play to which Fromm's theory of a patriarchal-vs.-matriarchal conflict might conceivably apply. Creon and Antigone in that play do seem to stand, as Fromm maintains, for the principle of order and authority, obedience and hierarchy on the one side, and on the other for the principle of blood relationship as the fundamental and indestructible tie. But this is only one aspect of their relationship to each other and to the total dramatic pattern. To overstress the dramatic conflict in these terms is to convert the *Antigone* into a sociological tract. Robert F. Goheen in his recent study of the play's dominant imagery adopts a more promising approach, examining (as Fromm never bothers to do) the specific language and imagery that constitute the play's symbolic action. "The imagery employed by Sophocles," Goheen writes, "is a functional means of communication in his dramas. It is aesthetic not simply in the sense of the decorative, but in the true sense of being a means of perception (*aisthêsis*) offered to the reader by the poet to take him into the meaning of the work." The recurrence of sight imagery, especially in the Haemon scene, throws the Creon-Antigone conflict into another perspective than the sociological. The drama becomes internalized: the emphasis is not merely on the question of domination by one sex or the other, nor even on the preferability of one or the other way of life; it is also, and far more subtly, upon the nature of human awareness. The conflict is primarily between two ways of grasping truth: Antigone's, the way of direct intuition, vs. Creon's, the way of sound sense and reason, or reliance on "right thinking" (*phronêsis*), on the linear, the measured, the plainly ordered. Each way of knowing has both its special reward and its special limitation of partial blindness. Fromm, to be sure, admits this spiritual antithesis as an aspect and derivative of the matriarchal-patriarchal conflict. But he errs, I believe, in two respects. He underrates Sophocles' artistic objectivity by assuming him to be taking sides. And he ignores the rich pattern of associated imagery—Goheen stresses in particular the images drawn from money and merchandising, from warfare, from animal life, and from seafaring—in which the characters of the two protagonists are caught up and given both fullness and concretion of meaning.

In any case, whatever our interpretation of the *Antigone,* there is no ground for drawing deductions from its supposed meaning to the meaning of the *Oedipus Tyrannus.* Fromm distorts the evidence by speaking repeatedly of the three Theban plays as a "trilogy"—despite his footnoted acknowledgment that they were not composed in the same order as the dramatic action represents. As a matter of fact they were written long intervals apart. The *Antigone* is generally accepted as having been written in or about 441 B.C., the *Oedipus Tyrannus* in 430 or later, and the *Oedipus at Colonus* shortly before Sophocles' death in 406. Moreover, each play was originally produced with two other Sophoclean tragedies, of which no record remains. Not in any sense, then, do the three extant Theban plays constitute a trilogy, and it is by no means permissible to deduce the purpose of the *Oedipus Tyrannus* from the purpose (if we know it) of the *Antigone.*

In the *Antigone* Creon is something of a melodramatic villain. In the plays written later his character becomes more ambivalent. Fromm, since he mistakenly treats the *Antigone* as if it had been written after the two other plays, misses the significance of the character change. He describes the figure of Creon as "indistinct" in the two Oedipus plays and as "becoming" colorful and definite in the *Antigone.* Since the *Antigone* was actually written first of the three, our critical problem is the reverse of the one he raises. Why does Sophocles blur the moral outlines of his Creon figure in the later plays? The likeliest answer surely is that with advancing maturity he no longer saw the moral issue in the relatively simple black-and-white terms of the *Antigone;* he had come to accept his characters as irresolvably ambivalent—no plain heroes and villains but multi-dimensional men steeped, like all of us, in moral ambiguities, which, though we see them in shifting perspectives, we must carry with us to the grave.

How, then, may a critical reader discover proper clues to the depth-meaning of *Oedipus Tyrannus*?

The first evidence is found in the title. You cannot perfectly rely on a writer to give you a major clue in the title of his work, but it is likely enough that he may want to do so, and the possibility should be explored. What is the meaning of the title *Oedipus Tyrannus?* Not, as in so many translations, "Oedipus Rex" or "King Oedipus." And of course not "Oedipus the Tyrant" either. Liddell and Scott's unabridged Greek lexicon declares that in classical Greek the word *tyrannos* was never applied to a hereditary monarch, for whom the word was *basileus;* it was restricted to those who had received the royal power by some means other than direct succession. Not even force or trickery was necessarily involved. Oedipus used none; he was offered the throne by the grateful Theban people. No matter: he was still a *tyrannos,* or usurper, within the accepted meaning of the word. The closest translation we can give for the play's title, then, is *Oedipus the Usurper.* And we must try to see a little further what *tyrannia* or "usurpation" connoted, and especially what its moral involvements were, to the mind of a fifth-century Greek.

To usurp is to overstep the measure, to erupt the proper limits of one's station in life, or of what is morally fitting, or (it may be) of the area of human as distinguished from divine prerogative. It is the vice or guilt or "tragic flaw" (*hamartia*) of arrogance (*hybris*). Cornford's alluring hypothesis that the rise of the idea may have been connected with the agricultural arrangements in prehistoric Greece has been mentioned in Chapter X. At all events, whatever its early history the idea of overstepping the boundary soon developed cosmic, moral, and political analogies. Just as (in the fragment quoted from Heraclitus) the sun dare not overstep his appointed path, lest the Furies, in their role as the handmaidens of Justice, find him out and punish him, so likewise a man dare not step beyond the path which Destiny has appointed him. Specifically he dare not emulate the gods, for divine indignation and vengeance (*nemesis*) will crash down upon him if he does. The primary *hamartia,* from this standpoint, is usurpation.

Oedipus was a usurper not only with respect to his father's throne and his mother's bed. That aspect is present in the play to be sure, and to a Greek audience Oedipus' ignorance of the relationships would not absolve him of guilt, nor does Oedipus ever expect that it will do so. Usurpation is still a half-physical, half-mythical thing; it happens and produces its terrible consequences regardless of motive. In this respect, therefore, so far as it goes, Freud would seem to have made a valid point after all. But there is another respect in which Oedipus was a usurper more consciously. His victory over the Sphinx was almost godlike, and for man to become too nearly godlike in any way at all (recall Hippolytus' tragic excess of chastity) is a display of *hybris,* arrogance, which by the inherent laws of destiny must be stricken down. The half-articulate usurpation imagery, then, together with the accusations of usurpation which the characters directly or obliquely hurl at one another, represents one depth-theme of the drama.

Next, there is the blight, afflicting the Theban countryside as the play opens. And here we meet with a quite different conception of moral law from the one involved in usurpation. The earlier idea is primarily an Olympian conception—an affair of clear boundary lines marked off in the bright vault of space. Blight and sickness, together with their opposite, which is health, are elements in the chthonic conception, appropriate to Mother Earth and the flora and fauna that grow out of her womb. Evil doing, from this standpoint, is felt as a kind of sickness, a malady in the individual, the commonwealth, and environing nature alike, and with terrible powers of contagion. When the blood of a murdered man seeps into the earth all vegetation sickens. And the same infection creeps into the human commonwealth, the *polis,* the city. What to do save lop off the offending member as one would lop off the diseased branch of a tree? The penalty of sin is at once a withering away in some sense of the individual and his exile from the commonwealth—not by arbitrary decree but by the sheer logic of the chthonic idea.

It is worth noting with what thematic effectiveness Sophocles introduces the word *polis* again and again at the beginnings and ends of lines, where it will have greatest prominence. Finally, after numerous such echoings Oedipus caps his emotional attack on Creon with the cry, "*O polis polis!*" ("O city city!") The contrasting word *xenos* (alien) is first used by Oedipus with unconscious irony when, in explaining why he did not know the details of King Laius' murder, he says "I'm just an alien here." The irony is a double one: he is not an alien in the way he thinks, since he is actually a son of the Theban royal house; but he is presently to be an alien in a more terrible sense, namely an exile.

The third and most central set of thematic images has to do with the blindness-vs.-vision antithesis and the solving of riddles. As the usurpation theme epitomizes Olympian morality and as the blight theme epitomizes chthonic morality, so I might venture the proposition that the blindness-riddle-vision theme epitomizes the morality of the mystery cults of Greece, and in a broader way one aspect of mystical religion generally. In the higher forms of Greek mystery cults, such as the worship of Demeter at Eleusis, the rebirth cycle of crops and seasons develop into the idea of spiritual rebirth. And when that happens the agency of rebirth is no longer magic, nor is it mere orgiastic ecstasy; it involves both inward purification and the imparting of a secret. The initiates at Eleusis performed a symbolic act of entering into darkness; in the inner shrine of the Eleusinian temple a new light was lit, and the sacred mysteries were revealed through such symbols as the sacred ear of grain. Oedipus, who solved the Sphinx's riddle and now would open up the dark mystery of his own origin, is inwardly blind, as the blind visionary Tiresias tries to tell him; and in putting out his eyes after his dreadful self-discovery he completes the symbolic pattern.

What can be concluded, then, as to the depth-meaning of **Oedipus Tyrannus?** Nothing in plain expository terms; of that I am sure. Sophocles was not at all the didactic and partisan writer that Fromm would have him. Francis Fergusson remarks in *The Idea of a Theatre* that "the peculiar virtue of Sophocles' presentation of the myth is that it preserves the ultimate mystery by focusing upon the tragic human at a level beneath, or prior to any rationalization whatever." I fully concur, and at the same time I think we can penetrate a little farther into the mystery—never to its heart—by awareness of the "concrete universals" that reside in the most characteristic uses of imagery. Our analyses are at best propaedeutic. They explain nothing essential, but do their work if they steer us to a fresh reading of the play with our visual and auditory imagination newly alerted.

Alister Cameron (essay date 1968)

SOURCE: "The Tragic Perspective," in *The Identity of Oedipus the King: Five Essays on the "Oedipus Tyrannus,"* New York University Press, 1968, pp. 125-54.

[*In the following excerpt, Cameron discusses what can be learned from* Oedipus Tyrannus *concerning guilt, the past, and fate.*]

In the middle of the **Oedipus** we find this juxtaposition: Oedipus and Creon quarrel, and before the scene is finished Oedipus has threatened to kill Creon, or at least to have him killed. Only the most strenuous pleading of both Jocasta and the chorus stops him. Then, in the next scene, Oedipus describes to Jocasta how he met Laius and his party, how he and they disputed the passage of the road, and how he killed them all.

Here, placed together, are Oedipus virtually on the point of killing now and Oedipus who did kill many years ago. An arresting juxtaposition, and surely not an accidental one. It immediately raises questions about the part played by Oedipus in the patricide. It also suggests that in this play crucial events of the past are in some sense being repeated in the present, and that is something about the play that has far-reaching implications for its interpretation.

Later we shall examine the relation of these two incidents to each other in detail, but let us look, for a moment, at another point of similarity between Oedipus' story of the past and the present action itself. In the scene with Teiresias, just before the quarrel with Creon, the following exchange occurs:[1] the old seer makes a mysterious reference to Oedipus' parents at which Oedipus pulls him up short, shouting, "Wait. What man gave me birth?" (437) Teiresias replies, but as Oedipus says bitterly, in nothing but "riddles." And Oedipus is right, because Teiresias, without meeting the question, goes on in his riddling talk to tell what in the end will become of Oedipus. The parallel to this, in event and situation, is of course the experience of the young Oedipus at Delphi. He had asked the god then who his parents were. Apollo had not answered his question. Instead, as Oedipus in his account of the incident says, again bitterly, the god had sent him away "dishonored" and given him "other things" in reply, saying that he would marry his mother, produce an accursed race, and kill his father. In short, as between these two moments the question is the same, the answer in each case is not directly to the question, but is instead, riddles and prophecies in which Teiresias repeats the role of Apollo. That should not surprise us, since we have already been told plainly about Teiresias that he is "the lord who sees most like the lord Phoebus" (284-85).

Repeating the past in this action then is not limited or peculiar to the two juxtaposed incidents we cited first. In fact, the perspective on time and events which the juxtaposition reflects is something that belongs to the whole action.[2]

How does the past in general stand in this play? When we put it all together, we find that there is a surprising lot of it, which in itself is an indication of its importance and relevance to the action. In the play, of course it is not all together. Different items are brought out at different times. This is common dramatic practice to be sure, but here the past is wholly dictated by the interests of the action; what is told about it, when and how it is told.

We often speak of events that have taken place in a given story before the play itself begins as being its "antecedents," almost as if they did not belong to the play. Aristotle categorizes certain things as lying "outside the drama," "the tragedy," "the *mythos*." Such terms, of themselves, settle nothing about how much or how little prior events belong to an action, and how much or little they mean to it. That remains a matter of the particular play. And about the ***Oedipus,*** it can certainly be said that the past is very little introduced for secondary purposes, such as to fill the audience in on the story, or to get things started, or to supply interesting information. Here, past and present are so

closely identified that there is no outside and inside. To anyone who knows the play, a simple catalogue of the past events involved is enough to prove the point: the oracle to Laius, the birth, the "exposure," the passing of the infant from hand to hand, the young prince in Corinth, and all that is contained in that narrative; the coming of Oedipus to Thebes, the Sphinx, the marriage and his elevation to the throne, the children, the plague, and the appeal to Delphi. This is all past and clearly all of it is taken thoroughly into the action. The past, in other words, becomes an integral part of the dramatist's formation of the subject.

We have already had some indication of how thoroughgoing this taking in of the past is. But it is time to see in detail what the repeating consists of, and the best place to do that is the juxtaposition we began with. What does the similarity between Oedipus on the stage quarreling with Creon and Oedipus in the pass fighting Laius consist of?

Let us divide the question into two basic components: first, the character, and second, the situation in which the character exists. Oedipus' character at any given moment in the action is the sum of what he has been shown to be from the beginning to that point. In the briefest kind of summary, thus. First, there is the noble king, "famous to all," who took up the challenging task that came to him from Delphi, and took it up as his deeply felt duty, with all the eager force of his nature. But then, no sooner had he done so than he was attacked, or so he thought, by Teiresias. This he resented, took as a personal affront, grew angry, arrogant, threatening, and dangerous.[3] That, let us say, is the character of Oedipus brought up to the time of the meeting with Creon. Then, in that meeting, suspicion and anger are accelerated to the point where he is ready to kill: "No indeed I do not want your exile," he cries to Creon, "It is your death I want" (623). The threat is far from idle. It is deadly serious; we must not fail to see that. Oedipus in this moment, before he is stopped by Jocasta and the chorus, is in the act of laying his hands on Creon.[4]

Now let us go on to the young man in the pass, as he is described shortly after this in the story Oedipus tells to Jocasta. As the prince of Corinth, he had enjoyed the highest esteem among his fellow countrymen. But the shocking incident at the banquet in Corinth, when he was taunted with being a bastard, "rankled" so that he went off secretly to Delphi. There he was "dishonored," as he says, by Apollo's prediction, and fled out into the world, away from Corinth. But, directly, he met Laius and his party in the mountain pass.

This then was the young Oedipus: in Corinth, proud, vulnerable to the personal affront; at Delphi, a figure of sympathy for the terrible predicament in which he found himself. But in both places, he was also a young man who relied on himself, made his own decisions, and acted on them. Then, in the encounter in the pass he showed himself resolute, high-tempered, indeed more than that. Quick to resent the affront that was offered him on the road, he acted with no second thoughts: "I struck in anger . . . and I killed the whole lot" (774-813).[5]

The point to be grasped is the simple one, that when in the course of the play we reach this story Oedipus tells about himself, the man we hear about, the young Oedipus in the story, is the same man acting in the same way as the Oedipus we have just now been watching in action upon the stage. I do not mean that the whole of Oedipus, in all his parts as he has been presented from the beginning of this action, is repeated. Only this, that enough of the essential Oedipus is there, and vividly there, so that we cannot fail to recognize him as unmistakably the same man, to recognize that the young man who at the moment of challenge to himself took things into his own hands and slew his father is indeed *this* Oedipus. The correspondence is that direct.

The question of situation is more complex. As between the young Oedipus, who was cut off from home by the god's prediction and driven out alone into the world, and the great king who stands very high in the eyes of the world, the contrast in external situation and circumstance is complete. But also, it is perfectly well understood that there is another situation, not the openly declared public one, but an undeclared real one behind it. And that is Oedipus' situation with Apollo. It was Apollo's words at Delphi that drove Oedipus out into the world; therefore, when immediately he met Laius face to face, we know perfectly well that this was no simple coincidence but something that had its place within the divine scheme of things for Oedipus. In other words, we know that Oedipus met his fate there. I have already suggested where Teiresias stands, and that he and Oedipus face to face are a repeating of Oedipus with Apollo. But we should notice now that it is the whole setting of the play that repeats itself. Thus, when the plague comes, Oedipus turns directly to Delphi; he does not go up himself, but Creon goes as his representative. The question asked is Oedipus' question, and the answer Creon brings back is Apollo's answer to Oedipus. It is also another "riddle," and one that again sets fateful action on its course. Moreover, this action is hardly well started when Oedipus once again finds the enemy across his path, or so he thinks, first in Teiresias and then Creon. In other words, while immediate circumstances change for Oedipus, the old situation remains, the fateful situation in which he lives and acts.

But a more specific question has to be reckoned with. Can we speak seriously of a fateful resemblance in situation between the incident in the pass and the quarrel with Creon on the stage, when it was Oedipus' fate on the former occasion to meet and kill not just anybody that blocked his way but his own father—not homicide but patricide? And if to that is added the necessary condition for the patricide, namely Oedipus' ignorance of the man he confronted, then are we left with any possible resemblance between Laius and Creon?

Let us consider Creon. Who is he? A prince of Thebes, of virtually equal standing with Oedipus himself (581 ff.).

The homicide in this case, in other words, would have serious political implications. But Creon is also a kinsman, by marriage to be sure, but still a man to whom Oedipus is bound by the closest ties. Oedipus had made a considerable point of the relationship earlier when he said, "For I sent my own brother-in-law to Phoebus' house." And the truth of the matter is that this is the man of all men alive to whom Oedipus is most closely bound, by public and private obligations alike.[6] Sophocles cannot repeat the patricide, but I suggest that by creating a situation in which a violation of the most sacred bonds is in prospect, he does the nearest thing to it.

There is also a resemblance in the point of ignorance. Naturally it falls short of the absolute ignorance of not knowing who a man is. Still, the fact is prominently held before us that Oedipus is as ignorant about Creon as a man could well be. He has delusions about him: that Creon is plotting against his life and throne, that Creon is a "murderer" and a "robber" (532 ff.). The ignorance, in short, is tragic ignorance, the familiar condition in which the hero, not knowing what he is up against, acts disastrously. One may, I think very properly, ask whether Oedipus' situation with Laius is anything more than this ignorance in its most extreme form. Certainly Oedipus on the stage acts constantly in blind ignorance.[7]

Where do we stand with our juxtaposition? The facts are these: we do not hear about Oedipus in the pass until we have come to know him well on the stage, and until we have been made thoroughly aware of the fateful situation in which he acts there; we do not hear how Oedipus killed Laius until after we have seen him brought to the point of killing on the stage. These are the plain facts of construction. But the point of this construction lies in the resemblance it contains and the parallel it makes. We have already seen enough to realize that this is a matter which involves the fundamental issues of the play.

Let me repeat. When we reach the point in the action where Oedipus tells his story, we recognize through his words and actions the character in it. The gestures made to us from the past, as it were, have a familiarity about them as being the gestures of a man we have already come to know remarkably well. This recognition is almost forced upon us and it has its obvious implications which, however, need to be stated pretty flatly. It is a commonplace to speak of Oedipus' fate being given. But, if the play makes a point of showing us as between past and present the same man acting in essentially the same situation, the implication is that whenever Oedipus' fate occurs, or can be said to occur, Oedipus is characteristically active in it. We cannot then speak of a given fate without also speaking of a given character. In fact, the implication seems to be that it is nonsense to speak of Oedipus' fate as if it at any time existed without his being active and alive in it.

Then where does this take us in the interpretation of the play? A perspective in which the past is seen through the present, we said, has important implications. And perhaps what comes to mind first is the controversial question of Oedipus' guilt or innocence in the patricide.

This debate always begins with Oedipus' account of what happened. Who pushed whom first? Didn't Laius mean to kill Oedipus and, therefore, didn't Oedipus resist and kill in self-defense?[8] If so, he cannot be guilty of homicide, let alone patricide. In brief, that is the argument for innocence. From the other side, it is argued that for a young man who has been warned by Apollo that he will one day kill his father (whom he has some reason to believe he does not know), Oedipus acts with criminal disregard of the possible consequences when he kills a man he does not know. Moreover, by his own account, he was hotheaded, proud. This points to guilt. True, in the eyes of the law, he cannot be guilty of patricide, for there is no denying the fact that he did not know that the man was his father; but in the eyes of gods and men he cannot be exonerated, which is to say, in some sense he must be guilty. To those who maintain Oedipus' innocence, this argument is feeble, indeed intolerable. All it has to say is that Oedipus is human, fallible like other men, and to suppose that Sophocles would advance that as proof of guilt, they argue, is absurd. On the other hand, the argument for innocence, in the eyes of those who see Oedipus as guilty, has to ignore those qualities which are simply obvious.

If I had to choose between these two positions I should choose the second.[9] Everybody would like Oedipus to be innocent if only because it is outrageous that a man placed in the position he was, and such a man, should be found guilty. But then one must remember that tragedy is outrageous; it is only the good man's suffering that is tragic and only the wicked man's that is reasonable. And what sort of innocent could Oedipus be? An "injured innocent"? The argument for innocence seems forced to say so, for it implies that the point we must see about him, very much the point of the play, is that in no sense does he deserve his fate, that he is either a man who simply sustains a terrible fate or who nobly resists it. I think we must see clearly that he is neither of these, the reason being that such a reading of Oedipus simply removes him from the action, takes him out of the play. Apart from the anachronism this view entails, making him a romantic hero rather than a Greek one, the fact is, the decisive one I think, that the play presents us with a character who is almost exactly the opposite of an "injured innocent." Oedipus is not a man who is assailed by fate or who waits until it comes to him; on the contrary, he seizes his fate and throws the whole force of his personality into it.[10]

It is the perspective that is wrong. The proponents of both sides of this argument, in making their case, start from the account of what happened in the pass and then, for confirmation, appeal to the rest of the play or to the parts of it which seem to support one or the other view. It is my point that we have no right to appeal to the present action except within the perspective that the action itself provides.

So let us follow the perspective. In an action where the past is taken into the present, it is the present that counts.

What we must judge, in other words, if we judge at all, is Oedipus faced with the command from Delphi, and Oedipus with the different forms that situation takes: with Teiresias, Creon, Jocasta, right through the blinding. The first questions one should ask then are these: is Oedipus innocent with Teiresias, with Creon, with Jocasta, with himself? After that we may ask who pushed whom. True, this does not make a legal case against him for patricide. But then, tragedy does not take place in the law courts.[11] Also true, and most startling in the whole sequence, is the evidence of our senses about this man that when aroused as he is by Teiresias he is capable of killing, and, as with Creon, of killing his own kinsman.[12]

Thus, if we are forced to choose between guilty and innocent in the patricide, the weight of evidence comes down for guilty, as guilty in the past as he is now. That, as I see it, is the bearing of the action, and not just of this or that part of it, but of the whole.

Yet, are we forced to choose? Have we any right to judge? There is at least the possibility that we import this issue into the play ourselves, since Sophocles makes no explicit statement here about guilt or innocence. That he took up in the *Coloneus,* a very different sort of play.[13] I myself believe he is intent in the *Tyrannus* on something more elementary.[14] That is, the fact that in the fullest sense Oedipus' fate belongs to him. For I do not think we can fail to see what I should call a fitness in him or even an aptitude for what happens. That judgment, I feel sure, the play does make, although perhaps more fact than judgment. But it is a fact which one comes upon in considering any major issue in the play, as we ourselves have found repeatedly. Earlier, we put it that the character appears to belong to this action as if by some profound natural right. The fitness we see now within the perspective of the play is exactly the same thing.

We had better look back now and take further note of the conclusion we reached earlier here; that whenever and wherever Oedipus' fate may be said to occur, Oedipus always appears to be an agent in it. And this carries with it an implication which we have also met before: that Sophocles shows us how Oedipus' fate *comes about.* The point is an important one to consider again, because it is so widely believed that fate in the Greek tragedy, whether in the past or in the present, does not come about but is simply given, and nowhere so clearly as in the *Oedipus.*

So let us consider once more the "givenness" of this play and the question of Oedipus' fate. Before the play begins, he had already done what Apollo had said he would do: kill his father and marry his mother. How then, in all conscience, can we speak of Sophocles as showing us Oedipus' fate coming about? Isn't his fate already complete? That is an obvious but not a simple question. And there are other related questions which have to be asked that have the opposite implication. Is it conceivable that Sophocles' interest in this play lies in the fact that Oedipus' fate already exists without his also asking how it came to exist? Can it be doubted that he is enormously interested in the acts into which Oedipus falls during the course of the action and could these be anything, therefore, but fateful acts?[15] In other words, if Sophocles is not showing us Oedipus' fate in the process of coming about, what could he be showing us? Again, if Oedipus' fate is complete before the play beings, then does the play stand somewhere outside his fate? Where? A sequel to his fate, an epilogue, a commentary on it? These are the possibilities, and I cannot see that they are not absurd.

Oedipus' fate is, of course, not complete before the play begins. Apollo commands the search for the guilty man, commands Oedipus, knowing him well, knowing both that he is guilty and will search and therefore find himself. This Oedipus does. That is the literal record of the action. Fate is, to be sure, an ambiguous word, but not so ambiguous that we cannot recognize it here; at least if this is not a fate and its fulfillment, then I do not know what a fate can be. And yet, it remains true that Oedipus' fate by the acts he has committed is, if not complete, already in existence and indeed sealed. How can his fate be in existence and coming into existence at the same time without contradiction? That is the question we have to ask now.

It is not a question to be limited to the *Oedipus*. It applies as well, for example, to the *Ajax* or to the *Hippolytus,* for the heroes of both these plays have also already committed irrevocable, fateful acts before action begins on the stage, and as between them and the *Oedipus* there is no essential difference in this matter. And actually, it is a matter which affects Greek tragedy as a whole. Always things have happened, or been done in the past from which the individual or individuals involved cannot escape. In other words, what we are talking about is a condition inherent for the Greek in the world of tragedy.[16] There are different ways of recognizing this world, some more explicit than others, and these two plays I have cited are perhaps the most explicit. With their formal opening divine declarations, they represent the world in which tragic action takes place less subtly than does the *Oedipus.* But the result is the same, for although the fateful situation of Oedipus—that he has killed his father and married his mother—is undeclared, it is no less well understood that it exists.

Then what about the action that does take place? As an example, let us again take the *Hippolytus.* What about the hero, his purity and his hauteur; about Phaedra's mad passion for him and his response (to say nothing about how bad his rhetoric is); about the revenge she took; about Theseus' blind anger, and the catastrophic death of Hippolytus that followed on it? In short, about the whole action, although Aphrodite had announced that the gates of hell were open for Hippolytus (56-57), can it be doubted that this play shows us a fate coming about? And what does the showing consist of? Clearly, the sealed world of tragic action is there, but also clearly within it the characters, their relations and responses to each other; in other words, a showing or a bringing out of the tragic necessities which together make the fate a reality. Thus, it

is not a contradiction to say of the same fate that it is in existence and that it is also coming about now.

Earlier, in following the tragic inevitability of Oedipus' self-discovery, we were dealing with the same problem. And we said then that this process was not among the things which were given in advance to the dramatist. Similarly, here, while it is a principle of the world of tragedy that a man cannot escape his acts, it remains for the dramatist to find the tragic necessities in the particular story which demonstrate the truth of the principle. Perhaps since the Greek tragic world, between the people who lived in it and the powers that governed it, was more clearly formulated, the tragic necessities about Oedipus were closer at hand; more given in that sense for Sophocles than they were for Shakespeare, say, about Macbeth. Even so there was nothing cut and dried about finding them. We said earlier that it seems a fate does not ever exist here without a character, for, as between Oedipus and his fate, we never find one without the other. And that is to say in other words, that the creating or the finding of the character who is necessary to his fate, that creative insight, was as much the business of tragedy then as it has been since.

Bearing in mind, then, the fact that a fate is not simply given, but that it comes about and that a character is necessary for it to become a reality, let us return to the patricide and to the point that we recognize Oedipus in it. What conclusions do we draw? We must try to state them as explicitly as possible. First, the one we have already drawn, that our recognition of Oedipus in the patricide means that we see the same character who is at work now in his fate was also at work in it in the past. It was in that perspective, we maintained, that the question of guilt or innocence in the patricide had to be assessed. But now, I think we must go a step further. Since that event is taken into the present action, and seen through it, we are in effect seeing the patricide coming about as if it were happening now. If that is true, since there can be no doubt that patricide is his fate, there can also be no doubt that we are seeing his fate come about. The perspective of the action, it seems to me, will admit no other conclusion. If it is agreed on the basis of the present action that a fate can never exist without a character, or characters, who execute it, the only alternative I can see would be to say that the play shows us Oedipus' fate as if it were coming about now, whereas, in reality, it had come about in the past. But this is inadmissible because it would take us back to the proposition that we have seen is false: that Oedipus' fate is complete before the play begins. It would also, in my opinion, imply a literary posture which is quite foreign to the spirit of the play, or to any other Greek play, saying, in effect, that Oedipus on the stage was acting symbolically or allegorically, not really acting. The conclusion we are left with then is simply this: that the patricide being taken into the present action, as if it were happening now, takes its place and its meaning in Oedipus' fate as a part of the process that is going on now. This is the process of Oedipus meeting his fate, still going on and completed nowhere but here.

We have said nothing about the marriage, the other act by which in the past Oedipus sealed his fate, and we should like to know how it was committed. Sophocles does not describe how it happened in the way he describes the murder. The theme of incest, however, is always present. Naturally, the action being concerned specifically with the search for Laius' murderer, as between the two issues, patricide and incest, it is the former that for most of the distance up to the recognition occupies the foreground. But the lines play ironically on the incest before Jocasta appears on the scene, and when she does appear, her presence of course keeps it before us. And then, when the action shifts its course from the search for Laius' murderer to the question of Oedipus' birth, with Jocasta on the stage throughout, the incest has displaced the patricide and become the first interest. And certainly, when we reach the discovery, and from there on, the lines make it clear that it is the thought of the marriage that haunts Oedipus and overwhelms him. Thus, in different ways, the marriage looms very large in the action, and if the play tells us how Oedipus' fate comes about it cannot be totally silent on this score.

We are, as I said, told nothing in detail about the event itself. There is, however, an understanding: that the people of Thebes, in gratitude and as the prize of victory for his conquest of the Sphinx, had offered Oedipus the throne and with it the queen, and he had accepted both.[17] Thus the victory and the marriage are, in effect, one event and, as a result, it is in connection with the Sphinx that we learn what we do learn about how the marriage happened. From the priest in the prologue we hear about the great reputation Oedipus has won in the eyes of the world for his conquest: he is the "noblest of men," the "savior" of his country, "first among men" in dealings with the gods, he overcame the monster "with the adherence of a god," etc. (31-51). But it is from Oedipus himself that we learn how it happened and, after the laudatory and pious remarks of the priest, it comes as a shock when we hear Oedipus saying angrily and arrogantly to Teiresias that he defeated the Sphinx himself, by his own wits:

> But I came, I Oedipus the ignorant one, and I stopped her, hitting the mark with my wit, not by learning from birds.

> (396-98)

Oedipus' point here in his duel with Teiresias is that whereas he, Teiresias, with all his mantic art could do nothing when the Sphinx was ravaging the country, he, the famous Oedipus, came along and "without birds" saved Thebes single-handed.

The clue to the marriage, I suggest, is found in this picture Oedipus gives of himself as the man who came along and where others had failed, risked all (presumably he risked his life) and won all. In other words, he is a man who trusts his luck and his wits and wins, or so he thinks. Don't we know that supreme self-confidence and the readiness to risk all very well?[18] And the image of the gambler

with fortune is not farfetched. Teiresias at one point refers directly to the marriage, thus:

> What harbor shall not be filled with your cries, what Cithaeron will not echo soon, when you shall realize what bad anchorage it was you entered in the marriage to this house, for all the luck of your fair voyage?

> (420-23)

A few lines later the reference is indirect but no less pointed, when again we here Teiresias say:

> And yet it was just that fortune (*tyche*) that destroyed you.

> (442)

Oedipus had won the game with the Sphinx, or so it seemed, and had picked up as his winnings the throne and the queen. Jocasta, in other words, he had won as a part of his political "fortune." What Teiresias puts to him here is that his fortune with the Sphinx had been his misfortune, and he is referring, of course, to the disastrous marriage.

Admittedly being told nothing directly about the marriage itself, we have to read between the lines to find Oedipus in this fateful event, But when we do, it is the same Oedipus we find, the one acting before our eyes, and the marriage takes its place in Oedipus' fate accordingly. We need only look at him in the moment before the scene of recognition to see how much the gambler with fortune is a part of the present action: "Let break what will . . . I deeming myself Fortune's child, generous Fortune, shall not be deprived of my inheritance" (1076-81). This is surely the gambler for high stakes, ready to risk all and reckless of the consequences.

Difficult as it was in the case of the patricide to say that Oedipus was guilty, it seems preposterous in the incest. Yet, the fact presented by the action cannot be denied, that Oedipus took Jocasta in the same way; blindly Teiresias would say,[19] arrogantly as Oedipus' own words betray him. He put his hand to his fate in this event as he had in others, and continues to do now.[20] This leaves us with the thought, however preposterous, that in the marriage he cannot be called innocent. And perhaps the most revealing thing in the whole matter and the most damaging, is what Oedipus does to Jocasta in that last scene. He treats her roughly, very roughly, so that when she leaves the stage there is a sense of her being driven off to her death by him. True, she has her own reasons for going, of which he is still unaware but, after all, what happens to her here at the hands of this "child of Fortune" is not totally different from what happened to Laius. She too looks like a casualty of his acting.

Earlier, we said that while it made no sense of the play to call Oedipus innocent to find him guilty was outrageous. Then, is it less outrageous to say about acts which in the eyes of gods and men are the most unnatural of all acts— and this the play makes very clear—that the noble Oedipus was somehow fit to perform them?[21] For whatever his faults, Oedipus is noble. And, after all, the acts he performs he is condemned to perform in ignorance. Therefore, whenever he acts, necessarily he acts blindly. Blindness is given him in his situation. The Greek word for it is *ate*.

All this is very true. However, what we have also seen many times is that Oedipus acts not only *in* blindness but *with* blindness. That is, there is not only the built-in ignorance of the situation, there is also a condition of the soul, a blindness which leads him, for example with Creon, to act with a passionate ignorance.[22] The Greek word for this is again *ate,* which is to say that the phenomenon we recognize here of a fitness in the soul for the tragic situation is common enough. The odds against Oedipus are certainly enormous, notoriously so. But tragedy always works with such odds, and it is nonetheless Oedipus who threatens Teiresias, who would kill Creon, and not Oedipus by name only, but the noble Oedipus with the whole force of his personality. In short, it is put down at the center of this story that this noble nature is somehow itself productive of a fantastically ugly tragedy. The chorus after the discovery see Oedipus' fate as the *paradeigma* (1193) of the great fall from blessedness. The appalling part of the lesson is how Oedipus brought it about. Oedipus, *even* Oedipus, is fit for his fate. That is the remarkable and tragic thing the play has to say.

Guilt and innocence are moral judgments which in their different ways resolve the problem of suffering. Tragedy has its limitations, one being that it does not provide solutions to the problems it poses. If it tried, or when it tries, it runs the risk of denying the fact by which it exists, that suffering is real and cannot be explained away. That does not mean that it leaves the problem alone. Sophocles does not leave the story of Oedipus where he found it, in Homer or in Aeschylus, or in fantasy, folklore, or nightmare, where it originated in the first place. He explores it, he has vision about it, and he illuminates it. The center of this vision which he leads us to recognize is Oedipus fully human and alive in the terrible story. This, as I say, solves no problems, but it does one thing which apparently never loses its fascination. It grasps the joint of the world at which tragedy arises, and that is nothing more nor less than what we have been seeing, here and elsewhere in these pages; that however monstrous the things given, the man has a capacity for them. This is, of course, for such a man as Oedipus an outrageous vision; it does not satisfy common sense; it is not comfortable. But Sophocles, neither in this nor any other play, thought he was making a world in which such a terrible fitness exists either acceptable or comfortable. What he was doing was presenting the world as he saw it. And this we must believe the "serene" Sophocles believed passionately he must show, and we must see. To some, this vision has been undeniably true. Others deny it, like Plato, and insist that the tragic necessities it poses are false. No one, I should think, Plato included, has been able to forget it.

We have had much to say about knowing the self and about Sophocles' Oedipus as the unforgettable exemplar

of this drive to the real world. But one thing remains to be added: that it is surely Sophocles who knows himself. Sophocles, it was said in antiquity, was the happy one, and the one "loved of the gods." He was also, as his plays show, the one beyond others who knew how to look unhappiness and suffering in the face. To be "loved of the gods" and to be "happy," as Aristotle said, is not easy. It means in Sophocles' writing finding one's true self in the real world. In Sophocles himself this happiness is an awesome achievement.[23]

Still, whether we are convinced or not by this vision, it is a matter of more than historical interest to consider further what sort of world it presents and what position it gives to man. Two things we said in connection with the blinding were excluded: first, the idea of a tragic Oedipus who is nothing but a victim struggling in the grip of his fate; and second, the other extreme conclusion, that he is a free agent. The only fitness of "the worm on the hook" for his fate would be, so far as I can see, his impotence. As for free agent, it means—if it means anything at all—freedom of choice, and although we have been able to say of Oedipus that he chose to act and that this was profoundly expressive of his nature,[24] it would be obvious nonsense to say that Oedipus would choose to kill his father of his own free will. And then further, perhaps it is necessary to say, just because we have been making much of Oedipus' fitness or capacity for tragedy, that this does not signify a world in which the fatality is lodged in the character, at least not in the sense of tragedy which would have no existence except as it is created out of the psyche. In other words, this is not private tragedy, but tragedy which takes place in a world which has fatality built into it, therefore objective, public tragedy.

Then how does this built-in fatality function? That is the question we should like to be able to answer. Naturally, nobody could pretend to be able to dispose of so vast a question, but, as Aristotle might put it, we can still try to say something about it. If we look back once more to the command from Delphi with which the play begins we can say this: that Apollo confronts Oedipus with a fate which he, being the man he is, cannot but take up.[25] Doesn't that mean then that the god knows the particular fate that belongs to the particular man and knows his capacity to take it up?[26] Perhaps we can say that this is tragedy's way of expressing the terrible fitness or symmetry it sees between what is given to a man and what he does. And it is abundantly clear in the play that Apollo knows Oedipus through and through. Therefore, what sort of a world? One in which the gods know men but know at least some men to their misfortune. In other words, it seems that this is a world where the man, or the woman, who is known to the gods, or of whom they take notice, is a man who is in for trouble, headed for disaster. A merciless sort of world for some people then. Is that the point?

It is part of the point, but not the whole of it. Certain things are left in this world for certain men or women beyond, or along with trouble. And two characteristic positive findings or interests of tragedy I think we can put a name to: honor for one, and for the second, the capacity of a man to act and declare himself in his own actions. Honor, to which the Greeks were acutely sensitive, is the public recognition of a man's achievements. Accordingly, the heroes of tragedy win honor from the gods. Even Aphrodite, perhaps the cruelest divinity, while she brings about Phaedra's death (in the *Hippolytus*) also gives her "glory." And, it might be added, Artemis in the same play goes beyond honor. She decrees perpetual honor for her devoted Hippolytus, but in explaining that she, being a goddess, may not weep for him, there is more than a suggestion that she gives him love and compassion as well as honor (1394). But it seems that honor is implicit in the tragic relation itself. For who are the men to whom the gods offer a fate and a destiny? They are the heroes. And what is a hero in tragedy? The man who has the capacity for tragedy. That is, the man who can and will take up his fate.[27] These are the men the gods know. Knowing them they see that they "walk proudly" (883-85), whereas only the gods have the right to be prond. Such men, it seems, the gods in their government of the world with its "high-footed laws" must bring down or, as in Artemis' case, keep hands off while they are brought down.[28] It is, to be sure, a merciless world but just as surely not one in which the gods act at random. Certain men the gods confront with a fate, and that in itself we are given to understand is a title of nobility.[29]

Human pity for Oedipus there is in the *Tyrannus,* but not divine, and no divine honors are decreed for him. Honor certainly, and perhaps compassion, are implicit in the divine summons and the "marvelous" departure from life in the *Coloneus* (1665). By comparison, the earlier play remains silent, painfully silent. Nevertheless, at the end, as I have said more than once, this play contains the classic example of the man who acts and declares himself in his own actions. All men may have the capacity for action, but Greek tragedy is not much concerned with that. Its concern is with the men and women who have this capacity in a heightened degree, and in the fact that for such men, the world is inevitably tragic.[30] For the heightened capacity for action does not enable the hero to escape tragedy, only to go further and further into it. The Greek tragic world allows no room for taking your life into your own hands and making it something different from what it is. Nonetheless, it is you in the last analysis who make it. In other words, we come to the crucial fact of which the play by its present action gives eloquent evidence: that the fate comes about, and that the actor is essential to the process, whether now or in the past. A fate, it follows, without an actor would exist only in a secondary sense, as something written in the books of the gods, not lived. The tragic poet was certainly not interested in such an abstraction. What fascinates him is the man, the kind of man who, with his actions, brings the universe alive. In showing this, he makes the point, I suggest, that there is room in this universe, or opportunity for such great action.

A play where situation and character remain constant, where the past is taken into what happens on the stage,

raises questions about time. And they are general questions affecting Greek tragedy as a whole; for the perspective on action in the *Oedipus* was not contrived for a single play. Ajax equally with Oedipus was active in his fate in the past. In fact, the perspective is an *optique* on the world that belongs to all. And a world in which Oedipus old or young remains the same and acts in the same situation must be a timeless world in some sense, at least one with no past in the historic sense; rather, since what it contains is a repeated enactment of the same factors, a world of a continuous present. This is thoroughly Greek, and to give it its Greek name, it is a world in *being*.[31] And then we must go further; if a world in being, then not only with no historic past but with no future either. And this too is profoundly true of Greek tragedy. As we watch the progress of events, we hope passionately that things will become different. But it is the central truth of these tragedies that hope precisely prevents men from seeing things as they are and must continue to be; that, in the tragic world, hope is a delusion.[32] The tragic function of the gods, for example, is very much that they force men to recognize and face the fact that there is no escape into the future from things as they are and must be.

Then, finally, we might raise the question: is it not true of all tragedy that it offers no escape into the future? I have referred earlier to the view that only later tragedy is capable of expressing a genuine interplay of character and circumstance, and I have tried to show that on the contrary nothing is more striking about this fixed world, this world in being as we are now calling it, than that by its repeated enactment or reenactment it is a being, fully alive, repeatedly enlivened by the actor. Not a Parmenidean world, therefore, which excludes motion and variety, for surely no one can deny the variety in Oedipus, or the fact that it registers itself on events. On the other hand, if it is claimed for other tragedy that it is capable of producing a new situation, is creative of wholly new events in a future, then that is another matter, for of this achievement the Greek was certainly not capable.

A Hellenist wonders, naturally, if the distinction is valid. What is the newness, the creative novelty, in Shakespeare? Is there a difference in kind from the *Oedipus*? Are Lear, Macbeth, Hamlet, Othello really changed, transformed in the course of the play, and do they by their choices and acts transform their world, the situation in which they act? Or, is tragedy there too the exploration of the fateful situation and the character or characters that fit it? And do we, the spectators, not hope that things will be different for this character or that, and yet know they will not? In whatever age, is it not just this point that tragedy makes to us—the ancient point that we cannot escape what is?

We are talking here about tragedy and tragedy alone. I do not believe that a fixed world of being was the only world the Greeks conceived of, and I am certainly not questioning the fact that since the Greeks, in history, religion, and science, a sense of change and novelty has been achieved which is not found in Greek tragedy. But I am asking if that sense of change is compatible with tragedy. In a world of genuine novelty, I myself find it difficult to imagine the kind of happening which the Greeks called by the name "tragedy." And if there is a later drama that we still call tragedy, which represents such a world, I should be inclined to give it some other name in recognition of the fact that it has broken out of the tragic world into some other world.[33] In short, I wonder whether men who no longer believe in a world in being can go on writing tragedy.[34] Perhaps that is what O'Neill felt when he said it was so difficult for a dramatist to capture a "classic fate" in a modern play.

Notes

1. See above, Chapter 2, pp. 48 ff., for the implications of this exchange in relation to the self-discovery.

2. This question of time so far as I know has not been discussed in the literature. Letters (p. 104) speaks of the "telescoping of the present with the past or the imminent which is the essence of classic irony." This is a suggestive remark but Letters does not follow it up. Knox (*Oedipus*, p. 41) says more: "The character of Oedipus in action in the present time of the play makes plausible and explains his actions in the past; it does this with especial force since one of the purposes of Oedipus' present action is precisely to reconstruct and understand his past." I agree. However, I cannot see Knox's further point that the situation in the present is different from the one that existed in the past, because if it were it simply could not explain the past. See also Kirkwood, pp. 69 ff.

3. "I think you and he who plots it (Creon) will have reason to lament your purging of the land. If you didn't look old to me you would have realized to your cost . . . what your plots deserve" (401-03). Knox (p. 28) is able to say on the basis of these lines that Oedipus "disclaims any intention of punishing Teiresias." The bald threat of physical violence here should not be minimized.

4. I cannot see Oedipus here as anything but a man acting in terrible excitement. But I can't agree with Reinhardt (p. 122) who thinks Oedipus' threat to kill Creon more a "passionate outburst" than a serious threat. Knox (pp. 17 ff.) thinks him deliberate and reflective. What Knox (p. 30) and Adams (pp. 95 ff.) are impressed with is not the fact that Oedipus wants Creon put to death but that Creon is not killed. To Knox this shows a "democratic temper" and, to Adams, Oedipus' "own essential goodness." I must say that these interpretations strike me as extraordinarily lighthearted. The fact is that Oedipus barely escapes a terrible deed and, as he says, by no will of his own (688). He is, in fact, what Creon says he is: "sullen" . . . , "over-bearing" . . . , "ignorant" . . . (673-77).

5. See Kirkwood's interesting note (p. 69 n) stressing the point that Laius, by Oedipus' own account, "paid no equal penalty."

6. Creon emphasizes the relationship: "For to cast off a noble friend I say is like casting off one's own life which is the thing he loves most" (611-12). This reminds one of Aristotle's statement, "a friend is another self" (*Nicomachean Ethics*, 1166a31). The lines, of course, bear ironically on the point that Oedipus is constantly injuring himself. See also Sheppard, p. lv, where he observes that a tyrant typically is unable to distinguish friend from foe. And Plato, *Republic* 575e, the tyrant "has no friends."

7. Sophocles, through Creon, stresses Oedipus' ignorance in different ways here, most subtly thus: "I do not know and where I do not understand it is my habit to be silent" (569). A contrast runs through the whole scene of course, between the man governed by prudence . . . and the man who acts blindly, thus emphasizing Oedipus' ignorance. The contrast between the two is maintained to the end: Creon, "What I do not mean, it is not my habit to say idly" (1520).

   Perhaps Sophocles, *Fr.* 238N 924P should be read in this context: "The hardest evil to wrestle with is ignorance." The sense seems to be that it is ignorance which makes a man most dangerous.

   One must remember that many things with Oedipus in the *Oedipus* are pushed to an extreme, and ignorance is one of them. But does his ignorance differ essentially from Ajax'? Ajax acted in madness sent upon him by Athena when he slaughtered the flocks. Deianeira certainly did not know any more than Oedipus what she was doing. What about Antigone? Could anyone make the plea of ignorance for her? It would hardly seem so. She knew the great risk when she chose to act. And yet when Creon makes it quite clear that she will in fact die, she like many another pleads that she too has been led by the gods. She speaks of herself as "ill-fated," as being carried off by Death, as being a victim of the blind follies of her race (857-928).

8. Letters (p. 218) justifies Oedipus as "having his head almost split open." This is fun, but for what happened see Jebb's comment on 804-12. The herald, and Laius, told Oedipus to get off the road. Evidently he wouldn't budge, so the driver pushed him, Oedipus hit him, and then Laius brought his stick down on Oedipus' head, etc. I would add from my own experience that it is very annoying and rather dangerous to meet someone who insists on having the road to himself, especially when you are driving a "narrow" . . . "hidden" . . . (1399) pass in the mountains in Europe.

9. Kirkwood, p. 276: "Scarcely anybody doubts that Oedipus is morally innocent." This I find a rather ambiguous statement especially in view of the fact that Kirkwood himself is also able to speak about Oedipus' responsibility. But perhaps all that is meant is that Oedipus is a good man, which I should think nobody at all would question.

Letters defends the innocence of Oedipus vigorously, and apparently thinks anybody who doesn't is a numbskull or worse. His case (p. 220) is based largely on the distinction between guilt and ritual uncleanness and on Oedipus' arguments in the *Coloneus.*

Waldock, p. 167: "Oedipus is indisputably a victim; that fact is at the very heart of the drama." He believes Oedipus' "deficiencies fade into nothingness." Oedipus, as he thinks, is "normal," and it is absurd that he should pay the price for being so (p. 146). Waldock does not want us to have anything to do with "the veritable matters behind human conflicts." They "abolish the drama," he believes. Sophocles, he says, "eschews thinking," and Waldock is down on anybody who tries "smuggling significance into *Oedipus Tyrannus*" (p. 159); "There is no meaning in the *Oedipus Tyrannus*" (p. 168); "the theme of Lear is universal, Oedipus is not."

10. See Whitman, pp. 122-46 for the opposite view, e.g., "Oedipus remains a type of human ability condemned to destruction by an external insufficiency in life itself." See Kirkwood, p. 171 on the interpretations of recent "hero-worshippers."

11. It has been argued that an Athenian jury would have acquitted Oedipus: see Sheppard, p. xxviii, and see Wilamowitz, *Hermes,* 34 (1899), pp. 55 ff. It seems to me that the only court Oedipus is judged by in the play is on Olympus (867). No doubt Creon too in the *Antigone,* for different reasons, would have been acquitted in law, but I think there can be no doubt that the gods find him guilty: the chorus does, he finds himself guilty (1257 ff.) and we, not as judges but as men, agree with him. To argue to a conclusion in the play from Athenian legal practice is open to the criticism of judging the play by criteria other than its own.

12. I am not sure whether Adams (p. 90) is justifying Oedipus' conduct toward Teiresias when he says that his suspicion of the seer is not unfounded. To say "they are the natural suspicions of any *tyrannos*" does not of course justify, although it does explain, and that may be all that Adams means. What his pages here (pp. 90-95) really bring out very well is the fact that given his situation (ruler) and his character (at this point tyrannical), Oedipus' conduct with Teiresias and Creon is thoroughly convincing. Letters on the other hand (p. 223) apparently thinks there is nothing tyrannical about Oedipus. I think Oedipus in certain circumstances behaves tyrannically. I do not mean by that he is a tyrant, and I think the play shows the word . . . as no more applicable to Oedipus than it would be to some other king when he behaves badly. See Knox, *passim,* for quite a different view. And for Knox' point (pp. 74 ff.) that an Athenian audience would have accepted Oedipus' suspicions of Creon with relish because they were familiar with such plots, to that I must say

that he (and Whitman whom he cites) are a good deal more complacent about the Athenian suspicion of plots and counterplots than, say, Thucydides, who regarded it as a sign of moral deterioration.

13. The difference between the two plays in this matter is, of course, very striking. We cannot read one play in terms of the other without getting into difficulties. Thus, for example, Sophocles, when he wrote the *Antigone,* had no thought of the *Coloneus* in his mind, for in the earlier play (50), Oedipus, according to Ismene, had died "odious and infamous" (also it seems to be the implication of 897 ff. that he had died in Thebes). On the other hand, no one can doubt that when he wrote the *Coloneus* he did have the *Oedipus* in mind.

Does Sophocles say in the *Coloneus* that Oedipus was innocent in the patricide and the marriage? Perhaps he does, though the question is open to some doubt on the grounds that it is Oedipus who is doing the talking and not Sophocles. Perhaps the whole question is a biographical one. Did Sophocles have second thoughts on the question of Oedipus' guilt, and did that question interest him in the later play in a way that it had not in the earlier one? It is also possible that he felt the *Oedipus* had been misunderstood, that people had drawn conclusions on this score (like mine, for example) which he had not intended and did not like. But equally possible is that he felt that he himself had done less than justice to Oedipus and therefore wrote the *Coloneus* as his palinode, the amend of the gods and his amend too. Did the old gentleman also see a dilemma on this question of guilt left by the *Oedipus* which confronted us and him with an obscure, unresolved, and terrifying problem? And did he now with other ideas about guilt and innocence, seeing perhaps more clearly—and less tragically—set about resolving the dilemma? These are different ways in which one can make sense of the difference between the two plays. Each of them, it is worth noting, implies that Sophocles, whether he meant it or not, had himself implied that Oedipus was guilty (and, of course, Oedipus in the *Coloneus* blames himself for thinking just that at the time: 437 ff., 768). The one thing we can be sure of is that the criterion for judging guilt or innocence in the *Oedipus* is not to be found in the *Coloneus* or in Sophocles' state of mind but in the play itself. See Nilsson, *Geschichte,* p. 758 on the "innocence" in the *Coloneus* as reflecting a change in Sophocles' attitude towards the gods. Letters (p. 295) finds that Sophocles "virtually remade his hero."

14. I do not think Sophocles wrote the *Oedipus* to show that Oedipus was guilty. What he is doing, as I see it, is putting before us the sort of man Oedipus was or must have been, and the sort of world it must have been that he lived in for such things to happen. Therefore he did not write the Creon scene with the idea of proving that after all Oedipus was guilty;

nevertheless, from the scene and the number of other things which show Oedipus' temper in the play it follows that he is guilty. And not guilty in a ritualistic sense . . . but guilty in a sense that his character and will, as demonstrated by the action, are implicated. Sheppard, pp. xxiv ff., puts all the emphasis on the blood-pollution. Oedipus certainly becomes pure . . . and the theme of purification is very strong in the play: cf. pp. 466 ff. See Jebb's excellent remarks *OC,* p. xxii) on the conclusion of the play. They imply, I believe, that not only is there justice in the "amend" but also in the suffering that the gods had led Oedipus through.

15. See Sheppard, p. xxii, for an example of the opposite view: "Sophocles has been at pains to make the hero innocent: and since the tragic truth was true before the play began, had Oedipus been as reasonable as Creon, and as modest as the chorus, the tragic result would, in Apollo's own time, have come to light." This amounts to saying that Oedipus' character has nothing to do with his fate and also that he is "the injured innocent"; to saying that the play says, in effect, "How good a man and how terrible and undeserved a fate," and I should think one would have to say if Sophocles had been at pains to make Oedipus innocent he could very easily have done a better job of it.

16. I do not believe there are really any exceptions to the rule. It might be argued that there is a difference in this respect between the *Oedipus* and, for example, the *Antigone.* However, I think it more apparent than real. Creon has already issued his edict before the play begins (and Antigone has already revolted against it). This does not mean that Creon's actions are not decisive in bringing about his fate; it means rather that his present conduct towards Antigone shows how he became fated in the first place. Further, at the end of the play the process of a man bringing about his fate is "repeated." When Creon through Teiresias comes to some realization of his position, then he is like Oedipus in his flight from Apollo's prediction, seeking to avoid his fate but precisely doing everything (the burial of Polyneices first, for example) to bring it to its final completion.

17. This is the account given in the *Phoenissae:* Jocasta speaking, "My brother Creon proclaimed my nuptials, to join my bed in marriage with him who could read the riddle of the subtle maiden" (47-49). Apollodorus, III, v. 8: "Creon proclaimed that he would give both kingdom and the wife of Laius to the one who solved the riddle." In the *Coloneus* (525 f.) Oedipus argues that Thebes "bound" him to the fatal marriage and when the chorus say "you did it," he replies that it was a "gift" which he wishes he had never "taken up" . . . (539-41). We must bear in mind that Oedipus in the *Coloneus* speaks proudly and passionately in his own defense, and we should be careful therefore about taking him exactly at his own estimate.

18. Compare 145-46: "For either with the god's help we shall turn out lucky . . . or lost. . . ."

19. So Teiresias, 413: "You have sight and you do not see where you are in evil."

20. It is what Oedipus did—the work of his "hands," "what things I wrought" (in the pass), and "what I did" (the marriage)—that haunts him later (1398-1403).

21. There are perhaps two points to be kept in mind about Oedipus from the *Coloneus.* The first from his defense of the patricide and the marriage, that his parents were the guilty ones, not he: "And yet how could I be really evil . . . ? I who acted in reply to what I had suffered, so that had I done those things knowingly I would not even then have been evil . . . ?" This is going pretty far. The second point has to do with the Polyneices' scene, in which it becomes so distressingly clear that Oedipus in his wrath is quite willing to send his son to certain and horrible death. And this is distressing not only to us of a later age, as Antigone's intercession for her brother at this point makes quite clear. One is loath to recognize the capacity in Oedipus to kill his father knowing that he was his father, but it is not out of the question.

There can be no doubt that Sophocles accepts the common view that these are the most unnatural and frightful acts and makes the most of it (for a mockery of this attitude see André Gide's *Oedipe*). The point, or one point of the plague is that what Oedipus has done causes a revulsion in nature herself. Other crimes. Ajax' for example, or Creon's in *Antigone,* are great offenses against the political, moral, and religious order but they are comprehensible, somehow contained within a context of law, the state etc. as Oedipus' cannot be. Ajax is finally tried in a sort of court of his peers. Oedipus is beyond that. He in his singular fate is a creature apart, beyond human judgment. This point is made much of. Thus Creon at the end says only a god can deal with Oedipus (1518). The public measure of his apartness is given in these horrendous words, also by Creon: "But if you no longer feel shame before the race of mortal men at least respect the flame of the lord Helios which pastures all creatures, so as not to show thus a naked pollution, one which neither the earth, nor the sacred rain, nor the light will receive" (1424-28).

22. Oedipus is what he charges Teiresias with (371), "blind in his [*noüs*]." This is a state of his being in contrast with what he appears to be, or thinks he is. See Reinhardt, pp. 116 ff. Reinhardt (p. 110) points out that Creon's suspicions in the *Antigone* are a matter of the external situation whereas with Oedipus they have to do with his soul.

See Dodds, p. 5 on *ate:* "Always, or practically always, *ate* is a state of mind"; but also (p. 38): "*Ate* always, I think, retains the implication that the ruin is supernaturally determined."

23. See Schadewaldt's brilliant treatment of this question (pp. 28 ff.).

24. Snell (p. 123) says of the tragedy that with it "for the first time in history man begins to look at himself as the maker of his own decisions." But "decision," "choice," etc. are terms I think which when applied to the Greek tragedy bring a good deal of ambiguity with them. There is little reflective decision pictured to us in the Greek. It is certainly more implicit than explicit. But see Snell, pp. 124 ff., on *Medea*. I prefer to limit myself to speaking of the decisive act which is expressive of the character. It is well known that what we commonly mean by "choice," "will," "decision" etc., is not easy to find even in Plato and Aristotle.

25. See Sophocles, Fr. 879N, 964P: "This is the gift of the god, and whatever gifts the gods give one must never flee, my child." Also *Philoctetes:* "The fortunes that are given men by the gods one must bear" (1316-17). Cf. *Homeric Hymn to Demeter,* 147: "The gifts of the gods we men endure of necessity however much we suffer." And Solon 12, 64 (Hiller): "and the gifts of the immortal gods are inescapable."

Plato's myth of Er (*Republic,* 614-21) offers an interesting comparison. The man who had the first lot, and therefore the first choice of the patterns of life which lay on the ground, sprang forward and blindly picked up the greatest tyranny. He discovered he had chosen a fate which among other evils led to the eating of his own children. He complained bitterly that the fault lay not with him but with the gods. Plato makes a point of saying that the man was not bad, but that he acted quickly and in ignorance. Plato does not deny a certain leading by the gods. Necessity and her daughters in Er preside over the disposition of the lots and the lives. These are the symbols of law and order. Over against them are the souls. The two sides meet, as it were, when the individual takes his place within the scheme and chooses. The choosing in other words takes place within a divine control and at the same time is dictated by the individual's character.

So much tragedy and Plato have in common. Oedipus is not "bad" . . . either; the quick, headlong acting in ignorance of the consequences by the first chooser in Er is like him, and it is clear that Plato here had the grisliest stories of tragedy in mind—from Cronos to Thyestes. Plato claims the chooser is responsible . . . and so in its own way, although to a lesser degree, does tragedy. The differences are, of course, deep. Plato gives a choice, not an unlimited one (the lots are to some extent fixed, if only by the series of numbers) but a choice which contains the real possibility in the immortal history of the soul, through knowledge, of escape from evil and suffering. Such a possibility is nothing but an illusion in tragedy. Also there is the difference between the two formulations that in tragedy the divine order is not abstract and unmoved like necessity. Apollo comes up close, in effect, personally, to the hero. The "offering" of a fate there is direct and active, and it is, so to speak, the "right" fate from which, therefore, there is no escape. Paradoxically in this rightness, the fact that it belongs to him, the character comes most fully alive.

26. "But Zeus and Apollo are sharp and they know the destiny of mortals" (*Oedipus* 497-99).

27. Antigone is a case in point. She goes beyond . . . (see Adams' observations on this point; p. 44) and yet compels the admiration of gods and men. None the less, in the justice of things which is honored and protected by the gods, she must pay the price of this greatness. This, it seems to me, is the point of the second *stasimon* at 613-14, although the lines are admittedly obscure and the text is not certain.

28. On the gods bringing heroes to their doom, cf. Herodotus, VI, 135 on Miltiades. Aeschylus expresses this relation between gods and men pretty clearly through Darius' ghost in the *Persians:* "Alas, swift indeed has the completion of the oracles come, and upon my son Zeus has brought them through. I for long have been confident the gods would work them out; but whenever a man hurries on himself the god too joins in." Athena to Ajax illustrates this in grim fashion when she says "Since it is your pleasure [to beat the imagined Odysseus] go ahead with your intent" (114-15). See Knox, *HCS,* LXV (1961) for a somewhat different view of Athena's relation to the hero.

Also the gods, it seems, must not only bring down but they must publish abroad the whole truth of the matter. So, in the second *stasimon* here, things must be clear so that all men "can point to them" (902); and in the fourth, "all-seeing time has found Oedipus out and judges the marriage that was no marriage, etc." Athena shows Ajax' crime to Odysseus for him to proclaim it to all the Argives (*Ajax* 66). And perhaps it is this function of the gods in the life of Oedipus we would recognize in the brief account of the *Odyssey:* "Suddenly the gods made these things known among men" (XI, 280).

29. See Sophocles, Fr., 703N, 770P: "And what a *daimon* you will come before . . . who knows neither what is fair-seeming, nor favor, but cleaves to Justice absolute alone."

And see Blumenthal (*RE.,* col. 1086) succinctly that it is an Hellenic law that "a great fate grips only the great."

30. The ancient sentiment is well-known, particularly in Aeschylus *Cho.,* 312. Cf. also Sophocles, *Fr.* 209N, 229P: "For the one who does something is bound to suffer."

And of course the capacity for action means also the capacity for suffering. Cf. Schadewaldt, p. 24:

"Oedipus ist gross durch seine Fähigkeit zum Leiden, zu einem Leid von grosser Art."

On Creon without the capacity either for acting or for suffering, see Reinhardt, p. 142 f.

31. The chorus of the *Trachiniae* express a similar thought: "The having of evils and the waiting on them are equal" (952).

32. In Sophocles, hope feeds men: "For it is hope that feeds the majority of men." (Fr., 862N, 948P), but again doom it is powerless: "Fow how shall I being a man fight with divine fortune where hope avails nothing in the face of terror?" (197N, 196P). In Aeschylus, *Suppl.*, p. 96f., Zeus hurls men from "their high-towered hopes" to ruin. For hope, the solace and the delusion, see Thucydides, 5.103.

33. On common ground between Christian tragedy and Greek, see Aylen, pp. 158-65. Enlightenment, Christianity, Naturalism, are often said to be hostile to tragedy. Cf. Saint Evremond (*De la tragédie ancienne et moderne*): "The spirit of our religion is directly opposite to that of tragedy." He disliked its "black ideas" and thought he had banished them.

34. Aylen (p. 186), far from believing that the possibility of tragedy has been eliminated, maintains that philosophy is dead, science limited in what it can say, and that for the future the best possibility of illuminating life lies with tragedy.

Works Cited

Adams, S. M. *Sophocles the Playwright*. Toronto, 1957.

Aylen, L. *Greek Tragedy and the Modern World*. London, 1964.

Dodds, E. R. *The Greeks and the Irrational*. Berkeley, 1951.

Jebb, Richard C. *Sophocles, Oedipus Tyrannus* (3rd ed.). Cambridge, 1893.

Kirkwood, G. M. *A Study of Sophoclean Drama*, Ithaca, N. Y., 1958.

Kitto, H. D. F. *Form and Meaning in Drama*. London, 1956.

Knox, B. M. W. *Oedipus at Thebes*. New Haven, 1957.

Letters, F. J. H. *The Life and Work of Sophocles*. London, 1953.

Nilsson, M. P. *Geschichte der Griechischen Religion*. Vol. 1. Munich, 1941.

Reinhardt, K. *Sophokles* (3rd ed.). Frankfurt am Main, 1948.

Schadewaldt, W. *Sophokles und das Leid*. Berlin, 1948.

Sheppard, J. T. *The Oedipus Tyrannus*. Cambridge, 1920.

Snell, B. *The Discovery of the Mind*. Translated by T. G. Rosenmeyer. Oxford, 1953.

Waldock, A. J. A. *Sophocles the Dramatist*. Cambridge, 1951.

Whitman, C. H. *Sophocles*. Cambridge, Mass., 1951.

Wilamowitz-Moellendorf, U. von. *Der Glaube der Hellenen*. Berlin, 1932.

Jonathan Culler (essay date 1981)

SOURCE: "Semiotic Consequences," in *Studies in Twentieth Century Literature*, Vol. 6, Nos. 1-2, Fall, 1981, pp. 5-15.

[*In the following essay, Culler uses* Oedipus Tyrannus *to illustrate some of his points concerning the importance of semiotics in literary criticism.*]

If one is interested in the consequences of semiotics for the study of literary signification, one needs a reliable account of what semiotics is or says; and for that it may be important to reflect on the strange consequentiality of semiotics itself, for semiotics is not a continuous discipline with a progressive historical evolution.[1] Thinkers have often produced major insights about signs and signification, but semiotics is not the sum of insights about the sign. It comes into being when the problem of the sign is brought to the fore, made to organize a field—a consequential intellectual development.

One consequence of the advent of semiotics is the creation of precursors and thus of a history. The history of semiotics involves not an ordinary causal sequence but that special historical relationship which Freud calls *Nachträglichkeit,* whereby an experience not understood at the time it took place (such as witnessing a Primal Scene) is later invested with traumatic meaning and, as trauma, can then be treated as a cause of later events.[2] Semiotics now identifies, as the trauma which determined its character, the activities in the early years of this century of a strange couple, Ferdinand de Saussure and Charles Sanders Peirce.

They are all ill-sorted couple. Saussure was a successful and respectable Swiss professor who had doubts about the foundations of linguistics as then practiced and therefore wrote practically nothing; but he did argue, in lectures that have come down to us through students' notes, that since language was a system of signs, linguistics ought to be part of a larger science of signs, «a science which would study the life of signs within society. We call it semiology from the Greek *semeion.* It would teach us what signs consist of, what laws govern them. Since it does not yet exist we cannot say what it will be, but it has a right to existence; its place is ensured in advance.»[3]

These suggestions were not taken up, and only later, when various disciplines had taken structural linguistics as a methodological model and become versions of structuralism, did it become evident that the semiology Saussure postulated had begun to develop. At this point he became a powerful influence, partly because he had written little and because the program outlined for semiotics seemed easy to grasp: linguistics was to serve as example and its basic concepts applied to other domains of social and cultural life. The semiotician is attempting to grasp the system (*langue*) which underlies and makes possible meaningful events (*parole*). He is concerned with the system as a functioning totality (*synchronic* analysis) not with the historical provenence of its various elements (*diachronic* analysis), and he must describe two kinds of relations: contrasts or oppositions between signs (*paradigmatic* relations) and possibilities of combination through which signs create larger units (*syntagmatic* relations).

Peirce is a very different case. A wayward philosophical genius, denied tenure by Johns Hopkins, he devoted himself wholeheartedly to «semeiotic,» as he called it, which would be the science of sciences, since «the entire universe is perfused with signs if it is not composed entirely of signs.»[4] If the universe consists entirely of signs (and he argued that even man was a sign—not the word *man* but man as category or individual), then there is a great deal of classifying to do. Peirce's voluminous writings on semiotics remained unpublished and unreadable until recently. Only with the growth of semiotics in the last few years have our levels of tolerance risen to the point where we can read Peirce, but it is still difficult, since the laboriously produced *Collected Papers* did not recognize semiotics as a field of enquiry and disrupted by their arrangement Peirce's attempts to constitute it through his writing. The failings of this edition have doubtless confirmed many in the view that «who steals my Peirce steals trash.» His revaluation will not be accomplished until the new, semiotically-oriented edition of his works appears.

Peirce's writings are full of proliferating categories (in arguing that men are like other signs he cited the fact that both men and signs procreate): distinctions combine to produce such species as «rhematic indexical sinsign.» There are, he decided, ten trichotomies by which signs can be distinguished, giving us 59,049 classes of sign. Fortunately, there are redundancies and dependencies so that one only need deal with 66 categories, but even this has proved too much for all but the most masochistic theorists, and this excessive or impractical character of Peirce's ambitious constructions has prevented him from exercizing the influence he might have. Today, it is becoming increasingly evident that he is a radical theorist of the first magnitude.

Peirce is a philosophical pragmatist. He defines truth not as correspondence with some objective reality but as what works: to call a judgement objectively valid is to predict that eventually «all the world will agree in it.»[5] Reality is what is presented in the opinion which will prevail. Peirce shows, in an argument worthy of Nietzsche or Derrida, that «external reality» is something we postulate in order to account for our conviction that investigation will lead to agreement. The reality of things is the postulate we make in order to explain our belief that people will, after discussion and investigation of alternatives, when all the evidence is in, reach agreement. We account for this conviction by assuming that there is an independent, external reality that will induce agreement. «This involves,» Peirce says, «no error, and is convenient for certain purposes, but it does not follow that it affords the point of view from which it is proper to look at the matter in order to understand its true philosophy.»[6]

Those who do not know Peirce well and simply cite him to buttress an argument sometimes assume that since he is known as a pragmatist he must be above all a practical man, a believer in brute facts, suitable guru for a practical American semiotics which would repudiate the excessive theorizing of Europeans, especially the French. On the contrary, Peirce, much more than Saussure, is the brilliant, speculative theorist, delighted to pursue ideas wherever they may take him. Deciding that the answer to the question «what is man?» is that he is a symbol or sign, Peirce works towards a more specific answer by asking in what respects a man differs from the word *six* (this is a fascinating lecture in which, incidentally, he concludes that the differences are primarily physiological).[7]

Peirce and Saussure are very different (at sixes and sevens, one might say) but recent theoretical work, such as Umberto Eco's *Theory of Semiotics* and the papers by Sebeok and Eco in the 1975 Peirce symposium, has shown that their teachings are congruent or complementary on a surprising number of matters.[8] Indeed, a major achievement of recent semiotic theory is to have made it impossible to oppose Peirce to Saussure in a simplistic way. As Thomas Sebeok, doyen of American semioticians, has noted, «the distinction between the traditions has lost its force.»[9] Occasionally someone still will appeal to one parent against the other, as children trying to get away with something will do, but usually this can be shown to rest on a misunderstanding of Peirce: that he is practical while Saussure is theoretical. There are at least four important points on which the approaches of these two founders of semiotics meet and form a tradition. The first two points are not directly related to the study of literature but the last two are.

1. The first point is presented by Peirce's claim that «the entire universe is perfused with signs if it is not composed entirely of signs.»[10] Since the late nineteenth century, a series of eminent thinkers has insisted that our world be discussed in terms not of physical objects and events but of social and cultural facts: objects and events with meaning, which is to say, signs. Philosophers, sociologists, psychologists have shown that even the most elementary processes of perception themselves are already semiotic, involving social and cultural matrices, categories, distinctions. It has become almost banal truth that there is no

perception, in the sense of unmediated presence of objects: the perceptual object is already a sign. We perceive an example of a chair.

Semiotics can take no credit for these discoveries about the symbolic nature of all human experience, which have been made in other fields. Semiotics is the systematic culmination of this perspective. As Peirce says, it is not that we have objects on the one hand and thoughts on the other; it is, rather, that we have signs everywhere, «some more mental and spontaneous, others more material and regular.»[11] The task of semiotics is to describe the various systems of signs and sign processes which make up the world and, in particular, to study the ways in which semiotic systems and activities create the cultural units which are the objects of our world.

Here the basic semiotic principle is what Saussure called the arbitrary nature of the sign. Occasionally people think this means only that the signifiers of forms used to express concepts are arbitrary: determined by convention rather than by any natural affinity between form and concept. To restrict the principle in this way is to fall into an error which Saussure frequently warned against, the error of thinking of a language as a nomenclature which supplies its own names or forms to denote concepts or classes given in advance. Students and teachers of languages are, of course, only too aware that each language has not only its own system of signifiers but also its own system of signifieds, its own concepts. Languages articulate the world in different ways, which is why translation cannot be undertaken by looking up each foreign word in a dictionary and writing down the English word which stands for the same concepts—it doesn't work because the concepts are never quite the same. Each language articulates a system of signifieds which are, in Saussure's terms, arbitrary and conventional: arbitrary because not determined by an independent reality (French and English are equally valid articulations of the world); conventional because however natural they seem they are always determined by social rule, semiotic convention. This is the fundamental principle of semiotics.

It is perhaps worth adding here that the principle of the arbitrary nature of the sign should not be confused with the so-called Sapir-Whorf hypothesis that language determines thought. On the contrary, semiotics insists that there is a whole range of cultural activities and practices—not just language—semiotic in nature, which create categories that will find a place as signifieds in natural languages. Thus the rules of basketball create categories which English then names as «dunk-shot» or «foul.» Clearly it is not the case that because «foul» is a sign of English there will be fouls in basketball. The rules of the game are a semiotic sub-system which interacts with the language. For semiotics, we live among a series of systems of this kind which articulate a world. What we think of as things or events are semiotic constructs, cultural units.

2. I have already broached the second point which defines the heritage of Peirce and Saussure and which bears on the relation of verbal signs to non-verbal signs. Peirce, in one of his tentrichotomies, distinguished *symbols* (which were purely conventional and best represented by linguistic signs) from *indices* (where signifier is related to signified by causality or contiguity) and *icons* (where there is a relation of resemblance). Saussure too noted that there were different sorts of signs, but he argued that however natural the relationship between signifier and signified may appear in non-verbal signs, there is always a convention which semiotics must investigate.[12] Semiotics must always resist the tendency among members of a culture to take their signs as natural, as based on a non-conventional relation. Recent work on Peirce's concept of the icon by Sebeok and Eco has shown how much Peirce agreed with Saussure:[13] whether we are dealing with maps, paintings or diagrams, every material image «is largely conventional in its mode of representation.»[14] It is only after taking for granted a great many complicated conventions that one can suggest that a map actually resembles what it represents. The task of semiotics is to uncover these conventions on which our everday activities depend. The principle of the arbitrary and conventional nature of all signs is the guarantee against sloppiness and delusion.

I have said that these two points did not relate directly to the study of literature, but they do confirm something which students of literature already know to be the case. If a poem tells us that the beloved wore a silver gown, we do not think that this sequence simply represents an extra-linguistic reality which has determined the sequence. We know that what is represented here is itself part of a sign system, so we ask what this means and how it fits in with the rest of the poem. In literature we are free from the delusion that signs are determined (and accounted for) by realities which are simply there prior to any semiosis. Semiotics is a codification of this understanding of sign systems which literary critics, for the most part, already have.

3. The third point on which Peirce and Saussure would agree is that semiotics is not a method of interpretation which can be applied to a text to produce new readings. It is, rather, a theoretical framework within which the study of signifying processes of all kinds takes place. It asks not «what does this work mean?» but «how is the process of signification organized here?» It is important to note, though, that rigorous attention to the signifying procedures that a work establishes and to the work's own representation of the signifying process can yield subtle and penetrating interpretations of literary works. This kind of criticism, which involves a scrupulous analysis or taking apart of the logic of signification in a text, is now often called «deconstruction.»

4. Finally, by posing the problem of what kind of sign processes are at work in texts, semiotics ought to have one very important consequence: it ought to make criticism confront a problem which it has always tried to sweep under the rug, the problem of the relationship between signification and communication.

This is a central issue in semiotics. Those who see semiotics as studying communication are content to think of meaning as what is communicated by signs, and this view has its virtues in some cases. We are not likely to object to the notion that a word's meaning is what it means to speakers of the language, but those who want semiotics to deal, as Peirce did, with all kinds of correlations among semiotic phenomena, find that the attempt to treat meaning as what is communicated does not suffice in practice. As soon as we look at actual texts or situations we begin to make discoveries, to see relationships and correlations which had not previously been noticed and which have not therefore been communicating anything to anyone. If one were to study the behavior of undergraduates—highly codified and ritualized, always communicating to those in the know—we might discover, for example, that the fad of «streaking» coincided with the Watergate cover-up.[15] Whatever we think of this correlation, it seems wrong to reject it on the grounds that this meaning was not communicated to spectators at the time. When we come to literature, the critic certainly will not be content to reject a pattern or correlation he has just discovered on the ground that it has not been communicating meaning to previous readers. On the contrary, literary criticism as a semiotic activity has been predicated on the attempt to discover and interpret new patterns, structures, and correlations.

However, criticism has usually tried to avoid facing this semiotic problem. The New Criticism, by identifying the intentional and affective fallacies, simply denied the relevance of a communicational perspective and assumed that literature involved signification which was inherent in the structures of the work and which patient study might discover. Recent ventures into what has come to be called «reader-response criticism,» whether sophisticated as in Stanley Fish or bathetic as in versions based on ego psychology, simply reverse the claim: there is no signification, no meaning to be discovered. Meaning is simply the experience of each reader, what is communicated to him. This is not only false to literary criticism, which has been able to make discoveries about meaning that have become part of our knowledge of literature, but also false to the classroom situation on which it claims to focus. What we find in a classroom, when you give a class a poem, is not 25 students projecting their unique personalities onto works and each producing a complex interpretation which precisely reflects his personality, but rather varying degrees of incomprehension, interpretations carried over from previous classes, etc.—until discussion begins; patterns, structures, and correlations are pointed out; and students begin to make discoveries about meaning and come to see interpretive possibilities which their teachers had not envisioned. That we are dealing with complex structures and an interpretive competence becomes clear in the work of Stanley Fish. Though Fish says he is recording the experience of an informed reader like himself, that is improbable, for any real reader, as he started on his 14th «self-consuming artifact,» would not have the experience Fish describes—the experience of being surprised and disturbed to see the work question its own categories and negate its own claims.[16] On the contrary, he would expect this and be pleasantly gratified to see his expectations confirmed. What Fish presents as meaning communicated is in fact significance discovered.

Semiotics, with its focus on the problem of meaning, ought to make critics aware of the necessity of working out a dialectic between signification and communication, constructing a theory that accounts for the possibility of discovering meaning, instead of either rejecting the communicational perspective or else arguing that criticism has been an elitist activity which ought to stop *studying* works and simply record what they mean to those who have not yet learned to read carefully and skillfully.

So far I have proceeded without examples, except for that bare reference to streaking, and to put some clothes on this naked form I should like to conclude with some remarks about a work well known to most readers, a work which our culture has interpreted as central to our definition of the nature and situation of man: **Oedipus Rex.** Freud, one of millions of enthusiastic readers, describes the play as follows:

> The action of the play consists of nothing other than the process of revealing, with cunning delays and ever-mounting excitement (a process that can be likened to the work of a psychoanalysis) that Oedipus himself is the murderer of Laius, but further that he is the son of the murdered man and of Jocasta. Appalled at the abomination he has unwittingly perpetrated, Oedipus blinds himself and forsakes his home.[17]

Freud emphasizes that the play involves the bringing to light, the revelation, of an awful deed—the event *par excellence*—and this event is so powerful that it imposes its meaning (Oedipus is «appalled»), irrespective of any intention by the actor. This is what has always been communicated by the play: the event is revealed; it makes Oedipus guilty; and he attains true human dignity in accepting the meaning imposed by the revealed event.

But this reading fails to account for an interesting element in the play, discussed in a different perspective by Sandor Goodhart.[18] When Oedipus first asks whether anyone witnessed Laius's death he is told, «All died save one who fled in terror and could tell us only one clear fact. He said that robbers, not one but many, fell in with the King's party and killed them.» And later, when Oedipus begins to wonder whether he may in fact have killed Laius, he tells Jocasta that all hangs on the testimony of this witness, whom they await. «You say he spoke of robbers, that robbers killed him. If he still says robbers, it was not I. One is not the same as many; but if he speaks of one lone traveller, there is no escape: the finger points to me.» To which Jocasta answers, «Oh, but I assure you, that was what he said. He cannot go back on it now; the whole town heard it, not only I.»

The only witness has publicly told a story that is incompatible with Oedipus's guilt. This possibility of innocence is never effectively eliminated, for by the time the witness arrives Oedipus is busy discovering that he is the son of Laius and asks only about his birth, not about the murder. The witness is never asked whether the murderers were one or many.

I am not suggesting that Oedipus was really innocent and has been falsely convicted for 2400 years. I am interested in the significance of the fact that the possibility of innocence is never properly dispelled: the whole action of this play is the revelation of the dastardly deed, but we are never confronted with the deed itself, given the testimony of the eyewitness. Oedipus himself and all his readers are convinced that he is guilty, but our conviction does not come from revelation of the deed. Where *does* it come from? From a repetition of prophecies, from signs. It was prophesied that Laius would be killed by his son; it was prophesied that Oedipus would kill his father; and Tiresias, asked who is guilty of murder, prophesies that it will prove to be Oedipus. Given this conjunction of signs, this textual interweaving of prophecies, when Oedipus discovers that he is the son of Laius he leaps to the conclusion that he is the murderer.

He becomes the murderer of his father not by a violent act that is brought to light but by deeming the act to have taken place: by assuming that what the signs claim must have happened, by appropriating what the signs represent. The network of signs which the prophecies have woven leads to the affirmation of the event which those signs predict. And we as readers cannot escape this process either: the text compels us to affirm the truth of the parricide.

I offer this beginning of a reading of ***Oedipus*** to support my claim that literary criticism must not limit itself to what has been communicated but must preserve the possibility of discovering meaning by reinterpreting elements previously disregarded. But from a semiotic point of view what is important here is the play's implicit commentary on the relation between meaning and event, between signs and the «realities» often thought to be independent of them. On the one hand, in working toward revelation of the murder, the play implicitly claims that the revealed event will determine meaning. If it took place, then Oedipus is a parricide; and the play compels readers to affirm, with Oedipus, that because it did, he is. But the play also shows that this deed is not revealed as such but inferred from signs. We are given not a deed from which we infer meaning but meaning from which we infer a deed. Peirce identified «external reality» as what is inferred from our belief in agreement, and we find much the same position here. We are not wrong to think Oedipus is guilty, but it can be shown that the event which we take as imposing is already a consequence of signs and not a reality independent of *semiosis*. In the beginning was the word. We are not wrong to think that there are events, that they create meaning, but whenever we try to grasp a thing or event said to have determined meaning, we discover that the thing or event is already a product of signs, already enmeshed in *semiosis*. We cannot get outside textuality.

What I offer here is not a semiotic reading of ***Oedipus***— there is no such thing—but a reading attentive to the logic of signification and in that sense a reading made possible by semiotics. Here as elsewhere, one consequence of semiotics is the demonstration that events, the originary events which we always seek to discover, are themselves already semiotic consequences.

Notes

1. This paper was originally written for a Forum on semiotics at the December 1977 meeting of the Modern Language Association in Chicago. It bears some traces of that occasion, particularly in its attempt to criticize proleptically the general position espoused by Robert Scholes in a paper, «Semiotics: The American Way,» for the same Forum—a position which I believe he no longer holds.

2. See Jonathan Culler, *The Pursuit of Signs* (Ithaca: Cornell University Press, 1981), chapter IX, «Story and Discourse in the Analysis of Narrative.»

3. Ferdinand de Saussure, *Cours de linguistique générale* (Paris: Payot, 1973), p. 33. *Course in General Linguistics,* trans. Wade Baskin (London: Fontana, 1974), p. 16. For further discussion see Jonathan Culler, *Saussure* (New York: Penguin, 1977).

4. Charles Sanders Peirce, *Collected Papers,* 8 vols. (Cambridge: Harvard University Press, 1931-58), V, 448.

5. Peirce, VII, 259.

6. Peirce, VII, 335.

7. Peirce, VII, 583-4. The lecture is entitled «Consciousness and Language,» VII, 579-596.

8. Umberto Eco, *A Theory of Semiotics,* (Bloomington: Indiana University Press, 1976); Eco, «Peirce's Notion of Interpretant,» *MLN,* 91, No. 6 (Dec. 1976), 1457-72; and Thomas Sebeok, «Iconicity,» *Ibid.,* pp. 1427-56.

9. Sebeok, «Ecumenicalism in Semiotics,» in *A Perfusion of Signs,* ed. Sebeok (Bloomington: Indiana University Press, 1977), p. 182.

10. Peirce, V, 448.

11. Peirce, VII, 570.

12. Saussure, *Cours,* pp. 100-101; *Course,* p. 68, Cf. Culler, *Saussure,* pp. 98-9.

13. In addition to the articles by Eco and Sebeok cited in note 8, see Michael McCanles, «Conventions,» *Diacritics,* 7, No. 3 (Fall 1977), 54-63.

14. Peirce, 2, 276.

15. Alan Dundes, «Projection in Folklore» *MLN,* 91, No. 6 (Dec. 1976), 1526.

16. For further discussion see Culler, *The Pursuit of Signs,* chapter 6.

17. Sigmund Freud, *The Interpretation of Dreams* (New York: Avon, 1965) p. 295.

18. Sandor Goodhart, «*Who Killed Laius*», unpublished Ph.D. dissertation SUNY-Buffalo, 1977. See also Goodhart, «Oedipus and Laius's Many Murderers,» *Diacritics,* 8, No. 1 (1978), 55-71; and my discussion in *The Pursuit of Signs,* chapter 9.

Eric A. Havelock (essay date 1984)

SOURCE: "Oral Composition in the *Oedipus Tyrannus* of Sophocles," in *New Literary History,* Vol. 16, No. 1, Autumn, 1984, pp. 175-97.

[In the following essay, Havelock describes elements of oral composition that can be found in the text of Oedipus Tyrannus.]

A stage play is by definition composed for performance by action and elocution. To argue for "oral" composition may seem to be arguing for the obvious. The "orality" of Greek drama, however, if it exists, goes deeper than a mere management of stage conventions. It would mean that what had to be spoken on the Greek stage in the fifth century before Christ was molded in a very special way. There are of course compositional rules common to all drama *qua* drama. But I shall argue that there were certain rules operating in classic Greek drama which were peculiar to it, and which stage production of later periods from the Hellenistic age to the present has, in the nature of things, been unable to share.

The surviving plays have come down to us as texts carefully read, copied, and transmitted over hazardous centuries and now at last printed in books. It is surely as texts that they deserve to be estimated, that is, as literate creations by literate authors. So runs the consensus of scholars, critics, translators, and adapters, to whom it would not occur that something like the "oralism" now accepted as inherent in the Homeric poems would survive in a Greek tragedy and be detectable there, let alone one so tightly constructed as the *Oedipus Tyrannus.* These plays were written down at the time of composition, else we would not have them. They were composed, so we usually think, with that kind of economy that is expected of the written word, and so rank as "literate" composition.

But suppose the case is more complicated than that? Allowing their share in literacy, does one also perceive a share in preliteracy? Historically speaking, these are admittedly unique productions. It has not occurred to any postclassical playwright to put anything quite like them on stage, or if he has tried this he has failed. Even as we translate, imitate, or adapt, we are aware of our modern distance from them. Could it be that the uniqueness of their nature derives from a uniqueness in their cultural position, poised midway between previous centuries of oral composition and coming centuries of literate composition?

The case for "orality" as a genre of verbal composition specifically distinct from the textual has now won critical acceptance, though not its possible application to Greek drama. It grew from seeds implanted by Milman Parry's perception that the Homeric poems were oral constructs, the work of nonliterates, and has been slowly strengthened by the cumulative weight of comparative studies of surviving pockets of orality in various parts of the world of today, notably the Balkans (where Parry and his assistant Albert Lord initiated the practice of recording local singers) and now also Africa, Polynesia, and other areas. The ground thus covered and the conclusions to be drawn have recently received masterly summation and interpretation by Walter J. Ong.[1] That the concept has needed vigorous defense of the kind he supplies is sufficiently indicated by the fact that his opening chapter devotes itself to an argument for "The Orality of Language." Why feel compelled to defend a concept which, when you think of it, seems obvious unless it be true that the written and printed word has become an obstacle to our understanding of the nonwritten as it was spoken and managed for millenia of human history? Might it even be true that it has prevented a full understanding of the ancient Greeks?

Arguments for orality in a Greek play must rely on evidences supplied by the text, for that is all we now have, but to recognize what these are one has to know first what one is looking for. Direct inspection as such cannot yield the secret. Recognition of what may be latent there depends upon guidance supplied by retrospection, into the history of human culture and of that particular Greek cultural experience which had preceded the appearance of Attic drama. One has to consider what orality really means both as a historical term representing a specific social condition and as a psychological one representing the use of certain restricted physical senses for purposes of communication.

Three books of my own previously published have proposed some answers,[2] of which I here shall offer a brief summation, a necessary detour which will bring us back in due course to consideration of Sophocles' most famous play.

The character of orality, a condition of the past, is best imagined in the light of its opposite in the present, namely literacy. Ever since late antiquity, the European peoples, including those who migrated overseas, have lived within the ambience of literacy and have taken its existence for granted, even under circumstances where its advantages were available only to minorities within their ranks. Its presence has relied on a technological invention, the Greek alphabet, which superseded all previous technologies of written communication, and the use of which, like literacy itself, has become an unconscious historical habit. It has supplied the means of documentation for the national cultures in which it is available, whether handwritten, printed, or electronically coded. Though documentation is used daily for ephemeral purposes—a letter to a friend or a throwaway leaflet—its fundamental use is to provide a receptacle, a storehouse, for the preservation and reuse of the "knowledge"—using the term in its broadest possible application—which allows the culture to "work." This knowledge is not a static body; its reuse implies continual replenishment, revision, and extension, also carried out by the same instrument, the alphabet. In an industrial society like ours it is easy to see, after a moment's reflection, how this works at the technical level, in production: the manufacture of an automobile depends ultimately upon the guidance supplied by previous documentation covering perhaps tens of thousands of items of technical information. But alphabetization works at a more fundamental level, to place in storage the legal system, the governmental apparatus, the religion and customs, the history and sense of identity of a given cultural group. Such information, in the widest sense, becomes the responsibility of the educational system to transmit between the generations while also interpreting, qualifying, amending, or enlarging it (a very slow process). The court of appeal has always to be a textbook, or a "program," or a work of what we call "literature"—in other words, an alphabetized document. It is there in the background. Enough people have read it to make it effective as a control over what may be ephemerally communicated, whether we are reading a newspaper, watching a televised program based on a previous script, or just conversing with our friends about what we have read or seen. A great deal of modern communications theory—and indeed, the term *communication* itself—deriving from the seminal ideas of Marshall McLuhan, has tended to concentrate upon the techniques of ephemeral transmission of ephemeral speech—as on radio or television—and what this does to speech, rather than on the technology of the storage of speech for reuse, and what this does to speech. It is of course possible that the introduction of the computer with its memory bank will redirect attention to these matters. All too often even the introduction of the written word is treated merely as an improved or at least altered form of "communication" rather than as a drastic revolution in the storage of information, producing a parallel revolution in its content. The temptation to see primary orality as a system devoted to the maintenance of interpersonal relationships in direct "human communication" (Ong, pp. 176-77) must be resisted. The clue to the character of any culture, oral or literate, lies in the character of what it saves up for reconsideration.

We think of knowledge—if we ever think of it at all—as something residing within our own heads, which of course is true. But in a structural sense knowledge is something shared by a community in varying degree in order to enable it to function, and we commonly refer to this shared resource as a "body" of knowledge. We would not use such an expression if the said knowledge did not exist in documented form as an artifact separable from ourselves

which we can "read," that is, physically survey with our eyes and handle with our hands, instead of merely hearing it with our ears and pronouncing it with our mouths. It is contained not in an acoustic and ephemeral medium like spoken language, but in a visible and material one, and a verifiable one, and as such acquires an objective existence independent of what goes on in our own heads.

The question arises: Has such a documented basis for human culture with all its concomitants always existed? It is very difficult for us to think otherwise, but in fact the historical evidence is overwhelming that for the larger part of our previous life as a species the answer has been no, which forces upon us the further question: In its absence, could human culture itself exist? If we restrict the reference of the term *culture* to a system of civil society, ordered government, and a recognizable architecture and art, the answer is unequivocally yes. Even in recent memory, the case of the Incas of Peru in the Western hemisphere furnishes an irrefutable example, as do many prehistoric societies of the Old World.

To reconstruct an image of such a society and how it would work requires an unusual effort of historical imagination, and one which at the same time has to be rigorous in insisting on the exclusions that are necessary. We must presuppose not only the nonexistence of writing and documentation, but also the absence of all those results of such documentation as have been described above. It is one among many merits of Ong's treatment of this problem that he insists that we accept the concept of a "primary orality" (p. 6 and passim) as a cultural condition which exists or has existed in its own right, in distinction from any of those mixed situations, partly oral, partly literate, which so often confront the investigator in the contemporary world. He has also placed his finger on the psychological cause which makes the necessary effort so difficult for us to accept, and particularly for the literate scholar to accept: "To dissociate words from writing is psychologically threatening, for literates' sense of control over language is closely tied to the visual transformations of language: without dictionaries, written grammar rules, punctuation, and all the rest of the apparatus that makes words into something you can 'look' up, how can literates live?" (p. 14).

How indeed! And how could nonliterates live at all! Since they undeniably did, one answers by asking the further question: In a society of totally oral communication, what is there that can take the place of documentation as a cultural underpinning? What if anything can constitute the equivalent of a "body" of objective knowledge on which the members of the community can rely for consultation and guidance? That they would need some such guidance would seem likely if such a society were to retain coherence and a historical sense of itself and a measure of law, government, and morality.

In dealing with other problems, scholar and scientist are used to testing hypotheses against physical or textual evidences. The difficulty with understanding the climate of primary orality is that in the nature of the case the investigator has to rely, to a quite unprecedented extent, upon a priori methods alone, guided only by insights derived from a mixture of anthropology, psychology, linguistics, and a common sense of how the human animal would behave or has to behave in given circumstances. It is of the essence of primary orality that it vanishes like a bubble when pricked by the arrival of literacy from the outside. This has happened in the Americas, to the societies destroyed by the Spaniards, and to the Red Indian societies destroyed by the French and English. It has happened to the Polynesians as their preliteracy gave way to the inroads of traders, missionaries, and colonial administrators. It is not merely a matter of the literate scholar arriving to investigate and pretending to reconstruct the oral original within his own concepts and language. The original itself succumbs with incredible swiftness from within, as it absorbs with eagerness the educational advantages of script, whether the text be that of its own tongue or that of the foreigner.

The anthropological literature which has sought to describe such societies and report their speech has done so only after their speech habits and thought habits have already been infected by literate contact. Understanding and interpretation have been supplied in terms of categories drawn from the literate presuppositions of Europeans, the basic one being that which assumes as a matter of course that the purpose of oral performance and therefore of oral composition is to entertain rather than instruct. That indeed is what it starts to do, once relieved of other responsibilities. The loss of contact with primary orality comes out very well in the otherwise invaluable reports of Ruth Finnegan,[3] when she writes: "At the same time, the increasing availability of these written versions fed into the oral literary tradition. In the South Pacific, it seems, these were not (as sometimes supposed) two separate and opposed modes but, both now and in the past, form part of one dynamic in which both written and oral forms interact."[4] This defense of literate manipulation of oral tradition certainly reflects a literary rather than an anthropological judgment, since it ignores, at least by implication, that deprivation of ethical, legal, and social function which overtakes orality once literacy intrudes and converts it into mere entertainment. As worded, her statement in effect dismisses the existence of Ong's "primary orality" as irrelevant to the Polynesian case. "It [oral literature, in her terms] may no longer be circulating in some pure 'natural' and 'uncontaminated' state—*if such ever existed* [my italics]—but in the perhaps even more interesting and variegated situation of the modern Pacific, interacting with writing, broadcasting, Christianity, education, entertainment. . . ."[5] This modern phenomenon of a mixed orality is thus evaluated as a more significant and interesting subject of study than an original which is hypothetical and in any case now beyond the reach of investigation.

Ong's view of this problem is very different, and his warning against the dangers of mental confusions arising from the use of an ambiguous nomenclature is well taken:

One might argue (as does Finnegan 1977, p. 16) that the term "literature", though devised primarily for works in writing, has simply been extended to include related phenomena such as traditional oral narrative in cultures untouched by writing. Many originally specific terms have been so generalized in this way. But concepts have a way of carrying their etymologies with them forever. The elements out of which a term is originally built usually and probably always linger somehow in subsequent meanings, sometimes obscurely, but often powerfully and even irreducibly. Writing moreover . . . is a particularly pre-emptive and imperialist activity that tends to assimilate other things to itself even without the aid of etymologies.

(P. 12)

On the other side of the world from the South Pacific, the investigation and recording of the oral poetry of the Balkans has been threatened by a similar confusion of interpretation and a similar misuse of nomenclature, which arises from the parallel existence of a body of revivalist poetry, some of it under Italian influence, pretending to be traditionalist and therefore to be a resurrection of oral tradition but in which the supposedly oral element is essentially spurious. In Albert Lord's words: "Once the oral technique is lost, it is never regained. The written technique on the other hand is not compatible with the oral technique and the two could not possibly combine to form another, a third 'transitional' technique. . . . When and how then does the 'literary' technique start? The poet of whom we have been speaking can read and write, but he is still an oral poet. To become a 'literary' poet he has to leave the oral tradition and learn a technique of composition that is impossible without writing or that is developed because of writing."[6]

However, not even Balkan oral poetry can supply the answers we are seeking. Primary orality is a social condition governing the consciousness and behavior of whole peoples, not merely a condition of personal nonliteracy existing as a survival in individual singers. The Parry-Lord collection of Jugo-Slav recorded songs, while shedding invaluable light on the methods of primary oral composition, fails to offer models of its content because for centuries such songs and their singers have been relieved of the responsibility of supporting the culture in which they are performed. The Balkans and Eastern Europe have ever since Rome been governed by literate elites. Law and religion, history and morals, have enjoyed the support and guidance of documented speech; oral poetry, practiced in pockets of these regions, no longer is asked to perform this magisterial, that is, Homeric, role. It is composed or rather improvised as a peasant survival to entertain but not to guide, govern, or instruct.

We return for a moment to the previous question: In a culture of primary orality, what if anything can constitute the equivalent of a body of objective, that is, documented knowledge? Since recourse to material evidence is impossible, the answer must rely on theory and on psychology. Since all communication is under these conditions acoustic, its storage, if it is to occur, must be acoustic also. Can a verbal technique suitable for this purpose be devised? Being acoustic, the content of communication is normally ephemeral as uttered, in contrast to the relative permanency of the written word. If it is to be reused, it must be not only uttered but remembered, and the instrument for guaranteeing this resides nowhere else but in the personal memories of individuals, which however are fallible and also impermanent since their owners will die. What is needed is a form of uttered speech not only memorizable by an individual but transmissible by him to his juniors.

It would seem that at an elemental level the ordinary language of a cultural group—its vernacular—as it is learned and transmitted would supply guidance for cultural continuity, and this is true, for any given vernacular comprises idioms which state and repeat relationships, behavior patterns, and beliefs common to the group using it. But at some indeterminable point in the social-evolutionary process, as relationships within the group and its common beliefs become more complex, it would feel the need for some reinforcement of these through a special statement or set of statements set apart from the vernacular so as to be treated with a kind of reverence and so learned and transmissible as such—an enclave of contrived speech existing within the current vernacular. This would require some acoustic stability to be effective as a transmittant. The acoustic device available for the purpose is rhythm, which can take a variety of forms. The origin of poetry, according to this theory, lies in social function: it is a preservative which ensures a degree—no doubt fluctuating—of acoustic storage; it is the mnemonic technique par excellence, and is used as such in all cultures of primary orality. Since rhythm is in the first instance melodic, the linguistic form being secondary, all such verbal poetry is also at the same time musical in varying degree and requires the services of musical instruments. The resultant product in primary orality consists of songs chanted or sung, continually recited and repeated within a given society, covering the formalities of social custom and belief. They are liable to coalesce into a single magisterial composition, or perhaps two, of a great many verses, which becomes the historical epic of the group. For this purpose, a stringed instrument alone becomes the appropriate assistant, wind and percussion being more serviceable for shorter compositions.

Rhythm as such only guarantees its own repetition. To preserve a lengthy sequence of verbalized statements requires further mnemonic assistance, and this is provided by the syntactical rule which requires they be cast in the form of a tale, a narrative of events performed by human agents within some kind of story line or plot, for it is the tale that we are biologically programmed to remember most easily. The nature of preserved speech in primary orality is therefore bifocal: it is committed to instruction, but this must be contained within the tale; it is at once didactic and recreational, but in social terms the didactic function is prior. The language contrived for this purpose is never the simple vernacular but one which, because of its commitment to preservation and therefore to the past, uses a vocabulary which is itself in varying degree archaic—that is, ritualistic, remote, venerable.

Rhythm used to assist memory need not be confined to sound. It can operate at the level of meaning when it takes the form of statements which either repeat or resemble each other or are balanced against each other. The most evident symptom of this oral habit lies in the verbal formulas—rhythmic units of two, sometimes three words. It is this formulary aspect of oral verse-making which, once noted by Milman Parry, has attracted most attention from scholars. One can say that it operates on the acoustic principle of the echo, which assists recall and so memorization by either repeating a verbal formula already used or giving its acoustic equivalent with some change of meaning which yet resembles a previous meaning. There is also the mnemonic advantage of encouraging economy in the vocabulary used—you do not need to remember an unlimited number of words—while allowing some degree of novel statement, not mere repetition, which yet resembles previous statement.

The same compositional principle extends itself to the construction of the tale as a whole; it will avoid sheer surprise and novel invention. It has been well observed that oral poetry employs recurrent themes[7] which progressively repeat each other with variations as the story progresses, even to the degree that versified descriptions of recurrent acts and intentions become standardized (e.g., "arming scenes," "embassy scenes," and the like). Insofar as they merely replicate, they fail to meet the challenge of stating a "meaning" which is new or distinct but which can nevertheless be preserved. The basic method for assisting the memory to retain a series of distinct meanings is to frame the first of them in a way which will suggest or forecast a later meaning which will recall the first without being identical with it. What is to be said and remembered later is cast in the form of an echo of something said already; the future is encoded in the present. All oral narrative is in structure continually both prophetic and retrospective, and it is this mode of composition—essentially an extension of the acoustic echo principle—which is used to preserve the instructional material of the tale by preserving an easier recollection of the narrative contexts in which the material is incorporated.

These correspondences, when observed, are usually explained as "patterns"—a visual term. More correctly, under conditions of primary orality they are acoustic responsions, sometimes involving wordplay. To speak therefore of a "story line" (Ong, ch. 6) as being just that can mislead, for though the narrative syntax is paratactic—the basic conjunction being "and then," "and next"—the narrative is not linear but turns back on itself in order to assist the memory to reach the end by having it anticipated somehow in the beginning.

This accretion of acoustic knowledge rhythmically framed and socially shared cannot arise spontaneously. It requires the services of professionals who have mastered the specialized formulaic language required, and at the same time have a comprehensive mentality tuned to the variety of the culture pattern they live in. They are not moralists with a single point of view—a luxury reserved for literate thinkers—but reporters with an instinct for the typical. Finally, unlike writers, they have to be not only composers but performers, for only by performance can such group poetry be published, known, and remembered. This professional ability becomes a craft dependent for its existence on continuous training in successive apprenticeship to master singers and master musicians and provides the technological basis for the power wielded in such societies by shamans, priesthoods, prophets, and "bards of the people" (*LRG,* p. 243). Often enough the singer who has stood at the king's elbow becomes the king himself, as in the case of David, King of the Hebrews, who "danced before the Lord."

I have said that such a reconstruction has to be hypothetical because material evidence or recorded testimony covering primary orality is, in the nature of the case, nonexistent. This is not quite true. There are accounts, meager enough, reported by European navigators who explored the Pacific before the days of colonial penetration or literate research. Fortunately for the present purposes, the data they were interested in collecting were in the main geographic, sometimes economic, which meant that if they cast an occasional curious eye on native customs and habits, it was with a naiveté which forbade over-interpretation. This is true of Captain Cook's encounter with Tahiti, which has given us some account of a cadre of professional singers, dancers, actors, and musicians revered by the society they served, using a specially contrived speech to celebrate the seasonal festivals and those that marked the great events of communal life (*GCJ,* pp. 31-32). More recently, what is probably the closest approximation to primary orality still surviving, if it still does survive, is located among some of the tribes of the central African hinterland.

The "Myth of the Bagre," recovered and recorded by Jack Goody and his associates, supplies a text which, though touched by the influence of literacy, still retains evidences of the mnemonic rules of oral composition, has a content which carries out the magisterial function of cultural guidance, and is recited and taught by a group of professionals (*GCJ,* p. 346, nn. 13, 14).

When we read the classics of what is styled Greek "literature," we confront written works which are rooted in a previous condition of primary orality. Whatever claims may be put forward for the Mycenaean culture, inflated as they have been by specialists in the field, they would dwindle were it not for the celebration of Mycenae in the oral poetry of Homer, an imaginative construct which arose within the compass of perhaps five centuries of complete nonliteracy that followed Mycenae's collapse. In parallel with the poetry there emerged in the same period corresponding achievements in visual art, architecture, and politics. These were the preconditions for that flowering of Athenian culture in the fifth century which produced Greek drama.

If the Homeric poems constitute one of these preconditions, it is natural to suppose that they also constitute the oral storage mechanism of the original culture, and this is borne out first by their compositional style—the verbal formulas metrically shaped, the archaic narrative, the patterns of anticipation and responsion; second, by social content—the typical situations and statements, the repeated moral formulas, the ritualized performances, the contained maxims; third, in manner of transmission—recited by professional singers on public occasions to audiences gathered for this purpose, and taught to the young in schools by these same professionals (*LRG,* p. 267). All these symptoms of cultural oralism will later reappear, in attenuated form, in Athenian drama.

The alphabet which enabled these epics and later poetry to achieve the status of artifacts by being written down seems to have been invented near the end of the eighth century. This "commitment to writing," as we say, occurred under unique circumstances which have never recurred, and in the nature of things never could recur. (1) An oral language was transcribed by a means invented by people who were themselves oralists and (2) who themselves spoke the language that was being transcribed and (3) who had to learn to apply the new technique from scratch unaided by the guidance of literate mentors either domestic or foreign. The result is that in the Homeric poems we are left an alphabetized report of a composition of primary orality unique in its integrity.

A further conclusion follows, concerning the transitional process which set in after Homer and led to literacy. This must have been equally unique in its gradualness, quite unlike what happens when literacy and nonliteracy either collide or coexist in modern situations. Between 700 and 400 B.C., roughly speaking, there were no ready-made models of literate composition, or habits of reading, or literate ways of thinking available to accelerate the transition. Alphabetization had to be introduced into a population which, having previously brought the oral manner of composition to a fine art, cherished it as a familiar companion to daily life. What was expected at first from alphabetized scripts as they became available was not a literate "literature" but an extending series of written versions of oral storage. Education remained oral; cultural expectations remained oral. Only as the teaching of letters was introduced into primary schools before adolescence could a population of readers become available; and this occurred about the time Plato went to school, or a little before. It had not yet occurred at the time when Aeschylus initiated the golden age of Athenian drama.

The long-term effects of a transfer of the balance of the senses used in communication, from ear to eye and from mouth to hand, were drastic. Conversion of an acoustic performance into a visible artifact fostered the conception of an ownership of the composed word and hence of authorship. Poetry could now be circulated with a name firmly attached to it. Previous modes of composition had been inherently collectivist; idiom and themes had to be shared; you could not copyright a recitation. With authorship came the potential for taking a more personal charge of what was uttered so as to manipulate and reorganize it according to the private intentions of the composer. To be sure, previous recitations of oral verse might differ in quality according to different levels of accomplishment in the singers, and would be recognized as such. But the material was drawn from a shared repertoire, not personally invented.

The *Oedipus* therefore is, under one aspect, a personally produced product embodying a degree of personal creativity. Nevertheless its composition, like that of all Greek drama, involves a partnership between the oral and the written, the acoustic and the visual, a dichotomy which can also be rendered in terms of tradition versus design, generic versus specific, communal versus personal. It is a combination which lies at the heart of all high classic Greek "literature" from Homer to Euripides.

This partnership was not mechanical but creative. Literacy did not take over from orality but slowly interpenetrated it. It is a mistake to suppose, as G. S. Kirk and others have argued we should, that once the Homeric poems were written down the results for the creative oral process became negative.[8] Under modern conditions this does occur when a mature literacy invades and takes over an original orality. The partnership concept, as applied to the Greek high classical, is at first hard to understand just because it is unique and calls for a critique not yet developed by comparativists. Nor does the Yugoslav analogy, for reasons already stated, offer any help.

In Greek drama we perceive the last flowering of this partnership, the supreme product of a creative tension between the needs and expectations of the oral and those of the written, of the listener and of the reader. Since the latter component has hitherto received the lion's share of critical attention, it seems appropriate in this place to shift focus in order to disclose the oral side of the partnership.

We now know what we are looking for—namely, a type of composition which at the level of style meets the mnemonic requirements: it will be versified and to a degree musical; its vocabulary will be grandiloquent and slightly archaic, in a manner superimposed upon the current vernacular; it may retain traces of formulaic idiom and is likely to use a syntax suitable to the actions of agents performing in a narrative context which itself is archaic, that is, drawn from past memory or what passes for memory. The story, however, is to be told in such a way as to avoid novelty; it will turn back on itself, through responsion or reversal, so that the conclusion is partially anticipated in the beginning. To this end we expect the use of prophetic anticipations and retrospective summations, employing the principle of acoustic echo which may extend as far as verbal assonance.

This style of composition is to be placed at the service of a content which, as it tells its tale, continually recalls and recommends the social *ethos* and *nomos* of the audiences to which it is addressed. We use these convenient Greek terms to comprehend the customs, beliefs, loyalties, proprieties, and rituals of that society to which the audience belongs.

Versified language is something the *Oedipus* shares with all Greek plays, and the scholarly critic taking the obvious in his stride automatically attributes the choice to the personalities of their authors: they all happened to be professional "poets." But was the choice of verse also socially conditioned, reflecting the pressure to compose speech suitable for nonreaders to remember? Plato in the next generation tried poetry but dropped it for prose, for he could expect a supply of readers not originally available for Sophocles. Drama's musical component, however, had now shrunk; dialogue is spoken without its help, and in a rhythm which, as the Greeks themselves noted, is closest to the cadences of ordinary speech. The hexametric formulas have disappeared; the vocabulary is Attic and contemporary, not archaic. And yet a flavor of the archaic is retained; the syntax is manipulated; ordinary usage is remodeled, intensified; the style is neither that of inherited oral epic on the one hand, nor that of written prose on the other. It can assume individuality when used by three different authors, and yet remain consistently "high classical" and somewhat remote, an effect assisted by an infusion of some Doric dialectical forms in the choruses.

Action is enclosed within an antique tale, in modern terms a "myth," employing a syntax which is largely performative—a natural result of drama's art form, a vehicle second only to epic as a suitable repository of memorized speech. The tale is culled from oral memory; the names of its agents and the settings within which they live or act are archaic, drawn from that same legendary Greek past which is presupposed in the Homeric poems. Only one extant play by Aeschylus breaks this rule, and even so assigns its personalities to a remote and mysterious kingdom.

These properties being common to Greek drama are not difficult to appreciate in themselves; only when viewed against the background of primary orality do they acquire a fresh dimension. The mnemonic rules that operate to control the way the plot is constructed are at first sight less evident and can best be tested by recourse to a specific text. The testing becomes the more stringent as applied to the *Oedipus,* a composition which on the surface appears to be unusually sophisticated, that is to say, constructed with a care that only a literate author composing for a literate audience might be expected to apply.

The plot is woven into an elaborate pattern of prophecies of what will happen and repetitions that it has happened. Among these, the utterances ascribed to Teiresias, oracular in tone, exercise dominant control. Reluctantly appearing in answer to summons (a recollection of the part played by a prophet in the opening of the *Iliad*) and provoked by his ruler's intemperate accusations, he breaks out at last into a defiant reply, or rather two replies, in which he spells out and then recapitulates a detailed definition of the real identity of the culprit who has caused Thebes' present distress, what his situation is, and what his fate will be:

I

You have eyes, but do not see
Where you are living or whose house is your home
Do you know your origins? Unawares you have
  become abhorrent
to your own kin, the dead and the living
Double-lashed the curse of mother and father both
that dire-footed will hound you from this land
clear your vision now but darkness soon—
Hark! hear Kithairon echoing to your anguished cries

II

This man, the object of your menaces
and inquisition, proclaimed the murderer
of Laius, is right here now,
styled foreigner and migrant, till as native
Theban exposed. No pleasure to him
in what will befall. Vision lost,
wealth lost, blind and beggared, to foreign land
will he fare forth with staff to feel his way.
Exposure will reveal him consorting with his own
  children
as brother and father combined, and as of her who
  gave him birth
both son and husband, and of his father
a partner in bed and in murder.

Viewed as oral management, the design of these overlapping declarations is to alert the listening audience to follow in detail the future course of the action. It knows perfectly well now what is going to happen to the protagonist; the words have been riveted on their attention. The barrier of impenetrability between what on the surface is said and what is really meant is placed between Oedipus and Teiresias, but not between the audience and Teiresias. The details as stated define both present circumstance and its future unraveling, and do it twice over, with repetitiousness characteristic of oral composition.

As the unraveling occurs, the various dramatic items promised in this disclosure are not only performed but compulsively recapitulated by way of retrospective comment and lamentation. The blinding previously predicted is announced as the moment for it arrives (l. 1183), and after performance through self-infliction is ceremoniously reported (ll. 1268-79) and then continually reviewed in words put into the sufferer's own mouth (ll. 1313-18, 1323, 1326, 1334, 1337, 1371, 1375, 1385, 1389, 1470, 1482-83, 1486). The complex set of sexual interrelations first laid out in all detail of possible permutations and combinations by Teiresias is elaborately and compulsively recapitulated by the victim in the last third of the play (ll. 1256-57, 1357-61, 1403-8, 1481-85, 1496-99). Even the predicted exile to Mount Kithaeron (l. 421), scene of his babyhood (l. 1090), is in the conclusion recalled, reasserted, and demanded (ll. 1451-54). The total effect is that of an extended ring composition. Initial statements in effect addressed to the audience are echoed and re-echoed in the conclusion, to assist the purpose of imprinting upon

acoustic memories the totality of what is said and done. This indeed might seem to be the main purpose served by the introduction on stage of the two daughters, still small children with no speaking parts, but providing occasion for a last obsessive retracing of Oedipus's complex sexual dilemma (ll. 1496-99).

The prophecies of Teiresias are only the most conspicuous portion of a series of oracular warnings, initiated by Creon's report of an oracular reply which supplies the first clue to the whereabouts of the slayer of Oedipus's father: he is here in Thebes (ll. 95-111). The implications are not understood. Teiresias follows with riddling descriptions of Oedipus himself, as already noted. Again they are not understood, even though Oedipus is challenged to understand them: "Go and think this out" (ll. 460-61). In the next instance we are transported into a past which has created the present. Laius and Jocasta had been given the original fateful oracle which threatened Laius's life, predicting he will be killed by his own son. They think to evade the prediction by exposing the infant (ll. 711-25). But this exercise of independent intelligence turns out to be mistaken, leading to a result the precise opposite of that intended. Their son as he grows up in his turn will commit himself to the same fatal sequence, by the same kind of error, against the same antagonist, for (as he recalls in response to prompting) he was given an oracle from the same source, prophesying parricide and incest on his part. He was in Corinth when he heard this, and like his real parents he thinks to cheat it by fleeing, this time from his supposed parents (ll. 787-97). The correct hint given to him that they are not his parents (ll. 779-80) is ignored. He has flunked all the tests and guaranteed first his fatal involvement and then its exposure.

In effect these statements, whether prophetic or oracular, are riddles. The entire play is composed so as to turn upon their pronouncements and attempted solutions. Oedipus himself is first introduced as a famous riddle solver (ll. 8, 35-40), and the title is echoed, with poignant irony, in the finale pronounced by the chorus (l. 1525). He had correctly understood and solved the riddle of the Sphinx. But the developing action soon casts him in the reverse role, as a man who fails to solve a series of further riddles. His second opponent has now in effect become Apollo, a more formidable antagonist in the battle of wits (ll. 1329-30).

Riddles are wordplays exchanged in competition between interlocutors, in this case between Apollo on the one hand and Oedipus's parents or Oedipus himself on the other; in two instances Apollo uses intermediaries. The diction employed can exploit not only correspondences between meanings, but acoustic assonances and responsion. This kind of dramaturgy reverts to the roots of orally communicated wisdom. It exploits matchings of similarities and contrasts at the two levels of meaning and of sound simultaneously, which because of the echo system employed are friendly to any effort of oral memorization. They constitute a kind of intellectual exercise—a dialectic—at the primary level of oral exchange and oral manners. The audience went home from the theater with their heads full of it.

Scene from a 1987 Indonesian production of Oedipus.

The riddling of the **Oedipus,** then, while giving to this particular play a peculiar degree of dramatic tension, can be seen as a revival of a traditional device, mnemonic in character and having its roots in the habits of primary orality. A complete critique of a play so cunningly constructed would have to grant also that the total effect could have been gained only as a level of literate intelligence came to operate upon a level of oral intelligence. In psychological terms, a verbal architecture, made possible by the visualization of words in script, is to be inferred as superimposed upon an echo system resounding in the author's ears.

The anthropological obligation to commemorate the social mores had been assigned in the first instance to the chorus as constituting the original element in dramatic composition. As a replacement for epic, it had the advantage that verbal mimesis (*PP,* ch. 2) (to use Plato's term) could be reinforced by dance and by a use of melody beyond the range of a stringed instrument (*PP,* ch. 9). Choric composition can best be defined by the term *generic* as opposed to personal. The art of the composer is devoted to expressing as poignantly as he can what his community feels or would

feel, as opposed to whatever unique and private thoughts he himself might be capable of contributing. This becomes conspicuous in the choric compositions of Aeschylus; and those of Sophocles, sophisticated as they may seem, still carry the same generic stamp. The five choruses of the **Oedipus** are ceremonial representations of five types of public ritualized performance. The *parodos* (ll. 151-215), responding to the delivery of Apollo's first oracle, is a hymn of ritual supplication, a prayer for succor from danger and death, addressed to five gods, including Athena. The first stasimon (ll. 463-511), responding to the dreadful riddle of Teiresias, is formulated as an averting prayer, and as a formal imprecation upon the unknown source of pollution, designed to protect the city from peril. The second (ll. 863-910) responds to the premature confidence expressed by Oedipus and Jocasta—and especially Jocasta—that they have outwitted the oracles addressed to them. This time it is not supplication or imprecation but deprecation, a solemn litany designed to avert what might be dangerous—namely, skepticism or impiety at the expense of a powerful god. The third stasimon (ll. 1086-1109) is in an altogether different key, though equally ritualistic, being a brief birthday song, of a rather special kind, surprisingly touching and tender, responding to the revelation that Oedipus was a foundling discovered on the mountainside. He is saluted as a true child of nature, of Kithairon, or of the nymphs, or perchance of Apollo or Pan? These sentiments have been widely misunderstood. They are not "ironic," on the one hand, or mistaken on the other. They anticipate the final reception of Oedipus by the earth, his true mother, in the last play of the Oedipus series, the **Oedipus at Colonus.** The fourth (ll. 1186-1222), following the culminating and catastrophic revelation of his true sexual situation, is a funeral dirge, a lament for the children of men in general (the Homeric echo is very plain here) and for Oedipus himself. He may still live on, but he has become dead to this world and its proprieties; by breaking a sexual taboo, he has become a kind of nonperson. Four of these five ritualized songs address themselves to preoccupations commonly experienced in early societies: the need to guard against plague, to identify sources of social pollution, to preserve esteem for oracles, to come to terms with the uncertain hazards of life. Their expression is generic, repeating normal components of an ethic orally preserved and celebrated.

The same four include observations which bear more directly upon the action. The *parodos* contains a vivid description of the plague's present and local effects (ll. 167-88); the first stasimon adds a meditation upon the possibility that Oedipus himself may after all be the culprit sought (ll. 483-511); the second concludes by criticizing the protagonists for their skeptical impiety (ll. 897-910); the fourth enlarges upon the personal reversal of fortune that Oedipus has suffered (ll. 1197-1222).

In these passages the chorus functions as a partner in the plot, furthering the process of the tale as it is told—the particular tale the dramatist has chosen. Accompanying as they do the generic statements, they serve to integrate generalized themes into the context of a given narrative, much as had occurred in epic composition, but with the difference that the themes have become more explicit, a natural result of being expressed in song rather than in the course of chanted narrative. Such meditation offers no innovative inventions designed to challenge existing views, prejudices, habits, and conventions. Nor on the other hand does it seek to expose or exploit them. It simply weaves a familiar texture in and out of a cautionary tale, clothed in a dress which the listening audience instinctively followed, accepted, and remembered because they recognized artistic versions of what they commonly performed, and commonly believed, week in and week out in their corporate and family capacities.

When Aristophanes in his comedy *The Frogs* chose to dramatize an imaginary poetic contest between Aeschylus and Euripides, the god Dionysus, acting appropriately as judge of their respective performances, submits them to a final examination, in which the contestants are required to offer for comparison rival *gnomae,* that is, maxims or aphorisms, of their own composition. "Though today we would not think of testing dramatic expertise in this way,

the texts (of both tragedians) demonstrate that the test was reasonable at the time" (*LRG,* p. 302). Wisdom of this sort is in fact a rooted characteristic of classic drama, symptomatic of its closeness to primary orality, in which the saying, couched as proverb, maxim, or aphorism, is such a conspicuous element, framed mnemonically by use of parallelism, antithesis, pithy compression, and acoustic balance to be repeated and reused on the lips of the people.

While it is relatively easy to identify maxims in the dramatic texts when they are framed as such, they more commonly appear in disguise, lurking within statements which appear to be addressed directly to what is happening. The iambic rhetoric which constitutes nine-tenths of what passes for "action" in a Greek play ordinarily prefers language which is normative, implying that "what I am doing or saying is only what is to be expected under the circumstances." In this way the sentiments of oral-cultural storage get into the text indirectly as part of the action, giving it that air of formality which separates it and always will separate it from the stagecraft of later centuries.

The prologue to the **Oedipus,** which gets the plot moving, is cast in the form of an exchange between the protagonist and a priest acting as spokesman for a delegation of citizens. Within the first fifty-seven lines there occur eight examples of statements apparently addressed to specifics, which can be transferred backwards into the generic oral formulas which are being echoed in them.

(Oedipus)		
2-3	[specific]:	What means this session of all of you before me with your suppliant boughs all wreathed?
	[generic]:	civic emergencies call for supplication offered to gods with appropriate equipment
6-7	[specific]:	here I am in person, preferring not to rely on messengers other than myself
	[generic]:	direct intelligence obtained personally is preferable to news communicated by others [cf. *Seven Against Thebes,* ll. 67-68]
9-10	[specific]:	aged sire, speak up, since it is natural and appropriate for you to speak on their behalf
	[generic]:	the older members of a community are its appropriate spokesmen
(Priest)		
15-20	[specific]:	you can see us in our respective age groups as we sit at your altars, some not yet strong enough to fly far, some burdened with age, priests like me, and here too the chosen of our young men. The rest of the populace crouches garlanded in the marketplaces.

	[generic]:	a civic population is made up of the children at one extreme, the aged at the other, the male youth [as the fighters] in the middle, and the rest of the population [i.e., the women; cf. *Seven*, ll. 10-16]
25-27	[specific]:	our city is dying as the fruits of its soil die and is dying as its flocks and herds die and as the pregnancies of its women are aborted.
	[generic]:	pestilence is a visitation which destroys plants and animals, and renders women barren.
41-45	[specific]:	we supplicate you of all men, for I can see that it is the counsels of men already experienced that have successful issue.
	[generic]:	here the maxim lacks disguise, aside from its application to present emergency.
49-50	[specific]:	let us never by any means have cause to remember your government as one under which we originally stood erect and then fell flat.
	[generic]:	stability and continuity of government is best [or: the measure of good government is the continuous prosperity of its subject]
54-55	[specific]:	if indeed you intend to govern this land as well as control it, better to control it in company with its men then control a land that is emptied of them.
	[generic]:	a governing power which destroys its own citizens is no government.

Equipped with this sample, the reader can thread his way through the remaining text, observing the recurrent intrusion of similar generic observations. It is interesting to compare their comparative density as between the *Seven Against Thebes* and the **Oedipus**. Nearly forty years of growing literacy have registered their effect, not only in decreasing the proportion but in increasing the degree of linguistic manipulation applied by the author to the language used (*LRG*, pp. 303-4).

The matrix enclosing these materials, giving opportunity for their enunciation, is provided by the myth chosen by the dramatist for exploitation. Because of modern preoccupation with the heroic ideal as it has been supposed to inform the life-style of ancient Hellas, and also under the influence of Freud, the Athenian stage has lately been viewed as providing an arena for the display of autonomous personalities grappling in depth with dilemmas personal to themselves.[9] Even Professor Ong, otherwise observant of the nuances of the transition from the oral to the "chirographic," succumbs to the temptation to see Oedipus as a

character cast in this mold, and therefore as a "chirographic" character represented "in depth" (pp. 152, 154), when in fact objectively speaking Sophocles' hero could be regarded as a rather stupid, or at least insensitive man in whose predicament we become involved because (a) he happens to be in a position of great authority and (b) has nevertheless entangled himself in circumstances beyond his control which are bound to destroy that authority.

Orally preserved communication committed to the preservation of social propriety favored stories which focused on the social and collective context within which individuals were allowed to operate. This is as true of Achilles as it is of Oedipus. The social matrix for Attic drama is the polis, the city-state, and in particular the city of Athens. Mycenaean and other antique fables furnished a backdrop, a kind of fantasy (*GCJ*, p. 56), which served to give to the dramatic statement a ritual and even religious flavor. But the overriding theme is the fortune and fate of the contemporary city; the social wisdom preserved in the text is that appropriate to civic preoccupations. In those preliminary fifty-seven lines already reviewed, the issue to be settled in the rest of the play is plainly stated to be the restoration of a city to a health it has lost. The image of its assembled population is there on stage and compulsively noted. The term *polis* itself, introduced by Oedipus in the fourth line of the play, is reiterated four times in the priest's reply (ll. 21, 28, 46, 51), not counting its synonyms (land, town, soil: ll. 14, 25, 35, 47, 54). As the plot winds down to its conclusion, it is announced that the source of the city's pollution, now discovered, is to be segregated from the community (ll. 1425-31). Oedipus's fate is not his own to decide, but waits upon a newly constituted political authority (l. 1523). Between these two terminal points, the plot as it proceeds continually places its chief actors against the background of a civic community in which they rule and in which their government is crucial. The fantasy element is supplied by the mythology of Thebes. The actual community which the audience feels is on trial before their eyes is their own. Need we wonder then that the plot turns on a practice of population control accepted silently, and we can guess uneasily, by this same community? So much that has been written about this play fails to note the relevance of the plot to contemporary practice. The omission is striking. How many of the audience shifted in their seats as the tale of the exposure of the infant Oedipus unfolded itself, an exposure implicitly condemned by the results to which it leads?

Social custom apart, there were historical memories both past and recent waiting to be stirred by what the play says. The prayer of supplication offered by the chorus as they enter sets up the ambivalent geographic context with which and within which the members of the audience are invited to identify themselves: it is at once ancient Thebes, a city of the imagined past, and contemporary Athens, a city experienced in the present. After first identifying Thebes as the location of the myth and the recipient of Apollo's oracle (ll. 151-57), their first invocation (marked as first) is addressed to Athena, Zeus's daughter, followed by Artemis and Apollo, whose previous succor of a city in dire peril is commemorated (ll. 165-66). Are we in the legendary Thebes rescued by Oedipus, or in the theater on that acropolis once occupied over fifty years ago by the Persians and rescued and reoccupied after Salamis? Such memories were always close to the surface in the Athens of the later fifth century. The audience begins to realize where it is and is made doubly sure when the next two stanzas describe in woeful detail a civic plague and its effects. They were now listening to verse composed for themselves, the recent survivors of just such a calamity, the Great Plague of Athens of 429—a present memory reinforced by Homeric memory of that plague which initiates the action of the *Iliad.*

Plague had occurred in the course of a war still being waged when the play was produced, and with oppressive results on the population. The chorus next names Ares as the war god whose presence terrifies them with thoughts of escaping from the city by sea eastward or westward (ll. 190-99). Against him they invoke the protection of Apollo's arrows and Artemis's flaming torches (ll. 203-8) before concluding with an appeal to Dionysus, patron deity of their present (mythical) location (ll. 210). The ode thus ends where it began, in Thebes. Overall, the effect once more is of ring composition, a standard oral form, used in this case to evoke contemporary concerns as they are enclosed within an envelope of the archaic and traditional.

The archaeology of Thebes is not likely to throw much light upon reasons for such inclusion. The imagined inhabitants of a Mycenaean capital in the Greek hinterland could not plausibly be represented as resorting to a long sea voyage as an immediate means of escape, nor would such a civic community be described by its priest as one not only of warriors but of ships (l. 56). The same speaker addresses himself to a ruler described as hitherto supremely successful, but who might now fall (l. 50) and who may face the prospect of ruling over a depopulated territory (ll. 54-57). His proper title is not one of divinity—*isotheos,* an unacceptable impiety—but "first of men" (ll. 31-33); we can hear an echo of this in the tribute paid later to Pericles by the historian Thucydides. As one takes in all the contemporary allusiveness of the play, the impression grows that in the role of the protagonist we hear a muted memory at once critical, mournful, and sympathetic of Athens's leading statesman, and his fate as a plague-stricken victim of his own policies.

After the same fashion, Aeschylus's *Seven Against Thebes,* drawing on the same cycle of Theban legend, had celebrated recent Athenian history within an antique tale (*LRG,* pp. 294, 295, 297). This is not to be understood as a departure from the anthropological function. Customs, rituals, and beliefs commemorated in oral storage can be perceived as rooted in a distant past, provided the perceiving is done by the literate historian. For the oral composer and his audience the material is felt to be contemporary. The memory of oral societies is short; the specific memories they are able to retain are recent. A Shakespeare could, if he chose, dramatize distant history—that of a Lear or Macbeth—because he could read documented sources which were historical in intention. The composers

of Attic tragedy had only the epic compositions of Homer and a few successors now alphabetized. The antique background of the plays—Trojan, Argive, Theban, Corinthian—remains formal and sketchy, a convenience for the commemoration of the present community represented in the audience, a commemoration of the way they are living now, presumed to be the traditional way, commingled with some experiences of the recent past. It is a theatrical situation well summed up in the words of Jean-Paul Vernant: "The performance of tragedy is not only an art form, it is a social institution . . . to which the city, by founding the tragic competitions, gives status along with its political and legal instruments. By establishing . . . a performance open to all citizens . . . the city makes itself into a theater, in a way it becomes an object of representation, and plays itself before the public."[10]

To this I would add that such a type of performance, unique to the Attic stage, becomes understandable when its causation is perceived to exist in the conditions governing poetic composition in a culture of oral communication requiring oral storage of cultural information.

Notes

1. Walter J. Ong, *Orality and Literacy: The Technologizing of the Word* (London and New York, 1982). Hereafter cited in text.

2. Eric A. Havelock, *Preface to Plato* (Cambridge, Mass. and Oxford, 1963), hereafter *PP; The Greek Concept of Justice* (Cambridge, Mass., 1978), hereafter *GCJ; The Literate Revolution in Greece* (Princeton, N.J., 1982), hereafter *LRG.* Ong, pp. 180-95, contains an extensive bibliography which "lists some significant works which can serve as entries into major fields."

3. Ruth Finnegan, *Oral Literature in Africa* (Oxford, 1970); *Oral Poetry: Its Nature, Significance and Social Context* (Cambridge, 1977); "Oral Literature and Writing in the South Pacific," in *Oral and Traditional Literatures,* ed. N. Simms, *Pacific Quarterly,* 7 (1982).

4. Finnegan, "Oral Literature and Writing," p. 34.

5. Finnegan, "Oral Literature and Writing," p. 34.

6. Albert B. Lord, *The Singer of Tales* (Cambridge, Mass., 1960), pp. 129-30.

7. Lord, ch. 4.

8. G. S. Kirk, *Songs of Homer* (Cambridge, 1962), p. 71: "The *Iliad* and the *Odyssey* are oral poems . . . an elaborate system which is quickly weakened when the poet begins to compose by writing"; p. 87: "Literacy destroys the virtue of an oral singer"; p. 319: "The weakest and most impure of the post-Homeric singers. . . ."

9. C. H. Whitman, *Sophocles: A Study of Heroic Humanism* (Cambridge, Mass., 1951).

10. Jean-Paul Vernant, "Tensions and Ambiguities in Greek Tragedy," in *Interpretation: Theory and Practice,* ed. Charles A. Singleton (Baltimore, 1967), pp. 107-8.

Bernhard Frank (essay date 1992)

SOURCE: "Sophocles's *Oedipus the King*," in *Explicator,* Vol. 51, No. 1, Fall, 1992, pp. 5-6.

[*In the following essay, Frank contends that during the climax of* Oedipus Tyrannus, *Oedipus reverses roles with Jocasta.*]

> . . . There, there, we saw his wife
> hanging, the twisted rope around her neck.
> When he saw her, he cried out fearfully
> and cut the dangling noose. Then, as she lay,
> poor woman, on the ground, what happened after
> was terrible to see. He tore the brooches—
> the gold chased brooches fastening her robe—
> away from her and lifting them up high
> dashed them on his own eyeballs, shrieking out
> such things as: they will never see the crime
> I have committed or had done upon me!
> Dark eyes, now in the days to come look on
> forbidden faces, do not recognize
> those whom you long for—with such imprecations
> he struck his eyes again and yet again
> with the brooches. And the bleeding eyeballs gushed
> and stained his beard—no sluggish oozing drops
> but a black rain and bloody hail poured down.

lines 1263-80; David Grene, trans.

The self-blinding of Oedipus, a scene that Harold Bloom, in his introduction to *Sophocles' **Oedipus Rex*** (New York: Chelsea House, 1988), singles out as "too terrible for acting out . . . [and] also too dreadful for representation in language," has been read, time and again, as the manifestation of *either* Apollo's (and secondarily, Teiresias') prophecy, *or* of Oedipus' free will. Bloom interprets the act as Oedipus' "protest against Apollo, who brings both the light and the plague" (3). He dismisses the Freudian theory of the act as a form of castration as "less relevant here than the outcry against the god" (4).

Another, very different interpretation of the scene emerges, however, which ultimately serves to explain, or at least mitigate, the lame ending, in which the blind Oedipus enters the house to await Apollo's further instructions.

When Oedipus bursts through the double doors, which to Bloom suggest the female labia (3), he is already inured to the knowledge of being a parricide. He had known for many years that he had killed a man and suspected early on in the play that it was Laius. His total preoccupation, that of a man gone amok, now centers on the discovery of his incestuous relationship with Jocasta. He intends to thrust his sword into her offending womb, which ironically would emulate the sexual act one last time. When he finds the queen dead by her own hand, however, a strange reversal occurs. Jocasta becomes the newborn, the dead infant that Oedipus should have been, if the tragedy was to have been averted. And it is Oedipus who delivers the child and, severing the "twisted" umbilical cord, lowers it to the ground.

It is significant that the brooches (or, as sometimes translated, pins) with which he then blinds himself come from Jocasta's dress. Oedipus could have used any nearby object for the purpose—why Jocasta's brooches? The act appears as another stage of their role reversal. Far from seeking to castrate himself, Oedipus takes on Jocasta's persona and rapes his own eyes with her "phalluses." The blood gushes down and stains his beard—the pubic region, as it were, of his pierced eyes. It is Jocasta's twofold revenge, reciprocating his oft-repeated coital act.

By their role reversal, Oedipus has avenged both the crime he committed and the one of which he was the victim. He has paid Jocasta back for sending him to his infant death and avenged the incest perpetrated on her. The climax of the play is here. The disposition of the Oedipus who survives the ordeal is really only of secondary importance. His exile, now, can wait.

Richard Fabrizio (essay date 1995)

SOURCE: "The Two Oedipuses: Sophocles, Anguillara, and the Renaissance Treatment of Myth," in *MLN,* Vol. 110, No. 1, January, 1995, pp. 178-91.

[*In the following essay, Fabrizio examines how Giovanni Andrea dell'Anguillara, a Renaissance writer, dealt with what he deemed inconsistencies of characterization in his adaptation of Sophocles's text.*]

To discuss so minor a writer as Giovanni Andrea dell'Anguillara (ca. 1517-1571) seems like an exercise in willful obscurantism or personal enthusiasm for what is better dead and buried. Of course, it could be claimed with Ernst Robert Curtius and Aby Warburg that "God lurks in detail," that only by a minute exploration of even the minor figures of a period can we achieve any synthesis and understanding of literary history. We are all aware from experience how often a second or even third rate writer illuminates more clearly than a master the mentality of a period. But a more tangible justification exists for conjuring up the name of Anguillara from the dusty tomes of the past. His *Edippo tragedia* was both the first performed and first printed vernacular version of the Oedipus story in the Renaissance. Called "among the most famous tragedies" by one of those eighteenth-century collectors of details, Crescimbeni (I. iv. 309), the *Edippo* was printed twice in 1565,[1] once in Padua and once in Venice. It was also performed twice, first in Padua in 1556 (Pelaez 77) or 1560 (Lorini 88) on a permanent stage designed by Falconetto for the home of Alvise Cornaro (Fiocco 142; "Idea" 219) and, I believe, a second time in Vicenza in 1561 on a temporary wooden stage designed by Palladio for the Olympic Academy. Both productions were done with a splendor and pomp befitting the famous story and befitting a text that would return the story of Oedipus to the stage after more than a thousand year hiatus.

While the stage history of the 1585 production of Sophocles' **Oedipus** for the inauguration of Palladio's Teatro Olimpico has been told repeatedly, both in its own time (Ingegneri) and after (Gallo, Puppi, Schrade), the tale of Anguillara's play is hardly known. And it probably will never be told, lacking as it does early MS or printed evidence and depending on contradictory reports in those ponderous but charming biographical and bibliographical texts of the seventeenth and eighteenth century: Castellini, Temanza, Mazzuchelli, Tiraboschi, Fontanini, Angiolgabriello, and others. That the *Edippo* has been confined to the dust bins of literature by an unfortunate loss of evidence is ironic, for Anguillara repeatedly complained, often with a broad smile, against his fate. In one poem, he said that while "Fortune" showed "Her smiling face" to his patron, he only saw "Her behind" ("culo": "Capitolo: Nella Sedia" 115). Yet according to our standards, he was quite fortunate: a poet of many witty poems in the style of Berni; a translator who even recently was called a star (Melczer 246-265); a letterato called upon by the Olympic Academy to write the preface for the first Italian performance of the first Italian tragedy, Trissino's *Sofonisba* (Corrigan 199); a writer who served at the court of King Henry II and Catherine de' Medici; and last but not least, an aspiring inventor ("Lettera alla Signoria").

And yet his reputation has become as small and misshaped as his body; he was, in fact, a dwarfish hunchback. Though he laughed at his deformity, calling his body a mess of mountains and valleys ("Capitolo al Cardinale di Trento" 301-302), he—I think—would have cried at his historical neglect, and especially at the neglect of his *Edippo,* which as his preface shows, he hoped would bring fame by association with the noble tragic genre. Not fame, but infamy came to it instead. His *Edippo* was damned by both contemporaries and by nineteenth- and twentieth-century critics, and by all for the same reason: its additions to Sophocles' text. A Latin letter by the priest Girolamo Negri mentions its first performance, complaining that its four hour production was "undecipherable" (tota . . . est etrusca; 120). De Nores, in his 1588 *Poetica,* called these added episodes that ran so counter to Aristotle's prescriptions little less than vicious. Later critics were no less kind, castigating Anguillara on the same basis: those dreaded episodes (D' Ovidio 277; Pelaez 79; Bosisio 83-84; Symonds II 244). But these additions are at the heart of Anguillara's vision. While all translation involves a degree of exegesis, particularly in the Renaissance (Norton 179), Anguillara literally recreated the figure of Oedipus. His *Edippo* is close to those types of imitations recognized by modern criticism, imitations that have a "dialectical relation" to their subtexts (Greene 39-40), works that retain the terms of their sources but "mean them in another sense" (Bloom 14). But the *Edippo* is really unique in what it attempts. Other Renaissance writers did one of two things: they translated Sophocles' text and left it as is;[2] or they mimicked its structures, as defined by Aristotle, in newly conceived plots and characters. No one else in the period completely redefined Oedipus.

Both Anguillara and his contemporaries start from the same point: the riddles embedded in Sophocles' text. Not what is understood there but what is incomprehensible forms the basis of the Renaissance Oedipus. While his contemporaries shun the textual riddles, Anguillara faces them head on. He accepts Sophocles' plot and modifies Oedipus' behavior. Into his second and third acts, Anguillara confines the whole of Sophocles' plot, interjecting into it new allusions that redefine its characters. In the rest of the text, Anguillara does the opposite: he expands the plot by inventing new material and by drawing bits and pieces from Euripides, Seneca, and Statius, and then interjects back into it material from Sophocles. At the same time, Anguillara maintains a link with the Middle Ages and the medieval Oedipus *romans:* their concern for pathos in particular. No wonder critics were dumbfounded and distraught. Nevertheless there is a sense to the whole, a reason for using such a variety of sources and motifs. Anguillara tried to solve a problem, a problem that he and his contemporaries noticed in Sophocles' *Oedipus* and its Aristotelian interpretation: Oedipus did not act consistently. Anguillara's object is to bring consistency to Edippo's life, to reconcile what I call the paradox of the two Oedipuses. With an almost Freudian fervor, Anguillara transforms his *Edippo* into a study of desire within the family, geometrically plotting its course from compassion and love to rivalry and incest. So what follows is not the story of the resuscitation of a dead body as much as an attempt to expose how a Renaissance writer understood or misunderstood the classic mind. And this story is very much the story of the two Oedipuses.

Oedipus is famous for his intelligence. To Sophocles (8) and Euripides (1506), he is glorious and wise for his ability to decipher a riddle. But in Sophocles' *Oedipus,* Oedipus is also obtuse. He is unable to put together elementary facts of his past with his present—facts of time, of place, of number, and of geneology. Every student has been perplexed and stimulated by this paradox, the paradox of the two Oedipuses. Elaborate theories have been devised to explain away the paradox of the two Oedipuses. In one theory Oedipus may be in fact neither parricide nor incestuous (Goodhardt; Ahl); he is guilty rather of misreading his past, his parentage, of blindly behaving as if the oracle must be his fate (Ahl). In another theory, Oedipus has always been sure of his past, of his patricide and incest; when the plague comes, he engages in a performance of ignorance in order to allow his people to ritually expiate themselves in the unravelling of his guilt (Vellacott). And of course, the most famous theory of our time, Freud's, explains away the paradox of the two Oedipuses by a dichotomy of the mind, a division between unconscious desire and conscious action, between suppression and anxiety. In each of these theories, the Oedipuses are reconciled, denying either that Oedipus commits a crime or accepting the crime and explaining it away. Whichever theory we accept, we realize that Sophocles' language is rich in paradox.

Against a backdrop of Aristotelian theory, Renaissance writers and critics also struggled to repair the split in the two Oedipuses. Some recognized that Aristotle's theory of character transformation rationalized the dichotomy, the theory of *peripeteia*—a reversal of fortune that forces one to face the past—and the theory of *anagnorisis*—a recognition of the meaning of one's past in terms of the present. Aristotle's rationalization provided little practical help. Oedipus' past was filled with so many inconsistencies that writers avoided the text and instead used its motifs. For example, in the tragedy *Alidoro* (1568) a baby is cast out of its royal home because of a dire oracle; later he returns and unknowingly commits incest with his sister (Neri 173-174). Gabriele Bombace, who probably wrote this tragedy, explains its creative methodology in his description of the play's first performance. He pinpoints the connections between Sophocles' text and Aristotle's theory: "There are no lack of literati who, comparing diligently the anagnorisis and peripeteia of *Oedipus* with that of *Alidoro,* dare for several reasons to affirm that this is better than that: and among other reasons because it is beyond belief that Oedipus . . . with so many signs of correspondence between place and time . . . had never thought that he was the murderer of Laius, the which error was sustained and defended by Aristotle the best he could as something outside the scenic action of the play itself. It is nevertheless very important and very far from the verisimilitude found in *Alidoro*" (*Tragedia* II 1004). There are three key elements here: 1) the reference to the passage in Aristotle that concerns a play's inner action and prior events (*Poetics.* XV. 1454b. 10d); 2) the intimation that Aristotle's theory of tragedy rationalizes the inconsistencies in *Oedipus;* and 3) the appeal to verisimilitude—fidelity to real life—as the standard that constitutes rationality.

Anguillara is unique in his use of the plot of Sophocles' *Oedipus* to solve what such writers saw as the irrationalities of the text. Most eliminated the plot of *Oedipus* and either imitated its handling of peripeteia and anagnorisis or competed with its horror by exploiting the shock of incest. Guarini's *Il Pastor Fido* (1590) imitates not the life of Oedipus but the way Oedipus came to recognize the meaning of his acts through reversals of fortune. Guarini so complicates and multiplies the reversals in plot that they outdo those in *Oedipus.* Each new twist foils the characters; they are blind to its meaning. But all finally becomes clear, for the world is rational once the secret design of Fate is revealed (Perella 257-259). Although concentrating on these reversals, Guarini retains certain elements of the plot of *Oedipus:* a child lost to its true parents, a dark fate for the state, an oracle that predicts a cure. Tasso's *Torrismondo* (1573) also manipulates and "renews" the story of Oedipus (Neri 147), while forsaking its plot. It retains a dire prediction, a child purposely separated from its parents, and incest. But here too the episodes are constructed so as to complicate the plot and thus rival the way its classical source, *Oedipus,* used peripeteia and anagnorisis. And again the hero, perfectly rational, is victimized by the irrationality of the daily world in which he lives (Dainard 45).

Rather than its complex structure, most Renaissance writers tried to imitate *Oedipus'* horror. Dramatists noticed

that Aristotle modeled his cathartic theory on *Oedipus;* therefore, they began to locate the catharsis of pity and fear in the attraction and repulsion for incest. Cesare della Porta, in his *Delpha* (1586), says that his subject is so terrible that "it will overwhelm (*involva*) Oedipus in perpetual silence" (Neri 157). Muzio Manfredi's *Semiramis* (ca. 1583; Herrick 206-209) was long praised for its exploitation of the "ferocious" passions (Neri 140). But it was Speroni's *Canace* (1542) that most exploited the incest theme. In fact, Speroni theorized that incest may not be an evil (Speroni 215); but even if it is, an evil hero may evoke a catharsis (Speroni 229). In the critical battle over the *Canace,* one thing is clear: incest is justified as a legitimate way to arouse pity and fear (Cf. Weinberg II. 925, 948-952). *Canace* was, nevertheless, castigated for its lasciviousness (Cinzio 139) and, like the *Edippo,* for its use of disparate episodes from a variety of sources (Cinzio 107-109; Roaf I-LI). Constructed according to those laws of Aristotle that explain *Oedipus* (Roaf XLVIII, n. 43), the *Canace* pays homage to Sophocles' but refuses to imitate its plot.

Anguillara does both. He takes on the great text; he takes on the problem of the two Oedipuses who act inconsistently. He does everything with the object of eliminating the contradictions in Sophocles' text and in Oedipus' character. Bombace, as already mentioned, pointed out not only the inconsistencies in *Oedipus,* but also the way in which Aristotle tried to justify them as material "outside the scenic action of the play" (*Tragedia* II 1004). Apparently alluding to the same passage in Aristotle, De Nores (*Poetica,* 1588) takes the opposite position. He attacks Anguillara based on a justification of Aristotle's theory. Aristotle says: "The irrational (*alogon*) must not be in the episodes/incidents (*pragmata*). If this can't be done, [the irrational must be kept] outside the tragedy" (*alogon de méden einai en tois pragmasin, ei de mē exso tēs tragoidias;* XV. 1454b. 10d). Aristotle, thus, distinguishes a double structure in every play: a structure of words referring to the past and a structure of acts performed in the present. The irrational (*alogon*) may exist in the verbal allusions to the past; so it is justifiable that in all his time in Thebes prior to the play's opening Oedipus had never mentioned Laius (see *Poetics,* p. 57, note d). To explain such prior matters would require material to be added to the play. De Nores, in his criticism of Anguillara, points out that verisimilitude demands that the episodes (*pragmata*) in a play be "few" and "necessary." Like "too many feet," too many episodes impede rather than improve movement (18 verso). According to De Nores, the episodes Anguillara added to Sophocles' *Oedipus* are "beside the point," violate "decorum," are "unnecessary" and "superfluous" (18 verso-19 recto).

For example, Anguillara reconciles events prior to the play's opening with each other and with those in the play. Polibo, whose wife is barren, prepares in advance for a foundling to be accepted as legitimate by having his wife feign pregnancy. Thus Edippo leaves Corinth not because he is accused of bastardy and doubts his parentage but because he wishes to know his future. Motivated by doubt, Sophocles' Oedipus goes to Delphi not to learn his future but to recover his past. Leaving Delphi still in doubt, Sophocles' Oedipus nevertheless acts as if he is sure of the identity of his parents by shunning Corinth. Edippo acts logically. After hearing the oracle, he refuses to return to Corinth because he is sure of his parentage, sure that he can control his future, sure that he will subvert the prophecy that he will kill his father and marry his mother.

The way Anguillara repairs what he must have thought as the illogic of Sophocles' text is apparent in the handling of Edippo's knowledge of his past as a prelude to his investigation of Laio's death. In spite of all his years in Thebes, Sophocles' Oedipus is strangely ignorant of the facts of Laius' death until he begins his relentless inquiry. Edippo knows everything; he talked many times about it. He knows when and how Laio was killed. Only one detail he does not know: where the murder took place, a detail that we may forgive anyone for overlooking. But at the end of every correction a new error pops up. Knowing the facts, why had Edippo never done anything? Every age seems to negotiate a path between tolerable and intolerable irrationalities.

Anguillara, like commentators today (Goodhardt; Ahl), noticed that the case Oedipus builds against himself is not reasonably strong. Therefore, Anguillara piles up so many clues to prove that Edippo killed Laio that all doubt vanishes. Not only are all the numbers correct: time, place, and witnesses, but new details are added. Edippo accepts that he has killed Laio only because the Theban shepherd, Forbante, proves he is a reliable witness by even more physical evidence, a distinctive wound on his head and distinctive words at the scene of the killing that Edippo recognizes. But it is a final clue that confirms his belief: at the time of the killing, Laio wore "a red cloak all adorned in gold and embroidery" (un manto rosso / Tutto guarnito d'oro, e di ricami; Act III, Sc. 2, 29 verso-30 recto). Discovery (anagnorisis) is a matter of purely physical evidence. Guilt is detached from a personal judgment of responsibility. Investigatory objectivity and expository balance are deemed the essence of rationality.

Irrational unbalance is an expository technique in Sophocles. While the murder investigation is in the foreground, incest floats in the background. As the one investigation turns into the other, many details of the first are left unanswered and of the second unasked. In Anguillara, the murder and the incest run along parallel but separate tracts. First, he establishes a history of familial love and simultaneously a mechanism to prevent its eruption into its opposite—incest and rivalry. Next he arranges a curse on incest to preface the curse on regicide. To introduce the incest, he carefully builds a family structure marked by compassion and love. Edippo flees Corinth when he is close to twenty. This allows Anguillara to stress Edippo's loving relationship to his supposed parents as well as the age difference between him and his wife, who is sixty when the play begins. Edippo has been loved by his Corinthian parents, has had a full childhood, has felt safe and sound in Corinth. As he has been loved, Edippo loves his own children, who when the play opens are old enough to rule and to marry, old enough to have a history of his guiding and protecting them. Anguillara was surely influenced in the matter of age by Euripides' *Phoenissae* and Statius' *Thebaid* and the medieval Oedipus *romans*. Sophocles hardly mentions age at all. When Oedipus talks about parents and family, he speaks about them in terms of unfulfilled desire. The "sweetest" (*hēdiston*) sight of all must be to see "the faces" (*ommata*) of one's parents (999), he conjectures.

Surely one of the episodes De Nores found "superfluous" is what may be called "the contracts scene" (Act I, Sc. 2): a scene that demonstrates Edippo's deep love for his children and his apprehension of the danger of familial love. Assuming that he controls two kingdoms, one that he will inherit (Corinth) and one that he has conquered (Thebes), Edippo draws up an elaborate contract in which one city is given to Polinice and the other to Eteocle. He then assures the future of his daughters, contracting each to a noble marriage. To a great extent any rivalry or jealousy within the family is prevented by these contracts before it begins. But is the attempt to block out such future conflicts a mark of their strength? Incest and civic rebellion, Edippo tells his children, are tied together, a connection found in every work on Oedipus from Statius' *Thebaid* to Lydgate's *Siege of Thebes,* from Silvestrius (76) to the works of the Medieval mythographers (Anderson 121-125). And thus, within this civic context, Edippo issues his first curse: "May God send his anger and vengeance / Against anyone who with his own flesh / Tries to vent his lasciviousness; / Let him live in misery, a beggar. / Deprived of light, and suffer / Every anguish, either in prison or in exile" (Act I, Sc. 2, 7 recto). Incest becomes a part of the foreground of Anguillara's play; it is tied not only to the prediction given to Laio and Edippo but paralleled to the later oracle about the cause of the plague (Act II, Sc. 3).

Thus Anguillara's Edippo issues a double curse, one against incest that balances the one against the murderer. Sophocles' curse is directed only against the murderer. Nor is incest, apparently, introduced as the cause of the plague in Sophocles, while in Anguillara the cause is linked both to murder and to incest. Nowhere is Sophocles' use of misdirection that leads to misinterpretation better seen than in the wording of the oracle about the plague's cause. To understand the Apollonian oracle in Sophocles, one is forced to devise a theory to put its clues together. Indeed, it is not very clear which words belong to the god and which to Creon (Bollack II. 59; Ahl 59). In a rather off-hand manner, Creon says:

> I'd like to say what I heard from the god.
> Phoibos, the king, clearly (*emphanōs*) commands us
> To drive out (*elaunein*) the *miasma* nourishing the
>   land,
> And not to nourish the incurable.
>
> (95-98)

Does the word "clearly" (*emphanōs*) refer to the manner of the command or to its content? Does it mean that Apollo commands openly or "unambiguously" (Kamerbeek 48)? The cause of the plague is not named. What or who should be driven out is not named. Are the words that follow Apollo's or Creon's interpretation of them?

> Driving out the man (*andrēlatountas*), or
>   for blood spilled paying back with spilled blood,
> For it is blood that has turned the city into a wintry
>   place.
>
>   (100-101)

The words "driving out the man" (*andrēlatountas*) are syntactically connected to Phoibos' commands in Creon's earlier report of the oracle (Kamerbeek 48). But are they logically connected? Creon's "driving out the man" is an exact parallel to Apollo's words "driving out . . . the *miasma*" (*elaunein*). Has Creon substituted his word "man" for the god's word "miasma"? Nowhere is the incest explicitly mentioned, for it is unclear whether *miasma*, which is almost always associated with a dead body (Parker 128-132), may ever be connected with incest (Parker 97; Oudemans 48, 50-51, 128).

All this is changed in Anguillara. His oracle is perfectly clear:

> These are Apollo's own remarks:
> An infamous foreigner (*peregrino*) inhabits Thebes,
> Who is not a foreigner, in fact he's Theban,
> But believes he's a foreigner, and all believe the
>   same of him.
> He's already killed Laius, King of Thebes,
> To whom he's closely tied by blood;
> And he does now, and has done even greater evil.
>
>   (Act II. Sc. 3, 14 recto)

One person committed the crime; that person is a Theban who thinks he is a stranger; he is a relative of the dead king; he has committed an even greater evil than regicide: clearly incest.

Incest, incorporated into a family structure filled with love, provokes constant talk of rivalry and jealousy. Edippo labels his Corinthian father "rival." He did not go back to Corinth "because the oracle had already predicted / That I must be . . . / . . . adulterer and rival to my father" (. . . perché già l'oracol mi predisse, / Ch'io . . . dovea . . . / di mio padre farmi / Adultero, e rival . . ."; Act III, Sc. 4, 35 recto). The accusation of adultery and rivalry is repeated over and over again in the text (e.g., Act 5, Sc. 2, 58 recto). In fact, all along Giocasta and Edippo have lived aware that their relationship is symbolically incestuous. After the discovery that Edippo has killed Laio, but before the discovery of the incest, Giocasta calls Edippo "son." To his question about why she calls him son rather than husband, Giocasta says: "Edippo, because I am much older than you / I may still call you son" (Edippo, per l'età c'haggio maggiore, / Di voi, posso figliuol chiamarvi anchora; Act III, Sc. 4, 36 recto). Edippo responds: "Out of the same kind of respect I have always / Treated you with the reverence I would have for a mother" (Per lo stesso rispetto anch'io v'ho sempre / Portato riverentia come a madre; 36 recto).

Creating a close family structure for Edippo forced Anguillara to psychologize its internal mechanism. Every family member's action dovetails with an appropriate motivation. And motives conform to rules of verisimilitude and decorum: fidelity to ordinary reality and popular manners. The blinding scene demonstrates this. In Sophocles, blinding is epistemological, tied to the question of how we know; in Anguillara, it is psychological, tied to the question of why we feel.

Anguillara, following Euripides, Seneca, and Statius, times Edippo's blinding prior to Giocasta's suicide. Sophocles alone orders the blinding after it, transforming it from an act of simple self-punishment to a stage in the discovery of truth. Knowing is a function of memory and so is action. If our memories are fantasies, how can we act intelligently? There are indeed two Oedipuses: the fictitious character created by circumstance and coincidence, and the real person created by "mis-memory" and misunderstanding. Oedipus acts foolishly because he thinks he is someone other than who he is. With eyes dependent on fiction, he failed to recognize a distinction most fundamental to self-knowledge: the meaning of his origin. But without eyes, and with memory re-formed, he sees in a new way. Does he now see the "real" Oedipus? His words at the scene of the blinding force us to consider the question of knowing:

> Because they [his eyes] did not see either
> the things (*outh'*) I suffered or the evil
> things (*outh'*) I did, but in darkness the
> remaining time, seeing the things (*ous*)
> that I wished not to see and seeing the
> things (*ous*) I wished to see but did not know.
>
>   (1271-1274)

To what does he refer by the paralleled set of four unidentified "things"? Do the first two refer to his past? Do the things he suffered refer to his exposition as a baby and the evil oracle he was given? Do the things he did refer to his patricide and incest? Does the third thing, the thing he wished not to see, refer to the future of his incestuous children? And finally does the fourth thing refer to his present, to his desire to have seen and to have known as a child his biological parents? Perhaps these "things," the particles (*outh'* . . . *outh'*, *ous* . . . *ous*), ought not to be taken as literally as they are here (Parry 269) or as Bassi does in his edition of the Greek text (129, note to ll. 1271-1273). We are misled by such traps and almost cannot prevent ourselves from falling into them. But to misunderstand is to enter the world of Oedipus and into the possibility of discovering error and therefore of realizing truth.

Anguillara avoids the traps. He concentrates on the psychological impact of the blinding, on the shock of learning that his loving Corinthian parents were not his real parents, on the guilt of discovering that the wife with whom he lived as if she were a mother and who treated him like a son was indeed his mother. Finding Giocasta screaming in their bedroom, he says to her: "Mother, wife, turn to me / Your eyes, and look at your son and husband / And you will see what penalty (*pena*) he has chosen / To punish himself (*punirsi*) for his sin" (Act IV, Sc. 1, 44 recto). Horror and passion dominate the description of the scene. Oedipus displays bloodied eyes to Giocasta. Timing his blinding before her suicide gives him the opportunity to act as if he were a child asking for approval or at least for acknowledgment that what he has done is right. The Edippo who closes the play is the same Edippo who opened it, except that he is in possession of a few more facts—however pertinent. His emotional and instinctual ties to Giocasta are as powerful as before he knew the truth. He still loves her. Everything in the scene highlights the deep-rooted ties of love that exist among family members. Edippo kisses Antigone and bloodies her face. Ismene runs for bandages to bind Edippo's bloodied eyes. Blood, tears, and screams replace the contracts at the beginning of the play that were meant to bring about calm and to achieve peaceful social and familial relationships. Edippo's reasonable concern and love for his children is mirrored in the logic of such legal devices. But the more Edippo tries to construct a logical world, the more Anguillara tries to find fitting reasons for action, the more reason fails and the unruly passions are released. The *Edippo* reflects the logic of Freud's version of the family drama more than anything we find in Sophocles.

What is really a minor play, rather melodramatic and unpoetic, pinpoints a Renaissance tendency: in spite of its reverence for the ancients, the Renaissance destroyed their myths in trying to understand them.

Notes

1. I believe that the earlier printed editions mentioned in the literature are all in error: 1556 (Mazzuchelli, Vol. I, Pt. 2, 789-790; Paitoni IV 60; Ginguené; Mutini); 1554 (Bárberi-Squarotti, who in a letter to me disavows this date); 1560 (Bosisio 80).

2. For example, see Alessandro Pazzi de' Medici, *Edipo principe,* 1526, existing only in MS (Neri 51, note 2, and 189; *Inventari* IV 225, No. 372; Quadrio IV 103); Guido Guidi, *Oedipus,* 1532 (Bolgar 525, listed without date); Bernardo Segni (d. 1559), *Edipo principe* (Quadrio IV 103), not printed until 1778 (Neri 96, note 1); Pietro Angelii Bargeo, *Edipo tiranno,* printed in 1589 (Quadrio IV 103; Schaaber 481).

Works Cited

Ahl, Frederick. *Sophocles' Oedipus: Evidence and Self-Conviction.* Ithaca, N.Y.: Cornell UP, 1991.

Anderson, David. "Mythography or Historiography? The Interpretation of Theban Myths in Late Medieval Literature." *Florilegium* 8 (1986): 113-139.

Anecdota Litteraria Ex MSS Codicibus Eruta . . . Vol. I. Rome: Apud A. Fulgonium, 1773-1783. 4 vols.

Angiolgabriello di Santa Maria, Padre. *Biblioteca e storia di quegli scrittori così della città come del territorio di Vicenza che pervennero fin'ad ora a notizia.* Vol. 4. Vicenza: C. B. Vendrammi Mosca, 1772-1792. 4 vols.

Anguillara, Giovanni Andrea Dell'. "Canzone a Catterina de' Medici, Reina di Francia." *Anecdota* I 427-439.

———. "Canzone di M. Gio: Andrea Alias Del Gobbo da Sutri." Pelaez 120-124.

———. "Capitolo al Cardinale di Trento." *Opere Burlesche* 294-303.

———. "Capitolo al Cardinale Farnese." Pelaez 107-110.

———. "Capitolo: Nella Sedia Vacante al Papa Futuro." Pelaez 110-117.

———. "Capitolo Delle Mosche." Pelaez 117-119.

———. *Edippo. Tragedia.* Padua: Per L. Pasquatto, 1565.

———. "Lettera al Duca Cosimo." Venice. 22 May 1563. With a note by C. Guasti. *Giornale Storico degli Archivi Toscani.* II (1858): 241-245.

———. "Lettera alla Signoria di Venezia." Received before 18 Sept. 1551. Rossi 435.

———. "Lettera al Francesco Bolognetti." Rome, 22 May 1566. *Anecdota* I. 407-408.

———. "Lettera al Francesco Bolognetti." Rome, 22 June 1566. *Anecdota* I. 427-439.

———. "Lettera al Benedetto Varchi." Lyon, 6 June 1560. Pelaez 106.

———. "Lettera al Benedetto Varchi." Venice, 13 June 1561. Pelaez 107.

———. *Prologo alla "Sofonisba" di Giangiorgio Trissino (1562).* Vicenza: G. Burato, 1879.

———. "Sonetto a Carlo IX." *Anecdota* I. 440.

———. "Sonetto al Cardinale di Trento." *Anecdota* I. 442.

———. "Sonetto al Medesimo Cardinale di Trento." *Anecdota* I. 442.

———. "Stanze per lo Natale di Monsignor Lo Duca di Angiov." *Delizie delli Eruditi Bibliofili Italiani.* Quarta Pubblicazione. Florence: Giacomo Molini, 1864.

Aristotle. *The Poetics.* Ed. W. Hamilton Fyfe. Loeb Classical Library. 1927. Cambridge, Mass.: Harvard UP, 1982.

Bárberi-Squarotti, Giorgio. "Anguillara." *Grande dizionario enciclopedico.* 1955 ed.

Bloom, Harold. *The Anxiety of Influence: A Theory of Poetry.* New York: Oxford UP, 1973.

Bolgar, R. R. *The Classical Heritage and Its Beneficiaries.* 1954. Cambridge: Cambridge UP, 1977.

Bollack, Jean. *L'Oedipe Roi de Sophocle.* Vol. 2. Lille: Presses Universitaires de Lille, 1990. 4 vols.

Bosisio, Paolo. "Il tema di Edipo nella tradizione della tragedia italiana." *Edipo in Francia.* Biblioteca dell'Archivum Romanicum, Series 1, Vol. 226: Studi di Letteratura Francese XV. Florence: Olschki, 1989. 78-122.

Castellini, Silvestro. *Storia della città di Vicenza . . . dall' origine . . . sino all'anno 1630.* Venice: F. V. Mosca, 1783-1822. Vol. XVIII. 90-91.

Cinzio, Giambattista Giraldi. *Il giudizio sopra la tragedia di Canace e Macareo.* Speroni 95-182.

Corrigan, Beatrice. "Two Renaissance Views of Carthage: Trissino's *Sofonisba* and Castellani's *Astrubale.*" *Comparative Drama* 5 (1971): 193-206.

Crescimbeni, Giovanni Mario. *Istoria della volgar poesia.* Vol. I, Lib. 4. Venice: Lorenzo Basegio, 1781.

Dainard, J. A. "A Seventeenth-Century French Translation of *Il Re Torrismondo.*" *Rivista di Studi Italiani* III. 1 (June 1985): 44-70.

De Nores, Iason. *Poetica.* Padua: Paulo Maietto, 1588.

D'Ovidio, Francesco. *Saggi critici.* Naples: Domenico Morano, 1878.

Euripides. *Phoenician Maidens.* Ed. Arthur S. Way. Loeb Classical Library. 1912. London: Heinemann, 1925.

Fiocco, Giuseppe. "Il Teatro di Alvise Cornaro." *Atti del convegno sul tema: Il teatro classico italiano nel '500 (Roma, 9-12 febbraio 1969).* Rome: Accademia Nazionale dei Lincei, 1971. 141-146.

Fontanini, Giusto. *Biblioteca dell'eloquenza italiana . . . con le annotazioni del Signor Apostolo Zeno.* 2 vols. Venice: G. Pasquali, 1753.

Gallo, Alberto. *La prima rappresentazione al Teatro Olimpico, con i progetti e le relazioni dei contemporanei.* Milan: Edizioni Il Polifilo, 1973.

Ginguené, P. L. "Anguillara." *Biografia universale antica e moderna.* 1811. Rev. ed. Venice, 1822: II 411-412.

Goodhardt, Sandor. "Lēistas Ephaske: Oedipus and Laius' Many Murderers." *Diacritics.* 8.1 (Spring 1978): 55-71.

Greene, T. *The Light in Troy: Imitation and Discovery in Renaissance Poetry.* New Haven: Yale UP, 1982.

Herrick, Marvin T. *Italian Tragedy in the Renaissance.* Urbana: University of Illinois, 1965.

"Idea del teatro. Schede iconografiche." *Il teatro italiano nel rinascimento.* Ed. Fabrizio Cruciani e Daniele Seragnoli. Bologna: Il Mulino, 1987. 199-224.

Ingegneri, Angelo. *Della poesia rappresentativa e del modo di rappresentare le favole sceniche* (1598). Ed. Maria Luisa Doglio. Ferrara: Edizioni Panini, 1989.

Inventari dei manoscritti delle biblioteche d'Italia. Vol. 4. Florence: Olschki, 1890-98 vols. to date.

Kamerbeek, J. C. *The Plays of Sophocles: Commentaries. Part IV: The Oedipus Tyrannus.* Leiden: Brill, 1967.

Lorini, Giulio. "Per la biografia di G. A. Dell'Anguillara." *Giornale storico della letteratura italiana.* CVI. 316-317 (1935): 81-93.

Lydgate, John. *Siege of Thebes.* Ed. Axel Erdmann and Eilert Ekwall. 2 vols. 1911-1930. Millwood, New York: Kraus Reprint, 1981.

Mazzuchelli, Conte Gianmaria. *Gli scrittori d'Italia, cioè notizie storiche e critiche intorno alle vite, e agli scritti dei letterati italiani.* Vol. I, Pt. 2. Brescia: Giambattista Bossini, 1758.

Melczer, William. "Towards the Dignification of the Vulgar Tongues: Humanistic Translations into Italian and Spanish in the Renaissance." *Canadian Review of Comparative Literature* 8.2 (Spring 1981): 256-271.

Mutini, Claudio. "Anguillara." *Dizionario biografico degli italiani.* Rome: Istituto della Enciclopedia Italiana, 1961.

Negri, Girolamo. *Hieronymi Nigri . . . Epistolae et Orationes.* Sadoleto 119-121.

Neri, Ferdinando. *La tragedia italiana.* 1904. Turin: Bottega d'Erasmo, 1971.

Norton, Glyn P. "Humanist Foundations of Translation Theory (1400-1450): A Study in the Dynamics of Word." *Canadian Review of Comparative Literature.* 8.2 (Spring 1981): 173-203.

Opere burlesche. Vol. 2. In Usecht al Reno (Venice): Jacopo Broedelet, 1771. 3 vols.

Oudemans, Th. C. W. and A. P. M. H. Lardinois. *Tragic Ambiguity: Anthropology, Philosophy and Sophocles' "Antigone."* Leiden: Brill, 1987.

Paitoni, Jacopomaria. *Biblioteca degli autori antichi greci e latini volgarizzati, che abbraccia la notizia delle loro edizioni: nella quale si esamina particolarmente quanto ne hanno scritto i celebri Maffei, Fontanini, Zeno, ed Argelati* (sic). Venice: S. Occhi, stamp., 1766-1767.

Parker, Robert. *Miasma: Pollution and Purification in Early Greek Religion.* Oxford: Clarendon Press, 1985.

Parry, Adam, "Sophocles, *Oedipus Rex,* 1271-1274." *Classical Quarterly.* n.s. 10.2 (Nov. 1960): 268-270.

Pelaez, M. "La vita e le opere di Giovanni Andrea Dell'Anguillara," *Il Propugnatore.* n.s. 4.1 (1891): 40-124.

Perella, Nicolas. "Fate, Blindness and Illusion in the *Pastor Fido.*" *Romantic Review* XLIX (1958): 252-268.

Puppi, Leonello. "Gli spettacoli all'Olimpico di Vicenza dal 1585 all'inizio del'600." *Studi sul teatro veneto fra rinascimento ed età barocca.* Ed. Maria Teresa Muraro. Florence: Olschki, 1971.

Quadrio, Francesco Saverio. *Della storia, e della ragione d'ogni poesia.* Vol. III, Libro I. Milan: Francesco Angelli, 1743.

Roaf, Christina. "Introduzione." Speroni, *Canace*. XIII-LXI.

Rossi, Vittorio. "Nuovi documenti su Giovanni Andrea Dell'Anguillara." *Giornale storico della letteratura italiana*. XVIII. 54 (1981): 435-438.

Sadoleto, Jacopo. *Jacobi Sadoleti Epistolarum Appendix, Accedunt Hieronymi Nigri et Pauli Sadoleti . . .* Ed. Vincenzo Alessandro Constanzi. Rome: G. Salomonius, 1767.

Schrade, Leo. *La représentation d'Edippo Tiranno au Teatro Olimpico (Vicence 1585).* Paris: Éditions du Centre National de la Recherche Scientifique, 1960.

Seneca. *Oedipus. Tragedies.* Ed. F. J. Miller. Vol. I. Loeb Classical Library. 1917. Cambridge, Mass.: Harvard UP, 1960. 2 vols.

Shaaber, M. A. *Sixteenth-century Imprints in the Libraries of the University of Pennsylvania.* Philadelphia: University of Pennsylvania Press, 1976.

Silvestris, Bernardus. *The Cosmographia.* Trans. Winthrop Wetherbee. New York: Columbia UP, 1973.

Sophocles. *Oedipus the King.* Ed. F. Storr. Loeb Classical Library. 1912. Cambridge, Mass.: Harvard UP, 1981.

———. *Edipo Re.* ΟΙΔΙΠΟΥΣ. Intro. e Commento di Domenico Bassi. Milan: Signorelli, 1977.

Speroni, Sperone. *Canace e scritti in sua difesa,* and Giambattista Giraldi Cinzio. *Scritti contro la "Canace," Giudizio ed Epistola latina.* Ed. Christina Roaf. Bologna: Commissione per i Testi di Lingua, 1982.

Statius. *Thebaid.* Ed. J. H. Mozley. 2 vols. Loeb Classical Library. 1928. Cambridge, Mass.: Harvard UP, 1961.

Symonds, John Addington. *The Renaissance in Italy.* 2 vols. New York: Modern Library, 1935.

Temanza, Tommaso. *Vita di Andrea Palladio Vicentino.* Venice: Giambattista Pasquali, 1767.

Tiraboschi, Girolamo. *Storia della letteratura italiana.* Vol. VII. 3. 1772. Florence: Molini, Landi, 1805-1813. 9 vols. in 20.

La tragedia del cinquecento. Ed. Marco Ariani. Turin: Einaudi, 1977. Vol. II. Part 2 of *Il teatro italiano.* 6 vols. to date. 1975-.

Vellacott, Philip. *Sophocles and Oedipus: A Study of "Oedipus Tyrannus" with a New Translation.* London: Macmillan, 1971.

Weinberg, Bernard. *A History of Literary Criticism in the Italian Renaissance.* 2 vols. Chicago: University of Chicago Press, 1961.

Charles Segal (essay date 1995)

SOURCE: "Time and Knowledge in the Tragedy of Oedipus," in *Sophocles's Tragic World: Divinity, Nature, Society,* Harvard University Press, 1995, pp. 138-60.

[*In the following excerpt, Segal discusses how indefinite descriptions of time in* Oedipus Tyrannus *are part of what obscures the identity of Laius's killer.*]

The story of Oedipus is the archetypal myth of personal identity in Western culture. It is the myth par excellence of self-knowledge, of human power and human weakness, of the determining forces of the accidents of birth that we can neither change nor escape. Its concerns are the interplay of supreme rationality and supreme ignorance, control and aggression in the human personality, and the relation of individual existence to order or chaos, meaning or meaninglessness in the world as we experience it and interpret it. Oedipus is a kind of black fairy tale; but, as Vladimir Nabokov remarks a propos of another fiction about self-discovery and self-deception, "Without these fairy tales the world would not be real."[1]

For the modern interpretation of the Oedipus myth three models have been the most influential. They are Nietzsche's proto-existentialist view, Freud's psychoanalytic reading, and Claude Lévi-Strauss's structuralist approach.[2] As the last is not concerned directly with the problem of knowledge or with a knowing subject, it is only incidental to my theme, and I shall here be concerned mostly with the Nietzschean and Freudian readings.

The existentialist interpretation of Oedipus in Nietzsche's *Birth of Tragedy,* whose influence can be traced in varying degrees in the work of Karl Reinhardt, Cedric Whitman, Bernard Knox, and R. P. Winnington-Ingram, sees in Sophocles' hero man alienated from the rest of nature and therefore cut off from his intellectual power, which probes nature's secrets and would wrench from nature even the secret of his place in nature. What Nietzsche distinguishes as the triple fate of Oedipus—answering the Sphinx's riddle, killing his father, and marrying his mother—marks the unnaturalness of this terrible wisdom. It is a look into the abyss from which, however, the tragic poet comes away with the "luminous after-image" that is the "metaphysical solace" of tragedy. This Oedipus is an anomaly, a monster. His "extreme unnaturalness" is symbolized by the incestuous union, a form of resisting nature, forcing her to "yield up her secrets." To seek such wisdom is itself "to break the consecrated tables of the natural order" and to experience the disintegration of nature in himself.[3] Oedipus, in this view, combines in himself the poles of the monstrous and the exemplary, a *unio oppositorum* parallel to his combination of intellectual power and ignorance.[4]

In Freud's reading this ambiguity of knowledge lies in the contrast between the hero's intellectual feats and a kind of "knowledge" that has become ignorance through the force of repression. The hidden violence in the past is not the accidental, unique event of an accursed family, but the aggressive and sexual drives of the libido in the deepest, oldest, and most intractable parts of our mental life. The necessity given in the oracle that Oedipus will marry his mother and murder his father is the "fate" or "destiny" to which each of us is subject in the repressed desires of the unconscious.[5] Freud's emphasis on the unbreakable chain of events that includes the incest and the parricide is true to the quiet objectivity of the oracle, which in Sophocles is merely a descriptive statement of what will happen, not, as in Aeschylus, a warning to Laius about the consequences of disobeying the oracle (*Seven against Thebes* 742-749).[6]

For Freud the fascination of the play lies in its unveiling of the impulses of our earliest childhood, repressed but still alive as archaic residues, and often troubling ones, in our unconscious. When the Corinthian Messenger tells Oedipus that Polybus and Merope are not his parents, he sets him free to explore his repressed knowledge of darker origins. In place of Polybus and Merope, whose names he knows, Oedipus discovers the parents whose names he does not yet (consciously) know, the father he killed and the mother he married. The guilt that we carry with us for having wished, and thus, in the uncompromising judgment of the superego, having performed those terrible crimes, is acted out, made visible, and expiated by the suffering of Oedipus. This suffering is a retribution that (as George Devereux and others have argued) strikes at the root of the crime by the symbolic substitution of eyes for phallus: the self-blinding is a symbolic self-castration, the fitting punishment for one who has used his sexual organ in the outrageous crime of intercourse with his mother.[7]

The fact that the Sophoclean Oedipus does not have an "oedipus complex" because he has never known his true mother or because his greatest desire is to avoid his mother and father, as some antipsychological interpreters have objected, does not invalidate the Freudian reading of the relation between conscious and unconscious knowledge in the *Tyrannus*. Jean-Pierre Vernant and others are right to point out that the psychological aspect of the myth so fully developed by later playwrights from Dryden to Cocteau receives little emphasis in Sophocles' work.[8] For a fully psychological rendering of the myth in antiquity we have to wait for Seneca. Yet Freud was by no means wrong to trace his reading of the myth to Sophocles. Whatever the *Tyrannus* may or may not reveal about the emotional life of its protagonist, the play remains valid and important for its presentation of a model of knowledge that Freud applied to the unconscious: a paradoxical kind of knowledge that at every point coexists with ignorance.

Jacques Lacan's rereading of Freud, with a stronger emphasis on the place of language in the blockage between conscious and unconscious knowledge, bypasses some of the objections to psychoanalyzing Oedipus as if he were a neurotic individual. On a Lacanian reading, the play constitutes a Discourse of the Other speaking as the hidden self from which Oedipus is irremediably alienated.[9] This is a part of himself whose language he will not allow himself to understand. The so-called ambiguity or "tragic irony" of Sophocles' double and triple meanings, therefore, serves as a model of the "intransitive" or "noncommunicating language" of the unconscious (to adopt the terms of Francesco Orlando). This is a language that conceals as much as it reveals, masks as well as unveils knowledge.[10] This language, thickened around the signifier rather than transparent to the signified, is both the medium and the condition of Oedipus' alienation from himself. It is a language that both contains and withholds; and the

knowledge in its realm is a knowledge that Oedipus cannot permit himself to know.

Sophocles makes the ambiguity of language impinge inescapably on the ambiguity of personal identity. In the play language and kinship function as parallel modes of situating oneself in the world and so of knowing who one is. To know the truth of what we are, we need to understand the discourse through which we create ourselves. We construct ourselves through our language about ourselves.

The mental order that language gives us about ourselves, however, cannot be separated from the mental order that it imposes on the world around us, and vice versa. For this relation between language and coherence that we find, or make, in our world, Lévi-Strauss' refocusing of the myth on logical classification—excess and deficiency in treating kin and nonkin, born from one and born from two, autochthony and incest—makes an important contribution.[11] By combining the verbal fusions of the riddle with the generational fusions of incest, Sophocles brings together language and personal identity as obverse and reverse of a single entity, man as a being in time and man as a maker of meanings, a user of language. Language, like Oedipus himself, becomes both exemplary and irregular. Oedipus is both the paradigm of man and the monster, the anomaly. He comprehends (in both senses) the essence of human identity by answering the Sphinx's riddle—what goes on four, two, and three feet at changing periods of strength and weakness; but he is the exception to his own formulation of the answer, for his own feet were "yoked" at birth (*Oedipus* 718), made one from two, because of the prediction that he would occupy two generations at the same time; and so he was never to progress on the path of life at all. The man who has solved the riddle of stability and progression that defines identity in time is ignorant of the coincident planes of diachrony and synchrony in his own life pattern.

The (con)fusion of kin terms in incest generates the (con)fusion of differences in language. Oedipus' very name, the primary word of the language of the self, incessantly confuses meanings instead of distinguishing the oneness of individuality made possible in human society. As Know-Foot (*oida, pous*), he is the exemplary hero of the victory of language and intelligence over the demonic monstrosity of the Sphinx. But Oedipus Swell-Foot (*oidein, pous*) or Oedipus Know-Where (*oida pou*) is exemplary of man's helplessness, despite his intellectual victories, before the greater mystery of who he "really" is and what violence his origins, maturation, and attainment of power may contain.[12]

For Freud that violence points to something below the level of conscious knowledge. The past is not a specific family curse but the expression of universally existing archaic strata in the self. For Nietzsche that violence is itself the intellectual power by which man asserts his dominion over nature. For ritualists like René Girard, it is the means by which a necessary social mechanism can be set into motion. The implications of Sophocles' play make all such universalizing extrapolations possible. The *Tyrannus* remains a founding text in European culture. It is one of the most revealing documents of Western man's determination to define self-knowledge in intellectual and rational terms, and one of the most powerful statements of the limitations of the enterprise.

Modern classical scholars, whether their orientation is philosophical like Karl Reinhardt, or linguistic like Bernard Knox, or anthropological like Jean-Pierre Vernant, often see their task as salvaging the historical specificity of the play from such universalizing interpretations. Like the *Oresteia* or *Hamlet,* however, the *Oedipus* will always be torn between the historicists and the universalizers. Each side needs to rescue the work from the other; and the play, like every such great work, needs so to be rescued, from both and either.

. . . . .

From Aristotle to Lévi-Strauss interpreters have analyzed the structure of *Oedipus Tyrannus* and admired the orderliness of the mental world which that structure exemplifies. Others have emphasized the contrast between the formal beauty of the play's logical design and the frightening role of chance and necessity in its contents. This division may be compared to (although it does not fully coincide with) that between the pious serenity that some have found in Sophocles and the deep questioning of all meaning seen by others. If we join the two sides in a dialectical rather than a disjunctive relation, we may be able to grasp better how the *Oedipus Tyrannus,* perhaps more than any other work of antiquity, forces us to consider both the order-imposing power of art and the arbitrariness of that imposition.

Put in other terms, this play is also about the origins of its own writing, that is, about the modes of representation through which the work of art imposes order upon experience in such a way that the disorder always remains a part of the order. This relation forms a Heraclitean *palintonos harmonia,* a "back-stretched fitting together," of opposites held in place by their reciprocal and counterbalancing tensions, "as in a bow or a lyre." The very perfection of the formal design of the plot sets off the disturbing imperfection of the world that the plot creates.

One attribute of tragic drama as developed by the Greeks is the fact that it inscribes into this very perfection of the form the destructive potential that dissolves the order back into chaos. Hence such tragedy calls attention to its own paradox, the paradox of its pleasurable pain. Like many great tragedies of reversal, from the *Bacchae* to *Hamlet,* the *Oedipus* is also "metatragedy," tragedy about tragedy. The proportional relation between tragedy and metatragedy, however, differs from the ancient to the modern author. Whereas Shakespeare or Pirandello uses the awareness of illusion to explore theatricality—the "wooden O" that holds "the vasty fields of France"—Sophocles uses

theatricality to explore the moral, religious, and metaphysical questions raised by the suffering of Oedipus.[13]

In chapter 14 of the *Poetics* Aristotle cites the story of Oedipus as an example of pity and fear that result not from the spectacle, from the stage effects, but from the composition of the plot, the way events are made to "stand together," *sunestanai.* Later in the chapter, in giving examples of such plots, Aristotle mentions two criteria: first, the terrifying or pitiable events should occur within the family; and, second, knowledge should be involved.[14] Subdividing the latter category, he observes that the terrifying or pitiable acts may be performed with knowledge or in ignorance, but the best action for tragedy occurs in ignorance followed by knowledge or recognition as in the *Tyrannus.*[15] In linking knowledge and terror, Aristotle puts his finger on an important element in the dynamics of the Oedipus plot. But these dynamics involve other elements that Aristotle's brief sketch does not include, particularly time and theatricality. By the latter I mean the self-consciousness of the play as a theatrical spectacle. This self-consciousness is a part of the texture and textuality of the work, inherent in the composition of the events, and is to be distinguished from the "external" effects of staging and scenery, what Aristotle calls *opsis.*

The *Oedipus* is a play about revealing the potential horror beneath the surface beauty of life, as of art. Oedipus' very person, the body of the king, is emblematic of this division between surface appearance and reality. Near the end he addresses Polybus and Corinth, "in name [*logōi*] the ancient home of (his) fathers," who have "nurtured me as a thing of beauty [*kallos*] with evils beneath the scars" (1395-96). When the chorus declares, "Here is Oedipus" (1297; cf. 1524), it calls attention to the play's theatricality, the act of parading forth on the stage a figure who is a paradigm of irrational suffering and malignant eventuality in human life. At the moment of discovery of the terrible truth beneath the surface, the chorus explicitly calls Oedipus an "example," *paradeigma,* of deceptive "seeming" and of the precariousness of happiness (1189-94). "In the present circumstances," the chorus says, "who is more wretched to hear about?" (1204).

"O you who hold the greatest honor in this land," the Messenger goes on after the choral ode, "such deeds will you *hear* and such will you *see,* and such grief will you gain, if in noble fashion you still feel concern for the Labdacid house" (1223-26).[16] The words are almost a programmatic announcement of the effect of the tragic spectacle. Yet the scene they introduce, as we shall observe later, still withholds the spectacle of Oedipus from the stage.

The next scene moves the paradigmatic "hearing" of 1204 to the exemplary "seeing" proper to the theater, "the pleasure proper to tragedy," as Aristotle would say. The Messenger now describes how Oedipus, still offstage and unseen, shouts out to "open the fastenings (of the doors)" (1287-88), to show him to all the Thebans as his father's killer. This anticipation of an imminent entrance of

Oedipus upon the stage heightens the tension between the verbal and the visual mimesis of the theatrical situation. The doors then open, as the Messenger says. As he goes on to describe this scenic action, he himself echoes, now in direct discourse, the earlier quoted words of Oedipus that the bolts be opened (1294-95): "For these fastenings of the doors are being opened" (cf. 1287-88). "Soon you will see a spectacle," the Messenger continues to the chorus, "such that even the one who loathes will feel pity" (1295-96). "Soon you will see a spectacle": it is almost as if the playwright/director were telling his audience how he is utilizing the visual effects proper to his medium. The chorus, like the audience that now beholds the palace doors opening up, gives voice to the proper theatrical response, again in visual terms: "O suffering terrible for men to look upon" (1297). The chorus' exclamation over the appearance of Oedipus onstage takes up the Messenger's account of the "things terrible to see" (1267) in his long narrative. The obverse of the present spectacle, namely the blinded king with his bloodied eyes, is the unseen "spectacle" of the closed interior: "it was not possible to behold as a spectacle her (Jocasta's) suffering" (1253).

Just at the moment when Oedipus' tragic knowing becomes realized visually as a spectacle full of terror, Oedipus himself moves away from a visual experience of the world. His inarticulate cries of pain, stylized in our text as *aiai, aiai, pheu, pheu* (1307-08), crystallize into the visually disoriented state of the blind man who does not know where he is (1309). His *daimōn*, the mysterious power of "divinity" that presides over his destiny, has leapt "into a place of terror, not to be heard, not to be seen," the chorus replies. But in contrast to this conjunction of sight and hearing in the theatrical experience is Oedipus' experience of the voice alone, now a quasi-animate entity, endowed with flight (like the Sphinx).[17] In the paradoxical overlay and separation of the visible and the invisible in the revelation of tragic truth, the unique theatrical collocation of sound and sight in the representation of the myth is brought to bear on a figure who has returned to an oral culture, surrounded by presences that he knows only by voice and hearing and having only aural knowledge of the world outside himself. A hundred lines later, however, Oedipus utters the impassioned wish that he had cut off the channels of sight and hearing both: so terrible is his sense of pollution and his feeling of utter separation from his world (1375-90).[18]

. . . . .

The *Oedipus* is unusual in Greek drama in that so much of the present action is concerned with the reconstruction of past events. No other Greek play presents quite this situation to such a degree. No other Greek play so drastically calls into question the reports and narratives of minor characters. Although lies and false reports are not unexampled in Greek tragedy, there is no situation quite analogous to that of the old Herdsman, the sole witness to Laius' death. From the facts given us in the play, his story—that many robbers, not one, killed Laius—has to be a lie, even though (contrary to the usual practice of Greek

tragedy) the audience is never so informed explicitly. The elaborate lies of Lichas in *Trachiniae,* of the Paedagogus in the *Electra,* or of Neoptolemus in the *Philoctetes* are handled very differently, for they give either direct or indirect indications of the true story.[19] In the case of Laius' death, however, the falsehood in the story is itself a major theme, part of the play's concern with the problem of knowledge. The contradictions also express the tension between the theatrical time of the performance in which the unities of time and place are observed and the represented or mimetic time indicated in the background.

The *Oedipus,* like no other Greek play, dramatizes this coming together of a complex past action into a single critical moment. When a modern playwright such as Jean Cocteau in his antiheroic version, *La machine infernale,* wishes to represent this situation, he preserves (more or less) the unity of time but abandons that of place, and he adds the supernatural elements of Laius' ghost on the battlements (an ironic glance at *Hamlet*) and Oedipus' encounter with the Sphinx outside the walls of Thebes. For all our predilection for regarding the Sophoclean *Oedipus* as a tragedy of fate, in its austere form it is remarkably sparing of direct supernatural intervention. Sophocles devotes most of the action to the problem of logical deduction in the present and thereby brings into focus the problem of the play's reflection on the problem of recovering the past and therefore on its own theatricality, that is, the means by which a dramatic work creates a plausible representation of the passage of time in a whole human life. The represented time of the fictional action is arranged so as to coincide plausibly with the "real" time that elapses during the performance. And yet this "real" interval of two or three hours serves as a symbolic condensation of an entire lifetime.

Time in the play has a dynamic quality of expansion and contraction, vagueness and density. It is both the indefinite and inert passing of years and the single moment of crisis in decision and action, the irreversible turning point of a man's life. In this sense Oedipus, who in the prologue calls the day "comeasured with time" (73), is also himself "comeasured with time" (another possible meaning of the phrase in Sophocles' dense syntax) and "found out by time" (1213).[20] Oedipus' innocent-looking "comeasured with time" in the prologue will recur to describe the death of Polybus, "comeasured by great time" (963), as time's pattern is beginning to clarify around Oedipus. The phrase is then echoed a second time to clinch the identification of the Herdsman whom Oedipus "has been seeking of old" (1112), "for in his great old age he is in harmony with this man here, of equal measure" (*summetros,* 1112-13). These "measurings," however, are now indeed coming "together" (*sum-metros);* and the result will be the futility of Oedipus' attempt to escape, by means of measuring distance, what will issue forth inescapably in time (794-796): "And I, on hearing these things, measuring the land of Corinth henceforth by the stars, took flight."[21]

Instead of being defined by his "kindred months" in a slow rhythm of waxing and waning, becoming small and great (1082-83), Oedipus is defined by the abrupt catastrophe of a single day (351, 478) that makes him both "great" and "small," king and beggar, in one instant. In this respect too he answers in his own life the Sphinx's riddle about human mortality in general: man is *ephēmeros,* the creature whose life can be determined by the events of a single day.

Time can have an unexpected fullness, as in Creon's account of past events in the prologue. Here there is an indefinite interval between the death of Laius and the arrival of Oedipus to vanquish the Sphinx, an interval in which the Thebans cannot investigate the death of their king because the Sphinx compels them to consider only the immediate present, "the things at their feet, letting go the things unclear" (131). Laius' death is suddenly pushed into the category of "the things unclear" or "the invisible things" *(ta aphanē).* The expression makes this major crisis in the present life of the city retreat into the obscurity of remote happenings, far beyond living memory.

There is the same vague plenitude in the time surrounding Laius' death. Oedipus asks, "How much time before did Laius (die?)" and Creon replies (561), "Times [literally, years, *chronoi*] great and old would be measured." As in the prologue, that determining event becomes surrounded by an aura of remote, almost mythical time, as if it were an act belonging to primordial beginnings (as in one sense it indeed is) and not to a specific historical moment in the life of an individual and a city. Yet at the peripety this vagueness of temporal duration is suddenly rent by the electrifying flash of the single moment of "terrible hearing" (1169). In the relaxed seasonal tempo of herdsmen's life on Cithaeron, before Oedipus' birth, only the changes of summer and winter, without events, mark the passage of time (1132-40). Time has a wholly different aspect in the single instant of recognition that suddenly changes the entire shape of a life, revealing it now in the true perspective of an "ill-fated birth" (1181; cf. 1068).

Sophocles' skillful handling of events moves us back to origins and forward to the dark future. The present is both a recapitulation of the past and a reenactment of the past in symbolic form. Knowledge in the play results from conjoining separate events of the past in a single moment of the present. Oedipus' intelligence, Jocasta suggests, consists in "inferring the new by means of the old" (916). When Oedipus does in fact bring together the "old things" of his remote infancy and early manhood with the "new things" of his present life and circumstance, he will know himself as both king and pollution, both the savior and the destroyer of Thebes.

As Oedipus begins his "tracking" of Laius' killer (221; cf. 109), he needs a *sumbolon,* usually translated "clue." But the word also means "tally," one of two parts of a token that fit together to prove one's rightful place in (say) a law-court. The investigative skill that Oedipus will demonstrate, then, consists in fitting pieces together. But the word *sumbolon* also has another meaning, namely the

"token" left with a child exposed at birth in order to establish later proof of his identity. It has this sense in Euripides' parallel foundling tale of Ion (a kind of Oedipus story in reverse). Presented with an old basket that contains the secret of his origins, Ion hesitates to open it and examine the "tokens from his mother" (*sumbola, Ion* 1386) lest he turn out to be the child of a slave (1382-83; cf. ***Oedipus*** 1063, 1168); but he takes the risk: "I must dare," he says (*tolmēteon,* 1387). Oedipus does the same: "I must hear," he declares at his critical moment of self-discovery (*akousteon,* 1170), though with a far different result. The initially objective and public task of "tracking down" by "clues" turns into the personal and intimate task of finding the "birth-tokens" that prove his identity.

Just as the forward push for knowledge begins to accelerate, there is a retarding movement that pulls back toward the mysteriously closed and veiled origins of the play's and of Oedipus' beginnings. It is appropriately the mother who takes on this retarding role. She who stands at the first beginning of his life and (as we learn) is involved in a contradictory pull between the birth and the death of her new child (cf. 1173-75) would still keep him from the terrible knowledge and so save his life. As in the case of all great plots, the play combines forward movement to the end with the pleasure of delaying and complicating that end.[22] But the play also reflects on the paradoxes of theatrical narrative as well as on the paradoxes of tragic knowledge. This is a kind of knowledge in which clarity and dimness coexist and our knowing of ourselves includes at its center a core of ignorance, the shadowy conjunction at our origins whose mystery we can never fully penetrate.

. . . . .

The contradictions inherent in this tragic knowledge are sharpest in the tension between Oedipus' intellect and something that is never fully explicable in rational terms. The element of the inexplicable is represented onstage in the person of the blind prophet of Apollo, Teiresias. It is through signs, not through speech, Heraclitus says, that Apollo indicates his messages to men at the Delphic Oracle: "The lord whose oracle is at Delphi," the fragment of Heraclitus reads, "neither speaks nor conceals, but uses signs" (*sēmainei*).[23] It is precisely in the interpretation of such signs that Oedipus has the greatest difficulty, for the word implies both "evidence" from which deductions may rationally be drawn and the mysterious "marks" of supernatural intervention in human life, the omens or bird-signs through which the gods send their messages to men. The double connotation of the word contains the conflict between human and divine knowledge, between aggressive rationality and inspired or innate understanding, that embroils Oedipus and Teiresias in their bitter quarrel (390-398). Oedipus boasts that he defeated the Sphinx without divine help, relying solely on his resolute intelligence, *gnomē;* he did not need signs from the birds (395-398).[24] The priest in the prologue has a different view of the matter: to him Oedipus solved the riddle "with the support of a god" (38). To the priest Oedipus is "not made *equal* to the gods" (31), whereas the chorus believes that lord Teiresias, divine prophet (298), "sees the *same* things as Lord Apollo" (284).[25]

The interpretation of "signs" or "evidence" brings human knowledge into its most problematical juxtaposition with divine knowledge. The noun *sēmeia*, "signs," and the verb *sēmainein*, "designate by signs," occur throughout the play at the points where communication among men brings something unknown and potentially dangerous from the gods. At line 710 Jocasta offers "signs" of the unreliability of oracles, namely the oracle about Laius' son that leads into the first fateful revelation of past. The Messenger from Corinth arrives to "indicate as by signs" (*sēmainein*) the news of Polybus' death (933, 957). After his news Oedipus asks the chorus to *sēmainein* whether the Old Herdsman is "from the fields or from here, since it is the right moment for these things to be found out" (1050). Rejecting Jocasta's plea to give up the search a few lines later, he affirms confidently, "Taking such signs [*sēmeia*], I shall not fail to reveal my birth" (1058-59).

Although Oedipus' first act is to consult Delphi, he never integrates what Apollo and Teiresias know into what he knows.[26] Not until it is too late does he put the oracles together by means of that intelligence whose special property it is to join past and present and connect disparate events, facts, experiences, stages of life. This failure in logical deduction was one of Voltaire's objections to the structure of the play.[27] But what was a fault for the rationalist of the Age of Enlightenment is the very essence of the tragic element for the ancient dramatist. Oedipus uses his human knowledge primarily in conflict with the divine, to block, deny, contradict, or evade it. All to no avail.

Knowledge veers not only between human and divine, but also between activity and passivity.[28] Human knowledge, the knowledge that seems the achievement of man's intellectual power, is actively sought and willed. Divine knowledge comes, it seems, by chance, on precarious and unpredictable paths. The mystery of divine knowledge takes the form of the blind prophet; and the knowledge that comes (or seems to come) by sheer coincidence takes the form of the Corinthian Messenger and the Old Herdsman. It is the latter who provides the clinching piece of knowledge, Oedipus' identity as the exposed child of Laius and Jocasta.

This figure makes his first appearance early in the play, unnamed except for the vital fact that he saw and "knows" details of Laius' death. When Oedipus asks Creon if any "messenger or companion of the journey saw [*kateide*] anything. . . (116-117), Creon responds (118-120):

> *Cr.* They are all dead, except for some one man [*plēn heis tis*], who, having fled in fear of what he saw [*eide*], had nothing to tell except *one* thing he knew [*plēn hen . . . eidōs*].

> *Oed.* What was that? For one thing would find out many [*hen . . . polla*] for (us) to learn.

The play on the similar-sounding Greek words for "saw" and "knew," *eide . . . eidōs*, in the dense syntax of 119,

suggests the identification of "knowing" with "seeing" that is to prove decisive for the play's large concern with intelligence and ignorance.[29] Just fifteen lines earlier Oedipus has said of Laius, "I know [*exoida*] (him) (only) by hearing [*akouōn*], for I have never seen [*eiseidon*] him" (105).

This first mention of one person who "knows" anything is as vague as possible: Creon refers to "some one man" (*heis tis*, 118). Oedipus makes no attempt to refine this description. Instead he shifts attention from "some one *man*" to "some one *thing*" in his next line: "What sort of thing (did he say)? For *one thing* would find out *many* for (us) to learn" (120). His "one thing . . . many (things)" here takes up Creon's "nothing except one thing" in the previous line; but it also replaces the masculine "some one man" (*heis tis*, 118) with the neuter "one thing" (*hen*, 119).[30] The grammatical categories of language itself, the ease of shifting from masculine to neuter in the inflection of the pronominal adjective "one," seem to lead the investigators astray from what will finally solve the mystery. Language itself encourages their deception in pursuing what will prove, in one sense, misinformation.

Forgotten for some six hundred lines, over a third of the play, this individual surfaces again in the tense scene when Jocasta's reference to the triple roads (another numerical problem) has aroused Oedipus' anxiety (730). "Alas, these things are now clear," he says. "Who was it who spoke these words to you, my wife?" (754-755). "A house-servant, [*oikeus tis*]," Jocasta replies, "who reached us, the only one saved [*eksōtheis monos*]" (756). This last expression is the other, objective side of Creon's description of the man's "having fled in fear" in the prologue (118). "Did he then happen to be present in the house [*en domoisin*]?" Oedipus presses on (757). "No," answers Jocasta; and she explains how he came to Thebes, found Oedipus already in possession of the royal power (*kratē*) and Laius dead. Touching Jocasta's hand, he asked to be sent to the fields (761) and to the pastures of the flocks, so that "he might be as far as possible out of sight of the town" (762). The contrast between house and field on the one hand and fields and pastures on the other (*agrous* and *nomas*, 756-757 and 761) recalls Oedipus' first specific point of investigation of Laius' death: "Was it in the house or in the fields?" (112).[31] The sole witness there was "some one man" (118); and Creon's terminology calls attention to his unitary identity. It now appears that he, like Oedipus, is two: he is the house-servant (*oikeus*, 756) and the Herdsman in the "pastures of the flocks" (*poimniōn nomas*, 761).[32] He is both the man described by Jocasta and the man described by Creon. The problem of counting and knowing and of the one and the many also links him with Oedipus, whose pride of knowledge lies in having counted correctly in answering the Sphinx's riddle.

The problem of the one and the many murderers of Laius that rests on this man's testimony also touches another crucial part of Oedipus' past, not only the son's killing of the father but also the father's killing of the son. When Jocasta recounts her tale of exposing the infant prophesied to be "his father's killer" (721), she says that Laius "cast him into the pathless mountain by the hands of others [allōn chersin]" (719). Yet according to the Old Herdsman the child was taken to the mountain by one, not by many.[33] This figure too possesses "knowing" from a crucial "seeing." It is after he "saw" Oedipus on the throne that he requested from Jocasta a kind of absence of vision, to be "away from the sight" (apoptos) of the palace (762). Like Oedipus in the future, he seeks a combination of negated vision (ap-optos) and exile from his place in house and city (1384-94, 1451-54).

The phraseology of 758-759, "He saw you having the (royal) power and Laius killed" suggestively conjoins Oedipus' power (kratos) with Laius' death. To the receptive listener, it could also suggest that he saw "Oedipus having (possessing) the power and having killed Laius," a vision truly terrible and truly dangerous.[34] The Old Herdsman has "seen" the double aspect of Oedipus' kratos, "rule" and "strength." The king whom this kratos has displaced, like the Old Herdsman himself, will also prove to be double: not just a ruler, but also a father. When the truth begins to emerge the kratos becomes increasingly clear as that of Zeus, who has "power over all things" (895).[35]

When Oedipus is still the confident king searching for the killer of Laius, however, he sends for the old servant, this only survivor of the attack on the former king (765-770). Now the initial "oneness" of that survivor bifurcates even more strikingly and ominously into two. Oedipus' statement in the prologue apropos of searching out this figure, "One thing would find out many for (us) to learn," proves truer than he knew. The man who survived the attack on Laius proves to be the old herdsman of Thebes who rescued the infant Oedipus from death by exposure on Cithaeron. The detail is sheer coincidence. And yet that coincidence contains a kind of symbolic necessity. Oedipus cannot progress in his role as ruler of the city, whose task it is to find and expel Laius' killer (96-146, 241-243), until he has solved the mystery of his own origins. The philosopher George Santayana remarked that those who do not know the past are compelled to repeat it. The *Oedipus* works out the truth of this statement on the level of personal knowledge: not to know who you are is to be compelled to search ceaselessly for your origins.

. . . . .

In his determined pursuit of these origins, Oedipus forces the figure who holds the missing piece to recapitulate an earlier stage of his life too, when he changed from house-servant (756) to herdsman (761), and in that latter role brought Oedipus to both doom and salvation on Mount Cithaeron (cf. 1349-52). This spatial shift, from the center of palace life (756) to the margins of the city on the mountains, is symmetrical with the movements of Oedipus himself. The Old Herdsman's life, governed by such a different rhythm of time, proves to be both causally and analogically related to Oedipus' life, parallel but more vaguely outlined and set into a larger and remoter frame.

The densely compacted synopsis of Oedipus' whole life in the limited mimetic time of the performance has behind it, like a larger shadow, the more expansive movement of the old Herdsman's passage through time. Both men are simultaneously saviors and destroyers. Oedipus is both the savior (sōtēr) and pollution (miasma) of Thebes. The Old Herdsman saves Oedipus but also destroys him: "I wish that he perished, he who loosed me from the fetter on my feet and rescued and saved me from death, for it was no act of kindness that he did" (1349-54).[36] Both men have an instinctive moment of pity toward what they would save. Oedipus at the beginning "pities" the citizens (katoiktiras, 13; cf. 58) as the Herdsman had "pitied" the helpless infant (katoiktiras, in the same metrical position, 1178).

Oedipus' life, like the Herdsman's, has its present shape determined by "flight in fear." "Frightened, he fled," says Creon of the Old Herdsman in the prologue, "with only one thing to say of what he saw" (118). "I fled," says Oedipus to Jocasta, "to where I might not see the insults of my oracles fulfilled" (796-797). In his subsequent conversation with Jocasta and the Corinthian Messenger he vividly recreates the mood of fear that hovered about that flight.[37] The Herdsman's "flight" brought him safely away from the city, into the mountains (756-762); Oedipus would return to the mountains (1451-54) from which he was saved, but the kind of "salvation" he finds proves far more ambiguous than that of the Messenger. "I would not have been saved [esōthēn] from dying," he says with new-found insight near the end, "except for some terrible suffering [deinon kakon]" (1456-57). The "terror" and the "salvation," antithetical terms for the Herdsman, come together in a characteristic paradox for Oedipus.

And yet the Old Herdsman who recurs as a figure dimly parallel to Oedipus in his life's movements and spontaneous impulse of pity is also in one essential point the opposite of Oedipus. Among the first specific details that Sophocles supplies about him are his "flight in fear" in order to be "the only one saved" (118, 756). His characteristic mode of action in the play is evasion through running away. This is what he did when Oedipus attacked Laius at the crossroads and what he does again when he returns from that episode to find Oedipus ruling in Thebes. He repeats the pattern a third and last time on the stage when Oedipus interrogates him. He tries to escape by evasion or denial,[38] but now Oedipus compels him to face and speak the "terrible thing" that is contained in the truth (1169-70).

This last scene brings Oedipus and his shadowy double together, finally, on the stage; and this coming together shows us their characteristic divergence. Here the herdsman-slave (cf. doulos, 1123; also 764, 1168) seeks survival by denying the truth, whereas the king goes to meet his destiny head-on, confronting the "necessity" that comes from the oracles surrounding his existence, even if that confrontation means his death. The herdsman-slave at the crossroads was "the only one to be saved" (756). King Oedipus is ready to become the sacrificial victim, the *pharmakos*, whose single death saves the whole city (1409-

15).[39] Here, as the ancient *Life* says, Sophocles "knows how to adapt the situation and the events so that from a small half-verse or from a single word he can draw an entire character" (section 21).

At the beginning of the play the king shows himself to the people as a potential savior, "to all called Oedipus the famed" (8). At the peripety the doors of the palace again open and Oedipus shows himself to the people as the curse and the pollution: "to all the Thebans the slayer of his father" (*patroktonon*, 1288). Now he is not only the polluter of Thebes as the killer of Laius, the original definition of the source of the plague by the oracle, but also the polluter of the symbolic center of the city, the royal house of Thebes, under the terms that he applies to himself in 1288, "father's slayer and mother's . . ." (*patroktonos kai metros . . .*). But these words of Oedipus are not spoken dramatically onstage; they are reported by the Messenger as part of Oedipus' shouted command that the gates be thrown open to reveal him to the Thebans as a spectacle of pity and fear (1288-89, 1294-97). The impassioned shout, however, contains a powerful silence. Oedipus calls himself "his father's killer," but he breaks off as he pronounces the rest of the terrible phrase, "and his mother's . . ." The Messenger fills in the lacuna with an indirect, explanatory phrase, as narrator: "He said things unholy that I may not speak" (1289).[40]

. . . . .

The partial suppression of speech parallels the partial suppression of sight. This theatrical spectacle works as much by what is not said and not shown as by the spoken and visible elements of the performance. Certain things are more powerful for being left unsaid and unseen. Such are the two long narratives, one by Oedipus and one by the Messenger. The first describes the death of the father at the blow of the son's *skēptron*, the "staff" carried by the wandering exile and also the "scepter" carried by the ruling monarch; the second describes the death of the mother and the self-blinding of the son. Both scenes are left hidden, without *opsis*, in order that they may be played out the more effectively in the interior theater of ourselves, the "other scene" that the theater can create.[41]

These two narratives of crucial past events are complementary primal scenes. Both are enacted in the nonvisual medium of a buried memory. In the first case, Oedipus tells his story when what has been "invisible" (*aphanē*, 131) becomes "clearly visible" (*aiai tad' ēdē diaphanē*, "alas, these things are already clearly visible," 754).[42] The cry *aiai* that accompanies this "clarification," however, shows knowledge shifting from intellect to emotion.[43] Oedipus will repeat that cry (*aiai, aiai, pheu, pheu*) when, after gaining full knowledge, he blinds himself, and "the things at the feet" (131) are at last fully "visible" (1307-08).

The second narrative, the tale of Jocasta's death, begins with the Messenger's qualification, "Of what was done the most painful things are absent, for vision was not present"

(1238-39). The absence of the pain is symmetrical with the nonpresence of the vision. But, the Messenger goes on, he will tell "the sufferings of that unhappy woman" insofar as his memory permits (1239). The collocation of presence and absence at 1238 is appropriate both to the indirect mode of narration here and to the necessarily partial recovery of lost events through memory.

In this crucial scene Sophocles takes pains to show us how we *know* what we *see*. The Messenger's "memory" leads us verbally into the interior chamber (*esō . . . es ta numphika*, 1241-42) of Jocasta's marriage bed.[44] He tells how Jocasta "closed the gates" with violence behind her "when she went in" (1244). The narrative relies on the medium of sound to reveal what has occurred in the chamber. Those outside have heard a voice from within. But the account includes also something more than the voice, namely memory (*mnēmē*, 1246), which includes both "memory" and "mention." This "remembering" by Jocasta is deeper and more painful than the Messenger's "memory" eight lines before (1239), and it takes us into the remoter past (1244-48):

> When she went inside the gates, she dashed the doors closed inside and called on Laius now long since a corpse, having memory (making mention) of the sowing (seeds) of old [*mnēmēn palaiōn spermatōn*], by which he himself died, but left behind the mother of a child for ill-starred childmaking with his own.[45]

The repetition "Laius now long since a corpse" and the "old seeds" (*palai, palaiōn*), combined with the emphasis on memory (*mnēmē*, 1239, 1246), reinforces the movement back to the past. At the same time Jocasta's reported gesture of closing the doors behind her as she calls up the "memory of the sowing of old," that is, the night when Laius made her pregnant with Oedipus, prepares for the symbolic reenactment of her second, incestuous marriage in the ensuing narrative, with the son now replacing the father.[46] She, recalling her union with Laius, her last "memory" in life, closes the "gates" of her marriage chamber, which should have remained closed. Oedipus bursts into the palace and asks for a sword, searching for Jocasta (1252-57).

The narrative that follows recalls the crimes of Oedipus' past too. The verb used at 1252 for his violent entry to the palace, *eisepaise*, "struck his way within," will recur twenty lines later for his piercing of his eyes (1270; cf. 1331). It is the same verb that he has used to describe his angry "striking" of Laius when the process of self-discovery began for him (*paio di' orgēs*, "I struck in anger," 807). The weapon he seeks now is one of penetration (1255), different from the staff/scepter, the weapon he used to club Laius at the crossroads (*skēptron*, 811). He then forcibly "drives into the double gates" (*pulais diplais enēlato*), "pushes at the doors" (*ekline koila kleithra*) so that they bend inward (literally, "pushes the hollow doors"), and "enters [literally, falls into, *empiptei*] the chamber" (1261-62). He thus forces his way into the mother's closed, interior space, the interiority being emphasized by the "hollow" doors. This is the private chamber that she has barred behind her as she remembers those "seeds" of Laius in the past.[47]

Sophocles gives us our glimpse of that "other scene" through narration rather than as part of the spectacle, through memory rather than in the immediacy of present event: "There was no vision," says the Messenger, "but yet, as far as lies in my memory [*mnēmēs*], you will learn her sufferings" (1238-39). The emphasis on memory is striking when one considers how much memory in the play has distorted the recollection of the past. Jocasta, Oedipus, and the Old Herdsman have all shown highly selective memories (1057, 1131; cf. 870-871).

Another blockage of vision highlights the indirectness of our access to this scene. Oedipus' very act of forcible entry deprives the Messenger of certain, visual knowledge of the details. "How after this she perished," the Messenger goes on, "I do not know [*ouket' oida*], for Oedipus, shouting, broke his way in, and by his act it was no longer possible to behold [as in a spectacle, *ektheasasthai*] her woe (1253). But rather we turned our gaze toward him as he roamed around" (1251-54).[48]

Vision again becomes blurred in the vagueness of the Messenger's report that "some divinity" (*daimōnōn tis*) showed Oedipus the way, "for it was not any one of us men [*andrōn*] who were present nearby" (1258-59). The men are concrete forms, "nearby," visible and familiar; the unknown *daimōn* is invisible, mysterious, undefined.

Sophocles makes our vision of the narrated events something deliberately elusive. Vision is blocked first by the closing of doors (1241-48), then by the violent acts and shouts of Oedipus in the palace (1252-53), and finally by his presence over the body of Jocasta (1265-77). After Oedipus has broken down the door, we, the onlookers, are allowed to "see into" (*eiseidomen*) the firmly shut chamber (1263). The penetration of the eye to increasingly inward and hidden space culminates in Oedipus' "seeing" of Jocasta (1265), the goal and result of his forced entry to the locked, forbidden place. From that point, vision is again permitted, though still in the indirect mode of third person narration. It is now a vision characterized by that quality of "the terrible," *to deinon,* that broods over the play from the beginning and finally becomes visible in the spectacle of "things terrible [*deina*] to look upon" (1267, "The things after that were terrible to look upon" or "From that point there were things terrible to see").[49]

This last object of sight, these "things terrible to look upon," is the physical act of putting an end to vision, Oedipus' tearing the pins from Jocasta's robes and striking them into his eyes. It is reported not as the result of an active verb of seeing, as at 1263 (*eiseidomen,* "we saw") and 1265 (*horai nin,* "he sees her"), but in an impersonal way: "From that point there were things terrible to see." It is as if this "seeing" is already formed into a tableau, a final memorable sight, fixed as the result of a narrative of

unforgettable power but not in fact shown on the stage. When that all-pervasive "terror" reaches it climax, "no spectacle is present" (*opsis ou para,* 1238). Such are *ta deina,* "the terrible things," that the unstaged spectacle has finally to "show."[50]

The horror of the sight is now matched by the horror of the sound. This too comes to us indirectly, by report. Jocasta's "call" to the dead Laius (1245) and her "lament" over her marriage bed (1249) fade into the silence of her still-mysterious death ("how after this she perished I do not know," 1251). The sounds we now hear come from Oedipus: he "shouts" (1252) as he breaks his way into the palace, "cries terrible things" (1260) as he forces his way into Jocasta's chamber, "roars terribly" (1265) at what he sees there, and "shouts" again as he strikes his eyes (1271).[51] This last cry recapitulates the crescendo of horror, for it repeats the "terrible shouting" as he has forced the doors ten lines earlier (1260), while the accompanying action, the "striking" of his eyes, repeats his first entry into the palace (*epaise,* 1270; *eisepaise,* 1252). The last shout (1271) is itself closely linked to vision, for it is a cry that "his eyes will never see the things that he has suffered or the things that he has done" (1271-72). The same verbs of shouting recur less than twenty lines later when Oedipus calls for the opening of another set of gates (*boāi, audōn,* 1287, 1289). These are no longer the doors of private, interior chambers, but the public gates of the palace, which reveal to all the Thebans the fearful spectacle that he has become. In both cases the messages of Oedipus' shouting are reported indirectly by the narrator, and both contain a denial or rejection of sight and of speech respectively (1271 and 1289). This most intense point of hearing and seeing in the play is surrounded by declarations of not speaking and not seeing.

This withholding of vision or partial access to vision in a story whose culmination contains the destruction of the power to see is one means by which Sophocles stamps this narration with its characteristic feature, a reluctance to emerge into the light, a horror that wants to remain hidden in the darkness of the unseen. Teiresias' blind seeing, reluctant speech, and uncomprehended utterances in the meeting with Oedipus early in the play form the first explicit model onstage for a story that refuses to be told and a knowledge that refuses to be known. Now, at the most intense point of the action, the suppression of vision and speech moves to the center of the narrative. Not only does the refusal to see and to say pervade this telling, but it is through this powerful "won't tell" that the story in fact gets itself told.

This climactic scene is recovered only by a series of recessive movements into the past and by a steady progression of acts of looking into a closed interior in the present. The discontinuous rhythm of exposure and concealment, vision and nonvision, closing and removing blocking objects is a symbolical condensation of Oedipus' past. In the narrative movement that retrospectively unfolds the story of his life, as in the patterning of events that constitute that life and give it its tragic form, synchrony and diachrony come together.

When Oedipus has broken down the doors and does at last "see" Jocasta's body in her chamber, the first thing he does after "releasing" her from the noose is to "pull off the gold-beaten pins from her garments, (the pins) with which she was dressed" (1268-69). This is the first of "the things terrible to see" (1267) that is described. *Peronai,* the pins that hold the robes together, are not merely the decorative "brooches," as the word is frequently translated. Their removal could suggest the gesture of undressing the queen in her "marriage chamber" (*ta numphika,* 1242) as she "lay there" (1267), a grotesque and horrible reenactment of the first night of their union. This is the act for which he "strikes the sockets of his eyes" in the next line.[52] As the body of the king becomes that through which the invisible truth is made reality instead of appearance, so the body of Jocasta points to something that remains inaccessible to vision and must remain hidden.

In folktales of this type, as Vladimir Propp has shown, the true identity of the incestuous husband/son is discovered by a scar or other mark in bed on the wedding night.[53] Jean Cocteau brilliantly plays with this age-old motif of the discovery on the wedding night in his *Machine infernale.*[54] Sophocles withholds that recognition until it can bring only the tragic recognition of indelible pollution. He retains the sexual component of that knowledge, however, by displacing the physical union onto a series of symbolic equivalents: the penetration of the queen's closed chambers and the removal of the pins from her recumbent body. These displacements are, in turn, part of that temporal enlargement and complication of the action that Sophocles everywhere exercises on the myth. He superimposes present acts on a remote past; he fuses, or confuses, the diachronic and the synchronic axes. By deepening the temporal perspective through the motif of discovering and remembering a long-forgotten past, he also calls attention to the representational power of drama, by which a single action unfolding before us on the stage can contain symbolically the meaning of an entire lifetime. In the condensed temporal frame of Oedipus' life the tragedian finds also a mirror image of his manipulation of time in the artistic construction of his play.

At the most intense moment of the stage action, Sophocles brings the forward movement of the play almost to a halt in order to allow his language to congeal, as it were, into a medium that shows both speech and time to us in a new light, revealing some things that we could not see before (1223-96). Speech and time become strange new entities wherein we see ourselves also as somehow strange and new. The otherness of the medium reflects back to us our own hitherto-unperceived strangeness as both subject and object of the message, as the alien content of a knowledge that resists being known, the hidden Other that we carry in ourselves. The external observer is also drawn into the action of self-discovery and becomes, with Oedipus, both the searcher and the one who is discovered.

Notes

1. Vladimir Nabokov, *Lectures on Don Quixote* (New York 1983) 1.

2. For fuller discussion of these readings of the Oedipus myth with further references see Segal, *OT* 57-66.

3. "Birth of Tragedy," chap. 9, in Friedrich Nietzsche, *The Birth of Tragedy and the Genealogy of Morals,* trans. F. Golffing (New York 1956) 60f.

4. This emphasis on the unnaturalness of Oedipus, his place apart, his monstrosity, reappears as a central element in the view of tragedy expounded by René Girard in *La violence et le sacré* (Paris 1972) = *Violence and the Sacred,* trans. Patrick Gregory (Baltimore 1979), especially 68-88. Here Oedipus is the model for the scapegoating process embodied in the sacred kingship and in the tragic hero: a figure who attracts to himself all the pollutions, all the excesses, all the most outrageous crimes in order to become the focal point and the central figure in the expulsion of violence from the social order, the re-sacralization of violence enacted in the terrible suffering of the hero-king. The arbitrary victim, chosen by fate, collects all the violence in himself and expels it in his sacred suffering that gives violence back to the gods. For brief discussion and criticism see Segal, *OT* 65f.

5. Sigmund Freud, *The Interpretation of Dreams* (1900), trans. and ed. James Strachey, in *The Standard Edition of the Complete Psychological Works of Sigmund Freud,* vol. 3 (London 1953) 260-264.

6. For a brief discussion of Sophocles' revisions of the Aeschylean version of the Oedipus myth see Segal, *OT* 43 and 46-48.

7. George Devereux, "The Self-Blinding of Oidipous in Sophokles: *Oidipous Tyrannos,*" *JHS* 93 (1973) 36-49; also Pietro Pucci, "On the 'Eye' and the 'Phallos' and Other Permutabilities in *Oedipus Rex,*" in *Arktouros: Studies Presented to Bernard M. W. Knox on the Occasion of His 65th Birthday,* ed. Glen W. Bowersock, Walter Burkert, and Michael C. J. Putnam (Berlin and New York 1979) 130-133, especially 131.

8. J.-P. Vernant, "Oedipe sans complexe," in J.-P. Vernant and Pierre Vidal-Naquet, *Mythe et tragédie en Grèce ancienne* (Paris 1972) 77-98, especially 95f. = *Myth and Tragedy* 85-111, especially 108f. For further discussion see Chapter 7 of this volume.

9. For Lacan's Discourse of the Other see, inter alia, Jacques Lacan, *Speech and Language in Psychoanalysis,* trans. Anthony Wilden (Baltimore 1968) 20ff., 106ff., 169ff.

10. Francesco Orlando, *Per una teoria freudiana della letteratura* (Turin 1973) 57ff.

11. Claude Lévi-Strauss, "The Structural Study of Myth," in *Structural Anthropology,* trans. Claire Jacobson

and B. C. Schoepf (Garden City, N.Y., 1967) 202-228; Terence Turner, "Narrative, Structure and Mythopoiesis," *Arethusa* 10 (1977) 103-163.

12. For the multiple implications of the name of Oedipus see Knox, *Oedipus* 182-184; Segal, *T&C* 211f., 243f.

13. For "metatragedy" see C. Segal, *Dionysiac Poetics and Euripides' Bacchae* (Princeton 1982), chap. 7.

14. Aristotle, *Poetics* 1453b14ff. See Gerald F. Else, *Aristotle's Poetics: The Argument* (Cambridge, Mass., 1957) 414ff.

15. Aristotle, *Poetics* 1453b30ff., 1454a2ff. See Diego Lanza, "La paura di Edipo," *Aut/Aut* 184-185 (1981) 25f.

16. At 1225 I read Hartung's emendation *eugenōs*, accepted by many editors, in place of the manuscripts' *engenōs*, "in kinsmanly fashion" or, more freely, "feel kinsmen's concern for the Labdacid house." If the manuscript reading is kept, the metaphorical familial feeling of the chorus would contrast with the horror of what is now revealed in the literal family of Oedipus.

17. Throughout the play the metaphor of flying is associated with man's helplessness before the unknown and the supernatural; see 16f., 175ff., 482, 488, 509. See also Chapter 9.

18. For the motif of vision in the play see R. G. A. Buxton, "Blindness and Limits: Sophocles and the Logic of Myth," *JHS* 100 (1980) 22-37, especially 22-25 and 35-37.

19. Ursula Parlavantza-Friedrich, *Täuschungsszenen in den Tragödien des Sophokles* (Berlin 1969), has no discussion of the Herdsman's narrative. The contradictions and falsehoods that it may contain are discussed by Philip Vellacott, *Sophocles and Oedipus* (London 1971) 177 and 187; Jebb on 756 and Kamerbeek on 758-759; and E. P. Arthur, "Sophocles' *Oedipus Tyrannus*: The Two Arrivals of the Herdsman," *Antichthon* 14 (1980) 9-17, especially 15ff.

20. On time in the *Tyrannus* see Segal, *T&C* 228-231; also Jacqueline de Romilly, *Time in Greek Tragedy* (Ithaca 1968) 108-110.

21. The relevant passages are as follows: *ēmar . . . xummetroumenon chronōi*, "the day comeasured with time" (73); *ephēure s' akonth' ho panth' horōn chronos*, "time, which sees all, found you out against your will" (1213); *tōi makrōi ge summetroumenos chronōi*, "comeasured by great time" (963); *en te gar makrōi / gērāi xunāidei tōide tàndri summetros*, "in his great age he is in harmony with this man here, of equal measure" (1112f.); *tēn Korinthian / astrois to loipon ekmetroumenos chthona*, "measuring the land of Corinth henceforth by the stars" (794f.). In this last passage the reasons for replacing the manuscript reading with Nauck's emendation, *tekmaroumenos*

("inferring"), as Lloyd-Jones and Wilson do in their OCT, do not seem to me decisive. For the manuscript reading see Dawe and Jebb ad loc. For other aspects of 794-796 see Chapter 9.

22. See Peter Brooks, "Freud's Masterplot," *Yale French Studies* 54/55 (1977) 280-300.

23. Fragment 22B93 in Hermann Diels and Walther Kranz, eds., *Die Fragmente der Vorsokratiker*, 5th ed. (Berlin 1952) 1.172.

24. Cf. also 965-967 and, on omens and augury, Knox, *Oedipus* 170ff. See also *Antigone* 998, 1005, 1013, 1021.

25. Buxton, "Blindness" 23, observes the contrast between lines 31 and 298 but understates the difference between equality and sameness.

26. See Mario Vegetti, "Forme di sapere nell' Edipo re," in *Tra Edipo e Euclide* (Milan 1983) 23ff.

27. Voltaire, *Lettres sur Oedipe*, letter 3.

28. On the movement between activity and passivity in the tragic hero, see Vernant, "Ebauches de la volonté dans la tragédie grecque," *Mythe et tragédie* 43-74, especially 68ff. = "Intimations of the Will in Greek Tragedy," in Vernant and Vidal-Naquet, *Myth and Tragedy* 49-84, especially 77-79.

29. Note also Oedipus' *kateide*, "saw," at 117.

30. That shift is also anticipated in Creon's movement from *plēn heis* at 118 to *plēn hen* at 119. On the question of "one" and "many" here see Segal, *T&C* 214f., with the further literature cited in the notes there.

31. For this movement between country and city see Segal, *T&C* 220ff.

32. Cf. also 1123, where the Old Herdsman is described as *oikoi trapheis*, "brought up in the house."

33. There is another discrepancy in Jocasta's account of the exposure of the child that the Old Herdsman's account brings out. She has said that it was Laius who cast out the infant (718), whereas when Oedipus asks whether it was the mother who gave him the child, the Herdsman answers in the affirmative (1173; cf. 1175). It is, of course, possible that Jocasta is correct after all and that the change from father to mother at 1173-75 reflects Oedipus' preoccupation here with rejection by his mother. In any case, the Herdsman plays an increasingly important role in giving different perspectives on what "really" happened in the past.

34. Lines 758f. have the second perfect (intransitive) participle, whereas the periphrastic construction requires the active (cf. *Ajax* 22, *Trachiniae* 412, *Electra* 590); but the double meaning is probably still within reach.

35. On Zeus and this passage see Chapter 8.

36. Note too the further irony in this double identity of the Old Herdsman as savior and destroyer: at 763f. Jocasta speaks of the Old Herdsman as Laius' companion, who "deserved to get a favor [*charis*] even greater than this" (i.e., than permission to leave the city for the pastures). At 1352f. Oedipus regrets that the Herdsman saved him from death by exposure on Cithaeron, "doing nothing to earn gratitude" *(ouden es charin prassōn)*.

37. Cf. 839ff., 988ff., 1002, 1010f.

38. Cf. 1129-1231, 1146-59, 1165.

39. See J.-P. Vernant, "Ambiguïté et renversement. Sur la structure énigmatique d'Oedipe-Roi," in *Mythe et tragédie* 99-131, especially 114ff. = Vernant and Vidal-Naquet, *Myth and Tragedy* 113-140, especially 127ff.; also Euripides, *Bacchae* 962f. and Pseudo-Gregory, *Christus Patiens* 1525. See Segal, *Dionysiac Poetics* 42-45. Even though Oedipus is not actually expelled from Thebes at the end of the play and the city is not clearly saved from the plague, his experiences in the play adumbrate the pattern of the *pharmakos*, particularly as he becomes the one man who takes upon himself all the pollutions of the city.

40. For the suppression of the tabooed words of patricide and incest see Diskin Clay, "Unspeakable Words in Greek Tragedy," *AJP* 103 (1982) 285-286, 288-292. Note too that at 1441 Oedipus calls himself *patrophontēs* and *asebēs*, again suppressing any reference to the incestuous union.

41. For Lacan's "other scene" ("anderer Schauplatz") see Jacques Lacan, *Ècrits: A Selection,* trans. Alan Sheridan (New York 1977) 193, 264, 284f.

42. As Knox notes, *diaphanē* occurs only here in tragedy (*Oedipus* 243, n. 87). See also his remarks on pp. 132ff. for the importance of *phainō* and related words in the play.

43. Note the similar exclamation, *iou, iou,* at 1182, with the related word of intellectual clarification *saphes.*

44. That movement "within" is subtly prepared for at 1171, when the Herdsman, about to reveal Oedipus' identity as the son of Jocasta, refers to her as "the one within," *hē d' esō.*

45. This translation attempts to bring out the force of the repetition *tiktousan . . . dusteknon* at 1247; the repeated root *tek-* hammers in the horror of the doubled "mothering." Note the triple repetition of the root *tek-* at 1250.

46. On the symbolic reenactment of the union, though with a very different interpretation, see John Hay, *Lame Knowledge and the Homosporic Womb* (Washington, D.C., 1978) 103ff. and 133f.

47. *Mnēmēn palaiōn spermatōn,* "memory of the sowing [or seed] of old," 1246. On the sexual meaning of gates see Hay, *Lame Knowledge* 103-105. The implications of sexual violence in the forcing of gates may have played a role in the first *Hippolytus* of Euripides, close in date to the *Tyrannus:* cf. Pseudo-Apollodorus, *Epitome* 1.18; and W. S. Barrett, *Euripides, Hippolytus,* (Oxford 1964) 38f.

48. In this extremely dense and important passage the phrase *huph' ou,* "by his (Oedipus') act," at 1252 may be a significant echo of *huph' hōn,* "by which seed" Laius would die, a few lines before at 1246, also at the end of the verse. If so, Laius' act of irresponsible begetting (the "seed of old") is brought into suggestive association with its eventual result, Oedipus' self-blinding, which in turn is a symbolic reenactment of the incest as a crime against both the father and the mother.

49. The motif of fearful seeing is emphasized by the repetitions at 1297, 1306, and 1312. For the atmosphere of fear in the play see Lanza, "La paura di Edipo," 28-33.

50. Hay, *Lame Knowledge* 76f., notes the importance of the denied "vision" here and the connection of *opsis* with the theatrical spectacle; but his emphasis is rather on the desire to see that such a denial creates in the spectator than on the contrast between the visualization inherent in theater and its firm negation in this climactic event. He observes, however, the possibility of a further play on spectacle in the reemergence of Oedipus from behind the closed gates, now "frightfully transformed by a new mask" (77)—an element of spectacle that is permitted in the midst of so much left unseen.

51. *Deina bruchētheis* at 1265 escalates *deinon aüsas* to a new level of violence.

52. Psychoanalytically oriented interpreters regard the eyes here as a substitute for the phallus, that is, as the punishment of castration for incest: see Hay, *Lame Knowledge* 125ff.; and Devereux, "Self-Blinding of Oidipous."

53. Vladimir Propp, *Edipo alla luce del folclore,* ed. C. S. Janovic (Turin 1975) 127f. = Lowell Edmunds and Alan Dundes, eds., *Oedipus: A Folklore Casebook* (New York 1983) 76-121, especially 113f. The sexual implications of the scene are deepened by its close parallel with Deianeira's enactment of "marriage" as death in *Trachiniae* 899-902 and 915-926: see Segal, *OT* 153f.

54. See Segal, *OT* 27-29.

Abbreviations

AJP: American Journal of Philology

Dawe: R. D. Dawe, ed., *Sophocles: Oedipus Tyrannus* (Cambridge 1982)

Jebb: Richard C. Jebb, ed., *Sophocles, The Plays of Sophocles,* 7 vols. (Cambridge 1893-1908)

JHS: Journal of Hellenic Studies

Kamerbeek: J. C. Kamerbeek, ed., *The Plays of Sophocles,* 7 vols. (Leiden 1953-1984); *Ajax,* 2nd ed., 1963

Knox, *Oedipus*: B. M. W. Knox, *Oedipus at Thebes* (New Haven 1957)

Lloyd-Jones and Wilson, OCT: Hugh Lloyd-Jones and N. G. Wilson, eds., *Sophoclis Fabulae,* Oxford Classical Texts (Oxford 1990)

Lloyd-Jones and Wilson, *Sophoclea*: Hugh Lloyd-Jones and N. G. Wilson, *Sophoclea* (Oxford 1990)

Nauck: Augustus Nauck, ed., *Tragicorum Graecorum Fragmenta,* 2nd ed. (Leipzig 1889)

Segal, *OT*: Charles Segal, *Sophocles' Oedipus Tyrannus: Tragic Heroism and the Limits of Knowledge* (New York 1993)

Segal, *T&C*: Charles Segal, *Tragedy and Civilization: An Interpretation of Sophocles* (Cambridge, Mass. 1981)

Vernant and Vidal-Naquet, *Myth and Tragedy*: Jean-Pierre Vernant and Pierre Vidal-Naquet, *Myth and Tragedy in Ancient Greece* (1972, 1986), trans. J. Lloyd (New York 1990)

R. Drew Griffith (essay date 1996)

SOURCE: "Asserting Eternal Providence: The Question of Guilt," in *The Theatre of Apollo: Divine Justice and Sophocles's "Oedipus the King,"* McGill-Queen's University Press, 1996, pp. 45-58.

[*In the following excerpt, Griffith examines the cases for and against Oedipus and explains why he is guilty of murder.*]

On the last occasion I had the good fortune to read E. R. Dodds' famous essay "On Misunderstanding the *Oedipus Rex*,"[1] I felt certain misgivings at some of his conclusions. Dodds is denouncing a view that he discovered in some undergraduate essays on the question "In what sense, if in any, does the *Oedipus Rex* attempt to justify the ways of God to man?" The offending view[2] holds that "we get what we deserve"[3]—that is, that Oedipus in some measure merits his suffering. Dodds' position in answer to this has an ethical aspect (Oedipus has an "essential moral innocence"[4]), a religious one (Sophocles' "gods are [not] in any human sense just"[5]), and a literary-critical one ("there is no reason at all why we should require a dramatist—even a Greek dramatist—to be for ever running about delivering banal 'messages'"[6] Many have anticipated Dodds in his position[7] and others have followed him,[8] with very few dissenting.[9] This position is consonant with the emotional reaction of anyone watching or reading the play. Our sympathies are with Oedipus: we feel terror and pity at his plight, and this makes us want him to be innocent and his nemesis, Apollo, to be unac-

countably vicious. This emotional reaction is important, because Greek tragedy is an emotional medium.[10]

Tragedy is also, however, an intellectual art-form, and the intellectual clarification of the concepts of terror and pity is arguably as much a part of tragic catharsis as is any psychological purgation through terror and pity.[11] As well as feeling for Oedipus, we must analyse his situation. Texts contemporary with Sophocles suggest that, while feeling about the play much as we do, many members of its original audience would have questioned Dodds' analysis. Oedipus has no essence beyond what we can infer from the deeds that he performs, and of these Sophocles' contemporaries would have found some morally innocent and others not. Apollo's actions, meanwhile, would have seemed to them to be just in an all-too-human sense. The first chapter argues that we should not constrain ourselves to historicist modes of understanding; nevertheless, the present chapter is devoted to the analysis of the roles of Oedipus and Apollo in the play along lines suggested by fifth-century thought in order to show that even within the terms of historicist interpretation, the guilt of Oedipus and the justice of Apollo are clear.

Beyond doubt, Oedipus suffers greatly in Sophocles' play. He has been living in a state of incest, and he blinds himself in order to be unable to see the children conceived in pollution (1273-4, 1369-70). Let us suppose that he is not responsible for his incest and the pain that he experiences is innocent suffering.[12] (We will return to the problem of innocent suffering in chapter 5.) The presence of this innocent suffering explains our sympathy for his actions but should not cloud our analysis of them.

If there is any additional suffering that Oedipus merits, it must be because he has done something. He is not likely punished for a character flaw,[13] because not all tragic heroes suffer a *hamartia*, which is in any case more likely an ignorance of fact than a moral flaw,[14] and because actions and not character traits cause things to happen in Greek tragedy.[15]

Oedipus does only one thing on stage: he "pursue[s] the truth at whatever personal cost" and "accept[s] and endure[s] it when found."[16] This is shown by the moment (1170) when he pauses in his course of action, having realized its implications, and chooses to follow Delphi's command and implicate himself by pursuing the truth. This decision recalls that moment in Aeschylus's *Libation Bearers* (899-903) where Orestes pauses briefly and then immediately chooses to follow Delphi's command and kill his mother. But this very self-prosecution points backward in condemnation to an earlier act, namely Oedipus's murder of his father Laius (which, on the basis of the arguments advanced in the last chapter, we are justified in considering him to have committed).

The murder of Laius might justify part of Oedipus's suffering, since it is a deed and not a character flaw and since it not only precedes but also paves the way for his suffering.[17] Laius's death makes Jocasta a widow, and so enables Oedipus to marry her[18] and reside in Thebes; the residence of the regicide in Thebes in turn causes the plague (106-7) that sets in motion the plot. Still, small causes can provoke disproportionately large effects, and our question remains.

The crime of parricide has two components: homicide and father abuse. The play enforces this distinction: the quests for Laius's killer and for Oedipus's father remain separate for most of it, not merging until the recognition scene (1182-5). Let us examine the crime under these two headings, beginning by considering the murder of Laius in the context of fifth-century Athenian law. This is relevant, given Greek tragedy's tendency to anachronism,[19] the audience's familiarity with the Athenian judicial apparatus, and the probability that the play draws heavily for its structure on the process of judicial inquiry.[20]

Classical Athenian jurisprudence recognizes three kinds of killing,[21] and different scholars have classified Laius's murder under all three. The first is the unintentional killing of an innocent victim (what we would call "manslaughter"). The hero of *Oedipus at Colonus* claims unintentionality to defend himself from the charge of parricide (273, 547-8, 988-99). Yet if Oedipus did not know that Laius was his father, he knew that he was a human being and that his act was homicide, in contrast to Deianira, who could (but, interestingly, does not) plead unintentional killing, having administered a poison believing it to be a love potion.

The second kind is justified homicide (which has no equivalent in, for example, Canadian jurisprudence), which is the intentional killing of a criminal caught in the act. The best-known example is the killing of an adulterer apprehended *in flagrante delicto*,[22] but another is the killing of a highwayman caught red-handed.[23] Oedipus does not claim to have thought that Laius was a robber.[24] Indeed, according to the admittedly none-too-factual report of Laius's surviving slave, Laius and company suspected Oedipus of intending to rob them (122), as he does in Euripides' version.[25]

The third kind is intentional homicide (ordinary murder). Self-defence[26] was a mitigating circumstance in a case of intentional homicide, rather than grounds for lawful homicide.[27] Demosthenes (21.71-5) tells how a certain Euaeon, who killed a man in retaliation for a single blow, was convicted by one vote. This case shows that, despite the considerable sympathy that the jury obviously felt for the killer, "the mere fact that the victim struck the first blow was not sufficient to acquit the killer."[28] One must show that the victim intended to kill the murderer. Yet Oedipus does not argue self-defence,[29] claiming, as he would have to do, that Laius was about to kill him,[30] stating in fact that on this occasion[31] Laius wanted only to drive him from the road (805). Moreover, according to Plato (*Leg.* 869b)—who may or may not be reflecting Attic law—parent murder is the only crime in which self-defence is not an extenuating circumstance.

One might suppose that Oedipus's act was a third-degree murder since he acted without malice aforethought (807), and that he was guilty of something less than premeditated homicide, but this claim would ignore fifth-century Attic law, which reserves no special category for homicide that is intentional but unpremeditated. "The Athenians used [the terms] 'unpremeditated' and 'unintentional' interchangeably . . . The practical effect of this was to narrow unintentional homicides to our category of accidental killings. This meant that all other killings were classified as intentional and were subject to the severest penalties. Sudden killings thus received no more lenient treatment than any other intentional killings unless some justification such as self-defence could be shown"[32] (which in Oedipus's case, as we have seen, it could not).

Again, one might argue that, whatever the judgment of a hypothetical fifth-century court, the heroic society in which Oedipus is imagined as having lived would have "acquitted" him. Not so. In Homer and Hesiod a murderer faces one of three penalties. He may either be killed by the victim's family,[33] go into exile,[34] or offer monetary compensation.[35] Only two of the murders mentioned in epic are not followed by such an atonement: one is the murder of Laius; the other is Heracles' murder of Iphitus.[36] When Sophocles recounts the latter (*Trach.* 38, 270-9), he supplies the penalty, exile, that is missing in Homer's account. Given Sophocles' supplement to this story, Oedipus stands alone among epic murderers[37] in escaping human retribution. We do not know why this is so in the epics, but Sophocles supplies an explanation: the Thebans were too distracted by the Sphinx to investigate the murder and try the killer (130-1). Although postponed by the Sphinx, punishment was as fitting for Laius's killer as for any other. This is why the oracle orders the murderer's exile (98) and why Oedipus pronounces this sentence upon him (236-43).

The audience's appreciation of Oedipus's act was conditioned by the precepts of ancient Greek popular morality.[38] For example, Laius's murder occurred at a crossroads (716, 730, 733, 800-1), an important fact since it is a constant in the myth, while the precise location is variable.[39] The crossroads is a place where a decision must be made, as in the story of the choice of Heracles.[40] As in that story, the alternatives confronting Oedipus were as much moral as directional: by turning one way, he would kill four strangers; either by retreating (an option available to Oedipus, but not to Heracles) or by deviating temporarily from his chosen path, he would spare them.

Three considerations make clear the judgment that morality passes upon these alternatives. First, since Laius was trying to push Oedipus from the road (804-5), which was narrow (1399), and since there was another path available, one party should step aside. According to Homer (*Il.* 9.69, 160-1), one should yield to the kinglier—that is, to him who commands more men[41]—and to the elder. The old might defer to the young of higher rank, but with both age and rank[42] on his side one would expect deference and try to exact it if not forthcoming. Laius (a king) is actually kinglier than Oedipus (a king's son) and obviously so, travelling in a mule-car (753, 803) with a retinue, while Oedipus goes alone on foot[43]. In the parallel incident in the *Iliad* (1.188-92), when Achilles is provoked by Agamemnon, who is both kinglier and elder, he contemplates homicide, revealing that the course actually chosen by Oedipus is not unnatural, but then wisely abstains from violence. Laius was also clearly older than Oedipus, for his hair was "a sable silver'd" (742) and Oedipus calls him "elder" (805, 807), not necessarily an old man, but a senior figure[44] deserving of respect. Oedipus should not have quarrelled with Laius, not because he might be his father[45] but because morality demanded respect for elders.[46]

Secondly, Laius was a stranger (813), whom it is wrong to kill,[47] for "all strangers are in the keeping of Zeus" (*Od.* 6.207-8 = 14.57-8) in his capacity as Zeus of Strangers.[48] Indeed, some may even be Zeus incognito.[49] These beliefs are grounded in social reality: the stranger lacks brotherhood, law, and hearth (*Il.* 9.63) and is very vulnerable. To limit this vulnerability and prevent a breakdown of society, the Greeks ritualized the behaviour proper towards strangers. When a stranger presents himself at one's house, he must be entertained no matter how inconvenient (cf Eur. *Alc.* 76ff). Even in battle one should not attack a man of unknown identity lest he be a god.[50] The proper behaviour of strangers meeting as wayfarers is shown in the *Iliad*, where Priam, the old man, travelling away from home with his herald, encounters the unrecognized young man, his surrogate son, who is Hermes in disguise and whom he suspects of being a brigand. In contrast to Oedipus, Hermes is a paragon of courtesy.[51] To murder strangers is extreme barbarity, fit for Laestrygonians or Cyclopes, each of whom is a law to himself and cares nothing for others (*Od.* 9.112-15), but unthinkable to a civilized Greek. Of potentially ironic application to Oedipus is Hesiod's observation (*Op.* 327-32) that whoever harms a stranger is as bad as a father abuser.

Thirdly, Laius was accompanied by a herald (753), recognizable as such (802), presumably through his caduceus.[52] The herald accompanied him because he was an "envoy sent to consult the oracle"[53] (114) on official religious and state business. Oedipus at first "[forebore] to strike the sacred herald"[54]—whom he does eventually kill—because heralds are inviolable.[55] To violate their rights was "sacrilegious"; to kill them was to break the customs of all men. Herodotus (7.133-7) tells how the Spartans killed Dareius's heralds and were incited by the hero Talthybius, in life the herald of Agamemnon, to send men to Xerxes to die to expiate the crime. Xerxes refused to act illegally like the Spartans; yet, although he spared them, their sons later died, Herodotus editorializes, in requital for Talthybius's wrath. Once, whenever Athenian youths assembled, they wore mourning for the herald Copreus, whom the Athenians had killed (Philostr. *VS* 2.1.5 = 2.59 Kayser). An Athenian herald murdered by the Megarians was buried with full honours at the Dipylon gate, while his murder caused enmity between the two states.[56]

Three arguments, all inadequate, might be raised in Oedipus's favour. The first is that he did not choose to kill Laius because, unlike Agamemnon's sacrifice of Iphigeneia (Aesch. *Ag.* 206-17), his deliberation is not reported. Lacking on his lips is "the characteristic cry of the tragic hero,"[57] "What should I do?"[58] Yet this is a feature of his character, not of his situation. The only one to hesitate in our play is Creon (91-2, 1443); Oedipus is full of Sophoclean self-assurance, impatient at others' slowness (74, 287, 1162) and always quick to jump to a suspicion (124-5, 139-40, 380-9). More quick-witted than Agamemnon, he will not laboriously deliberate before choosing the wrong course; it is his particular glory to rush "with characteristic decisiveness"[59] into actions whose outcome is ruinous.

Secondly, Oedipus was provoked. Laius was rude to him and seems by nature to share his temperament as well as his looks (743), as we would expect of kings, who laid great store by heredity.[60] Morality, far from counselling one to turn the other cheek, commands vengeance: helping friends and harming enemies is the oft-cited recipe for justice.[61] Still, the vengeance exacted by Oedipus exceeds the wrong done. Oedipus says, "[Laius] paid no equal penalty" (810),[62] a phrase reminiscent of the herald in Aeschylus's *Agamemnon* (532-3), who says that the Trojans "do not boast that they wrought more than they suffered." This reminiscence is ominous in view of the consequences that Agamemnon's excessive vengeance had for him. Of course, in all self-defence killings the victim gets more than he gave,[63] but this is only because he is less successful; in terms of intent the acts are equal, with one killing in order to avoid being killed. Yet by Oedipus's own admission Laius only sought to remove him—albeit forcibly—from the road (804-5). On this point again morality suggests that the vengeance should fit the offence, being equal to instead of greater than the crime, a principle enunciated by Antigone (Soph. *Ant.* 927-8).

If equality of retribution was not an absolute standard of morality, the Greeks were at least sensitive to the problems inherent in excessive retaliation (cf Soph. fr. 589 *TrGF*). This is clear in the present passage, where the escalating violence spirals rapidly out of control: Laius and his servant drive Oedipus away, perhaps using only words (804-5); Oedipus responds with a blow, evidently of his fist (806-7); Laius is then the first to use a weapon, coming down upon Oedipus's head with an ox-goad (807-9); Oedipus finally kills them all with a deadlier weapon, his staff (811-13).

Why, then, mention the provocation at all? (It is not in earlier or later accounts.[64]) The reason is that neither here nor anywhere else did Sophocles portray an irredeemably evil man. Faced with a dilemma, Oedipus chooses a crime that he would never have gone out of his way to commit.

Thirdly, it will be argued that no one censures Oedipus for murder as murder (as distinct from regicide and parricide). On a strict application of the principle that what is not mentioned in the play does not exist (schol. *Il.* 5.385d), such censure must be impossible. The answer to this lies in the play's structure. The rapid movement of the play between two distinct questions, the public one of who killed Laius (106-7) and the private worry of Oedipus over his parents' identity (437, 779-93, 1017), allows no time for the identity of Oedipus's victims to be raised in its own right. If a third question arises at all, it is the red herring of whether one can foreknow the future (720-2, 945-9, 981-2). Oedipus reveals to Jocasta and the audience his past, apparently for this first time, only when the play is half over (813), and in the context of the distracting search for Laius's killer.

If Oedipus chose to kill the old man and his act was no mere accident or reflex, what was his motive? None is explicit in the text, which gives an account remarkable for its succinctness (813); we must infer one from Oedipus's character.[65] Oedipus, exemplary in so many respects, is led to his crime because he has the Sophoclean hero's impulsive incapacity to yield,[66] as when he ignores the pleas of his wife and herdsman to stop his investigation (1060-1, 1165).[67] Read this trait as hubris[68] or heroism; it keeps him from yielding to the old man and thence leads him to murder. "Character is destiny."[69]

If Oedipus is unquestionably guilty of murder, we must turn to the question of whether he is guilty of the other component of parricide, harming his father. Oedipus does harm his father and this was a grave offence,[70] but he never would have done so knowingly, having taken elaborate, if futile, steps to avoid it. Therefore, he could[71] defend himself by saying that he did not know that Laius was his father. One can act in ignorance and still bear some blame, according to Pittacus of Mytilene, who enacted a law that one be fined double for an offence committed while drunk.[72] This law was not designed to discourage drunkenness,[73] or he would have outlawed wine, but rather, as Aristotle approvingly explains, because one is culpable of a crime committed in ignorance if this ignorance arises through negligence. Oedipus's abuse of his father is an extraordinary example of such a crime.

One would not have thought Oedipus negligent in harming his father. Indeed, his abandoning of his comfortable life in Corinth to embark upon the wandering that brought him to Thebes seems the opposite of negligence. Nevertheless, Oedipus was negligent in remaining ignorant of his father's identity, having been led into this negligence again by his impulsive character. He made the trek to Delphi to learn who his parents were and, upon hearing that he was destined to defile them, immediately abandoned the object of his journey, for the oracle manifestly did not resolve it (788-9), raising instead the separate (789) issue of parricide and incest, and Oedipus set off to flee Corinth. Far from distracting him from his parents' identity as it did,[74] the oracle's response made it imperative that he pursue just this quest. As a distant second best, he might have contemplated a life of non-violence and celibacy[75] rather than murdering the first people he met and marrying in the first city to which he came.

The failure to consult the oracle further is an essential ingredient in his downfall and shifts the blame on to his own shoulders, as is shown by Sophocles' friend (cf Soph. fr. 5 West *IEG*) Herodotus.[76] Herodotus tells how Croesus, having received the oracle that if he attacked Persia, he would destroy a mighty empire, caused his own misfortune by attacking without first determining which empire was meant (Hdt. 1.91.4). Delphi addressed a similar rebuke in like circumstances to the children of Heracles (290 Parke-Wormell = L63 Fontenrose). While repeated consultation of an oracle might seem an improbable pestering of the god, myth records many examples of just this phenomenon.[77] Like that of Croesus and the Heraclids, Oedipus's ignorance results from his negligence in failing either to understand Apollo's warning or to inquire further about a question that the oracle has just shown to be crucial. In this regard Creon is an important foil, showing constant reliance upon Delphi (603, 1442-3).

There are signs that Oedipus has not been told the truth: the scars on his feet that have always troubled him (1033) and the story of the drunk (780), which was widely circulated,[78] and which Polybus and Merope do not deny outright (783-4). Oedipus, a reader (though often, as we shall see in chapter 6, a misreader) of signs, has to his credit noted these and feels the uncertainty of his parentage as an impairment of his intellect (786); it motivates his hundred-kilometre walk on mountain roads from Corinth to Delphi and repeatedly rears its head during his quest for the regicide (437, 779-93, 1017). He elevates his ignorance into his governing principle, acknowledging that he is "the Know-Nothing Oedipus" (397) and relishing the irony of his apparent superiority over the divinely inspired Teiresias.

This man, who knows of his ignorance, acts not once but repeatedly as though he were privy even to hidden facts, treating the many phantasms of his imagination (124-5, 139-40, 380-9) as though they were manifest revelations (534-5). Likewise at the crossroads he acted—knowingly and yet as though unknowingly—in ignorance, recklessly failing to yield when it was moral and convenient to do so.

In light of these observations, we see that Oedipus is guilty of parricide as well as being an innocent victim of incest. But there is still one point to make in his favour, namely that his fate was unconditionally pre-ordained.[79] "Sophocles," writes Dodds, "has provided a conclusive answer to those who suggest that Oedipus could, and therefore should, have avoided his fate. The oracle was *unconditional* . . . And what an oracle predicts is bound to happen."[80]

While a conditional prediction allows for the play of free will, an unconditional prediction might be supposed to imply predestination. Even on this assumption the prediction does not exonerate Oedipus, for predestination does not, paradoxically, constitute a compulsion. Dodds knows this. His own book *The Greeks and the Irrational* made familiar the concept of overdetermination, whereby according to early Greek thought an event may be "doubly determined, on the natural and on the supernatural plane."[81] We cannot deny this overdetermined status to Oedipus's act: he killed Laius by free choice, thereby abdicating any claim to essential moral innocence. Oedipus's act is also determined on the supernatural plane by fate, and the Pythia says so (713), but fate is an impersonal force, not an Olympian deity or even a lackey of the gods like the Furies, and it is as binding upon gods as upon mortals (cf *Il.* 16.433-61).

Oedipus's unsuccessful attempt to elude his fate has been attributed to hubris,[82] but he would have invited greater condemnation either by rushing towards Corinth in homicidal and libidinous determination to fulfil the prophecy or by quietly going about his business like some Stoic *avant la lettre*. Moreover, Socrates is not hubristic in trying to disprove Delphi's claim that he is the wisest of men,[83] a less than total faith in the ineluctability of the Pythia's predictions being neither unusual at Athens nor in itself evidence of impiety.

Even apart from overdetermination, Oedipus's fate does not absolve him of blame, since he could have fulfilled it in total innocence. Laius could have "died at the hand of his son" (713) and Oedipus become the "murderer" (793) of his father had he killed him accidentally, for example while hunting or playing the javelin or discus (cf e.g. Hdt. 1.43, Apollod. *Bibl.* 1.3.3). One who kills by accident is readily called a "murderer" by a society that denies this name and the consequent legal proceedings neither to animals nor even to inanimate objects (Arist. *Ath. Pol.* 57.4; cf Soph. *OT* 969-70).

Furthermore, an unconditional prediction is not evidence for predestination if time for the agent making the prediction is not an abstract, inexorable forward flow. Consider this example: suppose I videotape a group of playing children and, before playing back the tape, I state that during the play-session Lee will steal Tom's teddy bear. My prediction is unconditional and will be brought to pass, and yet I did not compel Lee to act in this way; I may even wish that it had not happened (it has spoiled my movie). I am, in fact, incapable of imposing my will on the children or of removing theirs from them, but I can accurately predict how they will act because I do not experience time as they do, as a chronometric, impersonal medium. If Apollo has a relationship to time like that in this example, he could accurately predict events without ordaining them and he could have such a relationship to time only if Time itself is a free agent, moving forward or backward, quickly or slowly, for the benefit of those whom he would help. According to the Greek conception, such was in fact the nature of Time.[84] In our play Time is personified as "the All-seer" (1213).[85] The situation in the play is more complex than in the videotape example because Apollo does not predict the event to a disinterested third party but to the protagonist himself, and Oedipus reacts of his own free will to the god's prediction. Yet

such is the nature of fate that any action that Oedipus might have taken in response to any prediction that Apollo might have made would have ended in the same result, albeit brought about by a different chain of intermediary events.

To sum up: By murdering the belligerent stranger, his superior and elder, along with his retinue, including the sacred herald, while they were engaged upon official religious and state business, Oedipus violated the prerogatives of Zeus of Strangers, the respect due to superiors and elders, and the principle of fitting retaliation; he is therefore guilty of murder. He knew that he was acting in ignorance and yet behaved as though he did not know this; he is therefore guilty of father abuse. He was fated to commit his crime, but it cannot be shown that he was compelled to do so, and certainly not in the way he did.

What, then, of Apollo, who manifests himself in the story of Oedipus (1329)? If Oedipus had been, as the prevailing view holds, essentially morally innocent, then Apollo would have been unjust in allowing him to suffer as he does. Now that we have found Oedipus in fact responsible in some measure for some of the suffering that he incurs, the possibility arises that Apollo's actions may be just. There is no *a priori* reason to think that they are so; the gods of Greek myth lie, commit adultery, are gluttons. "Men find some things unjust, other things just; but in the eyes of God all things are beautiful and good and just."[86] Nevertheless, if the actions of Sophocles' Apollo conform to an accepted definition of justice, we should admit that he at least is in that sense a just god.

We have seen that he did not compel Oedipus to kill his father and sleep with his mother, but neither did he try to prevent him from doing so—for example, by giving him a straightforward answer to his question concerning his parents. The reason he did not is linked, perhaps, to the fundamental difference of power between god and man. Gods cannot reveal themselves undisguised to men without destroying them;[87] when they appear incognito they are often recognized only at the end of the encounter and only by the extremity of their body, their feet (*Il.* 13.71-2, Verg. *Aen.* 1.405, etc.). This disguise principle is intensified in connection with verbal communication. Gods have their own language and their own special intonation.[88] The inevitable process of translation needed to enable them to communicate with men is complex: at Delphi, when "the enquirer entered, the Pythia was already under the influence of Apollo, and was in some abnormal state of trance or ecstasy . . . [Her] answer would vary in its degree of coherence and intelligibility. When it had been given, the prophet would reduce it to some form, and dictate it to the enquirer."[89] The answer given by this convoluted process was perforce oblique: "The lord whose oracle is in Delphi neither speaks nor hides, but gives a sign" (Heraclitus 22 B 93 Diels-Kranz). It is scarcely surprising if the answer is not so straightforward as we would like.

Even so, Apollo does not lie to Oedipus. The cause of Oedipus's extraordinary ignorance of the events attendant upon his birth lies with Polybus and Merope. The drunk at the banquet accused Oedipus of being a supposititious child (780), but this is itself either a lie or an error, for Polybus was privy to the secret (1021). Even at the drunk's false charge the royal couple express anger, thereby effectively misleading Oedipus (783-4).[90] Later, a quick detection of the regicide is prevented by the lone survivor's mendacious description of "many robbers" (122-3).[91] In both cases humans, not gods, have lied.

Whether we find any justice in Apollo's actions will depend upon our definition of the term. Simonides' definition, cited by Polemarchus in Plato's *Republic,* is "giving back to each person what is owing." So conceived, justice is wholly reactive. It requires one not to initiate any action but only to respond in kind to the actions of others. It does not require one to help any person (by warning of impending disaster or by any other means) unless one has been helped first by him. True to the Greek's anthropomorphic conception of the gods, this rule applies to human-god relationships just as to relationships between humans. In the *Iliad* Apollo helps Chryses because he has roofed many temples for him (*Il.* 1.39). In the *Oresteia* the gods punish Agamemnon and Clytaemnestra in response to their breaking of laws.

According to this conception of justice, Apollo is under no obligation to help Oedipus by warning him of the impending catastrophe, for Oedipus has performed no prior service for him. Yet, once Oedipus has offended the gods by his sacrilegious behaviour at the crossroads, Apollo is obliged to intervene and ensure that the fitting penalty of exile is enforced. He does this through the plague and the oracle to Creon (97); we can also see him at work in the fortuitous arrival of the Corinthian messenger (924), who, again by a striking pseudo-coincidence, is the very man who rescued the infant Oedipus in the first place (1022). Compassionate and comforting Apollo is not, but he is just in this all-too-human sense.

At this point a further objection might be raised. Given that, from Oedipus's perspective, the murder of Laius is a crime justly punished by his subsequent suffering, is not the same act, when viewed from the perspective of Laius, merely an absurd suffering and, as such, evidence for the wanton cruelty of the gods that negates any other hint of divine justice in the play? When viewed from the perspective of Jocasta, does not the incestuous marriage, discovery of which provoked her suicide, also refute any claims of divine justice? I can meet this objection in two ways: first, Laius was not a wholly innocent bystander at the time of his murder, having actually provoked Oedipus to strike. Second, the suffering of Laius and Jocasta may be construed as punishment for an earlier crime of their own: that in which he "yoked" the feet of the infant Oedipus (718) and she gave the child to a herdsman to kill (1173-4).[92]

Opinion is divided over whether newborns were commonly exposed in fifth-century Athens.[93] Even if they were,

it would be rare to treat a healthy, legitimate, first-born son like Oedipus in this way.[94] Exposure did not constitute homicide, first because the newborn was not a legal person until its adoption into the family during the naming festival, which took place on about the tenth day of life,[95] and an unwanted child would be exposed before this time—Oedipus, for example, at three days (717-18); and secondly because the parent did not actually kill the child. Yet, while not criminal, the act was open to moral censure: Oedipus blames his parents for hurting him knowingly, while he committed his crimes in ignorance (Soph. *OC* 273, 547-8, 988-99); the servant saved him out of pity (1178), and Jocasta, thinking of the exposure, calls him "wretched" (855).[96] Furthermore, Oedipus's was no ordinary exposure. Ordinary exposure is not necessarily lethal, thrusting the newborn from the family only, not necessarily from life. All children exposed in myth[97] and, presumably, many in real life were saved and reared as foundlings, for the parents, callous enough to abandon their child, scruple actually to shed its blood. By contrast, Laius and Jocasta, intending actually to kill their son, left him on a trackless mountain (719) where the hope of rescue was slight and took the unprecedented step of maiming him, which both weakened him and made it unlikely that he would be rescued even if found. We note the symmetrical justice in the adult Oedipus's causing the deaths in fact of the parents who tried to kill him as an infant. If they had not exposed Oedipus and tried thereby to evade Apollo's oracle, then Oedipus would have known who they were and would not have unknowingly murdered the one and slept with the other (he shows a revulsion from doing so willingly).

Recognition that Oedipus's guilt and Apollo's justice are greater than is usually allowed for affects how we understand what—if any—is Sophocles' message. Sophocles' gods, like those of Aeschylus, are just in an obvious human sense. It is no longer true, on the basis of this play at least, to speak of "the incomprehensible ways of the divine will" or to hold that "one must not bring in false concepts of human morality involving good and evil."[98] These are precisely the concepts necessary to understand Apollo's role in Oedipus's suffering. It is even less true to say that "what causes his ruin is his own strength and courage, his loyalty to Thebes, and his loyalty to the truth."[99] This is only "the immediate cause"[100] of his ruin, and the Greeks are far more sensitive than we to ultimate causes, abounding as their myths do in nativities, inventors, aetiologies, and even an original sin or two.[101] This is especially true in a legal context: for example, in Plato's *Apology* (18a-b) Socrates identifies and refutes his "former accusers." Oedipus is himself an aficionado of ultimate causes, beginning with confident relish (132) the seemingly hopeless investigation into the regicide and extrapolating from Teiresias's claim that he, Oedipus, has committed parricide and incest not only an alleged proximate cause (Teiresias has been bribed to say this) but also a putative distant cause (Creon bribed him because he wants the kingship [380-9]). We must never forget the ultimate cause of Oedipus's ruin - the murder at the crossroads comes back after all these years (613, 1213) to haunt him.

The profound differences between Aeschylus and Sophocles are not theological, and it is difficult to agree with those who find in the god who tells Orestes, "You *must* kill your mother,"[102] a kinder, gentler Apollo than the god who tells Oedipus, "You *will* kill your father." What is new—and far from comforting—in Sophocles is his assessment, gloomy even by Greek standards, of the limits of human knowledge. The ignorance of Sophoclean characters runs through a broad spectrum: Oedipus mistakes his parents for strangers, homecoming for exile, and hereditary kingship for unconstitutional rule; Creon in *Antigone* twice mistakes the priorities of the living for those of the dead;[103] Deianira mistakes a poison for a love-potion; and Ajax mistakes a sheep for Agamemnon. In Sophocles humans deceive one another[104] and people act with a self-confidence unwarranted by their feeble grasp of reality. Only once does a god deceive—Athena in *Ajax* (51-2)—and her deception, motivated by retribution (762-77), prevents a crime from being committed. It is in his anthropology rather than his theology that the uncompromising quality of Sophocles' world consists.

The function of art, according to Dodds, quoting Dr Johnson, is "the enlargement of our sensibility."[105] This phrase is perhaps too broad to capture the specific virtue of tragic drama. The virtue of tragedy lies elsewhere, in a region suggested by the examination question set by Dodds for his undergraduates, namely, in adding understanding to our spontaneous emotional response, in order to assert eternal providence, and justify the ways of God to men.

Notes

1. Dodds 1966 = Dodds 1973, 64-77. The article has been cited frequently and anthologized several times, e.g. in O'Brien 1968, 17-29; Segal 1983, 177-88; and Bloom 1988, 35-47.

2. Dodds 1966 identifies and refutes two further views (that the *OT* is a tragedy of fate and that Sophocles, as a pure artist, does not concern himself with morality or religion at all), which, since they are mutually exclusive of the view I support, I join him in rejecting.

3. Dodds 1966, 37 = 1973, 64.

4. Ibid., 42 = 69.

5. Ibid., 47 = 75.

6. Ibid., 45 = 73. Dodds holds a similar view of Aesch. *Eum.*; he writes (1973, 47-8): "Nearly everyone agrees . . . that there is a political point here; but after a century of controversy there is still no agreement on what the point is. I believe myself that this is exactly what the poet would have wished: he was writing a political play, yes; but a propagandist play, no."

7. Of these Dodds mentions (1966, 38 = 1973, 65) especially Wilamowitz 1899. He also (1966, 42 = 1973, 69) sees similarities between his view and those of Whitman, Waldock, Letters, Ehrenberg, Knox, and Kirkwood.

8. Winnington-Ingram 1980, 203, and Dawe 1982, 4-5.

9. The view that Oedipus is guilty is expressed by Vellacott 1964, and Cameron 1968, 133.

10. See Stanford 1983, who cites bibliography at 174-6, to which add Kokolakis 1986, and Heath 1987, 5-36.

11. Golden 1976.

12. One could, however, argue (as Charles Daniels has pointed out to me) that by knowing he was acting in ignorance and yet, by marrying Jocasta, behaving as though he did not know this, Oedipus was as guilty of mother abuse as of father abuse.

13. Dodds 1966, 38-9 = 1973, 66.

14. On this question, see especially Bremer 1969, Stinton 1975, and Halliwell 1986a, 202-37.

15. On the general preference for plot over character, see Goldhill 1990, who cites bibliography at 111 n 32. On character in Sophocles, see Easterling 1977.

16. Dodds 1966, 48 = 1973, 76.

17. Ibid., 39 = 66.

18. There are no grounds on which to assess Oedipus's guilt or innocence in the case of his incest, for incest was not formally illegal at Athens; see Harrison 1968, 22 n 3, and Broadbent 1968, 155. What matters more than the legality or otherwise of incest is that incest is obviously a violation of motherhood, which the Greeks held in high esteem (see Sommerstein 1989 ad Aesch. *Eum.* 657-66), and apparently constituted a pollution (Parker 1983, 97-8).

19. Knox 1964, and Easterling 1985.

20. Garner 1987, 103-4, and Lewis 1989; cf Greiffenhagen 1966.

21. See MacDowell 1978, 113-18.

22. . . . e.g. Lys. 1.

23. . . . Dem. 23.53; cf Aeschin. 1.91.

24. Gagarin 1978, 118 n 32, *pace* Wilamowitz 1899, 55 = 1931-37, vi.209.

25. Eur. *Phoen.* 44-5. Even in Euripides' version the robbery is incidental to the murder and is not the motive for it.

26. . . . Lys. 4.11, Dem. 23.50, 47.7, Isoc. 20.1, Pl. *Leg.* 869d, Arist. *Rhet.* 2.24.9 (= 1402a), Apollod. *Bibl.* 2.4.9.

27. Gagarin 1978.

28. Ibid., 117.

29. As is claimed by Wilamowitz 1899, 55 = 1931-37, vi.209; Sheppard 1920, xxix; and Bowra 1944, 165.

30. Not even in the *OC* does he make this claim explicitly. . . .

31. For Laius had, of course, wanted to kill him when he exposed him years before, a point to which we shall return. . . .

32. Loomis 1972, 93.

33. *Od.* 1.35-43, 3.309-10, 11.422-30.

34. *Il.* 2.661-70, 13.694-7, 15.431-9, 16.572-6, 23.85-90, 24.480-3, *Od.* 13.259-75, 14.380-1, 15.271-82, [Hes.] *Aspis* 9-19, 80-5, Hes. fr. 257 Merkelbach-West.

35. . . . *Il.* 9.633, 18.497-508.

36. Laius: *Od.* 11.271-80; Iphitus: *Od.* 21.24-30.

37. There are other murderers known to Greek myth as we find it in Apollodorus who make no compensation or purification for murder; these are listed by Parker 1983, 375, sect. 2 and 3.

38. I shall henceforth use the term "morality" as a shorthand for "ancient Greek popular morality."

39. See App. B.

40. Pind. *Pyth.* 11.38, Theogn. 911-92, Prodicus apud Xen. *Mem.* 2.1.21-34 (= 84 B 2 Diels-Kranz), Hdt. 1.11.2, Pl. *Leg.* 799c. Beyond its empirical demonstrability, recent readers of the play are reminded of this fact by the commentary of Dawe 1982, 3, a scholar scarcely given to rash interpretative conjecture. See, too, Halliwell 1986, 189.

41. Agamemnon, . . . commands one hundred ships to Achilles' fifty (*Il.* 2.576, 685). See Drews 1983; Geddes 1984, 28-36; and Rihill 1986.

42. E.g. *Od.* 2.14, Tyrt. fr. 12.37 West, Theogn. 935-6. . . .

43. The king has naturally undertaken a mission to Delphi himself, rather than delegating it; cf Pind. *Ol.* 6.37-8. No motive for the mission is given or necessary in the play.

44. Dawe 1982, 174 ad 805.

45. As Vellacott 1964, 140, argues.

46. E.g. Ar. *Nub.* 993, Pl. *Resp.* 412c, 465a, Xen. *Rep. Lac.* 2.10.

47. See Gould 1973, 90-4.

48. *Il.* 13.624-5, *Od.* 9.270-1, 14.283-4. Burkert 1985, 130.

49. *Od.* 17.483-7, Ov. *Met.* 1.212-13, 8.611-724; cf Acts 14.12. Hollis 1970, 108-9, and 1990, 341-54.

50. *Il.* 6.119-236. This is a special case, since Glaucus and Diomedes are connected by earlier ties of family; but then so too were Oedipus and Laius, if they had only bothered to stop and find this out. . . .

51. The particular relevance of this story to my argument was pointed out to me by Emmet Robbins.

52. So Jebb 1887, 110 ad 804-12.

53. See Bill 1901.

54. Jebb 1887 ad 804-12.

55. See Wéry 1966. The relevance of this evidence to the case of Oedipus has been noted by Fitton Brown 1969, 308. . . .

56. Plut. *Per.* 30.3, Dem. 12.4. Oedipus, who killed a man engaged in a *theoria,* will easily insult a seer (386-9; cf his insulting of the Pythia, 964-5), since that is a relatively common form of disrespect for the god's servants (cf *Il.* 1.106, 12.231-50, Soph. *Ant.* 1033-8).

57. Garvie 1986 ad 899.

58. . . . Aesch. *Cho.* 899, Soph. *Phil.* 908, Eur. *Alc.* 380, cf Aesch. *Suppl.* 379-80, *Ag.* 206-7, Soph. *Aj.* 457, Hdt. 1.11.3-4, Eur. *Med.* 502, Ar. *Vesp.* 319a (paratragic). See further Fowler 1987b.

59. Bowra 1944, 190.

60. Cf Neoptolemus in Soph. *Phil.,* who shares the nature of the father he has never known.

61. E.g. *Ant.* 641-4. Blundell 1989, 26-59.

62. . . . Bowra 1944, 164, is wrong to say, "Laius was the aggressor and got what he deserved"; by Oedipus's own admission he got *more* than he deserved.

63. Gagarin 1978, 118 n 32. . . .

64. Earlier accounts: *Od.* 11.273, Pind. *Ol.* 2.38-9; later accounts: cf Eur. *Phoen.* 37-44, in which Oedipus is provoked, but not by Laius. . . .

65. Dodds 1966, 38-41 = 1974, 66-8, ridicules the scrutiny of character, but I would argue that much of this scrutiny has been rather insufficiently focused than misdirected.

66. See Knox 1964, 15-16.

67. He does yield once in the play, with great reluctance, at 669-72, when he spares Creon in response to the combined pleas of Jocasta and the chorus.

68. In chapter 7 we will see reason for preferring the hubris over the heroism interpretation. Some scholars such as Winnington-Ingram 1980 have tried to have an Oedipus at once arrogant (183) and innocent (203).

69. Heraclitus 22 B 119 Diels-Kranz, quoted by Winnington-Ingram 1980, 177.

70. Hes. *Op.* 331-2, Theogn. 821-2, Aesch. *Eum.* 269-71, Ar. *Ran.* 147-50.

71. As he does in Soph. *OC* 273, 547-8, 988-9.

72. Diog. Laert. 1.76, Ar. *Pol.* 2.9.9 (= 1274b), *Rhet.* 2.25.7 (= 1402b).

73. *Pace* Diog. Laert. . . .

74. He acts as though he knew that Polybus and Merope were undoubtedly his parents; cf 826-7.

75. Which can only with extreme latitude be character-ized as "compil[ing] a handlist of all the things he must not do" (Dodds 1966, 40 = 1974, 69, quoting Waldock); it would be a short list.

76. Sophocles and Herodotus shared views on many top-ics: e.g. *Ant.* 908-12 = Hdt. 3.119.6; *El.* 417-23 = Hdt. 1.108.1; *OC* 337-41 = Hdt. 2.35.2; *OT* 1528-30 = Hdt. 1.32.5; *El.* 62-4 = Hdt. 4.95; *OC* 1224-7 = Hdt. 7.46.3-4.

77. 4-5, 43-4, 94-5, 161, 216-21 Parke-Wormell = Q58A-B, Q28-9, Q146-7, Q191A-B, Q7-9 Fonten-rose.

78. See App. C.

79. 148, 149 Parke-Wormell = L17, L18 Fontenrose. Wilamowitz 1899, 55 = 1931-37, vi.209; Dodds 1966, 41 = 1973, 69.

80. Dodds 1966, 41 = 1973, 69 (Dodds' italics).

81. Dodds 1951, 31. In the present context he cites, after Knox 1957, 39, the case of Peter, who fulfilled Jesus' prediction that he would deny him (Matt. 26.34, 74-5) but "did so by an act of free choice" (Dodds 1966, 43 = 1973, 71). Kitto 1958, 60, is right in say-ing, "there was nothing compulsory about the affair at the cross-roads." Dodds uses the concept of over-determination in his study of the *Oresteia* 1973, 56. . . .

82. Halsted 1979, 77.

83. Pl. *Ap.* 21a-b (420 Parke-Wormell = H3 Fontenrose).

84. De Romilly 1968, 50, writes, "Even if things are supposed to exist through all eternity and to have been decided regardless of time, it is with time and in time that they come to be. He *uncovers* them." See also Vivante 1972, who cites bibliography at 130-1, to which add Komornicka 1976.

85. This is a title of Zeus (Aesch. *Eum.* 1045, Soph. *OC* 1085) and of Helios (Aesch. *PV* 91; cf *Il.* 3.277).

86. Heraclitus 22 B 102 Diels-Kranz, quoted by Dodds 1966, 47 = 1973, 76.

87. Zeus and Semele: Pind. *Ol.* 2.25-6, Eur. *Bacch.* 6-12; Yahweh and Moses: Exod. 33.18-23.

88. For their own language, see Hes. *Theog.* 831. . . . See also Watkins 1970, who cites bibliography at 1

nn 1 and 2, to which add Clay 1972 and 1974 and Calderón Felices 1982.

89. Parke and Wormell 1956, i.33.

90. Nothing would have prevented Polybus and Merope from openly adopting a child, but, as a foundling (1026), Oedipus cannot be adopted if Athenian laws are imagined as holding good in Corinth; hence they are forced to lie. See Harrison 1968, 71.

91. Goodhart 1978, 56 n 2. . . .

92. Lloyd-Jones 1983, 121, likewise believes that Laius must deserve his suffering, yet his own solution (that the suffering is provoked by Laius's rape of Chrysippus) violates Aristarchus's rule, "What is not mentioned in the play does not exist," and so is less economical than the view proposed here.

93. Cameron 1932 and Harris 1982 hold that exposure was common; Golden 1982 holds that the exposure of girls was common; van Hook 1920, Bolkestein 1922, Engels 1980, and Patterson 1985 are far more sceptical about the frequency of exposure of children of either sex.

94. Health: Patterson 1985, 113-14; legitimacy: ibid. 115-16; primogeniture: Cameron 1932, 106 (cf Pl. *Theat.* 161c); maleness: Golden 1981. Tyro in one of Sophocles' plays of that name exposed her twins because they were illegitimate. It would of course be rare in real life, if not unparalleled in legend (cf Paris: Apollod. *Bibl.* 3.12.5), that a child should be prophesied to kill his father (Soph. *OT* 712-13).

95. Richardson 1974, 231-4; Patterson 1985, 105-6; and Golden 1986, 252-6.

96. Golden 1981, 331; cf Pl. *Theat.* 161a.

97. On exposure as a motif in myth see Murray 1943 and Redford 1967. . . .

98. "Die unerforschlichen Wege des göttlichen Willens"; "man darf nicht gut und böse falsche Begriffe men-schlicher Sittlichkeit hineintragen," Wilamowitz 1899, 56 = 1931-37, vi.210.

99. Dodds 1966, 43 = 1973, 71.

100. Ibid., 43 = 71.

101. Nativities: Pind. *Ol.* 1.26-7, 6.39-47, 7.35-8, *Nem.* 1.35-47; inventors: Pind. *Ol.* 1.40-5, 7.42, 13.17-22, *Pyth.* 2.32, 4.217, 12.6-8, and see Kleingünther 1933 and Thraede 1962. . . .

102. Aesch. *Cho.* 269-96, 900-2, 953-6, 1029-30, *Eum.* 798-9.

103. First at *Ant.* 773-80, 1068-71; secondly at 1192-1205.

104. *Aj.* 646-92, *Trach.* 249-90, 569-77, *El.* 680-763, *Phil.* 343-90.

105. Dodds 1966, 45, 49 = 1973, 74, 77. This curious doctrine of enlarged sensibility was no mere temporary aberration of Dodds' thought, for he had enunciated it years before in Dodds 1944, xliii = 1960, xlvii. Dodds does not specify the source of this quotation, but David Sansone has most plausibly suggested to me that it is an inaccurate quotation from memory of Johnson's *Life of Waller* §139: "From poetry the reader justly expects, and from good poetry always obtains, the enlargement of his comprehension and elevation of his fancy."

Abbreviations

Abbreviations of the names of authors and titles follow those given in N.G.L. Hammond, *The Oxford Classical Dictionary,* 2nd ed. (Oxford: Clarendon 1970), ix-xxii.

AC: *L'Antiquité classique*

BICS: *Bulletin of the Institute of Classical Studies, University of London*

CB: *Classical Bulletin*

CP: *Classical Philology*

CQ: *Classical Quarterly*

CR: *Classical Review*

EMC/CV: *Echoes du Monde Classique/Classical Views*

G&R: *Greece and Rome*

GRBS: *Greek, Roman and Byzantine Studies*

HSCP: *Harvard Studies in Classical Philology*

IEG M.L. West, *Iambi et elegi Graeci.* Oxford: Clarendon 1971–72

JHS: *Journal of Hellenic Studies*

LCM: *Liverpool Classical Monthly*

RHMUS: *Rheinisches Museum*

TAPA: *Transactions of the American Philological Association*

TRGF B. Snell, *Tragicorum Graecorum fragmenta.* Göttingen: Vandenhoeck and Ruprecht 1971-

Works Cited

Bloom, H., ed. 1988. *Modern Critical Interpretations: Sophocles' Oedipus Rex.* New York: Chelsea House Publishers

Blundell, M.W. 1989. *Helping Friends and Harming Enemies.* Cambridge: Cambridge University Press

Bolkestein, H. 1922. "The Exposure of Children at Athens. . . ." CP 17.222-39

Bowra, C. M. 1944. *Sophoclean Tragedy.* Oxford: Clarendon

Bremer, J. M. 1969. *Hamartia.* Amsterdam: Adolf M. Hakkert

Broadbent, M. 1968. *Studies in Greek Genealogy.* Leiden: E. J. Brill

Burkert, W. 1985. *Greek Religion.* Trans. J. Raffan. London: Blackwell

Calderón Felices, J. 1982. "Lengua de los dioses—lengua de los hombres." *Faventia* 4.5-33

Cameron, A. 1932. "The Exposure of Children and Greek Ethics." CR 46.105-14

———. 1968. *The Identity of Oedipus the King.* New York and London: New York University Press

Clay, J. S. 1972. "The Planktai and Moly: Divine Naming and Knowing in Homer." *Hermes* 100.127-31

———. 1974. "Demas and Aude: The Nature of Divine Transformations in Homer." *Hermes* 102.129-36

Dawe, R. D. 1982. *Sophocles: Oedipus Rex.* Cambridge: Cambridge University Press

de Romilly, J. 1968. *Time in Greek Tragedy.* Ithaca: Cornell University Press

Dodds, E. R. 1966. "On Misunderstanding the *Oedipus Rex.*" G&R 13.37-49

———. 1973. *The Ancient Concept of Progress.* Oxford: Clarendon

Drews, R. 1983. *Basileus.* New Haven: Yale University Press

Easterling, P. E. 1985. "Anachronism in Greek Tragedy." JHS 105.1-10

Engles, D. 1980. "The Problem of Female Infanticide in the Greco-Roman World." CP 75.112-20

Fitton Brown, A. D. 1969. Review of W.-H. Friedrich, *Vorbild und Neugestaltung,* CR 19.307-9

Fowler, R. L. 1987b. "The Rhetoric of Desperation." HSCP 91.5-38

Gagarin, M. 1978. "Self-Defense in Athenian Homicide Law." GRBS 19.111-20

Garner, R. 1987. *Law and Society in Classical Athens.* London: Croom Helm

Garvie, A. F. 1986. *Aeschyli Choephori.* Oxford: Clarendon

Geddes, A. G. 1984. "Who's Who in Homeric Society?" CQ 34.17-36

Golden, L. 1976. "The Clarification Theory of *Katharsis.*" *Hermes* 104.437-52

Golden, M. 1981. "Demography and the Exposure of Girls at Athens." *Phoenix* 35.316-31

———. 1986. "Names and Naming at Athens: Three Studies." EMC/CV 5.245-69

Godhill, S. 1990. "Character and Action, Representation and Reading: Greek Tragedy and Its Critics." 100-27 in C. Pelling, ed., *Characterization and Individuality in Greek Literature*. Oxford: Clarendon

Goodhart, S. 1978. ". . . Oedipus and Laius' Many Murderers." *Diacritics* 8.55-71

Gould, J. 1973. "*Hiketeia*." JHS 93.74-103

Greiffenhagen, G. 1966. "Der Prozess des Ödipus." *Hermes* 94.147-76

Halliwell, S. 1986a. *Aristotle's Poetics*. London: Duckworth

Halsted, J. B. 1979. "Oedipus, in *Oedipus the King*, Commits Many Serious Errors." CB 55.73-7

Harris, W. V. 1982. "The Theoretical Possibility of Extensive Infanticide in the Graeco-Roman World." CQ 32.114-16

Harrison, A.R.W. 1968. *The Law of Athens* I: *The Family and Property*. Oxford: Clarendon

Heath, M. 1987. *The Poetics of Greek Tragedy*. London: Duckworth

Jebb, R. C. 1893. *Sophocles: The Oedipus Tyrannus*. Cambridge: Cambridge University Press

Kleingünther, A. 1933. . . . *Philologus* Supp. 26

Knox, B. M. W. 1964. *The Heroic Temper*. Berkeley: University of California Press

Kokolakis, M. M. 1986. "Greek Drama: The Stirring of Pity." Vol. 1.170-8 in J.H. Betts, et al., eds., *Studies = Festschrift T.B.L. Webster*. Bristol: Bristol Classical Press

Komornicka, A. M. 1976. "La Notion du temps chez Pindare." *Eos* 64.5-15

Lewis, R. G. 1989. "The Procedural Basis of Sophocles' *Oedipus Tyrannus*." GRBS 30.41-66

Lloyd-Jones, H. 1983. *The Justice of Zeus*. 2nd ed. Berkeley: University of California Press

Loomis, W. T. 1972. "The Nature of Premeditation in Athenian Homicide Law." JHS 92.86-95

MacDowell, D. M. 1978. *The Law in Classical Athens*. London: Thames and Hudson

Murray, G. 1943. "Ritual Elements in the New Comedy." CQ 37.46-54

O'Brien, M. J., ed. 1968. *Twentieth Century Interpretations of Oedipus Rex*. Englewood Cliffs, NJ: Prentice-Hall

Parke, H. W., and D. E. W. Wormell. 1956. *The Delphic Oracle* I *The History*. Oxford: Clarendon

Parker, R. 1983. *Miasma*. Oxford: Clarendon

Patterson, C. 1985. "'Not Worth the Rearing': The Causes of Infant Exposure in Ancient Greece." TAPA 115.103-23

Redford, D. B. 1967. "The Literary Motif of the Exposed Child." *Numen* 14.209-28

Richardson, N. J. 1974. *The Homeric Hymn to Demeter*. Oxford: Clarendon

Rihill, T. 1986. "Kings and Commoners in Homeric Society." LCM 11.81-91

Segal, E. 1983. *Oxford Readings in Greek Tragedy*. Oxford: Clarendon

Sheppard, J. T. 1920. *The Oedipus Tyrannus of Sophocles*. Cambridge: Cambridge University Press

Sommerstein, A. H. 1989. *Aeschylus: Eumenides*. Cambridge: Cambridge University Press

Stanford, W. B. 1983. *Greek Tragedy and the Emotions*. London: Routledge and Kegan Paul

Stinton, T. C. W. 1975. "*Hamartia* in Aristotle and Greek Tragedy." CQ 25.221-54 = *Collected Papers on Greek Tragedy*. Oxford: Clarendon 1990. 143-85

Thraede, K. 1962. "Das Lob des Erfinders: Bemerkungen zur Analyse der Heuremata-Kataloge." *RhMus* 105.158-86

van Hook, l. r. 1920. "the exposure of infants at athens." TAPA 51.134-45

Vellacott, P. H. 1964. "The Guilt of Oedipus." G&R 11.137-48

Vivante, P. 1972. "On Time in Pindar." *Arethusa* 5.107-31

Wéry, L. M. 1966. "Le Meurtre des hérauts de Darius en 491 et l'inviolabilité du héraut." AC 35.468-86

West, M. L. 1966. *Hesiod:* Theogony. Oxford: Clarendon

Wilamowitz-Moellendorff, U. von. 1899. "Excurse zum Oedipus des Sophokles." *Hermes* 34.55-80

Winnington-Ingram, R. P. 1980. *Sophocles: An Interpretation*. Cambridge: Cambridge University Press

Mark Ringer (essay date 1998)

SOURCE: "The Theban Plays: Illusion into Reality," in *Electra and the Empty Urn: Metatheater and Role Playing in Sophocles*, The University of North Carolina Press, 1998, pp. 67-99.

[*In the following excerpt, Ringer analyzes the different levels of illusion Sophocles uses in his Theban plays and discusses the audience's involvement in these illusions.*]

All of Sophocles' tragedies engage the spectator in the fundamental metatheatrical problem of appearance versus reality. The dichotomy of appearance and essence is one of the favorite subjects of serious drama. By its very nature, drama deals in illusion, in the creative tension of one person or object standing in for or representing something else. As one of the masters of dramatic irony,

Sophocles exhibits the keenest appreciation of the often invisible gulf that separates deeds from words and perception from reality. It is natural that someone so attuned to these fissures in experience would want to explore thoroughly the boundaries of his aesthetic medium. This exploration often calls attention to the irony of a character's situation in the story as well as the irony of the theatrical situation itself, the flickering "in and out" of illusion that is repeatedly created and destroyed in the course of a performance.

The so-called Theban Plays, *Antigone, Oedipus Tyrannus,* and *Oedipus at Colonus,* were not viewed by Sophocles as a deliberate cycle or trilogy. *Oedipus at Colonus* may be securely dated around 406, at the very end of the poet's long life; the other two plays came from earlier in Sophocles' career. There is evidence that *Antigone* dates from around 442, and *Oedipus Tyrannus* may have appeared between 429 and 425.[1] While Sophocles was not the only tragedian to return to a particular myth at different stages of his career, the story of Oedipus' family obviously held a special fascination for him, drawing the enormous concentration of his powers in these three plays. In varying degrees, Sophocles' three most famous tragedies represent drama about drama.

ANTIGONE

All three Theban Plays use the illusion-versus-reality motif as a major component of their thematics. *Antigone,* the earliest of the three tragedies, is built on two contrasting visions of reality: the brutal, corporal world of the literalist Creon and the invisible world of the dead, which Antigone seeks to honor. One critic observes that during the course of the play, "Death will finally reveal the true *apolis* [cityless one] and the true *hypsipolis* [person held in high esteem by the city] and separate the illusion from the reality."[2] These contrasting visions of reality are embodied by two characters who strive for dominance as playwrights-within-the-play.

Sophocles was elected as a general in 441/40. One of the ancient hypotheses of *Antigone* claims that Sophocles won this post due to the popularity of this play. If true, this would place *Antigone* close to 442. Even if the anonymous author of the hypothesis is incorrect, it seems plausible that such a detail would not have been recorded unless it were at least chronologically possible. As a growing imperial power, Athens would have found particular resonance in a tragedy dealing with conflicts between state authority and private or local traditions and beliefs. Few surviving tragedies suggest the notion of the poet as [*didáskalos*] or "teacher of the polis" as clearly as does *Antigone.* The verb derived from [*didáskalos*] serves literally as the play's last word . . . ("The old are taught wisdom," 1353). The tragedy serves as an object lesson in the dangers of tyrannical power—the kind of power that has come to the untested Creon and the expanding Athenian Empire.

Antigone is one of the few Sophoclean heroines who unequivocally sustains the weight of Cedric Whitman's vi-

sion of [*areté*]. Her self-image never suffers the kind of compromises that either threaten, injure, or overtake characters like Ajax or Electra. With Antigone, word and deed are never separate. Creon, on the other hand, offers a fine example of just such a fragmentation. The play ruthlessly exposes the dichotomy of Creon's noble-sounding speeches and sentiments and the hollowness that lies beneath them, a hollowness comparable with that of an egocentric actor.

It does not minimize Antigone's radiant moral purpose that the brunt of the dialogue and stage time is given to the character of Creon. *Antigone,* during the course of its action, strips away the illusion of Creon's integrity as a ruler, while affirming the real integrity of the heroine. The perception of his true identity as a petty, empty figure grows and develops throughout the play. In Creon's first appearance, his "ship of state" speech (162-210) is an impressive piece of self-representation. There is evidence that this speech was regarded in antiquity as a model of statesmanship. Demosthenes' great rival, Aeschines, had been an actor before turning to oratory; and one of his more notable roles had been Creon in *Antigone.* In order to bait his opponent about his deficiencies in citizenship, Demosthenes ordered that the "ship of state" speech be read over to Aeschines to remind him of the duties of a true statesman. Demosthenes' tactic would lack point unless Creon's speech were regarded by the average fourth-century audience as an idealistic statement of principle. In ridiculing the former actor, Demosthenes refers to him as "Creon-Aeschines" and berates him for not "repeating [the speech] over to himself to guide him as an ambassador." Demosthenes might even have seen a deeper similarity between Sophocles' tyrant and "Creon-Aeschines": both the dramatic character and the ex-actor have a fine patriotic speech in their "repertory" that only serves to illustrate their inner hollowness as politicians and as men.[3]

Sophocles' Creon provides his audience with the necessary criteria to appreciate how far he falls from his own standard for the ideal ruler and citizen. The play's central development takes this exemplary speech of Creon's as a starting point, then steadily reveals his actual character through his ensuing actions. On a metatheatrical plane, Creon sets himself a noble role to play but fails to live up to the part. His selfish and cruel deeds . . . jar with his noble sounding words. . . . His failure as a ruler and as a man is a kind of theatrical-performative failure. His blustering tirades and posturing disintegrate his own family, revealing him to be "one who does not exist, equal to nothing" (1325). The "big words of the excessively boastful are punished with great blows" (. . . 1350-53).

While *Ajax* afforded examples of stage tyranny in the bullying figures of Menelaus and Agamemnon (who, like Creon, concern themselves with obstructing a burial), Creon's tyranny is made all the more memorable for its added metatheatrical dimension. During his confrontation with the captured Antigone, the princess remarks that "tyranny is happy in many things / particularly in being able *to do* and say whatever it wants . . ." (506-7). Creon's power is theatrically or performatively defined throughout **Antigone.** Like an egotistical actor/playwright, he controls what may be done . . . or said . . . as well as what may be seen and heard. He even endeavors to control other characters' exits and entrances. His attempts at being the only actor or speaker within the theater meet with opposition and failure from early on in the tragedy. By the end of the play, Creon has lost all of his "theatrical" control. Other voices successfully contend with his. He ends the tragedy not as the master of what may be shown or discussed but as a spectatorial object standing amid the ruins of his own family.

Creon will deliver his first public address as ruler as a kind of self-styled herald. . . . Antigone warns Ismene that he is about to come "here . . . and make proclamation . . . to those who do not know his rulings" (33-34). Creon himself uses the same language of heralding in respect to his proclamation: "I make proclamation . . . to the citizens . . ." (192-93). Creon's authority as herald is challenged when Antigone tells him, "It was not Zeus who made *this proclamation*" (450). Creon's authority as a "speaker" or "announcer to all" is directly threatened.

The exposure of Polyneices' corpse is referred to as a kind of ghastly act of showmanship. The body is left "to be seen . . . as a feast for dogs and birds" (206). This same presentational or spectatorial language is adopted by the Sentry, who describes the mysterious first burial of the body as causing the corpse to "vanish" (. . . 255). Creon, the cruel showman, is incensed that the grotesque spectacle might be taken from the gaze of his captive audience, the Theban citizens. The worst extremes of Creon's hubris are attained when the king orders Antigone to be brought onstage so that she may be killed "right in front of her bridegroom" (760-61). Haemon averts this ghastly spectacle by leaving the stage.

As ruler, Creon views himself as the ultimate speaker or doer. The burial is referred to repeatedly as "the deed," that action which the chief "actor" will not allow (252, 262, 273). The presence of the comic Sentry serves to highlight the disparity between Creon's self-image and his real nature. The Sentry allows us to examine, in Reinhardt's words, "the mighty man . . . seen by a creature who shrieks and shakes, is chosen by lot, dilly-dallies, and comforts himself tragically with 'fate.'"[4] David Grene has described the role of the Sentry as "a remarkable experiment in Greek tragedy in the direction of naturalism of speech."[5] Grene seems to have mistaken the most remarkable aspect of the Sentry's words: his speech is notable not so much for "naturalism," an effect difficult to achieve in Greek tragic verse, as for the character's use of an inflated, pseudotragic tone (223-24, 235-36). The Sentry speaks as a comic figure, aware that he has been thrust into a tragic setting. He self-consciously views himself as a messenger . . . bearing bad news (. . . 277). His self-conscious status as a messenger puts him in contention with Creon who quickly tries to control this "rival"

performer, angrily ordering him to say his piece and leave quickly (244). But the Sentry cannot be controlled so easily. The Sentry's ability to share and dominate stage time helps to undermine Creon's authority on stage. Clearly Creon is not the only doer and speaker. In fact, he is powerless to silence even this lowliest of characters and drive him from the stage before the Sentry establishes an easy rapport with the theater audience. The Sentry also displays an ability to "stage" his arguments with himself for the audience's benefit.

> Often I was halted by my thoughts,
> making me turn myself around in circles.
> For my soul . . . found a voice, speaking many things
>   to me:
> "Wretch, why go where you'll pay the price on arrival?"
> "Poor one, stalling again? And if Creon learns this
> from another man, how could you not suffer for it?"
> Revolving like this, I made a short journey long . . .
>
> (225-31)

His description of "revolving," "turning in circles," and the reported speech of his "soul" suggests rich mimetic possibilities for the actor. For the passage to be effective, the contrast between the Sentry's persona and his "soul" needs to be strongly highlighted by the actor. This reenacted self-interrogation is full of comic potential and prefigures the self-interrogation performed by slave characters in Plautine comedy.[6]

By his words and body language, the lowly comic character calls attention to playacting. We see an actor playing a character who suddenly fragments into several "characters," all aspects of the same theatrically represented figure. The Sentry's tendency to "fragment" into different voices makes him appear a character of less dramatic integrity than Creon, with whom he shares the stage. But the Sentry's brief, comic role playing momentarily destabilizes Creon's illusory sense of power; and his ludicrous cringing before Creon somehow makes Creon share in his ridiculousness.

The Sentry's inept use of a tragic-style gnome ("For I come with a firm grasp on the hope / that one cannot suffer anything other than what is fated," 235-36) along with his explanation of his breathless entry ("My lord, I will not say that I have arrived breathless / due to speed, plying a nimble foot," 223-24) have a touch of the metatheatrical. They all suggest a consciousness of theatrical convention.[7] Speech and action . . . are the principal building blocks of all drama, and they are the things Creon most wants to monopolize and control. The Sentry's talkative personality is an affront to Creon's stage management. "You are a chatterer by nature, it is clear," the tyrant proclaims. Picking up on Creon's need for control, the Sentry responds, "Yes, but at least I'm not the one who *did this deed* . . ." (320-21). Another speaker is exasperating enough for Creon in his theater/state, but not as exasperating as another "doer."

As the Sentry leaves the stage under Creon's bitter mandate to find the criminal, he bids farewell to his monarch.

> Well, may [the criminal] be found, that's most
>   important. But
> whether he is caught or not, for fortune will decide
>   that,
> you shall certainly not see me coming here again.
> As it is, I have been saved beyond hope and my own
> expectation, and owe the gods much thanks.
>
> (327-31)

The force of these lines is directed not at Creon but to the audience. The Sentry's entertaining performance and his incongruous presence have undermined Creon's authority before the eyes of the theater spectators. His promise never to return "here" (. . . 329) is the remark not only of a character leaving the stage but of a comic actor self-consciously saying good-bye to his audience.

The Sentry's later reentry reminds the audience of his earlier promise.

> My lord, men should never swear an oath not to do
>   something.
> Afterthought belies intention. I could have sworn that
> it would be long before I came here again because of
> your threats which lashed at me.
>
> (388-91)

The comedy in the Sentry's reentrance is muted by the fact that he is bearing Antigone to her doom. It is typical of his ambiguous placement within the tragedy that, while offering momentary diversion from the rising tensions of the action, this peripheral figure hints so succinctly at the serious issue of Creon's dangerous stubbornness: unlike the Sentry, Creon will *not* learn to change his mind before it is too late.

The question of who is the central character of the play, Antigone or Creon, would probably have been of little interest to an ancient audience. Modern criticism has exerted much energy on this vexed question, which arises from Antigone's disappearance from the stage in the middle of the play and Creon's control of the rest of the tragedy. This structural feature has led the play to be termed a "diptych," the result of Sophocles' relative immaturity as a dramatist, before achieving structural perfection in his later plays. The same charge has been brought against *Ajax* and *Trachiniae*. These concerns vanish when the performance conditions of the ancient theater are taken into account in all three of these allegedly "diptych" dramatic structures. The allocation of roles between the three actors is particularly evocative in *Antigone*. One actor doubled as Antigone with Teiresias and either Eurydice or the Messenger. A second actor doubled as Ismene, the Sentry, Haemon, and either the Messenger or Eurydice. One actor played Creon only. The voice and physical presence which brought Antigone to life before the ancient audience would go on to assume the role of Teiresias, the seer who reveals the Gods' anger and leads Creon to yield belatedly to their will (and Antigone's). The same "Antigone" actor would also impersonate either the Messenger, who relates the heroine's fate, or Eurydice, whose brief appearance signals the final destruction of Creon's family wrought by his opposition to Antigone. The "Ismene" actor would enjoy a similar association with his later roles. The Sentry and Haemon represent sympathetic figures who, for all their many contrasts, are both falsely accused by Creon.[8]

These probable role assignments point to an aesthetic unity attained by the act of ancient theatrical performance. Viewed in this light, the tragedy is no longer a diptych when we can hear and see the "Antigone" actor absorbed into other characters who maintain the conflict "she" had instigated with Creon. Creon's function as a solo role defines that character's position in the play. He is isolated both by his extreme political stance and by the physical realities of performance within the Theater of Dionysus. His role is played by a single actor surrounded by colleagues who continually change their roles. As Creon is isolated from his surrounding actors, so too is he isolated from the polis of Thebes and the polis represented by the theater audience. The play makes frequent reference to the ruler and the polis, often contrasting the populous city-state and the isolated nature of the tyrant. This contrast contains a latent theatrical corollary, the opposition of a crowded *theatron* and a single actor performing before it.

The tragedy opens with Antigone and Ismene furtively entering from the skene door to discuss what Antigone has learned about Creon's decree. The skene becomes the Theban royal palace, and the two women see their situation as one that will potentially isolate them from their polis. That polis, the citizens who make up Thebes, is inescapably equated with the polis that fills the theater auditorium. Ismene balks at setting herself against the overwhelming force of Creon and the city. "What, you intend to bury [the corpse] when the polis has forbidden it?" (44). Ismene tells Antigone she is incapable of defying the citizens (. . . 79). The performative implications of these two theatrical figures, caught between the skene and the vast auditorium containing thousands of Athenian citizens, resonates throughout these lines.

Antigone proposes the clandestine burial to her sister as a kind of action which will reveal Ismene's inner nature. "You will show . . . / whether your nature is noble or if you are a coward sprung from a noble line" (37-38). Ismene refuses "to act against the citizens" (. . . 79). She argues that she is weak and incapable of defying those in power. While she may be as appalled as Antigone by the proclamation, Ismene counsels that the sisters keep their feelings to themselves and endure this and whatever worse may follow (61-64). Antigone's rage against her sister is charged with the performative language of action and deeds. "I would not tell you to do it, even if you were / willing to act . . . after all, nor would I be content for you to act . . . with me. / Rather you be . . . the sort of person that you decide, but for my part / I shall bury him. It's noble for me to do . . . this and die" (69-72). Antigone refuses to separate her inner and outer nature. She insists on acting or doing the deed dictated by her inherent nobility. By her insistence on action, she irrevocably breaks from her sister and sets in motion her challenge to Creon's political and performative authority. The tyrant's rule necessitates subjects who will be too intimidated to speak or act against the ruler. For Antigone, action and intention are inseparable. She will not be the fragmented, doubly theatrical figure her sister has become. When Ismene attempts to share her sister's punishment, Antigone rejects her. "I don't tolerate a loved one who only loves *in words* . . ." (543). Unlike Ismene or the Sentry, both of whom were undertaken by the same actor, Antigone is unafraid to link deed with word in challenging Creon's autocratic rule. "Did you do this deed?" . . . Creon demands when she is brought before him. "I *say* that I *did* it and I do not deny it" . . . (442-43). This conflict of inner and outer nature, of word and action, will be developed further by Sophocles in the relationship between Electra, Chrysothemis, and Clytemnestra.

Antigone will make frequent reference to the phenomenon of the single individual (or performer) opposing the will of a vast polis (or audience). At first it is Antigone who is portrayed as the lone outsider. But as the play progresses, Creon is presented increasingly as the lone individual whose folly leads him to oppose the polis and the gods. Antigone's arraignment before Creon marks a turning point in the audience's perception of the outsider or "cityless one," as well as a development of the conceit of the audience standing in for the Theban polis. Antigone says:

> How could I have achieved more glory
> Than by burying my brother?
> *These here all* . . . would
> Say this if fear didn't seal their mouths.
> But tyranny is happy in many things,
> Particularly in doing and saying whatever it wants.
> *Creon: You alone* . . . among these Cadmeans see this.
> *Antigone: They* . . . see it *too;* but *they* keep their mouths
> shut because of you.
>
> (502-9)

The "Theban citizens" or "polis" now becomes the Chorus and the theater audience as well. The theater audience's silence and attentiveness to the "actor" Creon blend into the stage illusion of the Chorus, the onstage audience. This passage begins Creon's isolation from all other stage figures, an isolation that will increase with Creon's condemnation of Antigone. The rhetorical figure of the single person opposing the polis, as enunciated by the Chorus's preceding songs (106, 370), now seems to be identified as Creon alone. In his argument with his father, Haemon cautions Creon: "I can hear in the dark how the city mourns for this girl" (692-93). Creon has replaced Antigone as the figure isolated from the audience and surrounding theatrical environment, the on- and offstage cities.

> *Haemon:* No city . . . belongs to one man.
> *Creon:* Isn't the city considered to belong to its rulers?
> *Haemon:* You would be an excellent monarch for a desert.
>
> (737-39)

Sophocles signals Creon's final collapse as the playwright/director-within-the-play when he crumbles before the Chorus and asks "What must I do then? Tell me, and I will obey" . . . (1099). Even after Creon learns his mistake and rushes to undo his error, the polis-audience relationship is maintained. When Eurydice silently exits to commit suicide after the Messenger's speech, the Messenger reasons that she does not think it proper to utter laments before the city (1246-50). The last scene, when Creon bears Haemon's body into the theater, is charged with the language of revelation and visual presentation. Creon, the arch realist, has come to acknowledge the unseen forces that drove Antigone. His folly is manifested in the dead son he bears and the dead wife revealed to him on the eccyclema. He and the characters on stage with him regard him and the carnage surrounding him as spectatorial objects or theatrical symbols exemplifying a moral lesson (1263-64, 1270, 1279-80, 1293-95, 1297-99).[9]

Twice during the course of the tragedy, the Chorus makes direct reference to the god of theater.[10] During the parodos celebrating the defeat of the Argive forces, the Chorus calls on Bacchus to be its leader in night-long celebratory dances at the gods' temples . . . (152-55). This passage is interesting not only for its references to the god but for the self-reflexive device of the Chorus discussing its primary performative function. . . . This image of Bacchus leading his dancing Theban countrymen is soon contrasted with Creon's first entrance and his proclamation. After Teiresias' warnings have finally prevailed upon Creon and he leaves to release Antigone, the Chorus bursts into an excited hymn to Dionysus (1115-52). As in comparable moments in *Ajax, Trachiniae,* and *Oedipus Tyrannus,* the Chorus prematurely predicts a happy resolution to the play's action. Dionysus, the "dance leader of the fire-breathing stars" (. . . 1146-47) is urged to appear "with cleansing foot" (1144).

These two references to Dionysus are rich in suggestiveness. Each is placed at a deciding moment in the drama: before Creon proclaims his fateful edict and after he has renounced his stance against Antigone. The passages encourage the listener to look for the theater god's literal or figurative manifestation on stage. After the parodos, Creon symbolically renounces Dionysus in his insistence upon punishing the dead Polyneices. Two of Dionysus' greatest attributes were as a dissolver of boundaries and as a god of ecstatic release. Creon's autocratic rule, with its insistence on male prerogative, stands opposed to any Dionysian impulse. Like Pentheus in the *Bacchae,* Creon refuses to be bested by a woman, lest he relinquish his masculine authority (484-85). Unlike the god who "makes no distinction of ages" (*Bacchae* 204-9), Creon refuses to learn from the ideas of the young (726-27). The god of role playing and masks forsakes the actor playing Creon, allowing him only the one role to play, while the other two actors are constantly changing characters.

By the time the Chorus pleads for Dionysus to appear as a redeemer (1115-54), it is already too late. The god's presence *is* felt in the closing scenes of **Antigone,** but it is in his role as destroyer and god of destructive madness. Dionysus, through his servant Sophocles, has attempted to teach Creon and the Athenian audience the limits of mortal power and masculine prerogative. By electing Sophocles to the generalship in 441/40, the Athenian audience signaled the playwright that, unlike Creon, it had grasped his lesson, at least for the moment.

OEDIPUS TYRANNUS

One can imagine the disturbing effect of **Oedipus Tyrannus** upon its original audience, if the consensus of scholarly opinion is correct in dating the play to the early or mid 420s. This period saw Athens, already enmeshed in the Peloponnesian War, undergoing bouts of plague that wiped out hundreds of citizens, including Sophocles' friend Pericles. Sophocles seems to have originated the plotting device of the Theban plague as the motivation behind Oedipus' fateful investigation. The Athenians wanted their tragic playwrights to create distance between the contemporary polis and the catastrophes represented in the theater. With their own plague fresh in the collective memory, the Theban plague would have reminded the Athenians of one of their worst civic calamities. Perhaps this is one of the reasons this play, so often regarded as the highest achievement of the ancient theater, only won second place.

In addition to its startling connection to contemporary events, the play harks back to the earlier **Antigone.** Jebb perceived an analogy between the first entrance of Creon in **Antigone** with the proclamation delivered by his ill-fated nephew near the beginning of **Oedipus Tyrannus** (216-75). "In each case a Theban king addresses Theban elders, announcing a stern decree, adopted in reliance on his own wisdom, and promulgated with haughty consciousness of power; the elders receive the decree with a submissive deference under which we can perceive traces of misgiving; and as the drama proceeds, the elders become spectators of calamities occasioned by the decree, while its author turns to them for comfort."[11] Both *tyrannoi* engage in similar arguments with Teiresias. Both learn harsh lessons concerning the limitations of human power and the unseen forces that move below the surface of nature. Like Creon in **Antigone,** Oedipus is a ruler described as a *"tyrannos,"* a word with associations of nonhereditary kingship and the pejorative sense of "tyranny." Both tragedies seem to play with the double implications of this word. Like the Creon in **Antigone,** King Oedipus can be rash and destructive when opposed; and his stubborn determination forces the action of the play to its horrible conclusion. But Oedipus is a far more complex figure than the earlier tyrant. It is as if Sophocles had fused elements of Anti-

gone's character, particularly her propensity to sacrifice herself for a higher cause, with that of her uncle.

Even more than the Creon of **Antigone,** the protagonist of **Oedipus Tyrannus** possesses qualities that are analogous to those of a theater artist. Oedipus is a dramatic figure obsessed with performing actions and speeches and revealing truths for the entire polis before his palace/skene. Oedipus promises his citizens and the theater audience that he "shall make manifest" (. . . 132) the mystery threatening his polis. Ironically, he himself becomes the object revealed (. . . 1184). His relentless search for the truth about the past ultimately exposes the searcher, much as a finished artwork reveals as much about its artificer as about its subject matter. Oedipus is presented as a master of action and deeds and a genius at the decipherment and manipulation of language. He attained his kingship after engaging in a deadly competition of quasi-literary and performative dimensions. Unaided by gods or men, Oedipus answered the riddle of the Sphinx, described as "the rhapsode hound" (. . . 391). This curious image of the Sphinx as "rhapsode" makes their encounter an *agon* not only between human being and monster but between two verbal and performative artists.

After his true parentage has been revealed, Oedipus asks the Shepherd why he had spared the crippled infant's life so many years before. The old man responds, "I pitied it, my lord" (. . . 1178). From the beginning, Oedipus has been an object of pity, either for the few who were aware of his cursed birth and subsequent mutilation or for the theater audience viewing a man who is blind to the horrid circumstances of his life. Pity, one of the cardinal tragic emotions in Aristotelian literary theory, is at the core of Oedipus' dramatic situation. The Shepherd's line at 1178 reveals that "pity" is, ironically enough, the reason Oedipus survived to experience the present catastrophe. Part of the irony rests in the self-reflexive nature of the Shepherd's "pity." Oedipus is the ultimate subject for tragedy. He stimulates pity in the theater audience and owes his existence to the pity he generated in the Shepherd.

After the Shepherd's final revelations, the Chorus literally refers to Oedipus as possessing a fate that is a "paradigm" . . . of humanity's unhappiness (1193). The Second Messenger's first lines, which introduce the tragedy's final revelation, are striking for their explicitly metatheatrical language. "O you who are held in greatest honor in this land, / what deeds you shall hear of, what deeds you shall see, and what / grief you shall endure . . . , if you still have a kinsmen's regard for the house of Labdacus" (1223-25). These words prepare the audience to view Oedipus' imminent reentry, stumbling and blinded, as a *theatrical* experience.[12] The Messenger will refer to him as a "sight" . . . the "beholding" . . . of which will lead to "pity" (. . . 1295-96).

Like **Antigone's** Creon, Oedipus is used to "doing and saying whatever he wants" which, as Antigone observed, is the prerogative of the *tyrannos* (***Ant.*** 506-7). Like the earlier Creon, Oedipus is a play-wright/director-within-the-play who displays formidable powers in controlling the stage space and other characters' performative behavior, as well as correctly perceiving a challenge to his dramaturgical authority. But in this later, far more ironic work, Oedipus misinterprets the source of this metatheatrical challenge. Oedipus wrongly perceives his rival dramatist to be Creon, who, in Oedipus' view, is scripting and directing subordinates like Teiresias to set the groundwork for a political coup.

After the scene with Teiresias, Oedipus suspects an insurrection is underway. It is particularly ironic that Oedipus, now in Creon's position in ***Antigone,*** suspects Creon as the instigator of the alleged plot. Creon, Oedipus charges, is a man with a "daring face" (. . . 533). The theatrical nature of Creon's alleged duplicity (his deceptive behavior and stage management of others) is registered by Oedipus' use of . . . a word that means both "face" and the actor's "mask." Oedipus charges Creon with behaving like a malevolent dramatist. Unlike Antigone's direct challenge to Creon in her play, utilizing defiant words and actions to subvert her uncle's authority, Oedipus perceives a subtler metatheatrical game. Creon, according to Oedipus, is disguising his handiwork and scripting others to do his dirty work for him. Oedipus asks Creon, "Did you think that I would not recognize the act . . . as yours?" (538). Oedipus is accusing his brother-in-law of dramatist-like behavior, sending (. . . 705) the "actor" Teiresias into the theater after "persuading him by speeches to tell lying words" (. . . 526). Creon has allegedly used Teiresias as a mouthpiece for slanderous accusations, which would have tainted his own lips had he spoken them directly (706). Teiresias has served Creon much as an actor serves his playwright. Even the reverend prophet's elderly behavior is challenged as a sham or "seeming" by Oedipus. The prophet will not be physically harmed, Oedipus reasons, because he "seems old" (. . . 402). Oedipus' position *is* under threat, but the threat does not come from any of his fellow characters within the play, as Creon had experienced in ***Antigone.*** In ***Oedipus Tyrannus,*** the threat to the *tyrannos*'s autonomy as playwright/director-within-the-play comes from outside the mimetic world of the tragedy. The challenge resides with the gods and with Sophocles.

Like Shakespeare's *Hamlet*, Sophocles' *Oedipus* is a character who has rejected the role thrust upon him by divine (or authorial) prophecy. Oedipus has endeavored to ward off the disasters predicted for him and to script his life in his own way. Oedipus is a character who discovers himself trapped within a play he does not want to write or act in. For all his eagerness to solve Laius' murder and discover his own identity, Oedipus has been "found out, unwillingly, by time, the all seeing" (. . . 1214). The true metatheatrical rivalry is between Oedipus, the playwright-within-the-play, who fulfills his traditional role "unwillingly" . . . as incest and parricide, and Sophocles, who enjoys omniscient power over his creations who are striving within the orchestra circle. Something of this character-

author conflict has been observed in the frustrating closure of ***Trachiniae.*** The idea of a character in conflict with his or her prescribed role has grown in complexity since Hyllus challenged the gods and the playwright for their treatment of their "children" on stage. Sophocles' metadramatic irony has deepened in the time since ***Trachiniae*** and ***Antigone.***

As in ***Antigone,*** the part of the *tyrannos* serves as the protagonist's only role in the play, accenting Oedipus' position as the unambiguous focal point of the tragedy. A second actor played the Priest, Jocasta, and the Shepherd. The second actor's parts share interesting resonances. It is fitting that the "Jocasta" actor also plays the Shepherd who received the infant Oedipus from her so many years before (1173). The casting presents Oedipus with the missing link with his mysterious past. It is a piece of extraordinary performative irony that the Priest who represents religious orthodoxy within the play literally speaks with the same voice as Jocasta, the religious skeptic. The third actor played Creon and the Corinthian Messenger, a fitting arrangement since both characters bring misleading "good" news to Oedipus.

The role of Teiresias could have been played by either the second or the third actor. Either assignment contains interesting performative resonances. If Teiresias is played by the "Creon" actor, the irony of Oedipus' accusations against Creon would be intensified. Teiresias would literally be speaking from the same "mouth" (705-6) as Creon. This theatrical situation would give Oedipus' mistaken accusations a delightfully paradoxical dimension. The other possibility, that the "Priest/Jocasta/Shepherd" actor plays Teiresias, is more likely. It is equally attractive in terms of ironic implications and appears more aesthetically elegant in terms of theatrical applicability. If the "Priest" actor plays the prophet, the tritagonist avoids having to rapidly change back and forth between Creon and Teiresias within a little over 350 lines (150-512), certainly a possible feat, but an awkward and unnecessary one, considering the availability of the deuteragonist, who has 480 lines between the Priest's exit and Jocasta's emergence from the skene (150-630). This latter schematic allows for a more equal allotment of acting responsibilities between deuteragonist and tritagonist in the first half of the play. In performative terms, it creates the effect of both the Priest and Teiresias, the two symbols of religious orthodoxy, inhabiting the body and voice of the "Jocasta" actor. Jocasta is the character whose disbelief in oracles and in any middlemen between humans and divinity will so scandalize the Chorus.

The Second Messenger also could have been played by either the second or third actor. Assigning the role to the third actor is attractive for reasons of balance, making his responsibilities more equal to the second in amount of lines and stage time. It also allows one actor to handle all of the messenger roles, a configuration encountered in the tritagonist's doubling of both messenger parts in Euripides' *Bacchae*.

Oedipus' character suggests the poet's refining vision of the Creon-Antigone opposition of some dozen years earlier; the play also affords a second glimpse of Creon himself. The Creon of this play is hardly the bully of the *Antigone,* but much of his presence in this later play carries intertextual, metatheatrical associations with the earlier character. Creon's speech about the disadvantages of kingly power (583-602) contains strong irony in light of his royal performance in *Antigone.* Creon's argument with Oedipus recalls the *agon* between Creon and Haemon. Stichomythic exchanges like

> *Oedipus:* I must be ruler.
> *Creon:* Not if you rule badly.
>
> (*OT [Oedipus Tyrannus]* 628-29)

or Creon's remark "I have a share in the city too, it's not yours alone" (630) could easily find a place in the *agon* scenes of *Antigone.* The audience member familiar with *Antigone* would appreciate the ironic role reversal in Creon's position. In Oedipus' tragedy, Creon seems to play Haemon's role by arguing with a tyrannical ruler. For all of Creon's protestations that kingship holds no attractions for him, he assumes kingly responsibility with great alacrity after Oedipus' downfall. Creon's newfound power is manifested by his stage management of his nephew and his children during the exodos. Creon readily tells the blinded Oedipus when and where he may exit the theater space (1429, 1515, 1521). "Do not desire to have power in everything," Creon admonishes, "for power did not accompany you through all your life" (1522-23). When Oedipus blesses Creon for bringing Antigone and Ismene to their father, it is impossible not to register the irony of Oedipus' wish that better fortune may attend Creon than has overseen Oedipus' fate (1478-79). That wish resonates with the catastrophe of the *Antigone* play.

Oedipus Tyrannus borrows from situations and characters in *Antigone* but rephrases them into entirely new configurations. Both tragedies are concerned with the limitations of a ruler's vision. *Oedipus Tyrannus,* as Karl Reinhardt has written, is a play devoted to the "tragedy of human illusion." In this play, "the danger to man lies not in the *hubris* of human self-assertion but in the *hubris* of seeming as opposed to being."[13] Reinhardt's view, with its obvious analog to the conditions of theater itself, an art form created out of appearances and deception, has influenced many subsequent interpreters. Seale, admitting his debt to the German scholar, envisions "the very matter of the tragedy" resting upon the protagonist's perception of his world in the play.[14]

Creon's "ship of state" speech in *Antigone* (162-90) gains ironic power only when viewed against his later actions. The *Oedipus Tyrannus* begins with the tacit assumption that the theater audience is thoroughly aware of the title character's genuine identity as incestuous parricide. The rich, obsessive irony of Oedipus' words is present from the play's opening speech (1-13). The play strips away the layers of illusion that surround the protagonist until he perceives his true identity, the identity the theater audience was aware of from the beginning.

Ajax and *Trachiniae* have already afforded examples of one of Sophocles' favorite metatheatrical devices, the phenomenon of the audience-within-the-play. With this strategy, the playwright focuses the spectators' attention on a character whom they watch in order to gauge their own responses to what they see and hear. *Oedipus Tyrannus* is structured so as to focus attention on how Oedipus receives and processes information. The audience is fascinated to watch how he reacts to the events occurring around him. Near the beginning of the play, Oedipus remarks that no one suffers as much as he does for his dying city (59-61). He insists that the investigation be conducted before the suppliants (and theater audience) who have assembled before the palace door. "Speak before all" (. . . 93), Oedipus urges, engaging both the characters surrounding him before the skene and the theater audience.[15] During much of the play's action, Oedipus self-consciously plays the part of the ideal monarch—a role he mistakenly believes he has won by merit rather than merely inherited. The suppliants, and, by extension, the theater audience, have come expecting him to act like a king, and his words and actions do not disappoint. He is an ideal audience and ideal actor, suffering with those he sees suffer and then offering himself as the agent and, ultimately, the scapegoat of his community. Throughout the play, the protagonist represents the ultimate actor, "the greatest in all men's eyes" (40).

When the final revelation occurs during the interrogation of the Shepherd, Oedipus turns from one who sees or reveals things for others (. . . 132) into the thing seen, the person revealed (. . . 1184). This new, terrible vision of himself as the most horrible of spectatorial objects paradoxically moves him out of the audience's sight with his exit into the skene. Once inside the palace/skene building, Oedipus destroys his eyes, the organs of Apollo and the principal means of perceiving theater, at least in the Greek imagination. The blinded Oedipus will later remark that he would have destroyed his hearing had that been possible (1386-89). Oedipus rejects the senses of sight and hearing, the two "theatrical" senses, ironically transforming himself into the most shocking of theatrical revelations. His self-conscious display of his own degradation at the end of the play is one of the most harrowing sequences in Western drama. Reinhardt observes: "Now there are no biers, no eccyclema, no apparatus. . . . instead of being brought in, put on show so that men can point him out, the victim is eager to put himself on show, to display the monstrous discovery that he has made in his search for himself: the blinded man he has been all along."[16] Oedipus is perhaps the greatest of Sophocles' internal director/playwrights. His final transformation into a blind pariah is the supreme example of the duality of human life, its dangerous instability, its ability to turn one being into its apparent opposite. Oedipus becomes the image of Teiresias, his former nemesis. The blinded king, once rooted in power and wealth, is reduced to "a voice" that "floats on the wings of the air" (. . . 1310). Just as disaster has brought Oedipus closer to his earlier opponent, Teiresias, the haunting image of the blinded Oedipus' "floating voice" suggests he has attained a mysterious parity with an even earlier enemy, the demonic, flying "rhapsode" (391) called the Sphinx.[17]

When Oedipus runs from the stage to confront Jocasta and blind himself, the Chorus sings its third stasimon, making Oedipus the "paradigm" of the tragedy of human "seeming." . . .

> O race of mortals,
> I count your life as no more than nothing.
> For what man, what man has
> more of happiness
> than so much as a seeming
> and after the seeming a falling away?
> As an example, you,
> your fate, you, o wretched Oedipus,
> I deem no mortal happy.
>
> (1186-96)

Illusion and seeming . . . are the bane and basis of existence. The horror of life may be seen in its parity with the theatrical experience, where seeming and representation are the foundation of perception. In *Oedipus Tyrannus,* theatrical seeming is employed to reveal *all* seeming. By analogy, the theatrical deception is yet another form of the "seeming" of human life. Human happiness, the very will to live, is portrayed as an illusion, as ephemeral as Oedipus' triumph and the present enactment that has recounted his story. The play exists as a means of revealing Oedipus. It is an illusion dependent on the destruction of Oedipus' illusion. Even after the apparent destruction of all "seeming" with Oedipus' self-discovery and blinding, the seeming-versus-reality dichotomy remains. The blinded Oedipus begs Creon to let him touch his children again. "If I lay my hands on them I can seem . . . to have them with me, as when I could see" (1469-70).

Seeming and duality are at the core of the *Oedipus* world. When announcing to the citizens his investigation into Laius' death, Oedipus promises: "I shall speak these words as both a stranger to the story, / and as a stranger to the deed" (. . . 219-20). Oedipus' relationship with the Laius story is as paradoxical as the relationship between the actor playing Oedipus and his role. The actor is a "stranger" to the words and deeds Sophocles has directed him to perform. Nevertheless, the actor says and does these things as if they were his own speeches and actions. Oedipus is actorlike in his taking upon himself words and deeds on the behalf of other characters. . . . Oedipus' ambiguous relationship to his theatrical environment is analogous to the theater audience's relationship to tragedy. In order to enjoy tragedy as an aesthetic experience, members of the audience must perceive the subject matter of tragedy as something strange . . . or "other" than their personal lives or experiences. At the same time, tragedy must partake of the deepest fears and anxieties of its audience if it is to excite the pity, fear, and catharsis that Aristotle articulated

as the primary results of the tragic experience in the theater. This implicit connection between the deception . . . of life and the medium of theater works to remove the distance between the play and its audience. Segal has suggested the ways in which "Oedipus' fate in the orchestra mirrors back to the members of the audience." Their absorption in his tragedy causes them to "temporarily lose [their] identity, [their] secure definition by house, position, friends, and become, like Oedipus, nameless and placeless."[18]

Oedipus is in a dilemma similar to that of Ajax. Both characters perform disastrous acts while under a deluded notion of reality. Both men are destroyed by a hostile cosmos. In *Ajax* the audience actually sees the divine instigator of the hero's downfall in the character of Athena. But in *Oedipus Tyrannus,* the metatheatrical role of the god, a playwright-within-the-play, has been absorbed into the fabric of the tragedy with breathtaking subtlety. In *Oedipus Tyrannus,* Sophocles enjoys a parity with Apollo, the divine artificer of Oedipus' misfortunes. The human playwright's craft portrays the operation of the god's design. Both divine and human artificers are paradoxically omnipresent yet unseen. Apollo's inscrutability and distance from the human characters whose actions he has manipulated serve as metaphors of the playwright's art. Sophocles also maneuvers his subjects into the patterns he desires while remaining outside of his creation. The relationship of Apollo to the playwright and the art of tragedy is suggested by the Chorus in its second stasimon.

In order to calm her husband's mounting anxiety, Jocasta has cast doubt upon the truthfulness of oracles. After the exit of Jocasta and Oedipus, the Chorus sings an ode denouncing impiety. The second strophe of the stasimon must be quoted in full. . . .

> If someone walks with haughtiness
> in deed or word,
> unafraid of Justice and without
> reverence for shrines of Gods,
> may an evil fate seize on him,
> for his unlucky pride,
> if he will not gain advantage justly
> and keep away from unholy things
> or rashly touches what should not be touched.
> Amid such things, what man shall contrive
> to defend his life against angry arrows?
> For if such deeds are honored
> why should I be in a chorus?
>
> (883-96)

In the antistrophe following, the Chorus remarks that it will no longer regard the important shrines of Delphi, Abae, or Olympia "unless these [oracles] do fit together / so as to be pointed at by all mortals" (902-3). Unless the oracles of Apollo are made manifest, an open, public spectacle which may be "pointed to" (. . . 902), the Chorus will lose its sense of religion and, as it intimates in the preceding strophe, will literally stop "being a chorus" (. . . 896). If god (or the tragic dramatist) does not bring his prophecies to fruition, the Chorus will give up its principal function in the tragedy being enacted. The words are a challenge both to Apollo and to the playwright.

These lines from the second stasimon are among the most controversial in Sophocles, due to their metatheatrical implications.[19] . . . Bernard Knox's summary of the parabasis-like effect of 896 eloquently states the implications of Sophocles' *trompe l'oeil.*

> "Why should I dance?" With this phrase the situation is brought out of the past and the myth into the present moment in the Theatre of Dionysus. For these words of the Chorus were accompanied not only by music but, as the Chorus's very name reminds us, by dancing: this is the choral dance and song from which tragedy developed, and which is still what it was in the beginning, an act of religious worship. If the oracles and the truth do not coincide the very performance of the tragedy has no meaning, for tragedy is itself a form of worship of the gods. The phrase "Why should I dance?" is a *tour de force* which makes the validity of the performance itself depend on the *dénouement* of the play.[20]

The placement of the stasimon after Jocasta's rejection of oracular power is telling. Her denunciation of the oracles and the religious beliefs surrounding them is tantamount to her rejecting her place as a character within the play. She and Oedipus have no more freedom from the prophecy than they have from the dramatic script of which they are a part. Neither script nor prophecy may exist without the validation of a higher, divine order. The members of the Chorus intimate that their lives within Thebes and as characters within the present play are in jeopardy. The passage jolts the audience's perceptions by simultaneously calling attention to the Chorus and the play's double nature as story and performance of that story. The Sophoclean stasimon may be compared with an equally self-referential passage in twentieth-century drama. In Beckett's *Endgame,* Clove threatens that play's continuance in a manner similar to the defiant actions of Oedipus and Jocasta.

> Clove: I'll leave you.
> Hamm: No!
> Clove: What is there to keep me here?
> Hamm: The dialogue.[21]

The Chorus will again draw attention to its performative function when singing the ode to Mount Cithaeron (1086-1109). As so often in Sophoclean tragedy, the poet heightens the impact of the final calamity by having the Chorus prematurely celebrate a happy resolution. The direct reference to dancing . . . at 1092 bestows a self-conscious artificiality upon the Chorus's merrymaking. The Chorus is following its dramatic function—it is "dancing"—but the audience may realize that it is celebrating only because it remains incapable of penetrating the illusion of Oedipus' identity. It is intriguing that the Chorus theorizes that the foundling Oedipus may be the child of Dionysus himself (1105). Earlier, during the parodos, the Chorus had called upon Dionysus to redeem his suffering homeland (211). The wine god's presence is discernible throughout this play. Apollo's brother, a god of role playing and reversal, the patron of the tragic competition itself, Dionysus may be a spiritual father of Oedipus, if not a biological one. A god who often wreaks havoc on the family, who revels in duality and contradiction, is the appropriate force compelling Oedipus to discover his true identity.

Somewhat earlier in the play, Oedipus discussed the claims made by the lone survivor of the attack on Laius at the place where three roads met. The man claimed a troop of robbers committed the crime. Oedipus takes comfort in the alleged plurality of the attackers. "I was not the killer," he reasons, "for one [man] is not the same as many" (845). Oedipus finally learns how "one may equal many" (845). In the Theater of Dionysus, one man performing actions (. . . 847) may stand in for any or all of his fellow men. It is this "standing in" that allows the performer and the spectators the scope and resonance that make *Oedipus Tyrannus* one of the masterpieces of metatheater.[22]

OEDIPUS AT COLONUS

In **Oedipus at Colonus,** the relationship of the play's world to the world of the audience has changed drastically. The title of the play suggests something of what is unique and different in this final work, written at the close of the fifth century. Athens and its immediate environs figure comparatively rarely as a setting for fifth-century tragedy.[23] The Athenian tragedians preferred setting their plays in areas other than Athens to create a sense of distance and perspective for their audiences. Tragedy, with its malfunctioning families and governments, often carries by its very nature an implicit critique of the society in which its action is set. While much of Greek tragedy may be said to offer a critique of fifth-century Athens, it does so obliquely through the comfortably distant mirrors of places like Thebes, Trachis, and Troy. The festival presentation of tragedy, an important propaganda tool of the Athenian Empire, could ill afford to openly criticize its host city by using it as an example of a "tragic" society. It is also probable that Athenian audiences themselves enjoyed the aesthetic distance that a foreign setting brought with it.[24] From this perspective we may begin to appreciate Sophocles' boldness in giving his final play an Athenian setting.

Throughout his career, Sophocles devoted careful attention to the physical environments in which he set his plays. We may remember Ajax' solitary tent on the shore. The Paedagogus' opening lines in **Electra** create a brief but significant entry point to that play. **Philoctetes,** written only a few years before **Oedipus at Colonus,** gives significant attention to the depiction of Lemnos, whose desolate landscape carries significance both for the play's action and the nature of the title character. Colonus, however, is given the most detailed and thorough place description in Greek tragedy.

Knowledge of fifth-century *skenographia* is virtually nonexistent. It will never be known how detailed or schematic the actual stage setting or decoration would have been for this or any fifth-century play in the Theater of Dionysus. Whatever the means of scenic representation, Sophocles is taking a great risk in compelling his audience to compare the stage space representing Colonus with the real model. As one scholar notes, the fifth-century actors and audience "shared the very daylight of the grove one mile away."[25] Antigone, in describing the place to which she and her father have arrived, remarks that "the towers that / shield the city are, to judge by the eye, far off" (14-16). "The towers" are none other than the temples of the Athenian Acropolis, which stood behind the audience in the Theater of Dionysus.[26] Sophocles' choice of setting, whatever its physical representation on the ancient stage, displays his confidence in the power of his theater to withstand the comparison of his created scene with the genuine article.

The deme of Colonus and the city of Athens almost constitute dramatic characters within the play. Sophocles' choice of setting was probably influenced by events during the closing years of the Peloponnesian War. A troop of Boeotians was repulsed by Athenian soldiers near the grove of Colonus Hippios in 407 B.C., an action that may well have reminded Athenians of Oedipus' legendary powers within the grove.[27] Colonus, like the Theater of Dionysus, is a sacred place where humanity may intermingle with the gods. Both the theater and the grove are located near the very heart of Athenian society. Colonus was Sophocles' own deme. His use of Colonus represents an example of an ancient dramatist "staging" his home and polis, endeavoring to preserve it, through dramatic action and poetry, from the ravages of war and time.

Critics have remarked on the idealizing nature of Sophocles' praise of his homeland, particularly the sublime encomium for Colonus and Athens contained within the first stasimon (668-719). It has been noted that many of the physical and moral features held up for admiration by the poet were already nearing destruction when Sophocles was writing the play. Kirkwood has compared the play's use of Athens with other near-contemporary texts such as Thucydides' version of Pericles' funeral oration and later fourth-century authors who would nostalgically describe the city as a utopia. Sophocles' emphasis on the "justness" or "fairness" . . . of Athens represents the playwright's attempt to restore this lost trait to his crippled society.[28] Athens is the one place capable of receiving a hero such as Oedipus. While Thebes desires possession of his body as a powerful talisman, Athens can accept all of the hero with his strange mixture of blessings and curses. Athens is civilized enough to understand and accept the contradictions inherent in Oedipus, as the city has symbolically accepted so many other tragic heroes into its community during performances at the Theater of Dionysus.

Just as Sophocles shows great daring in his choice of scene, his dramaturgical structure puts unprecedented demands on his three actors. Virtually all fifth-century tragedy may be comfortably performed by three actors without the necessity of a single role being shared between actors. Before **Oedipus at Colonus,** only a late work by Euripides, the *Phoenician Women* (411-409 B.C.), required a role to be shared by two actors and this text may well have been substantially altered for performances during the fourth century. In **Oedipus at Colonus,** Sophocles requires his deuteragonist and tritagonist to share the role of Antigone, while all three actors share the part of Theseus. This doubling feat sustains Sophocles' extraordinarily fluid dramatic structure and stands as a testimony to the versatility of late fifth-century actors, as well as to the innovative courage of the octogenarian playwright. Sophocles obviously wanted his last play to stand as a repository of spiritual and poetic vision as well as a testament to his unsurpassed technical skill. As so often occurs, Sophocles' doubling of roles will carry thematic and structural resonances for the tragedy's performative meaning. The protagonist played Oedipus throughout the play, returning, appropriately enough, to narrate his previous character's death in the guise of the Messenger. As if this were not enough, Sophocles required the protagonist to be recycled as Theseus for that character's final entrance from line 1750 to the end of the play. The deuteragonist played Antigone from lines 1-847, Theseus in that character's second and third scenes (886-1210 and 1500-1555), Polyneices, and Antigone again, from line 1670 to the end. The tritagonist played the Citizen, Ismene, Theseus at that character's first appearance (551-667), Creon, Antigone (1099-1555), and resumed the role of Ismene from line 1670 to the end.

If this scheme of doubling seems wildly complex and challenging, even for a cast of accomplished actors, it is. Some scholars, including Jebb, have postulated that Sophocles must have composed the play with a fourth actor in mind, but there is no evidence of a fourth actor being used for fifth-century tragedy. No other tragedy requires it; and the availability of a fourth actor would obviate the play's carefully orchestrated patterns of entrances and exits. Furthermore, this remarkable pattern of role allocation strongly suggests performative meaning. All three actors are allowed to play members of the Theban royal family. The role of Antigone, already one of the most popular heroines of classical tragedy, journeys from the deuteragonist to the tritagonist and back again to the original actor. The role of Theseus undergoes a far more remarkable journey with the role being played by all three actors in succession from the third, to the second, to the first agonist. Brian Johnston has written that "Theseus' role gradually increases in mimetic authority" during the course of the tragedy until, with Oedipus' transfiguration, Theseus stands as the last living link with Oedipus' heroism and as the custodian of Oedipus' legacy for Athens. At this point, Oedipus' voice literally speaks through the mask of Theseus. Theseus, by the end of the play, "has earned the right, as it were, to be 'performed' by the Oedipus actor. He has become the closest to Oedipus, underscored by the fact that he alone, and not Antigone nor Ismene, is privileged to witness Oedipus' wonderful death. . . . [The protagonist's assumption of Theseus at 1750] is the *theatrical* manifestation of Oedipus' gift to Athens."[29]

Sophocles' virtuosity as a playwright and the virtuosity he demands of his cast illustrate the void separating modern, naturalistic acting and production styles from those of classical Athens. They also reveal a playwright capable of great technical daring, even at the end of an unusually long and successful career. Only Verdi's stylistic self-recreation in his late operas, *Otello* and *Falstaff,* seems a comparable example of octogenarian creativity. The doubling and tripling of roles also points to the self-consciousness of Sophocles' dramaturgy, the way dramatic convention becomes part of a play's very meaning.

Unlike the Oedipus character in the *Tyrannus* play, the aged Oedipus has had from the opening moments of **Oedipus at Colonus** a clear perception of his true status and relation to the stage world that surrounds him. The "Oedipus" actor has stood his ground while the deuteragonist and tritagonist have each played deceptive characters like Creon and Polyneices, figures whose crafty and duplicitous speeches serve to disguise their ulterior motives. In the play's concluding moments, Theseus replaces Oedipus in the body and voice of the protagonist, whose voice and stage presence have, through the roles of Oedipus and the Messenger, represented the spiritual "reality" and integrity that lie at the core of Sophocles' play.

Were intertextual reference to other dramatic texts the sole criterion of metatheatricality, **Oedipus at Colonus** would rank among the most metatheatrical of ancient tragedies.[30] While tragedy frequently carries allusions to earlier texts, tragic or epic, **Oedipus at Colonus** is particularly "bookish."[31] Sophocles adopted the pattern of earlier tragedies based on the theme of the suppliant. These "suppliant" plays, Aeschylus' *Suppliants,* Euripides' *Children of Heracles* and *Suppliants,* and many lost examples, served as the models for **Oedipus at Colonus.** Suppliant dramas are made up of a fairly traditional set of encounters: the suppliant meets and pleads with the host; an enemy seriously challenges the suppliant's security; the host encounters and defeats the enemy in a military action, winning security for the suppliant. In addition to the suppliant play schematic, **Oedipus at Colonus** presupposes an audience familiar with the two earlier Sophoclean Theban tragedies as well as Aeschylus' *Seven Against Thebes* and Euripides' *Phoenician Women.* The wrangling between Eteocles and Polyneices, described by Ismene (*OC* 336, 365-81), and the chillingly prophetic scene where Polyneices begs Antigone to give him burial, should he die in his campaign (*OC* 1399-1446), all suggest these earlier plays, which were already very famous when **Oedipus at Colonus** was written. Echoes of the **Antigone** prologue are evident in the brief exchange between the two grieving sisters, when Ismene sensibly tries to restrain the impulsive Antigone from visiting her father's mysterious burial place (*OC* 1724-36). Creon's seizure of Oedipus' daughters and their eventual restoration by Theseus rephrases and

resolves the wrenching exodos of **Oedipus Tyrannus,** where the blind Oedipus is presented with his children and then is forcibly parted from them by Creon. Sophocles is compelling us to look not only beyond the closure of the present play into an uncertain future: he is compelling us to look into *other plays* as well; plays by himself and by other poets.

Sophocles devotes much important stage time in **Oedipus at Colonus** to debating issues raised by **Oedipus Tyrannus,** particularly Oedipus' speeches of self-defense before the ghoulishly inquisitive Chorus of Colonian elders and, later, his enemy Creon (510-48, 960-1000). The present play functions as a belated sequel to the earlier tragedy. Like the *Eumenides,* which closed Aeschylus' *Oresteia* by bringing the action to an Athenian setting, **Oedipus at Colonus** uses its Athenian locale as a site of final consummation both for Oedipus and, by extension, for Attic tragedy itself. By absorbing the contradictions inherent in Oedipus (and in tragedy), Athens reaps the benefit of a mysterious protective power.

In **Oedipus at Colonus,** Sophocles reverses the structure of dramatic irony that he used to such great effect in **Antigone** and **Oedipus Tyrannus.** In those earlier plays the audience beheld the struggle of two rulers, Creon and Oedipus, who each attempt to maintain a vision of the world based either on misapprehension or illusion. By the end of each tragedy, the rulers meet their downfall after finally seeing the truth of their situation, a truth that the audience has either known all along or has realized long before the character. In **Oedipus at Colonus** the protagonist moves from the lowest fortune to a state of deification. This last Sophoclean tragedy serves as a kind of "antitragedy," a work that self-consciously reverses the tragic pattern of earlier plays. The **Colonus** play begins with an Oedipus who seems in some ways similar to the figure who exits the stage at the end of the **Tyrannus.** Like the earlier rendering of the character, the aged Oedipus has a habit of blundering upon places that are not to be touched by ordinary humans. Soon after Oedipus' first entrance in the orchestra, the Chorus describes him as "Terrible to see, terrible to hear" (. . . 141). These theatrically charged words are reminiscent of the description given the newly blinded Oedipus by the Second Messenger in **Oedipus Tyrannus:** "what deeds you shall hear of, what deeds you shall see, and what / grief you shall endure" (. . . *OT* 1224-25). At the start of Sophocles' last play, Oedipus remains the paradigm of theatrical suffering and misfortune. But this similarity to his earlier self is superficial. The Chorus is soon won over by the old man's suffering. Antigone pleads for the Chorus and, by extension, the theater audience, to view the aged wanderer with "pity" (. . . 242). This "pity" will move the Colonians to sympathize with Oedipus to the point that they accept him into their community. . . . Ismene will wonder "when will the gods take pity . . . on [Oedipus'] sorrows?" (383-84). By the end of the play, even these distant, mysterious beings, Oedipus' cosmic audience, "take pity" and accept the old man into their company.

In Sophocles' last tragedy, the spectators and the protagonist share a "conspiracy of knowledge" from the opening moments of the play.[32] The audience is assured of the "reality" of Oedipus' ultimate destiny, and the assurance is maintained throughout all of the challenges that face the protagonist before his final apotheosis. As Peter Burian has shown, the play follows a pattern, discernible in other suppliant dramas, that helps to assure the audience of Oedipus' ultimate victory.[33]

The protagonist now represents a kind of "truth," while all the obstacles he faces (the initial rejection by the Chorus, the evil machinations of Creon, the pleas of Polyneices) almost seem illusory, since they "are waged against [the certain] knowledge" of Oedipus' redemption.[34] Oedipus' security seems so assured that the numerous threats posed to his position in the grove have about them the air of dramaturgical contrivance. Reinhardt notes the "baroque" tendencies of this final Sophoclean play with its fascination for minute detail representing a "struggle to create drama within drama itself." Reinhardt describes Ismene's arrival as "a whole recognition scene in miniature," as Antigone painstakingly describes her sister's distant approach from the parodos (310-21).[35]

Oedipus' certainty concerning his destiny and rightful place within the Eumenides' grove protects his character from the ironic separation of word and action that occurs so frequently in Sophoclean drama. Oedipus and Athens itself, as personified by Theseus and the Chorus, are incapable of subterfuge and are able to see through the hypocritical "performances" of outsiders such as Creon and the Theban government he represents. Oedipus, the last of the tragic protagonists of fifth-century drama, is accepted into a society where word and action go hand in hand. This helps to make *Oedipus at Colonus* into a "tragedy to end tragedy," a deliberate resolution of the nagging ambiguities at the core of so much fifth-century drama. Both Creon and the polis he represents reveal a false, "theatricalized" nature, in which appearance is more important than essence and where human beings are exploited as empty material objects. This is exemplified by Creon's scheme to force Oedipus back to Thebes, where he will live a prisoner outside the city perimeter. This cruel plot will enable Thebes to reap the benefit of Oedipus' physical presence while protecting the city from actual contact with the pariah. It may now be seen why Sophocles gives Ismene the grand entrance, which Reinhardt described as a "miniature recognition scene." Ismene reports the oracle, enabling Oedipus to unmask Creon even before he enters the stage and begins his elaborate "performance" of sympathy with his wretched cousin. This oracle will prove the final salvation for both Oedipus and Athens.

Eteocles and Polyneices share a good part of Creon's "theatrical" perfidy. For the sons of Oedipus, Reinhardt observes, "action has parted company with meaning," as has "the appearance of justice with its reality."[36] Athens represents a place where word and action exist in harmony,

a place that can accept the paradox of Oedipus and, by extension, the paradox of tragic drama itself, which uses masks to "unmask truth." Segal has argued that the character of Oedipus in this last play may be equated symbolically with the entire genre of tragedy. "By returning to this figure whose life contains the most extreme of tragic reversals, Sophocles seems to be consciously reflecting upon and transcending the tragic pattern which he did so much to develop."[37]

Just as Oedipus may be equated with the performative genre in which he appears, so too may the aged playwright be found reflected in his title character. In no other Greek tragedy is it so natural to speak of a personal identification between a character and a playwright. Like Oedipus and the Chorus, Sophocles was an old man by the time he wrote his last play. That Sophocles was held as a symbol of veneration during the latter stages of his life may be inferred by the fact that he was given the cult name of *Dexion* ("Receiver," or "Hospitable One") after his death and was worshiped as a beneficent deity (*Vita* 17). This curious historical fact unavoidably reminds the reader of the more spectacular deification that Oedipus undergoes in Sophocles' final play.

Several Greek and Roman sources preserve an anecdote that the octogenarian Sophocles was brought before a lawcourt by his middle-aged sons, who hoped to have the old man declared senile so that they might take control of his property. By way of self-defense, Sophocles was said to have read the jury the first stasimon of the play he was currently writing, *Oedipus at Colonus* (668-719), comprising the ode to Colonus and Athens. Sophocles won his case and "was escorted from the court as if from the theater . . . , with the applause and shouts of those present."[38] While such a story cannot be verified, its very existence suggests something of the remarkable personal identification perceived in the ancient world between *Oedipus at Colonus* and its creator. Whatever the reality of Sophocles' domestic situation in his last years, Oedipus' expression of love for Athens and his terrifying revilement of his son have encouraged ancient as well as modern readers to read an autobiographical element into the character. While this is a dubious practice at best, it would be impossible as well as absurd to attempt it with any other character from Greek tragedy.

Sophocles did not live to see the final capitulation of Athens to Sparta. His final play allows the playwright, through the voice of his protagonist, to utter a lasting benediction for his homeland. A conspiracy of knowledge has been forged between Oedipus and the spectators from the very first moments of the drama. The audience has been allowed to share with the aging hero a sure knowledge of his destiny. Now with his daughters and Theseus at his side, Oedipus hears the sound of thunder that presages his passing from this world.

> I will teach you, Aegeus' son, something which shall
> be a treasure for your city that age cannot hurt.
>
> (1518-19)

Oedipus commands Theseus not to describe his final moments to anyone, neither "to these citizens" . . . (1528),
nor "to my own children, though they are dear all the
same" (1529). By "citizens" Oedipus is ostensibly referring to the Chorus, but his words must surely carry to the
theater full of Athenian citizens who, until this moment,
have enjoyed their position as Oedipus' passive confidant.
Oedipus is now passing into a stage of his journey that
may be neither seen nor spoken about. It is impossible not
to hear in Oedipus' final lines, before his onstage audience, the aged poet's farewell to his theater audience and
to his city.[39]

> Come, dearest of friends,
> may you yourself and this land and your helpers
> be blessed, and in that prosperous state remember
> me, one of the dead, and be fortunate forever.

(1552-55)

Oedipus at Colonus was first performed in 401 B.C., some
four years after the death of Sophocles (406/5) and three
years after the capitulation of Athens (404). Contemporary
audiences must have been keenly aware of the play's
unique status as the author's posthumous farewell to his
community. The play forms a deliberate closure to
Sophocles' career as a tragedian. In telling the story of
Oedipus' final moments, Sophocles has found a means of
absorbing his own persona into the artifice of the play. In
effect, he "stages" himself before the citizens in the Theater
of Dionysus, fashioning a dramatic character that may
stand in for himself as artistic creator and defender of
Athenian society. By immortalizing himself in the stage
figure of Oedipus, Sophocles also seeks to give a mythic,
theatrical permanence to his city's greatness, just as that
greatness may well have seemed about to slip into the
realm of history and myth. Sophocles understood the
paradox of theatrical illusion as well as he did the paradox
of tragic heroism. When Oedipus, the aged pariah, learns
that his wretched body contains a beneficent power for
whatever land may claim him, he asks incredulously,
"When I am nothing, *then* am I a man?" (393). By transferring the image of a noble, stainless Athens into the seemingly fragile medium of a dramatic text, Sophocles bestows
the gift of eternity upon his polis and himself as an artistic
creator. Sophocles has learned the lessons of over sixty
years in the service of Dionysus, that stage illusion may
mirror spiritual truth. He knows that the craftsmen of Dionysus practice an art as magical as the deathless, self-
renewing Athenian olive trees.

Notes

1. Lesky, *Greek Tragic Poetry,* pp. 133, 152. For a more
   recent examination on the *Antigone* date, see the edition of Brown, p. 2.

2. Segal, *Tragedy and Civilization,* p. 444 n. 49. Both
   Segal and Seale have written about the play's
   inexorable revelation of truth. Rosevach, "The Two
   Worlds of the *Antigone*," pp. 16-26, is also interesting for its interpretation of the play's structure and
   thematics.

3. Demosthenes, "On the Embassy," 19.246.

4. Reinhardt, *Sophocles,* p. 71.

5. *Sophocles* (ed. Grene and Lattimore, 2nd ed.), 1:169.

6. See especially Niall Slater's view of the monologue
   from *Epidicus* (81-103), in *Plautus,* p. 21. A near
   contemporary parallel to Sophocles' Sentry may be
   found in Aristophanes' *Acharnians* when Dicaeopolis
   repeatedly addresses his "soul" (. . . 480, 483) and
   his "suffering heart" (. . . 485) in humorously
   melodramatic fashion. There is also an obvious
   similarity between the Sentry and a Shakespearean
   clown such as Lancelot Gobbo in *The Merchant of
   Venice.* Sophocles' bold juxtaposition of low- and
   high-born characters gives *Antigone* an unusually
   varied social view, comparable with Shakespeare's
   combination of Cleopatra and the asp salesman.

7. See also Brown, who cites the "out of breath messenger" motif as it appears in Euripides' *Medea*
   (1119-20) and Aristophanes' *Birds* (1121-22). *Antigone* 223-24 (ed. Brown).

8. See also Damen, "Actor and Character in Greek
   Tragedy," p. 322.

9. Seale writes of the closing moments, "All that
   remains is the tableau of corpses, Teiresias' prediction made good and the culmination of the whole
   process, concrete visualization." *Vision and Stagecraft,* pp. 108-9.

10. For the self-reflexive aspects of Dionysian allusion
    within this and other tragedies, see Bierl, "Was hat
    die Tragödie mit Dionysos zu tun? Rolle und Func-
    tion des Dionysos am Beispiel der 'Antigone' des
    Sophokles," pp. 43-58, and *Dionysos und die
    griechische Tragödie: Politische und
    'metatheatralische' Aspekte im Text.* On choral self-
    reference in Sophocles, see also Heikkilä, "'Now I
    have a Mind to Dance,'" and Henrichs, "Why Should
    I Dance?"

11. *Antigone* 162-210 (ed. Jebb).

12. See also Segal, "Time, Theatre, and Knowledge," p.
    465.

13. Reinhardt, *Sophocles,* pp. 98, 116.

14. Seale, *Vision and Stagecraft,* p. 218.

15. A similar drawing of the theater audience into the
    stage action occurs on Creon's second entrance when
    he speaks to the members of the Chorus and, over
    their heads, to the theater audience (. . . 513). The
    idea of the theater audience standing in for the The-
    ban population is further reinforced by Jocasta's first
    lines, warning Oedipus and Creon not to quarrel
    publicly before the "house" (634-38). Segal detects a
    theatrical self-consciousness in operation throughout
    the play, particularly in Sophocles' "visual" language,
    the way characters and situations are described as

spectatorial objects—or, as in the death of Jocasta or Oedipus' blinding, objects that must not or cannot "be seen." "Time, Theatre, and Knowledge," pp. 459-89.

16. Reinhardt, *Sophocles,* p. 130.

17. The hidden similarity between Oedipus and Teiresias is the subject of an interesting article by Lattimore, "Oedipus and Teiresias," pp. 105-11. The 1984 Greek National Theatre production directed by Minos Volanakis closed the play with Oedipus' ceremonial acceptance of a walking staff similar to the one used by Teiresias, allowing the audience to "see" Oedipus "become" Teiresias. For the comparison of Oedipus to the Sphinx, see Segal, "Time, Theatre, and Knowledge," p. 466.

18. Segal, *Tragedy and Civilization,* p. 247. Taplin has analyzed the frustrating, thwarted closure of the play. He describes Oedipus' futile plea to leave Thebes and his ignominious final exit into the skene as a deliberate disappointment of audience expectation and a subtle means of making the play continue unresolved within the spectator's consciousness (Taplin, "Sophocles in His Theatre," p. 174). . . .

19. . . . To Segal, the questions posed by the Chorus find no comforting answers in the protagonist's downfall. . . . Segal views the second stasimon as a self-conscious "ritual-within-ritual," a passage that is "parallel and homologous with the larger, enframing ritual structure of the festival in which the play itself has its own ceremonial function" (Segal, *Tragedy and Civilization,* p. 235). See also Henrichs, "Why Should I Dance?," pp. 65-73.

20. Knox, *Oedipus at Thebes,* p. 47. Knox has elsewhere referred to the passage as "a sort of Sophoclean *Verfremdungseffekt*" ("Oedipus Rex," in *Essays Ancient and Modern,* p. 139).

21. Beckett, *Endgame,* p. 58.

22. For the idea of Oedipus as a character self-consciously "standing in" for others, see also Wilshire, *Role Playing and Identity.*

23. Aeschylus' *Eumenides* shifts its scene midway through its action from the temple at Delphi to the Areopagus in Athens. Euripides' *Children of Heracles* is set in Marathon, a district near to and ruled by Athens.

24. Herodotus (6.21) relates the famous. . . [story] concerning Aeschylus' rival, Phrynichus, who was fined a thousand drachmas for reminding his audience of the recent fall of Miletus in his tragedy, *The Capture of Miletus.* The play was banned due to its unpleasant emotional effect on its audience. Phrynichus seems to have destroyed the aesthetic distance necessary for the calamities of tragedy to bring pleasure instead of pain. Lesky, however, notes that the incident may have been a political ruse aimed at

humiliating the archon, Themistocles. Lesky, *Greek Tragic Poetry,* p. 34.

25. Seale, *Vision and Stagecraft,* p. 113.

26. See also *Oedipus at Colonus* (ed. Blundell), p. 20 n. 4.

27. Birge, "The Grove of the Eumenides: Refuge and Hero Shrine in *Oedipus at Colonus,*" pp. 12-13.

28. Kirkwood, "From Melos to Colonus . . .," p. 103.

29. Johnston, "The Metamorphoses of Theseus in *Oedipus at Colonus,*" pp. 280, 283. See also Edmunds, *Theatrical Space and Historical Place in Sophocles' Oedipus at Colonus,* pp. 69-70.

30. One is reminded of Bruno Gentili's definition of metatheater as any play that is "constructed from previously existing plays." *Theatrical Performances in the Ancient World,* p. 15.

31. Gellie, *Sophocles,* p. 293 n. 4.

32. Seale, *Vision and Stagecraft,* p. 113.

33. Burian, "Suppliant and Savior: Oedipus at Colonus," pp. 408-29.

34. Seale, *Vision and Stagecraft,* p. 113.

35. Reinhardt, *Sophocles,* pp. 202, 200-201.

36. Ibid., p. 204.

37. Segal, *Tragedy and Civilization,* pp. 407, 406.

38. Plutarch, *Moralia* 785. See also *Oedipus at Colonus* (ed. Jebb), p. xl.

39. See also Reinhardt, *Sophocles,* pp. 220, 222.

FURTHER READING

Criticism

Ahl, Frederick. "Oracular Wordplay." In *Sophocles' Oedipus: Evidence and Self-Conviction,* pp. 244-59. Ithaca, N.Y.: Cornell University Press, 1991.
 Examines the wordplay in Sophocles's choice of names for his characters.

Arkins, Brian. "The Final Lines of Sophocles, *King Oedipus* (1524-30)." *Classical Quarterly* 38, No. 2 (1988): 555-58.
 Argues that the closing lines of *King Oedipus,* although often questioned by scholars, are, in fact, genuine.

Armstrong, Richard H. "*Oedipus* as Evidence: The Theatrical Background to Freud's Oedipus Complex." http://www.clas.ufl.edu/ipsa/journal/articles/psyart1999/oedipus/armstr01.htm.

Examines Freud's assertion that *Oedipus Tyrannus* moves modern audiences with as much intensity as it did ancient Greek audiences.

Berkowitz, Luci and Theodore F. Brunner, eds. *Sophocles: "Oedipus Tyrannus."* New York: W. W. Norton & Company, Inc., 1970, 261p.
   Includes religious and psychological studies of the play as well as several essays concerning the guilt or innocence of Oedipus. A selection from this work is printed above.

Bloom, Harold, ed. *Sophocles's Oedipus Rex.* New York: Chelsea House Publishers, 1988, 174 p.
   Includes nine essays covering assorted topics—among them the motives for Oedipus's self-blinding; the question of his guilt; the nature of illusion and truth; and the troublesome ambiguity of the play's language.

Fowler, B. H. "Thought and Underthought in Three Sophoclean Plays." *Eranos: Acta Philologica Suecana* 79, No. 1 (1981): 1-22.
   Discusses the use of metaphorical language in *Ajax, Antigone,* and *Oedipus Tyrannus.*

Gilula, Dwora. "The First Greek Drama on the Hebrew Stage: Tyrone Guthrie's *Oedipus Rex* at the Habima." *Theatre Research International* 13, No. 2 (Summer 1988): 131-46.
   Provides an overview of the 1947 Guthrie production and offers reasons for its failure.

Gregory, Justina. "The Encounter at the Crossroads in Sophocles' *Oedipus Tyrannus.*" *Journal of Hellenic Studies* 115 (1995): 141-46.
   Analyzes Oedipus's speech concerning his parentage, his response to the oracle, and the killing of Laius.

Halliwell, Stephen. "Where Three Roads Meet: A Neglected Detail in the *Oedipus Tyrannus.*" *Journal of Hellenic Studies* 106 (1986): 187-90.
   Discusses the significance of crossroads in Greek literature.

Lewis, R. G. "The Procedural Basis of Sophocles's *Oedipus Tyrannus.*" *Greek, Roman and Byzantine Studies* 30, No. 1 (Spring 1989): 41-66.

Investigates Attic legal procedures to determine the process Sophocles used as a framework for the play.

Nussbaum, Martha C. "The *Oedipus Rex* and the Ancient Unconscious." In *Freud and Forbidden Knowledge,* edited by Peter L. Rudnytsky and Ellen Handler Spitz, pp. 42-71. New York: New York University Press, 1994.
   Contrasts Greek accounts of the unconscious mind with those of Freud.

O'Brien, Michael J., ed. *Twentieth Century Interpretations of Oedipus Rex*: *A Collection of Critical Essays.* Englewood Cliffs, N.J.: Prentice-Hall, Inc., 1968, 119 p.
   Includes nine essays, covering dramatic elements; typical misunderstandings of the play; interpretation of the last scene; and other topics. A selection from this work is printed above.

Payne, M. E. "Three Double Messenger Scenes in Sophocles." *Mnemosyne* 53, No. 4 (August 2000): 403-18.
   Compares the structure and function of three messenger scenes from *Oedipus Tyrannus, Trachiniae,* and *Philoctetes.*

Rusten, Jeffrey. "Oedipus and Triviality." *Classical Philology* 91, No. 2 (April 1996): 97-112.
   Surveys some of the arguments concerning the significance of the crossroads, including possible sexual symbolism.

Segal, Charles. "*Oedipus Tyrannus.*" In *Tragedy and Civilization: An Interpretation of Sophocles,* pp. 207-48. Cambridge, Mass.: Harvard University Press, 1981.
   Provides an overview and analysis of the play.

Van Nortwick, Thomas. *Oedipus: The Meaning of a Masculine Life.* Norman: University of Oklahoma Press, 1998, 185p.
   Examines the nature of Oedipus's heroism and discusses the many ironic elements in the play.

Zelenak, Michael X. "The Troublesome Reign of King Oedipus: Civic Discourse and Civil Discord in Greek Tragedy." *Theatre Research International* 23, No. 1 (Spring 1998): 69-78.
   Provides an overview of Athenian drama, including the circumstances surrounding its origins.

Additional coverage of Sophocles's life and career is contained in the following sources published by the Gale Group: *Ancient Writers*; *Dictionary of Literary Biography,* **Vol. 176;** *DISCovering Authors*; *DISCovering Authors: British*; *DISCovering Augthors: Canadian*; *DISCovering Authors Modules: Dramatists* **and** *Most Studied Authors*; **and** *Drama Criticism,* **Vol. 1.**

How to Use This Index

The main references

> **Calvino, Italo**
> 1923-1985 .... CLC 5, 8, 11, 22, 33, 39,
> 73; SSC 3

list all author entries in the following Gale Literary Criticism series:

BLC = *Black Literature Criticism*
CLC = *Contemporary Literary Criticism*
CLR = *Children's Literature Review*
CMLC = *Classical and Medieval Literature Criticism*
DA = *DISCovering Authors*
DAB = *DISCovering Authors: British*
DAC = *DISCovering Authors: Canadian*
DAM = *DISCovering Authors: Modules*
  DRAM: *Dramatists Module;* *MST:* *Most-Studied Authors Module;*
  MULT: *Multicultural Authors Module;* *NOV:* *Novelists Module;*
  POET: *Poets Module;* *POP:* *Popular Fiction and Genre Authors Module*
DC = *Drama Criticism*
HLC = *Hispanic Literature Criticism*
LC = *Literature Criticism from 1400 to 1800*
NCLC = *Nineteenth-Century Literature Criticism*
NNAL = *Native North American Literature*
PC = *Poetry Criticism*
SSC = *Short Story Criticism*
TCLC = *Twentieth-Century Literary Criticism*
WLC = *World Literature Criticism, 1500 to the Present*

The cross-references

> See also CANR 23; CA 85-88;
> obituary CA116

list all author entries in the following Gale biographical and literary sources:

AAYA = *Authors & Artists for Young Adults*
AITN = *Authors in the News*
BEST = *Bestsellers*
BW = *Black Writers*
CA = *Contemporary Authors*
CAAS = *Contemporary Authors Autobiography Series*
CABS = *Contemporary Authors Bibliographical Series*
CANR = *Contemporary Authors New Revision Series*
CAP = *Contemporary Authors Permanent Series*
CDALB = *Concise Dictionary of American Literary Biography*
CDBLB = *Concise Dictionary of British Literary Biography*
DLB = *Dictionary of Literary Biography*
DLBD = *Dictionary of Literary Biography Documentary Series*
DLBY = *Dictionary of Literary Biography Yearbook*
HW = *Hispanic Writers*
JRDA = *Junior DISCovering Authors*
MAICYA = *Major Authors and Illustrators for Children and Young Adults*
MTCW = *Major 20th-Century Writers*
SAAS = *Something about the Author Autobiography Series*
SATA = *Something about the Author*
YABC = *Yesterday's Authors of Books for Children*

Literary Criticism Series
Cumulative Author Index

CYA; MTCW 1; RHW; SAAS 1; SATA
2, 30, 73; SATA-Essay 109; WYA; YAW

Ainsworth, William Harrison
1805-1882 .... **NCLC 13**
See also DLB 21; HGG; RGEL; SATA 24

Aitmatov, Chingiz (Torekulovich)
1928- .... **CLC 71**
See also CA 103; CANR 38; MTCW 1;
RGSF; SATA 56

Akers, Floyd
See Baum, L(yman) Frank

Akhmadulina, Bella Akhatovna
1937- .... **CLC 53; DAM POET**
See also CA 65-68; CWP; CWW 2

Akhmatova, Anna 1888-1966 ..... **CLC 11, 25,
64, 126; DAM POET; PC 2**
See also CA 19-20; 25-28R; CANR 35;
CAP 1; DA3; MTCW 1, 2; RGWL

Aksakov, Sergei Timofeyvich
1791-1859 .... **NCLC 2**
See also DLB 198

Aksenov, Vassily
See Aksyonov, Vassily (Pavlovich)

Akst, Daniel 1956- .... **CLC 109**
See also CA 161

Aksyonov, Vassily (Pavlovich)
1932- .... **CLC 22, 37, 101**
See also CA 53-56; CANR 12, 48, 77;
CWW 2

Akutagawa Ryunosuke
1892-1927 .... **TCLC 16; SSC 44**
See also CA 117; 154; DLB 180; MJW;
RGSF; RGWL

Alain 1868-1951 .... **TCLC 41**
See also CA 163; GFL 1789 to the Present

Alain-Fournier .... **TCLC 6**
See Fournier, Henri Alban
See also DLB 65; GFL 1789 to the Present;
RGWL

Alarcon, Pedro Antonio de
1833-1891 .... **NCLC 1**

Alas (y Urena), Leopoldo (Enrique Garcia)
1852-1901 .... **TCLC 29**
See also CA 113; 131; HW 1; RGSF

Albee, Edward (Franklin III) 1928- . **CLC 1,
2, 3, 5, 9, 11, 13, 25, 53, 86, 113; DA;
DAB; DAC; DAM DRAM, MST; DC
11; WLC**
See also AITN 1; AMW; CA 5-8R; CABS
3; CAD; CANR 8, 54, 74; CD; CDALB
1941-1968; DA3; DFS 2, 3, 8, 10, 13;
DLB 7; INT CANR-8; MTCW 1, 2;
RGAL; TUS

Alberti, Rafael 1902-1999 .... **CLC 7**
See also CA 85-88; 185; CANR 81; DLB
108; HW 2; RGWL

Albert the Great 1193(?)-1280 ...... **CMLC 16**
See also DLB 115

Alcala-Galiano, Juan Valera y
See Valera y Alcala-Galiano, Juan

Alcayaga, Lucila Godoy
See Godoy Alcayaga, Lucila

Alcott, Amos Bronson 1799-1888 .... **NCLC 1**
See also DLB 1, 223

Alcott, Louisa May 1832-1888 . **NCLC 6, 58,
83; DA; DAB; DAC; DAM MST, NOV;
SSC 27; WLC**
See also AAYA 20; AMWS 1; CDALB
1865-1917; CLR 1, 38; DA3; DLB 1, 42,
79, 223, 239, 242; DLBD 14; FW; JRDA;
MAICYA; NFS 12; RGAL; SATA 100;
YABC 1; YAW

Aldanov, M. A.
See Aldanov, Mark (Alexandrovich)

Aldanov, Mark (Alexandrovich)
1886(?)-1957 .... **TCLC 23**
See also CA 118; 181

Aldington, Richard 1892-1962 .... **CLC 49**
See also CA 85-88; CANR 45; DLB 20, 36,
100, 149; RGEL

Aldiss, Brian W(ilson) 1925- . **CLC 5, 14, 40;
DAM NOV; SSC 36**
See also CA 5-8R; CAAE 190; CAAS 2;
CANR 5, 28, 64; CN; DLB 14; MTCW 1,
2; SATA 34; SFW

Alegria, Claribel 1924- .... **CLC 75; DAM
MULT; HLCS 1; PC 26**
See also CA 131; CAAS 15; CANR 66, 94;
CWW 2; DLB 145; HW 1; MTCW 1

Alegria, Fernando 1918- .... **CLC 57**
See also CA 9-12R; CANR 5, 32, 72; HW
1, 2

Aleichem, Sholom .... **TCLC 1, 35; SSC 33**
See also Rabinovitch, Sholem

Aleixandre, Vicente 1898-1984 ... **TCLC 113;
HLCS 1**
See also CANR 81; HW 2; RGWL

Alepoudelis, Odysseus
See Elytis, Odysseus
See also CWW 2

Aleshkovsky, Joseph 1929-
See Aleshkovsky, Yuz
See also CA 121; 128

Aleshkovsky, Yuz .... **CLC 44**
See also Aleshkovsky, Joseph

Alexander, Lloyd (Chudley) 1924- ... **CLC 35**
See also AAYA 1, 27; CA 1-4R; CANR 1,
24, 38, 55; CLR 1, 5, 48; CWRI; DLB
52; FANT; JRDA; MAICYA; MTCW 1;
SAAS 19; SATA 3, 49, 81; SUFW; WYA;
YAW

Alexander, Meena 1951- .... **CLC 121**
See also CA 115; CANR 38, 70; CP; CWP;
FW

Alexander, Samuel 1859-1938 .... **TCLC 77**

Alexie, Sherman (Joseph, Jr.)
1966- .... **CLC 96; DAM MULT**
See also AAYA 28; CA 138; CANR 95;
DA3; DLB 175, 206; MTCW 1; NNAL

Alfau, Felipe 1902-1999 .... **CLC 66**
See also CA 137

Alfieri, Vittorio 1749-1803 .... **NCLC 101**
See also RGWL

Alfred, Jean Gaston
See Ponge, Francis

Alger, Horatio, Jr. 1832-1899 .... **NCLC 8, 83**
See also DLB 42; RGAL; SATA 16; TUS

Algren, Nelson 1909-1981 ..... **CLC 4, 10, 33;
SSC 33**
See also CA 13-16R; 103; CANR 20, 61;
CDALB 1941-1968; DLB 9; DLBY 81,
82; MTCW 1, 2; RGAL; RGSF

Ali, Ahmed 1908-1998 .... **CLC 69**
See also CA 25-28R; CANR 15, 34

Alighieri, Dante
See Dante

Allan, John B.
See Westlake, Donald E(dwin)

Allan, Sidney
See Hartmann, Sadakichi

Allan, Sydney
See Hartmann, Sadakichi

Allard, Janet .... **CLC 59**

Allen, Edward 1948- .... **CLC 59**

Allen, Fred 1894-1956 .... **TCLC 87**

Allen, Paula Gunn 1939- .... **CLC 84; DAM
MULT**
See also AMWS 4; CA 112; 143; CANR
63; CWP; DA3; DLB 175; FW; MTCW
1; NNAL; RGAL

Allen, Roland
See Ayckbourn, Alan

Allen, Sarah A.
See Hopkins, Pauline Elizabeth

Allen, Sidney H.
See Hartmann, Sadakichi

Allen, Woody 1935- .... **CLC 16, 52; DAM
POP**
See also AAYA 10; CA 33-36R; CANR 27,
38, 63; DLB 44; MTCW 1

Allende, Isabel 1942- . **CLC 39, 57, 97; DAM
MULT, NOV; HLC 1; WLCS**
See also AAYA 18; CA 125; 130; CANR
51, 74; CWW 2; DA3; DLB 145; DNFS;
FW; HW 1, 2; INT 130; MTCW 1, 2;
NCFS 1; NFS 6; RGSF; SSFS 11

Alleyn, Ellen
See Rossetti, Christina (Georgina)

Alleyne, Carla D. .... **CLC 65**

Allingham, Margery (Louise)
1904-1966 .... **CLC 19**
See also CA 5-8R; 25-28R; CANR 4, 58;
CMW; DLB 77; MSW; MTCW 1, 2

Allingham, William 1824-1889 ...... **NCLC 25**
See also DLB 35; RGEL

Allison, Dorothy E. 1949- .... **CLC 78**
See also CA 140; CANR 66; CSW; DA3;
FW; MTCW 1; NFS 11; RGAL

Alloula, Malek .... **CLC 65**

Allston, Washington 1779-1843 .... **NCLC 2**
See also DLB 1, 235

Almedingen, E. M. .... **CLC 12**
See also Almedingen, Martha Edith von
See also SATA 3

Almedingen, Martha Edith von 1898-1971
See Almedingen, E. M.
See also CA 1-4R; CANR 1

Almodovar, Pedro 1949(?)- .... **CLC 114;
HLCS 1**
See also CA 133; CANR 72; HW 2

Almqvist, Carl Jonas Love
1793-1866 .... **NCLC 42**

Alonso, Damaso 1898-1990 .... **CLC 14**
See also CA 110; 131; 130; CANR 72; DLB
108; HW 1, 2

Alov
See Gogol, Nikolai (Vasilyevich)

Alta 1942- .... **CLC 19**
See also CA 57-60

Alter, Robert B(ernard) 1935- .... **CLC 34**
See also CA 49-52; CANR 1, 47, 100

Alther, Lisa 1944- .... **CLC 7, 41**
See also CA 65-68; CAAS 30; CANR 12,
30, 51; CN; CSW; GLL 2; MTCW 1

Althusser, L.
See Althusser, Louis

Althusser, Louis 1918-1990 .... **CLC 106**
See also CA 131; 132; DLB 242

Altman, Robert 1925- .... **CLC 16, 116**
See also CA 73-76; CANR 43

Alurista
See Urista, Alberto H.
See also DLB 82; HLCS 1

Alvarez, A(lfred) 1929- .... **CLC 5, 13**
See also CA 1-4R; CANR 3, 33, 63, 100;
CN; CP; DLB 14, 40

Alvarez, Alejandro Rodriguez 1903-1965
See Casona, Alejandro
See also CA 131; 93-96; HW 1

Alvarez, Julia 1950- .... **CLC 93; HLCS 1**
See also AAYA 25; AMWS 7; CA 147;
CANR 69; DA3; MTCW 1; NFS 5, 9

Alvaro, Corrado 1896-1956 .... **TCLC 60**
See also CA 163

Amado, Jorge 1912-2001 ... **CLC 13, 40, 106;
DAM MULT, NOV; HLC 1**
See also CA 77-80; CANR 35, 74; DLB
113; HW 2; MTCW 1, 2; RGWL

Ambler, Eric 1909-1998 .... **CLC 4, 6, 9**
See also BRWS 4; CA 9-12R; 171; CANR
7, 38, 74; CMW; CN; DLB 77; MTCW
1, 2

Ambrose, Stephen E(dward)
1936- .... **CLC 145**
See also CA 1-4R; CANR 3, 43, 57, 83;
NCFS 2; SATA 40

Amichai, Yehuda 1924-2000 .. **CLC 9, 22, 57,
116**
See also CA 85-88; 189; CANR 46, 60, 99;
CWW 2; MTCW 1

Amichai, Yehudah
See Amichai, Yehuda

Amiel, Henri Frederic 1821-1881 .... **NCLC 4**

Amis, Kingsley (William)
1922-1995 ...... **CLC 1, 2, 3, 5, 8, 13, 40,
44, 129; DA; DAB; DAC; DAM MST,
NOV**
See also AITN 2; BRWS 2; CA 9-12R; 150;
CANR 8, 28, 54; CDBLB 1945-1960;
CN; CP; DA3; DLB 15, 27, 100, 139;
DLBY 96; HGG; INT CANR-8; MTCW
1, 2; RGEL; RGSF; SFW

Amis, Martin (Louis) 1949- .... **CLC 4, 9, 38,
62, 101**
See also BEST 90:3; BRWS 4; CA 65-68;
CANR 8, 27, 54, 73, 95; CN; DA3; DLB
14, 194; INT CANR-27; MTCW 1

Ammons, A(rchie) R(andolph)
1926-2001 ...... **CLC 2, 3, 5, 8, 9, 25, 57,
108; DAM POET; PC 16**
See also AITN 1; CA 9-12R; CANR 6, 36,
51, 73; CP; CSW; DLB 5, 165; MTCW 1,
2; RGAL

Amo, Tauraatua i
See Adams, Henry (Brooks)

Amory, Thomas 1691(?)-1788 .... **LC 48**

Anand, Mulk Raj 1905- .. **CLC 23, 93; DAM
NOV**
See also CA 65-68; CANR 32, 64; CN;
MTCW 1, 2; RGSF

Anatol
See Schnitzler, Arthur

Anaximander c. 611B.C.-c.
546B.C. .... **CMLC 22**

Anaya, Rudolfo A(lfonso) 1937- ...... **CLC 23,
148; DAM MULT, NOV; HLC 1**
See also AAYA 20; CA 45-48; CAAS 4;
CANR 1, 32, 51; CN; DLB 82, 206; HW
1; MTCW 1, 2; NFS 12; RGAL; RGSF

Andersen, Hans Christian
1805-1875 ...... **NCLC 7, 79; DA; DAB;
DAC; DAM MST, POP; SSC 6; WLC**
See also CLR 6; DA3; MAICYA; RGSF;
RGWL; SATA 100; YABC 1

Anderson, C. Farley
See Mencken, H(enry) L(ouis); Nathan,
George Jean

Anderson, Jessica (Margaret) Queale
1916- .... **CLC 37**
See also CA 9-12R; CANR 4, 62; CN

Anderson, Jon (Victor) 1940- . **CLC 9; DAM
POET**
See also CA 25-28R; CANR 20

Anderson, Lindsay (Gordon)
1923-1994 .... **CLC 20**
See also CA 125; 128; 146; CANR 77

Anderson, Maxwell 1888-1959 .... **TCLC 2;
DAM DRAM**
See also CA 105; 152; DLB 7, 228; MTCW
2; RGAL

Anderson, Poul (William)
1926-2001 .... **CLC 15**
See also AAYA 5, 34; CA 1-4R; 181; CAAE
181; CAAS 2; CANR 2, 15, 34, 64; CLR
58; DLB 8; FANT; INT CANR-15;
MTCW 1, 2; SATA 90; SATA-Brief 39;
SATA-Essay 106; SCFW 2; SFW; SUFW

Anderson, Robert (Woodruff)
1917- .... **CLC 23; DAM DRAM**
See also AITN 1; CA 21-24R; CANR 32;
DLB 7

Anderson, Sherwood 1876-1941 ..... **TCLC 1,
10, 24; DA; DAB; DAC; DAM MST,
NOV; SSC 1, 46; WLC**
See also AAYA 30; CA 104; 121; CANR
61; CDALB 1917-1929; DA3; DLB 4, 9,
86; DLBD 1; GLL 2; MTCW 1, 2; NFS
4; RGAL; RGSF; SSFS 4,10,11

Andier, Pierre
See Desnos, Robert

Andouard
See Giraudoux, Jean(-Hippolyte)

Andrade, Carlos Drummond de ..... **CLC 18**
See also Drummond de Andrade, Carlos
See also RGWL

Andrade, Mario de 1893-1945 .... **TCLC 43**
See also RGWL

Andreae, Johann V(alentin)
1586-1654 .... **LC 32**
See also DLB 164

Andreas Capellanus fl. c. 1185- .... **CMLC 45**
See also DLB 208

Andreas-Salome, Lou 1861-1937 ... **TCLC 56**
See also CA 178; DLB 66

Andress, Lesley
See Sanders, Lawrence

Andrewes, Lancelot 1555-1626 .... **LC 5**
See also DLB 151, 172

Andrews, Cicily Fairfield
See West, Rebecca

Andrews, Elton V.
See Pohl, Frederik

Andreyev, Leonid (Nikolaevich)
1871-1919 .... **TCLC 3**
See also CA 104; 185

Andric, Ivo 1892-1975 .... **CLC 8; SSC 36**
See also CA 81-84; 57-60; CANR 43, 60;
DLB 147; MTCW 1; RGSF; RGWL

Androvar
See Prado (Calvo), Pedro

Angelique, Pierre
See Bataille, Georges

Angell, Roger 1920- .... **CLC 26**
See also CA 57-60; CANR 13, 44, 70; DLB
171, 185

Angelou, Maya 1928- .... **CLC 12, 35, 64, 77;
BLC 1; DA; DAB; DAC; DAM MST,
MULT, POET, POP; PC 32; WLCS**
See also AAYA 7, 20; AMWS 4; BW 2, 3;
CA 65-68; CANR 19, 42, 65; CDALBS;
CLR 53; CP; CPW; CSW; CWP; DA3;
DLB 38; MTCW 1, 2; NCFS 2; NFS 2;
PFS 2, 3; RGAL; SATA 49; YAW

Anna Comnena 1083-1153 .... **CMLC 25**

Annensky, Innokenty (Fyodorovich)
1856-1909 .... **TCLC 14**
See also CA 110; 155

Annunzio, Gabriele d'
See D'Annunzio, Gabriele

Anodos
See Coleridge, Mary E(lizabeth)

Anon, Charles Robert
See Pessoa, Fernando (Ant

Anouilh, Jean (Marie Lucien Pierre)
1910-1987 .... **CLC 1, 3, 8, 13, 40, 50;
DAM DRAM; DC 8**
See also CA 17-20R; 123; CANR 32; DFS
9, 10; EW; GFL 1789 to the Present;
MTCW 1, 2; RGWL

Anthony, Florence
See Ai

Anthony, John
See Ciardi, John (Anthony)

Anthony, Peter
See Shaffer, Anthony (Joshua); Shaffer,
Peter (Levin)

Anthony, Piers 1934- .... **CLC 35; DAM POP**
See also AAYA 11; CA 21-24R; CANR 28,
56, 73; CPW; DLB 8; FANT; MTCW 1,
2; SAAS 22; SATA 84; SFW; YAW

Anthony, Susan B(rownell)
1820-1906 .... **TCLC 84**
See also FW

Antoine, Marc
See Proust, (Valentin-Louis-George-Eug

Antoninus, Brother
See Everson, William (Oliver)

Antoninus, Marcus Aurelius
121-180 .... **CMLC 45**
See also AW

Antonioni, Michelangelo 1912- .... **CLC 20,
144**
See also CA 73-76; CANR 45, 77

Antschel, Paul 1920-1970
See Celan, Paul
See also CA 85-88; CANR 33, 61; MTCW
1

Anwar, Chairil 1922-1949 .... **TCLC 22**
See also CA 121

Anzaldua, Gloria (Evanjelina) 1942-
See also CA 175; CSW; CWP; DLB 122;
FW; HLCS 1; RGAL

Apess, William 1798-1839(?) .... **NCLC 73;
DAM MULT**
See also DLB 175; NNAL

Apollinaire, Guillaume 1880-1918 .. **TCLC 3,
8, 51; DAM POET; PC 7**
See also CA 152; GFL 1789 to the Present;
MTCW 1; RGWL; WP

Appelfeld, Aharon 1932- ... **CLC 23, 47; SSC
42**
See also CA 112; 133; CANR 86; CWW 2;
RGSF

Apple, Max (Isaac) 1941- .... **CLC 9, 33**
See also CA 81-84; CANR 19, 54; DLB
130

Appleman, Philip (Dean) 1926- .... **CLC 51**
See also CA 13-16R; CAAS 18; CANR 6,
29, 56

Appleton, Lawrence
See Lovecraft, H(oward) P(hillips)

Apteryx
See Eliot, T(homas) S(tearns)

Apuleius, (Lucius Madaurensis)
125(?)-175(?) .... **CMLC 1**
See also AW; DLB 211; RGWL; SUFW

Aquin, Hubert 1929-1977 .... **CLC 15**
See also CA 105; DLB 53

Aquinas, Thomas 1224(?)-1274 ..... **CMLC 33**
See also DLB 115; EW

Aragon, Louis 1897-1982 .. **CLC 3, 22; DAM
NOV, POET**
See also CA 69-72; 108; CANR 28, 71;
DLB 72; GFL 1789 to the Present; GLL
2; MTCW 1, 2; RGWL

Arany, Janos 1817-1882 .... **NCLC 34**

Aranyos, Kakay 1847-1910
See Mikszath, Kalman

Arbuthnot, John 1667-1735 .... **LC 1**
See also DLB 101

Archer, Herbert Winslow
See Mencken, H(enry) L(ouis)

Archer, Jeffrey (Howard) 1940- ...... **CLC 28;
DAM POP**
See also AAYA 16; BEST 89:3; CA 77-80;
CANR 22, 52, 95; CPW; DA3; INT
CANR-22

Archer, Jules 1915- .... **CLC 12**
See also CA 9-12R; CANR 6, 69; SAAS 5;
SATA 4, 85

Archer, Lee
See Ellison, Harlan (Jay)

Archilochus c. 7th cent. B.C.- .... **CMLC 44**
See also DLB 176

Arden, John 1930- .... **CLC 6, 13, 15; DAM
DRAM**
See also BRWS 2; CA 13-16R; CAAS 4;
CANR 31, 65, 67; CBD; CD; DFS 9;
DLB 13; MTCW 1

Avison, Margaret 1918- .... **CLC 2, 4, 97;**
DAC; DAM POET
See also CA 17-20R; CP; DLB 53; MTCW
1

Axton, David
See Koontz, Dean R(ay)

Ayckbourn, Alan 1939- ...... **CLC 5, 8, 18, 33,**
74; DAB; DAM DRAM; DC 13
See also BRWS 5; CA 21-24R; CANR 31,
59; CBD; CD; DFS 7; DLB 13; MTCW
1, 2

Aydy, Catherine
See Tennant, Emma (Christina)

Ayme, Marcel (Andre) 1902-1967 ... **CLC 11;**
SSC 41
See also CA 89-92; CANR 67; CLR 25;
DLB 72; EW; GFL 1789 to the Present;
RGSF; RGWL; SATA 91

Ayrton, Michael 1921-1975 .... **CLC 7**
See also CA 5-8R; 61-64; CANR 9, 21

Azorin .... **CLC 11**
See also Martinez Ruiz, Jose

Azuela, Mariano 1873-1952 . **TCLC 3; DAM**
MULT; HLC 1
See also CA 104; 131; CANR 81; HW 1, 2;
MTCW 1, 2

Baastad, Babbis Friis
See Friis-Baastad, Babbis Ellinor

Bab
See Gilbert, W(illiam) S(chwenck)

Babbis, Eleanor
See Friis-Baastad, Babbis Ellinor

Babel, Isaac
See Babel, Isaak (Emmanuilovich)
See also SSFS 10

Babel, Isaak (Emmanuilovich)
1894-1941(?) .... **TCLC 2, 13; SSC 16**
See also Babel, Isaac
See also CA 104; 155; MTCW 1; RGSF;
RGWL

Babits, Mihaly 1883-1941 .... **TCLC 14**
See also CA 114

Babur 1483-1530 .... **LC 18**

Babylas 1898-1962
See Ghelderode, Michel de

Baca, Jimmy Santiago 1952-
See also CA 131; CANR 81, 90; CP; DAM
MULT; DLB 122; HLC 1; HW 1, 2

Bacchelli, Riccardo 1891-1985 .... **CLC 19**
See also CA 29-32R; 117

Bach, Richard (David) 1936- .... **CLC 14;**
DAM NOV, POP
See also AITN 1; BEST 89:2; CA 9-12R;
CANR 18, 93; CPW; FANT; MTCW 1;
SATA 13

Bachman, Richard
See King, Stephen (Edwin)

Bachmann, Ingeborg 1926-1973 .... **CLC 69**
See also CA 93-96; 45-48; CANR 69; DLB
85; RGWL

Bacon, Francis 1561-1626 .... **LC 18, 32**
See also CDBLB Before 1660; DLB 151,
236; RGEL

Bacon, Roger 1214(?)-1294 .... **CMLC 14**
See also DLB 115

Bacovia, George 1881-1957 .... **TCLC 24**
See also Bacovia, G.; Vasiliu, Gheorghe
See also DLB 220

Badanes, Jerome 1937- .... **CLC 59**

Bagehot, Walter 1826-1877 .... **NCLC 10**
See also DLB 55

Bagnold, Enid 1889-1981 ...... **CLC 25; DAM**
DRAM
See also CA 5-8R; 103; CANR 5, 40; CBD;
CWD; CWRI; DLB 13, 160, 191; FW;
MAICYA; RGEL; SATA 1, 25

Bagritsky, Eduard 1895-1934 .... **TCLC 60**

Bagrjana, Elisaveta
See Belcheva, Elisaveta

Bagryana, Elisaveta .... **CLC 10**
See also Belcheva, Elisaveta
See also CA 178; DLB 147

Bailey, Paul 1937- .... **CLC 45**
See also CA 21-24R; CANR 16, 62; CN;
DLB 14; GLL 2

Baillie, Joanna 1762-1851 .... **NCLC 71**
See also DLB 93; RGEL

Bainbridge, Beryl (Margaret) 1934- . **CLC 4,**
5, 8, 10, 14, 18, 22, 62, 130; DAM NOV
See also BRWS 6; CA 21-24R; CANR 24,
55, 75, 88; CN; DLB 14, 231; MTCW 1,
2

Baker, Elliott 1922- .... **CLC 8**
See also CA 45-48; CANR 2, 63; CN

Baker, Jean H. .... **TCLC 3, 10**
See also Russell, George William

Baker, Nicholson 1957- .... **CLC 61; DAM**
POP
See also CA 135; CANR 63; CN; CPW;
DA3; DLB 227

Baker, Ray Stannard 1870-1946 .... **TCLC 47**
See also CA 118

Baker, Russell (Wayne) 1925- .... **CLC 31**
See also BEST 89:4; CA 57-60; CANR 11,
41, 59; MTCW 1, 2

Bakhtin, M.
See Bakhtin, Mikhail Mikhailovich

Bakhtin, M. M.
See Bakhtin, Mikhail Mikhailovich

Bakhtin, Mikhail
See Bakhtin, Mikhail Mikhailovich

Bakhtin, Mikhail Mikhailovich
1895-1975 .... **CLC 83**
See also CA 128; 113; DLB 242

Bakshi, Ralph 1938(?)- .... **CLC 26**
See also CA 112; 138; IDFW 3

Bakunin, Mikhail (Alexandrovich)
1814-1876 .... **NCLC 25, 58**

Baldwin, James (Arthur) 1924-1987 . **CLC 1,**
2, 3, 4, 5, 8, 13, 15, 17, 42, 50, 67, 90,
127; BLC 1; DA; DAB; DAC; DAM
MST, MULT, NOV, POP; DC 1; SSC
10, 33; WLC
See also AAYA 4, 34; AFAW 1, 2; AMWS
1; BW 1; CA 1-4R; 124; CABS 1; CAD;
CANR 3, 24; CDALB 1941-1968; CPW;
DA3; DFS 11; DLB 2, 7, 33; DLBY 87;
MTCW 1, 2; NFS 4; RGAL; RGSF;
SATA 9; SATA-Obit 54; SSFS 2

Bale, John 1495-1563 .... **LC 62**
See also DLB 132; RGEL

Ball, Hugo 1886-1927 .... **TCLC 104**

Ballard, J(ames) G(raham) 1930- . **CLC 3, 6,**
14, 36, 137; DAM NOV, POP; SSC 1
See also AAYA 3; CA 5-8R; CANR 15, 39,
65; CN; DA3; DLB 14, 207; HGG;
MTCW 1, 2; NFS 8; RGEL; RGSF; SATA
93; SFW

Balmont, Konstantin (Dmitriyevich)
1867-1943 .... **TCLC 11**
See also CA 109; 155

Baltausis, Vincas 1847-1910
See Mikszath, Kalman

Balzac, Honore de 1799-1850 ... **NCLC 5, 35,**
53; DA; DAB; DAC; DAM MST, NOV;
SSC 5; WLC
See also DA3; DLB 119; GFL 1789 to the
Present; RGSF; RGWL; SSFS 10

Bambara, Toni Cade 1939-1995 ...... **CLC 19,**
88; BLC 1; DA; DAC; DAM MST,
MULT; SSC 35; WLCS
See also AAYA 5; AFAW 2; BW 2, 3; CA
29-32R; 150; CANR 24, 49, 81;
CDALBS; DA3; DLB 38; MTCW 1, 2;
RGAL; RGSF; SATA 112; SSFS 4, 7, 12

Bamdad, A.
See Shamlu, Ahmad

Banat, D. R.
See Bradbury, Ray (Douglas)

Bancroft, Laura
See Baum, L(yman) Frank

Banim, John 1798-1842 .... **NCLC 13**
See also DLB 116, 158, 159; RGEL

Banim, Michael 1796-1874 .... **NCLC 13**
See also DLB 158, 159

Banjo, The
See Paterson, A(ndrew) B(arton)

Banks, Iain
See Banks, Iain M(enzies)

Banks, Iain M(enzies) 1954- .... **CLC 34**
See also CA 123; 128; CANR 61; DLB 194;
HGG; INT 128; SFW

Banks, Lynne Reid .... **CLC 23**
See also Reid Banks, Lynne
See also AAYA 6

Banks, Russell 1940- .... **CLC 37, 72; SSC 42**
See also AMWS 5; CA 65-68; CAAS 15;
CANR 19, 52, 73; CN; DLB 130

Banville, John 1945- .... **CLC 46, 118**
See also CA 117; 128; CN; DLB 14; INT
128

Banville, Theodore (Faullain) de
1832-1891 .... **NCLC 9**
See also GFL 1789 to the Present

Baraka, Amiri 1934- . **CLC 1, 2, 3, 5, 10, 14,**
33, 115; BLC 1; DA; DAC; DAM MST,
MULT, POET, POP; DC 6; PC 4;
WLCS
See also Jones, LeRoi
See also AFAW 1, 2; AMWS 2; BW 2, 3;
CA 21-24R; CABS 3; CAD; CANR 27,
38, 61; CD; CDALB 1941-1968; CP;
CPW; DA3; DFS 3, 11; DLB 5, 7, 16, 38;
DLBD 8; MTCW 1, 2; PFS 9; RGAL; WP

Baratynsky, Evgenii Abramovich
1800-1844 .... **NCLC 103**
See also DLB 205

Barbauld, Anna Laetitia
1743-1825 .... **NCLC 50**
See also DLB 107, 109, 142, 158; RGEL

Barbellion, W. N. P. .... **TCLC 24**
See also Cummings, Bruce F(rederick)

Barber, Benjamin R. 1939- .... **CLC 141**
See also CA 29-32R; CANR 12, 32, 64

Barbera, Jack (Vincent) 1945- .... **CLC 44**
See also CA 110; CANR 45

Barbey d'Aurevilly, Jules-Amedee
1808-1889 .... **NCLC 1; SSC 17**
See also DLB 119; GFL 1789 to the Present

Barbour, John c. 1316-1395 .... **CMLC 33**
See also DLB 146

Barbusse, Henri 1873-1935 .... **TCLC 5**
See also CA 105; 154; DLB 65; RGWL

Barclay, Bill
See Moorcock, Michael (John)

Barclay, William Ewert
See Moorcock, Michael (John)

Barea, Arturo 1897-1957 .... **TCLC 14**
See also CA 111

Barfoot, Joan 1946- .... **CLC 18**
See also CA 105

Barham, Richard Harris
1788-1845 .... **NCLC 77**
See also DLB 159

Baring, Maurice 1874-1945 .... **TCLC 8**
See also CA 105; 168; DLB 34; HGG

Baring-Gould, Sabine 1834-1924 ... **TCLC 88**
See also DLB 156, 190

Barker, Clive 1952- ...... **CLC 52; DAM POP**
See also AAYA 10; BEST 90:3; CA 121;
129; CANR 71; CPW; DA3; HGG; INT
129; MTCW 1, 2

Barker, George Granville
1913-1991 .... **CLC 8, 48; DAM POET**
See also CA 9-12R; 135; CANR 7, 38; DLB
20; MTCW 1

Blasco Ibanez, Vicente
1867-1928 .... **TCLC 12; DAM NOV**
See also CA 110; 131; CANR 81; DA3;
EW; HW 1, 2; MTCW 1

Blatty, William Peter 1928- .... **CLC 2; DAM POP**
See also CA 5-8R; CANR 9; HGG

Bleeck, Oliver
See Thomas, Ross (Elmore)

Blessing, Lee 1949- .... **CLC 54**
See also CAD; CD

Blight, Rose
See Greer, Germaine

Blish, James (Benjamin) 1921-1975 . **CLC 14**
See also CA 1-4R; 57-60; CANR 3; DLB
8; MTCW 1; SATA 66; SCFW 2; SFW

Bliss, Reginald
See Wells, H(erbert) G(eorge)

Blixen, Karen (Christentze Dinesen)
1885-1962
See Dinesen, Isak
See also CA 25-28; CANR 22, 50; CAP 2;
DA3; MTCW 1, 2; NCFS 2; SATA 44

Bloch, Robert (Albert) 1917-1994 .... **CLC 33**
See also AAYA 29; CA 5-8R, 179; 146;
CAAE 179; CAAS 20; CANR 5, 78;
DA3; DLB 44; HGG; INT CANR-5;
MTCW 1; SATA 12; SATA-Obit 82; SFW;
SUFW

Blok, Alexander (Alexandrovich)
1880-1921 .... **TCLC 5; PC 21**
See also CA 104; 183; EW; RGWL

Blom, Jan
See Breytenbach, Breyten

Bloom, Harold 1930- .... **CLC 24, 103**
See also CA 13-16R; CANR 39, 75, 92;
DLB 67; MTCW 1; RGAL

Bloomfield, Aurelius
See Bourne, Randolph S(illiman)

Blount, Roy (Alton), Jr. 1941- .... **CLC 38**
See also CA 53-56; CANR 10, 28, 61;
CSW; INT CANR-28; MTCW 1, 2

Bloy, Leon 1846-1917 .... **TCLC 22**
See also CA 121; 183; DLB 123; GFL 1789
to the Present

Blume, Judy (Sussman) 1938- .. **CLC 12, 30;
DAM NOV, POP**
See also AAYA 3, 26; CA 29-32R; CANR
13, 37, 66; CLR 2, 15, 69; CPW; DA3;
DLB 52; JRDA; MAICYA; MTCW 1, 2;
SATA 2, 31, 79; WYA; YAW

Blunden, Edmund (Charles)
1896-1974 .... **CLC 2, 56**
See also CA 17-18; 45-48; CANR 54; CAP
2; DLB 20, 100, 155; MTCW 1; PAB

Bly, Robert (Elwood) 1926- .... **CLC 1, 2, 5,
10, 15, 38, 128; DAM POET**
See also AMWS 4; CA 5-8R; CANR 41,
73; CP; DA3; DLB 5; MTCW 1, 2; RGAL

Boas, Franz 1858-1942 .... **TCLC 56**
See also CA 115; 181

Bobette
See Simenon, Georges (Jacques Christian)

Boccaccio, Giovanni 1313-1375 ... **CMLC 13;
SSC 10**
See also RGSF; RGWL

Bochco, Steven 1943- .... **CLC 35**
See also AAYA 11; CA 124; 138

Bodel, Jean 1167(?)-1210 .... **CMLC 28**

Bodenheim, Maxwell 1892-1954 .... **TCLC 44**
See also CA 110; 187; DLB 9, 45; RGAL

Bodker, Cecil 1927- .... **CLC 21**
See also CA 73-76; CANR 13, 44; CLR 23;
MAICYA; SATA 14

Boell, Heinrich (Theodor)
1917-1985 ..... **CLC 2, 3, 6, 9, 11, 15, 27,
32, 72; DA; DAB; DAC; DAM MST,
NOV; SSC 23; WLC**
See also Boll, Heinrich
See also CA 21-24R; 116; CANR 24; DA3;
DLB 69; DLBY 85; EW; MTCW 1, 2

Boerne, Alfred
See Doeblin, Alfred

Boethius c. 480-c. 524 .... **CMLC 15**
See also DLB 115; RGWL

Boff, Leonardo (Genezio Darci)
1938- .... **CLC 70; DAM MULT; HLC 1**
See also CA 150; HW 2

Bogan, Louise 1897-1970 .... **CLC 4, 39, 46,
93; DAM POET; PC 12**
See also AMWS 3; CA 73-76; 25-28R;
CANR 33, 82; DLB 45, 169; MTCW 1,
2; RGAL

Bogarde, Dirk
See Van Den Bogarde, Derek Jules Gaspard
Ulric Niven

Bogosian, Eric 1953- .... **CLC 45, 141**
See also CA 138; CAD; CD

Bograd, Larry 1953- .... **CLC 35**
See also CA 93-96; CANR 57; SAAS 21;
SATA 33, 89

Boiardo, Matteo Maria 1441-1494 .... **LC 6**

Boileau-Despreaux, Nicolas 1636-1711 . **LC 3**
See also GFL Beginnings to 1789; RGWL

Bojer, Johan 1872-1959 .... **TCLC 64**
See also CA 189

Bok, Edward W. 1863-1930 .... **TCLC 101**
See also DLB 91; DLBD 16

Boland, Eavan (Aisling) 1944- .. **CLC 40, 67,
113; DAM POET**
See also BRWS 5; CA 143; CANR 61; CP;
CWP; DLB 40; FW; MTCW 2; PFS 12

Boll, Heinrich
See Boell, Heinrich (Theodor)
See also RGSF; RGWL

Bolt, Lee
See Faust, Frederick (Schiller)

Bolt, Robert (Oxton) 1924-1995 ...... **CLC 14;
DAM DRAM**
See also CA 17-20R; 147; CANR 35, 67;
CBD; DFS 2; DLB 13, 233; MTCW 1

Bombal, Maria Luisa 1910-1980 ...... **SSC 37;
HLCS 1**
See also CA 127; CANR 72; HW 1; RGSF

Bombet, Louis-Alexandre-Cesar
See Stendhal

Bomkauf
See Kaufman, Bob (Garnell)

Bonaventura .... **NCLC 35**
See also DLB 90

Bond, Edward 1934- .... **CLC 4, 6, 13, 23;
DAM DRAM**
See also BRWS 1; CA 25-28R; CANR 38,
67; CBD; CD; DFS 3,8; DLB 13; MTCW
1

Bonham, Frank 1914-1989 .... **CLC 12**
See also AAYA 1; CA 9-12R; CANR 4, 36;
JRDA; MAICYA; SAAS 3; SATA 1, 49;
SATA-Obit 62; TCWW 2; YAW

Bonnefoy, Yves 1923- .. **CLC 9, 15, 58; DAM
MST, POET**
See also CA 85-88; CANR 33, 75, 97;
CWW 2; GFL 1789 to the Present; MTCW
1, 2

Bontemps, Arna(ud Wendell)
1902-1973 ..... **CLC 1, 18; BLC 1; DAM
MULT, NOV, POET**
See also BW 1; CA 1-4R; 41-44R; CANR
4, 35; CLR 6; CWRI; DA3; DLB 48, 51;
JRDA; MAICYA; MTCW 1, 2; SATA 2,
44; SATA-Obit 24; WCH; WP

Booth, Martin 1944- .... **CLC 13**
See also CA 93-96; CAAE 188; CAAS 2;
CANR 92

Booth, Philip 1925- .... **CLC 23**
See also CA 5-8R; CANR 5, 88; CP; DLBY
82

Booth, Wayne C(layson) 1921- .... **CLC 24**
See also CA 1-4R; CAAS 5; CANR 3, 43;
DLB 67

Borchert, Wolfgang 1921-1947 .... **TCLC 5**
See also CA 104; 188; DLB 69, 124

Borel, Petrus 1809-1859 .... **NCLC 41**
See also GFL 1789 to the Present

Borges, Jorge Luis 1899-1986 ... **CLC 1, 2, 3,
4, 6, 8, 9, 10, 13, 19, 44, 48, 83; DA;
DAB; DAC; DAM MST, MULT; HLC
1; PC 22, 32; SSC 4, 41; WLC**
See also AAYA 26; CA 21-24R; CANR 19,
33, 75; DA3; DLB 113; DLBY 86; DNFS;
HW 1, 2; MTCW 1, 2; RGSF; RGWL;
SFW; SSFS 4,9; TCLC 109

Borowski, Tadeusz 1922-1951 .... **TCLC 9**
See also CA 106; 154; RGSF

Borrow, George (Henry)
1803-1881 .... **NCLC 9**
See also DLB 21, 55, 166

Bosch (Gavino), Juan 1909-
See also CA 151; DAM MST, MULT; DLB
145; HLCS 1; HW 1, 2

Bosman, Herman Charles
1905-1951 .... **TCLC 49**
See also Malan, Herman
See also CA 160; DLB 225; RGSF

Bosschere, Jean de 1878(?)-1953 ... **TCLC 19**
See also CA 115; 186

Boswell, James 1740-1795 .... **LC 4, 50; DA;
DAB; DAC; DAM MST; WLC**
See also CDBLB 1660-1789; DLB 104, 142

Bottomley, Gordon 1874-1948 ..... **TCLC 107**
See also CA 120; 192; DLB 10

Bottoms, David 1949- .... **CLC 53**
See also CA 105; CANR 22; CSW; DLB
120; DLBY 83

Boucicault, Dion 1820-1890 .... **NCLC 41**

Boucolon, Maryse
See Cond

Bourget, Paul (Charles Joseph)
1852-1935 .... **TCLC 12**
See also CA 107; DLB 123; GFL 1789 to
the Present

Bourjaily, Vance (Nye) 1922- .... **CLC 8, 62**
See also CA 1-4R; CAAS 1; CANR 2, 72;
CN; DLB 2, 143

Bourne, Randolph S(illiman)
1886-1918 .... **TCLC 16**
See also Aurelius
See also AMW; CA 117; 155; DLB 63

Bova, Ben(jamin William) 1932- ...... **CLC 45**
See also AAYA 16; CA 5-8R; CAAS 18;
CANR 11, 56, 94; CLR 3; DLBY 81; INT
CANR-11; MAICYA; MTCW 1; SATA 6,
68; SFW

Bowen, Elizabeth (Dorothea Cole)
1899-1973 . **CLC 1, 3, 6, 11, 15, 22, 118;
DAM NOV; SSC 3, 28**
See also BRWS 2; CA 17-18; 41-44R;
CANR 35; CAP 2; CDBLB 1945-1960;
DA3; DLB 15, 162; FW; HGG; MTCW
1, 2; RGSF; SSFS 5; SUFW

Bowering, George 1935- .... **CLC 15, 47**
See also CA 21-24R; CAAS 16; CANR 10;
DLB 53

Bowering, Marilyn R(uthe) 1949- .... **CLC 32**
See also CA 101; CANR 49; CP; CWP

Bowers, Edgar 1924-2000 .... **CLC 9**
See also CA 5-8R; 188; CANR 24; CP;
CSW; DLB 5

Bowie, David .... **CLC 17**
See also Jones, David Robert

Bowles, Jane (Sydney) 1917-1973 ..... **CLC 3, 68**
See also CA 19-20; 41-44R; CAP 2

Bowles, Paul (Frederick) 1910-1999 . **CLC 1, 2, 19, 53; SSC 3**
See also AMWS 4; CA 1-4R; 186; CAAS 1; CANR 1, 19, 50, 75; CN; DA3; DLB 5, 6; MTCW 1, 2; RGAL

Bowles, William Lisle 1762-1850 . **NCLC 103**
See also DLB 93

Box, Edgar
See Vidal, Gore
See also GLL 1

Boyd, Nancy
See Millay, Edna St. Vincent
See also GLL 1

Boyd, Thomas (Alexander) 1898-1935 .... **TCLC 111**
See also CA 111; 183; DLB 9; DLBD 16

Boyd, William 1952- .... **CLC 28, 53, 70**
See also CA 114; 120; CANR 51, 71; CN; DLB 231

Boyle, Kay 1902-1992 .... **CLC 1, 5, 19, 58, 121; SSC 5**
See also CA 13-16R; 140; CAAS 1; CANR 29, 61; DLB 4, 9, 48, 86; DLBY 93; MTCW 1, 2; RGAL; RGSF; SSFS 10

Boyle, Mark
See Kienzle, William X(avier)

Boyle, Patrick 1905-1982 .... **CLC 19**
See also CA 127

Boyle, T. C.
See Boyle, T(homas) Coraghessan
See also AMWS 8

Boyle, T(homas) Coraghessan 1948- .... **CLC 36, 55, 90; DAM POP; SSC 16**
See also Boyle, T. C.
See also BEST 90:4; CA 120; CANR 44, 76, 89; CN; CPW; DA3; DLBY 86; MTCW 2

Boz
See Dickens, Charles (John Huffam)

Brackenridge, Hugh Henry 1748-1816 .... **NCLC 7**
See also DLB 11, 37; RGAL

Bradbury, Edward P.
See Moorcock, Michael (John)
See also MTCW 2

Bradbury, Malcolm (Stanley) 1932-2000 .... **CLC 32, 61; DAM NOV**
See also CA 1-4R; CANR 1, 33, 91, 98; CN; DA3; DLB 14, 207; MTCW 1, 2

Bradbury, Ray (Douglas) 1920- .... **CLC 1, 3, 10, 15, 42, 98; DA; DAB; DAC; DAM MST, NOV, POP; SSC 29; WLC**
See also AAYA 15; AITN 1, 2; AMWS 4; CA 1-4R; CANR 2, 30, 75; CDALB 1968-1988; CN; CPW; DA3; DLB 2, 8; HGG; MTCW 1, 2; NFS 1; RGAL; RGSF; SATA 11, 64, 123; SCFW 2; SFW; SSFS 1; SUFW; YAW

Braddon, Mary Elizabeth 1837-1915 .... **TCLC 111**
See also Aunt Belinda; White, Babington
See also CA 108; 179; CMW; DLB 18, 70, 156; HGG

Bradford, Gamaliel 1863-1932 .... **TCLC 36**
See also CA 160; DLB 17

Bradford, William 1590-1657 .... **LC 64**
See also DLB 24, 30; RGAL

Bradley, David (Henry), Jr. 1950- ... **CLC 23, 118; BLC 1; DAM MULT**
See also BW 1, 3; CA 104; CANR 26, 81; CN; DLB 33

Bradley, John Ed(mund, Jr.) 1958- . **CLC 55**
See also CA 139; CANR 99; CN; CSW

Bradley, Marion Zimmer 1930-1999 .... **CLC 30; DAM POP**
See also Chapman, Lee; Dexter, John; Gardner, Miriam; Ives, Morgan; Rivers, Elfrida
See also AAYA 40; CA 57-60; 185; CAAS 10; CANR 7, 31, 51, 75; CPW; DA3; DLB 8; FANT; FW; MTCW 1, 2; SATA 90; SATA-Obit 116; SFW; YAW

Bradshaw, John 1933- .... **CLC 70**
See also CA 138; CANR 61

Bradstreet, Anne 1612(?)-1672 ...... **LC 4, 30; DA; DAC; DAM MST, POET; PC 10**
See also AMWS 1; CDALB 1640-1865; DA3; DLB 24; FW; PFS 6; RGAL; WP

Brady, Joan 1939- .... **CLC 86**
See also CA 141

Bragg, Melvyn 1939- .... **CLC 10**
See also BEST 89:3; CA 57-60; CANR 10, 48, 89; CN; DLB 14; RHW

Brahe, Tycho 1546-1601 .... **LC 45**

Braine, John (Gerard) 1922-1986 . **CLC 1, 3, 41**
See also CA 1-4R; 120; CANR 1, 33; CD-BLB 1945-1960; DLB 15; DLBY 86; MTCW 1

Bramah, Ernest 1868-1942 .... **TCLC 72**
See also CA 156; CMW; DLB 70; FANT

Brammer, William 1930(?)-1978 ...... **CLC 31**
See also CA 77-80

Brancati, Vitaliano 1907-1954 .... **TCLC 12**
See also CA 109

Brancato, Robin F(idler) 1936- .... **CLC 35**
See also AAYA 9; CA 69-72; CANR 11, 45; CLR 32; JRDA; SAAS 9; SATA 97; WYA; YAW

Brand, Max
See Faust, Frederick (Schiller)
See also TCWW 2

Brand, Millen 1906-1980 .... **CLC 7**
See also CA 21-24R; 97-100; CANR 72

Branden, Barbara .... **CLC 44**
See also CA 148

Brandes, Georg (Morris Cohen) 1842-1927 .... **TCLC 10**
See also CA 105; 189

Brandys, Kazimierz 1916-2000 .... **CLC 62**

Branley, Franklyn M(ansfield) 1915- .... **CLC 21**
See also CA 33-36R; CANR 14, 39; CLR 13; MAICYA; SAAS 16; SATA 4, 68

Brathwaite, Edward (Kamau) 1930- ...... **CLC 11; BLCS; DAM POET**
See also BW 2, 3; CA 25-28R; CANR 11, 26, 47; CP; DLB 125

Brautigan, Richard (Gary) 1935-1984 .... **CLC 1, 3, 5, 9, 12, 34, 42; DAM NOV**
See also CA 53-56; 113; CANR 34; DA3; DLB 2, 5, 206; DLBY 80, 84; FANT; MTCW 1; RGAL; SATA 56

Brave Bird, Mary
See Crow Dog, Mary (Ellen)
See also NNAL

Braverman, Kate 1950- .... **CLC 67**
See also CA 89-92

Brecht, (Eugen) Bertolt (Friedrich) 1898-1956 .... **TCLC 1, 6, 13, 35; DA; DAB; DAC; DAM DRAM, MST; DC 3; WLC**
See also CA 104; 133; CANR 62; DA3; DFS 4, 5, 9; DLB 56, 124; EW; IDTP; MTCW 1, 2; RGWL

Brecht, Eugen Berthold Friedrich
See Brecht, (Eugen) Bertolt (Friedrich)

Bremer, Fredrika 1801-1865 .... **NCLC 11**

Brennan, Christopher John 1870-1932 .... **TCLC 17**
See also CA 117; 188; DLB 230

Brennan, Maeve 1917-1993 .... **CLC 5**
See also CA 81-84; CANR 72, 100

Brent, Linda
See Jacobs, Harriet A(nn)

Brentano, Clemens (Maria) 1778-1842 .... **NCLC 1**
See also DLB 90; RGWL

Brent of Bin Bin
See Franklin, (Stella Maria Sarah) Miles (Lampe)

Brenton, Howard 1942- .... **CLC 31**
See also CA 69-72; CANR 33, 67; CBD; CD; DLB 13; MTCW 1

Breslin, James 1935-1996
See Breslin, Jimmy
See also CA 73-76; CANR 31, 75; DAM NOV; MTCW 1, 2

Breslin, Jimmy .... **CLC 4, 43**
See also Breslin, James
See also AITN 1; DLB 185; MTCW 2

Bresson, Robert 1901(?)-1999 .... **CLC 16**
See also CA 110; 187; CANR 49

Breton, Andre 1896-1966 .. **CLC 2, 9, 15, 54; PC 15**
See also CA 19-20; 25-28R; CANR 40, 60; CAP 2; DLB 65; GFL 1789 to the Present; MTCW 1, 2; RGWL; WP

Breytenbach, Breyten 1939(?)- .. **CLC 23, 37, 126; DAM POET**
See also CA 113; 129; CANR 61; CWW 2; DLB 225

Bridgers, Sue Ellen 1942- .... **CLC 26**
See also AAYA 8; CA 65-68; CANR 11, 36; CLR 18; DLB 52; JRDA; MAICYA; SAAS 1; SATA 22, 90; SATA-Essay 109; YAW

Bridges, Robert (Seymour) 1844-1930 ... **TCLC 1; DAM POET; PC 28**
See also BRW; CA 104; 152; CDBLB 1890-1914; DLB 19, 98

Bridie, James .... **TCLC 3**
See also Mavor, Osborne Henry
See also DLB 10

Brin, David 1950- .... **CLC 34**
See also AAYA 21; CA 102; CANR 24, 70; INT CANR-24; SATA 65; SCFW 2; SFW

Brink, Andre (Philippus) 1935- . **CLC 18, 36, 106**
See also AFW; BRWS 6; CA 104; CANR 39, 62; CN; DLB 225; INT CA-103; MTCW 1, 2

Brinsmead, H(esba) F(ay) 1922- ...... **CLC 21**
See also CA 21-24R; CANR 10; CLR 47; CWRI; MAICYA; SAAS 5; SATA 18, 78

Brittain, Vera (Mary) 1893(?)-1970 . **CLC 23**
See also CA 13-16; 25-28R; CANR 58; CAP 1; DLB 191; FW; MTCW 1, 2

Broch, Hermann 1886-1951 .... **TCLC 20**
See also CA 117; DLB 85, 124; RGWL

Brock, Rose
See Hansen, Joseph
See also GLL 1

Brodkey, Harold (Roy) 1930-1996 ... **CLC 56**
See also CA 111; 151; CANR 71; CN; DLB 130

Brodsky, Iosif Alexandrovich 1940-1996
See Brodsky, Joseph
See also AITN 1; CA 41-44R; 151; CANR 37; DAM POET; DA3; MTCW 1, 2

Brodsky, Joseph . **CLC 4, 6, 13, 36, 100; PC 9**
See also Brodsky, Iosif Alexandrovich
See also AMWS 8; CWW 2; MTCW 1

Brodsky, Michael (Mark) 1948- .... **CLC 19**
See also CA 102; CANR 18, 41, 58

Brodzki, Bella ed. .... **CLC 65**

Brome, Richard 1590(?)-1652 .... **LC 61**
See also DLB 58

Bromell, Henry 1947- .... **CLC 5**
See also CA 53-56; CANR 9

Bromfield, Louis (Brucker)
1896-1956 .... **TCLC 11**
See also CA 107; 155; DLB 4, 9, 86;
RGAL; RHW

Broner, E(sther) M(asserman)
1930- .... **CLC 19**
See also CA 17-20R; CANR 8, 25, 72; CN;
DLB 28

Bronk, William (M.) 1918-1999 .... **CLC 10**
See also CA 89-92; 177; CANR 23; CP;
DLB 165

Bronstein, Lev Davidovich
See Trotsky, Leon

Bronte, Anne 1820-1849 ..... **NCLC 4, 71, 102**
See also BRW; DA3; DLB 21, 199

Bronte, Charlotte 1816-1855 ...... **NCLC 3, 8,
33, 58; DA; DAB; DAC; DAM MST,
NOV; WLC**
See also AAYA 17; BRW; CDBLB 1832-
1890; DA3; DLB 21, 159, 199; NFS 4

Bronte, Emily (Jane) 1818-1848 ... **NCLC 16,
35; DA; DAB; DAC; DAM MST, NOV,
POET; PC 8; WLC**
See also AAYA 17; BRW; CDBLB 1832-
1890; DA3; DLB 21, 32, 199

Brontes
See Bront

Brooke, Frances 1724-1789 .... **LC 6, 48**
See also DLB 39, 99

Brooke, Henry 1703(?)-1783 .... **LC 1**
See also DLB 39

Brooke, Rupert (Chawner)
1887-1915 .... **TCLC 2, 7; DA; DAB;
DAC; DAM MST, POET; PC 24; WLC**
See also BRW; BRWS 3; CA 104; 132;
CANR 61; CDBLB 1914-1945; DLB 19;
GLL 2; MTCW 1, 2; PFS 7

Brooke-Haven, P.
See Wodehouse, P(elham) G(renville)

Brooke-Rose, Christine 1926(?)- .. **CLC 40**
See also BRWS 4; CA 13-16R; CANR 58;
CN; DLB 14, 231; SFW

Brookner, Anita 1928- .. **CLC 32, 34, 51, 136;
DAB; DAM POP**
See also BRWS 4; CA 114; 120; CANR 37,
56, 87; CN; CPW; DA3; DLB 194; DLBY
87; MTCW 1, 2

Brooks, Cleanth 1906-1994 . **CLC 24, 86, 110**
See also CA 17-20R; 145; CANR 33, 35;
CSW; DLB 63; DLBY 94; INT CANR-
35; MTCW 1, 2

Brooks, George
See Baum, L(yman) Frank

Brooks, Gwendolyn (Elizabeth)
1917-2000 .. **CLC 1, 2, 4, 5, 15, 49, 125;
BLC 1; DA; DAC; DAM MST, MULT,
POET; PC 7; WLC**
See also AAYA 20; AFAW 1, 2; AITN 1;
AMWS 3; BW 2, 3; CA 1-4R; 190; CANR
1, 27, 52, 75; CDALB 1941-1968; CLR
27; CP; CWP; DA3; DLB 5, 76, 165;
MTCW 1, 2; PFS 1, 2, 4, 6; RGAL; SATA
6; SATA-Obit 123; WP

Brooks, Mel .... **CLC 12**
See also Kaminsky, Melvin
See also AAYA 13; DLB 26

Brooks, Peter 1938- .... **CLC 34**
See also CA 45-48; CANR 1

Brooks, Van Wyck 1886-1963 .... **CLC 29**
See also CA 1-4R; CANR 6; DLB 45, 63,
103

Brophy, Brigid (Antonia)
1929-1995 .... **CLC 6, 11, 29, 105**
See also CA 5-8R; 149; CAAS 4; CANR
25, 53; CBD; CN; CWD; DA3; DLB 14;
MTCW 1, 2

Brosman, Catharine Savage 1934- ..... **CLC 9**
See also CA 61-64; CANR 21, 46

Brossard, Nicole 1943- .... **CLC 115**
See also CA 122; CAAS 16; CCA 1; CWP;
CWW 2; DLB 53; FW; GLL 2

Brother Antoninus
See Everson, William (Oliver)

The Brothers Quay
See Quay, Stephen; Quay, Timothy

Broughton, T(homas) Alan 1936- ..... **CLC 19**
See also CA 45-48; CANR 2, 23, 48

Broumas, Olga 1949- .... **CLC 10, 73**
See also CA 85-88; CANR 20, 69; CP;
CWP; GLL 2

Broun, Heywood 1888-1939 .... **TCLC 104**
See also DLB 29, 171

Brown, Alan 1950- .... **CLC 99**
See also CA 156

Brown, Charles Brockden
1771-1810 .... **NCLC 22, 74**
See also AMWS 1; CDALB 1640-1865;
DLB 37, 59, 73; FW; HGG; RGAL

Brown, Christy 1932-1981 .... **CLC 63**
See also CA 105; 104; CANR 72; DLB 14

Brown, Claude 1937- .... **CLC 30; BLC 1;
DAM MULT**
See also AAYA 7; BW 1, 3; CA 73-76;
CANR 81

Brown, Dee (Alexander) 1908- . **CLC 18, 47;
DAM POP**
See also AAYA 30; CA 13-16R; CAAS 6;
CANR 11, 45, 60; CPW; CSW; DA3;
DLBY 80; MTCW 1, 2; SATA 5, 110;
TCWW 2

Brown, George
See Wertmueller, Lina

Brown, George Douglas
1869-1902 .... **TCLC 28**
See Douglas, George
See also CA 162

Brown, George Mackay 1921-1996 ... **CLC 5,
48, 100**
See also BRWS 6; CA 21-24R; 151; CAAS
6; CANR 12, 37, 67; CN; CP; DLB 14,
27, 139; MTCW 1; RGSF; SATA 35

Brown, (William) Larry 1951- .... **CLC 73**
See also CA 130; 134; CSW; INT 133

Brown, Moses
See Barrett, William (Christopher)

Brown, Rita Mae 1944- .... **CLC 18, 43, 79;
DAM NOV, POP**
See also CA 45-48; CANR 2, 11, 35, 62,
95; CN; CPW; CSW; DA3; FW; INT
CANR-11; MTCW 1, 2; NFS 9; RGAL

Brown, Roderick (Langmere) Haig-
See Haig-Brown, Roderick (Langmere)

Brown, Rosellen 1939- .... **CLC 32**
See also CA 77-80; CAAS 10; CANR 14,
44, 98; CN

Brown, Sterling Allen 1901-1989 ...... **CLC 1,
23, 59; BLC 1; DAM MULT, POET**
See also AFAW 1, 2; BW 1, 3; CA 85-88;
127; CANR 26; DA3; DLB 48, 51, 63;
MTCW 1, 2; RGAL; WP

Brown, Will
See Ainsworth, William Harrison

Brown, William Wells 1815-1884 ... **NCLC 2,
89; BLC 1; DAM MULT; DC 1**
See also DLB 3, 50; RGAL

Browne, (Clyde) Jackson 1948(?)- ... **CLC 21**
See also CA 120

Browning, Elizabeth Barrett
1806-1861 ...... **NCLC 1, 16, 61, 66; DA;
DAB; DAC; DAM MST, POET; PC 6;
WLC**
See also CDBLB 1832-1890; DA3; DLB
32, 199; PAB; PFS 2; WP

Browning, Robert 1812-1889 . **NCLC 19, 79;
DA; DAB; DAC; DAM MST, POET;
PC 2; WLCS**
See also BRW; CDBLB 1832-1890; DA3;
DLB 32, 163; PAB; PFS 1; RGEL; TEA;
WP; YABC 1

Browning, Tod 1882-1962 .... **CLC 16**
See also CA 141; 117

Brownson, Orestes Augustus
1803-1876 .... **NCLC 50**
See also DLB 1, 59, 73

Bruccoli, Matthew J(oseph) 1931- ... **CLC 34**
See also CA 9-12R; CANR 7, 87; DLB 103

Bruce, Lenny .... **CLC 21**
See also Schneider, Leonard Alfred

Bruin, John
See Brutus, Dennis

Brulard, Henri
See Stendhal

Brulls, Christian
See Simenon, Georges (Jacques Christian)

Brunner, John (Kilian Houston)
1934-1995 .... **CLC 8, 10; DAM POP**
See also CA 1-4R; 149; CAAS 8; CANR 2,
37; CPW; MTCW 1, 2; SCFW 2; SFW

Bruno, Giordano 1548-1600 .... **LC 27**
See also RGWL

Brutus, Dennis 1924- .... **CLC 43; BLC 1;
DAM MULT, POET; PC 24**
See also BW 2, 3; CA 49-52; CAAS 14;
CANR 2, 27, 42, 81; CP; DLB 117, 225

Bryan, C(ourtlandt) D(ixon) B(arnes)
1936- .... **CLC 29**
See also CA 73-76; CANR 13, 68; DLB
185; INT CANR-13

Bryan, Michael
See Moore, Brian
See also CCA 1

Bryan, William Jennings
1860-1925 .... **TCLC 99**

Bryant, William Cullen 1794-1878 . **NCLC 6,
46; DA; DAB; DAC; DAM MST,
POET; PC 20**
See also AMWS 1; CDALB 1640-1865;
DLB 3, 43, 59, 189; PAB; RGAL

Bryusov, Valery Yakovlevich
1873-1924 .... **TCLC 10**
See also CA 107; 155; SFW

Buchan, John 1875-1940 .... **TCLC 41; DAB;
DAM POP**
See also CA 108; 145; CMW; DLB 34, 70,
156; HGG; MTCW 1; RGEL; RHW;
YABC 2

Buchanan, George 1506-1582 .... **LC 4**
See also DLB 152

Buchanan, Robert 1841-1901 .... **TCLC 107**
See also CA 179; DLB 18, 35

Buchheim, Lothar-Guenther 1918- .... **CLC 6**
See also CA 85-88

Buchner, (Karl) Georg 1813-1837 . **NCLC 26**
See also EW; RGSF; RGWL

Buchwald, Art(hur) 1925- .... **CLC 33**
See also AITN 1; CA 5-8R; CANR 21, 67;
MTCW 1, 2; SATA 10

Buck, Pearl S(ydenstricker)
1892-1973 ... **CLC 7, 11, 18, 127; DA;
DAB; DAC; DAM MST, NOV**
See also AITN 1; AMWS 2; CA 1-4R; 41-
44R; CANR 1, 34; CDALBS; DA3; DLB
9, 102; MTCW 1, 2; RGAL; RHW; SATA
1, 25

Buckler, Ernest 1908-1984 .... **CLC 13; DAC;
DAM MST**
See also CA 11-12; 114; CAP 1; CCA 1;
DLB 68; SATA 47

Buckley, Vincent (Thomas)
1925-1988 .... **CLC 57**
See also CA 101

Collier, Jeremy 1650-1726 .... **LC 6**

Collier, John 1901-1980 .... **SSC 19**
    See also CA 65-68; 97-100; CANR 10; DLB 77; FANT

Collingwood, R(obin) G(eorge) 1889(?)-1943 .... **TCLC 67**
    See also CA 117; 155

Collins, Hunt
    See Hunter, Evan

Collins, Linda 1931- .... **CLC 44**
    See also CA 125

Collins, (William) Wilkie 1824-1889 .... **NCLC 1, 18, 93**
    See also BRWS 6; CDBLB 1832-1890; CMW; DLB 18, 70, 159; MSW; RGEL; RGSF; SUFW

Collins, William 1721-1759 . **LC 4, 40; DAM POET**
    See also DLB 109; RGEL

Collodi, Carlo .... **NCLC 54**
    See also Lorenzini, Carlo
    See also CLR 5; WCH

Colman, George
    See Glassco, John

Colt, Winchester Remington
    See Hubbard, L(afayette) Ron(ald)

Colter, Cyrus 1910- .... **CLC 58**
    See also BW 1; CA 65-68; CANR 10, 66; CN; DLB 33

Colton, James
    See Hansen, Joseph
    See also GLL 1

Colum, Padraic 1881-1972 .... **CLC 28**
    See also CA 73-76; 33-36R; CANR 35; CLR 36; CWRI; MAICYA; MTCW 1; RGEL; SATA 15

Colvin, James
    See Moorcock, Michael (John)

Colwin, Laurie (E.) 1944-1992 .... **CLC 5, 13, 23, 84**
    See also CA 89-92; 139; CANR 20, 46; DLBY 80; MTCW 1

Comfort, Alex(ander) 1920-2000 .... **CLC 7; DAM POP**
    See also CA 1-4R; 190; CANR 1, 45; CP; MTCW 1

Comfort, Montgomery
    See Campbell, (John) Ramsey

Compton-Burnett, I(vy) 1892(?)-1969 .... **CLC 1, 3, 10, 15, 34; DAM NOV**
    See also BRW; CA 1-4R; 25-28R; CANR 4; DLB 36; MTCW 1; RGEL

Comstock, Anthony 1844-1915 ...... **TCLC 13**
    See also CA 110; 169

Comte, Auguste 1798-1857 .... **NCLC 54**

Conan Doyle, Arthur
    See Doyle, Arthur Conan

Conde (Abellan), Carmen 1901-
    See also CA 177; DLB 108; HLCS 1; HW 2

Conde, Maryse 1937- .... **CLC 52, 92; BLCS; DAM MULT**
    See also BW 2, 3; CA 110; CAAE 190; CANR 30, 53, 76; CWW 2; MTCW 1

Condillac, Etienne Bonnot de 1714-1780 .... **LC 26**

Condon, Richard (Thomas) 1915-1996 ...... **CLC 4, 6, 8, 10, 45, 100; DAM NOV**
    See also BEST 90:3; CA 1-4R; 151; CAAS 1; CANR 2, 23; CMW; CN; INT CANR-23; MTCW 1, 2

Confucius 551B.C.-479B.C. .. **CMLC 19; DA; DAB; DAC; DAM MST; WLCS**
    See also DA3

Congreve, William 1670-1729 .... **LC 5, 21; DA; DAB; DAC; DAM DRAM, MST, POET; DC 2; WLC**
    See also CDBLB 1660-1789; DLB 39, 84; RGEL

Connell, Evan S(helby), Jr. 1924- . **CLC 4, 6, 45; DAM NOV**
    See also AAYA 7; CA 1-4R; CAAS 2; CANR 2, 39, 76, 97; CN; DLB 2; DLBY 81; MTCW 1, 2

Connelly, Marc(us Cook) 1890-1980 . **CLC 7**
    See also CA 85-88; 102; CANR 30; DFS 12; DLB 7; DLBY 80; RGAL; SATA-Obit 25

Connor, Ralph .... **TCLC 31**
    See also Gordon, Charles William
    See also DLB 92; TCWW 2

Conrad, Joseph 1857-1924 .... **TCLC 1, 6, 13, 25, 43, 57; DA; DAB; DAC; DAM MST, NOV; SSC 9; WLC**
    See also AAYA 26; CA 104; 131; CANR 60; CDBLB 1890-1914; DA3; DLB 10, 34, 98, 156; MTCW 1, 2; NFS 2; RGEL; RGSF; SATA 27; SSFS 1, 12

Conrad, Robert Arnold
    See Hart, Moss

Conroy, Pat
    See Conroy, (Donald) Pat(rick)
    See also MTCW 2

Conroy, (Donald) Pat(rick) 1945- ... **CLC 30, 74; DAM NOV, POP**
    See also Conroy, Pat
    See also AAYA 8; AITN 1; CA 85-88; CANR 24, 53; CPW; CSW; DA3; DLB 6; MTCW 1

Constant (de Rebecque), (Henri) Benjamin 1767-1830 .... **NCLC 6**
    See also DLB 119; EW; GFL 1789 to the Present

Conybeare, Charles Augustus
    See Eliot, T(homas) S(tearns)

Cook, Michael 1933-1994 .... **CLC 58**
    See also CA 93-96; CANR 68; DLB 53

Cook, Robin 1940- .... **CLC 14; DAM POP**
    See also CA 32; BEST 90:2; CA 108; 111; CANR 41, 90; CPW; DA3; HGG; INT 111

Cook, Roy
    See Silverberg, Robert

Cooke, Elizabeth 1948- .... **CLC 55**
    See also CA 129

Cooke, John Esten 1830-1886 .... **NCLC 5**
    See also DLB 3; RGAL

Cooke, John Estes
    See Baum, L(yman) Frank

Cooke, M. E.
    See Creasey, John

Cooke, Margaret
    See Creasey, John

Cook-Lynn, Elizabeth 1930- . **CLC 93; DAM MULT**
    See also CA 133; DLB 175; NNAL

Cooney, Ray .... **CLC 62**
    See also CBD

Cooper, Douglas 1960- .... **CLC 86**

Cooper, Henry St. John
    See Creasey, John

Cooper, J(oan) California (?)- .... **CLC 56; DAM MULT**
    See also AAYA 12; BW 1; CA 125; CANR 55; DLB 212

Cooper, James Fenimore 1789-1851 .... **NCLC 1, 27, 54**
    See also AAYA 22; CDALB 1640-1865; DA3; DLB 3; NFS 9; RGAL; SATA 19

Coover, Robert (Lowell) 1932- ...... **CLC 3, 7, 15, 32, 46, 87; DAM NOV; SSC 15**
    See also AMWS 5; CA 45-48; CANR 3, 37, 58; CN; DLB 2, 227; DLBY 81; MTCW 1, 2; RGAL; RGSF

Copeland, Stewart (Armstrong) 1952- .... **CLC 26**

Copernicus, Nicolaus 1473-1543 .... **LC 45**

Coppard, A(lfred) E(dgar) 1878-1957 .... **TCLC 5; SSC 21**
    See also CA 114; 167; DLB 162; HGG; RGEL; RGSF; SUFW; YABC 1

Coppee, Francois 1842-1908 .... **TCLC 25**
    See also CA 170

Coppola, Francis Ford 1939- ... **CLC 16, 126**
    See also AAYA 39; CA 77-80; CANR 40, 78; DLB 44

Corbiere, Tristan 1845-1875 .... **NCLC 43**
    See also GFL 1789 to the Present

Corcoran, Barbara (Asenath) 1911- .... **CLC 17**
    See also AAYA 14; CA 21-24R; CAAE 191; CAAS 2; CANR 11, 28, 48; CLR 50; DLB 52; JRDA; RHW; SAAS 20; SATA 3, 77, 125

Cordelier, Maurice
    See Giraudoux, Jean(-Hippolyte)

Corelli, Marie .... **TCLC 51**
    See also Mackay, Mary
    See also DLB 34, 156; RGEL

Corman, Cid .... **CLC 9**
    See also Corman, Sidney
    See also CAAS 2; DLB 5, 193

Corman, Sidney 1924-
    See Corman, Cid
    See also CA 85-88; CANR 44; CP; DAM POET

Cormier, Robert (Edmund) 1925-2000 .... **CLC 12, 30; DA; DAB; DAC; DAM MST, NOV**
    See also AAYA 3, 19; CA 1-4R; CANR 5, 23, 76, 93; CDALB 1968-1988; CLR 12, 55; DLB 52; INT CANR-23; JRDA; MAI-CYA; MTCW 1, 2; NFS 2; SATA 10, 45, 83; SATA-Obit 122; WYA; YAW

Corn, Alfred (DeWitt III) 1943- .... **CLC 33**
    See also CA 179; CAAE 179; CAAS 25; CANR 44; CP; CSW; DLB 120; DLBY 80

Corneille, Pierre 1606-1684 ..... **LC 28; DAB; DAM MST**
    See also GFL Beginnings to 1789; RGWL

Cornwell, David (John Moore) 1931- .... **CLC 9, 15; DAM POP**
    See also le Carre, John
    See also CA 5-8R; CANR 13, 33, 59; DA3; MTCW 1, 2

Corso, (Nunzio) Gregory 1930-2001 . **CLC 1, 11; PC 33**
    See also CA 5-8R; CANR 41, 76; CP; DA3; DLB 5, 16; MTCW 1, 2; WP

Cortazar, Julio 1914-1984 ... **CLC 2, 3, 5, 10, 13, 15, 33, 34, 92; DAM MULT, NOV; HLC 1; SSC 7**
    See also CA 21-24R; CANR 12, 32, 81; DA3; DLB 113; HW 1, 2; MTCW 1, 2; RGSF; RGWL; SSFS 3

Cortes, Hernan 1485-1547 .... **LC 31**

Corvinus, Jakob
    See Raabe, Wilhelm (Karl)

Corvo, Baron
    See Rolfe, Frederick (William Serafino Austin Lewis Mary)
    See also GLL 1; RGEL

Corwin, Cecil
    See Kornbluth, C(yril) M.

Cosic, Dobrica 1921- .... **CLC 14**
    See also CA 122; 138; CWW 2; DLB 181

du Maurier, Daphne 1907-1989 .. **CLC 6, 11, 59; DAB; DAC; DAM MST, POP; SSC 18**
See also AAYA 37; BRWS 3; CA 5-8R; 128; CANR 6, 55; CMW; CPW; DA3; DLB 191; HGG; MTCW 1, 2; NFS 12; RGEL; RGSF; RHW; SATA 27; SATA-Obit 60

Du Maurier, George 1834-1896 ..... **NCLC 86**
See also DLB 153, 178; RGEL

Dunbar, Paul Laurence 1872-1906 . **TCLC 2, 12; BLC 1; DA; DAC; DAM MST, MULT, POET; PC 5; SSC 8; WLC**
See also AFAW 1, 2; AMWS 2; BW 1, 3; CA 104; 124; CANR 79; CDALB 1865-1917; DA3; DLB 50, 54, 78; RGAL; SATA 34

Dunbar, William 1460(?)-1520(?) .... **LC 20**
See also DLB 132, 146; RGEL

Duncan, Dora Angela
See Duncan, Isadora

Duncan, Isadora 1877(?)-1927 .... **TCLC 68**
See also CA 118; 149

Duncan, Lois 1934- .... **CLC 26**
See also AAYA 4, 34; CA 1-4R; CANR 2, 23, 36; CLR 29; JRDA; MAICYA; SAAS 2; SATA 1, 36, 75; YAW

Duncan, Robert (Edward)
1919-1988 .... **CLC 1, 2, 4, 7, 15, 41, 55; DAM POET; PC 2**
See also CA 9-12R; 124; CANR 28, 62; DLB 5, 16, 193; MTCW 1, 2; RGAL; WP

Duncan, Sara Jeannette
1861-1922 .... **TCLC 60**
See also CA 157; DLB 92

Dunlap, William 1766-1839 .... **NCLC 2**
See also DLB 30, 37, 59; RGAL

Dunn, Douglas (Eaglesham) 1942- .... **CLC 6, 40**
See also CA 45-48; CANR 2, 33; CP; DLB 40; MTCW 1

Dunn, Katherine (Karen) 1945- .... **CLC 71**
See also CA 33-36R; CANR 72; HGG; MTCW 1

Dunn, Stephen 1939- .... **CLC 36**
See also CA 33-36R; CANR 12, 48, 53; CP; DLB 105

Dunne, Finley Peter 1867-1936 ...... **TCLC 28**
See also CA 108; 178; DLB 11, 23; RGAL

Dunne, John Gregory 1932- .... **CLC 28**
See also CA 25-28R; CANR 14, 50; CN; DLBY 80

Dunsany, Edward John Moreton Drax Plunkett 1878-1957
See Dunsany, Lord
See also CA 104; 148; DLB 10; MTCW 1; SFW

Dunsany, Lord .... **TCLC 2, 59**
See also Dunsany, Edward John Moreton Drax Plunkett
See also DLB 77, 153, 156; FANT; RGEL

du Perry, Jean
See Simenon, Georges (Jacques Christian)

Durang, Christopher (Ferdinand)
1949- .... **CLC 27, 38**
See also CA 105; CAD; CANR 50, 76; CD; MTCW 1

Duras, Marguerite 1914-1996 . **CLC 3, 6, 11, 20, 34, 40, 68, 100; SSC 40**
See also CA 25-28R; 151; CANR 50; CWW 2; DLB 83; GFL 1789 to the Present; IDFW 4; MTCW 1, 2; RGWL

Durban, (Rosa) Pam 1947- .... **CLC 39**
See also CA 123; CANR 98; CSW

Durcan, Paul 1944- .... **CLC 43, 70; DAM POET**
See also CA 134; CP

Durkheim, Emile 1858-1917 .... **TCLC 55**

Durrell, Lawrence (George)
1912-1990 .... **CLC 1, 4, 6, 8, 13, 27, 41; DAM NOV**
See also BRWS 1; CA 9-12R; 132; CANR 40, 77; CDBLB 1945-1960; DLB 15, 27, 204; DLBY 90; MTCW 1, 2; RGEL; SFW

Durrenmatt, Friedrich
See Duerrenmatt, Friedrich
See also RGWL

Dutt, Toru 1856-1877 .... **NCLC 29**
See also DLB 240

Dwight, Timothy 1752-1817 .... **NCLC 13**
See also DLB 37; RGAL

Dworkin, Andrea 1946- .... **CLC 43, 123**
See also CA 77-80; CAAS 21; CANR 16, 39, 76, 96; FW; GLL 1; INT CANR-16; MTCW 1, 2

Dwyer, Deanna
See Koontz, Dean R(ay)

Dwyer, K. R.
See Koontz, Dean R(ay)

Dwyer, Thomas A. 1923- .... **CLC 114**
See also CA 115

Dybek, Stuart 1942- .... **CLC 114**
See also CA 97-100; CANR 39; DLB 130

Dye, Richard
See De Voto, Bernard (Augustine)

Dylan, Bob 1941- .... **CLC 3, 4, 6, 12, 77**
See also CA 41-44R; CP; DLB 16

Dyson, John 1943- .... **CLC 70**
See also CA 144

E. V. L.
See Lucas, E(dward) V(errall)

Eagleton, Terence (Francis) 1943- .. **CLC 63, 132**
See also CA 57-60; CANR 7, 23, 68; DLB 242; MTCW 1, 2

Eagleton, Terry
See Eagleton, Terence (Francis)

Early, Jack
See Scoppettone, Sandra
See also GLL 1

East, Michael
See West, Morris L(anglo)

Eastaway, Edward
See Thomas, (Philip) Edward

Eastlake, William (Derry)
1917-1997 .... **CLC 8**
See also CA 5-8R; 158; CAAS 1; CANR 5, 63; CN; DLB 6, 206; INT CANR-5; TCWW 2

Eastman, Charles A(lexander)
1858-1939 .... **TCLC 55; DAM MULT**
See also CA 179; CANR 91; DLB 175; NNAL; YABC 1

Eberhart, Richard (Ghormley)
1904- .. **CLC 3, 11, 19, 56; DAM POET**
See also AMW; CA 1-4R; CANR 2; CDALB 1941-1968; CP; DLB 48; MTCW 1; RGAL

Eberstadt, Fernanda 1960- .... **CLC 39**
See also CA 136; CANR 69

Echegaray (y Eizaguirre), Jose (Maria Waldo) 1832-1916 .... **TCLC 4; HLCS 1**
See also CA 104; CANR 32; HW 1; MTCW 1

Echeverria, (Jose) Esteban (Antonino)
1805-1851 .... **NCLC 18**
See also LAW

Echo
See Proust, (Valentin-Louis-George-Eug

Eckert, Allan W. 1931- .... **CLC 17**
See also AAYA 18; CA 13-16R; CANR 14, 45; INT CANR-14; SAAS 21; SATA 29, 91; SATA-Brief 27

Eckhart, Meister 1260(?)-1327(?) ... **CMLC 9**
See also DLB 115

Eckmar, F. R.
See de Hartog, Jan

Eco, Umberto 1932- .... **CLC 28, 60, 142; DAM NOV, POP**
See also BEST 90:1; CA 77-80; CANR 12, 33, 55; CPW; CWW 2; DA3; DLB 196, 242; MTCW 1, 2

Eddison, E(ric) R(ucker)
1882-1945 .... **TCLC 15**
See also CA 109; 156; FANT; SFW; SUFW

Eddy, Mary (Ann Morse) Baker
1821-1910 .... **TCLC 71**
See also CA 113; 174

Edel, (Joseph) Leon 1907-1997 .. **CLC 29, 34**
See also CA 1-4R; 161; CANR 1, 22; DLB 103; INT CANR-22

Eden, Emily 1797-1869 .... **NCLC 10**

Edgar, David 1948- .. **CLC 42; DAM DRAM**
See also CA 57-60; CANR 12, 61; CBD; CD; DLB 13, 233; MTCW 1

Edgerton, Clyde (Carlyle) 1944- ...... **CLC 39**
See also AAYA 17; CA 118; 134; CANR 64; CSW; INT 134; YAW

Edgeworth, Maria 1768-1849 .... **NCLC 1, 51**
See also BRWS 3; DLB 116, 159, 163; FW; RGEL; SATA 21

Edmonds, Paul
See Kuttner, Henry

Edmonds, Walter D(umaux)
1903-1998 .... **CLC 35**
See also CA 5-8R; CANR 2; CWRI; DLB 9; MAICYA; RHW; SAAS 4; SATA 1, 27; SATA-Obit 99

Edmondson, Wallace
See Ellison, Harlan (Jay)

Edson, Russell .... **CLC 13**
See also CA 33-36R; WP

Edwards, Bronwen Elizabeth
See Rose, Wendy

Edwards, G(erald) B(asil)
1899-1976 .... **CLC 25**
See also CA 110

Edwards, Gus 1939- .... **CLC 43**
See also CA 108; INT 108

Edwards, Jonathan 1703-1758 .... **LC 7, 54; DA; DAC; DAM MST**
See also DLB 24; RGAL

Efron, Marina Ivanovna Tsvetaeva
See Tsvetaeva (Efron), Marina (Ivanovna)

Ehle, John (Marsden, Jr.) 1925- ...... **CLC 27**
See also CA 9-12R; CSW

Ehrenbourg, Ilya (Grigoryevich)
See Ehrenburg, Ilya (Grigoryevich)

Ehrenburg, Ilya (Grigoryevich)
1891-1967 .... **CLC 18, 34, 62**
See also CA 102; 25-28R

Ehrenburg, Ilyo (Grigoryevich)
See Ehrenburg, Ilya (Grigoryevich)

Ehrenreich, Barbara 1941- .... **CLC 110**
See also BEST 90:4; CA 73-76; CANR 16, 37, 62; FW; MTCW 1, 2

Eich, Guenter 1907-1972 .... **CLC 15**
See also Eich, Gunter
See also CA 111; 93-96; DLB 69, 124

Eich, Gunter
See Eich, Guenter
See also RGWL

Eichendorff, Joseph 1788-1857 .... **NCLC 8**
See also DLB 90; RGWL

Eigner, Larry .... **CLC 9**
See also Eigner, Laurence (Joel)
See also CAAS 23; DLB 5; WP

Eigner, Laurence (Joel) 1927-1996
See Eigner, Larry
See also CA 9-12R; 151; CANR 6, 84; CP; DLB 193

Einstein, Albert 1879-1955 .... **TCLC 65**
See also CA 121; 133; MTCW 1, 2

Esenin, Sergei (Alexandrovich)
1895-1925 .... **TCLC 4**
See also CA 104; RGWL

Eshleman, Clayton 1935- .... **CLC 7**
See also CA 33-36R; CAAS 6; CANR 93;
CP; DLB 5

Espriella, Don Manuel Alvarez
See Southey, Robert

Espriu, Salvador 1913-1985 .... **CLC 9**
See also CA 154; 115; DLB 134

Espronceda, Jose de 1808-1842 ..... **NCLC 39**

Esquivel, Laura 1951(?)- ... **CLC 141; HLCS 1**
See also AAYA 29; CA 143; CANR 68;
DA3; DNFS; MTCW 1; NFS 5

Esse, James
See Stephens, James

Esterbrook, Tom
See Hubbard, L(afayette) Ron(ald)

Estleman, Loren D. 1952- ..... **CLC 48; DAM NOV, POP**
See also AAYA 27; CA 85-88; CANR 27,
74; CMW; CPW; DA3; DLB 226; INT
CANR-27; MTCW 1, 2

Euclid 306B.C.-283B.C. .... **CMLC 25**

Eugenides, Jeffrey 1960(?)- .... **CLC 81**
See also CA 144

Euripides c. 484B.C.-406B.C. .... **CMLC 23; DA; DAB; DAC; DAM DRAM, MST; DC 4; WLCS**
See also DA3; DFS 1, 4, 6; DLB 176;
RGWL

Evan, Evin
See Faust, Frederick (Schiller)

Evans, Caradoc 1878-1945 ... **TCLC 85; SSC 43**

Evans, Evan
See Faust, Frederick (Schiller)
See also TCWW 2

Evans, Marian
See Eliot, George

Evans, Mary Ann
See Eliot, George

Evarts, Esther
See Benson, Sally

Everett, Percival
See Everett, Percival L.
See also CSW

Everett, Percival L. 1956- .... **CLC 57**
See also Everett, Percival
See also BW 2; CA 129; CANR 94

Everson, R(onald) G(ilmour)
1903-1992 .... **CLC 27**
See also CA 17-20R; DLB 88

Everson, William (Oliver)
1912-1994 .... **CLC 1, 5, 14**
See also CA 9-12R; 145; CANR 20; DLB
212; MTCW 1

Evtushenko, Evgenii Aleksandrovich
See Yevtushenko, Yevgeny (Alexandrovich)
See also RGWL

Ewart, Gavin (Buchanan)
1916-1995 .... **CLC 13, 46**
See also BRWS 7; CA 89-92; 150; CANR
17, 46; CP; DLB 40; MTCW 1

Ewers, Hanns Heinz 1871-1943 ..... **TCLC 12**
See also CA 109; 149

Ewing, Frederick R.
See Sturgeon, Theodore (Hamilton)

Exley, Frederick (Earl) 1929-1992 .... **CLC 6, 11**
See also AITN 2; CA 81-84; 138; DLB 143;
DLBY 81

Eynhardt, Guillermo
See Quiroga, Horacio (Sylvestre)

Ezekiel, Nissim 1924- .... **CLC 61**
See also CA 61-64; CP

Ezekiel, Tish O'Dowd 1943- .... **CLC 34**
See also CA 129

Fadeyev, A.
See Bulgya, Alexander Alexandrovich

Fadeyev, Alexander .... **TCLC 53**
See also Bulgya, Alexander Alexandrovich

Fagen, Donald 1948- .... **CLC 26**

Fainzilberg, Ilya Arnoldovich 1897-1937
See Ilf, Ilya
See also CA 120; 165

Fair, Ronald L. 1932- .... **CLC 18**
See also BW 1; CA 69-72; CANR 25; DLB
33

Fairbairn, Roger
See Carr, John Dickson

Fairbairns, Zoe (Ann) 1948- .... **CLC 32**
See also CA 103; CANR 21, 85; CN

Fairman, Paul W. 1916-1977
See Queen, Ellery
See also CA 114; SFW

Falco, Gian
See Papini, Giovanni

Falconer, James
See Kirkup, James

Falconer, Kenneth
See Kornbluth, C(yril) M.

Falkland, Samuel
See Heijermans, Herman

Fallaci, Oriana 1930- .... **CLC 11, 110**
See also CA 77-80; CANR 15, 58; FW;
MTCW 1

Faludi, Susan 1959- .... **CLC 140**
See also CA 138; FW; MTCW 1

Faludy, George 1913- .... **CLC 42**
See also CA 21-24R

Faludy, Gyoergy
See Faludy, George

Fanon, Frantz 1925-1961 ... **CLC 74; BLC 2; DAM MULT**
See also BW 1; CA 116; 89-92

Fanshawe, Ann 1625-1680 .... **LC 11**

Fante, John (Thomas) 1911-1983 ..... **CLC 60**
See also CA 69-72; 109; CANR 23; DLB
130; DLBY 83

Farah, Nuruddin 1945- .. **CLC 53, 137; BLC 2; DAM MULT**
See also BW 2, 3; CA 106; CANR 81; CN;
DLB 125

Fargue, Leon-Paul 1876(?)-1947 .... **TCLC 11**
See also CA 109

Farigoule, Louis
See Romains, Jules

Farina, Richard 1936(?)-1966 .... **CLC 9**
See also CA 81-84; 25-28R

Farley, Walter (Lorimer)
1915-1989 .... **CLC 17**
See also CA 17-20R; CANR 8, 29, 84; DLB
22; JRDA; MAICYA; SATA 2, 43; YAW

Farmer, Philip Jose 1918- .... **CLC 1, 19**
See also AAYA 28; CA 1-4R; CANR 4, 35;
DLB 8; MTCW 1; SATA 93; SFW

Farquhar, George 1677-1707 ... **LC 21; DAM DRAM**
See also DLB 84; RGEL

Farrell, J(ames) G(ordon)
1935-1979 .... **CLC 6**
See also CA 73-76; 89-92; CANR 36; DLB
14; MTCW 1; RGEL; RHW

Farrell, James T(homas) 1904-1979 . **CLC 1, 4, 8, 11, 66; SSC 28**
See also AMW; CA 5-8R; 89-92; CANR 9,
61; DLB 4, 9, 86; DLBD 2; MTCW 1, 2;
RGAL

Farrell, Warren (Thomas) 1943- ...... **CLC 70**
See also CA 146

Farren, Richard J.
See Betjeman, John

Farren, Richard M.
See Betjeman, John

Fassbinder, Rainer Werner
1946-1982 .... **CLC 20**
See also CA 93-96; 106; CANR 31

Fast, Howard (Melvin) 1914- .. **CLC 23, 131; DAM NOV**
See also AAYA 16; CA 1-4R, 181; CAAE
181; CAAS 18; CANR 1, 33, 54, 75, 98;
CMW; CN; CPW; DLB 9; INT CANR-
33; MTCW 1; RHW; SATA 7; SATA-
Essay 107; TCWW 2; YAW

Faulcon, Robert
See Holdstock, Robert P.

Faulkner, William (Cuthbert)
1897-1962 .... **CLC 1, 3, 6, 8, 9, 11, 14, 18, 28, 52, 68; DA; DAB; DAC; DAM MST, NOV; SSC 1, 35, 42; WLC**
See also AAYA 7; AMW; AMWR; CA 81-
84; CANR 33; CDALB 1929-1941; DA3;
DLB 9, 11, 44, 102; DLBD 2; DLBY 86,
97; MTCW 1, 2; NFS 4, 8; RGAL; RGSF;
SSFS 2, 5, 6, 12

Fauset, Jessie Redmon
1882(?)-1961 .... **CLC 19, 54; BLC 2; DAM MULT**
See also AFAW 2; BW 1; CA 109; CANR
83; DLB 51; FW; MAWW

Faust, Frederick (Schiller)
1892-1944(?) .... **TCLC 49; DAM POP**
See also Austin, Frank; Brand, Max; Chal-
lis, George; Dawson, Peter; Dexter, Martin; Evans, Evan; Frederick, John; Frost,
Frederick; Manning, David; Silver, Nicholas
See also CA 108; 152

Faust, Irvin 1924- .... **CLC 8**
See also CA 33-36R; CANR 28, 67; CN;
DLB 2, 28; DLBY 80

Fawkes, Guy
See Benchley, Robert (Charles)

Fearing, Kenneth (Flexner)
1902-1961 .... **CLC 51**
See also CA 93-96; CANR 59; CMW; DLB
9; RGAL

Fecamps, Elise
See Creasey, John

Federman, Raymond 1928- .... **CLC 6, 47**
See also CA 17-20R; CAAS 8; CANR 10,
43, 83; CN; DLBY 80

Federspiel, J(uerg) F. 1931- .... **CLC 42**
See also CA 146

Feiffer, Jules (Ralph) 1929- ..... **CLC 2, 8, 64; DAM DRAM**
See also AAYA 3; CA 17-20R; CAD; CANR
30, 59; CD; DLB 7, 44; INT CANR-30;
MTCW 1; SATA 8, 61, 111

Feige, Hermann Albert Otto Maximilian
See Traven, B.

Feinberg, David B. 1956-1994 .... **CLC 59**
See also CA 135; 147

Feinstein, Elaine 1930- .... **CLC 36**
See also CA 69-72; CAAS 1; CANR 31,
68; CN; CP; CWP; DLB 14, 40; MTCW
1

Feke, Gilbert David .... **CLC 65**

Feldman, Irving (Mordecai) 1928- ..... **CLC 7**
See also CA 1-4R; CANR 1; CP; DLB 169

Felix-Tchicaya, Gerald
See Tchicaya, Gerald Felix

Fellini, Federico 1920-1993 .... **CLC 16, 85**
See also CA 65-68; 143; CANR 33

Felsen, Henry Gregor 1916-1995 ..... **CLC 17**
See also CA 1-4R; 180; CANR 1; SAAS 2;
SATA 1

Felski, Rita .... **CLC 65**

Fenno, Jack
See Calisher, Hortense

Fenollosa, Ernest (Francisco)
1853-1908 .... **TCLC 91**
Fenton, James Martin 1949- .... **CLC 32**
See also CA 102; CP; DLB 40; PFS 11
Ferber, Edna 1887-1968 .... **CLC 18, 93**
See also AITN 1; CA 5-8R; 25-28R; CANR 68; DLB 9, 28, 86; MTCW 1, 2; RGAL; RHW; SATA 7; TCWW 2
Ferdowsi, Abu'l Qasem 940-1020 . **CMLC 43**
See also RGWL
Ferguson, Helen
See Kavan, Anna
Ferguson, Niall 1964- .... **CLC 134**
See also CA 190
Ferguson, Samuel 1810-1886 .... **NCLC 33**
See also DLB 32; RGEL
Fergusson, Robert 1750-1774 .... **LC 29**
See also DLB 109; RGEL
Ferling, Lawrence
See Ferlinghetti, Lawrence (Monsanto)
Ferlinghetti, Lawrence (Monsanto)
1919(?)- .... **CLC 2, 6, 10, 27, 111; DAM POET; PC 1**
See also CA 5-8R; CANR 3, 41, 73; CDALB 1941-1968; CP; DA3; DLB 5, 16; MTCW 1, 2; RGAL; WP
Fern, Fanny
See Parton, Sara Payson Willis
Fernandez, Vicente Garcia Huidobro
See Huidobro Fernandez, Vicente Garcia
Fernandez-Armesto, Felipe .... **CLC 70**
Fernandez de Lizardi, Jose Joaquin
See Lizardi, Jose Joaquin Fernandez de
Ferre, Rosario 1942- ...... **CLC 139; HLCS 1; SSC 36**
See also CA 131; CANR 55, 81; CWW 2; DLB 145; HW 1, 2; MTCW 1
Ferrer, Gabriel (Francisco Victor) Miro
See Miro (Ferrer), Gabriel (Francisco Victor)
Ferrier, Susan (Edmonstone)
1782-1854 .... **NCLC 8**
See also DLB 116; RGEL
Ferrigno, Robert 1948(?)- .... **CLC 65**
See also CA 140
Ferron, Jacques 1921-1985 .... **CLC 94; DAC**
See also CA 117; 129; CCA 1; DLB 60
Feuchtwanger, Lion 1884-1958 .... **TCLC 3**
See also CA 104; 187; DLB 66
Feuillet, Octave 1821-1890 .... **NCLC 45**
See also DLB 192
Feydeau, Georges (Leon Jules Marie)
1862-1921 .... **TCLC 22; DAM DRAM**
See also CA 113; 152; CANR 84; DLB 192; EW; GFL 1789 to the Present; RGWL
Fichte, Johann Gottlieb
1762-1814 .... **NCLC 62**
See also DLB 90
Ficino, Marsilio 1433-1499 .... **LC 12**
Fiedeler, Hans
See Doeblin, Alfred
Fiedler, Leslie A(aron) 1917- .. **CLC 4, 13, 24**
See also CA 9-12R; CANR 7, 63; CN; DLB 28, 67; MTCW 1, 2; RGAL
Field, Andrew 1938- .... **CLC 44**
See also CA 97-100; CANR 25
Field, Eugene 1850-1895 .... **NCLC 3**
See also DLB 23, 42, 140; DLBD 13; MAICYA; RGAL; SATA 16
Field, Gans T.
See Wellman, Manly Wade
Field, Michael 1915-1971 .... **TCLC 43**
See also CA 29-32R
Field, Peter
See Hobson, Laura Z(ametkin)
See also TCWW 2
Fielding, Helen 1959(?)- .... **CLC 146**
See also CA 172; DLB 231

Fielding, Henry 1707-1754 ..... **LC 1, 46; DA; DAB; DAC; DAM DRAM, MST, NOV; WLC**
See also CDBLB 1660-1789; DA3; DLB 39, 84, 101; RGEL
Fielding, Sarah 1710-1768 .... **LC 1, 44**
See also DLB 39; RGEL
Fields, W. C. 1880-1946 .... **TCLC 80**
See also DLB 44
Fierstein, Harvey (Forbes) 1954- .... **CLC 33; DAM DRAM, POP**
See also CA 123; 129; CAD; CD; CPW; DA3; DFS 6; GLL
Figes, Eva 1932- .... **CLC 31**
See also CA 53-56; CANR 4, 44, 83; CN; DLB 14; FW
Finch, Anne 1661-1720 .... **LC 3; PC 21**
See also DLB 95
Finch, Robert (Duer Claydon)
1900- .... **CLC 18**
See also CA 57-60; CANR 9, 24, 49; CP; DLB 88
Findley, Timothy 1930- . **CLC 27, 102; DAC; DAM MST**
See also CA 25-28R; CANR 12, 42, 69; CCA 1; CN; DLB 53; FANT; RHW
Fink, William
See Mencken, H(enry) L(ouis)
Firbank, Louis 1942-
See Reed, Lou
See also CA 117
Firbank, (Arthur Annesley) Ronald
1886-1926 .... **TCLC 1**
See also BRWS 2; CA 104; 177; DLB 36; RGEL
Fish, Stanley
See Fish, Stanley Eugene
Fish, Stanley E.
See Fish, Stanley Eugene
Fish, Stanley Eugene 1938- .... **CLC 142**
See also CA 112; 132; CANR 90; DLB 67
Fisher, Dorothy (Frances) Canfield
1879-1958 .... **TCLC 87**
See also CA 114; 136; CANR 80; CLR 71,; CWRI; DLB 9, 102; MAICYA; YABC 1
Fisher, M(ary) F(rances) K(ennedy)
1908-1992 .... **CLC 76, 87**
See also CA 77-80; 138; CANR 44; MTCW 1
Fisher, Roy 1930- .... **CLC 25**
See also CA 81-84; CAAS 10; CANR 16; CP; DLB 40
Fisher, Rudolph 1897-1934 .. **TCLC 11; BLC 2; DAM MULT; SSC 25**
See also BW 1, 3; CA 107; 124; CANR 80; DLB 51, 102
Fisher, Vardis (Alvero) 1895-1968 ...... **CLC 7**
See also CA 5-8R; 25-28R; CANR 68; DLB 9, 206; RGAL; TCWW 2
Fiske, Tarleton
See Bloch, Robert (Albert)
Fitch, Clarke
See Sinclair, Upton (Beall)
Fitch, John IV
See Cormier, Robert (Edmund)
Fitzgerald, Captain Hugh
See Baum, L(yman) Frank
FitzGerald, Edward 1809-1883 .... **NCLC 9**
See also DLB 32; RGEL
Fitzgerald, F(rancis) Scott (Key)
1896-1940 .. **TCLC 1, 6, 14, 28, 55; DA; DAB; DAC; DAM MST, NOV; SSC 6, 31; WLC**
See also AAYA 24; AITN 1; AMW; AMWR; CA 110; 123; CDALB 1917-1929; DA3; DLB 4, 9, 86; DLBD 1, 15, 16; DLBY 81, 96; MTCW 1, 2; NFS 2; RGAL; RGSF; SSFS 4

Fitzgerald, Penelope 1916-2000 . **CLC 19, 51, 61, 143**
See also BRWS 5; CA 85-88; 190; CAAS 10; CANR 56, 86; CN; DLB 14, 194; MTCW 2
Fitzgerald, Robert (Stuart)
1910-1985 .... **CLC 39**
See also CA 1-4R; 114; CANR 1; DLBY 80
FitzGerald, Robert D(avid)
1902-1987 .... **CLC 19**
See also CA 17-20R; RGEL
Fitzgerald, Zelda (Sayre)
1900-1948 .... **TCLC 52**
See also CA 117; 126; DLBY 84
Flanagan, Thomas (James Bonner)
1923- .... **CLC 25, 52**
See also CA 108; CANR 55; CN; DLBY 80; INT 108; MTCW 1; RHW
Flaubert, Gustave 1821-1880 .... **NCLC 2, 10, 19, 62, 66; DA; DAB; DAC; DAM MST, NOV; SSC 11; WLC**
See also DA3; DLB 119; GFL 1789 to the Present; RGSF; RGWL; SSFS 6
Flavius Josephus
See Josephus, Flavius
Flecker, Herman Elroy
See Flecker, (Herman) James Elroy
Flecker, (Herman) James Elroy
1884-1915 .... **TCLC 43**
See also CA 109; 150; DLB 10, 19; RGEL
Fleming, Ian (Lancaster) 1908-1964 . **CLC 3, 30; DAM POP**
See also AAYA 26; CA 5-8R; CANR 59; CDBLB 1945-1960; CMW; CPW; DA3; DLB 87, 201; MSW; MTCW 1, 2; RGEL; SATA 9; YAW
Fleming, Thomas (James) 1927- ...... **CLC 37**
See also CA 5-8R; CANR 10; INT CANR-10; SATA 8
Fletcher, John 1579-1625 .... **LC 33; DC 6**
See also CDBLB Before 1660; DLB 58; RGEL
Fletcher, John Gould 1886-1950 .... **TCLC 35**
See also CA 107; 167; DLB 4, 45; RGAL
Fleur, Paul
See Pohl, Frederik
Flooglebuckle, Al
See Spiegelman, Art
Flora, Fletcher 1914-1969
See Queen, Ellery
See also CA 1-4R; CANR 3, 85
Flying Officer X
See Bates, H(erbert) E(rnest)
Fo, Dario 1926- .... **CLC 32, 109; DAM DRAM; DC 10**
See also CA 116; 128; CANR 68; CWW 2; DA3; DLBY 97; MTCW 1, 2
Fogarty, Jonathan Titulescu Esq.
See Farrell, James T(homas)
Follett, Ken(neth Martin) 1949- ..... **CLC 18; DAM NOV, POP**
See also AAYA 6; BEST 89:4; CA 81-84; CANR 13, 33, 54; CMW; CPW; DA3; DLB 87; DLBY 81; INT CANR-33; MTCW 1
Fontane, Theodor 1819-1898 .... **NCLC 26**
See also DLB 129; RGWL
Fontenot, Chester .... **CLC 65**
Foote, Horton 1916- .... **CLC 51, 91; DAM DRAM**
See also CA 73-76; CAD; CANR 34, 51; CD; CSW; DA3; DLB 26; INT CANR-34
Foote, Mary Hallock 1847-1938 .. **TCLC 108**
See also DLB 186, 188, 202, 221

Gardons, S. S.
See Snodgrass, W(illiam) D(e Witt)
Garfield, Leon 1921-1996 .... **CLC 12**
See also AAYA 8; CA 17-20R; 152; CANR 38, 41, 78; CLR 21; DLB 161; JRDA; MAICYA; SATA 1, 32, 76; SATA-Obit 90; YAW
Garland, (Hannibal) Hamlin
1860-1940 .... **TCLC 3; SSC 18**
See also CA 104; DLB 12, 71, 78, 186; RGAL; RGSF; TCWW 2
Garneau, (Hector de) Saint-Denys
1912-1943 .... **TCLC 13**
See also CA 111; DLB 88
Garner, Alan 1934- ..... **CLC 17; DAB; DAM POP**
See also AAYA 18; CA 73-76, 178; CAAE 178; CANR 15, 64; CLR 20; CPW; DLB 161; FANT; MAICYA; MTCW 1, 2; SATA 18, 69; SATA-Essay 108; YAW
Garner, Hugh 1913-1979 .... **CLC 13**
See also Warwick, Jarvis
See also CA 69-72; CANR 31; CCA 1; DLB 68
Garnett, David 1892-1981 .... **CLC 3**
See also CA 5-8R; 103; CANR 17, 79; DLB 34; FANT; MTCW 2; RGEL; SFW
Garos, Stephanie
See Katz, Steve
Garrett, George (Palmer) 1929- .. **CLC 3, 11, 51; SSC 30**
See also AMWS 7; CA 1-4R; CAAS 5; CANR 1, 42, 67; CN; CP; CSW; DLB 2, 5, 130, 152; DLBY 83
Garrick, David 1717-1779 .... **LC 15; DAM DRAM**
See also DLB 84; RGEL
Garrigue, Jean 1914-1972 .... **CLC 2, 8**
See also CA 5-8R; 37-40R; CANR 20
Garrison, Frederick
See Sinclair, Upton (Beall)
Garro, Elena 1920(?)-1998
See also CA 131; 169; CWW 2; DLB 145; HLCS 1; HW 1
Garth, Will
See Hamilton, Edmond; Kuttner, Henry
Garvey, Marcus (Moziah, Jr.)
1887-1940 ...... **TCLC 41; BLC 2; DAM MULT**
See also BW 1; CA 120; 124; CANR 79
Gary, Romain .... **CLC 25**
See also Kacew, Romain
See also DLB 83
Gascar, Pierre .... **CLC 11**
See also Fournier, Pierre
Gascoyne, David (Emery) 1916- .... **CLC 45**
See also CA 65-68; CANR 10, 28, 54; CP; DLB 20; MTCW 1; RGEL
Gaskell, Elizabeth Cleghorn
1810-1865 .... **NCLC 5, 70, 97; DAB; DAM MST; SSC 25**
See also BRW; CDBLB 1832-1890; DLB 21, 144, 159; RGEL; RGSF
Gass, William H(oward) 1924- . **CLC 1, 2, 8, 11, 15, 39, 132; SSC 12**
See also AMWS 6; CA 17-20R; CANR 30, 71, 100; CN; DLB 2, 227; MTCW 1, 2; RGAL
Gassendi, Pierre 1592-1655 .... **LC 54**
See also GFL Beginnings to 1789
Gasset, Jose Ortega y
See Ortega y Gasset, Jose
Gates, Henry Louis, Jr. 1950- .... **CLC 65; BLCS; DAM MULT**
See also BW 2, 3; CA 109; CANR 25, 53, 75; CSW; DA3; DLB 67; MTCW 1; RGAL

Gautier, Theophile 1811-1872 .. **NCLC 1, 59; DAM POET; PC 18; SSC 20**
See also DLB 119; GFL 1789 to the Present; RGWL
Gawsworth, John
See Bates, H(erbert) E(rnest)
Gay, John 1685-1732 .. **LC 49; DAM DRAM**
See also DLB 84, 95; RGEL
Gay, Oliver
See Gogarty, Oliver St. John
Gaye, Marvin (Penze) 1939-1984 ..... **CLC 26**
See also CA 112
Gebler, Carlo (Ernest) 1954- .... **CLC 39**
See also CA 119; 133; CANR 96
Gee, Maggie (Mary) 1948- .... **CLC 57**
See also CA 130; CN; DLB 207
Gee, Maurice (Gough) 1931- .... **CLC 29**
See also CA 97-100; CANR 67; CLR 56; CN; CWRI; RGSF; SATA 46, 101
Gelbart, Larry (Simon) 1928- .... **CLC 21, 61**
See also Gelbart, Larry
See also CA 73-76; CANR 45, 94
Gelbart, Larry 1928-
See Gelbart, Larry (Simon)
See also CAD; CD
Gelber, Jack 1932- .... **CLC 1, 6, 14, 79**
See also CA 1-4R; CAD; CANR 2; DLB 7, 228
Gellhorn, Martha (Ellis)
1908-1998 .... **CLC 14, 60**
See also CA 77-80; 164; CANR 44; CN; DLBY 82, 98
Genet, Jean 1910-1986 .. **CLC 1, 2, 5, 10, 14, 44, 46; DAM DRAM**
See also CA 13-16R; CANR 18; DA3; DFS 10; DLB 72; DLBY 86; GFL 1789 to the Present; GLL 1; MTCW 1, 2; RGWL
Gent, Peter 1942- .... **CLC 29**
See also AITN 1; CA 89-92; DLBY 82
Gentile, Giovanni 1875-1944 .... **TCLC 96**
See also CA 119
Gentlewoman in New England, A
See Bradstreet, Anne
Gentlewoman in Those Parts, A
See Bradstreet, Anne
Geoffrey of Monmouth c.
1100-1155 .... **CMLC 44**
See also DLB 146
George, Jean
See George, Jean Craighead
George, Jean Craighead 1919- .... **CLC 35**
See also AAYA 8; CA 5-8R; CANR 25; CLR 1; DLB 52; JRDA; MAICYA; SATA 2, 68, 124; YAW
George, Stefan (Anton) 1868-1933 . **TCLC 2, 14**
See also CA 104; EW
Georges, Georges Martin
See Simenon, Georges (Jacques Christian)
Gerhardi, William Alexander
See Gerhardie, William Alexander
Gerhardie, William Alexander
1895-1977 .... **CLC 5**
See also CA 25-28R; 73-76; CANR 18; DLB 36; RGEL
Gerstler, Amy 1956- .... **CLC 70**
See also CA 146; CANR 99
Gertler, T. .... **CLC 134**
See also CA 116; 121
Ghalib .... **NCLC 39, 78**
See also Ghalib, Asadullah Khan
Ghalib, Asadullah Khan 1797-1869
See Ghalib
See also DAM POET; RGWL
Ghelderode, Michel de 1898-1962 ..... **CLC 6, 11; DAM DRAM; DC 15**
See also CA 85-88; CANR 40, 77

Ghiselin, Brewster 1903- .... **CLC 23**
See also CA 13-16R; CAAS 10; CANR 13; CP
Ghose, Aurabinda 1872-1950 .... **TCLC 63**
See also CA 163
Ghose, Zulfikar 1935- .... **CLC 42**
See also CA 65-68; CANR 67; CN; CP
Ghosh, Amitav 1956- .... **CLC 44**
See also CA 147; CANR 80; CN
Giacosa, Giuseppe 1847-1906 .... **TCLC 7**
See also CA 104
Gibb, Lee
See Waterhouse, Keith (Spencer)
Gibbon, Lewis Grassic .... **TCLC 4**
See also Mitchell, James Leslie
See also RGEL
Gibbons, Kaye 1960- .... **CLC 50, 88, 145; DAM POP**
See also AAYA 34; CA 151; CANR 75; CSW; DA3; MTCW 1; NFS 3; RGAL; SATA 117
Gibran, Kahlil 1883-1931 .... **TCLC 1, 9; DAM POET, POP; PC 9**
See also CA 104; 150; DA3; MTCW 2
Gibran, Khalil
See Gibran, Kahlil
Gibson, William 1914- .. **CLC 23; DA; DAB; DAC; DAM DRAM, MST**
See also CA 9-12R; CAD; CANR 9, 42, 75; CD; CN; CPW; DFS 2; DLB 7; MTCW 1; SATA 66; SCFW 2; SFW; YAW
Gibson, William (Ford) 1948- ... **CLC 39, 63; DAM POP**
See also AAYA 12; CA 126; 133; CANR 52, 90; DA3; MTCW 1
Gide, Andre (Paul Guillaume)
1869-1951 . **TCLC 5, 12, 36; DA; DAB; DAC; DAM MST, NOV; SSC 13; WLC**
See also CA 104; 124; DA3; DLB 65; EW; GFL 1789 to the Present; MTCW 1, 2; RGSF; RGWL
Gifford, Barry (Colby) 1946- .... **CLC 34**
See also CA 65-68; CANR 9, 30, 40, 90
Gilbert, Frank
See De Voto, Bernard (Augustine)
Gilbert, W(illiam) S(chwenck)
1836-1911 .... **TCLC 3; DAM DRAM, POET**
See also CA 104; 173; RGEL; SATA 36
Gilbreth, Frank B., Jr. 1911-2001 .... **CLC 17**
See also CA 9-12R; SATA 2
Gilchrist, Ellen 1935- .... **CLC 34, 48, 143; DAM POP; SSC 14**
See also CA 113; 116; CANR 41, 61; CN; CPW; CSW; DLB 130; MTCW 1, 2; RGAL; RGSF; SSFS 9
Giles, Molly 1942- .... **CLC 39**
See also CA 126; CANR 98
Gill, Eric 1882-1940 .... **TCLC 85**
Gill, Patrick
See Creasey, John
Gillette, Douglas .... **CLC 70**
Gilliam, Terry (Vance) 1940- .... **CLC 21, 141**
See also Monty Python
See also AAYA 19; CA 108; 113; CANR 35; INT 113
Gillian, Jerry
See Gilliam, Terry (Vance)
Gilliatt, Penelope (Ann Douglass)
1932-1993 .... **CLC 2, 10, 13, 53**
See also AITN 2; CA 13-16R; 141; CANR 49; DLB 14
Gilman, Charlotte (Anna) Perkins (Stetson)
1860-1935 .... **TCLC 9, 37; SSC 13**
See also CA 106; 150; DLB 221; FW; HGG; MAWW; MTCW 1; RGAL; RGSF; SFW; SSFS 1

Gordon, Mary (Catherine) 1949- .... **CLC 13, 22, 128**
See also AMWS 4; CA 102; CANR 44, 92; CN; DLB 6; DLBY 81; FW; INT 102; MTCW 1

Gordon, N. J.
See Bosman, Herman Charles

Gordon, Sol 1923- .... **CLC 26**
See also CA 53-56; CANR 4; SATA 11

Gordone, Charles 1925-1995 .... **CLC 1, 4; DAM DRAM; DC 8**
See also BW 1, 3; CA 93-96; 180; 150; CAAE 180; CAD; CANR 55; DLB 7; INT 93-96; MTCW 1

Gore, Catherine 1800-1861 .... **NCLC 65**
See also DLB 116; RGEL

Gorenko, Anna Andreevna
See Akhmatova, Anna

Gorky, Maxim .... **TCLC 8; DAB; SSC 28; WLC**
See Peshkov, Alexei Maximovich
See also DFS 9; MTCW 2

Goryan, Sirak
See Saroyan, William

Gosse, Edmund (William)
1849-1928 .... **TCLC 28**
See also CA 117; DLB 57, 144, 184; RGEL

Gotlieb, Phyllis Fay (Bloom) 1926- .. **CLC 18**
See also CA 13-16R; CANR 7; DLB 88; SFW

Gottesman, S. D.
See Kornbluth, C(yril) M.; Pohl, Frederik

Gottfried von Strassburg fl. c.
1170-1215 .... **CMLC 10**
See also DLB 138; RGWL

Gould, Lois .... **CLC 4, 10**
See also CA 77-80; CANR 29; MTCW 1

Gourmont, Remy(-Marie-Charles) de
1858-1915 .... **TCLC 17**
See also CA 109; 150; GFL 1789 to the Present; MTCW 2

Govier, Katherine 1948- .... **CLC 51**
See also CA 101; CANR 18, 40; CCA 1

Goyen, (Charles) William
1915-1983 .... **CLC 5, 8, 14, 40**
See also AITN 2; CA 5-8R; 110; CANR 6, 71; DLB 2; DLBY 83; INT CANR-6

Goytisolo, Juan 1931- .... **CLC 5, 10, 23, 133; DAM MULT; HLC 1**
See also CA 85-88; CANR 32, 61; CWW 2; GLL 2; HW 1, 2; MTCW 1, 2

Gozzano, Guido 1883-1916 .... **PC 10**
See also CA 154; DLB 114

Gozzi, (Conte) Carlo 1720-1806 .... **NCLC 23**

Grabbe, Christian Dietrich
1801-1836 .... **NCLC 2**
See also DLB 133; RGWL

Grace, Patricia Frances 1937- .... **CLC 56**
See also CA 176; CN; RGSF

Gracian y Morales, Baltasar
1601-1658 .... **LC 15**

Gracq, Julien .... **CLC 11, 48**
See also Poirier, Louis
See also CWW 2; DLB 83; GFL 1789 to the Present

Grade, Chaim 1910-1982 .... **CLC 10**
See also CA 93-96; 107

Graduate of Oxford, A
See Ruskin, John

Grafton, Garth
See Duncan, Sara Jeannette

Graham, John
See Phillips, David Graham

Graham, Jorie 1951- .... **CLC 48, 118**
See also CA 111; CANR 63; CP; CWP; DLB 120; PFS 10

Graham, R(obert) B(ontine) Cunninghame
See Cunninghame Graham, Robert (Gallnigad) Bontine
See also DLB 98, 135, 174; RGEL; RGSF

Graham, Robert
See Haldeman, Joe (William)

Graham, Tom
See Lewis, (Harry) Sinclair

Graham, W(illiam) S(idney)
1918-1986 .... **CLC 29**
See also BRWS 7; CA 73-76; 118; DLB 20; RGEL

Graham, Winston (Mawdsley)
1910- .... **CLC 23**
See also CA 49-52; CANR 2, 22, 45, 66; CMW; CN; DLB 77; RHW

Grahame, Kenneth 1859-1932 ...... **TCLC 64; DAB**
See also CA 108; 136; CANR 80; CLR 5; CWRI; DA3; DLB 34, 141, 178; FANT; MAICYA; MTCW 2; RGEL; SATA 100; YABC 1

Granger, Darius John
See Marlowe, Stephen

Granin, Daniil .... **CLC 59**

Granovsky, Timofei Nikolaevich
1813-1855 .... **NCLC 75**
See also DLB 198

Grant, Skeeter
See Spiegelman, Art

Granville-Barker, Harley
1877-1946 .... **TCLC 2; DAM DRAM**
See also Barker, Harley Granville
See also CA 104; RGEL

Granzotto, Gianni
See Granzotto, Giovanni Battista

Granzotto, Giovanni Battista
1914-1985 .... **CLC 70**
See also CA 166

Grass, Guenter (Wilhelm) 1927- ... **CLC 1, 2, 4, 6, 11, 15, 22, 32, 49, 88; DA; DAB; DAC; DAM MST, NOV; WLC**
See also CA 13-16R; CANR 20, 75, 93; DA3; DLB 75, 124; EW; MTCW 1, 2; RGWL

Gratton, Thomas
See Hulme, T(homas) E(rnest)

Grau, Shirley Ann 1929- .... **CLC 4, 9, 146; SSC 15**
See also CA 89-92; CANR 22, 69; CN; CSW; DLB 2; INT CANR-22; MTCW 1

Gravel, Fern
See Hall, James Norman

Graver, Elizabeth 1964- .... **CLC 70**
See also CA 135; CANR 71

Graves, Richard Perceval
1895-1985 .... **CLC 44**
See also CA 65-68; CANR 9, 26, 51

Graves, Robert (von Ranke)
1895-1985 .. **CLC 1, 2, 6, 11, 39, 44, 45; DAB; DAC; DAM MST, POET; PC 6**
See also BRW; CA 5-8R; 117; CANR 5, 36; CDBLB 1914-1945; DA3; DLB 20, 100, 191; DLBD 18; DLBY 85; MTCW 1, 2; NCFS 2; RGEL; RHW; SATA 45

Graves, Valerie
See Bradley, Marion Zimmer

Gray, Alasdair (James) 1934- .... **CLC 41**
See also CA 126; CANR 47, 69; CN; DLB 194; HGG; INT CA-126; MTCW 1, 2; RGSF

Gray, Amlin 1946- .... **CLC 29**
See also CA 138

Gray, Francine du Plessix 1930- ..... **CLC 22; DAM NOV**
See also BEST 90:3; CA 61-64; CAAS 2; CANR 11, 33, 75, 81; INT CANR-11; MTCW 1, 2

Gray, John (Henry) 1866-1934 ...... **TCLC 19**
See also CA 119; 162; RGEL

Gray, Simon (James Holliday)
1936- .... **CLC 9, 14, 36**
See also AITN 1; CA 21-24R; CAAS 3; CANR 32, 69; CD; DLB 13; MTCW 1; RGEL

Gray, Spalding 1941- ..... **CLC 49, 112; DAM POP; DC 7**
See also CA 128; CAD; CANR 74; CD; CPW; MTCW 2

Gray, Thomas 1716-1771 .... **LC 4, 40; DA; DAB; DAC; DAM MST; PC 2; WLC**
See also CDBLB 1660-1789; DA3; DLB 109; PAB; PFS 9; RGEL; WP

Grayson, David
See Baker, Ray Stannard

Grayson, Richard (A.) 1951- .... **CLC 38**
See also CA 85-88; CANR 14, 31, 57; DLB 234

Greeley, Andrew M(oran) 1928- ..... **CLC 28; DAM POP**
See also CA 5-8R; CAAS 7; CANR 7, 43, 69; CMW; CPW; DA3; MTCW 1, 2

Green, Anna Katharine
1846-1935 .... **TCLC 63**
See also CA 112; 159; CMW; DLB 202, 221

Green, Brian
See Card, Orson Scott

Green, Hannah
See Greenberg, Joanne (Goldenberg)

Green, Hannah 1927(?)-1996 .... **CLC 3**
See also CA 73-76; CANR 59, 93; NFS 10

Green, Henry .... **CLC 2, 13, 97**
See also Yorke, Henry Vincent
See also BRWS 2; CA 175; DLB 15; RGEL

Green, Julian (Hartridge) 1900-1998
See Green, Julien
See also CA 21-24R; 169; CANR 33, 87; DLB 4, 72; MTCW 1

Green, Julien .... **CLC 3, 11, 77**
See also Green, Julian (Hartridge)
See also GFL 1789 to the Present; MTCW 2

Green, Paul (Eliot) 1894-1981 .... **CLC 25; DAM DRAM**
See also AITN 1; CA 5-8R; 103; CANR 3; DLB 7, 9; DLBY 81; RGAL

Greenberg, Ivan 1908-1973
See Rahv, Philip
See also CA 85-88

Greenberg, Joanne (Goldenberg)
1932- .... **CLC 7, 30**
See also AAYA 12; CA 5-8R; CANR 14, 32, 69; CN; SATA 25; YAW

Greenberg, Richard 1959(?)- .... **CLC 57**
See also CA 138; CAD; CD

Greenblatt, Stephen J(ay) 1943- ...... **CLC 70**
See also CA 49-52

Greene, Bette 1934- .... **CLC 30**
See also AAYA 7; CA 53-56; CANR 4; CLR 2; CWRI; JRDA; MAICYA; NFS 10; SAAS 16; SATA 8, 102; YAW

Greene, Gael .... **CLC 8**
See also CA 13-16R; CANR 10

Greene, Graham (Henry)
1904-1991 .... **CLC 1, 3, 6, 9, 14, 18, 27, 37, 70, 72, 125; DA; DAB; DAC; DAM MST, NOV; SSC 29; WLC**
See also AITN 2; BRWS 1; CA 13-16R; 133; CANR 35, 61; CDBLB 1945-1960; CMW; DA3; DLB 13, 15, 77, 100, 162, 201, 204; DLBY 91; MSW; MTCW 1, 2; RGEL; SATA 20

Greene, Robert 1558-1592 .... **LC 41**
See also DLB 62, 167; IDTP; RGEL; TEA

Greer, Germaine 1939- .... **CLC 131**
See also AITN 1; CA 81-84; CANR 33, 70;
FW; MTCW 1, 2

Greer, Richard
See Silverberg, Robert

Gregor, Arthur 1923- .... **CLC 9**
See also CA 25-28R; CAAS 10; CANR 11;
CP; SATA 36

Gregor, Lee
See Pohl, Frederik

Gregory, Isabella Augusta (Persse)
1852-1932 .... **TCLC 1**
See also BRW; CA 104; 184; DLB 10;
RGEL

Gregory, J. Dennis
See Williams, John A(lfred)

Grekova, I. .... **CLC 59**

Grendon, Stephen
See Derleth, August (William)

Grenville, Kate 1950- .... **CLC 61**
See also CA 118; CANR 53, 93

Grenville, Pelham
See Wodehouse, P(elham) G(renville)

Greve, Felix Paul (Berthold Friedrich)
1879-1948
See Grove, Frederick Philip
See also CA 104; 141; 175; CANR 79;
DAC; DAM MST

Grey, Zane 1872-1939 . **TCLC 6; DAM POP**
See also CA 104; 132; DA3; DLB 212;
MTCW 1, 2; RGAL; TCWW 2

Grieg, (Johan) Nordahl (Brun)
1902-1943 .... **TCLC 10**
See also CA 107; 189

Grieve, C(hristopher) M(urray)
1892-1978 ..... **CLC 11, 19; DAM POET**
See also MacDiarmid, Hugh; Pteleon
See also CA 5-8R; 85-88; CANR 33;
MTCW 1; RGEL

Griffin, Gerald 1803-1840 .... **NCLC 7**
See also DLB 159; RGEL

Griffin, John Howard 1920-1980 ..... **CLC 68**
See also AITN 1; CA 1-4R; 101; CANR 2

Griffin, Peter 1942- .... **CLC 39**
See also CA 136

Griffith, D(avid Lewelyn) W(ark)
1875(?)-1948 .... **TCLC 68**
See also CA 119; 150; CANR 80

Griffith, Lawrence
See Griffith, D(avid Lewelyn) W(ark)

Griffiths, Trevor 1935- .... **CLC 13, 52**
See also CA 97-100; CANR 45; CBD; CD;
DLB 13

Griggs, Sutton (Elbert)
1872-1930 .... **TCLC 77**
See also CA 123; 186; DLB 50

Grigson, Geoffrey (Edward Harvey)
1905-1985 .... **CLC 7, 39**
See also CA 25-28R; 118; CANR 20, 33;
DLB 27; MTCW 1, 2

Grillparzer, Franz 1791-1872 . **NCLC 1, 102;
DC 14; SSC 37**
See also DLB 133; RGWL

Grimble, Reverend Charles James
See Eliot, T(homas) S(tearns)

Grimke, Charlotte L(ottie) Forten
1837(?)-1914
See Forten, Charlotte L.
See also BW 1; CA 117; 124; DAM MULT,
POET; DLB 239

Grimm, Jacob Ludwig Karl
1785-1863 .... **NCLC 3, 77; SSC 36**
See also Grimm and Grimm
See also DLB 90; MAICYA; RGSF;
RGWL; SATA 22; WCH

Grimm, Wilhelm Karl 1786-1859 .. **NCLC 3,
77; SSC 36**
See also Grimm and Grimm
See also DLB 90; MAICYA; RGSF;
RGWL; SATA 22; WCH

**Grimmelshausen, Hans Jakob Christoffel
von**
See Grimmelshausen, Johann Jakob Christoffel von
See also RGWL

**Grimmelshausen, Johann Jakob Christoffel
von** 1621-1676 .... **LC 6**
See also Grimmelshausen, Hans Jakob
Christoffel von
See also DLB 168

Grindel, Eugene 1895-1952
See
See also CA 104

Grisham, John 1955- .... **CLC 84; DAM POP**
See also AAYA 14; CA 138; CANR 47, 69;
CMW; CN; CPW; CSW; DA3; MTCW 2

Grossman, David 1954- .... **CLC 67**
See also CA 138; CWW 2

Grossman, Vasily (Semenovich)
1905-1964 .... **CLC 41**
See also CA 124; 130; MTCW 1

Grove, Frederick Philip .... **TCLC 4**
See also Greve, Felix Paul (Berthold
Friedrich)
See also DLB 92; RGEL

Grubb
See Crumb, R(obert)

Grumbach, Doris (Isaac) 1918- . **CLC 13, 22,
64**
See also CA 5-8R; CAAS 2; CANR 9, 42,
70; CN; INT CANR-9; MTCW 2

Grundtvig, Nicolai Frederik Severin
1783-1872 .... **NCLC 1**

Grunge
See Crumb, R(obert)

Grunwald, Lisa 1959- .... **CLC 44**
See also CA 120

Guare, John 1938- .... **CLC 8, 14, 29, 67;
DAM DRAM**
See also CA 73-76; CAD; CANR 21, 69;
CD; DFS 8, 13; DLB 7; MTCW 1, 2;
RGAL

Gubar, Susan (David) 1944- .... **CLC 145**
See also CA 108; CANR 45, 70; FW;
MTCW 1; RGAL

Gudjonsson, Halldor Kiljan 1902-1998
See Laxness, Halld
See also CA 103; 164; CWW 2

Guenter, Erich
See Eich, Guenter

Guest, Barbara 1920- .... **CLC 34**
See also CA 25-28R; CANR 11, 44, 84; CP;
CWP; DLB 5, 193

Guest, Edgar A(lbert) 1881-1959 ... **TCLC 95**
See also CA 112; 168

Guest, Judith (Ann) 1936- .... **CLC 8, 30;
DAM NOV, POP**
See also AAYA 7; CA 77-80; CANR 15,
75; DA3; INT CANR-15; MTCW 1, 2;
NFS 1

Guevara, Che .... **CLC 87; HLC 1**
See also Guevara (Serna), Ernesto

Guevara (Serna), Ernesto
1928-1967 .... **CLC 87; DAM MULT;
HLC 1**
See also Guevara, Che
See also CA 127; 111; CANR 56; HW 1

Guicciardini, Francesco 1483-1540 ..... **LC 49**

Guild, Nicholas M. 1944- .... **CLC 33**
See also CA 93-96

Guillemin, Jacques
See Sartre, Jean-Paul

Guillen, Jorge 1893-1984 .... **CLC 11; DAM
MULT, POET; HLCS 1; PC 35**
See also CA 89-92; 112; DLB 108; HW 1;
RGWL

Guillen, Nicolas (Cristobal)
1902-1989 ... **CLC 48, 79; BLC 2; DAM
MST, MULT, POET; HLC 1; PC 23**
See also BW 2; CA 116; 125; 129; CANR
84; HW 1; LAW; RGWL; WP

Guillevic, (Eugene) 1907-1997 .... **CLC 33**
See also CA 93-96; CWW 2

Guillois
See Desnos, Robert

Guillois, Valentin
See Desnos, Robert

Guimaraes Rosa, Joao 1908-1967
See also CA 175; HLCS 2; LAW; RGSF;
RGWL

Guiney, Louise Imogen
1861-1920 .... **TCLC 41**
See also CA 160; DLB 54; RGAL

Guiraldes, Ricardo (Guillermo)
1886-1927 .... **TCLC 39**
See also CA 131; HW 1; LAW; MTCW 1

Gumilev, Nikolai (Stepanovich)
1886-1921 .... **TCLC 60**
See also CA 165

Gunesekera, Romesh 1954- .... **CLC 91**
See also CA 159; CN

Gunn, Bill .... **CLC 5**
See also Gunn, William Harrison
See also DLB 38

Gunn, Thom(son William) 1929- .. **CLC 3, 6,
18, 32, 81; DAM POET; PC 26**
See also BRWS 4; CA 17-20R; CANR 9,
33; CDBLB 1960 to Present; CP; DLB
27; INT CANR-33; MTCW 1; PFS 9;
RGEL

Gunn, William Harrison 1934(?)-1989
See Gunn, Bill
See also AITN 1; BW 1, 3; CA 13-16R;
128; CANR 12, 25, 76

Gunn Allen, Paula
See Allen, Paula Gunn

Gunnars, Kristjana 1948- .... **CLC 69**
See also CA 113; CCA 1; CP; CWP; DLB
60

Gurdjieff, G(eorgei) I(vanovich)
1877(?)-1949 .... **TCLC 71**
See also CA 157

Gurganus, Allan 1947- . **CLC 70; DAM POP**
See also BEST 90:1; CA 135; CN; CPW;
CSW; GLL 1

Gurney, A(lbert) R(amsdell), Jr.
1930- ..... **CLC 32, 50, 54; DAM DRAM**
See also CA 77-80; CAD; CANR 32, 64;
CD

Gurney, Ivor (Bertie) 1890-1937 ... **TCLC 33**
See also CA 167; PAB; RGEL

Gurney, Peter
See Gurney, A(lbert) R(amsdell), Jr.

Guro, Elena 1877-1913 .... **TCLC 56**

Gustafson, James M(oody) 1925- ... **CLC 100**
See also CA 25-28R; CANR 37

Gustafson, Ralph (Barker)
1909-1995 .... **CLC 36**
See also CA 21-24R; CANR 8, 45, 84; CP;
DLB 88; RGEL

Gut, Gom
See Simenon, Georges (Jacques Christian)

Guterson, David 1956- .... **CLC 91**
See also CA 132; CANR 73; MTCW 2

Guthrie, A(lfred) B(ertram), Jr.
1901-1991 .... **CLC 23**
See also CA 57-60; 134; CANR 24; DLB
212; SATA 62; SATA-Obit 67

Guthrie, Isobel
See Grieve, C(hristopher) M(urray)

Guthrie, Woodrow Wilson 1912-1967
See Guthrie, Woody
See also CA 113; 93-96

Guthrie, Woody .... **CLC 35**
See also Guthrie, Woodrow Wilson

Gutierrez Najera, Manuel 1859-1895
See also HLCS 2

Guy, Rosa (Cuthbert) 1928- .... **CLC 26**
See also AAYA 4, 37; BW 2; CA 17-20R;
CANR 14, 34, 83; CLR 13; DLB 33;
JRDA; MAICYA; SATA 14, 62, 122;
YAW

Gwendolyn
See Bennett, (Enoch) Arnold

H. D. .... **CLC 3, 8, 14, 31, 34, 73; PC 5**
See also Doolittle, Hilda

H. de V.
See Buchan, John

Haavikko, Paavo Juhani 1931- .. **CLC 18, 34**
See also CA 106

Habbema, Koos
See Heijermans, Herman

Habermas, Juergen 1929- .... **CLC 104**
See also CA 109; CANR 85; DLB 242

Habermas, Jurgen
See Habermas, Juergen

Hacker, Marilyn 1942- ...... **CLC 5, 9, 23, 72,
91; DAM POET**
See also CA 77-80; CANR 68; CP; CWP;
DLB 120; FW; GLL 2

Haeckel, Ernst Heinrich (Philipp August)
1834-1919 .... **TCLC 83**
See also CA 157

Hafiz c. 1326-1389(?) .... **CMLC 34**
See also RGWL

Haggard, H(enry) Rider
1856-1925 .... **TCLC 11**
See also BRWS 3; CA 108; 148; DLB 70,
156, 174, 178; FANT; MTCW 2; RGEL;
RHW; SATA 16; SFW; SUFW

Hagiosy, L.
See Larbaud, Valery (Nicolas)

Hagiwara, Sakutaro 1886-1942 .... **TCLC 60;
PC 18**

Haig, Fenil
See Ford, Ford Madox

Haig-Brown, Roderick (Langmere)
1908-1976 .... **CLC 21**
See also CA 5-8R; 69-72; CANR 4, 38, 83;
CLR 31; CWRI; DLB 88; MAICYA;
SATA 12

Hailey, Arthur 1920- ..... **CLC 5; DAM NOV,
POP**
See also AITN 2; BEST 90:3; CA 1-4R;
CANR 2, 36, 75; CCA 1; CN; CPW; DLB
88; DLBY 82; MTCW 1, 2

Hailey, Elizabeth Forsythe 1938- ..... **CLC 40**
See also CA 93-96; CAAE 188; CAAS 1;
CANR 15, 48; INT CANR-15

Haines, John (Meade) 1924- .... **CLC 58**
See also CA 17-20R; CANR 13, 34; CSW;
DLB 212

Hakluyt, Richard 1552-1616 .... **LC 31**
See also RGEL

Haldeman, Joe (William) 1943- .... **CLC 61**
See Graham, Robert
See also AAYA 38; CA 53-56, 179; CAAE
179; CAAS 25; CANR 6, 70, 72; DLB 8;
INT CANR-6; SCFW 2; SFW

Hale, Sarah Josepha (Buell)
1788-1879 .... **NCLC 75**
See also DLB 1, 42, 73

Halevy, Elie 1870-1937 .... **TCLC 104**

Haley, Alex(ander Murray Palmer)
1921-1992 . **CLC 8, 12, 76; BLC 2; DA;
DAB; DAC; DAM MST, MULT, POP**
See also AAYA 26; BW 2, 3; CA 77-80;
136; CANR 61; CDALBS; CPW; CSW;
DA3; DLB 38; MTCW 1, 2; NFS 9

Haliburton, Thomas Chandler
1796-1865 .... **NCLC 15**
See also DLB 11, 99; RGEL; RGSF

Hall, Donald (Andrew, Jr.) 1928- ...... **CLC 1,
13, 37, 59; DAM POET**
See also CA 5-8R; CAAS 7; CANR 2, 44,
64; CP; DLB 5; MTCW 1; RGAL; SATA
23, 97

Hall, Frederic Sauser
See Sauser-Hall, Frederic

Hall, James
See Kuttner, Henry

Hall, James Norman 1887-1951 ..... **TCLC 23**
See also CA 123; 173; RHW 1; SATA 21

Hall, (Marguerite) Radclyffe
1880-1943 .... **TCLC 12**
See also CA 110; 150; CANR 83; DLB 191;
RGEL

Hall, Radclyffe 1880-1943
See Hall, (Marguerite) Radclyffe
See also BRWS 6; MTCW 2; RHW

Hall, Rodney 1935- .... **CLC 51**
See also CA 109; CANR 69; CN; CP

Halleck, Fitz-Greene 1790-1867 .... **NCLC 47**
See also DLB 3; RGAL

Halliday, Michael
See Creasey, John

Halpern, Daniel 1945- .... **CLC 14**
See also CA 33-36R; CANR 93; CP

Hamburger, Michael (Peter Leopold)
1924- .... **CLC 5, 14**
See also CA 5-8R; CAAS 4; CANR 2, 47;
CP; DLB 27

Hamill, Pete 1935- .... **CLC 10**
See also CA 25-28R; CANR 18, 71

Hamilton, Alexander
1755(?)-1804 .... **NCLC 49**
See also DLB 37

Hamilton, Clive
See Lewis, C(live) S(taples)

Hamilton, Edmond 1904-1977 .... **CLC 1**
See also CA 1-4R; CANR 3, 84; DLB 8;
SATA 118; SFW

Hamilton, Eugene (Jacob) Lee
See Lee-Hamilton, Eugene (Jacob)

Hamilton, Franklin
See Silverberg, Robert

Hamilton, Gail
See Corcoran, Barbara (Asenath)

Hamilton, Mollie
See Kaye, M(ary) M(argaret)

Hamilton, (Anthony Walter) Patrick
1904-1962 .... **CLC 51**
See also CA 176; 113; DLB 191

Hamilton, Virginia (Esther) 1936- .. **CLC 26;
DAM MULT**
See also AAYA 2, 21; BW 2, 3; CA 25-28R;
CANR 20, 37, 73; CLR 1, 11, 40; DLB
33, 52; INT CANR-20; JRDA; MAICYA;
SATA 4, 56, 79, 123; YAW

Hammett, (Samuel) Dashiell
1894-1961 .... **CLC 3, 5, 10, 19, 47; SSC
17**
See also AITN 1; AMWS 4; CA 81-84;
CANR 42; CDALB 1929-1941; CMW;
DA3; DLB 226; DLBD 6; DLBY 96;
MSW; MTCW 1, 2; RGAL; RGSF

Hammon, Jupiter 1720(?)-1800(?) . **NCLC 5;
BLC 2; DAM MULT, POET; PC 16**
See also DLB 31, 50

Hammond, Keith
See Kuttner, Henry

Hamner, Earl (Henry), Jr. 1923- ...... **CLC 12**
See also AITN 2; CA 73-76; DLB 6

Hampton, Christopher (James)
1946- .... **CLC 4**
See also CA 25-28R; CD; DLB 13; MTCW
1

Hamsun, Knut .... **TCLC 2, 14, 49**
See also Pedersen, Knut
See also RGWL

Handke, Peter 1942- .... **CLC 5, 8, 10, 15, 38,
134; DAM DRAM, NOV**
See also CA 77-80; CANR 33, 75; CWW
2; DLB 85, 124; MTCW 1, 2

Handy, W(illiam) C(hristopher)
1873-1958 .... **TCLC 97**
See also BW 3; CA 121; 167

Hanley, James 1901-1985 ...... **CLC 3, 5, 8, 13**
See also CA 73-76; 117; CANR 36; CBD;
DLB 191; MTCW 1; RGEL

Hannah, Barry 1942- .... **CLC 23, 38, 90**
See also CA 108; 110; CANR 43, 68; CN;
CSW; DLB 6, 234; INT CA-110; MTCW
1; RGSF

Hannon, Ezra
See Hunter, Evan

Hansberry, Lorraine (Vivian)
1930-1965 ..... **CLC 17, 62; BLC 2; DA;
DAB; DAC; DAM DRAM, MST,
MULT; DC 2**
See also AAYA 25; AFAW 1, 2; AMWS 4;
BW 1, 3; CA 109; 25-28R; CABS 3;
CANR 58; CDALB 1941-1968; DA3;
DFS 2; DLB 7, 38; FW; MTCW 1, 2;
RGAL

Hansen, Joseph 1923- .... **CLC 38**
See also Brock, Rose; Colton, James
See also CA 29-32R; CAAS 17; CANR 16,
44, 66; CMW; DLB 226; GLL 1; INT
CANR-16

Hansen, Martin A(lfred)
1909-1955 .... **TCLC 32**
See also CA 167; DLB 214

Hansen and Philipson eds. .... **CLC 65**

Hanson, Kenneth O(stlin) 1922- .... **CLC 13**
See also CA 53-56; CANR 7

Hardwick, Elizabeth (Bruce)
1916- .... **CLC 13; DAM NOV**
See also AMWS 3; CA 5-8R; CANR 3, 32,
70, 100; CN; CSW; DA3; DLB 6;
MAWW; MTCW 1, 2

Hardy, Thomas 1840-1928 .. **TCLC 4, 10, 18,
32, 48, 53, 72; DA; DAB; DAC; DAM
MST, NOV, POET; PC 8; SSC 2; WLC**
See also CA 104; 123; CDBLB 1890-1914;
DA3; DLB 18, 19, 135; MTCW 1, 2; NFS
3, 11; PFS 3, 4; RGEL; RGSF

Hare, David 1947- .... **CLC 29, 58, 136**
See also BRWS 4; CA 97-100; CANR 39,
91; CBD; CD; DFS 4, 7; DLB 13; MTCW
1

Harewood, John
See Van Druten, John (William)

Harford, Henry
See Hudson, W(illiam) H(enry)

Hargrave, Leonie
See Disch, Thomas M(ichael)

Harjo, Joy 1951- ...... **CLC 83; DAM MULT;
PC 27**
See also CA 114; CANR 35, 67, 91; CP;
CWP; DLB 120, 175; MTCW 2; NNAL;
RGAL

Harlan, Louis R(udolph) 1922- .... **CLC 34**
See also CA 21-24R; CANR 25, 55, 80

Harling, Robert 1951(?)- .... **CLC 53**
See also CA 147

Harmon, William (Ruth) 1938- .... **CLC 38**
See also CA 33-36R; CANR 14, 32, 35;
SATA 65

Harper, F. E. W.
See Harper, Frances Ellen Watkins

Harper, Frances E. W.
See Harper, Frances Ellen Watkins

Harper, Frances E. Watkins
See Harper, Frances Ellen Watkins

Isler, Alan (David) 1934- .... CLC 91
See also CA 156
Ivan IV 1530-1584 .... LC 17
Ivanov, Vyacheslav Ivanovich
1866-1949 .... TCLC 33
See also CA 122
Ivask, Ivar Vidrik 1927-1992 .... CLC 14
See also CA 37-40R; 139; CANR 24
Ives, Morgan
See Bradley, Marion Zimmer
See also GLL 1
Izumi Shikibu c. 973-c. 1034 .... CMLC 33
J .... CLC 10, 36, 86; DAM NOV; SSC 20
See also CA 97-100; CANR 36, 50, 74;
DA3; DLB 182; DLBY 94; MTCW 1, 2
J. R. S.
See Gogarty, Oliver St. John
Jabran, Kahlil
See Gibran, Kahlil
Jabran, Khalil
See Gibran, Kahlil
Jackson, Daniel
See Wingrove, David (John)
Jackson, Helen Hunt 1830-1885 .... NCLC 90
See also DLB 42, 47, 186, 189; RGAL
Jackson, Jesse 1908-1983 .... CLC 12
See also BW 1; CA 25-28R; 109; CANR
27; CLR 28; CWRI; MAICYA; SATA 2,
29; SATA-Obit 48
Jackson, Laura (Riding) 1901-1991
See Riding, Laura
See also CA 65-68; 135; CANR 28, 89;
DLB 48
Jackson, Sam
See Trumbo, Dalton
Jackson, Sara
See Wingrove, David (John)
Jackson, Shirley 1919-1965 . CLC 11, 60, 87;
DA; DAC; DAM MST; SSC 9, 39;
WLC
See also AAYA 9; CA 1-4R; 25-28R; CANR
4, 52; CDALB 1941-1968; DA3; DLB 6,
234; HGG; MTCW 2; RGAL; RGSF;
SATA 2; SSFS 1
Jacob, (Cyprien-)Max 1876-1944 .... TCLC 6
See also CA 104; GFL 1789 to the Present;
GLL 2; RGWL
Jacobs, Harriet A(nn)
1813(?)-1897 .... NCLC 67
See also AFAW 1; DLB 239; RGAL
Jacobs, Jim 1942- .... CLC 12
See also CA 97-100; INT 97-100
Jacobs, W(illiam) W(ymark)
1863-1943 .... TCLC 22
See also CA 121; 167; DLB 135; HGG;
RGEL; RGSF; SSFS 2; SUFW
Jacobsen, Jens Peter 1847-1885 .... NCLC 34
Jacobsen, Josephine 1908- .... CLC 48, 102
See also CA 33-36R; CAAS 18; CANR 23,
48; CCA 1; CP
Jacobson, Dan 1929- .... CLC 4, 14
See also CA 1-4R; CANR 2, 25, 66; CN;
DLB 14, 207, 225; MTCW 1; RGSF
Jacqueline
See Carpentier (y Valmont), Alejo
Jagger, Mick 1944- .... CLC 17
Jahiz, al- c. 780-c. 869 .... CMLC 25
Jakes, John (William) 1932- . CLC 29; DAM
NOV, POP
See also AAYA 32; BEST 89:4; CA 57-60;
CANR 10, 43, 66; CPW; CSW; DA3;
DLBY 83; FANT; INT CANR-10; MTCW
1, 2; RHW; SATA 62; SFW; TCWW 2
James I 1394-1437 .... LC 20
See also RGEL
James, Andrew
See Kirkup, James

James, C(yril) L(ionel) R(obert)
1901-1989 .... CLC 33; BLCS
See also BW 2; CA 117; 125; 128; CANR
62; DLB 125; MTCW 1
James, Daniel (Lewis) 1911-1988
See Santiago, Danny
See also CA 174; 125
James, Dynely
See Mayne, William (James Carter)
James, Henry Sr. 1811-1882 .... NCLC 53
James, Henry 1843-1916 ..... TCLC 2, 11, 24,
40, 47, 64; DA; DAB; DAC; DAM
MST, NOV; SSC 8, 32; WLC
See also CA 104; 132; CDALB 1865-1917;
DA3; DLB 12, 71, 74, 189; DLBD 13;
HGG; MTCW 1, 2; NFS 12; RGAL;
RGEL; RGSF; SSFS 9
James, M. R.
See James, Montague (Rhodes)
See also DLB 156
James, Montague (Rhodes)
1862-1936 .... TCLC 6; SSC 16
See also CA 104; DLB 201; HGG; RGEL;
RGSF; SUFW
James, P. D. .... CLC 18, 46, 122
See also White, Phyllis Dorothy James
See also BEST 90:2; BRWS 4; CDBLB
1960 to Present; DLB 87; DLBD 17
James, Philip
See Moorcock, Michael (John)
James, Samuel
See Stephens, James
James, Seumas
See Stephens, James
James, Stephen
See Stephens, James
James, William 1842-1910 .... TCLC 15, 32
See also AMW; CA 109; RGAL
Jameson, Anna 1794-1860 .... NCLC 43
See also DLB 99, 166
Jameson, Fredric 1934- .... CLC 142
See also DLB 67
Jami, Nur al-Din 'Abd al-Rahman
1414-1492 .... LC 9
Jammes, Francis 1868-1938 .... TCLC 75
See also GFL 1789 to the Present
Jandl, Ernst 1925-2000 .... CLC 34
Janowitz, Tama 1957- ... CLC 43, 145; DAM
POP
See also CA 106; CANR 52, 89; CN; CPW
Japrisot, Sebastien 1931- .... CLC 90
See also CMW
Jarrell, Randall 1914-1965 .... CLC 1, 2, 6, 9,
13, 49; DAM POET
See also CA 5-8R; 25-28R; CABS 2; CANR
6, 34; CDALB 1941-1968; CLR 6; CWRI;
DLB 48, 52; MAICYA; MTCW 1, 2;
PAB; PFS 2; RGAL; SATA 7
Jarry, Alfred 1873-1907 . TCLC 2, 14; DAM
DRAM; SSC 20
See also CA 104; 153; DA3; DFS 8; DLB
192; GFL 1789 to the Present; RGWL
Jawien, Andrzej
See John Paul II, Pope
Jaynes, Roderick
See Coen, Ethan
Jeake, Samuel, Jr.
See Aiken, Conrad (Potter)
Jean Paul 1763-1825 .... NCLC 7
Jefferies, (John) Richard
1848-1887 .... NCLC 47
See also DLB 98, 141; RGEL; SATA 16;
SFW
Jeffers, (John) Robinson 1887-1962 .. CLC 2,
3, 11, 15, 54; DA; DAC; DAM MST,
POET; PC 17; WLC
See also AMWS 2; CA 85-88; CANR 35;
CDALB 1917-1929; DLB 45, 212;
MTCW 1, 2; PAB; PFS 3, 4; RGAL

Jefferson, Janet
See Mencken, H(enry) L(ouis)
Jefferson, Thomas 1743-1826 . NCLC 11, 103
See also CDALB 1640-1865; DA3; DLB
31; RGAL
Jeffrey, Francis 1773-1850 .... NCLC 33
See also DLB 107
Jelakowitch, Ivan
See Heijermans, Herman
Jellicoe, (Patricia) Ann 1927- .... CLC 27
See also CA 85-88; CBD; CD; CWD;
CWRI; DLB 13, 233; FW
Jemyma
See Holley, Marietta
Jen, Gish .... CLC 70
See also Jen, Lillian
Jen, Lillian 1956(?)-
See Jen, Gish
See also CA 135; CANR 89
Jenkins, (John) Robin 1912- .... CLC 52
See also CA 1-4R; CANR 1; CN; DLB 14
Jennings, Elizabeth (Joan) 1926- ...... CLC 5,
14, 131
See also BRWS 5; CA 61-64; CAAS 5;
CANR 8, 39, 66; CP; CWP; DLB 27;
MTCW 1; SATA 66
Jennings, Waylon 1937- .... CLC 21
Jensen, Johannes V. 1873-1950 ...... TCLC 41
See also CA 170; DLB 214
Jensen, Laura (Linnea) 1948- .... CLC 37
See also CA 103
Jerome, Saint 345-420 .... CMLC 30
See also RGWL
Jerome, Jerome K(lapka)
1859-1927 .... TCLC 23
See also CA 119; 177; DLB 10, 34, 135;
RGEL
Jerrold, Douglas William
1803-1857 .... NCLC 2
See also DLB 158, 159; RGEL
Jewett, (Theodora) Sarah Orne
1849-1909 .... TCLC 1, 22; SSC 6, 44
See also AMW; CA 108; 127; CANR 71;
DLB 12, 74, 221; FW; MAWW; RGAL;
RGSF; SATA 15; SSFS 4
Jewsbury, Geraldine (Endsor)
1812-1880 .... NCLC 22
See also DLB 21
Jhabvala, Ruth Prawer 1927- . CLC 4, 8, 29,
94, 138; DAB; DAM NOV
See also CA 1-4R; CANR 2, 29, 51, 74, 91;
CN; DLB 139, 194; IDFW 4; INT CANR-
29; MTCW 1, 2; RGSF; RGWL; RHW
Jibran, Kahlil
See Gibran, Kahlil
Jibran, Khalil
See Gibran, Kahlil
Jiles, Paulette 1943- .... CLC 13, 58
See also CA 101; CANR 70; CWP
Jimenez (Mantecon), Juan Ramon
1881-1958 .... TCLC 4; DAM MULT,
POET; HLC 1; PC 7
See also CA 104; 131; CANR 74; DLB 134;
EW; HW 1; MTCW 1, 2; RGWL
Jimenez, Ramon
See Jim
Jimenez Mantecon, Juan
See Jim
Jin, Ha
See Jin, Xuefei
Jin, Xuefei 1956- .... CLC 109
See also CA 152; CANR 91
Joel, Billy .... CLC 26
See also Joel, William Martin
Joel, William Martin 1949-
See Joel, Billy
See also CA 108

Kafka, Franz 1883-1924 . **TCLC 2, 6, 13, 29, 47, 53, 112; DA; DAB; DAC; DAM MST, NOV; SSC 5, 29, 35; WLC**
See also AAYA 31; CA 105; 126; DA3; DLB 81; MTCW 1, 2; NFS 7; RGSF; RGWL; SFW; SSFS 3, 7, 12

Kahanovitsch, Pinkhes
See Der Nister

Kahn, Roger 1927- .... **CLC 30**
See also CA 25-28R; CANR 44, 69; DLB 171; SATA 37

Kain, Saul
See Sassoon, Siegfried (Lorraine)

Kaiser, Georg 1878-1945 .... **TCLC 9**
See also CA 106; 190; DLB 124; RGWL

Kaledin, Sergei .... **CLC 59**

Kaletski, Alexander 1946- .... **CLC 39**
See also CA 118; 143

Kalidasa fl. c. 400-455 .... **CMLC 9; PC 22**
See also RGWL

Kallman, Chester (Simon)
1921-1975 .... **CLC 2**
See also CA 45-48; 53-56; CANR 3

Kaminsky, Melvin 1926-
See Brooks, Mel
See also CA 65-68; CANR 16

Kaminsky, Stuart M(elvin) 1934- ..... **CLC 59**
See also CA 73-76; CANR 29, 53, 89; CMW

Kandinsky, Wassily 1866-1944 .... **TCLC 92**
See also CA 118; 155

Kane, Francis
See Robbins, Harold

Kane, Henry 1918-
See Queen, Ellery
See also CA 156; CMW

Kane, Paul
See Simon, Paul (Frederick)

Kanin, Garson 1912-1999 .... **CLC 22**
See also AITN 1; CA 5-8R; 177; CAD; CANR 7, 78; DLB 7; IDFW 3, 4

Kaniuk, Yoram 1930- .... **CLC 19**
See also CA 134

Kant, Immanuel 1724-1804 ..... **NCLC 27, 67**
See also DLB 94

Kantor, MacKinlay 1904-1977 .... **CLC 7**
See also CA 61-64; 73-76; CANR 60, 63; DLB 9, 102; MTCW 2; RHW; TCWW 2

Kaplan, David Michael 1946- .... **CLC 50**
See also CA 187

Kaplan, James 1951- .... **CLC 59**
See also CA 135

Karageorge, Michael
See Anderson, Poul (William)

Karamzin, Nikolai Mikhailovich
1766-1826 .... **NCLC 3**
See also DLB 150; RGSF

Karapanou, Margarita 1946- .... **CLC 13**
See also CA 101

Karinthy, Frigyes 1887-1938 .... **TCLC 47**
See also CA 170

Karl, Frederick R(obert) 1927- .... **CLC 34**
See also CA 5-8R; CANR 3, 44

Kastel, Warren
See Silverberg, Robert

Kataev, Evgeny Petrovich 1903-1942
See Petrov, Evgeny
See also CA 120

Kataphusin
See Ruskin, John

Katz, Steve 1935- .... **CLC 47**
See also CA 25-28R; CAAS 14, 64; CANR 12; CN; DLBY 83

Kauffman, Janet 1945- .... **CLC 42**
See also CA 117; CANR 43, 84; DLBY 86

Kaufman, Bob (Garnell) 1925-1986 . **CLC 49**
See also BW 1; CA 41-44R; 118; CANR 22; DLB 16, 41

Kaufman, George S. 1889-1961 ...... **CLC 38; DAM DRAM**
See also CA 108; 93-96; DFS 1, 10; DLB 7; INT 108; MTCW 2; RGAL

Kaufman, Sue .... **CLC 3, 8**
See also Barondess, Sue K(aufman)

Kavafis, Konstantinos Petrou 1863-1933
See Cavafy, C(onstantine) P(eter)
See also CA 104

Kavan, Anna 1901-1968 .... **CLC 5, 13, 82**
See also BRWS 7; CA 5-8R; CANR 6, 57; MTCW 1; RGEL; SFW

Kavanagh, Dan
See Barnes, Julian (Patrick)

Kavanagh, Julie 1952- .... **CLC 119**
See also CA 163

Kavanagh, Patrick (Joseph)
1904-1967 .... **CLC 22; PC 33**
See also BRWS 7; CA 123; 25-28R; DLB 15, 20; MTCW 1; RGEL

Kawabata, Yasunari 1899-1972 ..... **CLC 2, 5, 9, 18, 107; DAM MULT; SSC 17**
See also CA 93-96; 33-36R; CANR 88; DLB 180; MJW; MTCW 2; RGSF; RGWL

Kaye, M(ary) M(argaret) 1909- ...... **CLC 28**
See also CA 89-92; CANR 24, 60; MTCW 1, 2; RHW; SATA 62

Kaye, Mollie
See Kaye, M(ary) M(argaret)

Kaye-Smith, Sheila 1887-1956 .... **TCLC 20**
See also CA 118; DLB 36

Kaymor, Patrice Maguilene
See Senghor, L

Kazakov, Yuri Pavlovich 1927-1982 . **SSC 43**
See also CA 5-8R; CANR 36; MTCW 1; RGSF

Kazan, Elia 1909- .... **CLC 6, 16, 63**
See also CA 21-24R; CANR 32, 78

Kazantzakis, Nikos 1883(?)-1957 .... **TCLC 2, 5, 33**
See also CA 105; 132; DA3; MTCW 1, 2; RGWL

Kazin, Alfred 1915-1998 ..... **CLC 34, 38, 119**
See also AMWS 8; CA 1-4R; CAAS 7; CANR 1, 45, 79; DLB 67

Keane, Mary Nesta (Skrine) 1904-1996
See Keane, Molly
See also CA 108; 114; 151; CN; RHW

Keane, Molly .... **CLC 31**
See also Keane, Mary Nesta (Skrine)
See also INT 114

Keates, Jonathan 1946(?)- .... **CLC 34**
See also CA 163

Keaton, Buster 1895-1966 .... **CLC 20**

Keats, John 1795-1821 ...... **NCLC 8, 73; DA; DAB; DAC; DAM MST, POET; PC 1; WLC**
See also CDBLB 1789-1832; DA3; DLB 96, 110; PAB; PFS 1, 2, 3, 9; RGEL; WP

Keble, John 1792-1866 .... **NCLC 87**
See also DLB 32, 55; RGEL

Keene, Donald 1922- .... **CLC 34**
See also CA 1-4R; CANR 5

Keillor, Garrison .... **CLC 40, 115**
See also Keillor, Gary (Edward)
See also AAYA 2; BEST 89:3; DLBY 87; SATA 58

Keillor, Gary (Edward) 1942-
See Keillor, Garrison
See also CA 111; 117; CANR 36, 59; CPW; DAM POP; DA3; MTCW 1, 2

Keith, Michael
See Hubbard, L(afayette) Ron(ald)

Keller, Gottfried 1819-1890 .... **NCLC 2; SSC 26**
See also DLB 129; RGSF; RGWL

Keller, Nora Okja 1965- .... **CLC 109**
See also CA 187

Kellerman, Jonathan 1949- .. **CLC 44; DAM POP**
See also AAYA 35; BEST 90:1; CA 106; CANR 29, 51; CMW; CPW; DA3; INT CANR-29

Kelley, William Melvin 1937- .... **CLC 22**
See also BW 1; CA 77-80; CANR 27, 83; CN; DLB 33

Kellogg, Marjorie 1922- .... **CLC 2**
See also CA 81-84

Kellow, Kathleen
See Hibbert, Eleanor Alice Burford

Kelly, M(ilton) T(errence) 1947- ...... **CLC 55**
See also CA 97-100; CAAS 22; CANR 19, 43, 84; CN

Kelman, James 1946- .... **CLC 58, 86**
See also BRWS 5; CA 148; CANR 85; CN; DLB 194; RGSF

Kemal, Yashar 1923- .... **CLC 14, 29**
See also CA 89-92; CANR 44; CWW 2

Kemble, Fanny 1809-1893 .... **NCLC 18**
See also DLB 32

Kemelman, Harry 1908-1996 .... **CLC 2**
See also AITN 1; CA 9-12R; 155; CANR 6, 71; CMW; DLB 28

Kempe, Margery 1373(?)-1440(?) ... **LC 6, 56**
See also DLB 146; RGEL

Kempis, Thomas a 1380-1471 .... **LC 11**

Kendall, Henry 1839-1882 .... **NCLC 12**
See also DLB 230

Keneally, Thomas (Michael) 1935- ... **CLC 5, 8, 10, 14, 19, 27, 43, 117; DAM NOV**
See also BRWS 4; CA 85-88; CANR 10, 50, 74; CN; CPW; DA3; MTCW 1, 2; RGEL; RHW

Kennedy, Adrienne (Lita) 1931- ..... **CLC 66; BLC 2; DAM MULT; DC 5**
See also AFAW 2; BW 2, 3; CA 103; CAAS 20; CABS 3; CANR 26, 53, 82; CD; DFS 9; DLB 38; FW

Kennedy, John Pendleton
1795-1870 .... **NCLC 2**
See also DLB 3; RGAL

Kennedy, Joseph Charles 1929-
See Kennedy, X. J.
See also CA 1-4R; CANR 4, 30, 40; CP; CWRI; SATA 14, 86

Kennedy, William 1928- .. **CLC 6, 28, 34, 53; DAM NOV**
See also AAYA 1; AMWS 7; CA 85-88; CANR 14, 31, 76; DA3; DLB 143; DLBY 85; INT CANR-31; MTCW 1, 2; SATA 57

Kennedy, X. J. .... **CLC 8, 42**
See also Kennedy, Joseph Charles
See also CAAS 9; CLR 27; DLB 5; SAAS 22

Kenny, Maurice (Francis) 1929- ..... **CLC 87; DAM MULT**
See also CA 144; CAAS 22; DLB 175; NNAL

Kent, Kelvin
See Kuttner, Henry

Kenton, Maxwell
See Southern, Terry

Kenyon, Robert O.
See Kuttner, Henry

Kepler, Johannes 1571-1630 .... **LC 45**

Kerouac, Jack ..... **CLC 1, 2, 3, 5, 14, 29, 61**
See also Kerouac, Jean-Louis Lebris de
See also AAYA 25; AMWS 3; CDALB 1941-1968; DLB 2, 16; DLBD 3; DLBY 95; GLL 1; MTCW 2; NFS 8; RGAL; WP

Kerouac, Jean-Louis Lebris de 1922-1969
See Kerouac, Jack
See also AITN 1; CA 5-8R; 25-28R; CANR 26, 54, 95; CPW; DA; DAB; DAC; DAM MST, NOV, POET, POP; DA3; MTCW 1, 2; WLC

Knowles, John 1926- . **CLC 1, 4, 10, 26; DA; DAC; DAM MST, NOV**
See also AAYA 10; CA 17-20R; CANR 40, 74, 76; CDALB 1968-1988; CN; DLB 6; MTCW 1, 2; NFS 2; RGAL; SATA 8, 89; YAW

Knox, Calvin M.
See Silverberg, Robert

Knox, John c. 1505-1572 .... **LC 37**
See also DLB 132

Knye, Cassandra
See Disch, Thomas M(ichael)

Koch, C(hristopher) J(ohn) 1932- .... **CLC 42**
See also CA 127; CANR 84; CN

Koch, Christopher
See Koch, C(hristopher) J(ohn)

Koch, Kenneth 1925- .... **CLC 5, 8, 44; DAM POET**
See also CA 1-4R; CAD; CANR 6, 36, 57, 97; CD; CP; DLB 5; INT CANR-36; MTCW 2; SATA 65; WP

Kochanowski, Jan 1530-1584 .... **LC 10**
See also RGWL

Kock, Charles Paul de 1794-1871 . **NCLC 16**

Koda Rohan
See Koda Shigeyuki

Koda Shigeyuki 1867-1947 .... **TCLC 22**
See also CA 121; 183; DLB 180

Koestler, Arthur 1905-1983 ... **CLC 1, 3, 6, 8, 15, 33**
See also BRWS 1; CA 1-4R; 109; CANR 1, 33; CDBLB 1945-1960; DLBY 83; MTCW 1, 2; RGEL

Kogawa, Joy Nozomi 1935- ..... **CLC 78, 129; DAC; DAM MST, MULT**
See also CA 101; CANR 19, 62; CN; CWP; FW; MTCW 2; NFS 3; SATA 99

Kohout, Pavel 1928- .... **CLC 13**
See also CA 45-48; CANR 3

Koizumi, Yakumo
See Hearn, (Patricio) Lafcadio (Tessima Carlos)

Kolmar, Gertrud 1894-1943 .... **TCLC 40**
See also CA 167

Komunyakaa, Yusef 1947- .... **CLC 86, 94; BLCS**
See also AFAW 2; CA 147; CANR 83; CP; CSW; DLB 120; PFS 5; RGAL

Konrad, George
See Konr
See also CWW 2

Konrad, Gyorgy 1933- .... **CLC 4, 10, 73**
See also Konrad, George
See also CA 85-88; CANR 97; CWW 2; DLB 232

Konwicki, Tadeusz 1926- .... **CLC 8, 28, 54, 117**
See also CA 101; CAAS 9; CANR 39, 59; CWW 2; DLB 232; IDFW 3; MTCW 1

Koontz, Dean R(ay) 1945- .... **CLC 78; DAM NOV, POP**
See also AAYA 9, 31; BEST 89:3, 90:2; CA 108; CANR 19, 36, 52, 95; CMW; CPW; DA3; HGG; MTCW 1; SATA 92; SFW; YAW

Kopernik, Mikolaj
See Copernicus, Nicolaus

Kopit, Arthur (Lee) 1937- ..... **CLC 1, 18, 33; DAM DRAM**
See also AITN 1; CA 81-84; CABS 3; CD; DFS 7; DLB 7; MTCW 1; RGAL

Kops, Bernard 1926- .... **CLC 4**
See also CA 5-8R; CANR 84; CBD; CN; CP; DLB 13

Kornbluth, C(yril) M. 1923-1958 .... **TCLC 8**
See also CA 105; 160; DLB 8; SFW

Korolenko, V. G.
See Korolenko, Vladimir Galaktionovich

Korolenko, Vladimir
See Korolenko, Vladimir Galaktionovich

Korolenko, Vladimir G.
See Korolenko, Vladimir Galaktionovich

Korolenko, Vladimir Galaktionovich
1853-1921 .... **TCLC 22**
See also CA 121

Korzybski, Alfred (Habdank Skarbek)
1879-1950 .... **TCLC 61**
See also CA 123; 160

Kosinski, Jerzy (Nikodem)
1933-1991 .... **CLC 1, 2, 3, 6, 10, 15, 53, 70; DAM NOV**
See also AMWS 7; CA 17-20R; 134; CANR 9, 46; DA3; DLB 2; DLBY 82; HGG; MTCW 1, 2; NFS 12; RGAL

Kostelanetz, Richard (Cory) 1940- .. **CLC 28**
See also CA 13-16R; CAAS 8; CANR 38, 77; CN; CP

Kotlowitz, Robert 1924- .... **CLC 4**
See also CA 33-36R; CANR 36

Kotzebue, August (Friedrich Ferdinand) von
1761-1819 .... **NCLC 25**
See also DLB 94

Kotzwinkle, William 1938- ..... **CLC 5, 14, 35**
See also CA 45-48; CANR 3, 44, 84; CLR 6; DLB 173; FANT; MAICYA; SATA 24, 70; SFW; YAW

Kowna, Stancy
See Szymborska, Wislawa

Kozol, Jonathan 1936- .... **CLC 17**
See also CA 61-64; CANR 16, 45, 96

Kozoll, Michael 1940(?)- .... **CLC 35**

Kramer, Kathryn 19(?)- .... **CLC 34**

Kramer, Larry 1935- .. **CLC 42; DAM POP; DC 8**
See also CA 124; 126; CANR 60; GLL 1

Krasicki, Ignacy 1735-1801 .... **NCLC 8**

Krasinski, Zygmunt 1812-1859 .... **NCLC 4**
See also RGWL

Kraus, Karl 1874-1936 .... **TCLC 5**
See also CA 104; DLB 118

Kreve (Mickevicius), Vincas
1882-1954 .... **TCLC 27**
See also CA 170; DLB 220

Kristeva, Julia 1941- .... **CLC 77, 140**
See also CA 154; CANR 99; DLB 242; FW

Kristofferson, Kris 1936- .... **CLC 26**
See also CA 104

Krizanc, John 1956- .... **CLC 57**
See also CA 187

Krleza, Miroslav 1893-1981 .... **CLC 8, 114**
See also CA 97-100; 105; CANR 50; DLB 147; RGWL

Kroetsch, Robert 1927- . **CLC 5, 23, 57, 132; DAC; DAM POET**
See also CA 17-20R; CANR 8, 38; CCA 1; CN; CP; DLB 53; MTCW 1

Kroetz, Franz
See Kroetz, Franz Xaver

Kroetz, Franz Xaver 1946- .... **CLC 41**
See also CA 130

Kroker, Arthur (W.) 1945- .... **CLC 77**
See also CA 161

Kropotkin, Peter (Alekseievich)
1842-1921 .... **TCLC 36**
See also CA 119

Krotkov, Yuri 1917-1981 .... **CLC 19**
See also CA 102

Krumb
See Crumb, R(obert)

Krumgold, Joseph (Quincy)
1908-1980 .... **CLC 12**
See also CA 9-12R; 101; CANR 7; MAI-CYA; SATA 1, 48; SATA-Obit 23; YAW

Krumwitz
See Crumb, R(obert)

Krutch, Joseph Wood 1893-1970 ..... **CLC 24**
See also CA 1-4R; 25-28R; CANR 4; DLB 63, 206

Krutzch, Gus
See Eliot, T(homas) S(tearns)

Krylov, Ivan Andreevich
1768(?)-1844 .... **NCLC 1**
See also DLB 150

Kubin, Alfred (Leopold Isidor)
1877-1959 .... **TCLC 23**
See also CA 112; 149; DLB 81

Kubrick, Stanley 1928-1999 .... **CLC 16**
See also AAYA 30; CA 81-84; 177; CANR 33; DLB 26; TCLC 112

Kueng, Hans 1928-
See Kung, Hans
See also CA 53-56; CANR 66; MTCW 1, 2

Kumin, Maxine (Winokur) 1925- ..... **CLC 5, 13, 28; DAM POET; PC 15**
See also AITN 2; AMWS 4; ANW; CA 1-4R; CAAS 8; CANR 1, 21, 69; CP; CWP; DA3; DLB 5; MTCW 1, 2; PAB; SATA 12

Kundera, Milan 1929- . **CLC 4, 9, 19, 32, 68, 115, 135; DAM NOV; SSC 24**
See also AAYA 2; CA 85-88; CANR 19, 52, 74; CWW 2; DA3; DLB 232; MTCW 1, 2; RGSF; SSFS 10

Kunene, Mazisi (Raymond) 1930- ... **CLC 85**
See also BW 1, 3; CA 125; CANR 81; DLB 117

Kung, Hans .... **CLC 130**
See also Kueng, Hans

Kunikida, Doppo 1869(?)-1908 ...... **TCLC 99**
See also DLB 180

Kunitz, Stanley (Jasspon) 1905- .. **CLC 6, 11, 14, 148; PC 19**
See also AMWS 3; CA 41-44R; CANR 26, 57, 98; CP; DA3; DLB 48; INT CANR-26; MTCW 1, 2; PFS 11; RGAL

Kunze, Reiner 1933- .... **CLC 10**
See also CA 93-96; CWW 2; DLB 75

Kuprin, Aleksander Ivanovich
1870-1938 .... **TCLC 5**
See also CA 104; 182

Kureishi, Hanif 1954(?)- .... **CLC 64, 135**
See also CA 139; CBD; CD; CN; DLB 194; GLL 2; IDFW 4

Kurosawa, Akira 1910-1998 .... **CLC 16, 119; DAM MULT**
See also AAYA 11; CA 101; 170; CANR 46

Kushner, Tony 1957(?)- .... **CLC 81; DAM DRAM; DC 10**
See also CA 144; CAD; CANR 74; CD; DA3; DFS 5; DLB 228; GLL 1; MTCW 2; RGAL

Kuttner, Henry 1915-1958 .... **TCLC 10**
See also CA 107; 157; DLB 8; FANT; SFW

Kuzma, Greg 1944- .... **CLC 7**
See also CA 33-36R; CANR 70

Kuzmin, Mikhail 1872(?)-1936 ...... **TCLC 40**
See also CA 170

Kyd, Thomas 1558-1594 .... **LC 22; DAM DRAM; DC 3**
See also BRW; DLB 62; RGEL; TEA

Kyprianos, Iossif
See Samarakis, Antonis

La Bruyere, Jean de 1645-1696 .... **LC 17**
See also GFL Beginnings to 1789

Lacan, Jacques (Marie Emile)
1901-1981 .... **CLC 75**
See also CA 121; 104

Laclos, Pierre Ambroise Francois
1741-1803 .... **NCLC 4, 87**
See also EW; GFL Beginnings to 1789; RGWL

Lacolere, Francois
See Aragon, Louis

Lawson, Henry (Archibald Hertzberg)
1867-1922 .... **TCLC 27; SSC 18**
See also CA 120; 181; DLB 230; RGEL;
RGSF

Lawton, Dennis
See Faust, Frederick (Schiller)

Laxness, Halldor .... **CLC 25**
See also Gudjonsson, Halldor Kiljan
See also RGWL

Layamon fl. c. 1200- .... **CMLC 10**
See also DLB 146; RGEL

Laye, Camara 1928-1980 ... **CLC 4, 38; BLC 2; DAM MULT**
See also BW 1; CA 85-88; 97-100; CANR
25; MTCW 1, 2

Layton, Irving (Peter) 1912- .... **CLC 2, 15; DAC; DAM MST, POET**
See also CA 1-4R; CANR 2, 33, 43, 66;
CP; DLB 88; MTCW 1, 2; PFS 12; RGEL

Lazarus, Emma 1849-1887 .... **NCLC 8**

Lazarus, Felix
See Cable, George Washington

Lazarus, Henry
See Slavitt, David R(ytman)

Lea, Joan
See Neufeld, John (Arthur)

Leacock, Stephen (Butler)
1869-1944 .... **TCLC 2; DAC; DAM MST; SSC 39**
See also CA 104; 141; CANR 80; DLB 92;
MTCW 2; RGEL; RGSF

Lear, Edward 1812-1888 .... **NCLC 3**
See also CLR 1; DLB 32, 163, 166; MAI-
CYA; RGEL; SATA 18, 100; WP

Lear, Norman (Milton) 1922- .... **CLC 12**
See also CA 73-76

Leautaud, Paul 1872-1956 .... **TCLC 83**
See also DLB 65; GFL 1789 to the Present

Leavis, F(rank) R(aymond)
1895-1978 .... **CLC 24**
See also BRW; CA 21-24R; 77-80; CANR
44; DLB 242; MTCW 1, 2; RGEL

Leavitt, David 1961- ..... **CLC 34; DAM POP**
See also CA 116; 122; CANR 50, 62; CPW;
DA3; DLB 130; GLL 1; INT 122; MTCW
2

Leblanc, Maurice (Marie Emile)
1864-1941 .... **TCLC 49**
See also CA 110; CMW

Lebowitz, Fran(ces Ann) 1951(?)- ... **CLC 11, 36**
See also CA 81-84; CANR 14, 60, 70; INT
CANR-14; MTCW 1

Lebrecht, Peter
See Tieck, (Johann) Ludwig

le Carre, John .... **CLC 3, 5, 9, 15, 28**
See also Cornwell, David (John Moore)
See also BEST 89:4; BRWS 2; CDBLB
1960 to Present; CMW; CN; CPW; DLB
87; MTCW 2; RGEL

Le Clezio, J(ean) M(arie) G(ustave)
1940- .... **CLC 31**
See also CA 116; 128; DLB 83; GFL 1789
to the Present; RGSF

Leconte de Lisle, Charles-Marie-Rene
1818-1894 .... **NCLC 29**
See also EW; GFL 1789 to the Present

Le Coq, Monsieur
See Simenon, Georges (Jacques Christian)

Leduc, Violette 1907-1972 .... **CLC 22**
See also CA 13-14; 33-36R; CANR 69;
CAP 1; GFL 1789 to the Present; GLL 1

Ledwidge, Francis 1887(?)-1917 .... **TCLC 23**
See also CA 123; DLB 20

Lee, Andrea 1953- ... **CLC 36; BLC 2; DAM MULT**
See also BW 1, 3; CA 125; CANR 82

Lee, Andrew
See Auchincloss, Louis (Stanton)

Lee, Chang-rae 1965- .... **CLC 91**
See also CA 148; CANR 89

Lee, Don L. .... **CLC 2**
See also Madhubuti, Haki R.

Lee, George W(ashington)
1894-1976 .... **CLC 52; BLC 2; DAM MULT**
See also BW 1; CA 125; CANR 83; DLB
51

Lee, (Nelle) Harper 1926- . **CLC 12, 60; DA; DAB; DAC; DAM MST, NOV; WLC**
See also AAYA 13; AMWS 8; CA 13-16R;
CANR 51; CDALB 1941-1968; CSW;
DA3; DLB 6; MTCW 1, 2; NFS 2; SATA
11; WYA; YAW

Lee, Helen Elaine 1959(?)- .... **CLC 86**
See also CA 148

Lee, John .... **CLC 70**

Lee, Julian
See Latham, Jean Lee

Lee, Larry
See Lee, Lawrence

Lee, Laurie 1914-1997 .... **CLC 90; DAB; DAM POP**
See also CA 77-80; 158; CANR 33, 73; CP;
CPW; DLB 27; MTCW 1; RGEL

Lee, Lawrence 1941-1990 .... **CLC 34**
See also CA 131; CANR 43

Lee, Li-Young 1957- .... **PC 24**
See also CA 153; CP; DLB 165; PFS 11

Lee, Manfred B(ennington)
1905-1971 .... **CLC 11**
See also Queen, Ellery
See also CA 1-4R; 29-32R; CANR 2;
CMW; DLB 137

Lee, Shelton Jackson 1957(?)- .... **CLC 105; BLCS; DAM MULT**
See also Lee, Spike
See also BW 2, 3; CA 125; CANR 42

Lee, Spike
See Lee, Shelton Jackson
See also AAYA 4, 29

Lee, Stan 1922- .... **CLC 17**
See also AAYA 5; CA 108; 111; INT 111

Lee, Tanith 1947- .... **CLC 46**
See also AAYA 15; CA 37-40R; CANR 53;
FANT; SATA 8, 88; SFW; YAW

Lee, Vernon .... **TCLC 5; SSC 33**
See also Paget, Violet
See also DLB 57, 153, 156, 174, 178; GLL
1

Lee, William
See Burroughs, William S(eward)
See also GLL 1

Lee, Willy
See Burroughs, William S(eward)
See also GLL 1

Lee-Hamilton, Eugene (Jacob)
1845-1907 .... **TCLC 22**
See also CA 117

Leet, Judith 1935- .... **CLC 11**
See also CA 187

Le Fanu, Joseph Sheridan
1814-1873 ..... **NCLC 9, 58; DAM POP; SSC 14**
See also CMW; DA3; DLB 21, 70, 159,
178; HGG; RGEL; RGSF; SUFW

Leffland, Ella 1931- .... **CLC 19**
See also CA 29-32R; CANR 35, 78, 82;
DLBY 84; INT CANR-35; SATA 65

Leger, Alexis
See Leger, (Marie-Rene Auguste) Alexis
Saint-Leger

Leger, (Marie-Rene Auguste) Alexis
Saint-Leger 1887-1975 .. **CLC 4, 11, 46; DAM POET; PC 23**
See also Saint-John Perse
See also CA 13-16R; 61-64; CANR 43; EW;
MTCW 1

Leger, Saintleger
See Leger, (Marie-Rene Auguste) Alexis
Saint-Leger

Le Guin, Ursula K(roeber) 1929- ..... **CLC 8, 13, 22, 45, 71, 136; DAB; DAC; DAM MST, POP; SSC 12**
See also AAYA 9, 27; AITN 1; ANW; CA
21-24R; CANR 9, 32, 52, 74; CDALB
1968-1988; CLR 3, 28; CN; CPW; DA3;
DLB 8, 52; FANT; FW; INT CANR-32;
JRDA; MAICYA; MTCW 1, 2; NFS 6, 9;
SATA 4, 52, 99; SFW; SSFS 2; SUFW;
WYA; YAW

Lehmann, Rosamond (Nina)
1901-1990 .... **CLC 5**
See also CA 77-80; 131; CANR 8, 73; DLB
15; MTCW 2; RGEL; RHW

Leiber, Fritz (Reuter, Jr.)
1910-1992 .... **CLC 25**
See also CA 45-48; 139; CANR 2, 40, 86;
DLB 8; FANT; HGG; MTCW 1, 2; SATA
45; SATA-Obit 73; SCFW 2; SFW; SUFW

Leibniz, Gottfried Wilhelm von
1646-1716 .... **LC 35**
See also DLB 168

Leimbach, Martha 1963-
See Leimbach, Marti
See also CA 130

Leimbach, Marti .... **CLC 65**
See also Leimbach, Martha

Leino, Eino .... **TCLC 24**
See also Loennbohm, Armas Eino Leopold

Leiris, Michel (Julien) 1901-1990 ..... **CLC 61**
See also CA 119; 128; 132; GFL 1789 to
the Present

Leithauser, Brad 1953- .... **CLC 27**
See also CA 107; CANR 27, 81; CP; DLB
120

Lelchuk, Alan 1938- .... **CLC 5**
See also CA 45-48; CAAS 20; CANR 1,
70; CN

Lem, Stanislaw 1921- .... **CLC 8, 15, 40**
See also CA 105; CAAS 1; CANR 32;
CWW 2; MTCW 1; SCFW 2; SFW

Lemann, Nancy 1956- .... **CLC 39**
See also CA 118; 136

Lemonnier, (Antoine Louis) Camille
1844-1913 .... **TCLC 22**
See also CA 121

Lenau, Nikolaus 1802-1850 .... **NCLC 16**

L'Engle, Madeleine (Camp Franklin)
1918- .... **CLC 12; DAM POP**
See also AAYA 28; AITN 2; CA 1-4R;
CANR 3, 21, 39, 66; CLR 1, 14, 57;
CPW; CWRI; DA3; DLB 52; JRDA;
MAICYA; MTCW 1, 2; SAAS 15; SATA
1, 27, 75; SFW; WYA; YAW

Lengyel, Jozsef 1896-1975 .... **CLC 7**
See also CA 85-88; 57-60; CANR 71;
RGSF

Lenin 1870-1924
See Lenin, V. I.
See also CA 121; 168

Lenin, V. I. .... **TCLC 67**
See also Lenin

Lennon, John (Ono) 1940-1980 .. **CLC 12, 35**
See also CA 102; SATA 114

Lennox, Charlotte Ramsay
1729(?)-1804 .... **NCLC 23**
See also DLB 39; RGEL

Lentricchia, Frank (Jr.) 1940- .... **CLC 34**
See also CA 25-28R; CANR 19

Lenz, Gunter .... **CLC 65**

Lenz, Siegfried 1926- .... **CLC 27; SSC 33**
See also CA 89-92; CANR 80; CWW 2;
DLB 75; RGSF; RGWL

Leon, David
See Jacob, (Cyprien-)Max

Maepenn, K. H.
See Kuttner, Henry

Maeterlinck, Maurice 1862-1949 ... **TCLC 3; DAM DRAM**
See also CA 104; 136; CANR 80; DLB 192; GFL 1789 to the Present; RGWL; SATA 66

Maginn, William 1794-1842 .... **NCLC 8**
See also DLB 110, 159

Mahapatra, Jayanta 1928- .... **CLC 33; DAM MULT**
See also CA 73-76; CAAS 9; CANR 15, 33, 66, 87; CP

Mahfouz, Naguib (Abdel Aziz Al-Sabilgi) 1911(?)-
See Mahf
See also BEST 89:2; CA 128; CANR 55; CWW 2; DAM NOV; DA3; MTCW 1, 2; RGWL; SSFS 9

Mahfuz, Najib (Abdel Aziz al-Sabilgi)
.... **CLC 52, 55**
See also Mahfouz, Naguib (Abdel Aziz Al-Sabilgi)
See also DLBY 88; RGSF

Mahon, Derek 1941- .... **CLC 27**
See also BRWS 6; CA 113; 128; CANR 88; CP; DLB 40

Maiakovskii, Vladimir
See Mayakovski, Vladimir (Vladimirovich)
See also RGWL

Mailer, Norman 1923- ... **CLC 1, 2, 3, 4, 5, 8, 11, 14, 28, 39, 74, 111; DA; DAB; DAC; DAM MST, NOV, POP**
See also AAYA 31; AITN 2; CA 9-12R; CABS 1; CANR 28, 74, 77; CDALB 1968-1988; CN; CPW; DA3; DLB 2, 16, 28, 185; DLBD 3; DLBY 80, 83; MTCW 1, 2; NFS 10; RGAL

Maillet, Antonine 1929- .. **CLC 54, 118; DAC**
See also CA 115; 120; CANR 46, 74, 77; CCA 1; CWW 2; DLB 60; INT 120; MTCW 2

Mais, Roger 1905-1955 .... **TCLC 8**
See also BW 1, 3; CA 105; 124; CANR 82; DLB 125; MTCW 1; RGEL

Maistre, Joseph 1753-1821 .... **NCLC 37**
See also GFL 1789 to the Present

Maitland, Frederic William 1850-1906 .... **TCLC 65**

Maitland, Sara (Louise) 1950- .... **CLC 49**
See also CA 69-72; CANR 13, 59; FW

Major, Clarence 1936- . **CLC 3, 19, 48; BLC 2; DAM MULT**
See also AFAW 2; BW 2, 3; CA 21-24R; CAAS 6; CANR 13, 25, 53, 82; CN; CP; CSW; DLB 33

Major, Kevin (Gerald) 1949- . **CLC 26; DAC**
See also AAYA 16; CA 97-100; CANR 21, 38; CLR 11; DLB 60; INT CANR-21; JRDA; MAICYA; SATA 32, 82; WYA; YAW

Maki, James
See Ozu, Yasujiro

Malabaila, Damiano
See Levi, Primo

Malamud, Bernard 1914-1986 .. **CLC 1, 2, 3, 5, 8, 9, 11, 18, 27, 44, 78, 85; DA; DAB; DAC; DAM MST, NOV, POP; SSC 15; WLC**
See also AAYA 16; AMWS 1; CA 5-8R; 118; CABS 1; CANR 28, 62; CDALB 1941-1968; CPW; DA3; DLB 2, 28, 152; DLBY 80, 86; MTCW 1, 2; NFS 4, 9; RGAL; RGSF; SSFS 8

Malan, Herman
See Bosman, Herman Charles; Bosman, Herman Charles

Malaparte, Curzio 1898-1957 .... **TCLC 52**

Malcolm, Dan
See Silverberg, Robert

Malcolm X .... **CLC 82, 117; BLC 2; WLCS**
See also Little, Malcolm

Malherbe, Francois de 1555-1628 .... **LC 5**
See also GFL Beginnings to 1789

Mallarme, Stephane 1842-1898 ...... **NCLC 4, 41; DAM POET; PC 4**
See also GFL 1789 to the Present; RGWL

Mallet-Joris, Francoise 1930- .... **CLC 11**
See also CA 65-68; CANR 17; DLB 83; GFL 1789 to the Present

Malley, Ern
See McAuley, James Phillip

Mallowan, Agatha Christie
See Christie, Agatha (Mary Clarissa)

Maloff, Saul 1922- .... **CLC 5**
See also CA 33-36R

Malone, Louis
See MacNeice, (Frederick) Louis

Malone, Michael (Christopher) 1942- .... **CLC 43**
See also CA 77-80; CANR 14, 32, 57

Malory, (Sir)Thomas 1410(?)-1471(?) .... **LC 11; DA; DAB; DAC; DAM MST; WLCS**
See also BRW; CDBLB Before 1660; DLB 146; EFS 2; RGEL; SATA 59; SATA-Brief 33; SUFW

Malouf, (George Joseph) David 1934- .... **CLC 28, 86**
See also CA 124; CANR 50, 76; CN; CP; MTCW 2

Malraux, (Georges-)Andre 1901-1976 .... **CLC 1, 4, 9, 13, 15, 57; DAM NOV**
See also CA 21-22; 69-72; CANR 34, 58; CAP 2; DA3; DLB 72; EW; GFL 1789 to the Present; MTCW 1, 2; RGWL

Malzberg, Barry N(athaniel) 1939- ... **CLC 7**
See also CA 61-64; CAAS 4; CANR 16; CMW; DLB 8; SFW

Mamet, David (Alan) 1947- .. **CLC 9, 15, 34, 46, 91; DAM DRAM; DC 4**
See also AAYA 3; CA 81-84; CABS 3; CANR 15, 41, 67, 72; CD; DA3; DFS 2, 3, 6, 12; DLB 7; IDFW 4; MTCW 1, 2; RGAL

Mamoulian, Rouben (Zachary) 1897-1987 .... **CLC 16**
See also CA 25-28R; 124; CANR 85

Mandelshtam, Osip
See Mandelstam, Osip (Emilievich)
See also RGWL

Mandelstam, Osip (Emilievich) 1891(?)-1943(?) .... **TCLC 2, 6; PC 14**
See also Mandelshtam, Osip
See also CA 104; 150; EW; MTCW 2

Mander, (Mary) Jane 1877-1949 ... **TCLC 31**
See also CA 162; RGEL

Mandeville, John fl. 1350- .... **CMLC 19**
See also DLB 146

Mandiargues, Andre Pieyre de .... **CLC 41**
See also Pieyre de Mandiargues, Andre
See also DLB 83

Mandrake, Ethel Belle
See Thurman, Wallace (Henry)

Mangan, James Clarence 1803-1849 .... **NCLC 27**
See also RGEL

Maniere, J.-E.
See Giraudoux, Jean(-Hippolyte)

Mankiewicz, Herman (Jacob) 1897-1953 .... **TCLC 85**
See also CA 120; 169; DLB 26; IDFW 3

Manley, (Mary) Delariviere 1672(?)-1724 .... **LC 1, 42**
See also DLB 39, 80; RGEL

Mann, Abel
See Creasey, John

Mann, Emily 1952- .... **DC 7**
See also CA 130; CAD; CANR 55; CD; CWD

Mann, (Luiz) Heinrich 1871-1950 ... **TCLC 9**
See also CA 106; 164, 181; DLB 66, 118; EW; RGWL

Mann, (Paul) Thomas 1875-1955 ... **TCLC 2, 8, 14, 21, 35, 44, 60; DA; DAB; DAC; DAM MST, NOV; SSC 5; WLC**
See also CA 104; 128; DA3; DLB 66; EW; GLL 1; MTCW 1, 2; RGSF; RGWL; SSFS 4, 9

Mannheim, Karl 1893-1947 .... **TCLC 65**

Manning, David
See Faust, Frederick (Schiller)
See also TCWW 2

Manning, Frederic 1887(?)-1935 ... **TCLC 25**
See also CA 124

Manning, Olivia 1915-1980 .... **CLC 5, 19**
See also CA 5-8R; 101; CANR 29; FW; MTCW 1; RGEL

Mano, D. Keith 1942- .... **CLC 2, 10**
See also CA 25-28R; CAAS 6; CANR 26, 57; DLB 6

Mansfield, Katherine .... **TCLC 2, 8, 39; DAB; SSC 9, 23, 38; WLC**
See also Beauchamp, Kathleen Mansfield
See also DLB 162; FW; GLL 1; RGEL; RGSF; SSFS 2,8,10,11

Manso, Peter 1940- .... **CLC 39**
See also CA 29-32R; CANR 44

Mantecon, Juan Jimenez
See Jim

Mantel, Hilary (Mary) 1952- .... **CLC 144**
See also CA 125; CANR 54; CN; RHW

Manton, Peter
See Creasey, John

Man Without a Spleen, A
See Chekhov, Anton (Pavlovich)

Manzoni, Alessandro 1785-1873 ... **NCLC 29, 98**
See also RGWL

Map, Walter 1140-1209 .... **CMLC 32**

Mapu, Abraham (ben Jekutiel) 1808-1867 .... **NCLC 18**

Mara, Sally
See Queneau, Raymond

Marat, Jean Paul 1743-1793 .... **LC 10**

Marcel, Gabriel Honore 1889-1973 . **CLC 15**
See also CA 102; 45-48; MTCW 1, 2

March, William 1893-1954 .... **TCLC 96**

Marchbanks, Samuel
See Davies, (William) Robertson
See also CCA 1

Marchi, Giacomo
See Bassani, Giorgio

Marcus Aurelius
See Antoninus, Marcus Aurelius

Marguerite
See de Navarre, Marguerite

Marguerite de Navarre
See de Navarre, Marguerite
See also RGWL

Margulies, Donald .... **CLC 76**
See also DFS 13; DLB 228

Marie de France c. 12th cent. - ..... **CMLC 8; PC 22**
See also DLB 208; FW; RGWL

Marie de l'Incarnation 1599-1672 ...... **LC 10**

Marier, Captain Victor
See Griffith, D(avid Lewelyn) W(ark)

Mariner, Scott
See Pohl, Frederik

Marinetti, Filippo Tommaso 1876-1944 .... **TCLC 10**
See also CA 107; DLB 114

Maugham, W(illiam) Somerset
1874-1965 ... **CLC 1, 11, 15, 67, 93; DA;
DAB; DAC; DAM DRAM, MST, NOV;
SSC 8; WLC**
See also BRW; CA 5-8R; 25-28R; CANR
40; CDBLB 1914-1945; CMW; DA3;
DLB 10, 36, 77, 100, 162, 195; MTCW
1, 2; RGEL; RGSF; SATA 54

Maugham, William Somerset
See Maugham, W(illiam) Somerset

Maupassant, (Henri Rene Albert) Guy de
1850-1893 . **NCLC 1, 42, 83; DA; DAB;
DAC; DAM MST; SSC 1; WLC**
See also DA3; DLB 123; EW; GFL 1789 to
the Present; RGSF; RGWL; SSFS 4;
SUFW; TWA

Maupin, Armistead 1944- ..... **CLC 95; DAM
POP**
See also CA 125; 130; CANR 58; CPW;
DA3; GLL 1; INT 130; MTCW 2

Maurhut, Richard
See Traven, B.

Mauriac, Claude 1914-1996 .... **CLC 9**
See also CA 89-92; 152; CWW 2; DLB 83;
GFL 1789 to the Present

Mauriac, Francois (Charles)
1885-1970 .... **CLC 4, 9, 56; SSC 24**
See also CA 25-28; CAP 2; DLB 65; EW;
GFL 1789 to the Present; MTCW 1, 2;
RGWL

Mavor, Osborne Henry 1888-1951
See Bridie, James
See also CA 104

Maxwell, William (Keepers, Jr.)
1908-2000 .... **CLC 19**
See also CA 93-96; 189; CANR 54, 95; CN;
DLBY 80; INT 93-96

May, Elaine 1932- .... **CLC 16**
See also CA 124; 142; CAD; CWD; DLB
44

Mayakovski, Vladimir (Vladimirovich)
1893-1930 .... **TCLC 4, 18**
See also Maiakovskii, Vladimir; Mayakovsky, Vladimir
See also CA 104; 158; EW; MTCW 2; SFW

Mayakovsky, Vladimir
See Mayakovski, Vladimir (Vladimirovich)
See also WP

Mayhew, Henry 1812-1887 .... **NCLC 31**
See also DLB 18, 55, 190

Mayle, Peter 1939(?)- .... **CLC 89**
See also CA 139; CANR 64

Maynard, Joyce 1953- .... **CLC 23**
See also CA 111; 129; CANR 64

Mayne, William (James Carter)
1928- .... **CLC 12**
See also AAYA 20; CA 9-12R; CANR 37,
80, 100; CLR 25; FANT; JRDA; MAI-
CYA; SAAS 11; SATA 6, 68, 122; YAW

Mayo, Jim
See L'Amour, Louis (Dearborn)
See also TCWW 2

Maysles, Albert 1926- .... **CLC 16**
See also CA 29-32R

Maysles, David 1932-1987 .... **CLC 16**
See also CA 191

Mazer, Norma Fox 1931- .... **CLC 26**
See also AAYA 5, 36; CA 69-72; CANR
12, 32, 66; CLR 23; JRDA; MAICYA;
SAAS 1; SATA 24, 67, 105; YAW

Mazzini, Guiseppe 1805-1872 .... **NCLC 34**

McAlmon, Robert (Menzies)
1895-1956 .... **TCLC 97**
See also CA 107; 168; DLB 4, 45; DLBD
15; GLL 1

McAuley, James Phillip 1917-1976 .. **CLC 45**
See also CA 97-100; RGEL

McBain, Ed
See Hunter, Evan

McBrien, William (Augustine)
1930- .... **CLC 44**
See also CA 107; CANR 90

McCabe, Patrick 1955- .... **CLC 133**
See also CA 130; CANR 50, 90; CN; DLB
194

McCaffrey, Anne (Inez) 1926- .... **CLC 17;
DAM NOV, POP**
See also AAYA 6, 34; AITN 2; BEST 89:2;
CA 25-28R; CANR 15, 35, 55, 96; CLR
49; CPW; DA3; DLB 8; JRDA; MAI-
CYA; MTCW 1, 2; SAAS 11; SATA 8,
70, 116; SFW; WYA; YAW

McCall, Nathan 1955(?)- .... **CLC 86**
See also BW 3; CA 146; CANR 88

McCann, Arthur
See Campbell, John W(ood, Jr.)

McCann, Edson
See Pohl, Frederik

McCarthy, Charles, Jr. 1933-
See McCarthy, Cormac
See also CANR 42, 69; CN; CPW; CSW;
DAM POP; DA3; MTCW 2

McCarthy, Cormac .... **CLC 4, 57, 59, 101**
See also McCarthy, Charles, Jr.
See also AMWS 8; CA 13-16R; CANR 10;
DLB 6, 143; MTCW 2; TCWW 2

McCarthy, Mary (Therese)
1912-1989 .. **CLC 1, 3, 5, 14, 24, 39, 59;
SSC 24**
See also AMW; CA 5-8R; 129; CANR 16,
50, 64; DA3; DLB 2; DLBY 81; FW; INT
CANR-16; MAWW; MTCW 1, 2; RGAL

McCartney, (James) Paul 1942- . **CLC 12, 35**
See also CA 146

McCauley, Stephen (D.) 1955- .... **CLC 50**
See also CA 141

McClaren, Peter .... **CLC 70**

McClure, Michael (Thomas) 1932- ... **CLC 6,
10**
See also CA 21-24R; CAD; CANR 17, 46,
77; CD; CP; DLB 16; WP

McCorkle, Jill (Collins) 1958- .... **CLC 51**
See also CA 121; CSW; DLB 234; DLBY
87

McCourt, Frank 1930- .... **CLC 109**
See also CA 157; CANR 97; NCFS 1

McCourt, James 1941- .... **CLC 5**
See also CA 57-60; CANR 98

McCourt, Malachy 1932- .... **CLC 119**

McCoy, Horace (Stanley)
1897-1955 .... **TCLC 28**
See also CA 108; 155; CMW; DLB 9

McCrae, John 1872-1918 .... **TCLC 12**
See also CA 109; DLB 92; PFS 5

McCreigh, James
See Pohl, Frederik

McCullers, (Lula) Carson (Smith)
1917-1967 .... **CLC 1, 4, 10, 12, 48, 100;
DA; DAB; DAC; DAM MST, NOV;
SSC 9, 24; WLC**
See also AAYA 21; AMW; CA 5-8R; 25-
28R; CABS 1, 3; CANR 18; CDALB
1941-1968; DA3; DFS 5; DLB 2, 7, 173,
228; FW; GLL 1; MAWW; MTCW 1, 2;
NFS 6; RGAL; RGSF; SATA 27; SSFS 5;
YAW

McCulloch, John Tyler
See Burroughs, Edgar Rice

McCullough, Colleen 1938(?)- .... **CLC 27,
107; DAM NOV, POP**
See also AAYA 36; CA 81-84; CANR 17,
46, 67, 98; CPW; DA3; MTCW 1, 2;
RHW

McDermott, Alice 1953- .... **CLC 90**
See also CA 109; CANR 40, 90

McElroy, Joseph 1930- .... **CLC 5, 47**
See also CA 17-20R; CN

McEwan, Ian (Russell) 1948- .... **CLC 13, 66;
DAM NOV**
See also BEST 90:4; BRWS 4; CA 61-64;
CANR 14, 41, 69, 87; CN; DLB 14, 194;
HGG; MTCW 1, 2; RGSF

McFadden, David 1940- .... **CLC 48**
See also CA 104; CP; DLB 60; INT 104

McFarland, Dennis 1950- .... **CLC 65**
See also CA 165

McGahern, John 1934- ... **CLC 5, 9, 48; SSC
17**
See also CA 17-20R; CANR 29, 68; CN;
DLB 14, 231; MTCW 1

McGinley, Patrick (Anthony) 1937- . **CLC 41**
See also CA 120; 127; CANR 56; INT 127

McGinley, Phyllis 1905-1978 .... **CLC 14**
See also CA 9-12R; 77-80; CANR 19;
CWRI; DLB 11, 48; PFS 9; SATA 2, 44;
SATA-Obit 24

McGinniss, Joe 1942- .... **CLC 32**
See also AITN 2; BEST 89:2; CA 25-28R;
CANR 26, 70; CPW; DLB 185; INT
CANR-26

McGivern, Maureen Daly
See Daly, Maureen

McGrath, Patrick 1950- .... **CLC 55**
See also CA 136; CANR 65; CN; DLB 231;
HGG

McGrath, Thomas (Matthew)
1916-1990 ..... **CLC 28, 59; DAM POET**
See also CA 9-12R; 132; CANR 6, 33, 95;
MTCW 1; SATA 41; SATA-Obit 66

McGuane, Thomas (Francis III)
1939- .... **CLC 3, 7, 18, 45, 127**
See also AITN 2; CA 49-52; CANR 5, 24,
49, 94; CN; DLB 2, 212; DLBY 80; INT
CANR-24; MTCW 1; TCWW 2

McGuckian, Medbh 1950- .... **CLC 48; DAM
POET; PC 27**
See also BRWS 5; CA 143; CP; CWP; DLB
40

McHale, Tom 1942(?)-1982 .... **CLC 3, 5**
See also AITN 1; CA 77-80; 106

McIlvanney, William 1936- .... **CLC 42**
See also CA 25-28R; CANR 61; CMW;
DLB 14, 207

McIlwraith, Maureen Mollie Hunter
See Hunter, Mollie
See also SATA 2

McInerney, Jay 1955- .... **CLC 34, 112; DAM
POP**
See also AAYA 18; CA 116; 123; CANR
45, 68; CN; CPW; DA3; INT 123; MTCW
2

McIntyre, Vonda N(eel) 1948- .... **CLC 18**
See also CA 81-84; CANR 17, 34, 69;
MTCW 1; SFW; YAW

McKay, Claude .... **TCLC 7, 41; BLC 3;
DAB; PC 2**
See also McKay, Festus Claudius
See also AFAW 1, 2; DLB 4, 45, 51, 117;
GLL 2; PAB; PFS 4; RGAL; WP

McKay, Festus Claudius 1889-1948
See McKay, Claude
See also BW 1, 3; CA 104; 124; CANR 73;
DA; DAC; DAM MST, MULT, NOV,
POET; MTCW 1, 2; WLC

McKuen, Rod 1933- .... **CLC 1, 3**
See also AITN 1; CA 41-44R; CANR 40

McLoughlin, R. B.
See Mencken, H(enry) L(ouis)

McLuhan, (Herbert) Marshall
1911-1980 .... **CLC 37, 83**
See also CA 9-12R; 102; CANR 12, 34, 61;
DLB 88; INT CANR-12; MTCW 1, 2

McMillan, Terry (L.) 1951- .... **CLC 50, 61, 112; BLCS; DAM MULT, NOV, POP**
See also AAYA 21; BW 2, 3; CA 140; CANR 60; CPW; DA3; MTCW 2; RGAL; YAW

McMurtry, Larry (Jeff) 1936- .. **CLC 2, 3, 7, 11, 27, 44, 127; DAM NOV, POP**
See also AAYA 15; AITN 2; AMWS 5; BEST 89:2; CA 5-8R; CANR 19, 43, 64; CDALB 1968-1988; CN; CPW; CSW; DA3; DLB 2, 143; DLBY 80, 87; MTCW 1, 2; RGAL; TCWW 2

McNally, T. M. 1961- .... **CLC 82**

McNally, Terrence 1939- ... **CLC 4, 7, 41, 91; DAM DRAM**
See also CA 45-48; CAD; CANR 2, 56; CD; DA3; DLB 7; GLL 1; MTCW 2

McNamer, Deirdre 1950- .... **CLC 70**

McNeal, Tom .... **CLC 119**

McNeile, Herman Cyril 1888-1937
See Sapper
See also CA 184; CMW; DLB 77

McNickle, (William) D'Arcy
1904-1977 .... **CLC 89; DAM MULT**
See also CA 9-12R; 85-88; CANR 5, 45; DLB 175, 212; NNAL; RGAL; SATA-Obit 22

McPhee, John (Angus) 1931- .... **CLC 36**
See also AMWS 3; ANW; BEST 90:1; CA 65-68; CANR 20, 46, 64, 69; CPW; DLB 185; MTCW 1, 2

McPherson, James Alan 1943- .. **CLC 19, 77; BLCS**
See also BW 1, 3; CA 25-28R; CAAS 17; CANR 24, 74; CN; CSW; DLB 38; MTCW 1, 2; RGAL; RGSF

McPherson, William (Alexander)
1933- .... **CLC 34**
See also CA 69-72; CANR 28; INT CANR-28

McTaggart, J. McT. Ellis
See McTaggart, John McTaggart Ellis

McTaggart, John McTaggart Ellis
1866-1925 .... **TCLC 105**
See also CA 120

Mead, George Herbert 1873-1958 . **TCLC 89**

Mead, Margaret 1901-1978 .... **CLC 37**
See also AITN 1; CA 1-4R; 81-84; CANR 4; DA3; FW; MTCW 1, 2; SATA-Obit 20

Meaker, Marijane (Agnes) 1927-
See Kerr, M. E.
See also CA 107; CANR 37, 63; INT 107; JRDA; MAICYA; MTCW 1; SATA 20, 61, 99; SATA-Essay 111; YAW

Medoff, Mark (Howard) 1940- ... **CLC 6, 23; DAM DRAM**
See also AITN 1; CA 53-56; CAD; CANR 5; CD; DFS 4; DLB 7; INT CANR-5

Medvedev, P. N.
See Bakhtin, Mikhail Mikhailovich

Meged, Aharon
See Megged, Aharon

Meged, Aron
See Megged, Aharon

Megged, Aharon 1920- .... **CLC 9**
See also CA 49-52; CAAS 13; CANR 1

Mehta, Ved (Parkash) 1934- .... **CLC 37**
See also CA 1-4R; CANR 2, 23, 69; MTCW 1

Melanter
See Blackmore, R(ichard) D(oddridge)

Melies, Georges 1861-1938 .... **TCLC 81**

Melikow, Loris
See Hofmannsthal, Hugo von

Melmoth, Sebastian
See Wilde, Oscar (Fingal O'Flahertie Wills)

Meltzer, Milton 1915- .... **CLC 26**
See also AAYA 8; CA 13-16R; CANR 38, 92; CLR 13; DLB 61; JRDA; MAICYA; SAAS 1; SATA 1, 50, 80; SATA-Essay 124; YAW

Melville, Herman 1819-1891 ..... **NCLC 3, 12, 29, 45, 49, 91, 93; DA; DAB; DAC; DAM MST, NOV; SSC 1, 17, 46; WLC**
See also AAYA 25; CDALB 1640-1865; DA3; DLB 3, 74; NFS 7, 9; RGAL; RGSF; SATA 59; SSFS 3

Membreno, Alejandro .... **CLC 59**

Menander c. 342B.C.-c. 293B.C. ... **CMLC 9; DAM DRAM; DC 3**
See also DLB 176; RGWL

Menchu, Rigoberta 1959-
See also CA 175; DNFS; HLCS 2

Mencken, H(enry) L(ouis)
1880-1956 .... **TCLC 13**
See also AMW; CA 105; 125; CDALB 1917-1929; DLB 11, 29, 63, 137, 222; MTCW 1, 2; RGAL

Mendelsohn, Jane 1965- .... **CLC 99**
See also CA 154; CANR 94

Mercer, David 1928-1980 .... **CLC 5; DAM DRAM**
See also CA 9-12R; 102; CANR 23; CBD; DLB 13; MTCW 1; RGEL

Merchant, Paul
See Ellison, Harlan (Jay)

Meredith, George 1828-1909 .. **TCLC 17, 43; DAM POET**
See also CA 117; 153; CANR 80; CDBLB 1832-1890; DLB 18, 35, 57, 159; RGEL

Meredith, William (Morris) 1919- .... **CLC 4, 13, 22, 55; DAM POET; PC 28**
See also CA 9-12R; CAAS 14; CANR 6, 40; CP; DLB 5

Merezhkovsky, Dmitry Sergeyevich
1865-1941 .... **TCLC 29**
See also CA 169

Merimee, Prosper 1803-1870 ... **NCLC 6, 65; SSC 7**
See also DLB 119, 192; GFL 1789 to the Present; RGSF; RGWL; SSFS 8

Merkin, Daphne 1954- .... **CLC 44**
See also CA 123

Merlin, Arthur
See Blish, James (Benjamin)

Merrill, James (Ingram) 1926-1995 .. **CLC 2, 3, 6, 8, 13, 18, 34, 91; DAM POET; PC 28**
See also AMWS 3; CA 13-16R; 147; CANR 10, 49, 63; DA3; DLB 5, 165; DLBY 85; INT CANR-10; MTCW 1, 2; PAB; RGAL

Merriman, Alex
See Silverberg, Robert

Merriman, Brian 1747-1805 .... **NCLC 70**

Merritt, E. B.
See Waddington, Miriam

Merton, Thomas 1915-1968 ..... **CLC 1, 3, 11, 34, 83; PC 10**
See also AMWS 8; CA 5-8R; 25-28R; CANR 22, 53; DA3; DLB 48; DLBY 81; MTCW 1, 2

Merwin, W(illiam) S(tanley) 1927- ... **CLC 1, 2, 3, 5, 8, 13, 18, 45, 88; DAM POET**
See also AMWS 3; CA 13-16R; CANR 15, 51; CP; DA3; DLB 5, 169; INT CANR-15; MTCW 1, 2; PAB; PFS 5; RGAL

Metcalf, John 1938- .... **CLC 37; SSC 43**
See also CA 113; CN; DLB 60; RGSF

Metcalf, Suzanne
See Baum, L(yman) Frank

Mew, Charlotte (Mary) 1870-1928 .. **TCLC 8**
See also CA 105; 189; DLB 19, 135; RGEL

Mewshaw, Michael 1943- .... **CLC 9**
See also CA 53-56; CANR 7, 47; DLBY 80

Meyer, Conrad Ferdinand
1825-1905 .... **NCLC 81**
See also DLB 129; RGWL

Meyer, Gustav 1868-1932
See Meyrink, Gustav
See also CA 117; 190

Meyer, June
See Jordan, June
See also GLL 2

Meyer, Lynn
See Slavitt, David R(ytman)

Meyers, Jeffrey 1939- .... **CLC 39**
See also CA 73-76; CAAE 186; CANR 54; DLB 111

Meynell, Alice (Christina Gertrude Thompson) 1847-1922 .... **TCLC 6**
See also CA 104; 177; DLB 19, 98; RGEL

Meyrink, Gustav .... **TCLC 21**
See also Meyer, Gustav
See also DLB 81

Michaels, Leonard 1933- .... **CLC 6, 25; SSC 16**
See also CA 61-64; CANR 21, 62; CN; DLB 130; MTCW 1

Michaux, Henri 1899-1984 .... **CLC 8, 19**
See also CA 85-88; 114; GFL 1789 to the Present; RGWL

Micheaux, Oscar (Devereaux)
1884-1951 .... **TCLC 76**
See also BW 3; CA 174; DLB 50; TCWW 2

Michelangelo 1475-1564 .... **LC 12**

Michelet, Jules 1798-1874 .... **NCLC 31**
See also GFL 1789 to the Present

Michels, Robert 1876-1936 .... **TCLC 88**

Michener, James A(lbert)
1907(?)-1997 .... **CLC 1, 5, 11, 29, 60, 109; DAM NOV, POP**
See also AAYA 27; AITN 1; BEST 90:1; CA 5-8R; 161; CANR 21, 45, 68; CN; CPW; DA3; DLB 6; MTCW 1, 2; RHW

Mickiewicz, Adam 1798-1855 .. **NCLC 3, 101**
See also RGWL

Middleton, Christopher 1926- .... **CLC 13**
See also CA 13-16R; CANR 29, 54; DLB 40

Middleton, Richard (Barham)
1882-1911 .... **TCLC 56**
See also CA 187; DLB 156; HGG

Middleton, Stanley 1919- .... **CLC 7, 38**
See also CA 25-28R; CAAS 23; CANR 21, 46, 81; CN; DLB 14

Middleton, Thomas 1580-1627 .... **LC 33; DAM DRAM, MST; DC 5**
See also DLB 58; RGEL

Migueis, Jose Rodrigues 1901- .... **CLC 10**

Mikszath, Kalman 1847-1910 .... **TCLC 31**
See also CA 170

Miles, Jack .... **CLC 100**

Miles, Josephine (Louise)
1911-1985 .. **CLC 1, 2, 14, 34, 39; DAM POET**
See also CA 1-4R; 116; CANR 2, 55; DLB 48

Militant
See Sandburg, Carl (August)

Mill, Harriet (Hardy) Taylor
1807-1858 .... **NCLC 102**
See also FW

Mill, John Stuart 1806-1873 .... **NCLC 11, 58**
See also CDBLB 1832-1890; DLB 55, 190; FW 1; RGEL

Millar, Kenneth 1915-1983 ... **CLC 14; DAM POP**
See also Macdonald, Ross
See also CA 9-12R; 110; CANR 16, 63; CMW; CPW; DA3; DLB 2, 226; DLBD 6; DLBY 83; MTCW 1, 2

Montherlant, Henry (Milon) de
1896-1972 ..... CLC 8, 19; DAM DRAM
See also CA 85-88; 37-40R; DLB 72; EW;
GFL 1789 to the Present; MTCW 1

Monty Python
See Chapman, Graham; Cleese, John
(Marwood); Gilliam, Terry (Vance); Idle,
Eric; Jones, Terence Graham Parry; Palin,
Michael (Edward)
See also AAYA 7

Moodie, Susanna (Strickland)
1803-1885 .... NCLC 14
See also DLB 99

Moody, Hiram F. III 1961-
See Moody, Rick
See also CA 138; CANR 64

Moody, Rick .... CLC 147
See also Moody, Hiram F. III

Moody, William Vaughan
1869-1910 .... TCLC 105
See also CA 110; 178; DLB 7, 54; RGAL

Mooney, Edward 1951-
See Mooney, Ted
See also CA 130

Mooney, Ted .... CLC 25
See also Mooney, Edward

Moorcock, Michael (John) 1939- ...... CLC 5,
27, 58
See also Bradbury, Edward P.
See also AAYA 26; CA 45-48; CAAS 5;
CANR 2, 17, 38, 64; CN; DLB 14, 231;
FANT; MTCW 1, 2; SATA 93; SFW;
SUFW

Moore, Brian 1921-1999 ... CLC 1, 3, 5, 7, 8,
19, 32, 90; DAB; DAC; DAM MST
See also Bryan, Michael
See also CA 1-4R; 174; CANR 1, 25, 42,
63; CCA 1; CN; FANT; MTCW 1, 2;
RGEL

Moore, Edward
See Muir, Edwin
See also RGEL

Moore, G. E. 1873-1958 .... TCLC 89

Moore, George Augustus
1852-1933 .... TCLC 7; SSC 19
See also BRW; CA 104; 177; DLB 10, 18,
57, 135; RGEL; RGSF

Moore, Lorrie .... CLC 39, 45, 68
See also Moore, Marie Lorena
See also DLB 234

Moore, Marianne (Craig)
1887-1972 .... CLC 1, 2, 4, 8, 10, 13, 19,
47; DA; DAB; DAC; DAM MST,
POET; PC 4; WLCS
See also AMW; CA 1-4R; 33-36R; CANR
3, 61; CDALB 1929-1941; DA3; DLB 45;
DLBD 7; MAWW; MTCW 1, 2; PAB;
RGAL; SATA 20; WP

Moore, Marie Lorena 1957-
See Moore, Lorrie
See also CA 116; CANR 39, 83; CN; DLB
234

Moore, Thomas 1779-1852 .... NCLC 6
See also DLB 96, 144; RGEL

Moorhouse, Frank 1938- .... SSC 40
See also CA 118; CANR 92; CN; RGSF

Mora, Pat(ricia) 1942-
See also CA 129; CANR 57, 81; CLR 58;
DAM MULT; DLB 209; HLC 2; HW 1,
2; SATA 92

Moraga, Cherríe 1952- .... CLC 126; DAM
MULT
See also CA 131; CANR 66; DLB 82; FW;
GLL 1; HW 1, 2

Morand, Paul 1888-1976 .... CLC 41; SSC 22
See also CA 184; 69-72; DLB 65

Morante, Elsa 1918-1985 .... CLC 8, 47
See also CA 85-88; 117; CANR 35; DLB
177; MTCW 1, 2; RGWL

Moravia, Alberto .... CLC 2, 7, 11, 27, 46;
SSC 26
See also Pincherle, Alberto
See also DLB 177; MTCW 2; RGSF;
RGWL

More, Hannah 1745-1833 .... NCLC 27
See also DLB 107, 109, 116, 158; RGEL

More, Henry 1614-1687 .... LC 9
See also DLB 126

More, SirThomas 1478-1535 .... LC 10, 32
See also BRWS 7; RGEL

Moreas, Jean .... TCLC 18
See also Papadiamantopoulos, Johannes
See also GFL 1789 to the Present

Morgan, Berry 1919- .... CLC 6
See also CA 49-52; DLB 6

Morgan, Claire
See Highsmith, (Mary) Patricia
See also GLL 1

Morgan, Edwin (George) 1920- .... CLC 31
See also CA 5-8R; CANR 3, 43, 90; CP;
DLB 27

Morgan, (George) Frederick 1922- .. CLC 23
See also CA 17-20R; CANR 21; CP

Morgan, Harriet
See Mencken, H(enry) L(ouis)

Morgan, Jane
See Cooper, James Fenimore

Morgan, Janet 1945- .... CLC 39
See also CA 65-68

Morgan, Lady 1776(?)-1859 .... NCLC 29
See also DLB 116, 158; RGEL

Morgan, Robin (Evonne) 1941- .... CLC 2
See also CA 69-72; CANR 29, 68; FW;
GLL 2; MTCW 1; SATA 80

Morgan, Scott
See Kuttner, Henry

Morgan, Seth 1949(?)-1990 .... CLC 65
See also CA 185; 132

Morgenstern, Christian (Otto Josef
Wolfgang) 1871-1914 .... TCLC 8
See also CA 105; 191

Morgenstern, S.
See Goldman, William (W.)

Mori, Rintaro
See Mori Ogai
See also CA 110

Moricz, Zsigmond 1879-1942 .... TCLC 33
See also CA 165

Morike, Eduard (Friedrich)
1804-1875 .... NCLC 10
See also DLB 133; RGWL

Mori Ogai 1862-1922 .... TCLC 14
See also CA 164; DLB 180; TWA

Moritz, Karl Philipp 1756-1793 .... LC 2
See also DLB 94

Morland, Peter Henry
See Faust, Frederick (Schiller)

Morley, Christopher (Darlington)
1890-1957 .... TCLC 87
See also CA 112; DLB 9; RGAL

Morren, Theophil
See Hofmannsthal, Hugo von

Morris, Bill 1952- .... CLC 76

Morris, Julian
See West, Morris L(anglo)

Morris, Steveland Judkins 1950(?)-
See Wonder, Stevie
See also CA 111

Morris, William 1834-1896 .... NCLC 4
See also BRW; CDBLB 1832-1890; DLB
18, 35, 57, 156, 178, 184; FANT; RGEL;
SFW; SUFW

Morris, Wright 1910-1998 .. CLC 1, 3, 7, 18,
37
See also CA 9-12R; 167; CANR 21, 81;
CN; DLB 2, 206; DLBY 81; MTCW 1, 2;
RGAL; TCLC 107; TCWW 2

Morrison, Arthur 1863-1945 .... TCLC 72;
SSC 40
See also CA 120; 157; CMW; DLB 70, 135,
197; RGEL

Morrison, Chloe Anthony Wofford
See Morrison, Toni

Morrison, James Douglas 1943-1971
See Morrison, Jim
See also CA 73-76; CANR 40

Morrison, Jim .... CLC 17
See also Morrison, James Douglas

Morrison, Toni 1931- . CLC 4, 10, 22, 55, 81,
87; BLC 3; DA; DAB; DAC; DAM
MST, MULT, NOV, POP
See also AAYA 1, 22; AFAW 1, 2; AMWS
3; BW 2, 3; CA 29-32R; CANR 27, 42,
67; CDALB 1968-1988; CN; CPW; DA3;
DLB 6, 33, 143; DLBY 81; FW; MTCW
1, 2; NFS 1, 6, 8; RGAL; RHW; SATA
57; SSFS 5; YAW

Morrison, Van 1945- .... CLC 21
See also CA 116; 168

Morrissy, Mary 1958- .... CLC 99

Mortimer, John (Clifford) 1923- ..... CLC 28,
43; DAM DRAM, POP
See also CA 13-16R; CANR 21, 69; CD;
CDBLB 1960 to Present; CMW; CN;
CPW; DA3; DLB 13; INT CANR-21;
MSW; MTCW 1, 2; RGEL

Mortimer, Penelope (Ruth)
1918-1999 .... CLC 5
See also CA 57-60; 187; CANR 45, 88; CN

Morton, Anthony
See Creasey, John

Mosca, Gaetano 1858-1941 .... TCLC 75

Mosher, Howard Frank 1943- .... CLC 62
See also CA 139; CANR 65

Mosley, Nicholas 1923- .... CLC 43, 70
See also CA 69-72; CANR 41, 60; CN;
DLB 14, 207

Mosley, Walter 1952- .... CLC 97; BLCS;
DAM MULT, POP
See also AAYA 17; BW 2; CA 142; CANR
57, 92; CMW; CPW; DA3; MTCW 2

Moss, Howard 1922-1987 ...... CLC 7, 14, 45,
50; DAM POET
See also CA 1-4R; 123; CANR 1, 44; DLB
5

Mossgiel, Rab
See Burns, Robert

Motion, Andrew (Peter) 1952- .... CLC 47
See also BRWS 7; CA 146; CANR 90; CP;
DLB 40

Motley, Willard (Francis)
1912-1965 .... CLC 18
See also BW 1; CA 117; 106; CANR 88;
DLB 76, 143

Motoori, Norinaga 1730-1801 .... NCLC 45

Mott, Michael (Charles Alston)
1930- .... CLC 15, 34
See also CA 5-8R; CAAS 7; CANR 7, 29

Mountain Wolf Woman 1884-1960 .. CLC 92
See also CA 144; CANR 90; NNAL

Moure, Erin 1955- .... CLC 88
See also CA 113; CP; CWP; DLB 60

Mowat, Farley (McGill) 1921- .... CLC 26;
DAC; DAM MST
See also AAYA 1; CA 1-4R; CANR 4, 24,
42, 68; CLR 20; CPW; DLB 68; INT
CANR-24; JRDA; MAICYA; MTCW 1,
2; SATA 3, 55; YAW

Mowatt, Anna Cora 1819-1870 ..... NCLC 74
See also RGAL

Moyers, Bill 1934- .... CLC 74
See also AITN 2; CA 61-64; CANR 31, 52

Mphahlele, Es'kia
See Mphahlele, Ezekiel
See also DLB 125, 225; RGSF; SSFS 11

Mphahlele, Ezekiel 1919- .... **CLC 25, 133; BLC 3; DAM MULT**
See also Mphahlele, Es'kia
See also BW 2, 3; CA 81-84; CANR 26, 76; CN; DA3; DLB 225; MTCW 2; SATA 119

Mqhayi, S(amuel) E(dward) K(rune Loliwe) 1875-1945 ...... **TCLC 25; BLC 3; DAM MULT**
See also CA 153; CANR 87

Mrozek, Slawomir 1930- .... **CLC 3, 13**
See also CA 13-16R; CAAS 10; CANR 29; CWW 2; DLB 232; MTCW 1

Mrs. Belloc-Lowndes
See Lowndes, Marie Adelaide (Belloc)

M'Taggart, John M'Taggart Ellis
See McTaggart, John McTaggart Ellis

Mtwa, Percy (?)- .... **CLC 47**

Mueller, Lisel 1924- .... **CLC 13, 51; PC 33**
See also CA 93-96; CP; DLB 105; PFS 9

Muir, Edwin 1887-1959 .... **TCLC 2, 87**
See also Moore, Edward
See also BRWS 6; CA 104; DLB 20, 100, 191; RGEL

Muir, John 1838-1914 .... **TCLC 28**
See also CA 165; DLB 186

Mujica Lainez, Manuel 1910-1984 ... **CLC 31**
See also Lainez, Manuel Mujica
See also CA 81-84; 112; CANR 32; HW 1

Mukherjee, Bharati 1940- ...... **CLC 53, 115; AAL; DAM NOV; SSC 38**
See also BEST 89:2; CA 107; CANR 45, 72; CN; DLB 60; DNFS; FW; MTCW 1, 2; RGAL; RGSF; SSFS 7

Muldoon, Paul 1951- .... **CLC 32, 72; DAM POET**
See also BRWS 4; CA 113; 129; CANR 52, 91; CP; DLB 40; INT 129; PFS 7

Mulisch, Harry 1927- .... **CLC 42**
See also CA 9-12R; CANR 6, 26, 56

Mull, Martin 1943- .... **CLC 17**
See also CA 105

Muller, Wilhelm .... **NCLC 73**

Mulock, Dinah Maria
See Craik, Dinah Maria (Mulock)
See also RGEL

Munford, Robert 1737(?)-1783 .... **LC 5**
See also DLB 31

Mungo, Raymond 1946- .... **CLC 72**
See also CA 49-52; CANR 2

Munro, Alice 1931- .... **CLC 6, 10, 19, 50, 95; DAC; DAM MST, NOV; SSC 3; WLCS**
See also AITN 2; CA 33-36R; CANR 33, 53, 75; CCA 1; CN; DA3; DLB 53; MTCW 1, 2; RGEL; RGSF; SATA 29; SSFS 5

Munro, H(ector) H(ugh) 1870-1916
See Saki
See also CA 104; 130; CDBLB 1890-1914; DA; DAB; DAC; DAM MST, NOV; DA3; DLB 34, 162; MTCW 1, 2; RGEL; WLC

Murasaki, Lady
See Murasaki Shikibu

Murasaki Shikibu 978(?)-1026(?) ... **CMLC 1**
See also EFS 2; RGWL

Murdoch, (Jean) Iris 1919-1999 ... **CLC 1, 2, 3, 4, 6, 8, 11, 15, 22, 31, 51; DAB; DAC; DAM MST, NOV**
See also BRWS 1; CA 13-16R; 179; CANR 8, 43, 68; CDBLB 1960 to Present; CN; DA3; DLB 14, 194, 233; INT CANR-8; MTCW 1, 2; RGEL

Murfree, Mary Noailles 1850-1922 ... **SSC 22**
See also CA 122; 176; DLB 12, 74; RGAL

Murnau, Friedrich Wilhelm
See Plumpe, Friedrich Wilhelm

Murphy, Richard 1927- .... **CLC 41**
See also BRWS 5; CA 29-32R; CP; DLB 40

Murphy, Sylvia 1937- .... **CLC 34**
See also CA 121

Murphy, Thomas (Bernard) 1935- ... **CLC 51**
See also CA 101

Murray, Albert L. 1916- .... **CLC 73**
See also BW 2; CA 49-52; CANR 26, 52, 78; CSW; DLB 38

Murray, Judith Sargent 1751-1820 .... **NCLC 63**
See also DLB 37, 200

Murray, Les(lie) A(llan) 1938- .... **CLC 40; DAM POET**
See also BRWS 7; CA 21-24R; CANR 11, 27, 56; CP; RGEL

Murry, J. Middleton
See Murry, John Middleton

Murry, John Middleton 1889-1957 .... **TCLC 16**
See also CA 118; DLB 149

Musgrave, Susan 1951- .... **CLC 13, 54**
See also CA 69-72; CANR 45, 84; CCA 1; CP; CWP

Musil, Robert (Edler von) 1880-1942 .... **TCLC 12, 68; SSC 18**
See also CA 109; CANR 55, 84; DLB 81, 124; EW; MTCW 2; RGSF; RGWL

Muske, Carol .... **CLC 90**
See also Muske-Dukes, Carol (Anne)

Muske-Dukes, Carol (Anne) 1945-
See Muske, Carol
See also CA 65-68; CANR 32, 70; CWP

Musset, (Louis Charles) Alfred de 1810-1857 .... **NCLC 7**
See also DLB 192; EW; GFL 1789 to the Present; RGWL; TWA

Mussolini, Benito (Amilcare Andrea) 1883-1945 .... **TCLC 96**
See also CA 116

My Brother's Brother
See Chekhov, Anton (Pavlovich)

Myers, L(eopold) H(amilton) 1881-1944 .... **TCLC 59**
See also CA 157; DLB 15; RGEL

Myers, Walter Dean 1937- ..... **CLC 35; BLC 3; DAM MULT, NOV**
See also AAYA 4, 23; BW 2; CA 33-36R; CANR 20, 42, 67; CLR 4, 16, 35; DLB 33; INT CANR-20; JRDA; MAICYA; MTCW 2; SAAS 2; SATA 41, 71, 109; SATA-Brief 27; YAW

Myers, Walter M.
See Myers, Walter Dean

Myles, Symon
See Follett, Ken(neth Martin)

Nabokov, Vladimir (Vladimirovich) 1899-1977 .... **CLC 1, 2, 3, 6, 8, 11, 15, 23, 44, 46, 64; DA; DAB; DAC; DAM MST, NOV; SSC 11; WLC**
See also AMW; AMWR; CA 5-8R; 69-72; CANR 20; CDALB 1941-1968; DA3; DLB 2; DLBD 3; DLBY 80, 91; MTCW 1, 2; NFS 9; RGAL; RGSF; SSFS 6; TCLC 108

Naevius c. 265B.C.-201B.C. .... **CMLC 37**
See also DLB 211

Nagai, Kafu .... **TCLC 51**
See also Nagai, Sokichi
See also DLB 180

Nagai, Sokichi 1879-1959
See Nagai, Kafu
See also CA 117

Nagy, Laszlo 1925-1978 .... **CLC 7**
See also CA 129; 112

Naidu, Sarojini 1879-1949 .... **TCLC 80**
See also RGEL

Naipaul, Shiva(dhar Srinivasa) 1945-1985 .... **CLC 32, 39; DAM NOV**
See also CA 110; 112; 116; CANR 33; DA3; DLB 157; DLBY 85; MTCW 1, 2

Naipaul, V(idiadhar) S(urajprasad) 1932- .... **CLC 4, 7, 9, 13, 18, 37, 105; DAB; DAC; DAM MST, NOV; SSC 38**
See also BRWS 1; CA 1-4R; CANR 1, 33, 51, 91; CDBLB 1960 to Present; CN; DA3; DLB 125, 204, 206; DLBY 85; MTCW 1, 2; RGEL; RGSF

Nakos, Lilika 1899(?)- .... **CLC 29**

Narayan, R(asipuram) K(rishnaswami) 1906-2001 .... **CLC 7, 28, 47, 121; DAM NOV; SSC 25**
See also CA 81-84; CANR 33, 61; CN; DA3; DNFS; MTCW 1, 2; RGEL; RGSF; SATA 62; SSFS 5

Nash, (Frediric) Ogden 1902-1971 . **CLC 23; DAM POET; PC 21**
See also CA 13-14; 29-32R; CANR 34, 61; CAP 1; DLB 11; MAICYA; MTCW 1, 2; RGAL; SATA 2, 46; TCLC 109; WP

Nashe, Thomas 1567-1601(?) .... **LC 41**
See also DLB 167; RGEL

Nathan, Daniel
See Dannay, Frederic

Nathan, George Jean 1882-1958 .... **TCLC 18**
See also Hatteras, Owen
See also CA 114; 169; DLB 137

Natsume, Kinnosuke 1867-1916
See Natsume, S
See also CA 104

Natsume, Soseki .... **TCLC 2, 10**
See also Natsume, Kinnosuke
See also DLB 180; RGWL

Natti, (Mary) Lee 1919-
See Kingman, Lee
See also CA 5-8R; CANR 2

Naylor, Gloria 1950- .... **CLC 28, 52; BLC 3; DA; DAC; DAM MST, MULT, NOV, POP; WLCS**
See also AAYA 6, 39; AFAW 1, 2; AMWS 8; BW 2, 3; CA 107; CANR 27, 51, 74; CN; CPW; DA3; DLB 173; FW; MTCW 1, 2; NFS 4, 7; RGAL

Neff, Debra .... **CLC 59**

Neihardt, John Gneisenau 1881-1973 .... **CLC 32**
See also CA 13-14; CANR 65; CAP 1; DLB 9, 54

Nekrasov, Nikolai Alekseevich 1821-1878 .... **NCLC 11**

Nelligan, Emile 1879-1941 .... **TCLC 14**
See also CA 114; DLB 92

Nelson, Willie 1933- .... **CLC 17**
See also CA 107

Nemerov, Howard (Stanley) 1920-1991 .... **CLC 2, 6, 9, 36; DAM POET; PC 24**
See also AMW; CA 1-4R; 134; CABS 2; CANR 1, 27, 53; DLB 5, 6; DLBY 83; INT CANR-27; MTCW 1, 2; PFS 10; RGAL

Neruda, Pablo 1904-1973 .. **CLC 1, 2, 5, 7, 9, 28, 62; DA; DAB; DAC; DAM MST, MULT, POET; HLC 2; PC 4; WLC**
See also CA 19-20; 45-48; CAP 2; DA3; DNFS; HW 1; MTCW 1, 2; PFS 11; RGWL; WP

Nerval, Gerard de 1808-1855 ... **NCLC 1, 67; PC 13; SSC 18**
See also GFL 1789 to the Present; RGSF; RGWL

Nervo, (Jose) Amado (Ruiz de) 1870-1919 .... **TCLC 11; HLCS 2**
See also CA 109; 131; HW 1; LAW

Nessi, Pio Baroja y
See Baroja (y Nessi), Pio

O'Brien, Flann .... **CLC 1, 4, 5, 7, 10, 47**
See also O Nuallain, Brian
See also BRWS 2; DLB 231; RGEL

O'Brien, Richard 1942- .... **CLC 17**
See also CA 124

O'Brien, (William) Tim(othy) 1946- . **CLC 7, 19, 40, 103; DAM POP**
See also AAYA 16; CA 85-88; CANR 40, 58; CDALBS; CN; CPW; DA3; DLB 152; DLBD 9; DLBY 80; MTCW 2; RGAL

Obstfelder, Sigbjoern 1866-1900 .... **TCLC 23**
See also CA 123

O'Casey, Sean 1880-1964 .... **CLC 1, 5, 9, 11, 15, 88; DAB; DAC; DAM DRAM, MST; DC 12; WLCS**
See also CA 89-92; CANR 62; CBD; CD-BLB 1914-1945; DA3; DLB 10; MTCW 1, 2; RGEL

O'Cathasaigh, Sean
See O'Casey, Sean

Occom, Samson 1723-1792 .... **LC 60**
See also DLB 175; NNAL

Ochs, Phil(ip David) 1940-1976 .... **CLC 17**
See also CA 185; 65-68

O'Connor, Edwin (Greene)
1918-1968 .... **CLC 14**
See also CA 93-96; 25-28R

O'Connor, (Mary) Flannery
1925-1964 .... **CLC 1, 2, 3, 6, 10, 13, 15, 21, 66, 104; DA; DAB; DAC; DAM MST, NOV; SSC 1, 23; WLC**
See also AAYA 7; AMW; CA 1-4R; CANR 3, 41; CDALB 1941-1968; DA3; DLB 2, 152; DLBD 12; DLBY 80; MAWW; MTCW 1, 2; NFS 3; RGAL; RGSF; SSFS 2, 7, 10

O'Connor, Frank .... **CLC 23; SSC 5**
See also O'Donovan, Michael John
See also DLB 162; RGSF; SSFS 5

O'Dell, Scott 1898-1989 .... **CLC 30**
See also AAYA 3; CA 61-64; 129; CANR 12, 30; CLR 1, 16; DLB 52; JRDA; MAI-CYA; SATA 12, 60; YAW

Odets, Clifford 1906-1963 .... **CLC 2, 28, 98; DAM DRAM; DC 6**
See also AMWS 2; CA 85-88; CAD; CANR 62; DFS 3; DLB 7, 26; MTCW 1, 2; RGAL

O'Doherty, Brian 1934- .... **CLC 76**
See also CA 105

O'Donnell, K. M.
See Malzberg, Barry N(athaniel)

O'Donnell, Lawrence
See Kuttner, Henry

O'Donovan, Michael John
1903-1966 .... **CLC 14**
See also O'Connor, Frank
See also CA 93-96; CANR 84

O'Faolain, Julia 1932- .... **CLC 6, 19, 47, 108**
See also CA 81-84; CAAS 2; CANR 12, 61; CN; DLB 14, 231; FW; MTCW 1; RHW

O'Faolain, Sean 1900-1991 ...... **CLC 1, 7, 14, 32, 70; SSC 13**
See also CA 61-64; 134; CANR 12, 66; DLB 15, 162; MTCW 1, 2; RGEL; RGSF

O'Flaherty, Liam 1896-1984 .... **CLC 5, 34; SSC 6**
See also CA 101; 113; CANR 35; DLB 36, 162; DLBY 84; MTCW 1, 2; RGEL; RGSF; SSFS 5

Ogilvy, Gavin
See Barrie, J(ames) M(atthew)

O'Grady, Standish (James)
1846-1928 .... **TCLC 5**
See also CA 104; 157

O'Grady, Timothy 1951- .... **CLC 59**
See also CA 138

O'Hara, Frank 1926-1966 .... **CLC 2, 5, 13, 78; DAM POET**
See also CA 9-12R; 25-28R; CANR 33; DA3; DLB 5, 16, 193; MTCW 1, 2; PFS 8; 12; RGAL; WP

O'Hara, John (Henry) 1905-1970 . **CLC 1, 2, 3, 6, 11, 42; DAM NOV; SSC 15**
See also AMW; CA 5-8R; 25-28R; CANR 31, 60; CDALB 1929-1941; DLB 9, 86; DLBD 2; MTCW 1, 2; NFS 11; RGAL; RGSF

O Hehir, Diana 1922- .... **CLC 41**
See also CA 93-96

Ohiyesa 1858-1939
See Eastman, Charles A(lexander)

Okigbo, Christopher (Ifenayichukwu)
1932-1967 ... **CLC 25, 84; BLC 3; DAM MULT, POET; PC 7**
See also AFW; BW 1, 3; CA 77-80; CANR 74; DLB 125; MTCW 1, 2; RGEL

Okri, Ben 1959- .... **CLC 87**
See also BRWS 5; BW 2, 3; CA 130; 138; CANR 65; CN; DLB 157, 231; INT 138; MTCW 2; RGSF

Olds, Sharon 1942- ... **CLC 32, 39, 85; DAM POET; PC 22**
See also CA 101; CANR 18, 41, 66, 98; CP; CPW; CWP; DLB 120; MTCW 2

Oldstyle, Jonathan
See Irving, Washington

Olesha, Iurii
See Olesha, Yuri (Karlovich)
See also RGWL

Olesha, Yuri (Karlovich) 1899-1960 .. **CLC 8**
See also Olesha, Iurii
See also CA 85-88; EW

Oliphant, Laurence 1829(?)-1888 .. **NCLC 47**
See also DLB 18, 166

Oliphant, Margaret (Oliphant Wilson)
1828-1897 .... **NCLC 11, 61; SSC 25**
See also Oliphant
See also DLB 18, 159, 190; HGG; RGEL; RGSF; SUFW

Oliver, Mary 1935- .... **CLC 19, 34, 98**
See also AMWS 7; CA 21-24R; CANR 9, 43, 84, 92; CP; CWP; DLB 5, 193

Olivier, Laurence (Kerr) 1907-1989 . **CLC 20**
See also CA 111; 150; 129

Olsen, Tillie 1912- .... **CLC 4, 13, 114; DA; DAB; DAC; DAM MST; SSC 11**
See also CA 1-4R; CANR 1, 43, 74; CDALBS; CN; DA3; DLB 28, 206; DLBY 80; FW; MTCW 1, 2; RGAL; RGSF; SSFS 1

Olson, Charles (John) 1910-1970 .. **CLC 1, 2, 5, 6, 9, 11, 29; DAM POET; PC 19**
See also AMWS 2; CA 13-16; 25-28R; CABS 2; CANR 35, 61; CAP 1; DLB 5, 16, 193; MTCW 1, 2; RGAL; WP

Olson, Toby 1937- .... **CLC 28**
See also CA 65-68; CANR 9, 31, 84; CP

Olyesha, Yuri
See Olesha, Yuri (Karlovich)

Omar Khayyam
See Khayyam, Omar
See also RGWL

Ondaatje, (Philip) Michael 1943- .... **CLC 14, 29, 51, 76; DAB; DAC; DAM MST; PC 28**
See also CA 77-80; CANR 42, 74; CN; CP; DA3; DLB 60; MTCW 2; PFS 8

Oneal, Elizabeth 1934-
See Oneal, Zibby
See also CA 106; CANR 28, 84; MAICYA; SATA 30, 82; YAW

Oneal, Zibby .... **CLC 30**
See also Oneal, Elizabeth
See also AAYA 5; CLR 13; JRDA

O'Neill, Eugene (Gladstone)
1888-1953 .... **TCLC 1, 6, 27, 49; DA; DAB; DAC; DAM DRAM, MST; WLC**
See also AITN 1; CA 110; 132; CDALB 1929-1941; DA3; DFS 9,11, 12; DLB 7; MTCW 1, 2

Onetti, Juan Carlos 1909-1994 ... **CLC 7, 10; DAM MULT, NOV; HLCS 2; SSC 23**
See also CA 85-88; 145; CANR 32, 63; DLB 113; HW 1, 2; MTCW 1, 2; RGSF

O Nuallain, Brian 1911-1966
See O'Brien, Flann
See also CA 21-22; 25-28R; CAP 2; DLB 231; FANT

Ophuls, Max 1902-1957 .... **TCLC 79**
See also CA 113

Opie, Amelia 1769-1853 .... **NCLC 65**
See also DLB 116, 159; RGEL

Oppen, George 1908-1984 ..... **CLC 7, 13, 34; PC 35**
See also CA 13-16R; 113; CANR 8, 82; DLB 5, 165; TCLC 107

Oppenheim, E(dward) Phillips
1866-1946 .... **TCLC 45**
See also CA 111; CMW; DLB 70

Opuls, Max
See Ophuls, Max

Origen c. 185-c. 254 .... **CMLC 19**

Orlovitz, Gil 1918-1973 .... **CLC 22**
See also CA 77-80; 45-48; DLB 2, 5

Orris
See Ingelow, Jean

Ortega y Gasset, Jose 1883-1955 ... **TCLC 9; DAM MULT; HLC 2**
See also CA 106; 130; HW 1, 2; MTCW 1, 2

Ortese, Anna Maria 1914- .... **CLC 89**
See also DLB 177

Ortiz, Simon J(oseph) 1941- . **CLC 45; DAM MULT, POET; PC 17**
See also AMWS 4; CA 134; CANR 69; CP; DLB 120, 175; NNAL; PFS 4; RGAL

Orton, Joe .... **CLC 4, 13, 43; DC 3**
See also Orton, John Kingsley
See also BRWS 5; CBD; CDBLB 1960 to Present; DFS 3, 6; DLB 13; GLL 1; MTCW 2; RGEL

Orton, John Kingsley 1933-1967
See Orton, Joe
See also CA 85-88; CANR 35, 66; DAM DRAM; MTCW 1, 2

Orwell, George .... **TCLC 2, 6, 15, 31, 51; DAB; WLC**
See also Blair, Eric (Arthur)
See also CDBLB 1945-1960; CLR 68; DLB 15, 98, 195; NFS 3, 7; RGEL; SCFW 2; SFW; SSFS 4; YAW

Osborne, David
See Silverberg, Robert

Osborne, George
See Silverberg, Robert

Osborne, John (James) 1929-1994 .... **CLC 1, 2, 5, 11, 45; DA; DAB; DAC; DAM DRAM, MST; WLC**
See also BRWS 1; CA 13-16R; 147; CANR 21, 56; CDBLB 1945-1960; DFS 4; DLB 13; MTCW 1, 2; RGEL

Osborne, Lawrence 1958- .... **CLC 50**
See also CA 189

Osbourne, Lloyd 1868-1947 .... **TCLC 93**

Oshima, Nagisa 1932- .... **CLC 20**
See also CA 116; 121; CANR 78

Oskison, John Milton 1874-1947 .. **TCLC 35; DAM MULT**
See also CA 144; CANR 84; DLB 175; NNAL

Ossian c. 3rd cent. - .... **CMLC 28**
See also Macpherson, James

Pope, Alexander 1688-1744 ...... **LC 3, 58, 60, 64; DA; DAB; DAC; DAM MST, POET; PC 26; WLC**
  See also CDBLB 1660-1789; DA3; DLB 95, 101; PAB; PFS 12; RGEL; WP

Popov, Yevgeny .... **CLC 59**

Porter, Connie (Rose) 1959(?)- .... **CLC 70**
  See also BW 2, 3; CA 142; CANR 90; SATA 81

Porter, Gene(va Grace) Stratton .. **TCLC 21**
  See also Stratton-Porter, Gene(va Grace)
  See also CA 112; CWRI; RHW

Porter, Katherine Anne 1890-1980 ... **CLC 1, 3, 7, 10, 13, 15, 27, 101; DA; DAB; DAC; DAM MST, NOV; SSC 4, 31, 43**
  See also AITN 2; CA 1-4R; 101; CANR 1, 65; CDALBS; DA3; DLB 4, 9, 102; DLBD 12; DLBY 80; MTCW 1, 2; RGAL; RGSF; SATA 39; SATA-Obit 23; SSFS 1,8,11

Porter, Peter (Neville Frederick)
  1929- .... **CLC 5, 13, 33**
  See also CA 85-88; CP; DLB 40

Porter, William Sydney 1862-1910
  See Henry, O.
  See also CA 104; 131; CDALB 1865-1917; DA; DAB; DAC; DAM MST; DA3; DLB 12, 78, 79; MTCW 1, 2; YABC 2

Portillo (y Pacheco), Jose Lopez
  See Lopez Portillo (y Pacheco), Jose

Portillo Trambley, Estela 1927-1998
  See Trambley, Estela Portillo
  See also CANR 32; DAM MULT; DLB 209; HLC 2; HW 1

Posse, Abel .... **CLC 70**

Post, Melville Davisson
  1869-1930 .... **TCLC 39**
  See also CA 110; CMW

Potok, Chaim 1929- ... **CLC 2, 7, 14, 26, 112; DAM NOV**
  See also AAYA 15; AITN 1, 2; CA 17-20R; CANR 19, 35, 64, 98; CN; DA3; DLB 28, 152; INT CANR-19; MTCW 1, 2; NFS 4; SATA 33, 106; YAW

Potter, Dennis (Christopher George)
  1935-1994 .... **CLC 58, 86, 123**
  See also CA 107; 145; CANR 33, 61; CBD; DLB 233; MTCW 1

Pound, Ezra (Weston Loomis)
  1885-1972 .. **CLC 1, 2, 3, 4, 5, 7, 10, 13, 18, 34, 48, 50, 112; DA; DAB; DAC; DAM MST, POET; PC 4; WLC**
  See also AMW; AMWR; CA 5-8R; 37-40R; CANR 40; CDALB 1917-1929; DA3; DLB 4, 45, 63; DLBD 15; EFS 2; MTCW 1, 2; PAB; PFS 2, 8; RGAL; WP

Povod, Reinaldo 1959-1994 .... **CLC 44**
  See also CA 136; 146; CANR 83

Powell, Adam Clayton, Jr.
  1908-1972 .... **CLC 89; BLC 3; DAM MULT**
  See also BW 1, 3; CA 102; 33-36R; CANR 86

Powell, Anthony (Dymoke)
  1905-2000 .... **CLC 1, 3, 7, 9, 10, 31**
  See also BRW; CA 1-4R; 189; CANR 1, 32, 62; CDBLB 1945-1960; CN; DLB 15; MTCW 1, 2; RGEL

Powell, Dawn 1897-1965 .... **CLC 66**
  See also CA 5-8R; DLBY 97

Powell, Padgett 1952- .... **CLC 34**
  See also CA 126; CANR 63; CSW; DLB 234

Powell, (Oval) Talmage 1920-2000
  See Queen, Ellery
  See also CA 5-8R; CANR 2, 80

Power, Susan 1961- .... **CLC 91**
  See also CA 160; NFS 11

Powers, J(ames) F(arl) 1917-1999 ..... **CLC 1, 4, 8, 57; SSC 4**
  See also CA 1-4R; 181; CANR 2, 61; CN; DLB 130; MTCW 1; RGAL; RGSF

Powers, John J(ames) 1945-
  See Powers, John R.
  See also CA 69-72

Powers, John R. .... **CLC 66**
  See also Powers, John J(ames)

Powers, Richard (S.) 1957- .... **CLC 93**
  See also CA 148; CANR 80; CN

Pownall, David 1938- .... **CLC 10**
  See also CA 89-92, 180; CAAS 18; CANR 49; CBD; CD; CN; DLB 14

Powys, John Cowper 1872-1963 ... **CLC 7, 9, 15, 46, 125**
  See also CA 85-88; DLB 15; FANT; MTCW 1, 2; RGEL

Powys, T(heodore) F(rancis)
  1875-1953 .... **TCLC 9**
  See also CA 106; 189; DLB 36, 162; FANT; RGEL; SUFW

Prado (Calvo), Pedro 1886-1952 ... **TCLC 75**
  See also CA 131; HW 1; LAW

Prager, Emily 1952- .... **CLC 56**

Pratt, E(dwin) J(ohn)
  1883(?)-1964 .... **CLC 19; DAC; DAM POET**
  See also CA 141; 93-96; CANR 77; DLB 92; RGEL

Premchand .... **TCLC 21**
  See also Srivastava, Dhanpat Rai

Preussler, Otfried 1923- .... **CLC 17**
  See also CA 77-80; SATA 24

Prevert, Jacques (Henri Marie)
  1900-1977 .... **CLC 15**
  See also CA 77-80; 69-72; CANR 29, 61; GFL 1789 to the Present; IDFW 3, 4; MTCW 1; RGWL; SATA-Obit 30

Prevost, (Antoine Francois)
  1697-1763 .... **LC 1**
  See also EW; GFL Beginnings to 1789; RGWL

Price, (Edward) Reynolds 1933- ... **CLC 3, 6, 13, 43, 50, 63; DAM NOV; SSC 22**
  See also AMWS 6; CA 1-4R; CANR 1, 37, 57, 87; CN; CSW; DLB 2, 218; INT CANR-37

Price, Richard 1949- .... **CLC 6, 12**
  See also CA 49-52; CANR 3; DLBY 81

Prichard, Katharine Susannah
  1883-1969 .... **CLC 46**
  See also CA 11-12; CANR 33; CAP 1; MTCW 1; RGEL; RGSF; SATA 66

Priestley, J(ohn) B(oynton)
  1894-1984 .... **CLC 2, 5, 9, 34; DAM DRAM, NOV**
  See also BRW; CA 9-12R; 113; CANR 33; CDBLB 1914-1945; DA3; DLB 10, 34, 77, 100, 139; DLBY 84; MTCW 1, 2; RGEL; SFW

Prince 1958(?)- .... **CLC 35**

Prince, F(rank) T(empleton) 1912- .. **CLC 22**
  See also CA 101; CANR 43, 79; CP; DLB 20

Prince Kropotkin
  See Kropotkin, Peter (Aleksieevich)

Prior, Matthew 1664-1721 .... **LC 4**
  See also DLB 95; RGEL

Prishvin, Mikhail 1873-1954 .... **TCLC 75**

Pritchard, William H(arrison)
  1932- .... **CLC 34**
  See also CA 65-68; CANR 23, 95; DLB 111

Pritchett, V(ictor) S(awdon)
  1900-1997 ...... **CLC 5, 13, 15, 41; DAM NOV; SSC 14**
  See also BRWS 3; CA 61-64; 157; CANR 31, 63; CN; DA3; DLB 15, 139; MTCW 1, 2; RGEL; RGSF

Private 19022
  See Manning, Frederic

Probst, Mark 1925- .... **CLC 59**
  See also CA 130

Prokosch, Frederic 1908-1989 ...... **CLC 4, 48**
  See also CA 73-76; 128; CANR 82; DLB 48; MTCW 2

Propertius, Sextus c. 50B.C.-c.
  16B.C. .... **CMLC 32**
  See also AW; DLB 211; RGWL

Prophet, The
  See Dreiser, Theodore (Herman Albert)

Prose, Francine 1947- .... **CLC 45**
  See also CA 109; 112; CANR 46, 95; DLB 234; SATA 101

Proudhon
  See Cunha, Euclides (Rodrigues Pimenta) da

Proulx, Annie
  See Proulx, E(dna) Annie
  See also AMWS 7

Proulx, E(dna) Annie 1935- .. **CLC 81; DAM POP**
  See also Proulx, Annie
  See also CA 145; CANR 65; CN; CPW 1; DA3; MTCW 2

Proust,
  (Valentin-Louis-George-Eugene-)Marcel 1871-1922 . **TCLC 7, 13, 33; DA; DAB; DAC; DAM MST, NOV; WLC**
  See also CA 104; 120; DA3; DLB 65; EW; GFL 1789 to the Present; MTCW 1, 2; RGWL

Prowler, Harley
  See Masters, Edgar Lee

Prus, Boleslaw 1845-1912 .... **TCLC 48**
  See also RGWL

Pryor, Richard (Franklin Lenox Thomas)
  1940- .... **CLC 26**
  See also CA 122; 152

Przybyszewski, Stanislaw
  1868-1927 .... **TCLC 36**
  See also CA 160; DLB 66

Pteleon
  See Grieve, C(hristopher) M(urray)
  See also DAM POET

Puckett, Lute
  See Masters, Edgar Lee

Puig, Manuel 1932-1990 .... **CLC 3, 5, 10, 28, 65, 133; DAM MULT; HLC 2**
  See also CA 45-48; CANR 2, 32, 63; DA3; DLB 113; DNFS; GLL 1; HW 1, 2; MTCW 1, 2; RGWL

Pulitzer, Joseph 1847-1911 .... **TCLC 76**
  See also CA 114; DLB 23

Purdy, A(lfred) W(ellington)
  1918-2000 .... **CLC 3, 6, 14, 50; DAC; DAM MST, POET**
  See also CA 81-84; 189; CAAS 17; CANR 42, 66; CP; DLB 88; PFS 5; RGEL

Purdy, James (Amos) 1923- .... **CLC 2, 4, 10, 28, 52**
  See also AMWS 7; CA 33-36R; CAAS 1; CANR 19, 51; CN; DLB 2; INT CANR-19; MTCW 1; RGAL

Pure, Simon
  See Swinnerton, Frank Arthur

Pushkin, Alexander (Sergeyevich)
  1799-1837 . **NCLC 3, 27, 83; DA; DAB; DAC; DAM DRAM, MST, POET; PC 10; SSC 27; WLC**
  See also DA3; DLB 205; EW; RGSF; RGWL; SATA 61; SSFS 9

P'u Sung-ling 1640-1715 .... **LC 49; SSC 31**

Putnam, Arthur Lee
  See Alger, Horatio, Jr.

Sokolov, Sasha .... **CLC 59**
Solo, Jay
   See Ellison, Harlan (Jay)
Sologub, Fyodor .... **TCLC 9**
   See also Teternikov, Fyodor Kuzmich
Solomons, Ikey Esquir
   See Thackeray, William Makepeace
Solomos, Dionysios 1798-1857 .... **NCLC 15**
Solwoska, Mara
   See French, Marilyn
Solzhenitsyn, Aleksandr I(sayevich)
   1918- .. **CLC 1, 2, 4, 7, 9, 10, 18, 26, 34,**
   78, 134; DA; DAB; DAC; DAM MST,
   NOV; SSC 32; WLC
   See also AITN 1; CA 69-72; CANR 40, 65;
   DA3; EW; MTCW 1, 2; NFS 6; RGSF;
   RGWL; SSFS 9
Somers, Jane
   See Lessing, Doris (May)
Somerville, Edith 1858-1949 .... **TCLC 51**
   See also DLB 135; RGEL; RGSF
Somerville & Ross
   See Martin, Violet Florence; Somerville,
   Edith
Sommer, Scott 1951- .... **CLC 25**
   See also CA 106
Sondheim, Stephen (Joshua) 1930- . **CLC 30,**
   39, 147; DAM DRAM
   See also AAYA 11; CA 103; CANR 47, 67
Song, Cathy 1955- .... **PC 21**
   See also AAL; CA 154; CWP; DLB 169;
   FW; PFS 5
Sontag, Susan 1933- .... **CLC 1, 2, 10, 13, 31,**
   105; DAM POP
   See also AMWS 3; CA 17-20R; CANR 25,
   51, 74, 97; CN; CPW; DA3; DLB 2, 67;
   MTCW 1, 2; RGAL; RHW; SSFS 10
Sophocles 496(?)B.C.-406(?)B.C. .... **CMLC 2,**
   47; DA; DAB; DAC; DAM DRAM,
   MST; DC 1; WLCS
   See also DA3; DFS 1, 4, 8; DLB 176;
   RGWL
Sordello 1189-1269 .... **CMLC 15**
Sorel, Georges 1847-1922 .... **TCLC 91**
   See also CA 118; 188
Sorel, Julia
   See Drexler, Rosalyn
Sorokin, Vladimir .... **CLC 59**
Sorrentino, Gilbert 1929- .. **CLC 3, 7, 14, 22,**
   40
   See also CA 77-80; CANR 14, 33; CN; CP;
   DLB 5, 173; DLBY 80; INT CANR-14
Soto, Gary 1952- .... **CLC 32, 80; DAM**
   MULT; HLC 2; PC 28
   See also AAYA 10, 37; CA 119; 125; CANR
   50, 74; CLR 38; CP; DLB 82; HW 1, 2;
   INT 125; JRDA; MTCW 2; PFS 7;
   RGAL; SATA 80, 120; YAW
Soupault, Philippe 1897-1990 .... **CLC 68**
   See also CA 116; 147; 131; GFL 1789 to
   the Present
Souster, (Holmes) Raymond 1921- .... **CLC 5,**
   14; DAC; DAM POET
   See also CA 13-16R; CAAS 14; CANR 13,
   29, 53; CP; DA3; DLB 88; RGEL; SATA
   63
Southern, Terry 1924(?)-1995 .... **CLC 7**
   See also CA 1-4R; 150; CANR 1, 55; CN;
   DLB 2; IDFW 3, 4
Southey, Robert 1774-1843 .... **NCLC 8, 97**
   See also DLB 93, 107, 142; RGEL; SATA
   54
Southworth, Emma Dorothy Eliza Nevitte
   1819-1899 .... **NCLC 26**
   See also DLB 239
Souza, Ernest
   See Scott, Evelyn

Soyinka, Wole 1934- .... **CLC 3, 5, 14, 36, 44;**
   BLC 3; DA; DAB; DAC; DAM
   DRAM, MST, MULT; DC 2; WLC
   See also BW 2, 3; CA 13-16R; CANR 27,
   39, 82; CD; CN; CP; DA3; DFS 10; DLB
   125; MTCW 1, 2; RGEL
Spackman, W(illiam) M(ode)
   1905-1990 .... **CLC 46**
   See also CA 81-84; 132
Spacks, Barry (Bernard) 1931- .... **CLC 14**
   See also CA 154; CANR 33; CP; DLB 105
Spanidou, Irini 1946- .... **CLC 44**
   See also CA 185
Spark, Muriel (Sarah) 1918- ..... **CLC 2, 3, 5,**
   8, 13, 18, 40, 94; DAB; DAC; DAM
   MST, NOV; SSC 10
   See also BRWS 1; CA 5-8R; CANR 12, 36,
   76, 89; CDBLB 1945-1960; CN; CP;
   DA3; DLB 15, 139; FW; INT CANR-12;
   MTCW 1, 2; RGEL; YAW
Spaulding, Douglas
   See Bradbury, Ray (Douglas)
Spaulding, Leonard
   See Bradbury, Ray (Douglas)
Spelman, Elizabeth .... **CLC 65**
Spence, J. A. D.
   See Eliot, T(homas) S(tearns)
Spencer, Elizabeth 1921- .... **CLC 22**
   See also CA 13-16R; CANR 32, 65, 87;
   CN; CSW; DLB 6; MTCW 1; RGAL;
   SATA 14
Spencer, Leonard G.
   See Silverberg, Robert
Spencer, Scott 1945- .... **CLC 30**
   See also CA 113; CANR 51; DLBY 86
Spender, Stephen (Harold)
   1909-1995 .... **CLC 1, 2, 5, 10, 41, 91;**
   DAM POET
   See also BRWS 2; CA 9-12R; 149; CANR
   31, 54; CDBLB 1945-1960; CP; DA3;
   DLB 20; MTCW 1, 2; PAB; RGEL
Spengler, Oswald (Arnold Gottfried)
   1880-1936 .... **TCLC 25**
   See also CA 118; 189
Spenser, Edmund 1552(?)-1599 ..... **LC 5, 39;**
   DA; DAB; DAC; DAM MST, POET;
   PC 8; WLC
   See also CDBLB Before 1660; DA3; DLB
   167; EFS 2; PAB; RGEL; WP
Spicer, Jack 1925-1965 .... **CLC 8, 18, 72;**
   DAM POET
   See also CA 85-88; DLB 5, 16, 193; GLL
   1; WP
Spiegelman, Art 1948- .... **CLC 76**
   See also AAYA 10; CA 125; CANR 41, 55,
   74; MTCW 2; SATA 109; YAW
Spielberg, Peter 1929- .... **CLC 6**
   See also CA 5-8R; CANR 4, 48; DLBY 81
Spielberg, Steven 1947- .... **CLC 20**
   See also AAYA 8, 24; CA 77-80; CANR
   32; SATA 32
Spillane, Frank Morrison 1918-
   See Spillane, Mickey
   See also CA 25-28R; CANR 28, 63; DA3;
   DLB 226; MTCW 1, 2; SATA 66
Spillane, Mickey .... **CLC 3, 13**
   See also Spillane, Frank Morrison
   See also CMW; DLB 226; MTCW 2
Spinoza, Benedictus de 1632-1677 .. **LC 9, 58**
Spinrad, Norman (Richard) 1940- ... **CLC 46**
   See also CA 37-40R; CAAS 19; CANR 20,
   91; DLB 8; INT CANR-20; SFW
Spitteler, Carl (Friedrich Georg)
   1845-1924 .... **TCLC 12**
   See also CA 109; DLB 129
Spivack, Kathleen (Romola Drucker)
   1938- .... **CLC 6**
   See also CA 49-52

Spoto, Donald 1941- .... **CLC 39**
   See also CA 65-68; CANR 11, 57, 93
Springsteen, Bruce (F.) 1949- .... **CLC 17**
   See also CA 111
Spurling, Hilary 1940- .... **CLC 34**
   See also CA 104; CANR 25, 52, 94
Spyker, John Howland
   See Elman, Richard (Martin)
Squires, (James) Radcliffe
   1917-1993 .... **CLC 51**
   See also CA 1-4R; 140; CANR 6, 21
Srivastava, Dhanpat Rai 1880(?)-1936
   See Premchand
   See also CA 118
Stacy, Donald
   See Pohl, Frederik
Stael
   See Sta
   See also RGWL
Stael, Germaine de .... **NCLC 91**
   See also Stael-Holstein, Anne Louise Ger-
   maine Necker
   See also DLB 119, 192; FW; GFL 1789 to
   the Present
Stael-Holstein, Anne Louise Germaine
   Necker 1766-1817 .... **NCLC 3**
   See also Stael; Stael, Germaine de
   See also EW; TWA
Stafford, Jean 1915-1979 .. **CLC 4, 7, 19, 68;**
   SSC 26
   See also CA 1-4R; 85-88; CANR 3, 65;
   DLB 2, 173; MTCW 1, 2; RGAL; RGSF;
   SATA-Obit 22; TCWW 2
Stafford, William (Edgar)
   1914-1993 .. **CLC 4, 7, 29; DAM POET**
   See also CA 5-8R; 142; CAAS 3; CANR 5,
   22; DLB 5, 206; INT CANR-22; PFS 2,
   8; RGAL; WP
Stagnelius, Eric Johan 1793-1823 . **NCLC 61**
Staines, Trevor
   See Brunner, John (Kilian Houston)
Stairs, Gordon
   See Austin, Mary (Hunter)
   See also TCWW 2
Stairs, Gordon 1868-1934
   See Austin, Mary (Hunter)
Stalin, Joseph 1879-1953 .... **TCLC 92**
Stancykowna
   See Szymborska, Wislawa
Stannard, Martin 1947- .... **CLC 44**
   See also CA 142; DLB 155
Stanton, Elizabeth Cady
   1815-1902 .... **TCLC 73**
   See also CA 171; DLB 79; FW
Stanton, Maura 1946- .... **CLC 9**
   See also CA 89-92; CANR 15; DLB 120
Stanton, Schuyler
   See Baum, L(yman) Frank
Stapledon, (William) Olaf
   1886-1950 .... **TCLC 22**
   See also CA 111; 162; DLB 15; SFW
Starbuck, George (Edwin)
   1931-1996 .... **CLC 53; DAM POET**
   See also CA 21-24R; 153; CANR 23
Stark, Richard
   See Westlake, Donald E(dwin)
Staunton, Schuyler
   See Baum, L(yman) Frank
Stead, Christina (Ellen) 1902-1983 ... **CLC 2,**
   5, 8, 32, 80
   See also BRWS 4; CA 13-16R; 109; CANR
   33, 40; FW; MTCW 1, 2; RGEL; RGSF
Stead, William Thomas
   1849-1912 .... **TCLC 48**
   See also CA 167
Steele, SirRichard 1672-1729 .... **LC 18**
   See also BRW; CDBLB 1660-1789; DLB
   84, 101; RGEL

Stribling, T(homas) S(igismund)
1881-1965 .... **CLC 23**
See also CA 189; 107; CMW; DLB 9;
RGAL

Strindberg, (Johan) August
1849-1912 .... **TCLC 1, 8, 21, 47; DA;**
DAB; DAC; DAM DRAM, MST; WLC
See also CA 104; 135; DA3; DFS 4, 9; EW;
MTCW 2; RGWL

Stringer, Arthur 1874-1950 .... **TCLC 37**
See also CA 161; DLB 92

Stringer, David
See Roberts, Keith (John Kingston)

Stroheim, Erich von 1885-1957 ..... **TCLC 71**

Strugatskii, Arkadii (Natanovich)
1925-1991 .... **CLC 27**
See also CA 106; 135; SFW

Strugatskii, Boris (Natanovich)
1933- .... **CLC 27**
See also CA 106; SFW

Strummer, Joe 1953(?)- .... **CLC 30**

Strunk, William, Jr. 1869-1946 ...... **TCLC 92**
See also CA 118; 164

Stryk, Lucien 1924- .... **PC 27**
See also CA 13-16R; CANR 10, 28, 55; CP

Stuart, Don A.
See Campbell, John W(ood, Jr.)

Stuart, Ian
See MacLean, Alistair (Stuart)

Stuart, Jesse (Hilton) 1906-1984 ... **CLC 1, 8,**
11, 14, 34; SSC 31
See also CA 5-8R; 112; CANR 31; DLB 9,
48, 102; DLBY 84; SATA 2; SATA-Obit
36

Sturgeon, Theodore (Hamilton)
1918-1985 .... **CLC 22, 39**
See also Queen, Ellery
See also CA 81-84; 116; CANR 32; DLB 8;
DLBY 85; HGG; MTCW 1, 2; SFW;
SUFW

Sturges, Preston 1898-1959 .... **TCLC 48**
See also CA 114; 149; DLB 26

Styron, William 1925- .... **CLC 1, 3, 5, 11, 15,**
60; DAM NOV, POP; SSC 25
See also BEST 90:4; CA 5-8R; CANR 6,
33, 74; CDALB 1968-1988; CN; CPW;
CSW; DA3; DLB 2, 143; DLBY 80; INT
CANR-6; MTCW 1, 2; NCFS 1; RGAL;
RHW

Su, Chien 1884-1918
See Su Man-shu
See also CA 123

Suarez Lynch, B.
See Bioy Casares, Adolfo; Borges, Jorge
Luis

Suassuna, Ariano Vilar 1927-
See also CA 178; HLCS 1; HW 2

Suckling, Sir John 1609-1642 .... **PC 30**
See also BRW; DAM POET; DLB 58, 126;
PAB; RGEL

Suckow, Ruth 1892-1960 .... **SSC 18**
See also CA 113; DLB 9, 102; RGAL;
TCWW 2

Sudermann, Hermann 1857-1928 .. **TCLC 15**
See also CA 107; DLB 118

Sue, Eugene 1804-1857 .... **NCLC 1**
See also DLB 119

Sueskind, Patrick 1949- .... **CLC 44**
See also Suskind, Patrick

Sukenick, Ronald 1932- .... **CLC 3, 4, 6, 48**
See also CA 25-28R; CAAS 8; CANR 32,
89; CN; DLB 173; DLBY 81

Suknaski, Andrew 1942- .... **CLC 19**
See also CA 101; CP; DLB 53

Sullivan, Vernon
See Vian, Boris

Sully Prudhomme, Rene-Francois-Armand
1839-1907 .... **TCLC 31**
See also GFL 1789 to the Present

Su Man-shu .... **TCLC 24**
See also Su, Chien

Summerforest, Ivy B.
See Kirkup, James

Summers, Andrew James 1942- .... **CLC 26**

Summers, Andy
See Summers, Andrew James

Summers, Hollis (Spurgeon, Jr.)
1916- .... **CLC 10**
See also CA 5-8R; CANR 3; DLB 6

Summers, (Alphonsus Joseph-Mary
Augustus) Montague
1880-1948 .... **TCLC 16**
See also CA 118; 163

Sumner, Gordon Matthew .... **CLC 26**
See also Sting

Surtees, Robert Smith 1805-1864 .. **NCLC 14**
See also DLB 21; RGEL

Susann, Jacqueline 1921-1974 .... **CLC 3**
See also AITN 1; CA 65-68; 53-56; MTCW
1, 2

Su Shi
See Su Shih
See also RGWL

Su Shih 1036-1101 .... **CMLC 15**
See also Su Shi

Suskind, Patrick
See Sueskind, Patrick
See also CA 145; CWW 2

Sutcliff, Rosemary 1920-1992 .... **CLC 26;**
DAB; DAC; DAM MST, POP
See also AAYA 10; CA 5-8R; 139; CANR
37; CLR 1, 37; CPW; JRDA; MAICYA;
RHW; SATA 6, 44, 78; SATA-Obit 73;
YAW

Sutro, Alfred 1863-1933 .... **TCLC 6**
See also CA 105; 185; DLB 10; RGEL

Sutton, Henry
See Slavitt, David R(ytman)

Suzuki, D. T.
See Suzuki, Daisetz Teitaro

Suzuki, Daisetz T.
See Suzuki, Daisetz Teitaro

Suzuki, Daisetz Teitaro
1870-1966 .... **TCLC 109**
See also CA 121; 111; MTCW 1, 2

Suzuki, Teitaro
See Suzuki, Daisetz Teitaro

Svevo, Italo .... **TCLC 2, 35; SSC 25**
See also Schmitz, Aron Hector
See also RGWL

Swados, Elizabeth (A.) 1951- .... **CLC 12**
See also CA 97-100; CANR 49; INT 97-
100

Swados, Harvey 1920-1972 .... **CLC 5**
See also CA 5-8R; 37-40R; CANR 6; DLB
2

Swan, Gladys 1934- .... **CLC 69**
See also CA 101; CANR 17, 39

Swanson, Logan
See Matheson, Richard (Burton)

Swarthout, Glendon (Fred)
1918-1992 .... **CLC 35**
See also CA 1-4R; 139; CANR 1, 47; SATA
26; TCWW 2; YAW

Sweet, Sarah C.
See Jewett, (Theodora) Sarah Orne

Swenson, May 1919-1989 ...... **CLC 4, 14, 61,**
106; DA; DAB; DAC; DAM MST,
POET; PC 14
See also AMWS 4; CA 5-8R; 130; CANR
36, 61; DLB 5; GLL 2; MTCW 1, 2;
SATA 15; WP

Swift, Augustus
See Lovecraft, H(oward) P(hillips)

Swift, Graham (Colin) 1949- ...... **CLC 41, 88**
See also BRWS 5; CA 117; 122; CANR 46,
71; CN; DLB 194; MTCW 2; RGSF

Swift, Jonathan 1667-1745 ..... **LC 1, 42; DA;**
DAB; DAC; DAM MST, NOV, POET;
PC 9; WLC
See also CDBLB 1660-1789; CLR 53;
DA3; DLB 39, 95, 101; NFS 6; RGEL;
SATA 19

Swinburne, Algernon Charles
1837-1909 .... **TCLC 8, 36; DA; DAB;**
DAC; DAM MST, POET; PC 24; WLC
See also CA 105; 140; CDBLB 1832-1890;
DA3; DLB 35, 57; PAB; RGEL

Swinfen, Ann .... **CLC 34**

Swinnerton, Frank Arthur
1884-1982 .... **CLC 31**
See also CA 108; DLB 34

Swithen, John
See King, Stephen (Edwin)

Sylvia
See Ashton-Warner, Sylvia (Constance)

Symmes, Robert Edward
See Duncan, Robert (Edward)

Symonds, John Addington
1840-1893 .... **NCLC 34**
See also DLB 57, 144

Symons, Arthur 1865-1945 .... **TCLC 11**
See also CA 107; 189; DLB 19, 57, 149;
RGEL

Symons, Julian (Gustave)
1912-1994 .... **CLC 2, 14, 32**
See also CA 49-52; 147; CAAS 3; CANR
3, 33, 59; CMW; DLB 87, 155; DLBY
92; MSW; MTCW 1

Synge, (Edmund) J(ohn) M(illington)
1871-1909 . **TCLC 6, 37; DAM DRAM;**
DC 2
See also BRW; CA 104; 141; CDBLB 1890-
1914; DLB 10, 19; RGEL

Syruc, J.
See Milosz, Czeslaw

Szirtes, George 1948- .... **CLC 46**
See also CA 109; CANR 27, 61; CP

Szymborska, Wislawa 1923- .... **CLC 99**
See also CA 154; CANR 91; CWP; CWW
2; DA3; DLB 232; DLBY 96; MTCW 2

T. O., Nik
See Annensky, Innokenty (Fyodorovich)

Tabori, George 1914- .... **CLC 19**
See also CA 49-52; CANR 4, 69; CBD; CD

Tagore, Rabindranath 1861-1941 ... **TCLC 3,**
53; DAM DRAM, POET; PC 8
See also CA 104; 120; DA3; MTCW 1, 2;
RGEL; RGSF; RGWL

Taine, Hippolyte Adolphe
1828-1893 .... **NCLC 15**
See also EW; GFL 1789 to the Present

Talese, Gay 1932- .... **CLC 37**
See also AITN 1; CA 1-4R; CANR 9, 58;
DLB 185; INT CANR-9; MTCW 1, 2

Tallent, Elizabeth (Ann) 1954- .... **CLC 45**
See also CA 117; CANR 72; DLB 130

Tally, Ted 1952- .... **CLC 42**
See also CA 120; 124; CAD; CD; INT 124

Talvik, Heiti 1904-1947 .... **TCLC 87**

Tamayo y Baus, Manuel
1829-1898 .... **NCLC 1**

Tammsaare, A(nton) H(ansen)
1878-1940 .... **TCLC 27**
See also CA 164; DLB 220

Tam'si, Tchicaya U
See Tchicaya, Gerald Felix

Tan, Amy (Ruth) 1952- . **CLC 59, 120; DAM**
MULT, NOV, POP
See also AAYA 9; BEST 89:3; CA 136;
CANR 54; CDALBS; CN; CPW 1; DA3;
DLB 173; FW; MTCW 2; NFS 1; RGAL;
SATA 75; SSFS 9; YAW

Tandem, Felix
See Spitteler, Carl (Friedrich Georg)

Author Index

Valera y Alcala-Galiano, Juan
1824-1905 .... **TCLC 10**
See also CA 106

Valery, (Ambroise) Paul (Toussaint Jules)
1871-1945 ... **TCLC 4, 15; DAM POET;
PC 9**
See also CA 104; 122; DA3; EW; GFL 1789
to the Present; MTCW 1, 2; RGWL

Valle-Inclan, Ramon (Maria) del
1866-1936 .... **TCLC 5; DAM MULT;
HLC 2**
See also CA 106; 153; CANR 80; DLB 134;
EW; HW 2; RGSF; RGWL

Vallejo, Antonio Buero
See Buero Vallejo, Antonio

Vallejo, Cesar (Abraham)
1892-1938 .. **TCLC 3, 56; DAM MULT;
HLC 2**
See also CA 105; 153; HW 1; LAW; RGWL

Valles, Jules 1832-1885 .... **NCLC 71**
See also DLB 123; GFL 1789 to the Present

Vallette, Marguerite Eymery
1860-1953 .... **TCLC 67**
See also CA 182; DLB 123, 192

Valle Y Pena, Ramon del
See Valle-Incl

Van Ash, Cay 1918- .... **CLC 34**

Vanbrugh, SirJohn 1664-1726 . **LC 21; DAM
DRAM**
See also DLB 80; IDTP; RGEL

Van Campen, Karl
See Campbell, John W(ood, Jr.)

Vance, Gerald
See Silverberg, Robert

Vance, Jack .... **CLC 35**
See also Vance, John Holbrook
See also DLB 8; SCFW 2

Vance, John Holbrook 1916-
See Queen, Ellery; Vance, Jack
See also CA 29-32R; CANR 17, 65; CMW;
FANT; MTCW 1; SFW

**Van Den Bogarde, Derek Jules Gaspard
Ulric Niven** 1921-1999 .... **CLC 14**
See also CA 77-80; 179; DLB 19

Vandenburgh, Jane .... **CLC 59**
See also CA 168

Vanderhaeghe, Guy 1951- .... **CLC 41**
See also CA 113; CANR 72

van der Post, Laurens (Jan)
1906-1996 .... **CLC 5**
See also AFW; CA 5-8R; 155; CANR 35;
CN; DLB 204; RGEL

van de Wetering, Janwillem 1931- ... **CLC 47**
See also CA 49-52; CANR 4, 62, 90; CMW

Van Dine, S. S. .... **TCLC 23**
See also Wright, Willard Huntington

Van Doren, Carl (Clinton)
1885-1950 .... **TCLC 18**
See also CA 111; 168

Van Doren, Mark 1894-1972 .... **CLC 6, 10**
See also CA 1-4R; 37-40R; CANR 3; DLB
45; MTCW 1, 2; RGAL

Van Druten, John (William)
1901-1957 .... **TCLC 2**
See also CA 104; 161; DLB 10; RGAL

Van Duyn, Mona (Jane) 1921- ...... **CLC 3, 7,
63, 116; DAM POET**
See also CA 9-12R; CANR 7, 38, 60; CP;
CWP; DLB 5

Van Dyne, Edith
See Baum, L(yman) Frank

van Itallie, Jean-Claude 1936- .... **CLC 3**
See also CA 45-48; CAAS 2; CAD; CANR
1, 48; CD; DLB 7

van Ostaijen, Paul 1896-1928 .... **TCLC 33**
See also CA 163

Van Peebles, Melvin 1932- .... **CLC 2, 20;
DAM MULT**
See also BW 2, 3; CA 85-88; CANR 27,
67, 82

van Schendel, Arthur(-Francois-emile)
1874-1946 .... **TCLC 56**

Vansittart, Peter 1920- .... **CLC 42**
See also CA 1-4R; CANR 3, 49, 90; CN;
RHW

Van Vechten, Carl 1880-1964 .... **CLC 33**
See also AMWS 2; CA 183; 89-92; DLB 4,
9, 51; RGAL

van Vogt, A(lfred) E(lton) 1912-2000 . **CLC 1**
See also CA 21-24R; 190; CANR 28; DLB
8; SATA 14; SATA-Obit 124; SFW

Varda, Agnes 1928- .... **CLC 16**
See also CA 116; 122

Vargas Llosa, (Jorge) Mario (Pedro)
1936- .... **CLC 3, 6, 9, 10, 15, 31, 42, 85;
DA; DAB; DAC; DAM MST, MULT,
NOV; HLC 2**
See also CA 73-76; CANR 18, 32, 42, 67;
DA3; DLB 145; DNFS; HW 1, 2; LAW;
MTCW 1, 2; RGWL

Vasiliu, Gheorghe
See Bacovia, George
See also CA 123; 189; DLB 220

Vassa, Gustavus
See Equiano, Olaudah

Vassilikos, Vassilis 1933- .... **CLC 4, 8**
See also CA 81-84; CANR 75

Vaughan, Henry 1621-1695 .... **LC 27**
See also DLB 131; PAB; RGEL

Vaughn, Stephanie .... **CLC 62**

Vazov, Ivan (Minchov) 1850-1921 . **TCLC 25**
See also CA 121; 167; DLB 147

Veblen, Thorstein B(unde)
1857-1929 .... **TCLC 31**
See also AMWS 1; CA 115; 165

Vega, Lope de 1562-1635 .... **LC 23; HLCS 2**
See also RGWL

Vendler, Helen (Hennessy) 1933- ... **CLC 138**
See also CA 41-44R; CANR 25, 72; MTCW
1, 2

Venison, Alfred
See Pound, Ezra (Weston Loomis)

Verdi, Marie de
See Mencken, H(enry) L(ouis)

Verdu, Matilde
See Cela, Camilo Jos

Verga, Giovanni (Carmelo)
1840-1922 .... **TCLC 3; SSC 21**
See also CA 104; 123; EW; RGSF; RGWL

Vergil 70B.C.-19B.C. .... **CMLC 9, 40; DA;
DAB; DAC; DAM MST, POET; PC
12; WLCS**
See also Virgil
See also DA3; DLB 211; EFS 1

Verhaeren, emile (Adolphe Gustave)
1855-1916 .... **TCLC 12**
See also CA 109; GFL 1789 to the Present

Verlaine, Paul (Marie) 1844-1896 .. **NCLC 2,
51; DAM POET; PC 2, 32**
See also EW; GFL 1789 to the Present;
RGWL

Verne, Jules (Gabriel) 1828-1905 ... **TCLC 6,
52**
See also AAYA 16; CA 110; 131; DA3;
DLB 123; GFL 1789 to the Present;
JRDA; MAICYA; RGWL; SATA 21;
SCFW; SFW; WCH

Verus, Marcus Annius
See Antoninus, Marcus Aurelius

Very, Jones 1813-1880 .... **NCLC 9**
See also DLB 1; RGAL

Vesaas, Tarjei 1897-1970 .... **CLC 48**
See also CA 190; 29-32R

Vialis, Gaston
See Simenon, Georges (Jacques Christian)

Vian, Boris 1920-1959 .... **TCLC 9**
See also CA 106; 164; DLB 72; GFL 1789
to the Present; MTCW 2; RGWL

Viaud, (Louis Marie) Julien 1850-1923
See Loti, Pierre
See also CA 107

Vicar, Henry
See Felsen, Henry Gregor

Vicker, Angus
See Felsen, Henry Gregor

Vidal, Gore 1925- ...... **CLC 2, 4, 6, 8, 10, 22,
33, 72, 142; DAM NOV, POP**
See also Box, Edgar
See also AITN 1; AMWS 4; BEST 90:2;
CA 5-8R; CAD; CANR 13, 45, 65, 100;
CD; CDALBS; CN; CPW; DA3; DFS 2;
DLB 6, 152; INT CANR-13; MTCW 1,
2; RGAL; RHW

Viereck, Peter (Robert Edwin)
1916- .... **CLC 4; PC 27**
See also CA 1-4R; CANR 1, 47; CP; DLB
5; PFS 9

Vigny, Alfred (Victor) de
1797-1863 . **NCLC 7, 102; DAM POET;
PC 26**
See also DLB 119, 192; EW; GFL 1789 to
the Present; RGWL

Vilakazi, Benedict Wallet
1906-1947 .... **TCLC 37**
See also CA 168

Villa, Jose Garcia 1914-1997 .... **PC 22**
See also AAL; CA 25-28R; CANR 12

Villarreal, Jose Antonio 1924-
See also CA 133; CANR 93; DAM MULT;
DLB 82; HLC 2; HW 1; RGAL

Villaurrutia, Xavier 1903-1950 ...... **TCLC 80**
See also CA 192; HW 1

Villehardouin, Geoffroi de
1150(?)-1218(?) .... **CMLC 38**

**Villiers de l'Isle Adam, Jean Marie Mathias
Philippe Auguste** 1838-1889 ... **NCLC 3;
SSC 14**
See also DLB 123; GFL 1789 to the Present;
RGSF

Villon, Francois 1431-1463(?) . **LC 62; PC 13**
See also DLB 208; EW; RGWL

Vine, Barbara .... **CLC 50**
See also Rendell, Ruth (Barbara)
See also BEST 90:4

Vinge, Joan (Carol) D(ennison)
1948- .... **CLC 30; SSC 24**
See also AAYA 32; CA 93-96; CANR 72;
SATA 36, 113; SFW; YAW

Viola, Herman J(oseph) 1938- .... **CLC 70**
See also CA 61-64; CANR 8, 23, 48, 91

Violis, G.
See Simenon, Georges (Jacques Christian)

Viramontes, Helena Maria 1954-
See also CA 159; DLB 122; HLCS 2; HW
2

Virgil
See Vergil
See also RGWL; WP

Visconti, Luchino 1906-1976 .... **CLC 16**
See also CA 81-84; 65-68; CANR 39

Vittorini, Elio 1908-1966 .... **CLC 6, 9, 14**
See also CA 133; 25-28R; RGWL

Vivekananda, Swami 1863-1902 .... **TCLC 88**

Vizenor, Gerald Robert 1934- .... **CLC 103;
DAM MULT**
See also CA 13-16R; CAAS 22; CANR 5,
21, 44, 67; DLB 175, 227; MTCW 2;
NNAL; TCWW 2

Vizinczey, Stephen 1933- .... **CLC 40**
See also CA 128; CCA 1; INT 128

Vliet, R(ussell) G(ordon)
1929-1984 .... **CLC 22**
See also CA 37-40R; 112; CANR 18

Warner, Marina 1946- .... **CLC 59**
See also CA 65-68; CANR 21, 55; CN;
DLB 194

Warner, Rex (Ernest) 1905-1986 ...... **CLC 45**
See also CA 89-92; 119; DLB 15; RGEL;
RHW

Warner, Susan (Bogert)
1819-1885 .... **NCLC 31**
See also DLB 3, 42, 239

Warner, Sylvia (Constance) Ashton
See Ashton-Warner, Sylvia (Constance)

Warner, Sylvia Townsend
1893-1978 .... **CLC 7, 19; SSC 23**
See also BRWS 7; CA 61-64; 77-80; CANR
16, 60; DLB 34, 139; FANT; FW; MTCW
1, 2; RGEL; RGSF; RHW

Warren, Mercy Otis 1728-1814 ..... **NCLC 13**
See also DLB 31, 200; RGAL

Warren, Robert Penn 1905-1989 .. **CLC 1, 4,
6, 8, 10, 13, 18, 39, 53, 59; DA; DAB;
DAC; DAM MST, NOV, POET; SSC 4;
WLC**
See also AITN 1; CA 13-16R; 129; CANR
10, 47; CDALB 1968-1988; DA3; DLB
2, 48, 152; DLBY 80, 89; INT CANR-10;
MTCW 1, 2; RGAL; RGSF; RHW; SATA
46; SATA-Obit 63; SSFS 8

Warshofsky, Isaac
See Singer, Isaac Bashevis

Warton, Thomas 1728-1790 ..... **LC 15; DAM
POET**
See also DLB 104, 109; RGEL

Waruk, Kona
See Harris, (Theodore) Wilson

Warung, Price .... **TCLC 45**
See also Astley, William
See also RGEL

Warwick, Jarvis
See Garner, Hugh
See also CCA 1

Washington, Alex
See Harris, Mark

Washington, Booker T(aliaferro)
1856-1915 ...... **TCLC 10; BLC 3; DAM
MULT**
See also BW 1; CA 114; 125; DA3; RGAL;
SATA 28

Washington, George 1732-1799 .... **LC 25**
See also DLB 31

Wassermann, (Karl) Jakob
1873-1934 .... **TCLC 6**
See also CA 104; 163; DLB 66

Wasserstein, Wendy 1950- .. **CLC 32, 59, 90;
DAM DRAM; DC 4**
See also CA 121; 129; CABS 3; CAD;
CANR 53, 75; CD; CWD; DA3; DFS 5;
DLB 228; FW; INT 129; MTCW 2; SATA
94

Waterhouse, Keith (Spencer) 1929- . **CLC 47**
See also CA 5-8R; CANR 38, 67; CBD;
CN; DLB 13, 15; MTCW 1, 2

Waters, Frank (Joseph) 1902-1995 .. **CLC 88**
See also CA 5-8R; 149; CAAS 13; CANR
3, 18, 63; DLB 212; DLBY 86; RGAL;
TCWW 2

Waters, Mary C. .... **CLC 70**

Waters, Roger 1944- .... **CLC 35**

Watkins, Frances Ellen
See Harper, Frances Ellen Watkins

Watkins, Gerrold
See Malzberg, Barry N(athaniel)

Watkins, Gloria Jean 1952(?)-
See hooks, bell
See also BW 2; CA 143; CANR 87; MTCW
2; SATA 115

Watkins, Paul 1964- .... **CLC 55**
See also CA 132; CANR 62, 98

Watkins, Vernon Phillips
1906-1967 .... **CLC 43**
See also CA 9-10; 25-28R; CAP 1; DLB
20; RGEL

Watson, Irving S.
See Mencken, H(enry) L(ouis)

Watson, John H.
See Farmer, Philip Jose

Watson, Richard F.
See Silverberg, Robert

Waugh, Auberon (Alexander)
1939-2001 .... **CLC 7**
See also CA 45-48; 192; CANR 6, 22, 92;
DLB 14, 194

Waugh, Evelyn (Arthur St. John)
1903-1966 .. **CLC 1, 3, 8, 13, 19, 27, 44,
107; DA; DAB; DAC; DAM MST,
NOV, POP; SSC 41; WLC**
See also BRW; CA 85-88; 25-28R; CANR
22; CDBLB 1914-1945; DA3; DLB 15,
162, 195; MTCW 1, 2; RGEL; RGSF

Waugh, Harriet 1944- .... **CLC 6**
See also CA 85-88; CANR 22

Ways, C. R.
See Blount, Roy (Alton), Jr.

Waystaff, Simon
See Swift, Jonathan

Webb, Beatrice (Martha Potter)
1858-1943 .... **TCLC 22**
See also CA 117; 162; DLB 190; FW

Webb, Charles (Richard) 1939- .... **CLC 7**
See also CA 25-28R

Webb, James H(enry), Jr. 1946- ...... **CLC 22**
See also CA 81-84

Webb, Mary Gladys (Meredith)
1881-1927 .... **TCLC 24**
See also CA 182; 123; DLB 34; FW

Webb, Mrs. Sidney
See Webb, Beatrice (Martha Potter)

Webb, Phyllis 1927- .... **CLC 18**
See also CA 104; CANR 23; CCA 1; CP;
CWP; DLB 53

Webb, Sidney (James) 1859-1947 .. **TCLC 22**
See also CA 117; 163; DLB 190

Webber, Andrew Lloyd .... **CLC 21**
See also Lloyd Webber, Andrew
See also DFS 7

Weber, Lenora Mattingly
1895-1971 .... **CLC 12**
See also CA 19-20; 29-32R; CAP 1; SATA
2; SATA-Obit 26

Weber, Max 1864-1920 .... **TCLC 69**
See also CA 109; 189

Webster, John 1580(?)-1634(?) ... **LC 33; DA;
DAB; DAC; DAM DRAM, MST; DC
2; WLC**
See also BRW; CDBLB Before 1660; DLB
58; IDTP; RGEL

Webster, Noah 1758-1843 .... **NCLC 30**
See also DLB 1, 37, 42, 43, 73

Wedekind, (Benjamin) Frank(lin)
1864-1918 .... **TCLC 7; DAM DRAM**
See also CA 104; 153; DLB 118; EW;
RGWL

Wehr, Demaris .... **CLC 65**

Weidman, Jerome 1913-1998 .... **CLC 7**
See also AITN 2; CA 1-4R; 171; CAD;
CANR 1; DLB 28

Weil, Simone (Adolphine)
1909-1943 .... **TCLC 23**
See also CA 117; 159; EW; FW; GFL 1789
to the Present; MTCW 2

Weininger, Otto 1880-1903 .... **TCLC 84**

Weinstein, Nathan
See West, Nathanael

Weinstein, Nathan von Wallenstein
See West, Nathanael

Weir, Peter (Lindsay) 1944- .... **CLC 20**
See also CA 113; 123

Weiss, Peter (Ulrich) 1916-1982 .. **CLC 3, 15,
51; DAM DRAM**
See also CA 45-48; 106; CANR 3; DFS 3;
DLB 69, 124; RGWL

Weiss, Theodore (Russell) 1916- ... **CLC 3, 8,
14**
See also CA 9-12R; CAAE 189; CAAS 2;
CANR 46, 94; CP; DLB 5

Welch, (Maurice) Denton
1915-1948 .... **TCLC 22**
See also CA 121; 148; RGEL

Welch, James 1940- ..... **CLC 6, 14, 52; DAM
MULT, POP**
See also CA 85-88; CANR 42, 66; CN; CP;
CPW; DLB 175; NNAL; RGAL; TCWW
2

Weldon, Fay 1931- . **CLC 6, 9, 11, 19, 36, 59,
122; DAM POP**
See also BRWS 4; CA 21-24R; CANR 16,
46, 63, 97; CDBLB 1960 to Present; CN;
CPW; DLB 14, 194; FW; HGG; INT
CANR-16; MTCW 1, 2; RGEL; RGSF

Wellek, Rene 1903-1995 .... **CLC 28**
See also CA 5-8R; 150; CAAS 7; CANR 8;
DLB 63; INT CANR-8

Weller, Michael 1942- .... **CLC 10, 53**
See also CA 85-88; CAD; CD

Weller, Paul 1958- .... **CLC 26**

Wellershoff, Dieter 1925- .... **CLC 46**
See also CA 89-92; CANR 16, 37

Welles, (George) Orson 1915-1985 .. **CLC 20,
80**
See also AAYA 40; CA 93-96; 117

Wellman, John McDowell 1945-
See Wellman, Mac
See also CA 166; CD

Wellman, Mac .... **CLC 65**
See also Wellman, John McDowell; Well-
man, John McDowell
See also CAD; RGAL

Wellman, Manly Wade 1903-1986 ... **CLC 49**
See also CA 1-4R; 118; CANR 6, 16, 44;
FANT; SATA 6; SATA-Obit 47; SFW

Wells, Carolyn 1869(?)-1942 .... **TCLC 35**
See also CA 113; 185; CMW; DLB 11

Wells, H(erbert) G(eorge)
1866-1946 . **TCLC 6, 12, 19; DA; DAB;
DAC; DAM MST, NOV; SSC 6; WLC**
See also AAYA 18; BRW; CA 110; 121;
CDBLB 1914-1945; CLR 64; DA3; DLB
34, 70, 156, 178; HGG; MTCW 1, 2;
RGEL; RGSF; SATA 20; SFW; SSFS 3;
SUFW; WCH; YAW

Wells, Rosemary 1943- .... **CLC 12**
See also AAYA 13; CA 85-88; CANR 48;
CLR 16, 69; CWRI; MAICYA; SAAS 1;
SATA 18, 69, 114; YAW

Welsh, Irvine 1958- .... **CLC 144**
See also CA 173

Welty, Eudora 1909-2001 .... **CLC 1, 2, 5, 14,
22, 33, 105; DA; DAB; DAC; DAM
MST, NOV; SSC 1, 27; WLC**
See also CA 9-12R; CABS 1; CANR 32,
65; CDALB 1941-1968; CN; CSW; DA3;
DLB 2, 102, 143; DLBD 12; DLBY 87;
HGG; MTCW 1, 2; RGAL; RGSF; RHW;
SSFS 2, 10

Wen I-to 1899-1946 .... **TCLC 28**

Wentworth, Robert
See Hamilton, Edmond

Werfel, Franz (Viktor) 1890-1945 ... **TCLC 8**
See also CA 104; 161; DLB 81, 124;
RGWL

Wergeland, Henrik Arnold
1808-1845 .... **NCLC 5**

Wersba, Barbara 1932- .... **CLC 30**
See also AAYA 2, 30; CA 29-32R, 182;
CAAE 182; CANR 16, 38; CLR 3; DLB
52; JRDA; MAICYA; SAAS 2; SATA 1,
58; SATA-Essay 103; YAW

Wilder, Samuel 1906-
See Wilder, Billy
See also CA 89-92

Wilder, Stephen
See Marlowe, Stephen

Wilder, Thornton (Niven)
1897-1975 .. CLC 1, 5, 6, 10, 15, 35, 82;
DA; DAB; DAC; DAM DRAM, MST,
NOV; DC 1; WLC
See also AAYA 29; AITN 2; AMW; CA 13-
16R; 61-64; CANR 40; CDALBS; DA3;
DFS 1, 4; DLB 4, 7, 9, 228; DLBY 97;
MTCW 1, 2; RGAL; RHW; WYAS 1

Wilding, Michael 1942- .... CLC 73
See also CA 104; CANR 24, 49; CN; RGSF

Wiley, Richard 1944- .... CLC 44
See also CA 121; 129; CANR 71

Wilhelm, Kate .... CLC 7
See also Wilhelm, Katie (Gertrude)
See also AAYA 20; CAAS 5; DLB 8; INT
CANR-17; SCFW 2

Wilhelm, Katie (Gertrude) 1928-
See Wilhelm, Kate
See also CA 37-40R; CANR 17, 36, 60, 94;
MTCW 1; SFW

Wilkins, Mary
See Freeman, Mary E(leanor) Wilkins

Willard, Nancy 1936- .... CLC 7, 37
See also CA 89-92; CANR 10, 39, 68; CLR
5; CWP; CWRI; DLB 5, 52; FANT; MAI-
CYA; MTCW 1; SATA 37, 71; SATA-
Brief 30

William of Ockham 1290-1349 ..... CMLC 32

Williams, Ben Ames 1889-1953 ..... TCLC 89
See also CA 183; DLB 102

Williams, C(harles) K(enneth)
1936- .... CLC 33, 56, 148; DAM POET
See also CA 37-40R; CAAS 26; CANR 57;
CP; DLB 5

Williams, Charles
See Collier, James Lincoln

Williams, Charles (Walter Stansby)
1886-1945 .... TCLC 1, 11
See also CA 104; 163; DLB 100, 153;
FANT; RGEL; SUFW

Williams, (George) Emlyn
1905-1987 .... CLC 15; DAM DRAM
See also CA 104; 123; CANR 36; DLB 10,
77; MTCW 1

Williams, Hank 1923-1953 .... TCLC 81

Williams, Hugo 1942- .... CLC 42
See also CA 17-20R; CANR 45; CP; DLB
40

Williams, J. Walker
See Wodehouse, P(elham) G(renville)

Williams, John A(lfred) 1925- ..... CLC 5, 13;
BLC 3; DAM MULT
See also AFAW 2; BW 2, 3; CA 53-56;
CAAS 3; CANR 6, 26, 51; CN; CSW;
DLB 2, 33; INT CANR-6; RGAL; SFW

Williams, Jonathan (Chamberlain)
1929- .... CLC 13
See also CA 9-12R; CAAS 12; CANR 8;
CP; DLB 5

Williams, Joy 1944- .... CLC 31
See also CA 41-44R; CANR 22, 48, 97

Williams, Norman 1952- .... CLC 39
See also CA 118

Williams, Sherley Anne 1944-1999 . CLC 89;
BLC 3; DAM MULT, POET
See also AFAW 2; BW 2, 3; CA 73-76; 185;
CANR 25, 82; DLB 41; INT CANR-25;
SATA 78; SATA-Obit 116

Williams, Shirley
See Williams, Sherley Anne

Williams, Tennessee 1914-1983 . CLC 1, 2, 5,
7, 8, 11, 15, 19, 30, 39, 45, 71, 111; DA;
DAB; DAC; DAM DRAM, MST; DC
4; WLC
See also AAYA 31; AITN 1, 2; CA 5-8R;
108; CABS 3; CAD; CANR 31; CDALB
1941-1968; DA3; DFS 1,3,7,12; DLB 7;
DLBD 4; DLBY 83; GLL 1; MTCW 1, 2;
RGAL

Williams, Thomas (Alonzo)
1926-1990 .... CLC 14
See also CA 1-4R; 132; CANR 2

Williams, William C.
See Williams, William Carlos

Williams, William Carlos
1883-1963 .... CLC 1, 2, 5, 9, 13, 22, 42,
67; DA; DAB; DAC; DAM MST,
POET; PC 7; SSC 31
See also CA 89-92; CANR 34; CDALB
1917-1929; DA3; DLB 4, 16, 54, 86;
MTCW 1, 2; PAB; PFS 1, 6, 11; RGAL;
RGSF; WP

Williamson, David (Keith) 1942- ..... CLC 56
See also CA 103; CANR 41; CD

Williamson, Ellen Douglas 1905-1984
See Douglas, Ellen
See also CA 17-20R; 114; CANR 39

Williamson, Jack .... CLC 29
See also Williamson, John Stewart
See also CAAS 8; DLB 8; SCFW 2

Williamson, John Stewart 1908-
See Williamson, Jack
See also CA 17-20R; CANR 23, 70; SFW

Willie, Frederick
See Lovecraft, H(oward) P(hillips)

Willingham, Calder (Baynard, Jr.)
1922-1995 .... CLC 5, 51
See also CA 5-8R; 147; CANR 3; CSW;
DLB 2, 44; IDFW 3; MTCW 1

Willis, Charles
See Clarke, Arthur C(harles)

Willy
See Colette, (Sidonie-Gabrielle)

Willy, Colette
See Colette, (Sidonie-Gabrielle)
See also GLL 1

Wilson, A(ndrew) N(orman) 1950- .. CLC 33
See also BRWS 6; CA 112; 122; CN; DLB
14, 155, 194; MTCW 2

Wilson, Angus (Frank Johnstone)
1913-1991 . CLC 2, 3, 5, 25, 34; SSC 21
See also BRWS 1; CA 5-8R; 134; CANR
21; DLB 15, 139, 155; MTCW 1, 2;
RGEL; RGSF

Wilson, August 1945- ... CLC 39, 50, 63, 118;
BLC 3; DA; DAB; DAC; DAM
DRAM, MST, MULT; DC 2; WLCS
See also AAYA 16; AFAW 2; AMWS 8; BW
2, 3; CA 115; 122; CAD; CANR 42, 54,
76; CD; DA3; DFS 3,7; DLB 228; MTCW
1, 2; RGAL

Wilson, Brian 1942- .... CLC 12

Wilson, Colin 1931- .... CLC 3, 14
See also CA 1-4R; CAAS 5; CANR 1, 22,
33, 77; CMW; CN; DLB 14, 194; HGG;
MTCW 1; SFW

Wilson, Dirk
See Pohl, Frederik

Wilson, Edmund 1895-1972 .. CLC 1, 2, 3, 8,
24
See also CA 1-4R; 37-40R; CANR 1, 46;
DLB 63; MTCW 1, 2; RGAL

Wilson, Ethel Davis (Bryant)
1888(?)-1980 .... CLC 13; DAC; DAM
POET
See also CA 102; DLB 68; MTCW 1;
RGEL

Wilson, Harriet E. Adams
1827(?)-1863(?) .... NCLC 78; BLC 3;
DAM MULT
See also DLB 50

Wilson, John 1785-1854 .... NCLC 5

Wilson, John (Anthony) Burgess 1917-1993
See Burgess, Anthony
See also CA 1-4R; 143; CANR 2, 46; DAC;
DAM NOV; DA3; MTCW 1, 2

Wilson, Lanford 1937- .... CLC 7, 14, 36;
DAM DRAM
See also CA 17-20R; CABS 3; CAD; CANR
45, 96; CD; DFS 4, 9, 12; DLB 7

Wilson, Robert M. 1944- .... CLC 7, 9
See also CA 49-52; CAD; CANR 2, 41; CD;
MTCW 1

Wilson, Robert McLiam 1964- .... CLC 59
See also CA 132

Wilson, Sloan 1920- .... CLC 32
See also CA 1-4R; CANR 1, 44; CN

Wilson, Snoo 1948- .... CLC 33
See also CA 69-72; CBD; CD

Wilson, William S(mith) 1932- .... CLC 49
See also CA 81-84

Wilson, (Thomas) Woodrow
1856-1924 .... TCLC 79
See also CA 166; DLB 47

Wilson and Warnke eds. .... CLC 65

Winchilsea, Anne (Kingsmill) Finch
1661-1720
See Finch, Anne
See also RGEL

Windham, Basil
See Wodehouse, P(elham) G(renville)

Wingrove, David (John) 1954- .... CLC 68
See also CA 133; SFW

Winnemucca, Sarah 1844-1891 .... NCLC 79;
DAM MULT
See also DLB 175; NNAL; RGAL

Winstanley, Gerrard 1609-1676 .... LC 52

Wintergreen, Jane
See Duncan, Sara Jeannette

Winters, Janet Lewis .... CLC 41
See also Lewis, Janet
See also DLBY 87

Winters, (Arthur) Yvor 1900-1968 .... CLC 4,
8, 32
See also AMWS 2; CA 11-12; 25-28R; CAP
1; DLB 48; MTCW 1; RGAL

Winterson, Jeanette 1959- .... CLC 64; DAM
POP
See also BRWS 4; CA 136; CANR 58; CN;
CPW; DA3; DLB 207; FANT; FW; GLL
1; MTCW 2; RHW

Winthrop, John 1588-1649 .... LC 31
See also DLB 24, 30

Wirth, Louis 1897-1952 .... TCLC 92

Wiseman, Frederick 1930- .... CLC 20
See also CA 159

Wister, Owen 1860-1938 .... TCLC 21
See also CA 108; 162; DLB 9, 78, 186;
RGAL; SATA 62; TCWW 2

Witkacy
See Witkiewicz, Stanislaw Ignacy

Witkiewicz, Stanislaw Ignacy
1885-1939 .... TCLC 8
See also CA 105; 162; DLB 215; RGWL;
SFW

Wittgenstein, Ludwig (Josef Johann)
1889-1951 .... TCLC 59
See also CA 113; 164; MTCW 2

Wittig, Monique 1935(?)- .... CLC 22
See also CA 116; 135; CWW 2; DLB 83;
FW; GLL 1

Wittlin, Jozef 1896-1976 .... CLC 25
See also CA 49-52; 65-68; CANR 3

Yevtushenko, Yevgeny (Alexandrovich)
1933- .. **CLC 1, 3, 13, 26, 51, 126; DAM POET**
See also Evtushenko, Evgenii Aleksandrovich
See also CA 81-84; CANR 33, 54; CWW 2; MTCW 1

Yezierska, Anzia 1885(?)-1970 .... **CLC 46**
See also CA 126; 89-92; DLB 28, 221; FW; MTCW 1; RGAL

Yglesias, Helen 1915- .... **CLC 7, 22**
See also CA 37-40R; CAAS 20; CANR 15, 65, 95; CN; INT CANR-15; MTCW 1

Yokomitsu, Riichi 1898-1947 .... **TCLC 47**
See also CA 170

Yonge, Charlotte (Mary)
1823-1901 .... **TCLC 48**
See also CA 109; 163; DLB 18, 163; RGEL; SATA 17; WCH

York, Jeremy
See Creasey, John

York, Simon
See Heinlein, Robert A(nson)

Yorke, Henry Vincent 1905-1974 ..... **CLC 13**
See also Green, Henry
See also CA 85-88; 49-52

Yosano Akiko 1878-1942 .... **TCLC 59; PC 11**
See also CA 161

Yoshimoto, Banana .... **CLC 84**
See also Yoshimoto, Mahoko
See also NFS 7

Yoshimoto, Mahoko 1964-
See Yoshimoto, Banana
See also CA 144; CANR 98

Young, Al(bert James) 1939- . **CLC 19; BLC 3; DAM MULT**
See also BW 2, 3; CA 29-32R; CANR 26, 65; CN; CP; DLB 33

Young, Andrew (John) 1885-1971 ...... **CLC 5**
See also CA 5-8R; CANR 7, 29; RGEL

Young, Collier
See Bloch, Robert (Albert)

Young, Edward 1683-1765 .... **LC 3, 40**
See also DLB 95; RGEL

Young, Marguerite (Vivian)
1909-1995 .... **CLC 82**
See also CA 13-16; 150; CAP 1; CN

Young, Neil 1945- .... **CLC 17**
See also CA 110; CCA 1

Young Bear, Ray A. 1950- ..... **CLC 94; DAM MULT**
See also CA 146; DLB 175; NNAL

Yourcenar, Marguerite 1903-1987 ... **CLC 19, 38, 50, 87; DAM NOV**
See also CA 69-72; CANR 23, 60, 93; DLB 72; DLBY 88; GFL 1789 to the Present; GLL 1; MTCW 1, 2; RGWL

Yuan, Chu 340(?)B.C.-278(?)B.C. . **CMLC 36**

Yurick, Sol 1925- .... **CLC 6**
See also CA 13-16R; CANR 25; CN

Zabolotsky, Nikolai Alekseevich
1903-1958 .... **TCLC 52**
See also CA 116; 164

Zagajewski, Adam 1945- .... **PC 27**
See also CA 186; DLB 232

Zalygin, Sergei -2000 .... **CLC 59**

Zamiatin, Evgenii
See Zamyatin, Evgeny Ivanovich
See also RGSF; RGWL

Zamiatin, Yevgenii
See Zamyatin, Evgeny Ivanovich

Zamora, Bernice (B. Ortiz) 1938- .. **CLC 89; DAM MULT; HLC 2**
See also CA 151; CANR 80; DLB 82; HW 1, 2

Zamyatin, Evgeny Ivanovich
1884-1937 .... **TCLC 8, 37**
See also Zamiatin, Evgenii
See also CA 105; 166; EW; SFW

Zangwill, Israel 1864-1926 ... **TCLC 16; SSC 44**
See also CA 109; 167; CMW; DLB 10, 135, 197; RGEL

Zappa, Francis Vincent, Jr. 1940-1993
See Zappa, Frank
See also CA 108; 143; CANR 57

Zappa, Frank .... **CLC 17**
See also Zappa, Francis Vincent, Jr.

Zaturenska, Marya 1902-1982 ..... **CLC 6, 11**
See also CA 13-16R; 105; CANR 22

Zeami 1363-1443 .... **DC 7**
See also RGWL

Zelazny, Roger (Joseph) 1937-1995 . **CLC 21**
See also AAYA 7; CA 21-24R; 148; CANR 26, 60; CN; DLB 8; FANT; MTCW 1, 2; SATA 57; SATA-Brief 39; SFW; SUFW

Zhdanov, Andrei Alexandrovich
1896-1948 .... **TCLC 18**
See also CA 117; 167

Zhukovsky, Vasily (Andreevich)
1783-1852 .... **NCLC 35**
See also DLB 205

Ziegenhagen, Eric .... **CLC 55**

Zimmer, Jill Schary
See Robinson, Jill

Zimmerman, Robert
See Dylan, Bob

Zindel, Paul 1936- ..... **CLC 6, 26; DA; DAB; DAC; DAM DRAM, MST, NOV; DC 5**
See also AAYA 2, 37; CA 73-76; CAD; CANR 31, 65; CD; CDALBS; CLR 3, 45; DA3; DFS 12; DLB 7, 52; JRDA; MAICYA; MTCW 1, 2; SATA 16, 58, 102; YAW

Zinov'Ev, A. A.
See Zinoviev, Alexander (Aleksandrovich)

Zinoviev, Alexander (Aleksandrovich)
1922- .... **CLC 19**
See also CA 116; 133; CAAS 10

Zoilus
See Lovecraft, H(oward) P(hillips)

Zola, emile (edouard Charles Antoine)
1840-1902 .... **TCLC 1, 6, 21, 41; DA; DAB; DAC; DAM MST, NOV; WLC**
See also CA 104; 138; DA3; DLB 123; EW; GFL 1789 to the Present; IDTP; RGWL

Zoline, Pamela 1941- .... **CLC 62**
See also CA 161; SFW

Zoroaster 628(?)B.C.-551(?)B.C. ... **CMLC 40**

Zorrilla y Moral, Jose 1817-1893 .... **NCLC 6**

Zoshchenko, Mikhail (Mikhailovich)
1895-1958 .... **TCLC 15; SSC 15**
See also CA 115; 160; RGSF

Zuckmayer, Carl 1896-1977 .... **CLC 18**
See also CA 69-72; DLB 56, 124; RGWL

Zuk, Georges
See Skelton, Robin
See also CCA 1

Zukofsky, Louis 1904-1978 ... **CLC 1, 2, 4, 7, 11, 18; DAM POET; PC 11**
See also AMWS 3; CA 9-12R; 77-80; CANR 39; DLB 5, 165; MTCW 1; RGAL

Zweig, Paul 1935-1984 .... **CLC 34, 42**
See also CA 85-88; 113

Zweig, Stefan 1881-1942 .... **TCLC 17**
See also CA 112; 170; DLB 81, 118

Zwingli, Huldreich 1484-1531 .... **LC 37**
See also DLB 179

Literary Criticism Series
Cumulative Topic Index

This index lists all topic entries in Gale's *Classical and Medieval Literature Criticism*, *Contemporary Literary Criticism*, *Literature Criticism from 1400 to 1800*, *Nineteenth-Century Literature Criticism*, and *Twentieth-Century Literary Criticism*.

Topic Index

LITERARY CRITICISM SERIES

CMLC Cumulative Nationality Index

CMLC Cumulative Title Index

Title Index

Title Index

Title Index

Title Index

Title Index

Title Index